# Employment Discrimination Law

## Second Edition

### Five-Year Cumulative Supplement

# FIVE-YEAR CUMULATIVE SUPPLEMENT

to

## Schlei & Grossman's

# Employment Discrimination Law

## Second Edition

Editor-in-Chief
**DAVID A. CATHCART**
*Gibson, Dunn & Crutcher*
*Los Angeles, CA*

Co-Editor
**R. LAWRENCE ASHE, JR.**
*Paul, Hastings, Janofsky & Walker*
*Atlanta, GA*

**American Bar Association**
**Section of Labor and Employment Law**

The Bureau of National Affairs, Inc., Washington, D.C.

Copyright © 1989

American Bar Association
Chicago, Ill.

**Library of Congress Cataloging-in-Publication Data**
(Revised for Five-Year Cumulative-Supplement)

Schlei, Barbara Lindemann, 1935—
  Employment discrimination law.

  Kept up to date by supplements.
  Includes index.
  1. Discrimination in employment—Law and
legislation—United States.   I. Grossman, Paul,
1939—       II. Title.
KF3464.S34   1983      344.73′01133      82-12801
ISBN 0-87179-386-5      347.3041133
ISBN 0-87179-387-3 (student ed.)


Published by BNA Books, 1231 25th St., N.W., Washington, D.C. 20037

International Standard Book Number: 0-87179-584-1
Printed in the United States of America

# Dedication to the 1983 Supplement

# BRUCE E. NELSON

The most relentless adversary in our profession also happens to be our single commodity—time. We guard it, sell it, crave it, and constantly ask for more. So the lawyer who gives it away freely to others and takes time to indulge in living is someone to remember.

With this book we remember Bruce E. Nelson, who helped conceive the idea of this Supplement and was to have been a co-editor. Bruce Nelson had managed to harness time—somehow he was always available for any extra job that needed to be done. He freely helped young colleagues. He made time to teach large and small seminars across the country. His commitment to advancing our profession was endless. And with all of that, Bruce Nelson took the time to celebrate life. Whether on the ski slopes or in a garden, he loved it all. Most of all Bruce loved people and he took the time to let them know it. The work always got done, but a huge bear hug or a midnight conversation came before a filing deadline.

Bruce packed so much living into his time that maybe his forty years were more than forty. Certainly, to all of us who loved him that unforgettable laughter lives on, and to others perhaps the lesson of his values has meaning. This Supplement is dedicated to Bruce Nelson, a colleague who made the time for living more worthwhile.

Bruce Nelson was a partner in the law firm of Morrison & Foerster, San Francisco. He chaired the subcommittee of the ABA Section of Labor and Employment Law which conceived of this Supplement as a project of the Equal Employment Opportunity Law Committee, and he also chaired the subcommittee which drafted the chapter on Related Causes of Action for this Supplement. Bruce Nelson died at the age of 40 on January 27, 1984.

MARK S. DICHTER

# FOREWORD

The Labor and Employment Law Section of the American Bar Association proudly welcomes its revised and greatly expanded *Five-Year Cumulative Supplement to Employment Discrimination Law* to its growing list of major publications covering today's different areas of labor and employment law.

This Supplement, published with the assistance of the members of the Section's Committee on Federal Labor Standards Legislation which drafted the chapters on the Age Discrimination in Employment Act and the Equal Pay Act, is a major publication of the Section's Committee on Equal Employment Opportunity Law and its various subcommittees.

The *Five-Year Cumulative Supplement* carries forward the tradition of the entire Section in providing reference materials intended to help all who concern themselves with American labor and employment law. Judges, arbitrators, practitioners, academicians, students, and others who seek guidance on the latest developments, trends, and legal nuances of equal employment law will be assisted greatly by the efforts of the hundreds of lawyers who gladly volunteered their services over the period of years covered by this Supplement.

The Section is deeply appreciative for the long-continuing work of those many members who have so generously given their time and talents to this immensely demanding effort. The many thousands who use this illuminating Supplement will be indebted to them and to their total commitment to excellence.

Special recognition and tribute are given to David A. Cathcart and R. Lawrence Ashe, Jr., Editor-in-Chief and Co-Editor, respectively, for their leadership, dedication, and tireless efforts in guiding this most difficult and complex writing and editorial process to fruition.

WILLIAM L. KELLER, *Chairman*
HERBERT L. SEGAL, *Chairman-Elect*
*Section of Labor and Employment Law*

# PREFACE

This book exists only because of the generous contributions of the many individuals whose combined efforts have brought this project to completion. We have acknowledged by name all those who we know at this writing helped with the final product. We are sure there are others, and we thank them as well. We owe much to all these friends and colleagues for thus joining in recording and celebrating the continuing vitality of American equal employment law. We are also grateful to all of our colleagues on the Equal Employment Opportunity Law Committee of the American Bar Association's Labor and Employment Law Section for the opportunity to assist in assembling the product of so much care by so many people.

As usual with large projects, a few individuals are owed special gratitude. Among many others, we thank the successive Chairs of the Section of Labor and Employment Law who have supported this project; the editors of BNA Books and particularly Anne Scott, who has tirelessly cajoled, encouraged, and corrected our efforts in excellent proportion at every turn; Barbara Schlei and Paul Grossman, who read every word and reacted with clarity and generous support; Geoff Weirich, of the Atlanta office of Paul, Hastings, Janofsky & Walker, a gifted lawyer who joined in the final editing of each chapter and has been our conscience and colleague in the latter phases of this project; Charles Shanor, General Counsel of the Equal Employment Opportunity Commission and George Salem, then Solicitor of Labor, who in their unofficial capacities read and commented on passages respectively covering the policies and activities of the EEOC and the Department of Labor; and the partners of Gibson, Dunn & Crutcher and Paul, Hastings, Janofsky & Walker who have given steadfast support to the completion of this effort.

This Cumulative Supplement and the latest press reports alike remind us that Title VII and the other federal equal employment statutes remain close to the center of public attention. As these words are written, the most recent Supreme Court decisions and legislative proposals pending in Congress are renewing and redefining our continuing national debate on the meaning and application of equal employment opportunity in the American workplace. Shifting balances between and within the Legislative and Executive Branches and the increasing importance of state and local jurisdictions all affect the continuing story. We should likely expect no less of a subject that is about jobs, about work, about fairness in the workplace—touching at once the personal hopes of millions of Americans and also the economic and industrial life of our country.

Title VII reaches its quarter century mark as this Cumulative Supplement is published, and we are entitled to reflect on its significance from that perspective. As we see again this season the dangers facing all hopes for peaceful constructive change around the world, we renew our gratitude for the generous purpose and steady vision reflected in these great national reform statutes first made law a quarter century ago. Among these Title VII stands in the first rank. It is hard to recall or, for the younger among us, even to imagine our country as it was before these changes. It is sobering to think of the tide of anxiety and hope on which these enactments carried the nation toward the future that we and our children now accept as commonplace. In this spirit we remember and celebrate the courage, imagination, and perseverance of all who thus helped renew the American promise, and all those who as lawyers and judges assist in the continuing evolution whose latest directions are chronicled in this book.

Our largest personal obligations are closest to home. We especially thank Janet, Sarah, and Rebecca Cathcart and Kathy, Robbie, and Sally Ashe, as well as Kelly and Nicole Weirich whose special generosity and patience will be instantly understood by all authors and editors and their families.

June 1989

DAVID A. CATHCART

R. LAWRENCE ASHE, JR.

# ACKNOWLEDGMENTS

This cumulative Supplement is the work of many attorneys throughout the country, principally members of the Committee on Equal Employment Opportunity Law, who devoted a great amount of time and effort and talent in drafting of the chapters. Those names with an asterisk are non-Committee members who made significant contributions. Chapters 13 and 14 were drafted by members of the Federal Labor Standards Legislation Committee. We express our deep gratitude to all of those attorneys listed below who contributed so much to this project.

## Chapters 2, 3, and 18

Chairperson: Charles C. Warner

| | |
|---|---|
| Michael V. Abcarian | James A. King, Jr. |
| Howard R. Barron | James P. Kohl |
| Mark Blondman | Frederick John Lewis |
| Brian Wegg Bulger | Paul Steven Mannweiler |
| Edward Lee Dale | Christopher Marlowe |
| Guy F. Driver, Jr. | Mitchell |
| Thomas William Duda | Gregory C. Parliman |
| Hugh M. Finneran | Bernard George Peter, Jr. |
| William F. Gardner | John Runyan |
| Barry A. Hartstein | Patrick H. Scanlon |
| Timothy W. Johnson | Brian A. Schaffer* |
| W. Carl Jordan | Timothy L. Stalnaker |
| Jeffrey Steven Karp | Russell G. Tisman |
| Melvin Stephen Katzman | Robert D. Weisman |

Lon R. Williams, Jr.

## Chapters 4, 5, and 6

Chairpersons: Catherine B. Hagen
R. Lawrence Ashe, Jr.

| | |
|---|---|
| B. Lee Crawford, Jr.* | John Murray* |
| Virginia Hoyt | Earl W. Putnam |
| Stephen W. Jones | Kay M. Todd |

Michael A. Warner

## Chapters 7 and 8

Chairperson: Thomas H. Barnard

Alexander K. Abraham
James A. Burstein
Robert Fletcher Childs, Jr.
Arthur K. Davis
Bernard M. Dworski
Denise Moore Fogg
Herbert Edward Gerson
Kay H. Hodge
Peyton S. Irby, Jr.
Roger B. Jacobs
Michael L. Jensen
Martin Klaper

Neil E. Klingshirn
Jeffrey Charles Londa
Donald J. Maroldy
Arlene Mayerson
Gary E. Murg
Irving Perlman
Barbara Ashley Phillips
Stephen David Shawe
David J. Somrak
Kenneth Douglas Stein
Hill B. Wellford, Jr.
David L. Williams

## Chapters 9, 10, 11, and 15

Chairperson: Charles L. Chester

Theresa Bustillos
Allen Butler
Arun Das
Heather E. Hudson
James A. Jablonski
Harris E. Kershnar
Edward R. Levin
Susan G. Lowenstam
Carl N. Martin II
Michael D. Moberly*

Jerry E. Nathan
David A. Rhem
Anne Marie Sferra
Cathie A. Shattuck
David M. Silberman
David L. Slate
Susan M. Solomon
Richard C. Stephenson
Harry N. Turk
Edward R. Young

James E. Youngdahl

## Chapter 12

Chairperson: David L. Slate

Robert J. Allen, Jr.
Terry S. Bickerton
Nancy K. Busch
Susan S. Cahoon
Coeta J. Chambers*
Richard Seth Cohen
Robert F. Conte
Walter P. DeForest III
Herbert C. Ehrhardt
William F. Ford

James W. Gladden
John Kevin Hennessy
James H. Kizziar, Jr.
Anne E. Libbin
John R. Low
Christopher Luis
Elton Bruce Mather
Marian Priest McCulloch
Francis J. Newton, Jr.
Steven J. Rothschild

Gordon Williams Schmidt　　Charles Austin Stewart
Bradd N. Siegel　　　　　　Eugene D. Ulterino
Claudia Withers

## Chapters 13 and 14

Chairpersons: J. Anthony Messina
Stephen W. Skrainka

Keith A. Ashmus　　　　Anthony B. Haller
Michael I. Bernstein　　Irving L. Hurwitz
Leo J. Bub　　　　　　Karl D. Johnston
Robert D. Cadish　　　Kathy L. Krieger
Jennifer A. Clark　　　Christine M. Ramatowski
Robert T. Fries　　　　Patrick M. Sanders
Leric J. Goodman　　　Harry Sangerman
Terry M. Yellig

## Chapters 16, 17, and 23

Chairperson: Gary R. Siniscalco

Luis F. Antonetti　　　　Harley Morris Kastner
E. Garth Black　　　　　Susan Krell
David P. Callet　　　　　Richard C. Mariani
Harry S. Chandler　　　Thomas Peter Moran
Francis J. Connell　　　George N. Nichols
William J. Cooney　　　Dean E. Peterson
Richard D. Deluce　　　Jay John Price
Rochelle S. Eisenberg　George C. Rozmarin
Barbara Rynicker Evans　Willis Stephen Ryza
Joel Lester Finger　　　Brad Seligman
Daniel W. Fouts　　　　H. Warren Siegel
Chris R. Gangemi, Jr.　Robert W. Stewart
Brock B. Gordon　　　　Susan G. Tanenbaum
Carol F. Graebner　　　Gregory J. Utken
William R. Hayden　　　Charles C. Warner
James Francis Henriot　John Patrick White

## Chapters 19, 20, 21, and 22

Chairperson: Jack L. Whitacre

J. David Andrews　　　Edward J. Dempsey
Tim Boe　　　　　　　Robert Saul Ellenport
Victoria Corcoran　　　Ronald M. Green

J. Walker Henry
Charles C. High, Jr.
Jay P. Krupin
Lawrence G. Mackowiak
M. Daniel McGinn
Michael R. Maine
Donald D. Oliver

David M. Pellow
Richard J. Reibstein
Jon Howard Rosen
Hayes C. Stover
Robert B. Terry
Lisa S. Van Amburg
Shelley J. Venick

## Chapters 24 and 25

Chairpersons: Ronald S. Cooper
John C. Fox

Richard Antonelli
Albert Calille
Robert Cannella
Milton C. Denbo
Jim Frank
James D. Henry
Helen D. Irvin
Stephen M. Kite-Powell
Ellen Kohn

John B. Langel
Malcolm Maclean
Samuel T. Perkins
Mitchell S. Rubin
John Sagaser
John Schnebly
Martin D. Schneiderman
William C. Strock
John Vering

Charles B. Wolf

## Chapters 26, 27, and 29

Chairperson: Debra A. Millenson

John W. Brahm
Martin K. Denis
Gerard J. DeWolf
Mark S. Greene
William Russell Hamilton III
J. Frederic Ingram
Robert L. Jauvits
Kent Jonas
Daniel E. Leach
David A. Maddux

Richard Masterson
William J. McMorrow
Louis Obdyke
Mary Aileen O'Callaghan
John L. Quinn
William E. Rachels, Jr.
W. Reed Scism
Jay T. Swett
Arlene F. Switzer
M. Kirby C. Wilcox

John B. Wolf

## Chapters 28 and 30

Chairperson: William F. Highberger

Richard R. Brann
Louis A. Cappadonna, Jr.

Michael F. Delaney
Joanne Dellaverson

Daniel G. Galant

Catherine Hagen

Sam Jensen

Lawrence M. Joseph

James K. L. Lawrence

Richard E. Lieberman

Thomas O. Magan

Laurel J. McKee

Stuart W. Miller

Emile C. Ott

Robert Rountree Reinhart

Sheldon J. Stark

Jeffrey A. Walker

John R. Wester

Zachary D. Fasman

## Chapters 31, 32, and 33

Chairperson: Keith M. Pyburn, Jr.

Jon P. Bachelder

James J. Bierbower

Patricia Brandin

Joseph P. Carey

William B. Dickinson

Sandra E. Durant

Donald Elisburg

Allen I. Fagin

Russell H. Gardner

Thomas M. Gonzales

Andrew W. Haines

Donald B. Harden

Sara Jay

Judith J. Johnson

Thomas T. Lawson

Richard F. Liebman

Joyce E. Margulies

Christine O. Merriman

Vance D. Miller

Kathlyn E. Noecker

Charles S. Ralston

Steve Ralston

Frederick T. Shea

Peter G. Smith

Richard P. Theis

## Chapters 34, 35, and 40

Chairperson: William A. Clineburg, Jr.

Madeline Balk

Max G. Brittain, Jr.

William P.H. Cary

Walter Cochran-Bond

Dennis G. Collins

John R. Crenshaw

Guy O. Farmer II

David F. Guldenschuh

Howard C. Harpham

Eric H. Joss

John H. Leddy

Thomas J. Manley

David L. McComb

George P. Parker

Wayne J. Positan

Richard A. Schneider

Robert E. Schreiber

Ronald R. Snyder

Michael M. Tarnow

Michael S. Thwaites

Frank P. Ward, Jr.

## Chapter 36

Chairperson: Philip J. Pfeiffer

| | |
|---|---|
| Mary Amanda Balch | Arthur E. Joyce |
| Thomas H. Barnard | Edward Katze |
| James S. Bramnick | Alan M. Lerner |
| Bernard J. Casey | Philip K. Lyon |
| David A. Copus | Kathleen M. Mills |
| Deborah Crandall | Perry Elizabeth Pearce |
| John J. Doyle, Jr. | Gregory L. Riggs |
| William H. Emer | John B. Rosenquest III |
| Barry L. Goldstein | Paul J. Russoniello |
| Steven S. Greene | Marc Alan Silverstein |
| Penda Hair | Kent Spriggs |
| Michael C. Hallerud | Joseph A. Teklits |
| Bruce S. Harrison | David L. Treat* |
| William F. Joy, Jr. | Ralph J. Zatzkis |

## Chapters 37, 38, and 39

Chairperson: Thomas A. Lemly

| | |
|---|---|
| Fred W. Alvarez | Emmett F. McGee, Jr.* |
| John F. Aslin | John M. Miller |
| Robert B. Barnhouse | Paul O. Miller III |
| Joel Paul Bennett | Scott C. Moriearty |
| Mark W. Berry* | Jeffrey Ivan Pasek |
| William R. Blane* | Christine H. Perdue |
| Rachel Simonoff Blechman | Ruth Raisfeld* |
| Thomas E. Brydges | David B. Ritter* |
| Barry L. Chaet | Kerry G. Robinson* |
| Philip W. Clements* | Henry W. Saad |
| Paul W. Drewitz | Guy T. Saperstein |
| Lee M. Finkel | Richard H. Schnadig |
| Mary Ann Fuchs* | David M. Selcer |
| Charles K. Howard, Jr. | Gary L. Smith |
| Hunter R. Hughes | Mona Spitz* |
| A. Thomas Hunt | Stuart Thomsen* |
| Laurie Johnston* | James C. Webber* |
| Donald J. Logie, Jr. | Thomas Hylton Williams |
| John P. Mann | William Witman |
| Mari Mayeda* | Sally Barian Yates* |

We express our particular appreciation to Barbara Lindemann Schlei and Paul Grossman, who authored the Second Edition. They were our inspiration throughout this project, and they offered invaluable guidance and insight through their review of every chapter in this Supplement.

And to Anita Barajas and Janet Yescas of Gibson, Dunn & Crutcher, and Toni Favors, Barbara Holmes, and Sallie Mathis of Paul, Hastings, Janofsky and Walker, a special tribute for extraordinary efforts and dedication. We also thank our own partners for their endless support in time, resources, and faith in this works' contribution to the legal profession.

DAVID A. CATHCART

R. LAWRENCE ASHE, JR.

# DETAILED TABLE OF CONTENTS

*Page*

### Third Category of Discrimination—Adverse Impact

## Litigation

## CHAPTER 1

# AN OVERVIEW

We highlight in this chapter the most significant developments covered in this Cumulative Supplement, which is current for lower-court cases through mid-1987 and for Supreme Court cases through March 1989. The reader should always check the subsequent history of all cases and other developments cited in this Supplement.

## Proof

Employment discrimination litigation continues to turn on four theories of proof: disparate treatment, adverse impact, perpetuation into the present of the effects of past discrimination, and failure to make reasonable accommodation.[1] In disparate treatment cases, courts still apply the shifting burden analysis announced in *McDonnell Douglas Corp. v. Green*[2] and *Texas Department of Community Affairs v. Burdine.*[3] The *McDonnell Douglas-Burdine* test is designed for litigation based on circumstantial evidence, however, and does not apply when a plaintiff presents direct evidence of discrimination that is sufficient in itself to sustain the plaintiff's burden of proof.[4] Where a plaintiff's prima facie case is established by direct evidence, a defendant bears a heavier burden and generally must either refute that evidence or demonstrate the absence of a causal connection between the biased decision maker and the adverse decision.[5]

The Supreme Court has emphasized, in *United States Postal Service Board of Governors v. Aikens,*[6] that the *McDonnell Douglas-Burdine* analysis must not obscure the ultimate issue: whether the plaintiff has sustained the burden of proving intentional discrimination by the defendant against the plaintiff. Courts continue to adapt the elements of the *McDonnell Douglas-Burdine* test to the facts of specific cases.[7]

Statistics continue to play an important role in both class disparate treatment and adverse impact actions.[8] A plaintiff's statistical evidence need

---

[1]*See* Chapter 36 (Proof).

[2]411 U.S. 792, 5 FEP 965 (1973).

[3]450 U.S. 248, 25 FEP 113 (1981). *See* Chapter 36 (Proof).

[4]Trans World Airlines v. Thurston, 469 U.S. 111, 121, 36 FEP 977, 982 (1985); Thompkins v. Morris Brown College, 752 F.2d 558, 563, 37 FEP 24, 28 (11th Cir. 1985).

[5]*Id.* Plaintiffs will argue that an employer may rebut direct evidence of a discriminatory policy only with "clear and convincing evidence that job decisions made when the discriminatory policy was in force were not made in pursuit of that policy." Cox v. American Cast Iron Pipe Co., 784 F.2d 1546, 40 FEP 678, 688 (11th Cir.), *cert. denied,* 479 U.S. 883, 41 FEP 1712 (1986). Plaintiffs also will argue that the *McDonnell Douglas-Burdine* framework does not apply where a pattern or practice of disparate treatment is demonstrated. 40 FEP at 689. *See also* Chapter 36 (Proof) at notes 73–85 and accompanying text.

[6]460 U.S. 711, 31 FEP 609 (1983).

[7]*See* Chapter 36 (Proof), notes 4–6 and accompanying text.

[8]*See generally* Mozee v. Jeffboat, Inc., 746 F.2d 365, 35 FEP 1810 (7th Cir. 1984); Segar v. Smith, 738 F.2d 1249, 35 FEP 31 (D.C. Cir. 1984), *cert. denied,* 471 U.S. 1115, 37 FEP 1312 (1985).

not account for every factor in order to establish a prima facie case.[9] However, even though sufficiently persuasive statistics can without more create a prima facie case of classwide discrimination, they cannot alone establish a case of individual disparate treatment.[10] A plaintiff claiming that the defendant's rebuttal statistics are contaminated by a potentially biased factor must demonstrate that the challenged factor is indeed biased.[11]

Within this analytical structure, the Supreme Court addressed and partially resolved in *Watson v. Fort Worth Bank & Trust*[12] a decade-old debate over whether the adverse impact theory of proof may properly be applied to employment decisions based upon subjective criteria. The Court unanimously held that subjective decisions could be challenged through an adverse impact analysis.[13] Although *Watson* thus held that a plaintiff need not prove discriminatory intent in order successfully to challenge subjective criteria, the Court was sharply divided on significant issues concerning evidentiary standards and allocation of the burden of proof. Two of these issues suggest the likelihood of future appellate litigation as the full Court—now including Justice Kennedy—defines its approach to employment discrimination law. First, Justice O'Connor's plurality opinion, joined by Justices Rehnquist, White, and Scalia, observed that extension of the adverse impact theory to subjective decisions in *Watson* "calls for a fresh and somewhat closer examination of the constraints that operate to keep that analysis within its proper bounds."[14] Second, the formulation of the "business necessity" test set out in *Watson* appears less stringent than that used by many lower courts. The *Watson* plurality declared that a defendant employer responding to a prima facie case of adverse impact has the "burden of producing evidence that its employment practices are based on legitimate business reasons," and of proving that legitimate goals are "significantly served by" the practice at issue.[15]

The *Watson* plurality also set forth "evidentiary guidelines" for lower courts in analyzing adverse impact challenges to subjective criteria. First, a plaintiff must show more than statistical disparities in the employer's work force. It must identify specific challenged employment practices allegedly responsible for any observed statistical disparities.[16] An employer then may show that a given employment requirement is lawful because it has a " 'manifest relationship to the employment in question,' "[17] but the plurality noted that this formulation "should not be interpreted as implying that the ultimate burden of proof can be shifted to the defendant," because that burden "remains with the plaintiff at all times."[18]

Justice Blackmun, joined by Justices Brennan and Marshall, vigorously disagreed with the plurality analysis, asserting that Justice O'Connor's views

---

[9]Bazemore v. Friday, 478 U.S. 385, 41 FEP 92 (1986).
[10]Carmichael v. Birmingham Saw Works, 738 F.2d 1126, 1131, 35 FEP 791, 795 (11th Cir. 1984).
[11]Coates v. Johnson & Johnson, 756 F.2d 524, 544, 37 FEP 467, 482 (7th Cir. 1985).
[12]487 U.S. _____, 47 FEP 102 (1988).
[13]47 FEP at 107 (eight Justices so held, Justice Kennedy not participating in the decision).
[14]*Id.*, 47 FEP at 108. *See* Chapter 36 (Proof) at note 16 and accompanying text.
[15]47 FEP at 110–11 (1988). *See* Chapter 36 (Proof), notes 154 and 199 and accompanying text.
[16]47 FEP at 109.
[17]*Id.*, 47 FEP at 110 (quoting Griggs v. Duke Power Co., 401 U.S. 424, 432, 3 FEP 175, 178 (1971)). *See* Chapter 36 (Proof) at notes 153–156 and accompanying text.
[18]47 FEP at 110.

on the allocation of burdens of proof and production in an adverse impact case were "flatly contradicted" by prior Supreme Court precedent, pursuant to which a plaintiff who successfully establishes a prima facie case of adverse impact shifts to the defendant the burden of proving that the employment practice in question is a business necessity.[19] Justice Blackmun further disagreed that the defendant may carry its burden "simply by 'producing evidence that its employment practices are based on legitimate business reasons.' "[20] Emphasizing the word "necessity," Justice Blackmun stated that employment criteria effectively excluding a protected class at a significantly disproportionate rate must relate directly to a prospective employee's ability to perform the job effectively, and not merely bear an indirect or minimal relationship to job performance.

Justice Stevens declined to join either Justice O'Connor's or Justice Blackmun's opinions in *Watson* regarding burdens of proof and evidentiary standards in adverse impact cases. Justice Kennedy did not participate in the *Watson* decision. Hence subsequent disposition of these issues may depend on Justice Kennedy.[21] The Supreme Court should resolve some of these issues in *Wards Cove Packing Co. v. Atonio.*[22]

Several decisions have clarified the relative probative value of different types of statistical proof. In *Bazemore v. Friday*[23] the Supreme Court approved the use of multiple regression analyses in proving compensation discrimination. The *Bazemore* Court held unanimously that a regression analysis had been erroneously excluded from evidence even though it did not include all measurable variables thought to have an effect on salary level. Such omissions affect the weight but not the admissibility of the study. The sufficiency of a regression analysis in carrying a plaintiff's ultimate burden of proof will depend on the factual context of each case in light of all the evidence.[24] In addition, courts continue to admit into evidence studies based on actual applicant flow data, which the Fifth Circuit has noted are generally superior to census or other general labor market statistics.[25] The Ninth Circuit has held that "[d]isparate impact should always be measured against the actual pool of applicants or eligible employees unless there is a characteristic of the challenged selection device that makes use of the actual pool of applicants or eligible employees inappropriate."[26] Where actual applicant

---

[19]*Id.,* 47 FEP at 111.

[20]*Id.,* 47 FEP at 113. *See* Chapter 36 (Proof) at notes 157–160 and accompanying text.

[21]Although Justice Kennedy has not addressed this question since ascending to the Supreme Court, he authored the majority opinion in *State, County & Mun. Employees v. Washington,* 770 F.2d 1401, 38 FEP 1353 (9th Cir. 1985), that "[adverse] impact analysis is confined to cases that challenge a specific, clearly delineated employment practice applied at a single point in the job selection process." *Id.* at 1405, 38 FEP at 1357–58.

[22]810 F.2d 1477, 43 FEP 130 (9th Cir. 1987), *cert. granted,* 487 U.S. _____ (1988).

[23]478 U.S. 385, 41 FEP 92 (1986).

[24]*Id.,* 41 FEP at 99. The Court stated that "[n]ormally, failure to include variables will affect the analysis' probativeness, not its admissibility," although "[t]here may, of course, be some regressions so incomplete as to be inadmissible as irrelevant." *Id.,* 41 FEP at 99 & n.10. *Bazemore* sets forth a list of characteristics in the regression analysis which the unanimous Court characterized as "an impressive array of evidence" in establishing compensation discrimination occurring with "each week's paycheck," although originally caused by pre-Act employment segregation within the challenged Civil Service system. *Id.,* 41 FEP at 100, 97.

[25]Payne v. Travenol Laboratories, 673 F.2d 798, 823–24, 28 FEP 1212, 1232 (5th Cir.), *cert. denied,* 459 U.S. 1038, 30 FEP 440 (1982).

[26]Moore v. Summa Corp., Hughes Helicopter Div., 708 F.2d 475, 482, 32 FEP 97, 102 (9th Cir. 1983). *See also* Chapter 36 (Proof), notes 221–222 and accompanying text.

flow data are unavailable or unreliable, courts prefer qualified labor market data, reflecting representation of relevant protected groups among those qualified for the positions at issue.[27] Courts limit general population data to situations where applicant flow or labor pool data are unavailable or flawed and where individual candidates are expected to resemble the qualifications within the population at large.[28]

The *Watson* Court's discussion of statistical proof confirms a continuing judicial uncertainty regarding the requisite sufficiency of statistical disparities.[29] Although standard deviation analysis continues to dominate in evaluating the legal significance of such disparities,[30] some courts utilize and others criticize the "four-fifths" or "80-percent" rule.[31] Courts disagree whether a disparity between two and three standard deviations adequately establishes adverse impact.[32]

### Reverse Discrimination and Affirmative Action

Several Supreme Court decisions have addressed the tension between permissible affirmative action and unlawful reverse discrimination. These cases have been at the leading edge of a national controversy over these issues. *Firefighters Local 1784 v. Stotts*[33] invalidated a trial court's order modifying a Title VII consent decree to protect blacks from seniority-based layoffs under a concededly bona fide seniority system. This decision generated substantial uncertainty whether the Court's restrictions on affirmative action overrides would extend beyond public employers, would cover voluntary plans or consent decrees, or would be limited to layoffs. In addition, many believed that *Stotts* presaged a limitation on affirmative action to identifiable victims of discrimination.

During the 1985–1986 term the Supreme Court issued a trilogy of

---

[27]*See, e.g.,* Domingo v. New England Fish Co., 727 F.2d 1429, 1436, 34 FEP 584, 592, *modified,* 742 F.2d 520, 37 FEP 1303 (9th Cir. 1984); Pegues v. Mississippi State Employment Serv., 699 F.2d 760, 766–68, 31 FEP 257, 261–63 (5th Cir.), *cert. denied,* 464 U.S. 991, 33 FEP 440 (1983).

[28]*See, e.g.,* Moore v. Summa Corp., Hughes Helicopter Div., *supra* note 26 ("[g]eneral population statistics are useful as a proxy for the pool of potential applicants, if ever, only where the challenged employer practice screens applicants for entry level jobs requiring little or no specialized skills"). The labor force participation of groups with above average birth rates will be somewhat overstated by use of general population data.

[29]Watson v. Fort Worth Bank & Trust, 487 U.S. _____, 47 FEP 102, 109 & n.3 (1988) ("[W]e have not suggested that any particular number of 'standard deviations' can determine whether a plaintiff has made out a prima facie case in the complex area of employment discrimination. * * * [C]ourts appear generally to have judged the 'significance' or 'substantiality' of numerical disparities on a case-by-case basis.").

[30]*See, e.g.,* EEOC v. Western Elec. Co., 713 F.2d 1011, 1018, 32 FEP 708, 714 (4th Cir. 1983) (requiring standard deviation analysis before drawing conclusions from straight percentages); Hazelwood School Dist. v. United States, 433 U.S. 299, 15 FEP 1 (1977); Castaneda v. Partida, 430 U.S. 482 (1977).

[31]*Compare* Bigby v. City of Chicago, 38 FEP 844 (N.D. Ill. 1984), *aff'd,* 766 F.2d 1053, 38 FEP 853 (7th Cir. 1985), *cert. denied,* 474 U.S. 1056, 39 FEP 1200 (1986) (utilized 80% test) *with* Fudge v. City of Providence Fire Dep't, 766 F.2d 650, 659 n.10, 38 FEP 648 (1st Cir. 1985) (80% test rejected where sample small) and Clady v. County of Los Angeles, 770 F.2d 1421, 38 FEP 1575 (9th Cir. 1985), *cert. denied,* 475 U.S. 1109, 40 FEP 792 (1986) (80% test rejected; Uniform Guidelines held not to have the force of law). *Cf.* Connecticut v. Teal, 457 U.S. 440, 29 FEP 1 (1982) (regarding the companion "bottom line" rule under the Uniform Guidelines).

[32]*See, e.g.,* Kilgo v. Bowman Transp., 789 F.2d 859, 40 FEP 1415 (11th Cir. 1986) (*per se* rule rejected; disparities below two to three standard deviations could still be discriminatory, and greater disparities might not foreclose chance); Clady v. County of Los Angeles, *supra* note 31, 770 F.2d at 1428–29 (neither two to three standard deviation test nor 80% rule should be applied uncritically).

[33]467 U.S. 561, 34 FEP 1702 (1984).

affirmative action decisions—*Wygant v. Jackson Board of Education,*[34] *Sheet Metal Workers Local 28 v. EEOC,*[35] and *Firefighters Local 93 v. Cleveland*[36] —which provided further guidance but left unanswered questions. These decisions provided a field day for Justice counters—seven Justices authored 14 opinions—and the Court's difficulty in assembling a consensus suggests the strain which these issues continue to impose.

In *Wygant,* a case decided under the Fourteenth Amendment, a five-to-four majority of the Court reversed—without a majority opinion—lower court decisions that had upheld a collective bargaining agreement providing the type of affirmative action "override" protection against layoff which had been imposed by decree in *Stotts.* The labor contract in *Wygant* itself provided that, in the event of layoff, no greater percentage of minority employees would be laid off than the current percentage of minorities employed. On varying grounds, five Justices held that this layoff override was unconstitutional, despite being collectively bargained.[37] Notwithstanding this result, opinions by majority Justices Powell and O'Connor both endorsed affirmative action by public employers under some circumstances,[38] thus providing support from at least six Justices on this general principle.

In *Cleveland Firefighters,* six Justices upheld a Title VII consent decree which granted race-conscious affirmative action relief in promoting firefighters, even though the decree's benefits flowed to persons not shown to have been victims of discrimination. All six majority Justices—Brennan, Marshall, Blackmun, Stevens, Powell, and O'Connor—expressly distinguished a consent decree from an "order of the court" within the meaning of § 706(g),[39] and concluded that a consent decree may benefit nonvictims even though the trial court might lack the authority to order this result after a trial.[40]

The egregious facts underlying the Court's decision in *Sheet Metal Workers* have been widely viewed as explaining its result and limiting its precedential effect. The union had been found in civil contempt for violating earlier court orders to remedy discrimination, and as part of the contempt remedy the court had ordered extensive affirmative relief, including a 29.23 percent nonwhite membership goal to be met by August 1987. Justice Powell's fifth vote, establishing the Court majority approving the lower court's order, was based expressly on the history of blatant Title VII violations in the factual record, and on his stated view that the membership goal was not a quota.[41]

The Supreme Court revisited this subject in *Johnson v. Transportation*

---

[34]476 U.S. 267, 40 FEP 1321 (1986).
[35]478 U.S. 421, 41 FEP 107 (1986).
[36]478 U.S. 501, 41 FEP 139 (1986).
[37]40 FEP at 1327.
[38]*Id.,* 40 FEP at 1328–29.
[39]Sec. 706(g), 42 U.S.C. § 2000e-5(g), provides that:
No order of the court shall require the admission or reinstatement of an individual as a member of a union, or the hiring, reinstatement, or promotion of an individual as an employee, or the payment to him of any back pay, if such individual was refused admission, suspended, or expelled, or was refused employment or advancement or was suspended or discharged for any reason other than discrimination on account of race, color, religion, sex, or national origin or in violation of section 2000e-3(a) of this title.
[40]41 FEP at 149.
[41]41 FEP at 132.

*Agency, Santa Clara County*[42] and *United States v. Paradise.*[43] In *Johnson,* the Court faced an attack by a disfavored male employee who lost a promotional opportunity to a female competitor selected after consideration of the county's affirmative action plan. The Court held that the defendant did not violate Title VII by this promotion, even though the promoted female employee was assigned to a road dispatcher position over a male employee who had similar but somewhat higher ratings based on tests, interviews, and prior experience. The Court held that *Steelworkers v. Weber*[44] applied to public as well as private employers, and that this public employer had adopted its affirmative action plan in response to a "manifest imbalance" in the representation of women in its work force within "traditionally segregated job classifications," reflected in this case by the absence of female employees in skilled craft positions.[45] Moreover, the Court found that the Santa Clara County plan did not "unnecessarily trammel" the interests of white males, who were still permitted to bid for promotions to these positions, and whose qualifications were considered along with affirmative action objectives.[46]

*Johnson* has been widely regarded as encouraging employers, both private and public, to adopt and act upon affirmative action plans designed to encourage work force diversification within "traditionally segregated job classifications," by permitting individual employee selection decisions to incorporate consideration of affirmative action objectives. However, the necessary factual predicate for an affirmative action plan remains unclear. Justice Powell's vote was necessary to the Court majority upholding the Santa Clara County plan. Justice O'Connor concurred, but on the basis that the facts established a prima facie case of employment discrimination.[47] The replacement of Justice Powell by Justice Kennedy leaves open the possibility that the Court may yet require that affirmative action plans adopted outside the consent decree context be based either on a colorable finding of employment discrimination or alternatively on facts that would support a prima facie case that Title VII had been violated.[48]

In *Paradise,* the Court upheld a promotion order requiring that one black state trooper be promoted for every white trooper until a 25 percent black representation rate was attained at the corporate level.[49] *Paradise* thus provides further support for the selective use of quotas as remedies in appropriate cases. The Justices supporting this result relied on the factual record of pervasive and systemic employment discrimination maintained over a long period.[50]

Finally, in *City of Richmond v. J.A. Croson  Co.,*[51] the Court recently affirmed the Fourth Circuit's invalidation of a Richmond minority set-aside plan that had required prime contractors on city construction contracts to

---

[42]480 U.S. 616, 43 FEP 411 (1987).

[43]480 U.S. 149, 43 FEP 1 (1987).

[44]443 U.S. 193, 20 FEP 1 (1979).

[45]43 FEP at 418.

[46]*Id.,* 43 FEP at 417–18.

[47]*Id.,* 43 FEP at 425.

[48]*See* City of Richmond v. J.A. Croson, Co., *infra* note 51, and accompanying text ("strict scrutiny" standard applied to MBE set-aside program of public employer, in opinion by Justice O'Connor, supported by Court majority including Justice Kennedy).

[49]43 FEP at 12.

[50]*Id.,* 43 FEP at 15.

[51]488 U.S. ____, 57  USLW 4132, 109 S. Ct. 706 (1989), *aff'g* 822 F.2d 1355 (4th Cir. 1987).

subcontract at least 30 percent of the dollar amount of each contract to one or more Minority Business Enterprises (MBEs). An MBE had been defined to include a business at least 51 percent of which was owned and controlled by black, Spanish-speaking, Oriental, Indian, Eskimo, or Aleut citizens. Under the plan, the City adopted rules requiring individualized consideration of each request for a waiver from the 30 percent set-aside requirement, and requiring that waivers be supported by proof that insufficient MBEs were available or willing to participate. Following remand by the Supreme Court for reconsideration of the plan in light of *Wygant,* the Fourth Circuit reversed its previous approval of the plan. The Supreme Court affirmed this decision, holding that the plan had to satisfy a standard of strict scrutiny, and that it failed to do so because it was not justified by a compelling governmental interest and because the 30 percent set-aside was not narrowly tailored to accomplish a legitimate remedial purpose.[52] Justice O'Connor wrote the Court's opinion, joined by Justices Rehnquist, White, Stevens, and Kennedy.

### Age Discrimination

Congress acted in late 1984 to end the controversy over the constitutionality of the transfer of authority for enforcement of the Age Discrimination in Employment Act (ADEA) and the Equal Pay Act (EPA) from the Department of Labor to the EEOC brought about by the Supreme Court's decision in *Immigration & Naturalization Service v. Chadha.*[53] Congress expressly confirmed the EEOC's authority. Congress also amended the ADEA to remove the age-70 coverage cap, to extend its coverage to U.S. citizens employed abroad by American companies[54] and to raise the retirement income level triggering the ADEA executive exemption from $27,000 to $44,000.[55]

The Supreme Court decided three cases under the ADEA holding that the bona fide occupational qualifications (BFOQ) exception must be narrowly construed.[56] In *Johnson v. Mayor of Baltimore*[57] the Supreme Court reversed the Fourth Circuit, rejecting an age 55 mandatory retirement for firefighters. Similarly, in *Western Air Lines v. Criswell*[58] the Court affirmed the Ninth Circuit's decision holding that the BFOQ exception did not permit the mandatory retirement of flight engineers at age 60. The Supreme Court emphasized in both *Johnson* and *Criswell* that competency decisions normally should be made on an individual basis. In *Trans World Airlines v. Thurston*[59] the Supreme Court affirmed the Second Circuit's decision that the ADEA required TWA to afford 60-year-old captains the same cockpit-transfer privileges given captains disqualified for reasons other than age.

The *Thurston* Court also addressed the standard for awarding liqui-

---

[52]*Id.* at _____, 109 S. Ct. at 708.
[53]462 U.S. 919, 51 USLW 4907 (1983). *Cf.* Steelworkers v. Weber, *supra* note 44 and Johnson v. Transportation Agency, Santa Clara County, *supra* note 42.
[54]Older Americans Act Amendments of 1984, Pub. L. No. 98-459, 98 Stat. 1767 (1984), amending 29 U.S.C. § 623(f)(1) and adding 29 U.S.C. § 623(g)(1)–(3).
[55]*Id.,* amending 29 U.S.C. § 631(c)(1).
[56]*See* Chapter 14 (Age).
[57]472 U.S. 353, 37 FEP 1839 (1985).
[58]472 U.S. 400, 37 FEP 1829 (1985).
[59]469 U.S. 111, 36 FEP 977 (1985).

dated damages for willful violations of the ADEA. The Court adopted the Second Circuit's "reckless disregard" standard: an employer's conduct is "willful" if it " 'knew or showed reckless disregard for the matter of whether its conduct was prohibited by the ADEA.' "[60] The Court specifically rejected the standard previously applied in some circuits that a violation is willful if an employer knew of the potential application of the ADEA.[61]

In more recent ADEA decisions, the courts of appeal have continued to support properly planned and competently administered work force reductions based on economic need.[62] Although upholding the validity of a release, the Sixth Circuit in *Runyan v. National Cash Register Corp.*[63] suggested caution in the preparation and administration of termination allowance plans that are coupled with releases of employment-related claims. A significant national controversy has arisen over whether private settlements of ADEA claims, made without EEOC participation, are enforceable as a bar to subsequent ADEA litigation. This controversy affects individual settlements and also the frequent use of termination allowance plans that condition additional severance payments in part on waivers of all employment-related claims, including claims of age discrimination. A consensus of circuit court decisions holds that severance policies are governed by the Employee Retirement Income Security Act (ERISA).[64] Releases of claims are usually intended also to protect the employer against employment termination claims under state law.[65] Such groups as the American Association of Retired Persons have opposed such "unsupervised" ADEA settlements on the asserted grounds that the ADEA itself requires government participation and supervision of settlements as a condition of enforceability.[66] Thus far, five circuit courts of appeal have upheld voluntary and knowing private ADEA releases.[67] The Ninth Circuit, however, has upheld a unique district court ruling that a proposed waiver of ADEA claims, not signed by the employee, is admissible evidence for a jury determination of whether the employer's layoff of the employee was motivated by willful age discrimination.[68] As this Supplement went to press, legislation pending in Congress would substantially prohibit waivers of unasserted ADEA claims and impose significant restrictions on waivers of asserted ADEA claims.[69]

---

[60]*Id.* at 128, 36 FEP at 985 (quoting Air Line Pilots Ass'n v. Trans World Airlines, 713 F.2d 940 (2d Cir. 1983), *aff'd in pertinent part,* 469 U.S. 111, 36 FEP 977 (1985)). *See* Chapter 14 (Age) and Chapter 38 (Monetary Relief).

[61]36 FEP at 985.

[62]*See, e.g.,* Ridenour v. Lawson Co., 791 F.2d 52, 40 FEP 1455 (6th Cir. 1986).

[63]787 F.2d 1039, 40 FEP 807 (6th Cir.) (en banc), *cert. denied,* 479 U.S. 850, 41 FEP 1712 (1986).

[64]*See, e.g.,* Scott v. Gulf Oil Corp., 754 F.2d 1499, 1503–04 (9th Cir. 1985); Blau v. Del Monte Corp., 748 F.2d 1348 (9th Cir. 1984), *cert. denied,* 474 U.S. 865 (1985); Donovan v. Dillingham, 688 F.2d 1367, 1370–73 (11th Cir. 1982). Subject to ERISA requirements, employers may adopt and publish termination allowance plans incorporating severance payments computed on standard formulas causing severance payments to increase with increasing salary or seniority or both. Such termination allowance plans are intended both to satisfy ERISA requirements of publication and fair administration and ADEA requirements that severance payments not be computed or paid on a discriminatory basis with respect to age.

[65]*See* Chapter 23 (Related Causes of Action).

[66]*See* Chapter 14 (Age) at notes 202–213 for a review of this issue.

[67]*See* Chapter 14 (Age) at note 210. Whether a particular factual situation constitutes a "voluntary and knowing waiver" is the source of much litigation. *See* Chapter 14 (Age), note 214.

[68]Cassino v. Reichhold Chems., 817 F.2d 1338, 47 FEP 865 (9th Cir. 1987), *cert. denied,* 484 U.S. _____, 47 FEP 1776 (1988). *See* Chapter 14 (Age) at note 217.

[69]*See* Age Discrimination in Employment Waiver Protection Act, S. 54 and HR 1432, 101st Cong., 1st Sess. (1989).

## Sex Discrimination

In a series of widely noted decisions, courts have addressed some of the major issues arising from the increased participation of women in the workplace. The Supreme Court issued its first major decision on sexual harassment in *Meritor Savings Bank v. Vinson,* [70] holding that an employer could be liable for harassment based either on a *quid pro quo* exchange of sexual favors for employment benefits, or on maintenance of a working environment which is pervasively hostile or abusive toward women. The Court held that a plaintiff's apparent consent to participation in sexual activities will not be a defense if the sexual advances were in fact unwelcome. [71] The Court also stated that in determining whether the employer would be liable for the harassing supervisor's transgressions, agency principles would be considered. [72] While not resolving the standard governing employer liability, the *Vinson* Court observed that an employer would be better insulated from liability if it had a specific policy proscribing sexual harassment and a grievance procedure permitting initial complaint to someone other than the person who allegedly harassed the complaining employee. [73] *Vinson* has thus clarified that: (1) liability for sexual harassment may be established without "economic" or "tangible" losses from alleged discrimination, (2) actionable harassment must be "sufficiently severe or pervasive 'to alter the conditions of [the victim's] employment and create an abusive working environment,' " [74] (3) apparently voluntary participation in sexual activities is not controlling, because the factual question will remain whether alleged sexual advances were "unwelcome," [75] and (4) appropriate employer policies should include publication of express opposition to sexual harassment and a grievance procedure permitting complaining employees to bypass the alleged harassing supervisor. [76] Following *Vinson,* the EEOC issued a Guidance Memorandum on Sexual Harassment, [77] and federal appellate courts have resolved numerous other issues. [78]

A divided Supreme Court held in *California Federal Savings & Loan Association v. Guerra* [79] that Title VII does not preempt a California statute requiring employers to provide up to four months unpaid leave to female

---

[70] 477 U.S. 57, 40 FEP 1822 (1986).

[71] *Id.,* 40 FEP at 1827.

[72] *Id.,* 40 FEP at 1829.

[73] *Id.*

[74] *Id.,* 40 FEP at 1827 (quoting Henson v. City of Dundee, 682 F.2d 897, 904, 29 FEP 787, 793 (11th Cir. 1982)).

[75] *Id.,* 40 FEP at 1827.

[76] *Id.,* 40 FEP at 1829.

[77] EEOC Policy Guidance on Sexual Harassment, reproduced at 401 FEP 6081 and 201 DAILY LAB. REP. E-1 (BNA, Oct. 18, 1988) (EEOC states that employers can insulate themselves from apparent authority of supervisors by implementing and publicizing policy expressly opposing sexual harassment and including an effective complaint procedure that does not require the victim to complain first to the allegedly offending supervisor; "[w]hen employees know that recourse is available, they cannot reasonably believe that a harassing work environment is authorized or condoned by the employer." *Id.* at E-7. EEOC also states that personnel policies will not insulate employers from quid pro quo sexual harassment charges, because "no matter what the employer's policy, the employer is always liable for any supervisory actions that affect the victim's employment status, such as hiring, firing, promotion or pay." *Id.* at n.32. The employer's sexual harassment policy "should ensure confidentiality as much as possible." *Id.* at E-7.).

[78] *See* Chapter 12 (Sex).

[79] 479 U.S. 272, 42 FEP 1073 (1987), *aff'g* 758 F.2d 390, 37 FEP 849 (9th Cir. 1985).

employees disabled by pregnancy, childbirth, or related medical conditions. The Court expressly endorsed the Ninth Circuit's conclusion that "Congress intended the [Pregnancy Discrimination Act] to be 'a floor beneath which pregnancy disability benefits may not drop—not a ceiling above which they may not rise.' "[80]

The Seventh and Ninth circuits each have rejected contentions that Title VII not only prohibits intentional sex discrimination in compensation, but also requires payment on a theory of "comparable worth." In *Nurses, ANA v. Illinois,* [81] the Seventh Circuit held that a state's failure to implement the results of a comparable worth study cannot be a basis for Title VII liability, noting that the theory of comparable worth "is not a legal concept, but a shorthand expression for the movement to raise the ratio of wages in traditionally women's jobs to wages in traditionally men's jobs."[82] In *State, County & Municipal Employees (AFSCME) v. Washington,* [83] the state employer had conducted its own study and concluded that its market-based prevailing wage policies had led to a compensation system in which jobs held predominantly by women were paid 20 percent less than jobs of comparable worth held predominantly by men. Washington had taken some steps to adjust these wage differences but had not funded the full implementation of this study's conclusions. The Ninth Circuit held that Washington had no obligation to do so under Title VII, expressly rejecting the union's contention that the state had become "committed to implement a new system of compensation based on comparable worth as defined by the study." The court held that "[i]t is insufficient for a plaintiff alleging discrimination under the disparate treatment theory to show the employer was merely aware of the adverse consequences the policy would have on a protected group," because the "plaintiff must show the employer chose the particular policy because of its effect on members of a protected class."[84]

Both the *Nurses'* and *AFSCME* decisions expressly rejected assertions that Title VII obliges employers to depart from market-based compensation.[85] It appears that comparable worth advocates are now left to pursue their cause chiefly in state forums, in collective bargaining, and in proposals for new legislation.

Circumstantial proof of intentional pay discrimination was given further definition by a unanimous Supreme Court in *Bazemore v. Friday.* [86] Although *Bazemore* involved race discrimination in compensation, it has wider implications for circumstantial proof of compensation discrimination in other contexts. In *Bazemore,* the Court held that a public employer was liable under Title VII for failing to eliminate color-based post-1972 salary disparities which arose from pre-1972 acts of employment discrimination against blacks—and thus based Title VII liability on continuation in the

---

[80]*Id.,* 42 FEP at 1079 (quoting 758 F.2d at 396, 37 FEP at 852).
[81]783 F.2d 716, 40 FEP 244 (7th Cir. 1986).
[82]*Id.* at 719, 40 FEP at 246.
[83]770 F.2d 1401, 38 FEP 1353, 1357, 1359–60 (9th Cir. 1985).
[84]*Id.,* 38 FEP at 1357.
[85]*See, e.g.,* State, County & Mun. Employees v. Washington, 770 F.2d 1401, 38 FEP 1353, 1359 (9th Cir. 1985) ("We find nothing in the language of Title VII or its legislative history to indicate Congress intended to abrogate fundamental economic principles such as the laws of supply and demand or to prevent employers from competing in the labor market.").
[86]478 U.S. 385, 41 FEP 92 (1986).

present of pre-Act employment discrimination. The *Bazemore* Court remanded for further proceedings, observing that each week's paycheck is a new violation of Title VII "regardless of the fact that this pattern was begun prior to the effective date of Title VII" and that "the present salary structure, . . . is illegal [, even though] it is a mere continuation of the pre-1965 discriminatory pay structure."[87]

The Court held in *Arizona Governing Committee v. Norris*[88] that under Title VII an employer may not provide lower periodic retirement benefits to female employees than to male employees when both sexes have made equal contributions toward a pension plan. This extension in *Norris* of the Court's 1978 ruling in *City of Los Angeles, Department of Water & Power v. Manhart*[89] effectively prohibits employer use of sex-based actuarial tables, whether directly or through the purchase of insurance funding a deferred compensation plan on sex-based actuarial assumptions.[90]

Two appellate cases applied Title VII to women engaged in professional employment. The Supreme Court held in *Hishon v. King & Spalding*[91] that Title VII prohibits sex discrimination in consideration for admission to law partnerships. A unanimous Court held that a female associate may sue a law firm under Title VII for allegedly discriminating against her on the basis of sex in considering her for partnership, where the firm had used the prospect of partnership to encourage lawyers to join the firm, allegedly had represented to the plaintiff that advancement to partnership after five or six years was "a matter of course" for associates with satisfactory evaluations, had promised that associates would be considered on a "fair and equal basis," and where the plaintiff had relied on these representations when she accepted employment with the firm.[92]

As this Supplement went to press, the Supreme Court issued its fragmented decision in *Price Waterhouse v. Hopkins,*[93] defining burdens of proof in a mixed-motive Title VII case. At trial, Ann Hopkins had persuaded the district court that sexual stereotypings in some partner evaluations had

---

[87]*Id.,* 41 FEP at 97, 97 n.6. In subsequent compensation discrimination cases, the Seventh and Eleventh circuits have split on whether employers may defend compensation differentials between incumbent male and female employees as based on a "factor other than sex" where they arise from the perpetuation of previous salaries upon transfer to new positions. *Compare* Glenn v. General Motors Corp., 841 F.2d 1567, 46 FEP 1331 (11th Cir.), *cert. denied,* 488 U.S. ____, 48 FEP 232 (1988) (employer paid men transferring to job position from hourly positions more than it paid women because of employer's policy of not reducing pay upon transfer to a salaried position; the employer policy does not qualify as "factor other than sex" and cannot be a defense to compensation discrimination; rejects analysis of Seventh Circuit's *Covington* decision) *with* Covington v. Southern Ill. Univ., 816 F.2d 317, 43 FEP 839 (7th Cir.), *cert. denied,* 484 U.S. 848, 44 FEP 1672 (1987) (university paid a female art advisor less than male who had been reassigned to art advisory position from more highly paid instructor position; policy of not reducing faculty member's salary on assignment change is "factor other than sex" and a defense to compensation discrimination, even where factor is unrelated to job performance or job requirements).

[88]463 U.S. 1073, 32 FEP 233 (1983).

[89]435 U.S. 702, 17 FEP 395 (1978), reproduced at p. 372 of the Second Edition.

[90]The *Norris* Court held that its decision would apply only prospectively to cover benefits derived from contributions made after the judgment, and delayed the effective date of the judgment until August 1, 1983. In *Florida v. Long,* 487 U.S. ____, 47 FEP 7 (1988), the Court held that individuals who retired after *Manhart* but before *Norris* were not entitled to an upward adjustment in their pensions.

[91]467 U.S. 69, 34 FEP 1406 (1984), *rev'g and remanding* 678 F.2d 1022, 29 FEP 51 (11th Cir. 1982).

[92]*Id.,* 467 U.S. at 72, 34 FEP at 1408.

[93]57 USLW 4469, 49 FEP 954 (1989). *Hopkins* was decided too late for discussion elsewhere in this Supplement, but its wide relevance must be carefully considered, especially with respect to issues concerning proof, sex discrimination, constructive discharge, and subjective factors. *Hopkins* will be discussed comprehensively in the next Supplement.

contributed to her rejection for partnership. Partners commenting on her candidacy had referred, for example, to her supposed need for a "course at charm school" and suggested that she "may have overcompensated for being a woman." However, Price Waterhouse had demonstrated that its partnership decision was also based on Hopkins' interpersonal difficulties at work, and these were held at trial and on appeal to be legitimate factors.[94] Six Justices concurred that Hopkins had sufficiently established Price Waterhouse's reliance on the impermissible factor of gender to require that Price Waterhouse prove, by a preponderance of the evidence, that the partnership decision would have been the same if based on wholly lawful factors Price Waterhouse actually considered. However, no majority opinion defined what a Title VII plaintiff must show to shift this burden of persuasion—proof by a preponderance "that her gender played a motivating part in an employment decision" (Justice Brennan's plurality opinion) or that the illegitimate criterion was a *"substantial* factor" in the employment decision (separate opinions by Justices White and O'Connor, concurring in the judgment).[95]

Courts have continued to reach varying results in cases involving pregnancy as a claimed BFOQ. The Eleventh Circuit has held that potential harm to a fetus or potential offspring of a female employee is not a BFOQ defense unless the employer "shows a direct relationship between the policy and the actual ability of a pregnant or fertile female to perform her job."[96] The Fifth Circuit has held that nonpregnancy could be reasonably necessary for passenger safety and therefore could be a legitimate BFOQ for the position of flight attendant.[97]

## National Origin and Citizenship

The Immigration Reform and Control Act of 1986[98] has transformed radically the role of employers in immigration matters. Employers now must verify that applicants and new employees either are citizens or are otherwise legally entitled to work in the United States.[99] In addition, employers may

---

[94]The Circuit Court for the District of Columbia had held that Hopkins' pass over for partnership and the later decision by her office's partners not to renominate her amounted to constructive discharge in view of her objectives and expectations. Price Waterhouse did not challenge this conclusion. 49 FEP at 956 n.1. The Supreme Court reversed and remanded, because Price Waterhouse had been required to prove by "clear and convincing evidence" that it would have made the same decision without taking gender into account. *Id.* at 966.

[95]As to burdens of proof, the Justices stated: "[W]hen a plaintiff in a Title VII case proves that her gender played a motivating part in an employment decision, the defendant may avoid a finding of liability only by proving by a preponderance of the evidence that it would have made the same decision even if it had not taken the plaintiff's gender into account[,]" (Brennan, Marshall, Blackmun, and Stevens, JJ.), 49 FEP at 966; "in order to justify shifting the burden on the issue of causation to the defendant, a disparate treatment plaintiff must show by direct evidence that an illegitimate criterion was a substantial factor in the decision," (O'Connor, J., concurring in judgment), *id.* at 973; "as Justice O'Connor states, "[the plaintiff's] burden was to show that the unlawful motive was a substantial factor in the adverse employment action," (White, J., concurring in judgment), *id.* at 906; "[t]he shift in the burden of persuasion occurs only where a plaintiff proves by direct evidence that an unlawful motive was a substantial factor actually relied upon in making the decision," (Kennedy, Rehnquist, and Scalia, JJ., dissenting and characterizing the Court's holding), *id.* at 975. Justice White would not require that the employer produce objective evidence supporting its "makes no difference" burden. *Id.* at 967.

[96]Hayes v. Shelby Memorial Hosp., 726 F.2d 1543, 1549, 34 FEP 444, 449 (11th Cir. 1984).

[97]Levin v. Delta Air Lines, 730 F.2d 994, 34 FEP 1192 (5th Cir. 1984), *aff'g* 34 FEP 1187 (S.D. Tex. 1982).

[98]Pub. L. No. 99-603, 100 Stat. 3359 (1986) (codified in scattered sections of 7, 8, 18, 20, and 24 U.S.C.A. (West Supp. 1988)).

[99]8 U.S.C. § 1324a.

not discriminate against individuals qualified to work in the United States on the basis of citizenship.[100] The integration of these requirements with Title VII obligations has required employers comprehensively to examine and revise their personnel practices.

In a pair of 1987 decisions, *St. Francis College v. Al-Khazraji*[101] and *Shaare Tefila Congregation v. Cobb,*[102] the Supreme Court held that 42 U.S.C. § 1981 covered allegations of discrimination based on "ancestry or ethnic characteristics."[103] The Fifth Circuit has now abandoned its earlier position that § 1981 prohibits discrimination based on alienage.[104]

The Ninth Circuit has twice addressed "English-only" rules. The court upheld as a non-discriminatory programming decision a radio station's order that a bilingual employee stop speaking Spanish on the air, in *Jurado v. 11-50 Corp.,*[105] while affirming, in *Gutierrez v. Municipal Court, County of L.A.,*[106] the issuance of a preliminary injunction restraining enforcement of an "English-only" requirement for state court employees on the grounds the employees had established a likelihood of eventual success on the merits and the possibility of irreparable injury. In *Gutierrez,* the Ninth Circuit stated that English-only rules are burdensome conditions of employment that frequently mask national origin discrimination and must be carefully scrutinized.

## Handicap

With *School Board of Nassau County v. Arline,*[107] the Supreme Court has led a developing line of authority holding that persons suffering from a contagious disease—tuberculosis in *Arline*—can be handicapped and thus entitled to reasonable accommodation by employers covered by the Vocational Rehabilitation Act of 1973 so long as they remain "qualified" to perform the duties of their positions. In *Arline,* the Court held that under § 504 of the Rehabilitation Act the following four factors must be considered in determining whether a handicapped person with a contagious disease remains "qualified" to perform the major elements of her or his job: (1) how the disease is transmitted, (2) how long the carrier remains infectious, (3) the severity of the potential harm to third persons, and (4) the probabilities that the disease will be transmitted and will cause harm.[108] The result of the *Arline* decision was codified by House and Senate vote on March 22, 1988, overriding a presidential veto and declaring that persons with contagious diseases are protected under § 504.[109] The Ninth Circuit has held in *Chalk v. United States District Court, Central District of California*[110] that a teacher suffering from AIDS must be returned to the classroom, because an overwhelming consensus of medical opinion establishes that casual contact between chil-

---

[100]8 U.S.C. § 1324b.

[101]481 U.S. 604, 43 FEP 1305 (1987).

[102]481 U.S. 615, 43 FEP 1309 (1987).

[103]*Supra* note 101, 43 FEP at 1308; *supra* note 102, 43 FEP at 1310.

[104]Bhandari v. First Nat'l Bank of Commerce, 829 F.2d 1343, 45 FEP 126 (5th Cir. 1987) (en banc), overruling Guerra v. Manchester Terminal Corp., 498 F.2d 641, 8 FEP 433 (5th Cir. 1974).

[105]813 F.2d 1406, 43 FEP 870 (9th Cir. 1987).

[106]838 F.2d 1031 (9th Cir. 1988).

[107]480 U.S. 273, 43 FEP 81 (1987).

[108]*Id.,* 43 FEP at 87.

[109]Civil Rights Restoration Act of 1987, Pub. L. 100-259, § 9, 102 Stat. 28, 31 (codified in pertinent part at 29 U.S.C. § 706).

[110]840 F.2d 701, 46 FEP 279 (9th Cir. 1988).

dren and AIDS victims is not dangerous, and AIDS therefore is a handicap under the Rehabilitation Act. California appears to be reaching a similar result under the California Fair Employment and Housing Act.[111]

Determining whether a person is handicapped continues to be an issue. In *Jasany v. United States Postal Service,*[112] the Sixth Circuit held that an individual is not limited in a "major life activity" under the Rehabilitation Act unless the physical or mental impairment affects a range of jobs. In *Jasany,* an individual who suffered from eye strain while working on a letter-sorting machine was held not protected as a handicapped person under the Rehabilitation Act because the impairment was job-specific.[113]

The Department of Labor has continued to insist that alleged disabilities based on back problems must be shown to cause a reasonable probability of substantial present harm in order to justify a job requirement that screens out otherwise qualified handicapped persons.[114]

The Supreme Court held in *Atascadero State Hospital v. Scanlon*[115] that the Eleventh Amendment to the U.S. Constitution precluded suit in federal court against the State of California for allegedly denying employment on the basis of handicap in violation of the federal Rehabilitation Act. The Court held that California did not lose its immunity by accepting federal financial assistance and that Congress had not intended to exercise its Fourteenth Amendment power to override California's constitutional immunity.[116] The Seventh Circuit has joined other circuits holding that no private right of action exists under § 503, and has also held that the decision of the Department of Labor on a § 503 claim is not reviewable.[117] The Supreme Court has held that actions under § 504 are not limited to circumstances in which the primary objective of the federal financial assistance is to provide employment.[118]

## Religious Preference

The Supreme Court held in *Ansonia Board of Education v. Philbrook*[119] that an employer could satisfy its duty of accommodating religious preferences by offering an accommodation which is in fact reasonable, even if the employer rejects other reasonable accommodations which the employee prefers. The Court rejected EEOC guidelines which stated that the employer

---

[111] *See* Raytheon Co. v. Fair Employment & Hous. Comm'n, 46 FEP 1089 (Cal. Super. Ct. 1988) (affirming on mandamus review a determination of the Fair Employment and Housing Commission that AIDS is a handicap, that medical consensus has established that casual contact foreseeable in industrial setting cannot transmit AIDS virus, that anticipated anxiety among co-workers that might be detrimental to company morale is insufficient basis for keeping an AIDS victim from work, and that such persons must be permitted to remain in employment as long as they are able to do their jobs).

[112] 755 F.2d 1244, 37 FEP 210 (6th Cir. 1985).

[113] *Id.,* 37 FEP at 215.

[114] *See* OFCCP v. Texas Indus., 47 FEP 18 (1988) (Secretary of Labor determined that despite evidence that individual's back problems made her a safety risk as truck driver, employer did not establish reasonable probability she would suffer impairment that would cause her to lose control while driving).

[115] 473 U.S. 234, 38 FEP 97 (1985).

[116] *Id.,* 38 FEP at 102.

[117] Andrews v. Consolidated Rail Corp., 831 F.2d 678, 44 FEP 786 (7th Cir. 1987).

[118] Consolidated Rail Corp. v. Darrone, 465 U.S. 624, 34 FEP 79 (1984).

[119] 479 U.S. 60, 42 FEP 359 (1986).

must accept any alternative offered by the employee which does not impose undue hardship.[120]

The Ninth Circuit has twice upheld the reasonableness of accommodations provided in the context of collective bargaining relationships. In *Hudson v. Western Airlines*[121] the Ninth Circuit approved, as a reasonable accommodation to a Sabbatarian, a provision in a collective bargaining agreement for vacation and leave time which allowed flight attendants to trade blocks of flights, days off, specific trips and transfers to other bases. The Court held that the attendant's failure to use the reasonable means available to her under the agreement undermined her claim that her employer had violated Title VII by discharging her for refusing a flight assignment that would have required her to work on her Sabbath. The Ninth Circuit revisited the question of conscientious religious objections to union dues payments in *Machinists v. Boeing Co.,*[122] holding that employees who are subject to union-security provisions in a collective bargaining agreement and have religious objections to labor unions may contribute to charities instead of paying union dues.[123] The Fourth Circuit upheld an employer's discharge of a Sabbatarian without an attempted accommodation in *EEOC v. Ithaca Industries,*[124] where the employee proposed, as an accommodation, that the employee be exempt from Sunday work and that other employees be required to take Sunday shifts or be discharged.

### Scored Tests

The Uniform Guidelines on Employee Selection Procedures (Uniform Guidelines) continue to be questioned. The General Accounting Office (GAO) has responded to "public criticisms of the Guidelines by some of their users" by calling for their review and revision.[125] In July 1984 the EEOC voted to begin a comprehensive review of the Guidelines.[126] The American Psychological Association (APA) published a revision of its 1974 testing standards during 1985.[127] The APA's Division of Industrial and Organizational Psychology revised its principles for validation and the use of personnel selection procedures in 1987.[128] Although several cases reflect a continuing general acceptance of the principles of the Uniform Guidelines,[129] the

---

[120]*Id.,* 42 FEP at 363.

[121]851 F.2d 261, 47 FEP 295 (9th Cir. 1988).

[122]833 F.2d 165, 45 FEP 791 (9th Cir. 1987).

[123]The Court held that the charitable contribution provision in § 19 of the Labor-Management Relations Act, 29 U.S.C. § 169, providing for a charitable contribution substitute only for employees who are members of religious denominations historically objecting to labor unions, did not control the scope of reasonable accommodations under § 701(j) of Title VII, 42 U.S.C. § 2000e(j).

[124]829 F.2d 519, 44 FEP 1575 (4th Cir. 1987).

[125]General Accounting Office, *Uniform Guidelines on Employee Selection Procedures Should be Reviewed and Revised,* Rep. No. GAO/FPCD-82-86 (July 30, 1982), reviewed in 150 DAILY LAB. REP. A-1 (BNA, Aug. 4, 1982); *see also* other criticism noted in Chapter 4 (Scored Tests) at note 16 and accompanying text.

[126]*See* 242 DAILY LAB. REP. D-1 (BNA, Dec. 17, 1984); 221 DAILY LAB. REP. A-6 (BNA, Nov. 15, 1984); *see also* Chapter 4 (Scored Tests) at note 17 and accompanying text.

[127]American Psychological Association, Standards for Educational and Psychological Testing (1985). *See* 79 DAILY LAB. REP. A-5 (BNA, Apr. 24, 1984); 93 DAILY LAB. REP. A-4 (BNA, May 12, 1983); *see also* Chapter 4 (Scored Tests) at note 19 and accompanying text.

[128]*Principles for the Validation and Use of Personnel Selection Procedures* (3d ed. 1987).

[129]Nash v. Consolidated City of Jacksonville, Duval County, Fla., 763 F.2d 1393, 1395, 38 FEP 151, 152 (11th Cir. 1985) (use of the "80% rule" under 29 C.F.R. § 1607.4(d) (1985), "as well as statistical

Ninth Circuit held in *Clady v. County of Los Angeles*[130] that the Uniform Guidelines are not legally binding, were not promulgated as regulations, and do not have the force of law.

The Fifth and Seventh circuits have suggested that job-relatedness may be established by demonstrating a "manifest and legitimate business relationship" between the challenged tests and the jobs for which they were used,[131] and by evidence showing that the test "measures traits that are significantly related to the applicant's ability to perform the job."[132] Courts generally continue to hold that a validation study may provide a valid defense to a disparate impact claim even though the study does not fully comply with the Uniform Guidelines.[133] Expert testimony has been questioned, however, where the expert had not seen the actual text of the examination and had never correlated the test with successful job performance.[134]

The question whether race-conscious remedies may be utilized after a finding of prior testing discrimination continues to generate controversy. The Fifth Circuit held in *Williams v. City of New Orleans*[135] that Title VII does not prohibit use of a quota to remedy past discrimination, even though the quota's benefits are not limited to actual victims. The Sixth Circuit held a proposed consent decree illegal and contrary to the public interest because the decree relied unduly upon promotion examinations that had been shown to have an adverse impact.[136] The Second Circuit remanded one challenged consent decree with a race-conscious remedy for a determination whether the proposed remedy unnecessarily trampled upon the interests of nonminority employees[137] under the standards announced in *Steelworkers v. Weber.*[138]

---

evidence produced by [plaintiff's] expert witness," was sufficient to establish prima facie case of discriminatory impact); Hill v. Metropolitan Atlanta Rapid Transit Auth., 591 F. Supp. 125, 45 FEP 782 (N.D. Ga. 1984), *aff'd in part, rev'd and remanded in part,* 841 F.2d 1533, 46 FEP 930 (11th Cir. 1988) (in summary judgment posture, plaintiff fails to establish adverse impact where pass rate for minority group is over 80% of pass rate of majority group taking same test); Evans v. City of Evanston, 621 F. Supp. 710, 712, 37 FEP 1290, 1292 (N.D. Ill. 1985) (§ 4(d) of Uniform Guidelines cited as "evidence" of adverse impact); Reid v. New York, 570 F. Supp. 1003, 1005–6, 38 FEP 266, 267–68 (S.D.N.Y. 1983) (violation of 80% rule held sufficient evidence of discrimination to show "probability of success on the merits" in approving class action consent decree); Brunet v. City of Columbus, 642 F. Supp. 1214, 1227, 42 FEP 1846, 1857 (S.D. Ohio 1986), *cert. denied,* 485 U.S. _____, 46 FEP 1080 (1988); Police Officers for Equal Rights v. City of Columbus, 644 F. Supp. 393, 407, 42 FEP 1752, 1763 (S.D. Ohio 1985); *see also* Chapter 4 (Scored Tests) at note 23 and accompanying text.

[130]770 F.2d 1421, 38 FEP 1575 (9th Cir. 1985), *cert. denied,* 475 U.S. 1109, 40 FEP 792 (1986). *But see* Allen v. Isaac, 39 FEP 1142, 1157 (N.D. Ill. 1986); Brunet v. City of Columbus, 642 F. Supp. 1214, 1236–37, 42 FEP 1846, 1865 (S.D. Ohio 1986), *cert. denied,* 485 U.S. _____, 46 FEP 1080 (1988).

[131]Rivera v. City of Wichita Falls, 665 F.2d 531, 537, 27 FEP 1352, 1357 (5th Cir. 1982); Cormier v. P.P.G. Indus., 702 F.2d 567, 568, 31 FEP 1039 (5th Cir. 1983); *see also* Chapter 4 (Scored Tests) at notes 58 and 61 and accompanying text.

[132]Gillespie v. Wisconsin, 771 F.2d 1035, 1040, 38 FEP 1487, 1490 (7th Cir. 1985), *cert. denied,* 474 U.S. 1083, 39 FEP 1424 (1986); *see* Watson v. Fort Worth Bank & Trust, 487 U.S. _____, 47 FEP 102 (1988); *see also* Chapter 4 (Scored Tests) at note 62 and accompanying text.

[133]Clady v. County of Los Angeles, *supra* note 130; *see also* Chapter 4 (Scored Tests) at note 64 and accompanying text. *But see* Allen v. Isaac, *supra* note 130; Brunet v. City of Columbus, *supra* note 129.

[134]Nash v. Consolidated City of Jacksonville, Duval County, Fla., *supra* note 129; *see also* Chapter 4 (Scored Tests) at Section IX.A.

[135]729 F.2d 1554, 34 FEP 1009 (5th Cir. 1984) (en banc), *appeal dismissed,* 763 F.2d 667 (5th Cir. 1985); *see infra* Chapter 4 at note 96 and accompanying text; *see also supra* notes 33 through 52 and accompanying text for discussion of affirmative action and reverse discrimination, including Supreme Court decisions post-dating decisions cited in this paragraph.

[136]Williams v. Vukovich, 720 F.2d 909, 925–26, 33 FEP 238, 251–52 (6th Cir. 1983); *see infra* Chapter 4 at note 97 and accompanying text.

[137]Bushey v. New York State Civil Serv. Comm'n, 733 F.2d 220, 228, 34 FEP 1065, 1071–72 (2nd Cir. 1984), *cert. denied,* 469 U.S. 1117, 36 FEP 1166 (1985); *see also infra* Chapter 4 at notes 100–102 and accompanying text.

[138]443 U.S. 193, 20 FEP 1 (1979); *see infra* Chapter 24.

## Seniority

*California Brewers Association v. Bryant*[139] continues to govern the determination whether employment systems are seniority systems within the meaning of § 703(h).[140] Several courts have applied the factors set forth in *James v. Stockham Valves & Fittings Co.*[141] to determine under § 703(h) that a seniority provision is[142] or is not[143] bona fide.

Major decisions affecting seniority under Title VII during the period covered by this Supplement have addressed the relationship between court-ordered or voluntarily adopted quotas and goals adopted as part of Title VII consent decrees or affirmative action plans. The Supreme Court held in *Firefighters Local 1784 v. Stotts*[144] that a court could not unilaterally modify a consent decree to override a collectively bargained bona fide seniority system for the purpose of insulating recently hired minorities from a last-hired, first-fired seniority layoff rule. The Court reached the same result in *Wygant v. Jackson Board of Education,*[145] where the Court invalidated as unconstitutional state action a collectively bargained affirmative action provision between a public school board and a teacher's union that apportioned layoffs between minority and nonminority employees in order to preserve the nonminority work force representation attained under an affirmative action program. The Court also clarified in *Firefighters Local 93 v. City of Cleveland*[146] that a consent decree may apportion certain promotions to minority candidates, even though a court could not under § 706(g) of Title VII impose such apportionment if the case were litigated to judgment, because § 706(g) "by itself does not restrict the ability of employers or unions to enter into voluntary agreements [such as consent decrees] providing for race-conscious remedial action."[147] The Court distinguished *Stotts* because it involved an involuntary modification of a consent decree. Finally, in *Sheet Metal Workers*

---

[139]444 U.S. 598, 22 FEP 1 (1980).

[140]Allen v. Prince George's County, Md., 737 F.2d 1299, 38 FEP 1220 (4th Cir. 1984) (essence of seniority system is preference for longer employed person, and policy of filling vacancies from within by promotion or transfer before resorting to new hires is "seniority system"); United States v. City of Cincinnati, 771 F.2d 161, 38 FEP 1402 (6th Cir. 1985) (where employer's rule provided that persons hired on same day would be given seniority rankings based on pre-employment test scores, tie-breaking rule was merely an appendage and not a seniority system under § 703(h); relief granted to minority and female employees laid off based on test score rankings).

[141]559 F.2d 310, 15 FEP 827 (5th Cir. 1977), *cert. denied,* 434 U.S. 1034, 16 FEP 501 (1978).

[142]Gantlin v. Westvaco Corp., 526 F. Supp. 1356, 29 FEP 1406 (D.S.C. 1981), *aff'd,* 734 F.2d 980, 34 FEP 1316 (4th Cir. 1984) (seniority system bona fide under § 703(h) despite tripartite seniority allocation (job, department, and mill) where rational breakdown and no evidence of improper motive); Bernard v. Gulf Oil Corp., 643 F. Supp. 1494 (E.D. Tex. 1986), *aff'd in part, vacated and remanded in part,* 841 F.2d 547 (5th Cir. 1988) (district court upheld seniority provision providing one-day seniority as craftsmen for laborers in previously all-black unit wishing to transfer to previously all-white craft division; case remanded for determination of post-Act bona fides).

[143]United States v. Georgia Power Co., 695 F.2d 890, 30 FEP 1305 (5th Cir. 1983) (on remand for reconsideration in light of *Pullman-Standard v. Swint,* 456 U.S. 273, 28 FEP 1073 (1982), Fifth Circuit reaffirmed prior holding that (1) seniority system penalized blacks more than whites, (2) unequal treatment was not attributable to legitimate division of bargaining units, and (3) seniority system originated in a period of discrimination and was maintained for unlawful purpose); *see also* Wattleton v. Boilermakers Local 1509, 686 F.2d 586, 29 FEP 1389 (7th Cir. 1982), *cert. denied,* 459 U.S. 1208, 30 FEP 1856 (1983) (seniority system negotiated and maintained for purpose of excluding blacks from bargaining unit, and changed when employer first began to hire blacks, unlawful because resulted in transfers of whites to bargaining unit jobs with full carryover seniority, while blacks were discouraged and prohibited from doing so); *see also* Chapter 3.

[144]467 U.S. 561, 34 FEP 1702 (1984).

[145]476 U.S. 267, 40 FEP 1321 (1986).

[146]478 U.S. 501, 41 FEP 139 (1986).

[147]*Id.,* 41 FEP at 148.

*Local 28 v. EEOC,*[148] the Court held that a court may under certain appropriate circumstances order preferential relief benefiting individuals who are not actual victims of discrimination as a remedy for violations of Title VII, without violating either § 706(g) or the Equal Protection Clause, and that such relief may be necessary where an employer's reputation for employment discrimination discourages minorities from seeking available employment, or where such relief may operate as an interim measure until nondiscriminatory hiring and promotion procedures can be developed and implemented.[149]

## Preemption and Related Causes of Action

Congress did not give Title VII the preemptive effect enjoyed by the Labor Management Relations Act[150] and by the Employee Retirement Income Security Act.[151] Differences of procedure and remedy between Title VII and state claims have led to multiple litigation. These tendencies have been accelerated by the explosive expansion of employment litigation on wrongful termination and collateral tort theories under state law. Courts continue to grapple with the application of the doctrines of *res judicata* and collateral estoppel in the litigation of employment claims in multiple forums, particularly following the Supreme Court's decisions in *Kremer v. Chemical Construction Corp.,*[152] *Migra v. Warren City School District Board of Education,*[153] and *McDonald v. City of West Branch, Michigan.*[154] In contrast to these attempts to limit multiple litigation of employment-related claims, the Supreme Court held in *Cooper v. Federal Reserve Bank of Richmond*[155] that a judgment for an employer in an employment discrimination class action does not preclude individual class members from bringing subsequent actions raising individual claims of discrimination.[156] The Court also ratified multiple litigation of some employment claims in *University of Tennessee v. Elliot,*[157] holding that a state administrative law judge's determination that a discharge was free of race bias did not preclude a later Title VII action, though it did foreclose claims under 42 U.S.C. §§ 1981 and 1983.[158]

Common law developments within the several states continue to expand

---

[148]478 U.S. 421, 41 FEP 107 (1986); *see* United States v. Paradise, 480 U.S. 149, 43 FEP 1 (1987) (upholding consent decree that instituted promotion quota for blacks who had not been identified as actual victims of discrimination, where state employer had long and pervasive history of discrimination and failure to comply with court-ordered remedies and promotion quota was enforced as part of court's broad remedial authority to require compliance with its own decree).

[149]41 FEP at 117–18.

[150]*See* § 301, Labor Management Relations Act, 29 U.S.C. 185(a); Allis-Chalmers Corp. v. Lueck, 471 U.S. 202, 118 LRRM 3345 (1985).

[151]*See* § 514, Employee Retirement Income Security Act of 1974, as amended, 29 U.S.C. § 1144; Shaw v. Delta Air Lines, 463 U.S. 85, 32 FEP 121 (1983); Blau v. Del Monte Corp., 748 F.2d 1348, 5 EBC 2744 (9th Cir. 1984), *cert. denied,* 474 U.S. 865 (1985).

[152]456 U.S. 461, 28 FEP 1412 (1982) (state court review of state administrative decision must be given full faith and credit in subsequent Title VII suit).

[153]465 U.S. 75, 33 FEP 1345 (1984) (plaintiff barred by *res judicata* from raising §§ 1983 and 1985 claims in federal lawsuit that she failed to raise in prior state court action for breach of employment contract).

[154]466 U.S. 284, 115 LRRM 3646 (1984); *see also* Chapter 29 (Election and Exhaustion of Remedies) (arbitration award under collective bargaining agreement does not preclude a § 1983 claim).

[155]467 U.S. 867, 35 FEP 1 (1984).

[156]*See* Chapters 29 (Election and Exhaustion of Remedies) and 34 (Class Action).

[157]478 U.S. 788, 41 FEP 177 (1986).

[158]The Court distinguished Title VII because it expressly provides that the EEOC give weight to state administrative rulings, from which the Court inferred that Title VII was not intended to be preclusive.

the opportunities for plaintiffs to allege employment-related contract and tort claims. California has continued to be a pace-setting jurisdiction. In *Foley v. Interactive Data Corp.,* [159] the California Supreme Court broadly recognized an oral or implied contract cause of action and a tort cause of action for a discharge contrary to fundamental public policy, while rejecting a tort recovery for breach of an implied covenant of good faith and fair dealing in the employment context.[160]

The preemptive effect of Section 301 of the Labor Management Relations Act[161] on state law claims was at issue in *Lingle v. Norge Division, Magic Chef,* [162] where the Court held that a tort remedy under state law for discharge in retaliation for filing a workers' compensation claim was not preempted by Section 301. The Court reaffirmed its longstanding doctrine that "if the resolution of a state-law claim depends upon the meaning of a collective-bargaining agreement, the application of state law * * * is preempted and federal labor law principles—necessarily uniform throughout the nation—must be employed to resolve the dispute."[163] Applying this principle, the Court unanimously held that the facts relevant to the retaliatory discharge claim in *Lingle* could be tried without interpreting any provision of the collective bargaining agreement, including the provision requiring that employees only be discharged for "proper" or "just" cause.[164] The Court acknowledged that the state-law analysis of the retaliation issue "might well involve attention to the same factual considerations as the contractual determination of whether Lingle was fired for just cause," but "disagree[d] * * * that such parallelism renders the state-law analysis dependent upon the contractual analysis," because "§ 301 preemption merely ensures that federal law will be the basis for interpreting collective-bargaining agreements, and says nothing about the substantive rights a State may provide to workers when adjudication of those rights does not depend upon the interpretation of such agreements."[165]

## EEOC Procedure

The ability of the EEOC to pursue discrimination claims through the issuance of Commissioner's charges and administrative subpoenas was strengthened by the Supreme Court's decision in *EEOC v. Shell Oil Co.* [166] The *Shell Oil* decision effectively has broadened the utility of the Commissioner's charge by limiting the information which must be contained in the charge and thereby allowing for a broader scope of investigation.[167] The

---

[159]47 Cal.3d 654, 765 P.2d 373, 254 Cal. Rptr. 211, 3 IER 1729 (Cal. S. Ct. 1988).

[160]*Id.,* 3 IER at 1751.

[161]29 U.S.C. § 185(a); *see also supra* note 137.

[162]486 U.S. _____, 46 FEP 1553 (1988).

[163]*Id.,* 46 FEP at 1555.

[164]*Id.,* 46 FEP at 1553.

[165]*Id.,* 46 FEP at 1557. The Court's generalized statement has raised questions about the possible reach of *Lingle* beyond its facts. *See infra* Chapter 23, note 6; *see also* Newberry v. Pacific Racing Ass'n, 854 F.2d 1142, 3 IER 959 (9th Cir. 1988) (post-*Lingle* decision affirming summary judgment dismissing removed state tort law claims, including claim for alleged infliction of emotion distress; emotional distress claim relating to discharge would require determination whether discharge was justified under collective bargaining agreement; portion of emotional distress claim arising from alleged false post-discharge statements not preempted, but statements not sufficiently outrageous to support action).

[166]466 U.S. 54, 34 FEP 709 (1984).

[167]*See* Chapters 26 (EEOC Administrative Process) and 31 (EEOC Litigation).

EEOC has undergone substantial internal development and reform, including the issuance of Policy Statements on Remedies and Relief for Individual Cases of Unlawful Discrimination,[168] Investigative Compliance,[169] the Relationship of Title VII of the Civil Rights Act to the Immigration Reform and Control Act of 1986,[170] and Enforcement Policy.[171]

## Attorney's Fees

The Supreme Court in *Webb v. County Board of Education of Dyer County, Tennessee*[172] resolved a conflict in the circuits and held that attorney's fees could not be recovered for time spent in nonmandatory administrative proceedings.[173] Other questions of attorney's fees and settlement were resolved by the Supreme Court in *Marek v. Chesny,*[174] *Evans v. Jeff D.,*[175] and *City of Riverside v. Rivera.*[176] In *Marek,* the Court held that plaintiffs who reject an offer of judgment under Fed. R. Civ. P. 68 and do not ultimately receive a judgment greater than was offered not only must pay the defendant's post-offer costs but also must forego attorney's fees for the same period. Moreover, the word "costs" in Rule 68 was defined to include attorney's fees, with no obligation for the offeror to itemize separately the amount tendered to settle the underlying claims and claims for attorney's fees.[177] In *Jeff D.,* the Court held that a district court could properly approve a settlement in which the plaintiff waives his rights to attorney's fees under the Civil Rights Attorney's Fee Awards Act, and that counsel are not ethically prohibited from simultaneously negotiating a settlement of both merits and fees.[178] The Court left open the extent to which state and local bar associations may regulate such simultaneous negotiations.[179] Finally, in *Rivera* the Court approved a fee award substantially exceeding the underlying damages, and thus established that fees for prevailing parties need not be limited to the amount of damages awarded where factual findings establish that hours and hourly rates were reasonable, that counsel's skill was exceptional, and that facts litigated on those claims on which the parties did not prevail were drawn from a common core.[180]

---

[168]Policy Statement on Remedies and Relief for Individual Cases of Unlawful Discrimination, Equal Employment Opportunity Commission, approved Feb. 5, 1985.

[169]Policy Statement on Investigative Compliance, Equal Employment Opportunity Commission, adopted July 14, 1986.

[170]Policy Statement on the Relationship of Title VII of the Civil Rights Act to the Immigration Reform and Control Act of 1986, Equal Employment Opportunity Commission, adopted Feb. 26, 1987.

[171]Statement of Enforcement Policy, Equal Employment Opportunity Commission, adopted Sept. 11, 1984.

[172]471 U.S. 234, 37 FEP 785 (1985).

[173]*See* Chapter 39 (Attorney's Fees).

[174]473 U.S. 1, 38 FEP 124 (1985).

[175]475 U.S. 717, 40 FEP 860 (1986).

[176]477 U.S. 561, 41 FEP 65 (1986).

[177]38 FEP at 124.

[178]40 FEP at 866–68.

[179]40 FEP at 865 n.15.

[180]41 FEP at 70.

CHAPTER 2

# DISPARATE TREATMENT

## II. Proof of Disparate Treatment

The basic allocation and order of proof to be used in most cases alleging discriminatory treatment were established by the Supreme Court in *McDonnell Douglas Corp. v. Green*[1] and *Texas Department of Community Affairs v. Burdine.*[2] The plaintiff must establish a prima facie case; the employer then must articulate a legitimate, nondiscriminatory reason for its actions; and, finally, the plaintiff must then prove that this proffered reason is a pretext for intentional discrimination. The burden of proof remains with the plaintiff at all times.[3] The courts have continued to apply these well-established principles.[4]

---

[1]411 U.S. 792, 5 FEP 965 (1973).

[2]450 U.S. 248, 25 FEP 113 (1981).

[3]*E.g.,* Boudreaux v. Helena-West Helena School Dist., 819 F.2d 854 (8th Cir. 1987) (plaintiff always bears ultimate burden of persuasion that employer intentionally discriminated); Burton v. Ohio Adult Parole Auth., 798 F.2d 164, 41 FEP 1799 (6th Cir. 1986) (if appellate court determines that plaintiff was at any time relieved of burden of persuasion, decision must be reversed and remanded for correct allocation of burdens); Hill v. Seaboard Coast Line R.R., 767 F.2d 771, 39 FEP 1656 (11th Cir. 1985) (defendant never has burden of persuasion). *But see* Evans v. Harnett County Bd. of Educ., 684 F.2d 304, 29 FEP 672 (4th Cir. 1982) (shifting burden of persuasion to defendant proper where either intentional segregative action or recent history of racial discrimination in school system is found).

[4]Legrand v. University of Ark. at Pine Bluff Trustees, 821 F.2d 478, 44 FEP 60 (8th Cir. 1987) (plaintiffs had established prima facie case and defendant's proffered explanation was pretextual); Beatty v. Chesapeake Center, 818 F.2d 318, 43 FEP 1472 (4th Cir. 1987) (articulated reason inherently incredible as a matter of law and, therefore, regarded as pretext for discrimination); Johnson v. Legal Servs. of Ark., 813 F.2d 893, 43 FEP 343 (8th Cir. 1987) (same procedure for order and allocation of proof is followed in Title VII and § 1981 actions); Sylvester v. Callon Energy Servs., 781 F.2d 520, 39 FEP 1660 (5th Cir. 1986) (articulated reasons lacked support in reason or in record); O'Connor v. Peru State College, 781 F.2d 632, 39 FEP 1241, *aff'd,* 781 F.2d 632, 39 FEP 1241 (8th Cir. 1986) (articulated reason legitimate and not pretextual where conduct of female employee was dissimilar to that of male employees); White v. Colgan Elec. Co., 781 F.2d 1214, 39 FEP 1599 (6th Cir. 1986) (district court erred in holding that employer failed to advance legitimate nondiscriminatory reason for its actions; there was insufficient evidence in record to conclude that proffered explanation was pretextual); Tulloss v. Near N. Montessori School, 776 F.2d 150, 39 FEP 418 (7th Cir. 1985) (even if plaintiff established prima facie case of discrimination, defendant demonstrated valid nondiscriminatory reason for her dismissal, and district court adequately addressed whether proffered reason for termination was pretextual); Moore v. Devine, 767 F.2d 1541, 38 FEP 1196 (11th Cir. 1985), *modified on other grounds,* 780 F.2d 1559, 39 FEP 1644 (11th Cir. 1986) (having failed to establish prima facie case, plaintiff cannot prevail by showing that defendant has failed to articulate legitimate nondiscriminatory reason or that proffered reason was probably not true reason); Joshi v. Florida State Univ. Health Center, 763 F.2d 1227, 38 FEP 38 (11th Cir.), *cert. denied,* 474 U.S. 948, 39 FEP 384 (1985) (defendant failed to articulate legitimate nondiscriminatory reason for action; thus discrimination was established); Miller v. WFLI Radio, 687 F.2d 136, 29 FEP 929 (6th Cir. 1982) (case remanded to give plaintiff opportunity to disprove nondiscriminatory reason relied upon by magistrate but not advanced by defendant); Halsell v. Kimberly-Clark Corp., 683 F.2d 285, 29 FEP 1185 (8th Cir. 1982), *cert. denied,* 459 U.S. 1205, 30 FEP 1856 (1983) (directed verdict for defendant where defendant's evidence rebutted any inference of discrimination); Sumner v. San Diego Urban League, 681 F.2d 1140, 29 FEP 707 (9th Cir. 1982) (case remanded for findings showing three-step analysis rather than just ultimate issue); Montgomery v. Yellow Freight Sys., 671 F.2d 412, 28 FEP 831 (10th Cir. 1982) (no violation in discharging black employee but not white employees where situations not comparable); Holden v. Commission Against Discrimination, 671 F.2d 30, 28 FEP 47 (1st Cir.), *cert. denied,* 459 U.S. 843, 29 FEP 1560 (1982)

21

The Supreme Court reaffirmed the *McDonnell Douglas* and *Burdine* framework in *United States Postal Service Board of Governors v. Aikens,*[5] a failure-to-promote case. However, the Supreme Court held that, since the case was fully tried on the merits, the court of appeals and the parties erroneously focused on the procedural question of whether the plaintiff succeeded in establishing a prima facie case, rather than the ultimate question of discrimination:

> "But when the defendant fails to persuade the district court to dismiss the action for lack of a *prima facie* case, and responds to the plaintiff's proof by offering evidence of the reason for the plaintiff's rejection, the fact finder must then decide whether the rejection was discriminatory within the meaning of Title VII. At this stage, the McDonnell-Burdine presumption 'drops from the case,' and 'the factual inquiry proceeds to a new level of specificity. * * *'
>
> "* * * Where the defendant has done everything that would be required of him if the plaintiff had properly made out a *prima facie* case, whether the plaintiff really did so is no longer relevant. The district court has before it all the evidence it needs to decide whether 'the defendant intentionally discriminated against the plaintiff.' "[6]

The Court also reaffirmed in *Aikens* that the plaintiff is not limited to proving his case by direct evidence. Rather, the plaintiff may prove his case by direct or circumstantial evidence just as in any lawsuit. The Court stated:

> "The trier of fact should consider all the evidence, giving it whatever weight and credence it deserves. Thus, we agree with the Court of Appeals that the District Court should not have required Aikens to submit direct evidence of discriminatory intent."[7]

The three-step framework of *McDonnell Douglas* and *Burdine* does not necessarily mean that the evidence must be presented to the court in that order. In *Dance v. Ripley*[8] the court held that the plaintiff was not deprived of her opportunity to demonstrate pretext when the district court granted

---

(evidence of disparate treatment not sufficient to show pretext); Haynes v. Miller, 669 F.2d 1125, 27 FEP 1611 (6th Cir. 1982) (plaintiff failed to establish prima facie case of discrimination). *Compare* Barnes v. Yellow Freight Sys., 778 F.2d 1096, 39 FEP 1050 (5th Cir. 1985) (presumption of discriminatory intent arises when a supervisor of one race treats employees of same race more favorably than similarly situated employees of another race under circumstances that are essentially identical; district court erred in dismissing complaint because plaintiff could not meet straight *McDonnell Douglas* analysis).

[5]460 U.S. 711, 31 FEP 609 (1983). *See also* Cooper v. Federal Reserve Bank of Richmond, 467 U.S. 867, 35 FEP 1 (1984).

[6]*Id.* at 714–15, 31 FEP at 611 (citations and footnote omitted). *See also* Pollard v. Rea Magnet Wire Co., 824 F.2d 557, 44 FEP 1137 (7th Cir.), *cert. denied,* 484 U.S. —, 45 FEP 648 (1987) (once trial of disparate treatment case is over, rules governing prima facie cases, order of proof, etc., no longer apply); Yowell v. United States Postal Serv., 810 F.2d 644, 42 FEP 1294 (7th Cir. 1987) (once case has been fully tried, whether plaintiff established prima facie case is irrelevant); Tulloss v. Near N. Montessori School, *supra* note 4 (no error for district court not to state whether plaintiff made out prima facie case, since defendant articulated legitimate nondiscriminatory reason for dismissal); Cunningham v. Housing Auth. of the City of Opelousas dba Opelousas Hous. Auth., 764 F.2d 1097, 38 FEP 417 (5th Cir.), *cert. denied,* 474 U.S. 1007, 39 FEP 720 (1985) (on appeal of fully tried case, only issue is ultimate finding of discrimination; court need not address allegations of failure to articulate reason or whether that reason is legitimate). *But see* Legrand v. University of Ark. at Pine Bluff Trustees, *supra* note 4 (district court error in failing to recognize plaintiff's prima facie case was not remedied by finding on ultimate issue of discrimination in defendant's favor).

[7]*Id.* at 714, n.3, 31 FEP at 610 (citations omitted).

[8]776 F.2d 370, 39 FEP 466 (1st Cir. 1985).

a Rule 41(b) dismissal of her claim at the close of her case-in-chief. Concluding that the district court had addressed the ultimate question of discrimination and that the *McDonnell Douglas* analysis does not require a three-step process ending with plaintiff's rebuttal case, the court held that "the district court may dismiss the complaint at the close of plaintiff's case if: one, during plaintiff's case, the defendant's nondiscriminatory reason was articulated; two, plaintiff had notice and an opportunity to rebut the proffered nondiscriminatory reason; and three, plaintiff failed to rebut the reason persuasively."[9] The court, finding that the plaintiff had ample notice of the defendant's reasons, which were contained in a memorandum introduced into evidence as a joint exhibit, and the opportunity to rebut the defendant's reasons, concluded that the Rule 41(b) dismissal did not deprive the plaintiff of an opportunity to demonstrate that the defendant's proffered reasons for her not receiving a promotion were pretextual.[10]

The *McDonnell Douglas* framework also does not require that evidence be presented in distinct compartments of proof. Thus, the plaintiff's evidence used to establish a prima facie case may also sufficiently demonstrate the pretextual nature of the defendant's articulated reasons.[11]

Several courts have noted that the three-part analysis is not appropriate in all situations. If the plaintiff presents direct evidence *sufficient to support a finding* of intentional discrimination, the defendant, rather than merely articulating a legitimate nondiscriminatory reason, can rebut only by either defeating such evidence or by showing by a preponderance of the evidence that the same decision would have been reached even absent the presence of the discriminatory motive.[12] Similarly, where plaintiff's prima facie case has shown a history of recent institution-wide discrimination, some circuits have approved shifting the ultimate burden of persuasion to the defendant to show that the challenged personnel action was not undertaken with discriminatory intent.[13]

---

[9]*Id.* at 374, 39 FEP at 469.

[10]*Id. See also* Robinson v. Montgomery Ward & Co., 823 F.2d 793, 44 FEP 491 (4th Cir. 1987); Mitchell v. Baldrige, 759 F.2d 80, 37 FEP 689 (D.C. Cir. 1985); McDaniel v. Temple Indep. School Dist., 770 F.2d 1340, 38 FEP 1567, 1570, n.3 (5th Cir. 1985); Holden v. Commission Against Discrimination, *supra* note 4; Gaballah v. Johnson, 629 F.2d 1191, 23 FEP 46 (7th Cir. 1980); Sime v. California State Univ. & Colleges Trustees, 526 F.2d 1112, 11 FEP 1104 (9th Cir. 1975).

[11]Monroe v. Burlington Indus., 784 F.2d 568, 40 FEP 273 (4th Cir. 1986) (trier of fact allowed to consider evidence used to demonstrate prima facie case on issue of whether defendant's explanation was pretextual).

[12]*Price Waterhouse v. Hopkins,* 57 U.S.L.W. 4469, 49 FEP 954 (1989), must be considered carefully in evaluating prior decisions such as Terbovitz v. Fiscal Court of Adair County, Ky., 825 F.2d 111, 44 FEP 841 (6th Cir. 1987) (direct evidence required conclusion that unlawful discrimination was at least a "motivating factor," and employer failed to show that same decision would have been made absent any discriminatory animus); Carney v. Martin Luther Home, Inc., 824 F.2d 643, 44 FEP 683 (8th Cir. 1987) (district court erred in applying *McDonnell Douglas* analysis where female employee presented direct evidence of discrimination); Wilson v. City of Aliceville, 779 F.2d 631, 39 FEP 1290 (11th Cir. 1986) (case remanded to allow evidence of racial slur to be admitted as direct evidence of discrimination); Blalock v. Metals Trades, 775 F.2d 703, 39 FEP 140 (6th Cir. 1985) (district court erred in not finding direct evidence of religious discrimination). *Cf.* Kendall v. Block, 821 F.2d 1142 (5th Cir. 1987) (direct evidence inconclusive); Craft v. Metromedia, 766 F.2d 1205, 38 FEP 404 (8th Cir. 1985), *cert. denied,* 475 U.S. 1058, 40 FEP 272 (1986) (where district court did not accept any direct evidence of discrimination, court correctly failed to shift burden to defendant to prove by preponderance of the evidence that it would have taken the challenged action even in the absence of gender bias).

[13]*See* Knighton v. Laurens County School Dist. No. 56, 721 F.2d 976, 33 FEP 299 (4th Cir. 1983); Harris v. Birmingham Bd. of Educ., 712 F.2d 1377, 32 FEP 1198 (11th Cir. 1983). *Cf.* Lujan v. Franklin

In *Lewis v. University of Pittsburgh,* [14] the Third Circuit held that the trial court properly instructed the jury hearing the plaintiff's § 1981 claim that the plaintiff had the burden of proving that she would have been promoted *but for* her race. In rejecting the plaintiff's argument that race need only be a substantial or contributing factor in the adverse decision, the court of appeals relied on the Supreme Court's holding in *McDonald v. Santa Fe Trail Transportation Co.* [15] that a Title VII plaintiff bears the burden of proving intentional, "but for" discrimination.[16] The court reasoned that, since § 1981 actions require the same elements of proof as Title VII claims, the plaintiff's burden of proof is the same under both statutes.[17]

In *Blalock v. Metals Trades,* [18] the court relied on the causation standard applied in *Mt. Healthy School District Board of Education v. Doyle* [19] in determining the causation requirements in a dual motive employment case. Recognizing that *McDonald* requires intentional, "but for" discrimination, but that the plaintiff need not show he was rejected solely on the basis of race, the Sixth Circuit held:

> "[I]n order to prove a violation of Title VII, a plaintiff need demonstrate by a preponderance of the evidence that the employer's decision to take an adverse employment action was more likely than not motivated by a criterion proscribed by the statute. Upon such proof, the employer has the burden to prove that the adverse employment action would have been taken even in the absence of the impermissible motivation, and that, therefore, the discriminatory animus was not the cause of the adverse employment action."[20]

Other courts have declined to follow this rule[21] or applied it only in determining appropriate relief.[22]

---

County Bd. of Educ., 766 F.2d 917, 38 FEP 9 (6th Cir. 1985) (*Burdine* requires that burden of persuasion not shift to defendant unless challenged employment decision had adverse impact on protected group at issue).

[14] 725 F.2d 910, 33 FEP 1091 (3d Cir. 1983), *cert. denied,* 469 U.S. 892, 35 FEP 1688 (1984).

[15] 427 U.S. 273, 12 FEP 1577 (1976).

[16] *See also* EEOC v. Prudential Fed. Sav. & Loan Ass'n, 763 F.2d 1166, 37 FEP 1691 (10th Cir.), *cert. denied,* 474 U.S. 946, 39 FEP 384 (1985); La Montagne v. American Convenience Prod., 750 F.2d 1405, 36 FEP 913 (7th Cir. 1984); Jack v. Texaco Research Center, 743 F.2d 1129, 35 FEP 1818 (5th Cir. 1984); Fadhl v. City & County of San Francisco, 741 F.2d 1163, 35 FEP 1291 (9th Cir. 1984). *Cf.* Dillon v. Coles, 746 F.2d 998, 36 FEP 159 (3d Cir. 1984) (court's standard of whether gender was "a" determinative factor, instead of explicit reference to a "but for" test, is not reversible error because instructions as a whole made plain plaintiff was to prove that the impermissible factor made a difference).

[17] *Supra* note 14, at 915 n.5, 33 FEP at 1095.

[18] *Supra* note 12.

[19] 429 U.S. 274 (1977). *See also* Price Waterhouse v. Hopkins, *Supra* note 12 (White, J., concurring in judgment).

[20] *Supra* note 12, at 712, 39 FEP at 147. *See also* Underwood v. District of Columbia Armory Bd., 816 F.2d 769, 43 FEP 965 (D.C. Cir. 1987) (district court decision to discount direct evidence of discrimination and find that legitimate reason was in fact the real motivation not clearly erroneous); Hill v. Seaboard Coast Line R.R., 767 F.2d 771, 39 FEP 1656 (11th Cir. 1985) (case remanded to determine if defendant proved that those promoted were more qualified).

[21] Wheeler v. Snyder Buick, Inc., 794 F.2d 1228, 41 FEP 341 (7th Cir. 1986) ("same decision" rule not appropriate under *McDonnell Douglas* framework, since requirement that impermissible factor must have been sufficiently large component of challenged decision is already part of determining pretext).

[22] Bibbs v. Department of Agriculture, 778 F.2d 1318, 39 FEP 970 (8th Cir. 1985) (plaintiff need only show that race is discernible factor to establish liability of employer and obtain injunctive and declaratory relief; however, in order to receive reinstatement and back pay, plaintiff must show race was "but for" factor with burden of production and persuasion shifting to defendant to show that plaintiff would not have been hired or promoted in the absence of the proven discrimination). *See also* Haskins v. Department

The vast majority of disparate treatment cases continue to depend on the issue of pretext, with comparative evidence being the primary type of proof.[23]

---

of the Army, 808 F.2d 1192, 42 FEP 1120 (6th Cir.), *cert. denied,* 484 U.S. —, 44 FEP 1672 (1987) (*Blalock* does not preclude district court from applying "same decision" test in fashioning a remedy, when that court has proceeded under assumption that such an inquiry is not part of liability determination).

[23]*E.g.,* Grigsby v. Reynolds Metals Co., 821 F.2d 590, 44 FEP 449 (11th Cir. 1987) (no evidence showed that plaintiff was affected by reduction-in-force any more severely than other employees involved); Smith v. Texas Dep't of Water Resources, 818 F.2d 363, 43 FEP 1727 (5th Cir. 1987) (conduct for which female employee was discharged found to be dissimilar to that of male employee who was allegedly not disciplined for engaging in similar behavior); Smith v. Papp Clinic, P.A., 808 F.2d 1449, 42 FEP 1553 (11th Cir. 1987) (district court finding of no pretext not clearly erroneous when it was determined that plaintiff deserved more severe punishment than white employee because she was supervisor that day and had received previous warnings); Loeffler v. Carlin, 780 F.2d 1365, 39 FEP 1089 (8th Cir. 1985), *denial of prejudgment interest aff'd en banc sub nom.* Loeffler v. Tisch, 806 F.2d 817, 42 FEP 792 (8th Cir. 1986), *rev'd and remanded on issues of prejudgment interest sub nom.* Loeffler v. Frank, 486 U.S. —, 46 FEP 1659 (1988) (circuit court had affirmed as not clearly erroneous district court's finding that plaintiff established pretext by showing that female employees openly violated same rule for which he was discharged yet did not receive discipline of comparable severity); Namenwirth v. University of Wis. Sys. Bd. of Regents, 769 F.2d 1235, 38 FEP 1155 (7th Cir. 1985), *cert. denied,* 474 U.S. 1061, 39 FEP 1200 (1986) (magistrate explicitly found that men in plaintiff's position would not have been treated differently); Smith v. Monsanto Chem. Co., 770 F.2d 719, 38 FEP 1141 (8th Cir. 1985), *cert. denied,* 475 U.S. 1050, 40 FEP 272 (1986) (district court finding of pretext clearly erroneous where all white employees similarly situated under company's policy were treated as harshly for stealing as black employee); Talley v. United States Postal Serv., 720 F.2d 505, 33 FEP 361 (8th Cir. 1983), *cert. denied,* 466 U.S. 952, 37 FEP 592 (1984) (plaintiff attempted to prove pretext by presenting statistical evidence of general racial disparaties within St. Louis postal system; this evidence inadequate to prove pretext, since plaintiff must show specifically how she was treated differently from similarly situated individuals). *Compare* Zahorik v. Cornell Univ., 729 F.2d 85, 34 FEP 165 (2d Cir. 1984) (tenure decisions are highly individualized and subjective; plaintiff must show that significant portion of scholars in that field believe she should be tenured and that discrimination influenced denial of tenure).

## CHAPTER 3

# SENIORITY

## II. SENIORITY AND TRANSFER RIGHTS

### B. The Bona Fide Seniority System Defense

The protection of § 703(h) is not available where the action complained of results from defendant's failure to apply the collective bargaining agreement's seniority provisions to plaintiffs, as distinguished from results of the application of the provisions.[1]

In *Freeman v. Motor Convoy,*[2] the Eleventh Circuit joined the majority of the circuits in holding that § 703(h) is available as a defense to claims brought under 42 U.S.C. § 1981. Noting that a split between the circuits exists on this issue,[3] the court stated that

> "[a] construction of Section 703(h) which limits the application of the statute to Title VII actions would produce anomalous results. In certain cases, seniority systems could be lawful under Title VII but unlawful under Section 1981. As the Fourth Circuit noted in *Johnson v. Ryder Truck Lines, Inc.,* * * * it is unlikely 'that Congress intended to create conflicting and contradictory standards for determining what constitutes illegal discrimination.' * * * Accordingly, we * * * conclude that the district court correctly applied Section 703(h) to plaintiff's claim under Section 1981."[4]

The Supreme Court held in *Trans World Airlines v. Thurston*[5] that any seniority system that includes a discriminatory practice (*e.g.,* mandatory retirement for members of the protected age group) does not qualify for the bona fide seniority system defense contained in the Age Discrimination in Employment Act.[6]

---

[1]Scarlett v. Seaboard Coast Line R.R., 676 F.2d 1043, 29 FEP 433 (5th Cir. 1982) (differing treatment of black trainmen did not stem from application of facially neutral seniority system, but was result of defendant's failure to apply seniority and promotion provisions of collective bargaining agreement to such employees; bona fide seniority system defense therefore not available to defendant).

[2]700 F.2d 1339, 31 FEP 517 (11th Cir. 1983).

[3]*Id.* at 1349, 31 FEP at 521. *Compare* Pettway v. American Cast Iron Pipe Co., 576 F.2d 1157, 17 FEP 1712 (5th Cir. 1978), *cert. denied,* 439 U.S. 1115 (1979) (§ 703(h) available as defense to § 1981 claims) *and* Johnson v. Ryder Truck Lines, 575 F.2d 471, 17 FEP 571 (4th Cir. 1978), *cert. denied,* 440 U.S. 979, 19 FEP 467 (1979) (same) *with* Bolden v. Pennsylvania State Police, 578 F.2d 912, 17 FEP 687 (3d Cir. 1978) (§ 703(h) *not* available as defense to § 1981 claim).

[4]*Id.* at 1349, 31 FEP at 525 (citations omitted). In light of the holding in *General Bldg. Contractors Ass'n v. Pennsylvania,* 458 U.S. 375, 29 FEP 139 (1982), a showing of discriminatory intent is necessary to prove a § 1981 violation; the result would be the same whether or not the seniority system was bona fide if it was created or maintained with a discriminatory purpose. Teamsters v. United States, 431 U.S. 324, 14 FEP 1514 (1977).

[5]469 U.S. 111, 36 FEP 977 (1985).

[6]*Id.* at 124, 36 FEP at 983 (bona fide seniority system defense to mandatory retirement unavailable where captains, disqualified to pilot for reasons other than age, automatically are allowed to "bump" less senior flight engineers, whereas captains disqualified when reaching age 60 must bid for flight engineer vacancies). *See also* Chapter 14 (Age).

## C. Proving and Disproving the Existence of a Bona Fide Seniority System After *Teamsters*

### 1. What Constitutes a "Seniority System"

Two circuit courts have applied *California Brewers Association v. Bryant* [7] to determine whether employment systems are seniority systems within the meaning of § 703(h). The Fourth Circuit[8] noted that the essence of a seniority system is a preference for persons who have been employed longer. Thus, a policy of filling vacancies from within by promotion or transfer before resorting to hiring was a "seniority system" because it granted a preference to employees over those who had never been employed. The Sixth Circuit[9] was required to determine whether a method used to break seniority "ties" was an ancillary rule necessary to the operation of the seniority system and therefore protected by § 703(h), or merely an appendage. The rule in question provided that persons hired on the same day would be ranked, for seniority purposes, based on their scores on a preemployment test. Holding that the tie-breaking rule was merely an appendage that was not a seniority system within the meaning of § 703(h), the court granted relief to minority and female employees who had been laid off based on their test score rankings.

### 2. Bona Fides or Lack Thereof

The courts continue to rely on the factors set forth in *James v. Stockham Valves & Fittings Co.* [10] for determining whether a seniority provision qualifies under § 703(h) as a bona fide seniority system.[11]

a. *Seniority System Not Bona Fide.* In *United States v. Georgia Power Co.,* [12] on remand from the Supreme Court for reconsideration in light of *Pullman-Standard v. Swint,* [13] the Fifth Circuit reaffirmed its prior holding

---

[7]444 U.S. 598, 22 FEP 1 (1980).

[8]Allen v. Prince George's County, Md., 737 F.2d 1299, 38 FEP 1220 (4th Cir. 1984). *See also* Calloway v. Westinghouse Elec. Corp., 642 F. Supp. 663, 41 FEP 1715 (M.D. Ga. 1986) (provision in collective bargaining agreement that an employee's length of employment governs promotions or upgrading within bargaining units is a seniority system); Moore v. Stage Employees, IATSE, Local 659, 29 FEP 542 (C.D. Cal. 1982) ("experience roster" used as multi-employer hiring list was a seniority system where a minimal period of service was required for listing on roster and where greater length of time on roster increased an individual's hiring priority).

[9]United States v. City of Cincinnati, 771 F.2d 161, 38 FEP 1402 (6th Cir. 1985).

[10]559 F.2d 310, 15 FEP 827 (5th Cir. 1977), *cert. denied,* 434 U.S. 1034, 16 FEP 501 (1978).

[11]Gantlin v. West Virginia Pulp & Paper Co., 734 F.2d 980, 34 FEP 1316 (4th Cir. 1984), *aff'g* 526 F. Supp. 1356, 29 FEP 1406 (D.S.C. 1981) (seniority system bona fide); Firefighters for Racial Equality v. Bach, 611 F. Supp. 166, 38 FEP 19 (D. Colo. 1985) (on remand for consideration of four factors in *Stockham Valves,* district court held that § 703(h) constitutes an affirmative defense and adopted a three-step analysis: plaintiff must establish prima facie case of discriminatory treatment or impact resulting from application of seniority system; defendant then has burden of establishing that system is racially neutral and that it rationally furthers some legitimate employer or employee purpose; plaintiff then has burden of proving that system was implemented with intent to discriminate); Jones v. Cassens Transp., 617 F. Supp. 869, 39 FEP 1341 (E.D. Mich. 1985) (on remand, district court reaffirmed earlier holding that seniority system was not bona fide since it operated to preclude women from interunit transfers); Faulkner v. Republic Steel Corp., 30 FEP 555 (N.D. Ala. 1979) (on remand for consideration of four factors in *Stockham Valves*).

[12]695 F.2d 890, 30 FEP 1305 (5th Cir. 1983).

[13]456 U.S. 273, 28 FEP 1073 (1982). In *Swint,* the Supreme Court held that a finding of discriminatory intent, necessary for finding that a seniority system is not bona fide, is a finding of fact subject to the "clearly erroneous" standard of review. The Court therefore rejected the Fifth Circuit view that, as the ultimate issue, discriminatory intent *vel non* may be independently determined by an appellate court.

that (1) the seniority system at issue penalized blacks more than whites, (2) the unequal treatment was not attributable to a legitimate division of bargaining units, and (3) the seniority system not only originated in a period of discrimination, but was also maintained for an unlawful purpose.[14] The court distinguished *Swint,* where the Supreme Court had held that the "clearly erroneous" rule applied to a district court's finding as to whether the differential impact of a seniority system reflected an intent to discriminate, by determining that subsidiary findings of the trial court " 'demonstrate[d] that this system *could not be found* to be bona fide * * *.' "[15] In *Wattleton v. Boilermakers Local 1509,*[16] the Seventh Circuit held that a seniority system was negotiated and maintained for the purpose of excluding blacks from the bargaining unit and therefore was not bona fide. Tracing the history of the union's collective bargaining agreement with the employer, the district court had found that modifications were made in the agreement's seniority provisions when the employer first began to hire blacks. As the result of these changes, whites were transferred to jobs within the bargaining unit represented by the defendant union with full carryover seniority, while blacks were discouraged and prohibited from doing so.[17]

*b. Seniority System Bona Fide. Gantlin v. Westvaco Corp.*[18] involved a seniority system in which bargaining unit employees accumulated three types of seniority, respectively reflecting time in their job, department, and the mill.[19] Under this system, job seniority applied to promotions and demotions within lines of progression; departmental seniority was used as a tiebreaker between employees in the same line of progression with identical job seniority, and applied to layoffs from the department; and mill seniority applied to transfers between departments and to mill layoffs. Applying the standards set forth in *James v. Stockham Valves & Fittings Co.,*[20] the district court concluded that (1) the seniority consequences of transferring were the

---

[14]*Id.* at 893, 30 FEP at 1306–07.

[15]*Id.* at 892, 30 FEP at 1306 (emphasis in original) (quoting United States v. Georgia Power Co., 634 F.2d 929, 935, 24 FEP 1398, 1402 (5th Cir. 1981)). In *Swint,* on remand from the Supreme Court, the Fifth Circuit vacated and remanded the case to the district court for further proceedings to determine whether discriminatory job assignments occurred after 1964, what impact the "locking in" of blacks to the least remunerative departments had on discouraging transfer between seniority units, and the significance of the discriminatory motivation of Machinists with respect to the institution of Steelworker's seniority system, and any other proceedings that were deemed necessary. Swint v. Pullman-Standard, 692 F.2d 1031, 30 FEP 867 (5th Cir. 1982). Similarly, in *Terrell v. United States Pipe & Foundry Co.,* 696 F.2d 1132, 30 FEP 1515 (5th Cir. 1983), the Fifth Circuit, again on remand from the Supreme Court for reconsideration in light of *Swint,* vacated its judgment regarding the seniority system issue and remanded the case to the district court for further proceedings to consider evidence of intentional discrimination in the creation and maintenance of the defendant's seniority system. On remand, the district court found that the seniority system was created and maintained with the intent to discriminate against blacks and therefore was not bona fide. 39 FEP 571 (N.D. Ala. 1985).

[16]686 F.2d 586, 29 FEP 1389 (7th Cir. 1982), *cert. denied,* 459 U.S. 1208, 30 FEP 1856 (1983).

[17]*See also* Jones v. Cassens Transp., 538 F. Supp. 929, 32 FEP 1713 (E.D. Mich.), *appeal dismissed mem.,* 705 F.2d 454, 33 FEP 1696 (6th Cir. 1982), *on remand,* 617 F. Supp. 869, 39 FEP 1341 (E.D. Mich. 1985) (seniority system not bona fide since operated only to prevent women from pursuing transfers between units; all female employees were included in office unit regardless of actual duties and only members of office unit were prohibited from transferring to other, more desirable units within company) (reaffirming finding of liability on remand).

[18]526 F. Supp. 1356, 29 FEP 1406 (D.S.C. 1981), *aff'd,* 734 F.2d 980, 34 FEP 1316 (4th Cir. 1984).

[19]The defendant's seniority system was established pursuant to three separate collective bargaining agreements stemming from separate bargaining units for machinists, electricians/power production employees, and other production and maintenance personnel.

[20]*Supra* note 10.

same for all employees—black or white; (2) the establishment of separate bargaining units for machinists, electricians/power production employees, and other production and maintenance personnel was rational; (3) there was no evidence that the seniority system was adopted for the purpose of discriminating against employees because of race; and (4) the evidence did not establish that the seniority system had been maintained for a discriminatory purpose.[21] The court noted that the mere fact that the seniority system was established at a time when discrimination in job assignments was a custom does not render the system non-bona-fide or compel a finding that the system had its genesis in racial discrimination.[22] In *Faulkner v. Republic Steel Corp.,*[23] the court found that, while the pre-1963 seniority system did not meet all the requirements of a bona fide system under § 703(h) set out in *Stockham Valves,* the modifications incorporated into the system in 1963 were intended to provide blacks with opportunities to escape the consequences of their original discriminatory assignments by the employer. Consequently, notwithstanding residual post-1963 inhibitions to transfer, the court found the seniority system, as it operated after 1963, to be bona fide within the meaning of § 703(h). In *Bernard v. Gulf Oil Corp.,*[24] the court upheld a seniority provision according one-day seniority as a craftsman to laborers in a previously all-black unit who wished to transfer to the previously all-white craft division, finding that the purpose and effect of the provision was to maintain quality, that it did not discourage transfers, and that the other *Stockham Valves* standards were met.

## D. Remedies for Unlawful Restrictions on Transfer and Promotion

In *Ingram v. Madison Square Garden Center,*[25] the Second Circuit recognized that remedies cannot be created in a vacuum, and that, in granting retroactive seniority, a district court must attempt to recreate the *actual, not hypothetical,* circumstances that would have existed without discrimination. In other words, relief could only be granted to those members of the class who would actually, and not those who merely could, have been promoted under a nondiscriminatory scheme. Title VII does not require, and the district court cannot, as a remedial measure, create, a preference for class members that would result in a promotion rate exceeding that which would have existed if no discrimination had occurred.[26]

---

[21]526 F. Supp. at 1374–75, 29 FEP at 1420.

[22]*Id. See also* Calloway v. Westinghouse Elec. Corp., 642 F. Supp. 663, 41 FEP 1715 (M.D. Ga. 1986) (seniority system held bona fide where discriminatory intent not proven, even though statistical evidence showed de facto discrimination); Black Law Enforcement Officers Ass'n v. City of Akron, 40 FEP 322 (N.D. Ohio 1986), *aff'd in pertinent part and rev'd in part,* 824 F.2d 475, 44 FEP 1477 (6th Cir. 1987) (on preliminary injunction motion, court held that accumulated-point system for up to 14 years' service, in determining promotions of officers to sergeant, was neutral and legitimate, since no evidence that system had its genesis in racial discrimination or that it was negotiated or maintained for that or any other illegal purpose; further, the fact that system may ultimately be found to perpetuate past discrimination does not make it unlawful).

[23]30 FEP 555 (N.D. Ala. 1979).

[24]643 F. Supp. 1494 (E.D. Tex. 1986), *aff'd in part, vacated and remanded in part,* 841 F.2d 547 (5th Cir. 1988) (remanding for determination of post-Act bona fides).

[25]709 F.2d 807, 32 FEP 641 (2d Cir.), *cert. denied,* 464 U.S. 937, 33 FEP 48 (1983).

[26]*Id.,* 709 F.2d at 812, 32 FEP at 645–46. *See also* Campbell v. Tennessee Valley Auth., 613 F. Supp. 611, 38 FEP 779 (E.D. Tenn. 1985) (plaintiff who was discriminated against in promotion procedures

## III. SENIORITY AND LAYOFF

The courts have been frequently confronted with determining whether minority employment gains achieved under judicially ordered hiring quotas must be preserved in the event of layoffs that otherwise would have been seniority-based. The Supreme Court, in *Firefighters Local 1784 v. Stotts,* [27] resolved at least one aspect of the conflict between the rights of minorities and nonminorities where layoffs are necessary subsequent to a Title VII consent decree. [28] The consent decree in *Stotts* did not award retroactive seniority, nor did it contain a plan to be followed in the event a reduction in force was necessary. For other purposes, seniority was to be based on each individual's total length of service with the city.

The city proposed layoffs based on a last-hired, first-fired rule, with seniority defined as each individual's continuous service with the city. The respondent black firefighters then brought suit and obtained an injunction against the proposed layoffs. On appeal, the Sixth Circuit held that the district court erred in holding that the seniority system was not bona fide, but affirmed the lower court's order as a valid modification of the consent decree.

The Supreme Court resolved the issue of the district court's authority, pursuant to a consent decree, to override the seniority provisions of the collective bargaining agreement against the respondents on two bases. First, the Court held that the injunction was not, as respondents argued, simply an enforcement of the existing consent decree. [29] Second, the Court concluded that, even if the order were viewed as a modification of the consent decree, § 703(h) precluded such modification. In reaching this second conclusion, the Court affirmed the Sixth Circuit's holding that the seniority system was bona fide. The Court then proceeded to address the question whether, consistent with § 703(h), the district court could order the petitioners to disregard a bona fide seniority system in order to protect the beneficiaries of the consent decree.

The Sixth Circuit had reasoned that, since the district court could have ordered relief overriding the seniority system if the case had gone to trial, it had corresponding authority to modify the consent decree in the same fashion. In reviewing and reversing this holding, the Supreme Court construed § 703(h) as an express limitation on the district court's remedial authority. The Court noted that, although a district court has authority to award actual victims of discrimination competitive seniority and place them accordingly on the seniority roster, such an award cannot be based simply upon membership in a disadvantaged class. The Court relied on its holding in *Teamsters v. United States* [30] that retroactive competitive seniority can only

---

entitled only to equal opportunity to consideration for the position and is not entitled to position when turned down after being allowed to compete for position nondiscriminatorily).

[27] 467 U.S. 561, 34 FEP 1702 (1984).

[28] The court also addressed and rejected the respondents' argument that, since the white firefighters had been recalled, the case was moot. Justices Blackmun, Brennan, and Marshall dissented sharply on this issue.

[29] 467 U.S. at 575–76, 34 FEP at 1709.

[30] 431 U.S. 324, 14 FEP 1514 (1977).

be awarded to individual class members who prove that the discriminatory practice affected them adversely.

The Court noted that, in formulating the consent decree, the parties had not identified specific employees entitled to individual relief from the challenged practices. This fact narrowed the range of remedial action subsequently available to the class. The Court stated: "It therefore seems to us in light of *Teamsters,* the Court of Appeals imposed on the parties as an adjunct of settlement something that could not have been ordered had the case gone to trial and the plaintiffs proved that a pattern or practice of discrimination existed."[31]

*Stotts* prevents a court from "enter[ing] a disputed modification of a consent decree in Title VII litigation if the resulting order is inconsistent with that statute."[32] Of course, members of the injured class may still be entitled to relief upon either a showing that the seniority system is not bona fide or proof of individual discrimination:

> "Since * * * Title VII precludes a district court from displacing a non-minority employee with seniority under the contractually established seniority system absent either a finding that the seniority system was adopted with discriminatory intent or a determination that such a remedy was necessary to make whole a proven victim of discrimination, the district court was precluded from granting such relief over the city's objection in this case."[33]

Since the Supreme Court's decision in *Stotts,* the courts have continued to wrestle with some of the issues left open by the decision, particularly the scope to be given to the Court's finding that minority employees were not entitled to relief absent a finding that they were proven victims of discrimination.

Another more recent Supreme Court decision taking an approach similar to *Stotts* concerning layoffs is *Wygant v. Jackson Board of Education.*[34] The Court there ruled that a provision of a collective bargaining agreement between a school board and teachers' union apportioning layoffs between minority and nonminority employees in order to preserve the effects of an affirmative action program violated the Equal Protection Clause of the federal constitution.[35]

---

[31]467 U.S. at 579, 34 FEP at 1711.

[32]*Id.* at 576 n.9, 34 FEP at 1710.

[33]*Id.* Immediately following the Supreme Court's decision in *Stotts,* two district courts dissolved injunctions prohibiting implementation of seniority-based layoff plans having a disproportionate impact on minority employees. United States v. City of Cincinnati, 35 FEP 676 (S.D. Ohio 1984), *aff'd in part, reversed in part,* 771 F.2d 161, 38 FEP 1402 (6th Cir. 1985) (a municipality cannot ignore seniority under Civil Service regulations in determining order of layoffs); Vulcan Pioneers v. New Jersey Dep't of Civil Serv., 588 F. Supp. 732, 35 FEP 24 (D.N.J. 1984), *aff'd,* 770 F.2d 1077 (3d Cir. 1985) (seniority rights must prevail by virtue of Supreme Court decision).

[34]476 U.S. 267, 40 FEP 1321 (1986).

[35]The *Wygant* decision must be compared with two other contemporaneous Supreme Court decisions which, although not involving layoffs, suggested limitations to the scope of *Stotts. See* Firefighters Local 93 v. City of Cleveland, 478 U.S. 501, 41 FEP 139 (1986) *and* Sheet Metal Workers Local 28 v. EEOC, 478 U.S. 421, 41 FEP 107 (1986). In *Firefighters Local 93,* in which a consent decree apportioned certain promotions to minority candidates, the Supreme Court held that the relief afforded by a consent decree may be broader than that which a court could impose under § 706(g) of Title VII if the case were litigated to judgment, although such a decree remains subject to challenges under other sections of Title VII and the Equal Protection Clause of the Constitution. The Court underscored that § 706(g) "by itself does not restrict the ability of employers or unions to enter into voluntary agreements [such as consent decrees] providing for race-conscious remedial action." *Stotts* was distinguished, in relevant part, because it involved a nonvoluntary modification of a consent decree. In *Sheet Metal Workers Local 28,* the Supreme

At issue in *Wygant* was a collective bargaining agreement negotiated after a period of racial unrest, in which layoffs were apportioned between affirmative action hirees (pursuant to a negotiated affirmative action plan) and nonminority teachers. The collective bargaining agreement provided:

> "In the event that it becomes necessary to reduce the number of teachers through layoff from employment by the Board, teachers with the most seniority in the district shall be retained, except that at no time will there be a greater percentage of minority personnel laid off than the current percentage of minority personnel employed at the time of the layoff."[36]

When layoffs subsequently became necessary and the Board refused to displace nonminority teachers in order to retain minority probationary teachers, two minority teachers and the teachers' union successfully brought suit in state court to compel compliance with the agreement. The displaced nonminority teachers then brought suit in federal court, challenging the layoff provision as violative of the Civil Rights Act and the Equal Protection Clause. While the District Court and Sixth Circuit upheld the layoff provision,[37] the Supreme Court reversed.[38] In considering the equal protection challenge, the Court held that the layoff provision, like all classifications based on race or ethnic status, was subject to strict judicial scrutiny and could be upheld only if it were narrowly tailored to achieve a compelling governmental interest. The Court concluded that the school board had not established a compelling interest and, even if it had, the layoff provision "was not a legally appropriate means of achieving even a compelling purpose."[39]

The Court emphasized that it has never upheld a racial classification against an equal protection challenge without some showing of prior discrimination by the governmental unit involved. While acknowledging the legitimacy of the school board's interest in eradicating discrimination, citing *Brown v. Board of Education of Topeka, Kansas,*[40] the Court was unwilling to recognize a compelling governmental interest underlying the layoff provision, since the trial court failed to "make a factual determination that the employer had a strong basis in evidence for its conclusion that remedial action was necessary."[41]

The Court further recognized that the standard for reviewing the means

---

Court held that, under appropriate circumstances, neither § 706(g) nor the Equal Protection Clause prohibits a court from ordering preferential relief that benefits individuals who are not actual victims of discrimination as a remedy for violation of Title VII, and such relief would be necessary in cases in which an employer's reputation for discrimination operates to discourage minorities from seeking available employment, or as an interim measure pending the development and implementation of nondiscriminatory hiring or promotion procedures. *See also* United States v. Paradise, 480 U.S. 149, 43 FEP 1 (1987) (consent decree upheld which instituted promotion quota for blacks who had not been identified as actual victims of discrimination, where state employer had long and pervasive history of discrimination and failure to comply with court-ordered remedies).

[36]40 FEP at 1322.

[37]*See* 746 F.2d 1152, 36 FEP 153 (6th Cir. 1984).

[38]Justice O'Connor concurred in the judgment and in most of the Court's opinion rendered by Justice Rehnquist, but felt it unnecessary to evaluate the constitutionality of the layoff provision since she found that the governmental interest underlying the plan was insufficient to survive equal protection scrutiny. 40 FEP at 1328–32. Justice White viewed the layoff provision as equivalent to "the discharge of white teachers to make room for blacks, none of whom has been shown to be a victim of any racial discrimination," and filed a one-paragraph opinion concurring in the judgment. *Id.,* 40 FEP at 1332–33.

[39]40 FEP at 1326.

[40]349 U.S. 294 (1955).

[41]40 FEP at 1325.

of accomplishing a race-conscious purpose has been articulated in various ways ("necessary," "narrowly tailored," "specifically and narrowly framed," "the most exact connection between justification and classification") and involves a consideration of alternative and less restrictive means. While acknowledging that race could be taken into account when "effectuating a limited and properly tailored remedy to cure the effects of prior discrimination," even though innocent parties might be affected,[42] the burden imposed on innocent parties by a preferential layoff scheme was too intrusive. The Court expressly stated:

> "We have previously expressed concern over the burden that a preferential layoff scheme imposes on innocent parties. * * * In cases involving valid *hiring* goals, the burden to be borne by innocent individuals is diffused to a considerable extent among society generally. Though hiring goals may burden some innocent individuals, they simply do not impose the same kind of injury that layoffs impose. Denial of a future employment opportunity is not as intrusive as loss of an existing job."[43]

Thus, because less intrusive means of accomplishing racial equality, such as hiring goals, were available, the Board's layoff procedure violated the Equal Protection Clause.[44]

Aside from the *Wygant* decision, various courts of appeals also have dealt with the scope of *Stotts*. Some courts have followed *Stotts* and upheld layoffs based on seniority provisions in a collective bargaining agreement where the consent decree did not mention or deal with layoffs or demotions.[45] Several courts of appeal, however, have read *Stotts* narrowly to prohibit courts only from modifying consent decrees, entered without a finding of discrimination, in such manner as to override bona fide seniority systems.[46] Other courts have permitted preferential treatment, despite seniority provi-

---

[42]*See* Franks v. Bowman Transp. Co., 424 U.S. 747, 12 FEP 549 (1976).

[43]40 FEP at 1327.

[44]*See also* Britton v. South Bend Community School Corp., 819 F.2d 766, 43 FEP 1483 (7th Cir.), *cert. denied*, 484 U.S. —, 45 FEP 648 (1987) (en banc) (collective bargaining agreement provision requiring layoff of all white teachers before black teachers was not "narrowly tailored" to remedy previous discrimination and therefore violated Fourteenth Amendment; moreover, the ultimate teacher ratio goal was tied to student population and not to teacher availability, so that the remedy did not specifically address *employment* discrimination).

[45]United States v. City of Cincinnati, 771 F.2d 161, 38 FEP 1402 (6th Cir. 1985) (court is bound by seniority provisions in collective bargaining agreement, but case remanded for further findings whether using "composite scores" for determining layoffs for employees hired on same date discriminated against black and female officers); White v. Colgan Elec. Co., 781 F.2d 1214, 39 FEP 1599 (6th Cir. 1986) (explanation for laying off plaintiff, to wit, conformity with inverse layoff procedure dictated by collective bargaining agreement, was a legitimate basis for employer's action).

[46]Pennsylvania v. Operating Engineers Local 542, 770 F.2d 1068, 38 FEP 673 (3d Cir. 1985), *cert. denied*, 474 U.S. 1060, 39 FEP 1200 (1986) (distinguishing *Stotts* because here there was a judicial finding of intentional discrimination and no bona fide seniority system); Deveraux v. Geary, 765 F.2d 268, 38 FEP 23 (1st Cir. 1985), *cert. denied*, 471 U.S. 1115, 41 FEP 272 (1986) (distinguishing *Stotts* because there is no claimed conflict between a seniority plan and the remedies provided for in the decree, thus § 703(h) not involved); Turner v. Orr, 759 F.2d 817, 37 FEP 1186 (11th Cir. 1985), *cert. denied*, 478 U.S. 1020, 41 FEP 272 (1986) (distinguishing *Stotts* because this case did not involve infringement of bona fide seniority system, and no nonminority worker had to step down to accommodate a minority); Diaz v. AT&T, 752 F.2d 1356, 36 FEP 1742 (9th Cir. 1985) (limited *Stotts* to its facts); Van Aken v. Young, 750 F.2d 43, 36 FEP 777 (6th Cir. 1984) (distinguishing *Stotts* because this case involved affirmative action plan voluntarily applied by the city at point of hiring, unrelated to seniority rights); Kromnick v. Philadelphia School Dist., 739 F.2d 894, 35 FEP 538 (3d Cir. 1984), *cert. denied*, 469 U.S. 1107, 36 FEP 976 (1985) (distinguishing *Stotts* because here there is no overriding of bona fide seniority plan); Grann v. City of Madison, 738 F.2d 786, 35 FEP 296 (7th Cir.), *cert. denied*, 469 U.S. 918, 35 FEP 1800 (1984) (distinguishing *Stotts* in part because *Stotts* did not involve a judicial finding of intentional discrimination).

sions, where it was concluded that layoff protection was implied in the settlement agreement.[47]

## IV. CONSTRUCTIVE SENIORITY AS A REMEDY TO IDENTIFIABLE VICTIMS OF DISCRIMINATION

Where a court finds classwide discrimination in hiring, retroactive seniority can be granted only to those class members who, in the absence of discrimination, would have actually been hired and not to the entire class.[48] However, the extent to which relief must be limited to identifiable victims, or can also benefit nonvictims, is a matter of ongoing debate.[49]

Different views have also been expressed as to what facts or circumstances must be present to meet the test set forth in *Franks v. Bowman Transportation*[50] requiring the presence of "unusual adverse impact" to justify the denial of retroactive seniority. The Seventh Circuit approved the district court's refusal to grant full retroactive competitive seniority on being rehired to a class of 1,400 female flight attendants who were terminated on the basis of a no-marriage rule, finding that such seniority would result in unusual adverse impact on incumbents in terms of furloughs, terminations, and involuntary transfers, whether or not the discriminates were immediately reinstated.[51] In finding that immediate reinstatement would cause unusual adverse impact, the Seventh Circuit noted that immediate reinstatement would decrease the percentage of minority-group flight attendants from 15 to 10 percent and that furloughs of incumbents would preclude new hires by the airline, including minority-group persons, for several years.[52] The Seventh Circuit also held that the defendants had carried the burden of showing that reinstatement with full competitive seniority would result in unusual adverse impact.[53]

---

[47]Miller v. Fairchild Indus., 797 F.2d 727, 41 FEP 809 (9th Cir. 1986) (*Stotts* did not preclude preferential treatment and layoff protection where it was implied in settlement agreement).

[48]Ingram v. Madison Square Garden Center, 709 F.2d 807, 32 FEP 641 (2d Cir.), *cert. denied,* 464 U.S. 937, 33 FEP 48 (1983).

[49]Decisions requiring that individuals be identified as actual victims of discrimination to be awarded constructive seniority may be of questionable value as precedent in light of the Supreme Court's decisions in *Firefighters Local 93 v. City of Cleveland,* 478 U.S. 501, 41 FEP 139 (1986) and *Sheet Metal Workers Local 28 v. EEOC,* 478 U.S. 421, 41 FEP 107 (1986). In the latter case the Court held that a district court may award preferential relief (in that case the benefits of coverage under an affirmative action plan) even to minorities who were not identified as victims of discrimination, "where an employer or a labor union has engaged in persistent or egregious discrimination, or where necessary to dissipate the lingering effects of pervasive discrimination." *Id.,* 41 FEP at 116. In support of its decision, the Court determined from the legislative history of Title VII that Congress "did not intend to prohibit a court from exercising its remedial authority" in a manner to benefit victims of discrimination who have not been specifically identified. *Id.,* 41 FEP at 124. The Court also declined the petitioner's invitation "to read *Stotts* to prohibit a court from ordering any kind of race conscious affirmative relief that might benefit nonvictims." *Id.,* 41 FEP at 128.

On the same day, the Supreme Court held in *Firefighters Local 93* that a district court could enter a consent decree "which provides relief that may benefit individuals who are not the actual victims of the defendant's discriminatory practices." 41 FEP at 141. There, the city had agreed to create promotional opportunities for firefighters of all races, with the only 10 minorities that had qualified for upper-level positions to be promoted, regardless of seniority.

[50]*Supra* note 42.

[51]Romasanta v. United Airlines, 717 F.2d 1140, 32 FEP 1545 (7th Cir. 1983), *cert. denied,* 466 U.S. 944, 34 FEP 920 (1984).

[52]*Id.*

[53]*Id.*

The Eighth Circuit found a district court's findings of adverse impact unpersuasive and granted retroactive seniority to female employees who had been unlawfully denied employment.[54] The district court had refused the plaintiff's request for retroactive seniority, holding that this relief would result in the bumping of long-time employees into less desirable jobs, lead to low employee morale and labor-management problems, and place pressure and strain on employees. In reversing the district court, the Eighth Circuit held that such consequences are to be expected in Title VII cases and do not constitute the type of unusual adverse impact contemplated by *Franks v. Bowman Transportation* as sufficient to justify the denial of retroactive seniority.[55]

---

[54]EEOC v. Rath Packing Co., 787 F.2d 318, 40 FEP 580 (8th Cir. 1986), *cert. denied,* 479 U.S. 910, 41 FEP 1712 (1986). *See also* Jones v. Memphis Light, Gas & Water Div., 642 F. Supp. 644, 41 FEP 1165 (W.D. Tenn. 1986) (although priority provisions of public utility's affirmative action plan may have conflicted with seniority system established in memorandum of understanding with the union, the affirmative action plan was narrowly tailored and substantially related to goal of remedying past discrimination against black and female employees; it was narrow in scope and impact, temporary and satisfied the "strict scrutiny" test; thus, the provision superseded the seniority system and did not violate equal protection or Title VII).

[55]787 F.2d at 335, 40 FEP at 594. *See also* EEOC v. M.D. Pneumatics, Inc., 779 F.2d 21, 44 FEP 530 (8th Cir. 1985) (employer's "effort to remedy the effects of its past discrimination, although commendable, are not the kind of compelling reasons which justify the denial of retroactive seniority").

## CHAPTER 4

# SCORED TESTS

## II. STATUTORY PROVISION

Early in the development of the law of scored tests, the Supreme Court rejected claims that professionally developed employment tests should be automatically insulated from liability under the provisions of § 703(h) of Title VII.[1] Similarly, the Fifth Circuit has rejected a claim that, absent intentional discrimination, scored tests are protected from liability under the "bona fide merit system" provision of § 703(h).[2]

In analyzing equal protection claims under the Fourteenth Amendment arising from use of scored tests, the Supreme Court has long held that proof of adverse impact alone is insufficient to state a constitutional claim of discrimination.[3] Overruling its earlier opinion, the Seventh Circuit has recently held under a similar analysis that "an exam might fail to survive the exacting scrutiny to which Title VII subjects examinations that have a disproportionate impact on a protected group such as blacks yet still not be so unreasonable as to create constitutional doubts unrelated to discrimination."[4]

## III. BASIC ANALYSIS OF TESTING CASES

Most courts have continued to apply classic disparate impact analysis to testing cases[5] and to hold that, absent proof of adverse impact, an employer has no duty to validate its employment test.[6] However, there are isolated exceptions. One trial court analyzed a hiring case, in which the three plaintiffs were rejected for their failure to pass a written examination, under

---

[1]*See* Griggs v. Duke Power Co., 401 U.S. 424, 435–36, 3 FEP 175, 179–80 (1971), reproduced at p. 6 of the Second Edition.

[2]Walls v. Mississippi State Dep't of Pub. Welfare, 730 F.2d 306, 320, 34 FEP 1114, 1124 (5th Cir. 1984), *aff'g in relevant part* 542 F. Supp. 281, 310–11, 31 FEP 1795, 1819–20 (N.D. Miss. 1982) ("an invalid test cannot measure 'merit' ").

[3]*See* Washington v. Davis, 426 U.S. 229, 237, 12 FEP 1415, 1418 (1976), reproduced at p. 116 of the Second Edition.

[4]Bigby v. City of Chicago, 766 F.2d 1053, 1055, 38 FEP 853, 854 (7th Cir. 1985), *cert. denied,* 474 U.S. 1056, 39 FEP 1200 (1986) (overruling DiIulio v. City of Northlake Bd. of Fire & Police Comm'rs, 682 F.2d 666 (7th Cir.), *cert. denied,* 459 U.S. 1038 (1982)).

[5]*See, e.g.,* Carroll v. Sears, Roebuck & Co., 708 F.2d 183, 32 FEP 286 (5th Cir. 1983) (employment tests are "the kind of employment practice to which the disparate impact model traditionally has applied"); Bunch v. Bullard, 795 F.2d 384, 395, 41 FEP 515, 524 (5th Cir. 1986) ("without the aid of disparate impact theory, a plaintiff faces an almost insuperable handicap in challenging a facially neutral employment requirement"); Allen v. Isaac, 39 FEP 1142, 1155 (N.D. Ill. 1986).

[6]*See* Clady v. County of Los Angeles, 770 F.2d 1421, 38 FEP 1575 (9th Cir. 1985), *cert. denied,* 475 U.S. 1109, 40 FEP 792 (1986); Kraszewski v. State Farm Gen. Ins. Co., 38 FEP 197 (N.D. Cal. 1985); Evans v. City of Evanston, 621 F. Supp. 710, 37 FEP 1290 (N.D. Ill. 1985); Rivera v. City of Wichita Falls, 665 F.2d 531, 538, 27 FEP 1352, 1358 (5th Cir. 1982) ("the duty to validate * * * arises only when the test has a disparate impact"); Brunet v. City of Columbus, 642 F. Supp. 1214, 1229, 42 FEP 1846, 1859 (S.D. Ohio 1986), *cert. denied,* 485 U.S. — (1988).

disparate treatment analysis.[7] The defendant contested the plaintiff's ability to satisfy the "qualifications" prong of the *McDonnell Douglas* test. The plaintiffs claimed they nevertheless were qualified for the opening, because the test was invalid and had an adverse impact on blacks or women.[8] The court applied adverse impact analysis with regard to this portion of the disparate treatment prima facie case.

The circuit courts do not agree on the scope of review of disparate impact determinations. The Ninth Circuit has held that the proper scope of appellate review for determining whether plaintiffs have established a prima facie case of disparate impact is *de novo* review, rather than the "clearly erroneous" standard.[9] However, more recently, the Fifth Circuit has used the "clearly erroneous" rule.[10]

The courts have continued to reject testing claims attempted under the Civil Rights Acts of 1866 and 1871 or the Fifth and Fourteenth amendments absent some showing that the test was intentionally used to discriminate.[11] Reversing a district court decision, the Eighth Circuit held that a finding that an employer implemented a test which it knew had an adverse impact on blacks was not alone sufficient to support a finding of "intentional discrimination under disparate treatment analysis."[12]

In what appears to be the first case of its kind, the Eleventh Circuit held that an employer has a duty of "reasonable accommodation" of the handicapped under the Rehabilitation Act of 1973 when it "uses a test which cannot and does not accurately reflect the abilities of the handicapped person."[13]

## IV. THE UNIFORM GUIDELINES ON EMPLOYEE SELECTION PROCEDURES

In a report said to have been prompted by "public criticisms of the

---

[7]Hill v. Metropolitan Atlanta Rapid Transit Auth., 591 F. Supp. 125, 45 FEP 782 (N.D. Ga. 1984), *aff'd in part, rev'd and remanded in part,* 841 F.2d 1533, 46 FEP 930 (11th Cir. 1988).

[8]*Id.* See also Fudge v. City of Providence Fire Dep't, 766 F.2d 650, 655, 38 FEP 648, 652 (1st Cir. 1985) (utilizing a similar disparate treatment analysis, but without specific reference to *McDonnell Douglas Corp. v. Green,* 411 U.S. 792, 5 FEP 965 (1973)).

[9]Clady v. County of Los Angeles, *supra* note 6, 770 F.2d at 1427, 38 FEP at 1580.

[10]Bunch v. Bullard, 795 F.2d 384, 392, 41 FEP 515, 522 (5th Cir. 1986) (citing Walls v. Mississippi State Dep't of Pub. Welfare, 730 F.2d 306, 34 FEP 1114 (5th Cir. 1984)).

[11]Walls v. Mississippi State Dep't of Pub. Welfare, 542 F. Supp. 281, 313, 31 FEP 1795, 1821 (N.D. Miss. 1982), *aff'd in relevant part,* 730 F.2d 306, 34 FEP 1114 (5th Cir. 1984) ("[U]nder *Connecticut v. Teal,* 457 U.S. 440, 452, 29 FEP 1, 6 (1982), 'no special haven for discriminatory tests' that are not job-related is offered the employer by Section 703(h);" district court therefore correct in holding that "[a]s to the testing challenges based on § 1981, § 1983, and the fourteenth amendment, we conclude that plaintiffs failed to establish that the racially neutral testing devices may be 'traced to a racially discriminatory purpose.' "). *But see* DiIulio v. Board of Fire & Police Comm'rs, *supra* note 4, 682 F.2d at 669 (a panel of the Seventh Circuit, in a highly unusual opinion, held that "constitutional due process" required that police sergeant promotion exam have "a direct and substantial relation to appellants' qualifications to be police sergeants"). In *Bigby v. City of Chicago, supra* note 4, another panel of the Seventh Circuit overruled *DiIulio.*

[12]Easley v. Anheuser-Busch, 758 F.2d 251, 261 n.22, 37 FEP 549, 556 (8th Cir. 1985), *rev'g in relevant part* 572 F. Supp. 402, 414, 34 FEP 380, 389 (E.D. Mo. 1983). This conclusion was based in part on a finding that it is "widely known" by those in the testing and employee selection fields that a written paper-and-pencil test generally disqualifies a higher percentage of blacks than whites. 572 F. Supp. at 406, 34 FEP at 382. *But see* Black Shield Police Ass'n v. City of Cleveland, 42 FEP 270, 277 (N.D. Ohio 1986) (plaintiffs unsuccessfully attempted to show discriminatory intent based on city's administration of test very shortly after expiration of consent decree).

[13]Stutts v. Freeman, 694 F.2d 666, 669, 669 n.3, 30 FEP 1121, 1123 (11th Cir. 1983) (reversing summary judgment for employer where there was "strong evidence" that plaintiff, who had failed test owing to dyslexia, could "probably perform most competently" in job at issue).

guidelines by some of their users," the General Accounting Office (GAO) has made a strong call for the review and revision of the Uniform Guidelines on Employee Selection Procedures (Uniform Guidelines).[14] In so doing the GAO joined the ranks of numerous professional groups as well as personnel management associations that have criticized the Uniform Guidelines as "not provid[ing] an up-to-date framework for validating selection procedures"[15] and that have publicly urged revisions.[16]

In July 1984 the EEOC voted to begin a comprehensive review of the Uniform Guidelines.[17] This review is still in progress, and the latest regulatory agenda for the agency shows no projected end date.[18] In another development of interest, the American Psychological Association published a long-awaited revision of its 1974 testing standards during 1985.[19]

## C. The Weight to Be Accorded Administrative Guidelines on Employee Testing

Recent judicial opinions generally refer to the Uniform Guidelines in determining whether a given testing device has adverse impact and in assessing both its job-relatedness and any validation efforts. Although few recent decisions have followed *Griggs*[20] in according the Guidelines "great deference,"[21] and although some courts have applied them less than rigorously,[22] throughout the majority of cases there is a general acceptance of their

---

[14]General Accounting Office, *Uniform Guidelines on Employee Selection Procedures Should Be Reviewed and Revised,* Rep. No. GAO/FPCD-82-26 (July 30, 1982), reviewed in 150 DAILY LAB. REP. A-1 (BNA, August 4, 1982). The Uniform Guidelines are published at 29 C.F.R. §1607 (1988).
[15]*Id.*
[16]In 1981 both the Committee on Psychological Tests and Assessment of the American Psychological Association (APA) and the Executive Committee of APA's Division of Industrial and Organizational Psychology (Division 14) made public calls for the revision of the Guidelines "consistent with current research, knowledge and professional standards." *See* Second Edition at p. 94 n.48. *See also* 150 DAILY LAB. REP. A-1 (BNA, August 4, 1982). The International Personnel Management Association, an organization of public personnel managers, has also urged revision of the Guidelines. *See* 146 DAILY LAB. REP. A-4 (BNA, July 29, 1982).
[17]*See* 242 DAILY LAB. REP. D-1 (BNA, December 17, 1984); 221 DAILY LAB. REP. A-6 (BNA, November 15, 1984).
[18]52 FED. REG. 40,919 (1987).
[19]American Psychological Ass'n, *Standards for Educational and Psychological Testing* (1985). *See* 79 DAILY LAB. REP. A-5 (BNA, April 24, 1984). *See also* 93 DAILY LAB. REP. A-4 (BNA, May 12, 1983).
[20]Griggs v. Duke Power Co., 401 U.S. 424, 434, 3 FEP 175, 179 (1971).
[21]Walls v. Mississippi State Dep't of Pub. Welfare, 542 F. Supp. 281, 312, 31 FEP 1795, 1820 (N.D. Miss. 1982), *aff'd in relevant part,* 730 F.2d 306, 34 FEP 1114 (5th Cir. 1984); Wilmore v. City of Wilmington, 533 F. Supp. 844, 854 n.25, 30 FEP 1764, 1771 (D. Del. 1982), *rev'd on other grounds,* 699 F.2d 667, 31 FEP 2 (3d Cir. 1983) (Uniform Guidelines entitled to "great deference" but courts "not bound" by them). *See also* Burney v. City of Pawtucket, 559 F. Supp. 1089, 1101 n.18, 34 FEP 1274, 1284 (D.R.I. 1983), *appeal dismissed,* 728 F.2d 547, 34 FEP 1295 (1st Cir. 1984) ("Defendants' burden to prove job relatedness is much higher when the Guidelines are ignored.").
[22]*See, e.g.,* Eison v. City of Knoxville, 570 F. Supp. 11, 13, 33 FEP 1141, 1142–43 (E.D. Tenn. 1983) (while citing Uniform Guideline standards for determining adverse impact, court made no reference to Uniform Guidelines in finding certain physical tests for police applicants "job-related"); Berkman v. City of New York, 536 F. Supp. 177, 206, 28 FEP 856, 882 (E.D.N.Y. 1982), *aff'd,* 705 F.2d 584, 31 FEP 767 (2d Cir. 1983) (contrasting "somewhat mechanical fact/inference distinction of Guidelines § 14(c)(2)" with "the more realistic view of *Guardians IV* [Guardians Ass'n v. Civil Serv. Comm'n, 630 F.2d 79, 23 FEP 909 (2d Cir. 1980), *cert. denied,* 452 U.S. 940 (1981)]"); Clady v. County of Los Angeles, 770 F.2d 1421, 1428–29, 38 FEP 1575, 1580–81 (9th Cir. 1985), *cert. denied,* 475 U.S. 1109, 40 FEP 792 (1986) (while citing Uniform Guidelines, court noted they are not legally binding and acknowledged there is no "consensus on a threshold mathematical showing of variance to constitute substantial disproportionate impact," and analyzes "whether the statistical disparity is 'substantial' or 'significant' in a given case").

principles.[23] A few courts have resolved testing issues without reference to the Guidelines,[24] but this is the exception rather than the rule. The trend in the Eighth Circuit toward reliance on the Guidelines (noted in the Second Edition at page 96) has continued.[25] The Seventh Circuit has also endorsed the Guidelines as drawing "upon current psychological literature on psychometrics as well as standards of test validation established by the American Psychological Association."[26]

Some courts have found ways to distinguish them in a particular case. One court avoided strict application of the Uniform Guidelines to a disparate impact case arising from a high school diploma requirement, holding that the "exacting criteria" of the Uniform Guidelines are more applicable to testing cases than educational requirements.[27] Other courts have used different techniques for analyzing discriminatory impact where the sample population is small.[28]

## V. Triggering Defendant's Duty to Prove Job-Relatedness: Plaintiff's Proof of Adverse Impact

### A. Quantum of Adverse Impact Necessary to Establish Plaintiff's Prima Facie Case

To support a finding of sufficient statistical significance to establish a prima facie case of adverse impact, courts continue to cite both the 80-percent (or "four-fifths") rule of the Uniform Guidelines[29] and the *Castaneda*

---

[23]Nash v. Consolidated City of Jacksonville, 763 F.2d 1393, 1395, 38 FEP 151, 152 (11th Cir. 1985) (use of the "80% rule" under 29 C.F.R. § 1607.4(d) (1985), "as well as statistical evidence produced by [plaintiff's] expert witness," was sufficient to establish prima facie case of discriminatory impact); Evans v. City of Evanston, 621 F. Supp. 710, 712, 37 FEP 1290, 1292 (N.D. Ill. 1985) (§ 4(d) of Uniform Guidelines cited as "evidence" of adverse impact); Reid v. New York, 570 F. Supp. 1003, 1005–06, 38 FEP 266, 267–68 (S.D.N.Y. 1983) (violation of 80% rule held sufficient evidence of discrimination to show "probability of success on the merits" in approving class action consent decree); Brunet v. City of Columbus, 642 F. Supp. 1214, 1227, 42 FEP 1846, 1857 (S.D. Ohio 1986), *appeal dismissed mem.,* 826 F.2d 1062, 44 FEP 1671 (6th Cir. 1987), cert. denied, 485 U.S. — (1988); Police Officers for Equal Rights v. City of Columbus, 644 F. Supp 393, 407, 42 FEP 1752, 1763 (S.D. Ohio 1985). *But see* Clady v. County of Los Angeles, *supra* note 22.

[24]*See, e.g.,* Washington v. Kroger Co., 671 F.2d 1072, 1077, 29 FEP 1739, 1744 (8th Cir. 1982) (finding math test valid on its face for grocery store checkers).

[25]Gilbert v. City of Little Rock, 799 F.2d 1210, 1214, 44 FEP 509, 513 (8th Cir. 1986).

[26]Gillespie v. Wisconsin, 771 F.2d 1035, 1040, 38 FEP 1487 (7th Cir. 1985), *cert. denied,* 474 U.S. 1083, 39 FEP 1424 (1986); *see also* Allen v. Isaac, 39 FEP 1142, 1154 (N.D. Ill. 1986).

[27]Aguilera v. Cook County Police & Corrections Merit Bd., 760 F.2d 844, 37 FEP 1140 (7th Cir.), *cert. denied,* 474 U.S. 907 (1985).

[28]Fudge v. City of Providence Fire Dep't, 766 F.2d 650, 658, 38 FEP 648, 654–55 (1st Cir. 1985); Bunch v. Bullard, 795 F.2d 384, 395, 41 FEP 515, 524 (5th Cir. 1986); Black Shield Police Ass'n v. City of Cleveland, 42 FEP 270, 279 (N.D. Ohio 1986).

[29]Bushey v. New York State Civil Serv. Comm'n, 733 F.2d 220, 225–26, 34 FEP 1065, 1069 (2d Cir. 1984), *cert. denied,* 469 U.S. 1117, 36 FEP 1166 (1985) (minority pass rate of 25% compared with nonminority pass rate of 50% established adverse impact under Uniform Guidelines' "four-fifths" rule); Easley v. Anheuser-Busch, 572 F. Supp. 402, 406, 34 FEP 380, 382–83 (E.D. Mo. 1983), *aff'd in part on other grounds,* 758 F.2d 251, 37 FEP 549 (8th Cir. 1985) (out of total of 1,500 applicants, only 30% of black applicants passed, whereas 50% of white applicants passed, so black pass rate less than 80% of white pass rate; there was difference of 6.64 standard deviations between expected pass rate for blacks and actual pass rate for blacks); Eison v. City of Knoxville, *supra* note 22 (no adverse impact under "four-fifths" rule when selection rate for all candidates, not just one year's candidates, compared); Williams v. City & County of San Francisco, 31 FEP 885 (N.D. Cal. 1983) (80% rule of Uniform Guidelines used because it was "law of the case" owing to prior partial summary judgment decision). *See also* Wilmore v. City of Wilmington, 533 F. Supp. 844, 853, 30 FEP 1764, 1771 (D. Del. 1982) ("Four-fifths is a rule of thumb which must be considered along with the size of the sample, to form the

*v. Partida*[30] "two or three standard deviations" principle.[31] However, the 80-percent rule has drawn criticism.[32] In one case a trial court declined to follow the 80-percent rule where the acceptance rate for minorities was 81.55 percent of that of majority candidates, but there was expert testimony that the disparity nevertheless was statistically significant.[33] At the other extreme, another trial court found a clearly "significant discriminatory pattern" of selection from a test which eliminated about one-fourth of female applicants, but only about 1 percent of male applicants.[34]

None of the recent decisions made a finding of adverse impact where the ratio of pass or failure rates was less than 1.5:1.[35] One court, in dicta, without citing any significance test, found adverse impact based simply on testimony as to the small number of blacks who achieved high enough test scores to be considered and the fact that the same tests were found in another proceeding to have had an adverse impact at another of the defendant's plants.[36]

## B. Appropriate Method of Comparison

In making adverse impact determinations, the courts continue to rely on comparisons of both pass rates and failure rates.[37] As in the prior testing

---

basis for a conclusion about the statistical likelihood of such a disparity"); Allen v. Isaac, 39 FEP 1142, 1155 (N.D. Ill. 1986); Police Officers for Equal Rights v. City of Columbus, 644 F. Supp. 393, 433, 42 FEP 1752, 1783 (S.D. Ohio 1985); Bernard v. Gulf Oil Corp., 643 F. Supp. 1494, 1501 (E.D. Tex. 1986), *aff'd in part, vacated and remanded in part,* 841 F.2d 547 (5th Cir. 1988) (remanding for determination of post-Act bona fides); Brunet v. City of Columbus, 642 F. Supp. 1214, 1230, 42 FEP 1846, 1859–60 (S.D. Ohio 1986), *appeal dismissed mem.,* 826 F.2d 1062, 44 FEP 1671 (6th Cir. 1987), *cert. denied,* 485 U.S. — (1988).

[30]430 U.S. 482, 496 n.17 (1977).

[31]*See, e.g.,* Rivera v. City of Wichita Falls, 665 F.2d 531, 536 n.7, 27 FEP 1352, 1357 (5th Cir. 1982) (finding adverse impact where there was a nine standard deviations difference between expected and observed failure rates, citing *Castaneda v. Partida, supra* note 30). *See also* Berkman v. City of New York, 536 F. Supp. 177, 205, 28 FEP 856, 881 (E.D.N.Y. 1982), *aff'd,* 705 F.2d 584, 31 FEP 767 (2d Cir. 1983) (finding in case of "the inexorable zero" disparate impact "by any reasonable measure including * * * *Castaneda* [and the] Uniform Guidelines"); Easley v. Anheuser-Busch, *supra* note 29; Police Officers for Equal Rights v. City of Columbus, 644 F. Supp. 393, 432 n.13, 42 FEP 1752, 1783 n.13 (S.D. Ohio 1985); Berger v. Iron Workers Local 201, 42 FEP 1161, 1174 (D.D.C. 1985).

[32]*See* Clady v. County of Los Angeles, *supra* note 22.

[33]Hill v. Metropolitan Atlanta Rapid Transit Auth., 591 F. Supp. 125, 129, 45 FEP 782 (N.D. Ga. 1984), *aff'd in part and rev'd and remanded in part,* 841 F.2d 1533, 46 FEP 930 (11th Cir. 1988) (not reaching ultimate impact determination, however, because test had been validated).

[34]Thomas v. City of Evanston, 610 F. Supp. 422, 42 FEP 1795 (N.D. Ill. 1985).

[35]*See* Second Edition at p. 99. Those recent decisions finding impact and their respective pass or failure ratios are as follows: Bushey v. New York State Civil Serv. Comm'n, *supra* note 29 (passing ratio of 2:1); Easley v. Anheuser-Busch, *supra* note 29 (passing ratio of 1.67:1); Rivera v. City of Wichita Falls, *supra* note 31 (failure ratio of 7.4:1); Berkman v. City of New York, 536 F. Supp. 177, 206, 28 FEP 856, 882 (E.D.N.Y. 1982), *aff'd,* 705 F.2d 584, 31 FEP 767 (2d Cir. 1983) (46% of men passed while no women did); Van Aken v. Young, 541 F. Supp. 448, 28 FEP 1669 (E.D. Mich. 1982), *aff'd,* 750 F.2d 43, 36 FEP 777 (6th Cir. 1984) (failure ratios of 3.0:1 and 4.5:1); Walls v. Mississippi State Dep't of Pub. Welfare, 542 F. Supp. 281, 312, 31 FEP 1795, 1820 (N.D. Miss. 1982), *aff'd in relevant part,* 730 F.2d 306, 34 FEP 1114 (5th Cir. 1984) (failure ratios of 32:1, 5.56:1, and 7.25:1); Burney v. City of Pawtucket, 559 F. Supp. 1089, 1101 n.18, 34 FEP 1274, 1284 (D.R.I. 1983), *appeal dismissed,* 728 F.2d 547, 34 FEP 1295 (1st Cir. 1984) (pass ratio of 1.8:1).

[36]Jones v. International Paper Co., 720 F.2d 496, 499, 33 FEP 430, 432 (8th Cir. 1983) (despite finding of adverse impact, however, district court decision in favor of defendant affirmed because plaintiffs could not establish that they were otherwise qualified for positions).

[37]Bushey v. New York Civil Serv. Comm'n, *supra* note 29 (pass rates); Easley v. Anheuser-Busch, *supra* note 29 (pass rates); Eison v. Knoxville, 570 F. Supp. 11, 13, 33 FEP 1141, 1142–43 (E.D. Tenn. 1983) (pass rates); Rivera v. City of Wichita Falls, *supra* note 31 (failure rates); Van Aken v. Young, *supra* note 35 (failure rates); Berkman v. City of New York, *supra* note 35 (failure rates); Tillery v. Pacific Tel. Co., 34 FEP 54 (N.D. Cal. 1982) (pass rates); Burney v. City of Pawtucket, *supra* note 35 (pass rates); Walls v. Mississippi State Dep't of Pub. Welfare, *supra* note 35 (comparing failure rates on one of tests at issue and pass rates on others).

cases, none of the recent cases discussed the choice of pass versus failure rates or noted its potential importance. A few of the recent testing cases compared mean test scores in addition to comparing pass or failure rates.[38] One case was reversed and remanded, even though the rates at which the applicants were placed on the selection list were comparable, because the actual selections were based upon an applicant's ranking on the list, a factor the district court did not consider.[39]

In a Ninth Circuit case,[40] the court approved the county's test validation study, which compared test scores from a written examination with the performance of recruits during their firefighting academy training period.[41] Significantly, the plaintiffs did not contest the comparison between test scores and graduation from the training academy.[42]

## C. The "Bottom Line"

A number of cases have expressly considered "bottom line" arguments in the wake of the Supreme Court's decision in *Connecticut v. Teal,*[43] which rejected this defense, at least where the test at issue operates as a barrier to further consideration in the selection process. In one case the Fifth Circuit found that the district court's reliance on the bottom line theory had been rejected by the Supreme Court in *Teal,* but nonetheless affirmed on the ground that the prima facie case was rebutted by a showing that the tests were job-related.[44] In another case *Teal* was not followed where the challenged portions of the selection process were scored numerically, unlike the pass/fail grading in *Teal.*[45]

Other trial courts found that the "bottom line" was not determinative where, although not an absolute barrier, the test "could have had a major impact" on further consideration[46] or where it provided a "ready potential for * * * decisive consequences."[47]

---

[38]*See, e.g.,* Walls v. Mississippi State Dep't of Pub. Welfare, *supra* note 35 (finding adverse impact based in part on "significant differences" in mean test scores); Police Officers for Equal Rights v. City of Columbus, 644 F. Supp. 393, 408, 42 FEP 1752, 1763 (S.D. Ohio 1985) (mean scores compared in addition to analysis of pass rates). *But see* Brunet v. City of Columbus, 642 F. Supp. 1214, 1227–28, 42 FEP 1846, 1858 (S.D. Ohio 1986), *appeal dismissed mem.,* 826 F.2d 1062, 44 FEP 1671 (6th Cir. 1987), *cert. denied,* 485 U.S. — (1988) (mean score comparison not accepted in female firefighters case where women were actually hired at a higher rate than men and where there were many applicants for only a few positions).

[39]Gilbert v. City of Little Rock, 722 F.2d 1390, 1397–98, 33 FEP 557, 562 (8th Cir. 1983), *cert. denied,* 466 U.S. 972, 34 FEP 1312 (1984).

[40]Clady v. County of Los Angeles, 770 F.2d 1421, 38 FEP 1575 (9th Cir. 1985), *cert. denied,* 475 U.S. 1109, 40 FEP 792 (1986).

[41]*Id.,* 770 F.2d at 1426, 38 FEP at 1579.

[42]*Id. But see* Brunet v. City of Columbus, 642 F. Supp. 1214, 1247, 42 FEP 1846, 1873 (S.D. Ohio 1986), *appeal dismissed mem.,* 826 F.2d 1062, 44 FEP 1671 (6th Cir. 1987), *cert. denied,* 485 U.S. — (1988).

[43]457 U.S. 440, 29 FEP 1 (1982), reproduced at p. 1378 of the Second Edition.

[44]Cormier v. P.P.G. Indus., 702 F.2d 567, 31 FEP 1039 (5th Cir. 1983).

[45]Brunet v. City of Columbus, 642 F. Supp. 1214, 1224–27, 42 FEP 1846 (S.D. Ohio 1986), *appeal dismissed mem.,* 826 F.2d 1062, 44 FEP 1671 (6th Cir. 1987), *cert. denied,* 485 U.S. — (1988) (citing the Second Edition in support of this holding, as well as Smith v. Troyan, 562 F.2d 492, 10 FEP 1380 (6th Cir. 1975), *cert. denied,* 426 U.S. 934, 12 FEP 1560 (1976)).

[46]Williams v. City & County of San Francisco, 31 FEP 885, 887 (N.D. Cal. 1983).

[47]Burney v. City of Pawtucket, 559 F. Supp. 1089, 1100, 34 FEP 1274, 1283 (D.R.I. 1983), *appeal dismissed mem.,* 728 F.2d 547, 34 FEP 1295 (1st Cir. 1984). *See also* Wilmore v. City of Wilmington, 699 F.2d 667, 31 FEP 2 (3d Cir. 1983) (finding comparable test scores of blacks and whites not determinative where there was evidence that administrative experience—from which blacks had been barred—affected results of tests).

Generally the courts have continued to evaluate each selection device separately for adverse impact.[48] In an unusual variation, one court found that a written examination could have an adverse impact on Hispanics even though their pass rate on the exam was higher than that of whites, because the written examination was coupled with a high school diploma or equivalency certificate requirement.[49]

## D. Rebuttal of Plaintiff's Statistics

Two cases from the Fifth Circuit have emphasized that without proof of a causal connection between success or failure on the test and lower selection rates for the job or jobs at issue, there can be no prima facie showing of discrimination. In one case, the court refused to find a prima facie case where plaintiffs' proof failed to establish the required causal connection.[50] The test in the case did not have a cutoff and was only one of many factors considered in hiring and promotion decisions. The court went on to note that the plaintiffs had alleged that a racial disparity in hiring was due to both testing and use of subjective hiring criteria. The plaintiffs' failure to isolate the adverse effect of testing was held fatal to their challenge of it. Similarly, the Fifth Circuit found that a prima facie case had not been established where the plaintiffs failed to link lower scores on the test at issue with lower referral rates by the defendant employment service.[51]

Courts have continued to reject a statistical showing of disparate impact where the data base used is too small to factor out the element of chance, or for that reason along with others.[52] In one case, the court refrained from combining test scores for three different years after analyzing differences among the tests in each year.[53] After subdividing test results for the three years in question, the court found that plaintiff's data base, comprising 248 applicants, was too small to eliminate chance as a reason for the disparity, and rejected the statistical analysis.[54] In another case,[55] the court rejected plaintiff's attempted statistical showing based upon: (1) too small a data base

---

[48]Vanguard Justice Soc'y v. Hughes, 592 F. Supp. 245, 36 FEP 1494 (D. Md. 1984) (while actual promotions made did not violate 80% rule of Uniform Guidelines, court finds, and defendant concedes, that written exam in question had a disparate impact under Uniform Guidelines); Clady v. County of Los Angeles, *supra* note 40 (written examinations held to have discriminatory impact against blacks, although plaintiffs concede there is no "bottom line" adverse impact when evaluating "total selection process"). *But see* Brunet v. City of Columbus, *supra* note 45.

[49]Aguilera v. Cook County Police & Corrections Merit Bd., 760 F.2d 844, 37 FEP 1140 (7th Cir.), *cert. denied,* 474 U.S. 907 (1985).

[50]Carroll v. Sears, Roebuck & Co., 708 F.2d 183, 32 FEP 286 (5th Cir. 1983).

[51]Pegues v. Mississippi State Employment Serv., 699 F.2d 760, 31 FEP 257 (5th Cir.), *cert. denied,* 464 U.S. 991, 33 FEP 440 (1983).

[52]*See, e.g.,* Tillery v. Pacific Tel. Co., 34 FEP 54 (N.D. Cal. 1982) (no disparate impact where 10 of 35 blacks passed test at issue as compared with 50 of 110 whites); Pegues v. Mississippi State Employment Serv., *supra* note 51, at 774, 31 FEP at 268 ("Where the sample size is small, few test scores may significantly skew the overall disparity, thus reducing the reliability of any inference which might be drawn from any minority 'fail' rates"); Bunch v. Bullard, 795 F.2d 384, 395, 41 FEP 515, 524 (5th Cir. 1986) ("the district court did not perform, nor do we attempt, the application of probability theories to a sample size as small as this"); Black Shield Police Ass'n v. City of Cleveland, 42 FEP 270, 279 (N.D. Ohio 1986) ("because these statistics reflect the results of a single employment action, effecting [sic] the opportunities of a small number of Blacks for a small number of promotions, they are not significantly probative of a disparate impact").

[53]Fudge v. City of Providence Fire Dep't, 766 F.2d 650, 38 FEP 648 (1st Cir. 1985).

[54]*Id.* at 657–58, 38 FEP at 654.

[55]Smith v. Western Elec. Co., 35 EPD ¶ 34,656 (N.D. Tex. 1984), *aff'd,* 770 F.2d 520, 38 FEP 1605 (5th Cir. 1985).

to be significant (without reciting the specific numbers), (2) "procedures * * * justified by legitimate business reasons;" and (3) "total unacceptability of plaintiff's statistical proof."[56]

## VI. VALIDATION OF TESTS WITH ADVERSE IMPACT: DEFENDANT'S PROOF OF JOB-RELATEDNESS

### A. Standard of Proof of Job-Relatedness

The courts continue the trend toward requiring a specific showing of job-relatedness, including all relevant factors in a job selection system.[57] Although not expressly addressing the issue, the Fifth Circuit appeared in its recent opinions to take a decided step away from its previous "strict business necessity" standard of proving job-relatedness.[58] In one case, for example, the court affirmed a trial court's finding of job-relatedness where the defendants showed that the tests at issue validly predicted job performance,[59] but apparently did not make the further showing that the tests were essential to the safety and efficiency of the plant.[60] Similarly, in a later case, the Fifth Circuit affirmed the district court's decision that a prima facie case had been rebutted, because the employer showed that the tests "have a manifest and legitimate and [sic] business relationship to the jobs for which the tests were used."[61] The Seventh Circuit has used a similar standard for job-relatedness in *Gillespie v. Wisconsin,* where it held a test to be valid, "if it measures traits that are significantly related to the applicant's ability to perform the job."[62] One district court found that physical tests were job-related, because the "exercises used on the tests were related to physical traits deemed necessary in police officers."[63]

### B. Choice of Validation Strategy

While noting that noncompliance with the Uniform Guidelines "diminishes the probative value of the defendant's validation study," the Ninth Circuit followed the general trend of cases holding that a validation study may provide a valid defense to a disparate impact claim even though it does not comply fully with the Uniform Guidelines.[64] In that case the court

[56]*Id.* at p. 34,963.

[57]*See, e.g.,* Kraszewski v. State Farm Gen. Ins. Co., 38 FEP 197 (N.D. Cal. 1985). Employer's attempted reliance upon flow statistics from its Aptitude Index Battery (AIB) test for agent trainee positions was severely criticized and discounted by the court in a sex-based class action because of other subjective hiring factors, word-of-mouth recruitment by all-male managers, male-oriented negativism in recruiting policies, and male-dominated advertising; court found the cumulative effect of these practices to create a disparate impact, and held that the employer's other recruiting practices precluded it from showing, based upon the AIB test only, that its hiring procedure was job-related.

[58]Rivera v. City of Wichita Falls, 665 F.2d 531, 537, 27 FEP 1352, 1357 (5th Cir. 1982); Cormier v. PPG Indus., 702 F.2d 567, 31 FEP 1039 (5th Cir. 1983).

[59]Rivera v. City of Wichita Falls, *supra* note 58.

[60]The latter standard was utilized in *Watkins v. Scott Paper Co.,* 530 F.2d 1159, 1168, 12 FEP 1191, 1197 (5th Cir.), *cert. denied,* 429 U.S. 861 (1976).

[61]Cormier v. PPG Indus., *supra* note 58, at 568, 31 FEP at 1039.

[62]Gillespie v. Wisconsin, 771 F.2d 1035, 1040, 38 FEP 1487, 1490 (7th Cir. 1985), *cert. denied,* 474 U.S. 1083, 39 FEP 1424 (1986).

[63]Eison v. City of Knoxville, 570 F. Supp. 11, 13, 33 FEP 1141, 1143 (E.D. Tenn. 1983).

[64]Clady v. County of Los Angeles, 770 F.2d 1421, 38 FEP 1575 (9th Cir. 1985), *cert. denied,* 475 U.S. 1109, 40 FEP 792 (1986). *But see* Allen v. Isaac, 39 FEP 1142, 1157 (N.D. Ill. 1986); Brunet v.

rejected the plaintiffs' argument that the employer's validation studies were unreliable because they were prepared *post hoc* as a defense to litigation. The court observed that it was impossible in that case to assess the written exam's validity until after it had been given and the job performance of successful applicants measured.[65]

## C. Criterion-Related Validation

Correlation coefficients of 0.36[66] and 0.38[67] were found sufficient in the recent decisions to support a finding of criterion-related validity.[68]

Criterion-related validation was held by one court to be the most accurate method of validating a test,[69] but the Seventh Circuit in evaluating an essay test for personnel specialists concluded that a "review of the Uniform Guidelines and the relevant psychological literature reveals no preference for criterion-related validity."[70]

Two cases affirmed a finding of criterion-related validity for a test which was correlated solely to success in training. "It is sufficient," said the Fifth Circuit in one, "that the test validly predicts performance at the police academy. It need not also bear a positive correlation to satisfactory performance as a police officer."[71]

In the other case, the Ninth Circuit approved the employer's criterion-related validation study, which compared test scores from the written exam in question with performance of firefighter recruits in training programs.[72] The court also approved the employer's validation studies, which showed a positive correlation of 0.3838 between success on the written exam in question and graduation from the firefighter training program.[73]

## D. Content Validation

The courts continue to stress the necessity, for content-validity purposes, of a thorough job analysis which indicates the importance of the work behaviors identified.[74] One district court underscored the value of a valida-

---

City of Columbus, 642 F. Supp. 1214, 1236–37, 42 FEP 1846, 1865 (S.D. Ohio 1986), *appeal dismissed mem.*, 826 F.2d 1062, 44 FEP 1671 (6th Cir. 1987), *cert. denied,* 485 U.S. — (1988).

[65]Clady v. County of Los Angeles, *supra* note 64, 770 F.2d at 1431, 38 FEP at 1583.

[66]Tillery v. Pacific Tel. Co., 34 FEP 54 (N.D. Cal. 1982).

[67]Rivera v. City of Wichita Falls, *supra* note 58, at 538 n.9, 27 FEP at 1358.

[68]*But see* Walls v. Mississippi State Dep't of Pub. Welfare, 542 F. Supp. 281, 300, 31 FEP 1795, 1811 (N.D. Miss. 1982), *aff'd in relevant part,* 730 F.2d 306, 34 FEP 1114 (5th Cir. 1984) (although test has some "positive correlation" to job performance, not "useful" in predicting performance where there was evidence that "the proportion of successful employees who would have been selected by the test (70%)" very close to "proportion successful without the use of the test (68%)").

[69]Bernard v. Gulf Oil Corp., 643 F. Supp. 1494, 1501 (E.D. Tex. 1986), *aff'd in part, vacated and remanded in part,* 841 F.2d 547 (5th Cir. 1988) (remanding for determination of post-Act bona fides). (citing United States v. Georgia Power Co., 474 F.2d 906, 912, 5 FEP 587 (5th Cir. 1973)).

[70]Gillespie v. Wisconsin, 771 F.2d 1035, 1040–41, 38 FEP 1487, 1491 (7th Cir. 1985), *cert. denied,* 474 U.S. 1083, 39 FEP 1424 (1986).

[71]Rivera v. City of Wichita Falls, 665 F.2d 531, 538 n.9, 27 FEP 1352, 1358 n.9 (5th Cir. 1982).

[72]Clady v. County of Los Angeles, *supra* note 64, 770 F.2d at 1426, 38 FEP at 1579.

[73]*Id.* at 1426 & n.5, 38 FEP at 1579.

[74]*See, e.g.,* Easley v. Anheuser-Busch, 572 F. Supp. 402, 414–15, 34 FEP 380, 389 (E.D. Mo. 1983), *rev'd in part on other grounds,* 758 F.2d 251, 37 FEP 549 (8th Cir. 1985) (attempt to validate preemployment test for bottlers failed to meet content-validity rules of Uniform Guidelines in virtually all respects);

tion study which tested for all important knowledge areas of the job.[75] In that case the employer had developed a 1982 promotional exam based upon a content-valid 1981 exam, but had reworked the 1981 exam in such a way that "significant knowledge areas, comprising up to 30% of the job" had been eliminated.[76] In this light, the court found the test was not content-valid, because it did not "measure all, or nearly all, of the significant knowledge areas of a job in approximate proportion to each knowledge area's relative importance to the job."[77] This latter holding overstates both the case law and relevant principles of industrial psychology. For example, a flight simulator test of landing skills would undoubtedly be content-valid for commercial airline pilot candidates, even though less than five percent of the job duties were sampled. Other courts have held a sampling of job duties to be adequate for content-validity studies.[78]

## F. Differential, Single Group, and Situational Validity

The Fifth Circuit implicitly rejected the notion that validity is necessarily geographically specific where the court affirmed validation of a test used to predict training performance at a police academy based on correlations established at two other academies elsewhere in the state.[79] "[V]alidity studies conducted by one test user," said the court, "will justify use of that test by others when the jobs of the two users are substantially similar and the test was clearly validated by the first user."[80]

The Ninth Circuit affirmed a trial court's factual finding that differential validation for blacks and Hispanics in the context of a written hiring exam was "*contra* the consensus of the professionals in [plaintiff's expert's] field of expertise; and *contra* the opinion of defendant's witnesses, both expert and lay, which were supported by substantial relevant experience, sufficient data, analyses of data, or relevant authority."[81]

---

Berkman v. City of New York, 536 F. Supp. 177, 195, 28 FEP 856, 872 (E.D.N.Y. 1982), *aff'd,* 705 F.2d 584, 31 FEP 767 (2d Cir. 1983) (rejecting employer's content-validity study in large part because of paucity of evidence that physical skills and abilities being measured were relatively important to performance of job of firefighter); Burney v. City of Pawtucket, 559 F. Supp. 1089, 1102, 34 FEP 1274, 1284 (D.R.I. 1983), *appeal dismissed,* 728 F.2d 547, 34 FEP 1295 (1st Cir. 1984) ("Job functions must be individually identified. The importance of these functions in relation to each other must also be determined.").

[75]Vanguard Justice Soc'y v. Hughes, 592 F. Supp. 245, 36 FEP 1494 (D. Md. 1984).

[76]*Id.* at 266, 36 FEP at 1512.

[77]*Id.*

[78]Bernard v. Gulf Oil Corp., 643 F. Supp. 1494, 1502 (E.D. Tex. 1986), *aff'd in part, vacated and remanded in part,* 841 F.2d 547 (5th Cir. 1988) (rejecting plaintiff's contention that a one-to-one relationship between test and actual duties was required); Gillespie v. Wisconsin, 771 F.2d 1035, 1044, 38 FEP 1487, 1493 (7th Cir. 1985), *cert. denied,* 474 U.S. 1083, 39 FEP 1424 (1986) ("Title VII does not require an employer to test all or nearly all skills required for the occupation."). *But see* Brunet v. City of Columbus, 642 F. Supp. 1214, 1248, 42 FEP 1846, 1874 (S.D. Ohio 1986), *appeal dismissed mem.,* 826 F.2d 1062, 44 FEP 1671 (6th Cir. 1987), *cert. denied,* 485 U.S. — (1988) ("a test, to be content valid, must reflect all or nearly all the important aspects of the job").

[79]Rivera v. City of Wichita Falls, 665 F.2d 531, 537, 27 FEP 1352, 1357 (5th Cir. 1982); Brunet v. City of Columbus, 642 F. Supp. 1214, 1247, 42 FEP 1846, 1873 (S.D. Ohio 1986), *appeal dismissed mem.,* 826 F.2d 1062, 44 FEP 1671 (6th Cir. 1987), *cert. denied,* 485 U.S. — (1988) (validation study in Akron accepted where positions were similar).

[80]Rivera v. City of Wichita Falls, 665 F.2d 531, 538 n.10, 27 FEP 1352, 1358 (5th Cir. 1982).

[81]Clady v. County of Los Angeles, 770 F.2d 1421, 1431, 38 FEP 1575, 1583 (9th Cir. 1985), *cert. denied,* 475 U.S. 1109, 40 FEP 792 (1986) (plaintiff's expert was Dr. James Kirkpatrick, an experienced expert witness).

## G. Validity Problems in the Application of Scored Tests

Selection decisions based on strict rank-ordering of test scores continue to attract judicial disapproval in the absence of appropriate validation of the rank-ordering. In one case a trial court observed that because slight differences in scores are virtually meaningless in measuring the merits of candidates, ranking by zones is far more realistic.[82]

While no recent reported cases flatly reject the use of rank-ordering by test scores for all purposes, the cases clearly continue the trend disfavoring use of rank-ordering without specific and well-documented justification.[83] One court rejected rank-ordering where a test was not sufficiently precise and there was no evidence presented to show that scores on the test varied directly with job performance.[84] On the other hand, one trial court found that relative rank orders of scores between minority and majority applicants would not "necessarily be irrelevant" in determining whether white applicants with higher test scores were victims of reverse discrimination in favor of black applicants with lower test scores.[85] The court cautioned: "That while a test may be valid for both screening and ranking purposes does not mean that as between two individuals the one with the higher score is better qualified;" but it nonetheless found that test scores, along with "additional proof regarding the validity of the test," may be sufficient to support an inference of reverse discrimination.[86]

The courts continue to agree with the Uniform Guidelines that cutoff scores "should be set so as to be reasonable and consistent with normal expectations of acceptable proficiency within the workforce."[87] In one case, for example, the court affirmed, over a union's objections, a cutoff score set by reference to the average scores of job incumbents, citing this provision.[88] In another challenge to a cutoff score, the Seventh Circuit affirmed its use where it was based on a testing expert's estimates of minimal ability levels needed and had further been set to maximize the number of minorities who would proceed to the interview stage.[89]

---

[82]Kirkland v. New York State Dep't of Correctional Servs., 552 F. Supp. 667, 671, 32 FEP 446, 450 (S.D.N.Y. 1982), aff'd, 711 F.2d 1117, 32 FEP 509 (2d Cir. 1983), cert. denied, 465 U.S. 1005, 33 FEP 1344 (1984). See also Walls v. Mississippi State Dep't of Pub. Welfare, 542 F. Supp. 281, 300, 31 FEP 1795, 1811 (N.D. Miss. 1982), aff'd in relevant part, 730 F.2d 306, 34 FEP 1114 (5th Cir. 1984); Gilbert v. City of Little Rock, 722 F.2d 1390, 1397–98, 33 FEP 557, 562 (8th Cir. 1983), cert. denied, 466 U.S. 972, 34 FEP 1312 (1984); Berkman v. City of New York, supra note 74.

[83]Vanguard Justice Soc'y v. Hughes, supra note 75, at 266–68, 36 FEP at 1512–14; Thomas v. City of Evanston, 610 F. Supp. 422, 430–31, 42 FEP 1795 (N.D. Ill. 1985); Kraszewski v. State Farm Gen. Ins. Co., 38 FEP 197 (N.D. Cal. 1985).

[84]Brunet v. City of Columbus, supra note 78 ("if a test is to be used to rank-order applicants, it must be more than merely content valid").

[85]In re Birmingham Reverse Discrimination Employment Litig., 37 FEP 1 (N.D. Ala. 1985).

[86]Id. at 6, 7.

[87]29 C.F.R. § 1607.5(h)(1985).

[88]Berkman v. City of New York, 536 F. Supp. 177, 28 FEP 856 (E.D.N.Y. 1982), aff'd, 705 F.2d 584, 31 FEP 767 (2d Cir. 1983). See also Burney v. City of Pawtucket, 559 F. Supp. 1089, 1103, 34 FEP 1274, 1285 (D.R.I. 1983), appeal dismissed, 728 F.2d 547, 34 FEP 1295 (1st Cir. 1984) (rejecting admittedly arbitrarily set cutoff, citing 29 C.F.R. § 1607.5(h)(1985)); Brunet v. City of Columbus, 642 F. Supp. 1214, 1257, 42 FEP 1846 (S.D. Ohio 1986), appeal dismissed mem., 826 F.2d 1062, 44 FEP 1671 (6th Cir. 1987), cert. denied, 485 U.S. — (1988) (requiring that cutoff scores be based upon scores of incumbent firefighters).

[89]Gillespie v. Wisconsin, 771 F.2d 1035, 1045, 38 FEP 1487, 1494 (7th Cir. 1985), cert. denied, 474 U.S. 1083, 34 FEP 1424 (1986).

## VII. DEMONSTRATION OF ALTERNATIVE SELECTION DEVICES HAVING LESS DISPARATE IMPACT: PRETEXTUAL USE OF SCORED TESTS

Among the reasons one court found for invalidating a preemployment test was that an alternative selection procedure without equivalent adverse impact was available to the defendant. The court found that, prior to institution of the tests, applicants were hired simply on the basis of a review of their applications and interviews, without an adverse impact, and there was no substantial evidence that employees hired under that system did not perform satisfactorily.[90]

Few cases have discussed in detail the plaintiff's burden of identifying and proving alternative selection devices meeting the employer's legitimate needs, but having less adverse impact. In one important discussion of the issue, the Ninth Circuit held two alternative suggestions by plaintiffs to be inadequate.[91] First, the plaintiffs argued that a hiring procedure in effect prior to the contested examination itself was a suitable alternative. The employer countered that argument by (1) expert testimony showing the prior hiring pattern resulted from an "atypical" applicant pool during earlier years, due, in part, to a remedial hiring order from prior litigation, and (2) a utility analysis which demonstrated significant training cost savings by using the contested written examination.[92] Second, the plaintiffs suggested a civil service banding rule as a more benign alternative; however, the court found insufficient evidence in the record to assess the impact of the banding rule on minority hiring and, accordingly, dismissed that alternative as well.[93]

The Seventh Circuit found a plaintiff's "bare assertion" that an employer could have developed a multiple-choice test (rather than an essay examination) or used a commercially developed test failed to satisfy its burden of demonstrating the existence of alternative tests with less adverse impact.[94]

## VIII. REMEDIES

The question of whether race-conscious remedies may be utilized as a remedy for prior testing discrimination continues to be hotly debated, particularly in light of the Supreme Court's decision in *Firefighters Local 1784 v. Stotts.*[95] In *Williams v. City of New Orleans,*[96] a decision which preceded the

---

[90]Easley v. Anheuser-Busch, 572 F. Supp. 402, 410, 34 FEP 380, 385 (E.D. Mo. 1983), *rev'd in relevant part,* 758 F.2d 251, 37 FEP 549 (8th Cir. 1985).

[91]Clady v. County of Los Angeles, *supra* note 81, 770 F.2d at 1432–33, 38 FEP at 1584–85.

[92]*Id.* at 1426 & n.6, 38 FEP at 1579.

[93]*Id.* at 1433, 38 FEP at 1585.

[94]Gillespie v. Wisconsin, *supra* note 89.

[95]467 U.S. 561, 34 FEP 1702 (1984). *See* Chapter 24 (Reverse Discrimination and Affirmative Action).

[96]729 F.2d 1554, 34 FEP 1009 (5th Cir. 1984) (en banc), *appeal dismissed,* 763 F.2d 667 (5th Cir. 1985).

Supreme Court's decision in *Stotts,* the Fifth Circuit in an en banc opinion held that the imposition of a quota to remedy past discrimination is not forbidden by Title VII even though it is not limited to actual victims of discrimination.

A proposed consent decree was held by the Sixth Circuit to be illegal and contrary to the public interest because of an undue reliance upon promotion examinations which had been shown to have an adverse impact.[97] Moreover, the discriminatory testing procedure cannot be saved by an ad hoc arbitrary promotion of minority candidates to achieve some sort of "bottom line" racial balance.[98] In *Firefighters Local 1590 (Wilmington) v. City of Wilmington,* [99] the city had unilaterally altered the scoring procedure to improve blacks' chances of promotion, after administering a promotion test which showed disparate impact. It based this decision on its interpretation of a consent decree, but the court held that the decree said only that if disparate impact was later determined, plaintiffs could file suit again. The Second Circuit has held that a consent decree with a race-conscious remedy may be appropriate on the sole basis of a finding of adverse impact and that there is no obligation to decide whether or not the prima facie case is rebuttable through job-related explanations.[100] However, the case was remanded for a determination of whether the proposed remedy unnecessarily trammeled the interests of nonminority employees[101] under the standards adopted in *Steelworkers v. Weber.* [102]

The courts routinely continue to award compliance relief, requiring employers to reformulate tests in accord with the Uniform Guidelines or other specific direction.[103] In one case, the trial court declined to impose mandatory promotion of minorities after a finding of discrimination, where the disparity between minority and majority promotions historically had not constituted "significant prior discrimination."[104] Another trial court awarded back pay relief over the employer's contention that it had relied in good faith on a state statute requiring rank-ordering of applicants.[105] The court rejected the employer's good-faith defense, finding that the state statute did not relieve the employer of the burden of constructing a test which is content-valid under Title VII.[106]

---

[97]Williams v. Vukovich, 720 F.2d 909, 925–26, 33 FEP 238, 251–52 (6th Cir. 1983).

[98]*Id.* (citing Connecticut v. Teal, 457 U.S. 440, 442, 29 FEP 1, 2 (1982), which rejected the "bottom line" concept).

[99]Firefighters Local 1590 (Wilmington) v. City of Wilmington, 632 F. Supp. 1177, 40 FEP 1078 (D. Del. 1986).

[100]Bushey v. New York State Civil Serv. Comm'n, 733 F.2d 220, 226, 34 FEP 1065, 1070 (2d Cir. 1984), *cert. denied,* 469 U.S. 1117, 36 FEP 1166 (1985) (if defendant had to prove inability to rebut prima facie case, no Title VII case would be settled without judicial determination of validity, which would seriously undermine preference for voluntary settlement).

[101]*Id.,* 733 F.2d at 228, 34 FEP at 1071–72.

[102]443 U.S. 193, 20 FEP 1 (1979).

[103]Kraszewski v. State Farm Gen. Ins. Co., 38 FEP 197 (N.D. Cal. 1985); Vanguard Justice Soc'y v. Hughes, 592 F. Supp. 245, 36 FEP 1494 (D. Md. 1984).

[104]Vanguard Justice Soc'y v. Hughes, *supra* note 103, at 271–72, 36 FEP at 1516–17.

[105]Thomas v. City of Evanston, 610 F. Supp. 422, 42 FEP 1795 (N.D. Ill. 1985).

[106]*Id.* at 433.

## IX. Practical Litigation Issues and Considerations

### A. The Industrial Psychologist as an Expert Witness

*3. Trial Role of the Expert*

The Eleventh Circuit found the testimony of plaintiff's expert not relevant to the job-relatedness of the employer's test, because the expert had not seen the actual examination and had never correlated the test with successful job performance.[107] Thus, because the expert had not performed a job-relatedness test himself, the plaintiffs found they had no evidence to rebut the expert testimony and other evidence of the employer on job-relatedness issues.[108] Another court rejected an expert's validation study where the expert had not studied the job, but instead based his analysis on the abilities tested by the examination.[109]

### B. Use of Test Questions

Some courts have engaged in an analysis of specific test questions, requiring that the tests themselves become part of the record, despite claims of confidentiality.[110] The Uniform Guidelines make provisions for security concerns in retesting in any event.[111]

### C. Job Analysis

The courts continue to place a higher burden on employers to demonstrate content validity of a written examination when the underlying job analysis is of dubious accuracy.[112] One trial court underscored the importance of developing and maintaining documentation on job analysis where the employer asserted that a more thorough job analysis had been performed, but lacked documentation to prove it.[113] The court found that, since the employer "carries the burden of showing content validity, its near total lack of substantiation means that it has not met its burden."[114]

---

[107]Nash v. Consolidated City of Jacksonville, 763 F.2d 1393, 38 FEP 151 (11th Cir. 1985).

[108]*Id.* at 1396, 38 FEP at 152–53.

[109]Allen v. Isaac, 39 FEP 1142, 1153 (N.D. Ill. 1986).

[110]Fudge v. City of Providence Fire Dep't, 766 F.2d 650, 38 FEP 648 (1st Cir. 1985) (extensive discussion of specific test questions on firefighters examination at pp. 653–54); Vanguard Justice Soc'y v. Hughes, *supra* note 103, at 262–63, 36 FEP at 1507–08 (detailed discussion of expert testimony on job-relatedness and construction of test questions); Nash v. Consolidated City of Jacksonville, *supra* note 107, at 1398 (court observes that it is "hopeless" for trier of fact to determine content validity or job-relatedness of a test without the questions themselves placed into evidence).

[111]29 C.F.R. § 1607.12 (1985). *See also* Question No. 61, *Questions and Answers on Uniform Guidelines on Employee Selection Procedures,* 44 Fed. Reg. 11996 (1979).

[112]Vanguard Justice Soc'y v. Hughes, *supra* note 103, at 260, 36 FEP at 1507.

[113]Thomas v. City of Evanston, *supra* note 105.

[114]*Id.* at 430 n.16. *See also* Allen v. Isaac, 39 FEP 1142, 1157 (N.D. Ill. 1986).

## CHAPTER 5

# NONSCORED OBJECTIVE CRITERIA

## I. GENERAL ANALYTICAL CONSIDERATIONS

No major changes in the analytical framework used in evaluating non-scored objective criteria have occurred since the publication of the Second Edition. *Griggs v. Duke Power Co.*[1] continues to be the seminal decision regarding the analysis of such criteria.

There is still some uncertainty in the decisions with respect to the proper analysis of the third part of the tripartite test for analyzing disparate impact claims. Some decisions appear to hold that if the employer demonstrates that the questioned employment practice is job-related, the plaintiff may prevail by demonstrating that there were suitable alternatives with a lesser discriminatory impact.[2] Other decisions have held that the evidence of alternatives with lesser discriminatory impact is not conclusive, but rather evidence that the practice may be a mere pretext for discrimination.[3] In any event, the ultimate burden of proof at this stage is on the plaintiff.[4]

---

[1]401 U.S. 424, 3 FEP 175 (1971), reproduced at p. 6 of the Second Edition.

[2]*E.g.,* Dothard v. Rawlinson, 433 U.S. 321, 329, 15 FEP 10, 14 (1977); Brunet v. City of Columbus, 642 F. Supp. 1214, 1245, 42 FEP 1846, 1872 (S.D. Ohio 1986), *appeal dismissed mem.,* 826 F.2d 1062, 44 FEP 1671 (6th Cir. 1987), *cert. denied,* 485 U.S. — (1988).

[3]*E.g.,* Connecticut v. Teal, 457 U.S. 440, 447, 29 FEP 1, 4 (1982); United States v. Town of Cicero, Ill., 786 F.2d 331, 333, 40 FEP 537, 539 (7th Cir. 1986); EEOC v. Governor Mifflin School Dist., 623 F. Supp. 734, 743, 39 FEP 1059, 1059 (E.D. Pa. 1985). The Seventh Circuit has held that a plaintiff may prevail if it comes forward with evidence either of mere pretext or can demonstrate that there are suitable alternatives with a lesser discriminatory injury, implying that the standards are not synonymous. Griffin v. Regency Univs. Bd. of Regents, 795 F.2d 1281, 1287, 41 FEP 228, 234–35 (7th Cir. 1986); *see also* Jordan v. Wilson, 649 F. Supp. 1038, 42 FEP 950 (M.D. Ala. 1986). The Eighth Circuit has held that if the plaintiff shows a suitable alternative with lesser discriminatory effect, this would be evidence that the employer's practice was a mere pretext for discrimination, implying that there are other ways to meet the "mere pretext" standard. Easley v. Anheuser-Busch, 758 F.2d 251, 255 n.7, 37 FEP 549, 552 n.7 (8th Cir. 1985).

[4]*E.g.,* Connecticut v. Teal, *supra* note 3 ("[T]he plaintiff may prevail, if he shows that employer was using the practice as a mere pretext for discrimination."); Griffin v. Regency Univs. Bd. of Regents, *supra* note 3 (if defendant proves job-relatedness, plaintiff may show mere pretext or a suitable alternative); United States v. Town of Cicero, Ill., *supra* note 3 (if defendant proves job-relatedness, plaintiff may present evidence to show a suitable alternative); Brunet v. City of Columbus, *supra* note 2 ("If, but only if, the employer meets the burden of establishing manifest relationship, the burden shifts back to the plaintiff to show that there is an alternative selection device with less disparate impact * * *."); Chambers v. Omaha Girls Club, 629 F. Supp. 925, 951, 40 FEP 362, 382 (D. Neb. 1986), *aff'd,* 834 F.2d 697, 45 FEP 698 (8th Cir. 1987) (plaintiff failed to meet her burden of showing that policy against employing single pregnant females was mere pretext for discrimination); Smith v. Western Elec. Co., 35 EPD ¶ 34,656 (N.D. Tex. 1984), *aff'd on other grounds,* 770 F.2d 520, 38 FEP 1605 (5th Cir. 1985) (plaintiff failed to prove existence of effective and not too costly alternative with less discriminatory impact).

## II. SPECIFIC EDUCATIONAL, EXPERIENCE, PERFORMANCE, AND LICENSURE REQUIREMENTS

### A. Educational Requirements

Decisions continue to follow the trend of relaxing stringent validation requirements for highly skilled and professional jobs while maintaining such requirements for relatively low-skilled positions.[5]

Courts have upheld a high school education requirement as a valid, and perhaps even necessary, precondition for employment as a law enforcement or corrections officer.[6] The Fifth Circuit has held that the danger to public safety of hiring unqualified police officers and the high degree of individual initiative and responsibility the job entails validate such a hiring criterion.[7] The court also rejected the argument that the requirement did not adequately relate to the skills necessary for performance as a police officer, noting that, unlike craftsman and laborer positions, the factors that combine to create a qualified police officer are less susceptible to quantification and testing. The Seventh Circuit has also upheld a high school education requirement for correction officers, citing the complex and demanding skills, knowledge areas, and personal attributes necessary to handle the job.[8]

---

[5]*Compare* Carpenter v. Stephen F. Austin State Univ., 706 F.2d 608, 622, 31 FEP 1758, 1769–70 (5th Cir. 1983) (court rejects high school educational requirement for university's administrative and clerical employees where requirement had disparate impact on black males and where university failed to offer any evidence of job-relatedness) *with* Hawkins v. Anheuser-Busch, 697 F.2d 810, 30 FEP 1170 (8th Cir. 1983) (college degree requirement for Supervisor of Trade Returns justified by business necessity) *and* Walls v. Mississippi State Dep't of Pub. Welfare, 730 F.2d 306, 316–17, 34 FEP 1114, 1121 (5th Cir. 1984) (lower court not clearly erroneous in finding certain educational requirements for public welfare positions job-related: college degree for social workers who handle child neglect and abuse cases; two years of college credit for "eligibility workers" who interview and assist clients who apply for government assistance; and high school diploma or its equivalent for clerk-typist). *See also* Merwine v. State Insts. of Higher Learning Bd. of Trustees, 754 F.2d 631, 37 FEP 340 (5th Cir.), *cert. denied,* 474 U.S. 823, 38 FEP 1727 (1985) (master's degree in library science was valid requirement for entry level university librarian); McKenney v. Marsh, 31 FEP 178 (D.D.C. 1983) (U.S. Center for Military History's preference for Ph.D. in position of deputy division chief held to be pretext for discrimination when there was no evidence that a Ph.D. was of value in position, a Ph.D. was not mentioned in position description, and plaintiffs' experience showed they had necessary expertise for the position); Briggs v. Anderson, 796 F.2d 1009, 1023 (8th Cir. 1986) (college degree in psychology or related field valid requirement for position as counselor, which required advanced knowledge of human behavior and skills in testing and dealing with groups).

[6]Aguilera v. Cook County Police & Corrections Merit Bd., 760 F.2d 844, 37 FEP 1140 (7th Cir.), *cert. denied,* 474 U.S. 907 (1985) (requirement that police officers and corrections officers have high school diplomas is clearly valid, and employers should not be required to prove over and over again that such a requirement is really necessary).

[7]Davis v. City of Dallas, 777 F.2d 205, 39 FEP 744 (5th Cir. 1985), *cert. denied,* 476 U.S. 1116, 40 FEP 1320 (1986) (city required that police officer applicants had completed 45 semester hours with at least "C" average in college).

[8]Aguilera v. Cook County Police & Corrections Merit Bd., *supra* note 6.

## B. Experience Requirements

In determining whether an experience requirement is valid, the courts continue to weigh the degree of exclusion versus the degree of business utility[9] and also consider the employer's past discrimination record.[10]

The First Circuit has held that a rule which automatically exempted from layoff employees with more than 10 years of experience was recognized as "amenable to disparate impact analysis" when it was shown that proportionately fewer blacks than whites had the requisite 10 years of experience. However, the court refused to find a prima facie case from the mere articulation of the policy in the absence of a showing that the "ten year rule," independent of other factors, actually caused a disproportionate number of blacks to be laid off.[11]

In an interesting twist on the typical case, it was held that a hotel's refusal to hire a black applicant for a bellman's position at a new hotel because that applicant had prior experience was not a pretext for discrimination.[12] The court accepted the defendant's explanation that the hotel did not want individuals already programmed from previous experience, but instead needed employees who were willing to learn and be trained in accordance with the procedures developed specifically for the new hotel.

## C. Performance and Licensure Requirements

Female applicants for firefighter positions have successfully shown that prehire physical examinations purportedly designed to test the applicants' ability to handle the physical demands of the job have a disparate impact on women.[13] When such a test is not adequately related to the physical attributes

---

[9]Kilgo v. Bowman Transp., 570 F. Supp. 1509, 31 FEP 1451 (N.D. Ga. 1983), *modified*, 576 F. Supp. 600, 40 FEP 1412 (N.D. Ga. 1984), *aff'd*, 789 F.2d 859, 40 FEP 1415 (11th Cir. 1986) (court found that one-year experience requirement for over-the-road truck driver positions had disparate impact on class of women and that requirement had not been shown to be justified by business necessity, particularly where defendant's validation attempts, which were not commenced until after litigation, failed to show correlation between prior experience and fewer accidents).

[10]Walker v. Jefferson County Home, 726 F.2d 1554, 34 FEP 465 (11th Cir. 1984) (requirement of prior supervisory experience for position of housekeeping department supervisor held to be discriminatory in light of defendant's past policy of favoring whites over blacks for movement into positions in which they could gain initial supervisory experience and defendant's failure to meet "business necessity" test because it could not prove that position was highly skilled or that economic and human risks involved in hiring unqualified applicant were great); Curl v. Reavis, 35 FEP 917 (W.D.N.C. 1983), *aff'd in relevant part*, 740 F.2d 1323, 35 FEP 930 (4th Cir. 1984) (although lack of road experience or jail supervision would be legitimate nondiscriminatory reason for rejecting applicant for position of police detective, employer violated Title VII where employer offered such experience only to male employees); Boudreaux v. Helena-West Helena School Dist., 819 F.2d 854 (8th Cir. 1987) (educational and business experience requirements not discriminatory in light of U.S. Department of Education's Office of Civil Rights 1985 finding that school district had developed and implemented objective nondiscriminatory hiring criteria and practices).

[11]Robinson v. Polaroid Corp., 732 F.2d 1010, 34 FEP 1134 (1st Cir. 1984).

[12]Clay v. Hyatt Regency Hotel, 724 F.2d 721, 33 FEP 1364 (8th Cir. 1984).

[13]*See* Berkman v. City of New York, 536 F. Supp. 177, 28 FEP 856 (E.D.N.Y. 1982), *aff'd*, 705 F.2d 584, 31 FEP 767 (2d Cir. 1983) *(Berkman I)*. In *Berkman I* the court held that, where none of the female applicants for New York City's fire department passed the seven-part physical agility test, in view of "the inexorable zero" pass rate, the test had a disparate impact on females. In *Brunet v. City of Columbus*, 642 F. Supp. 1214, 42 FEP 1846 (S.D. Ohio 1986), *appeal dismissed mem.*, 826 F.2d 1062, 44 FEP 1671 (6th Cir. 1987), *cert. denied*, 485 U.S. — (1988), plaintiffs challenged the 1980 and 1984 written and physical examinations for firefighter positions. The court held that where the percentages of males and females who completed the 1980 testing process and were ultimately hired were virtually the same, plaintiffs failed to show disparate impact, despite the fact that females had a lower average score.

actually required for performance as a firefighter, and is not validated by either a content- or criterion-related validation study, courts have concluded that the test was not justified by business necessity.[14]

## III. ARREST AND CONVICTION

### A. Arrest Records

Suspension or termination of an employee arrested for a crime will not be found to violate the antidiscrimination laws where the employer takes the action on a case-by-case basis after investigating the circumstances.[15]

### B. Convictions

In the absence of proof of adverse impact, the courts continue to uphold an employer's refusal to hire persons who give false or incomplete answers to inquiries concerning previous convictions.[16] The Fifth Circuit has upheld a requirement that candidates for police officer positions must not have been convicted of more than three moving traffic violations in the preceding 12 months, citing the public interest in the safe operation of squad cars and evidence that moving violations are a reliable predictor of future accident involvement.[17]

## IV. GARNISHMENTS AND OTHER FINANCIAL CRITERIA

The Eleventh Circuit has held that a district court erred in considering the legality of an employer's garnishment policy when it limited its analysis to discharged employees and failed to consider employees, disproportion-

---

With respect to the 1984 exam, however, where the ultimate selection rate for females was only about 22% that for male applicants, plaintiffs made out a prima facie case of disparate impact.

[14]*Compare Berkman I, supra* note 13 (further use of invalidated test enjoined) *and* Brunet, *supra* note 13 (four of seven events in physical exam placed undue emphasis on strength and speed as opposed to endurance and agility, and were therefore inadequately job-related) *with* Berkman v. City of New York, 626 F. Supp. 591, 43 FEP 305 (E.D.N.Y. 1985), *aff'd in relevant part,* 812 F.2d 52, 43 FEP 318 (2d Cir. 1987) *(Berkman II)* (subsequent physical exam, while still placing overemphasis on strength over stamina, was related to physical requirements of firefighting, and city allowed to use exam results with modifications in scoring).

[15]McCray v. Alexander, 29 FEP 653, 658 (D. Colo. 1982), *aff'd,* 38 EPD ¶ 35,509 (10th Cir. 1985) (Plaintiff, a black guard at an Army arsenal facility, was suspended and subsequently discharged for fatally shooting an unarmed motorist during an off-duty traffic altercation. The plaintiff contended, *inter alia,* that his employer discharged him because he had been arrested. Although the court took judicial notice that a disproportionate number of blacks are arrested for serious crimes, it held that plaintiff was discharged for the act of killing the motorist and not for his subsequent arrest.); State Div. of Human Rights v. Xerox Corp., 49 A.D.2d 21, 370 N.Y.S.2d 962, 37 FEP 1801 (1975), *aff'd,* 39 N.Y.2d 873, 386 N.Y.S.2d 221, 352 N.E.2d 139, 37 FEP 1806 (1976) (employer's suspension of arrested employee was permissible where it was shown that suspension was not automatic upon arrest but that such decisions were made on case-by-case basis after inquiry triggered by arrest); Kinoshita v. Canadian Pac. Airlines, 803 F.2d 471, 2 IER 971 (9th Cir. 1986) (employer who terminated two employees who had been arrested for trafficking in cocaine did not violate public policy since employees were terminated based on underlying facts of the arrest, not the arrest itself).

[16]Avant v. South Cent. Bell Tel. Co., 716 F.2d 1083, 32 FEP 1853 (5th Cir. 1983) (employer's refusal to hire plaintiff for lineman's position after learning of his prior petty larceny conviction upheld where applicant knowingly failed to disclose conviction on his application and there was no evidence that policy of refusing to hire applicants with criminal convictions had adverse impact upon blacks); Trapp v. State Univ. College at Buffalo, 30 FEP 1499, 1500 (W.D.N.Y. 1983) (employer did not discriminate against black applicant who falsely represented that he had led law-abiding life since his parole).

[17]Davis v. City of Dallas, *supra* note 7, 777 F.2d at 225–26, 39 FEP at 759–60.

ately black, who received reprimands for garnishments.[18] Because so few employees were discharged under the defendant's garnishment policy, a consideration of the discharge data alone prevented the plaintiffs from proving that the policy had a discriminatory effect. The court ruled that reprimands should also be considered because Title VII protects an employee's psychological as well as economic well-being, and discriminatory reprimands that have a meaningful adverse effect on employees' working conditions may be prohibited.

## V. Miscellaneous Criteria

### A. Pregnancy and Family Relationships

Courts have recently applied the *Griggs*[19] disparate impact analysis to employment rules regarding pregnancy and no-spouse rules. The discharge by a girls' club of an unmarried black female employee who became pregnant has been upheld.[20] The court held that the club's policy against retaining single employees who become pregnant had an adverse impact on black women. The club successfully proved a business necessity for the rule, however, stressing its unique role in exposing young girls to the greatest number of options in life, and showing that teenage pregnancy is contrary to that purpose and that the discharged employee would therefore have been a negative role model.

The Eighth Circuit has held that an employer failed to establish a business necessity for a rule barring employment of spouses of current employees.[21] Ninety-five percent of the defendants' employees were male, and 26 females had been denied employment because they were married to current employees.

The court held that the employer's concerns over dual absenteeism, scheduling vacations, supervision by one spouse over the other, and pressure to hire spouses was not supported by the evidence, and that the employer therefore failed to show a "compelling need" for the no-spouse rule.

### B. Drug Use

The Fifth Circuit has upheld a requirement that applicants for police officer positions not have a history of "recent or excessive marijuana usage."[22] The defendant city conceded that the requirement had a significant disparate impact on blacks, but the Fifth Circuit upheld the lower court's finding that prior marijuana use affected an officer's propensity to use it in the future and the willingness to enforce marijuana laws, and that the requirement was therefore job-related.

---

[18]Keenan v. American Cast Iron Pipe Co., 707 F.2d 1274, 32 FEP 142 (11th Cir. 1983).
[19]Griggs v. Duke Power Co., 401 U.S. 424, 3 FEP 175 (1971).
[20]Chambers v. Omaha Girls Club, 629 F. Supp. 925, 951, 40 FEP 362, 382 (D. Neb. 1986), *aff'd*, 834 F.2d 697, 45 FEP 698 (8th Cir. 1987).
[21]EEOC v. Rath Packing Co., 787 F.2d 318, 40 FEP 580 (8th Cir.), *cert. denied*, 479 U.S. 910, 41 FEP 1712 (1986).
[22]Davis v. City of Dallas, 777 F.2d 205, 223–25, 39 FEP 744, 758–59 (5th Cir. 1985), *cert. denied*, 476 U.S. 1116, 40 FEP 1320 (1986).

CHAPTER 6

# SUBJECTIVE CRITERIA

## I. METHOD OF ANALYSIS

In *Watson v. Fort Worth Bank & Trust,*[1] the Supreme Court held that claims of discrimination under a subjective promotion system may properly be analyzed under the adverse impact model as well as under the order and allocation of proof for disparate treatment cases.[2] The Court was divided, however, on the appropriate evidentiary standards to apply in the adverse impact analysis of such subjective employment practices.[3] Four of the Court's eight Justices opined that the application of the burden on plaintiff to prove a prima facie case and to overcome the employer's "business necessity" or "job-relatedness" defense should be sufficiently stringent "to avoid giving employers incentives to modify any normal and legitimate practices by introducing quotas or preferential treatment," because "the ultimate burden of proving that discrimination against a protected group has been caused by a specific employment practice remains with the plaintiff at all times."[4] Three Justices flatly rejected this analysis, asserting that established Title VII precedent makes it clear that in adverse impact cases the burden of proof shifts to the employer once plaintiff establishes a prima facie case.[5] Justice Stevens opined simply that these issues must await subsequent resolution in a factually appropriate case.[6]

Prior to *Watson* courts continued to hold that the use of subjective criteria to make employment decisions was not *per se* unlawful,[7] but recognized that it may create or strengthen an inference of discrimination.[8] The

---

[1]487 U.S. —, 47 FEP 102 (1988).

[2]*Id.,* 47 FEP at 107.

[3]*Id.,* 47 FEP at 108 (opinion of O'Connor, J.); *id.,* 47 FEP at 114–15 (opinion of Blackmun, J.); *id.,* 47 FEP at 116 (opinion of Stevens, J.).

[4]*Id.,* 47 FEP at 110–11 (opinion of O'Connor, J.).

[5]*Id.,* 47 FEP at 112–14 (opinion of Blackmun, J.).

[6]*Id.,* 47 FEP at 116 (opinion of Stevens, J.).

[7]*See, e.g.,* Casillas v. United States Navy, 735 F.2d 338, 345, 34 FEP 1493, 1497 (9th Cir. 1984) ("We have explicitly rejected the idea that an employer's use of subjective employment criteria has a talismanic significance"); Page v. U.S. Indus., 726 F.2d 1038, 1046, 34 FEP 430, 435 (5th Cir. 1984) ("It is clear that a promotional system which is based upon subjective selection criteria is not discriminatory per se."); Atonio v. Wards Cove Packing Co., 810 F.2d 1477, 1481, 43 FEP 130, 133 (9th Cir. 1987) (en banc); EEOC v. Rath Packing Co., 787 F.2d 318, 328, 40 FEP 580, 589 (8th Cir.), *cert. denied,* 479 U.S. 910, 41 FEP 1712 (1986) ("some subjectivity is inevitable in the hiring process"); Smith v. Western Elec. Co., 770 F.2d 520, 528, 38 FEP 1605, 1611 (5th Cir. 1985) ("An opportunity to discriminate, standing alone, will not establish discriminatory impact or treatment"). *See also* Nation v. Winn-Dixie Stores, 567 F. Supp. 997, 1005–06 n.20, 32 FEP 493, 500, *aff'd on reh'g,* 570 F. Supp. 1473, 32 FEP 1602 (N.D. Ga. 1983) ("[I]t is especially difficult in the context of promotions to formulate employer decision-making criteria that are completely free of subjectivity."); Judge v. Marsh, 649 F. Supp. 770, 42 FEP 1003 (D.D.C. 1986) (subjective criteria in hiring or promotion process are not to be condemned as unlawful *per se*).

[8]Burrus v. United Tel. Co. of Kan., 683 F.2d 339, 29 FEP 663 (10th Cir.), *cert. denied,* 459 U.S. 1071, 30 FEP 592 (1982) (rejection of otherwise qualified individual on basis of subjective considerations provides opportunity for unlawful discrimination and entitles plaintiff to inference of discrimination); Miles v. M.N.C. Corp., 750 F.2d 867, 36 FEP 1289 (11th Cir. 1985) (employer did not recall black

55

Second,[9] Third,[10] Sixth,[11] Ninth,[12] Tenth,[13] Eleventh,[14] and District of Columbia[15] circuits applied disparate impact analysis to subjective employment criteria. The Fourth,[16] Fifth,[17] Seventh,[18] and Eighth[19] circuits did not.

---

employee, stating it subjectively preferred others; court held that subjective evaluations were ready mechanism for discrimination and insufficient to rebut prima facie case, at least in light of evidence of tainted evaluation process).

[9]Zahorik v. Cornell Univ., 729 F.2d 85, 34 FEP 165 (2d Cir. 1984) (highly subjective tenure decision process analyzed under disparate impact theory); Grant v. Bethlehem Steel Corp., 635 F.2d 1007, 24 FEP 798 (2d Cir. 1980), cert. denied, 452 U.S. 940, 25 FEP 1683 (1981) (word-of-mouth hiring practice for foreman positions).

[10]Wilmore v. City of Wilmington, 699 F.2d 667, 31 FEP 2 (3d Cir. 1983) (subjective selection process for administrative firefighting positions disparately impaired minority performance on written promotional exams, which included administrative task analysis section).

[11]Rowe v. Cleveland Pneumatic Co., Numerical Control, 690 F.2d 88, 29 FEP 1682 (6th Cir. 1982) (rehire procedure which relied solely on subjective evaluations by white supervisory personnel).

[12]Atonio v. Wards Cove Packing Co., supra note 7 (word-of-mouth recruitment, lack of objective job qualifications, subjective hiring and promotion practices at cannery).

[13]Hawkins v. Bounds, 752 F.2d 500, 36 FEP 1285 (10th Cir. 1985) (subjective promotion procedures in Postal Service); Lasso v. Woodmen of the World Life Ins. Co., 741 F.2d 1241, 1246, 35 FEP 1417, 1420 (10th Cir. 1984), cert. denied, 471 U.S. 1099, 37 FEP 1216 (1985) (promotion policy based on "leadership ability, getting along with the person's peers, and the person's experience background"); Williams v. Colorado Springs School Dist. No. 11, 641 F.2d 835, 25 FEP 256 (10th Cir. 1981) (subjective hiring decisions by school principal); Bauer v. Bailar, 647 F.2d 1037, 25 FEP 963 (10th Cir. 1981) (subjective promotion procedures in Postal Service); Coe v. Yellow Freight Sys., 646 F.2d 407, 25 FEP 900 (10th Cir. 1981) (employer habitually used subjective criteria for determining employee qualification for jobs, promotions, or transfers). But see Heward v. Western Elec. Co., 35 FEP 807 (10th Cir. 1984) (impact analysis inapplicable to completely subjective decisions to terminate employees) (distinguishing Bauer v. Bailar, supra).

[14]Griffin v. Carlin, 755 F.2d 1516, 37 FEP 741 (11th Cir. 1985) (failure to apply disparate impact analysis to subjective promotion procedures would encourage employers to use subjective, rather than objective, employment criteria); Maddox v. Claytor, 764 F.2d 1539, 38 FEP 713 (11th Cir. 1985) (impact analysis applicable to use of selecting and ranking panels for promotions within Marine Corps).

[15]Segar v. Smith, 738 F.2d 1249, 1288 n.34, 35 FEP 31, 59 (D.C. Cir. 1984), cert. denied, 471 U.S. 1115, 37 FEP 1312 (1985) (impact analysis applicable to supervisory evaluation, discipline, and promotion systems involving subjective judgments).

[16]Compare Lewis v. Bloomsburg Mills, 773 F.2d 561, 38 FEP 1692, corrected on other grounds, 40 FEP 1615 (4th Cir. 1985) (subjective hiring practices at textile mill had disparate impact on black women, district court erred in finding impact due to job-related objective experience criteria) with Pope v. City of Hickory, N.C., 679 F.2d 20, 29 FEP 405 (4th Cir. 1982) (police department disciplinary actions did not fit within disparate impact model).

[17]Compare Smith v. Western Elec. Co., supra note 7 (plaintiffs failed to make prima facie case of disparate treatment or impact with respect to "largely subjective" promotion procedure) and Page v. U.S. Indus., supra note 7 (impact analysis appropriate for subjective promotional systems which could have classwide effect) with Bunch v. Bullard, 795 F.2d 384, 394, 41 FEP 515, 524 (5th Cir. 1986) ("allegedly discretionary promotion procedure fits within the disparate treatment analysis, rather than the disparate impact analysis"), Watson v. Fort Worth Bank & Trust, 798 F.2d 791, 797, 41 FEP 1179, 1183 (5th Cir. 1986), vacated and remanded, 487 U.S. —, 47 FEP 102 (1988) ("allegedly discretionary promotion system is properly analyzed under the disparate treatment model rather than the disparate impact model"), Walls v. Mississippi State Dep't of Pub. Welfare, 730 F.2d 306, 321–22, 34 FEP 1114 (5th Cir. 1984) (subjective evaluation process analyzed under disparate treatment model), Vuyanich v. Republic Nat'l Bank of Dallas, 723 F.2d 1195, 33 FEP 1521 (5th Cir.), cert. denied, 469 U.S. 1073, 36 FEP 568 (1984) (disparate treatment proper model for challenge to partially objective and subjective hiring process), Pegues v. Mississippi State Employment Serv., 699 F.2d 760, 31 FEP 257 (5th Cir.), cert. denied, 464 U.S. 991, 33 FEP 440 (1983) (discretionary classification and referral decisions not facially neutral procedure to which impact analysis applies), Carroll v. Sears, Roebuck & Co., 708 F.2d 183, 188, 32 FEP 286, 290 (5th Cir. 1983) (subjective evaluation for hiring and job placement should not be analyzed under disparate impact theory), Carpenter v. Stephen F. Austin State Univ., 706 F.2d 608, 620, 31 FEP 1758, 1768 (5th Cir. 1983) (discretionary classification not facially neutral practice to which impact analysis applies), Hill v. K-Mart Corp., 699 F.2d 776, 31 FEP 269 (5th Cir. 1983) (statistical evidence of discrimination through subjective decisions analyzed as disparate treatment problem), Payne v. Travenol Laboratories, 673 F.2d 798, 28 FEP 1212 (5th Cir.), cert. denied, 459 U.S. 1038, 30 FEP 440 (1982) (subjective interview process analyzed under disparate treatment model) and Pouncy v. Prudential Ins. Co. of Am., 668 F.2d 795, 28 FEP 121 (5th Cir. 1982) (impact analysis inapplicable to failure to post job openings, segregation of employees into levels, and subjective employment evaluations).

[18]Compare Regner v. City of Chicago, 789 F.2d 534, 40 FEP 1027 (7th Cir. 1986) (Cudahy, J.) (applying impact analysis to subjective employment practices "appropriate for claims considered at the early stages of the trial process") with Griffin v. Regency Univs. Bd. of Regents, 795 F.2d 1281, 1288 n.14, 41 FEP 228, 235 (7th Cir. 1986) (Cudahy, J.) ("We have previously noted, without deciding the issue, that a 'disparate impact claim is more problematic when subjective factors are present in the decision-making process'") (citing Regner v. City of Chicago, supra) and Namenwirth v. University of

## II. EMPLOYMENT DISCRIMINATION VIOLATIONS INVOLVING THE USE OF SUBJECTIVE CRITERIA

### A. Blue-Collar Jobs

Courts are most likely to find employers liable where employment decisions regarding blue-collar jobs are based on vague, subjective criteria, and where the plaintiff can show prima facie evidence of adverse impact or disparate treatment.[20] Where the employer relies on the discretion of its supervisors, without defined criteria, to determine which employees to rehire after layoffs,[21] or where a disproportionately white or male supervisory work force makes adverse discretionary employment decisions without clear guidelines, particularly where there is evidence that they manifest racist or sexist attitudes,[22] courts have found discrimination.

Similarly, management's practice of determining the potential physical strength of female applicants based solely upon visual evaluation of the

---

Wis. Sys. Bd. of Regents, 769 F.2d 1235, 38 FEP 1155 (7th Cir. 1985), *cert. denied*, 474 U.S. 1061, 39 FEP 1200 (1986) (courts have no choice but to defer to academic judgments with respect to tenure decisions).

[19]*Compare* EEOC v. Rath Packing Co., 787 F.2d 318, 40 FEP 580 (8th Cir.), *cert. denied*, 479 U.S. 910, 41 FEP 1712 (1986) (subjective hiring practices had disparate impact on women, not justified by business necessity) *and* Gilbert v. City of Little Rock, 722 F.2d 1390, 33 FEP 557 (8th Cir. 1983), *cert. denied*, 466 U.S. 972, 34 FEP 1312 (1984) (promotion process involving oral interviews, performance appraisals, and supervisor ratings analyzed under both disparate treatment and disparate impact models) *with* Talley v. United States Postal Serv., 720 F.2d 505, 33 FEP 361 (8th Cir. 1983), *cert. denied*, 466 U.S. 952, 37 FEP 592 (1984) (subjective decision-making by primarily white supervisory force not subject to challenge under disparate impact analysis), Harris v. Ford Motor Co., 651 F.2d 609, 28 FEP 537 (8th Cir. 1981) (subjective workmanship evaluation system alone not foundation for disparate impact case) *and* Emanuel v. Marsh, 828 F.2d 438, 45 FEP 666 (8th Cir. 1987) (disparate impact claim may not be based on subjective evaluation and promotion procedures).

[20]*E.g.*, Boykin v. Georgia-Pacific Corp., 706 F.2d 1384, 32 FEP 25 (5th Cir. 1983), *cert. denied*, 465 U.S. 1006, 33 FEP 1344 (1984) (promotion discrimination allegations involving skilled jobs in lumber mill); EEOC v. Rath Packing Co., *supra* note 19 (subjective hiring practices at meat processing facility had disparate impact on women); Lewis v. Bloomsburg Mills, *supra* note 16 (plaintiff showed disparate impact on blacks where initial screening of applications for job at textile mill done by receptionist without guidelines); Hill v. Seaboard Coast Line R.R., 767 F.2d 771, 775, 39 FEP 1656, 1659 (11th Cir. 1985) ("It is difficult to imagine how a large corporation with a numerous work force can expect to satisfy its legal duties towards minorities when its selections for promotion are made in such an unstructured and unguided manner.").

[21]Rowe v. Cleveland Pneumatic Co., Numerical Control, 690 F.2d 88, 29 FEP 1682 (6th Cir. 1982) (unexplained and unreviewed subjective decisions of foremen relied on in selecting employees for rehire improper).

[22]*E.g.*, Harris v. Birmingham Bd. of Educ., 712 F.2d 1377, 32 FEP 1198 (11th Cir. 1983) (high school coaching jobs not posted, no objective hiring standards, combined with unfettered discretion vested in two white decision makers); Carroll v. Sears, Roebuck & Co., 708 F.2d 183, 192, 32 FEP 286, 293 (5th Cir. 1983) ("Sears has no written criteria or guidelines for promotion, and does not post notices concerning specific job openings or promotion opportunities. It is undisputed that a majority of the supervisors are white. Given the importance of supervisory ratings and opinions and the presence of unwritten, subjective criteria for promotion, black employees face a greater risk of discrimination at Sears."); Harrell v. Northern Elec. Co., 672 F.2d 444, 28 FEP 911 (5th Cir.), *cert. denied*, 459 U.S. 1037, 30 FEP 440 (1982) (company's use of all-white personnel to make subjective determinations regarding black applicants for hire failed to refute prima facie showing of discrimination); EEOC v. United States Steel Corp., 34 FEP 978, 981 (N.D. Ga. 1984), *aff'd in pertinent part sub nom.* Nord v. United States Steel Corp., 758 F.2d 1462, 37 FEP 1232 (11th Cir. 1985) (claim of sex discrimination in promotions where all management personnel were male, principal factor in promotion decisions was supervisor's recommendation, vacancies were not posted, and there were no established standards or procedures governing promotions); Lams v. General Waterworks Corp., 766 F.2d 386, 38 FEP 516 (8th Cir. 1985) (white department head responsible for promoting predominantly black construction and maintenance workers believed blacks were not interested in promotions); Osahar v. Carlin, 642 F. Supp. 448 (S.D. Fla. 1986) (liability found where promotion system in post office administered by white supervisors in "racially charged atmosphere"). *See also* Price Waterhouse v. Hopkins, 57 U.S.L.W. 4469, 49 FEP 954 (1989), *rev'g and remanding* 825 F.2d 458, 44 FEP 458 (D.C. Cir. 1987) and discussion *supra* Chapter 1 (Overview).

applicant's appearance has been held improper.[23] However, defendants have prevailed where they based hiring decisions on such factors as past work experience in choosing one applicant over another[24] and on the initiative and articulation of an applicant in the interview procedure.[25]

## B. White-Collar Jobs

Courts are more likely to accept the use of subjective criteria in making employment decisions when the jobs are white collar, particularly professional, managerial, and academic positions.[26]

However, courts have found liability where subjective criteria were not used fairly and uniformly with procedural safeguards,[27] or where the employer relies on naked "good-faith" and "best-qualified" defenses.[28]

## III. FACTORS TO CONSIDER IN STRUCTURING, ATTACKING, OR DEFENDING SUBJECTIVE CRITERIA

Most cases finding liability have involved multiple deficiencies in the creation or use of subjective evaluation criteria, combined with convincing statistical evidence of disparate impact or treatment,[29] while cases rejecting

---

[23]EEOC v. Spokane Concrete Prods., 534 F. Supp. 518, 28 FEP 423 (E.D. Wash. 1982) ("eyeball" test of strength is not "professionally acceptable method" that fairly tests applicants).

[24]Lerma v. Bolger, 689 F.2d 589, 29 FEP 1828 (5th Cir. 1982) (evaluation based upon work experience and made in good faith is legally sufficient explanation).

[25]Pierce v. Owens-Corning Fiberglas Corp., 30 FEP 53 (D. Kan. 1982).

[26]See Jayasinghe v. Bethlehem Steel Corp., 760 F.2d 132, 37 FEP 817 (7th Cir. 1985) (employer properly relied on subjective considerations in choosing less academically qualified chemist for supervisory chemist position); Zahorik v. Cornell Univ., 729 F.2d 85, 34 FEP 165 (2d Cir. 1984); Mason v. Continental Ill. Nat'l Bank, 704 F.2d 361, 31 FEP 629 (7th Cir. 1983) (subjective evaluations for managerial position utilized without challenge); MacDonald v. Ferguson Reorganized School Dist. R-2, 711 F.2d 80, 31 FEP 184 (8th Cir.), cert. denied, 464 U.S. 961 (1983) (subjective criteria necessary to fill leadership position of assistant principal); see also Anderson v. City of Albuquerque, 690 F.2d 796, 29 FEP 1689 (10th Cir. 1982) (management position); Burrus v. United Tel. Co. of Kan., 683 F.2d 339, 29 FEP 663 (10th Cir.), cert. denied, 459 U.S. 1071, 30 FEP 592 (1982) (accountant); Johnson v. Michigan State Univ., 547 F. Supp. 429, 30 FEP 260 (W.D. Mich. 1982), aff'd mem., 723 F.2d 909, 35 FEP 1522 (6th Cir. 1983) (faculty position); McCarthney v. Griffin-Spalding County Bd. of Educ., 791 F.2d 1549, 41 FEP 245 (11th Cir. 1986) (use of recommendations, inquiry into teaching record, and ability to get along with others did not invalidate system for promoting teachers to administrative positions); Estepa v. Shad, 652 F. Supp. 567, 571 n.6 (E.D.N.Y. 1987) ("[w]here an employer considers candidates for a supervisory position, it may rely on subjective criteria"). Similarly, such a subjective evaluation process, used in the appropriate context, is not a basis for a finding of pretext. Royal v. State Highway Comm'n of Mo., 549 F. Supp. 681, 30 FEP 220 (E.D. Mo. 1982), aff'd, 714 F.2d 867, 32 FEP 1389 (8th Cir. 1983) (subjective analysis of leadership ability, supervisory skills, effectiveness of judgment, and willingness to cooperate and work with others not a pretext).

[27]Pouncy v. Prudential Ins. Co. of Am., supra note 17 (safeguards included meaningful instructions for evaluations, upper-level review of evaluations, and opportunity for each employee to review evaluation); Allen v. Isaac, 39 FEP 1142 (N.D. Ill. 1986) (performance evaluation used in promotion decisions for bank examiners did not conform to applicable EEOC guidelines); Stallworth v. Shuler, 777 F.2d 1431, 39 FEP 983 (11th Cir. 1985) (informal system of appointment to administrative and principal positions in school district without notice of vacancies). See also Allesberry v. Pennsylvania, 30 FEP 1634 (M.D. Pa. 1981); Womack v. Shell Chem. Co., 514 F. Supp. 1062, 28 FEP 224 (S.D. Ala. 1981). But see Price Waterhouse v. Hopkins, supra note 22.

[28]See Payne v. Travenol Laboratories, 673 F.2d 798, 28 FEP 1212 (5th Cir.), cert. denied, 459 U.S. 1038, 30 FEP 440 (1982) (general assertions of good faith and hiring only best qualified applicants insufficient); Wheeler v. City of Columbus, Miss., 686 F.2d 1144, 29 FEP 1699 (5th Cir. 1982) (general statements that employer hired only best qualified applicants insufficient).

[29]See Harris v. Birmingham Bd. of Educ., supra note 22 (failure to promulgate objective standards or policies regarding hiring, failure to post vacancies, lack of objective standards for evaluating candidates, and use of principals' recommendations without objective criteria all support finding of discrimination); Paxton v. Union Nat'l Bank, 688 F.2d 552, 563, 29 FEP 1233, 1243 (8th Cir. 1982), cert. denied, 460 U.S. 1083, 31 FEP 824 (1983) (utilization of primarily subjective criteria by white supervisors,

liability generally have involved statistics of only limited value or impact, together with multiple safeguards.[30] Where a subjective system creates no adverse effect on the subject class, such subjectivity is insufficient by itself to sustain the plaintiff's case.[31] At the same time, the existence of a subjective evaluation system lacking appropriate safeguards generates a greater risk of liability in cases where the statistical disparity is a matter of dispute.[32]

More recent cases provide additional examples of factors, identified in the Second Edition, used in evaluating the legality of subjective appraisal systems. Failure to articulate clear job-related qualifications[33] or consistent

---

affirmative action program not emphasized, and vacancies not posted or effectively communicated); Payne v. Travenol Laboratories, *supra* note 28 (virtually all-white work force above operations level, failure to post notices, reliance on recommendations of white supervisors without objective standards to guide them, length of service requirements, and other educational requirements); EEOC v. H.S. Camp & Sons, 542 F. Supp. 411, 33 FEP 330 (M.D. Fla. 1982) (no promotions prior to charge; requirements unwritten, vague, and subjective; no notices of vacancies posted; no safeguard procedures); EEOC v. Rath Packing Co., 787 F.2d 318, 40 FEP 580 (8th Cir.), *cert. denied,* 479 U.S. 910, 41 FEP 1712 (1986) (supervisor unable to articulate criteria for hiring decisions which had disparate impact on women); Lewis v. Bloomsburg Mills, 773 F.2d 561, 38 FEP 1692, *corrected on other grounds,* 40 FEP 1615 (4th Cir. 1985) (employer had no monitoring or safeguards on procedure whereby receptionist forwarded employment applications to supervisor, evidence showed disparate impact on blacks); Osahar v. Carlin, *supra* note 22 (employer rejected use of validated objective test as main promotion criteria; evidence of disparate treatment and impact against blacks in "atmosphere of racial tension and animosity"); Allen v. Isaac, *supra* note 27 (employer failed to follow EEOC guidelines on developing subjective performance evaluation procedure, with significant impact on blacks); Winfield v. St. Joe Paper Co., 38 EPD ¶ 35,580 (N.D. Fla. 1985) (plaintiff's statistical evidence of disparate treatment "compelling," no structured process for personnel director's hiring decisions); Lams v. General Waterworks Corp., *supra* note 22 (statistics showed blacks concentrated in construction and maintenance divisions, kept from other divisions through word-of-mouth hiring and promotion by white supervisors); Atonio v. Wards Cove Packing Co., 810 F.2d 1477, 43 FEP 130 (9th Cir. 1987) (comparative statistics supported inference of discriminatory impact and, because certain practices shown to cause that impact, *i.e.,* nepotism, separate hiring channels, word-of-mouth recruiting and race-labeling, housing and messing, incumbent upon employer to prove business necessity of those practices); Black Law Enforcement Officers Ass'n v. City of Akron, 824 F.2d 475, 44 FEP 1477 (6th Cir. 1987) (statistical proof that white officers regularly received higher ratings than black officers on performance appraisal test, combined with evidence that rating guidelines were not followed and that ratings were manipulated, showed discriminatory impact).

[30]*See* Page v. U.S. Indus., 726 F.2d 1038, 34 FEP 430 (5th Cir. 1984) (statistics did not show gross disparity; supervisors required to make promotional decisions in accordance with standards set out in collective bargaining agreement); Wilson v. Michigan Bell Tel. Co., 550 F. Supp. 1296, 1299, 30 FEP 427, 430 (E.D. Mich. 1982) (statistics only marginally reliable, assessment procedure job-related, and evaluation review process contained safety procedures); Maddox v. Claytor, 764 F.2d 1539, 38 FEP 713 (11th Cir. 1985) (plaintiffs failed to make prima facie case of either disparate impact or treatment; several objective safeguards checked discretion of promotion ranking panel); Atonio v. Wards Cove Packing Co., 768 F.2d 1120, 38 FEP 1170 (9th Cir. 1985), *vacated on other grounds,* 810 F.2d 1477, 43 FEP 130 (9th Cir. 1987) (plaintiff failed to make prima facie case of disparate treatment with respect to hiring, promotion, pay, and termination of cannery employees, employer showed reason for differences other than discriminatory animus); Smith v. Western Elec. Co., 770 F.2d 520, 38 FEP 1605 (5th Cir. 1985) (plaintiff's statistical evidence of disparate impact and treatment unconvincing, employer maintained detailed objective checks on promotion procedure, including process for grieving decisions).

[31]*See* Metrocare v. Washington Metro. Area Transit Auth., 679 F.2d 922, 929, 28 FEP 1585, 1591 (D.C. Cir. 1982) (subjectivity is applicable "only where the proof adequately shows a negative disparity in the employment or promotion opportunities of blacks"); Phillips v. Amoco Oil Co., 34 FEP 137 (S.D. Tex. 1982) (no evidence that subjective criteria selected applicants for hire in significantly discriminatory pattern); Ferguson v. E.I. du Pont de Nemours & Co., 560 F. Supp. 1172, 1194, 31 FEP 795, 810 (D. Del. 1983) ("Simply establishing that one prong of a promotion system invokes subjectivity, without more, does not demonstrate disparate impact."); Maddox v. Claytor, *supra* note 30; Smith v. Western Elec. Co., *supra* note 30; Lucero v. Continental Oil Co., 38 EPD ¶ 35,582 (S.D. Tex. 1985) (statistics showed no gross disparity in promotion of female employees to administrative assistant jobs); Hillis v. Marsh, 40 EPD ¶ 36,462 (E.D. Tex. 1986) (statistics showed black employees selected for promotion at Army depot at rates which exceeded their representation in the work force).

[32]*Compare* Carroll v. Sears, Roebuck & Co., *supra* note 22 (absence of written criteria or guidelines for promotion, failure to post notices concerning specific job openings for promotional opportunities, and unwritten subjective criteria for promotions warrant strict scrutiny of promotional practices) *with* Wilson v. Michigan Bell Tel. Co., *supra* note 30 (assumed statistical disparity insufficient to create prima facie case because of safeguards in applicant review process).

[33]*See* EEOC v. Rath Packing Co., *supra* note 29 (supervisor primarily responsible for hiring unable to articulate any particular qualification or attributes he looked for in an applicant). *But see* Phillips v. Amoco Oil Co., *supra* note 31 (defendant's ability to articulate at least some reason, *i.e.,* "a belief that

hiring and promotion guidelines[34] creates the impression of unfettered subjectivity and increases the probability of employer liability. Selection systems that combine objective with subjective elements, or that provide for significant procedural safeguards against discrimination are more likely to withstand attack than entirely subjective systems with unfettered discretion vested in one level of management.[35] Failure to provide adequate notice of job opportunities may impact negatively on subjective promotional systems.[36]

---

the plaintiff lacked sufficient ability to learn the required materials," sufficient to rebut prima facie case absent any evidence of pretext).

[34]*Compare* Paxton v. Union Nat'l Bank, *supra* note 29 (liability found with respect to promotion practices in part because of ad hoc contradictory and conflicting explanations), Payne v. Travenol Laboratories, *supra* note 28 (supervisor's recommendation delivered without guidance by any objective standards and operated to discriminate) *and* Winfield v. St. Joe Paper Co., *supra* note 29 (supervisor hired who he wished without benefit of process for evaluating applicants) *with* Wilson v. Michigan Bell Tel. Co., *supra* note 30 (evaluations by individuals assessing applicants required to be fully justified, in written form, and explained during supervised discussions involving each evaluator) *and* Johnson v. Michigan State Univ., *supra* note 26 (although subjective, determination of granting tenure was subject to specific stated criteria).

[35]In *Boykin v. Georgia-Pacific Corp.,* 706 F.2d 1384, 1390, 32 FEP 25, 29 (5th Cir. 1983), *cert. denied,* 465 U.S. 1006, 33 FEP 1344 (1984), the court found liability stating: "Although proof of discriminatory motive is generally required in disparate treatment cases, the evidence of subjective, standardless decision-making by company officials, which is a convenient mechanism for discrimination, satisfies this requirement." Thereafter, in *Page v. U.S. Indus., supra* note 30, at 1053, 34 FEP at 441, the Fifth Circuit distinguished *Boykin,* stating: "The record clearly shows that defendant did not maintain the type of *standardless* subjective system envisioned by the Court in *Boykin.* The employment system at issue in *Boykin* was devoid of any objective bases for judging possible applicants." Among the factors which the court held distinguished *Page* from *Boykin* were the use of collectively bargained job classifications and qualifications, and the fact that employees could seek review of decisions made by foremen. *See also* Bell v. Bolger, 708 F.2d 1312, 32 FEP 32 (8th Cir. 1983) (declining to find liability notwithstanding employer's use of evaluation form calling for subjective judgments, where decision makers also considered promotion interview, applicant's personnel folder, and promotion application); Parker v. Mississippi State Dep't. of Pub. Welfare, 811 F.2d 925, 43 FEP 243 (5th Cir. 1987) (declining to find liability notwithstanding employer's use of interview calling for subjective judgments, where employer also based decisions on objective factors, including test scores and tenure). In *Maddox v. Claytor, supra* note 30, the court approved use of a promotion ranking panel, noting that it proceeded under the supervision of a personnel specialist, evaluated relevant elements of each applicant's file on a mathematical scale, then resolved their differences and sent each applicant's scores to the personnel office, and that it played no further role in the selection process. The court suggested that the discretion of an interviewing panel which was also involved in the promotion process could have been checked by requiring a record explaining why one employee was selected over another. In *Smith v. Western Elec. Co., supra* note 30, an employer which based promotions on a work code system and an index ranking of employees showed that it kept a written manual which provided detailed instructions for the index plan's administration and a complete description of work codes, weekly records of employee time in different work codes, and a four-stage process to hear grievances from employees who felt they had been unfairly denied promotions. *Compare* Paxton v. Union Nat'l Bank, *supra* note 29 (white supervisors make most promotional decisions) *and* Payne v. Travenol Laboratories, *supra* note 28 (masking of racially motivated decisions by using subjective judgments particularly likely when all-white supervisory staff conducts interviews) *with* Wilson v. Michigan Bell Tel. Co., *supra* note 30 (black member of reviewing team provided very probative testimony regarding propriety of review procedure).

[36]*See* Paxton v. Union Nat'l Bank, *supra* note 29 (system to communicate vacancies to employees incomplete and untimely); Kraszewski v. State Farm Gen. Ins. Co., 38 FEP 197 (N.D. Cal. 1985) (citing *inter alia* defendant's reliance on word-of-mouth recruiting and failure to post notice of job openings in finding employment discrimination); Davis v. Richmond, Fredericksburg & Potomac R.R., 593 F. Supp. 271, 35 FEP 1140 (E.D. Va. 1984), *aff'd, rev'd and vacated in part on other grounds,* 803 F.2d 1322, 42 FEP 69 (4th Cir. 1986) (defendant's use of word-of-mouth recruiting and failure to notify employees formally of openings supported finding of discrimination in hiring and promotion); EEOC v. United States Steel Corp., 34 FEP 978, 981 (N.D. Ga. 1984), *aff'd in pertinent part sub nom.* Nord v. United States Steel Corp., 758 F.2d 1462, 37 FEP 1232 (11th Cir. 1985) (no posting of notices of job openings or promotion opportunities and no information provided to employees as to necessary qualifications for promotion); Ivy v. Meridian Coca-Cola Bottling Co., 641 F. Supp. 157 (S.D. Miss. 1986) (black employees not informed of promotion opportunities by white supervisors); Stallworth v. Shuler, *supra* note 27 (school district failed to advertise or post openings for administrative and principal positions); Lams v. General Waterworks Corp., 766 F.2d 386, 38 FEP 516 (8th Cir. 1985) (white supervisors maintained word-of-mouth policy on job openings).

CHAPTER 7

# RELIGION

## I. WHAT IS PROTECTED AS RELIGION

Trial courts have addressed in varying contexts the scope of activity protected as "religious observances." The plaintiff in *Wessling v. Kroger Co.*[1] was a lay religious school teacher who had left work on December 24 before the end of her shift, after having been denied permission to do so by her supervisor. The court found that her reasons for leaving—to decorate her church hall and prepare the religious school students for their Christmas play—did not constitute religious observances protected by Title VII or the state statute, but instead were social and family obligations. Although the court thought the employer "extraordinarily harsh" in discharging the plaintiff for walking off her job, no violation was found.

The plaintiffs in *McCrory v. Rapides Regional Medical Center,*[2] argued that they were discharged in violation of Title VII because their supervisor's religious belief proscribing extramarital relationships conflicted with their private right to have such relationships. However, The Court held that Title VII prohibits discrimination based upon an individual's own religious beliefs and not those of his or her employer. The Court concluded that adultery is not an expression of religious belief entitled to protection under Title VII. The court granted summary judgment to the employer and awarded attorneys' fees against the plaintiffs and their counsel pursuant to Title VII and Rule 11 of the Federal Rules of Civil Procedure.

## II. THE EMPLOYER'S DUTY TO ACCOMMODATE

### B. The Constitutionality of the Duty

The Supreme Court has held in *Estate of Thornton v. Caldor, Inc.*[3] that a Connecticut statute requiring employers to provide employees with an absolute and unqualified right not to work on their chosen Sabbath day had the primary effect of advancing a particular religious practice. It therefore violated the Establishment Clause of the First Amendment to the Constitution. Though the statute was a revision of the Connecticut Sunday-closing laws, any similar blanket mandate in a fair employment context would appear unconstitutional on the Court's analysis in *Thornton.* Consistent with *Thornton,* a court may determine on the facts of the case before it that

---

[1]554 F. Supp. 548, 30 FEP 1222 (E.D. Mich. 1982).
[2]635 F. Supp. 975, 40 FEP 750 (W.D. La.), *aff'd,* 801 F.2d 396, 44 FEP 1243 (5th Cir. 1986).
[3]472 U.S. 703, 38 FEP 1 (1985).

Sabbath leave imposes no more than a *de minimis* burden on the employer, and that ordering such leave under Title VII constitutes no violation of the First Amendment.[4]

Earlier, the constitutionality issues raised by *Cummins v. Parker Seal, Inc.*[5] were presented again to the Sixth Circuit in *McDaniel v. Essex International.*[6] The plaintiff, a Seventh-Day Adventist, was prohibited by her religion from paying union dues. The court followed its holding in *Cummins* that § 701(j) had a clearly secular purpose, not violative of the Establishment Clause, and dismissed the employer's and the union's constitutionality arguments, finding nothing in this case "which compels a re-examination of *Cummins.*"[7] The court then upheld the trial court's finding of unlawful failure to accommodate.

It is unclear whether courts may resolve on pretrial motions the constitutionality of employer practices advanced as reasonable accommodations. At least one trial court has done so with circuit court approval. In *EEOC v. Fremont Christian School,*[8] the court granted the plaintiff's motion for summary judgment, holding that the school violated Title VII by providing health insurance benefits to men that were not allowed to women. Uncontradicted evidence established that the school's policy was to provide health insurance only to a full-time employee who was the "head of the household." The school then conclusively presumed that this person is the husband, thus depriving similarly situated women of health insurance benefits. The school sought to justify its policy by religious beliefs regarding "differentiated roles of the sexes."[9] The school argued that its policy was grounded in religious belief, and that Title VII did not apply because the policy was protected by the Free Exercise and Establishment clauses. Citing *EEOC v. Mississippi College,*[10] the court enunciated three factors to be weighed in determining a violation of the Free Exercise Clause:

> "(1) [T]he magnitude of the statute's impact on the exercise of a religious belief; (2) the existence of a compelling state interest justifying the burden imposed upon the exercise of the religious belief; and (3) the extent to which recognition of the exemption from the statute would impede objectives sought to be advanced by the statute."[11]

Implementing this test, the court found (1) requiring the school to refrain from discriminating against female employees does not infringe the school's free exercise of its religious beliefs; (2) Title VII was enacted to eliminate all forms of discrimination as a "high priority"; and (3) permitting the school to discriminate on the basis of sex in health insurance benefits would defeat the intention of Congress to protect the employees of religious institutions.

---

[4]Protos v. Volkswagen of Am., 797 F.2d 129, 41 FEP 598 (3d Cir.), *cert. denied,* 479 U.S. 972, 44 FEP 216 (1986).

[5]516 F.2d 544, 10 FEP 974 (6th Cir. 1975), *aff'd by an equally divided court,* 429 U.S. 65, 13 FEP 1178 (1976), *vacated and remanded,* 433 U.S. 903, 15 FEP 31 (1977).

[6]696 F.2d 34, 30 FEP 831 (6th Cir. 1982).

[7]*Id.* at 37, 30 FEP at 833.

[8]609 F. Supp. 344, 34 FEP 1038 (N.D. Cal. 1984), *aff'd,* 781 F.2d 1362, 39 FEP 1815 (9th Cir. 1986). *See infra* notes 75 and 77 and accompanying text.

[9]*Id.,* 34 FEP at 1040, 1043.

[10]626 F.2d 477, 23 FEP 1501 (5th Cir. 1980), *cert. denied,* 453 U.S. 912 (1981).

[11]34 FEP at 1041. *See also* EEOC v. Pacific Press Publishing Ass'n, 676 F.2d 1272, 1279, 28 FEP 1596 (9th Cir. 1982).

In its Establishment Clause defense, the school contended that application of Title VII would unduly entangle church and state, and that its allegedly religious-based "head of household" policy is immune from government regulation since the policy represents the school's exercise of its Establishment Clause rights. The court recited another three-part test applicable to this defense:

"(1) the statute must have a secular purpose; (2) the primary effect of the statute must neither advance nor inhibit religion; and (3) the statute must not foster excessive entanglement with religion."[12]

The district court found the Fremont School "arguably" less sectarian than the seminary which the Fifth Circuit had required to comply with EEOC filing requirements in *EEOC v. Southwestern Baptist Theological Seminary*.[13] It found also that compliance with Title VII would not require the degree of ongoing close scrutiny over the school's operations that had led the Supreme Court to exempt the employer from enforcement of the collective bargaining requirements of the National Labor Relations Act in *NLRB v. Catholic Bishop of Chicago*.[14] Hence, the district court found insufficient risk of excessive entanglement with religion to support exemption from Title VII.[15]

On appeal, the Ninth Circuit affirmed the district court's ruling both on the Free Exercise and Establishment clauses, expressly holding that summary judgment was appropriate.[16] The court first concluded that the application of Title VII to the challenged employment practice would raise "serious constitutional questions," but that Congress had "clearly expressed" the intention that Title VII be so applied.[17] The court broadly reaffirmed that religious institutions are not immune from Title VII coverage; that the final version of § 702 of Title VII enacted in 1964 only excluded such employers with respect to discrimination based on religion, and then only with respect to persons hired to carry out the employer's "religious activities";[18] and that the 1972 amendments deleted the word "religious" but without further broadening the exemption in § 702. Hence, such employers "remain subject to the provisions of Title VII with regard to race, color, sex or national origin."[19]

Other courts have held that this type of careful balancing is not possible in a summary judgment proceeding.[20]

---

[12]*Supra* note 8, 34 FEP at 1041–42 (citing Lemon v. Kurtzman, 403 U.S. 602, 612 (1971) and EEOC v. Pacific Press Publishing Ass'n, *supra* note 11). This three-part test was again endorsed by the Supreme Court in *Corporation of the Presiding Bishop of the Church of Jesus Christ of Latter-Day Saints v. Amos*, 483 U.S. 327, 44 FEP 20 (1987). *See infra* at note 65.

[13]651 F.2d 277, 26 FEP 558 (5th Cir. 1981), *cert. denied*, 456 U.S. 905, 28 FEP 584 (1982).

[14]440 U.S. 490, 100 LRRM 2913 (1979).

[15]*Supra* note 8, 34 FEP at 1042.

[16]*Id.*, 39 FEP at 1819 n.1.

[17]*Id.*, 39 FEP at 1818.

[18]*Id.*

[19]*Id.*, quoting from the Section-by-Section Analysis of the Equal Employment Opportunity Act of 1972.

[20]*See* McCormick v. Belvidere School Dist. No. 100 Bd. of Educ., 32 FEP 504 (N.D. Ill. 1983) (defendant's motion for summary judgment denied because question of what constitutes reasonable accommodation is a case-by-case factual determination).

## C. The Extent of the Duty to Accommodate

### 1. The Elements of Proof

In *Ansonia Board of Education v. Philbrook,*[21] the Supreme Court declined to reach the question whether an employer's liability for religious accommodation claims should be measured under a proof scheme analogous to that established in other Title VII contexts, delineating the plaintiff's prima facie case and shifting production burdens. The Court held that— assuming an obligation to accommodate had been shown—an employer is not required to choose a reasonable accommodation preferred by the employee, but meets its obligations under § 701(j) of Title VII "when it demonstrates that it has offered a reasonable accommodation to the employee," and that "[t]he employer need not show that each of the employee's alternative accommodations would result in undue hardship."[22]

The Fifth Circuit held in *Brener v. Diagnostic Center Hospital*[23] that, while the plaintiff may not have the burden of proposing to the employer a workable accommodation, he does have a duty to cooperate with accommodation measures suggested by his employer: "a reasonable accommodation need not be on the employee's terms only."[24] Addressing a similar issue, a district court held that a plaintiff failed to establish a prima facie case of religious discrimination where he had not communicated his bona fide religious belief to his employer.[25]

### 2. The Scope of the Duty to Accommodate and the Degree of Hardship Required

As noted above, the Supreme Court ruled in *Ansonia Board of Education v. Philbrook*[26] that an employer meets its Title VII obligations by offering a reasonable accommodation of an employee's religious beliefs and need not implement a different reasonable accommodation proposed and preferred by the employee.[27] In *Ansonia,* the school district's collective bargaining agreement with the teachers' union contained a leave policy which specified allowable leave periods for various purposes and included three days annual leave for observance of mandatory religious holidays, as defined in the contract, and up to three days of accumulated leave each year for "necessary personal business." However, personal business leave could only be used for purposes not otherwise specified in the contract. Hence teachers desiring additional leave for secular or religious purposes covered by specific leave provisions of the contract could not draw from the personal business leave allowance. Under these provisions, teacher Philbrook had observed manda-

---

[21]479 U.S. 60, 42 FEP 359 (1986).

[22]*Id.,* 42 FEP at 363.

[23]671 F.2d 141, 28 FEP 907 (5th Cir. 1982).

[24]*Id.* at 146, 28 FEP at 910. The court did note, however, that "an employee is not required to modify his religious beliefs, only to attempt to satisfy them within the procedures offered by the employer." *Id.* at 146 n.3 28 FEP at 910 n.3 (citation omitted).

[25]Byrd v. Johnson, 31 FEP 1651 (D.D.C. 1983) (plaintiff testified that no one at his place of employment asked him about his religious affiliation, and he never volunteered it).

[26]*Supra* note 21.

[27]*Supra* note 22.

tory holy days of the Worldwide Church of God by using the three days granted in the labor contract and then taking unauthorized leave, with a corresponding pay reduction, or had scheduled hospital visits on church holy days or had worked on holy days. Philbrook had objected to this arrangement and proposed that he use personal business leave for religious observances or that he pay the cost of a substitute and receive full pay for the additional days of leave for religious observances. The school district declined these accommodations, and Philbrook claimed religious discrimination. The Second Circuit had held that, even assuming that the district's leave policy constituted a reasonable accommodation to Philbrook's belief, "Title VII requires the employer to accept the proposal the employee prefers unless that accommodation causes undue hardship on the employer's conduct of his business."[28] That court had remanded for consideration of the hardship resulting from Philbrook's proposed accommodations. The Supreme Court rejected the Second Circuit's reasoning and held that "an employer has met its obligation under § 701(j) when it demonstrates that it has offered a reasonable accommodation to the employee,"[29] and affirmed the order of remand to the district court for a "factual inquiry into past and present administration of the personal leave provisions of the collective-bargaining agreement."[30] The Court emphasized that unpaid leave would not be a reasonable accommodation if paid leave were provided on a discriminatory basis "for all purposes *except* religious ones."[31]

The Ninth Circuit has addressed the scope of required accommodation in two decisions. In *Proctor v. Consolidated Freightways Corp. of Delaware*[32] the court held that an employer's duty to offer a reasonable accommodation applies to each position to which an employee transfers, and that the employer must therefore offer a new accommodation tailored to the new job. The Ninth Circuit has also held that an employer need not implement employee-proposed alternatives where the employer's proposal effectively eliminates any religious conflict, reasonably preserves the employee's employment status, and the employee's rejection of the proposal is based on secular considerations.[33]

The Tenth Circuit affirmed the lower court's decision in *Pinsker v. Adams & Arapahoe Counties Joint District 28J,*[34] holding that where the employer's policies and practices jeopardized neither the employee's job nor his observation of religious holidays, the employer had not been unreasonable in accommodation of a teacher's religious practices, and that there was no prima facie showing of discrimination.[35]

One court has held that the duty to accommodate exists even where the employee's religious practices temporarily render him unfit to perform re-

---

[28]757 F.2d 476, 484, 37 FEP 404, 411 (2d Cir. 1985).

[29]*Supra* note 22.

[30]*Supra* note 21, 42 FEP at 364.

[31]*Id.* (emphasis by the Court).

[32]795 F.2d 1472, 41 FEP 704 (9th Cir. 1986).

[33]Postal Workers, San Francisco Local v. Postmaster Gen., 781 F.2d 772, 776, 39 FEP 1847, 1850 (9th Cir. 1986).

[34]735 F.2d 388, 34 FEP 1570 (10th Cir. 1984).

[35]*See* Di Pasquale v. Williamsville Cent. School Dist. Bd. of Educ., 626 F. Supp. 457, 37 FEP 1301 (W.D.N.Y. 1985).

quired duties safely. In *Toledo v. Nobel-Sysco,*[36] the court held that an employer had a duty to attempt accommodation of an employee's occasional off-the-job use of peyote (mescaline) by a member of the Native American religion who sought employment as a tractor-trailer driver. Though a violation of Title VII will usually be found where an employer makes no attempt to accommodate, the employer has no duty to tender accommodation proposals where the employee creates a reasonable belief that the proposals will be rejected.[37]

Courts have reached varying conclusions on the degree of accommodation required if the proposed accommodation would vary the terms of an established bargaining agreement.[38] In affirming the order of remand in *Ansonia Board of Education v. Philbrook,*[39] the Supreme Court directed a factual inquiry into the administration of the leave provisions of the school district's collective bargaining agreement and observed that provisions for unpaid leave would be an insufficient accommodation if paid leave were discriminatorily provided "for all purposes *except* religious ones."[40] The Eighth Circuit has upheld a collective bargaining agreement which allowed 16 days of absence in 12 months before discharge as a reasonable accommodation of an employee's religious beliefs.[41]

A "reverse religious discrimination" claim was recognized in *Ka Nam Kuan v. City of Chicago.*[42] There, a district court held that a Chicago police officer had stated a Title VII claim against the city for granting more paid religious holiday leave to certain non-Protestant employees than to him. As a result, the plaintiff had to work more overtime and accept a greater number of undesirable assignments. Denying the defendant's motion to dismiss, the court interpreted *Hardison*[43] as meaning that "[w]hen an employer bears more than a *de minimis* cost to accommodate a religious belief, it in effect discriminates against its other employees on the basis of their religious beliefs."[44] The court stated that the question whether the defendants have imposed an undue burden or a *de minimis* burden on the plaintiff is a question of fact, which could not be resolved without information such as the number of employees accommodated, the magnitude of the overtime the employer must pay, the impact of the policy on the employer's budget, and the work schedules of the employees who were not accommodated.[45]

Whether an employer has satisfied the duty to accommodate will frequently turn on what efforts the employer has attempted. In *Brener v. Diagnostic Center Hospital,*[46] the plaintiff, an Orthodox Jew, refused to work on

[36]651 F. Supp. 483, 41 FEP 282 (D.N.M. 1986).

[37]Wisner v. Truck Cent. Subsidiary of Saunders Leasing Sys., 784 F.2d 1571, 40 FEP 613 (11th Cir. 1986).

[38]*Compare* McDonald v. McDonnell Douglas Corp., 35 FEP 1661 (N.D. Okla. 1984) *and* EEOC v. Caribe Hilton Int'l, 597 F. Supp. 1007, 36 FEP 420 (D.P.R. 1984) *with* Philbrook v. Ansonia Bd. of Educ., 757 F.2d 476, 37 FEP 404 (2nd Cir. 1985), *aff'd and remanded,* 479 U.S. 60, 42 FEP 359 (1986).

[39]479 U.S. 60, 42 FEP 359 (1986).

[40]*Id.,* 42 FEP at 364.

[41]Johnson v. Angelica Uniform Group, 762 F.2d 671, 37 FEP 1409 (8th Cir. 1985).

[42]563 F. Supp. 255, 32 FEP 566 (N.D. Ill. 1983).

[43]Trans World Airlines v. Hardison, 432 U.S. 63, 14 FEP 1697 (1977).

[44]563 F. Supp. at 258, 32 FEP at 568.

[45]*Id.* at 259, 32 FEP at 569.

[46]671 F.2d 141, 28 FEP 907 (5th Cir. 1982).

Saturdays and religious holidays. The hospital at first directed shift changes for the plaintiff; but after complaints of preferential treatment, the hospital informed the plaintiff that any shift changes he could make would be approved but that the hospital could no longer direct shift changes, as this unfairly deviated from the normal practice. When the plaintiff did not appear for work on a religious holiday, after failing to arrange for a replacement, his employment was terminated. The court found that the hospital's efforts to accommodate the plaintiff were similar to, and in fact exceeded, those instituted by the employer in *Trans World Airlines v. Hardison*. [47] The court affirmed the district court's findings that the plaintiff failed to cooperate with the hospital's efforts to accommodate him within the established neutral scheduling system, and that accommodations proposed by the plaintiff would cause the hospital undue hardship.

Where an employer makes no attempt to accommodate, a violation is frequently found.[48]

While an employer may have a duty to accommodate by providing time off for religious observances, an employer is not necessarily obligated to provide the time off with pay.[49] An obligation to provide time off may be distinguished from an accommodation to religious activities at work: undue hardship to the employer was found when the employee read the Bible during working time; the employer could reasonably request her to cease this activity.[50]

The Fifth Circuit has affirmed a ruling that the efforts of an employer to help a plaintiff find another job were not an essential element of accommodation, particularly where the plaintiff was hired temporarily.[51]

### 3. Work-Scheduling Accommodations

As noted above, the Supreme Court has held in *Estate of Thornton v. Caldor, Inc.*[52] that a state may not require employers to provide Sabbath observers with an absolute and unqualified right not to work on their chosen Sabbath day.

Post-*Hardison* cases continue to focus on the objections or rights of other employees who object to deviations from a neutral scheduling system and/or the costs of accommodation.[53] Some courts, in denying summary

---

[47] *Supra* note 43.

[48] Wangsness v. Watertown School Dist. 14-4, Codington County, S.D., 541 F. Supp. 332, 29 FEP 375 (D.S.D. 1982) (plaintiff was refused leave of absence to attend week-long religious festival and then was discharged when he failed to report to work during that week; evidence showed board made no attempt to accommodate plaintiff's request on grounds that it would set precedent for other requests for leave).

[49] Pinsker v. Adams & Arapahoe Counties Joint Dist. 28J, 735 F.2d 388, 34 FEP 1570 (10th Cir. 1984) (policy did not cause plaintiff to risk job or prevent him from attending services since plaintiff free to take as many unpaid absences as needed). *See also* Reichman v. Bureau of Affirmative Action, 536 F. Supp. 1149, 30 FEP 1644 (M.D. Pa. 1982) (scheduling a meeting on Yom Kippur, a Jewish holiday, did not constitute religious discrimination where plaintiff was given paid day off).

[50] Gillard v. Sears, Roebuck & Co., 32 FEP 1274 (E.D. Pa. 1983) ("working hours" did not include lunch time or breaks).

[51] Turpen v. Missouri-Kansas-Texas R.R., 573 F. Supp. 820, 33 FEP 30 (N.D. Tex. 1983), *aff'd*, 736 F.2d 1022, 35 FEP 492 (5th Cir. 1984).

[52] 472 U.S. 703, 38 FEP 1 (1985). *See* text at *supra* note 3.

[53] Murphy v. Edge Memorial Hosp., 550 F. Supp. 1185, 30 FEP 1756 (M.D. Ala. 1982) (not required to alter neutral scheduling system by denying benefits of system to other employees nor to incur regular overtime expenditures); Brener v. Diagnostic Center Hosp., *supra* note 46.

judgment, have done so on the basis that the reasonableness of the attempted accommodation is a question of fact.[54]

In accommodating an employee who objects to working on Sundays it may not be enough simply to permit the employee to trade his Sunday shifts for the weekday shifts of other employees. Where religious scruples inhibit the employee from asking others to work on Sundays, an employer has been required to take reasonable steps to arrange the trades for the employee.[55]

The Eighth Circuit in *Mann v. Milgram Food Stores*[56] affirmed a finding of reasonable accommodation efforts when the employer transferred the plaintiff in order to accommodate his religious beliefs and give him maximum work hours. The employer's refusal to accept the plaintiff's suggestions for accommodation did not establish that the district court's findings were clearly erroneous.

In *Turpen v. Missouri-Kansas-Texas Railroad,*[57] the court considered one and one-half hours to be a reasonable amount of time to spend in considering the rescheduling of employees to accommodate the plaintiff. The court also found it unreasonable to force an employer to breach a collective bargaining agreement in order to pursue an involuntary switch of assignments with the plaintiff. The court held that the costs of requiring other employees to protect the plaintiff's assignment would have been more than *de minimis.*

### 4. Accommodation and Union Membership

Courts continue to require employers to accommodate an employee's religious objection to paying union dues notwithstanding a union security agreement.[58]

### 5. Accommodation and Personal Appearance

In *Bhatia v. Chevron U.S.A.,*[59] the Ninth Circuit permitted an employer to require the plaintiff to shave off facial hair in order to achieve a gas-tight face seal while wearing the respirator required by his employer. The plaintiff had refused to shave because he was a "devout Sikh and the Sikh religion proscribes the cutting or shaving of any body hair";[60] the plaintiff claimed that his employer did not pursue a reasonable accommodation for his religious beliefs. Affirming the lower court's decision, the Ninth Circuit held that the employer had made a reasonable accommodation by suspending rather than discharging the plaintiff, offering the plaintiff four different positions that did not require respirators, and promising to return the plaintiff to his old job if a respirator were developed that could be used safely with a beard. Furthermore, the court affirmed that retaining the plaintiff in his former position would cause undue hardship because the employer would

---

[54]McCormick v. Belvidere School Dist. No. 100, Bd. of Educ., 32 FEP 504 (N.D. Ill. 1983).
[55]Smith v. Pyro Mining Co., 827 F.2d 1081, 44 FEP 1152 (6th Cir. 1987).
[56]730 F.2d 1186, 34 FEP 735 (8th Cir. 1984).
[57]*Supra* note 51.
[58]McDaniel v. Essex Int'l, 696 F.2d 34, 30 FEP 831 (6th Cir. 1982).
[59]734 F.2d 1382, 34 FEP 1816 (9th Cir. 1984).
[60]*Id.* at 1383, 34 FEP at 1817.

either risk liability under the California OSHA standards or would have to revamp its system of duty assignments and impose on co-workers the plaintiff's share of potentially hazardous work.

## III. DISPARATE TREATMENT PROHIBITED

The District of Columbia Circuit has held that denial of promotion based on discriminatory evaluations motivated by religious animus constitutes illegal disparate treatment.[61] However, no disparate treatment was found in *Baz v. Walters*[62] where the plaintiff, a government hospital chaplain, was discharged because his evangelical approach interfered with his therapeutic duties at a Veterans Administration hospital.

No disparate treatment was found in *Fike v. United Methodist Children's Home*[63] where the plaintiff, a Methodist layman, was discharged and replaced by a Methodist minister in the position of director of the home. The plaintiff's discharge had been recommended by the Methodist Church, on the basis of dissatisfaction with the plaintiff's changes in the home's operation. The district court had found that the home was a secular institution not exempt from Title VII coverage under § 702, but had held that the home did not discriminate against Fike. The Eighth Circuit affirmed, holding that the minister was "not hired for the religious influence he might exert over the children or the Home's employees, but for the administrative advantage of his experience and contacts with the church. * * * [Therefore,] the difference * * * is not a religious difference,"[64] and therefore not sufficient to prove religious discrimination.

## IV. PERMISSIBLE RELIGIOUS DISCRIMINATION—SPECIAL EXEMPTIONS

### A. Educational and Religious Institutions Under § 702

In *Corporation of the Presiding Bishop of the Church of Jesus Christ of Latter-Day Saints v. Amos,*[65] the Supreme Court held that § 702's exemption applies to the secular, nonprofit activities of a religious organization. The Court held that such "benevolent neutrality" does not violate the Establishment Clause of the First Amendment under the Court's three-part analysis—reaffirmed in *Amos*—concluding that the statutory exemption (1) serves a secular purpose; (2) neither advances nor inhibits religion; and (3) does not entangle church and state.

In *Ohio Civil Rights Committee v. Dayton Christian Schools,*[66] the Su-

---

[61]Stoller v. Marsh, 682 F.2d 971, 29 FEP 85 (D.C. Cir. 1982), *cert. denied,* 460 U.S. 1037, 31 FEP 368 (1983) (after deciding part of plaintiff's claims not time-barred, court remanded case to district court for further determination).

[62]782 F.2d 701, 40 FEP 173 (7th Cir. 1986).

[63]709 F.2d 284, 32 FEP 60 (4th Cir. 1983).

[64]*Id.* at 286, 32 FEP at 62.

[65]483 U.S. 327, 44 FEP 20 (1987).

[66]477 U.S. 619, 41 FEP 78 (1986).

preme Court rejected the religious school's contention that Ohio state fair employment proceedings should be enjoined because the mere exercise of jurisdiction over it by the Ohio Civil Rights Commission violated its First Amendment rights. The religious school had argued that the Ohio Civil Rights Act[67] was unconstitutional because it did not provide an exemption parallel with § 702 of Title VII, allowing a limited scope for employment and hiring practices of religious institutions based on religious convictions. The Court majority declined to reach the constitutional issue, holding instead that the federal district court should have abstained from exercising its jurisdiction. The Court divided on the constitutional grounds for its ruling that abstention was proper. Five Justices, including Justices Powell and Burger, held that the district court should have abstained under *Younger v. Harris,*[68] because the pending Ohio administrative proceedings implicated important state interests and provided a full and fair opportunity for the federal plaintiff to litigate the constitutional claim. Four Justices based their concurrence in the Court's judgment on their view that it was then premature to base federal injunction proceedings on a risk that a state remedy could be unconstitutionally intrusive, where the school's liability had not yet been determined and the state agency had shown its willingness to tailor its remedies to accommodate religious freedoms.

In *Feldstein v. Christian Science Monitor,*[69] the court held the plaintiff's application for employment was lawfully rejected because he was not a Christian Scientist. The court declined to rule on the constitutionality of § 2000e-1 as it applies to all activities of religious organizations, secular and religious, finding the Monitor newspaper to be a religious activity of a religious organization.[70]

In an attempt to define that which constitutes a religious organization, the EEOC in Decision 83-6[71] analyzed *Fike v. United Methodist Children's Home of Virginia*[72] and *McClure v. Salvation Army*[73] and determined that the two controlling factors in such determinations are whether the organization had been created to serve a religious purpose and whether that purpose had remained unchanged. In Decision 83-6, the organization was held to have been established for the purpose of disseminating religious literature in order to interest the public in the Bible and the Christian faith. Since these purposes remained unchanged, the organization was therefore a religious association. The decision also extended the term "employment" in § 702 to include not only hiring, but also discharge based on religious beliefs. The EEOC stated:

> "In [enacting § 702,] Congress' intent was to allow such an organization to create and maintain a work force composed of individuals of compatible religious belief. That purpose would be frustrated if the religious organization was not permitted * * * to discharge individuals because their religious be-

---

[67]Ohio R.C. § 4112.01 *et seq.*
[68]401 U.S. 37 (1971).
[69]555 F. Supp. 974, 30 FEP 1842 (D. Mass. 1983).
[70]The court stated, however, that it had "grave doubts as to its ability to pass constitutional muster under the Establishment clause of the First Amendment." *Id.* at 978, 30 FEP at 1846.
[71]31 FEP 1858 (1983).
[72]547 F. Supp. 286, 31 FEP 594 (E.D. Va. 1982).
[73]323 F. Supp. 1100, 3 FEP 289 (N.D. Ga. 1971), *aff'd,* 460 F.2d 553, 4 FEP 490 (5th Cir.), *cert. denied,* 409 U.S. 896 (1972).

liefs were or became incompatible with those of the employing religious organization."[74]

Although § 702 protects a religious organization from charges of discrimination based on religion by its employees, the exemption does not exempt the organization from charges of employment discrimination on other grounds, such as sex bias in compensation.[75]

## B. Educational Institutions Under § 703(e)(2)

In *Pime v. Loyola University of Chicago,*[76] the university reserved three tenured positions for Jesuits and claimed that it was exempt under § 703(e)(2) as a university supported, controlled, or managed in whole or in substantial part by a religious society. The president of the university was a Jesuit, as were more than one-third of the trustees and several university officers and administrators. However, the Society of Jesus did not instruct the president or trustees with regard to university matters, and did not control the decisions of other Jesuits who served as university officers or administrators. Hence, the university was not exempt under § 703(e)(2).

## C. Religion as a Bona Fide Occupational Qualification

The Ninth Circuit held in *EEOC v. Fremont Christian School*[77] that the BFOQ exception in § 703(e) does not apply to discrimination in the provision of benefits because the BFOQ exception "does not apply to the full range of possibly discriminatory actions" and uses only the terms "hire and employ" while the broad prohibition against employment discrimination in § 703(a) additionally covers acts such as "discharge" and prohibits discrimination "against any individual with respect to his compensation, terms, conditions, or privileges of employment."[78] Thus, even though an employer contended that its policy of providing health insurance benefits only to a "head of household" was scripturally based, the BFOQ exception did not shield the school from Title VII liability.

In *Kern v. Dynalectron Corp.,*[79] the court held the BFOQ exception applicable where the plaintiff himself would be endangered because of his religion. The plaintiff was required to fly over a holy area which, under Saudi Arabian law, is prohibited to non-Moslems under penalty of death. When the plaintiff refused to convert to Islam, the defendant offered him a position not requiring his conversion. The plaintiff refused and claimed constructive discharge. The court distinguished this case from those involving claims of "customer preference," since converting to Islam was an "absolute prerequisite to doing this job,"[80] and accordingly held that the BFOQ exception was clearly applicable.

---

[74] 31 FEP at 1860.

[75] EEOC v. Fremont Christian School, 609 F. Supp. 344, 34 FEP 1038 (N.D. Cal. 1984), *aff'd,* 781 F.2d 1362, 39 FEP 1815 (9th Cir. 1986). *See supra* note 8 and *infra* note 77 and accompanying text.

[76] 585 F. Supp. 435, 34 FEP 1156 (N.D. Ill. 1984), *aff'd,* 803 F.2d 351, 42 FEP 1 (7th Cir. 1986).

[77] *Supra* note 75.

[78] *Id.,* 39 FEP at 1818.

[79] 577 F. Supp. 1196, 33 FEP 255 (N.D. Tex. 1983), *aff'd mem.,* 746 F.2d 810, 36 FEP 1716 (5th Cir. 1984).

[80] *Id.,* 577 F. Supp. at 1202, 33 FEP at 258.

In *Abrams v. Baylor College of Medicine,* [81] however, where two physicians were denied rotations in Saudi Arabia because they were Jewish, the court found that Jews were not excluded based on bona fide occupational qualification, but merely by Baylor's unilateral decision, and that this practice therefore violated Title VII.

Although rejecting the § 703(e)(2) argument in *Pime v. Loyola University,* [82] the court accepted the BFOQ argument under § 703(e)(1). Reviewing *Kern* and *Abrams,* the *Pime* court constructed a three-part test for the application of § 703(e)(1):

> "(1) hiring of an employee on the basis of religion, sex, or national origin; (2) religion, sex, or national origin is a *bona fide* occupational qualification; and (3) the occupational qualification being reasonably necessary to the normal operation of the employer's business or enterprise."[83]

In *Pime,* the philosophy department faculty had decided that Jesuits were required for the positions, since it was necessary for the future of both the department and Loyola that a "Jesuit presence" in the university be maintained and that the designated areas of teaching be done by competent Jesuit philosophers. The court held that this was, therefore, a bona fide occupational qualification.

[81]581 F. Supp. 1570, 34 FEP 229, *later proceeding,* 35 FEP 695 (S.D. Tex. 1984).
[82]*Supra* note 76 and accompanying text.
[83]*Supra* note 76, 585 F. Supp. at 442–43, 34 FEP at 1162.

## CHAPTER 8

# HANDICAP

## I. REHABILITATION ACT OF 1973, AS AMENDED

### B. Federal Contractors—§ 503

#### 1. Covered Contractors

The Eleventh Circuit has held that a newspaper which publishes various advertisements for the United States Air Force Reserve properly was found not to be a government contractor: each advertising purchase order was held to be a separate contract, and since no purchase order was in effect on the date of the plaintiff's discharge the OFCCP lacked jurisdiction over his complaint.[1]

#### 2. OFCCP Enforcement

*c. Individual Complaints and Compliance Reviews.* At least one Department of Labor Decision has held that there is no time limit within which the OFCCP must file an administrative complaint.[2]

#### 3. Private Right of Action

The Third and Tenth circuits have joined the majority opinion that there is no private right of action under § 503.[3]

In a similar analysis, the Eleventh Circuit held in *Howard v. Uniroyal*[4] that § 503 preempts a qualified handicapped individual's claim under state law as a third party beneficiary of the affirmative action clause contained in contracts between the employer and the federal government. The court reasoned that the remedy provided in detail by Congress in enacting § 503(b) was intended to be the plaintiff's sole means of enforcing the affirmative action clause contained in such contracts. The Ninth Circuit has also held that a plaintiff cannot circumvent this preemption rule by asserting his § 503 claim via § 1983,[5] because § 1983 is not applicable to a statutory violation

---

[1]Burnett v. Brock, 806 F.2d 265 (11th Cir. 1986).

[2]OFCCP v. Ozark Airlines, No. 80-OFCCP-24, 40 FEP 1859 (June 13, 1986). Although the OFCCP did not file an administrative complaint against the employer until 41 months after the employer denied employment to a handicapped individual, the Undersecretary decided that the proceedings were not time barred by the applicable state statute of limitations, since such statutes do not apply to federal antidiscrimination laws.

[3]Beam v. Sun Shipbuilding & Dry Dock Co., 679 F.2d 1077, 28 FEP 1725 (3d Cir. 1982); Hodges v. Atchison, Topeka & Santa Fe Ry., 728 F.2d 414, 34 FEP 457 (10th Cir.), *cert. denied,* 469 US 822, 35 FEP 1607 (1984).

[4]719 F.2d 1552, 33 FEP 453 (11th Cir. 1983); *see also* Chaplin v. Consolidated Edison Co. of New York, 579 F. Supp. 1470, 34 FEP 50 (S.D.N.Y. 1984) (third party beneficiary status may be inferred only when the parties intended to confer direct benefit on third party in contracting with each other; § 503 not intended to create private right for victims of discrimination).

[5]Meyerson v. Arizona, 709 F.2d 1235, 31 FEP 1183 (9th Cir. 1983), *vacated and remanded,* 465 U.S. 1095, 34 FEP 416 (1984), *on remand,* 740 F.2d 684, 35 FEP 127 (9th Cir. 1984).

"(1) where Congress has foreclosed private enforcement of that statute in the enactment itself, and (2) where the statute does not create 'enforceable rights.' "[6] The second exception applies to § 503 claims because Congress has foreclosed private enforcement of § 503 by providing, in 29 U.S.C. § 793(b), a comprehensive remedial scheme under the authority of the Department of Labor.[7]

The Seventh Circuit reached a similar result in *D'Amato v. Wisconsin Gas Co.,*[8] holding that handicapped individuals were not intended to be direct beneficiaries of government contracts containing the affirmative action provisions required by § 503, and therefore could not sue employers under a third-party beneficiary theory. Because the primary purpose of most covered contracts is unrelated to the affirmative action clauses they contain, the court reasoned that handicapped individuals were only incidental beneficiaries, and as such had no legally cognizable rights under the contracts.[9]

One California court has held that the language of § 503 does not create a "federal question" under 28 U.S.C. § 1331 for the purposes of removing state law causes of action to federal district court, since Congress has expressly declined to establish federal court jurisdiction over such claims.[10]

At least two courts have held that an employee has standing to seek to compel the Secretary of Labor to institute administrative enforcement proceedings against his employer for a § 503 violation.[11] The courts relied upon the employee's right to judicial review under the Administrative Procedure Act, 5 U.S.C. § 701(a).[12]

While courts continue to allow individuals to seek judicial review of both OFCCP actions and decisions regarding § 503 claims,[13] at least one court has held that the Department of Labor's decision not to prosecute a

---

[6]*Id.,* 709 F.2d at 1238, 31 FEP at 1185 (quoting Middlesex County Sewerage Auth. v. National Sea Clammers Ass'n, 453 U.S. 1, 19 (1981)).
[7]*Id.,* 709 F.2d at 1240, 31 FEP at 1187.
[8]760 F.2d 1474, 37 FEP 1092 (7th Cir. 1985).
[9]*Id.* at 1479, 37 FEP at 1095. The *D'Amato* court also cited favorably the Eleventh Circuit's opinion in *Howard v. Uniroyal, supra* note 4 (pervasive federal enforcement scheme preempts state law third party beneficiary claim) but noted that the *Howard* preemption analysis was distinct from its own.
[10]Johnson v. Smith dba Diversified Contract Servs., 630 F. Supp. 1, 40 FEP 1044 (N.D. Cal. 1986). In this case, the handicapped employee had brought suit in state court, alleging various state law causes of action. The employer removed the case to federal court, claiming that the state laws encompassed the broad federal policy in § 503 and thus created a basis for removal under 28 U.S.C. § 1331. In remanding the case to state court, the court held that the fact that Congress had expressly declined to create jurisdiction in any court for claims of § 503 violations was a conclusive indication that the employee's cause of action did not involve a "substantial" federal issue and therefore did not "arise under" federal law within the meaning of § 1331. *Id.* at 3–4, 40 FEP at 1047.
[11]Costner v. United States, 555 F. Supp. 146, 30 FEP 1301 (E.D. Mo. 1982), *rev'd,* 720 F.2d 539, 33 FEP 292 (8th Cir. 1983); Moon v. Donovan, 29 FEP 1780 (N.D. Ga. 1982), *aff'd,* 747 F.2d 599, 36 FEP 477 (11th Cir. 1984), *cert. denied,* 471 U.S. 1055, 37 FEP 848 (1985). In the latter case, the Secretary of Labor had determined that insufficient evidence existed to support the plaintiff's claim that he was terminated because of his handicap and consequently had closed his file. The plaintiff then sued his employer, but the court dismissed his case on the grounds that he had no private cause of action under § 503. *See also* Moon v. Roadway Express, 439 F. Supp. 1308, 16 FEP 20 (N.D. Ga. 1977), *aff'd sub nom.* Rogers v. Frito-Lay, 611 F.2d 1074, 24 FEP 16 (5th Cir.), *cert. denied,* 449 U.S. 889 (1980).
[12]The court in *Moon v. Donovan, supra* note 11, refused to issue a writ of mandamus under the Mandamus Act, 28 U.S.C. § 1361, recognizing that the Secretary's enforcement decisions are discretionary. In *Costner v. United States, supra* note 11, the district court found that the Secretary's decision not to commence enforcement proceedings on the basis of an administrative agency's regulation permitting the employer's action was not an abuse of discretion. For a further discussion of this case, *see* Section V.B, *infra.*
[13]Communications Workers v. Donovan, 37 FEP 1362 (S.D.N.Y. 1985).

handicap discrimination claim is within the Department's absolute discretion and thus unreviewable.[14]

## C. Recipients of Federal Financial Assistance—§ 504

### 1. Agency Enforcement

Section 505 requires exhaustion of administrative remedies before an action under that section may be filed.[15]

### 2. Private Enforcement

Recent cases have further defined what may constitute federal financial assistance. The Supreme Court[16] has adopted the approach of lower courts refusing to find "financial assistance" in a federal agency's mere certification[17] or licensing,[18] or in a state apprenticeship committee's "routing" of apprentices to federal contractors.[19] Likewise the availability of investment tax credits for airlines[20] or compensation to airlines for mail carriage[21] does not constitute federal financial assistance under § 504. However, the D.C. and Ninth circuits appear split as to whether or not an airline is a recipient of § 504 "federal financial assistance" by virtue of its use of services provided by airports receiving federal funding from the Airport and Airway Trust Fund.[22]

Recent cases from the Fifth Circuit hold that Medicare and Medicaid payments subject a hospital to the coverage of § 504.[23] Furthermore, a private

---

[14] Andrews v. Conrail, 40 FEP 492 (S.D. Ind. 1986). Interpreting the Administrative Procedure Act, 5 U.S.C. § 701 (a), the court followed *Heckler v. Chaney,* 470 U.S. 821, 53 USLW 4385 (1985) and found that the language of § 503 provides no meaningful standards or guidelines against which to judge the agency's exercise of discretion. Therefore, the court inferred a congressional intent to preclude judicial review. 40 FEP at 495. In so holding, the court expressly disfavored the Third Circuit's reasoning in *Moon v. Donovan,* 747 F.2d 599, 36 FEP 477 (11th Cir. 1984), *cert. denied,* 471 U.S. 1055, 37 FEP 848 (1985).

[15] Boyd v. United States Postal Serv., 752 F.2d 410, 36 FEP 1417 (9th Cir. 1985); Smith v. United States Postal Serv., 742 F.2d 257, 35 FEP 1304 (6th Cir. 1984); Johnson v. Orr, 747 F.2d 1352, 36 FEP 515 (10th Cir. 1984).

[16] Department of Transp. v. Paralyzed Veterans of Am., 477 U.S. 597, 54 USLW 4854 (1986) (no federal financial assistance under Rehabilitation Act in grants from airport trust funds or federally operated nationwide air traffic control system).

[17] Lemmo v. Willson, 583 F. Supp. 557, 34 FEP 1079 (D. Colo. 1984) (certification by Department of Labor for apprenticeship program not "financial assistance").

[18] California Ass'n of the Physically Handicapped v. Federal Communications Comm'n, 721 F.2d 667, 33 FEP 802 (9th Cir. 1983), *cert. denied,* 469 U.S. 832, 35 FEP 1608 (1984) (FCC broadcast licenses not federal financial assistance).

[19] Lemmo v. Willson, *supra* note 17.

[20] Paralyzed Veterans of Am. v. Civil Aeronautics Bd., 752 F.2d 694, 708–09, 53 USLW 2381 (D.C. Cir. 1985) (availability of investment tax credit under 26 U.S.C. § 46(a)(8) does not trigger coverage by § 504).

[21] Hingson v. Pacific Sw. Airlines, 743 F.2d 1408, 1414–15 (9th Cir. 1984) (government mail contracts constitute federal financial assistance only if they involve "subsidy" to the airline); Jacobson v. Delta Air Lines, 742 F.2d 1202, 1208–10 (9th Cir. 1984), *cert. dismissed,* 471 U.S. 1062 (1985) (discussion of when compensation for mail carriage constitutes "subsidy" and therefore is federal financial assistance for § 504 purposes).

[22] *Compare* Paralyzed Veterans of Am. v. Civil Aeronautics Bd., 752 F.2d 694, 712–15, 53 USLW 2381 (D.C. Cir. 1985) (Federal funding of airports and airway systems is federal financial assistance rendering § 504 applicable "to all air carriers using federally-funded airports in their 'program or activity' of providing commercial air transportation.") *with* Jacobson v. Delta Air Lines, 742 F.2d 1202, 1211–15 (9th Cir. 1984) (concluding that an airport's receipt of federal monies under Airport and Airway Trust Fund is insufficient to subject an airline to § 504 since airlines are taxed for these services).

[23] United States v. Baylor Univ. Medical Center, 736 F.2d 1039 (5th Cir. 1984), *cert. denied,* 469 U.S. 1189 (1985) (receipt of Medicare and Medicaid payments constitutes § 504 federal financial assistance);

contractor is also a recipient of federal financial assistance for § 504 purposes, if it provides services that are integral to the operation of a recipient hospital and directly contributes to claims for reimbursement under Medicare and Medicaid.[24]

The Seventh Circuit considered whether the non-earmarked federal grants were federal financial assistance in *Foss v. City of Chicago,* [25] and held that general revenue-sharing funds received by the City of Chicago, but not spent on the fire department, could not bring the fire department within the reach of § 504. However, the court based its ruling on the specific language and legislative history of the revenue sharing act, and suggested that in the case of other non-earmarked grants the use made of the grant by the local government may not be controlling.

The timing of the federal financial assistance may affect the plaintiff's standing to sue. Although federal financial assistance is not being provided at the time of the alleged discrimination, a plaintiff arguably still has standing if he proves he was subject to discrimination under the program for which those funds were received.[26] In this situation, the court may award the plaintiff affirmative injunctive relief and compensatory damages.[27] However, the Tenth Circuit has held that a finding of federal financial assistance during the period of employment was precluded because the employer had last received federal funding eight months before hiring the handicapped plaintiff. Furthermore, such receipt could not be inferred from the fact that the employer had used those federal funds to repay a loan during the plaintiff's employment.[28]

Though Congress has power to abrogate a state's immunity under the Eleventh Amendment when acting pursuant to Section 5 of the Fourteenth Amendment, such abrogation requires an unequivocal expression of congressional intent. Accordingly, the Supreme Court held in *Astascadero State Hospital v. Scanlon*[29] that the general authorization of § 504 of the Rehabilitation Act of 1973 for suit against a "recipient" of federal aid does not unequivocally abrogate states' immunity. In addition, the Court found that California did not consent to suit by its acceptance of funds since the Act does not manifest clear congressional intent to condition participation in Rehabilitation Act programs on a state's consent to waive immunity.

In *Consolidated Rail Corp. v. Darrone,* [30] the Supreme Court held that under § 504 an action can be maintained even where the primary purpose of the federal funding is not to promote employment. In *Darrone,* the Supreme Court specifically rejected the argument that Congress intended to enact the "primary objective" requirement of § 604 of the Civil Rights Act

---

Frazier v. Northwest Miss. Regional Medical Center Bd. of Trustees, 765 F.2d 1278, 38 FEP 783 (5th Cir. 1985).

[24]Frazier v. Northwest Miss. Regional Center Bd. of Trustees, *supra* note 23, 765 F.2d at 1289–91.

[25]817 F.2d 34, 43 FEP 1030 (7th Cir. 1987).

[26]Bachman v. American Soc'y of Clinical Pathologists, 577 F. Supp. 1257 (D.N.J. 1983) (federal grants earmarked for alcohol abuse seminars not related to program that allegedly discriminated against plaintiff).

[27]*Id.* at 1262.

[28]Niehaus v. Kansas Bar Ass'n, 793 F.2d 1159, 41 FEP 13 (10th Cir. 1986).

[29]473 U.S. 234, 38 FEP 97 (1985).

[30]465 U.S. 624, 34 FEP 79 (1984).

of 1964[31] when it added § 505(a)(2)[32] to the Rehabilitation Act in 1978.[33] The Court noted that the legislative history reveals that § 505(a)(2) was intended to codify regulations governing enforcement of § 504 that prohibited employment discrimination regardless of the purpose of federal financial assistance.[34] The Supreme Court further noted that the actual language of § 504 as well as the legislative history, executive interpretation, and the Rehabilitation Act's purpose—to promote and expand employment opportunities for the handicapped—are all consistent with the conclusion that § 504's bar on employment discrimination should not be limited to programs whose primary purpose is to promote employment.[35]

The Supreme Court in *Darrone* also stated that § 504 "limits the ban on discrimination to the specific program or activity receiving federal funds."[36] Thus, under *Darrone,* an employer receiving federal funds for certain programs or activities, but not for others, could not be held liable under § 504 unless the plaintiff could show that the program or activity with which he was involved received such funding.[37] The court did not resolve whether all of an employer's employees were covered by § 504 where the employer received generalized federal assistance not earmarked for any particular program.[38] Congress recently legislatively overruled *Darrone* and similar decisions by overriding President Reagan's veto of the Civil Rights Restoration Act of 1987. This extended nondiscrimination requirements to the entire institution receiving federal aid.

Standing to sue under § 504 is limited to persons who are proper proponents of the handicapped individual's rights.[39]

Administrative exhaustion is required under both § 504 and § 501.[40]

Following the Supreme Court's earlier conclusion that a private plaintiff under Title VI could recover back pay,[41] the Court in *Darrone* held that back

---

[31]§ 604 of Title VI, 42 U.S.C. § 2000d-3.

[32]The Rehabilitation, Comprehensive Services and Developmental Disabilities Amendments of 1978, Pub. L. No. 95-602, 92 Stat. 2955, *reprinted in* 1978 U.S. CODE CONG. & AD. NEWS 7312, § 505(a)(2), 29 U.S.C. § 795a(a)(2).

[33]Consolidated Rail Corp, v. Darrone, *supra* note 30, 34 FEP at 84.

[34]*Id.*

[35]*Id.,* 34 FEP at 83–84.

[36]*Id.,* 34 FEP at 84. *See, e.g.,* Lemmo v. Willson, 583 F. Supp. 557, 34 FEP 1079 (D. Colo. 1984) (funds to finance apprenticeship program do not give standing to plaintiff in apprenticeship program; fact that defendant received CETA funds for preapprentice program does not give plaintiff standing where he was employed as apprentice but did not participate in program receiving CETA assistance).

[37]Doyle v. University of Ala. in Birmingham, 680 F.2d 1323, 1326–27, 29 FEP 777, 779 (11th Cir. 1982).

[38]In *Darrone, supra* note 30, the Court did not consider whether the plaintiff below had sought and been denied employment in a program or activity receiving federal financial assistance because that question had not been considered by the court below. 34 FEP at 85. The Court noted that it had on two occasions considered the meaning of a "program or activity" as used in Title IX but that neither opinion provides particular guidance in cases like *Darrone* where there are nonearmarked direct grants. Grove City College v. Bell, 465 U.S. 555 (1984); North Haven Bd. of Educ. v. Bell, 456 U.S. 512, 535–40 28 FEP 1393 (1982). In *Grove City* the Court specifically declined to analogize grants of financial aid to students to non-earmarked direct grants and characterized such grants as "sui generis." 465 U.S. at 573.

[39]Hoyt v. St. Mary's Rehabilitation Center, 711 F.2d 864 (8th Cir. 1983) (plaintiff was not related to nor guardian of handicapped individual and did not claim handicapped individual's guardians were corrupt or incompetent; therefore, plaintiff lacked standing to pursue § 504 claim on behalf of handicapped individual).

[40]Smith v. United States Postal Serv., 766 F.2d 205, 37 FEP 1854 (6th Cir. 1985).

[41]Guardians Ass'n of New York City Police Dep't v. Civil Serv Comm'n, 463 U.S. 582, 32 FEP 250 (1983).

pay was available as a remedy for intentional discrimination under § 504.[42] While *Darrone* did not reach the question whether compensatory or punitive damages were available as a remedy under § 504, one court, relying upon cases under Title VI, has found that compensatory damages, but not punitive damages, may be assessed.[43]

## D. Definition of "Handicapped"

The Supreme Court has now held, in *Nassau County, Florida, School Board v. Arline,*[44] that the coverage of the Rehabilitation Act is not withdrawn where the disease which substantially limits one or more major life functions of an otherwise covered handicapped person is also contagious. The health and safety implications of employing a person with a contagious disease are properly analyzed by considering whether such a person is "otherwise qualified" for the job in question.[45]

An individual who raises a handicapped discrimination claim under the Rehabilitation Act of 1973 is required to establish the existence of an impairment that substantially limits a major life activity as an element of the prima facie case. The Act does not encompass characteristics that merely render an individual incapable of performing particular jobs,[46] or transitory illnesses that have no permanent effect on the person's health.[47] Although a district court in the District of Columbia has recognized transsexualism as a handicap,[48] the D.C. Circuit has held that sexual preference is not, and that an individual who was not hired because of homosexuality as opposed to his transvestism is not entitled to relief under the Rehabilitation Act.[49] Left handedness has been held not a handicap.[50] Likewise, acrophobia (fear of heights) was not a handicap where the plaintiff's stipulation that the "condition had never had any effect whatsoever on any of his activities"[51] supported the court's holding that the plaintiff had failed to allege a "substantial impairment of a major life function."[52]

A physician's diagnosis of an individual's health can be utilized in determining whether the individual is handicapped within the meaning of the Act.[53]

---

[42]Consolidated Rail Corp. v. Darrone, 465 U.S. 624, 34 FEP 79 (1984).

[43]Gelman v. Department of Educ., 544 F. Supp. 651, 29 FEP 926 (D. Colo. 1982). In *Guardians v. Civil Service Comm'n, supra* note 41, only four Supreme Court justices indicated that they would support monetary relief in a private action under Title VI in the absence of proof of intentional discrimination. See Consolidated Rail Corp. v. Darrone, *supra* note 42, 34 FEP at 82 n. 9.

[44]480 U.S. 273, 43 FEP 81 (1987).

[45]*Id.,* 43 FEP at 86–87.

[46]Jasany v. United States Postal Serv., 755 F.2d 1244, 37 FEP 210 (6th Cir. 1985).

[47]Stevens v. Stubbs, 576 F. Supp. 1409, 33 FEP 1249 (N.D. Ga. 1983) (plaintiff failed to prove he was qualified handicapped person and therefore was not entitled to protection). *But see* Arline v. Nassau County School Bd., 772 F.2d 759, 39 FEP 9 (11th Cir. 1985), *aff'd,* 480 U.S. 273, 43 FEP 81 (1987) (a chronic contagious disease such as tuberculosis is a handicap within the Act).

[48]Doe v. United States Postal Serv., 37 FEP 1867 (D.D.C. 1985).

[49] Blackwell v. Department of the Treasury, 639 F. Supp. 289, 41 FEP 1586 (D.D.C. 1986), *aff'd,* 830 F.2d 1183, 44 FEP 1856 (D.C. Cir. 1987).

[50]De la Torres v. United States Postal Serv., 781 F.2d 1134, 39 FEP 1795 (5th Cir. 1986) (plaintiff failed to show that being left-handed is impairment).

[51]Forrisi v. Department of Health & Human Servs., 794 F.2d 931, 41 FEP 190 (4th Cir. 1986).

[52]*Id.* at 934, 41 FEP at 191.

[53]Oesterling v. Walters, 760 F.2d 859, 37 FEP 865 (8th Cir. 1985) (condition of varicose veins does not constitute handicap where physicians described condition as mild to moderate and she could perform

The Sixth Circuit analyzed the definition of a handicapped individual by considering the hypothetical case of a person too short to play professional basketball.[54] The court argued that such a person fell without the definition of handicapped since the person was not "impaired," rejecting the approach that such a person would not be capable of performing the job (basketball competition) and hence would not be an "otherwise qualified handicapped individual."[55] The difference in the definitional approach may be significant: a finding of impairment shifts the burden of proof to the employer to prove the person was *not* qualified to perform the job with reasonable accommodation in spite of his or her "handicap."[56]

Although alcoholism is a handicapping condition under § 501 of the Rehabilitation Act,[57] an individual whose alcoholism affects his or her ability to perform a job safely is not a "qualified" handicapped person under the Rehabilitation Act of 1973: a qualified handicapped person is one who, with or without reasonable accommodation, can perform the essential functions of a position without endangering the health and safety of the individual or others.[58] Two courts addressing federal employment claims have held that where there is evidence that a leave of absence without pay or some other specific arrangement might be beneficial to the alcoholic employee, the federal employer must evaluate whether such a leave or alternative arrangement would impose an undue hardship on the federal employer.[59]

## II. VIETNAM ERA VETERANS' READJUSTMENT ASSISTANCE ACT—§ 402

In *Clementson v. Department of Labor,*[60] the District Court for the District of Hawaii granted summary judgment to the Department of Labor, dismissing an action brought by a disabled Vietnam-era veteran to review the Department of Labor's determination that the plaintiff's employer had not violated its affirmative action obligations under § 402 of the Vietnam Era Veterans' Readjustment Assistance Act of 1974, 38 U.S.C. § 2012. The

---

jobs that allowed her to sit and stand alternately throughout the day). *See infra* note 90 and accompanying text.

[54]Jasany v. United States Postal Serv., *supra* note 46.

[55]*Id.* at 1249–50, 37 FEP at 213.

[56]*Id.* at 1249–50 n.5, 37 FEP at 213–14 n.5.

[57]*See* Simpson v. Reynolds Metals Co., 629 F.2d 1226, 1231 n.8, 23 FEP 868 (7th Cir. 1980); Whitlock v. Department of Labor, 598 F. Supp. 126, 36 FEP 425 (D.D.C. 1984), *aff'd,* 790 F.2d 964 (D.C. Cir. 1986).

[58]As amended in 1978, § 706(7) of the Act generally defines the term "handicapped individual" and specifies that: "For purposes of sections 793 [§ 503] and 794 [§ 504] * * * as such sections relate to employment, such term does not include any individual who is an alcoholic or drug abuser whose current use of alcohol or drugs prevents such individual from performing the duties of the job in question or whose employment, by reason of such current alcohol or drug abuse, would constitute a direct threat to property or the safety of others. *See* 29 C.F.R. § 1613.702(4); Robinson v. Devine, 37 FEP 728 (D.D.C. 1985) (plaintiff's repeated instances of intoxication rendered him unqualified to safely and adequately perform job at time of his termination; agency fulfilled its reasonable accommodation obligation between receipt of notice of plaintiff's condition and point when plaintiff became unqualified for job). *See infra* notes 60 & 61 and accompanying text.

[59]Whitlock v. Department of Labor, *supra* note 57; Walker v. Weinberger, 600 F. Supp. 757, 36 FEP 1527 (D.D.C. 1985).

[60]608 F. Supp. 152, 121 LRRM 3118 (D. Hawaii 1985), *aff'd,* 806 F.2d 1402, 124 LRRM 2422 (9th Cir. 1986).

plaintiff had resigned his position and had then attempted to rescind his resignation. The employer did not allow him to rescind but permitted him to submit a new application. The job was later awarded to another Vietnam-era veteran. The facts also disclosed a poor working relationship between the plaintiff and his supervisor during his term of employment, despite his satisfactory rating, and the OFCCP did not find any evidence that this arose from discrimination based on the plaintiff's status as a disabled Vietnam-era veteran.

The court held that the action was reviewable under the Administrative Procedure Act but that there was no basis for overturning the agency's action in this case since the decision was based on the relevant factors and there was no clear error of judgment.

## III. Revenue Sharing

The State and Local Fiscal Assistance Act of 1976, 31 U.S.C. § 6701 *et seq.,* has been repealed.

## IV. State Law Protections

Virginia's nondiscrimination provisions now apply to all employers and also impose obligations analogous to those created by §§ 503 and 504 of the Federal Rehabilitation Act.[61] Other changes in state law are reflected in footnotes 62 through 67, which, respectively, substitute for footnotes 87, 88, 91, 93, 95, and 98 in Chapter 8 of the Second Edition.

## V. Governmental Employers

### A. Federal Government

A Department of Health and Human Service regulation which provided for special hiring of former mental patients without their taking civil service examinations violated § 501 to the extent it denied those patients certain benefits enjoyed by other civil service employees.[68]

Assuming, without deciding, that the Rehabilitation Act applies to the

---

[61]Va. Code § 51.01 *et seq.* (1980) (Supp. 1986).

[62]Only Delaware has no statutory or executive order prohibitions against discrimination on the basis of handicap.

[63]*E.g.,* Hawaii Rev. Stat. § 378-1 *et seq.* (1976); Kan. Stat. Ann. § 44-1001 *et seq.* (Supp. 1980). Other states have bypassed the state fair employment practices act and enacted a separate statute—*e.g.,* Idaho Code §56-701 *et seq.* (1976).

[64]*See supra* note 39 and accompanying text.

[65]Ariz. Exec. Order 77-11 (1977) was superseded by Ariz. Exec. Order 83-5 (1983), which repealed the requirements analogous to those imposed by §§ 503 and 504 of the Federal Rehabilitation Act.

[66]*E.g.,* Tex. Human Res. Code Ann. § 121.001 et seq. (Vernon 1980); Or. Rev. Stat. § 659.400 et seq. (1979); Tenn. Code Ann. §§ 8-50-103 and 104 (1979).

[67]*E.g.,* Kan. Stat. Ann. § 44-1002(j) (Supp. 1980) (" 'physical handicap' means the physical conditions of a person, whether congential or acquired by accident, injury, disease, which constitutes a substantial disability, but is unrelated to such person's ability to engage in a particular job or occupation").

[68]Allen v. Department of Health & Human Servs., 780 F.2d 64, 39 FEP 1108 (D.C. Cir. 1985).

Foreign Service, the District Court for the District of Columbia found that an officer's need for rehabilitation services available only in the United States demonstrated that he was not an "otherwise qualified" individual so that his discharge did not violate the Act.[69]

The Eleventh Amendment proscribes action by a handicapped person under § 504 against a state agency.[70] A government employee is not excused from misconduct or unsatisfactory performance that does not relate to his handicap even where the employer may have failed to reasonably accommodate that handicap. There must be some sufficient relationship between the loss of the employee's job and the violation of the duty due to the employee.[71]

Timeliness and procedural requirements of Title VII, rather than those of Title VI, apply to a job applicant's action under § 504, since it would be inconsistent to restrict most federal government employees to Title VII time limitations while permitting persons to whom § 504 applies to be governed by state statutes of limitation.[72]

## B. Disability as a Suspect or Quasi-Suspect Class

Under the rational relationship test, a Department of Transportation regulation prohibiting persons with a medical history or clinical diagnosis of epilepsy from driving in interstate or foreign commerce[73] has been upheld as applied to a driver who had not had a seizure in over 20 years.[74] However, a federal district court held that a plaintiff stated a claim for denial of equal protection where the Postal Service withdrew an offer of employment after it discovered her to be transsexual, because the Postal Service identified no rational relationship between the action and a legitimate government interest.[75]

## VI. PROOF AND DEFENSES

Generally, under § 504, plaintiffs must establish initially that they were employed by a recipient of federal financial assistance and that they were discriminated against in the context of a specific program or activity supported by such assistance.[76] Where a plaintiff was not denied employment in a program receiving federal financial assistance he or she cannot maintain a discrimination claim under the Act.[77]

With regard to the merits of a handicap claim under § 504, the basic elements that must be shown by the plaintiff are

"that (i) he [or she] is a 'handicapped person' under the Act, (ii) he [or she] is 'otherwise qualified' for the position, (iii) he [or she] is being excluded from

---

[69]Guerriero v. Schultz, 557 F. Supp. 511, 31 FEP 196 (D.D.C. 1983).
[70]Atascadero State Hosp. v. Scanlon, 473 U.S. 234, 38 FEP 97 (1985).
[71]Butler v. Department of the Navy, 595 F. Supp. 1063, 36 FEP 35 (D. Md. 1984).
[72]Cooper v. Federal Reserve Bank of Philadelphia, 36 FEP 989 (E.D. Pa. 1984).
[73]49 C.F.R. § 391.42(b)(8).
[74]Costner v. United States, 720 F.2d 539, 33 FEP 292 (8th Cir. 1983).
[75]Doe v. United States Postal Serv., 37 FEP 1867 (D.D.C. 1985).
[76]See Section I.C.2, supra.
[77]See supra notes 36–38 and accompanying text.

the position solely by reason of his [or her] handicap, and (iv) the position exists as part of a program or activity receiving federal financial assistance."[78]

In a variation on this proof, one district court required that the plaintiff show in his prima facie case that (1) he could perform essential functions of the position without endangering the health and safety of himself and others; (2) he met the experience and education requirements of the position; (3) he had a handicap preventing him from meeting the physical criteria for the position; (4) the challenged physical standards had a disproportionate impact on people with his particular handicap; and (5) there were plausible reasons to believe that the handicap could be accommodated or that the physical criteria were not job-related.[79]

The Eighth Circuit has held that the shifting burdens applicable to Title VII disparate treatment actions may, in some circumstances, also apply to cases brought under the Rehabilitation Act.[80] Where an employer conceded that the plaintiff was qualified for employment despite her visual handicap, but asserted that the applicant who was hired was better qualified, the Eighth Circuit applied the burdens of persuasion and production that apply in Title VII cases,[81] and held that the plaintiff had failed to rebut the employer's evidence of a legitimate, nondiscriminatory reason for rejecting her application. Judgment for the employer was affirmed.[82]

Courts are split as to whether a showing of disparate impact will suffice to prove a prima facie case under § 504.[83]

One court has held that where the only facts before the employer establish without contradiction that the plaintiff was not otherwise qualified, an employer does not have a duty to question the truthfulness of these facts before choosing to discharge the plaintiff.[84]

However, where the plaintiff proves that the employer has offered conflicting reasons for nonrestoration to duty, this evidences that these reasons were a pretext for discrimination.[85]

The Rehabilitation Act does not require employers to rewrite job descriptions materially in order to accommodate the handicap of an employee. The Act "does not demand that an employer settle for a worker who cannot effectively perform essential functions of the position."[86]

Similarly, the accommodation requirement refers to adjustments within the position for which the handicapped individual was employed, not that

---

[78]Bento v. I.T.O. Corp. of R.I., 599 F. Supp. 731, 36 FEP 1031, 1038 (D.R.I. 1984) (citing Doe v. New York Univ., 666 F.2d 761, 774–75 (2d Cir. 1981) and, as to factor (iv), relying on Consolidated Rail Corp. v. Darrone, 465 U.S. 624, 34 FEP 79 (1984)).

[79]Dexler v. United States Postal Serv., 40 FEP 633 (D. Conn. 1986).

[80]Norcross v. Sneed, 755 F.2d 113, 37 FEP 77 (8th Cir. 1985).

[81]*Id.* at 116, 37 FEP at 79.

[82]*Id.* at 118, 37 FEP at 80.

[83]*Compare* Jennings v. Alexander, 715 F.2d 1036 (6th Cir. 1983), *rev'd sub nom.* Alexander v. Choate, 469 U.S. 287, 53 USLW 4072 (1985) (proposed reductions in Medicaid coverage for inpatient hospital care from 20 days to 14 days had disparate impact on handicapped Medicaid recipients) (assuming that § 504 and its implementing regulations reach some claims of disparate impact, effect of Tennessee's reduction in annual inpatient hospital coverage is not among them) *with* Joyner v. Dumpson, 712 F.2d 770 (2d Cir. 1983) (district court erred in finding that plaintiff's adverse impact theory sufficed to state a prima facie violation of Rehabilitation Act).

[84]Walker v. Attorney Gen. of the United States, 572 F. Supp. 100, 32 FEP 1857 (D.D.C. 1983).

[85]Smith v. Administrator, Veterans Affairs, 32 FEP 986 (C.D. Cal. 1983).

[86]Bento v. I.T.O. Corp., *supra* note 78.

the hiring agency create a new position or that other workers perform the handicapped individual's duties.[87]

## A. Business Necessity and Job-Relatedness

### 1. Categorical Exclusion and Job-Relatedness

Persons with contagious diseases are within the coverage of § 504 of the Rehabilitation Act of 1973.[88] Thus, the Supreme Court held that the Eleventh Circuit erred in upholding a teacher's discharge because of her susceptibility to tuberculosis. Basing its decision on that part of the Act which protects those merely perceived to be handicapped,[89] the Supreme Court remanded the case for determination as to whether the teacher was "otherwise qualified" for her job. The decision thus forces individualized inquiry into the effects of impairments rather than allowing employment decisions based on generalized perceptions of an impairment's effects.

An employer was found to have justifiably relied upon the plaintiff's description of his handicap, as verified by a physician, in choosing to discharge him, regardless of subsequent medical evidence that he was not handicapped.[90]

Persons who are unable to perform the essential requirements of the job, even with a reasonable accommodation, have been found not to be "otherwise qualified."[91] A requirement that plaintiff prove that he is no longer handicapped to determine whether plaintiff is "otherwise qualified" violates § 504.[92]

Plaintiffs who have been rejected or discharged for alcoholism or drug addiction are generally not protected by the Act because § 706(7) provides that the term handicap does not include "any individual whose current use of alcohol or drugs prevents such individual from performing" his job duties.[93] This is particularly so where the individual's employment "would constitute a direct threat to the property or safety of others."[94] A district court has held that individuals rejected for firefighters' jobs as a result of drug

---

[87]Jasany v. United States Postal Serv., 33 FEP 1115 (N.D. Ohio 1983), aff'd, 755 F.2d 1244, 37 FEP 210 (6th Cir. 1985); accord Treadwell v. Alexander, 707 F.2d 473, 478, 32 FEP 62 (11th Cir. 1983).

[88]School Bd. of Nassau County v. Arline, 480 U.S. 273, 43 FEP 81 (1987).

[89]Id.

[90]Cook v. Department of Labor, 688 F.2d 669, 29 FEP 1558 (9th Cir. 1982), cert. denied, 464 U.S. 832, 32 FEP 1672 (1983) (the plaintiff, who had complained of chest pain and angina, conceded in this case that such a condition would disqualify him for the job). See supra note 53 and accompanying text.

[91]Schmidt v. Bell, 33 FEP 839 (E.D. Pa. 1983) (plaintiff's contention of being "otherwise qualified" rejected since plaintiff could not perform essential requirements of position, with or without reasonable accommodation); Jasany v. United States Postal Serv., 755 F.2d 1244, 37 FEP 210 (6th Cir. 1985) (employee hired specifically as distribution clerk-machine trainee, who is unable to work effectively at machine because of handicap, not "otherwise qualified"). See also supra Section I.D. and note 57.

[92]Cook v. United States, 36 FEP 1260 (D. Colo. 1983).

[93]29 U.S.C. § 706(7); see supra notes 57–59 and accompanying text.

[94]Id. See Robinson v. Devine, 37 FEP 728 (D.D.C. 1985). But see Huff v. Israel, 573 F. Supp. 107, 33 FEP 253 (M.D. Ga. 1983), vacated mem., 732 F.2d 943, 37 FEP 1816 (11th Cir. 1984). The plaintiff was discharged from his position as a public officer in a small city because of his third conviction for driving while under the influence. The city asserted that, because of the public nature of his office, the convictions reduced the plaintiff's effectiveness in his job. However, the plaintiff argued that he was discharged for being an alcoholic, even though his alcoholism had not interfered with his job performance. The lower court rejected the plaintiff's argument and held in favor of the city. The Eleventh Circuit, however, vacated the district court order without further comment.

screening for use of marijuana are not handicapped within the meaning of § 7 of the Rehabilitation Act, because there is no evidence that being a firefighter was a major life activity,[95] and one particular job for one particular employer cannot qualify as a major life activity.[96] Furthermore, even if the plaintiffs had established the existence of an impairment from the use of marijuana that substantially limited a major life activity, the court held that they would still not be covered by the Act, since marijuana can adversely affect the ability of firefighters to do their job.[97]

### 2. Risk of Future Injury or Incapacity

Courts have imposed a relatively heavy burden on the employer to show that the plaintiff's presence in the position in question posed a "reasonable probability of substantial harm."[98] In some cases, the issue of safety becomes interwoven with the duty to provide "reasonable accommodation" to the individual. In one such instance, a federal court found a special obligation where the employer was the recipient of funds under the Education of the Handicapped Act.[99] Risk of future injury may be used as a defense to a handicap action only where the risk is specifically related to the position for which the plaintiff is being considered.[100] In reversing a decision of the Department of Labor, the Ninth Circuit found that the disqualification of all "uncontrolled" diabetics for construction positions could not be justified by an alleged increased risk of future injury, because the risks associated with the job were not substantially different for diabetics in general.[101] In determining when under state statutes a qualified handicapped person could be excluded on the basis of a risk of future injury, courts continue to look at the likelihood of injury, the seriousness of the possible injury, and the imminence of the injury.[102]

In *Doe v. Region 13 Mental Health-Mental Retardation Commission,*[103] the Fifth Circuit affirmed the district court's judgment against the plaintiff notwithstanding the verdict, where the plaintiff had several psychiatric prob-

---

[95]McCleod v. City of Detroit, 39 FEP 225 (E.D. Mich. 1985).

[96]*See also* Jasany v. United States Postal Serv., *supra* note 91.

[97]McCleod v. City of Detroit, *supra* note 95.

[98]Mantolete v. United States Postal Serv., 767 F.2d 1416, 1422, 38 FEP 1081, 1086 (9th Cir. 1985). While Mantolete involved an action under § 501 of the Rehabilitation Act, the court found there to be no reason for a different definition of "qualified handicapped person" and thus, the same standard for the safety defense would appear to apply as well. 767 F.2d 1416, 1421, 38 FEP 1081, 1085.

[99]Fitzgerald v. Green Valley Area Educ. Agency, 589 F. Supp. 1130, 39 FEP 899 (S.D. Iowa 1984) (insistence on bus driver's license as requirement for school teacher may not be consistent with reasonable accommodation duty).

[100]*See* Doe v. New York Univ., 666 F.2d 761 (2d Cir. 1981) (upholding rejection of prospective medical student based on self-destructive behavior); Pushkin v. University of Colo. Regents, 658 F.2d 1372 (10th Cir. 1981) (psychological theories adduced against applicant for psychiatric residency with multiple sclerosis insufficient to show applicant not qualified).

[101]Bentivegna v. Department of Labor, 694 F.2d 619, 30 FEP 875 (9th Cir. 1982). Judge Anderson dissented on the grounds that sufficient evidence existed to support the determination of the Secretary of Labor that plaintiff's lack of control over his glucose level resulted in the potential for future injury and health complications. *Id.* at 623–25, 30 FEP at 879–80.

[102]*See* Maine Human Rights Comm'n v. Canadian Pac., Ltd., 458 A.2d 1225, 31 FEP 1028 (Me. Sup. Jud. Ct. 1983) (employer must show it had factual basis to believe, to reasonable probability, that employee's physical handicap would cause future deterioration of employee's health or endanger health and safety of others within forseeable future); Bey v. Bolger, 540 F. Supp. 910, 32 FEP 1652 (E.D. Pa. 1982) (risk of stroke and heart attack associated with uncontrolled hypertension and cardiovascular disease sufficient basis to deny reemployment to former Postal Service clerk because he could not perform "essential functions" of job without endangering his health and safety).

[103]704 F.2d 1402, 31 FEP 1332 (5th Cir. 1983).

lems and was a mental health associate with the Child Youth Service program. The court stated:

> "We believe that in cases of this sort where, as here, there has been no showing of discriminatory animus, and where there is uncontroverted evidence of a chronic deteriorating situation which is reasonably interpreted to pose a threat to the patients with whom the employee must work, no violation of Section 504 could reasonably be found."[104]

The court held that, although the plaintiff's work record was outstanding, the overwhelming evidence of her psychiatric condition made her no longer "otherwise qualified."

### 3. Fringe Benefits

In the few cases where the issue has arisen, federal and state courts have rejected employers' defenses based on increased health or life insurance costs[105] or the greater risk of potentially troublesome health problems.[106]

### B. Reasonable Accommodation and Undue Hardship

Courts continue to decide whether there has been reasonable accommodation pursuant to the obligations of the Rehabilitation Act on a case-by-case basis.[107] The Eleventh Circuit has held that a "duty to the public" does not excuse an employer from its duty to reasonably accommodate a handicapped employee.[108] Two courts have recently found that reasonable accommodation does not require an employer to place a handicapped worker in a new or different position.[109] One court has held that in order for a handicapped employee to prevail there must be a reasonable "causation" between the employer's failure to accommodate and the employee's termination.[110]

---

[104]*Id.* at 1412, 31 FEP at 1340.

[105]*See, e.g.,* State Div. of Human Rights v. Xerox Corp., 65 N.Y.2d 213, 218, 491 N.Y.S.2d 106, 480 N.E.2d 695, 37 FEP 1389, 1391 (Ct. App. 1985) (dicta); Sterling Transit Co. v. Fair Employment Practice Comm'n, Cal., 121 Cal.App.3d 791, 28 FEP 1351 (1981) (court, applying state law, directly rejected a defense of adverse financial impact based on potentially high medical, disability, and related costs.)

[106]*See supra* notes 98–104 and accompanying text.

[107]Trimble v. United States Postal Serv., 633 F. Supp. 367, 40 FEP 1101 (E.D. Pa. 1986) (company found liable since it had failed to demonstrate that certain duties of injured employee could not be performed without accommodation, e.g., assistance of equipment). *But cf.* Baker v. Department of Environmental Conservation, N.Y., 634 F. Supp. 1460, 1466 (N.D.N.Y. 1986) (granting special permission for use of motorized vehicles by handicapped plaintiffs in areas designated as wilderness not required under concept of "reasonable accommodation" since use of such vehicles would be "inimical to the [pristine] nature of these areas."

[108]Arline v. Nassau County, Florida, School Bd., 772 F.2d 759, 39 FEP 9 (11th Cir. 1985), *aff'd,* 480 U.S. 273, 43 FEP 81 (1987). Arline was a teacher fired because she was susceptible to tuberculosis. Her termination was upheld by the district court since the school board "was exempt from any duty whatever to weigh the actual costs and risks involved in accommodating Arline because of an overriding 'duty to the public it serves.' " *Id.,* 772 F.2d at 765, 39 FEP at 14. The Eleventh Circuit reversed this finding, concluding that "Section 504 * * * establishes that * * * a [public] duty cannot be used to shield an entity." The issue of accommodation was not reached by the Supreme Court.

[109]Dexler v. United States Postal Serv., 40 FEP 633 (D. Conn. 1986) (reasonable accommodation does not require the employer to "consider handicapped applicants for jobs for which they have not applied, assuming that the employer does not do so for applicants who are not handicapped"); Carty v. United States Postal Serv., 623 F. Supp. 1181, 39 FEP 1217, 1222 (D. Md. 1985) (Reasonable accommodation "does not include a requirement to reassign or transfer an employee to another position. Preferential reassignment for handicapped employees was not intended by the Rehabilitation Act.").

[110]Richardson v. United States Postal Serv., 613 F. Supp. 1213, 40 FEP 703 (D.D.C. 1985). Mr. Richardson, a Postal employee, was terminated because of an off-duty criminal conviction. Mr. Richardson claimed that his conviction resulted from his alcoholism, which, he alleged, his employer had an obligation to accommodate. The court found: "The nexus between the crime and the alcohol is, of course,

Controversy continues over the "line between a lawful refusal to extend affirmative action and illegal discrimination against handicapped persons."[111] Under § 504, the government grantee must provide meaningful access to the federally funded benefit which that grantee offers; to insure meaningful access, reasonable accommodations in the grantee's program or benefit may have to be made. The benefit itself cannot be defined in a way that effectively denies otherwise qualified handicapped individuals the meaningful access to which they are entitled.[112]

Undue hardship may be shown where the accommodation would require the defendant employer to assign other employees to perform many of the plaintiff's duties.[113]

Where an employer had information showing that a job applicant was able to perform a job despite his handicap, the Eleventh Circuit held that it failed to reasonably accommodate the applicant by rejecting him solely on the basis of a written general aptitude test score.[114]

A collective bargaining agreement which prohibits an employer from taking certain steps of accommodation has been held to constitute a legitimate business reason making such accommodation impracticable.[115]

The Third Circuit has declared that a handicapped person will not be "otherwise qualified" for employment if accommodating that person's limitation would be an undue hardship:

> "A handicapped individual who cannot meet all of a program's requirements is not otherwise qualified if there is a factual basis in the record reasonably demonstrating that accommodating that individual would require either a modification of the essential nature of the program, or impose an undue burden on the recipient of federal funds."[116]

Finding no basis in this standard for finding the accommodation unreasonable, the Third Circuit vacated the decision of the district court, which had held that the plaintiff's need to wear a hearing aid prevented him from driving a bus. The plaintiff had rebutted each supposed danger—mechanical failure, inability to localize sound, and the like—with a practical solution. Therefore, the lower court should have found that such accommodations were reasonable.[117]

---

highly conjectural. But even if events of 1978 and earlier were to be examined to untangle the reasons underlying Richardson's mental difficulties and alcohol use and Richardson's alcoholism was shown to be a substantial cause of his criminal conduct, it would not benefit Richardson here. Richardson was discharged for his criminal conduct, not because of alcoholism or poor job performance due to alcohol. He does not claim otherwise. The Rehabilitation Act only protects against removal solely because of alcohol abuse."*Id.* at 1215, 40 FEP at 704.

[111]Southeastern Community College v. Davis, 442 U.S. 397 (1979).

[112]Alexander v. Choate, 469 U.S. 287, 53 USLW 4072 (1985).

[113]Treadwell v. Alexander, 707 F.2d 473, 32 FEP 62 (11th Cir. 1983) (necessity of Army Corps of Engineers to require other park technicians to perform many of plaintiff's duties, in light of agency's limited resources and fact that only two to four other workers were available to patrol the 150,000 acres at Clark's Hill Lake, constituted undue hardship).

[114]Stutts v. Freeman, 694 F.2d 666, 30 FEP 1121 (11th Cir. 1983). Handicap cases turning upon reasonable accommodation are decided on a case-by-case basis. *See, e.g.,* Vickers v. Veterans Admin., 549 F. Supp. 85, 29 FEP 1197 (W.D. Wash. 1982) (employer sufficiently accommodated employee with hypersensitivity to smoke by offering transfer or desk partition to plaintiff, separating desks of smokers and nonsmokers, and seeking improvements in ventilation and exhaust systems).

[115]Daubert v. United States Postal Serv., 31 FEP 459 (D. Colo. 1982), *aff'd,* 733 F.2d 1367, 34 FEP 1260 (10th Cir. 1984) (discharge upheld on finding that accommodation was impossible based on union contract which effectively prohibited assignment of light duty job to plaintiff).

[116]Strathie v. Department of Transp., 716 F.2d 227, 32 FEP 1561 (3d Cir. 1983).

[117]*Id.*

One district court has weighed the social cost of refusing an accommodation against the economic cost of the accommodation to the employer, in finding that providing readers to blind income maintenance workers was a reasonable state accommodation.[118] These employees were first-level welfare agency workers, responsible for receiving and recording information from welfare applicants and determining eligibility for benefits. Their duties involved extensive paperwork with standardized forms. The court explained:

> "When one considers the social costs which would flow from the exclusion of persons such as plaintiffs from the pursuit of their profession, the modest cost of accommodation—a cost which seems likely to diminish, as technology advances and proliferates—seems, by comparison, quite small."[119]

The court in *Curry v. United States Postal Service*[120] held that defendant's failure to make reasonable accommodations for her arthritic condition constituted a continuing violation which excused her from filing for each violation.

Hiring a full-time physician to provide on-site blood testing facilities to accommodate a manic depressive in an underdeveloped area with poor communication, transportation, and medical facilities was an undue hardship, not a reasonable accommodation.[121]

---

[118]Nelson v. Thornburgh, 567 F. Supp. 369, 32 FEP 1640 (E.D. Pa. 1983), *aff'd mem.*, 732 F.2d 146, 34 FEP 835 (3d Cir. 1984), *cert. denied,* 469 U.S. 1188, 36 FEP 1264 (1985). The court relied on the regulations that specify the following factors to assess the reasonableness of an accommodation:

"(1) The overall size of recipient's program with respect to number of employees, number and type of facilities, and size of budget;

"(2) The type of the recipient's operation, including the composition and structure of the recipient's work force; and

"(3) The nature and cost of the accommodation needed." 45 C.F.R. § 81-12(c)(1–3) (1982).

[119]*Id.,* 567 F. Supp. at 382, 32 FEP at 1650.

[120]583 F. Supp. 334, 36 FEP 1312 (S.D. Ohio 1984).

[121]Gardner v. Morris, 752 F.2d 1271, 36 FEP 1272 (8th Cir. 1985).

## CHAPTER 9

# RACE AND COLOR

## I. COLOR AND OTHER RACE-LINKED CHARACTERISTICS

Employers' no-beard policies continue to be a subject of disparate impact analysis by the courts and the EEOC.[1]

## II. CULTURAL IDENTIFICATION AND GROOMING

The termination of a black employee who failed to list two city ordinance violations in response to an inquiry regarding traffic, misdemeanor, or felony offenses was held to be discriminatory because the employer concluded that the omission was indicative of "typical" black dishonesty.[2] The failure of a supervisor to recommend blacks for promotion based upon his belief that black employees were not interested in being promoted to other jobs also violated Title VII.[3]

## III. DISCRIMINATION EVIDENCED BY DEPRECATORY EMPLOYMENT ATMOSPHERE

While courts continue to find that an employer violates Title VII by tolerating racially offensive or derogatory language in the workplace,[4] no

---

[1]Haynes v. E.I. du Pont de Nemours & Co., 33 FEP 496 (S.D. Tex. 1983) (prima facie case not established by discharged black employee claiming need to grow beard because of pseudofolliculitis when he presented no evidence of the impact of the rule on other employees, did not advise his employer of his condition, and the employer pleaded with him to comply so he could keep his job); EEOC Dec. 83-17, 33 FEP 1884 (1983) (disparate impact found in security guard case when, in spite of the fact that 50% of the employer's security guards were black, employer could not show its no-beard policy was necessary for attracting or retaining customers or for hygiene purposes); EEOC v. Trailways, 530 F. Supp. 54, 27 FEP 801 (D. Colo. 1981) (policy violated Title VII because it effectively excluded 25% of black male work force from employment because of a racial trait—high susceptibility of blacks to skin disorder known as pseudofolliculitis barbae).

[2]EEOC v. Riss Int'l Corp., 525 F. Supp. 1094, 35 FEP 416 (W.D. Mo. 1981).

[3]Lams v. General Waterworks Corp., 766 F.2d 386, 38 FEP 516 (8th Cir. 1985) (employer relied heavily on supervisor's subjective evaluation of candidates for promotion).

[4]Snell v. Suffolk County, N.Y., 782 F.2d 1094, 39 FEP 1590 (2d Cir. 1986) (employer responsible for working environment so heavily polluted with discrimination that it destroyed emotional and psychological stability of minority group workers); Hamilton v. Rodgers, 791 F.2d 439, 40 FEP 1814 (5th Cir. 1986) (under Title VII, city responsible for conduct of supervisors who ignored racist antics of co-workers and intentionally discriminated against plaintiff, although city not liable under § 1983 since offensive conditions not so widespread that they could be deemed official policy); Hunter v. Allis-Chalmers Corp., Engine Div., 797 F.2d 1417, 41 FEP 721 (7th Cir. 1986) (employer liable for not dealing more effectively with what management level employees knew to be vicious campaign of racial harassment against black employee by co-workers); Erebia v. Chrysler Plastic Prods. Corp., 772 F.2d 1250, 37 FEP 1820 (6th Cir. 1985), *cert. denied,* 475 U.S. 1015, 40 FEP 192 (1986) (employer maintained hostile work environment by refusing to act on complaints by Hispanic supervisor that he was subjected to racial epithets from hourly employees whom he supervised); Walker v. Ford Motor Co., 684 F.2d 1355, 29 FEP 1259 (11th

violations were found where there existed extenuating circumstances such as an absence of hostility or racial animus and the rowdy nature of the work force,[5] where the challenged conduct was isolated and steps taken by the employer to prevent racial harassment,[6] where the conduct had only a slight effect on the complaining employees,[7] where the allegedly hostile statement was not made in furtherance of the employer's policies or tolerated by the employer,[8] where the challenged conduct occurred in and was condoned by a supervisor in a different plant and who played no role in the plaintiff's termination,[9] or where the plaintiff and supervisors complained of were of the same race.[10]

A growing body of cases shows judicial application of the principle that sporadic racial slurs in the workplace are not sufficient to establish a violation of Title VII,[11] but that the existence of a hostile racial environment may be established by evidence of the continuous use of racial epithets or the

---

Cir. 1982) (employer tolerated pervasive use of racial slurs at automobile dealership and when plaintiff objected, employer advised him that racial slurs were "just something a black man would have to deal with in the South"); Oden v. Southern Ry., 35 FEP 913 (N.D. Ga. 1984) (employer discriminated against black plaintiff by condoning and encouraging racially hostile environment); Moffett v. Gene B. Glick Co., 621 F. Supp. 244, 41 FEP 671 (N.D. Ind. 1985) (plaintiff subjected to continuous pattern of harassment by co-employees over several months).

[5]Vaughn v. Pool Co. of Tex., Pool Offshore Co. Div., 683 F.2d 922, 29 FEP 1017 (5th Cir. 1982) (no violation where black oil rig workers were subject to raw pranks, crude jokes, and verbal abuse, some of which had racial overtones, since racial slurs were bantered about without hostility or racial animus and all employees suffered the same unpleasantness which is a part of life on an offshore oil rig).

[6]Gilbert v. City of Little Rock, 722 F.2d 1390, 33 FEP 557 (8th Cir. 1983), aff'g 544 F. Supp. 1231, 29 FEP 969 (E.D. Ark. 1982), cert. denied, 466 U.S. 972, 34 FEP 1312 (1984) (allegations of racial harassment in city police department involved isolated events, reprimands were issued to those involved in racial incidents, and prompt action was taken to correct the situation by officers in charge).

[7]Hill v. K-Mart Corp., 699 F.2d 776, 31 FEP 269 (5th Cir. 1983) (black assistant store manager failed to show that racial slurs by two of her subordinates had any significant discriminatory impact on her authority or resulted in any loss of respect or dignity); Gilchrist v. Bolger, 35 FEP 75 (S.D. Ga. 1983), aff'd, 733 F.2d 1551, 35 FEP 81 (11th Cir. 1984) (use of the word "nigger" by two supervisors was not used in any slur, epithet, or insult directed at plaintiff, and was therefore only considered a judgment error by court).

[8]Amro v. St. Luke's Hosp. of Bethlehem, Pa., 39 FEP 1574 (E.D. Pa. 1986) (racial statement by staff physician could not be attributed to hospital in Title VII complaint by surgical resident alleging national origin discrimination in denial of staff privileges).

[9]Tate v. Dravo Corp., 623 F. Supp. 1090, 39 FEP 1544 (W.D.N.C. 1985) (no connection between evidence of racial slurs and plaintiff's discharge).

[10]Moore v. Inmont Corp., 608 F. Supp. 919, 39 FEP 1382 (W.D.N.C. 1985) (evidence failed to establish disparate treatment in enforcement of plant rules or that plaintiff's supervisors, who were black as was plaintiff, had harassed plaintiff).

[11]Briggs v. Anderson, 787 F.2d 1262, 40 FEP 883 (8th Cir. 1986) (a few instances of racial slurs do not constitute evidence of racially discriminatory atmosphere of which employer was aware); Gairola v. Virginia Dep't of Gen. Servs., 753 F.2d 1281, 36 FEP 1800 (4th Cir. 1985) (mocking of Hindu employee's attire by co-workers not sufficient to prove discriminatory discharge); Nichelson v. Quaker Oats Co., 752 F.2d 1153, 36 FEP 1534 (6th Cir.), vacated, 472 U.S. 1004, 37 FEP 1728 (1985) (isolated racial slur several years earlier not sufficient to establish discrimination in disciplinary action); Torres v. County of Oakland, 758 F.2d 147, 37 FEP 535 (6th Cir. 1985) (continuing use of racial slurs is required for a violation of Title VII); Barber v. Boilermakers Dist. Lodge 57, 778 F.2d 750, 39 FEP 1092 (11th Cir. 1985) (mere utterance of racial slur is not sufficient to carry plaintiff's ultimate burden of proof); Tolliver v. Yeargan, 728 F.2d 1076, 39 FEP 1179 (8th Cir. 1984) (plaintiff not victim of racial harassment; hostility was directed toward him because he was an "outsider" who would be resented regardless of race); Minority Police Officers Ass'n of South Bend v. City of South Bend, Ind., 617 F. Supp. 1330, 42 FEP 503 (N.D. Ind. 1985), aff'd, 801 F.2d 964, 42 FEP 525 (7th Cir. 1986) (isolated incidents of harassment by unknown persons insufficient to support an award against employer); Pierson v. Norcliff Thayer, Inc., 605 F. Supp. 273, 42 FEP 528 (E.D. Mo. 1985) (four specific instances of racially derogatory language not sufficient to establish Title VII violation); Tate v. Dravo, supra note 9 (racial slurs are not direct evidence that supervisors involved in black employee's termination intentionally discriminated against him); Easley v. Northern Shipping Co., 597 F. Supp. 954, 37 FEP 1055 (E.D. Pa. 1984) (evidence failed to show that remarks were motivated by racial discrimination or were in fact racially insulting); Ellison v. C.P.C. Int'l, Best Foods Div., 598 F. Supp. 159, 36 FEP 643 (E.D. Ark. 1984) (evidence of isolated racial slurs not sufficient to establish a violation of Title VII).

telling of racial jokes at upper levels of management, coupled with insufficient remedial action by the employer.[12]

Evidence of a single egregious racial slur is sufficient to present a triable issue of fact, thus defeating an employer's motion for summary judgment.[13] It is error for the trial court not to admit evidence of racial slurs, made under circumstances giving them relevance, in deciding issues of discharge and promotion.[14]

In two cases involving employees of police departments, the Fifth and Eighth circuits applied the "clearly erroneous" standard of review and affirmed trial court factual determinations that racially discriminatory comments and conduct did not rise to the level necessary to constitute a violation under Title VII.[15] Repeated subjection of an employee to discrete instances of disparate treatment by supervisors increases the likelihood that a finding of discriminatory treatment will be made based upon a racially hostile atmosphere created by the employer.[16] However, racial slurs by co-workers or derogatory remarks by supervisors may not be sufficient to establish disparate treatment in promotion or termination.[17]

---

[12]Hunter v. Allis-Chalmers Corp., Engine Div., *supra* note 4 (employer liable for not dealing more effectively with what management level employees knew to be vicious campaign of racial harassment against black employee by co-workers); Snell v. Suffolk County, N.Y., *supra* note 4 (county and sheriff's department had duty to take forceful action once it became aware that there was a racially discriminatory environment and an atmosphere of racial harassment—posting a notice was insufficient); Butler v. Coral Volkswagen, 629 F. Supp. 1034, 41 FEP 432 (S.D. Fla. 1986) (employer's tolerance of and participation in racial jokes and racial epithets sufficient to establish hostile environment, in view of employer's refusal to take sufficient remedial action).

[13]Bailey v. Binyon, 583 F. Supp. 923, 36 FEP 1236 (N.D. Ill. 1984); *cf.* Wilson v. City of Aliceville, 779 F.2d 631, 39 FEP 1290 (11th Cir. 1986) (it was error not to admit a witness' signed statement about a racial slur as direct evidence of discrimination in hiring).

[14]Leonard v. City of Frankfort Elec. & Water Plant Bd., 752 F.2d 189, 36 FEP 1181 (6th Cir. 1985) (it was error not to admit evidence of racial slurs in determining whether plaintiff's insubordination which led to his discharge was provoked); Bibbs v. Department of Agriculture, 778 F.2d 1318, 39 FEP 970 (8th Cir. 1985) (case remanded for entry of judgment in favor of plaintiff on denial of promotion by committee dominated by manager who called plaintiff a "black militant" and uttered racial slurs about another black employee); Miles v. M.N.C. Corp., 750 F.2d 867, 36 FEP 1289 (11th Cir. 1985) (error not to admit evidence of racial slurs to prove disparate treatment of blacks in employer's evaluation process).

[15]Gilbert v. City of Little Rock, *supra* note 6; Everitt v. City of Marshall, 703 F.2d 207, 31 FEP 985 (5th Cir.), *cert. denied,* 464 U.S. 894, 32 FEP 1768 (1983) (in spite of "persuasive evidence" racially prejudiced colleagues had trapped black female employee into committing a dereliction of duty, plaintiff failed to establish pretextual reason for her discharge); *cf.* United States v. New York, 593 F. Supp. 1216, 35 FEP 1535 (N.D.N.Y. 1984) (no violation of final decree mandating hiring goals for minorities in telling of racial jokes, including ethnic jokes other than those relating to blacks and hispanics, to break classroom monotony).

[16]Snell v. Suffolk County, N.Y., 782 F.2d 1094, 39 FEP 1590 (2d Cir. 1986); Carter v. Duncan-Huggins, Ltd., 727 F.2d 1225, 34 FEP 25 (D.C. Cir. 1984) (jury verdict for $10,000 compensatory damages in § 1981 suit upheld; particular attention was given to fact that employer's president had found humor in a racist joke and no reprimand was given to narrator); Shipes v. Trinity Indus., 40 FEP 1136 (E.D. Tex. 1985) (employer's promotion policies were discriminatory because blacks were not notified of openings and supervisors making promotional decisions made racist remarks); Coley v. Potters Indus., 35 FEP 1015 (D.N.J. 1984) (menial tasks required of discharged black secretary that were not required of former white secretaries created fact issue as to whether plaintiff was discharged because of her race); Pinkney v. Weinberger, 31 FEP 1278 (D.D.C. 1983) (discriminatory atmosphere endured almost daily by plaintiff had demeaning and demoralizing effect and constituted blatant racism).

[17]Hervey v. City of Little Rock, 787 F.2d 1223, 40 FEP 928 (8th Cir. 1986), *aff'g* 101 F.R.D. 45, 40 FEP 784 (E.D. Ark. 1984) (comments attributed to supervisor were not racial and were probably not harassing); Aikens v. Bolger, 33 FEP 1697 (D.D.C. 1984) (postmaster's derogatory remarks, not directed at black plaintiff or related to selection of an employee for a position, did not warrant a finding that promotion was denied because of race); Adams v. United Airlines, 578 F. Supp. 26, 35 FEP 618 (N.D. Ill. 1983) (racially demeaning comments by supervisors not involved in plaintiff's termination are not evidence of employer's discriminatory motive); Gillard v. Sears, Roebuck & Co., 32 FEP 1274 (E.D. Pa. 1983) (though co-workers may have directed racial and religious slurs against and toward employee, she did not prove that her discharge was motivated by race or religious beliefs).

A union which fails to file grievances on behalf of employees complaining of racial discrimination or intentionally avoids asserting discrimination claims on their behalf contributes to the establishment of a racially hostile work environment.[18]

## IV. DISCRIMINATION BECAUSE OF RACIAL ATTITUDES OR ASSOCIATION WITH BLACKS OR BLACK ORGANIZATIONS

Courts have afforded protection to both black and white employees who protest reverse discriminatory action against a white employee.[19]

At least one court has held, however, that a white employee may not bring suit under 42 U.S.C. § 1981 for alleged retaliation because of her support for minority group members.[20]

The First Amendment rights of free speech were held to provide protection from employer discipline for police officers whose conduct in protesting perceived racial discrimination in employment may have violated a city ordinance.[21]

In other contexts, courts have held that a white employee states a cause of action under Title VII and 42 U.S.C. § 1981 if she is discharged for marrying a black[22] or does not have her employment contract renewed because of close association with the Hispanic community.[23] In another case brought under 42 U.S.C. § 1981, the Seventh Circuit held that a district court did not abuse its discretion by permitting a plaintiff who was denied a promotion in 1980 to introduce evidence of a notation made on his employment application in 1966 that he had been arrested for marching in a demonstration.[24]

Courts have reached different results when assessing whether promo-

---

[18]Goodman v. Lukens Steel Co., 482 U.S. 656, 44 FEP 1 (1987) (a union which does not assert discrimination to avoid antagonizing employer and thus improve chances of success on other issues or in deference to wishes of white employees is liable under Title VII and 42 U.S.C. § 1981). *But see* Johnson v. Artim Transp. Sys., 826 F.2d 538, 44 FEP 772 (7th Cir. 1987) (no evidence that union treated grievances of similarly situated white employees differently from grievances of plaintiff; dismissal of Title VII claim against union upheld).

[19]Rucker v. Higher Educ. Aids Bd., 669 F.2d 1179, 1182, 27 FEP 1553, 1555–56 (7th Cir. 1982) (black supervisory employee unlawfully terminated for protesting employer's refusal to hire guidance counselor because she was white); Clark v. R.J. Reynolds Tobacco Co., 27 FEP 1628 (E.D. La. 1982) (employer violated Title VII when it retaliated against white employee because he was related to another employee who filed a reverse discrimination charge).

[20]Saldivar v. Cadena, 622 F. Supp. 949, 39 FEP 836 (W.D. Wis. 1985) (42 U.S.C. § 1981 affords protection only to members of minority race, not to white advocates for the protected race).

[21]Leonard v. City of Columbus, 705 F.2d 1299, 31 FEP 1441 (11th Cir. 1983), *cert. denied*, 468 U.S. 1204, 35 FEP 213 (1984) (although removal of American flag from uniform sleeves of six black policemen violated city ordinance when done in symbolic protest against alleged racially discriminatory practices of police department, such action was protected by the First Amendment, particularly where there was evidence that management had been inconsistent in its discipline of those who failed to wear the flag).

[22]Parr v. Woodmen of the World Life Ins. Co., 791 F.2d 888, 41 FEP 22 (11th Cir. 1986) (allegation that employer refused to hire white applicant because of interracial marriage states claim under Title VII and 42 U.S.C. § 1981); Gresham v. Waffle House, 586 F. Supp. 1442, 35 FEP 763 (N.D. Ga. 1984) (court held that plaintiff would not have been discharged for marrying a black if she had not been white). *Contra* Parr v. United Family Life Ins. Co., 35 FEP 95 (N.D. Ga. 1983) (white male who was not hired because he was married to a black female had no cause of action under Title VII because of his wife's race).

[23]Reiter v. Central Consol. School Dist. 26-JT, 618 F. Supp. 1458, 39 FEP 833 (D. Colo. 1985) (discriminatory employment practices based on an individual's association with people of a particular race are prohibited by Title VII).

[24]Ramsey v. American Air Filter Co., 772 F.2d 1303, 38 FEP 1612 (7th Cir. 1985) (employee's counsel was permitted to examine witness about notation on an employment application over employer's objection of undue prejudice).

tions based on friendship and political patronage are outside the coverage of Title VII.[25]

## V. SEGREGATED EMPLOYMENT AND EMPLOYMENT FACILITIES

Courts have continued to provide relief when employer-provided housing is segregated,[26] when black employees are isolated from customer contact,[27] or when blacks are excluded from certain positions.[28] Discrimination can also be proved by evidence of segregated sleeping arrangements on business trips, coupled with racial slurs.[29]

## VI. DEFENSES TO RACE AND COLOR DISCRIMINATION

Consistent with the express provisions of Title VII, courts have generally rejected bona fide occupational qualification as a defense to racial preferences in favor of blacks.[30]

---

[25]Autry v. North Carolina Dep't of Human Resources, 820 F.2d 1384, 44 FEP 169 (4th Cir. 1987) (evidence that successful candidate for promotion was a friend of the decision-maker and that her mother had political ties with Democratic party does not show, directly or indirectly, any evidence of race discrimination); Bohen v. City of E. Chicago, Ind., 622 F. Supp. 1234, 39 FEP 917 (N.D. Ind. 1985), aff'd in part, 799 F.2d 1180, 41 FEP 1108 (7th Cir. 1986) (males received promotions rather than females because they were friends of higher-ups). Contra King v. Smith, 39 FEP 614 (E.D. Ark. 1985) (white county clerk violated Title VII by not promoting black employee perceived to be friendly with and supporter of county clerk's black opponent in Democratic primary).

[26]Domingo v. New England Fish Co., 727 F.2d 1429, 34 FEP 584, modified, 742 F.2d 520, 37 FEP 1303 (9th Cir. 1984) (measurable difference in quality of segregated housing provided to nonwhites could be characterized as wage differential to be remedied by back pay award). See also Atonio v. Wards Cove Packing Co., 810 F.2d 1477, 43 FEP 130 (9th Cir. 1987) (en banc) (cannery workers alleged racial stratification of jobs and that nonwhites were provided segregated and inferior housing and food as compared with whites).

[27]Carter v. Duncan-Huggins, Ltd., 727 F.2d 1225, 34 FEP 25 (D.C. Cir. 1984) (black employee's work station was in isolated area and away from any customer contact; employee also was denied benefits such as parking space and key to the office).

[28]Lams v. General Waterworks Corp., 766 F.2d 386, 38 FEP 516 (8th Cir. 1985) (concentration of blacks in nonsupervisory positions was sufficient to raise inference of discrimination in promotion and hiring for those positions); Wilmore v. City of Wilmington, 699 F.2d 667, 31 FEP 2 (3d Cir. 1983) (fire department's exclusion of blacks from administrative jobs had detrimental effect on their professional development and resulted in poorer scores on promotional examinations). But see Nash v. City of Houston Civic Center, 800 F.2d 491, 41 FEP 1480 (5th Cir. 1986) (no unlawful discrimination shown by evidence that most of City's parking attendants are black and that all parking attendants are classified as part-time employees).

[29]Sylvester v. Callon Energy Servs., 781 F.2d 520, 39 FEP 1660 (5th Cir. 1986) (white supervisor terminated black employee two days after sharing hotel room with him when other white employees refused to do so).

[30]42 U.S.C. § 2000e-2(e); Lilly v. City of Beckley, W. Va., 797 F.2d 191, 41 FEP 772 (4th Cir. 1986), aff'g 615 F. Supp. 137, 40 FEP 1213 (S.D. W. Va. 1985) (white applicant unlawfully denied employment although city was attempting to implement its affirmative action plan); Parson v. Kaiser Aluminum & Chem. Corp., 727 F.2d 473, 34 FEP 505 (5th Cir.), cert. denied, 467 U.S. 1243, 34 FEP 1688 (1984); Rucker v. Higher Educ. Aids Bd., 669 F.2d 1179, 1181, 27 FEP 1553, 1554–55 (7th Cir. 1982) (improper for state agency that provides counseling services to disadvantaged youths to consider preferences of local black community for a counselor of the same race); Planells v. Howard Univ., 32 FEP 336, 345 n.1 (D.D.C. 1983) (court rejected as a mockery of Title VII assertion that because of their uniqueness in history, black colleges were subject to different legal standard in discrimination cases and awarded relief to a white teacher who was dismissed); Turgeon v. Howard Univ., 571 F. Supp. 679, 32 FEP 925 (D.D.C. 1983) (statistical evidence used to establish prima facie case and to rebut the defendant's attempt to defend its actions). But see Chaline v. KCOH, 693 F.2d 477, 30 FEP 834 (5th Cir. 1982) (although employer's proffered reason for discharge found to be pretextual, court apparently accepted premise that black-oriented radio station could rely on customer preference to rebut prima facie case of reverse discrimination by showing that white employee who wanted to be a disc jockey lacked proper "black voice" quality and sensitivity to listening tastes of black audience); Golden v. Lutheran Family Servs. in N.C., 601 F. Supp. 383, 39 FEP 1422 (W.D.N.C. 1984) (race may be a BFOQ for particular child care and supervisory employees employed by child care facility because of perception that children deserved white and black role models).

CHAPTER 10

# NATIONAL ORIGIN

## I. Scope of Protection

The decisional law regarding national origin continues to evolve in patterns similar to those reflected in decisions concerning sex and race discrimination. Courts have considered both claims of disparate treatment on the basis of national origin[1] and claims that ostensibly neu-

---

[1] *See, e.g.,* Agarwal v. University of Minn. Regents, 788 F.2d 504, 40 FEP 937 (8th Cir. 1986) (East Indian professor's dismissal was based on plagiarism and students' grievance rather than discrimination under Title VII); Kumar v. University of Mass. Bd. of Trustees, 38 FEP 1735 (1st Cir. 1985), *rev'g* 566 F. Supp. 1299, 32 FEP 306 (D. Mass. 1983) (university's reasons for denying tenure to East Asian Indian faculty member not pretextual); Bluebeard's Castle Hotel v. Virgin Islands Dep't of Labor, 786 F.2d 168, 40 FEP 603 (3d Cir. 1986) (white male of French ancestry failed to show his discharge by hotel was based on national origin discrimination); Alires v. Amoco Prod. Co., 774 F.2d 409, 38 FEP 1731 (10th Cir. 1985) (Hispanic failed to establish prima facie case of national origin discrimination); Carbonell v. Louisiana Dep't of Health & Human Resources, 772 F.2d 185, 38 FEP 1792 (5th Cir. 1985) (discharge of native of Cuba for repeatedly refusing direct orders of reassignment did not violate Title VII); Gairola v. Virginia Dep't of Gen. Servs., 753 F.2d 1281, 36 FEP 1800 (4th Cir. 1985) (Hindu employee failed to establish prima facie case of discrimination as to discharge); Diaz v. AT&T, 752 F.2d 1356, 36 FEP 1742 (9th Cir. 1985) (case reversed and remanded for failure of lower court to allow Mexican-American employee to establish prima facie case and discover relevant material); Carino v. University of Okla. Bd. of Regents, 750 F.2d 815, 36 FEP 826 (10th Cir. 1984) (Filipino-American employee made out prima facie case of discrimination against him by his employer based on his national origin); Uviedo v. Steves Sash & Door Co., 738 F.2d 1425, 35 FEP 906 (5th Cir. 1984), *cert. denied,* 474 U.S. 1054, 39 FEP 1200 (1986) (failure to promote Mexican and pay plaintiff wage equivalent to Anglo employees on basis of plaintiff's national origin held discriminatory); Almendral v. New York State Office of Mental Health, 743 F.2d 963, 34 FEP 1680 (2d Cir. 1984) (failure to promote claim of Filipino psychiatric social worker remanded because trial court failed to consider many of plaintiff's allegations); Casillas v. United States Navy, 735 F.2d 338, 34 FEP 1493 (9th Cir. 1984) (Hispanic industrial engineer employed by Navy failed to receive promotion owing to lack of sufficient job-related experience); Colon-Sanchez v. Marsh, 733 F.2d 78, 34 FEP 1144 (10th Cir.), *cert. denied,* 469 U.S. 855, 35 FEP 1608 (1984) (Hispanic civil service civilian employed by Army not promoted because non-Hispanic more qualified); Firefighters for Racial Equality v. Bach, 731 F.2d 664, 34 FEP 1005 (10th Cir. 1984), *remanded,* 611 F. Supp. 166, 38 FEP 19 (D. Colo. 1985) (case reversed and remanded because lower court evaluated components of bona fide seniority system under disparate impact theory, not disparate treatment theory; for clarification purposes, court held that employer has burden to show personnel decisions were made pursuant to bona fide seniority system, and, if met, plaintiff bears burden of proving bona fide system results from intent to discriminate); Morvay v. Maghielse Tool & Die Co., 708 F.2d 229, 31 FEP 1471 (6th Cir.), *cert. denied,* 464 U.S. 1011, 33 FEP 552 (1983) (Hungarian plaintiff properly discharged for insubordination and refusal to cooperate); Soria v. Ozinga Bros., 704 F.2d 990, 31 FEP 720 (7th Cir. 1983) (discharge by persons of Dutch ancestry due to poor employment record, not employee's Italian origin); Wagh v. Nimmo, 705 F.2d 1020, 33 FEP 232 (8th Cir. 1983) (employment terminated because of failure to perform job, not because of Indian national origin); Lartius v. Iowa Dep't of Transp., 705 F.2d 1018, 31 FEP 1120 (8th Cir. 1983) (jury determination that employee of Indian origin denied promotion for nondiscriminatory reasons sustained); Mohammed v. Callaway, 698 F.2d 395, 30 FEP 1315 (10th Cir. 1983) (lower court determination of no discrimination reversed where Hispanic U.S. Army employee better qualified than nonminority selected, where other irregularities present, and affirmative action programs not implemented); Canino v. EEOC, 707 F.2d 468, 32 FEP 139 (11th Cir. 1983) (Hispanic EEOC employee failed to make out prima facie case of discrimination in selection of EEOC district director because he was not qualified for position); Hamm v. Board of Regents of Fla., 708 F.2d 647, 32 FEP 441 (11th Cir. 1983) (failure to pay Hispanic special teaching assistant same salary as other special assistants due to additional duties, not national origin); Lerma v. Bolger, 689 F.2d 589, 29 FEP 1828 (5th Cir. 1982) (employer hired non-Hispanic over Mexican-American because of higher objective test score and prior work record with same employer); Gutierrez v. Denver Post, 691 F.2d 945, 30 FEP 105 (10th Cir. 1982) (Mexican-American failed to establish prima facie case of discrimination as to promotion and wage claims); Bell v. Home Life Ins. Co., 596 F. Supp. 1549, 36 FEP 440 (M.D.N.C. 1984) (employee

tral practices have had an adverse impact upon national origin groups.[2]

In two cases involving persons of Arabic[3] and Jewish[4] backgrounds, respectively, the Supreme Court has held that discrimination based on "ancestry or ethnic characteristics" constitutes a cognizable claim under 42 U.S.C. §§ 1981 and 1982. The Court appears to have recognized §§ 1981 and 1982 as covering most though likely not all claims of national origin discrimination.[5] Based on an historical analysis of shifting perceptions and definitions

---

of New Zealand origin failed to prove disparate treatment); Chaves v. Thomas, 35 FEP 397 (D.D.C. 1984) (Hispanic employee failed to meet burden of persuasion in selection of EEOC attorney position); Barreyro v. Garfinckel's, 34 FEP 1743 (D. Md. 1984), *appeal dismissed*, 758 F.2d 645, 37 FEP 1408 (4th Cir. 1985) (seamstress discharged because of personality conflicts with supervisors, not Filipino origin); Ramon v. Smith, 34 FEP 404 (S.D. Tex. 1984) (EEOC Hispanic employee failed to make out prima facie case of discrimination as to promotions and work assignments); Loiseau v. Department of Human Resources, 567 F. Supp. 1211, 39 FEP 289 (D. Or. 1983) (French-speaking West Indian denied promotion based on national origin, not performance, where he was not well treated by supervisors even to point of attempts at behavior modification to change plaintiff's style); Ghalam v. Tesson Ferry, Inc., 560 F. Supp. 631, 31 FEP 1074 (E.D. Mo. 1983) (Iranian general manager's employment terminated during Iranian hostage crisis because of performance not national origin); Stanford v. New York City Comm'n on Human Rights, 554 F. Supp. 413, 30 FEP 1299 (S.D.N.Y.), *remanded*, 742 F.2d 1433, 37 FEP 1816 (2d Cir. 1983) (provisional human rights specialist from Anguilla failed to establish prima facie case as to suspension where neither her appearance nor accent indicated she was anything but American and employer had no knowledge otherwise); Vicedomini v. Alitalia Airlines, 37 FEP 1381 (S.D.N.Y. 1983) (no national origin discrimination where Italian-American's replacement was of same national origin); Earnhardt v. Puerto Rico, 582 F. Supp. 25, 34 FEP 1837 (D.P.R. 1983), *aff'd*, 744 F.2d 1, 35 FEP 1406 (1st Cir. 1984) (mainland American, often referred to as gringo, treated as outsider, and subject to other derogatory national origin nicknames and criticisms, had employment contract prematurely terminated because of national origin); Whatley v. Skaggs Cos., 707 F.2d 1129, 31 FEP 1202 (10th Cir.), *cert. denied*, 464 U.S. 938, 33 FEP 48 (1983) (employer's discharge of Hispanic employee unlawful, despite contentions that court did not consider overwhelming evidence that employee was discharged because of performance); Robino v. Norton, 682 F.2d 192, 29 FEP 256 (8th Cir. 1982) (isolated instances of offhand, joking references to Italian personnel, made by a supervisor, insufficient to establish national origin discrimination).

[2]*See, e.g.*, Kim v. Commandant, Defense Language Inst., Foreign Language Center, 772 F.2d 521, 38 FEP 1710 (9th Cir. 1985) (Korean national failed to make showing that English Language and Proficiency Test (ELOPT) had disparate impact upon Koreans where all applicants for position of Korean Administrator who took ELOPT were Korean); Clady v. County of Los Angeles, 770 F.2d 1421, 38 FEP 1575 (9th Cir. 1985), *cert. denied*, 475 U.S. 1109, 40 FEP 792 (1986) (black and Hispanic applicants established prima facie case of disparate impact as to county fire department's written exam, but exam was job-related and there was no alternative selection device having comparable business utility and a less adverse impact); Firefighters for Racial Equality v. Bach, *supra* note 1 (determination that fire department's four-year seniority requirement for eligibility to take lieutenant's promotion examination is excessive reversed and remanded because lower court failed to determine whether requirement was part of bona fide seniority system); Soria v. Ozinga Bros., *supra* note 1 (plaintiff of Italian national origin failed to establish statistical proof that company's employment and disciplinary practices had disparate impact on non-Dutch and non-Christian Reformed Church persons); Beavers v. Iron Workers Local 1, 701 F.2d 601, 31 FEP 242 (7th Cir. 1982) (union's apprenticeship and ad hoc hiring policies for temporary work had disparate impact on skilled Hispanic ironworkers); Regner v. City of Chicago, 601 F. Supp. 830, 36 FEP 1734 (N.D. Ill. 1985), *rev'd*, 789 F.2d 534, 40 FEP 1027 (7th Cir. 1986) (Filipino librarian failed to establish prima facie case under disparate impact theory) (summary judgment for defendant improper; plaintiff met initial burden of disparate impact case and case was remanded for defendant to attempt to rebut plaintiff's case); Talev v. Reinhardt, 662 F.2d 888, 26 FEP 1185 (D.C. Cir. 1981) (promotion and wage policies of Voice of America challenged by Bulgarian employee did not have disparate impact on non-American-born employees); Stokes v. New York State Dep't of Correctional Servs., 569 F. Supp. 918, 33 FEP 1074 (S.D.N.Y. 1982) (seniority system for intradepartmental transfers not discriminatory even though system had disparate impact on Hispanic correctional officers owing to reasonable purpose of system); Bonilla v. Oakland Scavenger Co., 697 F.2d 1297, 31 FEP 50 (9th Cir. 1982), *cert. denied*, 467 U.S. 1251, 34 FEP 1800 (1984) (nepotism policy favoring Italians had disparate impact on Hispanics); Ramirez v. City of Omaha, 678 F.2d 751, 30 FEP 477 (8th Cir. 1982) (no disparate impact found in use of polygraph); Rivera v. City of Wichita Falls, 665 F.2d 531, 27 FEP 1352 (5th Cir. 1982) (reading comprehension test valid for selection of police recruits despite substantially lower Hispanic pass rate); Wang v. Hoffman, 694 F.2d 1146, 30 FEP 703 (9th Cir. 1982) (language skills requirement has potential adverse impact).

[3]St. Francis College v. Al-Khazraji, 481 U.S. 604, 43 FEP 1305, 1307–8 (1987).

[4]Shaare Tefila Congregation v. Cobb, 481 U.S. 615, 43 FEP 1309, 1310 (1987).

[5]*See* concurring opinion of Justice Brennan in *St. Francis College v. Al-Khazraji, supra* note 3: "I write separately only to point out that the line between discrimination based on 'ancestry or ethnic characteristics' and discrimination based on 'place or nation of * * * origin' is not a bright one. * * *

of concepts of "race" since the mid-19th century, the Court emphasized the older connection between "race" and ethnic origin. While expressly rejecting "a distinctive physiognomy" as an essential element in qualifying for protection under § 1981,[6] the Court in *St. Francis College* v. *Al-Khazraji* held that the plaintiff would make out a § 1981 claim on remand by proving that he was subjected to intentional discrimination "based on the fact that he was born an Arab, rather than solely on the place or nation of his origin or religion * * * ."[7] In *Shaare Tefila Congregation v. Cobb,*[8] a suit for alleged desecration of a synagogue, the Court expressly applied the same analysis as in *Al-Khazraji* and held that both § 1981 and § 1982 were "intended to protect from discrimination identifiable classes of persons who are subjected to intentional discrimination solely because of their ancestry or ethnic characteristics."

In *Weinberger v. Rossi,*[9] the Supreme Court held that executive agreements between the President and the host country providing for preferential employment of the host country's nationals were lawful, even though not a formal treaty within the meaning of 5 U.S.C. § 201, which prohibits employment discrimination against U.S. citizens on military bases overseas unless permitted by "treaty."

In a case having national origin overtones, a medical school was held to have unilaterally excluded American-Jewish physicians from participation in medical program teams sent to Saudi Arabia and thereby to have violated the antiboycott provisions of the Export Administration Act of 1979.[10]

The Ninth Circuit extended the protection of Title VII to discrimination which interferes with employment relations in a case where the Hispanic owner of a professional medical corporation sued a hospital which refused to hire his corporation to operate its hospital emergency room.[11] The courts, however, are continuing to attempt to unravel the employee/independent contractor conundrum for purposes of Title VII.[12]

---

Often * * * the two are identical as a factual matter. * * * I therefore read the Court's opinion to state only that discrimination based on birthplace alone is insufficient to state a claim under § 1981." *Id.,* 43 FEP at 1309 (citations omitted).

[6]*Id.,* 43 FEP at 1308.

[7]*Id.,* 43 FEP at 1308–9.

[8]*Supra* note 4, 43 FEP at 1310.

[9]456 U.S. 25, 28 FEP 585 (1982).

[10]Abrams v. Baylor College of Medicine, 581 F. Supp. 1570, 34 FEP 229 (S.D. Tex. 1984). *See also* Thomas v. Rohner-Gehrig & Co., 582 F. Supp. 669, 34 FEP 887 (N.D. Ill. 1984) (Title VII covers claim brought by American citizens against Swiss-owned company after they were discharged and replaced by individuals from Switzerland and Germany).

[11]Gomez v. Alexian Bros. Hosp. of San Jose, 698 F.2d 1019, 30 FEP 1705 (9th Cir. 1983).

[12]*Compare* Gomez v. Alexian Bros. Hosp. of San Jose, *supra* note 11 (alleged failure to award Hispanic doctors professional corporation consisting of numerous contracts to operate emergency room of hospital actionable under Title VII) *and* Amro v. St. Lukes Hosp. of Bethlehem, Pa., 39 FEP 1574 (E.D. Pa. 1986) (Palestine-born doctor in residency program at hospital who was denied staff privileges states claim under Title VII because, although doctor is an independent contractor, staff privileges is benefit which flows from being a resident, and therefore, cannot be applied in a discriminatory fashion) *with* Mares v. Marsh, 777 F.2d 1066, 40 FEP 858 (5th Cir. 1985) (Chinese grocery bagger at Army commissary held not employee of Army because Army did not have right of control over employee, and therefore, allegations of race and national origin claims not actionable).

## II. VARIOUS TYPES OF EMPLOYMENT PRACTICES

### A. Ability to Speak English as a Job Requirement

The courts and the EEOC continue to grapple with questions dealing with the ability to speak English fluently.[13] When the rule has a reasonable business justification and is not overly broad in coverage, it has been upheld.[14] However, a foreign accent which does not interfere with the employee's job duties has been held not a legitimate justification for adverse employment decisions.[15]

### D. Derogatory Epithets or Stereotype Images

Derogatory epithets based on national origin have played a significant role in determining that an employer prematurely terminated an employment contract based on national origin.[16]

Where derogatory epithets are uttered by co-workers, the question whether the employer has violated Title VII depends upon the frequency and egregiousness of the comments and upon the employer's knowledge.[17]

---

[13]*Compare, e.g.,* Stallcop v. Kaiser Found. Hosps., 820 F.2d 1044, 44 FEP 237, 125 LRRM 3075 (9th Cir.), *cert. denied,* 484 U.S. —, 45 FEP 776 (1987) (statement by supervisor that plaintiff did not know English language was not proof of discriminatory conduct; "Ethnicity and status as a non-English speaking person are not necessarily linked") *with* Carino v. University of Okla. Bd. of Regents, 750 F.2d 815, 36 FEP 826 (10th Cir. 1984) (a foreign accent that does not interfere with job duties is not legitimate justification for adverse employment decisions).

[14]Jurado aka Valentine v. Eleven-Fifty Corp., 813 F.2d 1406, 43 FEP 870 (9th Cir. 1987) (radio station's English-only rule was limited, reasonable, and business-related and therefore not racially motivated); Tran v. City of Houston, 35 FEP 471 (S.D. Tex. 1983) (Vietnamese who had worked as interpreter for U.S. Forces not hired because of lack of fluency in speaking English, not national origin); Desai v. Tompkins County Trust Co., 34 FEP 938 (N.D.N.Y.), *aff'd,* 37 FEP 1312 (2d Cir. 1984), *cert. denied,* 471 U.S. 1125, 37 FEP 1408 (1985) (bank's refusal to promote employee from India to head teller due, in part, to language difficulties in dealing with customers and co-workers); Kureshy v. City Univ. of N.Y., 561 F. Supp. 1098, 31 FEP 1264 (E.D.N.Y. 1983), *aff'd,* 742 F.2d 1431, 37 FEP 280 (2d Cir. 1984) (university lawfully denied tenure to associate professor because, in part, of lack of fluency in English which made him less effective as teacher); Casas v. First Am. Bank, 31 FEP 1479 (D.D.C. 1983) (poor communication skills caused by imprecise, confusing word choice and usage, not Filipino origin, was reason for denial of promotion); Hou v. Pennsylvania Dep't of Educ., Slippery Rock State College, 573 F. Supp. 1539, 33 FEP 513 (W.D. Pa. 1983) (Chinese professor denied promotion because accent and inability to communicate hindered teaching effectiveness); Smith v. District of Columbia, 29 FEP 1129 (D.D.C. 1982) (upholds bilingual requirement where job involves interfacing with non-English-speaking persons). *But see* Loiseau v. Department of Human Resources, 567 F. Supp. 1211, 39 FEP 289 (D. Or. 1983) (French-speaking West Indian's national origin, not heavy accent and different style of writing and speaking, basis for denial of promotion).

In EEOC Dec. 81-25, 27 FEP 1820 (1981), the employer had posted a notice and specifically informed its employees "when you are on the payroll, all conversation will be in English. Either work and speak English or work and don't talk." The employer contended that the rule was only applicable to particular areas. The EEOC decided that although the enforcement and application of the employer's rule may be limited in scope, the rule was presented to its employees as an absolute prohibition against speaking any language other than English while on the job. The EEOC concluded that there would rarely be, if ever, a need for an absolute prohibition against speaking any language other than English at all times and all circumstances in the workplace. On the other hand, the EEOC in Dec. 83-7, 31 FEP 1861 (1983), did not find reasonable cause to believe that a petroleum company violated Title VII when it adopted a rule requiring that only English be spoken by refinery employees who worked in a laboratory and processing area where the potential for fires and explosions existed and by all refinery employees during emergencies. The rule was narrowly drawn to assure effective communication during specified times and in specified areas.

[15]Carino v. University of Okla. Bd. of Regents, *supra* note 13.

[16]Earnhardt v. Puerto Rico, 582 F. Supp. 25, 34 FEP 1837 (D.P.R. 1983), *aff'd,* 744 F.2d 1, 35 FEP 1406 (1st Cir. 1984) (American citizen from mainland called "gringo," "muy American," and other derogatory national origin nicknames by Puerto Rican employer).

[17]*See, e.g.,* Snell v. Suffolk County, N.Y., 782 F.2d 1094, 39 FEP 1590 (2d Cir. 1986) (proliferation of demeaning literature and epithets against black and Hispanic correction officers constituted concerted

One court has extended protection against national origin discrimination to include a prohibition against employment discrimination based on an individual's association with people of a particular national origin.[18]

## F. Citizenship

Two courts have rejected the argument that § 1981 prohibits discrimination based on alienage.[19] In several cases, courts held that Title VII does not apply to claims of employment discrimination based on citizenship.[20]

In *Bernal v. Fainter*,[21] the Supreme Court clarified the scope of the political function equal protection exception. *Bernal* involved the constitutionality of a Texas statute requiring notaries to be U.S. citizens. In striking the statute down, the Court pointed out that the political function exception has been restricted to occupations involving significant amounts of discretion, such as teaching and police work. The work of a notary, however, is ministerial rather than discretionary. For this reason, the Court refused to extend the political function exception and held that the Texas statute violated the equal protection clause.

The Supreme Court in *Cabell v. Chavez-Salido*[22] applied the political function exception in upholding state legislation that required U.S. citizenship for public officers or employees declared by law to be "peace officers." The Court found the state scheme for designating those employees exercising important government functions "sufficiently tailored to withstand a facial challenge" and that for the positions specifically at issue, probation officers, "a citizenship requirement may seem an appropriate limitation on those who would exercise and * * * symbolize * * * power of the political community."[23]

Given the practical risks of exposure under the immigration laws, illegal aliens have generally not sought, let alone found, protection from employ-

---

pattern of harassment in violation of Title VII); Erebia v. Chrysler Plastic Prods. Corp., 772 F.2d 1250, 37 FEP 1820 (6th Cir. 1985), *cert. denied,* 475 U.S. 1015, 40 FEP 192 (1986) (repeated slurs against Mexican-American and management's tolerance and condonation constitute hostile work environment); Brown v. Parker-Hannifin Corp., 746 F.2d 1407, 36 FEP 127 (10th Cir. 1984) (harassment of employee of German origin whose employer failed to take steps to stop such behavior held actionable); Bell v. Home Life Ins. Co., 596 F. Supp. 1549, 36 FEP 440 (M.D.N.C. 1984) (plaintiff failed to show any alleged disparaging remarks were made with frequency or severity to constitute discriminatory conduct); United States v. New York, 593 F. Supp. 1216, 35 FEP 1535 (N.D.N.Y. 1984) (evidence failed to establish an atmosphere of discrimination where telling of jokes was isolated and not tolerated or condoned).

[18]Reiter v. Central Consol. School Dist. 26-JT, 618 F. Supp. 1458, 39 FEP 833 (D. Colo. 1985) (refusing to dismiss plaintiff's claim of employment discrimination based on her association with Hispanic community denied because such discriminatory practices prohibited under Title VII).

[19]Bhandari v. First Nat'l Bank of Commerce, 829 F.2d 1343, 45 FEP 126 (5th Cir. 1987) (en banc) (private discrimination based on alienage not prohibited under § 1981) *overruling* Guerra v. Manchester Terminal Corp., 498 F.2d 641, 8 FEP 433 (5th Cir. 1974); Ben-Yakir v. Gaylinn Assocs., 535 F. Supp. 543, 29 FEP 113 (S.D.N.Y. 1982) (Israeli citizen).

[20]Espinoza v. Farah Mfg. Co., 414 U.S. 86, 6 FEP 933 (1973) (Mexican's alleged denial of employment based on lack of citizenship or alienage does not constitute cause of action under Title VII); *see also* Longnecker v. Ore Sorters, (N. Am.), 634 F. Supp. 1077 (N.D. Ga. 1986) (plaintiff's claim that he was discharged because he was American and noncitizens were given preferential treatment is allegation of discrimination based on citizenship and therefore not cognizable under Title VII); Vicedomini v. Alitalia Airlines, 37 FEP 1381 (S.D.N.Y. 1983) (discrimination based on citizenship not actionable under Title VII); Dowling v. United States, 476 F. Supp. 1018, 22 FEP 442 (D. Mass. 1979) (U.S. citizen cannot sue hockey leagues that hire only Canadian referees); Mahdavi v. Fair Employment Practice Comm'n, 67 Cal. App.3d 326, 136 Cal. Rptr. 421, 33 FEP 755 (Ct. App. 1977) (California human rights law does not cover claims of discrimination based on alienage).

[21]467 U.S. 216 (1984).

[22]454 U.S. 432, 27 FEP 1129 (1982).

[23]*Id.* at 434–39, 27 FEP at 1131–35.

ment discrimination under the Constitution or federal or state discrimination laws. However, the Supreme Court in *Sure-Tan v. NLRB*[24] held that once hired, illegal aliens are "employees" under the National Labor Relations Act, and that it is an unfair labor practice under § 8(a)(3) of the Act to report undocumented employees to the Immigration and Naturalization Service in retaliation for their union activities. Crucial to the Court's decision was that the Immigration and Nationality Act did not then prohibit the employment of undocumented or illegal aliens.[25] Therefore, there was no conflict between the two statutes. Enactment of the Immigration Reform and Control Act of 1986[26] (IRCA) has changed the basis of the Court's pre-IRCA analysis in *Sure-Tan,* because IRCA expressly prohibits the employment of undocumented aliens and imposes comprehensive monitoring and enforcement responsibilities on employers.[27]

A division of authorities has already emerged on whether undocumented aliens may now recover damages and penalties provided under the Fair Labor Standards Act.[28]

## III. EXCEPTIONS

### A. Security Clearance

In a unique case, it was held that certain positions classified as "security positions" under the laws governing the Canal Zone had to be filled by U.S. citizens only. The term "security" was designed to ensure that certain positions crucial to the continuity and capability of operations and administration of activities in the Canal Zone be handled only by U.S. citizens and had nothing to do with the protection of military or political secrets. Accordingly, the fact that Panamanian noncitizens within the Canal Zone were excluded from these positions did not violate any fair employment law.[29]

---

[24]467 U.S. 883, 116 LRRM 2857 (1984).

[25]*Id.* at 891: "The [Immigration and Naturalization Act] evinces 'at best evidence of a peripheral concern with employment of illegal entrants.' "

[26]Pub. L. No. 99-603, 100 Stat. 3359 (1986).

[27]*See* text *infra.* Notably, however, there is a "grandfather clause" under IRCA for current employees. The statute's prohibitions do not apply to the hiring of an employee before its enactment, nor to the continuing employment of such an individual. IRCA §§ 274A.(a)(3)(A) and 274.(a)(3)(B).

The National Labor Relations Board's General Counsel has signaled one adjustment in policy following IRCA. The General Counsel's Memorandum GC 87-8, issued October 27, 1987, outlines the General Counsel's post-IRCA policy on seeking reinstatement and back pay for persons who are undocumented aliens but would otherwise be entitled to such relief. The memorandum states guidelines by which the General Counsel will condition efforts to seek reinstatement and back pay on (1) confirmation that the undocumented discriminatee has filed or intends to file for Temporary Resident Status (TRS) with the Immigration and Naturalization Service (INS), and (2) an INS determination that the undocumented discriminatee has made a prima facie showing of entitlement to TRS and has been issued a work permit, or an ultimate determination by the INS of TRS eligibility. Entitlement to back pay and reinstatement would be cut off by an INS determination that the undocumented discriminatee is not entitled to TRS.

[28]*Compare* In re Reyes, 814 F.2d 168, 170 (5th Cir. 1987) ("[I]t is well established that the protections of the Fair Labor Standards Act are applicable to citizens and aliens alike and whether the alien is documented or undocumented is irrelevant") *with* Patel v. Sumani Corp., 660 F. Supp. 1528 (N.D. Ala. 1987) (unreported), *appeal pending* (summary judgment denying minimum wage, overtime, and liquidated damages to admitted illegal alien; court holds post-IRCA immigration policies do not require full relief to illegal aliens in order to discourage their employment, and that access to remedies would encourage illegal immigration for employment contrary to national policy).

[29]Caton v. Canal Zone Gov't, 522 F. Supp. 1, 29 FEP 1803 (D.C.Z. 1981), *aff'd,* 669 F.2d 218, 29 FEP 1817 (5th Cir. 1982). *See also* Molerio v. Federal Bureau of Investigation, 749 F.2d 815, 36 FEP 586 (D.C. Cir. 1984) (Cuban plaintiff of Hispanic origin not hired by FBI due to plaintiff's inability to pass top secret security clearance, not due to discrimination).

## C. Legislative Immunity

In *Agromayor v. Colberg,* [30] the First Circuit applied the doctrine of absolute legislative immunity to withhold scrutiny of a claim of discrimination based on national origin. The plaintiff was denied a position as a press officer by a legislator, allegedly due, in part, to his national origin. The court reasoned that "barring outright patronage or mere party affiliation," once an employment position falls within a class wherein the legislature is given a right of choice, factual inquiry by the judiciary would encroach upon legislative wisdom and destroy the immunity.[31]

## D. First Amendment

In *Jurado aka Valentine v. Eleven-Fifty Corp.,* [32] the court applied First Amendment rights to hold that a discharged radio announcer had not been discriminated against on the basis of national origin. In this case, plaintiff began using Spanish words and phrases in part of his English-language radio program. The program director requested the plaintiff to stop using Spanish because it was bad for the ratings. Plaintiff refused and subsequently was discharged. The court reasoned that the acts complained of are protected programming decisions under the First Amendment and the Communications Act. On appeal, the Ninth Circuit held that there was insufficient evidence to establish discharge based on discriminatory motives, and, therefore, failed to address whether the radio station's actions were protected under the First Amendment and the Communications Act.[33]

## IV. THE IMMIGRATION REFORM AND CONTROL ACT OF 1986

In its final hours, the 99th Congress passed the most important immigration legislation since the McCarran-Walter Act of 1952. The Immigration Reform and Control Act of 1986 (IRCA)[34] is of special interest to all employers and referral agencies because the Act requires that employers (1) take specific steps intended to verify whether an individual applicant seeking employment after November 6, 1986, is legally entitled to work in the United States, (2) refuse to employ persons who cannot substantiate such entitlement, and (3) preserve records substantiating the mandatory verification. A special provision of IRCA requires that employers make these determinations of entitlement to work without discrimination based on national origin or citizenship. IRCA also provides special enforcement procedures incorporating civil and criminal sanctions.[35]

---

[30]738 F.2d 55, 35 FEP 239 (1st Cir.), *cert. denied,* 469 U.S. 1037, 36 FEP 464 (1984).

[31]*Id.,* 738 F.2d at 61, 35 FEP at 243.

[32]630 F. Supp. 569, 39 FEP 1459 (C.D. Cal. 1985), *aff'd,* 813 F.2d 1406, 43 FEP 870 (9th Cir. 1987).

[33]813 F.2d 1406, 43 FEP 870 (9th Cir. 1987).

[34]Pub. L. No. 99-603, 100 Stat. 3359 (to be codified at 8 U.S.C. § 1324A. Hereinafter, all further references to the Act are cited as IRCA and the applicable section of the Act). The final rules of § 274a of the Act are published in 52 FED REG. No. 84 (1987) (to be codified at 8 C.F.R. § 274a. Hereinafter, all further references to the Federal Regulations are cited to the Codification).

[35]This discussion analyzes most of Title I of the Act. It does not address other parts of the Act, such as changes pertaining to temporary agriculture workers and legalization of aliens.

## A. Section 101—Employment of Aliens

### 1. Coverage

*a. In General.* Section 101 of IRCA amends the Immigration and Nationality Act, 8 U.S.C. § 1101 *et seq.,* by adding a new section, 274A, regarding the employment of aliens. The section applies to all persons or entities[36] and provides that it is unlawful to hire, recruit, or refer for a fee an alien known not to be lawfully admitted for permanent residence or authorized to be so employed.[37] It is also unlawful to continue the employment of an alien hired after the enactment of IRCA knowing the alien is or has become an unauthorized alien.[38] An employer must be able to attest under penalty of perjury that it has examined the employee's documents evidencing employment authorization and identity. The individual being recruited, referred for a fee, or hired also must attest that he or she is a citizen or national of the United States, an alien lawfully admitted for permanent residence, or an alien authorized by the Attorney General for employment in the United States.[39]

*b. Employers Covered.* All employers are covered by the verification and recordkeeping requirements of IRCA and by the prohibition against the hiring of unauthorized aliens. IRCA itself covers individuals, partnerships, corporations and other organizations, nonprofit and profit, private and public, which employ, recruit, or refer persons for employment in the United States.[40] Regulations issued under IRCA further include joint ventures, governmental bodies, agencies, proprietorships, associations, and any other legal entities.[41] The Regulations include in the definition of an "employer" "an agent or anyone acting directly or indirectly in the interest" of an employer.[42]

*c. Types of Employment Covered. i. Hiring for Employment.* The Act covers all individuals hired for employment, and the Regulations define the term "hire" to mean "the actual commencement of employment of an employee for wages or other remuneration."[43] "Employment" is defined in the Regulations as "any service or labor performed by an employee for an employer within the United States, including service or labor performed on a U.S. vessel or aircraft which touches at a port in the United States."[44]

The term "employee" means an individual who provides services or labor for an employer for wages or other remuneration.[45] Independent con-

---

[36]The Act covers employers, recruiters, and referral agencies. For purposes of this discussion, all such entities covered by the Act will be referred to as Employers.

[37]IRCA § 274A.(a)(1)(A).

[38]IRCA §§ 274A.(a)(2) and 274A.(a)(3)(B).

[39]IRCA §§ 274A.(a)(1)(B) and 274A.(b).

[40]S. Rep. No. 99-132, 99th Cong., 1st Sess. 32 (1985).

[41]8 C.F.R. § 274a.1(b).

[42]8 C.F.R. § 274a.1(g).

[43]8 C.F.R. § 274a.1(c).

[44]8 C.F.R. § 274a.1(h).

[45]8 C.F.R. § 274a.1(f).

tractors are expressly excluded from the definition of "employee."[46] "Independent contractors" include:

> "Individuals or entities who carry on independent business, contract to do a piece of work according to their own means and methods, and are subject to control only as to results. Whether an individual or entity is an independent contractor, regardless of what the individual or entity calls itself, will be determined on a case-by-case basis. Factors to be considered in that determination include, but are not limited to, whether the individual or entity: supplies the tools or material; makes services available to the general public; works for a number of clients at the same time; directs the order or sequence in which the work is to be done and determines the hours during which the work is to be done."[47]

If the individual or entity is an independent contractor, the employee verification requirements do not apply. However, the employer is responsible if it knows that the independent contractor is an unauthorized alien or employs unauthorized aliens.[48]

*ii. Recruiting or referring for a fee.* The Act regulates two activities in addition to hiring: recruiting for a fee and referring for a fee. The term "recruit for a fee" means "the act of soliciting a person, directly or indirectly, and referring that person to another with the intent of obtaining employment for that person, for remuneration whether on a retainer or contingency basis."[49] The term "refer for a fee" is defined as "the act of sending or directing a person or transmitting documentation or information to another, directly or indirectly, with the intent of obtaining employment in the United States for such person, for remuneration whether on a retainer or contingency basis."[50] With respect to contract service referrals, it appears that the contract service is the employer and must perform the verification function.[51]

Two referring relationships are expressly excluded from the law's coverage:

(1) Labor Union Hiring Halls—The regulations exclude "Union hiring halls that refer union members or non-union individuals who pay union membership dues."[52]

(2) State Employment Agencies—State Employment Agencies[53] are not required to verify the identity and employability of those referred for jobs.[54] However, if a state employment agency chooses to do so, and if it complies with special rules, the employer will be relieved of verification responsibility.[55]

---

[46]*Id.*

[47]8 C.F.R. § 274a.1(j).

[48]IRCA § 274A.(a)(4); 8 C.F.R. § 274a.5.

[49]8 C.F.R. § 274a.1(e).

[50]8 C.F.R. § 274a.1(d).

[51]8 C.F.R. § 274a.1(g). However, the company using the temporary help could still be subject to sanctions if it knows the temporary help is an unauthorized alien.

[52]8 C.F.R. § 274a.1(d) and (e).

[53]State employment agency is defined as "Any state government Unit designated to cooperate with the United States Employment Service in the operation of the public employment service system." 8 C.F.R. § 274a.1(i).

[54]*Joint Explanatory Statement of the Committee of Conference, Conference Report,* H.R. Rep. No. 99-1000, 99th Cong., 2d Sess. 89 (1986); 8 C.F.R. § 274a.6(a).

[55]IRCA § 274A.(a)(5). If a state employment agency chooses to complete the verification process, the procedure that must be followed is set forth in 8 C.F.R. § 274a.6.

## 2. Verification Requirements

*a. Employee Verification Requirements.* The regulations set forth the outer permissible time limits for completing the verification process and presentation of documents. An employer may have a different policy with respect to different groups of employees based on job classification but may not maintain different policies based on national origin, citizenship, or other factors prohibited as a basis for employer action by Title VII.

An individual who is hired, recruited, or referred for a fee for employment must complete Section I—"Employee Information and Verification"—on a new U.S. Government Form I-9[56] at the time of hiring, *i.e.,* not later than the first day of work.[57] A preparer or translator may assist an individual by reading the form to the individual, assisting in completing the employee portion of the form, and having the individual sign or mark the form in the appropriate place. The preparer or translator should then complete the "Preparer/Translator Certification" portion of Form I-9.[58]

Completion of Form I-9 after acceptance of an offer of employment avoids unnecessary prehire collection of information that will likely reflect national origin and possibly other facts which cannot properly be the basis of employment selection decisions. In this respect, information needed to complete Form I-9 may be treated like information the employer requires for employee benefit enrollment or other legitimate business purposes, but which the employer collects only after employment is offered and accepted.[59]

An employee must present to the employer, recruiter, or referrer for a fee, within three business days of hire, the required documentation establishing his or her identity and employment eligibility.[60] If an individual is unable to provide the required documentation within the 3-day period, the time period will be extended to 21 business days after hire, providing the individual presents a "receipt for the application" of the documentation within 3 days of hire.[61]

*b. Employer Verification Requirements.* Within three business days of the hire, an employer, recruiter, or referrer for a fee must physically examine the documentation presented by the individual establishing identity and employment eligibility and complete Section 2—"Employer Review and

---

[56]Original of Form I-9 may be obtained from an INS district office or the Government Printing Office. Employers may photocopy Form I-9 from an original.

[57]8 C.F.R. §§ 274a.2(b)(1)(i)(A) and § 274a.1(c).

[58]8 C.F.R. § 274a.2(b)(1)(i)(A).

[59]*See, e.g., EEOC Guidelines on Prehire Inquiries:* "Data on such matters as marital status, number and age of children, and similar issues, which could be used in a discriminatory manner in making employment decisions but which are necessary for insurance, reporting requirements, or other business purposes can and should be obtained after a person has been employed, not by means of an application form or pre-employment interview." State law or regulation may similarly discourage or even prohibit such prehire inquiry. However, the following type of prehire inquiry is widely accepted and, for example, is expressly approved by the California Department of Fair Employment and Housing: "Can you, after employment, submit verification of your legal right to work in the United States?"

[60]8 C.F.R. §§ 274a.2(b)(1)(i)(B) and 274a.2(b)(1)(ii) and (iv). *See* Section IV.A.3., *infra,* for documentation requirements.

[61]8 C.F.R. §§ 274a.2(b)(1)(iii), (iv), and (vi).

Verification"—on Form I-9.[62] If an employee is hired for less than three days, the employer must complete its portion of Form I-9 before the end of the employee's first working day.[63]

A recruiter or referrer does not need to perform the verification process unless and until a recruited or referred individual is actually hired by an employer.[64] If a hired employee was recruited or referred for a fee, both the employer and the recruiter or referrer are responsible for verification.[65] A recruiter or referrer may designate agents to complete the employment verification process, including employers, in which case the employer must provide the recruiter or referrer with a photocopy of Form I-9.[66] Employers who hire persons referred to them from a state employment agency may comply with the act by retaining documentation to the effect that such a referral was made by the agency and that the agency certified that it has complied with the provisions of the Act.[67]

Employers must perform the required verification and recordkeeping for all employees hired on or after November 7, 1986, who continued to be employed as of June 1, 1987.[68]

An employer must monitor the expiration date and update Form I-9 for employees whose employment authorization document expires. On or before the expiration, the employee must present a document that shows continuing permission to work or is a new grant of work authorization.[69] The employer should review the document, and if it appears to be genuine and to relate to the individual, the employer must update the form by noting the document's identification number and expiration date on Form I-9.[70]

An employer is not required to reverify an employee's employment eligibility if the employee is continuing his or her employment and at all times has a reasonable expectation of employment. The regulations provide examples of situations that constitute "Continuing Employment" and thus do not require reverification:

(1) An employee takes approved paid or unpaid leave on account of study, illness or disability of a family member, illness or pregnancy, maternity or paternity leave, vacation, union business, or other temporary leave approved by the employer;

(2) An employee is promoted, demoted, or receives a pay raise;

(3) An employee is laid off for lack of work;

(4) An employee is on strike or in a labor dispute;

(5) An employee is reinstated after disciplinary suspension or wrongful termination which is found unjustified by any court, arbitrator,

---

[62] 8 C.F.R. §§ 274a.2(b)(1)(ii) and (iv).
[63] 8 C.F.R. § 274a.2(b)(1)(iii).
[64] 8 C.F.R. § 274a.2(b)(1)(iv).
[65] IRCA § 274A.(a)(1).
[66] 8 C.F.R. § 274a.2(b)(1)(iv).
[67] IRCA § 274A.(a)(5). State agency compliance provisions are set forth in 8 C.F.R. § 274a.6.
[68] 8 C.F.R. § 274a.2(a).
[69] A nonimmigrant whose document has expired but who has filed a timely application for an extension may continue employment for the same employer for up to 120 days. 8 C.F.R. § 274a.12(b)(15).
[70] 8 C.F.R. § 274a.2(b)(1)(vii).

or administrative body or is otherwise resolved through reinstatement or settlement;

(6) An employee transfers from one distinct unit of an employer to another distinct unit of the same employer; or

(7) An employee continues his or her employment with a related, successor, or reorganized employer providing the related, successor, or reorganized employer obtains Form I-9 from the predecessor company. Situations referenced in this provision include: the same employer at another location; an employer who continues to employ some or all of another employer's work force in cases involving a corporate reorganization, merger, or a sale of stock or assets; or an employer who continues to employ some or all of another employer's work force where both employers belong to the same multi-employer association and employees continue to work in the same bargaining unit under the same collective bargaining agreement.[71]

The foregoing enumeration is not all-encompassing. Other similar situations could constitute continuing employment.

An employer need not comply with the verification requirements for an employee who is rehired within three years of initial execution of Form I-9, providing the employer inspects the initial Form I-9 and determines that it relates to the employee and the employee is eligible to work.[72] Thus, if an individual is rehired more than three years after the initial execution of Form I-9, or the individual has not previously completed Form I-9, or the initial Form I-9 shows the individual is no longer eligible to work, then the employer must repeat the documentation procedure.

### 3. Documents to Be Examined

The Act and Regulations list those documents which verify employability and identity. With the exception of birth certificates, the regulations provide that employers must see original documents.[73] Documents designated as Group A Documents establish both employment authorization and identity. If one of these documents is presented, an employer need not check any further documentation.[74] If an employee does not have or choose to present a Group A Document, he or she must present one document which establishes identity, designated as a Group B Document, and one document which establishes employment eligibility, designated as a Group C Document.[75]

Employees may produce whichever documents they choose as long as the statutory requirements are satisfied. Employers are prohibited from specifying which of the Group A, B, or C documents are acceptable,[76] so long as the documents presented by the employee appear to be genuine.

---

[71]8 C.F.R. § 274a.2(b)(1)(viii).
[72]8 C.F.R. § 274a.2(c)(1).
[73]8 C.F.R. §§ 274a.2(b)(1)(v) and 274a.2(b)(1)(v)(C)(6).
[74]IRCA § 274A.(b)(1)(A)(i); 8 C.F.R. § 274a.2(b)(1)(v).
[75]IRCA § 274A.(b)(1)(A)(ii); 8 C.F.R. § 274a.2(b)(1)(v).
[76]8 C.F.R. § 274a.2(b)(1)(v).

*a. Documents Establishing Employment Authorization and Identity.* The following documents establish both employment authorization and identity (Group A Documents):

(1)   United States passport;

(2)   Certificate of United States Citizenship (Form N-560 or N-561);

(3)   Certificate of naturalization (Form N-550 or N-570);

(4)   Unexpired foreign passport which contains an unexpired Form I-551 stamp which reads "temporary evidence of lawful admission for permanent residence. Valid until *(Date)*. Employment authorized," or has attached a Form I-94 which contains an unexpired employment authorization stamp provided the proposed employment is authorized;

(5)   Resident alien card with a photograph (Form I-151 or I-551) (colloquially called "green cards");

(6)   Temporary resident card (Form I-688); or

(7)   Employment authorization card (Form I-688A).[77]

*b. Documents Establishing Identity Only.* The following documents establish an individual's identity (Group B Documents):

For individuals 16 years or older:

(1)   A driver's license or similar document issued for the purposes of identification by a state, which document contains a photograph of the individual or name, date of birth, sex, height, color of eyes, and address;

(2)   Driver's license issued by a Canadian government authority;[78]

(3)   School identification card with a photograph;

(4)   Voter's registration card;

(5)   U.S. military card or draft record;

(6)   Identification card issued by federal, state, or local government agencies, or a military dependent's identification card;

(7)   Native American tribal documents; or

(8)   U.S. Coastguard Merchant Mariner card.[79]

For individuals under 16 years of age who are unable to produce a document listed above, the following documents establish identity:

(1)   School record or report card;

(2)   Clinic, doctor, or hospital record; or

(3)   Day care or nursery school record.[80]

Minors under the age of 16 who are unable to produce one of the above identity documents are exempt from producing one if

(1)   the minor's parent or legal guardian completes Section 1 of Form I-9 and in the space for the minor's signature, the parent or legal guardian writes "minor under age 16;"

(2)   the parent or legal guardian completes on Form I-9 the preparer/translator certification; and

---

[77]IRCA § 274A.(b)(1)(B); 8 C.F.R. § 274a.2(b)(v)(A).

[78]The regulations do not impose any special requirement for Canadian driver's licenses, such as a photograph or other identifying information, which are required for U.S. citizens. 8 C.F.R. § 274a.2(b)(1)(v)(B)(1)(ix).

[79]IRCA § 274A.(b)(1)(D)(i); 8 C.F.R. § 274a.2(b)(1)(v)(B)(1).

[80]IRCA § 274A.(b)(1)(D)(ii); 8 C.F.R. § 274a.2(b)(1)(v)(B)(2).

(3) the employer writes on Section 2 of Form I-9 under the "List B, Identity" column "Minor under age 16."[81]

There are special regulations regarding acceptable documents from handicapped persons who are unable to produce complete documentation.[82]

*c. Documents Establishing Employment Authorization Only.* The following documents establish an individual's employment authorization (Group C Documents):

(1) An individual's social security account number card (other than such a card which specifies on the face that the issuance of the card does not authorize employment in the United States);

(2) An unexpired reentry permit (Form I-327);

(3) An unexpired refugee travel document (Form I-571);

(4) A certificate of birth issued by the Department of State (Form FS-545);

(5) A certificate of birth abroad issued by the Department of State (Form DS-1350);

(6) An original or certified copy of a birth certificate issued by a state, county, or municipal authority bearing a seal;

(7) An employment authorization document issued by the Immigration and Naturalization Service;

(8) Native American tribal document, or United States citizen identification card (Form I-197); or

(9) Identification card for use of resident citizen in the United States (Form I-179).[83]

*d. The Employer's Burden in Reviewing Documentation.* The employer, recruiter, or referrer meets its obligations "if the document reasonably appears on its face to be genuine."[84] The employer or referrer is not obliged to make an ultimate determination that prescribed documents are genuine. The Immigration and Naturalization Service (INS) is expected to establish a program to investigate and respond to inquiries from employers who are presented with questionable documents.[85] If a document seems questionable before such a program is established, employers may consider accepting the document conditionally and sending a certified letter to the local INS office requesting its opinion of the document. It is important that employers establish and apply one standard in reviewing all documents in order to avoid the potential for charges of employment discrimination.

### 4. Recordkeeping and Inspection

*a. Retention of Form I-9.* Employers are required to retain the I-9 forms and make them available for inspection by officers of the INS or the Department of Labor for a minimum of three years after the date of hire, or one year after the date the individual's employment is terminated, whichever occurs later.[86] For example, if an employer employs employee A for seven

---

[81] 8 C.F.R. § 274a.2(b)(1)(v)(B)(3).
[82] *See* 8 C.F.R. § 279a.2(b)(1)(v)(B)(4).
[83] IRCA § 274A.(b)(1)(C); 8 C.F.R. § 274a.2(b)(1)(v)(C).
[84] IRCA § 274A.(b)(1)(A); H.R. Rep. No. 99-682 Part 1, 99th Cong., 2d Sess. 62 (1986).
[85] H.R. Rep. No. 99-682 Part 1, 99th Cong., 2d Sess. 61 (1986).
[86] IRCA § 274A.(b)(3)(B); 8 C.F.R. § 274a.2(b)(2)(i)(A).

months and employee B for five years, the retention period for employee A is three years and the retention period for employee B is six years. The time period for retention of Form I-9 for a rehired employee commences from the date of the initial execution of Form I-9 or one year after termination, whichever is later.[87]

A recruiter or referrer for a fee must retain the documents for three years after the date of the referral.[88]

Employers may but need not supplement their documentary evidence of verification by making and retaining copies of documents presented by individuals to establish either identity or employment authorization.[89] An employer should maintain a uniform policy with respect to such supplementary document retention. Such retained copies should be held separately with Form I-9. The retention requirements do not apply to copies retained by the employer.[90]

*b. Inspection of Form I-9 by the Government.* Officers of the INS and the Department of Labor have authority to inspect I-9 forms.[91] The Regulations provide that the government must give an employer a minimum of three days' advance notice prior to an inspection of the forms.[92] No subpoena or warrant is required for an inspection.[93] However, if the INS chooses to obtain a warrant, it may enter an employer's premises without advance notice.[94] The I-9 forms generally must be made available at the location where the request was made. If the I-9 forms are kept at another location, the documents must be produced at the INS office nearest to the location where the documents are maintained.[95] Refusal or delay in presenting the forms for inspection is a violation of the retention requirements and, in that event, the INS may compel production by issuance of a subpoena.[96]

To ease the burden of producing I-9 forms for INS reviews, and because the forms may contain information reflecting national origin or other data not properly used for employment selections, employers may elect to keep these records in a central location separate from information used in employment determinations.

### 5. Effect of Compliance With Verification and Recordkeeping Requirements

The employer must comply in good faith with the certification and recordkeeping requirements of § 274A.(b). The Act itself also provides that an employer need do no *more* than comply with those requirements in order to comply with the Act:

> "(3) Defense—A person or entity that establishes that it has complied in good faith with the requirements of subsection (b) with respect to the hiring, recruit-

---

[87] 8 C.F.R. § 274a.2(c)(2).
[88] IRCA § 274A.(b)(3)(A); 8 C.F.R. § 274a.2(b)(2)(i)(B).
[89] IRCA § 274A.(b)(4); 8 C.F.R. § 274a.2(b)(3).
[90] 8 C.F.R. § 274a.2(b)(3).
[91] IRCA § 274A.(b)(3).
[92] 8 C.F.R. § 274a.2(b)(2)(ii).
[93] *Id.*
[94] 52 FED. REG. 16219 (1987).
[95] 8 C.F.R. § 274a.2(b)(2)(ii).
[96] *Id.*

ing, or referral for employment of an alien in the United States has established an affirmative defense that the person or entity has not violated paragraph (1)(A) with respect to such hiring, recruiting, or referral."[97]

Notwithstanding the unqualified statutory defense, the regulation which parallels this subsection states that compliance with the verification requirements establishes a *"rebuttable* affirmative defense."[98] The Regulations do not specify what kinds of facts would rebut such a presumption. However, legislative history indicates that to rebut the presumption, the government must prove that:

(1)   The documents did not reasonably appear on their face to be genuine;

(2)   The verification process was pretextual;

(3)   The employer collaborated with the employee in falsifying documents; or

(4)   Other similar circumstances.[99]

## 6. Sanctions

a. *Penalties for Knowingly Hiring, Recruiting, Referring, or Continuing to Employ an Unauthorized Alien.* Upon a finding that an employer knowingly hired, recruited, or referred an unauthorized alien for employment, or knowingly continued to employ an unauthorized alien, the INS or administrative law judge shall order that an employer cease and desist from violations of the Act and shall impose civil penalties for each unauthorized alien in an amount of (1) not less than $250 and not more than $2,000 for a first violation; (2) not less than $2,000 and not more than $5,000 for a second violation; and (3) not less than $3,000 and not more than $10,000 for the third and subsequent violations. In addition, the INS or administrative law judge may require an employer to abide by the verification requirements of the Act with respect to individuals hired and may also direct such other remedial action as is deemed appropriate.[100]

b. *Penalties for Violation of Verification and Recordkeeping Requirements.* Upon finding a violation of the verification and recordkeeping requirements, the INS or administrative law judge shall order civil penalties in an amount of not less than $100 and not more than $1,000 for each individual with respect to whom such violation occurred. In determining the amount of penalty for such violations, consideration is to be given to the size of the business of the employer being charged, the good faith of the employer, the seriousness of the violation, whether or not the individual was an unauthorized alien, and the history of previous violations of the employer.[101]

It is also unlawful for an employer to require individuals to post a bond or security, to pay or agree to pay an amount or otherwise to provide a

---

[97]IRCA § 274A.(a)(3).
[98]8 C.F.R. § 274a.4.
[99]H.R. Rep. No. 99-682, 99th Cong., 2d Sess. 57 (1986).
[100]IRCA § 274A.(e)(4); 8 C.F.R. § 274a.10(b)(1).
[101]IRCA § 274A.(e)(5); 8 C.F.R. § 274a.10(b)(2).

financial guarantee or indemnity against any potential liability arising from the act of hiring, recruiting, or referring an individual. The civil penalty for a violation of this provision is $1,000 for each violation.[102]

## 7. Pattern or Practice of Employment Discrimination

If the Attorney General has reasonable cause to believe that an employer is engaged in a pattern or practice of employment discrimination, the Attorney General may bring a civil action in the appropriate district court of the United States requesting a permanent or temporary injunction, restraining order, or such other order as the Attorney General believes is necessary.[103] In addition, any employer which is found to have engaged in the unlawful pattern or practice of discrimination may be fined not more that $3,000 as a criminal penalty for each unauthorized alien, imprisoned for not more than six months, or both, notwithstanding the provisions of any other federal law relating to fine levels.[104] The term "pattern or practice" is defined as regular, repeated, and intentional activities, but does not include isolated, sporadic, or accidental acts.[105] Criminal penalties cannot be imposed for violations of the verification or recordkeeping requirements.[106]

## 8. Enforcement Procedures

a. Investigation. The Act provides for a separate unit within the INS with the primary duty of prosecuting violations of the Act.[107] The INS will enforce the Act through independent investigations of violations by the INS as well as private complaints filed with the INS.[108]

The regulations set forth specific procedures for individuals and entities to file signed, written complaints alleging violations of the provisions of the Act making employment of unauthorized aliens unlawful.[109] The complaint must contain sufficient information to identify the complainant and the potential violator, including their names and addresses, as well as detailed factual allegations relating to the potential violation, including the date, time, and place the alleged violation occurred and the specific Act or conduct alleged to constitute a violation of the Act. The complaint may be submitted in person or by mail to the INS office having jurisdiction over the business or residence of the potential violator or by personally appearing before any immigration officer at an INS office.[110] Pursuant to the Act, the INS may conduct an investigation of a complaint it receives if the complaint has a "substantial probability of validity."[111]

The INS may conduct investigations for violations on its own initiative

---

[102]IRCA § 274A.(g)(1) and (2); 8 C.F.R. § 274a.8.
[103]IRCA § 274A.(f)(2); 8 C.F.R. § 274a.10(c).
[104]IRCA § 274A.(f)(1); 8 C.F.R. § 274a.10(a).
[105]8 C.F.R. § 274a.1(k).
[106]IRCA § 274A.(f)(1); 8 C.F.R. § 274a.10(a).
[107]IRCA § 274A.(e)(1)(D).
[108]IRCA §§ 274A.(e)(1)(A) and (C); 8 C.F.R. §§ 274a.9(a) and (b).
[109]IRCA § 274A.(e)(1)(A); 8 C.F.R. § 274a.9(a).
[110]8 C.F.R. § 274a.9(a).
[111]IRCA § 274A.(e)(1)(B). However, 8 C.F.R. § 274a.9(b) states that "[W]hen the [INS] receives a complaint from a third party, it shall investigate only those complaints which have 'a reasonable probability' of validity."

without having received a complaint and is authorized to investigate those complaints that have a "substantial probability of validity."[112]

The INS has reasonable access to examine any relevant evidence of any person or entity being investigated.[113] The Act also authorizes the INS to seek subpoenas from administrative law judges for purposes of investigation.[114]

*b. Notice of Intent to Fine.* If it is determined after investigation that the person or entity has violated § 274A of the Act, the Service shall issue and serve the alleged violator with a citation or a notice of intent to fine.[115] The contents of the notice of intent to fine must include: a concise statement of the factual allegations informing the respondent (employer) of the conduct alleged to be in violation of the law, the charges against respondent, the statutory provisions alleged to have been violated, and the penalty that may be imposed.

The notice of intent also must provide the following information to the respondent:

> "(a) that the Respondent has a right to representation by counsel of his or her own choice at no expense to the government;
> (b) that any statement given may be used against Respondent;
> (c) that Respondent has the right to request a hearing before an administrative law judge which must be requested within 30 days from service of the notice of intent to fine; and
> (d) The INS will issue a final order in 45 days if a written request for a hearing is not timely received and there is no appeal of the final order."[116]

Thus, if a respondent desires to contest the issuance of a Notice of Intent to Fine, a respondent must, by mail, serve a written answer responding to each allegation listed in the notice and request a hearing within 30 days from service of the notice. If an answer is not filed within the 30-day period, the INS will issue a final order to which there is no appeal.[117]

The hearing is held before an administrative law judge.[118] Administrative law judges have reasonable access to examine evidence and may compel by issuance of subpoena the attendance of witnesses and the production of evidence at a hearing.[119]

*c. Administrative Hearing.* The hearing shall be conducted in accordance with the requirements of the Administrative Procedure Act.[120] The government has the burden of proving by a preponderance of the evidence that a violation has occurred.[121] In the case of criminal penalties, the burden is "beyond a reasonable doubt."[122] After conclusion of the hearing, the

---

[112]IRCA § 274A.(e)(1)(B).

[113]IRCA § 274A.(e)(2)(A); 8 C.F.R. § 274a.9(b).

[114]IRCA § 274A.(e)(2)(B).

[115]8 C.F.R. § 274a.9(c). This is issued on Form I-762. The citation period is from June 1, 1987 until May 31, 1988, for first-time offenders of the Act. After May 31, 1988, the citation period is over and all offenders will be given notice of intent to fine. *Id.*

[116]8 C.F.R. § 274a.9(c)(1). Although the regulations provide no procedures for informal settlement or conciliation, the INS and the Office of Special Counsel have in practice entered into such agreements.

[117]8 C.F.R. § 274a.9(d).

[118]IRCA § 274A.(e)(3)(B).

[119]IRCA § 274A.(e)(2).

[120]5 U.S.C. § 554 (1982); IRCA § 274A.(e)(3)(B).

[121]IRCA § 274A.(e)(3)(C).

[122]H.R. Rep. No. 99-682 Part 1, 99th Cong., 2d Sess. 57 (1986).

administrative law judge issues an order which will include findings of fact and, if a violation is found, the amount and nature of the penalty.[123]

*d. Appeal of Administrative Order.* An order of an administrative law judge is subject to administrative appellate review and judicial review in the federal courts.[124] With respect to administrative review, the Act simply provides that the decision and order of the administrative law judge shall become the final agency decision, unless within 30 days the Attorney General modifies or vacates the decision and order. Judicial review is available as a matter of right only in a circuit court of appeals. If an employer wishes judicial review of an administrative order, an employer must file a petition for review in a circuit court of appeals within 45 days after the day the final administrative order is issued.[125]

An order of the INS, administrative law judge, or Attorney General is not enforceable against a party that does not voluntarily comply with the order. The Attorney General is required to file suit in an appropriate federal district court to seek compliance with the final order.[126]

## 9. Preemption

The Act expressly preempts all state and local laws imposing civil or criminal sanctions upon those who employ, recruit, or refer for a fee unauthorized aliens.[127] State or local laws imposing civil or criminal sanctions through licensing and similar laws are not preempted.[128]

## B. Section 102—Discrimination

Before passage of the Act, an employee's status as an undocumented alien had little legal significance to an employer, since it was not unlawful to employ such persons.[129] Now the Act *requires* employment discrimination against undocumented aliens seeking employment after November 6, 1986, the effective date of the Act.

## 1. Prohibited Practices

A major concern of many in Congress in considering immigration reform legislation was that the prohibition against hiring unauthorized aliens and the sanctions created by the Act to enforce it may lead to employment discrimination against "foreign looking" or "foreign sounding" persons or against persons who, although not citizens, are legally in the United

---

[123]IRCA § 274A.(e)(3)(C).
[124]IRCA §§ 274A.(e)(6) and (7).
[125]IRCA §§ 274A.(e)(6) and (7).
[126]IRCA § 274A.(e)(8).
[127]IRCA § 274A.(h)(2).
[128]*Id.*
[129]Under the Supreme Court's decision in *Sure-Tan v. NLRB,* 467 U.S. 883, 891, 116 LRRM 2857 (1984), for example, undocumented aliens have been included as employees under the National Labor Relations Act, and it has been an unfair labor practice under § 8(a)(3) of the NLRA to report undocumented employees to the INS in retaliation for their union activity. *Id.* at 895–96. A basic assumption in the Court's decision in *Sure-Tan* was that under the Immigration and Naturalization Act as it existed before IRCA, it was not unlawful for employers to hire illegal aliens. *See supra* notes 23–26 and accompanying text.

States.[130] This led to the inclusion of the Frank Amendment, the Act's antidiscrimination provision, which expressly prohibits discrimination based on national origin or citizenship status. Specifically, § 102 provides:

> "It is an unfair immigration-related employment practice for a person or other entity to discriminate against any individual (other than an unauthorized alien) with respect to the hiring, or recruitment or referral for a fee, of the individual for employment or the discharging of the individual from employment—
> (A) because of such individual's national origin, or
> (B) in the case of a citizen or intending citizen[131] * * * because of such individual's citizenship status."[132]

In *League of United Latin American Citizens v. Pasadena Independent School District,*[133] the district court preliminarily enjoined the school district from discharging any employee who qualified for legalization because he or she had earlier provided a false social security number.[134] The plaintiffs were hired before the enactment of the Immigration Reform and Control Act, while they were illegal aliens, and had provided false social security numbers on their applications. In February 1987, when reviewing new W-4 Withholding Forms, the employer discovered the false information and discharged the plaintiffs pursuant to the employer's established policy that falsifying information on an employment application constituted grounds for termination.

The court reasoned that a policy of terminating undocumented aliens for no other reason than that they have given employers a false social security number constitutes discrimination solely based on citizenship status because plaintiffs, at the time of hiring, were unable to secure valid social security numbers. The court reasoned that if the employer's employment practice was allowed to stand, plaintiffs "would be placed in the unfortunate and untenable position of deciding between prospective citizenship and present employment. In order to qualify for legalization, they must come forward and reveal their past misdeeds, misstatements, and falsifications. Once made, these revelations will automatically result in the termination of many qualified aliens now working with [the employer]." The court concluded that such a request would render the Act ineffectual. Accordingly, the court concluded that there is a substantial likelihood that plaintiffs will prevail on their claim that the employer violated the antidiscrimination provisions of the Act. The court ordered reinstatement and, upon issuance of a permanent injunction, back pay.

---

[130]Joint Explanatory Statement of the Committee of Conference, H.R. Rep. No. 1000, 99th Cong. 2d Sess. (1986); 53 FED. REG. 37402 (1987).

[131]The term "intending citizen" generally is defined as aliens who are lawfully admitted and who complete a Declaration of Intention to Become a Citizen. An alien must meet the definition of "intending citizen" at the time of the alleged discriminatory acts. IRCA § 274B.(a)(3)(B); 28 C.F.R. § 44.101(c).

[132]IRCA § 274B.(a)(1). Note that the Act applies only to hiring or discharging or recruitment or referral for a fee. It does not apply to wages, promotions, employee benefits, or other terms or conditions of employment.

[133]662 F. Supp. 443, 43 FEP 945 (S.D. Tex. 1987).

[134]Since the administrative structure had not been established under the Act at the time of this lawsuit, the court took jurisdiction without exhaustion of administrative remedies. *Id.* at 446, 43 FEP at 948.

## 2. Exceptions

*a. Covered Employers.* Section 102 does not apply to an employer that employs three or fewer employees.[135] An entity's number of employees is calculated as of the date of the alleged discrimination and includes part-time and full-time employees.[136]

*b. Preference for Equally Qualified U.S. Citizens.* It is not an unfair immigration-related employment practice for an employer to prefer to hire, recruit, or refer an individual who is a citizen or a national of the United States over another individual who is an alien if the two individuals are equally qualified.[137] However, the EEOC cautions employers to be aware that such citizenship preferences may still violate Title VII, if they have the purpose or effect of discriminating on the basis of national origin.[138]

*c. Exception Pertaining to National Origin Discrimination Covered Under Title VII.* Under the Act, the EEOC has exclusive jurisdiction of any case in which an individual alleges national origin discrimination and the employer is covered under § 703 of the Civil Rights Act of 1964 (National Origin).[139] In general, Title VII coverage extends to employers whose work force reaches 15 or more employees in each of 20 or more weeks during a 12-month period.[140] The definition of a covered "person or other entity" under §§ 274(B)(a)(1) and (2) of the Act is more broad than the definition of "employer" under Title VII and contains, for example, no exclusion for "a bona fide private membership club."[141] Thus, employers of four or more employees who are not covered by Title VII are covered by the prohibitions against national origin discrimination contained in the Act.[142]

*d. Exceptions Pertaining to Certain Citizenship Discrimination.* An employer may hire only citizens or otherwise make hiring decisions based on citizenship status if required to do so by law, regulation, or executive order;[143] may discriminate if required by a contract with the federal, state, or local government;[144] and may also hire only citizens if the Attorney General

---

[135]IRCA § 274B.(a)(2)(A); 28 C.F.R. § 44.200.(b)(1)(i).

[136]52 FED. REG. 37402 (1987).

[137]IRCA § 274B(a)(4); 28 C.F.R. § 44.200(b)(2).

[138]EEOC policy statement on the relationship of Title VII to the Act, reprinted in full at Lab. Rel. Rep., Fair Employment Practices Manual (BNA) 401:445 (1987).

[139]IRCA § 274B.(a)(2)(B); 28 C.F.R. § 44.200(b)(1)(ii).

[140]42 U.S.C. §2000e(b) (1964). For a more thorough discussion of Title VII coverage, *see* Chapter 27 (Title VII Coverage).

[141]*Compare* 8 C.F.R. § 274A.(1)(b) *with* 42 U.S.C. § 2000e(b) (1964).

[142]The EEOC has reaffirmed that the Immigration Reform and Control Act left intact the prohibitions of Title VII against employment discrimination based on national origin, and has warned that "[e]mployers should not mistakenly conclude either that they can avoid problems under the Immigration Act by ceasing to employ individuals of a particular national origin, or that the Act in any way sanctions less than full equal opportunity for employees of all ethnic backgrounds." *EEOC Policy Statement,* "Relationship of the Civil Rights Act to the Immigration Reform and Control Act of 1986," adopted February 26, 1987. The Policy Statement reviews several employment practices which in the EEOC's view raise special risks of national origin discrimination including, *e.g.,* employer policies on accents, speak-English-only rules, English fluency requirements, and citizenship requirements or preferences. The Policy Statement essentially restates long-standing EEOC policy on national origin discrimination in these and other covered areas, and should be consulted on points of specific interest.

[143]IRCA § 274B.(a)(2)(C); 28 C.F.R. § 44.200(b)(1)(iii)(A).

[144]IRCA § 274B.(a)(2)(C); 28 C.F.R. § 44.200(b)(1)(iii)(B).

determines it to be essential for the employer to do business with an agency or department of the federal, state, or local government.[145] However, the Regulations provide no guidelines defining what constitutes "essential" discrimination.

### 3. Standard of Proof

While the language of the Act suggests that both disparate treatment and disparate impact theories of liability apply to IRCA, the Reagan Administration and the Office of the Special Counsel took the position that the Act only prohibits intentional discrimination.[146] The Office of the Special Counsel asserted that discriminatory intent may be proved by both direct and circumstantial evidence, and the Act prohibits facially neutral policies which are intended to discriminate on prohibited bases and have that effect. The preamble to the Regulations specifically states that the appropriate models of proof[147] for claims of unlawful discrimination under the Act are *McDonnell Douglas Corp. v. Green*[148] and *Texas Department of Community Affairs v. Burdine.*[149]

### 4. EEOC Charge Pending

The Special Counsel and the EEOC cannot simultaneously entertain a charge based on the same set of facts. Thus, no charge may be filed alleging an unfair immigration-related employment practice if a charge with respect to that practice based on the same set of facts has been filed with the EEOC under Title VII of the Civil Rights Act of 1964, unless the charge is dismissed as being outside the scope of Title VII. Similarly, no charge alleging an unfair employment practice may be filed with the EEOC if a charge based on the same set of facts has been filed with the Special Counsel, unless the charge is dismissed as being outside the scope of § 102.[150] The preface to the final rules indicates that the Office of the Special Counsel will refer to the EEOC charges of national origin discrimination which it determines are covered by § 703 of Title VII.[151]

### 5. Antiretaliation Provisions

Although the Act does not provide for sanctions against those who engage in intimidation or retaliation against persons seeking to exercise their rights under the Act, the Regulations contain such a prohibition. Specifically, the Regulations provide that no person or entity covered by the unfair immigration-related employment practice legislation shall "intimidate, threaten, coerce or retaliate against any individual for the purpose of interfer-

---

[145] IRCA § 274B.(a)(2)(C); 28 C.F.R. § 44.200(b)(1)(iii)(C).
[146] 52 FED. REG. at 37404.
[147] *Id.* For a discussion of the Title VII disparate treatment standard of proof, *see* Chapter 2 (Disparate Treatment).
[148] 411 U.S. 792, 5 FEP 965 (1973).
[149] 450 U.S. 248, 25 FEP 113 (1981).
[150] IRCA § 274B.(b)(2); 28 C.F.R. § 44.300(d).
[151] 52 FED. REG. at 37402. The Office of Special Counsel indicates that it will make determinations concerning number of employees and calendar weeks to determine whether the charge should be filed with the EEOC instead of the special counsel.

ing with any right or privilege secured under [this section of the Act] or because he or she intends to file or has filed a charge or a complaint, testified, assisted, or participated in any manner in an investigation, proceeding, or hearing * * * ."[152]

### 6. Compliance

The Act creates a new claim for "Immigration-Related Unfair Employment Practices," and creates a "Special Counsel" in the Department of Justice to receive and process such claims.[153] The Special Counsel serves a term of four years. The Special Counsel will establish regional offices which will be staffed to investigate charges and issue and prosecute complaints before administrative law judges.[154]

*a. Procedure.* Charges may be filed with the Special Counsel either by individuals personally, by a person on another person's behalf, or by an officer of the INS alleging that an unfair immigration-related employment practice has occurred.[155] The charge may be filed by mail or hand delivery with the Office of the Special Counsel.[156]

*b. Content of Charge.* Charges must be written and sworn and must contain the following information:

(1) The charging party's[157] name, address, and telephone number;

(2) If different, the injured party's[158] name, address, and telephone number;

(3) The name and address of the person or entity against whom the charge is being made;

(4) A statement sufficient to describe the circumstances, place, and date of the alleged unfair immigration-related employment practice;

(5) A statement whether the charge alleges discrimination based on national origin, citizenship status, or both;

(6) A statement whether the injured party is a U.S. citizen, U.S. national, or alien authorized to work in the United States;

(7) If the injured party is an alien authorized to work, a statement whether the injured party

(a) Has been:

(i) Lawfully admitted for permanent residence;

(ii) Granted the status of an alien lawfully admitted for temporary residence under 8 U.S.C. § 1255a(a)(1);

(iii) Admitted as a refugee under 8 U.S.C. § 1157; or

(iv) Granted asylum under 8 U.S.C. § 1158; and

---

[152] 28 C.F.R. § 44.201.
[153] IRCA § 274B.(c)(1).
[154] IRCA §§ 274B.(c)(2) and (4); 28 C.F.R. § 44.305.
[155] IRCA § 274B.(b)(1); 28 C.F.R. §§ 44.300(a)(1) and (2).
[156] The mailing address is: Office of the Special Counsel for Immigration-Related Unfair Employment Practices, P.O. Box 65490, Washington, D.C. 20035-5490; The address for hand-delivered charges is: 1100 Connecticut Avenue, N.W., Suite 800, Washington, D.C. 20036. 28 C.F.R. § 44.300(c).
[157] The charging party is the individual who files a charge, or who is authorized by an individual to file a charge on an individual's behalf, or an INS officer who files a charge. 28 C.F.R. § 44.101(b).
[158] Injured party means a person who claims or is alleged to have been adversely affected directly by an unfair immigration-related employment practice. 28 C.F.R. § 44.101(e).

(b) Has completed a Declaration of Intention to become a citizen (INS Form N-315, "Declaration of Intention"; or INS Form I-772, "Declaration of Intending Citizen") and, if so, indicates the date of the declaration; and

(c) Has applied for naturalization, and, if so, indicates the date of the application;

(8) If the injured party is an alien authorized to work, the identification of the injured party's alien registration number and date of birth;

(9) A statement, if possible, of the number of persons employed on the date of the alleged discrimination by the person or entity against whom the charge is being made;

(10) A signature by the charging party and, if the charging party is neither the injured party nor an officer of the INS, a statement that the charging party has the authorization of the injured party to file the charge;

(11) A statement whether a charge based on the same set of facts has been filed with the EEOC, and, if so, the specific office and contact person (if known); and

(12) Authorization for the Special Counsel to reveal the identity of the injured or charging party when necessary to carry out the purposes of this section of the Act.[159]

c. *Service of Charge.* Notice of the charge will be served to the respondent by the Special Counsel by certified mail within 10 days of its receipt. The notice of the charge must include the date, place, and circumstances of the alleged unfair immigration-related employment practice.[160] The charging party will also receive a notice from the special counsel specifying the date on which the charge was received, advising the party that he or she has the right to file a complaint with an administrative law judge if the special counsel does not do so within 120 days of receipt of the charge, and stating the last date a complaint may be filed.[161]

d. *Improper Filing.* The Special Counsel may, in its discretion, deem a charging party's submission that fails to contain all of the required information sufficient to constitute a filed charge as of the date of receipt and obtain the remainder of the information during the investigation.[162] If the charging party's submission as filed is deficient and is deemed by the Special Counsel inadequate to constitute a charge, the Special Counsel shall notify the charging party that specific additional information is needed. The charge is deemed filed by the Special Counsel as of the date of receipt of the adequate information.[163]

e. *Statute of Limitations.* An aggrieved party must file a charge with the Special Counsel within 180 days of the occurrence of the unfair immigration-related employment practice. If a charge is mailed, it is deemed filed on the date it is postmarked.[164] A charge filed after that time will be dismissed with prejudice by the Special Counsel.[165] If a deficient charge is filed and is deemed

---

[159]IRCA § 274B.(b)(1); 28 C.F.R. § 44.101(a).
[160]IRCA § 274B.(b)(1); 28 C.F.R. § 44.301(e).
[161]28 C.F.R. §§ 44.301(a) and (b).
[162]28 C.F.R. § 44.301(c)(2).
[163]28 C.F.R. § 44.301(c)(1).
[164]IRCA § 274B.(d)(3); 28 C.F.R. § 44.300(b).
[165]28 C.F.R. § 44.301(d)(1).

an inadequate submission by the Special Counsel, such charge will be considered timely filed so long as the original charge is filed within the 180-day period and any additional information requested by the Special Counsel is provided in writing to the Special Counsel within the 180-day period or within 45 days of the date on which the charging party received the Special Counsel's request for additional information, whichever is later.[166]

*f. Tolling of the Statute of Limitations.* The issue of whether the statute of limitations is tolled under any given circumstances was not addressed in the Act, regulations, or legislative history. It remains to be seen whether tolling will be applied.[167]

### 7. Enforcement

*a. Investigation and Determination.* The Special Counsel may propound interrogatories, requests for production of documents, and requests for admissions.[168] Under § 274B(f) the Special Counsel also has authority to obtain "reasonable access to examine evidence of any person or entity being investigated," and under accompanying regulations, this includes access to the books, records, and accounts. The Regulations require that the respondent permit access by the Special Counsel during normal business hours to such sources of information as the special counsel decides are pertinent.[169] The respondent has no right of discovery during the investigative stage but may be entitled to discovery once the complaint is filed with the administrative law judge.[170]

The Special Counsel shall investigate each charge within 120 days of its receipt, and shall determine whether there is "reasonable cause" to believe the charge is true and whether a complaint will be brought before an administrative law judge.[171] When the Special Counsel deems charges deficient, and the charges are supplemented by the charging party, the 120-day investigation period commences when the Special Counsel receives the supplemental information.[172]

Within the 120-day period, the Special Counsel may issue a Letter of Determination notifying the charging party and respondent of the Special Counsel's determination that there is no reasonable cause to believe that the charge is true and that no complaint will be filed with an administrative law judge.[173] In that event, the charging party (other than an INS officer) may, within 90 days after the end of the 120-day period, file a complaint with an administrative law judge.[174]

If the Special Counsel does not issue a Letter of Determination within

---

[166]28 C.F.R. § 44.301(d)(2).

[167]The statutory time period for filing charges under Title VII has been held to be subject to equitable tolling. *See* Zipes v. Trans World Airlines, 455 U.S. 385, 28 FEP 1 (1982). For a more thorough discussion under Title VII, *see* Chapter 28 (Timeliness).

[168]28 C.F.R. § 44.302(a).

[169]28 C.F.R. § 44.302(b). The special counsel relies on 8 U.S.C. § 1324b(f)(2), which gives the special counsel reasonable access to examine the evidence of any person or entity being investigated.

[170]52 FED. REG. at 37408.

[171]IRCA § 274B.(d); 28 C.F.R. § 44.303(a). Attempts at informal resolution, if appropriate, should be made within this 120-day period. *See supra* note 108.

[172]28 C.F.R. § 44.301(c)(1).

[173]28 C.F.R. § 44.303(b).

[174]28 C.F.R. § 44.303(c)(2).

the 120-day period and fails to bring a complaint before an administrative law judge within 120 days of receipt of the charge, the charging party (other than an INS officer) may, within 90 days after the end of the 120-day period, file a complaint directly before an administrative law judge.[175] The Special Counsel may also, at any time within 90 days after the end of the 120-day period, file a complaint with an administrative law judge, provided the charging party has not yet done so. The Special Counsel may also seek to intervene in any proceeding before an administrative law judge brought by the charging party.[176]

The Special Counsel is authorized, "on his own initiative," to "conduct investigations respecting unfair immigration-related employment practices," and the "reasonable access" provision of § 274B(f) applies to such independent investigations. Based on such an investigation, the Special Counsel may file a complaint before an administrative law judge.[177]

*b. Hearings.* Both parties have a right to a hearing before an administrative law judge.[178] The process before the administrative law judge begins by service of the complaint on the respondent accompanied by a notice giving the time and place of the hearing. The hearing may not be held sooner than five days after the complaint is served.[179] Complaints may be amended by the administrative law judge conducting the hearing, or, upon motion of the party filing the complaint, any time prior to the issuance of an order.[180] A complaint is defined as a written submission "based on the same set of facts as in the charge filed with the Special Counsel."[181] It is unclear whether a hearing will be limited to only those events included in the charge filed with the Special Counsel.[182] The respondent has the right to file an answer to the complaint and to any amendments to the complaint.[183]

The Special Counsel (or the complainant in a private case) must prove his or her case by a "preponderance of the evidence."[184] The administrative law judge may receive evidence and hear testimony.[185] Like the Special Counsel, the administrative law judge shall have "reasonable access to examine evidence of any person or entity being investigated."[186] The administrative law judge also has the right to issue subpoenas to require that witnesses attend the hearing and that documents be produced. Compliance with such a subpoena may be enforced upon application of the administrative law judge to a U.S. District Court. Failure to obey the order of that court may constitute contempt.[187]

---

[175]IRCA § 274B.(d)(2); 28 C.F.R. § 44.303(c)(1).
[176]28 C.F.R. § 44.303(d).
[177]IRCA § 274B.(d)(1); 28 C.F.R. §§ 44.304(a) and (b).
[178]IRCA § 274B.(e)(1).
[179]*Id.*
[180]IRCA § 274B.(e)(1).
[181]28 C.F.R. § 44.101(d).
[182]This issue has been litigated in Title VII lawsuits. *See* Chapter 30 (Litigation Procedure).
[183]IRCA § 274B.(e)(1).
[184]IRCA § 274B.(g)(2)(A).
[185]IRCA § 274B.(f)(1).
[186]IRCA § 274B.(f).
[187]IRCA § 274B.(f)(2).

Detailed rules and regulations governing the hearing procedure will be issued by the Executive Office of Immigration Review.

c. *Decision of the Administrative Law Judge.* (1) *Generally.* The Act requires an administrative law judge to issue and serve an order which will be final unless appealed.[188] The order must state the facts of the case as determined by the administrative law judge based on the evidence presented at the hearing.[189]

If the administrative law judge finds in favor of the respondent, the administrative law judge will issue an order dismissing the complaint.[190]

(2) *Remedies.* (i) *In general.* If the administrative law judge finds that discrimination has occurred, the order will contain a cease-and-desist order and may contain one or more of the following:

(a) That the respondent comply with the employer verification obligations for up to three years;

(b) That the respondent retain for a period of three years the name and address of each person who applies for hiring for an existing position, or applies for recruiting, or referring for a fee, for employment in the United States;

(c) An award of reinstatement;

(d) That the respondent hire individuals directly and adversely affected by the discrimination with or without back pay; and/or

(e) That the respondent pay a civil penalty of not more than $1,000 for each individual discriminated against for a first offender and not more than $2,000 for each individual discriminated against for repeat offenders.[191]

(ii) *Limitation on back pay and hiring.* An administrative law judge may only order back pay from a date not more than two years prior to the date "of the filing of a charge with an administrative law judge"[192] (but no earlier than the effective date of the Act on November 6, 1986). The Act provides for mitigation of damages by amounts which could have been earned "with reasonable diligence." If an individual was refused employment for any reason other than discrimination based on national origin or citizenship status, an administrative law judge is not permitted to order that the person be hired or that he receive back pay.[193]

(iii) *Award of attorneys' fees.* An administrative law judge, in his discretion, may award reasonable attorneys' fees to a prevailing party other than the Government if the losing party's argument was "without reasonable foundation in law and fact."[194]

(3) *Judicial Review of an Administrative Law Judge Order.* Any person, including the Special Counsel, may appeal an administrative law judge's order to a court of appeals in the circuit in which the violation occurred or in which the employer resides or transacts business.[195] The notice of appeal

---

[188] IRCA § 274B.(g)(1).
[189] *Id.*
[190] IRCA § 274B.(g)(3).
[191] IRCA § 274B.(g)(2)(B).
[192] IRCA § 274B.(g)(2)(C).
[193] *Id.*
[194] IRCA § 274B.(h).
[195] IRCA § 274B.(i)(1).

must be filed within 60 days after the entry of the administrative law judge's order.[196] The jurisdiction of the court of appeals is exclusive and its judgment final, subject only to review by the Supreme Court upon a writ of certiorari or certification.[197]

If the court of appeals does not reverse the order, it may make and enter a decree enforcing it.[198] The court of appeals may award reasonable attorneys' fees to a prevailing party as a part of the costs of the action. The same standard applies for an award of attorneys' fees in the court of appeals as before the administrative law judge; an award is available only if the losing party's argument is "without reasonable foundation in law and fact."[199]

If an employer does not appeal an administrative law judge's order and fails to comply with the order, the special counsel or, if special counsel fails to act, the person filing the charge, may file a petition with the federal district court seeking enforcement in the district in which the violation occurred or in which the respondent resides or transacts business.[200] In an enforcement proceeding the merits of the administrative law judge's order are not subject to review.[201]

## C. Sunset Provisions

Section 101 of the Act requires the General Accounting Office (GAO) to submit to Congress three annual reports regarding, among other things, whether a pattern of employment discrimination has resulted against citizens or nationals of the United States or against eligible workers seeking employment from the Act's employer sanctions.[202] The Act further specifies that the employer sanctions shall cease 30 days after receipt of the last annual report, if: (1) GAO has reported that a widespread pattern of discrimination has resulted solely from the employer sanctions; and (2) there is enacted within such 30-day period a joint resolution stating that Congress approves the finding of the GAO report.[203]

---

[196]*Id.*
[197]IRCA § 274B.(i)(2).
[198]IRCA § 274B.(j)(3).
[199]IRCA § 274B.(j)(4).
[200]IRCA § 274B.(j)(1).
[201]IRCA § 274B.(j)(2).
[202]IRCA § 274A.(j).
[203]IRCA § 274B.(k).

## CHAPTER 11

# NATIVE AMERICANS

## II. SECTION 701(B) EXEMPTION FOR NATIVE AMERICANS

The Tenth Circuit has held that a nonprofit corporation whose membership is limited to Indian tribes is covered by the exclusion of "an Indian tribe" from the term "employer" within § 701(b).[1] The court held that the purposes of the Council of Energy Resource Tribes to manage the members' tribal energy resources reflect "precisely the type of activity that Congress sought to encourage by exempting Indian tribes" from Title VII.[2]

The decision in *Wardle v. Ute Indian Tribe*[3] holding that the § 701(b) exemption controls over more general civil rights statutes continues to be followed.[4]

## III. SECTION 703(I) EXEMPTION FOR NATIVE AMERICANS

A corporate employer was held exempt from Title VII under § 703(i) where the employer is 51 percent owned by the Sioux Indian Tribe, is located on the Devils Lake Sioux Indian Reservation in North Dakota, and maintains within the meaning of § 703(i) a "publicly announced employment practice * * * under which a preferential treatment is given to any individual because he is an Indian living on or near a reservation."[5]

The Title VII exemption for Indian preferences echoes preferences in other statutes. For example, the preference provisions of the Indian Preference Act apply to layoffs as well as hiring situations within the Bureau of Indian Affairs and the Indian Health Service.[6]

---

[1]Dille v. Council of Energy Resources Tribes, 801 F.2d 373, 41 FEP 1345 (10th Cir. 1986), *aff'g* 610 F. Supp 157, 39 FEP 1007 (D. Colo. 1985) (affirming dismissal of sex discrimination charges by five white female plaintiffs; defendant Council was composed of 39 exempt tribes and was formed to advance economic conditions of its members through energy resource management; Council's decisions are made by designated representatives of tribes).

[2]*Id.,* 41 FEP at 1346.

[3]623 F.2d 670, 23 FEP 35 (10th Cir. 1980).

[4]Stroud v. Seminole Tribe of Fla., 606 F. Supp. 678 (S.D. Fla. 1985) (Title VII express exemption for Indian tribes controls over 41 U.S.C. § 1981 broad civil rights provisions).

[5]Little v. Devils Lake Sioux Mfg. Corp., 607 F. Supp 700, 37 FEP 1282 (D.N.D. 1985) (discharged white female alleged she had been denied internal grievance conference regularly granted to native American employees; quoted language is from § 703(i), cited by the court).

[6]Preston v. Heckler, 734 F.2d 1359 n.15 (9th Cir. 1984) (court applied Indian Preference Act to require adoption of special standards apart from civil service requirements for evaluating Indians for employment in Indian Health Service; court also recognized that Congress enacted 25 U.S.C. § 472(a) to require Indian preference during layoffs of Bureau of Indian Affairs employees).

CHAPTER 12

# SEX

## MAJOR DEVELOPMENTS

In the years since publication of the Second Edition, courts have addressed major issues regarding sex discrimination in employment and the rights of women in the workplace.[1] The Supreme Court has upheld a state law requiring employers to provide pregnancy leave and qualified reinstatement rights to female employees disabled by pregnancy,[2] affirmed that sexual harassment constitutes sex discrimination,[3] prohibited sex discrimination in consideration for admission to professional partnerships,[4] and required equality in pay-outs from retirement plans.[5]

In *California Federal Savings & Loan Association v. Guerra,*[6] a divided Supreme Court held that Title VII does not preempt a California statute that requires employers to provide up to four months unpaid leave to female employees disabled by pregnancy, childbirth, or related medical conditions.[7]

The Court's majority of six Justices produced three opinions. Justice Marshall's opinion[8] offered two bases for the Court's conclusion that the California statute is not preempted by Title VII. First, the Court rejected the view that in passing the PDA, Congress intended to prohibit employment practices that favor pregnant employees. The Court specifically endorsed the Ninth Circuit's conclusion that "Congress intended the PDA to be 'a floor beneath which pregnancy disability benefits may not drop—not a ceiling above which they may not rise.' "[9] The Court noted that the California

---

[1] Significant decisions involving disparate treatment and adverse impact analysis, equal pay, and affirmative action are covered in other parts of this Supplement. *See, e.g.,* Chapters 2 (Disparate Treatment), 6 (Subjective Criteria), 3 (Equal Pay), and 24 (Reverse Discrimination and Affirmative Action).

[2] California Fed. Sav. & Loan Ass'n v. Guerra, 479 U.S. 272, 42 FEP 1073 (1987), *aff'g* 758 F.2d 390, 37 FEP 849 (9th Cir. 1985).

[3] Meritor Sav. Bank v. Vinson, 477 U.S. 57, 40 FEP 1822 (1986), *aff'g in part and remanding sub nom.* Vinson v. Taylor, 753 F.2d 141, 36 FEP 1423 (D.C. Cir. 1985).

[4] Price Waterhouse v. Hopkins, 57 USLW 4469, 49 FEP 954 (1989); Hishon v. King & Spalding, 467 U.S. 69, 34 FEP 1406 (1984), *rev'g and remanding* 678 F.2d 1022, 29 FEP 51 (11th Cir. 1982). *See* Chapter 1 (Overview).

[5] Arizona Governing Comm. v. Norris, 463 U.S. 1073, 32 FEP 233 (1983), *aff'g in part and rev'g in part* 671 F.2d 330, 28 FEP 369 (9th Cir. 1982).

[6] *Supra* note 2.

[7] 42 U.S.C. § 2000e(k). The California Department of Fair Employment and Housing had applied the state statute and accompanying regulations to require reinstatement to the employee's previous job, unless that job were no longer available due to business necessity and, in that case, to require that the employer make a reasonable, good-faith effort to place the employee in a substantially similar job. California Federal Savings & Loan and several employer groups challenged the California statute and its application as mandating preferential treatment of women disabled by pregnancy compared with other disabled employees, contrary to a standard of equal treatment argued to be contained in the Pregnancy Discrimination Act of 1978 (the PDA). On those grounds, California Federal argued that the California statute was preempted by Title VII as amended by the PDA.

[8] For himself and Justices Brennan, Blackmun, O'Connor, and, except as to the Title VII preemption analysis, Justice Stevens. *See* text, *infra.*

[9] 42 FEP at 1079 (quoting 758 F.2d at 396, 37 FEP at 852).

statute is "narrowly drawn to cover only the period of *actual physical disability* on account of pregnancy, childbirth, or related medical conditions,"[10] and thus, "unlike the protective labor legislation prevalent earlier in this century," does not reflect "archaic or stereotypical notions about pregnancy and the abilities of pregnant workers."[11] Moreover, the Court concluded that the California statute promotes rather than conflicts with the Title VII goal of achieving equality of employment opportunity: by " 'taking pregnancy into account,' California's pregnancy disability leave statute allows women, as well as men, to have families without losing their jobs."[12]

Second, the Court added that even if the PDA prohibited preferential treatment, the California statute would not be preempted because it does not *require* preferential treatment and therefore does not conflict with Title VII.[13] Reasoning that employers are free to extend the same benefits to employees disabled for other reasons, the Court concluded that compliance with both Title VII and the California statute is not "a physical impossibility" and that the California statute therefore does not compel an employer to violate Title VII.

Justice Stevens declined to join in the portion of Justice Marshall's opinion which generally reviewed the preemptive provisions of § 708 and § 1104 of Title VII,[14] but formed a five Justice majority—with Justices Marshall, Brennan, Blackmun, and O'Connor—on the remainder of Justice Marshall's opinion. Viewing the PDA "as part of Title VII," Justice Stevens rejected Justice White's dissenting argument that the "PDA mandates complete neutrality and forbids all beneficial treatment of pregnancy."[15] Likening the Court's rationale and the underlying evidence in *California Federal* to *Steelworkers v. Weber,*[16] Justice Stevens followed what he characterized as the Court's distinction in *Weber* "between discrimination *against* members of the protected class and special preferences *in favor of* members of that class," and on that basis concluded "that Justice Marshall's view, which holds that the PDA allows some preferential treatment of pregnancy, is more consistent with our interpretation of Title VII than Justice White's view is."[17] Qualifying this conclusion, Justice Stevens noted that "this is not to say, however, that all preferential treatment of pregnancy is automatically beyond the scope of the PDA"[18] and reaffirmed that "preferential treatment of the disadvantaged class is only permissible so long as it is consistent with 'accomplish[ing] the goal that Congress designated Title VII to achieve,' "[19] which is "seeking 'to achieve equality of employment opportunities and to remove barriers that have operated in the past to favor an identifiable group of * * * employees over other employees.' "[20]

---

[10]*Id.,* 42 FEP at 1081.
[11]*Id.*
[12]*Id.*
[13]*Id.*
[14]42 U.S.C. §§ 2000e-7 and 2000h-4.
[15]42 FEP at 1082.
[16]443 U.S. 193, 20 FEP 1 (1979). *See* p. 820 of the Second Edition.
[17]*Supra* note 2, 42 FEP at 1082.
[18]*Id.*
[19]*Id.,* 42 FEP at 1083 (quoting Steelworkers v. Weber, *supra* note 16, at 204, 20 FEP at 6).
[20]*Id.* (quoting Griggs v. Duke Power Co., 401 U.S. 424, 429–30, 3 FEP 175, 177 (1971)).

Justice Scalia concurred in the Court's judgment, on the ground that the California statute was not preempted by Title VII, "since it does not remotely purport to require or permit any refusal to accord federally mandated equal treatment to others similarly situated."[21]

Justice White, in dissent, joined by the Chief Justice and Justice Powell, contended that the plain meaning of the PDA "leaves no room for preferential treatment of pregnant workers."[22] He rejected the majority's view that Congress intended to permit preferential treatment and thereby to "put pregnancy in a class by itself within Title VII,"[23] and dismissed as "untenable" the majority's alternative conclusion that even if the PDA prohibits preferential treatment, an employer can still comply with both California law and Title VII. According to Justice White, "California surely had no intent to require employers to provide general disability leave benefits. It intended to prefer pregnancy and went no farther. Extension of these benefits to the entire work force would be a dramatic increase in the scope of the state law and would impose a significantly greater burden on California employers. That is the province of the California Legislature."[24] Thus, he would have found the California statute preempted by Title VII.

In its first decision concerning sexual harassment, the Supreme Court in *Meritor Savings Bank v. Vinson*[25] unanimously ruled that a Title VII violation may be premised on a claim of "hostile environment" without regard to whether the plaintiff suffered tangible job detriment as a result of the harassment. In adopting the "hostile environment" theory, the Court expressly rejected the defendants' position that Title VII is limited to "economic" or "tangible" discrimination, and instead endorsed the EEOC Guidelines and prior court decisions holding "that a plaintiff may establish a violation of Title VII by proving that discrimination based on sex has created a hostile or abusive work environment."[26] Actionable harassment "must be sufficiently severe or pervasive 'to alter the conditions of [the victim's] employment and create an abusive working environment.' "[27] Because the district court ruled for the defendants without considering the "hostile environment" theory, the case was remanded.

The Court rejected the district court's conclusion that the plaintiff was not a victim of sexual harassment because her intimate relationship with her supervisor was voluntary.[28] According to the Supreme Court, "the fact that sex-related conduct was 'voluntary,' in the sense that the complainant was not forced to participate against her will, is not a defense to a sexual harassment suit brought under Title VII. The gravamen of any sexual harassment claim is that the alleged sexual advances were 'unwelcome.' "[29] The "correct

---

[21]*Id.*

[22]*Id.*, 42 FEP at 1084 (White, J., dissenting).

[23]*Id.*, 42 FEP at 1084.

[24]*Id.*, 42 FEP at 1086.

[25]477 U.S. 57, 40 FEP 1822 (1986), *aff'g in part and remanding sub nom.* Vinson v. Taylor, 753 F.2d 141, 36 FEP 1423 (D.C. Cir. 1985).

[26]*Id.*, 40 FEP at 1827.

[27]*Id.* (quoting Henson v. City of Dundee, 682 F.2d 897, 904, 29 FEP 787, 793 (11th Cir. 1982)).

[28]Vinson v. Taylor, 23 FEP 37, 42 (D.D.C. 1980).

[29]40 FEP at 1827.

inquiry," said the Court, "is whether [the victim] by her conduct indicated that the alleged sexual advances were unwelcome, not whether her actual participation in sexual intercourse was voluntary."[30] In addition, the Court held that there is no *per se* rule against admitting testimony regarding the plaintiff's provocative dress and publicly expressed sexual fantasies, because "such evidence is obviously relevant" to the issue of whether the alleged sexual advances were unwelcome.[31]

The Court divided on the question whether an employer is strictly liable for sexual harassment by its supervisors. Although federal courts apply strict liability in Title VII cases where sexual harassment is directly linked to the grant or denial of an economic quid pro quo, in "hostile environment" cases most courts have held that the employer is not liable in the absence of actual or constructive notice of the supervisor's conduct.[32] The District of Columbia Circuit in *Vinson,* however, had held that Title VII imposes absolute liability in all cases of sexual harassment.[33] The Supreme Court majority rejected both rules. Citing the Restatement of Agency,[34] the majority held that while employers are not "always automatically liable for sexual harassment by their supervisors," lack of notice does not necessarily insulate employers from liability.[35]

In addition to claiming insufficient notice, the employer in *Vinson* sought insulation from liability because it had adopted a policy against discrimination and had a grievance procedure which the plaintiff did not use. The majority rejected that defense based on the facts of this case, but commented that such an argument "might be substantially stronger" if the employer had a specific policy proscribing sexual harassment and a grievance procedure "better calculated to encourage victims of harassment to come forward."[36] The concurring Justices, on the other hand, concluded that employer policies and procedures might be relevant to issues such as whether to award back pay, but are irrelevant to the underlying issue of employer liability.[37]

In *Hishon v. King & Spalding,* [38] a unanimous Supreme Court held that a female associate may bring a sex discrimination action under Title VII against a law firm which allegedly discriminated against her on the basis of sex in consideration of her for partnership. The female associate alleged that

---

[30]*Id.*

[31]*Id.,* 40 FEP at 1827, 1828. The Court relied on the EEOC Guidelines to the effect that the trier of fact must determine the existence of the harassment in light of "the record as a whole" and "the totality of circumstances, such as the nature of the sexual advances and the context in which the alleged incidents occurred." 29 C.F.R. § 1604.11(b) (1985).

[32]*See* cases cited in notes 184 and 186, *infra.*

[33]Vinson v. Taylor, 753 F.2d 141, 36 FEP 1423, *reh'g denied en banc,* 760 F.2d 1330, 37 FEP 1266 (D.C. Cir. 1985).

[34]Restatement (Second) of Agency §§ 219–37 (1958).

[35]40 FEP at 1829. Four Justices, concurring in the judgment, endorsed the EEOC Guidelines which provide that an employer is liable for the acts of its supervisors " 'regardless of whether the specific acts complained of were authorized or even forbidden by the employer and regardless of whether the employer knew or should have known of their occurrence.' " 40 FEP at 1830 (Marshall, J., concurring) (quoting 29 C.F.R. §§ 1604.11(c), (d) (1985)).

[36]*Id.,* 40 FEP at 1829.

[37]*Id.,* 40 FEP at 1831 (Marshall, J., concurring).

[38]467 U.S. 69, 34 FEP 1406 (1984).

the law firm used the prospect of partnership to induce young lawyers to join the firm; that the firm had represented to her that advancement to partnership after five or six years was "a matter of course" for associates who received satisfactory evaluations; that the firm had promised that associates would be considered on a "fair and equal basis"; that she had relied on these representations when she accepted employment with the firm; and that the firm's promise to consider her for partnership on a fair and equal basis created a binding employment contract.

The district court dismissed the complaint, holding that Title VII does not apply to the selection of partners by a partnership, and the Eleventh Circuit affirmed. The Supreme Court reversed, holding that the alleged contractual nature of the employment relationship was sufficient to trigger the provision of Title VII governing "terms, conditions, or privileges of employment." The Court stated that if the evidence at trial established that the parties had contracted to have the female associate considered for partnership, that promise is clearly a term, condition, and privilege of her employment. Title VII would therefore bind the firm to consider the associate for partnership without regard to sex.

Lastly, in *Arizona Governing Committee v. Norris,* [39] the Supreme Court extended its 1978 ruling in *City of Los Angeles, Department of Water & Power v. Manhart* [40] by holding that it is a violation of Title VII for an employer to provide lower retirement benefits to female employees than to male employees after both sexes have made equal contributions toward a pension plan. The Court decided that its reasoning in *Manhart*—that disparate treatment of male and female employees due to the greater life span of women violates Title VII—applied to the pay-out stage of a retirement plan as well as to the pay-in stage, and applied to pension benefits provided by employers who utilize third-party insurers, not just to an employer-operated plan as in *Manhart.*

In *Norris,* the State of Arizona offered its employees the opportunity to enroll in a deferred pension plan which allowed male and female employees to choose among three basic retirement options offered by several private insurance companies chosen by the State. If the employee chose a lump sum payment upon retirement or periodic payments of a fixed sum for a fixed period after retirement, the benefits provided to male and female employees were identical. If, however, an employee chose monthly annuity payments for the remainder of his or her life, all of the companies selected by the State used sex-based mortality tables to determine the annuity payments. Such tables yield lower monthly payments to women than to men of the same age because women on the average live longer than men. The Court held the annuity option to be illegal based on its decision in *Manhart,* because (as in *Manhart*) a woman participating in the Arizona plan who wished to obtain monthly annuity benefits equal to those obtained by a man would have to make greater contributions.

The Court viewed as irrelevant both the employees' voluntary participa-

---

[39]463 U.S. 1073, 32 FEP 233 (1983).
[40]435 U.S. 702, 17 FEP 395 (1978), reproduced at p. 372 of the Second Edition.

tion in the plan and the employees' opportunity to choose among different plans. Nor did the Court allow a defense based upon Arizona's inability to locate any companies that would provide benefits on a sex-neutral basis. The Court reasoned that since the deferred compensation benefits were only available to employees if they chose a benefit plan with an insurer selected by the State, the State itself was a party to the contracts and could not disclaim responsibility for the discriminatory features of the insurers' benefit plans. The Court stated that employers who cannot locate a third-party insurer willing to provide nondiscriminatory benefits must supply such benefits themselves or not provide them at all.

The Court cushioned the potential financial impact of the decision on employers and on the insurance industry, caused by the cost of equalizing benefits for men and women, by applying its decision prospectively to cover only benefits derived from contributions made after the judgment, and by delaying the effective date of the judgment until August 1, 1983.

## I. Bona Fide Occupational Qualification (BFOQ)

### C. The Theories of BFOQ

#### 1. Ability to Perform

Courts continue to reject BFOQ defenses based on sex where there is insufficient evidence that the excluded category could not perform the relevant work acceptably. For example, in *EEOC v. Spokane Concrete Products*,[41] the court refused to find male gender a BFOQ for the job of truck driver where there was no evidence that women could not perform the job. Since not even the *Weeks*[42] test—that all or substantially all women would be unable safely and efficiently to perform the duties of the job involved—was satisfied, the court was not required to decide whether the *Rosenfeld*[43] individual determination test was applicable.

The application of Title VII to the uniformed military services continues to generate controversy. The district court in *Hill v. Berkman*[44] determined in a lengthy analysis that Title VII applies to the "uniformed services"—a position contrary to what the court itself described as an "unbroken line of authority"[45]—and then decided that the Army had a BFOQ defense to the

---

[41]534 F. Supp. 518, 28 FEP 423 (E.D. Wash. 1982); *see also* Ulane v. Eastern Airlines, 581 F. Supp. 821, 35 FEP 1332 (N.D. Ill. 1983), *rev'd*, 742 F.2d 1081, 35 FEP 1348 (7th Cir. 1984), *cert. denied*. 471 U.S. 1017, 37 FEP 784 (1985) (district court rejected defendant's BFOQ defense because evidence did not show that all transsexuals, as a category, are unsafe airline pilots; Seventh Circuit reversed, holding that Title VII does not proscribe discrimination against transsexuals). *Ulane* is also discussed in Section IX, *infra*.

[42]Weeks v. Southern Bell Tel. & Tel. Co., 408 F.2d 228, 1 FEP 656 (5th Cir. 1969), excerpted at p. 342 of the Second Edition.

[43]Rosenfeld v. Southern Pac., 444 F.2d 1219, 3 FEP 604 (9th Cir. 1971), reproduced at p. 344 of the Second Edition. The California Industrial Welfare Commission Order at issue in *Rosenfeld*—prohibiting the assignment of women to jobs requiring regular lifting of more than 25 pounds—was again before the Ninth Circuit in 1986. In *Alaniz v. California Processors,* 785 F.2d 1412, 40 FEP 768 (9th Cir. 1986), the court concluded that whereas the IWC Order could not constitute a BFOQ defense to discrimination, good-faith reliance on the Order did provide a defense to claims for back pay.

[44]635 F. Supp. 1228, 40 FEP 1444 (E.D.N.Y. 1986).

[45]*Id.,* 40 FEP at 1447.

claimed discrimination. The case involved a woman who had joined the Army in order to become a Nuclear Biological and Chemical Specialist, a position from which she was later excluded when the position was reclassified by the Army into a "combat support role." The court concluded that the military "may exclude women from combat and combat support positions, because being male is a bona fide occupational qualification for a job that is by federal law and present national policy restricted to men."[46] On the other hand, civilian employees of the military services are protected by Title VII. Citing § 717(a),[47] the EEOC in a recent decision rejected the Navy's argument that its refusal to permit a female employee to participate in submarine sea trials was " 'not within the purview' of Title VII because [its action] was 'a military decision, not a personnel decision.' "[48] Moreover, the EEOC held that the Navy failed to establish its BFOQ defense because its own investigation had shown that the plaintiff's participation in previous sea trials had "had no deleterious effect on crew efficiency and that her future embarkations would create only minor inconveniences" and because "the agency *has already shown* that it could accommodate [her] with minimal infringement of crew privacy."[49]

Cases involving pregnancy as a BFOQ continue to show mixed results.[50] The Eleventh Circuit affirmed a district court's decision that potential harm to a fetus or potential offspring of a female employee is not a BFOQ defense "unless the employer shows a direct relationship between the policy and the actual ability of a pregnant or fertile female to perform her job."[51] By contrast, the Fifth Circuit held that nonpregnancy could be reasonably necessary to passenger safety and therefore could be a legitimate BFOQ for the position of flight attendant.[52] Moreover, that court rejected the argument that Title VII imposed a duty to transfer pregnant flight attendants to ground positions.

## 2. Same Sex

Courts continue to reject a same-sex BFOQ for law enforcement and prison guard positions based on prisoner privacy rights. The Eleventh Circuit rejected the contention that same-sex gender was a BFOQ defense for a sheriff's department's policy of considering female applicants for entry-level deputy positions only when positions were open in the women's section of the jail.[53] The court noted that the department's policy of assigning entry-

---

[46]*Id.* at 1243, 40 FEP at 1455.

[47]42 U.S.C. § 2000e-16(a).

[48]Doviak v. Department of the Navy, Employment Practices Dec. (CCH) ¶¶6867 at 7102, 7103 (EEOC Dec. 1986).

[49]*Id.* at 7106 (emphasis in original).

[50]Pregnancy cases are discussed in Section V, *infra.*

[51]Hayes v. Shelby Memorial Hosp., 726 F.2d 1543, 1549, 34 FEP 444, 449 (11th Cir. 1984). The court added: "Such a case should be rare." *Id.* at 1549 n.9, 34 FEP at 449 n.9.

[52]Levin v. Delta Air Lines, 730 F.2d 994, 34 FEP 1192 (5th Cir. 1984), *aff'g* 34 FEP 1187 (S.D. Tex. 1982).

[53]Hardin v. Stynchcomb, 691 F.2d 1364, 30 FEP 624 (11th Cir. 1982); *see also* Garrett v. Okaloosa County, Fla., 734 F.2d 621 (11th Cir. 1984) (prior exclusion of women from position of correction officer invalid where county could demonstrate no operational problems after women began serving in position); Edwards v. Alabama Dep't of Corrections, 615 F. Supp. 804, 810 (M.D. Ala. 1985) (femaleness not a BFOQ for position of shift commander at women's prison; shift commander can perform essential duties "without frequent patrolling of dormitories, restrooms or showers or regular searches of or contact with inmates"); Torres v. Wisconsin Dep't of Health & Social Servs., 639 F. Supp. 279, 40 FEP 1748 (E.D.

level deputies to the county jail was only sporadic. Further, the department had failed to prove that "the essence of its business" required the policy or that it could not assign new deputies to positions other than at the jail or rearrange scheduling to prevent female deputies assigned to the male section of the jail from performing duties violative of the prisoners' privacy rights.[54]

On the other hand, the Third Circuit dissolved a preliminary injunction against an employer's involuntary transfer of a woman guard to a less desirable shift so that there would be a woman available to assist female students during that particular shift.[55] The court held that the BFOQ defense is available to employers who require transfers of employees into a position staffed by employees of a particular sex, and remanded for consideration of whether sex was actually a BFOQ in this situation.

In other limited factual situations, courts have recently recognized a same-sex BFOQ, based in part on privacy rights. One court has sustained an employer's policy of using only men to clean men's washrooms and women to clean women's washrooms during periods when those washrooms would be in use by employees of a large office building.[56] Another court has upheld another employer's policy of hiring only women for the position of staff nurse in a hospital's labor and delivery area.[57]

A same-sex role model BFOQ has been rejected where role modeling was not found specifically essential to the purpose of the program. Male gender was found not to be a BFOQ for the position of child care worker

---

Wis. 1986), aff'd, 838 F.2d 944, 45 FEP 1652 (7th Cir. 1988) (security, privacy, and rehabilitation concerns do not justify BFOQ plan requiring only women be hired in Correctional Officer-3 positions at women's prison where there was no showing of adverse effects during prior years when men served in such positions and where prison already had in place adequate procedures for protecting inmate privacy); cf. Grummett v. Rushen, 779 F.2d 491, 496 (9th Cir. 1985) (inmates' privacy rights not infringed by presence of female guards; although potential for viewing unclothed inmates was great, record indicated actual viewing was infrequent and women were not assigned to positions requiring close or prolonged surveillance of disrobed inmates; officials "have struck an acceptable balance among the inmates' privacy interests, the institution's security requirements, and the female guards' employment rights"). And see Bagley v. Watson, 579 F. Supp. 1099, 35 FEP 1250 (D. Or. 1983), where the court found that sex was not a BFOQ for guard positions in an Oregon male maximum security correctional institution. Unlike the Supreme Court in Dothard v. Rawlinson, 433 U.S. 321, 15 FEP 10 (1977), reproduced at p. 349 of the Second Edition, the Bagley court did not discuss the BFOQ in terms of security. Rather, it considered the issue in terms of whether the male prisoners had a right not to be subjected to "pat-down" searches by women guards or to be free from visual observation by women guards (since the male prisoners would inevitably be in a state of undress during a guard's shift). The court found that those considerations did not justify a BFOQ.

[54]Supra note 53. See also Griffin v. Michigan Dep't of Corrections, 654 F. Supp. 690, 30 FEP 638 (E.D. Mich. 1982) (rejecting same-sex BFOQ based on alleged constitutional privacy rights of male inmates); Harden v. Dayton Human Rehabilitation Center, 520 F. Supp. 769, 27 FEP 1575 (S.D. Ohio 1981), aff'd, 779 F.2d 50, 45 FEP 1895 (6th Cir. 1985) (restriction of security guard positions to males unlawful).

[55]Moteles v. University of Pa., 730 F.2d 913, 34 FEP 424 (3d Cir.), cert. denied, 469 U.S. 855, 35 FEP 1800 (1984).

[56]Norwood v. Dale Maintenance Sys., 590 F. Supp. 1410, 35 FEP 1835 (N.D. Ill. 1984) (infringement of privacy combined with lost working time under alternative policies); see also Brooks v. ACF Indus., 537 F. Supp. 1122, 28 FEP 1373 (S.D. W. Va. 1982) (male employees' rights would be infringed by female janitor entering and performing duties in male bathhouse while it was being used).

[57]EEOC v. Mercy Health Center, 29 FEP 159 (W.D. Okla. 1982) (potential for life threatening complications justified not employing male delivery nurses in order to reduce stress, based on survey results and other evidence); see also Jones v. Hinds Gen. Hosp., 666 F. Supp. 933, 44 FEP 1076 (S.D. Miss. 1987) (male gender is BFOQ for position of orderly where duties include catheterization of male patients and significant number of male patients object to being exposed to female nurse assistants); State, County & Municipal Employees Local 567 v. Michigan Council 25, 635 F. Supp. 1010, 1014, 40 FEP 1648, 1655 (E.D. Mich. 1986) (privacy rights of mental health patients can justify a BFOQ, but defendants must show that "essence of their operation would be undermined by failing to have these sex-based classifications and * * * that no reasonable alternatives exist").

in a sheltered workshop for mentally ill young adults with a predominantly black male population.[58] The court recognized that same-sex gender could be a BFOQ where providing role models or providing sex education was necessary to the essential function of a program, but that it was not necessary to the essential purpose of the workshop in question, which was to teach work skills and appropriate workplace behavior.

### 3. Customer Preference

An asserted BFOQ defense usually will be treated skeptically if based on supposed customer preferences. A federal court in New York held that a school district's refusal to assign female bus drivers to routes serving an all-male religious school violated Title VII.[59] Noting that the BFOQ defense applies only in very narrow circumstances, the court concluded that "the fact that the Hasidic clientele strongly prefer male drivers does not make being male a BFOQ."[60]

### D. BFOQ and Business Necessity

The Eighth Circuit has reached different results in two recent cases showing the interplay of the BFOQ defense and the employer's burden of showing business necessity in impact discrimination cases. In *EEOC v. Rath Packing Co.,*[61] the Eighth Circuit held that the district court had correctly applied the business necessity test, rather than the BFOQ test, to the defendant's use of subjective hiring practices. The court stated that a "neutral employment practice may be justified by business necessity only if the practice not only fosters safety and efficiency but is essential to that goal."[62] Finding that "Rath was unable to identify the criteria and qualifications which were considered in the hiring decisions,"[63] the court upheld the district court's ruling that the company's use of subjective hiring practices was not justified by business necessity.

On the other hand, the district court had upheld Rath's no-spouse rule, stating the issue to be "whether management's response to the *perceived* production problems * * * was *reasonable* * * * and designed to improve conditions in the plant."[64] The Eighth Circuit reversed, holding that the

---

[58]Jatczak v. Ochburg, 540 F. Supp. 698, 28 FEP 1773 (E.D. Mich. 1982); *see also* EEOC Dec. 82-4, 28 FEP 1845 (1982) (same-sex BFOQ not applicable for position of group leader in male unit of youth home detention facility). *But see* Chambers v. Omaha Girls Club, 629 F. Supp. 925, 40 FEP 362 (D. Neb. 1986), *aff'd,* 834 F.2d 697, 45 FEP 698 (8th Cir. 1987).

[59]Bollenbach v. Monroe-Woodbury Cent. School Dist. Bd. of Educ., 659 F. Supp. 1450, 43 FEP 1205 (S.D.N.Y. 1987).

[60]*Id.* at 1472, 43 FEP at 1222.

[61]787 F.2d 318, 40 FEP 580 (8th Cir. 1986), *aff'g in part, rev'g in part and remanding* 40 FEP 559 (S.D. Iowa 1979), 37 BR 614, 40 FEP 574, *and* 40 FEP 576 (S.D. Iowa 1984), *cert. denied,* 479 U.S. 910, 41 FEP 1712 (1986).

[62]*Id.,* 787 F.2d at 328 n.10, 40 FEP at 588; *see also* Davis v. Richmond, Fredericksburg & Potomac R.R., 803 F.2d 1322, 42 FEP 69 (4th Cir. 1986) (requirement that trainees for locomotive engineers have "train service" experience effectively excluded all female employees and not justified by business necessity).

[63]*Id.,* 787 F.2d at 328, 40 FEP at 589.

[64]*Id.* at 331, 40 FEP at 591 (omissions and emphasis by the Eighth Circuit); *see also* note 151, *infra,* and accompanying text.

district court had applied the wrong standard because it had failed to consider whether there was a compelling need for the rule. Moreover, the court held that Rath had failed to show that the rule was required because of actual dual absenteeism, vacation scheduling, spousal supervision, employee pressure to hire spouses, or problems of employee morale.

The Eighth Circuit affirmed a district court ruling in *Chambers v. Omaha Girls Club*[65] that the Club's rule prohibiting employment of persons who became pregnant or caused pregnancy did not violate Title VII under either the disparate treatment or the disparate impact theory. As to the disparate treatment theory, the court determined that the Club had articulated a legitimate, nondiscriminatory reason for its rule—that is, "to provide positive role models in an attempt to discourage teenagers from becoming pregnant."[66]

Under the disparate impact theory the court said that the defendants could rely upon either business necessity or a BFOQ to rebut the plaintiff's case, and that the burden was essentially the same under either defense: either to demonstrate "a close nexus between the policy * * * and a 'substantial end goal' of the employer" or to show that the BFOQ was "related and necessary to the operation of the defendant's business."[67] Here, because the purpose of the Club was to foster growth and maturity in young girls by exposing them to "the greatest number of available positive options in life," and because the policy was based on the belief "that teenage pregnancies severely limit the available opportunities for teenage girls," the court concluded that "a manifest relationship exists between the Girls Club's fundamental purpose and its single pregnancy policy."[68] Because the finding of business necessity was dispositive of the case, the court observed that it was "not necessary to determine whether the evidence would satisfy a bfoq, although presumably it would."[69]

## III. Separate Lines of Progression and Seniority Systems

### B. Seniority and Transfer

In *American Tobacco Co. v. Patterson,*[70] the Supreme Court held, in a case alleging both racial and sex discrimination, that § 703(h) applies to seniority systems adopted after the effective date of Title VII, as well as to those adopted before that date. Reiterating its analysis in *Teamsters v. United States,*[71] the Court stated, "[t]o be cognizable, a claim that a seniority system has a discriminatory impact must be accompanied by proof of a discriminatory purpose."[72]

---

[65]*Supra* note 58.
[66]*Id.,* 629 F. Supp. at 947, 40 FEP at 379.
[67]*Id.* at 949–50, 40 FEP at 381.
[68]*Id.* at 950, 40 FEP at 381.
[69]*Id.* at 951 n.51, 40 FEP at 382.
[70]456 U.S. 63, 28 FEP 713 (1982).
[71]431 U.S. 324, 14 FEP 1514 (1977).
[72]456 U.S. at 69, 28 FEP at 716.

*Teamsters* and *American Tobacco* have been applied in several sex discrimination cases.[73] For example, in *Wright v. Olin Corp.,*[74] the plaintiff, claiming that defendant's line seniority system was adopted in 1968, argued that the system had a disparate impact upon blacks and females by locking them into undesirable jobs and departments. Analyzing the system under *Teamsters* and *American Tobacco,* the Fourth Circuit adopted the district court's findings that the system was bona fide within the meaning of § 703(h) since the system had been in effect since 1942, although modified in 1968 and 1971; it was rational and in accordance with industry practice and NLRB unit determinations; it applied equally to all employees regardless of race or sex; and it was instituted, maintained, and administered free of any purpose or intent to discriminate against blacks or females.

## IV. Fringe Benefits

### A. Statutory Authority and EEOC Guidelines

The Retirement Equity Act of 1984, effective December 31, 1984, amended the Employee Retirement Income Security Act (ERISA) to require liberalized "break in service" rules and lowered eligibility ages for pension benefits.[75] The amendments protect pension rights of workers who take time

---

[73]EEOC v. 34 FEP 943 (W.D. Mo. 1984); (separate nonfood dept. established as separate bargaining unit, based on business purpose); *see also* Allen v. Prince George's County, Md., 737 F.2d 1299, 38 FEP 1220 (4th Cir. 1984) (county's practice of granting preference to internal applicants for county jobs was valid seniority system under § 703(h) because it, in effect, granted seniority to all current employees, regardless of race or sex); Durant v. Owens-Illinois Glass Co., 517 F. Supp. 710, 31 FEP 215 (E.D. La. 1980), *aff'd,* 656 F.2d 89, 31 FEP 228 (5th Cir. 1981) (both departmental seniority system and subsequent plant seniority system bona fide; job segregation continued to exist not because of seniority system but because of employee choice); *cf.* Curl v. Reavis, 35 FEP 917 (W.D.N.C. 1983), *aff'd in part, rev'd in part on other grounds and remanded,* 740 F.2d 1323, 35 FEP 930 (4th Cir. 1984), *on remand,* 608 F. Supp. 1265, 45 FEP 1846 (W.D.N.C. 1985) (sheriff's department maintained segregated lines of progression); Jones v. Cassens Transp., 538 F. Supp. 929, 32 FEP 1713 (E.D. Mich.), *appeal dismissed mem.,* 705 F.2d 454, 33 FEP 1696 (6th Cir. 1982), *rev'd in part on other grounds and remanded sub nom.* Jones v. Teamsters Local 299, 748 F.2d 1083, 36 FEP 569 (6th Cir. 1984), *on remand,* 617 F. Supp. 869, 39 FEP 1341 (E.D. Mich. 1985) (seniority system in collective bargaining agreement did not preclude transfer of plaintiffs as alleged and de facto system, which did, was not immunized by § 703(h) because only purpose of de facto system was to provide best available job opportunities for males and deny them to females) (Title VII claim barred by failure to file EEOC charge against union, and breach of duty of fair representation claim time barred) (on pendent state claim, held that separate bargaining units for office workers and for others not bona fide).

[74]697 F.2d 1172, 30 FEP 889 (4th Cir. 1982). *See also* Moore v. Stage Employees, IATSE, Local 659, 29 FEP 542 (C.D. Cal. 1982) (summary judgment granted to defendant where all competent evidence indicated absence of discriminatory purpose in establishment and maintenance of seniority system); Brooks v. ACF Indus., 537 F. Supp. 1122, 28 FEP 1373 (S.D. W. Va. 1982) (seniority system long in effect but only recently reduced to writing upheld under § 703(h)); Mewshaw v. City of New York Police Dep't, 493 F. Supp. 838, 30 FEP 656 (S.D.N.Y.), *aff'd mem.,* 639 F.2d 769, 30 FEP 872 (2d Cir. 1980) (summary judgment granted defendant where *pro se* plaintiff failed to allege seniority system not bona fide within meaning of *Teamsters*); Bohm v. L.B. Hartz Wholesale Corp., 370 N.W.2d 901, 906, 38 FEP 495, 499 (Minn. App. 1985) (relying on Title VII precedent, court upheld departmental seniority system against state law claim that system locked women into lower paying clerical jobs; court found that system was "agreed upon by the majority of employees, presumably to perpetuate the autonomy of individual departments" and that there was no evidence of intentional discrimination in creation or maintenance of the system); *cf.* Edmonson v. United States Steel Corp., 659 F.2d 582, 27 FEP 39 (5th Cir. 1981) (rejecting challenge to seniority system established by consent decree). *But see* Jones v. Cassens Transp., *supra* note 73 (de facto seniority system no defense where system did not impact equally and evidence established discriminatory purpose in its maintenance).

[75]Pub. L. No. 98-397, 98 Stat. 1426 (1984).

off for childbirth and parenting and also give increased protection to a spouse's right to survivor benefits and annuities. Although the 99th Congress considered a number of bills concerning other aspects of sex discrimination and fringe benefits, none of those measures was enacted.

## B. Retirement Plans

### 1. Contributions and Benefits

In the landmark case of *Arizona Governing Committee v. Norris,* [76] the Supreme Court held that Title VII is violated when an employer provides lower retirement benefits to female employees than to male employees after both have made equal contributions to a pension plan. In the wake of *Norris,* several decisions involving similar facts were vacated. [77]

The Supreme Court in *Norris,* as in *City of Los Angeles, Department of Water & Power v. Manhart,* [78] refused to apply its holding retroactively. However, the Second Circuit in *Spirt v. Teachers Insurance & Annuity Association,* [79] on remand, distinguished *Norris* on that point and ordered retroactive application of its ruling invalidating the use of gender-based mortality tables in calculating retirement annuity payments. According to the *Spirt* court, *Norris* was based on the Supreme Court's desire to avoid imposing heavy financial burdens on the state employer and the plan itself, which would result if they were required to "top up" the benefits to female annuitants. [80] The *Spirt* court found that, because the plans in *Spirt* were defined contribution plans, rather than defined benefit plans as in *Norris,* retroactive relief would not impose such a burden. The court also concluded that the possible reduction in benefits paid to male annuitants was not unjust because, under the defined contribution plan, they had no settled expectation about the level of their future benefits. [81]

Retroactivity was also addressed by the Ninth Circuit in *Probe v. State Teachers' Retirement System.* [82] Although the plan's basic retirement benefit was calculated using gender-neutral criteria, the plan also offered a joint and survivor annuity option which utilized sex-segregated mortality tables. The court affirmed the district court's holding that the option violated Title VII because it resulted in lower benefits for male retirees than for female retirees. Full retroactive relief was not warranted, however, because after *Manhart* and before *Norris,* the defendant "reasonably could have assumed that it was lawful to provide an optional annuity system that reflected plans offered by

---

[76]463 U.S. 1073, 32 FEP 233 (1983), *aff'g in part and rev'g in part* 671 F.2d 330, 28 FEP 369 (9th Cir. 1982). This case is discussed in greater detail in the introductory remarks to this chapter.

[77]Spirt v. Teachers Ins. & Annuity Ass'n, 691 F.2d 1054, 29 FEP 1599 (2d Cir. 1982), *vacated,* 463 U.S. 1223, 32 FEP 359 (1983), *on remand,* 735 F.2d 23, 34 FEP 1510 (2d Cir.), *cert. denied,* 469 U.S. 881, 35 FEP 1688 (1984); Peters v. Wayne State Univ., 691 F.2d 235, 29 FEP 1753 (6th Cir. 1982), *vacated,* 463 U.S. 1223, 32 FEP 359 (1983); Retired Pub. Employees' Ass'n v. California, 677 F.2d 733, 28 FEP 1609 (9th Cir. 1982), *vacated,* 463 U.S. 1222, 32 FEP 359 (1983).

[78]435 U.S. 702, 17 FEP 395 (1978), reproduced at p. 372 of the Second Edition.

[79]*Supra* note 77.

[80]*Id.,* 735 F.2d at 26–27, 34 FEP at 1513–14.

[81]*Id.* at 28, 34 FEP at 1514.

[82]780 F.2d 776, 40 FEP 102 (9th Cir. 1986), *aff'g in part, rev'g in part and remanding* 27 FEP 1306 (C.D. Cal. 1981), *cert. denied,* 476 U.S. 1170, 40 FEP 1873 (1986).

insurance companies on the open market."[83] After *Norris,* on the other hand, the defendant should have known that any use of sex-segregated tables to calculate benefits was unlawful, even if the employee freely chose those benefits instead of an alternative, gender-neutral benefit. Thus, the court concluded that benefits derived from contributions made to the retirement fund before the *Norris* decision could be calculated in accordance with the original plan, but benefits derived from contributions after *Norris* must be calculated without regard to sex.[84]

The Eleventh Circuit has expressly refused to adopt the approach taken in *Probe.* In *Long v. Florida,*[85] the court specifically rejected the contention that the Florida Retirement System reasonably could have relied on the open market exception created in *Manhart.* Reasoning that the exception "applies exclusively to third parties," such as insurance companies, the court concluded that *Manhart* "put all pension funds on notice that benefits could not be based on sex-distinct mortality tables [and so] all funds, like the FRS, were forewarned and should have converted to sex-neutral mortality tables at that time."[86] Accordingly, after determining that topping up benefits would "not be devastating" to the fund or to third parties, the court affirmed an award of full retroactive relief for retirees who had retired after 1978, the year in which *Manhart* was decided.

Aside from its ruling under Title VII, the Supreme Court in *Norris* also settled the effect of the McCarran-Ferguson Act[87] on benefit plans administered by third-party insurers. In *Norris,* where the third-party insurers were not named defendants, the Court held that the McCarran-Ferguson Act was inapplicable because none of the named defendants was an "insurer," and because the Court's ruling merely prohibited the employer from offering fringe benefits that differed on the basis of sex.[88] In theory at least, the Court did not prohibit insurers from using sex-segregated annuity tables, but simply precluded employers from offering benefit plans to their employees which utilized insurers who used such sex-segregated annuity tables. Thus, application of Title VII did not "invalidate, impair, or supersede" any state insurance laws.

In contrast, in *Spirit v. Teachers Insurance & Annuity Association,*[89] the district court had held, and the appellate court had assumed, that one of the named defendants was an "insurer" otherwise subject to state insurance laws. Relying on legislative history and "historical context," the Second

---

[83]*Id.,* 780 F.2d at 782–83, 40 FEP at 107.

[84]The Ninth Circuit has affirmed the district court's decision in *Norris* on remand that gender-neutral tables be used for determining benefits based on contributions after August 1, 1983, the effective date of the Supreme Court's decision. The court held that neither the Supreme Court's opinion nor the Equal Pay Act requires that prospective relief to female retirees be based on the amount previously paid to men, using male actuarial tables. Norris v. Arizona Governing Comm., 796 F.2d 1119, 41 FEP 820 (9th Cir. 1986).

[85]805 F.2d 1542, 42 FEP 1058 (11th Cir. 1986), *cert. denied,* 484 U.S. —, 44 FEP 1672 (1987).

[86]*Id.,* 805 F.2d at 1551, 42 FEP at 1065.

[87]15 U.S.C. § 1011 *et seq.* Section 2 of that Act states: "No Act of Congress shall be construed to invalidate, impair, or supersede any law enacted by any State for the purpose of regulating the business of insurance, * * * unless such Act specifically relates to the business of insurance." 15 U.S.C. § 1012(b).

[88]Arizona Governing Comm. v. Norris, 463 U.S. 1073, 1087–88 n.17, 32 FEP 233, 239–40 (1983).

[89]691 F.2d 1054, 29 FEP 1599 (2d Cir. 1982), *vacated,* 463 U.S. 1223, 32 FEP 359 (1983), *on remand,* 735 F.2d 23, 34 FEP 1510 (2d Cir.), *cert. denied,* 469 U.S. 881, 35 FEP 1688 (1984).

Circuit concluded that the McCarran-Ferguson Act was never meant to exempt insurance companies from "federal policies in such fields as civil rights, labor and other areas of national concern," and held that "Title VII explicitly pre-empts New York insurance laws to the extent that they 'require or permit' a method of calculating pension benefits" which is improper under Title VII.[90]

Some programs that rely on gender-based distinctions have met with success. In *Heckler v. Mathews*[91] the Supreme Court held that a temporary gender-based distinction under which husbands but not wives were required to show dependency to receive spousal benefits and be exempted from a "pension offset" provision, does not violate equal protection requirements. The Court decided that the pension offset exception was justified by the legitimate governmental purpose of protecting the expectations of persons who had planned their retirements based on earlier sex-based dependency requirements. The Court noted that the narrowly tailored exception was based on reasoned analysis, rather than stereotypical assumptions, about the roles of men and women.

Likewise, the use of gender-based mortality tables by the IRS was upheld by the Second Circuit in *Manufacturers Hanover Trust Co. v. United States.*[92] The court held that the Commissioner's use of such tables in calculating the value of a decedent's reversionary interest in a trust was a constitutionally permissible classification because it was "substantially related to the important governmental objective of promoting equity and fairness in estate taxes by accurately valuing reversionary interests."[93]

The present effects of past discrimination were addressed by the Fifth Circuit in *Carpenter v. Stephen F. Austin State University.*[94] Before the effective date of Title VII, the employer had discriminatorily channeled black and female employees into lower-level positions; as hourly employees, they were excluded from participating in the university's retirement plan. After passage of Title VII, hourly employees were made eligible for the retirement plan, but only if they paid a lump sum contribution to the plan in the accrued amount that they would have paid had they been previously included. This requirement adversely and disproportionately affected black and female employees, who claimed that the eligibility requirement was a continuing violation of Title VII. The court held that the disparate effect of the financial hardship was not the result of discriminatory eligibility criteria,[95] and it found no present gender- or race-based impact and no unequal treatment of similarly situated pre-Title VII hourly employees.[96]

---

[90]*Id.,* 691 F.2d at 1066, 29 FEP at 1608 (applying Title VII's preemption clause, 42 U.S.C. § 2000e-7); *see also* Women in City Gov't United v. City of New York, 515 F. Supp. 295, 330, 25 FEP 927, 932–33 (S.D.N.Y. 1981) ("Congress did not intend the McCarran-Ferguson Act as a limitation on its power to enact civil rights legislation that might incidentally affect the business of insurance.").

[91]465 U.S. 728 (1984) (analyzing the Social Security Amendments Act of 1977, 42 U.S.C. § 402 (1976 & Supp. V 1981)).

[92]775 F.2d 459 (2d Cir. 1985), *rev'g* 576 F. Supp. 837 (S.D.N.Y. 1983), *cert. denied,* 475 U.S. 1095 (1986).

[93]*Id.,* 775 F.2d at 461.

[94]706 F.2d 608, 31 FEP 1758 (5th Cir. 1983).

[95]*Id.* at 629, 31 FEP at 1775.

[96]*Id.,* 31 FEP at 1776.

## 2. Retirement Eligibility Age

Female corrections officers filed a class action suit in *Marcoux v. Maine,*[97] alleging that a special retirement program available only to state prison guards, predominantly male, made them eligible to retire at age 50 with 20 years of service, while the plaintiff female corrections officers were covered by the general state employee retirement program and could not retire until age 60 with 25 years of service. The court applied Equal Pay Act standards for determining that the jobs were substantially equal, despite the fact that the plaintiffs did not meet the Equal Pay Act single-establishment criterion,[98] and held that the State[99] had violated Title VII by providing the special plan for the state prison guards.

## D. Insurance, Medical, and Disability Plans

In *Shaw v. Delta Air Lines,*[100] the Supreme Court clarified the preemptive nature of ERISA as it applies to state laws which govern employment discrimination and disability benefits. The Court ruled that state laws which are designed to prohibit discriminatory practices relating to employee benefit plans are preempted only insofar as they prohibit practices that are lawful under federal law. The Court reasoned that if ERISA were interpreted to preempt state discrimination laws entirely simply because they related to benefit plans, the goal of joint state and federal enforcement of Title VII would be frustrated.

The Court also held that § 4(b)(3) of ERISA, which exempts from ERISA coverage "any employee benefit plan * * * maintained solely for the purpose of complying with applicable * * * disability insurance laws," was intended to exclude entire "plans," not portions of plans, from ERISA coverage. Thus, those portions of the employer's multi-benefit plan maintained to comply with state law "are not exempt from ERISA and are not subject to state regulation."[101] This, however, does not mean that employers are thereby free of state regulation. The Court held that a state may require an employer to maintain a separate disability plan, exempt under § 4(b)(3), and may permit employers to meet their state law obligations by including required benefits in a multi-benefit ERISA plan. "In other words, while the State may not require an employer to alter its ERISA plan, it may force the employer to choose between providing disability benefits in a separately administered plan and including the state-mandated benefits in its ERISA plan."[102]

Courts are still struggling with the question of whether employers may

---

[97]35 FEP 553 (D. Me. 1984), *aff'd,* 797 F.2d 1100, 41 FEP 636 (1st Cir. 1986).

[98]*Id.,* 35 FEP at 563. On review, the court of appeals expressly declined to rule on whether the district court had erred in applying Equal Pay Act burdens of proof and persuasion to the Title VII claim. 797 F.2d at 1106, 41 FEP at 641.

[99]Relying on *Fitzpatrick v. Bitzer,* 427 U.S. 445, 12 FEP 1586 (1976), the court held that the Eleventh Amendment does not bar Title VII claims against state officials for injunctive relief and retroactive benefits. 35 FEP at 554.

[100]463 U.S. 85, 32 FEP 121 (1983).

[101]*Id.* at 107, 32 FEP at 129.

[102]*Id.* at 108, 32 FEP at 130.

condition benefits on meeting a "head of household" test. In the first of several cases involving the J.C. Penney "head of household" medical insurance plan, the Ninth Circuit in *Wambheim v. J.C. Penney Co.* [103] analyzed the employer's medical insurance policy under a disparate impact theory. The policy required that an employee be the "head of the household" (*i.e.,* earn more than half of the couple's combined income) before a spouse would be covered. Despite the disparate impact on female employees,[104] the court found no Title VII violation because the employer had a legitimate business justification of providing insurance for the largest number of employees with the greatest need for dependent coverage. The same head of household provision was upheld in *EEOC v. J.C. Penney Co.,* [105] although the district court expressly disagreed with the Ninth Circuit's conclusion that disparate impact analysis is applicable to such cases.[106] Relying on *Nashville Gas Co. v. Satty* [107] and *General Electric Co. v. Gilbert,* [108] the court held that disparate impact analysis applies only to cases arising under § 703(a)(2),[109] and found that this case did not arise under that section because the challenged provision had "no effect upon either employment opportunities or job status."[110] Thus, although the employer's rule had a disparate impact on female employees, there was no Title VII violation because the EEOC had failed to demonstrate the intent to discriminate which is required for a disparate treatment claim.[111]

More recently, the Ninth Circuit held in *EEOC v. Fremont Christian School*[112] that a religious school violated Title VII by providing a health insurance plan only for employees who were heads of households, defined in this case not as the spouse earning more than a certain proportion of the

---

[103]705 F.2d 1492, 31 FEP 1297 (9th Cir. 1983), *cert. denied,* 467 U.S. 1255, 34 FEP 1800 (1984) *(Wambheim II).*

[104]In an earlier proceeding, the Ninth Circuit reversed summary judgment for the employer, ruling that plaintiffs had established a prima facie case under disparate impact analysis. Wambheim v. J.C. Penney Co., 642 F.2d 362, 27 FEP 1495 (9th Cir. 1981) *(Wambheim I).* In *Wambheim II,* the Ninth Circuit acknowledged that this "is an unusual disparate impact case because it alleges a violation of § 703(a)(1)," but nevertheless reaffirmed its position that disparate impact analysis is applicable to such cases. 705 F.2d at 1494, 31 FEP at 1298.

[105]632 F. Supp. 871, 40 FEP 231 (E.D. Mich. 1985), *aff'd,* 843 F.2d 249, 46 FEP 815 (6th Cir. 1988).

[106]*Id.* at 877, 40 FEP at 237 (Appendix).

[107]434 U.S. 136, 16 FEP 136 (1977).

[108]429 U.S. 125, 13 FEP 1657 (1976).

[109]42 U.S.C. § 2000e-2(a)(2).

[110]632 F. Supp. at 878, 40 FEP at 238; *see also* Seville v. Martin Marietta Corp., 638 F. Supp. 590, 41 FEP 572 (D. Md. 1986) (complaint that employer offered fringe benefits to technical employees and not to clerical employees constitutes a claim under § 703(a)(1), but not under § 703(a)(2); thus, adverse impact analysis is not applicable, and in absence of showing of intent to discriminate, policy does not violate Title VII).

[111]In yet another case involving Penney's head of household provision, the Seventh Circuit has reversed a grant of summary judgment to the company. The court ruled that the district court was not bound by the decision in *EEOC v. J.C. Penney Co., supra* note 105, that the plaintiff could proceed under a disparate impact approach, and that the plaintiff was not bound by the Ninth Circuit's decision in *Wambheim II, supra* note 103, that the company had a good business justification for the rule. Colby v. J.C. Penney Co., 811 F.2d 1119, 43 FEP 47 (7th Cir. 1987).

[112]781 F.2d 1362, 39 FEP 1815 (9th Cir. 1986), *aff'g* 609 F. Supp. 344, 34 FEP 1038 (N.D. Cal. 1984); *see also* Grove v. Frostburg Nat'l Bank, 549 F. Supp. 922, 940, 31 FEP 1675, 1689 (D. Md. 1982) ("breadwinner" test used to determine coverage for female employees in health insurance plan improper when no attempt is made to determine if male employees are "breadwinners"); *cf.* Northeast Dep't, Ladies Garment Workers, ILGWU v. Teamsters Local 229 Welfare Fund, 764 F.2d 147 (3d Cir. 1985), *rev'g* 584 F. Supp. 68, 36 FEP 196 (M.D. Pa. 1983) ("escape clause" in ERISA benefit plan providing for no medical coverage if employee is covered by spouse's plan and if insured pays less than 50% of cost of that coverage, is invalid; inclusion of such a clause was arbitrary and capricious conduct by plan trustees).

family's combined income, but as single persons and married men. The court rejected the school's claim that its practice fell within the religious exemption created in § 702[113], reasoning that the exemption applies to hiring decisions, but does not permit discrimination based on sex with respect to compensation and benefits. Similarly, the court rejected the school's BFOQ defense, noting that the specific language of the statute extends the defense only to decisions "to hire or employ."[114] In addition, the court rejected the school's First Amendment claim, because compliance with Title VII with respect to health insurance would not interfere with religious belief and would interfere "minimally, if at all," with religious practice.[115]

The liability of insurance companies who market discriminatory policies was addressed by the court in *Crowder v. Fieldcrest Mills.*[116] Because the insurer only gave advice concerning the policy and exercised no control over the operation of the plan, the court held that it was not an employer within the meaning of § 2000e(b) and was thus not subject to liability under Title VII.

## V. Pregnancy, Childbirth, and Parenting

### A. General Theory

#### 1. Gilbert *and* Satty *Decisions*

The benefit/burden analysis used in *Nashville Gas Co. v. Satty*[117] has continued to be applied in cases that arose before the effective date of the Pregnancy Discrimination Act.[118]

#### 2. *Pregnancy Discrimination Act*

In *Newport News Shipbuilding & Dry Dock Co. v. EEOC,*[119] the Supreme Court decided that the Pregnancy Discrimination Act provides protection not only for female employees on a company payroll but also for the spouses of male employees. Accordingly, the Court held that an employer's health benefit plan which provided more extensive pregnancy coverage to female employees than to spouses of male employees violated § 703(a)(1) of Title VII, because such a plan provided a less inclusive benefits package to married male employees than that provided to married female employees. The Court rejected the employer's assertion that the Pregnancy Discrimination Act protects only employees and not spouses of employees. Several courts have

---

[113]42 U.S.C. § 2000e-1.

[114]781 F.2d at 1367, 39 FEP at 1819 (citing 42 U.S.C. § 2000e-2(e)).

[115]*Id.* at 1364, 39 FEP at 1816.

[116]569 F. Supp. 825, 36 FEP 394 (M.D.N.C. 1983) (policy provided primary coverage for dependents of male employees, but only secondary coverage for dependents of female employees; merits of the Title VII claim were not addressed; court also noted that insurer was not an employer under the Equal Pay Act).

[117]*Supra* note 107.

[118]*E.g.,* Zuniga v. Kleberg County Hosp., Kingsville, Tex., 692 F.2d 986, 989 n.6, 30 FEP 650, 652 (5th Cir. 1982).

[119]462 U.S. 669, 32 FEP 1 (1983), *aff'g* 682 F.2d 113, 29 FEP 200 (4th Cir. 1982) (en banc).

applied *Newport News* retroactively to the date of the Pregnancy Discrimination Act.[120]

Emphasizing the unique nature of the facts before it, the district court in *Chambers v. Omaha Girls Club*[121] upheld a club rule prohibiting the employment of single persons who become pregnant or cause pregnancy. Based on its findings that "the policy is a legitimate attempt by a private service organization to attack a significant problem within our society * * * [and] is related to the Girls Club's central purpose of fostering growth and maturity of young girls,"[122] the court held that the Club did not violate Title VII in its discharge of an unmarried black employee who had become pregnant.

## B. Mandatory Maternity Leaves

Courts have continued to sustain mandatory maternity leave policies under narrow circumstances when pregnancy creates a risk of serious harm to third parties because it adversely affects the employee's ability to fully perform her job or when pregnancy creates a serious risk of harm to the employee herself.[123]

## C. Right to Voluntary Leave

### 1. Pregnancy and Childbirth-Related Disability Leave

As discussed in the introduction to this chapter, the Supreme Court in *California Federal Savings & Loan Association v. Guerra*[124] upheld a state statute that requires employers to grant to employees disabled by pregnancy up to four months unpaid leave with qualified reinstatement rights. The Court rejected the position that the Pregnancy Discrimination Act (PDA) requires employers to treat employees disabled by pregnancy the same as, but

---

[120]*See* EEOC v. Texas Indus., 782 F.2d 547, 40 FEP 118 (5th Cir. 1986); EEOC v. Puget Sound Log Scaling & Grading Bureau, 752 F.2d 1389, 36 FEP 1664 (9th Cir. 1985); Schiffman v. Cimarron Aircraft Corp., 615 F. Supp. 382, 38 FEP 1245 (W.D. Okla. 1985); EEOC v. MTC Gear Corp., 595 F. Supp. 712, 36 FEP 1738 (N.D. Ill. 1984); EEOC v. Atlanta Gas Light Co., 36 FEP 1669 (N.D. Ga. 1983), *aff'd,* 751 F.2d 1188, 36 FEP 1671 (11th Cir.), *cert. denied,* 474 U.S. 968, 39 FEP 384 (1985).

[121]629 F. Supp. 925, 40 FEP 362 (D. Neb. 1986), *aff'd,* 834 F.2d 697, 45 FEP 698 (8th Cir. 1987).

[122]*Id.* at 951, 40 FEP at 382.

[123]*See* Levin v. Delta Air Lines, 730 F.2d 994, 34 FEP 1192 (5th Cir. 1984), *aff'g* 34 FEP 1187 (S.D. Tex. 1982) (mandatory maternity leave policy upheld based on findings that "many pregnant stewardesses will suffer severe or disabling pregnancy-related problems that would prevent their assisting passengers to safety in an emergency" and that occurrence of such problems is "unpredictable"); Fields v. Bolger, 723 F.2d 1216, 33 FEP 1109 (6th Cir. 1984) (reversing district court's award of back pay and attorney's fees to postal service employee who claimed she was forced to take maternity leave in violation of Title VII upon receipt of her own doctor's letter placing 35–40 pound restriction on her job-related lifting); In re National Airlines, 700 F.2d 695, 31 FEP 369 (11th Cir.), *cert. denied,* 464 U.S. 933, 33 FEP 48 (1983) (district court did not abuse its discretion by refusing to enjoin Pan American World Airways from applying mandatory maternity leave policy to former National Airlines flight attendants after merger, where Pan Am policy had been upheld by federal court as justified by considerations of passenger safety, even though similar National Airlines policy had been rejected by a different court); *cf.* Zuniga v. Kleberg County Hosp., Kingsville, Tex., *supra* note 120 (suggesting in dictum that mandatory leave of absence with guaranteed reinstatement might be appropriate where fetus was potentially endangered by pregnant woman's mere presence in workplace containing reproductive hazard).

[124]479 U.S. 272, 42 FEP 1073 (1987); *see also* Miller-Wohl Co. v. Commissioner of Labor & Indus., Mont., 692 P.2d 1243, 36 FEP 1010 (Mont. 1984) (Montana Maternity Leave Act not preempted even though it requires employers to grant reasonable leave of absence for pregnancy).

no better than other disabled employees. Indeed, the Court specifically held that the Act did not prohibit preferential treatment and embraced the Ninth Circuit's conclusion that the PDA establishes " 'a floor beneath which pregnancy disability benefits may not fall—not a ceiling above which they may not rise.' "[125]

In the absence of statutory preferences, courts generally have held that pregnancy-related disability leaves must be treated like other disability leaves.[126] Thus, an employer may lawfully refuse to hire a pregnant applicant who will not be on the payroll long enough to accrue sufficient sick leave and vacation time to cover her planned four- to six-week leave of absence following childbirth where the employer would not hire any applicant who planned to interrupt employment for that length of time before completion of training.[127]

## 2. Parenting Leave

Courts continue to hold that an employer is not required under Title VII or the Pregnancy Discrimination Act to provide parental leaves of absence except to the extent that leaves are provided for other personal reasons.[128] However, a bill has been introduced in Congress which, if enacted, would require employers of 50 or more employees to grant up to 10 weeks of unpaid leave to care for children or seriously ill dependent parents during any 24-month period and up to 15 weeks during any 12-month period for the employee's own serious illness.[129]

## 3. Reinstatement After Leave

The pregnancy disability leave statute upheld by the Supreme Court in *California Federal Savings & Loan Association v. Guerra*[130] has been interpreted to require reinstatement to the employee's previous job, unless that job is no longer available due to a business necessity. In such a case, the California statute and regulations require that the employer must make a reasonable, good-faith effort to place the employee in a substantially similar job. The Court concluded that this interpretation "promotes equal employment opportunity" because requiring reinstatement "ensures that [women] will not lose their jobs on account of pregnancy disability."[131] Thus, in upholding the statute, the majority determined that the PDA does not prohibit "the States from requiring employers to provide reinstatement to pregnant workers, regardless of their policy for disabled workers generally.[132]

---

[125]42 FEP at 1079 (quoting 758 F.2d 390, 396, 37 FEP 849, 852 (9th Cir. 1985)).

[126]*See* Schiffman v. Cimarron Aircraft Corp., *supra* note 120 (disability policy which excluded maternity benefits for both female employees and spouses of male employees, but provided full coverage for spouses of female employees, was *per se* violation of Title VII); Maddox v. Grandview Care Center, 607 F. Supp. 1404, 37 FEP 1263 (M.D. Ga. 1985), *aff'd,* 780 F.2d 987, 39 FEP 1456 (11th Cir. 1986) (employer's policy restricting pregnancy leave to maximum of three months is facially discriminatory in absence of similar restriction on other types of medical leave).

[127]Marafino v. St. Louis County Circuit Court, 537 F. Supp. 206, 29 FEP 621 (E.D. Mo. 1982), *aff'd per curiam,* 707 F.2d 1005, 31 FEP 1536 (8th Cir. 1983).

[128]Record v. Mill Neck Manor Lutheran School for the Deaf, 611 F. Supp. 905, 38 FEP 387 (E.D.N.Y. 1985); *see also* EEOC Guidelines, 29 C.F.R. § 1604 App. (1986).

[129]H.R. 770, The Family and Medical Leave Act of 1989, 101st Cong., 1st Session (1989).

[130]*Supra* note 124.

[131]*Id.,* 42 FEP at 1080.

[132]*Id.,* 42 FEP at 1078.

On the other hand, an employer that guarantees reinstatement to an employee who takes non-pregnancy-related disability leave must guarantee reinstatement to an employee who takes leave to deliver a child.[133] However, it appears to be lawful to end the accrual of seniority on the date on which the employee is physically capable of returning to work following the delivery of a child, by converting the employee's leave status from disability to personal leave on that date.[134]

## D. Benefits

### 1. State Disability Insurance

A state's disability insurance law which treats female employees who are temporarily disabled due to pregnancy less favorably than employees with other disabilities may violate the Pregnancy Discrimination Act.[135]

### 2. State Unemployment Compensation

In *Wimberly v. Labor & Industrial Relations Commission of Missouri,*[136] the Supreme Court unanimously upheld the denial of unemployment benefits to a woman who left work due to pregnancy. Under Missouri's eligibility requirements, unemployment benefits are denied to all claimants who leave work "for reasons not attributable to the employer or connected with the work."[137] Under this rule, employees who leave work due to a temporary disability, including pregnancy, are ineligible for benefits. The court rejected the plaintiff's contention that the Federal Unemployment Tax Act mandates preferential treatment for employees who leave work due to pregnancy, concluding instead that the law simply "prohibits states from singling out pregnancy for unfavorable treatment."[138]

Similarly, the Massachusetts Supreme Judicial Court has held that the base period earnings requirement for unemployment insurance is not, on its face, a violation of the state's Equal Rights Amendment.[139] Even though the requirement may operate to deny benefits to pregnant employees who take extended maternity leaves, it is not unconstitutional if it contains no sex-

---

[133]EEOC v. Western Elec. Co., 28 FEP 1122 (M.D.N.C. 1982).

[134]*Id.*

[135]Barone v. Hackett, 602 F. Supp. 481, 40 FEP 961 (D.R.I. 1984), *later proceeding sub nom.* United States v. Rhode Island Dep't of Employment Sec., 619 F. Supp. 509 (D.R.I. 1985) (Department of Employment Security and its director held liable under Title VII where Rhode Island Temporary Disability Act treated pregnancy less favorably than other covered disabilities) (back pay and prejudgment interest both appropriate). In an earlier proceeding, the plaintiff's employer was dismissed as a defendant in the case on the basis that the employer was not vicariously liable for the unequal treatment by the state. 28 FEP 1765 (D.R.I. 1982); *cf.* Section V.C.1 and notes 124–27, *supra.*

[136]479 U.S. 511, 42 FEP 1261 (1987).

[137]*Id.,* 42 FEP at 1262.

[138]*Id.,* 42 FEP at 1263 (construing a 1976 amendment to the Federal Unemployment Tax Act, 26 U.S.C. § 304(a)(12)). As discussed above, in construing Title VII the Supreme Court said that the Pregnancy Discrimination Act does not *prohibit* a state from *favoring* employees disabled because of pregnancy. *See* California Fed. Sav. & Loan Ass'n v. Guerra, *supra* notes 2, 6–12, and accompanying text. In this case, the Court simply concluded that the Federal Unemployment Tax Act's provision that benefits not be denied "solely on the basis of pregnancy or termination of pregnancy" does not *require* preferential treatment.

[139]Buchanan v. Director, Employment Sec. Div., 393 Mass. 329, 36 FEP 1884 (1984) (court concluded that the record was insufficient to determine whether base period earnings requirement had been *applied* in discriminatory fashion).

based distinctions and is applied uniformly to all claimants regardless of gender or purpose of absence.[140]

### 3. Employer Disability Insurance

In *Shaw v. Delta Air Lines,*[141] the Supreme Court held that ERISA preempts state discrimination statutes to the extent that they affect payment of pregnancy-related disability benefits and prohibit that which is permitted by federal discrimination statutes. However, the Court has held that the Pregnancy Discrimination Act does not invalidate a California statute requiring employers to provide up to four months of leave during a "period of *actual physical disability* on account of pregnancy."[142]

Lastly, an employee will be covered by the Pregnancy Discrimination Act even where the employer uses a benefits plan operated by a third party.[143]

### E. The Fertile or Pregnant Employee in a Hazardous Work Area

A uniform approach to the issues posed in these cases has not yet emerged. The Fourth Circuit has held that an employer may exclude fertile women workers from a toxic environment if such restrictions are reasonably required to protect the health of unborn children, but must show that the exclusion is necessary to avoid a demonstrated negative effect on the unborn child.[144] In contrast, the Eleventh Circuit affirmed an award of damages to a pregnant x-ray technician who claimed that her dismissal pursuant to a hospital's fetus protection policy violated the Pregnancy Discrimination Act of 1978.[145] In so holding, the court discouraged employer reliance on a BFOQ defense holding that "when a policy designed to protect employee offspring from workplace hazards proves facially discriminatory, there is, in effect, no defense, unless the employer shows a direct

---

[140]The district court decision discussed on pp. 400–01 of the Second Edition has been affirmed by the Fourth Circuit and the Supreme Court has refused to hear the case. *See* Brown v. Porcher, 502 F. Supp. 946 (D.S.C. 1980), *aff'd in relevant part,* 660 F.2d 1001 (4th Cir. 1981), *cert. denied,* 459 U.S. 1150 (1983).

[141]463 U.S. 85, 32 FEP 121 (1983); *see* text accompanying note 100, *supra.*

[142]California Fed. Sav. & Loan Ass'n v. Guerra, 479 U.S. 272, 42 FEP 1073, 1081 (1987). *See* note 124, *supra,* and accompanying text.

[143]*See* Arizona Governing Comm. v. Norris, 463 U.S. 1073, 1089–91, 32 FEP 233, 240–41 (1983) (Court, evaluating employee life insurance program, stated that "an employer that adopts a fringe-benefit scheme that discriminates among its employees on the basis of * * * sex * * * violates Title VII regardless of whether third parties are also involved in the discrimination."); EEOC v. Wooster Brush Co. Employees Relief Ass'n, 727 F.2d 566, 33 FEP 1823 (6th Cir. 1984) (employer could participate in disability benefits plan operated by independent employees' relief association only if it made up for plan's failure to provide pregnancy disability benefits); *cf.* Schiffman v. Cimarron Aircraft Corp., 615 F. Supp. 382, 38 FEP 1245 (W.D. Okla. 1985) (fact that employees voted to determine policy coverage does not insulate employer from responsibility for failure to treat pregnancy same as other conditions under disability policy).

[144]Wright v. Olin Corp., 697 F.2d 1172, 30 FEP 889 (4th Cir. 1982). On remand, in an opinion that has been vacated, the district court held that the company had demonstrated a valid business necessity for its policy because of the significant risk of harm to the unborn children of female employees exposed to certain chemicals and physical agents. The court stated, "An employer such as Olin can justifiably choose a policy of fetal protection as a moral obligation to protect the next generation from injury, and it is a social good that should be encouraged and not penalized." 585 F. Supp. 1447, 1453, 34 FEP 1226, 1231 (W.D.N.C.), *vacated,* 767 F.2d 915, 40 FEP 192 (4th Cir. 1984).

[145]Hayes v. Shelby Memorial Hosp., 726 F.2d 1543, 34 FEP 444 (11th Cir. 1984).

relationship between the policy and the actual ability of a pregnant fertile female to perform her job."[146] The court also suggested that even if analyzed as a disparate impact case, the employer's business necessity defense "may be rebutted by proof that there are acceptable alternative policies that would better accomplish the purposes of promoting fetal health, or that would accomplish the purpose with a less adverse impact on one sex."[147] As applied to this case, the court found that the plaintiff had here demonstrated that the hospital failed to consider acceptable alternatives, including reassignment or rearrangement of duties.[148]

## VI. Sex Plus

### B. Sex Plus Marriage

As noted above,[149] a district court upheld a private girls club policy prohibiting the employment of single persons who became pregnant or caused pregnancy on the basis that the policy was adequately related to the core purpose of the club—that is, providing young girls with positive role models.[150]

Although antinepotism rules have often been upheld by the courts,[151] the Eighth Circuit in *EEOC v. Rath Packing Co.*[152] held that the defendant's no-spouse rule had a disparate impact on women, since 95 percent of current employees were men, and that the discriminatory policy was not justified by business necessity.

Finally, as discussed above, the Ninth Circuit held that a church-operated school violated Title VII when it provided health coverage to married men but not to married women.[153]

---

[146]*Id.* at 1549, 34 FEP at 449 (footnote omitted). The court stated in note 9: "Such a case should be rare." *Id.* In addition, the court quoted the following with approval from the district court opinion: " 'Potential for fetal harm, unless it adversely affects a mother's job performance, is irrelevant to the BFOQ issue.' " *Id.* (quoting 546 F. Supp. 259, 264, 29 FEP 1173, 1176 (N.D. Ala. 1982)).

[147]*Id.* at 1553, 34 FEP at 453.

[148]*Id.* at 1553–54, 34 FEP at 453. In addition, in a footnote, the court questioned whether the hospital's desire to avoid litigation that might arise from injury to the fetus could constitute a business necessity. *Id.* at 1552–53 n.15, 34 FEP at 452. *See also* Zuniga v. Kleberg County Hosp., Kingsville, Tex., 692 F.2d 986, 994, 30 FEP 650, 656 (5th Cir. 1982) (business necessity defense was pretextual because hospital failed to utilize its leave of absence policy which was "an alternative, less discriminatory means of achieving its stated goal"). *But see* Levin v. Delta Air Lines, 730 F.2d 994, 34 FEP 1192 (5th Cir. 1984) (*Zuniga* does not require that defendant transfer pregnant flight attendants to ground positions in lieu of requiring mandatory leaves of absence).

[149]*See* text accompanying note 65, *supra.*

[150]Chambers v. Omaha Girls Club, 629 F. Supp. 925, 40 FEP 362 (D. Neb. 1986), *aff'd,* 834 F.2d 697, 45 FEP 698 (8th Cir. 1987).

[151]*See* text accompanying and cases cited at p. 410, n.179, of the Second Edition. In addition, it should be noted that the district court decision in *Vuyanich v. Republic Nat'l Bank of Dallas,* cited in that footnote, has been vacated and remanded. *See* 723 F.2d 1195, 33 FEP 1521 (5th Cir.), *cert. denied,* 469 U.S. 1073 36 FEP 568 (1984). *See also* Thomas v. Metroflight dba Metro Airlines, 814 F.2d 1506, 43 FEP 703 (10th Cir. 1987) (in a case of first impression in the circuit, the court, while acknowledging that no-spouse rules often result in discrimination against women, upheld trial court's determination that plaintiff's evidence in this case was insufficient).

[152]787 F.2d 318, 40 FEP 580 (8th Cir.), *cert. denied,* 479 U.S. 910, 41 FEP 1712 (1986). This case also is discussed in Section I.D., *supra.*

[153]EEOC v. Fremont Christian School, 781 F.2d 1362, 39 FEP 1815 (9th Cir. 1986). *See* text accompanying note 102, *supra.*

## D. Sex Plus Appearance and Grooming Standards

In *Gerdom v. Continental Airlines*, [154] the court specifically distinguished the permissible grooming standards cases in holding that strict weight requirements imposed upon flight hostesses constituted sex discrimination under Title VII. The court rejected Continental's claim that, under *Stroud*, [155] the airline was immune from discriminatory treatment claims because the weight requirements applied only to an exclusively female job classification. [156]

The focal issue in the highly publicized case of *Craft v. Metromedia* [157] was whether a Kansas City television station applied higher standards of appearance to female on-the-air personnel than to males. While conceding that "there may have been some emphasis on the feminine stereotype of 'softness' and bows and ruffles," the Eighth Circuit affirmed the district court's determination that the standards were based on permissible factors— "a true focus on consistency of appearance, proper coordination of colors and textures, the effects of studio lighting on clothing and makeup, and the greater degree of conservatism thought necessary in the Kansas City market." [158]

Courts continue to find that Title VII is violated when an employer requires its female employees to wear sexually suggestive attire as a condition of employment. [159]

## VII. Height, Weight, and Physical Agility Requirements

Courts strike down height and physical agility requirements that adversely affect women and are not shown to be job-related. [160] A police academy's physical agility tests were held unlawful because they adversely affected female applicants and trainees and had not been validated in a manner

---

[154] 692 F.2d 602, 30 FEP 235 (9th Cir. 1982), *en banc reconsideration of* 648 F.2d 1223, 26 FEP 601 (1981), *cert. dismissed*, 460 U.S. 1074 (1983).

[155] Stroud v. Delta Air Lines, 544 F.2d 892, 894, 14 FEP 206, 208 (5th Cir.), *cert. denied*, 434 U.S. 844, 15 FEP 1184 (1977) (no-marriage rule applied to flight attendants not discriminatory because no men hired for job). *See* pp. 408–09 of the Second Edition.

[156] 692 F.2d at 607, 30 FEP at 239–40 (citing County of Washington, Or. v. Gunther, 452 U.S. 161, 25 FEP 1521 (1981)).

[157] 766 F.2d 1205, 38 FEP 404 (8th Cir. 1985), *cert. denied*, 475 U.S. 1058, 40 FEP 272 (1986).

[158] *Id.*, 766 F.2d at 1215, 38 FEP at 411. *But see* Tamimi v. Howard Johnson Co., 807 F.2d 1550, 42 FEP 1289 (11th Cir. 1987) (Title VII violated where employer discharged employee who refused to comply with new rule requiring female employees to wear makeup); O'Donnell v. Burlington Coat Factory Warehouse, 656 F. Supp. 263, 266, 43 FEP 150, 152 (S.D. Ohio 1987) (Title VII violated where women salesclerks are required to wear smocks when men are permitted to wear slacks and shirt; rule perpetuates sexual stereotypes; "it is demeaning for one sex to wear a uniform when members of the other sex holding the same positions are allowed to wear professional business attire").

[159] *See* Priest v. Rotary dba Fireside Motel & Coffee Shoppe, 634 F. Supp. 571, 581, 40 FEP 208, 215 (N.D. Cal. 1986) (although primarily a sexual harassment case, court also held that defendant violated Title VII by removing plaintiff from her job as a cocktail waitress because of her refusal to wear sexually suggestive attire).

[160] *E.g.*, Berkman v. City of New York, 536 F. Supp. 177, 28 FEP 856 (E.D.N.Y. 1982), *aff'd*, 705 F.2d 584, 31 FEP 767 (2d Cir. 1983) (physical agility test for firefighter); United States v. North Carolina, 512 F. Supp. 968, 28 FEP 566 (E.D.N.C. 1981), *aff'd*, 679 F.2d 890, 30 FEP 824 (4th Cir. 1982), *cert. denied*, 459 U.S. 1103, 30 FEP 1048 (1983) (5'6" minimum height requirement for highway trooper); *cf.* EEOC v. Spokane Concrete Prods., 534 F. Supp. 518, 28 FEP 423 (E.D. Wash. 1982) ("eyeball" test of physical strength insufficient grounds for rejecting female truck driver applicant).

consistent with the Uniform Guidelines.[161] Similarly, in a class action suit, female flight attendants who were discharged or suspended for exceeding maximum weight limits were awarded summary judgment, on a disparate treatment analysis, where the weight limits (applied only to females) were designed to gain a competitive edge by featuring slim females and were not a BFOQ.[162]

On the other hand, the First Circuit held that a hiring barrier cannot have a disparate impact on a protected group when job competition is only among members of that group; thus an unvalidated height requirement for police officers is lawful when applied to hiring vacancies set aside for females only.[163]

## VIII. Sexual Harassment

### A. What Conduct Is Illegal

#### 1. Adverse Employment Decisions and Discriminatory Work Environment

Employers continue to be held liable under Title VII for hostile work environments resulting from sexual harassment in the workplace, irrespective of whether the employee suffered tangible job detriment.[164] The Supreme Court endorsed this view in *Meritor Savings Bank v. Vinson.*[165]

The EEOC and federal courts in interpreting EEOC Guidelines have begun to delineate the level of activity that constitutes unlawful sexual harassment. According to the Supreme Court in *Vinson,* sexual harassment actionable under a "hostile environment" theory "must be sufficiently severe or pervasive to 'alter the conditions of [the victim's] employment and create an abusive working environment.' "[166] The plaintiff's allegations in that

---

[161]Burney v. City of Pawtucket, 559 F. Supp. 1089, 34 FEP 1274 (D.R.I. 1983), *aff'd,* 728 F.2d 547, 34 FEP 1295 (1st Cir. 1984) (granting injunctive relief). *But see* Livingston v. Roadway Express, 802 F.2d 1250, 41 FEP 1713 (10th Cir. 1986) (6'4" maximum height limitation does not unlawfully discriminate against men; noting that company had hired 189 men and 2 women drivers during relevant time period, court concluded that the restriction discriminates based on height, not sex); EEOC v. Ryder/ P.I.E. Nationwide, 649 F. Supp. 1282, 42 FEP 929 (W.D.N.C. 1986) (in the absence of a specific weight requirement, refusal to hire 113-pound female truck driver was based on legitimate business considerations where safety manager recommended against hiring after she had difficulty handling a Jifflox, a heavy piece of equipment used to connect two trailers).

[162]Gerdom v. Continental Airlines, *supra* note 154.

[163]Costa v. Markey, 706 F.2d 1, 31 FEP 1324 (1st Cir. 1983), *on reh'g en banc of* 694 F.2d 876, 30 FEP 593 (1st Cir. 1982), *cert. denied,* 464 U.S. 1017, 32 FEP 656 (1983).

[164]*See* Moylan v. Maries County, 792 F.2d 746, 40 FEP 1788 (8th Cir. 1986); Horn v. Windsor Mobile Homes, Duke Homes Div., 755 F.2d 599, 37 FEP 228 (7th Cir. 1985); Katz v. Dole, 709 F.2d 251, 31 FEP 1521 (4th Cir. 1983); Henson v. City of Dundee, 682 F.2d 897, 29 FEP 787 (11th Cir. 1982); Hayden v. Cox Enters., 534 F. Supp. 1166, 28 FEP 1315 (N.D. Ga. 1982); Robson v. Eva's Super Mkt., 538 F. Supp. 857, 30 FEP 1212 (N.D. Ohio 1982); Rimedio v. Revlon, 528 F. Supp. 1380, 30 FEP 1205 (S.D. Ohio 1982); Reichman v. Bureau of Affirmative Action, 536 F. Supp. 1149, 30 FEP 1644 (M.D. Pa. 1982); *cf.* Bohen v. City of E. Chicago, Ind., 799 F.2d 1180, 41 FEP 1108 (7th Cir. 1986) (plaintiff may maintain equal protection claim where supervisory personnel engaged in sexual harassment and other management personnel had notice of the conduct). *But see* Arnold v. United States, 816 F.2d 1306, 43 FEP 1256 (9th Cir. 1987) (allegations that supervisor sexually harassed, assaulted, and touched plaintiff "do not rise to the level of constitutional violations").

[165]477 U.S. 57, 40 FEP 1822 (1986). This case is discussed more fully in the introduction to this chapter.

[166]*Id.,* 40 FEP at 1827 (quoting Henson v. City of Dundee, *supra* note 164, at 904, 29 FEP at 793).

case—that the supervisor made repeated demands upon the plaintiff for sexual favors, fondled her in front of other employees, exposed himself to her, and forcibly raped her on several occasions—were held "plainly sufficient to state a claim for 'hostile environment' sexual harassment."[167]

By contrast, in a post-*Vinson* case, a divided panel of the Sixth Circuit held in *Rabidue v. Texas-American Petrochemicals, Osceola Refining Co. Division*[168] that occasional obscene comments about the plaintiff and other women made by a co-employee who was "an extremely vulgar and crude individual"[169] and the posting of "pictures, of nude or scantily clad women" in work areas by other male employees "did not result in a working environment that could be considered intimidating, hostile, or offensive" under the EEOC Guidelines.[170] This conclusion was based on the court's determination that the obscenities were "annoying" but did not "seriously [affect] the psyches" of the female employees and that the posters had a "de minimis" effect on the plaintiff's work environment "when considered in the context of a society that condones and publicly features and commercially exploits open displays of * * * erotica."[171] In comments that were severely criticized by the dissent, the court suggested that Title VII was not "designed to bring about a magical transformation in the social mores of American workers"[172] and further implied that the plaintiff had assumed the risk by voluntarily entering a work environment "pervaded" by "the lexicon of obscenity."[173]

Participation in or consent to workplace sexual conduct may affect an employee's Title VII claim. Although the Supreme Court in *Vinson* held that the *fact* that a plaintiff "voluntarily" participated in sex-related conduct is not a defense to a Title VII claim, the Court also held that the "correct

---

[167]*Id.*, 40 FEP at 1827. That holding is consistent with earlier decisions of the lower courts. For example, the Fourth Circuit in *Katz v. Dole, supra* note 164, held that the plaintiff was entitled to prevail where the record indicated that she was "the object of sustained and non-trivial harassment * * * of [a] pervasive character." *Id.* at 256, 31 FEP at 1524. In that case a female air traffic controller, the only woman on the crew, was subjected to harassment by supervisory personnel and other controllers which "took the form of extremely vulgar and offensive sexually related epithets." *Id.* at 254, 31 FEP at 1522. When she complained to her superiors, they reacted with further sexual harassment or indifference. *See also* Arnold v. City of Seminole, Okla., 614 F. Supp. 853, 40 FEP 1539 (N.D. Okla. 1985) (court found that plaintiff suffered continuous barrage of harassment for almost six years beginning in 1977 when she became city's first woman police officer; incidents included derogatory and vicious jokes directed at her; pornographic and demeaning cartoons and nude photos with plaintiff's name written on them, posted in public view in police station; false charges of misconduct filed against her; dead, coiled snake placed in patrol car she normally drove; picture of plaintiff's face placed on punching bag in officers' exercise room—despite her complaints, the picture remained there for two years; her son arrested on false charges).

[168]805 F.2d 611, 42 FEP 631 (6th Cir. 1986), *cert. denied,* 481 U.S. 1041, 43 FEP 1056 (1987).

[169]*Id.* 805 F.2d at 615, 42 FEP at 634.

[170]*Id.* at 622, 42 FEP at 639; *see also* Downes v. Federal Aviation Admin., 775 F.2d 288, 39 FEP 70 (Fed. Cir. 1985) (five incidents, some of which were "trivial," over three-year period do not establish pattern of harassment; incidents were not representative of supervisor's conduct and were not routine); Scott v. Sears, Roebuck & Co., 605 F. Supp. 1047, 1055–56, 37 FEP 878, 884 (N.D. Ill. 1985), *aff'd,* 798 F.2d 210, 41 FEP 805 (7th Cir. 1986) (social invitations, flirting, and isolated incidents of rude behavior by co-employees that made plaintiff "uncomfortable" insufficient to alter a "term, condition or privilege" of employment); Joyner v. AAA Cooper Transp., 597 F. Supp. 537, 36 FEP 1644 (M.D. Ala. 1983) (although plaintiff prevailed on quid pro quo theory based on one incident of unwelcome homosexual advances, court said single incident was insufficient to establish claim of hostile environment); EEOC Dec. 82-2, 28 FEP 1843 (1982) (supervisor's unwelcome invitation for a drink and a compliment concerning an employee's figure in the context of a conversation on dieting did not make out a violation and therefore did not support claim of constructive discharge).

[171]805 F.2d at 622; 42 FEP at 639.

[172]*Id.* at 621, 42 FEP at 638 (quoting 584 F. Supp. 419, 430, 36 FEP 183, 191 (E.D. Mich. 1984)).

[173]*Id.* at 620, 42 FEP at 638.

inquiry" is whether the victim "by her conduct indicated that the alleged sexual advances were unwelcome."[174] The Court's focus on the plaintiff's entire conduct in determining whether the alleged advances were unwelcome is consistent with several earlier cases.[175]

Two courts have emphasized that harassment may constitute sex discrimination even if the offending conduct or language is not sexual in nature. Relying on race harassment cases, the Eleventh Circuit in *Bell v. Crakin Good Bakers, Inc.* [176] held that a Title VII claim could be based on "threatening, bellicose, demeaning, hostile or offensive conduct by a supervisor in the workplace because of the sex of the victim" and that a showing of "sexual advances" is not required.[177] Similarly, the D.C. Circuit, reversing a grant of summary judgment to the defendants in *McKinney v. Dole,* [178] stated that the trial court's error was its apparent assumption "that an incident of physical force toward an employee by a supervisor cannot constitute sexual discrimination or harassment unless it is for the purpose of obtaining sexual favors or is otherwise blatantly sexually oriented."[179]

Finally, the courts have not yet developed a consistent approach to cases in which an employer promotes or otherwise favors an employee because of a sexual relationship between the employer (or supervisor) and the employee. One district court has held that Title VII was violated when an employer provided tangible benefits to employees who submitted to his sexual advances and withheld those benefits from employees who rejected his overtures.[180] However, the Second Circuit held that Title VII was not violated when a manager hired the woman with whom he was romantically involved rather than male applicants who were similarly qualified.[181] The court reasoned that Title VII bars "disparate treatment premised on one's gender" but does not bar disparate treatment premised on "sexual liaisons" and "sexual

---

[174]Meritor Sav. Bank v. Vinson, 477 U.S. 57, 40 FEP 1822, 1827 (using the term voluntary "in the sense that the complainant was not forced to participate against her will"). The EEOC has taken the position that active participation creates a presumption that any continuing conduct is welcome. The presumption can be overcome only by giving specific notice to the alleged harasser that such conduct is no longer welcome; merely ceasing participation in the conduct is not sufficient. EEOC Dec. 84-1, 33 FEP 1887 (1983). *See also* discussion in Section B.1, *infra.*

[175]*E.g.,* Loftin-Boggs v. City of Meridian, Miss., 633 F. Supp. 1323, 41 FEP 532 (S.D. Miss. 1986), *aff'd,* 824 F.2d 971 (5th Cir. 1987), *cert. denied,* 484 U.S. 1063 (1988) (case dismissed where general unprofessional conduct was prevalent in department and plaintiff participated in and even initiated use of vulgar language and telling of crude stories); Evans v. Mail Handlers, 32 FEP 634, 637 (D.D.C. 1983) (although work environment was "very distasteful," plaintiff failed to establish prima facie case where evidence showed that "the alleged harassing conduct was substantially welcome by Plaintiff;" "Plaintiff did not consider the conduct * * * to be offensive or intimidating until the relationship began to deteriorate"); Ukarish v. Magnesium Elektron, 31 FEP 1315 (D.N.J. 1983) (employee who engaged in sexual conversations with co-employee not victim of sexual harassment because she did not seriously disagree with the language used and the language did not single her out as a target); Gan v. Kepro Circuit Sys., 28 FEP 639, 640, 641 (E.D. Mo. 1982) (although work environment "was permeated by an extensive amount of lewd and vulgar conversation and conduct," plaintiff failed to establish prima facie case because "the allegedly harassing conduct was substantially welcome and encouraged by plaintiff. She actively contributed to the distasteful working environment by her own profane and sexually suggestive conduct.").

[176]777 F.2d 1497, 39 FEP 948 (11th Cir. 1985).

[177]*Id.* at 1503, 39 FEP at 953.

[178]765 F.2d 1129, 38 FEP 364 (D.C. Cir. 1985).

[179]*Id.* at 1138, 38 FEP at 370.

[180]Priest v. Rotary dba Fireside Motel & Coffee Shoppe, 634 F. Supp. 571, 40 FEP 208 (N.D. Cal. 1986); *see also* King v. Palmer, 778 F.2d 878, 39 FEP 877 (D.C. Cir. 1985); Toscano v. Nimmo, 570 F. Supp. 1197, 32 FEP 1401 (D. Del. 1983).

[181]DeCintio v. Westchester County Medical Center, 807 F.2d 304, 42 FEP 921 (2d Cir. 1986), *cert. denied,* 484 U.S. —, 44 FEP 1672 (1987).

attractions."[182] The court specifically distinguished cases in which benefits had been awarded to an employee who had been coerced into submitting to the employer's advances or otherwise sexually harassed, and declined to define " 'sex,' for Title VII purposes, so broadly as to include an ongoing, voluntary, romantic engagement."[183]

## 2. Liability for Supervisor Harassment

Federal courts apply strict liability in Title VII cases where a job benefit or detriment is linked to discriminatory behavior.[184] However, before the Supreme Court's decision in *Vinson,*[185] the federal courts were split on the issue of strict liability in cases premised on a "hostile environment" theory. Most federal courts had refused to impose liability on the employer in such cases in the absence of notice of the alleged conduct.[186] However, the District of Columbia Circuit, in *Vinson v. Taylor,*[187] noting that the EEOC Guidelines are "unambiguous" on this issue, held that Title VII imposes strict liability in all cases of sexual harassment, without regard to whether the plaintiff has suffered job detriment and without regard to employer knowledge. Three district courts adopted that view.[188]

The Supreme Court in *Vinson* split on the strict liability issue. The majority expressly declined to adopt any categorical rule which automatically would impose liability on the employer for harassment by a supervisor or which necessarily would insulate an employer who had no notice of the conduct. Instead, the Court concluded that Congress "surely" intended to "place some limits on the acts of employees for which employers under Title VII are to be held responsible. For this reason, we hold that the Court of Appeals erred in concluding that employers are always automatically liable for sexual harassment by their supervisors. * * * For the same reason, absence of notice to an employer does not necessarily insulate that employer from liability."[189] In a separate opinion, four Justices concluded that there

---

[182]*Id.,* 807 F.2d at 306, 42 FEP at 922.

[183]*Id.* at 307, 42 FEP at 923.

[184]*See* Horn v. Windsor Mobile Homes, Duke Homes Div., 755 F.2d 599, 37 FEP 228 (7th Cir. 1985) (employer strictly liable for discrimination by supervisor who had "absolute" authority to hire and fire and used that authority to "extort" sexual favors); Crimm v. Missouri Pac. R.R., 750 F.2d 703, 36 FEP 883 (8th Cir. 1984) (in "quid pro quo" case, strict liability applies); Craig v. Y&Y Snacks, 721 F.2d 77, 33 FEP 187 (3d Cir. 1983); Katz v. Dole, 709 F.2d 251, 31 FEP 1521 (4th Cir. 1983); Henson v. City of Dundee, 682 F.2d 897, 29 FEP 787 (11th Cir. 1982); EEOC v. Judson Steel Co., 33 FEP 1286 (N.D. Cal. 1982).

[185]Meritor Sav. Bank v. Vinson, 477 U.S. 57, 40 FEP 1822 (1986).

[186]*See* Moylan v. Maries County, 792 F.2d 746, 40 FEP 1788 (8th Cir. 1986); Katz v. Dole, *supra* note 184; Henson v. City of Dundee, *supra* note 184; Davis v. Western-Southern Life Ins. Co., 34 FEP 97 (N.D. Ohio 1984); Ferguson v. E.I. du Pont de Nemours & Co., 560 F. Supp. 1172, 31 FEP 795 (D. Del. 1983); Meyers v. I.T.T. Diversified Credit Corp., 527 F. Supp. 1064, 27 FEP 995 (E.D. Mo. 1981).

[187]753 F.2d 141, 146, 36 FEP 1423, 1427, *reh'g denied en banc,* 760 F.2d 1330, 37 FEP 1266 (D.C. Cir. 1985), *aff'd on other grounds sub nom.* Meritor Sav. Bank v. Vinson, 477 U.S. 57, 40 FEP 1822 (1986).

[188]Mitchell v. OsAir, 629 F. Supp. 636, 45 FEP 580 (N.D. Ohio 1986), *appeal dismissed,* 816 F.2d 681 (6th Cir. 1987); Jeppsen v. Wunnicke, 611 F. Supp. 78, 83, 37 FEP 994, 997 (D. Alaska 1985) (court expressly rejected *Henson* and adopted *Vinson,* noting that the distinction between "tangible job benefit" or "quid pro quo" cases and "hostile work environment" cases is an "extremely slippery concept"); Ambrose v. United States Steel Corp., 39 FEP 30 (N.D. Cal. 1985); *cf.* College-Town v. Massachusetts Comm'n Against Discrimination, 400 Mass. 156, 508 N.E.2d 587 (1987) (under state fair employment law, employer is liable for discrimination by supervisor; "harassment by a supervisor carries an implied threat that the supervisor will punish resistance through exercising supervisory powers").

[189]40 FEP at 1829 (citing Restatement (Second) of Agency §§ 219–237 (1958)).

is "no justification for a special rule, to be applied *only* in 'hostile environment' cases, that sexual harassment does not create employer liability" until the employer is notified of the discriminatory conduct.[190]

The Supreme Court's decision in *Vinson* suggests that the inquiry concerning employer liability in cases not involving quid pro quo allegations should focus on (1) whether the employer had an established and specific policy prohibiting sexual harassment in the workplace, (2) whether the policy was communicated to employees, (3) whether and when the employer learned of the alleged harassment, and (4) if the employer knew of the conduct, whether the employer's response was adequate. The majority opinion in *Vinson* suggests that an employer who can establish the requisite facts as to each of these inquiries should not be liable for the supervisor's conduct. With respect to the third and fourth questions, the existence and adequacy of a grievance procedure and the victim's use or nonuse of the procedure also are relevant inquiries.[191]

In addition to the employer, in some cases supervisors have been held personally liable where the supervisor acquiesces in or condones unlawful acts by subordinates[192] or where the supervisor's actions involve an independent claim of tortious conduct.[193]

### 3. Liability for Co-Employee Harassment

Cases have turned on whether the employer knew or should have known of the harassment and on the employer's apparent willingness to reaffirm and enforce a policy prohibiting harassment. Supervisory indifference in the face of verbal harassment by co-workers was a basis for liability in *Katz v. Dole.*[194] Another court found an employer violated Title VII when the employer decided that, on the basis of a single uncorroborated complaint, it had no duty to reassign an over-the-road truck driver accused by his co-driver of sexual harassment. The court held that that was an insufficient response to the complaint.[195]

---

[190]*Id.,* 40 FEP at 1831 (Marshall, J., concurring) (emphasis in original).

[191]*See Sparks v. Pilot Freight Carriers,* 830 F.2d 1554, 45 FEP 160 (11th Cir. 1987), where the court reversed a grant of summary judgment for the employer, holding that the employer may be liable for a single supervisor's working environment sexual harassment even if only the supervisor and the victim knew of the harassment.

[192]*See* Yates v. Avco Corp., 819 F.2d 630, 43 FEP 1595 (6th Cir. 1987) (supervisor, as well as employer, held liable); Robson v. Eva's Super Mkt., 538 F. Supp. 857, 30 FEP 1212 (N.D. Ohio 1982) (noting that term "employer" as defined in 42 U.S.C. § 2000e(b) includes "any agent" of employer). *But see* Huebschen v. Wisconsin Dep't of Health & Social Servs., 716 F.2d 1167, 32 FEP 1582 (7th Cir. 1983) (overturning plaintiff's verdict against harassing supervisor because supervisor was not an employer within meaning of § 703(a)(1) of Title VII).

[193]*E.g.,* Otto v. Department of Health & Human Servs., 781 F.2d 754, 39 FEP 1754 (9th Cir. 1986) (supervisor not immune from liability for defamation and invasion of privacy if conduct was beyond his authority); Murphy v. Chicago Transit Auth., 638 F. Supp. 464 (N.D. Ill. 1986) (§ 1983 action for compensatory and punitive damages will lie against supervisors for deliberate indifference to sexual harassment by co-workers); Stewart v. Thomas, 538 F. Supp. 891, 895, 30 FEP 1609, 1612 (D.D.C. 1982) (refusing to dismiss plaintiff's supervisor as a defendant, court held that Title VII was not plaintiff's exclusive remedy because she was seeking to vindicate "two distinct and independent rights: her right to be free from discriminatory treatment at her jobsite and her right to be free from bodily or emotional injury caused by another person").

[194]*Supra* note 184, at 254, 31 FEP at 1522.

[195]Martin v. Norbar, Inc., 537 F. Supp. 1260, 30 FEP 103 (S.D. Ohio 1982); *see also* Zabkowicz v. Dart Indus., West Bend Co. Div., 589 F. Supp. 780, 35 FEP 610 (E.D. Wis. 1984), *aff'd in part and rev'd in part,* 789 F.2d 540, 40 FEP 1171 (7th Cir. 1986) (despite notice of prolonged, crude, explicit oral and

On the other hand, the Fourth and Eighth circuits have held that an employer's prompt investigation followed by disciplinary action against harassing co-workers is sufficient to avoid Title VII liability.[196]

### 4. Harassment by Nonemployees

In what was described by the EEOC as a case of first impression, the Commission declared that an employer may be held liable for sexual harassment by a nonemployee "where the employer fails to take corrective measures within its control once it knows or has reason to know of the nonemployee's conduct."[197] In this case, the harasser was a "regular and frequent customer" who had a "friendly personal relationship" with the employer.[198] Thus, the employer could have taken at least two appropriate corrective measures following knowledge of the charging party's complaints: informing the harasser that further offensive conduct toward the waitress would not be tolerated and relieving the charging party of the duty to wait on this particular customer in the future. The employer had done neither.[199]

### 5. Dress Requirements

Title VII is violated when an employer requires its female employees to wear sexually suggestive attire as a condition of employment.[200]

## B. Proof

### 1. General Considerations

According to the Supreme Court in *Vinson,* the "gravamen of any sexual harassment claim is that the alleged sexual advances were 'unwelcome.' "[201] The Court recognized that the question whether particular conduct was in fact unwelcome "presents difficult problems of proof and

---

pictorial harassment, employer failed to investigate or discipline offending co-workers until after plaintiff filed her EEOC charge; holding occasional meetings at which rules against use of abusive language were recited was insufficient response to plaintiff's complaints).

[196]Swentek v. USAir, 830 F.2d 552, 44 FEP 1808 (4th Cir. 1987); Barrett v. Omaha Nat'l Bank, 726 F.2d 424, 35 FEP 593 (8th Cir. 1984); *see also* Scott v. Sears, Roebuck & Co., 605 F. Supp. 1047, 1055, 37 FEP 878, 883 (N.D. Ill. 1985), *aff'd on other grounds,* 798 F.2d 210, 41 FEP 805 (7th Cir. 1986) (employer not liable absent actual knowledge or "harassment * * * so pervasive or so severe that constructive knowledge could be imputed to [employer]") (court of appeals found evidence insufficient to establish prima facie case of hostile environment, so expressly declined to rule on issue of employer liability for acts of co-workers); Ross v. Communications Satellite Corp., 34 FEP 260 (D. Md. 1984), *rev'd and remanded on other grounds,* 759 F.2d 355, 37 FEP 797 (4th Cir. 1985) (no sexual harassment where alleged co-worker harassment consisted of verbal flirtations without any evidence of physical actions and where employer company offered to take actions to ameliorate the situation and its effects).

[197]EEOC Dec. 84-3, 34 FEP 1887, 1890–91 (1984).

[198]*Id.* at 1891.

[199]Applying a variation of this principle, a New York court affirmed imposition of a penalty under state law against an employer because of the sexual harassment of employees by a polygraph examiner hired by the employer to test job applicants and employees suspected of theft. New York v. Hamilton dba American Truth Verification Serv., 125 A.D.2d 588, 509 N.Y.S.2d 779, 42 FEP 1069 (App. Div. 1986).

[200]*See* Priest v. Rotary dba Fireside Motel & Coffee Shoppe, 634 F. Supp. 571, 40 FEP 208 (N.D. Cal. 1986) (plaintiff established prima facie violation of Title VII by showing that defendant had removed her from her position as cocktail waitress because she refused to wear sexually suggestive clothes).

[201]Meritor Sav. Bank v. Vinson, 477 U.S. 57, 40 FEP 1822, 1827 (1986).

turns largely on credibility determination [sic] committed to the trier of fact. * * *"[202] While the fact that a plaintiff's participation in sex-related conduct was not "forced" against her will is not a defense to a claim of sexual harassment, evidence that the plaintiff dressed or spoke in a sexually provocative manner or otherwise "voluntarily" participated in sex-related conduct is relevant to the issue of whether the alleged advances were unwelcome. The Supreme Court expressly rejected the District of Columbia Circuit's view that testimony concerning the plaintiff's "provocative dress and publicly expressed fantasies 'had no place in this litigation.' "[203] On the "voluntariness" issue, testimony regarding the employer's knowledge of the plaintiff's financial needs was admitted by one court as evidence of the victim's economic vulnerability where it also was shown that that knowledge was used "to persuade her to perform the sexual acts."[204] On the other hand, two courts have held that psychiatric or psychological records concerning the plaintiff are not discoverable in sexual harassment cases.[205]

Although the Supreme Court's holding in *Vinson* makes clear that the plaintiff in a "hostile environment" case must prove that the conduct was "sufficiently severe or pervasive 'to alter the conditions of * * * employment and create an abusive working environment,' "[206] the Court did not address the type or quantum of evidence necessary to meet this standard. On this issue, some courts have permitted the plaintiff to introduce the testimony of other alleged victims of the harassment[207] or other "pattern" evidence concerning a supervisor's conduct.[208] The EEOC has held that a bare assertion of a manager's unwelcome sexual advances, unsupported by witnesses or corroborative evidence, is insufficient to establish sexual harassment.[209]

As noted above,[210] the Supreme Court in *Vinson* rejected the view that in a "hostile environment" case the plaintiff necessarily must show that the employer knew or should have known of the harassment and failed to take prompt remedial action. The Court also rejected the view that employers are automatically liable for a supervisor's conduct without regard to notice; instead, employer liability is premised on agency principles.[211] Thus, al-

---

[202]*Id.,* 40 FEP at 1827.

[203]*Id.,* 40 FEP at 1828 (quoting Vinson v. Taylor, 753 F.2d 141, 146 n.36, 36 FEP 1423, 1427 (D.C. Cir. 1985)).

[204]Phillips v. Smalley Maintenance Servs., 711 F.2d 1524, 1532, 32 FEP 975, 981 (11th Cir. 1983).

[205]*See* Jennings v. D.H.L. Airlines, 101 F.R.D. 549, 34 FEP 1423 (N.D. Ill. 1984); Priest v. Rotary dba Fireside Motel & Coffee Shoppe, 98 F.R.D. 755, 32 FEP 1064 (N.D. Cal. 1983), *decision on merits,* 634 F. Supp. 571, 40 FEP 208 (N.D. Cal. 1986) (plaintiff's sexual history not discoverable); *see also* Mitchell v. Hutchings, 116 F.R.D. 481, 44 FEP 615 (D. Utah 1987) (evidence of sexual behavior in workplace is discoverable, but information about victims' sexual proclivities and behavior or past sexual conduct is not discoverable).

[206]*Supra* note 201, 40 FEP at 1827 (quoting Henson v. City of Dundee, 682 F.2d 897, 904, 29 FEP 787, 793 (11th Cir. 1982)).

[207]Phillips v. Smalley Maintenance Servs., *supra* note 204.

[208]Vinson v. Taylor, 753 F.2d 141, 36 FEP 1423 (D.C. Cir. 1985), *aff'd in part and remanded sub nom.* Meritor Sav. Bank v. Vinson, 477 U.S. 57, 40 FEP 1822 (1986).

[209]EEOC Dec. 82-13, 29 FEP 1855 (1982).

[210]*See* text accompanying notes 185–190, *supra.*

[211]The difficulty courts are likely to face when applying common law agency principles in such cases is illustrated by *Davis v. United States Steel Corp.,* 779 F.2d 209, 39 FEP 955 (4th Cir. 1985). Addressing the issue of the employer's liability for state tort claims (after the plaintiff had dismissed her Title VII claim), the court split three ways on the issue of respondeat superior. The majority reversed the trial court's grant of summary judgment to the employer, concluding that a manager's failure to take any

though employer knowledge and response are relevant, the inquiry in such cases also may focus on whether the offending employee was acting within the scope of employment and on behalf of the employer or simply following the employee's own whim or interest. That, of course, creates the potential for serious conflicts of interest between the employer and the accused supervisory employee in hostile environment cases.

Finally, on a procedural issue, one district court has applied the Fifth Circuit's tolling doctrine on Title VII claims by requiring that an employee file her Title VII charge of sexual harassment within the 180-day statutory limitation period following the last claimed incident of harassment.[212] The plaintiff's failure to do so, without advising the court through complaint or affidavit of facts that would justify application of the tolling doctrine, resulted in dismissal of her complaint.

### 2. Order and Allocation of Proof

Although the Supreme Court did not address the issue in *Vinson,* it is possible to draw some conclusions concerning the order and allocation of proof in hostile environment sexual harassment cases. First, the approach formulated by the D.C. Circuit in *Bundy v. Jackson,*[213] patterned after *McDonnell Douglas Corp. v. Green,*[214] does not easily fit non-quid-pro-quo cases: by definition, in a hostile environment case, there has been no "decision" affecting a tangible economic benefit that the employer would seek to prove was based on legitimate, nondiscriminatory grounds, or which the plaintiff would then attempt to prove was "pretextual."

Based on *Vinson* and other recent cases, then, the order and allocation of proof in hostile environment cases appears to be as follows:

(1)   First, the employee must establish a prima facie case by proving (a) that the alleged sexual harassment occurred, (b) that the conduct was sufficiently severe or pervasive to "alter the conditions of employment and create an abusive work environment," and (c) that the conduct or advances were unwelcome. Proof of these elements is sufficient to establish a prima facie case against the offending supervisor; whether it is sufficient to establish a prima facie case against the employer as well is unclear. On the other

---

action after observing a supervisor's improper conduct could expose the company to liability because at that point "the matter could be said to have progressed from a frolic of [the supervisor's] own to behavior known to [the company] and condoned by it." *Id.* at 211, 39 FEP at 956. One judge, while concurring in the reversal, would have adopted a broader rule of liability: "I would hold that where acts of harassment are pervasively intermingled with the performance of supervisory duties, the supervisor does not cease as matter of law to be acting within the scope of his employment." *Id.* at 213, 39 FEP at 957 (Butzner, J., concurring and dissenting). Another judge, dissenting, contended that the supervisor's acts were "wholly prompted by personal sexual desires, even though committed on the employer's premises during work hours, [thus] cannot constitute acts done 'in furtherance of the employer's business,' within fair contemplation of the controlling common law principle." *Id.* at 214, 39 FEP at 958 (Phillips, J., concurring in part and dissenting in part).

[212]Forde v. Royal's, 537 F. Supp. 1173, 1175–76, 31 FEP 213, 215 (S.D. Fla. 1982) (court also rejected plaintiff's common law claims of breach of contract and intentional infliction of emotional distress).

[213]641 F.2d 934, 24 FEP 1155 (D.C. Cir. 1981), discussed at p. 426 of the Second Edition.

[214]411 U.S. 792, 5 FEP 965 (1973).

hand, proof by the plaintiff that the employer knew of the conduct and failed to take remedial action clearly will be sufficient to shift to the employer the burden of going forward with the evidence.

(2)    Once the burden of production has shifted, the employer (and/or the supervisor) may rebut the plaintiff's case by producing evidence that the conduct did not occur, or that it was genuinely "trivial" in nature or was an isolated incident, or that the plaintiff did not indicate that the conduct was unwelcome (or, conversely, that the plaintiff's conduct demonstrated that the behavior was welcome).

(3)    In order to insulate itself from liability for the acts of a supervisor, the employer should establish (a) that it had a specific published policy prohibiting sexual harassment in the workplace, (b) that it had established a grievance procedure "calculated to encourage victims of harassment to come forward," and (c) that it did not know (and had no reason to know) that the conduct occurred (e.g., the plaintiff failed to resort to the grievance procedure) or (d) if it had knowledge, that it took prompt and appropriate remedial action.

At least two other issues remain unresolved. First, while the court in *Bundy v. Jackson*[215] imposed the stringent "clear and convincing" evidence standard on employers in quid pro quo cases, it remains unclear whether the "preponderance of the evidence" test or the more stringent burden will be imposed on employers in hostile environment cases.[216] Second, while the Court in *Vinson* observed that employer liability in hostile environment cases would be premised on agency principles, the Court left unanswered whether the plaintiff or defendant carries the burden on this issue.

### 3. Effect of Employer Failure to Investigate

The burden remains on the employer to investigate cases of sexual harassment upon notice. Failure to investigate and take appropriate remedial action following notice will certainly be a significant factor with respect to employer liability.[217] In *Vinson,* the Court commented that the employer's argument against liability in that case might have been substantially stronger "if its procedures were better calculated to encourage victims of harassment to come forward."[218]

---

[215]*Supra* note 213.

[216]The Sixth Circuit recently adopted the preponderance of the evidence test in a case in which the plaintiff failed to establish a prima facie case. Rabidue v. Texas-American Petrochemicals, Osceola Ref. Co. Div., 805 F.2d 611, 621, 42 FEP 631, 639 (6th Cir. 1986), *cert. denied,* 481 U.S. 1041, 43 FEP 1056 (1987).

[217]*See* Craig v. Y&Y Snacks, 721 F.2d 77, 33 FEP 187 (3d Cir. 1983); Katz v. Dole, 709 F.2d 251, 31 FEP 1521 (4th Cir. 1983); Zabkowicz v. West Bend Co., 589 F. Supp. 780, 35 FEP 610 (E.D. Wis. 1984), *aff'd in part and rev'd in part,* 789 F.2d 540, 40 FEP 1171 (7th Cir. 1986) (periodic meetings that had only limited effect held insufficient corrective action); Lamb v. Smith Int'l, Drilco Div., 32 FEP 105 (S.D. Tex. 1983); EEOC v. Judson Steel Co., 33 FEP 1286 (N.D. Cal. 1982); Robson v. Eva's Super Mkt., 538 F. Supp. 857, 30 FEP 1212 (N.D. Ohio 1982); Martin v. Norbar, Inc., 537 F. Supp. 1260, 30 FEP 103 (S.D. Ohio 1982).

[218]Meritor Sav. Bank v. Vinson, 477 U.S. 57, 40 FEP 1822, 1829 (1986).

In addition, the employer's response following investigation may be tested for adequacy. The Sixth Circuit recently held that even though the employer "drastically demoted" the harasser following an investigation, "the matter was not dealt with effectively" in that the employer asked the victims not to go to the EEOC, failed to provide the victims with requested written assurances that their jobs would be protected, failed to correct the victims' personnel files regarding sick leave that each had taken because of the harassment, and failed to reinstate their sick leave.[219]

Employer investigations must be conducted carefully in order to avoid creating actionable claims for defamation or other torts by the allegedly offending supervisor or co-worker.[220]

## 4. Effect of Employer Antiharassment Policy

The Supreme Court in *Vinson* expressly rejected the position that the "mere existence of a grievance procedure and a policy against discrimination, coupled with [a plaintiff's] failure to invoke that procedure," insulates the employer from liability for harassment by a supervisor.[221] However, the importance of adopting and publicizing a specific antiharassment policy was emphasized by the *Vinson* majority when it observed that the defendant's "general nondiscrimination policy did not address sexual harassment in particular, and thus did not alert employees to their employer's interest in correcting that form of discrimination,"[222] and that the employer's defense might have been "substantially stronger if its procedures were better calculated to encourage victims of harassment to come forward."[223]

The Sixth Circuit has stated that a policy which gives the supervisor responsibility for receiving reports and correcting the harassment, "must necessarily discourage reporting and diminish an employee's faith in the system" when the supervisor is the harasser.[224] The court also commented that the employer's policy of not placing documentation about sexual harassment in personnel files had the effect of protecting the employer and the harasser rather than the victims. For example, in this case, the plaintiffs' files documented excessive absenteeism, but provided no explanation that the absences were due to harassment by the supervisor. The court commended the intent of the employer's antiharassment policy, but concluded that the policy "did not function effectively to eliminate harassment."[225]

---

[219]Yates v. Avco Corp., 819 F.2d 630, 43 FEP 1595 (6th Cir. 1987).

[220]See Johnson v. International Minerals & Chem. Corp., 40 FEP 1651 (D.S.D. 1986) (granting summary judgment to employer against three supervisory employees who had been discharged after company settled and investigated claims of sexual harassment by supervisors, dismissing their claims of wrongful discharge, breach of contract, defamation, and intentional infliction of emotional distress on findings that investigation was thorough, extensive, and conducted in good faith); Garziano v. E.I. du Pont de Nemours & Co., 818 F.2d 380, 43 FEP 1790 (5th Cir. 1987) (employer protected by qualified privilege for publishing description of incident in "sexual harassment bulletin" distributed to supervisors); see also cases cited in notes 234–36, infra.

[221]Supra note 218, 40 FEP at 1829.

[222]Id.

[223]Id. See Section D, infra.

[224]Yates v. Avco Corp., supra note 219, at 635, 43 FEP at 1599; see also Vinson, supra notes 221–23 and accompanying text.

[225]Id.

## C. Causes of Action Under State Law

Federal courts continue to exercise pendent jurisdiction over tort claims associated with allegations of sexual harassment. The tort claim most often recognized is intentional infliction of emotional distress.[226] The Eighth Circuit has held that an employee-at-will who alleged that she was discharged for refusing to sleep with her foreman had stated a claim for breach of contract and tort under Arkansas law.[227] Similarly, a district court in New Hampshire held that dismissal of a female employee for rejecting the sexual advances of her employer would support a claim for wrongful discharge.[228] The court reasoned that conditioning continued employment on submission to sexual harassment would offend public policy.

States vary as regards common law claims. Pennsylvania's Fair Employment Practices Act bars a common law "wrongful discharge" action based upon sexual harassment, but the Act does not preclude a claim of intentional infliction of emotional distress based on harassing activities.[229]

In a California case which has not been officially published,[230] a local union and its chief executive officer were held liable for compensatory and punitive damages resulting from the union chief's practice of conditioning future union-referred work for waitresses on their acceptance of "jobs" as prostitutes as well as their providing sexual favors to the union chief. The court held that the suit was not preempted by the NLRA and also affirmed an award of punitive damages for breach of the duty of fair representation.

Courts have recently split on the effect of state workers' compensation laws on claims of sexual harassment. One court denied an employer's motion for summary judgment based upon the contention that workers' compensation provided the exclusive remedy for all injuries arising out of or in the course of employment, because the court found that sexual harassment was not related to the risks inherent in the position of "management trainee."[231] Other courts, however, have dismissed pendent tort claims on the basis that

---

[226]*E.g.,* Priest v. Rotary dba Fireside Motel & Coffee Shoppe, 634 F. Supp. 571, 40 FEP 208 (N.D. Cal. 1986) (awarding $95,000 for intentional infliction of emotional distress, battery, and false imprisonment, plus $15,000 punitive damages); Arnold v. City of Seminole, Okla., 614 F. Supp. 853, 40 FEP 1539 (E.D. Okla. 1985) (verdict of $150,000 for claims under 42 U.S.C. § 1983, state discrimination law, and intentional infliction of emotional distress); Cummings v. Walsh Constr. Co., 561 F. Supp. 872, 31 FEP 930 (S.D. Ga. 1983); Frykberg v. State Farm Mut. Auto. Ins. Co., 557 F. Supp. 517, 32 FEP 575 (W.D.N.C. 1983); Vegh v. General Elec. Co., 34 FEP 135 (E.D. Pa. 1983); Stewart v. Thomas, 538 F. Supp. 891, 30 FEP 1609 (D.D.C. 1982) (court permitted joinder of assault, battery, and intentional infliction of emotional distress to Title VII claim); *cf.* Phillips v. Smalley Maintenance Servs., 711 F.2d 1524, 32 FEP 975 (11th Cir. 1983) (plaintiff awarded $25,000 for invasion of privacy; pendent jurisdiction proper); Hunt v. Weatherbee, 626 F. Supp. 1097, 39 FEP 1469 (D. Mass. 1986) (denying motion to dismiss civil RICO and conspiracy claims against union officials who allegedly condoned sexual harassment). *See generally* Chapter 23 (Related Causes of Action).

[227]Lucas v. Brown & Root, 736 F.2d 1202, 35 FEP 1855 (8th Cir. 1984).

[228]Chamberlin v. 101 Realty, 626 F. Supp. 865 (D.N.H. 1985); *see also* Holien v. Sears, Roebuck & Co., 298 Or. 76, 689 P.2d 1292, 36 FEP 137 (1984). *But see* Lui v. Intercontinental Hotels Corp., 634 F. Supp. 684 (D. Haw. 1986) (common law constructive discharge action barred by employee's failure to file sexual harassment charge under state antidiscrimination statute).

[229]Shaffer v. National Can Corp., 565 F. Supp. 909, 34 FEP 172 (E.D. Pa. 1983). *See also infra* Chapter 23 at note 9 and accompanying text.

[230]Seritis v. Hotel & Restaurant Employees Local 28, 167 Cal.App.3d 78, 213 Cal. Rptr. 588, 37 FEP 1501, *hearing denied and ordered not to be officially published,* 120 LRRM 2342 (Cal. 1985), *cert. denied,* 474 U.S. 1060, 121 LRRM 2208 (1986).

[231]Bennett v. Furr's Cafeterias, 549 F. Supp. 887, 30 FEP 93 (D. Colo. 1982).

the state's workers' compensation act was intended to substitute entirely for the common law.[232]

In several cases, courts have ruled that an employee who quits her job because of sexual harassment is not disqualified from receiving compensation by her resignation.[233]

Courts continue to uphold actions of employers who terminate the employment of managers or supervisors for engaging in sexual harassment.[234] One case involved the termination of a tenured professor for "immoral conduct" (a statutory offense under state law) in permitting male students to sexually harass a female student.[235] The Missouri Supreme Court held that a person of "ordinary intelligence" should have known that the acts were prohibited.

Finally, the Fifth Circuit recently reversed a verdict in favor of an employee who had been discharged for harassment and had sued his employer for defamation.[236] The employer had issued a "Management Information Bulletin" to supervisors which included statements that an employee (who was not named) had been discharged because of a sexual harassment incident and that "deliberate, repeated, and unsolicited physical contact as well as significant verbal abuse was involved in this case."[237] Although the bulletin apparently was not posted at the plant, it was read to some employees and summarized to most other employees. Noting that "federal law imposes a specific duty upon employers to protect the workplace and workers from sexual harassment," the court concluded that a qualified privilege applied to the employer's conduct because the bulletin was a legitimate means of informing the employees of the employer's anti-harassment policy.[238]

---

[232]See Lui v. Intercontinental Hotels Corp., *supra* note 228 (assault and battery claims dismissed because worker's compensation was plaintiff's exclusive remedy); Miller v. Lindenwood Female College, 616 F. Supp. 860, 40 FEP 510 (E.D. Mo. 1985) (if harasser acted within scope of his employment, then plaintiff's claim for intentional infliction of emotional distress was barred by workers' compensation); Harrison v. Reed Rubber Co., 603 F. Supp. 1456, 37 FEP 1544 (E.D. Mo. 1984) (barring causes of action for assault, battery, and negligent and intentional infliction of emotional distress).

[233]Dura Supreme v. Kienholz, 381 N.W.2d 92 (Minn. App. 1986); Doering v. Board of Review, 203 N.J. Super. 241, 496 A.2d 720 (1985); Weissmann v. Commonwealth Unemployment Compensation Bd. of Review, 502 A.2d 782 (Pa. Cmwlth. 1986); Sweitzer v. State Dep't of Employment Sec., 43 Wash.App. 511, 718 P.2d 3 (1986).

[234]See Carosella v. United States Postal Serv., 816 F.2d 638, 643, 43 FEP 845, 849 (Fed. Cir. 1987) (employer not required "to tolerate the disruption and inefficiencies caused by a hostile workplace environment until the wrongdoer has so clearly violated the law that the victims are sure to prevail in a Title VII action"); Crimm v. Missouri Pac. R.R., 750 F.2d 703, 36 FEP 883 (8th Cir. 1984) (showing that supervisor's discharge was based on recommendation of counsel after detailed investigation of charge of sexual harassment, constituted a good defense to supervisor's claim of age discrimination); Snipes v. United States Postal Serv., 677 F.2d 375, 30 FEP 1257 (4th Cir. 1982) (no breach of government merit system protection when postal supervisor who engaged in four incidents of sexual harassment was discharged); Johnson v. International Minerals & Chem. Corp., 40 FEP 1651 (D.S.D. 1986) (employer did not wrongfully discharge three supervisors following extensive investigation of sexual harassment charges); French v. Mead Corp., 33 FEP 635 (S.D. Ohio 1983), aff'd, 758 F.2d 652, 37 FEP 1408 (6th Cir.), cert. denied, 474 U.S. 820, 38 FEP 1727 (1985) (reasonable belief that supervisor harassed employee sufficient basis for termination, rebutting supervisor's claim of sex discrimination); County of Santa Clara v. Willis, 179 Cal.App.3d 1240, 225 Cal. Rptr. 244 (1986); Thomas v. Petrulis, 125 Ill.App.3d 415, 465 N.E.2d 1059, 35 FEP 190 (1984); Ramsey County Community Human Servs. v. Davila, 387 N.W.2d 421 (Minn. 1986); Petties v. New York State Dep't of Mental Retardation, 93 A.D.2d 960, 463 N.Y.S.2d 284, 31 FEP 1164 (App. Div. 1983), later proceeding, 106 A.D.2d 739, 483 N.Y.S.2d 775 (1984).

[235]Ross v. Robb, 662 S.W.2d 257 (Mo. 1983).

[236]Garziano v. E.I. du Pont de Nemours & Co., 818 F.2d 380, 43 FEP 1790 (5th Cir. 1987).

[237]Id. at 384, 43 FEP at 1793.

[238]Id. at 387, 43 FEP at 1796. The case was remanded for determination of whether the privilege had been abused. See also Barnes v. Oody, 514 F. Supp. 23, 28 FEP 816 (E.D. Tenn. 1981) (summary judgment for defendant employee in defamation action brought by fellow employee whom defendant had accused of harassment; arbitrator earlier had determined that allegations of harassment were true).

## D. Preventive Suggestions

The Supreme Court's majority opinion in *Vinson*[239] underscores the importance of the preventive suggestions contained in the Second Edition.[240] In order to shield themselves from liability in hostile environment cases, employers should adopt and publicize to their employees specific policies defining and prohibiting sexual harassment in the workplace. The policy should include a grievance procedure "calculated to encourage victims of harassment to come forward,"[241] by designating someone who is not the supervisor of the complaining employee to receive and investigate such complaints.[242]

Each complaint should be investigated promptly and thoroughly, and appropriate action should be taken at the conclusion of the investigation. However, as the Supreme Court observed in *Vinson*, claims of sexual harassment present "difficult problems of proof" and often turn on credibility determinations.[243] The employer must be aware of the interests of the accused supervisor, as well as the interests of the alleged victim of the harassment.[244] As noted in the Second Edition, the EEOC Guidelines advise that "[p]revention is the best tool for the elimination of sexual harassment."[245] Because of the dilemma employers may face when confronted with claims of sexual harassment, employers are well advised to augment their prohibitive policies by adequate supervisory training and educational programs.

## IX. Homosexuals and Transsexuals

### B. Transsexuals

The Seventh Circuit has joined those courts holding that Title VII does not prohibit discrimination against transsexuals.[246] Disagreeing with the reasoning of the district judge who had found a violation of Title VII, the court of appeals concluded that "a prohibition against discrimination based on an individual's sex is not synonymous with a prohibition against discrimination based on an individual's sexual identity disorder or discontent with the sex into which they were born."[247]

### C. Constitutional Issues in Public Employment

In *Under 21 v. City of New York,*[248] a state appellate court upheld an executive order issued by the Mayor of New York City which prohibited city

---

[239]Meritor Sav. Bank v. Vinson, 477 U.S. 57, 40 FEP 1822 (1986).
[240]*See* p. 429 of the Second Edition.
[241]40 FEP at 1829.
[242]*See* text accompanying note 224, *supra.*
[243]40 FEP at 1827.
[244]*See* notes 220 and 236, *supra,* and accompanying text.
[245]29 C.F.R. §1604.11 (f); *see* p. 422 of the Second Edition.
[246]Ulane v. Eastern Airlines, 742 F.2d 1081, 35 FEP 1348 (7th Cir. 1984), *rev'g* 581 F. Supp. 821, 35 FEP 1332 (N.D. Ill. 1983), *cert. denied,* 471 U.S. 1017, 37 FEP 784 (1985) (district court found sex discrimination and rejected BFOQ defense); *see also earlier proceedings,* 35 FEP 330 (N.D. Ill. 1983), *and* 28 FEP 1438 (N.D. Ill. 1982) (denying summary judgment and denying motion to dismiss).
[247]*Id.,* 742 F.2d at 1085, 35 FEP at 1351.
[248]108 A.D.2d 250, 488 N.Y.S.2d 669 (N.Y. 1985).

contractors from refusing to hire individuals on the basis of sexual orientation or affectional preference. Basing its decision on the equal protection clauses of both the state and federal constitutions, the court concluded that "[w]here sexual proclivity does not relate to job function, it seems clearly unconstitutional to penalize an individual in one of the most imperative of life's endeavors, the right to earn one's daily bread."[249]

The Sixth Circuit rejected both the First Amendment and the equal protection claims of a school counselor who contended that she was unconstitutionally suspended, transferred to other duties, then not rehired, because she had revealed to co-workers that she was bisexual.[250] First, as to her speech claim, the court concluded that "she was speaking only in her personal interest [since there was] no evidence of any public concern * * * with the issue of bisexuality * * *."[251] Secondly, the court held that the plaintiff failed on her equal protection claim because she could not show "that heterosexual school employees in situations similar to hers have been, or would be, treated differently for making their personal sexual preferences the topic of comment and discussion in the high school community."[252] In a sharp dissent, Judge Edwards stated that the plaintiff was "deprived of her job solely because she let it be known * * * that her sexual preference was for another woman."[253] He would have upheld the jury verdict because the "Constitution protects all citizens [including homosexuals] * * * certainly to the extent of being homosexual and stating their sexual preference in a factual manner where there is no invasion of any other person's rights."[254]

## X. Veterans Preference

Voluntarily initiated veterans preferences continue to be analyzed by the courts for adverse impact in light of the principles established in *Griggs v. Duke Power Co.*[255] One court found that a policy of awarding bonus points to applicants to an apprenticeship program if they had prior military service had an adverse impact on women and therefore violated Title VII.[256] On the other hand, the Ninth Circuit upheld an apprenticeship program which required applicants to be under the age of 26 and allowed veterans to deduct up to four years from their age for military service.[257] The court reasoned that

---

[249]*Id.* at 671.
[250]Rowland v. Mad River Local School Dist., 730 F.2d 444, 37 FEP 175 (6th Cir. 1984), *cert. denied,* 470 U.S. 1009, 37 FEP 188 (1985). *But see* National Gay Task Force v. Oklahoma City Bd. of Educ., 729 F.2d 1270, 34 FEP 459 (10th Cir. 1984), *aff'd by evenly divided court,* 470 U.S. 903, 37 FEP 505 (1985) (holding unconstitutional that part of state law which authorized dismissal of teachers who advocated or encouraged homosexuality, but upholding that part of statute permitting dismissal for engaging in "public homosexual activity").
[251]730 F.2d at 449, 37 FEP at 178.
[252]*Id.* at 452, 37 FEP at 180.
[253]*Id.* (dissenting opinion).
[254]*Id.*
[255]401 U.S. 424, 3 FEP 175 (1971).
[256]Bailey v. Southeastern Area Joint Apprenticeship Comm., 561 F. Supp. 895, 31 FEP 752 (N.D. W. Va. 1983).
[257]Brown v. Puget Sound Elec. Apprenticeship & Training Trust, 732 F.2d 726, 34 FEP 1201 (9th Cir. 1984), *cert. denied,* 469 U.S. 1108, 36 FEP 976 (1985); *see also* EEOC v. Sears, Roebuck & Co., 628 F. Supp. 1264, 1349, 39 FEP 1672, 1737 (N.D. Ill. 1986), *aff'd,* 839 F.2d 302, 45 FEP 1257 (7th Cir. 1988) (approving defendant's inclusion of veteran's status variable in its regression analyses demon-

the extension of the time limit for veterans who were unable to apply while in military service had no effect on the ability of women to apply for the program. The age credits simply afforded veterans the same opportunity to apply for the apprenticeship training as was available to nonveterans.[258]

In a case in which veterans preference rights were asserted by a widow of a veteran, the D.C. Circuit noted the inconsistency inherent in the plaintiff's position of asserting a sex discrimination claim while at the same time seeking the benefit of veterans preference rights, in light of the fact that those rights tend to disproportionately favor male employees.[259]

---

strating that differences in compensation were based on factors other than sex and stating that military service, like other pre-Sears experience, can lawfully affect starting salary).

   [258]732 F.2d at 732, 34 FEP at 1205.

   [259]Valentino v. United States Postal Serv., 674 F.2d 56, 28 FEP 593 (D.C. Cir. 1982).

CHAPTER 13

# EQUAL PAY

## II. THE ACT'S COVERAGE

The Equal Pay Act has been held not to apply to job applicants[1] and not to encompass employment conditions and opportunities.[2] The Act does, however, cover differentials in fringe benefits.[3] The existence of an employment contract is no bar to a claim for recovery under the Act.[4] Members of a state legislature are protected by legislative immunity from claims under the Equal Pay Act where the claimant performs work which is integral to the legislative process.[5] A church-controlled college with a strong religious atmosphere is an employer subject to the Equal Pay Act and has no immunity from its provisions under the Free Exercise and Establishment clauses of the First Amendment.[6]

## III. APPLICATION ON AN ESTABLISHMENT BASIS

The term "establishment" under the Act has been construed as a "distinct physical place of business" rather than "an entire business or enterprise."[7] However, in a case of first impression, a district court concluded that

[1]Torres v. Action for Boston Community Dev., 32 FEP 1516 (D. Mass. 1981).

[2]Lancaster v. Holt, Rinehart & Winston, 31 FEP 1389 (N.D. Fla. 1982), *later proceeding*, 31 FEP 1390 (N.D. Fla. 1983) (timeliness issue). *See also* Berry v. Louisiana State Univ. Bd. of Supervisors, 715 F.2d 971, 32 FEP 1567 (5th Cir. 1983), *aff'd*, 783 F.2d 1270, 42 FEP 917 (5th Cir.), *cert. denied*, 479 U.S. 868, 44 FEP 848 (1986) (Act does not cover claim of heavier workload for equal pay, but does apply where heavier workload results in indirect financial disadvantage); True v. New York State Dep't of Correctional Servs., 613 F. Supp. 27, 36 FEP 1048, 1050 (W.D.N.Y. 1984) (denial of overtime opportunities to female employees does not constitute valid claim under Equal Pay Act).

[3]EEOC v. Fremont Christian School, 609 F. Supp. 344, 351, 34 FEP 1038, 1044 (N.D. Cal. 1984), *aff'd*, 781 F.2d 1362, 39 FEP 1815 (9th Cir. 1986) (citing and relying on Laffey v. Northwest Airlines, 567 F.2d 429, 455 n.175, 13 FEP 1068, 1086 (D.C. Cir. 1976), *cert. denied*, 434 U.S. 1086, 16 FEP 998 (1978)). *But see* Probe v. State Teacher's Retirement Sys., 780 F.2d 776, 783–84, 40 FEP 102, 108 (9th Cir.), *cert. denied*, 476 U.S. 1170, 40 FEP 1873 (1986). The Ninth Circuit declined to decide whether a retirement plan's use of sex-segregated mortality tables violated the Equal Pay Act, since the court had found that this practice violated Title VII, the Supreme Court has not yet decided whether retirement benefits qualify as "wages" under the Equal Pay Act, and because, in any event, the decision would not apply retroactively to the plaintiffs, who had already retired when they brought their claims.

[4]Van Heest v. McNeilab, Inc., 624 F. Supp. 891, 895, 39 FEP 1190, 1193 (D. Del. 1985).

[5]Bostick v. Rappleyea, 629 F. Supp. 1328, 38 FEP 658 (N.D.N.Y. 1985) (decisions by legislature regarding position of legislative budget analyst protected by legislative immunity from Equal Pay Act suit where analyst performs work closely connected with legislative process).

[6]Russell v. Belmont College, 554 F. Supp. 667, 30 FEP 1111 (M.D. Tenn. 1982). In reaching its decision, the court distinguished *NLRB v. Catholic Bishop of Chicago*, 440 U.S. 490, 100 LRRM 2913 (1979), where the Supreme Court held that the National Labor Relations Act does not apply to lay teachers in church-operated schools. *See also* EEOC v. Fremont Christian School, *supra* note 3, 609 F. Supp. at 347–49, 34 FEP at 1040–43 (same result; relying on EEOC v. Mississippi College, 626 F.2d 477, 23 FEP 1501 (5th Cir. 1980), *cert. denied*, 453 U.S. 912, 26 FEP 64 (1981) *and* EEOC v. Pacific Press Publishing Ass'n, 676 F.2d 1272, 28 FEP 1596 (9th Cir. 1982)).

[7]29 C.F.R. § 800.108 (1983).

such geographical distinctions do not apply to the Civil Service.[8] Thus, the court held that a government entity which has centralized personnel administration cannot prevent comparisons being made between employees in various regional offices.[9] Similarly, courts have held that a county as a whole constitutes a single establishment in view of the county's centralized administration of personnel functions and the "significant functional interrelationship between the work of the employees in various locations."[10] This analysis has also been applied to private employers.[11]

## A. Application to Employers and Employees

Individual defendants who control some aspect of a plaintiff's condition of employment have been found within the statutory purview of an "employer."[12] A general partner is not an "employee" under the Act.[13] The Tenth Circuit has rejected the argument that discrimination itself defines the application of the antidiscrimination laws, *i.e.,* that any partner who can be discriminated against is, by that fact, an employee.[14] A nonprofit state corporation which received personnel from a federal organization and disbursed federal funds had employees engaged in commerce under the test for an employer under the Equal Pay Act.[15] The "personal staff" exception for employees is determined on a case-by-case basis and is intended to apply only

---

[8]Grumbine v. United States, 586 F. Supp. 1144, 34 FEP 847 (D.D.C. 1984).

[9]*Id.* at 1147–48, 34 FEP at 849.

[10]Tomchek-May v. Brown County, 581 F. Supp. 1163, 35 FEP 119 (E.D. Wis. 1984) (female personnel coordinator at county mental health center and male personnel coordinator at county transportation department employed in same establishment); State, County & Municipal Employees v. County of Nassau, N.Y., 609 F. Supp. 695, 706–07, 37 FEP 1424, 1432–33 (E.D.N.Y. 1985) (court refused to dismiss plaintiff's claims because it did not appear "beyond a doubt" that they could not prove that county operations were sufficiently centralized and interrelated so that entire county constituted a single establishment under Equal Pay Act.)

[11]*See* Forsberg v. Pacific Nw. Bell Tel. Co., 623 F. Supp. 117, 125–26, *on reconsideration of* 622 F. Supp. 1147 (D. Or. 1985). *See also* Foster v. Arcata Assocs., 772 F.2d 1453, 1464–65, 38 FEP 1850, 1858 (9th Cir. 1985), *cert. denied,* 475 U.S. 1048, 40 FEP 272 (1986) (offices hundreds of miles apart with no operational or functional overlap were not same establishment under Equal Pay Act).

[12]*See* Tuber v. Continental Grain Co., 36 FEP 933 (S.D.N.Y. 1984) (five individual officers who were employees of corporation but served as plaintiff's supervisors and as company policy makers could be considered plaintiff's employers pursuant to the definition set forth in 29 U.S.C. § 203(d)). *But see* Fury v. County Court of Wood County, W. Va., 608 F. Supp. 198, 200, 37 FEP 1881, 1883 (S.D. W. Va. 1985) (fact that County Commission set *total* budget for a given office did not render it an employer under Equal Pay Act, although it was a necessary party defendant in order to accord plaintiffs complete relief; instead, individual elected county officials who had primary responsibility for hiring, firing, and compensation of their employees were employers for purposes of Equal Pay Act).

*See also* Kennedy v. McDonald's Corp., 610 F. Supp. 203, 204–05, 37 FEP 1813, 1814–15 (S.D. W. Va. 1985) (McDonald's not employer for purposes of Title VII or Equal Pay Act where Franchise Development Corporation (FDC) owned and operated five local McDonald's restaurants, instructed plaintiff and paid her salary, and FDC's officers, agents, or employees made decisions to hire, discipline, and fire her).

[13]Wheeler v. Main Hurdman, 825 F.2d 257, 44 FEP 707 (10th Cir.), *cert. denied,* 484 U.S. —, 45 FEP 776 (1987).

[14]*Id.,* 44 FEP at 722.

[15]Ferguson v. Neighborhood Hous. Servs. of Cleveland, 780 F.2d 549, 552–53, 39 FEP 1163, 1165–66 (6th Cir. 1986). The court noted the fact that Neighborhood Housing Services (NHS) did not receive the federal funds directly, but said "[i]t cannot hide behind the city of Cleveland, for the origin of the funds is what is significant." *Id.* at 553, 39 FEP at 1166. The court also found that NHS met the second criterion for an employer under the Fair Labor Standards Act, since it was engaged in the business of construction or reconstruction—in this case for housing in the city of Cleveland—one of the six categories set forth in § 203(s) that define an "enterprise engaged in commerce or in the production of goods for commerce" for the purposes of the Fair Labor Standards and Equal Pay acts. *Id.* at 553–54, 39 FEP at 1166–67.

to individuals in "highly intimate and sensitive positions of responsibility on the staff of an elected official."[16]

## IV. ADMINISTRATIVE ENFORCEMENT

The EEOC's authority to carry out Equal Pay Act functions has been conclusively established.[17] The Reorganization Act of 1977, under which the authority to enforce the Act was transferred from the Secretary of Labor to the EEOC, contained a one-house veto provision, but the Supreme Court, in *Immigration & Naturalization Service v. Chadha,*[18] held the one-house legislative veto system unconstitutional. Subsequent to *Chadha,* the courts split on the validity of the transfer.[19] Recognizing the crisis presented by this split in authority, Congress passed legislation which ratifies all existing reorganization plans and validates all prior action taken pursuant to authority transferred by a reorganization plan.[20]

The EEOC is not required to engage in the same prelitigation concilia-tion efforts before bringing an enforcement action which it is required to undertake before suing under Title VII.[21] In addition, the EEOC may be permitted to continue a Title VII and Equal Pay Act action notwithstanding a settlement agreement between the employer and a state civil rights commis-sion.[22] Similarly, the Equal Pay Act also provides for immediate judicial review of private claims for equal pay, and there is no requirement that an aggrieved employee exhaust his administrative remedies before filing suit.[23]

## V. COURT ENFORCEMENT

### A. Relief Available

Front pay may be awarded as a remedy not only for claims based on Title VII but also for claims brought under the Equal Pay Act, notwithstand-

---

[16]Brewster v. Barnes, 788 F.2d 985, 990 (4th Cir. 1986) (quoting Curl v. Reavis, 740 F.2d 1323, 1370, 35 FEP 930 (4th Cir. 1984) (Title VII case) and Owens v. Rush, 654 F.2d 1370, 1375, 26 FEP 226 (10th Cir. 1981)) (where plaintiff did not occupy a high-level or intimate position or make policy decisions during the period of alleged unequal treatment she was not on the personal staff of the sheriff and qualified as an "employee" for purposes of the Equal Pay Act).

[17]Pub. L. No. 98-532, 98 Stat. 2705 (1984). *See, e.g.,* EEOC v. Westinghouse Elec. Corp., 765 F.2d 389, 391, 45 FEP 1342 (3d Cir. 1985) (Pub. L. No. 98–532 applies to EEOC Equal Pay Act enforcement authority); Santos v. Stanley Home Prods., 36 FEP 319 (D. Mass. 1984) (EEOC's authority to carry out ADEA functions conclusively established by Pub. L. No. 98-532).

[18]462 U.S. 919, 51 USLW 4907 (1983).

[19]A significant minority of courts held that the legislative veto provision of the Reorganization Act is not severable from the remainder of the Act, thus rendering the entire statute unconstitutional. *See, e.g.,* EEOC v. Martin Indus., 581 F. Supp. 1029, 34 FEP 201 (N.D. Ala.), *appeal dismissed,* 469 U.S. 806, 35 FEP 1607 (1984). The majority of courts, however, sustained the EEOC's authority over the Equal Pay Act, holding that the unconstitutional one-house veto provision is severable from the Reorga-nization Act. *See, e.g.,* EEOC v. Hernando Bank, 724 F.2d 1188, 34 FEP 15 (5th Cir. 1984). In addition to finding the provision severable, some courts ruled that Congress ratified the transfer of enforcement authority to the EEOC through subsequent appropriation measures. EEOC v. Dayton Power & Light Co., 605 F. Supp. 13, 35 FEP 401 (S.D. Ohio 1984); EEOC v. Radio Montgomery, 588 F. Supp. 567, 34 FEP 378 (W.D. Va. 1984).

[20]Pub. L. No. 98–532, 98 Stat. 2705 (1984).

[21]EEOC v. Hernando Bank, *supra* note 19; EEOC v. Home of Economy, 712 F.2d 356, 32 FEP 599 (8th Cir. 1983).

[22]EEOC v. Dayton Tire & Rubber Co., 573 F. Supp. 782, 33 FEP 318 (S.D. Ohio 1983).

[23]Ososky v. Wick, 704 F.2d 1264, 31 FEP 777 (D.C. Cir. 1983).

ing the different remedial provisions of the two statutes.[24] Where wage differences are due in part to sex discrimination, but are also due in part to lawful factors (e.g., experience), a district court may fashion a back pay award which takes into account the legitimate basis for the disparity.[25]

In determining whether an employer acted in good faith and with reasonable grounds to believe it was not violating the law for purposes of assessing liquidated damages under the Equal Pay Act, one court has concluded that reliance on a legal opinion insulates a defendant from such liability.[26] However, another court has stated that neither conformity to industry practices nor concurrence by the union in contract negotiations on wages suffices to establish an employer's good faith.[27] Liquidated damages may be awarded for the period during which a discriminatory wage differential existed, despite a retroactive pay adjustment covering that period.[28] Back pay under both Title VII and the Equal Pay Act may be based on longevity credit accumulated prior to the enactment of either statute.[29]

An award of attorney's fees in an equal pay case as authorized under the Equal Pay Act[30] is governed by the standards recently set out by the Supreme Court in *Hensley v. Eckerhart*[31] and should be based upon the number of hours reasonably expended, multiplied by a reasonable hourly rate.[32] A district court is obliged to apply "billing judgment" to the number of hours spent.[33] Excessive or redundant hours should be discounted.[34] In reaching an appropriate award, the result obtained in the litigation is given substantial weight.[35] Under *Christiansburg Garment Co. v. EEOC*,[36] attorney's fees may be awarded to prevailing civil rights defendants only where the plaintiff's claim is "frivolous, unreasonable, or groundless." Applying this standard to a Title VII/Equal Pay Act case, the Fifth Circuit has

---

[24]Thompson v. Sawyer, 678 F.2d 257, 293, 28 FEP 1614, 1645 (D.C. Cir. 1982). In this case, the appellate court explored the consequences of the overlapping remedies available to a plaintiff who alleges intentional wage discrimination under both the Equal Pay Act and Title VII.

[25]EEOC v. Whitin Mach. Works, 699 F.2d 688, 35 FEP 583 (4th Cir. 1983) (district court reached equitable result when it found that 20% of male's higher salary was due to his six years of seniority and then ordered employer to pay plaintiffs' back pay based on 80% of his salary until they too obtained six years' experience in position).

[26]Hill v. J.C. Penney Co., 688 F.2d 370, 29 FEP 1757 (5th Cir. 1982).

[27]Thompson v. Sawyer, 678 F.2d 257, 282, 28 FEP 1614, 1634–35 (D.C. Cir. 1982).

[28]Laffey v. Northwest Airlines, 740 F.2d 1071, 35 FEP 508 (D.C. Cir. 1984), *cert. denied*, 469 U.S. 1181, 36 FEP 1168 (1985).

[29]*Id.*, 740 F.2d at 1099, 35 FEP at 531–32. The airline had provided salary increases on the basis of length of service, so that a male purser hired in 1957 would have accumulated 10 years' longevity by 1967. Under the district court's ruling, a stewardess hired in 1957 would be entitled to the pay of a purser with only three years' longevity were she recovering under the Equal Pay Act and with only two years' longevity were she recovering under Title VII. Accordingly, the circuit court concluded that to deny the stewardesses longevity credit for their pre-Act services would differentiate between similarly situated males and females, and therefore would be violative of Title VII. *Id.* at 1101, 35 FEP at 532.

[30]42 U.S.C. § 2000e-5(k)(1982).

[31]461 U.S. 424, 31 FEP 1169 (1983). *See also Laffey v. Northwest Airlines,* 746 F.2d 4, 35 FEP 1609 (D.C. Cir. 1984), *cert. denied,* 472 U.S. 1021, 37 FEP 1816 (1985), for a detailed analysis of an appropriate fee calculation under the general standards of *Hensley.*

[32]Hensley v. Eckerhart, *supra* note 31 at 433, 31 FEP at 1173. *See also* Laffey v. Northwest Airlines, *supra* note 31 at 24–25, 35 FEP at 1624 (basis of fee should be firm's established billing rates).

[33]461 U.S. at 433, 31 FEP at 1173.

[34]*Id.*

[35]*Id. Compare* King v. McCord, 707 F.2d 466, 35 FEP 831 (11th Cir. 1983) (district court had properly reduced fee because plaintiff succeeded only on her Equal Pay Act claims but failed on all her Title VII claims) *with* Morgado v. Birmingham-Jefferson County Civil Defense Corps, 706 F.2d 1184, 32 FEP 12 (11th Cir. 1983), *cert. denied,* 464 U.S. 1045, 33 FEP 1084 (1984) (district court abused its discretion by reducing fee award for hours spent on unsuccessful claims because they were closely related to claims upon which plaintiff prevailed).

[36]434 U.S. 412, 16 FEP 502 (1978).

disapproved and reversed a fee award where a plaintiff makes out a prima facie equal pay case, but does not prevail.[37]

An award of liquidated damages is inappropriate where the employer relied on an invalid but plausible wage comparison.[38] Where appropriate, liquidated damages may be assessed against a government entity.[39]

An employer ordered to pay back pay and liquidated damages is entitled to a stay to prevent collection of the judgment debt pending appeal.[40]

The courts have diverged on the issue of prejudgment interest on back pay.[41] Postjudgment interest should be calculated pursuant to the formula in 28 U.S.C. § 1961.[42] One circuit court upheld a lower court's award of six percent prejudgment interest on back pay as to the period of time following a remedial order issued in the course of litigation, despite the plaintiff's contention that interest rates had risen after the initial award.[43] However, the court reversed the lower court's decision not to award postjudgment interest on liquidated damages, based upon 28 U.S.C. § 1961, which provides for an award of interest "on any money judgment in a civil case recovered in district court."[44]

Prejudgment interest may be awarded against a governmental entity.[45]

A recovery of back pay is statutorily limited to the two-year period prior to the filing of the complaint, or to three years if a willful violation is proven.[46]

Under certain circumstances, a job promotion may constitute a proper remedy to an Equal Pay Act violation.[47]

## B. The Statute of Limitations

An action under the Equal Pay Act is not time-barred as to employees listed in the prayer for relief of the initial complaint, but not specifically named as plaintiffs before the expiration of the two-year limitations period

---

[37]Plemer v. Parsons-Gilbane, 713 F.2d 1127, 32 FEP 1351 (5th Cir. 1983).

[38]Clymore v. Far-Mar-Co., 709 F.2d 499, 42 FEP 439 (8th Cir. 1983).

[39]Morgado v. Birmingham-Jefferson County Civil Defense Corps, *supra* note 35, at 1189, 32 FEP at 15–16.

[40]Laffey v. Northwest Airlines, 582 F. Supp. 280, 32 FEP 754 (D.D.C. 1982), *aff'd in part and rev'd in part,* 740 F.2d 1071, 35 FEP 508 (D.C. Cir. 1984), *cert. denied,* 469 U.S. 1168 (1985).

[41]*Compare* Marshall v. Central Kan. Medical Center, 29 FEP 1817 (D. Kan. 1981), *aff'd sub nom.* EEOC v. Central Kan. Medical Center, 705 F.2d 1270, 31 FEP 1510 (10th Cir. 1983) (court awarded prejudgment interest on back pay in suit by Secretary of Labor reasoning that defendant had been unjustly enriched by use of the money during time female employees were damaged) *with* Hill v. J.C. Penney Co., 688 F.2d 370, 29 FEP 1757 (5th Cir. 1982) (Fifth Circuit denied award to private plaintiffs under its rule precluding prejudgment interest in Fair Labor Standards Act cases.)

[42]*See* Laffey v. Northwest Airlines, 740 F.2d 1071, 1101, 35 FEP 508, 533 (D.C. Cir. 1984), *cert. denied,* 469 U.S. 1181, 36 FEP 1168 (1985). Interest in pending actions and judgments is also governed by 28 U.S. § 1961.

[43]*Id.,* 740 F.2d at 1103, 35 FEP at 532.

[44]*Id.,* 35 FEP at 533.

[45]EEOC v. County of Erie, 751 F.2d 79, 36 FEP 830 (2d Cir. 1984).

[46]Hudson v. Moore Business Forms, 609 F. Supp. 467, 37 FEP 1672 (N.D. Cal. 1985), *aff'd in part and vacated in part on other grounds,* 827 F.2d 450, 44 FEP 1310 (9th Cir. 1987), opinion superseded by opinion published at 836 F.2d 1156 (district court imposed established statutory limitations period despite plaintiff's contention that "continuous" violations throughout eight-year period entitled her to recovery for entire period in which discrimination took place.)

[47]Jehle v. Heckler, 603 F. Supp. 124, 127, 37 FEP 1310, 1312 (D.D.C. 1985) (promotion of female employee to higher classification where she had already been performing work required in that classification could be granted as a remedy to Equal Pay Act violation, despite fact that statute does not expressly call for such a remedy).

set forth in 29 U.S.C. § 216(c).[48] According to the Fifth Circuit, the "named as party plaintiff" requirement of 29 U.S.C. § 256, a statute similar to § 216(c), requires only that the employee be identified in the complaint or in a pleading equivalent to it.[49] One court held that the naming of three employees in the prayer of the complaint satisfied this test and permitted the inclusion of the employees in the action.[50]

Each time an employer issues a paycheck to a woman performing equal work for lower pay than a man would receive, a separate act of discrimination occurs which, for statute of limitations purposes, may be a separate basis for liability.[51]

## C. Jury Trial

One court held that an employer is entitled to separate hearings on equal pay and Title VII claims where joint trial might cause prejudice and confuse the issues before the jury.[52]

## F. Evidence Admissible

Where employees suffer an actionable present or continuing violation, the Equal Pay Act does not bar consideration of relevant evidence concerning their employment prior to the period of back pay.[53]

## VI. DETERMINING THE EQUALITY OF JOBS

### A. The Standard to Be Applied

The "substantially equal" test, first enunciated in *Schultz v. Wheaton Glass Co.,*[54] remains the appropriate standard for judging the equality of jobs under the Equal Pay Act. The Court of Appeals for the District of Columbia in *Thompson v. Sawyer,*[55] after reviewing the legislative history of the Equal Pay Act, interpreted this standard as embodying the middle course intended by Congress between a requirement that the jobs in question be exactly alike and a requirement that they merely be comparable.[56] The application of this test is not restricted to comparisons between an employee's immediate predecessor or successor;[57] an appropriate comparison must be made in light of

---

[48]EEOC v. Hernando Bank, 724 F.2d 1188, 34 FEP 15 (5th Cir. 1984).
[49]*Id.* at 1193, 34 FEP at 16.
[50]*Id.* The court also relied partially on the EEOC's references to the three employees in answers to the defendants' interrogatories. *Id.*
[51]Hall v. Ledex, Inc., 669 F.2d 397, 30 FEP 82 (6th Cir. 1982) (limitations defense rejected where plaintiff filed EEOC charge 330 days after she was promoted to her former supervisor's job at salary two-thirds lower than he had received); Billings v. Wichita State Univ., 557 F. Supp. 1348, 39 FEP 489 (D. Kan. 1983); Bazemore v. Friday, 478 U.S. 385, 41 FEP 92 (1986) (same; Title VII race discrimination claim).
[52]Davis v. Burlington Indus., 34 FEP 917 (N.D. Ga. 1983).
[53]EEOC v. McCarthy, 768 F.2d 1, 38 FEP 536 (1st Cir. 1985) (data relating to earlier years were relevant to historical treatment of salaries as well as in determining terms of increasing disparity) (citing Lamphere v. Brown Univ., 685 F.2d 743, 747, 29 FEP 701 (1st Cir. 1982)).
[54]421 F.2d 259, 9 FEP 502 (3d Cir.), *cert. denied,* 398 U.S. 905, 9 FEP 1408 (1970).
[55]678 F.2d 257, 28 FEP 1614 (D.C. Cir. 1982).
[56]*Id.* at 271–72, 28 FEP at 1624–27.
[57]Clymore v. Far-Mar-Co., 709 F.2d 499, 502, 42 FEP 439 (8th Cir. 1983).

all the circumstances and this may include comparing employees of similar experience who have worked in the relevant position.[58] The District of Columbia Circuit held that in proving a violation of the Act, the plaintiff need not compare herself to all similarly classified male employees but may choose one or more among those allegedly doing substantially equal work.[59]

## B. Equal Skill, Effort, and Responsibility

In *Thompson v. Sawyer,*[60] the court held that jobs could be "substantially equal" for the purposes of the Equal Pay Act even though performed on different machines, since the evidence demonstrated they were sufficiently related and sufficiently similar with respect to skill, effort, responsibility, and working conditions.

In determining whether jobs are substantially equal, the focus of the inquiry is overall job content. Thus, the Ninth Circuit rejected a university's argument that jobs from different academic disciplines can *never* be substantially equal, but held that the absence of substantial equality may be established by demonstrating that separate disciplines require a different emphasis on research, training, and community service.[61] According to one court, the *plaintiff* must show that any job differences are so insignificant that they do not contribute to the pay disparity.[62] The courts will look behind job classifications to the substance of the work.[63] Traditional distinctions between jobs may fade over time, and the erosion of differences may render such positions substantially equal for purposes of imposing liability.[64] Differences in job duties and responsibilities must be real; a nominal designation of an employee as a supervisor will not protect an employer from an Equal Pay Act claim.[65] The provisions of the Equal Pay Act apply to jobs that require equal skills, not to employees who possess equal skills.[66] The mere fact that jobs have similar titles or descriptions is not adequate to prove substantial equality.[67] Disparities may be found, however,

---

[58]*Id.,* 709 F.2d 499, 503 (8th Cir. 1983). For recent cases applying the "substantially equal test," *see generally* Laffey v. Northwest Airlines, 740 F.2d 1071, 35 FEP 508 (D.C. Cir. 1984), *cert. denied,* 469 U.S. 1181, 36 FEP 1168 (1985); EEOC v. Maricopa County Community College Dist., 736 F.2d 510, 35 FEP 234 (9th Cir. 1984); Epstein v. Secretary of the Treasury, 739 F.2d 274, 35 FEP 677 (7th Cir. 1984); Waterman v. New York Tel. Co., 36 FEP 41 (S.D.N.Y. 1984); EEOC v. Affiliated Foods, 34 FEP 943 (W.D. Mo. 1984).

[59]Goodrich v. Electrical Workers, IBEW, 815 F.2d 1519, 43 FEP 727, 731 (D.C. Cir. 1987).

[60]*Supra* note 55, at 274–76, 28 FEP at 1629–30. In deciding that the female workers had stated a prima facie case of unequal treatment in compensation, the court relied on the plaintiffs' expert testimony with respect to the similarity of the jobs in question.

[61]Spaulding v. University of Wash., 740 F.2d 686, 697–99, 708–09, 35 FEP 217, 224–25 (9th Cir.), *cert. denied,* 469 U.S. 1036, 36 FEP 464 (1984).

[62]EEOC v. Hay Assocs., 545 F. Supp. 1064, 1083, 29 FEP 994, 1008–09 (E.D. Pa. 1982) (plaintiff's financial consulting work substantially equal to work of one of her male co-workers, but not to work of two other co-workers, who had different consulting duties and played much greater role in financial planning seminars held for clients).

[63]*Id.*

[64]*See* Morgado v. Birmingham-Jefferson County Civil Defense Corps, 706 F.2d 1184, 1188–89, 32 FEP 12, 15 (11th Cir. 1983), *cert. denied,* 464 U.S. 1045, 33 FEP 1084 (1984).

[65]Hill v. J.C. Penney Co., 688 F.2d 370, 373–74, 29 FEP 1757, 1759–60 (5th Cir. 1982) (nominal designation as supervisor involved no real added responsibility).

[66]Hein v. Oregon College of Educ., 718 F.2d 910, 919–20, 33 FEP 1538, 1541 (9th Cir. 1983).

[67]Epstein v. Secretary of the Treasury, *supra* note 58.

not only in the type of work performed, but in the level of physical effort required to perform it.[68] Where there are additional job duties or the work is more difficult, a court may legitimately determine that the plaintiff has failed to prove his case.[69] Additionally, a difference in levels of training has been considered significant in finding that jobs are not substantially equal.[70]

Where an employer consolidates work previously performed in a higher-paid, predominantly male classification with work previously performed in a lower-paid, predominantly female classification, and pays all employees the lower rate, the consolidation will constitute a violation of the Equal Pay Act if it can be shown that the two jobs were substantially equal.[71]

## VII. STATUTORY DEFENSES

### A. "Differences * * * Pursuant to (i) a Seniority System"

In *EEOC v. Cleveland State University,* [72] the court found that certain salary differences were justified by a de facto seniority system based upon years in academic ranks. The Fourth Circuit has confirmed that seniority is a legitimate basis for wage differentials even where there is no formal seniority system in effect.[73]

Higher paying and "easier" jobs obtained through a bidding procedure in which employees were permitted to engage based upon their seniority can constitute a form of seniority premium within the scope of the seniority system exception to the Equal Pay Act.[74]

### B. "Differences * * * Pursuant to (ii) a Merit System"

Wage differences under this defense must be based on a bona fide merit system.[75] Generally, courts require the employer to show objective written

---

[68]EEOC v. Affiliated Foods, *supra* note 58 (wage differential justified where male employees required to lift and carry heavier items than those moved by female employees).

[69]*See, e.g.,* Grove v. Frostburg Nat'l Bank, 549 F. Supp. 922, 31 FEP 1675 (D. Md. 1982). *See also* Jacobs v. College of William & Mary, 517 F. Supp. 791, 28 FEP 1105 (E.D. Va. 1980), *aff'd mem.,* 661 F.2d 922, 28 FEP 1818 (4th Cir.), *cert. denied,* 454 U.S. 1033, 33 FEP 1696 (1981) (increased pressure and responsibility of coaching revenue-producing sport justified male sports coaches in a college being paid more than female coaches).

[70]Waterman v. New York Tel. Co., 36 FEP 41 (S.D.N.Y. 1984) (work of clerical instructors not substantially equal to that of technical instructors where technical instructors had many years of training in their field and clerical instructors did not).

[71]Brobst v. Columbus Servs. Int'l, 761 F.2d 148, 37 FEP 1253 (3d Cir. 1985), *cert. denied,* 484 U.S. —, 45 FEP 1256 (1988). The Third Circuit reversed a decision by the lower court which had not addressed the issue of the equality of the male laborers' and female custodians' jobs (which had been consolidated within the custodian category at the lower wage rate) but which granted the employer's motion *in limine* precluding the plaintiffs from presenting evidence on the issue. Because the procedures utilized by the lower court were defective, essentially converting the motion *in limine* into a summary judgment motion, the court remanded the case for further proceedings on the question of the substantial equality of the two jobs. Pursuant to its remand, the court stated that if it were found that prior to the consolidation either of the two wage differentials previously maintained were discriminatory in accordance with statutory requirements, a violation of the Act would be established.

[72]29 FEP 1782, 1792–95 (N.D. Ohio 1982) (system applied in fair and sex-neutral manner).

[73]EEOC v. Whitin Mach. Works, 699 F.2d 688, 689–90, 35 FEP 583, 584 (4th Cir. 1983).

[74]EEOC v. Affiliated Foods, 34 FEP 943 (W.D. Mo. 1984).

[75]Job descriptions that differentiate between positions but provide no means for advancement or reward based on merit do not constitute a bona fide merit system. Morgado v. Birmingham-Jefferson

standards, and a system based purely on subjective criteria is insufficient.[76] One court has held that matching a wage offer given to an employee by another employer does not constitute a merit system, even where the offer reflects the value of the employee's services.[77]

The merit system defense is not available where the employer's job classification system on its face indicates no significant differences between the grade levels of the jobs in issue and the system as applied to a lower grade female employee provides no means of advancement nor reward for merit.[78] However, the merit system defense may be applicable where there has been a significant change in a position previously filled by a male employee into which a female employee is promoted.[79] Thus, where an employer reclassified a position previously held by a male employee to a lower merit system grade because the work and responsibility involved had been considerably diminished at the time the female employee took over, the Ninth Circuit upheld the change under the Equal Pay Act with one judge in the panel majority holding that the merit system defense was applicable.[80]

If employees' salaries upon promotion were established through a discriminatory policy, then the practice of basing merit increases upon the initial salary is also discriminatory.[81]

## C. "Differences * * * Pursuant to (iii) a System Which Measures Earnings by Quantity or Quality of Production"

Under this defense, an employer must show the existence of a bona fide incentive system based on either the amount of work produced or the quality of the work produced. In *Bence v. Detroit Health Corp.,*[82] the appellate court held that the quantity test "refers to equal dollar per unit compensation rates."[83] Thus, there is no discrimination if two employees receive the same rate of pay for the same product but one receives more total compensation because he produces more.[84] However, an employer may not pay a *lesser* rate

---

County Civil Defense Corps, 706 F.2d 1184, 1188–89, 32 FEP 12, 15 (11th Cir. 1983), *cert. denied,* 464 U.S. 1045, 33 FEP 1084 (1984); *compare* EEOC v. Cleveland State Univ., *supra* note 72 (merit system based on competent teaching and research justified salary differentials between male and female professors).

[76]*See* Grove v. Frostburg Nat'l Bank, *supra* note 69 (bank's system of evaluating employees not a merit system because neither organized and structured nor based on systemic evaluation using predetermined criteria; primary consideration in pay decisions was "gut feeling" about employees by high-ranking official).

[77]Winkes v. Brown Univ., 32 FEP 1041, 1046–47 (D.R.I. 1983), *rev'd on other grounds,* 747 F.2d 792, 36 FEP 120 (1st Cir. 1984). *See infra* notes 101 and 102 and accompanying text.

[78]Grayboff v. Pendelton, 36 FEP 350 (N.D. Ga. 1984) (classification system which provides female employee no means of advancement is not bona fide merit system).

[79]Maxwell v. City of Tucson, 35 FEP 355, *opinion withdrawn and appeal dismissed mem.,* 749 F.2d 37, 36 FEP 576 (9th Cir. 1984). This opinion was withdrawn because the court determined it lacked jurisdiction because of an unresolved Title VII claim. However, it does indicate how a court might rule in this area.

[80]*Id.,* 35 FEP at 360. The other judge in the panel majority endorsed the change as based on business necessity which he held was a reasonable factor other than sex. The dissenting judge rejected both approaches.

[81]Derouin v. Litton Indus. Prods., Louis Allis Div., 618 F. Supp. 221, 37 FEP 941 (E.D. Wis. 1984). But since the court concluded that the pay policies of the employer were justified by factors other than sex, it found there was no basis for holding that the merit plan itself was unlawful.

[82]712 F.2d 1024, 32 FEP 434 (6th Cir. 1983), *cert. denied,* 465 U.S. 1025, 33 FEP 1884 (1984).

[83]*Id.,* 712 F.2d at 1029, 32 FEP at 438.

[84]*Id.*

to females per unit in order to equalize total compensation between men and women where there is no qualitative difference between men and women with respect to the work being performed.[85]

## D. "Differences * * * Pursuant to (iv) a Differential Based on Any Other Factor Other Than Sex"

In *Bence v. Detroit Health Corp.,*[86] the court raised but did not conclusively answer the question whether this defense encompasses literally any factor other than sex or whether it is confined to factors traditionally used in job evaluation systems.[87] On the facts of the case, the employer, a health club, argued that where sales opportunities were sex-segregated, it was justified in paying lower commission rates to women because the membership market for women was larger than for men and that it had a legitimate policy of equalizing the total remuneration of its employees.[88] The court rejected this argument on the grounds that male employees selling memberships did not provide a greater economic benefit that would justify commission differences,[89] that the policy therefore was not justified as based on a "factor other than sex," and that it unfairly locked female employees, and only female employees, into an inferior position "regardless of their effort or productivity."[90]

### 4. Market Rate

The Eleventh Circuit has affirmed a district court decision refusing to accept "market forces" alone as a factor other than sex so as to justify pay differentials. In *Beall v. Curtis,*[91] the district court rejected the employer's market forces defense, reasoning that the Equal Pay Act was intended specifically to counteract those forces in the market which "place a different value on the work of persons of different genders."[92] Thus, only where the market forces accord different values because of factors other than sex can they constitute a viable defense. Accordingly, the court concluded that market forces themselves have no intrinsic value under the Equal Pay Act, and to the extent that such forces recognize actual differences in jobs, those differences themselves must be examined.

The Eleventh Circuit has refused to accept, as a defense to Equal Pay Act liability, reliance on supply-and-demand as a factor other than sex justifying higher salaries for male teachers than for female teachers, where the state college paid women with equal or greater qualifications less than men who taught the same subjects and those who did the hiring did not

---

[85]*Id.* at 1030–31, 32 FEP at 438–39.

[86]*Supra* note 82.

[87]*Id.,* 712 F.2d at 1030–31, 32 FEP at 438–39. According to the appellate court, the legislative history of the Act tends to support the broader interpretation. *Id.*

[88]*Id.* at 1030, 32 FEP at 438.

[89]*Id.* at 1031, 32 FEP at 439; *compare* Hodgson v. Robert Hall Clothes, 473 F.2d 589, 597, 11 FEP 1271, 1277 (3d Cir.), *cert. denied,* 414 U.S. 866, 11 FEP 1310 (1973) (payment of higher salary to men assigned exclusively, for legitimate business reasons, to men's clothing department justified because of overwhelming evidence that men's department was more profitable than women's).

[90]*Id.*

[91]603 F. Supp. 1563, 37 FEP 644 (M.D. Ga.), *aff'd mem.,* 778 F.2d 791, 40 FEP 984 (11th Cir. 1985).

[92]*Id.,* 603 F. Supp. at 1579, 37 FEP at 656.

inform themselves of market rates for teachers of particular expertise, experience, or skills.[93]

In *Kouba v. Allstate Insurance Co.,*[94] the court reversed and remanded a district court judgment which had held that prior salary may *never* be a factor other than sex under the Act because its use perpetuates historic sex discrimination. The court held that the employer must use the factor reasonably in light of its business purposes. Thus, on remand, the court gave detailed instructions for examination of the reasonableness of the employer's use of prior salary in setting the minimum monthly salary for commission sales agents. The employer claimed that the prior salary base for commissions helped to motivate the agent to make commission sales and aided the employer in measuring a new sales agent's potential.

On the other hand, in *Covington v. Southern Illinois Univ.,*[95] the Seventh Circuit upheld a differential resulting from a sex-neutral policy of maintaining an employee's salary upon a change of assignment within the university. The court reasoned that such a salary retention policy qualifies as a factor other than sex because the Act does not preclude "an employer from implementing a policy aimed at improving employee morale when there is no evidence that that policy is either discriminatorily applied or has a discriminatory effect."[96] According to the court, an employer should be allowed to take into consideration the wage it paid an employee in another position "unless this policy is discriminatorily applied or unless there is evidence independent of the policy which establishes that the employer discriminates on the basis of sex."[97] The court also rejected the requirement that a "factor other than sex" must be related to the requirements of the particular position in question, noting that such a requirement has not been adopted by the Seventh Circuit.[98]

A district court has held, however, that the fact that a female employee performing work substantially equal to male employees is willing to accept a lower classification and had a salary history lower than that of male employees does not constitute a factor other than sex so as to justify a wage differential.[99]

In *Briggs v. City of Madison,*[100] the city upgraded pay ranges of male public health sanitarians but not pay ranges of female public health nurses. In a class action under Title VII by the nurses, the court held that the disparity was legitimately based on the city's perception of the market demands and designed to attract qualified applicants. According to the court, although this defense is untenable where skill requirements are essentially identical for both jobs, it is valid where different skills are required.

Wage differentials based on the force of the marketplace must be substantiated. The First Circuit has approved a compensation decision by

---

[93]Department of Labor v. Georgia Sw. College, 765 F.2d 1026, 43 FEP 1525 (11th Cir. 1985).
[94]691 F.2d 873, 30 FEP 57 (9th Cir. 1982).
[95]816 F.2d 317, 43 FEP 839 (7th Cir.), *cert. denied,* 484 U.S. 848, 44 FEP 1672 (1987).
[96]*Id.* at 322, 43 FEP at 843.
[97]*Id.* at 323, 43 FEP at 844–45 The court also noted that the salary retention policy "avoids the serious problem of 'unmerited' pay reductions." *Id.*
[98]*Id.* at 322, 43 FEP at 843.
[99]Grayboff v. Pendelton, 36 FEP 350, 358 (N.D. Ga. 1984).
[100]536 F. Supp. 435, 447, 28 FEP 739, 750 (W.D. Wis. 1982).

Brown University to increase the salary of a female associate professor over her male peer in the same field, in order to meet a competing offer from another university attempting to recruit her.[101] The court's decision was also influenced by a consent decree that had been recently imposed on Brown, requiring the university to undertake affirmative action to increase the tenured female faculty.[102]

### 5. Miscellaneous Exceptions

Prior sales experience in the pharmaceutical industry furnished a proper basis for apparent salary differentials between the plaintiff, who was terminated for poor sales performance, and certain of her male colleagues and her male successor, each of whom possessed substantial experience as a drug salesman.[103] However, although differences in starting salaries may be justified by differences in experience, courts are skeptical if the experience factor precludes women employees from catching up with their male counterparts as they gain greater experience.[104]

In *Maxwell v. City of Tucson,* [105] the Ninth Circuit rejected the employer's defense of a salary disparity based upon "business necessity." The court acknowledged that a pay differential resulting from the implementation of a sound business policy requiring a reduction in pay for higher level employees as their responsibilities were reduced would be legitimate, if established. The employer failed to meet its burden of proof, however, and the court noted that the assertion of "business necessity" *per se* was not an adequate defense under the Equal Pay Act.[106]

In *EEOC v. Hay Associates,* [107] the court rejected the employer's defense that a salary disparity was based on the expectation of greater economic benefit from the male employee. Although the court recognized that such a defense might exist, the employer failed to provide any basis for the difference in expectations. In addition, the court rejected for lack of supporting evidence a defense that the male was hired for training into a leadership role as a factor other than sex.

Differences in profitability between an all-male department and an all-female department may justify differentials in base salary between the two departments.[108]

An airline's "good faith" but erroneous belief that jobs performed by female stewardesses and male pursers were significantly different and, therefore, that its payment of lower wages to stewardesses was not in violation of the law, does not constitute a defense to an Equal Pay Act viola-

---

[101]Winkes v. Brown Univ., 32 FEP 1041, 1046–47 (D.R.I. 1983), *rev'd on other grounds,* 747 F.2d 792, 36 FEP 120 (1st Cir. 1984). *See also* Grove v. Frostburg Nat'l Bank, 549 F. Supp. 922, 934, 31 FEP 1675, 1684–85 (D. Md. 1982) ("patriotism" not a valid basis for wage differential where male and female would not have been eligible for draft).

[102]Winkes v. Brown Univ., *supra* note 101, 747 F.2d at 795–97, 36 FEP at 122–24.

[103]Trent v. Adria Laboratories, 28 FEP 353, 360–61 (N.D. Ga. 1982).

[104]Perryman v. Johnson Prods. Co., 532 F. Supp. 373, 376, 28 FEP 299, 302 (N.D. Ga. 1981), *vacated on other grounds,* 698 F.2d 1138, 31 FEP 93 (11th Cir. 1983) (experience defense rejected on facts).

[105]35 FEP 355, *opinion withdrawn and appeal dismissed mem.,* 749 F.2d 37, 36 FEP 576 (9th Cir. 1984).

[106]*Id.,* 35 FEP at 360.

[107]545 F. Supp. 1064, 1084, 29 FEP 994, 1008 (E.D. Pa. 1982).

[108]EEOC v. Affiliated Foods, 34 FEP 943, 957–58 (W.D. Mo. 1984).

tion.[109] Thus, although liquidated damages may be denied when an employer in good faith wrongly believes that its conduct conforms to legal requirements, such a belief does not permit a court to eliminate liability entirely.[110]

In *Wambheim v. J.C. Penney Co. (II)*[111] the court ruled that the employer's "head of household" rule, under which employees could only obtain medical and dental coverage for a spouse if the employee earns more than half of the couple's combined income, did not violate the Act. The court found that the employer had a legitimate and overriding business justification in shaping its insurance coverage to benefit dependent spouses who have the greatest need for coverage and in keeping the cost of its plan as low as possible.[112]

A freeze on job reclassifications within a gender-neutral classification system does not constitute a defense to an Equal Pay Act violation. In *EEOC v. Maricopa County Community College District,*[113] the court rejected this defense where the plaintiff had been performing work beyond her classification so that her job was substantially equal to that of male employees. The court ruled that where an employee takes on responsibilities beyond those in her job description, an employer has an affirmative duty to evaluate the employee's work and the employee's position to determine if reclassification is warranted.[114]

However, a formula utilized to bring female employees' salaries up to those of male employees occupying substantially equal positions does constitute a defense to an Equal Pay Act claim brought by the male employees, according to the Seventh Circuit. In *Ende v. Regency Universities Board of Regents,*[115] the court viewed the formula as a remedial method, determining the level of incremental adjustments necessary to bring female faculty members' salaries in line with those of male faculty members. As such, the application of the same formula to male employees would only perpetuate the pay inequity which it was designed to combat. On this basis, the court concluded that the formula fell within the Equal Pay Act defense authorizing pay differentials based on a factor other than sex.

In *Patkus v. Sangamon-Cass Consortium,*[116] the court held that an em-

---

[109]Laffey v. Northwest Airlines, 740 F.2d 1071, 35 FEP 508 (D.C. Cir. 1984), *cert. denied,* 469 U.S. 1181, 36 FEP 1168 (1985).

[110]*Id.,* 740 F.2d at 1099, 35 FEP at 529.

[111]705 F.2d 1492, 31 FEP 1297 (9th Cir. 1983), *cert. denied,* 467 U.S. 1255, 34 FEP 1800 (1984).

[112]*Id.,* 705 F.2d at 1495, 31 FEP at 1299.

[113]736 F.2d 510, 35 FEP 234 (9th Cir. 1984).

[114]*Id.* at 514, 35 FEP at 238.

[115]757 F.2d 176, 181, 37 FEP 575, 578 (7th Cir. 1985). The court stated that the claim by male faculty members that they were entitled to have the formula applied to them and to receive raises in accordance with it misconstrued the nature of the pay adjustments made under the formula as one establishing a "rate" of pay for female employees. *Id.*

[116]796 F.2d 1251, 38 FEP 1272 (7th Cir. 1985). The facts showed that prior to the termination of the plaintiff, a female administrator employed by an agency responsible for the management of the Comprehensive Employment and Training Act for two counties, the plaintiff had drafted a plan which upgraded the administrator's position and created a new position of assistant administrator. Following the plaintiff's termination on the grounds of insubordinate and abusive behavior toward agency personnel, a plan which was substantially the equivalent of the plan drafted by the plaintiff was implemented and a male administrator installed at a salary above that which the plaintiff had received. Under these circumstances, the court viewed the reorganization plan as a factor other than sex justifying the pay differential, reasoning that the new position and the elevated salary had been planned prior to the termination of the plaintiff and were unrelated to the sex of the person occupying the position. *Id.* at 1261, 38 FEP at 1278.

ployer did not violate the Equal Pay Act by paying a higher salary to a male administrator than was paid to his female predecessor where the salary change was based upon a corresponding change in the job itself, due to a reorganization plan. The court reasoned that the "factor other than sex" exception was intended by Congress to be a "broad general exception," included in the statute to ensure that bona fide job evaluation systems not be disrupted, and the right of an employer to change and revise a job evaluation and pay system fell within the scope of this congressional concern.[117]

Traditional industry practice may be a factor other than sex and therefore a defense to a prima facie case under the Equal Pay Act, but it will not avail an employer where the industry concerned has a pervasive history of sex segregation.[118]

The mere fact that a higher paid male employee in the same classification as a lower paid female employee leaves his job does not cure an Equal Pay Act violation. In *Jehle v. Heckler,*[119] the court rejected an argument by the Department of Health and Human Services that the departure of a male program analyst who had been performing substantially the same work as a female program analyst, but was paid a higher salary, constitutes a defense to an Equal Pay Act claim on the basis that no pay inequity remained within the department after the male employee had left. The court found that a violation of the Act occurred when the plaintiff and the male program analyst were both performing essentially the same work for unequal pay. Additionally, the court found that the violation would be continuing until the plaintiff received the same pay as the male program analyst had been receiving prior to his departure.

A state regulation permitting one classification of employee to perform any function beyond the written confines of specifically enumerated powers, as long as the employee has the education and competence to do so, permits the payment of a higher salary to such employees than to employees whose functions are similar, but whose conduct is limited to written guidelines. In *Beall v. Curtis,*[120] the court concluded that although there were many similarities between the nurse practitioners' and physicians' assistants' jobs, a significant difference in the law existed which itself provided the defendants with a valid defense. While nurse practitioners were limited in their practice to written protocols mutually agreed to by the nurse practitioner and the physician, physicians' assistants were permitted under state law to perform "any functions performed by the applying physician which the physician's assistant is qualified to perform."[121] Consequently, the court concluded that the distinction in job functions articulated under the applicable state law constituted a factor other than sex so as to justify a pay differential, over and

---

[117]*Id.* at 1261, 38 FEP at 1278.

[118]Thompson v. Sawyer, 678 F.2d 257, 276–77, 28 FEP 1614, 1629–30 (D.C. Cir. 1982).

[119]603 F. Supp. 124, 37 FEP 1310 (D.D.C. 1985). The court noted that the department had not argued that the male program analyst's job was overgraded. If in the course of a full classification review it were determined that the position should be reclassified, the court concluded that a prospective change in salary might be appropriate. Until such time, however, the plaintiff would be entitled to receive the established rating and salary. *Id.* at 127, 37 FEP at 1312.

[120]603 F. Supp. 1563, 37 FEP 644 (M.D. Ga.), *aff'd mem.,* 778 F.2d 791, 40 FEP 984 (11th Cir. 1985).

[121]*Id.,* 603 F. Supp. at 1579, 37 FEP at 656 (quoting from OFF. CODE GA. ANN. § 43-34-103(d)).

above the fact that the plaintiffs had failed to establish that their jobs were substantially equal to those of the male physicians' assistants.

However, a claim of violation of state law was held not to be a factor other than sex which would prohibit a unilateral increase in female clerical/jailers' wages, because the state law would be preempted by federal law.[122]

In *Derouin v. Litton Industrial Products, Louis Allis Division,*[123] the court held that a policy of basing a promoted employee's salary upon the employee's prepromotion salary was a factor other than sex justifying the difference between male and female employees' salaries, even though the policy operated to the disadvantage of persons initially hired at lower salaries. The court observed that there were several non-sex-related reasons underlying the employer's policy, including budgetary control, incentives for employee performance, the ability to compete with other employers for new hires, the ability to provide distinctions in supervisory salaries between supervisors in different departments, and other equitable considerations. Since the same policy was applied to all employees regardless of sex, and the facts did not reveal that the policy had a significantly greater adverse impact upon women, the court concluded that the policy was legitimate and provided a valid defense to the plaintiff's claims.

However, a defense claiming differences in rank as a factor other than sex justifying salary differentials is not valid where the employer discriminated against women with respect to rank placement at hire.[124]

## VIII. "COMPARABLE WORTH"

After six years of controversy over comparable worth, following the Supreme Court's decision in *County of Washington, Or. v. Gunther,*[125] the doctrine has been rejected by several courts, most significantly by the Ninth Circuit.

### A. The Bennett Amendment

In *State, County & Municipal Employees v. Washington,*[126] the Ninth Circuit reversed the district court ruling that Washington violated Title VII by setting salaries on the basis of "prevailing" or "market" rates, where that state had earlier conducted a study revealing that jobs filled primarily by women were paid less than those filled primarily by men, in job classes determined by a consultant to be of "comparable worth." Concluding that the history of the Civil Rights Act of 1964 and the Bennett Amendment contain no explicit discussion of compensation for either comparable or equal work, the court held that the state's reliance upon market rates, rather than upon the results of its job study, was not a form of sex-based wage discrimination cognizable under Title VII.[127]

---

[122]EEOC v. Green County, Wis., 618 F. Supp. 91, 94, 41 FEP 61, 63 (W.D. Wis. 1985).
[123]618 F. Supp. 221, 37 FEP 941 (E.D. Wis. 1984).
[124]Chang v. University of R.I., 606 F. Supp. 1161, 1229, 40 FEP 3, 58 (D.R.I. 1985).
[125]452 U.S. 161, 25 FEP 1521 (1981), reproduced at p. 464 of the Second Edition.
[126]770 F.2d 1401, 38 FEP 1353 (9th Cir. 1985).
[127]*Id.*

In *Power v. Barry County, Michigan,* [128] a class of female prison matrons brought suit alleging that they were underpaid in comparison with male correction officers, even though the respective jobs were of allegedly comparable and equal worth. The district court dismissed the allegation, holding that the theory of comparable worth is not cognizable under Title VII without proof of intentional discrimination. In addition to relying on post-*Gunther* judicial authority to the same effect and finding support in the legislative histories of the Equal Pay Act and Title VII, the court emphasized the onerous task that would be required in subjectively evaluating the intrinsic worth of different jobs. [129]

## B. The Prima Facie "Comparable Worth" Case

In *State, County & Municipal Employees,* the Ninth Circuit found no violation of Title VII under either the disparate impact or disparate treatment theory. In the court's view, disparate impact analysis is appropriate only in cases involving a specific practice on the part of the employer applied at a particular point in the job selection process, such as a height and weight requirement which has an adverse effect upon women. Accordingly, the court concluded that disparate impact analysis was inapplicable in the case before it, where the employer had taken into account several complex factors relating to the economics of the marketplace in establishing its salary levels. [130] In addition, the court held that Washington's practice of setting salary levels on market rates and not in accordance with a theory of comparable worth was insufficient to prove intentional discrimination, since Washington did not create the disparity existing in the market and Title VII imposed no duty to rectify a preexisting economic inequality. [131]

In *Spaulding v. University of Washington,* [132] the Ninth Circuit rejected a plaintiff's theory that intentional sex-based compensation discrimination under Title VII may be based on a plaintiff's showing of some degree of job comparability plus a combination of other factors, including direct or circumstantial evidence of discriminatory conduct and pay disparities. [133] In rejecting this view, the court held that the theory would allow an inadequate showing of comparability to be bolstered "with a confusing potpourri" of other factors, plunging the courts into standardless supervision of employment relations. [134]

The Ninth Circuit further held in *Spaulding* that an employer's reliance on competitive market prices to set wages cannot be regarded as a facially

---

[128]539 F. Supp. 721, 29 FEP 559 (W.D. Mich. 1982).

[129]*Compare EEOC v. Hay Assocs.,* 545 F. Supp. 1064, 1084, 29 FEP 994, 1008 (E.D. Pa. 1982), where the court, in dicta and in apparent conflict with *Power* explained its belief that the *Gunther* decision allows comparable worth claims under Title VII. The court did not reach the issue, however, because of the plaintiff's failure to show that her work was comparable or equally valuable to that performed by the male employees in question.

[130]*Supra* note 126. *But see* Watson v. Fort Worth Bank & Trust, 487 U.S. —, 47 FEP 102 (1988).

[131]*Id.* The court stated that "[n]either law nor logic deems the free market system a suspect enterprise," *id.* at 1407, 38 FEP at 1358–59, and, accordingly, that the law does not allow federal courts to "interfere in the market-based system for the compensation of Washington's employees." *Id.* at 1408, 38 FEP at 1360.

[132]740 F.2d 686, 35 FEP 217 (9th Cir.), *cert. denied,* 469 U.S. 1036, 36 FEP 464 (1984).

[133]*Id.,* 740 F.2d at 701, 35 FEP at 226.

[134]*Id.*

neutral policy or practice, and therefore cannot lead to a disparate impact analysis testing whether any demonstrated adverse impact of such reliance can be justified by business necessity.[135] According to the Ninth Circuit's analysis in *Spaulding,* employers "deal with the market as a given, and do not meaningfully have a 'policy' about it in the relevant Title VII sense;" hence liability under a disparate impact theory—where employers have relied on the market in setting compensation—would improperly subject employers to liability for pay differences over which they have no independent control and on which they have made no independent decision.[136]

The court in *Connecticut State Employees Association v. Connecticut*[137] rejected the notion that the judiciary in Title VII suits should be engaging in a subjective analysis of the value of different jobs, but held that a showing by the plaintiff that the *employer* had determined certain different jobs to have equivalent value may be used as evidence of intentional discrimination in order to state a claim under Title VII.[138] Thus, according to the court, a prima facie case may be established by proof (1) that the employer attributes equal or comparable values to various dissimilar jobs; and (2) that the female plaintiff is employed in one of these jobs and paid a smaller amount.

## C.  Defenses

Left undecided by *Gunther*[139] were the respective burdens in sex-based wage discrimination claims brought under Title VII. In *Kouba v. Allstate Insurance Co.,*[140] the employer argued that the standard Title VII rules announced in *Texas Department of Community Affairs v. Burdine*[141] govern, *i.e.,* that the plaintiff bears at all times the burden of proving that the wage differential was unlawful. In *Kouba,* the Ninth Circuit rejected this argument and held that once a prima facie case has been made out under *both* the Equal Pay Act and Title VII, the employer bears the affirmative burden of proving its actions justified by one of the Equal Pay Act defenses. The employer cannot under either statute merely come forward with evidence of some business reason and then shift the burden back to the plaintiff to prove

---

[135]*Id.* at 705–09, 35 FEP at 230–33. *But cf.* Watson v. Fort Worth Bank & Trust, *supra* note 130.
[136]*Id.* at 708, 35 FEP at 232–33. *See also* Briggs v. City of Madison, 536 F. Supp. 435, 447, 28 FEP 739, 750 (W.D. Wis. 1982) ("Nothing in [Title VII] indicates that the employer's liability extends to conditions of the marketplace which it did not create. Nothing indicates that it is improper for an employer to pay the wage rates necessary to compete in the marketplace for qualified job applicants.").
[137]31 FEP 191 (D. Conn. 1983).
[138]*See also* Nurses, ANA v. Illinois, 783 F.2d 716, 40 FEP 244 (7th Cir. 1986). The Seventh Circuit reversed the district court, which had dismissed a complaint based on rejection of what it deemed to be a comparable worth theory. Applying *Gunther* and *State, County & Municipal Employees,* the circuit court stated that if plaintiffs were complaining of Illinois' mere failure to implement a comparable worth study, their claim was properly dismissed. *Id.* at 723, 40 FEP at 249. However, the court found that the complaint was drafted in such a manner and supported with facts which might show intentional discrimination in either the state's failure to implement the study or in paying higher wages to men because of their sex and keeping women out of male job categories, and hence, would support a claim under Title VII. *See also Waterman v. New York Tel. Co.,* 36 FEP 41 (S.D.N.Y. 1984), in which the court rejected by implication the applicability of comparable worth under Title VII, stating that the theory is inapplicable under the Equal Pay Act and that the analysis of a claim of unequal pay for equal work is essentially the same under the Equal Pay Act and Title VII. *Id.* at 44–45.
[139]County of Washington, Or. v. Gunther, 452 U.S. 161, 25 FEP 1521 (1981), reproduced at p. 464 of the Second Edition.
[140]691 F.2d 873, 30 FEP 57 (9th Cir. 1982).
[141]450 U.S. 248, 25 FEP 113 (1981), reproduced at p. 1307 of the Second Edition.

pretext. The employer must show that "the factor of sex provided no basis for wage differential."[142]

However, the Eleventh Circuit has acknowledged that parties may stipulate the principles which will govern their claims and that the stipulation will be enforced by the courts.[143]

In *Peters v. City of Shreveport*[144] while agreeing with the proposition that, as a general matter, the Equal Pay Act should be interpreted consistently with Title VII in view of the Bennett Amendment, the Fifth Circuit hesitated "to rely exclusively upon this principle to interpret as substantially identical the causal element of a Title VII plaintiff's case and the showing an employer must make under the [Equal Pay] Act's fourth defense."[145] In concluding that a differential is 'based on' the factor of sex only if the factor of sex was a "but for" cause of the differential, the Fifth Circuit relied upon "a fundamental precept of * * * justice that it is unfair to impose liability for a result that would have occurred; in other words, the defendant's wrongful conduct must be a 'but for' cause of the complained of result." The court rejected the argument that liability automatically ensues if the factor of sex plays any part whatsoever in the employer's decision.[146]

The market rate defense can be raised in both disparate impact and disparate treatment cases under Title VII where plaintiffs rely upon comparable worth studies to make out a prima facie case.[147]

---

[142]Schwartz v. Florida Bd. of Regents, 807 F.2d 901, 43 FEP 1856, 1860 (11th Cir. 1987).

[143]Where the parties entered into a pretrial stipulation in which they agreed that the burdens of proof and production on the Title VII claims were governed by the principles enunciated in *Texas Dep't of Community Affairs v. Burdine, supra* note 141, the Eleventh Circuit upheld the application of the rules announced in *Burdine,* holding that a stipulation is binding on the parties unless modified. Feazell v. Tropicana Prods., 819 F.2d 1036, 44 FEP 101 (11th Cir. 1987).

[144]818 F.2d 1148, 43 FEP 1822 (5th Cir. 1987).

[145]*Id.* at 1161, 43 FEP at 1831.

[146]*Id.*

[147]*See* State, County & Municipal Employees v. Washington, 770 F.2d 1401, 38 FEP 1353 (9th Cir. 1985).

CHAPTER 14

# AGE

## I. Jurisdiction

### A. Protected Groups

Effective generally on January 1, 1987, the Age Discrimination in Employment Amendments of 1986[1] removed the age 70 upper limit of the protected class for all employees except "firefighters;"[2] "law enforcement officers,"[3] who may both continue to be hired or terminated pursuant to bona fide hiring or retirement plans adopted pursuant to state or local laws in effect on March 3, 1983; and employees age 70 or over who are "serving under a contract of unlimited tenure" at an institution of higher education.[4] These exceptions are repealed effective December 31, 1993,[5] and in the meantime are to be the subject of various studies, reports, and recommendations mandated by Congress.[6] Previous lawful mandatory retirement or other discriminatory provisions in collective bargaining agreements in effect on June 30, 1986, remain valid until the earlier of contract termination or January 1, 1990.[7]

Amendments[8] effective October 9, 1984, granted ADEA protection to U.S. citizens who are extraterritorial employees of U.S. corporations or their subsidiaries unless such protection would violate host country law, and raised the nonforfeitable retirement income triggering the executive exemption to $44,000. Previously, the ADEA had not been applied to employment outside the United States,[9] despite initial employment in, supervision from, and occasional business trips to the United States.[10] The limited extension of these amendments is not retroactive and does not apply to claims accruing prior to

---

[1]Age Discrimination in Employment Amendments of 1986, Pub. L. No. 99-592, 29 U.S.C. §§ 623 et seq. and 631(a).

[2]29 U.S.C. §§ 623(4)(i)(sic)(1) (both the previous section and the section added by Pub. L. No. 99-592 were designated as § 4(i) by the language of the public law that added them) and 630(11)(j).

[3]29 U.S.C. §§ 623(4)(i)(sic)(1) and 630(11)(k).

[4]29 U.S.C. § 631(12)(d).

[5]Age Discrimination in Employment Amendments of 1986, Pub. L. No. 99-592, § 3(b), 29 U.S.C. §§ 623(4)(i)(sic)(1) and (2).

[6]Age Discrimination in Employment Amendments of 1986, Pub. L. No. 99-592, §§ 5(a), (b), (c), and 6(c).

[7]Age Discrimination in Employment Amendments of 1986, Pub. L. No. 99-592, § 7(a).

[8]Older Americans Act Amendments of 1984, Pub. L. No. 98-459, 98 Stat. 1767; § 802, 98 Stat. 1792 (1984), 29 U.S.C. §§ 623(f)(1), (g), 630(f), and 631(c)(1).

[9]Cleary v. United States Lines, 728 F.2d 607, 34 FEP 333 (3d Cir. 1984); Thomas v. Brown & Root, 745 F.2d 279, 281, 35 FEP 1648 (4th Cir. 1984); Zahourek v. Arthur Young & Co., 750 F.2d 827, 36 FEP 865 (10th Cir. 1984); DeYoreo v. Bell Helicopter Textron, 785 F.2d 1282, 40 FEP 725 (5th Cir. 1986); see also Pfeiffer v. Wm. Wrigley Jr. Co., 755 F.2d 554, 37 FEP 85 (7th Cir. 1985).

[10]Wolf v. J.I. Case Co., 617 F. Supp. 858, 38 FEP 1647 (E.D. Wis. 1985) (responsibilities entirely foreign).

its effective date.[11] Retaliation claims by extraterritorially based employees are, however, cognizable.[12] Two cases suggest that pendent state law claims may be applied to such employment even though the federal claim fails.[13]

The Third Circuit, in a case of first impression, embraced the hybrid "right to control"/"economic realities" test traditionally applied in Title VII cases, and found district sales managers to be independent contractors not protected by the ADEA.[14] The Fourth Circuit, also applying this test to a salesman, reached the same conclusion.[15] The Fifth Circuit had earlier found a manufacturer's sales representative to be an independent contractor, and not an "employee" protected by the Act.[16]

Under the "economic realities" test for employees, protection was also denied a retail store manager under a terminated franchise agreement.[17] On the other hand, the Second Circuit refused to apply the "economic realities" test to deny protection to a radiologist who was a shareholder of a four-person professional corporation and instead focused on that individual's actual duties and status.[18] This approach comports with the concept that "partners" may sometimes be "employees" within the meaning of the ADEA.[19]

In cases "among the first to test the scope of the exemption" permitting retirement of a "bona fide executive" or a "high policymaking" employee at age 65, a chief labor counsel who had been forced to retire at age 65 was deemed protected by the ADEA in light of his minimal executive responsibility and contribution to the formulation of employer policy, while a senior vice president of finance and administration who was also forced to retire at age 65 was deemed *not* protected by the ADEA because of his extensive executive responsibilities. These included being one of the four people who constituted the company's management team and his entitlement to a company car and a paid membership to the country club.[20] The president of a

---

[11]DeYoreo v. Bell Helicopter Textron, *supra* note 9; Pfeiffer v. Wm. Wrigley Jr. Co., *supra* note 9; Ralis v. RFE/RL, 770 F.2d 1121, 38 FEP 1073 (D.C. Cir. 1985); Wolf v. J.I. Case, *supra* note 10 (extensive discussion).

[12]Wolf v. J.I. Case Co., *supra* note 10 (conduct or failed complaint must be based on reasonable good faith that Act applies).

[13]Wolf v. J.I. Case, *supra* note 10; Belanger v. Keydril Co., 596 F. Supp. 823, 36 FEP 132 (E.D. La. 1984), *aff'd mem.,* 772 F.2d 902, 41 FEP 64 (5th Cir. 1985). *But see* 29 U.S.C. § 213(f).

[14]EEOC v. Zippo Mfg. Co., 713 F.2d 32, 32 FEP 682 (3d Cir. 1983). *See also* Dake v. Mutual of Omaha Ins. Co., 600 F. Supp. 63, 36 FEP 1106 (N.D. Ohio 1984). *But see* Armbruster v. Quinn, 711 F.2d 1332, 32 FEP 369 (6th Cir. 1983) (Title VII case applying "economic realities" test to manufacturer's representative).

[15]Garrett v. Phillips Mills, Inc., 721 F.2d 979, 33 FEP 487 (4th Cir. 1983).

[16]Hickey v. Arkla Indus., 688 F.2d 1009, 29 FEP 1719 (5th Cir. 1982), *vacated without change in result and opinion replaced,* 699 F.2d 748, 31 FEP 238 (5th Cir. 1983).

[17]Singer v. Uni-Marts, 37 FEP 1197 (W.D. Pa. 1985) (however, claim stated for failure to "rehire" after franchise termination).

[18]Hyland v. New Haven Radiology Assocs., 794 F.2d 793, 41 FEP 183 (2d Cir. 1986). *Accord* Caruso v. Peat, Marwick, Mitchell & Co., 664 F. Supp. 144, 44 FEP 544 (S.D.N.Y. 1987) (individual denoted as "partner" does not *per se* fall outside protection of ADEA); Gorman v. North Pittsburgh Oral Surgery Assocs., Ltd., 664 F. Supp. 212 (W.D. Pa. 1987) (recognizing unique status of professional corporations under tax laws which allow a professional to employ him or herself). *But see* EEOC v. Dowd & Dowd, Ltd., 736 F.2d 1177, 1178, 34 FEP 1815 (7th Cir. 1984) (Title VII case applying partnership rules to shareholder in eight-attorney professional organization).

[19]EEOC v. Peat, Marwick, Mitchell & Co., 589 F. Supp. 534, 38 FEP 1843 (E.D. Mo. 1984), *aff'd,* 775 F.2d 928, 38 FEP 1846 (8th Cir. 1985), *cert. denied,* 475 U.S. 1046, 40 FEP 272 (1986) (enforcing EEOC subpoena to investigate possible violations in mandatory retirement policies in national accounting firm).

[20]Whittlesey v. Union Carbide Corp., 567 F. Supp. 1320, 32 FEP 473, *later proceeding,* 35 FEP 1085 (S.D.N.Y. 1983), *aff'd,* 742 F.2d 724, 35 FEP 1089 (2d Cir. 1984) (chief labor counsel); Colby

county community college[21] and an assistant state attorney,[22] on the other hand, both fell within the ADEA exemption applicable to a governmental "appointee on the policymaking level."

Legal representatives of deceased employees have standing to sue under the Act.[23] A union also has standing to sue as a "person" aggrieved.[24]

## B. Respondents Subject to Prohibitions

In *EEOC v. Wyoming,*[25] the Supreme Court, reversing a lower court determination,[26] held that the Tenth Amendment does not preclude application of the ADEA to state and local government employers. Since then, the proscriptions of the ADEA have been applied to municipalities,[27] a borough,[28] and a tristate regional planning commission.[29]

The Eleventh Amendment was held to bar neither an EEOC suit against a state (monetary damages and injunctive relief)[30] nor private suits against the Commonwealth of Puerto Rico (injunctive relief),[31] state courts (damages),[32] a county transportation agency (damages),[33] or a local school board (damages).[34]

The number employed at the time a cause of action arose, not the year in which the action was brought, determines whether an employer employs a number sufficient to invoke the coverage of the ADEA.[35] Members of a corporation's board of directors, if not otherwise employees, have not been so counted even though compensated for attending directors' meetings.[36]

---

v. Graniteville Co., 635 F. Supp. 381, 40 FEP 1513 (S.D.N.Y. 1986) (senior vice president of finance).

[21]EEOC v. Wayne County Community College Bd. of Trustees, 723 F.2d 509, 33 FEP 911 (6th Cir. 1983).

[22]EEOC v. Reno, 758 F.2d 581, 37 FEP 985 (11th Cir. 1985).

[23]Fariss v. Lynchburg Foundry, 769 F.2d 958, 38 FEP 992 (4th Cir. 1985); *accord* Worsowicz v. Nashua Corp., 612 F. Supp. 310, 38 FEP 1444 (D.N.H. 1985).

[24]29 U.S.C. §§ 626(c), 630(a); Electrical Workers, IBEW, Local 1439 v. Union Elec. Co., 761 F.2d 1257 n.1, 37 FEP 1346 (8th Cir. 1985), *aff'g* 585 F. Supp. 261, 37 FEP 1343 (E.D. Mo. 1984).

[25]460 U.S. 226, 31 FEP 74 (1983).

[26]EEOC v. Wyoming, 514 F. Supp. 595, 25 FEP 1392 (D. Wyo. 1981).

[27]EEOC v. City of Altoona, 723 F.2d 4, 33 FEP 888 (3d Cir. 1983), *cert. denied,* 467 U.S. 1204, 34 FEP 1400 (1984); Hahn v. City of Buffalo, 596 F. Supp. 939, 36 FEP 379 (W.D.N.Y. 1984), *aff'd,* 770 F.2d 12, 38 FEP 1069 (2d Cir. 1985). *But see* Kelly v. Wauconda Park Dist., 801 F.2d 269, 41 FEP 1376 (7th Cir. 1986), *cert. denied,* 480 U.S. 940, 43 FEP 560 (1987) (state or political subdivision, like private employer, must meet 20-employee standard of 29 U.S.C. § 630(b) to be held as an "employer" under the Act).

[28]Stember v. Borough of Baldwin, 31 FEP 690 (W.D. Pa. 1983).

[29]Kulick v. Tri-State Regional Planning Comm'n, 33 FEP 741 (S.D.N.Y. 1983).

[30]EEOC v. Wyoming, 32 FEP 1270 (D. Wyo. 1983); Coffin v. South Carolina Dep't of Social Servs., 562 F. Supp. 579, 33 FEP 1267 (D.S.C. 1983).

[31]Ramirez v. Puerto Rico Fire Serv., 715 F.2d 694, 32 FEP 1239 (1st Cir. 1983).

[32]Heiar v. Crawford County, 746 F.2d 1190, 35 FEP 1458, *amended,* 36 FEP 112 (7th Cir. 1984), *cert. denied,* 472 U.S. 1027, 37 FEP 1883 (1985).

[33]Barrett v. Suffolk Transp. Servs., 600 F. Supp. 81, 37 FEP 725 (E.D.N.Y. 1984).

[34]Kenny v. Valley County School Dists. No. 1 & 1A Bd. of Trustees, 563 F. Supp. 95, 31 FEP 1502 (D. Mont. 1983), *aff'd mem.,* 770 F.2d 170 (9th Cir. 1985). *Cf.* Johnson v. Mayor of Baltimore, 731 F.2d 209, 34 FEP 854 (4th Cir. 1984), *cert. granted,* 469 U.S. 1156, *rev'd and remanded on other grounds,* 472 U.S. 353, 37 FEP 1839 (1985) (issue whether § 5, Fourteenth Amendment, provides basis for extension of ADEA to states and their political subdivisions).

[35]McGraw v. Warren County Oil Co., 32 FEP 1798 (S.D. Iowa 1982), *aff'd per curiam,* 707 F.2d 990, 32 FEP 1801 (8th Cir. 1983).

[36]*Id.;* Zimmerman v. North Am. Signal Co., 704 F.2d 347, 31 FEP 634 (7th Cir. 1983) (unpaid, inactive officers not counted as well).

Similarly, according to the Seventh Circuit, part-time hourly employees may not be counted for days they neither worked nor were on paid leave.[37]

The joint employer doctrine, derived ultimately from decisions under the National Labor Relations Act, continues to be a basis for testing whether a parent corporation and its subsidiary may both be treated as proper respondents to a claim by an employee of the subsidiary. A parent corporation has been considered an employer of a subsidiary's employee where the parent was regularly and intimately involved with business decisions concerning the management of personnel, and the two acted jointly.[38]

Employees were barred from notifying persons employed by their parent corporation and other divisions of their subsidiary of the right to opt in, where the alleged discriminatory policy and practice did not emanate from or otherwise involve either the parent or the subsidiary.[39] Similarly, an employee of a trade association failed in his attempt to establish jurisdiction on the basis of an alleged agency or integrated enterprise relationship between the association and its individual corporate members,[40] while a sales representative failed to establish such a relationship between his broker employer and a manufacturer with whom the broker primarily did business.[41] On the other hand, a township was held not to be a separate employer from its police district.[42] The ADEA applies to a corporation wholly owned by a foreign government with respect to a U.S. resident employed here.[43]

## C. Apprenticeship Programs

An EEOC regulation[44] permits employers to incorporate into an apprenticeship program an entry age limitation, without regard for whether that limitation is a bona fide occupational qualification. A district court has held this regulation contravenes the ADEA.[45] Subsequently, the court granted summary judgment for the defendant based on a Portal-to-Portal Act good-faith reliance defense.[46]

---

[37]Zimmerman v. North Am. Signal Co., *supra* note 36; Weber v. George Cook Ltd., 563 F. Supp. 598, 31 FEP 1240 (S.D.N.Y. 1983). *See also* McGraw v. Warren County Oil Co., *supra* note 35. *Contra* Pedreyra v. Cornell Prescription Pharmacies, 465 F. Supp. 936, 21 FEP 1207 (D. Colo. 1979) (Title VII); Pascutoi v. Washburn-McReavy Mortuary, 11 FEP 1325, 1326–27 (D. Minn. 1975) (Title VII).

[38]Kamens v. Summit Stainless, 586 F. Supp. 324, 36 FEP 220, 116 LRRM 2778 (E.D. Pa. 1984); Lang v. El Paso Natural Gas Co., 35 FEP 1161 (W.D. Tex. 1984); Brenimer v. Great W. Sugar Co., 567 F. Supp. 218, 33 FEP 281, 115 LRRM 4278 (D. Colo. 1983); Berkowitz v. Allied Stores of Penn-Ohio, 541 F. Supp. 1209, 31 FEP 337 (E.D. Pa. 1982).

[39]Frank v. Capital Cities Communications, 88 F.R.D. 674, 25 FEP 1186, *amended,* 509 F. Supp. 1352, 25 FEP 1762 (S.D.N.Y. 1981). *But see* Odriozola v. Superior Cosmetic Distribs., 531 F. Supp. 1070, 29 FEP 503 (D.P.R. 1982) (relationship between two subsidiary companies sufficient to warrant dismissal of motion for summary judgment by one of two defendant subsidiaries).

[40]York v. Tennessee Crushed Stone Ass'n, 684 F.2d 360, 29 FEP 735 (6th Cir. 1982).

[41]Hague v. Spencer Turbine Co., 28 FEP 450 (M.D.N.C. 1982).

[42]EEOC v. Hudson Township, 40 FEP 691 (N.D. Ohio 1986).

[43]Gazder v. Air India, 574 F. Supp. 134, 33 FEP 427 (S.D.N.Y. 1983).

[44]29 C.F.R. § 1625.13

[45]Quinn v. New York State Elec. & Gas Corp., 569 F. Supp. 655, 32 FEP 1070 (N.D.N.Y. 1983).

[46]Quinn v. New York State Elec. & Gas Corp., 621 F. Supp. 1086, 39 FEP 690 (N.D.N.Y. 1985).

## II. Prohibited Practices

A plaintiff need not always demonstrate replacement by an individual outside the protected class in order to establish a violation of the ADEA.[47] Courts have also begun to recognize constructive discharge in the ADEA context.[48]

By amendment to the ADEA effective January 1, 1983, employers were required to offer their employees aged 65–69 the same group health insurance coverage they provide their younger employees.[49] This requirement must be read in conjunction with an amendment to the Social Security Act which subjugates Medicare benefits to employer group health plan benefits payable to employees (or their spouses) aged 65–69.[50] By the 1986 ADEA amendment effective January 1, 1987, this requirement was extended to employees and spouses who are 70 years of age and older and who are not covered by a collective bargaining agreement.[51]

Public employers continue to face not only challenges under the ADEA, but age-based constitutional challenges as well.[52]

---

[47]Pace v. Southern Ry. Sys., 701 F.2d 1383, 31 FEP 710 (11th Cir.), *cert. denied,* 464 U.S. 1018, 33 FEP 656 (1983), *reh'g denied,* 465 U.S. 1054 (1984) (demotion of 51-year-old plaintiff and replacement by 49-year-old employee); Meschino v. IT&T Corp., 563 F. Supp. 1066, 34 FEP 1634 (S.D.N.Y. 1983) (discharge during reduction in force); Allison v. Western Union Tel. Co., 680 F.2d 1318, 29 FEP 393 (11th Cir. 1982) (reduction in force); Douglas v. Anderson, 656 F.2d 528, 27 FEP 47, 115 LRRM 4906 (9th Cir. 1981) (discharge); Williams v. General Motors Corp., 656 F.2d 120, 26 FEP 1381 (5th Cir. 1981), *cert. denied,* 455 U.S. 943, 27 FEP 1765 (1982) (reduction in force).

[48]Guthrie v. J.C. Penney Co., 803 F.2d 202, 42 FEP 185 (5th Cir. 1986); Cockrell v. Boise Cascade Corp., 781 F.2d 173, 39 FEP 1201 (10th Cir. 1986). Bristow v. Daily Press, 770 F.2d 1251, 38 FEP 1145 (4th Cir. 1985), *cert. denied.,* 475 U.S. 1082, 40 FEP 608 (1986).

[49]§ 4(g), 29 U.S.C. § 623(g) (1982) (Tax Equity and Fiscal Responsibility Act of 1982 (TEFRA), Pub. L. No. 97-248, § 116(a), 96 Stat. 324, 353 (1982)). ADEA of 1986 deletes age 69 upper limit (from January 1, 1987 through January 1, 1990), *infra,* note 51.

[50]42 U.S.C. § 1395y(b)(3) (1982) (TEFRA, § 116(b), 96 Stat. 324, 353–54 (1982)). *See also* EEOC Regulations, 29 C.F.R. § 1625.20 (1983); Health Care Financing Admin. Regs., 42 C.F.R. §§ 405.340–405.344 (1983). Age Discrimination in Employment Amendments of 1986 (ADEA of 1986), Pub. L. No. 99-592, 29 U.S.C. §§ 623 *et seq.* and 631(a), deletes age 69 upper limit, *infra* note 51.

[51]Age Discrimination in Employment Amendments of 1986 (ADEA of 1986), Pub. L. No. 99-592, 29 U.S.C. §§ 623 *et seq.* and 631(a). Employees covered by a collective bargaining agreement in effect on June 30, 1986, must be covered by the earlier of termination (after January 1, 1987) or on January 1, 1990. Age Discrimination in Employment Act, 29 U.S.C. § 731(a).

[52]*See, e.g.,* Johnson v. Mayor of Baltimore, 472 U.S. 353, 37 FEP 1839 (1985) (BFOQ exception to be narrowly construed); Heiar v. Crawford County, 558 F. Supp. 1175, 35 FEP 1435, *later proceedings,* 35 FEP 1441 *and* 35 FEP 1455 (W.D. Wis. 1983), *aff'd in part, vacated and remanded in part,* 746 F.2d 1190, 35 FEP 1458, *amended,* 36 FEP 112 (7th Cir. 1984), *cert. denied,* 472 U.S. 1027, 37 FEP 1883 (1985) (equal protection afforded where county mandated retirement at age 55 of all nonelective protective occupation employees participating in retirement fund; no ruling on statutory claims under ADEA) (mandatory age 55 retirement not justified by BFOQ under ADEA; county failed to show substantially all deputy sheriffs over age 55 unable to perform duties safely and efficiently, or that it is impossible or impracticable to make individualized determination) (attorney's fees awarded) (trial court rejection of BFOQ defense for age 55 retirement rule not clearly erroneous); Bowman v. Department of Justice, Fed. Prison Sys., 510 F. Supp. 1183, 25 FEP 1178 (E.D. Va. 1981), *aff'd,* 679 F.2d 876, 29 FEP 1472 (4th Cir.), *cert. denied,* 459 U.S. 1072, 30 FEP 592 (1982) (mandatory retirement of correctional officers at age 55 upheld); Beck v. Borough of Manheim, 505 F. Supp. 923, 926–27, 24 FEP 1300, 1302 (E.D. Pa. 1981) (mandatory retirement of policeman at age 60 upheld, "[p]articularly where the law enforcement department is small and the abilities and characteristics of individuals therein consequently have disproportionate effects on each other"); Maresca v. Cuomo, 64 N.Y.2d 242, 485 N.Y.S.2d 724, 475 N.E.2d 95, 45 FEP 1606 (1984), *appeal dismissed,* 474 U.S. 802, 45 FEP 1896 (1985) (equal protection challenge to state constitutional and statutory provisions mandating retirement of certain judges at age 70 rejected). *Cf.* Western Airlines v. Criswell, 472 U.S. 400, 37 FEP 1829 (1985), *aff'g* 709 F.2d 544, 32 FEP 1204 (9th Cir. 1983) *and* EEOC v. County of Los Angeles, 706 F.2d 1039, 31 FEP 1474 (9th Cir. 1983), *cert. denied,* 464 U.S. 1073, 33 FEP 1224 (1984).

## III. PROCEDURE

### B. Accrual of Cause of Action

Following Title VII guidelines enunciated by the Supreme Court in *Delaware State College v. Ricks*[53] and *Chardon v. Fernandez,*[54] courts have held that the alleged discriminatory act was deemed to occur (and the claim therefore to accrue) on the date the plaintiff was unequivocally notified of the decision, rather than the date employment actually was affected or officially changed.[55]

Applications or requests for rehire,[56] requests for other employment within the company,[57] or similar efforts by the employee to ameliorate the effects of the employer's decision[58] do not extend the time for filing. However, termination and subsequent failure to rehire into a new position can be two

---

[53]449 U.S. 250, 24 FEP 827 (1980).

[54]454 U.S. 6, 27 FEP 57 (1981).

[55]Miller v. IT&T Corp., 755 F.2d 20, 37 FEP 8 (2d Cir.), *cert. denied,* 474 U.S. 851, 38 FEP 1728 (1985); O'Malley v. GTE Serv. Corp., 758 F.2d 818, 37 FEP 697 (2d Cir. 1985); Cook v. Pan Am. World Airways, 771 F.2d 635, 38 FEP 1344 (2d Cir. 1985), *cert. denied,* 474 U.S. 1109, 39 FEP 1568 (1986) (pilot seniority compromise, continuing violation until applied to a specific employee); Kriegesmann v. Barry-Wehmiller Co., 739 F.2d 357, 35 FEP 651 (8th Cir.), *cert. denied,* 469 U.S. 1036, 36 FEP 464 (1984); Heiar v. Crawford County; 746 F.2d 1190, 35 FEP 1458, *amended,* 36 FEP 112 (7th Cir. 1984), *cert. denied,* 472 U.S. 1027, 37 FEP 1883 (1985); Vaught v. R.R. Donnelley & Sons Co., 745 F.2d 407, 35 FEP 1820 (7th Cir. 1984); Bratton v. American Nat'l Ins. Co., 32 FEP 953 (N.D. Ga. 1983), *aff'd mem.,* 740 F.2d 978 (11th Cir. 1984); Kazanzas v. Walt Disney World Co., 704 F.2d 1527, 31 FEP 1590 (11th Cir.), *cert. denied,* 464 U.S. 982, 33 FEP 280 (1983); Leite v. Kennecott Copper Corp., 558 F. Supp. 1170, 31 FEP 390 (D. Mass.), *aff'd mem.,* 720 F.2d 658, 33 FEP 1520 (1st Cir. 1983) (issue left open, until trial, as to whether oral notice received by two of the plaintiffs was sufficiently clear); Price v. Litton Business Sys., 694 F.2d 963, 30 FEP 803 (4th Cir. 1982); Aronsen v. Crown Zellerbach, 662 F.2d 584, 27 FEP 518 (9th Cir. 1981), *cert. denied,* 459 U.S. 1290, 30 FEP 1856 (1983); Shipper v. Avon Prods., 605 F. Supp. 701, 44 FEP 257 (S.D.N.Y. 1985); Chambers v. European Am. Bank & Trust Co., 601 F. Supp. 630, 36 FEP 1550 (E.D.N.Y. 1985); Welty v. S.F.&G. dba Mercury, 605 F. Supp. 1548, 37 FEP 926 (N.D. Ala. 1985); Janikowski v. Bendix Co., 603 F. Supp. 1284, 39 FEP 1482 (E.D. Mich. 1985), *aff'd on this issue, rev'd in part,* 823 F.2d 945, 43 EPD ¶ 37,221 (6th Cir. 1987); Yokum v. St. Johnsbury Trucking Co., 595 F. Supp. 1532, 36 FEP 529 (D. Conn. 1984); Sprott v. Avon Prods., 596 F. Supp. 178, 36 FEP 538 (S.D.N.Y. 1984); Mull v. Arco Durethene Plastics, 784 F.2d 284, 40 FEP 311 (7th Cir. 1986); Lewis v. General Elec. Co., 34 FEP 1756 (W.D. Ky. 1983); Pfister v. Allied Corp., 539 F. Supp. 224, 30 FEP 838 (S.D.N.Y. 1982); Lippert v. General Elec. Co., 27 FEP 1427 (W.D. Ky. 1982). *But see* Elliott v. Group Medical & Surgical Serv., 714 F.2d 556, 32 FEP 1451 (5th Cir. 1983), *cert. denied,* 467 U.S. 1215, 34 FEP 1472 (1984) (timeliness determined under law in effect prior to Supreme Court decision holding that notice of termination is determinative); Monnig v. Kennecott Corp., 603 F. Supp. 1035, 37 FEP 193 (D. Conn. 1985) (equivocal letter, with no specified termination date, does not commence filing period); Verschuuren v. Equitable Life Assurance Soc'y, 554 F. Supp. 1188, 30 FEP 1309 (S.D.N.Y. 1983) ("termination letter" which conditioned dismissal upon inability of employer to find plaintiff another position held not final).

[56]Welty v. S.F.&G. dba Mercury, *supra* note 55; Nelson v. Massey-Ferguson, 36 FEP 365 (E.D. Wis. 1984); Burnam v. Amoco Container Co., 34 EPD ¶ 34,482 (N.D. Ga. 1984), *aff'd,* 755 F.2d 893, 45 FEP 1180 (11th Cir. 1985); Haupt v. International Harvester Co., 571 F. Supp. 1043, 32 FEP 1886 (N.D. Ill. 1983); Kinniry v. Aetna Ins. Co., 35 FEP 1474 (D. Conn. 1984); Moon v. Aeronca, Inc., 541 F. Supp. 747, 31 FEP 331 (S.D. Ohio 1982); Lewan v. Department of the Navy, Military Sealift Command, Atlantic, 35 FEP 1009 (D.N.J. 1982).

[57]Janikowski v. Bendix Co., *supra* note 55; Quinn v. Amoco Fabrics Co. dba Hazelhurst Mills, 35 FEP 1791 (S.D. Ga. 1984); Mull v. Arco Durethene Plastics, *supra* note 55.

[58]Kriegesmann v. Barry-Wehmiller Co., *supra* note 55. *But see* McConnell v. General Tel. of Cal., 814 F.2d 1311, 43 FEP 887 (9th Cir. 1987), *cert. denied,* 484 U.S. —, 45 FEP 1895 (1988); Cocke v. Merrill Lynch & Co., 817 F.2d 1559, 43 FEP 1724 (11th Cir. 1987) (representations of alternate employment and efforts by employer to relocate employee within company justify equitable tolling); Zebedeo v. Martin E. Segal Co., 582 F. Supp. 1394, 37 FEP 128 (D. Conn. 1984); Franci v. Avco Corp., Avco Lycoming Div., 538 F. Supp. 250, 31 FEP 347 (D. Conn. 1982); Colby v. Graniteville Co., 635 F. Supp. 381, 40 FEP 1513 (S.D.N.Y. 1986) (hopes of recall, requests for transfer, and request for reconsideration, respectively, kindled in part by employer, tolled time for filing).

separate acts of discrimination where the individual is told he is being considered.[59] Where the employee remains employed, the denial of promotion or transfer may be deemed "continuing" for filing purposes.[60] On the other hand, employment decisions such as the failure to adopt a pension plan have been deemed completed when announced.[61] While neither a layoff nor an employer's failure to recall or rehire establishes the basis for a continuing violation,[62] an unlawful discriminatory policy may have that effect in practice.[63] Thus, an employee need not file a charge upon first learning of the discriminatory policy; the filing period commences upon application of that policy to the individual employee.[64] Once a cause of action for unlawful discharge accrues, it survives the death of the plaintiff and the deceased former employee's executrix may therefore be substituted as a party plaintiff.[65]

## C. Deferral to State Proceedings

As held in *Oscar Mayer & Co. v. Evans,*[66] the failure to file a timely charge in a deferral state is not fatal to an action under the ADEA.[67]

---

[59]Caldwell v. National Ass'n of Home Builders, 771 F.2d 1051, 38 FEP 1398 (7th Cir. 1985) (summary judgment reversed).

[60]Taylor v. Home Ins. Co., 777 F.2d 849, 39 FEP 769 (4th Cir. 1985), *cert. denied,* 476 U.S. 1142, 40 FEP 1512 (1986) (successive demotions, two years apart, deemed continuing); Cory v. SmithKline Beckman Corp., 585 F. Supp. 871, 35 FEP 1682, 116 LRRM 3361 (E.D. Pa. 1984) (denial of job bids); Zewde v. Elgin Community College, 601 F. Supp. 1237, 37 FEP 895 (N.D. Ill. 1984); Small v. Bethlehem Steel Corp., 33 FEP 414 (D. Md. 1983) (demotion and denial of promotion part of alleged "plan"); Coleman v. Apex Acquisition, Clark Oil & Ref. Co. Div., 568 F. Supp. 1035, 36 FEP 758 (E.D. Wis. 1983) (continuing violation as to denial of promotion and refusal to reassign runs only until employee is discharged). *Cf.* Miller v. IT&T Corp., *supra* note 55 (ongoing reorganization irrelevant when plaintiff has notice of his own termination).

[61]Rothenberger v. Douglas County, 586 F. Supp. 210, 35 FEP 1376 (D.S.D. 1983), *aff'd,* 736 F.2d 1240, 35 FEP 1377 (8th Cir. 1984), *cert. denied,* 469 U.S. 1213, 37 FEP 64 (1985).

[62]Lawson v. Burlington Indus., 683 F.2d 862, 29 FEP 1224 (4th Cir.), *cert. denied,* 459 U.S. 944 (1982); Shultz v. Dempster Sys., 561 F. Supp. 1230, 32 FEP 1766 (E.D. Tenn. 1983).

[63]Electrical Workers (IBEW) Local 1439 v. Union Elec. Co., 761 F.2d 1257, 37 FEP 1346 (8th Cir. 1985) (cause of action timely, insurance plan illegal practice continuing violation); EEOC v. Westinghouse Elec. Corp., 725 F.2d 211, 33 FEP 945 (3d Cir. 1983), *amended,* 33 FEP 1816 (3d Cir.), *cert. denied,* 469 U.S. 820, 35 FEP 1607 (1984); (cause of action accrued not at time of notification of policy but at time of plant closing, when employees became eligible for claimed layoff and retirement benefits); Crosland v. Charlotte Eye, Ear & Throat Hosp., 686 F.2d 208, 29 FEP 1178 (4th Cir. 1982) (cause of action accrued at time of plaintiff's retirement because defendant did not finally decide plaintiff's pension status and benefit entitlement until he actually retired); EEOC v. Home Ins. Co., 553 F. Supp. 704, 30 FEP 841 (S.D.N.Y. 1982) (earlier of either last day of employment or, if applicable, date employer withdrew challenged policy provision).

[64]O'Malley v. GTE Serv. Corp., *supra* note 55 (discriminatory retirement policy); Heiar v. Crawford County, *supra* note 55 (same); *see also* EEOC v. Goodyear Tire & Rubber Co., 34 EPD ¶ 34,596 (N.D. Ohio 1984).

[65]Asklar v. Honeywell, 95 F.R.D. 419, 29 FEP 1596 (D. Conn. 1982) (executrix did not, however, have independent action for retaliation in view of absence of any employer-employee relationship between her and defendant).

[66]441 U.S. 750, 19 FEP 1167 (1979).

[67]Anderson v. Illinois Tool Works, 753 F.2d 622, 36 FEP 1693 (7th Cir. 1985); Agostine v. Iowa Beef Processors, 35 FEP 328 (D. Neb. 1984); Haller v. Butler Shoe Corp., 595 F. Supp. 998, 36 FEP 30 (D. Md. 1984); Nestor v. Quaker State Coca-Cola Bottling Co., 579 F. Supp. 289, 40 FEP 412 (W.D. Pa. 1984); McKelvy v. Metal Container Corp., 37 FEP 270 (M.D. Fla. 1984) (but pendent state claim dismissed as untimely filed); Clark v. American Home Prods. Corp., American Home Foods Div., 34 FEP 813 (D. Mass. 1982), *aff'd,* 743 F.2d 52, 35 FEP 1401 (1st Cir. 1984) (court noted, however, it would dismiss case if plaintiff failed to file complaint with state agency within 30 days of decision. *See also* Dixon v. Stephenson, Inc., 614 F. Supp. 60, 36 FEP 1861 (D.D.C. 1985) (ADEA refers to "state" law and, accordingly, no deferral on basis of county ordinance); Galvin v. Vermont, 598 F. Supp. 144, 36 FEP 1674 (D. Vt. 1984) (300-day period inapplicable where state police retirement systems excluded from coverage under state statute); Barrett v. Suffolk Transp. Servs., 37 FEP 724, *reconsideration denied,* 600

However, this does not mean that the state proceeding is optional or that it may be brought at any time. The state proceeding is mandatory and must be initiated with the time limitations set by § 626(d)(2).[68] Plaintiff's cooperation with the state's enforcement agency is not, however, a prerequisite to maintenance of an ADEA action.[69]

## D. Filing With the EEOC

### 1. Administration

On January 3, 1983, the EEOC published final ADEA procedural regulations,[70] including regulations governing the issuance of opinion letters.[71]

By legislation,[72] Congress confirmed the transfer of authority from the Secretary of Labor to the EEOC under the Reorganization Act of 1977,[73] and with it the jurisdiction of the EEOC to enforce the ADEA.[74] This legislative clarification made previous judicial decisions on this issue obsolete. Earlier challenges to such authority had been predicated upon a provision in the Reorganization Act for one-house congressional veto similar to that struck down in *Immigration & Naturalization Service v. Chadha.*[75] One court had held that this issue need not be addressed in a private action to which the EEOC was not a party.[76] A majority, however, had upheld the transfer of authority to the EEOC.[77]

---

F. Supp. 81, 37 FEP 725 (E.D.N.Y. 1984) (no need to file with state where state law ceiling is age 65). *But see* Koman v. Sears, Roebuck & Co., 595 F. Supp. 935, 36 FEP 1690 (N.D. Ill. 1984). *And see* Kinniry v. Aetna Ins. Co., 35 FEP 1474 (D. Conn. 1984) (state agency not "agent" for EEOC).

[68]Anderson v. Illinois Tool Works, *supra* note 67; Meschino v. IT&T Corp., 563 F. Supp. 1066, 34 FEP 1634 (S.D.N.Y. 1983). *See also* Isaac v. Harvard Univ., 603 F. Supp. 22, 37 FEP 369 (D. Mass. 1984), *aff'd in part, vacated in part,* rev'd in part, 769 F.2d 817, 38 FEP 764 (1st Cir. 1985) (Title VII charge); Morris v. Kaiser Eng'rs, 14 Ohio St. 3d 45, 471 N.E.2d 471, 36 FEP 807 (1984) (state's election-of-remedies doctrine cannot bar filing with Ohio Civil Rights Commission for purpose of satisfying ADEA prerequisite); James v. Miller-Wohl Co., 35 FEP 1846 (W.D.N.Y. 1984); Hay v. Wells Cargo, 596 F. Supp. 635, 36 FEP 166 (D. Nev. 1984), *aff'd mem.,* 796 F.2d 478, 41 FEP 1888 (9th Cir. 1986) (failure to commence state claim does not extend time for filing beyond 300-day period); Shanahan v. WITI-TV, 565 F. Supp. 219, 37 FEP 1118, 115 LRRM 4208 (E.D. Wis. 1982); Whitfield v. City of Knoxville, 567 F. Supp. 1344, 32 FEP 1052 (E.D. Tenn. 1983), *aff'd,* 756 F.2d 455, 37 FEP 288 (6th Cir. 1985). *See also* Stoecklein v. Illinois Tool Works, 589 F. Supp. 139, 36 FEP 1154 (N.D. Ill. 1984) (stay of federal case so plaintiff can comply with state commencement requirement and 60-day deferral period); Van Atta v. Kal-Aero, 555 F. Supp. 912, 32 FEP 1627 (W.D. Mich. 1983) (state law claims entertained as well); Clark v. American Home Prods. Corp., American Home Foods Div., *supra* note 67.

[69]MacGill v. Johns Hopkins Univ., 33 FEP 1254 (D. Md. 1983); Curto v. Sears, Roebuck & Co., 552 F. Supp. 891, 30 FEP 1196 (N.D. Ill. 1982), *summary judgment for defendant granted,* 38 FEP 547 (N.D. Ill. 1984).

[70]29 C.F.R. § 1626 (1983).

[71]*Id.,* § 1626.17.

[72]Pub. L. No. 98-532 (signed October 19, 1984).

[73]5 U.S.C. §§ 901–12 (1977).

[74]*See* EEOC v. First Citizens Bank of Billings, 758 F.2d 397, 45 FEP 1337 (9th Cir.), *cert. denied,* 474 U.S. 902 (1985); EEOC v. CBS, 748 F.2d 124, 36 FEP 575, *rev'g* 743 F.2d 969, 35 FEP 1127 (2d Cir. 1984).

[75]462 U.S. 919, 51 USLW 4907 (1983).

[76]Lopez v. Bulova Watch Co., 582 F. Supp. 755, 34 FEP 575 (D.R.I. 1984).

[77]*Transfer of authority upheld:* EEOC v. Hernando Bank, 724 F.2d 1188, 34 FEP 15 (5th Cir. 1984); Muller Optical Co. v. EEOC, 743 F.2d 380, 35 FEP 1147 (6th Cir. 1984); *see also* EEOC v. Allstate Ins. Co., 570 F. Supp. 1224, 32 FEP 1337 (S.D. Miss. 1983); EEOC v. United States Steel Corp., 34 FEP 1091 (W.D. Pa. 1984); EEOC v. International Mill Serv., 34 FEP 392 (E.D. Pa. 1984) (subpoena enforced); EEOC v. Radio Montgomery, 588 F. Supp. 567, 34 FEP 378 (W.D. Va. 1984); EEOC v. Pan Am. World Airways, 34 FEP 321 (N.D. Cal. 1984); EEOC v. Ingersoll Johnson Steel Co., 583 F. Supp. 983, 34 FEP 875 (S.D. Ind. 1984); EEOC v. Old Dominion Freight Line, 587 F. Supp. 1128, 35 FEP 1854 (M.D.N.C. 1984); EEOC v. Plessey, Inc., 34 FEP 500 (D. Kan. 1984); EEOC v. Chrysler Corp.,

When disputes arise over the timeliness of the filing of a charge, the EEOC's intake questionnaire may be introduced as an official record.[78] And while technical failures by the charging party[79] or the EEOC intake officer[80] normally will not preclude the assertion of statutory rights, the charge[81] or the particular circumstances[82] must give reasonable notice of a complaint, and cannot be used as a basis for suit over later-occurring events unless such occurrences are deemed to be a continuation of the matters complained of in the charge.[83]

## 2. 180/300-Day Filing Limit

The Second and Eighth circuits, both citing *Oscar Mayer*, followed the Ninth Circuit in holding that the 300-day period, rather than the 180-day period, applies to a plaintiff who, in a deferral state, has filed an untimely claim with the state agency.[84]

The timely charge of a former employee was held sufficient to satisfy the filing requirements for similarly situated employees who had failed to file a timely charge.[85] The failure of an individual to file a timely administrative charge at the state level,[86] or to meet the federal filing deadlines,[87] does not preclude the EEOC on its own from initiating a federal action. Further, in an EEOC-initiated class-type action, there is no requirement that all individ-

---

34 FEP 1862 (N.D. Ga. 1984), *aff'd on other grounds*, 759 F.2d 1523, 37 FEP 1244 (11th Cir. 1985); EEOC v. New York, 590 F. Supp. 37, 34 FEP 379 (N.D.N.Y. 1984); EEOC v. Armour & Co., 35 FEP 1262 (N.D.N.Y. 1984); EEOC v. Pennsylvania, 596 F. Supp. 1333, 36 FEP 234 (M.D. Pa. 1984); EEOC v. Dayton Power & Light Co., 605 F. Supp. 13, 35 FEP 401 (S.D. Ohio 1984); EEOC v. El Paso Natural Gas Co., 33 FEP 1837 (W.D. Tex. 1984); EEOC v. Delaware Dep't of Health & Social Servs., 595 F. Supp. 568 (D. Del. 1984); EEOC v. Goodyear Tire & Rubber Co., 34 EPD ¶ 34,596 (N.D. Ohio 1984); Santos v. Stanley Home Prods., 36 FEP 319 (D. Mass 1984); EEOC v. City of Memphis, 581 F. Supp. 179, 33 FEP 1089 (W.D. Tenn. 1983); EEOC v. Cudahy Foods Co., 588 F. Supp. 13, 33 FEP 1836 (W.D. Wash. 1983); EEOC v. Jackson County, 33 FEP 963 (W.D. Mo. 1983).
  *Transfer of authority held unconstitutional:* EEOC v. Chrysler Corp., 595 F. Supp. 344, 33 FEP 1838 (E.D. Mich. 1984) (but not retroactively applied); EEOC v. Martin Indus., 581 F. Supp. 1029, 34 FEP 201 (N.D. Ala.), *appeal dismissed*, 469 U.S. 806, 35 FEP 1607 (1984); EEOC v. Westinghouse Elec. Corp., 576 F. Supp. 1530, 33 FEP 1232 (W.D. Pa.), *appeal dismissed*, 469 U.S. 806, 35 FEP 1608 (1984); EEOC v. Allstate Ins. Co., 570 F. Supp. 1224, 32 FEP 1337 (S.D. Miss. 1983), *appeal dismissed for want of jurisdiction*, 467 U.S. 1232, 34 FEP 1785 (1984), *remanded mem.*, 740 F.2d 966, 35 FEP 1892 (5th Cir. 1984); EEOC v. Pan Am. World Airways, 576 F. Supp. 1530, 33 FEP 1232 (S.D.N.Y. 1984). *Cf.* EEOC v. CBS, 743 F.2d 969, 35 FEP 1127 (2d Cir.), *rev'g* 34 FEP 257 (S.D.N.Y.), *motion denied*, 748 F.2d 124, 36 FEP 575 (2d Cir. 1984).
  [78]Holly v. City of Naperville, 571 F. Supp. 668, 34 FEP 1788 (N.D. Ill. 1983).
  [79]Anness v. Steelworkers, 707 F.2d 917, 31 FEP 1447 (6th Cir. 1983) (wrong form).
  [80]Galvan v. Bexar County, Tex., 785 F.2d 1298, 40 FEP 710 (5th Cir. 1986).
  [81]Davis v. Devine, 736 F.2d 1108, 34 FEP 1807 (6th Cir.), *cert. denied*, 469 U.S. 1020, 36 FEP 320 (1984) (letters to agency applying for administrative law judge position asked reconsideration of appointments policy as conflicting with ADEA, but did not state complaint of age discrimination and had preceded plaintiff's rejection); Vinson v. Ford Motor Co., 806 F.2d 686, 42 FEP 681 (6th Cir. 1986), *cert. denied*, 482 U.S. 906, 43 FEP 1896 (1987) (plaintiff must identify conduct constituting age discrimination in "charge" to satisfy charge-filing requirement); Michelson v. Exxon Research & Eng'g Co., 808 F.2d 1005, 42 FEP 1031 (3d Cir. 1987) (telephone call to EEOC does not constitute a "charge" for purpose of statute).
  [82]Galvan v. Bexar County, Tex., *supra* note 80.
  [83]Davis v. Devine, *supra* note 81; Thomas v. Brown & Root, 745 F.2d 279, 35 FEP 1648 (4th Cir. 1984).
  [84]Goodman v. Heublein, 645 F.2d 127, 25 FEP 645 (2d Cir. 1981); EEOC v. Shamrock Optical Co., 788 F.2d 491, 40 FEP 880 (8th Cir. 1986); Bean v. Crocker Nat'l Bank, 600 F.2d 754, 20 FEP 533 (9th Cir. 1979). *See also* Aronsen v. Crown Zellerbach, 662 F.2d 584, 27 FEP 518 (9th Cir. 1981), *cert. denied*, 459 U.S. 1290, 30 FEP 1856 (1983).
  [85]Shuster v. Federated Dep't Stores, 508 F. Supp. 118, 29 FEP 324 (N.D. Ga. 1980).
  [86]EEOC v. Home Ins. Co., 553 F. Supp. 704, 30 FEP 841 (S.D.N.Y. 1982).
  [87]*See* EEOC v. Kansas, 28 FEP 1036 (D. Kan. 1982).

ual claimants file written consents in order to toll the filing period as to each claimant.[88] Otherwise, the courts have continued to be reluctant to toll the filing period,[89] absent misconduct, bad faith, or other circumstances attributable to the defendant.[90] In any event, an argument such as the failure to post

---

[88]EEOC v. Chrysler Corp., 546 F. Supp. 54, 29 FEP 284, *clarified,* 546 F. Supp. 73, 29 FEP 1385 (E.D. Mich. 1982), *aff'd,* 733 F.2d 1183, 34 FEP 1401 (6th Cir. 1984). Where additional plaintiffs do "opt in" by filing the requisite written consents, it has been held they are not required to satisfy the § 626(d) filing requirements so long as the named representative has satisfactorily complied with the applicable notice provisions and they in turn could have complied with the filing requirements in a timely manner. Johnson v. American Airlines, 531 F. Supp. 957, 29 FEP 330 (N.D. Tex. 1982), *aff'd on other grounds,* 745 F.2d 988, 36 FEP 321 (5th Cir. 1984), *cert. denied,* 472 U.S. 1027, 37 FEP 1883 (1985).

[89]Taylor v. General Tel. Co. of the Sw., 759 F.2d 437, 37 FEP 1228 (5th Cir. 1985) (filing requirement not met by mailing charge to EEOC on 180th day); Kriegesmann v. Barry-Wehmiller Co., 739 F.2d 357, 35 FEP 651 (8th Cir.), *cert. denied,* 469 U.S. 1036, 36 FEP 464 (1984) (no tolling because of extension of severance benefits over 25 weeks and offer to assist in outplacement); Kazanzas v. Walt Disney World Co., 704 F.2d 1527, 31 FEP 1590 (11th Cir.), *cert. denied,* 464 U.S. 982, 33 FEP 280 (1983); Vaught v. R.R. Donnelley & Sons Co., 745 F.2d 407, 35 FEP 1820 (7th Cir. 1984); Downey v. Firestone Tire & Rubber Co., 35 FEP 30 (D.D.C. 1984), *aff'd in part, rev'd in part and remanded,* 762 F.2d 137, 37 FEP 1072 (D.C. Cir. 1985) (failure to post ADEA notice and other circumstances did not warrant tolling); Mogley v. Chicago Title Ins. Co., 719 F.2d 289, 33 FEP 10 (8th Cir. 1983) (refusing to excuse failure to file earlier merely because timely filing might have resulted in substantially decreased retirement benefits); Posey v. Skyline Corp., 702 F.2d 102, 31 FEP 274 (7th Cir.), *cert. denied,* 464 U.S. 960, 33 FEP 152 (1983); Greene v. Whirlpool Corp., 708 F.2d 128, 31 FEP 1779 (4th Cir. 1983), *cert. denied,* 464 U.S. 1042, 33 FEP 1084 (1984) (failure to post ADEA notice did not warrant tolling in view of employee's otherwise acquired knowledge); Chambers v. European Am. Bank & Trust Co., 601 F. Supp. 630, 36 FEP 1550 (E.D.N.Y. 1985) (no tolling on basis of feared loss of severance benefits); Perazzo v. Top Value Enters., 590 F. Supp. 428, 41 FEP 401 (S.D. Ohio 1984) (employer silence regarding stock option plan not misleading); Bassett v. Sterling Drug, 578 F. Supp. 1244, 35 FEP 382 (S.D. Ohio 1984), *appeal dismissed,* 770 F.2d 165, 40 FEP 1617 (6th Cir. 1985) (hospitalization began only 17 days short of extended 300-day filing period); Fressel v. AT&T Technologies, 35 FEP 658 (N.D. Ga. 1984) (no tolling despite assurances of promotion to old position "if business improved"); Quinn v. Amoco Fabrics Co. dba Hazelhurst Mills, 35 FEP 1791 (S.D. Ga. 1984) (self-initiated conversations regarding other jobs, no basis for tolling); Hay v. Wells Cargo, 596 F. Supp. 635, 36 FEP 166 (D. Nev. 1984), *aff'd mem.,* 796 F.2d 478, 41 FEP 1888 (9th Cir. 1986) ("preoccupation with personal affairs" insufficient); Sprott v. Avon Prods., 596 F. Supp. 178, 36 FEP 538 (S.D.N.Y. 1984) (reliance on advice of counsel, settlement negotiations insufficient); Senkow v. Department of Energy, 35 FEP 26 (D.D.C. 1984), *aff'd,* 762 F.2d 138, 38 FEP 672 (D.C. Cir. 1985) (charge regarding reduction in force cannot encompass earlier denial of promotion); Rothenberger v. Douglas County, 586 F. Supp. 210, 35 FEP 1376 (D.S.D. 1983), *aff'd,* 736 F.2d 1240, 35 FEP 1377 (8th Cir. 1984), *cert. denied,* 469 U.S. 1213, 37 FEP 64 (1985) (no continuing violation when county did not adopt state's pension plan); Mull v. Arco Durethene Plastics, 784 F.2d 284, 40 FEP 311 (7th Cir. 1986) (oral notice of demotion and discharge commences limitations period); Miller v. IT&T Corp., 755 F.2d 20, 37 FEP 8 (2d Cir.), *cert. denied,* 474 U.S. 851, 38 FEP 1728 (1985) (mere possibility that dismissal might be reversed did not make it advisory or ineffective); O'Malley v. GTE Serv. Corp., 758 F.2d 818, 37 FEP 697 (2d Cir. 1985) (no continuing violation in facially proper retirement policy; employee's written acknowledgment of retirement begins limitation period); Herman v. National Broadcasting Co., 569 F. Supp. 282, 33 FEP 1278 (N.D. Ill. 1983), *aff'd in relevant part and rev'd in part,* 744 F.2d 604, 35 FEP 1653 (7th Cir. 1984), *cert. denied,* 470 U.S. 1028, 37 FEP 192 (1985) (new violations occurring after plaintiff's rehire but brought to EEOC's attention during its investigation did not warrant tolling); Leite v. Kennecott Copper Corp., 558 F. Supp. 1170, 31 FEP 390 (D. Mass.), *aff'd mem.,* 720 F.2d 658, 33 FEP 1520 (1st Cir. 1983) (tolling disallowed where plaintiffs, represented by counsel, claimed to have delayed filing suit based upon government's erroneous representations); Shultz v. Dempster Sys., 561 F. Supp. 1230, 32 FEP 1766 (E.D. Tenn. 1983) (no tolling where employer did not receive notice of alleged discrimination after filing period expired). *But see* Vance v. Whirlpool Corp., 707 F.2d 483, 31 FEP 1115, *modified on other grounds,* 716 F.2d 1010, 32 FEP 1391 (4th Cir. 1983), *cert. denied,* 465 U.S. 1102, 34 FEP 416 *and* 467 U.S. 1226, 34 FEP 1560 (1984) (action dismissed for failure to comply with jurisdictional 60-day waiting period, but plaintiff permitted to refile in view of dearth of clear precedent and absence of any demonstrated prejudice to defendant); James v. Miller-Wohl Co., 35 FEP 1846 (W.D.N.Y. 1984) (equitable tolling due to letter to employer, pendency of state agency proceedings; fact that plaintiff was store manager not controlling).

[90]Several decisions involving the tolling issue turn on whether the employer posted the required ADEA notice. *Compare* Elliott v. Group Medical & Surgical Serv., 714 F.2d 556, 32 FEP 1451 (5th Cir. 1983), *cert. denied,* 467 U.S. 1215, 34 FEP 1472 (1984) (failure to post ADEA notice warrants tolling), McClinton v. Alabama By-Products Corp., 743 F.2d 1483, 35 FEP 1893 (11th Cir. 1984) (same), Galvin v. Vermont, 598 F. Supp. 144, 36 FEP 1674 (D. Vt. 1984) (same) *and* Knight v. County of Dane, 30 FEP 1107 (W.D. Wis. 1982) *with* Hrzenak v. White-Westinghouse Appliance Co., 682 F.2d 714, 29 FEP 1278, 111 LRRM 2335 (8th Cir. 1982) (employee's assertion he never saw requisite notices insufficient to justify tolling where employer complied with posting regulations). For other circumstances, *see, e.g.,* Meyer v. Riegel Prods. Corp., 720 F.2d 303, 33 FEP 165 (3d Cir. 1983), *cert. dismissed,* 465 U.S. 1091

a statutorily required notice cannot be raised for the first time on appeal.[91]

### 3. Is Timely Filing a Jurisdictional Prerequisite?

Timely filing of an age discrimination charge is not a jurisdictional prerequisite. Some courts have held it is a condition precedent subject to equitable tolling based on the plaintiff's ignorance of statutory rights, found to be excusable under the circumstances.[92] The employer's failure to display a poster advising employees of ADEA rights continues to be advanced with mixed results as an excuse for untimely filing of charges.[93]

Delay in filing because of "depression or other psychological impairment" does not toll the filing period where the plaintiff did not claim he was rendered legally incompetent.[94] Representation by counsel shortly after the complained-of event negates any claim of ignorance of the filing requirements.[95] Discussions of and acceptance of a special assignment following an unambiguous termination notice are not circumstances sufficient to toll the filing period, even if the oral notice was not in proper written form in compliance with the employer's standard policies.[96]

---

(1984) (employer's misrepresentations regarding reason for employee's discharge, if relied upon, warrants tolling, even where employee represented by attorney); Price v. Litton Business Sys., 694 F.2d 963, 30 FEP 803 (4th Cir. 1982) (tolling unwarranted unless employee's failure to file in timely fashion due either to defendant's deliberate design or to actions defendant unmistakably should have understood would lead to delay); Lawson v. Burlington Indus., 683 F.2d 862, 864, 29 FEP 1224, 1226 (4th Cir.), *cert. denied*, 459 U.S. 944, 29 FEP 1752 (1982) (plaintiff's hope he would be recalled insufficient to establish "reasonable reliance on the defendant's conduct or representations" necessary to justify tolling); Monnig v. Kennecott Corp., 603 F. Supp. 1035, 37 FEP 193 (D. Conn. 1985) (employees believed they might remain employed after reorganization); Connor v. Hodel, 36 FEP 362 (D.D.C. 1984) (tolled until identity of person selected for promotion known); Agostine v. Iowa Beef Processors, 35 FEP 328 (D. Neb. 1984) (tolled due to "employer's actions following the termination"); Golletti v. Arco/Polymers, 35 FEP 1325 (W.D. Pa. 1984); Kinniry v. Aetna Ins. Co., 35 FEP 1474 (D. Conn. 1984); Franci v. Avco Corp., Avco Lycoming Div., 538 F. Supp. 250, 31 FEP 347 (D. Conn. 1982); EEOC v. City of Memphis, 581 F. Supp. 179, 33 FEP 1089 (W.D. Tenn. 1983) (statute of limitations tolled until EEOC obtained, through court action, compliance with subpoena). *See also* Felty v. Graves-Humphreys Co., 785 F.2d 516, 40 FEP 447 (4th Cir. 1986), *appeal after remand*, 818 F.2d 1126, 43 FEP 1507 (4th Cir. 1987) (claim that employer told plaintiff not to discuss pending termination with anyone or risk instant dismissal; *see infra* notes 101 and 102 and accompanying text).

[91]Kriegesmann v. Barry-Wehmiller Co., *supra* note 89.

[92]Jones v. Premier Indus. Corp., 611 F. Supp. 142, 38 FEP 277 (N.D. Ga. 1985); Felty v. Graves-Humphreys Co., *supra* note 90, at 576; Cerbone v. Ladies Garment Workers, 768 F.2d 45, 38 FEP 801 (2d Cir. 1985).

[93]McKinney v. Dole, 765 F.2d 1129, 38 FEP 364 (D.C. Cir. 1985) (plaintiff visited office where notice was posted only "infrequently"; no tolling); Byers v. Follmer Trucking Co., 763 F.2d 599, 37 FEP 1871 (3d Cir. 1985) (employer's testimony regarding policy to post notices suffices, in absence of contrary proof; precludes tolling for failure to post); Klausing v. Whirlpool Corp., 623 F. Supp. 156, 38 FEP 667 (S.D. Ohio 1985), *aff'd*, 785 F.2d 309, 40 FEP 984 (6th Cir. 1986) (discussion of facts surrounding posting of notice—suit barred by three-year statute of limitations); Slenkamp v. Borough of Brentwood, 603 F. Supp. 1298, 38 FEP 73 (W.D. Pa. 1985), *aff'd*, 826 F.2d 1057, 45 FEP 299 (3d Cir. 1987) (failure to post, coupled with other circumstances, tolls filing period); Pruet Prod. Co. v. Ayles, 784 F.2d 1275, 40 FEP 619 (5th Cir. 1986) (accountant with law degree who performed most of employer's personnel functions cannot rely on lack of posting); DeBrunner v. Midway Equip. Co., 803 F.2d 950, 42 FEP 65 (8th Cir. 1986) (posting failure did not justify tolling when employee learned of ADEA rights prior to discharge); Bomberger v. Consolidated Coal Co., 623 F. Supp. 89, 39 FEP 908 (W.D. Pa. 1985) (plaintiff's allegation that he "couldn't recall" seeing a poster not sufficient to toll filing period); Brudne v. Amalgamated Trust & Sav. Bank, 627 F. Supp. 458, 39 FEP 1607 (N.D. Ill. 1986); Kraus v. Canteen Serv. Co., 39 FEP 1377 (E.D. Mich. 1985) (employer's detailed factual assertions not rebutted by claim that plaintiff "never saw" or "never looked" at notices). *See also* cases cited, *supra*, notes 89 and 90.

[94]Kerver v. Exxon Prod. Research Co., 40 FEP 1567 (S.D. Tex. 1986), *aff'd*, 810 F.2d 196 (5th Cir. 1987).

[95]Jacobson v. Pitman-Moore, 624 F. Supp. 937, 39 FEP 1274 (D. Minn. 1985), *aff'd*, 786 F.2d 1172, 41 FEP 928 (8th Cir. 1986).

[96]Mull v. Arco Durethene Plastics, *supra* note 89.

Appeal of a dismissal under a grievance procedure does not toll the filing period.[97]

Concealment of facts from the plaintiff may be used to toll the deadline.[98] However, "suspicion" of discriminatory motivation triggers the commencement of the filing period.[99] Arguments that employers should be estopped from relying on the statutory filing period due to their unconscionable conduct generally continue to be unsuccessful.[100]

An unusual departure from this general rule is found in *Felty v. Graves-Humphreys Co.*[101] A panel majority concluded that an offer of a generous severance arrangement, conditioned upon the employee not discussing his discharge with "anyone" upon pain of immediate dismissal during the four and one-half month period prior to his termination date, "would be [a] powerful inducement that might well lull an older worker into failing to defend his rights" and would constitute an "equitable estoppel" based on the defendant's improper conduct (rather than the plaintiff's lack of knowledge) and extend the filing period. Upon remand and after an evidentiary hearing, however, the court found equitable estoppel inapplicable in this case because the plaintiff's decision to delay filing with the EEOC was not the result of the employer's conduct.[102]

Filing or service of the notice of intent to sue is, however, jurisdictional.[103] Suit prior to expiration of the 60-day period may be permitted if the EEOC has had an opportunity to review the charge.[104]

## E. EEOC Conciliation

An ADEA action brought by the EEOC on behalf of an employee is conditioned upon the requirement that the government satisfy its conciliation obligations.[105] A minimum of effort on the part of the EEOC has been required in order to satisfy such obligations.[106] One court has held that

---

[97]Shockley v. Vermont State Colleges, 793 F.2d 478, 45 FEP 923 (2d Cir. 1986); Dyer v. Jefferson Parish, La., 619 F. Supp. 284, 38 FEP 698 (E.D. La. 1985).

[98]Jones v. Premier Indus. Corp., *supra* note 92.

[99]Caldwell v. National Ass'n of Home Builders, 771 F.2d 1051, 38 FEP 1398 (7th Cir. 1985).

[100]Cook v. Pan Am. World Airways, 771 F.2d 635, 38 FEP 1344 (2d Cir. 1985), *cert. denied,* 474 U.S. 1109, 39 FEP 1568 (1986); Cerbone v. Ladies Garment Workers, *supra* note 92 (alleged offer of part-time job not fulfilled); Dillman v. Combustion Eng'g, 784 F.2d 57, 39 FEP 1750 (2d Cir. 1986) (good-faith discussion of retirement and severance benefits works no estoppel).

[101]785 F.2d 516, 40 FEP 447 (4th Cir. 1986).

[102]Felty v. Graves-Humphreys Co., 818 F.2d 1126, 43 FEP 1507 (4th Cir. 1987) *(Felty II).*

[103]McTighe v. Mechanics Local 19, 772 F.2d 210, 38 FEP 1477, 120 LRRM 2364 (6th Cir. 1985); Castro v. United States, 775 F.2d 399, 39 FEP 162 (1st Cir. 1985); Dempsey v. Pacific Bell Co., 789 F.2d 1451, 40 FEP 1575 (9th Cir. 1986). *But see* Popkins v. Zagel, 611 F. Supp. 809, 39 FEP 611 (C.D. Ill. 1985) (excused plaintiff's failure to file because defendants acted pursuant to state statute and any efforts to conciliate would have been meaningless).

[104]Morris v. Russell, Burdsall & Ward Corp., 577 F. Supp. 147, 38 FEP 1453 (N.D. Ohio 1983).

[105]EEOC v. Kansas, 28 FEP 1036 (D. Kan. 1982).

[106]*See, e.g.,* EEOC v. Chrysler Corp., 546 F. Supp. 54, 29 FEP 284, *clarified,* 546 F. Supp. 73, 29 FEP 1385 (E.D. Mich. 1982), *aff'd,* 733 F.2d 1183, 34 FEP 1401 (6th Cir. 1984) (failure of EEOC to identify many of individuals on behalf of whom it sought relief did not render EEOC's conciliation efforts defective where EEOC alleged systemwide discrimination); EEOC v. Prudential Fed. Sav. & Loan Ass'n, 741 F.2d 1225, 35 FEP 783 (10th Cir. 1984), *vacated and remanded for reconsideration in light of* Trans World Airlines v. Thurston, 469 U.S. 1154, 36 FEP 1168 (1985), *opinion withdrawn on remand,* 753 F.2d 851, 37 FEP 378 (10th Cir.), *cert. denied,* 474 U.S. 946, 39 FEP 384 (1985) (especially where employer's response to conciliation has been "intransigent").

prospective defendants who are afforded notice of the charge and an opportunity to conciliate need not be named in the charge.[107]

During attempts to conciliate, the statute of limitations is tolled while the EEOC is actively seeking conciliation for a period of up to one year,[108] but only for the EEOC, not in a private action. It has been held, however, that failure on the part of the EEOC to conciliate in good faith does not prevent such tolling; and that the remedy for failure to conciliate in good faith is not dismissal, but a stay of the proceedings in order to permit further conciliation efforts.[109]

## F. ADEA Suit

While the filing of an action by the EEOC (formerly the Secretary of Labor) extinguishes the right of individuals to institute their own ADEA actions, such government suits do not extinguish state claims.[110] The Second[111] and Eleventh[112] circuits have held, moreover, that a pending private ADEA action is not extinguished by the EEOC's filing of its own enforcement action.

According to the Fifth Circuit—the first circuit court to address the question—an ADEA action initiated in state court is removable.[113] In another case of first impression, a district court ruled that ADEA claims are not subject to arbitration even if such claims fell within the scope of an arbitration clause of an employment contract.[114]

Joinder was permitted of pattern and practice claims by three terminated employees who had worked in different facilities and divisions of an employer;[115] of both a parent and the subsidiary which employed a plaintiff, notwithstanding the plaintiff's failure to comply with ADEA procedural requirements with respect to the parent;[116] of an individual "informally

---

[107]Barkley v. Carraux, 533 F. Supp. 242, 28 FEP 544 (S.D. Tex. 1982).

[108]29 U.S.C. § 626(e)(2); EEOC v. Colgate-Palmolive Co., 586 F. Supp. 1341, 34 FEP 1749 (S.D.N.Y. 1984) (tolling only available while EEOC actively is attempting conciliation); Leite v. Kennecott Copper Corp., 558 F. Supp. 1170, 31 FEP 390 (D. Mass.), aff'd without opinion, 720 F.2d 658, 33 FEP 1520 (1st Cir. 1983). Cf. EEOC v. United States Steel Corp., 583 F. Supp. 1357, 34 FEP 973 (W.D. Pa. 1984) (preliminary injunction against employer's requirement that former employees sign release of claims as prerequisite of obtaining special pension).

[109]See EEOC v. Kansas, supra note 105; EEOC v. Colgate-Palmolive Co., 34 FEP 1551, 1555 (S.D.N.Y. 1983) (failure to conciliate not a jurisdictional defect; proper remedy is to stay proceedings "pending proper conciliation attempts," id.; based on claims of EEOC bad faith, conciliation record reviewed but discovery on issue of good faith denied "at this juncture").

[110]Dunlop v. Pan Am. World Airways, 672 F.2d 1044, 28 FEP 290 (2d Cir. 1982). But see Lettich v. Kenway, 590 F. Supp. 1225, 35 FEP 1289 (D. Mass. 1984) (declining pendent jurisdiction of individual age plaintiff's state law claims because, inter alia, "the ADEA appears to be an exclusive remedy," 35 FEP at 1290).

[111]Burns v. Equitable Life Assurance Soc'y, 696 F.2d 21, 30 FEP 873 (2d Cir. 1982), cert. denied, 464 U.S. 933, 33 FEP 48 (1983).

[112]Castle v. Sangamo Weston, Inc., 744 F.2d 1464, 36 FEP 113 (11th Cir. 1984), rev'g 31 FEP 324 (M.D. Fla. 1983). Cf. Mitchell v. McCorstin, 728 F.2d 1422, 34 FEP 886 (11th Cir. 1984) (individual who has brought own action does not have unconditional right to intervene in another's action).

[113]Baldwin v. Sears, Roebuck & Co., 667 F.2d 458, 27 FEP 1624 (5th Cir. 1982).

[114]Steck v. Smith Barney, Harris Upham & Co., 661 F. Supp. 543, 43 FEP 1736 (D.N.J. 1987).

[115]King v. Ralston Purina Co., 97 F.R.D. 477, 31 FEP 373, 115 LRRM 4951 (W.D.N.C. 1983) (claims logically related and same evidence cited).

[116]Watson v. Fuller Brush Co., 570 F. Supp. 1299, 33 FEP 585 (W.D. Mich. 1983); Brenimer v. Great W. Sugar Co., 567 F. Supp. 218, 33 FEP 281 (D. Colo. 1983). Cf. Clouser v. Cooperweld Steel Co., 38 FEP 1807 (N.D. Ohio 1985) (mere existence of parent-subsidiary relationship alone is not sufficient to warrant assertion of jurisdiction over parent corporation).

referred to in the body of the charge" but not named in it;[117] of the individual partners in a law firm where only the partnership was named to the EEOC in the notice of intent to sue;[118] and of claims as to both demotion and performance evaluation, even though only one of the claims was raised administratively, because the other claim grew out of or was reasonably related to the EEOC investigation and the employer had general notice of the matter.[119]

A plaintiff must plead "willfulness" in order to obtain the benefit of the three-year statute of limitations.[120] On the other hand, the defendant must plead the defense, and even then thereafter may be deemed to have waived it.[121] In *Trans World Airlines v. Thurston,*[122] the Supreme Court has now defined willfulness for purposes of determining liquidated damages as requiring either knowledge or reckless disregard of whether the conduct is prohibited. Although the "in the picture" standard of willfulness has still been applied by some courts in determining the relevant statute of limitations, the *Thurston* standard appears more likely to prevail.[123]

## G. Jury Trial

In two pre-*Thurston* decisions, different district courts held respectively that the jury should decide whether the violation was willful to determine the propriety of liquidated damages[124] and the appropriate limitations period.[125] *Thurston* left open the question whether different standards of willfulness would govern the availability of liquidated damages and the applicable statute of limitations, and also did not address the possibility of jury confusion in applying different standards of willfulness.

The availability of pension and profit-sharing benefits to an unlawfully rejected job applicant, like the front pay versus reinstatement issue, is an equitable issue to be decided by the court, rather than a legal issue to be presented to the jury.[126]

The EEOC is "a person" entitled to a trial by jury under § 7(c)(2), given

---

[117]Borumka v. Rocky Mountain Hosp. & Medical Serv. dba Blue Cross/Blue Shield of Colo., 599 F. Supp. 857, 37 FEP 685 (D. Colo. 1984). *See also* Pauls v. Elaine Revell, Inc., 571 F. Supp. 1018, 33 FEP 1182 (N.D. Ill. 1983) (corporate officers joined though not named in administrative charge).

[118]Lettich v. Kenway, *supra* note 110.

[119]EEOC v. Ford Motor Co., 529 F. Supp. 643, 33 FEP 863 (D. Colo. 1982), *later proceeding,* 573 F. Supp. 755, 33 FEP 868 (D. Colo. 1983), *aff'd,* 732 F.2d 120, 34 FEP 1034 (10th Cir. 1984); *see also* Borumka v. Rocky Mountain Hosp. & Medical Serv. dba Blue Cross/Blue Shield of Colo., *supra* note 117.

[120]Nelson v. Massey-Ferguson, 36 FEP 365 (E.D. Wis. 1984) (failure to plead).

[121]Heiar v. Crawford County, 746 F.2d 1190, 35 FEP 1458, *amended,* 36 FEP 112 (7th Cir. 1984), *cert. denied,* 472 U.S. 1027, 37 FEP 1883 (1985).

[122]469 U.S. 111, 36 FEP 977 (1985). For cases applying *Thurston* retroactively, *see* EEOC v. Prudential Fed. Sav. & Loan Ass'n, 763 F.2d 1116, 37 FEP 1691 (10th Cir.), *cert. denied,* 474 U.S. 946, 39 FEP 384 (1985); Berndt v. Kaiser Aluminum & Chem. Sales, 789 F.2d 253, 40 FEP 1252 (3d Cir. 1986); Gilkerson v. Toastmaster, Inc., 770 F.2d 133, 38 FEP 1167 (8th Cir. 1985); Gilchrist v. Jim Slemons Imports, 803 F.2d 1488, 42 FEP 314 (9th Cir. 1986); Archambault v. United Computing Sys., 786 F.2d 1507, 40 FEP 1050 (11th Cir. 1986).

[123]Trans World Airlines v. Thurston, *supra* note 122, at 127, 36 FEP at 985 n.21 (citing divided courts of appeal cases and reviewing the proper standard for statute of limitation purposes).

[124]Cowen v. Standard Brands, 572 F. Supp. 1576, 33 FEP 53 (N.D. Ala. 1983).

[125]Agostine v. Iowa Beef Processors, 35 FEP 328 (D. Neb. 1984).

[126]Dickerson v. Deluxe Check Printers, 703 F.2d 276, 31 FEP 621 (8th Cir. 1983), *later proceedings,* 783 F.2d 149, 40 FEP 960 (8th Cir. 1986) (post-remand appeal on other issues). *Cf.* EEOC v. Ford Motor Co., *supra* note 119 (right to jury trial as to legal claim not waived because plaintiff also seeks equitable relief).

its representative capacity.[127] The Foreign Sovereign Immunities Act of 1976 has been held to deny a jury trial to a former employee in an ADEA suit against an airline owned by a foreign state.[128]

Ignorance of the right to a jury trial has been deemed no excuse for failure to make a timely demand.[129] The Circuit Court for the District of Columbia has applied retroactively *Lehman v. Nakshian,*[130] holding that federal employees are not entitled to a jury trial in an ADEA suit against the federal government.[131]

A motion for judgment notwithstanding the verdict in an ADEA jury trial is contingent, according to the Fourth Circuit, upon identification of the substantive elements of the particular ADEA claim asserted and of the specific burdens of production applicable to the claim; identification of the appropriate standard for assessing the evidence; and application of that standard to the particular evidence adduced in light of the applicable production burdens.[132] A number of other courts, like the Fourth Circuit, have granted motions for directed verdict or judgment notwithstanding the verdict.[133] The propriety of specific instructions to the jury, such as the test to be applied by the jury in its evaluation of age as a factor, also has been challenged.[134]

## H. Class Action

A class action under Rule 23 of the Federal Rules of Civil Procedure is not available under the ADEA, and an individual included in a private ADEA suit must opt in and obtain the written consent of the court to such

---

[127]EEOC v. Brown & Root, 725 F.2d 348, 34 FEP 73 (5th Cir. 1984); EEOC v. Corry Jamestown Corp., 719 F.2d 1219, 33 FEP 871 (3d Cir. 1983); EEOC v. Colgate-Palmolive Co., 586 F. Supp. 1341, 34 FEP 1749 (S.D.N.Y. 1984); EEOC v. Chrysler Corp., 759 F.2d 1523, 37 FEP 1244 (11th Cir. 1985); EEOC v. Cudahy Foods Co., 588 F. Supp. 13, 33 FEP 1836 (W.D. Wash. 1983); EEOC v. Ford Motor Co., *supra* note 119.

[128]Carponcy v. Air France, 38 FEP 1518 (S.D.N.Y. 1985).

[129]Scharnhorst v. Independent School Dist. 710, 686 F.2d 637, 32 FEP 51 (8th Cir. 1982), *cert. denied,* 462 U.S. 1109, 38 FEP 1536 (1983); Washington v. New York City Bd. of Estimate, 709 F.2d 792, 32 FEP 45 (2d Cir.), *cert. denied,* 464 U.S. 1013, 35 FEP 1893 (1983); EEOC v. El Paso Natural Gas Co., 33 FEP 1837 (W.D. Tex. 1984) (prejudice to defendant); Simon v. Wiremold Co., 35 FEP 1819 (W.D. Pa. 1984) (counsel's inadvertence insufficient excuse); Spear v. Dayton's, 771 F.2d 1140, 38 FEP 1463 (8th Cir. 1985). *But see* Abbe v. Allen's Store for Men, 94 F.R.D. 295, 31 FEP 60 (N.D. Ill. 1982) (jury trial permitted even though plaintiff failed to make demand where plaintiff, a foreigner, had no prior exposure to our legal system and was represented by counsel who misapprehended his desire for trial by jury).

[130]453 U.S. 156, 26 FEP 65 (1981).

[131]Johnson v. Lehman, 679 F.2d 918, 28 FEP 1485 (D.C. Cir. 1982); Cuddy v. Carmen, 694 F.2d 853, 30 FEP 600 (D.C. Cir. 1982), *on remand,* 580 F. Supp. 788, 37 FEP 946 (D.D.C. 1984), *aff'd,* 762 F.2d 119, 37 FEP 1335 (D.C. Cir.), *cert. denied,* — U.S. —, 39 FEP 944 (1985).

[132]Lovelace v. Sherwin-Williams Co., 681 F.2d 230, 29 FEP 172 (4th Cir. 1982) (j.n.o.v. sustained).

[133]*See, e.g.,* Halsell v. Kimberly-Clark Corp., 683 F.2d 285, 29 FEP 1185 (8th Cir. 1982), *cert. denied,* 459 U.S. 1205, 30 FEP 1856 (1983); Stendebach v. CPC Int'l, 691 F.2d 735, 30 FEP 233 (5th Cir. 1982), *cert. denied,* 461 U.S. 944, 31 FEP 1296 (1983); Douglas v. Anderson, 656 F.2d 528, 27 FEP 47 (9th Cir. 1981); Ford v. General Motors Corp., 656 F.2d 117, 26 FEP 1389 (5th Cir. 1981); Stanojev v. Ebasco Servs., 643 F.2d 914, 25 FEP 355 (2d Cir. 1981); Trainer v. Philadelphia Nat'l Bank, 541 F. Supp. 195, 29 FEP 1460 (E.D. Pa. 1982), *aff'd,* 707 F.2d 1395, 32 FEP 680 (3d Cir. 1983). *See also* EEOC v. University of Okla., 554 F. Supp. 735, 30 FEP 1252 (W.D. Okla. 1982), *rev'd,* 774 F.2d 999, 38 FEP 1751 (10th Cir. 1985), *cert. denied,* 475 U.S. 1120, 40 FEP 856 (1986) (district court grant of j.n.o.v. reversed on grounds district court "reweighed" the evidence and factored in its view of the credibility of the witnesses.)

[134]*See* Cancellier v. Federated Dep't Stores, 672 F.2d 1312, 1316, 28 FEP 1151, 1153 (9th Cir.), *cert. denied,* 459 U.S. 859, 31 FEP 704 (1982) (instruction that "age must be a determining factor" in order to establish violation failed to provide guidance as to meaning of "determining factor"; error deemed harmless, however, in light of ample evidence that age made a difference in employee's termination).

inclusion.[135] A conflict persists, however, as to whether the courts are empowered under appropriate circumstances to permit or order notice to potential claimants informing them of their right to opt into an ADEA action.[136] Some district court authority supports the proposition that a plaintiff in an ADEA claim may be entitled to potential "opt-in" plaintiffs' names, addresses, and certain other employment information from the employer.[137]

The EEOC, in initiating suit, has been relieved from obtaining the consent of individual claimants to representation by the EEOC or to joinder as party plaintiffs.[138] The EEOC may move, however, to dismiss the claims of individuals who prefer to pursue the matter on their own.[139]

## I. Declaratory Judgment

The ADEA does not contemplate or permit a declaratory judgment action by a union or employer to establish a bona fide occupational qualification or other statutory defense.[140]

---

[135]*See, e.g.,* Woods v. New York Life Ins. Co., 686 F.2d 578, 29 FEP 1160 (7th Cir. 1982). Although adopting the option procedure, the circuits have split as to who may opt into an ADEA action. The Fifth Circuit requires that each opt-in plaintiff must timely file his or her own charge of discrimination. McCorstin v. United States Steel Corp., 621 F.2d 749, 755, 23 FEP 320 (5th Cir. 1980). The Ninth and Tenth circuits have held that similarly situated plaintiffs may opt into an ADEA action challenging systemic policies if the named plaintiff timely complied with the ADEA notice requirements in 29 U.S.C. § 626(d). Naton v. Bank of Cal., 649 F.2d 691, 697, 27 FEP 510 (9th Cir. 1981); Mistretta v. Sandia Corp., 639 F.2d 588, 593–95, 24 FEP 316 (10th Cir. 1980); Bean v. Crocker Nat'l Bank, 600 F.2d 754, 759–60, 20 FEP 533 (9th Cir. 1979). *See* Hopper v. Timex Corp., 595 F. Supp. 668, 35 FEP 1858 (E.D. Ark. 1984) (reviewing this split in authorities, and refusing to allow plaintiff to opt into ADEA action because underlying administrative change had been individualized and never gave defendant opportunity to conciliate class-type claims). *See also* Coventry v. United States Steel Corp., 34 FEP 971 (W.D. Pa. 1984) (acknowledging that opt-in criteria are unsettled, and allowing plaintiff who had withdrawn his EEOC charge to opt into another's action).

[136]In favor of such authority, *see* Sperling v. Hoffman-La Roche, Inc., 862 F.2d 439, 48 FEP 1010 (3d Cir. 1988) (authorizing neutral mailing inviting opt-ins, rejecting positions of the Eighth, Ninth, and Tenth circuits; following Second Circuit approach, but stating court approval of action should not be implied); Braunstein v. Eastern Photographic Laboratories, 600 F.2d 335 (2d Cir. 1978) (per curiam), *cert. denied,* 441 U.S. 944 (1979); Lusardi v. Xerox Corp., 99 F.R.D. 89, 33 FEP 1143 (D.N.J. 1983), *appeal dismissed,* 747 F.2d 174, 36 FEP 258 (3d Cir. 1984) (though recognizing divided authority on issue, court permitted notice to putative class members of their right to opt in and retention of pendent state claims) (not immediately appealable); Woods v. New York Life Ins. Co., *supra* note 135 (content of notice may be subject to court's approval); Johnson v. American Airlines, 531 F. Supp. 957, 29 FEP 330 (N.D. Tex. 1982), *aff'd on other grounds,* 745 F.2d 988, 36 FEP 321 (5th Cir. 1984), *cert. denied,* 472 U.S. 1027, 37 FEP 1883 (1985) (notice appropriate even in action maintained by employees occupying most prestigious and high-paying positions, provided it is informative, neutral, and makes clear prospective plaintiffs are free to select own counsel and will be bound, if they opt in, by judgment). *Contra* McKenna v. Champion Int'l Corp., 747 F.2d 1211, 36 FEP 325 (8th Cir. 1984); Woods v. New York Life Ins. Co., *supra;* Dolan v. Project Constr. Corp., 725 F.2d 1263, 26 WH 984 (10th Cir. 1984) (FLSA); Partlow v. Jewish Orphans' Home of S. Cal. dba Vista Del Mar Child Care Serv., 645 F.2d 757, 24 WH 1369 (9th Cir. 1981) (FLSA); Kinney Shoe Corp. v. Vorhes, 564 F.2d 859 (9th Cir. 1977).

[137]Vivone v. Acme Mkts., 105 F.R.D. 65, 37 FEP 561 (E.D. Pa. 1985) (notice issues reserved, information relevant to individual claim in any event); Palmer v. Reader's Digest Ass'n, 42 FEP 209 (S.D.N.Y. 1986) (discovery granted, notice to potential opt-in plaintiffs ordered, interlocutory appeal certified; notice ordered restricted to former employees terminated outside time frame of allegedly pretextual restructuring).

[138]EEOC v. Westinghouse Elec. Corp., 725 F.2d 211, 33 FEP 945 (3d Cir. 1983), *amended,* 33 FEP 1816 (3d Cir.), *cert. denied,* 469 U.S. 820, 35 FEP 1607 (1984) (action under § 17 commences for all purposes when complaint is filed and need not name individual employees for whom relief is sought; in § 16(c) action employees not specifically named in original complaint may be barred from relief).

[139]EEOC v. Chrysler Corp., 546 F. Supp. 54, 29 FEP 284, *clarified,* 546 F. Supp. 73, 29 FEP 1385 (E.D. Mich. 1982), *aff'd,* 733 F.2d 1183, 34 FEP 1401, *petition for reh'g en banc denied,* 738 F.2d 167, 41 FEP 1011 (6th Cir. 1984) (availability of this dismissal procedure does not convert ADEA enforcement actions under § 16(c) into Rule 23 "opt-out" class actions). *See also* EEOC v. Home Ins. Co., 553 F. Supp. 704, 30 FEP 841 (S.D.N.Y. 1982).

[140]Air Line Pilots v. Trans World Airlines, 713 F.2d 940, 32 FEP 1185 (2d Cir. 1983), *aff'd in part and rev'd in part on other grounds sub nom.* Trans World Airlines v. Thurston, 469 U.S. 111, 36 FEP 977 (1985).

## IV. PROOF

### A. Disparate Treatment

Generally, courts have continued to apply to ADEA cases,[141] with appropriate modifications, the Title VII standards for the allocation of burdens and ordering of proof first enunciated in *McDonnell Douglas Corp. v. Green,* [142] and later reaffirmed and clarified in *Texas Department of Community Affairs v. Burdine.* [143] Several courts have offered guidelines for applying these Title VII criteria—which were established in the context of a bench

---

[141]*For circuit decisions, see, e.g.,* Wildman v. Lerner Stores Corp., 771 F.2d 605, 38 FEP 1377 (1st Cir. 1985); Dugan v. Martin Marietta Aerospace, 760 F.2d 397, 37 FEP 833 (2d Cir. 1985); Haskell v. Kaman Corp., 743 F.2d 113, 35 FEP 941 (2d Cir. 1984); Hagelthorn v. Kennecott Corp., 710 F.2d 76, 33 FEP 977 (2d Cir. 1983); Goodman v. Heublein, 645 F.2d 127, 25 FEP 645 (2d Cir. 1981); Graham v. F. B. Leopold Co., 779 F.2d 170, 39 FEP 1025 (3d Cir. 1985); EEOC v. Western Elec. Co., 713 F.2d 1011, 32 FEP 708 (4th Cir. 1983); Fink v. Western Elec. Co., 708 F.2d 909, 31 FEP 1299 (4th Cir. 1983); Thornbrough v. Columbus & Greenville R.R., 760 F.2d 633, 37 FEP 1414 (5th Cir. 1985); Bohrer v. Hanes Corp., 715 F.2d 213, 32 FEP 1578 (5th Cir. 1983), *cert. denied,* 465 U.S. 1026, 33 FEP 1884 (1984); Elliott v. Group Medical & Surgical Serv., 714 F.2d 556, 32 FEP 1451 (5th Cir. 1983), *cert. denied,* 467 U.S. 1215, 34 FEP 1472 (1984); Reeves v. General Foods Corp., 682 F.2d 515, 29 FEP 779 (5th Cir. 1982); Davis v. Combustion Eng'g, 742 F.2d 916, 35 FEP 975 (6th Cir. 1984); Trembath v. St. Regis Paper Co., 753 F.2d 603, 36 FEP 1485, 118 LRRM 2585 (7th Cir. 1985); La Montagne v. American Convenience Prods., 750 F.2d 1405, 36 FEP 913 (7th Cir. 1984); Huhn v. Koehring Co., 718 F.2d 239, 32 FEP 1684 (7th Cir. 1983) (summary judgment on behalf of employer appropriate where plaintiff unable to show he met employer's qualifications); Golomb v. Prudential Ins. Co. of Am., 688 F.2d 547, 29 FEP 1491 (7th Cir. 1982); Ray v. MacMillian Bloedel Containers, 738 F.2d 965, 35 FEP 628 (8th Cir. 1984); Dace v. ACF Indus., 722 F.2d 374, 33 FEP 788 (8th Cir. 1983), *op. adhered to as supplemented by* 728 F.2d 976, 40 FEP 1604 (8th Cir. 1984); Bell v. Bolger, 708 F.2d 1312, 32 FEP 32 (8th Cir. 1983); EEOC v. Borden's, 724 F.2d 1390, 33 FEP 1708 (9th Cir. 1984); Daubert v. United States Postal Serv., 733 F.2d 1367, 34 FEP 1260 (10th Cir. 1984); Goldstein v. Manhattan Indus., 758 F.2d 1435, 37 FEP 1217 (11th Cir.), *cert. denied,* 474 U.S. 1005, 39 FEP 720 (1985); Pace v. Southern Ry. Sys., 701 F.2d 1383, 31 FEP 710 (11th Cir.), *cert. denied,* 464 U.S. 1018, 33 FEP 656 (1983), *reh'g denied,* 465 U.S. 1054 (1984); Allison v. Western Union Tel. Co., 680 F.2d 1318, 29 FEP 393 (11th Cir. 1982); Garner v. Boorstin, 690 F.2d 1034, 1035–36, 29 FEP 1765, 1766–67 (D.C. Cir. 1982).

*For district court decisions, see, e.g.,* Turner v. Food Giant, 36 FEP 1887 (M.D. Ga. 1985); Askin v. Firestone Tire & Rubber Co., 600 F. Supp. 751, 36 FEP 1487 (E.D. Ky. 1985), *aff'd without opinion,* 785 F.2d 307, 40 FEP 984 (6th Cir. 1986); Sharry v. Hanover Ins. Co., 36 FEP 1822 (D. Mass. 1985); Corrigan v. New York Univ. Medical Center, 606 F. Supp. 345, 37 FEP 715 (S.D.N.Y. 1985); Singer v. Uni-Marts, 37 FEP 1197 (W.D. Pa. 1985); Zebedeo v. Martin E. Segal Co., 582 F. Supp. 1394, 37 FEP 128 (D. Conn. 1984); Cope v. McPherson, 594 F. Supp. 171, 36 FEP 1075 (D.D.C. 1984), *aff'd per curiam,* 781 F.2d 207, 39 FEP 1560 (D.C. Cir. 1985); Cuddy v. Carmen, supra note 131; Snyder v. Washington Hosp. Center, 36 FEP 445 (D.D.C. 1984); Thomas v. Barry, 34 FEP 402 (D.D.C. 1984); Fugate v. Allied Corp., 582 F. Supp. 780, 34 FEP 1745 (N.D. Ill. 1984); Matthews v. Allis-Chalmers, 614 F. Supp. 11, 35 FEP 1404 (N.D. Ill. 1984), *aff'd,* 769 F.2d 1215, 38 FEP 1118 (7th Cir. 1985); Douglass v. Lehman, 581 F. Supp. 704, 34 FEP 1876 (D. Me. 1984); Morley v. County of Union, 35 FEP 1269 (D.N.J. 1984), *aff'd without opinion,* 760 F.2d 259, 41 FEP 64 (3d Cir. 1985); Friedman v. Bolger, 599 F. Supp. 306, 36 FEP 1125 (S.D.N.Y. 1984); Cory v. SmithKline Beckman Corp., 585 F. Supp. 871, 35 FEP 1682 (E.D. Pa. 1984); Woodfield v. Heckler, 591 F. Supp. 1390, 36 FEP 457 (E.D. Pa. 1984); Wilbur v. Southern Galvanizing Co., 34 FEP 1468 (D. Md. 1983); Leite v. Kennecott Copper Corp., 558 F. Supp. 1170, 31 FEP 390 (D. Mass.), *aff'd without opinion,* 720 F.2d 658, 33 FEP 1520 (1st Cir. 1983); Meschino v. IT&T Corp., 563 F. Supp. 1066, 34 FEP 1634 (S.D.N.Y. 1983); Bower v. Secorp Nat'l, State Equip. Div., 31 FEP 825 (W.D. Pa. 1983); Leibovitch v. Administrator, Veterans Admin., 33 FEP 777 (D.D.C. 1982); Smith v. World Book-Childcraft Int'l, 31 FEP 457 (N.D. Ill. 1982); Kahn v. Pepsi Cola Bottling Group, 547 F. Supp. 736, 34 FEP 815 (E.D.N.Y. 1982); Berkowitz v. Allied Stores of Penn-Ohio, 541 F. Supp. 1209, 31 FEP 337 (E.D. Pa. 1982); Sack v. Kimberly-Clark Corp., 33 FEP 624 (E.D. Wis. 1982); Deutsch v. Carl Zeiss, Inc., 529 F. Supp. 215, 32 FEP 890 (S.D.N.Y. 1981). *See also* West v. Fred Wright Constr. Co., 756 F.2d 31, 37 FEP 274 (6th Cir. 1985); LaGrant v. Gulf & W. Mfg. Co., 748 F.2d 1087, 36 FEP 465 (6th Cir. 1984); Stacey v. Allied Stores Corp., 581 F. Supp. 1103, 34 FEP 615 (D.D.C. 1984); Franklin v. Greenwood Mills Mktg. Co., 33 FEP 1847 (S.D.N.Y. 1983); Miller v. General Elec. Co., 562 F. Supp. 610, 33 FEP 1637 (E.D. Pa. 1983); Haxton v. Regan, 33 FEP 675 (M.D. Fla. 1983); Krodel v. Department of Health & Human Servs., 33 FEP 689 (D.D.C. 1983), *aff'd sub nom.* Krodel v. Young, 748 F.2d 701, 36 FEP 468 (D.C. Cir. 1984), *cert. denied,* 474 U.S. 817, 38 FEP 1727 (1985).

[142]411 U.S. 792, 5 FEP 965 (1973).

[143]450 U.S. 248, 25 FEP 113 (1981). *See also* United States Postal Serv. Bd. of Governors v. Aikens, 460 U.S. 711, 31 FEP 609 (1983).

trial—to an ADEA jury trial.[144] The Supreme Court affirmed in *Trans World Airlines v. Thurston*[145] a judgment in favor of plaintiffs who presented direct evidence that the defendant denied transfer rights to employees based on age, even though the plaintiffs failed to identify any vacancy to which they could transfer.

## 1. The Prima Facie Case

Courts have continued to modify the Title VII formula used in establishing a prima facie case to fit the particular fact situation at hand.[146] In

---

[144]*See, e.g.,* La Montagne v. American Convenience Prods., *supra* note 141 (j.n.o.v. affirmed upon finding plaintiff failed to prove pretext; court may inquire only as to whether evidence in favor of verdict is sufficiently substantial to support jury verdict in that party's favor); Davis v. Combustion Eng'g *supra* note 141 (court did not err in instructing jury that, in its rebuttal of plaintiff's prima facie case, defendant must present "credible" evidence rather than "admissible" evidence); Haskell v. Kaman Corp., *supra* note 141 (jury should be instructed that person who replaces discharged plaintiff should ordinarily be substantially younger than plaintiff to warrant inference of age discrimination); Criswell v. Western Airlines, 709 F.2d 544, 32 FEP 1204 (9th Cir. 1983), *aff'd,* 472 U.S. 400, 37 FEP 1829 (1985); Dace v. ACF Indus., *supra* note 141, at 375–76, 377 n.7, 33 FEP at 789–90, 791 n.7 (in deciding motion for directed verdict, court cannot consider evidence favorable to moving party, because of risk of assessing credibility of movant's witnesses; unlike Title VII litigation where inference of discrimination is removed once defendant offers evidence of nondiscriminatory motive, in ADEA jury trial case "it is open to argue that respect for the jury's role as factfinder requires the court to maintain the presumption of discrimination established by the prima facie case"); Elliott v. Group Medical & Surgical Serv., *supra* note 141 (motion to dismiss for failure to state prima facie case, made at close of jury trial, treated as motion for directed verdict); Bohrer v. Hanes Corp., *supra* note 141 (j.n.o.v.); Hagelthorn v. Kennecott Corp., *supra* note 141, at 82, 85, 33 FEP at 982, 984–85 (criticizing direct adaptation of *McDonnell Douglas* and *Burdine* to jury instructions; "defendant's proposed instructions, couched in such lawyerly cant as '*prima facie* case' and 'shifting burden of proof' would only have confused the jury"); Massarsky v. General Motors Corp., 706 F.2d 111, 31 FEP 832 (3d Cir.), *cert. denied,* 464 U.S. 937, 33 FEP 48 (1983); Stacey v. Allied Stores Corp., *supra* note 141 (j.n.o.v.); Franklin v. Greenwood Mills Mktg. Co., *supra* note 141 (same); Halsell v. Kimberly-Clark Corp., 683 F.2d 285, 29 FEP 1185 (8th Cir. 1982), *cert. denied,* 459 U.S. 1205, 30 FEP 1856 (1983) (directed verdict in favor of defendant appropriate where defendant, in satisfying its burden of production, undercut any inference of discrimination that may have been raised by plaintiff); Reeves v. General Foods Corp., *supra* note 141, at 521–23, 29 FEP at 782–85 (evidence sufficient to prove prima facie case does not automatically raise inference of intentional discrimination which requires submission of case to jury; rather, it creates only "legally mandatory 'rebuttable presumption'" which "'drops from the case'" if defendant articulates legitimate, nondiscriminatory reason for its act); Lovelace v. Sherwin-Williams Co., 681 F.2d 230, 244, 29 FEP 172, 181 (4th Cir. 1982) (j.n.o.v. properly granted where defendant's "internally consistent, corroborated" evidence not refuted by plaintiff's self-serving uncorroborated subjective opinion).

[145]469 U.S. 111, 36 FEP 977 (1985). *See also* Lindsey v. American Cast Iron Pipe Co., 772 F.2d 799, 39 FEP 14 (11th Cir. 1985).

[146]*See, e.g.,* Goldstein v. Manhattan Indus., *supra* note 141 (discharge); Trembath v. St. Regis Paper Co., *supra* note 141 (same); Herman v. National Broadcasting Co., 569 F. Supp. 282, 33 FEP 1278 (N.D. Ill. 1983) (hiring); Haskell v. Kaman Corp., *supra* note 141 (discharge); Dace v. ACF Indus., *supra* note 141 (demotion); Huhn v. Koehring Co., *supra* note 141 (discharge); Elliott v. Group Medical & Surgical Serv., *supra* note 141 (same); Hagelthorn v. Kennecott Corp., *supra* note 141 (same); Stumph v. Thomas & Skinner, 770 F.2d 93, 38 FEP 1114 (7th Cir. 1985) (reduction in force); Singer v. Uni-Marts, *supra* note 141 (hiring); Zebedeo v. Martin E. Segal Co., *supra* note 141 (failure to renew employment contract); Fugate v. Allied Corp., *supra* note 141 (reduction in force); Matthews v. Allis-Chalmers, *supra* note 141 (same); Douglass v. Lehman, *supra* note 141 (promotion); Woodfield v. Heckler, *supra* note 141 (demotion); Wildman v. Lerner Stores Corp., *supra* note 141 (discharge); Wilbur v. Southern Galvanizing Co., *supra* note 141 (same); Leite v. Kennecott Copper Corp., *supra* note 141 (reduction in force); Smith v. World Book-Childcraft Int'l, *supra* note 141 (discharge); Kahn v. Pepsi Cola Bottling Group, *supra* note 141 (same); Sack v. Kimberly-Clark Corp., *supra* note 141 (same); Deutsch v. Carl Zeiss, Inc., *supra* note 141 (reduction in force); Everett v. Communications Satellite Corp., 33 FEP 793 (D.D.C. 1983) (discharge); Kneisley v. Hercules, Inc., 577 F. Supp. 726, 33 FEP 1579 (D. Del. 1983) (reduction in force); Garner v. Boorstin, 690 F.2d 1034, 1036 n.4, 29 FEP 1765, 1767 n.4 (D.C. Cir. 1982) (promotion: plaintiff need not prove positions remained open; sufficient to "show that the available positions were filled by individuals with comparable qualifications who were not members of the classes protected by the relevant statutes"); Lovelace v. Sherwin-Williams Co., 681 F.2d 230, 239, 29 FEP 172, 176–77 (4th Cir. 1982) (demotion: plaintiff may establish prima facie case "by evidence (i) that he was at the time of demotion 'performing his job at a level that met his employer's legitimate expectations' and (ii) that following his demotion his employer sought someone to perform the same work"); Allison v. Western Union Tel. Co., *supra* note 141, at 1321, 29 FEP at

attempting to establish such a case, statistical evidence may be used, both to prove a prima facie case[147] and to demonstrate pretext.[148] However, such statistical evidence must be reliable and presented in a relevant framework, and the sample must be sufficiently large.[149]

## 2. Defendant's Articulation of a Legitimate, Nondiscriminatory Reason for Its Actions

Even when a defendant presents evidence of a legitimate, nondiscriminatory reason for its actions, a jury that reviewed all the evidence could still "find that the wrong occurred in the manner established by the plain-

---

394 (reduction in force: plaintiff can establish prima facie case by "(1) satisfying the 'standing requirements under the statute,' * * * i.e., showing that he is within the protected age group and that he has been adversely affected—discharged or demoted—by defendant's employment decision; (2) showing that he was qualified to assume another position at the time of discharge or demotion; and (3) producing evidence, circumstantial or direct, from which a factfinder might reasonably conclude that the employer intended to discriminate in reaching the decision at issue"); Holley v. Sanyo Mfg., 771 F.2d 1161, 38 FEP 1317 (8th Cir. 1985) (prima facie case cannot be made in reduction case without showing age a factor in discharge). Cf. Blackwell v. Sun Elec. Corp., 696 F.2d 1176, 1179, 30 FEP 1177, 1179 (6th Cir. 1983) (favoring "case-by-case" approach rather than "mechanical" application of McDonnell Douglas guidelines); Cline v. Roadway Express, 689 F.2d 481, 485, 29 FEP 1365, 1368 (4th Cir. 1982) (one need not resort to "McDonnell Douglas presumption-based proof scheme" where there is direct evidence indicating age was "a determining factor," or where there is circumstantial evidence "including but not limited to proof of the claimant's general qualifications, from which the inference of age discrimination may rationally be drawn independently of any presumption").

[147]See, e.g., Goldstein v. Manhattan Indus., supra note 141; LaGrant v. Gulf & W. Mfg. Co., supra note 141; Pace v. Southern Ry. Sys., supra note 141; Leftwich v. Harris-Stowe State College, 702 F.2d 686, 31 FEP 376 (8th Cir. 1983); Palmer v. United States, 794 F.2d 534, 539, 41 FEP 559, 563 (9th Cir. 1986) (stark pattern of discrimination, unexplainable on grounds other than age must be shown to establish prima facie case using only statistics); Elliott v. Group Medical & Surgical Serv., supra note 141; EEOC v. Western Elec. Co., supra note 141; Hagelthorn v. Kennecott Corp., supra note 141; Chern v. Ogden Food Serv. Corp., 33 FEP 1547 (E.D. Pa. 1984) (does not mean plaintiff can conduct discovery "as a de facto class action"); Kneisley v. Hercules, Inc., supra note 146; Franklin v. Greenwood Mills Mktg. Co., supra note 141; Miller v. General Elec. Co., supra note 141; EEOC v. Tecumseh Prods. Co., 33 FEP 1437 (W.D. Tenn. 1983).

[148]See, e.g., Goldstein v. Manhattan Indus., supra note 141; Krieg v. Paul Revere Life Ins. Co., 718 F.2d 998, 33 FEP 594 (11th Cir. 1983) (per curiam), cert. denied, 466 U.S. 929, 34 FEP 696 (1984) (insignificant that majority of managers terminated were in protected group because majority of managers employed were in protected group); Bell v. Bolger, supra note 141; Elliott v. Group Medical & Surgical Serv., supra note 141 (statistics inconclusive); Haxton v. Regan, supra note 141 (defendant's statistics at least as probative as plaintiff's); Krodel v. Department of Health & Human Servs., supra note 141; Brenimer v. Great W. Sugar Co., 567 F. Supp. 218, 33 FEP 281 (D. Colo. 1983); Pirone v. Home Ins. Co., 559 F. Supp. 306, 31 FEP 311 (S.D.N.Y.), aff'd, 742 F.2d 1430, 37 FEP 280 (2d Cir. 1983).

[149]See, e.g., Blackwell v. Sun Elec. Corp., supra note 146; Palmer v. United States, supra note 147 (inaccuracies in and small size of sample render study without persuasive value); Allison v. Western Union Tel. Co., supra note 141. But see Williams v. General Motors Corp., 656 F.2d 120, 26 FEP 1381 (5th Cir. 1981), cert. denied, 455 U.S. 943 (1982) (evidence can be circumstantial, including statistical, but statistical evidence has no magic properties). See also Pace v. Southern Ry. Sys., supra note 141 (sample too small and improper comparisons made); Bell v. Bolger, supra note 141 (sample too small and statistics inconclusive); Elliott v. Group Medical & Surgical Serv., supra note 141 (ADEA plaintiffs showed all were over 40, all were terminated, and all but one were replaced by persons under 40; expert concluded, on statistical analysis, that "age could neither be ruled in nor ruled out statistically as the factor leading to the discharges," id., 714 F.2d at 565); EEOC v. Western Elec. Co., supra note 141 (no statistically significant difference between number affected and those who would have expected to be affected; new theory not stressed at trial); Fink v. Western Elec. Co., supra note 141 (unreliability of small numbers, irrelevance of placements within Bell system but outside defendant company, inaccurate classification of terminations, and improper exclusion of others); Stendebach v. CPC Int'l, 691 F.2d 735, 738, 30 FEP 233, 235 (5th Cir. 1982), cert. denied, 461 U.S. 944, 31 FEP 1296 (1983) (in ruling on reduction in force and reorganization, court noted that smaller sample sizes increase likelihood that underrepresentation reflects chance rather than discriminatory practices); Parker v. Federal Nat'l Mortgage Ass'n, 567 F. Supp. 265, 271, 33 FEP 1207, 1212 (N.D. Ill. 1983), aff'd, 741 F.2d 975, 35 FEP 893 (7th Cir. 1984) (reduction in force; numbers within relevant division too small for "statistically valid inferences of discriminatory intent"); Rodriguez v. CPC Int'l, 31 FEP 455 (S.D. Tex. 1983) (reduction in force); Haxton v. Regan, supra note 141 (not placed within relevant framework); Cowen v. Standard Brands, 572 F. Supp. 1576, 33 FEP 53 (N.D. Ala. 1983) (very small group).

tiff.''[150] Once a defendant has articulated a justification for its actions, it has met its burden of production; the burden of persuasion remains with the plaintiff.[151]

### 3. Plaintiff's Proof of Pretext

If the defendant satisfies its burden of producing evidence of a legitimate, nondiscriminatory reason for its actions, the plaintiff is entitled to demonstrate that the reason asserted by the defendant is a pretext for discrimination.[152] To establish pretext, a plaintiff must prove more than that the employer's stated reasons were not true.[153] Direct evidence of age discrimination, however, obviates the need in some cases to show pretext.[154]

### 4. The Degree of Proof—Age Must Be a Determining Factor

The degree of proof a plaintiff must present in establishing a causal connection between age and the alleged discriminatory action has been described in varying ways. The courts have continued to emphasize, however, that age need not be the sole determining factor; it is sufficient that it is *a* determining factor.[155]

---

[150]Spagnuolo v. Whirlpool Corp., 641 F.2d 1109, 1112, 25 FEP 376, 378 (4th Cir.), *cert. denied,* 454 U.S. 860, 26 FEP 1688 (1981) (employer alleged that plaintiff's demotion resulted from legitimate reorganization efforts).

[151]*See, e.g.,* Trembath v. St. Regis Paper Co., *supra* note 141; La Montagne v. American Convenience Prods., *supra* note 141; West v. Fred Wright Constr. Co., *supra* note 141; Davis v. Combustion Eng'g, *supra* note 141; Haskell v. Kaman Corp., *supra* note 141; Locke v. Commercial Union Ins. Co., 676 F.2d 205, 28 FEP 1127 (6th Cir. 1982); Douglas v. Anderson, 656 F.2d 528, 27 FEP 47 (9th Cir. 1981); Sutton v. Atlantic Richfield Co., 646 F.2d 407, 25 FEP 1619 (9th Cir. 1981); Jackson v. Sears, Roebuck & Co., 648 F.2d 225, 25 FEP 1684 (5th Cir. 1981); Crosland v. Charlotte Eye, Ear & Throat Hosp., 686 F.2d 208, 29 FEP 1178 (4th Cir. 1982); Goodman v. Heublein, *supra* note 141; Turner v. Food Giant, *supra* note 141; Askin v. Firestone Tire & Rubber Co., *supra* note 141; Sharry v. Hanover Ins. Co., *supra* note 141; Corrigan v. New York Univ. Medical Center, *supra* note 141; Zebedeo v. Martin E. Segal Co., *supra* note 141; Cope v. McPherson, *supra* note 141; Cuddy v. Carmen, 694 F.2d 853, 30 FEP 600 (D.C. Cir. 1982), *on remand,* 580 F. Supp. 788, 37 FEP 946 (D.D.C. 1984), *aff'd,* 762 F.2d 119, 37 FEP 1335 (D.C. Cir.), *cert. denied,* 474 U.S. 1034, 39 FEP 944 (1985); Snyder v. Washington Hosp. Center, *supra* note 141; Thomas v. Barry, *supra* note 141; Douglass v. Lehman, *supra* note 141; Morley v. County of Union, *supra* note 141; Friedman v. Bolger, *supra* note 141; Herman v. National Broadcasting Co., *supra* note 146; Woodfield v. Heckler, *supra* note 141; Wildman v. Lerner Stores Corp., *supra* note 141; Wilbur v. Southern Galvanizing Co., *supra* note 141; Franklin v. Greenwood Mills Mktg. Co., *supra* note 141; Meschino v. IT&T Corp., *supra* note 141; Miller v. General Elec. Co., *supra* note 141; Bower v. Secorp Nat'l, State Equip. Div., *supra* note 141; Leibovitch v. Administrator Veterans Admin., *supra,* note 141; Berkowitz v. Allied Stores of Penn-Ohio, *supra* note 141; Sack v. Kimberly-Clark Corp., *supra* note 141; Caravetta v. Goulding, 33 FEP 796 (D.D.C. 1980).

[152]*See* cases cited *supra* note 151. *See also* EEOC v. Prudential Fed. Sav. & Loan Ass'n, 763 F.2d 1116, 37 FEP 1691 (10th Cir.), *cert. denied,* 474 U.S. 946, 39 FEP 384 (1985) (jury instruction on pretext).

[153]Krodel v. Young, 748 F.2d 701, 36 FEP 468 (D.C. Cir. 1984), *cert. denied,* 474 U.S. 817, 38 FEP 1727 (1985); Johnson v. University of Wis.-Milwaukee, 783 F.2d 59, 39 FEP 1822 (7th Cir. 1986) (plaintiff must show that proffered reason is not just pretext, but pretext for discrimination); Snyder v. Washington Hosp. Center, 36 FEP 445 (D.D.C. 1984); Belanger v. Keydril Co., 596 F. Supp. 823, 36 FEP 132 (E.D. La 1984).

[154]Wilhelm v. Blue Bell, 773 F.2d 1429, 38 FEP 1600 (4th Cir. 1985), *cert. denied,* 475 U.S. 1016, 40 FEP 272 (1986).

[155]*See, e.g.,* La Montagne v. American Convenience Prods., 750 F.2d 1405, 36 FEP 913 (7th Cir. 1984) (j.n.o.v. for defendant); Krodel v. Young, *supra* note 153, 748 F.2d at 706, 36 FEP at 472 (age must make a difference "in the sense that 'but for' the discriminatory motive, the employee would have been hired, promoted or retained"); Herman v. National Broadcasting Co., *supra* note 146 (sufficient evidence for plaintiff to avoid summary judgment); EEOC v. Prudential Fed. Sav. & Loan Ass'n, 741 F.2d 1225, 1230, 35 FEP 783, 787 (10th Cir. 1984) ("plaintiff need not prove that the reasons offered by the defendant are false if he proves that age was also a reason and that age was the factor that made a difference"); Grubb v. W.A. Foote Memorial Hosp., 741 F.2d 1486, 1498, 35 FEP 1048, 1057 (6th Cir. 1984), *first panel decision vacated and district court decision aff'd,* 759 F.2d 546, 37 FEP 867 (6th Cir.), *cert. denied,* 474 U.S. 946, 39 FEP 384 (1985); Parker v. Federal Nat'l Mortgage Ass'n, *supra* note 149

## 5. Statistics

While courts have continued to recognize the use of statistical evidence in ADEA cases, such evidence is being scrutinized carefully and several courts have indicated that statistical evidence is less persuasive with respect to age discrimination claims than in other types of discrimination cases.[156] The Tenth and District of Columbia circuits have held that statistical evidence is less significant in disparate treatment than in disparate impact cases.[157]

## B. Adverse Impact

Although the applicability of a disparate impact analysis to an age discrimination claim has been questioned,[158] a number of circuit courts have

---

(summary judgment for defendant); Monroe v. United Airlines, 736 F.2d 394, 402, 34 FEP 1622, 1628 (7th Cir. 1984), *cert. denied,* 470 U.S. 1004, 37 FEP 64 (1985) (circuit approval for "a determining factor" jury instruction); Cuddy v. Carmen, *supra* note 151, 694 F.2d at 857–58, 30 FEP at 603–04 (plaintiff must "show by a preponderance of the evidence that age was 'a determining factor' in the employer's decision" or that age "made a difference"); Coburn v. Pan Am. World Airways, 711 F.2d 339, 32 FEP 843 (D.C. Cir.), *cert. denied,* 464 U.S. 994, 33 FEP 440 (1983) (reduction in force); Perrell v. Finance America Corp., 726 F.2d 654, 656, 33 FEP 1728, 1729 (10th Cir. 1984) ("age must 'make a difference' * * * in the sense that, 'but for' the factor of age discrimination, the employee would not have been adversely affected"); Cancellier v. Federated Dep't Stores, 672 F.2d 1312, 1316, 28 FEP 1151, 1153 (9th Cir.), *cert. denied,* 459 U.S. 859, 31 FEP 704 (1982) ("age must 'make a difference' between termination and retention of the employee in the sense that, but for the presence of age discrimination, the employee would not have been discharged"); Steckl v. Motorola, 703 F.2d 392, 31 FEP 705 (9th Cir. 1983); Golomb v. Prudential Ins. Co. of Am., 688 F.2d 547, 550, 29 FEP 1491, 1492 (7th Cir. 1982) *("a determining factor")* (emphasis in original); Blackwell v. Sun Elec. Corp., *supra* note 146; Ackerman v. Diamond Shamrock Corp., 670 F.2d 66, 70, 27 FEP 1563, 1566 (6th Cir. 1982) ("whether age was a factor * * * and * * * made a difference"); Bohrer v. Hanes Corp., 715 F.2d 213, 32 FEP 1578 (5th Cir. 1983), *cert. denied,* 465 U.S. 1026, 33 FEP 1884 (1984); Fink v. Western Elec. Co., 708 F.2d 909, 31 FEP 1299 (4th Cir. 1983) ("but for"); Hagelthorn v. Kennecott Corp., 710 F.2d 76, 33 FEP 977 (2d Cir. 1983); Reardon v. Sharon Steel Corp., 36 FEP 1824 (W.D. Pa. 1985); Woodfield v. Heckler, 591 F. Supp. 1390, 36 FEP 457 (E.D. Pa. 1984); Williamson v. Owens-Illinois, 589 F. Supp. 1051, 1058, 34 FEP 1656, 1660 (N.D. Ohio 1984) (j.n.o.v. for defendant); Lombardo v. Columbia Dentoform Corp., 103 F.R.D. 630, 634–35, 36 FEP 869, 871–72 (S.D.N.Y. 1984) (defendant's motion for j.n.o.v. denied where jury had sufficient evidence from which to conclude age was factor in decision to discharge; defendant's motion for new trial granted in view of evidence that plaintiff's discharge was made in "good faith"); Matthews v. Allis-Chalmers, 614 F. Supp. 11, 14, 35 FEP 1404, 1405 (N.D. Ill. 1984), *aff'd,* 769 F.2d 1215, 38 FEP 1118 (7th Cir. 1985) ("plaintiff must show enough to make it appear more likely than not that age was a factor in the discharge, * * * 'that he was discriminated against *because* of his age' "); Stacey v. Allied Stores Corp., 581 F. Supp. 1103, 34 FEP 615 (D.D.C. 1984); Dallas v. Department of Environmental Quality Eng'g, Mass., 34 FEP 543 (D. Mass. 1984); Miller v. General Elec. Co., 562 F. Supp. 610, 33 FEP 1637 (E.D. Pa. 1983); Franklin v. Greenwood Mills Mktg. Co., 33 FEP 1847 (S.D.N.Y. 1983) ("but for"); Kiel v. Goodyear Tire & Rubber Co., 575 F. Supp. 847, 848, 33 FEP 1122, 1123 (N.D. Ohio 1983), *aff'd,* 762 F.2d 1008 (6th Cir. 1985) ("significant, major factor * * * as contrasted to a minor or insignificant reason"); EEOC v. City of New Castle, 32 FEP 1409 (W.D. Pa. 1983), *aff'd without opinion,* 740 F.2d 956, 34 FEP 836 (3d Cir. 1984); Popko v. City of Clairton, 570 F. Supp. 446, 450, 32 FEP 1414, 1417 (W.D. Pa. 1983) (discharge violates Act if age a "determinative factor, even in the presence of other, perhaps more compelling factors"); Krodel v. Department of Health & Human Servs., 33 FEP 689 (D.D.C. 1983), *aff'd sub nom.* Krodel v. Young, 748 F.2d 701, 36 FEP 468 (D.C. Cir. 1984), *cert. denied,* 474 U.S. 817, 38 FEP 1727 (1985); Duffy v. Wheeling Pittsburgh Steel Corp., 33 FEP 730 (E.D. Pa. 1983), *aff'd,* 738 F.2d 1393, 35 FEP 246 (3d Cir.), *cert. denied,* 469 U.S. 1087, 36 FEP 712 (1984).

[156]*See, e.g.,* Herman v. National Broadcasting Co., *supra* note 146; Haskell v. Kaman Corp., 743 F.2d 113, 35 FEP 941 (2d Cir. 1984) (reversal and new trial where statistical evidence based on too small a sample); Parker v. Federal Nat'l Mortgage Ass'n, *supra* note 149 (small sample and selective categorization); Williamson v. Owens-Illinois, 589 F. Supp. 1051, 1059–60, 34 FEP 1656, 1661–62 (N.D. Ohio 1984); Matthews v. Allis-Chalmers, *supra* note 155 (statistical evidence discounted); Moore v. McGraw Edison Co., 804 F.2d 1026, 1031, 42 FEP 229, 232 (8th Cir. 1986) (statistical evidence generally discounted in age cases).

[157]Heward v. Western Elec. Co., 35 FEP 807 (10th Cir. 1984); Krodel v. Young, *supra* note 153; *and compare* Cowen v. Standard Brands, *supra* note 149, at 1579, 33 FEP at 55 (defensive use of particular statistics rejected in disparate treatment case) *with* Ridenour v. Lawson Co., 791 F.2d 52, 40 FEP 1455 (6th Cir. 1986) (defensive use of statistical evidence, persuasive in disparate treatment case).

[158]Markham v. Geller, 451 U.S. 945, 947–48, 25 FEP 847 (1981) (Rehnquist, J., dissenting) (majority of court denying *certiorari,* Justice Rehnquist opposing denial); Dorsch v. L.B. Foster Co., 782 F.2d 1421,

held that such an analysis is appropriate.[159] An employer's denial of severance pay to employees eligible for retirement benefits[160] and an employer's policy prohibiting its pilots from downbidding to a flight engineer position[161] were each invalidated on the basis of both disparate treatment and disparate impact. Reservation by a college of certain positions for nontenured faculty was held to have a disparate impact upon the protected age class of employees,[162] while a directed verdict for the defendant was deemed improper where plaintiff presented evidence from which the jury could conclude that he was selected for demotion because of his greater seniority, a factor which could have a disparate impact on older employees.[163] An employer's hiring policy which precluded considering work experience in excess of 10 years was found to have a disparate impact on older individuals.[164] Even those circuits recognizing the disparate impact analysis differ, however, as to whether it is applicable to subjective employment decisions.[165]

An employer's reliance upon subjective criteria in implementing a reduction in force (*e.g.,* "choose the person you will miss the least") is not in and of itself violative of the ADEA; it is "only when such criteria result in discriminatory impact that a violation occurs."[166] Similarly, an employer's practice of encouraging the employment of recent college and technical school graduates in its work force has been held lawful where such persons were not insulated from challenged reductions.[167] However, a state law re-

---

40 FEP 201 (7th Cir. 1986) (adverse impact analysis developed in Title VII cases cannot be extended easily to age cases); Akins v. South Cent. Bell Tel. Co., 744 F.2d 1133, 1136, 36 FEP 151, 153 (5th Cir. 1984) (court declined to rule whether disparate impact theory available, but instructed district court to consider the issue for future decision on appeal); Massarsky v. General Motors Corp., 706 F.2d 111, 120, 31 FEP 832, 837 (3d Cir.), *cert. denied,* 464 U.S. 937, 33 FEP 48 (1983) (court declined to rule whether ADEA violation can be based solely on disparate impact theory, but assumed "without deciding" application of the theory). *See* Stacy, *A Case Against Extending the Adverse Impact Doctrine to ADEA,* 10 EMPLOYEE REL. L.J. 438 (1985); Note, *Age Discrimination and the Disparate Impact Analysis,* 34 STAN. L. REV. 837 (1982).

[159]Holt v. Gamewell Corp., 797 F.2d 36, 41 FEP 585 (1st Cir. 1986); Heward v. Western Elec. Co., *supra* note 157 (ADEA action may be brought under either disparate treatment or disparate impact theory); Monroe v. United Airlines, 736 F.2d 394, 404 n.3, 34 FEP 1622, 1629 n.3 (7th Cir. 1984), *cert. denied,* 470 U.S. 1004, 37 FEP 64 (1985) (court rejects defendant's claim "that it is questionable whether a plaintiff may prove violation of the ADEA by showing disparate impact on other workers of a facially neutral policy"); EEOC v. Borden's, 724 F.2d 1390, 33 FEP 1708 (9th Cir. 1984); EEOC v. Westinghouse Elec. Corp., 725 F.2d 211, 33 FEP 945 (3d Cir. 1983); EEOC v. Governor Mifflin School Dist., 623 F. Supp. 734, 39 FEP 1059 (E.D. Pa. 1985) (ADEA does reach to disparate impact type of case); Flight Officers v. United Airlines, 572 F. Supp. 1494, 1505–06, 36 FEP 173, 180–81, 114 LRRM 3347 (N.D. Ill. 1983), *aff'd,* 756 F.2d 1274, 119 LRRM 2301 (7th Cir. 1985).

[160]EEOC v. Borden's, *supra* note 159; EEOC v. Westinghouse Elec. Corp., *supra* note 159.

[161]Criswell v. Western Airlines, 709 F.2d 544, 32 FEP 1204 (9th Cir. 1983), *aff'd,* 472 U.S. 400, 37 FEP 1829 (1985).

[162]Leftwich v. Harris-Stowe State College, 702 F.2d 686, 31 FEP 376 (8th Cir. 1983) (statistical evidence, used to establish prima facie case of disparate impact, withstood college's asserted need for cost savings, flexibility, innovation, and quality in hiring of nontenured faculty).

[163]Dace v. ACF Indus., 722 F.2d 374, 378, 33 FEP 788, 791 (8th Cir. 1983), *op. adhered to as supplemented by* 728 F.2d 976, 40 FEP 1604 (8th Cir. 1984) ("discrimination on the basis of factors, like seniority, that invariably would have a disparate impact on older employees is improper under the ADEA").

[164]Haskins v. Department of Health & Human Servs., 35 FEP 256 (E.D. Mo. 1984); *but see* Sakellar v. Lockeed Missiles & Space Co., 765 F.2d 1453, 38 FEP 1860 (9th Cir. 1985), *cert. denied,* 474 U.S. 1084, 39 FEP 1424 (1986) (plaintiff could not show impact on anyone other than himself).

[165]*Compare* Heward v. Western Elec. Co., *supra* note 157 (not applicable) *with* Yartzoff v. Oregon, Employment Div., Dep't of Human Resources, 745 F.2d 557, 559, 36 FEP 16, 17 (9th Cir. 1984) (per curiam). *But see* Watson v. Fort Worth Bank & Trust, 487 U.S. —, 47 FEP 102 (1988) (Title VII).

[166]Allison v. Western Union Tel. Co., 680 F.2d 1318, 1322, 29 FEP 393, 395 (11th Cir. 1982) (plaintiff's motion for directed verdict denied in light of defendant's expert testimony rebutting statistical evidence used by plaintiffs to help establish prima facie case of disparate impact).

[167]Williams v. General Motors Corp., 656 F.2d 120, 130 n.17, 26 FEP 1381, 1388 n.17 (5th Cir. 1981), *cert. denied,* 455 U.S. 943, 27 FEP 1765 (1982).

quiring selection, in a reduction in force, of the oldest and most senior in service among those eligible for pension violated the ADEA in view of its disproportionate impact on the protected class.[168] A defendant's attempt to establish through statistical evidence the absence of any adverse impact during a reorganization of its sales force was rejected as "arguably skewed," where it presented statistics on the age of the total sales force after reorganization, rather than focusing on the ages of salespersons who were relocated or terminated.[169]

## V. AFFIRMATIVE DEFENSES

### A. The Statutory Provision

Congress amended § 4(f)(1) of the Act to add a sixth statutory affirmative defense which applies to certain overseas employees:[170]

"[It shall not be unlawful * * * ]
   (1)   to take any action otherwise prohibited * * * where such practices involve an employee in a workplace in a foreign country, and compliance with such subsections would cause such employer, or a corporation controlled by such employer, to violate the laws of the country in which such workplace is located. * * *"

### B. Reasonable Factors Other Than Age and Good Cause

An employment decision based upon reasonable factors other than age is valid and will be upheld.[171] Reliance upon a state statute which conflicts with the ADEA is not, however, a valid defense.[172] Nor is eligibility for early retirement[173] or nontenured faculty status[174] a valid excuse where that status

---

[168]Popko v. City of Clairton, 570 F. Supp. 446, 450, 32 FEP 1414, 1417 (W.D. Pa. 1983); EEOC v. City of New Castle, 32 FEP 1409 (W.D. Pa. 1983), aff'd without opinion, 740 F.2d 956, 34 FEP 836 (3d Cir. 1984).

[169]Cowen v. Standard Brands, 572 F. Supp. 1576, 1579, 33 FEP 53, 55 (N.D. Ala. 1983).

[170]Older Americans Act Amendments of 1984, Pub. L. No. 98–459, Title VIII, § 802(b), 98 Stat. 1792 (1984).

[171]See, e.g., Crimm v. Missouri Pacific R.R., 750 F.2d 703, 36 FEP 883 (8th Cir. 1984) (good-faith belief, after investigation, plaintiff guilty of sexual harassment); Anderson v. Savage Laboratories, 675 F.2d 1221, 28 FEP 1473 (11th Cir. 1982) (falsification of records); Iervolino v. Delta Air Lines, 796 F.2d 1408, 41 FEP 1017 (11th Cir. 1986), cert. denied, 479 U.S. 1090, 43 FEP 80 (1987) (company policy prohibiting captains from transferring to flight engineer—two-step downbid—for even safety reasons); Moore v. Sears, Roebuck & Co., 683 F.2d 1321, 29 FEP 931 (11th Cir. 1982) (performance); Allison v. Western Union Tel. Co., 680 F.2d 1318, 1322, 29 FEP 393, 394 (11th Cir. 1982) ("person you will miss the least"); Halsell v. Kimberly-Clark Corp., 683 F.2d 285, 29 FEP 1185 (8th Cir. 1982), cert. denied, 459 U.S. 1205, 30 FEP 1856 (1983) (qualifications); Stendebach v. CPC Int'l, 691 F.2d 735, 30 FEP 233 (5th Cir. 1982), cert. denied, 461 U.S. 944, 31 FEP 1296 (1983) (plant reorganization); Massarsky v. General Motors Corp., 706 F.2d 111, 119–20, 31 FEP 832, 836–37 (3d Cir.), cert. denied, 464 U.S. 937, 33 FEP 48 (1983) (exemption of students from layoff, notwithstanding disparate impact upon employees in protected class, where "nothing to indicate that older persons were precluded from becoming GMI students"); Lovelace v. Sherwin-Williams Co., 681 F.2d 230, 29 FEP 172 (4th Cir. 1982).

[172]EEOC v. County of Allegheny, 705 F.2d 679, 31 FEP 920 (3d Cir. 1983) (statutory requirement that applicants for police officer exam be less than 35 years of age); EEOC v. City of Altoona, 723 F.2d 4, 33 FEP 888 (3d Cir. 1983), cert. denied, 467 U.S. 1204, 34 FEP 1400 (1984); Popko v. City of Clairton, supra note 168; EEOC v. City of New Castle, supra note 168 (statutory mandate, in layoff situations, of early retirement for firefighters eligible for pension benefits).

[173]EEOC v. Westinghouse Elec. Corp., 725 F.2d 11, 33 FEP 945 (3d Cir. 1983), amended, 33 FEP 1816 (3d. Cir.), cert. denied, 469 U.S. 820, 35 FEP 1607 (1984); EEOC v. City of New Castle, supra note 168; EEOC v. Great Atl. & Pac. Tea Co., 618 F. Supp. 115, 38 FEP 827 (N.D. Ohio 1985).

[174]Leftwich v. Harris-Stowe State College, 702 F.2d 686, 31 FEP 376 (8th Cir. 1983) (neither cost savings nor purported goal of increased quality accepted).

has an adverse impact upon those in the protected age class. Further, reference to a bottom-line average age is not sufficient to show that reasonable factors other than age were utilized if, in fact, the employment decisions were discriminatory.[175]

The Eleventh Circuit has approved the *Mt. Healthy*[176] defense in ADEA cases under which an employer found to have discriminated may escape liability by showing that it would have treated the employee in the same manner even if it had not discriminated.[177]

## C. Bona Fide Occupational Qualifications

The BFOQ exception to the ADEA is narrowly construed. In *Johnson v. Mayor of Baltimore,*[178] the Court held that Baltimore must assess whether its age 55 mandatory retirement for firefighters was based on a BFOQ appropriate for that job, and that the Fourth Circuit could not validate Baltimore's mandatory retirement age for firefighters by reference to a federal civil service statute which adopted an age 55 mandatory retirement for federal firefighters. In *Western Airlines v. Criswell,*[179] the Court affirmed the Ninth Circuit's decision holding that the BFOQ exception did not permit the mandatory retirement of flight engineers at age 60. Adopting a two-step test expressly derived from *Usery v. Tamiami Trail Tours,*[180] the Court ruled that an employer must determine, first, whether the challenged job qualification is " 'reasonably necessary to the essence of [the employer's] business,' "[181] acknowledging that " '[t]he greater the safety factor, measured by the likelihood of harm and the probable severity of that harm in case of an accident, the more stringent may be the job qualifications designed to insure safe driving.' "[182] Second, the Court held that the employer could establish either that it had " 'a factual basis for believing * * * that all or substantially all [persons over the age qualification] would be unable to perform safely and efficiently the duties of the job involved,' "[183] or that it is " 'impossible or highly impractical' to deal with the older employees on an individualized basis."[184]

Finally, in *Trans World Airlines v. Thurston,*[185] the Court affirmed the Second Circuit's decision that the ADEA required TWA to afford 60-year-old captains the same transfer privileges that it provides to captains disqualified for reasons other than age.

The Supreme Court's 1985 BFOQ trilogy confirmed a narrow construction of the BFOQ exception in lower court decisions, along with the impor-

---

[175]*Id.*
[176]Mt. Healthy School Dist. Bd. of Educ. v. Doyle, 429 U.S. 274 (1977).
[177]Spanier v. Morrison's Mgmt. Servs., 822 F.2d 975, 44 FEP 628 (11th Cir. 1987).
[178]472 U.S. 353, 37 FEP 1839 (1985). Later proceeding, Johnson v. Mayor of Baltimore, 637 F. Supp. 903, 41 FEP 17 (D. Md. 1986), *aff'd,* 829 F.2d 35, 45 FEP 1895 (4th Cir. 1987) (age 60 mandatory retirement invalid, as is "no retirement plan credit after age 60" policy).
[179]472 U.S. 400, 37 FEP 1829 (1985).
[180]531 F.2d 224, 12 FEP 1233 (5th Cir. 1976). *See* Second Edition, Chapter 14 (Age), at pp. 507–17.
[181]37 FEP at 1835, quoting from Usery v. Tamiami Trail Tours, *supra* note 180, at 236, 12 FEP at 1241.
[182]*Id.*
[183]*Id.*
[184]*Id.*
[185]469 U.S. 111, 36 FEP 977 (1985).

tance of defendants' safety claims.[186] Often at issue in evaluating such claims is the ability of the employer to test its employees individually.[187] Also at issue is the proper focal point of inquiry. The Eighth Circuit, in conflict with the First and Seventh circuits, has deemed the BFOQ defense available only if applicable to the individual occupation in question (*e.g.,* district fire chief), as opposed to the generic class of employees employed by the business (firefighters).[188]

---

[186]*Decisions rejecting age limits as BFOQs:* Trans World Airlines v. Thurston, *supra* note 185 (no BFOQ where employer permitted captains disqualified for reasons other than age to bump flight engineers, but denied such option to those precluded from flying under FAA age-60 rule); Johnson v. Mayor of Baltimore, 731 F.2d 209, 34 FEP 854 (4th Cir. 1984) (city not entitled to rely on federal mandatory retirement age of 55 as BFOQ for firefighters); Criswell v. Western Airlines, 709 F.2d 544, 32 FEP 1204 (9th Cir. 1983), *aff'd,* 472 U.S. 400, 37 FEP 1829 (1985) (mandatory retirement of flight engineers at age 60 not BFOQ); EEOC v. County of Los Angeles, 706 F.2d 1039, 31 FEP 1474 (9th Cir. 1983), *cert. denied,* 464 U.S. 1073, 33 FEP 1224 (1984) (refusal to hire as sheriffs and helicopter pilots those over age 35, predicated upon more limited time such persons would remain fit for positions, improper); Hahn v. City of Buffalo, 770 F.2d 12, 38 FEP 1069 (2d Cir. 1985) (invalidating New York civil service law setting age 29 as maximum hiring age for police officers). *See also* EEOC v. County of Allegheny, 705 F.2d 679, 31 FEP 920 (3d Cir. 1983); Heiar v. Crawford County, 746 F.2d 1190, 35 FEP 1458, *amended,* 36 FEP 112 (7th Cir. 1984), *cert. denied,* 472 U.S. 1027, 37 FEP 1883 (1985); Orzel v. City of Wauwatosa Fire Dep't, 697 F.2d 743, 755, 30 FEP 1070, 1079 (7th Cir.), *cert. denied,* 464 U.S. 992, 33 FEP 440 (1983) (mandatory retirement of firefighters at age 55 not BFOQ, notwithstanding that public safety is "essence" of business); EEOC v. County of Santa Barbara, 666 F.2d 373, 377, 27 FEP 1481, 1484 (9th Cir. 1982) (mandatory retirement of corrections officers at age 60 not BFOQ, despite safety issues); Smallwood v. United Airlines, 661 F.2d 303, 26 FEP 1376 (4th Cir. 1981), *cert. denied,* 456 U.S. 1007, 28 FEP 1656 (1982) (safety and economic considerations rejected as basis for denying employment to pilot applicants over age 35); EEOC v. Florida, Dep't of Highway Safety & Motor Vehicles, 660 F. Supp. 1104 (N.D. Fla. 1986) (mandatory retirement of all highway patrol officers at age 62 not BFOQ); EEOC v. Pennsylvania Liquor Control Bd., 565 F. Supp. 520, 32 FEP 57 (E.D. Pa. 1983) (mandatory retirement of enforcement officers of state liquor control board at age 65 invalid); Whitfield v. City of Knoxville, 567 F. Supp. 1344, 32 FEP 1052 (E.D. Tenn. 1983), *aff'd,* 756 F.2d 455, 37 FEP 288 (6th Cir. 1985) (involuntary retirement of policemen and firemen age 50 or over held improper, even though reduction in force due to revenue shortfalls).

*Decisions accepting age limits as BFOQs:* EEOC v. Missouri Highway Patrol, 748 F.2d 447, 36 FEP 401 (8th Cir. 1984), *cert. denied,* 474 U.S. 828, 38 FEP 1728 (1985) (officers and radio operators, maximum hiring age of 32 a BFOQ, but mandatory retirement at age 60 for all uniform personnel unlawful); Gathercole v. Global Assocs., 727 F.2d 1485, 34 FEP 502 (9th Cir. 1984), *rev'g* 560 F. Supp. 642, 31 FEP 736 (N.D. Cal. 1983), *cert. denied,* 469 U.S. 1087, 36 FEP 712 (1984) (discharge of 60-year-old pilots to comply with Army contract and FAA regulation upheld); Williams v. Hughes Helicopters, 806 F.2d 1387, 42 FEP 1035 (9th Cir. 1986) (permitted reliance on FAA age-60 rule to validate stop flying policy for test pilots); Hoefelman v. Conservation Comm'n of Mo. Dep't of Conservation, 718 F.2d 281, 32 FEP 1773 (8th Cir. 1983) (BFOQ in requiring pilot, because of age, to transfer to position of equipment supervisor); EEOC v. University of Tex. Health Science Center at San Antonio, 710 F.2d 1091, 32 FEP 944 (5th Cir. 1983) (age a BFOQ in excluding applicants over age 45 from hire as campus police officer); Maki v. New York State Comm'r of Educ., 568 F. Supp. 252, 32 FEP 630 (N.D.N.Y. 1983), *aff'd without opinion,* 742 F.2d 1437, 37 FEP 280 (2d Cir. 1984) (mandatory retirement of school bus drivers at age 65 a BFOQ); Murnane v. American Airlines, 667 F.2d 98, 26 FEP 1537 (D.C. Cir. 1981), *cert. denied,* 456 U.S. 915 (1982) (refusal to hire pilot applicants over 40 upheld). *See also* Quinn v. New York State Elec. & Gas Corp., 569 F. Supp. 655, 32 FEP 1070 (N.D.N.Y. 1983); Tuohy v. Ford Motor Co., 675 F.2d 842, 28 FEP 1116 (6th Cir. 1982) (whether retirement of pilots at age 60 is BFOQ inappropriate for summary judgment).

[187]*See, e.g.,* Hoefelman v. Conservation Comm'n of Mo. Dep't of Conservation, 541 F. Supp. 272, 30 FEP 1104 (W.D. Mo. 1982), *aff'd,* 718 F.2d 281, 32 FEP 1773 (8th Cir. 1983) (individualized testing of pilots not possible). *But see* EEOC v. Pennsylvania, 768 F.2d 514, 39 FEP 591 (3d Cir. 1985) (financial and administrative burden of individual testing insufficient to justify age as BFOQ for state police officers).

[188]*Compare* EEOC v. City of St. Paul, 671 F.2d 1162, 28 FEP 312 (8th Cir. 1982) *with* Mahoney v. Trabucco, 738 F.2d 35, 35 FEP 97 (1st Cir.), *cert. denied,* 469 U.S. 1036, 36 FEP 464 (1984) (administrative work/police officers) *and* EEOC v. City of Janesville, 630 F.2d 1254, 1258, 24 FEP 1294, 1297 (7th Cir. 1980) (police chief/law enforcement personnel).

## D. Bona Fide Employment Benefits Plan

### 1. Pre-amendment Rule

It generally has been held that the 1978 Amendment to § 4(f)(2) of the ADEA does not retroactively apply to mandatory retirements pursuant to a bona fide retirement plan occurring prior to April 6, 1978 (the effective date of the amendment).[189] Even as to pre-amendment retirements, however, it has been held unlawful to mandate retirement, prior to age 65, of employees who are not plan participants;[190] to mandate early retirement under a plan which provides only for voluntary early retirement at the employees' option;[191] or to require employees to retire pursuant to a retirement plan found to be a subterfuge to evade the purposes of the ADEA.[192] It also has been held unlawful to attempt to bind an employee to a pre-amendment election of early retirement.[193]

Though the effective date of the 1978 ADEA amendment was extended for those employees covered by a collective bargaining agreement in effect on September 1, 1977 (*i.e.,* until the termination of the agreement or January 1, 1980, whichever occurred first), this exception has been narrowly construed.[194]

Age-based exclusions from various benefit plans, found in plans separate from and unrelated to the employer's bona fide retirement plans, have been held unlawful.[195]

### 3. 1986 Amendment Rule

The 1986 amendment to the ADEA[196] removed the age 70 upper limit for all employees, except firefighters, law enforcement personnel, and tenured teachers who continue under the current rules and plans until December 31, 1993. The effective date of the 1986 ADEA amendment was

---

[189]*See, e.g.,* EEOC v. County of Santa Barbara, *supra* note 186.

[190]*Id.*

[191]EEOC v. Liggett & Meyers, 29 FEP 1611 (E.D.N.C. 1982).

[192]EEOC v. Home Ins. Co., 672 F.2d 252, 27 FEP 1665 (2d Cir.), *on remand,* 553 F. Supp. 704, 30 FEP 841 (S.D.N.Y. 1982) (mandatory retirement age reduced from 65 to 62 subsequent to enactment of ADEA but prior to 1978 amendment). *But see* Alford v. City of Lubbock, Tex., 664 F.2d 1263, 27 FEP 1075 (5th Cir.), *cert. denied,* 456 U.S. 975, 28 FEP 1392 (1982); Crosland v. Charlotte Eye, Ear & Throat Hosp., 686 F.2d 208, 29 FEP 1178 (4th Cir. 1982).

[193]Campbell v. Connelie, 542 F. Supp. 275, 28 FEP 1726 (N.D.N.Y. 1982) (one may not intentionally relinquish right that did not arise until after alleged waiver).

[194]*See* EEOC v. County of Calumet, 686 F.2d 1249, 29 FEP 1020 (7th Cir. 1982); Knight v. County of Dane, 30 FEP 1107 (W.D. Wis. 1982). *But see* Graczyk v. Steelworkers, 763 F.2d 256, 37 FEP 1456 (7th Cir.), *cert. denied,* 474 U.S. 970, 39 FEP 384 (1985) (agreement signed after September 1, 1977, but made retroactive to termination of prior agreement on August 1, 1977, was within exemption); EEOC v. United Airlines, 755 F.2d 94, 37 FEP 36 (7th Cir. 1985) (collective bargaining agreement did not expire when union struck on March 31, 1979, and, accordingly, mandatory retirement pursuant to 1975 agreement held lawful).

[195]Alford v. City of Lubbock, Tex., *supra* note 192 (sick leave formed no part of retirement plan); EEOC v. Westinghouse Elec. Corp., 725 F.2d 211, 33 FEP 945 (3d Cir. 1983), *amended,* 33 FEP 1816 (3d Cir.), *cert. denied,* 469 U.S. 820, 35 FEP 1607 (1984) (layoff income and benefit plan limited to several employees under age 55, unlawful); EEOC v. Borden's, 551 F. Supp. 1095, 30 FEP 933 (D. Ariz. 1982), *aff'd,* 724 F.2d 1390, 33 FEP 1708 (9th Cir. 1984) (exclusion of employees eligible for early retirement from severance pay benefit plan had disparate impact upon those age 55 or over).

[196]*Supra* notes 1–5.

extended for employees covered by a collective bargaining agreement in effect on June 30, 1986, until the expiration of the agreement or January 1, 1990, whichever occurs first.[197]

### E. Bona Fide Seniority System

Courts continue to look to the EEOC regulations for guidance in determining the validity of seniority systems.[198]

### F. Settlement and Release

A substantial controversy has arisen whether private settlements of ADEA claims, made without EEOC participation, are enforceable as a bar to subsequent ADEA litigation. The controversy has acquired special significance because of a widespread practice by which some employers condition severance payments on waivers of employment termination claims including claims of age discrimination under the ADEA.[199] A consensus of circuit court decisions holds that severance policies are governed by the Employee Retirement Income Security Act (ERISA).[200] Pursuant to ERISA requirements, employers carrying out a reduction in force or voluntary early retirement program may adopt and publish termination allowance plans under which severance payments are often fixed in amount or computed by standard formulas causing the severance payments to increase with increasing salary or seniority or both. Such termination allowance plans are intended both to satisfy ERISA requirements of publication and fair administration and ADEA requirements that severance payments not be computed or paid on a discriminatory basis with respect to age. The release of claims frequently required as part of such plans is also intended to provide the employer with protection against employment termination claims under state law.[201]

Some plaintiffs and, as *amicus curiae,* the American Association of Retired Persons have argued that the ADEA was enacted as part of the Fair Labor Standards Act, adopting certain of the FLSA's enforcement procedures;[202] that the Supreme Court has held that private wage settlements under the FLSA are not enforceable if reached before litigation has commenced;[203] that this same requirement should generally apply to ADEA

---

[197]*Supra* note 7.

[198]Cook v. Pan Am. World Airways, 771 F.2d 635, 38 FEP 1344 (2d Cir. 1985), *cert. denied,* 474 U.S. 1109, 39 FEP 1568 (1986) (merged airline's integrated seniority list not subterfuge where it represented a compromise of conflicting positions).

[199]*See, e.g.,* Runyan v. National Cash Register Corp., 787 F.2d 1039, 40 FEP 807 (6th Cir.) (en banc), *cert. denied,* 479 U.S. 850, 41 FEP 1712 (1986).

[200]*See, e.g.,* Scott v. Gulf Oil Corp., 754 F.2d 1499, 1503–04 (9th Cir. 1955); Blau v. Del Monte Corp., 748 F.2d 1348, 5 EBC 2744 (9th Cir. 1984), *cert. denied,* 474 U.S. 865 (1985); Donovan v. Dillingham, 688 F.2d 1367, 1370–73 (11th Cir. 1982).

[201]*See* Chapter 23 (Related Causes of Action).

[202]*See* 29 U.S.C. §§ 621 and 626(b) (1982).

[203]*See* Brooklyn Sav. Bank v. O'Neil, 324 U.S. 697, 5 WH 232 (1945) (employee cannot privately release rights to liquidated damages, at least where no bona fide dispute exists between parties regarding FLSA coverage; "some policy considerations which forbid waiver of basic minimum and overtime wages under the Act also prohibit waiver of the employee's right to liquidated damages." *Id.* at 706–07 (footnote omitted); Schulte, Inc. v. Gangi, 328 U.S. 108, 4 WH 104 (1946) (private settlement of disputes over coverage of Act are invalid).

settlements so as to make EEOC participation and approval a condition precedent to their enforcement;[204] and that such "supervision" by the EEOC carries forward original congressional intent that unsupervised ADEA waivers are not enforceable.[205]

Employers have argued in support of private ADEA releases that their validity should depend on whether they are knowing and voluntary, under a standard long applied to settlements of equal employment claims under Title VII;[206] that the FLSA authorizes federal supervision of FLSA settlements but does not require it;[207] that the Supreme Court's decisions invalidating private FLSA settlements of coverage disputes did not preclude private settlements of factual issues such as ADEA cases commonly present;[208] and that the common practice of providing severance payments in return for releases of ADEA claims can confer significant benefits on participating employees which EEOC supervision would not significantly advance and might inhibit.[209]

As this Supplement went to press, five circuit courts had upheld voluntary and knowing private ADEA releases.[210] These and other decisions also reflect judicial concern that a waiver of ADEA claims be reviewed with care to determine whether the settlement of ADEA claims is knowing and voluntary in substance as well as form,[211] and whether the terms and conditions of such settlements are clearly understandable[212] and do

---

[204]For a decision adopting this analysis, see Runyan v. National Cash Register Corp., 759 F.2d 1253, 37 FEP 1086, vacated, 38 FEP 5 (6th Cir. 1985), and superseded, supra note 199.

[205]The American Association of Retired Persons has pressed this view, e.g., in a brief amicus curiae in Valenti v. International Mill Servs., 45 FEP 1054 (3d Cir. 1987), vacated and reh'g en banc granted (panel decision that unsupervised releases of disputed ADEA factual issues could be enforced, but that specific release at issue must be set aside because signed involuntarily; case was settled before en banc determination).

[206]See, e.g., Alexander v. Gardner-Denver Co., 415 U.S. 36, 52 n.15, 7 FEP 81, 87 n.15 (1974); Lancaster v. Buerkle Buick Honda Co., 809 F.2d 539, 42 FEP 1472 (8th Cir.), cert. denied, 482 U.S. 928, 43 FEP 1896 (1987); Runyan v. National Cash Register Corp., supra note 204; United States v. Allegheny-Ludlum Indus., 517 F.2d 826, 857–59, 11 FEP 167, 191–93 (5th Cir. 1975), cert. denied, 425 U.S. 944, 12 FEP 1090 (1976).

[207]29 U.S.C. §§ 621, 626(b).

[208]See Runyan v. National Cash Register Corp., supra note 199, 787 F.2d at 1043, 40 FEP at 810 (noting that factual issues in FLSA cases concern "the number of hours worked and the base pay rate" which can be determined "with some precision" while "[i]n ADEA cases * * * the factual issues frequently concern determination of motive and intent" which are "more difficult to resolve." Id. at 1044 n.8, 40 FEP at 811 n.8; also holding that the Supreme Court in Schulte, Inc. v. Gangi supra note 203, specifically did not consider the " 'possibility of compromises in other situations which may arise, such as a dispute over the number of hours worked or the regular rate of employment,' " 40 FEP at 810, quoting from Schulte, Inc. v. Gangi, supra, at 114–15.

[209]See, e.g., Runyan v. National Cash Register Corp., supra note 199, 787 F.2d at 1045, 40 FEP at 811–12; R. Silberman and C. Bolick, The EEOC's Proposed Rule on Releases of Claims Under the ADEA, 37 LAB. L.J. 195, 200 (April 1986); EEOC Notice of Final Rule, 52 FED. REG. 32293 (August 27, 1987) (to be codified at 29 C.F.R. § 1627(c)), suspended for fiscal year 1988 by amendment to EEOC budget appropriation for 1988, see infra note 215.

[210]Runyan v. National Cash Register Corp., 787 F.2d 1039, 1045, 40 FEP 807, 811–12 (6th Cir.), (en banc), cert. denied, 479 U.S. 850, 41 FEP 1712 (1986); Sullivan v. Boron Oil Co., 831 F.2d 288, 8 EBC 2590 (3d Cir. 1987); Dorosiewicz v. Kayser-Roth Hosiery, 823 F.2d 546 (4th Cir. 1987); EEOC v. Cosmair, Inc., L'Oreal Hair Care Div., 821 F.2d 1085, 44 FEP 569 (5th Cir. 1987); Lancaster v. Buerkle Buick Honda Co., supra note 206.

[211]See, e.g., Runyan v. National Cash Register Corp., supra note 210; EEOC v. United States Steel Corp., 671 F. Supp. 351, 44 FEP 1801 (W.D. Pa. 1987) (enjoining release and waiver); Anderson v. Montgomery Ward & Co., 650 F. Supp. 1480 (N.D. Ill. 1987) (denying summary judgment where employees provided evidence of pressure to accept purportedly voluntary separation program with release of claims).

[212]Runyan v. National Cash Register Corp., supra note 210; cf. Pilon v. University of Minn. Regents, 710 F.2d 466, 32 FEP 508 (8th Cir. 1983).

not impair the legitimate enforcement mission of the EEOC.[213]

In 1985, the EEOC proposed a special rule to permit waivers or releases of ADEA rights without the Commission's supervision or approval, provided that such waivers or releases are knowing and voluntary.[214] The EEOC subsequently published a final rule permitting unsupervised releases of ADEA rights provided releases are knowing and voluntary, do not provide for the release of prospective rights, and are not in exchange for benefits to which the employee is already entitled. Absent circumstances of fraud or duress, the EEOC's final rule stated that in evaluating such releases, the EEOC would consider whether the waiver of ADEA rights was (1) a written understandable clear waiver, (2) provided a reasonable period for employee deliberation, and (3) encouraged the employee to consult with counsel.[215]

While waivers of private actions and individual recovery under the ADEA have been approved, the Fifth Circuit has held that waivers of the right to file a charge with the EEOC are void because they conflict with the public policy favoring an independent agency enforcement interest with respect to employment discrimination charges.[216] The Ninth Circuit has affirmed a district court ruling that an employer's offered waiver of ADEA claims, not signed by the employee, is admissible evidence for a jury determination of the question whether the employer's layoff of the employee was motivated by willful age discrimination.[217]

Courts have refused to grant motions for summary judgment based upon releases where issues of fact have been presented as to knowledge, intent, or volition.[218]

## VI. REMEDIES

### A. Sovereign Immunity

The Eleventh Amendment precludes retrospective, but not prospective, relief against a state.[219] Further, in extending the ADEA in 1974 to state employees, Congress abrogated the immunity from monetary awards in an

---

[213]EEOC v. Cosmair, Inc., L'Oreal Hair Care Div., *supra* note 210; EEOC v. United States Steel Corp., *supra* note 211.

[214]50 FED. REG. 40870 (October 7, 1985).

[215]52 FED. REG. 32293 (August 27, 1987). However, Congress suspended implementation of the EEOC's proposed rule in fiscal years 1988 and 1989 by language in appropriations bills. *See* Pub. L. No. 100-202, 101 Stat. 1329-31 (1987). Legislation to ban most unsupervised age waivers was pending as this Supplement went to press. *See* S. 54, 101st Cong., 1st Sess. (1989), introduced by Sen. Metzenbaum (R-Ohio) on January 25, 1989.

[216]EEOC v. Cosmair, Inc., L'Oreal Hair Care Div., *supra* note 210; EEOC v. United States Steel Corp., 583 F. Supp. 1357, 34 FEP 973 (W.D. Pa. 1984) (execution as a prerequisite to pension benefits enjoined).

[217]Cassino v. Reichhold Chems., 817 F.2d 1338 (9th Cir. 1987), *cert. denied*, 484 U.S. — (1988) (proposed agreement not excluded as settlement offer because no claim had been asserted by employee before agreement was proposed by employer; requirement that ADEA claims be waived as condition of severance pay could support finding of willful age discrimination justifying liquidated damages under ADEA).

[218]*See, e.g.,* Ogelsby v. Coca-Cola Bottling Co. of Chicago/Wis., 620 F. Supp. 1336, 39 FEP 327 (N.D. Ill. 1985); Valenti v. International Mill Servs., 45 FEP 1054 (3d Cir. 1987), *vacated and reh'g en banc granted.*

[219]Ramirez v. Puerto Rico Fire Serv., 715 F.2d 694, 32 FEP 1239 (1st Cir. 1983) (error to deny claim for injunctive relief in form of reclassification and placement on employment roster); Barrett v. Suffolk Transp. Servs., 600 F. Supp. 81, 37 FEP 725 (E.D.N.Y. 1984).

age discrimination claim (*e.g.,* back pay and liquidated damages) which the states had previously enjoyed.[220]

## B. Equitable Relief

### 1. Injunctions

The Ninth Circuit has held systemwide injunctive relief appropriate where an airline's discriminatory actions were found to have been taken pursuant to a classwide policy.[221] Injunctive relief may be denied where a substantial monetary judgment serves as an adequate deterrent[222] or, in an individual action, the plaintiff fails to seek reinstatement.[223] Courts have split on whether the consequences of mandatory retirement such as inability to keep job skills current, loss of position or esteem, and the resulting emotional problems constitute irreparable harm which justifies injunctive relief.[224] The Sixth Circuit has upheld a preliminary injunction requiring an employer to offer forced retirees the option of layoff instead of retirement which the employer already afforded those under age 55.[225] An employer has been restrained from requiring employees to sign a broad release including waiver of their ADEA rights as a prerequisite for obtaining special pension benefits[226] and from requiring the retirement of an employee at age 57.[227]

### 2. Reinstatement

Reinstatement lies within the discretion of the trial court after consideration of all pertinent facts.[228] The same considerations applicable to reinstate-

---

[220]Ramirez v. Puerto Rico Fire Serv., *supra* note 219; Heiar v. Crawford County, 746 F.2d 1190, 35 FEP 1458, *amended,* 36 FEP 112 (7th Cir. 1984), *cert. denied,* 472 U.S. 1027, 37 FEP 1883 (1985) (Eleventh Amendment does not preclude ADEA money judgments against county governments).

[221]Criswell v. Western Airlines, 709 F.2d 544, 32 FEP 1204 (9th Cir. 1983), *aff'd,* 472 U.S. 400, 37 FEP 1829 (1985).

[222]Cancellier v. Federated Dep't Stores, 672 F.2d 1312, 1316, 28 FEP 1151, 1153 (9th Cir.), *cert. denied,* 459 U.S. 859, 31 FEP 704 (1982).

[223]Seidel v. Chicago Sav. & Loan Ass'n, 544 F. Supp. 508, 34 FEP 297 (N.D. Ill. 1982).

[224]EEOC v. New Jersey, 620 F. Supp. 977, 39 FEP 516 (D.N.J. 1985), *aff'd without opinion,* 815 F.2d 694, 43 FEP 653 (3d Cir. 1987) (alleged consequences of mandatory retirement held not sufficient to constitute irreparable harm); *but see* EEOC v. City of Bowling Green, Ky., 607 F. Supp. 524, 37 FEP 963 (W.D. Ky. 1985) (when officer alleged he would suffer from anxiety, emotional problems, and inability to keep up with job skills, court found sufficient irreparable harm); EEOC v. Pennsylvania, 39 FEP 587 (M.D. Pa. 1984).

[225]EEOC v. Chrysler Corp., 546 F. Supp. 54, 29 FEP 284, *clarified,* 546 F. Supp. 73, 29 FEP 1385 (E.D. Mich. 1982), *aff'd,* 733 F.2d 1183, 34 FEP 1401, *petition for reh'g en banc denied,* 738 F.2d 167, 41 FEP 1011 (6th Cir. 1984).

[226]EEOC v. United States Steel Corp., *supra* note 216 (release executed under conditions found to make release neither voluntary nor knowing; release also contained noncooperation covenant which would have hindered and impeded EEOC investigation). *See supra* notes 210–215 and accompanying text.

[227]EEOC v. City of Bowling Green, *supra* note 224; *see also* James v. Miller-Wohl Co., 35 FEP 1846 (W.D.N.Y. 1984) (injunctive relief available to individuals).

[228]*See, e.g.,* Goldstein v. Manhattan Indus., 758 F.2d 1435, 37 FEP 1217 (11th Cir.), *cert. denied,* 474 U.S. 1005, 39 FEP 720 (1985) (reinstatement appropriate despite plaintiff's reluctance to accept such, where employer indicated willingness to take plaintiff back on terms advantageous to plaintiff); Leftwich v. Harris-Stowe State College, 702 F.2d 686, 31 FEP 376 (8th Cir. 1983) (reinstatement to old position of associate professor with retroactive seniority appropriate, even though plaintiff would have been eligible for full professorship had he not been discharged); Kiel v. Goodyear Tire & Rubber Co., 575 F. Supp. 847, 33 FEP 1122 (N.D. Ohio 1983), *aff'd,* 762 F.2d 1008 (6th Cir. 1985) (reinstatement inappropriate, despite jury's finding that age was determining factor in plaintiff's discharge, where court ruled

ment apply as well, according to the Eighth Circuit, to a plaintiff whose application for an entry-level position had been denied unlawfully.[229] However, reinstatement has been held not to encompass the reassignment of particular sales accounts lost due to age discrimination.[230] Accrual of damages ceases to continue upon plaintiff's refusal of a good-faith offer of reinstatement.[231] A discriminatee is not required, however, to accept an offer of reinstatement to a position which the court concludes is essentially different from that formerly held.[232] While an unlawfully discharged plaintiff is not obligated to accept his employer's offers if they are not for a position reasonably comparable to that from which he was discharged, the Fourth Circuit has held that a district court may not require the bumping of the plaintiff's successor to satisfy an order of reinstatement and that, rather, the district court should have adopted the "rightful place" theory, utilized in Title VII cases, according the plaintiff full seniority rights, the next available vacancy "by means of that seniority," and back pay during the interim period to compensate for lost earnings.[233]

## C. Back Pay/Front Pay

Back pay encompasses what the plaintiff would have received in compensation but for the violation.[234] It must be calculated, according to the Eighth Circuit, on a year-by-year approach and, accordingly, any "excess" interim earnings in any one year cannot be deducted from back pay entitle-

---

employer had other legitimate reasons for its action); Duffy v. Wheeling Pittsburgh Steel Corp., 33 FEP 730 (E.D. Pa. 1983), aff'd, 738 F.2d 1393, 35 FEP 246 (3d Cir.), cert. denied, 469 U.S. 1087, 36 FEP 712 (1984) (no evidence suggesting unconscionable difficulties on reinstatement); Cancellier v. Federated Dep't Stores, supra note 222 (reinstatement denied because of acrimonious relationship between plaintiffs and defendants, as well as substantial verdict received by plaintiffs); Cline v. Roadway Express, 689 F.2d 481, 485, 29 FEP 1365, 1368 (4th Cir. 1982) (reinstatement upheld, notwithstanding defendant's claim of incompatability and plaintiff's lengthy absence from industry, in light of difficulties in fashioning appropriate award of damages alone); Bailey v. Container Corp. of Am., 660 F. Supp. 1048 (S.D. Ohio 1986) (reinstatement into pension plan).

[229]Dickerson v. Deluxe Check Printers, 703 F.2d 276, 31 FEP 621 (8th Cir. 1983), later proceedings, 783 F.2d 149, 40 FEP 960 (8th Cir. 1986) (post-remand appeal on other issues).

[230]Ingram v. Cox Communications, fka Cox Broadcasting Corp., 611 F. Supp. 150, 154, 38 FEP 1594, 1597 (N.D. Ga. 1985) ("reinstatement" means reinstatement to particular position, not restoration of particular aspects of job).

[231]Fiedler v. Indianhead Truck Line, 670 F.2d 806, 28 FEP 849 (8th Cir. 1982); Giandonato v. Sybron Corp. dba Taylor Instrument Co., 804 F.2d 120, 42 FEP 219 (10th Cir. 1986).

[232]Spagnuolo v. Whirlpool Corp., 641 F.2d 1109, 25 FEP 376 (4th Cir.), cert. denied, 454 U.S. 860, 26 FEP 1688 (1981).

[233]Spagnuolo v. Whirlpool Corp., 717 F.2d 114, 117–21, 32 FEP 1382, 1384–88 (4th Cir. 1983). But see Miller v. Lyng, 660 F. Supp. 1375, 44 FEP 696 (D.D.C. 1987) (bumping appropriate when necessary to make whole).

[234]See, e.g., Blim v. Western Elec. Co., 731 F.2d 1473, 1480, 34 FEP 757, 762 (10th Cir.), cert. denied, 469 U.S. 874, 36 FEP 816 (1984) (lost social security benefits, but not damages for increased tax liability allegedly caused by lump-sum back pay damages, where five-year averaging provisions of tax laws will eliminate "nearly all of any penalty that would otherwise result from receipt of a lump sum payment"); Coleman v. City of Omaha, 714 F.2d 804, 33 FEP 1462 (8th Cir. 1983) (accumulated sick leave and vacation time); Blackwell v. Sun Elec. Corp., 696 F.2d 1176, 30 FEP 1177 (6th Cir. 1983) (accrued health benefits, but not pension benefits, because plaintiff did not seek or gain reinstatement and at time of discharge had no vested rights); Hagelthorn v. Kennecott Corp., 710 F.2d 76, 33 FEP 977 (2d Cir. 1983) (back pay liability offset by difference between lump-sum pension payment plaintiff received when discharged and pension sum he would have received had he retired at age 65); Duffy v. Wheeling Pittsburgh Steel Corp., supra note 228 (cost-of-living increases; amount equal to employer's contribution to thrift plan; reimbursement for automobile, health, and dental care and insurance coverage that would have been paid for or covered by employer's insurance); Jacobson v. Pitman-Moore, 582 F. Supp. 169, 34 FEP 1267 (D. Minn. 1984) (cost of replacing insurance benefits). See also Chapter 38 (Monetary Relief).

ments for other years.[235] Back pay compensation awards may include lost wages[236] and lost benefits in the areas of pension,[237] insurance,[238] vacation,[239] and other terms and conditions of employment.[240] Damages have been deemed to accrue from the date of the discriminatory act until "the date damages are settled."[241] Damages, however, have been cut off by the elimination of a position resulting from a legitimate nondiscriminatory business decision, where the defendant employer carries its burden of proving that employment would not have continued in some other capacity.[242]

Plaintiffs have a duty, under the ADEA, to mitigate their damages by seeking other employment with reasonable diligence.[243] However, this obligation normally does not require acceptance of employment, even on a temporary basis, at a location unreasonably distant from plaintiff's home.[244] Neither does it require acceptance of defendant's offer of a position less than substantially equivalent to the position plaintiff was seeking.[245]

Courts have also considered whether to apply various offsets in the computation of damages.[246]

---

[235]Leftwich v. Harris-Stowe State College, *supra* note 228.

[236]*See, e.g.,* Kolb v. Goldring, Inc., 694 F.2d 869, 30 FEP 633 (1st Cir. 1982); O'Donnell v. Georgia Osteopathic Hosp., 574 F. Supp. 214, 36 FEP 944 (N.D. Ga. 1983), *aff'd in part, rev'd in part and remanded on other grounds,* 748 F.2d 1543, 36 FEP 953 (11th Cir. 1984) (cost of living and merit evaluation raises through date of trial); Syvock v. Milwaukee Boiler Mfg. Co., 665 F.2d 149, 27 FEP 610 (7th Cir. 1981).

[237]Bleakley v. Jekyll Island-State Park Auth., 536 F. Supp. 236, 29 FEP 1525 (S.D. Ga. 1982) (plaintiff, if she prevailed, entitled to be treated as though her pension benefits had vested as of trial date; pension benefits would be based upon anticipated earnings through date of trial).

[238]Fariss v. Lynchburg Foundry, 588 F. Supp. 1369, 35 FEP 1470 (W.D. Va. 1984), *aff'd,* 769 F.2d 958, 38 FEP 992 (4th Cir. 1985) (life insurance should be valued according to employer's replacement cost, not amount of proceeds that might have been available to deceased employees); Spagnuolo v. Whirlpool Corp., 550 F. Supp. 432, 32 FEP 1377 (W.D.N.C. 1982), *aff'd in part on other grounds,* 717 F.2d 114, 32 FEP 1382 (4th Cir. 1983). *But see* Foster v. Excelsior Springs City Hosp. & Convalescent Center, 631 F. Supp. 174, 40 FEP 1616 (W.D. Mo. 1986) (proceeds rather than premiums recoverable).

[239]Spagnuolo v. Whirlpool Corp., *supra* note 232.

[240]Goldstein v. Manhattan Indus., 758 F.2d 1435, 37 FEP 1217 (11th Cir.), *cert. denied,* 474 U.S. 1005, 39 FEP 720 (1985) ("concomitants of employment," *i.e.,* lost outside earnings from noncompeting lines plaintiff authorized to sell); Kolb v. Goldring, Inc., *supra* note 236; Spagnuolo v. Whirlpool Corp., *supra* note 238.

[241]*See, e.g.,* Kolb v. Goldring, Inc., *supra* note 236.

[242]Archambault v. United Computing Sys., 786 F.2d 1507, 40 FEP 1050 (11th Cir. 1986). *But see* Bonura v. Chase Manhattan Bank, N.A., 629 F. Supp. 353, 43 FEP 163 (S.D.N.Y.), *aff'd,* 795 F.2d 276, 43 FEP 173 (2d Cir. 1986) (employer liability did not end with sale of division).

[243]Fiedler v. Indianhead Truck Line, 670 F.2d 806, 28 FEP 849 (8th Cir. 1982); Cline v. Roadway Express, 689 F.2d 481, 485, 29 FEP 1365, 1368 (4th Cir. 1982); Kolb v. Goldring, Inc., *supra* note 236; Coleman v. City of Omaha, *supra* note 234 (evidence warranted presenting question of plaintiff's failure to mitigate damages to jury); Jacobson v. Pitman-Moore, 573 F. Supp. 565, 33 FEP 49 (D. Minn. 1983), *motions for new trial and j.n.o.v. denied,* 582 F. Supp. 169, 34 FEP 1267 (D. Minn. 1984); Whittlesey v. Union Carbide Corp., 567 F. Supp. 1320, 32 FEP 473, *later proceeding,* 35 FEP 1085 (S.D.N.Y. 1983), *aff'd,* 742 F.2d 724, 35 FEP 1089 (2d Cir. 1984) (on damages, including mitigation and front pay); Koyen v. Consolidated Edison Co. of N.Y., 560 F. Supp. 1161, 31 FEP 488 (S.D.N.Y. 1983).

[244]Spagnuolo v. Whirlpool Corp., 641 F.2d 1109, 25 FEP 376 (4th Cir.), *cert. denied,* 454 U.S. 860, 26 FEP 1688 (1981).

[245]Dickerson v. Deluxe Check Printers, 703 F.2d 276, 31 FEP 621 (8th Cir. 1983), later proceedings, 783 F.2d 149, 40 FEP 960 (8th Cir. 1986) (post-remand appeal on other issues); O'Donnell v. Georgia Osteopathic Hosp., *supra* note 236 (endorsing " 'duty of the trier of fact to weigh the evidence to determine whether a reasonable person would refuse the offer of reinstatement,' " quoting with approval from *Fiedler v. Indianhead Truck Line, supra* note 243 at 808. *Cf.* Cowen v. Standard Brands, 572 F. Supp. 1576, 33 FEP 53 (N.D. Ala. 1983) (unacceptable that plaintiff rejected offer of comparable employment because of hurt feelings or disbelief in bona fides of offer).

[246]*See, e.g.,* McDowell v. Avtex Fibers, 740 F.2d 214, 35 FEP 371 (3d Cir. 1984), *vacated on other grounds and remanded,* 469 U.S. 1202, 37 FEP 64 (1985) (neither unemployment insurance compensation benefits nor pension plan benefits received during period suit pending may be deducted from back pay award); Hagelthorn v. Kennecott Corp., 710 F.2d 76, 33 FEP 977 (2d Cir. 1983) (pension benefits paid to plaintiff at time of unlawful discharge at age 63 reduced by difference between lump sum received

Back pay is inappropriate, according to the Fourth Circuit, where the employer establishes it would not have hired the plaintiff even absent age discrimination.[247] However, back pay has been deemed appropriate in one case even though the plaintiff admitted to falsification of expense vouchers on two occasions, where no reinstatement was sought, and the falsification did not result in the securing of a position the plaintiff was not otherwise qualified to hold.[248]

While the Second Circuit has held that back pay is an equitable remedy which may be recovered against a labor organization, that Circuit has precluded recovery under the ADEA of money damages against such organizations.[249]

Although some controversy still persists over front pay in ADEA cases, front pay has been endorsed as an available remedy under appropriate circumstances by the First, Second, Third, Sixth, Eighth, Ninth, Tenth, and Eleventh circuits.[250]

---

and sum he would have received at age 65); Fariss v. Lynchburg Foundry, *supra* note 238, (lump-sum pension benefits offset against damages claimed); Maxfield v. Sinclair Int'l, 766 F.2d 788, 38 FEP 442 (3d Cir. 1985), *cert. denied,* 474 U.S. 1057, 39 FEP 1200 (1986) (social security benefits received following termination should not be deducted from back pay and front pay award); *But see* Crosby v. New England Tel. & Tel. Co., 624 F. Supp. 487, 39 FEP 1271 (D. Mass. 1985); EEOC v. Wyoming Retirement Sys., 771 F.2d 1425, 38 FEP 1544 (10th Cir. 1985) (offset for social security benefits received appropriate when defendant a public body); Whitfield v. City of Knoxville, 567 F. Supp. 1344, 32 FEP 1052 (E.D. Tenn. 1983), *aff'd,* 756 F.2d 455, 37 FEP 288 (6th Cir. 1985) (back pay offset by retirement incentive bonus); Smith v. Office of Personnel Mgmt., 778 F.2d 258, 39 FEP 1851 (5th Cir. 1985), *cert. denied,* 476 U.S. 1105, 40 FEP 1048 (1986) (recovery offset by disability compensation); Duffy v. Wheeling Pittsburgh Steel Corp., 33 FEP 730, (E.D. Pa. 1983), *aff'd,* 738 F.2d 1393, 35 FEP 246 (3d Cir.), *cert. denied,* 469 U.S. 1087, 36 FEP 712 (1984) (back pay offset by unemployment insurance benefits). *See also* Merkel v. Scovill, Inc., 570 F. Supp. 133, 38 FEP 1020 (S.D. Ohio 1983); Wilson v. Wehadkee Yarn Mills, 32 FEP 847 (M.D. Ala. 1983) (settlement offset by unemployment compensation benefits). *Cf.* Gathercole v. Global Assocs., 560 F. Supp. 642, 31 FEP 736 (N.D. Cal. 1983), *rev'd on other grounds,* 727 F.2d 1485, 34 FEP 502 (9th Cir.), *cert. denied,* 469 U.S. 1087, 36 FEP 712 (1984) (no deduction for social security early retirement benefits received after discharge since plaintiff would have received them had he retired voluntarily, but deduction for unemployment compensation benefits); *see also* Chapter 38 (Monetary Relief).

[247]Smallwood v. United States Airlines, 728 F.2d 614, 624, 34 FEP 217, 226 (4th Cir.), *cert. denied,* 469 U.S. 832, 35 FEP 1608 (1984) (such disqualification "may be established by evidence which had not been developed at the time the claimant was denied employment, provided such evidence is proved at trial of the remedy issue").

[248]Kneisley v. Hercules, Inc., 577 F. Supp. 726, 33 FEP 1579 (D. Del. 1983).

[249]Air Line Pilots v. Trans World Airlines, 713 F.2d 940, 32 FEP 1185 (2d Cir. 1983), *dismissed as to this issue for want of jurisdiction sub nom.* Trans World Airlines v. Thurston, 469 U.S. 111, 119 n.14, 36 FEP 977, 981 n.14 (1985) (TWA not the proper party to present this question).

[250]*Front pay permissible:* Wildman v. Lerner Stores Corp., 771 F.2d 605, 38 FEP 1377 (1st Cir. 1985) (where reinstatement impracticable or impossible, future damages "often speculative" and district court should consider circumstances of case including availability of liquidated damages); Whittlesey v. Union Carbide Corp., 742 F.2d 724, 727, 35 FEP 1089, 1091 (2d Cir. 1984) (front pay appropriate under ADEA "in limited circumstances" where factfinder can "reasonably predict that the plaintiff has no reasonable prospect of obtaining comparable alternative employment"); Maxfield v. Sinclair Int'l, *supra* note 246 (where reinstatement not feasible); Blum v. Witco Chem. Corp., 829 F.2d 367, 46 FEP 306 (3d Cir. 1987) (damages for lost pension benefits in the form of front pay); Davis v. Combustion Eng'g, 742 F.2d 916, 923, 35 FEP 975, 980 (6th Cir. 1984) (*per se* rule not appropriate; front pay left to trial court's discretion under facts of individual case); Gibson v. Mohawk Rubber Co., 695 F.2d 1093, 1100, 30 FEP 859 (8th Cir. 1982); Cancellier v. Federated Dep't Stores, 672 F.2d 1312, 1319, 28 FEP 1151 (9th Cir.), *cert. denied,* 459 U.S. 859, 31 FEP 704 (1982) (in dicta, court stated front pay might be available in addition to liquidated damages, but that value of reinstatement is often speculative and availability of substantial liquidated damages award may be proper consideration in denying additional damages in lieu of reinstatement; court omitted reference to its own decision in *Naton v. Bank of Cal.,* 649 F.2d 691, 27 FEP 510 (9th Cir. 1981), affirming without discussion a modest front pay award; EEOC v. Prudential Fed. Sav. & Loan Ass'n, 763 F.2d 1116, 37 FEP 1691 (10th Cir.), *cert. denied,* 474 U.S. 946, 39 FEP 384 (1985) (future damages in lieu of reinstatement furthers purpose of ADEA where reinstatement impossible as a practical matter); reaffirmed in Smith v. Consolidated Mut. Water Co., 787 F.2d 1441, 1443, 40 FEP 843, 844 (10th Cir. 1986); Goldstein v. Manhattan Indus., *supra* note 240, 758 F.2d at 1448–49 (where reinstatement impracticable or inadequate). *See also* Chern v. Ogden Food Serv. Corp., 33 FEP 1547 (E.D. Pa. 1984) (front pay within court's power to grant legal and equitable relief); Koyen v. Consolidated

## D. Liquidated Damages

Until resolved by the Supreme Court in *Trans World Airlines v. Thurston*[251] in 1985, the standard of willfulness necessary to establish entitlement to liquidated damages was unclear. In *Thurston,* the Supreme Court rejected definitions that had permitted some courts to find willfulness where the employer knew that the ADEA was "in the picture" or was potentially applicable. Such a standard, the Court stated, would lead to double damages awards in almost every case, even if the employer had acted reasonably and in good faith, and this was contrary to Congress' intent. The standard approved by the Court permits a finding of willfulness if "the employer * * * knew or showed reckless disregard for the matter of whether its conduct was prohibited by the ADEA."[252]

In applying the *Thurston* standard, some courts have focused on whether an employer acted with knowledge that such actions contravened the Act.[253] Others have required evidence of an intentional knowing violation in addition to the evidence necessary to establish a violation of the Act.[254] It has been suggested that an employer's age-related comments,[255] discrepancies in responses to governmental agencies investigating the charge,[256] or other extensive and unwarranted dilatory tactics[257] could provide sufficient grounds for a finding of willfulness. Emotional distress allegedly caused by an employer's action, however, has been held irrelevant to the issue of willfulness.[258] The Seventh Circuit reversed and remanded one case in which a jury determined that an employer had retaliated against an employee for filing an age charge because of the jury's inconsistent finding that the employer's action was not willful.[259]

Relying on the Supreme Court's discussion of the good-faith defense under the Portal-to-Portal Act and its application to the ADEA,[260] the Sixth and Tenth circuits have specifically ruled that good faith is a defense to a claim for liquidated damages under § 7(b) of the Act.[261] Another court held

---

Edison Co., *supra* note 243 (front pay awarded to 68-year-old plaintiff up to age 70); Fite v. First Tennessee Production Credit Ass'n, 861 F.2d 884, 48 FEP 449 (6th Cir. 1988) (court decides whether front pay appropiate, jury decides amount); Dominic v. Consolidated Edison Co., 822 F.2d 1249, 44 FEP 268 (2d Cir. 1987) (court also determines amount);

*Front pay impermissible:* Helwig v. Suburban Chevrolet, 33 FEP 1261 (D. Md. 1983) (front pay overly speculative and beyond ADEA remedial scheme); MacGill v. Johns Hopkins Univ., 33 FEP 1254 (D. Md. 1983) (front pay too speculative and would interfere with conciliatory purposes of statute).

[251]469 U.S. 111, 36 FEP 977 (1985). *See also* cases cited therein for retroactive application of *Thurston.*

[252]*Id.*

[253]Gilkerson v. Toastmaster, Inc., 770 F.2d 133, 38 FEP 1167 (8th Cir. 1985); Spanier v. Morrison's Mgmt. Servs., 611 F. Supp. 642, 38 FEP 177 (N.D. Ala. 1985).

[254]Spanier v. Morrison's Mgmt. Servs., *supra* note 253 (aggravated circumstances or evidence of a defiant attitude); Smith v. Consolidated Mut. Water Co., 787 F.2d 1441, 40 FEP 843 (10th Cir. 1986) (circumstantial evidence establishing ADEA violation insufficient to show willful conduct).

[255]Archambault v. United Computing Sys., 786 F.2d 1507, 40 FEP 1050 (11th Cir. 1986) ("too old for the position," "industry was a young man's game" which had "outgrown" plaintiff).

[256]*Id.*

[257]Dickerson v. Deluxe Check Printers, 703 F.2d 276, 31 FEP 621 (8th Cir. 1983), *later proceedings,* 783 F.2d 149, 40 FEP 960 (8th Cir. 1986) (post-remand appeal on other issues).

[258]Taylor v. Home Ins. Co., 777 F.2d 849, 39 FEP 769 (4th Cir. 1985), *cert. denied,* 476 U.S. 1142, 40 FEP 1512 (1986).

[259]Rose v. Hearst Corp., Hearst Magazines Div., 814 F.2d 491, 43 FEP 641 (7th Cir. 1987).

[260]Trans World Airlines v. Thurston, *supra* note 251, at 128, 36 FEP at 985.

[261]Whitfield v. City of Knoxville, 756 F.2d 455, 37 FEP 288 (6th Cir. 1985) (good-faith reliance on a split in legal authority); EEOC v. Wyoming Retirement Sys., 771 F.2d 1425, 38 FEP 1544 (10th Cir. 1985) (reliance on a state attorney general's opinion).

that in determining willfulness, consideration must be given to an employer's business justification defense.[262]

Because liquidated damages are compensatory in nature and not punitive, it has been held that such damages should be assessed only upon the net loss after offsets.[263] Awards of front pay have also been excluded in determination of liquidated damages.[264] Amounts awarded as compensatory damages under state law claims have been reduced by the amount of liquidated damages awarded under the ADEA to prevent double recovery for damages such as loss of reputation, humiliation, and mental anguish.[265]

In light of *Lehman v. Nakshian,*[266] it has been held that liquidated damages are not available in an action against the government in its capacity as an employer.[267]

### E. Compensatory Damages

The Tenth Circuit has joined the eight courts of appeal cited in the Second Edition in holding that compensatory damages for pain and suffering are not recoverable under the ADEA.[268] However, such damages may be recovered on the basis of a pendent state claim,[269] although some courts have declined to exercise such pendent jurisdiction on the ground this would circumvent the scope of remedies available under the ADEA.[270] Defendant employers will argue that such compensatory dam-

---

[262]Gilliam v. Armtex, Inc., 820 F.2d 1387, 44 FEP 113 (4th Cir. 1987).

[263]Fariss v. Lynchburg Foundry, 588 F. Supp. 1369, 35 FEP 1470 (W.D. Va. 1984).

[264]Dominic v. Consolidated Edison Co. of N.Y., 822 F.2d 1249, 44 FEP 268 (2d Cir. 1987).

[265]Merkel v. Scovill, Inc., 570 F. Supp. 141, 38 FEP 1026 (S.D. Ohio 1983).

[266]453 U.S. 156, 26 FEP 65 (1981).

[267]Wilkes v. United States Postal Serv., 548 F. Supp. 642, 30 FEP 20 (N.D. Ill. 1982); Leibovitch v. Administrator, Veterans Admin., 33 FEP 777 (D.D.C. 1982).

[268]Perell v. FinanceAmerica Corp., 726 F.2d 654, 33 FEP 1728 (10th Cir. 1984). *See also* Air Line Pilots v. Trans World Airlines, 713 F.2d 940, 32 FEP 1185 (2d Cir. 1983), *dismissed as to this issue for want of jurisdiction sub nom.* Trans World Airlines v. Thurston, 469 U.S. 111, 119 n.14, 36 FEP 977, 981 n.14 (1985) (not disturbed on this point on *certiorari* in *Trans World Airlines v. Thurston, supra;* Haskell v. Kaman Corp., 743 F.2d 113, 35 FEP 941 (2d Cir. 1984); Borumka v. Rocky Mountain Hosp. & Medical Serv. dba Blue Cross/Blue Shield of Colo., 599 F. Supp. 857, 37 FEP 685 (D. Colo. 1984); James v. Miller-Wohl Co., 35 FEP 1846 (W.D.N.Y. 1984); Karr v. Township of Lower Merion, 582 F. Supp. 410, 34 FEP 1557 (E.D. Pa. 1983); Meschino v. IT&T Corp., 563 F. Supp. 1066, 34 FEP 1634 (S.D.N.Y. 1983); Kempe v. Prince Gardner, Inc., 569 F. Supp. 779, 36 FEP 969 (E.D. Mo. 1983); Johnson v. Al Tech Specialty Steel Corp., 33 FEP 1684 (N.D.N.Y. 1983), *aff'd,* 731 F.2d 143, 34 FEP 861 (2d Cir. 1984); Prouty v. National R.R. Passenger Corp., 572 F. Supp. 200, 33 FEP 849 (D.D.C. 1983); Helwig v. Suburban Chevrolet, 33 FEP 1261 (D. Md. 1983); Pfeiffer v. Essex Wire Corp., 682 F.2d 684, 29 FEP 420 (7th Cir.), *cert. denied,* 459 U.S. 1039, 30 FEP 440 (1982); Fiedler v. Indianhead Truck Line, 670 F.2d 806, 28 FEP 849 (8th Cir. 1982). *Contra* Brenimer v. Great W. Sugar Co., 567 F. Supp. 218, 33 FEP 281 (D. Colo. 1983).

[269]New York v. Holiday Inns, 35 FEP 1308 (W.D.N.Y. 1984) (state antidiscrimination law and intentional infliction of emotional distress claims, not dismissed at preliminary stages); Venezia v. Scovill, Inc., 592 F. Supp. 3, 38 FEP 1263 (S.D. Ohio 1983) (pendent state discrimination action under Ohio statute permitting compensatory and punitive damages); *but see* Lettich v. Kenway, 590 F. Supp. 1225, 35 FEP 1289 (D. Mass. 1984) (likelihood of jury confusion and belief that ADEA precludes joinder of pendent claims cited as basis for dismissal of wrongful termination and intentional infliction of emotional distress claims); Arnell v. Pan Am. World Airways, 611 F. Supp. 908, 38 FEP 1451 (S.D.N.Y. 1985) (questions of plaintiff's mental state and airline's malice involved in state claims irrelevant to ADEA claim and could cause jury confusion); James v. KID Broadcasting Corp., 559 F. Supp. 1153, 38 FEP 439 (D. Utah 1983) (likelihood of jury confusion from divergent theories of relief). *Cf.* Cancellier v. Federated Dep't Stores, 672 F.2d 1312, 1316, 28 FEP 1151, 1153 (9th Cir.), *cert. denied,* 459 U.S. 859, 31 FEP 704 (1982); Hrzenak v. White-Westinghouse Appliance Co., 682 F.2d 714, 29 FEP 1278 (8th Cir. 1982); Shanahan v. WITI-TV, 565 F. Supp. 219, 37 FEP 1118, 115 LRRM 4208 (E.D. Wis. 1982).

[270]Borumka v. Rocky Mountain Hosp. & Medical Serv. dba Blue Cross/Blue Shield of Colo., *supra* note 268; Kempe v. Prince Gardner, Inc., *supra* note 268.

ages under state law must be reduced in any event by the amount of liquidated damages awarded under the ADEA.[271]

## F. Punitive Damages

Courts continue to hold that punitive damages are unavailable under the ADEA.[272]

## G. Attorney's Fees

Prevailing plaintiffs remain entitled to reasonable attorney's fees[273] and costs.[274] A plaintiff need not be entirely successful, either at trial or on appeal, in order to be entitled to an award of attorney's fees.[275] Nor is a prevailing plaintiff entitled to an enhancement of the lodestar amount simply for prevailing on all claims, according to the Eleventh Circuit, because total success does not necessarily demonstrate exceptional services.[276] The impact of private fee arrangements remains unsettled.[277] Fees may or may not be awarded for services before an administrative agency.[278]

---

[271]*See* Merkel v. Scovill, Inc., *supra* note 265 and accompanying text.

[272]Pfeiffer v. Essex Wire Corp., *supra* note 268; Fiedler v. Indianhead Truck Line, *supra* note 268; Borumka v. Rocky Mountain Hosp. & Medical Serv. dba Blue Cross/Blue Shield of Colo., *supra* note 268; James v. KID Broadcasting Corp., *supra* note 269; Wasilchuk v. Harvey's Wagon Wheel, 610 F. Supp. 206, 39 FEP 237 (D. Nev. 1985); Karr v. Township of Lower Merion, *supra* note 268; Rawson v. Sears, Roebuck & Co., 585 F. Supp. 1393, 35 FEP 113 (D. Colo. 1984); James v. Miller-Wohl Co., *supra* note 268; Johnson v. Al Tech Specialty Steel Corp., *supra* note 268; Prouty v. National R.R. Passenger Corp., *supra* note 268; Helwig v. Suburban Chevrolet, *supra* note 268 (even to victim of retaliation).

[273]*See, e.g.,* Heiar v. Crawford County, 746 F.2d 1190, 35 FEP 1458, *amended,* 36 FEP 112 (7th Cir. 1984), *cert. denied,* 472 U.S. 1027, 37 FEP 1883 (1985) (litigation expenses distinct from statutory costs or a lawyer's hourly billing rate, *e.g.,* postage, long distance phone calls, photocopying, travel, paralegal time, and expert witnesses included in reasonable attorney's fee); Leftwich v. Harris-Stowe State College, 702 F.2d 686, 31 FEP 376 (8th Cir. 1983); Hagelthorn v. Kennecott Corp., 710 F.2d 76, 33 FEP 977 (2d Cir. 1983) (court has no discretion to deny fees to prevailing plaintiff, only discretion as to amount of allowable fees); Monroe v. United Airlines, 736 F.2d 394, 34 FEP 1622 (7th Cir. 1984), *cert. denied,* 470 U.S. 1004, 37 FEP 64 (1985) (difficulty of issues, skill demonstrated by counsel, and size of recovery warranted enhancement of fee by $75 per hour); Babb v. Sun Co., 562 F. Supp. 491, 31 FEP 1340 (D. Minn. 1983) (legal assistant fees awardable as attorney's fees, not costs, but at reduced rate of $22.50 per hour).

[274]*See, e.g.,* Coleman v. City of Omaha, 714 F.2d 804, 33 FEP 1462 (8th Cir. 1983) (plaintiff should not have been denied, as costs, expert witness fees beyond statutory minimum because he failed to obtain prior court approval for his use of expert witness; remanded for finding concerning necessity or usefulness of evidence). *But see* Leftwich v. Harris-Stowe State College, *supra* note 273 (Lexis is component of attorney's fees which cannot be taxed independently as cost item in addition to attorney's fees award).

[275]Cancellier v. Federated Dep't Stores, *supra* note 269; Bruno v. Western Elec. Co., 618 F. Supp. 398, 38 FEP 1679 (D. Colo. 1985); *See* Chapter 39 (Attorney's Fees).

[276]Jones v. Central Soya Co., 748 F.2d 586, 38 FEP 1386 (11th Cir. 1984).

[277]*See, e.g.,* Cooper v. Singer, 719 F.2d 1496, 114 LRRM 3667 (10th Cir. 1983), *on reh'g of* 689 F.2d 929 (10th Cir. 1982) (en banc) (contingent fee arrangement does not limit client's recovery for attorney's fees under civil rights statute; if client's recovery is less than amount owed to attorney under fee arrangement, lawyer should reduce fee to amount of court award; if award is greater than fee arrangement, lawyer entitled to full amount); Criswell v. Western Airlines, 709 F.2d 544, 32 FEP 1204 (9th Cir. 1983), *aff'd,* 472 U.S. 400, 37 FEP 1829 (1985) (district court did not abuse its discretion in awarding fees in amount greater than that contracted for by plaintiffs); Spagnuolo v. Whirlpool Corp., 717 F.2d 114, 32 FEP 1382 (4th Cir. 1983) (attorney's fee award, which amounted to 43% more than that requested by plaintiff's attorneys, excessive); Sullivan v. Crown Paper Bd. Co., 719 F.2d 667, 33 FEP 13 (3d Cir. 1983) (recovery of both statutory and contingent fees might be allowed in appropriate circumstances, but here trial court must on remand permit recovery only of greater of the two).

[278]*See, e.g.,* Koyen v. Consolidated Edison Co. of N.Y., 560 F. Supp. 1161, 31 FEP 488 (S.D.N.Y. 1983). *See also* Bleakley v. Jekyll Island-State Park Auth., 536 F. Supp. 236, 29 FEP 1525 (S.D. Ga. 1982) (upheld); Kennedy v. Whitehurst, 690 F.2d 951, 29 FEP 1373 (D.C. Cir. 1982); Palmer v. General Servs. Admin., 787 F.2d 300, 40 FEP 630 (8th Cir. 1986) (unauthorized).

Attorney's fees have been awarded under the Equal Access to Justice Act[279] to an employer that prevailed in an ADEA action brought by the EEOC.[280] Defendants have also been given their attorney's fees where the action was maintained in bad faith[281] or after it became clear that there were no grounds upon which the plaintiff could prevail.[282] Costs have also been granted to prevailing defendants.[283]

An award that exceeds the amount of attorney's fees requested may be set aside as punitive.[284] Moreover, an award against an intervenor who attempted to block a settlement between the plaintiff and his employer was deemed impermissible.[285] The Eleventh Circuit has held that absent a controlling local rule, "only unfair surprise or prejudice may render untimely a postjudgment motion for attorney's fees."[286]

## H. Prejudgment Interest

Most courts agree that prejudgment interest is not allowable under the ADEA where liquidated damages have been awarded to the plaintiff.[287] Absent liquidated damages, prejudgment interest has been awarded where deemed necessary to make the plaintiff whole.[288] The failure to request prejudgment interest of the jury has been held to preclude a subsequent request for such an award from the district court judge.[289]

---

[279] 28 U.S.C. § 2412 (1981).

[280] EEOC v. Western Elec. Co., 33 FEP 1259 (S.D. Tex. 1983) (full expert witness fees also awarded in light of EEOC's bad faith in bringing case).

[281] Morgan v. Union Metal Mfg. Co., 757 F.2d 792, 37 FEP 625 (6th Cir. 1985); Gray v. New England Tel. & Tel. Co., 792 F.2d 251, 260 n.1, 40 FEP 1597, 1604 n.1 (1st Cir. 1986) (recognizing, but denying fee recovery, under bad-faith exception to American rule as discussed in *Alyeska Pipeline Serv. Co. v. Wilderness Soc'y,* 421 U.S. 240, 10 FEP 826 (1975). See Second Edition at p. 528.

[282] Cote v. James River Corp., 761 F.2d 60, 37 FEP 1243 (1st Cir. 1985). *See also* Carvahlo v. MacArthur Corp., 615 F. Supp. 164, 37 FEP 1587 (S.D. Fla. 1985) (fees for obtaining dismissal of claims for compensatory or punitive damages); Gianfriddo v. Western Union Tel. Co., 787 F.2d 6 (1st Cir. 1986) (frivolous appeal).

[283] Matthews v. Allis-Chalmers, 769 F.2d 1215, 38 FEP 1118 (7th Cir. 1985).

[284] *See, e.g.,* Kolb v. Goldring, Inc., 694 F.2d 869, 30 FEP 633 (1st Cir. 1982); Spagnuolo v. Whirlpool Corp., *supra* note 277 (attorney's fee excessive where 43% more than requested).

[285] Richardson v. Alaska Airlines, 750 F.2d 763, 36 FEP 986 (9th Cir. 1984).

[286] O'Donnell v. Georgia Osteopathic Hosp., 574 F. Supp. 214, 36 FEP 944 (N.D. Ga. 1983), *aff'd in part, rev'd in part and remanded on other grounds,* 748 F.2d 1543, 36 FEP 953 (11th Cir. 1984).

[287] *Compare* Blim v. Western Elec. Co., 731 F.2d 1473, 1479, 34 FEP 757, 761 (10th Cir.), *cert. denied,* 469 U.S. 874, 36 FEP 816 (1984) (not allowed), Kossman v. Calumet County, 800 F.2d 697, 41 FEP 1355 (7th Cir. 1986), *cert. denied,* 479 U.S. 1088, 43 FEP 80 (1987) (not entitled) *with* Reichman v. Bonsignore, Brignati & Mazzotta P.C., 818 F.2d 278, 43 FEP 1384 (2d Cir. 1987), Lindsey v. American Cast Iron Pipe Co., 810 F.2d 1094, 43 FEP 143 (11th Cir. 1987), Criswell v. Western Airlines, *supra* note 277 (allowed) *and* James v. KID Broadcasting Corp., 559 F. Supp. 1153, 38 FEP 439 (D. Utah 1983) (refused to strike from complaint). *See also* Rose v. National Cash Register Corp., 703 F.2d 225, 31 FEP 706 (6th Cir.), *cert. denied,* 464 U.S. 939, 33 FEP 48 (1983).

[288] Cline v. Roadway Express, 689 F.2d 481, 29 FEP 1365 (4th Cir. 1982). *See also* Heiar v. Crawford County, 746 F.2d 1190, 35 FEP 1458, *amended,* 36 FEP 112 (7th Cir. 1984), *cert. denied,* 472 U.S. 1027, 37 FEP 1883 (1985) (Seventh Circuit ordered trial court to consider factors including whether plaintiffs had to borrow money to maintain standard of living so that back pay award would go toward retiring loan, whether plaintiffs had refrained from borrowing but had lowered their standard of living instead, and employer's financial status); Berndt v. Kaiser Aluminum & Chem. Sales, 604 F. Supp. 962, 38 FEP 182 (E.D. Pa. 1985) (where liquidated damages not appropriate, but not on profit-sharing or pension benefits if these amounts would not have been payable until retirement).

[289] *See, e.g.,* Kolb v. Goldring, Inc., *supra* note 284.

## VII. BENEFITS

In 1983, the EEOC issued final regulations interpreting § 623(g) of the ADEA as amended by the Tax Equity and Fiscal Responsibility Act of 1982 (TEFRA), requiring that employers provide employees aged 65–69 with the same health care benefits they provide their younger employees.[290] Interim EEOC regulations interpreting provisions of the Deficit Reduction Act (DEFRA) affecting § 623(g) required that employers provide the same health care benefits to employee spouses aged 65–69 as to spouses under age 65.[291] Although initially approved by the EEOC, neither regulation was published in the *Federal Register.* On September 30, 1985, the EEOC voted to withdraw both the final TEFRA and interim DEFRA regulations.[292]

Early retirement incentive plans have been widely utilized by employers in recent years,[293] and challenges to their purposes and impact have generated a growing body of case law on the status of those plans under § 4(a)(1) and § 4(f)(2) of the ADEA. One question has been whether such plans are a prima facie violation of the ADEA under § 4(a)(1) if early retirement incentives are offered voluntarily and across-the-board. The Seventh Circuit held in *Henn v. National Geographic Society*[294] that such an early retirement plan was not presumptively discriminatory. In *Henn,* every advertising salesman of the National Geographic Society over age 55 was offered the option of early retirement with benefits including one year's salary, retirement benefits calculated as if the retiree had quit at 65, lifetime medical coverage as if the employee were still on the payroll, and some supplemental life insurance coverage. The recipients had two months to consider the offer. On such facts, the Seventh Circuit held that an employee to whom the offer of early retirement was extended was the beneficiary of any distinction based on age, and that "none can claim to be adversely affected by discrimination in the design or offer of the early retirement package."[295] The court held that "voluntariness" was established by the employees' opportunity to make an informed choice free from fraud or other misconduct, and that an employee's asserted difficulty in choosing between two desirable choices—here, between continued employment and early retirement—does not preclude a finding that the employee's decision was voluntary.[296] In *Paolillo v. Dresser Industries*

---

[290]These regulations were intended to implement statutory changes incorporated in the Tax Equity and Fiscal Responsibility Act of 1982, Pub. L. No. 97-248, 96 Stat. 324 (TEFRA) (approved September 3, 1982), as a new amendment to the ADEA, 29 U.S.C. § 623(g).

[291]These interim regulations were intended to implement the provisions of the Deficit Reduction Act, Pub. L. No. 98-369 (DEFRA) (1984).

[292]50 FED. REG. 50614 (1985). The EEOC began the rulemaking process again in 1988, in an advance notice of proposed rulemaking, but no proposed rules had been issued as this Supplement went to press. *See* 53 FED. REG. 26789 (1988).

[293]*See Offering of Early Retirement Windows on Rise at Top Industrials, Wyatt Says,* 134 DAILY LAB. REP. A-12 (BNA, July 15, 1987), summarizing the Wyatt Company's, "Top 50: A Survey of Retirement, Thrift and Profit-Sharing Plans Covering Salaried Employees of 50 Large U.S. Industrial Companies as of January 1, 1987."

[294]819 F.2d 824, 43 FEP 1620 (7th Cir.), *cert. denied,* 484 U.S. —, 45 FEP 520 (1987). *See also* Gray v. New England Tel. & Tel. Co., 792 F.2d 251, 40 FEP 1597 (1st Cir. 1986); Coburn v. Pan Am. World Airways, 711 F.2d 339, 32 FEP 843 (D.C. Cir.), *cert. denied,* 464 U.S. 994, 33 FEP 440 (1983); Bodnar v. Synpol, Inc., 843 F.2d 190, 46 FEP 1086 (5th Cir. 1988); Ackerman v. Diamond Shamrock Corp., 670 F.2d 66, 27 FEP 1563 (6th Cir. 1982).

[295]*Id.,* 43 FEP at 1623.

[296]*Id.*

*(Paolillo II),* [297] after withdrawing an earlier decision *(Paolillo I)* [298] holding that voluntary early retirement programs by definition establish prima facie violations of the ADEA under § 4(a)(1), the Second Circuit reversed summary judgment for the employer, and remanded the case for trial of whether the employees participated voluntarily and whether the plan was a subterfuge under § 4(f)(2). In the *Paolillo* litigation, the employer had offered elective termination to all employees aged 60 and over, providing severance pay and other benefits to employees who agreed to retire early. The notice period varied from one to six days, measured from the date each participant received full information about the plan. [299]

Early retirement plans which exclude employees eligible for early retirement benefits have been held unprotected under § 4(f)(2) by the Third and Ninth Circuits. The Third Circuit held in *EEOC v. Westinghouse Electric Corp.* [300] that a layoff income and benefit plan which excluded those eligible for early retirement pension benefits was not a bona fide benefit plan protected by § 4(f)(2) and, accordingly, was unlawful under § 4(a)(1) because it operated to penalize older employees. Similarly, the Ninth Circuit held in *EEOC v. Borden's* [301] that a severance pay plan which excluded employees beyond age 55 in light of their eligibility for early retirement benefits was not a bona fide employee benefit plan under § 4(f)(2), and was unlawful under § 4(a)(1) on the theory of both disparate treatment and disparate impact. On the other hand, the Seventh Circuit affirmed a finding of no violation where the plaintiff himself opted for retirement status instead of layoff. [302]

Voluntary early retirement plans providing lower benefits for older employees are not for that reason precluded from protection under § 4(f)(2). The Eighth Circuit held in *Patterson v. Independent School District 709* [303] that a pension plan providing diminishing incentives for early retirement as one passed the age of 55 was a bona fide employee benefit plan within the meaning of § 4(f)(2), where the plan was entirely voluntary and the time and manner of payment were determined by the mutual agreement of the employer and the employee. While not foreclosing a similar ultimate result, the Second Circuit reversed summary judgment for the employer in *Cipriano v. North Tonawanda, N.Y., Board of Education* [304] under a § 4(f)(2) defense with

---

[297] 821 F.2d 81, 44 FEP 71 (2d Cir. 1987).

[298] Paolillo v. Dresser Indus., 813 F.2d 583, 43 FEP 338 (2d Cir. 1987).

[299] *Id.*

[300] 725 F.2d 211, 224, 33 FEP 945, 954 (3d Cir. 1983), *amended,* 33 FEP 1816 (3d Cir.), *cert. denied,* 469 U.S. 820, 35 FEP 1607 (1984) ("the thread common to [Section 4(f)(2)] retirement, insurance and pension plans, but not found in the * * * [challenged] plan, is the age related cost factor") (Belleville, N.J. plant). *See also* EEOC v. Westinghouse Elec. Corp., 632 F. Supp. 343, 40 FEP 643 (E.D. Pa. 1986) (Lester, Pa. plant); EEOC v. Babcock & Wilcox Co., 43 FEP 736 (E.D.N.C. 1987).

[301] 724 F.2d 1390, 33 FEP 1708 (9th Cir. 1984). *And compare* EEOC v. Great Atl. & Pac. Tea Co., 618 F. Supp. 115, 38 FEP 827 (W.D. Ohio 1985) (same result as in *Borden's*) *with* Britt v. E.I. du Pont de Nemours & Co., 768 F.2d 593, 38 FEP 833 (4th Cir. 1985) (no violation of ADEA by making severance pay contingent on deferral of pension benefits; severance payments held to defer pension benefits just as would continuing to work, making severance payments a wage equivalent; court distinguished *EEOC v. Borden's, supra* and *EEOC v. Westinghouse Elec. Corp., supra* note 300, because severance payments there functioned as fringe benefits connected with plant closing and not as compensation for foregoing an entitlement to continue working).

[302] Parker v. Federal Nat'l Mortgage Ass'n, 567 F. Supp. 265, 33 FEP 1207 (N.D. Ill. 1983), *aff'd,* 741 F.2d 975, 35 FEP 893 (7th Cir. 1984).

[303] 742 F.2d 465, 35 FEP 1236 (8th Cir. 1984) (plan intended to "furnish an incentive for teachers to trigger or activate the general pension plan at an earlier age * * * ." 35 FEP at 1238; "sliding scale of diminishing benefits is manifestly appropriate." *Id.* at 1239).

[304] 785 F.2d 51, 40 FEP 355 (2d Cir. 1986) (Friendly, J.).

respect to a retirement plan offering retirement incentives to members of a bargaining unit between the ages of 55 and 60. The court held that the plan was bona fide under § 4(f)(2), "in the sense that employees benefited and substantial benefits were paid to employees who were covered by it." However, the Second Circuit remanded the case for further proceedings to determine whether the defendant employer and the defendant union could prove that the plan was not a subterfuge to evade the purposes of the ADEA, and thus meet the second requirement of the § 4(f)(2) defense.[305]

The Circuit Court for the District of Columbia has rejected an attempt by former and present employees of various employers to sue the EEOC on the ground their pension benefits were lower than required by the ADEA because of their employer's alleged refusal, in reliance upon an EEOC interpretative bulletin, to make contributions or provide service credits for work performed following their 65th birthday. The court held the plaintiffs lacked standing to sue the EEOC. The plaintiffs' purported injuries, the court ruled, were not fairly traceable to the bulletin, but resulted from independent actions of the employers.[306]

Preemption of state law age discrimination claims by the Employee Retirement Income Security Act (ERISA) has received judicial attention. The Ninth Circuit has concluded that ERISA preempted a state age discrimination law requiring an employer to provide pension credit or contributions for services rendered beyond age 65. The court held that the plan in question did not violate the ADEA and that preemption would therefore not impair the purposes of the ADEA.[307] The New Jersey Supreme Court has similarly found ERISA preemption where the plan complied with ERISA and, although the plan allegedly violated state age discrimination law, federal ADEA remedies were unavailable because the claim was untimely under that Act. Under those circumstances, the court concluded that the plan was preempted under § 514(a) of ERISA because it "relate[s] to" an "employee benefit plan" covered by ERISA, and that such preemption was not exempted by § 514(d) of ERISA because such preemption did not "impair" the ADEA, whose application was precluded in any event by the plaintiffs' untimely claim.[308]

---

[305]*Id.* at 57–59, 40 FEP at 360–62 ("All that we now decide is that even in the case of voluntary early retirement plans the employer—and also here the union—must come up with some evidence that the plan is not a subterfuge to evade the purposes of the ADEA by showing a legitimate business reason for structuring the plan as it did. * * * We would not wish our decision here to be read as a disapproval of voluntary early retirement plans in general or of this plan in particular. The evidence of business reasons required to show that a voluntary plan is not a subterfuge would almost necessarily be less than what was required to make such a showing in the case of a mandatory plan." *Id.* at 58–59, 40 FEP at 361–62.).

[306]Von Aulock v. Smith, 720 F.2d 176, 33 FEP 3 (D.C. Cir. 1983). Bell v. Purdue Univ. Trustees, 658 F. Supp. 184, 43 FEP 901 (N.D. Ind. 1987). *But see* American Ass'n of Retired Persons v. EEOC, 655 F. Supp. 228, 43 FEP 119 (D.D.C. 1987) (writ of mandamus issued ordering EEOC to rescind bulletin and publish for notice and comment proposed new rule).

[307]Champion Int'l Corp. v. Brown, 731 F.2d 1406, 34 FEP 1154 (9th Cir. 1984). In the Omnibus Budget Reconciliation Act of 1986, Congress added § 4(i), requiring employers to make pension contributions, allocations, and accruals without regard to age. The EEOC issued proposed rules under § 4(i) in November 1987, but their finalization has been delayed pending Treasury Department review. 52 FED. REG. 45360 (1987).

[308]Nolan v. Otis Elevator Corp., 102 N.J. 30, 505 A.2d 580, 40 FEP 281 (N.J. 1986), *rev'g* 197 N.J. Super. 468, 485 A.2d 312, 36 FEP 1109 (App. Div. 1984).

## VIII. THE REDUCTION IN FORCE

Cases involving reductions in force (RIFs) have multiplied during the economic recession of the early 1980s and the corporate mergers, acquisitions, and reorganizations which have continued in more recent years.[309] Courts generally recognize that the central issue raised by a challenged layoff is usually not whether the economic or corporate decision to cut back the work force has a substantial business-related basis, but whether the employer appropriately selected particular individuals to be separated, especially where some individuals are transferred while others are discharged.[310]

Employers confronted with forced cost reductions have based selections for employment termination on various factors. RIFs using seniority,[311] total job elimination,[312] or reasonable production standards[313] as the selection criterion tend to avoid significant ADEA problems because the standard is objectively defined without incorporating age as a factor. However, factors such as compensation,[314] pension eligibility,[315] or apparently subjective performance appraisals[316] are more likely to be challenged. Employer selections for termination and retention based on proven performance[317] or upon skill and ability[318] have been sustained where the rating system was fair and the selection criteria were consistently applied. RIFs by inverse seniority are almost universally accepted within the workplace and usually withstand challenge under the ADEA because they generally favor older workers.[319] Total job elimination typically does not raise ADEA issues unless job func-

---

[309]For decisions involving RIFs, *see supra* notes 48, 58, 63, 146, 148, 154, 158–159, 165–168, 170, 171, and 174.

[310]*Compare* Kirk v. Potter & Brumfield, 42 EPD ¶ 36,883 (S.D. Ind. 1986) (summary judgment denied to company which cut 500 employees) *with* Washburne v. Potter & Brumfield, 41 EPD ¶ 36,650 (S.D. Ind. 1986) (summary judgment granted in the same RIF).

[311]EEOC v. Wyoming Retirement Sys., 771 F.2d 1425, 38 FEP 1544 (10th Cir. 1985) (seniority rights honored).

[312]Holley v. Sanyo Mfg., 771 F.2d 1161, 38 FEP 1317 (8th Cir. 1985) (RIF involving eliminated positions).

[313]Surrisi v. Conwed Corp., 510 F.2d 1088, 10 FEP 707 (8th Cir. 1975) (failure to meet new sales goals).

[314]Dace v. ACF Indus., 722 F.2d 374, 33 FEP 788 (8th Cir. 1983), op. adhered to as supplemented by 728 F.2d 976, 40 FEP 1604 (8th Cir. 1984) (under specific facts held not discriminatory); Duffy v. Wheeling Pittsburgh Steel Corp., 738 F.2d 1393, 35 FEP 246 (3d Cir.), *cert. denied,* 469 U.S. 1087, 36 FEP 712 (1984) (termination of higher-paid employees linked to age where steel company terminated four oldest and most highly paid salesmen).

[315]EEOC v. Chrysler Corp., 546 F. Supp. 54, 29 FEP 284, *clarified,* 546 F. Supp. 73, 29 FEP 1385 (E.D. Mich. 1982), *aff'd,* 733 F.2d 1183, 34 FEP 1401, *petition for reh'g en banc denied,* 738 F.2d 167, 41 FEP 1011 (6th Cir. 1984) (involuntary retirement for employees over 55). *See also* notes 300–302 and accompanying text.

[316]Kirk v. Potter & Brumfield, *supra* note 310.

[317]Chappell v. GTE Prods. Corp., 803 F.2d 261, 42 FEP 23 (6th Cir. 1986), *cert. denied,* 480 U.S. 919, 43 FEP 160 (1987) (termination of personnel with lowest personnel evaluations, approved).

[318]Grigsby v. Reynolds Metals Co., 821 F.2d 590, 44 FEP 449 (11th Cir. 1987); Stendebach v. CPC Int'l, 691 F.2d 735, 30 FEP 233 (5th Cir. 1982), *cert. denied,* 461 U.S. 944, 31 FEP 1296 (1983) (committee developed job qualifications for all remaining positions and then objectively ranked current employees based on job-related skills; employer granted summary judgment in six other cases arising from same RIF based on Fifth Circuit's approval of selection methods utilized in this case); Massarsky v. General Motors Corp., 706 F.2d 111, 31 FEP 832 (3d Cir.), *cert. denied,* 464 U.S. 937, 33 FEP 48 (1983) (layoff selection process approved); Bossalina v. Lever Bros. Co., 40 EPD ¶ 36,259 (D. Md. 1986) (comparison of job performance and skills approved where employee negligently destroyed entire production line); Hansen v. Continental Ill. Nat'l Bank & Trust, No. 83-C-8961 (N.D. Ill. 1986) (least skilled employee released); Arnell v. Pan Am. World Airways, 41 EPD ¶ 36,506 (S.D.N.Y. 1986) (peer analysis system for judging performance upheld).

[319]Gill v. Union Carbide Corp., 368 F. Supp. 364, 7 FEP 571 (E.D. Tenn. 1973).

tion or personnel transfers also occur.[320] Reasonable production quantities have been held to be valid criteria where they are attainable and equally applied.[321] Use of pension eligibility or compensation levels as the criteria for termination, however, risks ADEA liability under a disparate impact analysis.[322]

Voluntary early retirement programs have generally met with court approval except when the alternative is constructive discharge.[323]

An employer is likely to be at risk where there are no clearly articulated selection standards or review processes, and circumstantial evidence (including derogatory age-related remarks) exists from which age discrimination could be inferred.[324] On the other hand, mere subjective qualification assessments, based on the discretionary judgments of supervisors, do not make such assessments illegal.[325]

Litigation concerning RIFs may be affected by confusion between seniority and age discrimination.[326] The Fifth Circuit has emphasized that "the seniority a given plaintiff has accumulated entitles him to no better or worse treatment in an age discrimination suit."[327]

RIF cases continue to create special difficulties for the *McDonnell Douglas* analysis of whether a prima facie case has been established and, if so, what is required to rebut the prima facie case.[328] Recognizing the special circumstances of RIF cases, the Fifth Circuit in *Williams v. General Motors Corp.*[329] established a three-prong test for establishing a prima facie case: (1) the plaintiff was within the protected age group and was discharged or

---

[320]Massarsky v. General Motors Corp., *supra* note 318.

[321]Nolting v. Yellow Freight Sys., 799 F.2d 1192, 41 FEP 1068 (8th Cir. 1986).

[322]EEOC v. Chrysler Corp., *supra* note 315 (involuntary retirement for employees over 55 while all employees under 55 were laid off subject to recall in order of seniority, clearly illegal); Kneisley v. Hercules, Inc., 577 F. Supp. 726, 33 FEP 1579 (D. Del. 1983). *But see* Holt v. Gamewell Corp., 797 F.2d 36, 41 FEP 585 (1st Cir. 1986) (RIF required to reduce costs; use of high salary as criterion along with ability to absorb work of eliminated position elsewhere did not establish discriminatory impact).

[323]Henn v. National Geographic Soc'y, 819 F.2d 824, 43 FEP 1620 (7th Cir.), *cert. denied*, 484 U.S. —, 45 FEP 520 (1987); Calhoun v. Acme Cleveland Corp., 798 F.2d 559, 41 FEP 1121 (1st Cir. 1986). *See* Section VII and accompanying notes, *supra*.

[324]*See, e.g.,* Duffy v. Wheeling Pittsburgh Steel Corp., 33 FEP 730 (E.D. Pa. 1983), *aff'd*, 738 F.2d 1393, 35 FEP 246 (3d Cir.), *cert. denied*, 469 U.S. 1087, 36 FEP 712 (1984) (employees laid off whose performances were superior to those retained; statements attributed to officer that company "was anxious to get younger and more aggressive people"; performance-based selection not sustained by testimony; court's finding of pretext held not clearly erroneous); Rose v. National Cash Register Corp., 703 F.2d 225, 31 FEP 706 (6th Cir.), *cert. denied*, 464 U.S. 939, 33 FEP 48 (1983) (no clearly defined selection criteria and age-related remarks); Franci v. Avco Corp., Avco Lycoming Div., 538 F. Supp. 250, 258, 31 FEP 347 (D. Conn. 1982) (direct evidence of age discrimination as well as impermissible selection criteria including cutting higher salaries). *But see* Haskell v. Kaman Corp., 743 F.2d 113, 35 FEP 941 (2d Cir. 1984) (district court erred in allowing testimony concerning remarks: (1) uttered over a 15-year period and (2) by former company officers concerning their own terminations; remand for new trial).

[325]EEOC v. Western Elec. Co., 713 F.2d 1011, 32 FEP 708 (4th Cir. 1983).

[326]*See* Barber v. American Airlines, 791 F.2d 658, 660–61, 40 FEP 1565 (8th Cir.), *cert. denied*, 479 U.S. 885, 41 FEP 1712 (1986).

[327]Williams v. General Motors Corp., 656 F.2d 120, 130 n.17, 26 FEP 1381, 1388–89 n.17 (5th Cir. 1981), *cert. denied*, 455 U.S. 943, 27 FEP 1765 (1982).

[328]McCorstin v. United States Steel Corp., 621 F.2d 749, 754, 23 FEP 320 (5th Cir. 1980) (in RIF situations threshold requirement of replacement inappropriate); *accord* Stumph v. Thomas & Skinner, 770 F.2d 93, 38 FEP 1114 (7th Cir. 1985) (replacement not required, summary judgment reversed) *and* Holley v. Sanyo Mfg., 771 F.2d 1161, 38 FEP 1317 (8th Cir. 1985) (confused analysis of replacement issue).

[329]*Supra* note 327. *See also* Stendebach v. CPC Int'l, 691 F.2d 735, 30 FEP 233 (5th Cir. 1982), *cert. denied*, 461 U.S. 944, 31 FEP 1296 (1983); Allison v. Western Union Tel. Co., 680 F.2d 1318, 29 FEP 393 (11th Cir. 1982); Branson v. Price River Coal Co., 627 F. Supp. 1324, 45 FEP 833 (D. Utah 1986). *But see* Sherrod v. Sears, Roebuck & Co., 785 F.2d 1312, 40 FEP 717 (5th Cir. 1986) (age not a factor).

demoted by defendant's employment decision; (2) the plaintiff was qualified to assume another position at the time of the discharge or demotion; and (3) the plaintiff produced evidence, circumstantial or direct, from which the trier of fact might reasonably conclude that the employer intended to discriminate in reaching the decision at issue. In *Williams,* the court held that the third element required that the evidence must lead the trier of fact reasonably to conclude either (1) that defendant consciously refused to consider retaining a plaintiff because of age, or (2) defendant regarded age as a negative factor in such consideration.[330] The Fifth Circuit held in *Thornbrough v. Columbus & Greenville Railroad*[331] that the third requirement of *Williams* could be read as either heightening or lessening the proof required for a prima facie case, and that discharge, coupled with the retention of younger employees, created a presumption of discrimination. The court also pointed out in *Thornbrough* that the plaintiff could show that an employer's proffered reason for termination of the older employee was pretextual, if the plaintiff was "clearly" better qualified than the employee who was retained.[332]

Several RIF cases suggest that courts may prefer to rely on comparative evidence[333] or statistical evidence[334] instead of circumstantial evidence[335] and that admissions or other direct evidence of age discrimination will make a disparate treatment analysis unnecessary.[336]

---

[330]Williams v. General Motors Corp., *supra* note 327.

[331]760 F.2d 633, 37 FEP 1414 (5th Cir. 1985).

[332]*Id.*

[333]Christie v. Foremost Ins. Co., 785 F.2d 584, 40 FEP 508 (7th Cir. 1986) (comparative evidence used—performance RIFs); LaGrant v. Gulf & W. Mfg., Co., 748 F.2d 1087, 36 FEP 465 (6th Cir. 1984); Thornbrough v. Columbus & Greenville R.R., *supra* note 331; Rosengarten v. J.C. Penney Co., 605 F. Supp. 154, 37 FEP 670 (E.D.N.Y. 1985); Szymczak v. Jones & Laughlin Steel Corp., 614 F. Supp. 532, 39 FEP 126 (W.D. Pa. 1985), *aff'd,* 791 F.2d 922 (3d Cir. 1986).

[334]Ridenour v. Lawson Co., 791 F.2d 52, 40 FEP 1455 (6th Cir. 1986) (statistical analysis based on FLSA-exempt employees retained refuted inference of age discrimination as average of remaining employees increased from 41.28 to 41.72 years); Hawks v. Ingersoll Johnson Steel Co., 583 F. Supp. 983, 38 FEP 93 (S.D. Ind. 1984) (statistics and desire to seek younger image). *But see* Kittredge v. Parker Hannifin Corp., 597 F. Supp. 605, 38 FEP 476 (W.D. Mich. 1984) (statistical sample too small).

[335]Haskell v. Kaman Corp., 743 F.2d 113, 35 FEP 941 (2d Cir. 1984); Sorosky v. Burroughs Corp., 37 FEP 1510 (C.D. Cal. 1985); Parker v. Federal Nat'l Mortgage Ass'n, 741 F.2d 975, 35 FEP 893 (7th Cir. 1984).

[336]Lindsey v. American Cast Iron Pipe Co., 772 F.2d 799, 39 FEP 14 (11th Cir. 1985) (direct statements that employer is looking for "younger person" coupled with a decision adverse to protected class member is substantial direct evidence to support jury verdict; disparate treatment analysis in *McDonnell Douglas* cannot be used to override jury verdict.

CHAPTER 15

# REPRISAL AND RETALIATION

## I. An Overview of the Two Clauses of § 704(a)

Several courts have held that a plaintiff need not file a separate charge of retaliation under § 704(a) before including a retaliation claim in a complaint filed in the district court.[1]

The Fifth Circuit has joined other courts in holding that the protections of § 704(a) apply to former employees.[2]

Courts have addressed litigation in multiple forums with respect to the retaliation provisions of § 704(a), with varying results. The Fourth Circuit has refused, in *Ross v. Communications Satellite Corp.,*[3] to allow the adverse findings of a state unemployment compensation proceeding to collaterally estop a plaintiff's Title VII claim of retaliatory discharge. In *Benton v. Kroger*

---

[1]Gupta v. East Tex. State Univ., 654 F.2d 411, 26 FEP 1081 (5th Cir. 1981) (a former employee who had filed an EEOC charge was not required to file subsequent charge to litigate allegations that his employer retaliated against him for filing the first charge); Waiters v. Parsons, 729 F.2d 233, 34 FEP 178 (3d Cir. 1984) (where EEOC investigation went beyond the specific retaliation alleged in charge and found evidence of retaliatory intent in pattern of actions, complaint based upon this pattern may not be dismissed for failure to exhaust administrative remedies); Howze v. Jones & Laughlin Steel Corp., 750 F.2d 1208, 36 FEP 1026 (3d Cir. 1984) (mere adding of claim of retaliation in amended complaint not sufficient reason to deny motion to amend where employer did not argue it would be prejudiced); EEOC v. West Co., 40 FEP 1024 (E.D. Pa. 1986) (plaintiff allowed to intervene in EEOC action on her behalf; further EEOC conciliation unlikely to produce results; no purpose in requiring new charge of discrimination); Thompson v. Machinists, 33 FEP 641 (D.D.C. 1983) (plaintiff allowed to amend her complaint by adding claim of retaliatory discharge, although only race and sex discrimination alleged in her EEOC charge, because facts presented to EEOC were the same facts on which retaliation claim was based); Lazic v. University of Pa., 513 F. Supp. 761, 29 FEP 1652 (E.D. Pa. 1981) (failure of former university faculty member to raise her retaliation claim before EEOC did not preclude her from litigating that issue in her Title VII action where claim was related to original charge and reasonably might be expected to grow out of investigation of that charge); Stiessberger v. Rockwell Int'l Corp., 29 FEP 1273 (E.D. Wash. 1982) (because retaliation is alleged to have stemmed from filing of original EEOC charge, subsequent charge is unnecessary); Scott v. City of Overland Park, 595 F. Supp. 520, 41 FEP 1211 (D. Kan. 1984) (failure to use term "retaliation" in EEOC charge does not bar its litigation in Title VII failure to promote case). *Compare* Malave v. Bolger, 599 F. Supp. 221, 41 FEP 226 (D. Conn. 1984) (plaintiff allowed to amend complaint to add allegations of retaliatory conduct against federal employer in spite of sovereign immunity principles) *with* Sims v. Heckler, 725 F.2d 1143, 33 FEP 1786 (7th Cir. 1984) (plaintiff's failure to comply with 29 C.F.R. § 1613.214(a)(1)(i) bars him from bringing Title VII action against federal employer where principles of sovereign immunity control). *But see* Carter v. County of Allegheny, 498 F. Supp. 1298, 30 FEP 478 (W.D. Pa. 1980) (complaint filed more than 90 days after issuance of right to sue notice, alleging retaliation based on original EEOC charge, was barred); Wrenn v. New York City Health & Hosps. Corp., No. 82-CIV 6363, slip op. (S.D.N.Y. 1986) (since plaintiff's claim of retaliation concerned matters which reasonably could be expected to grow out of plaintiff's charge of race discrimination with the EEOC, plaintiff need not file subsequent retaliation claim).

It has been held under the ADEA that a plaintiff need not file a separate charge of retaliation before including a retaliation claim in a complaint under the ADEA. Jacobson v. American Home Prods. Corp., 36 FEP 559 (N.D. Ill. 1982).

[2]EEOC v. Cosmair, Inc., L'Oreal Hair Care Div., 821 F.2d 1085, 44 FEP 569 (5th Cir. 1987); *see also* Bilka v. Pepe's, Inc., 601 F. Supp. 1254, 38 FEP 1655 (N.D. Ill. 1985).

[3]759 F.2d 355, 37 FEP 797 (4th Cir. 1985), *rev'g* 34 FEP 260 (D. Md. 1984). *See also* Battle v. Isaac, 624 F. Supp. 1109, 40 FEP 1664 (N.D. Ill. 1986) (if plaintiff in Title VII retaliatory discharge action can make prima facie case by proving that employer did not discharge others for the same misconduct when it should have done so, plaintiff is not estopped by adverse state unemployment compensation ruling).

221

*Co.,*[4] the court held that issues litigated in a termination of employment case filed under Title VII are not applicable to a retaliatory discharge claim filed under the state workers' compensation laws. Since there is no issue of collateral estoppel, plaintiff could not join the unrelated claims. In *Brown v. Manufacturers Hanover Trust Co.,*[5] the court barred a plaintiff, under the doctrine of *res judicata,* from relitigating her Title VII retaliation claim in federal court when she had previously sought judicial redress in state court, even though the state court action was still on appeal.

The Fifth Circuit limited the employer's discovery objections in *Whitaker v. Carney,*[6] holding that the retaliation clause does not impose upon the employer the duty of preventing nonworkplace retaliation by nonemployees. The employer thus was compelled to disclose to an alleged sexual harasser who had since resigned the names of those who had complained.

## II. The Participation Clause

The Eleventh Circuit has held that an employee who allegedly was refused a promotion after having testified in favor of a female co-worker during a sex discrimination hearing could seek relief under the participation clause of § 704(a).[7] Protection against retaliation under § 704(a) has been extended to the spouse of an employee who was also an employee of the same company, and who supported and aided his wife in the filing of an EEOC charge.[8] Courts continue to hold that the plaintiff may establish a violation of the participation clause without proving that the underlying claim of discrimination was valid.[9]

The participation clause has been interpreted broadly enough to cover the case of an employee who had informed his employer of his intent to file a charge of reverse discrimination.[10] The court in that case also noted the problems arising from a claim of protection under the participation clause before the charge is filed:

> "[W]hen the conduct of the plaintiff that produces the retaliation predates the actual filing of a charge, that conduct must have a sufficiently close connection with EEOC charge-filing before it will be protected by the 'participation' clause."[11]

## III. The Opposition Clause

The Seventh Circuit has interpreted the opposition clause to cover a hospital employee who was terminated for hiring a black security department employee whose employment prompted an anonymous bomb threat.[12]

---

[4]635 F. Supp. 56, 122 LRRM 2734 (S.D. Tex. 1986).
[5]602 F. Supp. 549, 36 FEP 1830 (S.D.N.Y. 1984).
[6]778 F.2d 216, 39 FEP 987 (5th Cir. 1985), *cert. denied,* 479 U.S. 813, 41 FEP 1711 (1986).
[7]Smith v. Georgia, 684 F.2d 729, 29 FEP 1134 (11th Cir. 1982), *appeal after remand,* 749 F.2d 683, 36 FEP 1176 (11th Cir. 1985).
[8]Mandia v. Arco Chem. Co., 618 F. Supp. 1248, 39 FEP 793 (W.D. Pa. 1985).
[9]Novotny v. Great Am. Fed. Sav. & Loan Ass'n, 539 F. Supp. 437, 28 FEP 1796 (W.D. Pa. 1982), *on remand from* 442 U.S. 366, 19 FEP 1482 (1979).
[10]Croushorn v. University of Tenn. Bd. of Trustees, 518 F. Supp. 9, 30 FEP 168 (M.D. Tenn. 1980).
[11]*Id.* at 22, 30 FEP at 174.
[12]EEOC v. St. Anne's Hosp., 664 F.2d 128, 27 FEP 170 (7th Cir. 1981).

The protection of the opposition clause has also been extended to an administrative foreman who took vacation and picketed, for apparently discrimination-related reasons, an annual meeting of the company's supervisory staff that she should have attended.[13] A waitress who had complained to her employer about sexual harassment from customers was determined by the EEOC to have engaged in protected activity opposing unlawful sexual harassment when she contacted an attorney about the harassment. Thus, her termination for contacting the attorney constituted retaliatory action by the employer.[14] Similarly, a complaint by a loan officer to a bank vice president that she was sexually harassed by a co-employee was deemed to constitute protected opposition to an unlawful employment practice.[15]

Courts have declined to protect employees under the opposition clause where their activities appear unrelated to protests against discriminatory practices. The opposition clause thus did not cover the conduct of an employee who was discharged for protesting his employer's decision not to transfer his secretary after he was transferred to a new job, because the employee had not protested the transfer policies of his employer as being discriminatory.[16] The actions of two college professors also were denied protection under the opposition clause where their involvement in a labor dispute with the school administration and in union organizing activities was viewed as unrelated to the protestation of discriminatory policies.[17] Similarly, the Ninth Circuit has held that a radio announcer who was discharged for violating a station's programming decision not to permit Spanish to be spoken on the air had not engaged in protected activity, where he had opposed the format change for personal reasons rather than because he believed it to be discriminatory.[18]

The Sixth Circuit has distinguished between activities related to affirmative action under Executive Order 11246 and employee actions opposing practices violating Title VII, and extended § 704(a) protection only to the latter. In *Holden v. Owens-Illinois,*[19] the Sixth Circuit held that an employee's overly aggressive attempts to force her employer into implementing a specific affirmative action program to comply with Executive Order 11246 did not constitute "opposition" protected by Title VII. Executive Order 11246 requires government contractors to establish affirmative action programs, but since Title VII does not mandate any affirmative action, the employee was not opposing a "practice" which violated Title VII.

## A. The Requirement That the Employment Practice Opposed Be "made * * * unlawful * * * by [Title VII]"

The Fifth, Seventh, and Ninth circuits have continued to hold that it is only necessary that an employee believe, in good faith, that the employ-

---

[13]Price v. Cannon Mills Co., 607 F. Supp. 1146, 39 FEP 708 (M.D.N.C. 1985).
[14]EEOC Dec. 84-3, 34 FEP 1887 (1984).
[15]Barrett v. Omaha Nat'l Bank, 584 F. Supp. 22, 35 FEP 585 (D. Neb. 1983), aff'd, 726 F.2d 424, 35 FEP 593 (8th Cir. 1984).
[16]McCluney v. Joseph Schlitz Brewing Co., 728 F.2d 924, 34 FEP 273 (7th Cir. 1984).
[17]Turner v. Barber-Scotia College, 604 F. Supp. 1450, 37 FEP 1642 (M.D.N.C. 1985).
[18]Jurado aka Valentine v. Eleven-Fifty Corp., 813 F.2d 1406, 43 FEP 870 (9th Cir. 1987).
[19]793 F.2d 745, 41 FEP 49 (6th Cir.), cert. denied, 479 U.S. 1008, 42 FEP 1536 (1986).

ment practice he or she opposes violates Title VII.[20] Recently, the Tenth Circuit also agreed that the existence of a good-faith belief that the practice opposed constitutes a Title VII violation is sufficient.[21]

## B. Whether Ambiguous Protests Constitute Protected Opposition

In *Gifford v. Atchison, Topeka & Santa Fe Railway*,[22] the plaintiff complained that a provision in the company's collective bargaining agreement with the union was disadvantageous to some female employees. Not until two years later did the plaintiff label her opposition as constituting opposition to "sex discrimination," leading the district court to conclude that the plaintiff's opposition to the collective bargaining agreement was not protected by the opposition clause. In reversing the district court on this point, the Ninth Circuit stated:

> "It does not follow that the employee must be aware that the practice is *unlawful under Title VII* at the time of the opposition in order for opposition to be protected. It requires a certain sophistication for an employee to recognize that an offensive employment practice may represent sex or race discrimination that is against the law. Here, Gifford argued from the outset that the collective bargaining agreement had a harsher impact on some of the women than it had on men."[23]

The Fourth Circuit held in *Holsey v. Armour & Co.*[24] that a black employee who had been frustrated in her effort to achieve a permanent position, having been bypassed in favor of less senior employees for work recalls, had engaged in protected opposition when she asked the employer whether her race influenced its treatment of her. One court determined that criticism of an alleged discriminatory hiring practice made to a supervisor in an informal "quasi-social setting" constituted opposition upon which a claim of retaliation could be based.[25] Similarly, where an employee was discharged after he gave a statement on behalf of a black employee involved in a pension dispute with their employer, the court held that the statement, which recounted racist comments by the employer-union, was protected activity under the opposition clause.[26] The Ninth Circuit reached a different result in *Jurado aka Valentine v. Eleven-Fifty Corp.*[27] with respect to a radio announcer who claimed that his discharge for speaking Spanish on the air was retaliation for participating in collective bargaining activities and for opposing an "English only" rule. The court found no evidence that the announcer had opposed any such rule prior to his termination, and concluded that his only concern was severance pay.

---

[20]DeAnda v. St. Joseph Hosp., 671 F.2d 850, 28 FEP 317 (5th Cir. 1982); Rucker v. Higher Educ. Aids Bd., 669 F.2d 1179, 27 FEP 1553 (7th Cir. 1982); EEOC v. Crown Zellerbach Corp., 720 F.2d 1008, 32 FEP 809 (9th Cir. 1983); Gifford v. Atchinson, Topeka & Santa Fe Ry., 685 F.2d 1149, 29 FEP 1345 *and* 34 FEP 240 (9th Cir. 1982); accord Croushorn v. University of Tenn. Bd. of Trustees, *supra* note 10; Zack v. City of Minneapolis, 35 FEP 1672 (D. Minn. 1984).

[21]Love v. Re/Max of Am., 738 F.2d 383, 35 FEP 565 (10th Cir. 1984). *See also* Mandia v. Arco Chem. Co., 618 F. Supp. 1248, 39 FEP 793 (W.D. Pa. 1985).

[22]*Supra* note 20.

[23]*Id.* at 1157, 29 FEP at 1350 (emphasis in original).

[24]743 F.2d 199, 35 FEP 1064 (4th Cir. 1984), *cert. denied,* 470 U.S. 1028, 37 FEP 192 (1985).

[25]Spence v. Auto Workers Local 1250, 595 F. Supp. 6, 35 FEP 1666 (N.D. Ohio 1984).

[26]Memmolo v. Commodore Business Machs., 36 FEP 1140 (E.D. Pa. 1984), *aff'd without opinion,* 770 F.2d 1072, 41 FEP 64 (3d Cir. 1985).

[27]630 F. Supp. 569, 39 FEP 1459 (C.D. Cal. 1985), *aff'd,* 813 F.2d 1406, 43 FEP 870 (9th Cir. 1987).

## C. Weighing the Disruption and Protection of Various Forms of Opposition

### 2. Serious, Public Opposition to the Employer's Goals

A black nurse engaged in protected activity by calling a press conference to highlight the poor care black patients received in a hospital.[28] Subsequent criticism of her work and her termination were found to be retaliatory in the absence of evidence to support the hospital's claim of poor work performance and lack of cooperation. Similarly, the Ninth Circuit held that a four-month disciplinary suspension constituted illegal retaliation when it was imposed on seven employees who publicly protested by sending a letter when a local school board, which was a major customer of their employer, gave an "affirmative action award" to the personnel manager of their employer.[29] The court held that the protest was not unreasonable even though it threatened the employer with economic harm, because the letter had no effect on the employees' job performance or on the workplace environment.[30] However, Title VII was held not to protect the public dissemination by a professor of letters and memoranda ridiculing school officials, where the professor felt he was the victim of racial discrimination. This was held to be conduct falling outside the protection of Title VII, and the ensuing reprimand did not constitute unlawful retaliation.[31]

### 4. Intra-Office Disruption

Where employee conduct in opposing employer practices has so interfered with that employee's job performance that it has rendered him ineffective, the EEOC determined that his discharge based upon that ineffectiveness is not retaliatory conduct by the employer.[32] Similarly, employees who are disruptive influences in their offices or who are unable to get along with co-workers may be terminated even if they have engaged in protected activity.[33] An employee also is not protected by Title VII when he or she violates legitimate company rules, knowingly disobeys company orders, disrupts the work environment of his or her employer, or willfully interferes with the attainment of the employer's goals.[34]

---

[28]Wrighten v. Metropolitan Hosps., 726 F.2d 1346, 33 FEP 1714 (9th Cir. 1984).

[29]EEOC v. Crown Zellerbach Corp., *supra* note 20.

[30]*Id.* at 1015–16, 32 FEP at 814–15.

[31]Araujo v. Boston College Trustees, 34 EPD ¶ 34,409 (D. Mass. 1983).

[32]EEOC Dec. 82–14, 31 FEP 1850 (1982); *see also* Jones v. Flagship Int'l dba Sky Chefs, 793 F.2d 714, 41 FEP 358 (5th Cir. 1986), *cert. denied,* 479 U.S. 1065, 43 FEP 80 (1987) (EEO personnel manager's action of filing a discrimination lawsuit against employer, suggesting class action suit and inviting others to sue or join in suit, rendered Jones ineffective in position for which she was employed).

[33]Johnson v. Allyn & Bacon, 34 FEP 795 (D. Mass. 1982), *aff'd,* 731 F.2d 64, 34 FEP 804 (1st Cir.), *cert. denied,* 469 U.S. 1018, 36 FEP 320 (1984).

[34]Unt v. Aerospace Corp., 765 F.2d 1440, 38 FEP 999 (9th Cir. 1985). ("It is apparent that Aerospace disciplined the appellant because of well documented performance deficiencies that were of a legitimate concern to Aerospace management and not because of any motive of reprisal for appellant's exercise of Title VII rights."); Smith v. Texas Dep't of Water Resources, 818 F.2d 363, 43 FEP 1727 (5th Cir. 1987), *cert. denied,* — U.S. — (refusal to perform specific job task despite being asked more than once under penalty of termination is not protected, despite the fact that task was unpalatable to employee, where it was not immoral, degrading, or dangerous to her health, nor did it have an immediate adverse effect on her salary or other terms of employment); Davis v. State Univ. of N.Y., 802 F.2d 638, 42 FEP 77 (2d Cir. 1986) (denial of merit increase and disciplinary documentation was result of atmosphere of acrimony, threatening integrity of institution, and not retaliation for filing charge).

Where a tenured economics professor claimed retaliation by the defendant for imposing various limitations upon him after the plaintiff had participated in an investigation of a job applicant's charge of sex discrimination, the court held that the defendant was justified in placing certain limitations on the plaintiff because of his history of disruptive and unprofessional conduct, and that the plaintiff's resignation after the limitations were imposed did not constitute a constructive discharge.[35] Similarly, another court held that a female office manager had not been demoted in retaliation for filing charges; the cause of her demotion was her disruption of the employer's operation and failure to cooperate with her superiors.[36] One court cautioned that employees higher on the management ladder should be more circumspect in expressing opposition to employment practices and that a high level official's poor judgment in confronting other management in front of employees therefore justified his termination.[37]

The Seventh Circuit has formulated a balancing test to assist in determining whether concerted absence from work to oppose alleged unlawful discrimination is protected against an employer's adverse action.

In *Mozee v. Jeffboat, Inc.*,[38] a class action was brought by black employees who had missed work to participate in "Black Days," a series of protests organized to combat employer treatment believed to be discriminatory. The court stated that if a prima facie case of retaliation is established, the district court should "balance any disruption caused by plaintiffs' absences against Black Days' advancement of Title VII's policy of eliminating discrimination."[39]

## IV. Whether Protection Extends to Persons Holding Special Kinds of Jobs

An equal opportunity specialist employed to serve as an advisor to a university's vice president owed a duty of loyalty to him and was expected to perform her duties within the framework of her position.[40] Therefore, releasing investigative reports concerning employment discrimination to a campus newspaper without her supervisor's prior approval and supplying information contained in personnel files without approval was not protected activity.

The Sixth Circuit has concluded that an employee hired to manage, design, and implement affirmative action programs is not entitled to special protection under Title VII when she instead acts like an EEOC Compliance Officer insisting that her employer implement a specific program.[41] The court

---

[35]Mitchell v. Visser, 529 F. Supp. 1034, 27 FEP 1312 (D. Kan. 1981).
[36]EEOC v. Mead Foods, 466 F. Supp. 1, 29 FEP 677 (W.D. Okla. 1977).
[37]Novotny v. Great Am. Fed. Sav. & Loan Ass'n, 539 F. Supp. 437, 28 FEP 1796 (W.D. Pa. 1982), *on remand from* 442 U.S. 366, 19 FEP 1482 (1979).
[38]746 F.2d 365, 35 FEP 1810 (7th Cir. 1984).
[39]*Id.* at 374, 35 FEP at 1817.
[40]Hamm v. Board of Regents of Fla., 708 F.2d 647, 32 FEP 441, *reh'g denied,* 715 F.2d 580 (11th Cir. 1983).
[41]Holden v. Owens-Illinois, 793 F.2d 745, 41 FEP 49 (6th Cir.), *cert. denied,* 479 U.S. 1008, 42 FEP 1536 (1986).

held that it was the employer's prerogative to decide how and when to implement an affirmative action program.[42]

In *Novotny v. Great American Federal Savings & Loan Association,*[43] the defendant's board, being upset with the plaintiff's public opposition to certain employment practices, did not reelect him as treasurer at its annual meeting and terminated his employment. In determining whether the plaintiff had properly channeled his disagreement with management's practices, the court

> "see[s] the test to be applied to Mr. Novotny as balancing the setting in which his opposition arose and was expressed against the interests, duties and motivations of both Novotny and the Association."[44]

After noting that it was "axiomatic" that the higher an employee was on the management ladder, the more circumspect he should be in expressing opposition to employment practices, the court concluded that the board had decided to terminate the plaintiff because he had conducted his opposition to management's practices in a manner and for a reason which would be unacceptable to even the fairest of managements.[45]

In considering an application for a preliminary injunction seeking reinstatement, a court may consider hostility between the plaintiff and his former colleagues as well as the potential that reinstatement could precipitate a breach of confidence or a conflict of interest.[46]

## V. TYPES OF ADVERSE TREATMENT COGNIZABLE UNDER § 704(a)

Claims of retaliatory conduct include, for example, actions of a supervisor in telephoning an employee at home, failing to provide her with information needed for her job, and attempting to create a false impression among co-workers that he had engaged in an affair with her;[47] constructively discharging an employee by reducing her hours of work by two-thirds;[48] giving an employee low marks on a promotion evaluation which prevented the employee's promotion;[49] disciplining an employee for violating the employer's unwritten rule against revealing confidential salary information necessary to process a discrimination charge filed by the employee;[50] giving an employee harder work assignments and finally discharging him after he refused to withdraw an EEOC charge at the employer's request;[51] destroying

---

[42]*Id.* at 753, 41 FEP at 56.

[43]*Supra* note 37.

[44]*Id.,* 539 F. Supp. at 450–51, 28 FEP at 1809.

[45]*Id.* at 451–52, 28 FEP at 1809–10.

[46]Holt v. Continental Group, 708 F.2d 87, 31 FEP 1468 (2d Cir. 1983), *rev'g* 542 F. Supp. 16, 29 FEP 618 (D. Conn. 1982), *cert. denied,* 465 U.S. 1030, 33 FEP 1884 (1984).

[47]Toscano v. Nimmo, 570 F. Supp. 1197, 32 FEP 1401 (D. Del. 1983).

[48]Thurber v. Jack Reilly's, Inc., 521 F. Supp. 238, 32 FEP 1508 (D. Mass. 1981), *aff'd,* 717 F.2d 633, 32 FEP 1511 (1st Cir. 1983), *cert. denied,* 466 U.S. 904, 34 FEP 544 (1984); Holsey v. Armour & Co., 743 F.2d 199, 35 FEP 1064 (4th Cir. 1984), *cert. denied,* 470 U.S. 1028, 37 FEP 192 (1985).

[49]Loiseau v. Department of Human Resources, 567 F. Supp. 1211, 39 FEP 289 (D. Or. 1983).

[50]EEOC v. Kansas City Power & Light Co., 32 FEP 1396 (W.D. Mo. 1981).

[51]Brady v. Thurston Motor Lines, 726 F.2d 136, 33 FEP 1370 (4th Cir.), *cert. denied,* 469 U.S. 827, 35 FEP 1608 (1984); Dominic v. Consolidated Edison Co. of N.Y., 822 F.2d 1249, 44 FEP 268, *reh'g denied,* 44 FEP 1048 (2d Cir. 1987) (deluging employee with work that was impossible to complete and designed to cause him to fail).

relevant documents prior to a Title VII trial, attempting to cover up the document destruction, demoting the plaintiff to a lower position, and assigning her to an isolated office;[52] denial of a grant to a university professor;[53] transfer to a meaningless and menial job;[54] deletion of positive references from a professional dossier maintained on a former university faculty member;[55] delaying a bonus and failing to grant a customary annual wage increase;[56] denial of a request for reimbursement of job-related law school courses;[57] termination of a trainee from an automobile dealership training program on the basis of incorrect absentee reports;[58] false accusations, unwarranted reprimands, removal from a job without explanation, intimidating comments, harassment, and threats of termination of employment;[59] laying off a male employee because of charges filed by female employees claiming that the male was paid a higher salary than they;[60] altering work assignments and giving an employee unsatisfactory performance evaluations[61] and threatening the employee with discharge for filing a charge of discrimination with the EEOC;[62] refusal to rehire and furnishing unfavorable references;[63] manipulating bumping rights;[64] denial of a position;[65] altering an employee's work schedule;[66] removal from office, exclusion from production meetings, and an attempt to persuade co-workers to file sexual harassment charges;[67] failure to approve a doctoral dissertation proposal;[68] refusal to provide any recommendation;[69] posting a copy of a newspaper article regarding the filing of the complaint and making derogatory comments;[70] imposing discipline that clearly outweighs the employee's misconduct;[71] retroactively altering an employee's performance ratings, giving the employee an unacceptable rating on a new evaluation, and transferring the employee to a location with poor

---

[52]Clemente v. United States, 568 F. Supp. 1150, 36 FEP 1716 (C.D. Cal. 1983), *vacated in part and rev'd in part,* 766 F.2d 1358, 38 FEP 808 (9th Cir. 1985), *cert. denied,* 474 U.S. 1101, 39 FEP 1424 (1986).

[53]Acosta v. University of the D.C., 528 F. Supp. 1215, 27 FEP 963 (D.D.C. 1981).

[54]Perry v. Metropolitan Dist. Comm'n, 27 FEP 1651 (D. Mass. 1981).

[55]Lazic v. University of Pa., 513 F. Supp. 761, 29 FEP 1652 (E.D. Pa. 1981).

[56]Hickman v. Flood & Peterson Ins., 29 FEP 1467 (D. Colo. 1982), *aff'd,* 766 F.2d 422, 38 FEP 186 (10th Cir. 1985).

[57]Reilly v. Califano, 537 F. Supp. 349, 29 FEP 1437 (N.D. Ill.), *aff'd,* 673 F.2d 1333, 30 FEP 120 (7th Cir. 1981), *cert. denied,* 456 U.S. 916, 30 FEP 120 (1982).

[58]Walker v. Ford Motor Co., 684 F.2d 1355, 29 FEP 1259 (11th Cir. 1982).

[59]Griffin v. Michigan Dep't of Corrections, 654 F. Supp. 690, 30 FEP 638 (E.D. Mich. 1982).

[60]Smith v. Joseph Horne Co., 30 FEP 486 (W.D. Pa. 1980), *aff'd,* 691 F.2d 491, 30 FEP 579 (3d Cir. 1982), *cert. denied,* 459 U.S. 1107, 30 FEP 1048 (1983).

[61]Yartzoff v. Thomas, 809 F.2d 1371, 42 FEP 1660 (9th Cir. 1987); Batts v. NLT Corp., 34 EPD ¶ 34,444 (M.D. Tenn. 1984).

[62]EEOC v. Atlantic Richfield Co., 30 FEP 551 (C.D. Cal. 1979). *See also* Lewis v. NLRB, 750 F.2d 1266, 36 FEP 1388 (5th Cir. 1985); Weiss v. United States, 595 F. Supp. 1050, 36 FEP 1 (E.D. Va. 1984).

[63]O'Brien v. Sky Chefs, 670 F.2d 864, 28 FEP 661, *amended,* 28 FEP 1690 (9th Cir. 1982); Curl v. Reavis, 35 FEP 917 (W.D.N.C. 1983), *aff'd,* 740 F.2d 1323, 35 FEP 930 (4th Cir. 1984); Waddell v. Small Tube Prods., 799 F.2d 69, 41 FEP 988 (3d Cir. 1986) (retaliatory motive inferred from fact that employer directed former employee not to report back to work after it learned that state agency had dismissed charge).

[64]Holsey v. Armour & Co., 743 F.2d 199, 35 FEP 1064 (4th Cir. 1984), *cert. denied,* 470 U.S. 1028, 37 FEP 192 (1985); Graham v. Adams, 640 F. Supp. 535, 40 FEP 1797 (D.D.C. 1986).

[65]Curl v. Reavis, *supra* note 63.

[66]Klein v. Indiana Univ. Trustees, 35 FEP 271 (S.D. Ind. 1984), *aff'd,* 766 F.2d 275, 38 FEP 290 (7th Cir. 1985); Sims v. Mme. Paulette Dry Cleaners, 580 F. Supp. 593, 34 FEP 305 (S.D.N.Y. 1984).

[67]Jackson v. RKO Bottlers of Toledo, 743 F.2d 370, 35 FEP 1318 (6th Cir. 1984), *cert. denied,* 478 U.S. — (1986).

[68]Lewis v. St. Louis Univ., 744 F.2d 1368 (8th Cir. 1984).

[69]Sparrow v. Piedmont Health Sys. Agency, 593 F. Supp. 1107, 38 FEP 1621 (M.D.N.C. 1984).

[70]Batts v. NLT Corp., *supra* note 61.

[71]Moss v. Southern Ry., 41 FEP 553 (N.D. Ga. 1986).

working conditions;[72] and suspending severance payments to a former employee.[73]

Instances where employers have been exonerated of retaliatory conduct include a transfer to a secretarial pool because the transfer was temporary and the plaintiff retained all pay and benefits;[74] transfers justified by departmental needs;[75] the redesignation of a job title and a temporary grade reduction which did not result in a reduction in salary;[76] temporary transfer to a lower grade and requesting the employee to sign a document acknowledging that the transfer was at her request, where the employee had requested not to work for a certain supervisor who she believed had sexually harassed her, and where she received the same salary and benefits as before and was assured that she would receive the next available position at her former grade;[77] suspension of a grievance appeal upon commencement of a Title VII suit in accordance with a university's informal practices;[78] the employer's private, informal, and noncoercive attempt to settle a discrimination charge;[79] a refusal to rehire an employee because the employee refuses to accept a settlement offer;[80] budgetary constraints freezing temporary faculty salaries while permanent faculty received salary increases;[81] and an applicant's claim that a prospective employer failed to hire him because he had filed an EEOC charge against his former employer.[82] Supervisory questioning of a charging party has been held not to be retaliatory in nature[83] as has failure to separate a charging party from a co-employee, conducting a work measurement study, and reviewing an employee's work.[84] Discharges were held not to be retaliatory where the evidence showed that they were based upon excessive absenteeism, physical limitations of the complainants, and increased workload at the defendant's plant rather than retaliation for race discrimination allegations.[85]

## VI. PROOF

### A. General Principles

Most courts have utilized a three-pronged burden of proof for establishing a prima facie case of retaliation: (1) the employee engaged in a protected

---

[72]Dominic v. Consolidated Edison Co. of N.Y., 822 F.2d 1249, 44 FEP 268, *reh'g denied,* 44 FEP 1048 (2d Cir. 1987).
[73]EEOC v. Cosmair, Inc., L'Oreal Hair Care Div., 821 F.2d 1085, 44 FEP 569 (5th Cir. 1987).
[74]Ferguson v. E.I. du Pont de Nemours & Co., 560 F. Supp. 1172, 31 FEP 795 (D. Del. 1983).
[75]Bishopp v. District of Columbia, 602 F. Supp. 1401, 37 FEP 235 (D.D.C. 1985), *rev'd in part, vacated in part, and remanded,* 788 F.2d 781, 40 FEP 903 (D.C. Cir. 1986) (remanded for reconsideration of retaliation claims in light of reversal on other issues).
[76]Burrows v. Chemed Corp. dba Vestal Laboratories, 743 F.2d 612, 35 FEP 1410 (8th Cir. 1984).
[77]Yates v. Avco Corp., 819 F.2d 630, 43 FEP 1595 (6th Cir. 1987).
[78]Kumar v. University of Mass. Bd. of Trustees, 566 F. Supp. 1299, 32 FEP 306 (D. Mass. 1983), *cert. denied,* 475 U.S. 1097, 40 FEP 792 (1986).
[79]McCarthney v. Griffin-Spalding County Bd. of Educ., 791 F.2d 1549, 41 FEP 245 (11th Cir. 1986).
[80]Longworth v. National Supermkts., 41 FEP 30 (E.D. Mo. 1986).
[81]Griffin v. Regency Univs. Bd. of Regents, 795 F.2d 1281, 41 FEP 228 (7th Cir. 1986).
[82]Clay v. Hyatt Regency Hotel, 724 F.2d 721, 33 FEP 1364 (8th Cir. 1984).
[83]Burrows v. Chemed Corp. dba Vestal Laboratories, 567 F. Supp. 978, 32 FEP 851 (E.D. Mo. 1983), *aff'd,* 743 F.2d 612, 35 FEP 1410 (8th Cir. 1984); Wintz v. Port Auth. of N.Y. & N.J., 551 F. Supp. 1323, 32 FEP 1621 (S.D.N.Y. 1982).
[84]Barrett v. Omaha Nat'l Bank, 584 F. Supp. 22, 35 FEP 585 (D. Neb. 1983), *aff'd,* 726 F.2d 424, 35 FEP 593 (8th Cir. 1984).
[85]Mitchell v. Safeway Stores, 624 F. Supp. 932, 39 FEP 1213 (D. Kan. 1985).

activity; (2) the employee was subjected to an adverse employment decision; and (3) there is a causal connection between (1) and (2).[86] Other courts have required that the plaintiff prove as part of his prima facie case that the employer knew of his participation in the protected activity.[87] In *Hartman v. Wick,*[88] the second prong of the prima facie test was modified for class claims of retaliation. The court held that a showing must be made that the "adverse actions must have been taken pursuant to a general practice or policy of the defendant."[89]

A prima facie case cannot be established by a plaintiff who cannot prove that he was the victim of an adverse personnel decision;[90] nor can a plaintiff who has not complained of discrimination establish a prima facie case of retaliation.[91]

The appropriateness of a retaliation analysis was addressed by the Eleventh Circuit in *Lee v. Russell County Board of Education.*[92] The court questioned whether the case before it should be analyzed under *McDonnell Douglas Corp. v. Green*[93] or the retaliatory discharge analysis of *Lindsey v.*

---

[86]McKenna v. Weinberger, 729 F.2d 783, 791, 34 FEP 509, 515 (D.C. Cir. 1984) (citing Second Edition) (supervisors did not know of EEO complaint but knew of investigation related to sexist treatment at time employee was discharged); Canino v. EEOC, 707 F.2d 468, 471, 32 FEP 139, 141 (11th Cir. 1983) (plaintiff failed to establish causal connection between complaints of discrimination and denial of promotion); Lamb v. Rantoul, 538 F. Supp. 34, 32 FEP 1016 (D.R.I. 1981) (standard of proof in claim of retaliation same as in proof of discrimination); DeAnda v. St. Joseph Hosp., 671 F.2d 850, 28 FEP 317 (5th Cir. 1982), *appeal after remand,* 749 F.2d 683, 36 FEP 1176 (11th Cir. 1985); Smith v. Georgia, 684 F.2d 729, 29 FEP 1134 (11th Cir. 1982); Reilly v. Califano, 537 F. Supp. 349, 29 FEP 1437 (N.D. Ill.), *aff'd,* 673 F.2d 1333, 30 FEP 120 (7th Cir. 1981), *cert. denied,* 456 U.S. 916, 30 FEP 120 (1982); Hickman v. Flood & Peterson Ins., 29 FEP 1467 (D. Colo. 1982), *aff'd,* 766 F.2d 422, 38 FEP 186 (10th Cir. 1985); Swint v. Volusia County, Dep't of Pub. Works, 36 FEP 1412 (M.D. Fla. 1984) (plaintiff made no showing of causal relationship between filing of EEOC charge and discharge from employment); McKinney v. Dole, 765 F.2d 1129, 38 FEP 364 (D.C. Cir. 1985); Underwood v. District of Columbia Armory Bd., 38 FEP 1713 (D.D.C. 1985); Mannikko v. Harrah's Reno, 630 F. Supp. 191 (D. Nev. 1986) (order and allocation of proof in retaliation case is same as in other Title VII actions); Kellner v. General Refractories Co., 631 F. Supp. 939, 41 FEP 538 (N.D. Ind. 1986) (employer failed to carry its burden of affirmatively putting forth evidence of nondiscriminatory reason for plaintiff's constructive discharge).

[87]Dean v. Civiletti, 29 FEP 881 (D.N.D. 1981), *aff'd in part, vacated and remanded in part,* 670 F.2d 99, 29 FEP 890 (8th Cir. 1982); Kellin v. ACF Indus., 517 F. Supp. 226, 27 FEP 1234 (E.D. Mo. 1981), *aff'd,* 671 F.2d 279, 29 FEP 1467 (8th Cir. 1982); Gilbreath v. Butler Mfg. Co., 750 F.2d 701, 36 FEP 833 (8th Cir. 1984); Weems v. Ball Metal & Chem. Div., 753 F.2d 527, 36 FEP 1606 (6th Cir. 1985); Wright v. Udell Dental Lab, 35 FEP 668 (D. Minn. 1984); Singh v. Bowsher, 609 F. Supp. 454, 41 FEP 202 (D.D.C. 1984), *aff'd,* 786 F.2d 432 (D.C. Cir. 1986) (no retaliation where supervisor unaware that employee had been hired pursuant to EEOC settlement agreement).

[88]600 F. Supp. 361, 36 FEP 622 (D.D.C. 1984).

[89]*Id.* at 367, 36 FEP at 627.

[90]Ferguson v. E.I. du Pont de Nemours & Co., 560 F. Supp. 1172, 31 FEP 795 (D. Del. 1983) (temporarily transferred plaintiff whose pay and benefits not reduced had not been subjected to adverse employment decision); Ekanem v. Health Hosp. Corp. of Marion County, Ind., 724 F.2d 563, 33 FEP 1497 (7th Cir. 1983), *cert. denied,* 469 U.S. 821, 35 FEP 1607 (1984) (plaintiff who continued to receive raises and promotions not subjected to adverse personnel action); Barrett v. Omaha Nat'l Bank, 726 F.2d 424, 35 FEP 593 (8th Cir. 1984) (plaintiff assigned to less stressful position after filing EEOC charge alleging sexual harassment); Geisler v. Folsom, 735 F.2d 991, 34 FEP 1581 (6th Cir. 1984) (no adverse action shown where plaintiff was instructed not to communicate directly with department director, but to lower level employee); Beall v. Curtis, 603 F. Supp. 1563, 37 FEP 644 (M.D. Ga.), *aff'd,* 778 F.2d 791, 40 FEP 984 (11th Cir. 1985) (configuration of part-time work schedule arranged after childbirth provides no basis for retaliation claim where similar in pattern to work schedule prior to childbirth).

[91]Theiss v. John Fabick Tractor Co., 532 F. Supp. 453, 34 FEP 266 (E.D. Mo. 1982) (plaintiff never complained to anyone with defendant that she was victim of discrimination); Talley v. United States Postal Serv., 720 F.2d 505, 33 FEP 361 (8th Cir. 1983), *cert. denied,* 466 U.S. 952, 37 FEP 592 (1984) (supervisor responsible for adverse personnel action had no knowledge that employee engaged in protected activity); Neale v. Dillon, 534 F. Supp. 1381, 32 FEP 1604 (E.D.N.Y.), *aff'd,* 714 F.2d 116, 37 FEP 1216 (2d Cir. 1982) (same).

[92]684 F.2d 769, 29 FEP 1508 (11th Cir. 1982), *appeal after remand,* 744 F.2d 768, 36 FEP 22 (11th Cir. 1984).

[93]411 U.S. 792, 5 FEP 965 (1973).

*Mississippi Research & Development Center.*[94] If the plaintiff could prove by direct evidence that his support of racial minorities was a significant factor in the Board's decision not to reemploy him, the court reasoned, the Board must then prove by a preponderance of the evidence that its decision not to reemploy the plaintiff would have been made absent the retaliatory factor. However, if the plaintiff did not prove retaliation by direct evidence, he may establish a prima facie case for retaliation under *McDonnell Douglas,* at which time the Board must then articulate a valid nondiscriminatory reason for its decision not to reemploy the plaintiff.[95] However, a district court has since suggested that the *Lee* analysis may be applicable only to claims alleging a violation of § 1983.[96]

The basic retaliation analysis may be modified in an appropriate case. In *Ruggles v. California Polytechnic State University, San Luis Obispo,*[97] dealing with a failure to hire, the Ninth Circuit modified the elements of a prima facie retaliatory discharge case in the failure to hire context to require that the plaintiff demonstrate that (1) she engaged in protected activities and that (2) she was eliminated from consideration, (3) because of her protected activities.

A plaintiff claiming a continuing pattern of discrimination and retaliation for protected activity need not file charges as to each act that is alleged to be part of the continuing discrimination.[98]

Since retaliation can include virtually any type of conduct and typically does not spring from a common source, and since claims of retaliation are usually not numerous, such claims do not lend themselves to class treatment.[99]

## B. Establishing the Causal Connection

Evidence that an employee was treated differently from employees who had not engaged in protected activity has been held sufficient to establish the causal connection.[100] If an employer treats an employee differently after learning that the employee has engaged in protected activity, that difference in treatment is sufficient to establish a causal connection between the protected activity and the adverse personnel action.[101] A causal connection may

---

[94]652 F.2d 488, 27 FEP 200 (5th Cir. 1981).

[95]Clay v. Hyatt Regency Hotel, 724 F.2d 721, 33 FEP 1364 (8th Cir. 1984) (court applied *McDonnell Douglas* framework in absence of direct evidence of retaliation); Simmons v. Camden County Bd. of Educ., 757 F.2d 1187, 37 FEP 795 (11th Cir.), *cert. denied,* 474 U.S. 981, 39 FEP 384 (1985) (burden of proof properly on plaintiffs to rebut legitimate reason for discharge where only circumstantial evidence offered).

[96]Iodice v. Southeastern Packing & Gaskets, 572 F. Supp. 1370, 33 FEP 275 (N.D. Ga. 1983).

[97]797 F.2d 782, 41 FEP 997 (9th Cir. 1986).

[98]Beckler v. Kreps, 541 F. Supp. 1311, 30 FEP 248 (E.D. Pa. 1982).

[99]Colbert v. City of Wichita, 33 FEP 218 (D. Kan. 1983).

[100]Loiseau v. Department of Human Resources, 567 F. Supp. 1211, 39 FEP 289 (D. Or. 1983) (employee received low marks on evaluation after filing charge); Curl v. Reavis, 35 FEP 917 (W.D.N.C. 1983), *aff'd in part and rev'd in part,* 740 F.2d 1323, 35 FEP 930 (4th Cir. 1984) (plaintiff fired after filing charge); *see also* DeCintio v. Westchester County Medical Center, 821 F.2d 111, 44 FEP 33 (2d Cir.), *cert. denied,* 484 U.S. —, 45 FEP 520 (1987) (causal connection can be established by showing similarly situated employees were treated disparately).

[101]Sims v. Mme. Paulette Dry Cleaners, 580 F. Supp. 593, 34 FEP 305 (S.D.N.Y. 1984) (employee warned and fired for tardiness after filing charge). *See also* Capaci v. Katz & Besthoff, 525 F. Supp. 317, 30 FEP 1541 (E.D. La. 1981), *aff'd in part and rev'd in part,* 711 F.2d 647, 32 FEP 961 (5th Cir. 1983), *cert. denied,* 466 U.S. 927, 34 FEP 696 (1984) (employer issued approximately 100 disciplinary slips after

also be established when only a short period of time passes between the protected activity and the adverse personnel action complained of.[102]

Defendants have sought to rebut evidence of a causal connection between protected activity and an adverse employment decision in a variety of ways. Evidence that an employee engaging in protected activity was treated no differently from nonprotesting employees has been sufficient to exonerate an employer accused of retaliation.[103] Frequently, defendants have argued that a plaintiff's job performance is the reason for the adverse employment decision.[104] Lack of knowledge of the protected activity has also been urged

---

employee filed charge); Kauffman v. Sidereal Corp., 695 F.2d 343, 32 FEP 1710 (9th Cir. 1982) (employer's attitude toward employee changed after she filed charge); Robinson v. Middendorf, 34 FEP 310 (D.D.C. 1976) (after charge was filed, employer refused to provide plaintiff with adequate work instructions, placed memoranda in her file criticizing her work, evaluated her on basis of job grade other than her own, and instructed co-workers not to associate with her); Price v. Cannon Mills Co., 607 F. Supp. 1146, 39 FEP 708 (M.D.N.C. 1985) (after filing an EEOC charge, employer deviated from standard procedure by refusing to allow plaintiff to explain her alleged misconduct at meeting which ended in her termination).

[102]Ferguson v. E.I. du Pont de Nemours & Co., 560 F. Supp. 1172, 31 FEP 795 (D. Del. 1983) (short period of time between protected act and discharge); Francoeur v. Corroon & Black Co., 552 F. Supp. 403, 34 FEP 323 (S.D.N.Y. 1982) (same); Love v. Re/Max of Am., 738 F.2d 383, 35 FEP 565 (10th Cir. 1984) (same); EEOC v. Midwestern Maintenance Corp., 36 EPD ¶ 34,977 (N.D. Ohio 1985) (same); Batts v. NLT Corp., 34 EPD ¶ 34,444 (M.D. Tenn. 1984) (adverse change in job duties and increased scrutiny of performance initiated soon after employer learned of lawsuit); Donnellon v. Fruehauf Corp., 794 F.2d 598, 41 FEP 569 (11th Cir. 1986) (prima facie case established where discharge occurred one month after filing charge); DeCintio v. Westchester County Medical Center, *supra* note 100 (causal connection can be established by showing that protected activity is followed closely by adverse treatment). *But see* McNeil v. Greyhound Lines, 31 FEP 1068 (S.D. Fla. 1983) (short passage of time not sufficient, without more, to meet causal link requirement of prima facie case); Griffin v. Regency Univs. Bd. of Regents, 795 F.2d 1281, 41 FEP 228 (7th Cir. 1986) (same); Jennings v. Tinley Park Community Consol. School Dist. 146, 796 F.2d 962, 41 FEP 497 (7th Cir. 1986), *cert. denied,* 481 U.S. 1017, 43 FEP 856 (1987) (discharge four months after filing of charge was not sufficient); Cooper v. City of N. Olmstead, 795 F.2d 1265, 41 FEP 425 (6th Cir. 1986) (citations for rules violations on nine occasions during four months following filing of charge is insufficient, where employee had been cited six times in seven months preceding filing of charge); Karriem v. Oliver T. Carr Co., 38 FEP 882 (D.D.C. 1985) (causal connection demonstrated by fact that plaintiff was discharged shortly after plaintiff wrote letter in response to charges made against him by upper level management).

[103]Melanson v. Rantoul, 536 F. Supp. 271, 32 FEP 1025 (D.R.I. 1982) (reassignment was common rotation within plaintiff's academic department); Lamb v. Rantoul, 538 F. Supp. 34, 32 FEP 1016 (D.R.I. 1981) (policy of not hiring own graduates without outside experience also applied to nonprotesting person); Colucci v. New York Times Co., 533 F. Supp. 1005, 32 FEP 1812 (S.D.N.Y. 1982) (employee filing charge not promoted, but another employee who filed charge at same time was promoted); Kumar v. University of Mass. Bd. of Trustees, 566 F. Supp. 1299, 32 FEP 306 (D. Mass 1983), *cert. denied,* — U.S. —, 40 FEP 792 (1986) (suspension of internal grievance procedure after discrimination suit filed pursuant to established custom); Clay v. Consumer Programs, 576 F. Supp. 185, 35 FEP 1497 (E.D. Mo. 1983), *aff'd,* 745 F.2d 501, 35 FEP 1502 (8th Cir. 1984) (restriction imposed on plaintiff's freedom to leave work area part of broader rules changes applicable to work force as a whole); *but cf.* Mozee v. Jeffboat, Inc., 746 F.2d 365, 35 FEP 1810 (7th Cir. 1984) (employer could not justify retaliatory action against black employees who were absent from work to protest employer's discriminatory policies by showing similarly harsh treatment of white employees who had missed work to protest against school busing).

[104]Mitchell v. Baldrige, 34 FEP 187 (D.D.C. 1984), *aff'd in part and vacated in part,* 759 F.2d 80, 37 FEP 689 (D.C. Cir. 1985) (plaintiff's job performance deteriorated after he filed charge); Desai v. Tompkins County Trust Co., 34 FEP 938 (N.D.N.Y.), *aff'd,* 37 FEP 1312 (2d Cir. 1984), *cert. denied,* 471 U.S. 1125, 37 FEP 1408 (1985) (unsatisfactory job performance and poor attitude caused employer to terminate employee); Manabat v. Columbus-Cuneo-Cabrini Medical Center, 34 FEP 254 (N.D. Ill. 1984) (plaintiffs' reliability as security guards questionable); Capaci v. Katz & Besthoff, *supra* note 101 (employee's superiors had endeavored to have her terminated because of performance problems on four occasions prior to her filing charge); Cazalas v. Department of Justice, 569 F. Supp. 213, 36 FEP 1698 (E.D. La. 1983), *aff'd,* 731 F.2d 280, 36 FEP 1713 (5th Cir. 1984), *cert. denied,* 469 U.S. 1207, 37 FEP 64 (1985) (employee's work problems caused termination); Clark v. R.J. Reynolds Tobacco Co., 27 FEP 1628 (E.D. La. 1982); EEOC v. Union Camp Corp., 27 FEP 1393 (W.D. Mich. 1981); Brown v. Delta Air Lines, 522 F. Supp. 1218, 30 FEP 38 (S.D. Tex. 1980), *aff'd without opinion,* 673 F.2d 1325, 30 FEP 120 (5th Cir. 1982); Stancil v. Claytor, 30 FEP 730 (D.D.C. 1978); Perry v. Prudential Ins. Co. of Am., 29 FEP 1837 (S.D. Tex. 1982); Payne v. Heckler, 604 F. Supp. 334, 39 FEP 1866 (E.D. Pa. 1985) (employee's job performance clearly inferior to standard set by her co-employees); Lee v. Joseph T. Ryerson & Son, 36 FEP 449 (W.D.N.C.), *aff'd,* 745 F.2d 51, 37 FEP

by defendants in rebuttal to a charge of retaliation.[105] A prolonged period of time between the plaintiff's engaging in protected activity and the alleged retaliatory action has also been advanced by defendants in urging the absence of a causal connection.[106] Other reasons stated by defendants include lack of job qualifications,[107] superior qualifications of other candidates,[108] insubordination,[109] improper conduct and poor relationships with other employees,[110] failure to express an interest in the job position allegedly sought,[111] depart-

---

1216 (4th Cir. 1984) (employee's excessive absenteeism had detrimental effect upon his own and work unit's productivity); Balicao v. University of Minn., 737 F.2d 747, 35 FEP 110 (8th Cir. 1984); Almendral v. New York State Office of Mental Health, 568 F. Supp. 571, 34 FEP 1536 (S.D.N.Y. 1983), aff'd in part and rev'd in part, 743 F.2d 963, 34 FEP 1680 (2d Cir. 1984) (several deficiencies in job performance noted prior to discrimination charges); Mannikko v. Harrah's Reno, 630 F. Supp. 191 (D. Nev. 1986) (plaintiff's maid work was substandard both as to quality and quantity); Davis v. Lambert of Ark., 781 F.2d 658, 39 FEP 1410 (8th Cir. 1986) (employer demonstrated that recalled employees performed better than plaintiff, who was not recalled); Vermett v. Hough, 627 F. Supp. 587, 42 FEP 1432 (W.D. Mich. 1986) (plaintiff discharged from police force for substandard performance); Gilbert v. West Ga. Medical Center Auth., 784 F.2d 402 (11th Cir. 1986) (plaintiff altered work schedule without authorization and falsified supervisor's initials); LeCompte v. Chrysler Credit Corp., 780 F.2d 1260, 27 WH 841 (5th Cir. 1986) (plaintiff prepared false audit reports and violated company policy).

[105]Acosta v. University of the D.C., 528 F. Supp. 1215, 27 FEP 963 (D.D.C. 1981); Hayden v. Cox Enters., Atlanta Newspapers Div., 534 F. Supp. 1166, 28 FEP 1315 (N.D. Ga. 1982); Cohen v. Fred Meyer, Inc., 686 F.2d 793, 29 FEP 1268 (9th Cir. 1982); Berke v. Ohio Dep't of Pub. Welfare, 30 FEP 387 (S.D. Ohio 1978), aff'd, 628 F.2d 980, 30 FEP 395 (6th Cir. 1980); Balicao v. University of Minn., supra note 104; Almendral v. New York State Office of Mental Health, supra note 104.

[106]Clark v. Chrysler Corp., 673 F.2d 921, 28 FEP 342 (7th Cir.), cert. denied, 459 U.S. 873, 29 FEP 1560 (1982) (two years); Burrus v. United Tel. Co. of Kan., 683 F.2d 339, 29 FEP 663 (10th Cir.), cert. denied, 459 U.S. 1071, 30 FEP 592 (1982) (three years); Jackson v. RKO Bottlers of Toledo, Pepsi-Cola, Dr. Pepper Bottling Co. Div., 783 F.2d 50, 40 FEP 222 (6th Cir.), cert. denied, 478 U.S. 1006, 41 FEP 271 (1986) (one year); Nelson v. Department of Commerce, No. 83–1528 (D.D.C. 1986) (seven years); but see Moss v. Southern Ry., 41 FEP 553 (N.D. Ga. 1986) (causal connection established despite one and one-half year period between EEOC complaint and discharge).

[107]Beckler v. Kreps, supra note 98; Beall v. Curtis, 603 F. Supp. 1563, 37 FEP 644 (M.D. Ga.), aff'd without opinion, 778 F.2d 791, 40 FEP 984 (11th Cir. 1985); McCloud v. Fairchild Indus., 582 F. Supp. 1478, 34 FEP 1881 (M.D.N.C. 1984); Araujo v. Boston College Trustees, 34 EPD ¶ 34,409 (D. Mass. 1983); Farlow v. University of N.C., 624 F. Supp. 434, 39 FEP 1418 (M.D.N.C. 1985) (college professor's qualifications for promotion did not change significantly from denial in 1980 to reapplication in 1981, so no retaliation in refusing promotion in 1981).

[108]Hamm v. University of S. Fla., 35 FEP 1879 (M.D. Fla. 1984).

[109]Benson v. Little Rock Hilton Inn, 742 F.2d 414, 35 FEP 1362 (8th Cir. 1984) (termination based solely on stealing application forms and making false statements to her employer and lawyer); Ferguson v. AT&T Co., 564 F. Supp. 1429, 31 FEP 1638 (W.D. Mo. 1983) (insubordination made termination necessary); Brown v. Delta Air Lines, supra note 104 (insubordination and poor performance); Payne v. Heckler, supra note 104 (contemptuous attitude and repeated refusals to conform to directives of supervisors supported decision to terminate); Gordon v. National R.R. Passenger Corp., 564 F. Supp. 199, 34 FEP 315 (E.D. Pa. 1983) (discharge followed injury sustained by plaintiff because of failure to obey orders, culminating incident given history of disciplinary action following acts of insubordination); Clay v. Consumer Programs, supra note 103 (plaintiff continually ignored employer's request to perform assignment); EEOC v. Kendon of Dallas, 34 EPD ¶ 35,393 (E.D. Tex. 1984) (employee impermissibly left overtime shift following confrontation with supervisor); Payne v. Dillard Paper Co., 34 EPD ¶ 34,491 (M.D.N.C. 1984) (failure to obey instructions triggered discharge). But see Pinkard v. Pullman-Standard, 678 F.2d 1211, 29 FEP 216 (5th Cir. 1982), cert. denied, 459 U.S. 1105, 30 FEP 1048 (1983) (claim of insubordination rejected as pretextual where other similar incidents had resulted in reprimands, not discharge); Mitchell v. Safeway Stores, 624 F. Supp. 932, 39 FEP 1213 (D. Kan. 1985).

[110]Jones v. Lumberjack Meats, 680 F.2d 98, 29 FEP 396 (11th Cir. 1982) (carrying tear gas pistol at work); Benson v. Little Rock Hilton Inn, supra note 109; Irby v. Sullivan, 737 F.2d 1418, 35 FEP 697 (5th Cir. 1984) (use of profanity and improper attire led to reprimands in months preceding discharge); Jackson v. RKO Bottlers of Toledo, Pepsi-Cola, Dr. Pepper Bottling Co. Div., supra note 106 (shoving match with another employee); Wajda v. Penn Mut. Life Ins. Co., 528 F. Supp 548, 32 FEP 1741 (E.D. Pa. 1981) (employee's contentious personality led to her discharge); Joshi v. Professional Health Servs., 606 F. Supp. 302, 43 FEP 1092 (D.D.C. 1985) (employee's disruptive behavior alienated fellow staff members and management); Otey v. Delta Air Lines, 36 FEP 1749 (S.D. Fla. 1985) (termination followed employee's unreasonable reaction to playful act of his supervisor); Leveen v. Stratford Hous. Auth., 629 F. Supp. 228, 42 FEP 1685 (D. Conn. 1986) (poor attitude and failure to provide timely and accurate reports and inventories).

[111]Hearn v. R.R. Donnelley & Sons Co., 739 F.2d 304, 42 FEP 1677 (7th Cir. 1984), cert. denied, 469 U.S. 1223, 42 FEP 1696 (1985) (employer inferred lack of interest in sales position).

mental reorganization,[112] disciplinary provisions in the collective bargaining agreement,[113] and the fact that the employee did not get along with his supervisor and had threatened to leave the employer and work for its competitor.[114] One court has held that the fact that an employee filed an EEOC charge made it likely that the employer treated him more favorably than other employees, since he was given four opportunities to pass a welding test before termination, so no causal connection was established.[115]

## C. Burden of Proof—The Degree of Causation Which Must Be Shown and the Risk of Nonpersuasion on That Issue

Courts now generally apply the "but for" test when faced with a "mixed motive" case.[116] Retaliation is not proved unless the plaintiff establishes by a preponderance of the evidence that the employer's proffered reason for its adverse personnel action is pretextual.[117]

---

[112]Burrows v. Chemed Corp. dba Vestal Laboratories, 743 F.2d 612, 35 FEP 1410 (8th Cir. 1984) (valid reorganization of company division caused change in job title and grade reclassification).

[113]Mozee v. Jeffboat, Inc., 746 F.2d 365, 35 FEP 1810 (7th Cir. 1984) (participation in opposition activity resulted in job absences punishable under the collective bargaining agreement).

[114]Donnellon v. Fruehauf Corp., 794 F.2d 598, 41 FEP 569 (11th Cir. 1986).

[115]Tate v. Dravo Corp., 623 F. Supp. 1090, 39 FEP 1544 (W.D.N.C. 1985).

[116]McMillan v. Rust College, 710 F.2d 1112, 32 FEP 939 (5th Cir. 1983); Kauffman v. Sidereal Corp., 695 F.2d 343, 345, 32 FEP 1710, 1711 (9th Cir. 1982) ("Under this test, it must be established by a preponderance of the evidence that engaging in the protected activity was one of the reasons for the firing and that but for such activity the plaintiff would not have been fired."); Jack v. Texaco Research Center, 743 F.2d 1129, 35 FEP 1818 (5th Cir. 1984); Ross v. Communications Satellite Corp., 759 F.2d 355, 37 FEP 797 (4th Cir. 1985) (employee "must show that the adverse action would not have occurred 'but for' the protected conduct. We reject the view that Title VII has been violated if retaliation for protected activity was merely 'in part' a reason for the adverse action."); Cobb v. Dufresne-Henry, 603 F. Supp. 1048, 37 FEP 1287 (D. Vt. 1985) ("[T]he employee need not prove that her activity was the sole basis for the employer's action, but the employee must prove that 'but for' the activity, he or she would not have been fired."). See also Shanley v. Youngstown Sheet & Tube Co., 552 F. Supp. 4, 30 FEP 1531 (N.D. Ind. 1982) (where there is hostility toward employee because of race or support of alleged victim of racial discrimination, and at same time there is some unlawful motive for terminating employee, there is no violation of Title VII if employee would have been terminated in any event); Robinson v. Monsanto Co., 758 F.2d 331, 37 FEP 875 (8th Cir. 1985) (court upheld jury instruction which made illegality contingent upon whether protected activity was a "determining factor" in decision to terminate); Robinson v. City of Lake Station, 630 F. Supp. 1052 (N.D. Ind. 1986) (evidence did not show that plaintiff would have been hired but for her previous participation in Title VII proceedings); Johnson v. Legal Servs. of Ark., 813 F.2d 893, 43 FEP 343 (8th Cir. 1987) (where retaliation played some part in discharge decision, employer must establish by preponderance of evidence that same decision would have been made absent a charge of discrimination).

[117]Ramon v. Smith, 34 FEP 404 (S.D. Tex. 1984) (loss of promotional opportunity not caused by protected activity); McKenna v. Weinberger, 34 FEP 284 (D.D.C. 1983), aff'd, 729 F.2d 783, 34 FEP 509 (D.C. Cir. 1984) (stated reason for terminating employee not pretext); Theiss v. John Fabick Tractor Co., 532 F. Supp. 453, 34 FEP 266 (E.D. Mo. 1982) (same); Simmons v. Camden County Bd. of Educ., 757 F.2d 1187, 37 FEP 795 (11th Cir.), cert. denied, 474 U.S. 981, 39 FEP 384 (1985) (plaintiffs' circumstantial evidence of retaliation not sufficient to show claims of misconduct and poor performance were pretextual); Mays v. Williamson & Sons Janitorial Servs., 591 F. Supp. 1518, 35 FEP 1868 (E.D. Ark. 1984), aff'd, 775 F.2d 258, 39 FEP 106 (8th Cir. 1985) (pretext established where employer's justification of employee's discharge not credible, given no prior reprimands for absenteeism and questionable validity of internal memoranda critical of her work performance); Oden v. Southern Ry., 35 FEP 913 (N.D. Ga. 1984) (legitimate reasons offered for discharge overcome where employer engaged in organized harassment of employee); EEOC v. Midwestern Maintenance Corp., 36 EPD ¶ 34,977 (N.D. Ohio 1985) (statements by supervisor evidencing retaliatory motive supported finding of pretext); Curl v. Reavis, 35 FEP 917 (W.D.N.C. 1983), aff'd in part and rev'd in part, 740 F.2d 1323, 35 FEP 930 (4th Cir. 1984) (reasons urged to justify series of adverse actions against employee shown to be pretextual); Farlow v. University of N.C., 624 F. Supp. 434, 39 FEP 1418 (M.D.N.C. 1985) (college professor who was not promoted based on lack of qualifications rather than sex discrimination in 1980 cannot claim retaliation in 1981 reapplication when basic qualifications have not changed); Clemente v. United States, 766 F.2d 1358, 38 FEP 808 (9th Cir. 1985), cert. denied, 474 U.S. 1101, 39 FEP 1424 (1986); Hohe v. Midland Corp., 613 F. Supp. 210, 38 FEP 664 (E.D. Mo. 1985), aff'd, 786 F.2d 1172 (8th Cir. 1986); Gold v. Gallaudet College, 630 F. Supp. 1176, 40 FEP 730 (D.D.C. 1986); McDaniel v. Temple Indep. School Dist. 770 F.2d 1340, 38 FEP 1567 (5th Cir. 1985).

## VII. RELIEF ISSUES OF SPECIAL INTEREST IN RETALIATION CASES

An employer has been enjoined from interfering with the employment of a discharged plaintiff's husband because of his support of his wife's suit against the employer.[118]

### A. Reinstatement

The Circuit Court for the District of Columbia affirmed the district court's preliminary injunction requiring the reinstatement of an employee who had been allegedly demoted and transferred following his testimony in a Title VII class action against his employer.[119] The lower court acknowledged that the plaintiff, a class member, had an adequate remedy at law if he could prove that his transfer and demotion were retaliatory in nature, but the court still entered the injunction since it was concerned that other class members would be fearful of presenting claims in the remedy phase of the class action proceeding if the injunction was not issued.

Although a court has the authority to grant a preliminary injunction to preserve the status quo pending exhaustion of EEOC procedures, it will not do so if the plaintiff is unable to demonstrate a probability of success on the merits of his claim.[120] The Second Circuit has held that there is a presumption of irreparable injury in every retaliation case and that the risk of weakened enforcement of Title VII is a factor to be considered in assessing irreparable injury.[121]

One court ordered a discharged probationary employee reinstated as a regular employee on the basis that she would have survived her probationary period but for the retaliatory discharge.[122] In another case, the Fifth Circuit approved an order reinstating a plaintiff to a position she had never formally held but had exercised on a de facto basis.[123]

### B. Preliminary Injunctive Relief Available to EEOC in § 704(a) Cases Pending Completion of the Administrative Process—§ 706(f)(2)

The EEOC's application for injunctive relief to compel reinstatement where the court found that the employer had legitimate reasons for discharging the nurse who had missed work, failed to perform duties, and left the job without notice was denied.[124]

However, another court granted the EEOC's motion for a preliminary injunction and reinstated a dischargee pending completion of the EEOC's

---

[118]Bledsoe v. Wilker Bros., 33 FEP 127 (W.D. Tenn. 1980).

[119]Segar v. Civiletti, 516 F. Supp. 314, 32 FEP 1308 (D.D.C. 1981), aff'd sub nom. Segar v. Smith, 738 F.2d 1249, 35 FEP 31 (D.C. Cir. 1984), cert. denied, 471 U.S. 1115, 37 FEP 1312 (1985).

[120]Haines v. Knight-Ridder Broadcasting, 32 FEP 1113 (D.R.I. 1980); Berman v. New York City Ballet, 616 F. Supp. 555, 38 FEP 1286 (S.D.N.Y. 1985); Stallings v. Manhattan Life Ins. Co., 39 EPD ¶ 36,061 (S.D.N.Y. 1986).

[121]Holt v. Continental Group, 708 F.2d 87, 31 FEP 1468 (2d Cir. 1983), rev'g 542 F. Supp. 16, 29 FEP 618 (D. Conn. 1982), cert. denied, 465 U.S. 1030, 33 FEP 1884 (1984).

[122]Zack v. City of Minneapolis, 35 FEP 1672 (D. Minn. 1984).

[123]McClure v. Mexia Indep. School Dist., 750 F.2d 396, 36 FEP 1402 (5th Cir. 1985).

[124]EEOC v. Bronson Methodist Hosp., 489 F. Supp. 1066, 27 FEP 884 (W.D. Mich. 1979).

investigation because the court concluded that other persons who became aware of the alleged retaliatory discharge of a high level black manager would be chilled from either opposing discriminatory practices or participating in the EEOC's processes and that this was sufficient to constitute irreparable harm.[125] Another court has held that where a plaintiff alleges significant retaliatory conduct by the employer, a court has jurisdiction to entertain an application for a preliminary injunction to preserve the status quo pending the EEOC's investigative and conciliatory processes, and that jurisdiction does not depend in those circumstances upon the issuance of a "right to sue" letter.[126]

## VIII. ALTERNATIVE CAUSES OF ACTION

### A. Private Employer

#### 1. The Civil Rights Act of 1866—42 U.S.C. § 1981

The Fifth[127] and Second[128] circuits have held that a plaintiff may state a claim under § 1981 for relief based on alleged retaliatory action. The Eighth Circuit continues to hold that a § 1981 action may be based upon retaliatory discharge, though a § 1983 action may not.[129]

A district court held that opposition to an employer's racial discrimination which falls short of filing a formal charge is protected under § 1981.[130] However, another trial court has stated that retaliation for advocacy of equal protection does not give rise to a cause of action under § 1981.[131]

#### 2. The Civil Rights Act of 1871—42 U.S.C. §§ 1983, 1985(3), and 1986

The Fifth and Sixth circuits have held that where a retaliation claim is based on a violation of Title VII and no other constitutional or federal statutory provision predating Title VII, there is no claim for a violation of § 1983.[132]

#### 3. National Labor Relations Act—28 U.S.C. §§ 157, 158(a)(1)

The Sixth Circuit granted the NLRB's petition to enforce its decision and order finding that the defendant employer discriminated against the plaintiff because of her union activity.[133] The Board's complaint alleged a violation of §§ 8(a)(1) and 8(a)(3) of the National Labor Relations Act

---

[125]EEOC v. Target Stores, 36 FEP 543, 544 (D. Minn. 1984).

[126]Berman v. New York City Ballet, *supra* note 120.

[127]Pinkard v. Pullman-Standard, 678 F.2d 1211, 1241 n.15, 29 FEP 216, 231 n.15 (5th Cir. 1982), *cert. denied,* 459 U.S. 1105, 30 FEP 1048 (1983); Goff v. Continental Oil Co., 678 F.2d 593, 29 FEP 79 (5th Cir. 1982).

[128]Choudhury v. Polytechnic Inst. of N.Y., 735 F.2d 38, 34 FEP 1572 (2d Cir. 1984) (court held that claim of racial discrimination *per se* is not essential to § 1981 retaliatory action).

[129]Greenwood v. Ross, 778 F.2d 448, 40 FEP 435 (8th Cir. 1985).

[130]Gresham v. Waffle House, 586 F. Supp. 1442, 35 FEP 763 (N.D. Ga. 1984).

[131]Saldivar v. Cadena, 622 F. Supp. 949, 39 FEP 836 (W.D. Wis. 1985).

[132]Irby v. Sullivan, 737 F.2d 1418, 35 FEP 697 (5th Cir. 1984); Day v. Wayne County Bd. of Auditors, 749 F.2d 1199, 1205, 36 FEP 743 (6th Cir. 1984); *see also* Greenwood v. Ross, *supra* note 129.

[133]NLRB v. Magnetics Int'l, 699 F.2d 806, 112 LRRM 2658, 30 FEP 1524 (6th Cir. 1983).

because of the employer's actions, including issuance of a disciplinary warning to the employee for excessive absences. On two of the days considered to be among those absences, the employee had been giving her deposition and attending the deposition of the employer's personnel manager in connection with her pending Title VII suit against the employer. Without referring to Title VII or § 704(a) of the Act, and without explanation or discussion, the court of appeals, citing *Eastex, Inc. v. NLRB,* [134] affirmed the Board's finding of an unfair labor practice when, for purposes of discriminating against the employee, the company counted the days she was absent from work while attempting to vindicate her Title VII rights.

### 5. Other Federal Avenues

The Circuit Court for the District of Columbia has held, in *Frazier v. Merit Systems Protection Board,* [135] that pursuant to the Civil Service Reform Act of 1978, four former U.S. Marshals could challenge the Marshals Service's decision to transfer them which they claim was in retaliation for filing equal employment opportunity complaints.

Under the ADEA, one court, relying on Title VII cases, has held that a plaintiff need not file a separate charge of retaliation before including a retaliation claim in a complaint alleging age discrimination.[136] In another ADEA case, the employee failed to state a prima facie case of retaliation under ADEA because she was unable to demonstrate that the selecting official knew she had filed complaints.[137]

A district court has stated that protection from retaliation under the ADEA covers an employee who holds a reasonable belief in good faith that the challenged employment practice violates the ADEA, even if the belief is later found to be mistaken, and that the plaintiff's retaliation claim does not necessarily fail simply because the plaintiff's claim of age discrimination cannot stand.[138]

ADEA defendants have sought to rebut evidence of a causal connection between protected activity and an adverse employment decision by alleging, for example, that the plaintiff was discharged because his work was scarce and there was no need for his specialty;[139] that the employee engaging in the protected activity was treated no differently from those who had not engaged in protected activity;[140] and that the employer's action was consistent with a collective bargaining agreement.[141]

### 6. Common Law Duties—State Law

The Seventh Circuit has held that a plaintiff who had litigated a claim of retaliation in the state court could not relitigate that issue in federal

---

[134]437 U.S. 556, 98 LRRM 2712 (1978).
[135]672 F.2d 150, 28 FEP 185 (D.C. Cir. 1982).
[136]Jacobson v. American Home Prods. Corp., 36 FEP 559 (N.D. Ill. 1982).
[137]Friedman v. Bolger, 599 F. Supp. 306, 36 FEP 1125 (S.D.N.Y. 1984).
[138]Wolf v. J.I. Case Co., 617 F. Supp. 858, 38 FEP 1647 (E.D. Wis. 1985).
[139]West v. Fred Wright Constr. Co., 756 F.2d 31, 37 FEP 274 (6th Cir. 1985).
[140]Zebedeo v. Martin E. Segal Co., 582 F. Supp. 1394, 37 FEP 128 (D. Conn. 1984).
[141]*Id.*

court.[142] A district court has refused to imply a cause of action under the common law of Wisconsin in favor of an employee claiming a retaliatory discharge for opposing his employer's employment practices.[143] Another district court has held that a plaintiff claiming retaliatory discharge must exhaust administrative procedures under the state discrimination statute before proceeding to court.[144]

## B. State and Local Government Employers

The Fifth Circuit has held that the employee must show a custom or pattern of retaliation to recover under § 1983[145] and that § 1983 did not provide a remedy for violation of the retaliation provisions of Title VII.[146] Where a female state employee alleged sex and race discrimination, the district court held that retaliation for advocacy of equal protection did not give rise to a § 1981 cause of action.[147] The Third Circuit has held that § 1983 provides a remedy to a city health official subjected to retaliation for exercise of his free speech rights.[148]

### 1. First Amendment Right of Free Speech

The limitation upon First Amendment rights in the workplace was reinforced by the Supreme Court in *Connick v. Myers.*[149] In *Connick,* an assistant district attorney was informed that she would be transferred to prosecute cases in a different section of the criminal court. She then prepared and distributed a questionnaire soliciting views of her fellow staff members concerning office transfer policy, office morale, the need for a grievance committee, the level of confidence in supervisors, and whether employees felt pressured to work in political campaigns. Shortly thereafter she was discharged because of her refusal to accept the transfer which the district attorney considered an act of insubordination. The Court held that

> "when a public employee speaks not as a citizen upon matters of public concern, but instead as an employee upon matters only of personal interest, absent the most unusual circumstances, a federal court is not the appropriate forum in which to review the wisdom of a personnel decision taken by a public agency allegedly in reaction to the employee's behavior."[150]

The Court concluded that the question of whether speech is a matter of public concern must be determined by the content, form, and context of a statement and if, when using this test, a statement is not of public concern, there is no requirement that a court engage in the balancing procedure associated with *Pickering v. Board of Education.*[151]

---

[142]Unger v. Consolidated Foods Corp., 693 F.2d 703, 30 FEP 441 (7th Cir. 1982), *cert. denied,* 460 U.S. 1102, 31 FEP 904 (1983).
[143]McCluney v. Joseph Schlitz Brewing Co., 489 F. Supp. 24, 29 FEP 1284 (E.D. Wis. 1980). *See also* Chapter 23 (Related Causes of Action).
[144]Merkel v. Scovill, Inc., 570 F. Supp. 133, 38 FEP 1020 (S.D. Ohio 1983).
[145]Lopez v. City of Austin, 710 F.2d 196, 32 FEP 601 (5th Cir. 1983).
[146]Irby v. Sullivan, 737 F.2d 1418, 35 FEP 697 (5th Cir. 1984).
[147]Saldivar v. Cadena, 622 F. Supp. 949, 39 FEP 836 (W.D. Wis. 1985).
[148]Bartholomew v. Fischl, 782 F.2d 1148 (3d Cir. 1986).
[149]461 U.S. 138, 1 IER 178 (1983).
[150]*Id.* at 147.
[151]*Id.* at 147–49. Pickering v. Township High School Dist. 205, Will County, Ill., Board of Educ., 391 U.S. 563, 1 IER 8 (1968).

A court has found that plaintiff's participation in a rally protesting racial discrimination was speech entitled to First Amendment protection, as was plaintiff's filing with the Office of Human Rights.[152]

Courts continue to assess whether the alleged retaliation of an employer involved matters of public interest or only matters of personal concern. In *Grossman v. Schwartz*,[153] an employer's retaliation toward a civil service lawyer raised no constitutional claim since it did not involve matters of public interest. In *Callaway v. Hafeman*,[154] plaintiff's efforts to keep her complaint of sexual harassment confidential rendered her speech personal and not of public concern, and accordingly there was no First Amendment protection.

---

[152]Dougherty v. Barry, 604 F. Supp. 1424, 37 FEP 1169 (D.D.C. 1985).

[153]No. CV-86-0209 (S.D.N.Y. 1986); *see also* Ferrara v. Mills, 781 F.2d 1508 (11th Cir. 1986) (public employee could not transform personal grievance into matter of public concern solely by involving a supposed popular interest in manner in which public institutions are run).

[154]628 F. Supp. 1478 (W.D. Wis. 1986), *aff'd*, 832 F.2d 414, 45 FEP 154 (7th Cir. 1987).

## CHAPTER 16

# ENTERING THE WORK FORCE

## II. CREATING THE APPLICANT POOL

### A. Word-of-Mouth Recruitment

Courts have continued to hold that word-of-mouth recruitment is not *per se* illegal, and that plaintiffs must establish liability by demonstrating that the practice is part of a pattern of intentional discrimination or, alternatively, that there exists a causal relationship between word-of-mouth recruitment and a demonstrated significant disparate impact on a protected class.[1]

---

[1]Atonio v. Wards Cove Packing Co., 810 F.2d 1477, 43 FEP 130 (9th Cir. 1987) (en banc) (word-of-mouth hiring and other challenged employment practices should be evaluated not only for possible disparate treatment but also under discriminatory impact analysis provided plaintiffs have satisfied "[t]he three elements of the plaintiffs' prima facie case [which] are that they must (1) show a significant disparate impact on a protected class, (2) identify specific employment practices or selection criteria and (3) show the [causal] relationship between the identified practices and the impact." 43 FEP at 134). *And compare* Markey v. Tenneco Oil Co., 707 F.2d 172, 32 FEP 148 (5th Cir. 1983) (word-of-mouth recruiting not discriminatory where trial court's labor market definition not clearly erroneous; market was based upon percentage of black applicants from each of four parishes within SMSA during relevant time period adopted by trial court); Clark v. Chrysler Corp., 673 F.2d 921, 927, 28 FEP 342, 347 (7th Cir.), *cert. denied,* 459 U.S. 873, 29 FEP 1560 (1982) (where percentage of minority applicants hired exceeded their representation in applicant pool and relevant labor market, use of word-of-mouth methods to publicize job openings, together with predominantly white work force, found not to have had disparate impact on minorities); Cage v. IMF dba Interstate Motor Freight Sys., 36 FEP 1085 (W.D. Tenn. 1984) (word-of-mouth recruitment not in violation of Title VII where it was not only medium used and resulted in racially balanced and representative applicant pool); *and* Gay v. Waiters' & Dairy Lunchmen's Local 30, 694 F.2d 531, 554, 30 FEP 605, 623 (9th Cir. 1982) (word-of-mouth recruiting along with subjective hiring criteria found not to make out prima facie case of intentional discrimination); Smith v. Western Elec. Co., 770 F.2d 520, 38 FEP 1605 (5th Cir. 1985) (word-of-mouth recruiting not unlawful where employer proved it listed jobs with State Employment Commission and large numbers of blacks applied for entry-level positions); Cuellar v. City of Cuero Police Dep't, 40 FEP 1188 (S.D. Tex. 1985) (informal, word-of-mouth recruitment and hiring procedures of police department in small rural community reflect size and life style of the area rather than intent to discriminate against Hispanic patrolman candidate) *with* Carmichael v. Birmingham Saw Works, 738 F.2d 1126, 35 FEP 791 (11th Cir. 1984) (word-of-mouth hiring policy suspect when black plaintiff told no work available, is hired as part-time janitor, and in same month white is hired as a salesperson); Domingo v. New England Fish Co., 727 F.2d 1429, 34 FEP 584, *modified,* 742 F.2d 520, 37 FEP 1303 (9th Cir. 1984) (word-of-mouth recruiting, nepotism, subjective criteria, and separate hiring channels for different job categories all support conclusion of race discrimination); Harris v. Birmingham Bd. of Educ., 712 F.2d 1377, 32 FEP 1198 (11th Cir. 1983) (same); NAACP v. City of Evergreen, Ala., 693 F.2d 1367, 1369, 30 FEP 925, 926 (11th Cir. 1982) (lack of system of advertising job vacancies other than by word-of-mouth "undoubtedly operated to the benefit of white applicants and to reduce the number of potential black applicants" by excluding blacks from access to such information); Cox v. American Cast Iron Pipe Co., 784 F.2d 1546, 40 FEP 678 (11th Cir.), *cert. denied,* 479 U.S. 883, 41 FEP 1712 (1986) (where employer no longer maintains clear policy of exclusion but continues to hire by word-of-mouth, or through other informal procedures, court holds that nonapplicant establishes prima facie case of discrimination in hiring by showing that employer had some reason to consider him for the post); Lams v. General Waterworks Corp., 766 F.2d 386, 38 FEP 516 (8th Cir. 1985) (reliance on word-of-mouth recruitment and other factors including isolation of black candidate pool in segregated work force required finding of Title VII liability); *and* EEOC v. Chicago Miniature Lamp Works, 622 F. Supp. 1281, 39 FEP 297 (N.D. Ill. 1985) (extensive statistical analysis in district court findings and conclusions under disparate treatment and disparate impact models; employer liable under disparate impact theory where heavy reliance on word-of-mouth recruiting resulted in exclusion of blacks from network of information concerning jobs and gross underrepresentation in both applicant flow and work force).

## B. Nepotism

Hiring policies that favor family members are subject to close scrutiny because of their inherent tendency to "select out" prospective applicants who may be members of a protected class. Courts have found nepotism illegal under a disparate impact analysis.[2]

Antinepotism policies, on the other hand, have survived a sex discrimination analysis in several cases involving husband-wife situations, and generally have been allowed absent proof that implementation of the policies has a disparate impact on males or females.[3]

## C. Walk-In Applications

Direct or "walk-in" application remains the most common method of obtaining employment. Courts have generally found this recruiting method lawful in the absence of a significant disparity between an employer's applicant pool and the relevant labor market.[4]

---

[2]George v. Farmers Elec. Coop., 715 F.2d 175, 32 FEP 1801 (5th Cir. 1983); Domingo v. New England Fish Co., *supra* note 1; Bonilla v. Oakland Scavenger Co., 697 F.2d 1297, 31 FEP 50 (9th Cir. 1982), *cert. denied,* 467 U.S. 1251, 34 FEP 1800 (1984) (company policy which restricted ownership of company stock to "family members," all of whom were of Italian ancestry, and reserved higher paying jobs for shareholder-employees, had clear disparate impact upon black and Spanish-surname employees; court rejected argument that company's legitimate interest in protecting family members outweighed national interest in eliminating employment discrimination based on race and national origin); Kraszewski v. State Farm Gen. Ins. Co., 38 FEP 197 (N.D. Cal. 1985) (insurance company's extensive use of nepotism in appointment of male trainee agents ensured gross underrepresentation of women in its sales force by deterring women who knew of this practice). *But see* Scott v. Pacific Maritime Ass'n, 695 F.2d 1199, 30 FEP 1517 (9th Cir. 1983) (company's "permissive rule" offering employment advantage to sons and daughters of deceased longshoremen or ships' clerks under certain circumstances did not have disparate impact on minorities; effects of rule were *de minimis* and there was no evidence that minorities were underrepresented in clerks' union) *and* Green v. Edward J. Bettinger Co., 608 F. Supp. 35, 36 FEP 452 (E.D. Pa. 1984), *aff'd without opinion,* 791 F.2d 917, 41 FEP 1888 (3d Cir. 1986), *cert. denied,* 479 U.S. 1069 (1987) (sole proprietorship employer did not discriminate against 42-year-old female employee by failing to consider her for position created specifically for employer's son; employee did not meet requirement of position of being employer's son and employer articulated nondiscriminatory justification for his choice; employer's grooming of son to take over business does not violate Title VII).

[3]Parsons v. County of Del Norte, 728 F.2d 1234, 34 FEP 571 (9th Cir.), *cert. denied,* 469 U.S. 846, 35 FEP 1608 (1984) (county's no-nepotism hiring policy not subject to strict scrutiny under Equal Protection and Due Process clauses since no fundamental rights involved; policy held constitutional); Cutts v. Fowler, 692 F.2d 138, 34 FEP 698 (D.C. Cir. 1982) (court rejected claim of female plaintiff that antinepotism provision of Civil Service Reform Act was unconstitutional as applied to her, in that her transfer to new division after her husband became head of division in which she worked imposed unconstitutional burden on her freedom to marry; burden minimized by her reassignment to new division at her same grade and salary); Slater v. Guest Servs., 33 FEP 886 (D.D.C. 1981) (female's access to confidential information constituted legitimate, nondiscriminatory reason for her termination where she was employed in same department as her nonmanagement spouse, even though company rules permitted male relatives to work together in same department); Fitzpatrick v. Duquesne Light Co., 601 F. Supp. 160, 37 FEP 843 (W.D. Pa.), *aff'd without opinion,* 779 F.2d 42 (3d Cir. 1985) (antinepotism policy requiring transfer of less senior employee who marries another employee upheld); Thomson v. Sanborn's Motor Express, 154 N.J. Super. 555, 382 A.2d 53, 30 FEP 33 (App. Div. 1977) (employer's policy prohibiting contemporaneous full-time employment of relatives in same department as applied to spouses does not constitute discrimination because of marital status); Miller v. C.A. Muer Corp., 420 Mich. 355, 362 N.W.2d 650, 43 FEP 1195 (Sup. Ct. 1984) (same); City of Simi Valley, Cal. v. Fair Employment & Hous. Comm. of Cal., 172 Cal. App. 3d 1254, 39 FEP 863 (1985) (although policies barring employment of spouses of employees may violate California Fair Employment and Housing Act prohibition against discrimination on account of marital status, employer may refuse to hire spouse where jobs in question might involve greater potential conflicts of interest or other hazards for married couples than for other persons). *But see* EEOC v. Rath Packing Co., 787 F.2d 318, 40 FEP 580 (8th Cir.), *cert. denied,* 479 U.S. 910, 41 FEP 1712 (1986) (no-spouse rule subject to "compelling need" standard where work force predominantly male); Kilgo v. Bowman Transp., 576 F. Supp. 600, 40 FEP 1412 (N.D. Ga. 1984), *aff'd,* 789 F.2d 859, 40 FEP 1415 (11th Cir. 1986) (defendant enjoined from enforcing antinepotism rule against female spouses of employees).

[4]Clark v. Chrysler Corp., *supra* note 1 (employer's recruiting practices, including posting sign above plant door to indicate applications were being taken, had no disparate impact on blacks, where plaintiff

## E. Chilling

The Seventh and Eleventh circuits have reaffirmed the principle that even plaintiffs who never formally applied for employment may state a claim under Title VII where recruiting methods never brought the opening to their attention or where the employer creates "an atmosphere in which employees understand their applying for certain positions is fruitless."[5]

In *General Contractors Association of New York v. Teamsters Local 282,*[6] a federal district court vacated an arbitrator's award providing for the stationing of teamsters equipped with radios to control access to each construction site and direct job applicants to an adjacent employment office. The award was the aftermath of a dispute between a construction worker and a minority job applicant. The court found that employment in the New York construction industry was obtained in three ways, the first two of which were not freely available to nonwhites: union hiring hall; referral by relatives and friends to available jobs; and the shape-up system, by which applicants went directly to the job site and applied to the foreman or superintendent of their particular skill. Here, evidence showed that in seeking the arbitrator's award, Local 282 intended to exclude minorities from construction sites, ostensibly for safety reasons. The court found this had "some impact, although not controlling impact," on whether the award violated public policy and federal law.[7] The court found that the award would have a discriminatory impact on nonwhites seeking construction work as well as a chilling effect on future minority applicants; and referral to an adjacent employment office would, for practical purposes, be illegally based on race, since white applicants would have additional access to hiring halls and referrals. The court vacated the award and directed the arbitrator to explore possible alternative remedies that would address the union's legitimate safety concerns without infringing upon the rights of minority applicants.

Courts have continued to assess the possible chilling effect on applicants of other apparently neutral job requirements.[8]

---

failed to demonstrate disparity in minority hiring); Waters v. Furnco Constr. Corp., 688 F.2d 39, 29 FEP 1256 (7th Cir. 1982), *on remand from* 438 U.S. 567, 17 FEP 1062 (1978) (no evidence of pretext in employer's proffered reason for refusal to hire at the gate, namely, need to obtain workers known from past experience to be sufficiently qualified).

[5]Babrocky v. Jewel Food Co., 773 F.2d 857, 867, 38 FEP 1667, 1674 (7th Cir. 1985) (reversing district court's dismissal of claim where plaintiffs failed to prove they applied for position; rigid insistence on *McDonnell Douglas* requirement of application was erroneous where employer filled position through union hiring hall, never posted notices of vacancies, and union never recommended female members for position in question); Cox v. American Cast Iron Pipe Co., *supra* note 1.

[6]28 FEP 1203 (S.D.N.Y. 1982). *See also* Andrews v. Bechtel Power Corp., 780 F.2d 124, 39 FEP 1033 (1st Cir. 1985), *cert. denied,* 476 U.S. 1172, 40 FEP 1873 (1986) (affirmed trial judgment dismissing Title VII race discrimination claim by *pro se* plaintiff against a union which had no black members and which followed a policy of referring union members to jobs ahead of nonmembers and then referring nonmembers on first-come-first-served basis).

[7]*Id.* at 1207.

[8]Kilgo v. Bowman Transp., 570 F. Supp. 1509, 31 FEP 1451 (N.D. Ga. 1983), *modified as to remedy,* 576 F. Supp. 600, 40 FEP 1412 (N.D. Ga. 1984), *aff'd,* 789 F.2d 859, 40 FEP 1415 (11th Cir. 1986) (applicant flow for posted driver positions not an appropriate labor pool because, *inter alia,* defendant's requirement of one year's experience in over-the-road driving was more likely to dissuade women than men from applying) (defendant to take "aggressive and determined" steps to recruit qualified women); Gavagan v. Danbury Civil Serv. Comm'n, 32 EPD ¶33,674 (D. Conn. 1983) (municipality enjoined from making appointments from eligibility list that awarded preference points to candidates with voluntary firefighting experience; court found, *inter alia,* hostility in private, volunteer fire companies toward women and minorities becoming members, thereby causing drastic chilling effect). *See also* Kraszewski

Exclusion from the applicant pool can also be grounds for a finding of bias. In *Building & Construction Trades Council v. Mayor of Camden*,[9] the Court held invalid a local ordinance adopted as part of the city's affirmative action program that would require that not less than 40 percent of the employees working on city construction projects be residents. Such exclusion of nonresidents from employment violated their constitutionally protected privilege to pursue a common calling to work.

Courts have continued to rule that age, height, and weight limits are in some circumstances not lawful.[10]

## III. Selecting From the Applicant Pool

### A. Selection Criteria

Although courts continue to scrutinize allegedly subjective hiring criteria with particular care, and the Supreme Court has held that such criteria are subject to the disparate impact test, the use of subjective criteria continues to be only marginally relevant where discriminatory intent is at issue, unless the criteria were actually applied in a discriminatory manner.[11]

---

v. State Farm Gen. Ins. Co., *supra* note 2 (applicants as class members were deterred and deterrance was not the result of an objective job requirement).

[9]465 U.S. 208 (1984). *Cf.* Pegues v. Mississippi State Employment Serv., 699 F.2d 760, 31 FEP 257 (5th Cir.), *cert. denied,* 464 U.S. 991, 33 FEP 440 (1983) (state employment service's discretionary and subjective classification and referral system may provide opportunity for intentional discrimination); Dillon v. Coles, 746 F.2d 998, 36 FEP 159 (3d Cir. 1984), *aff'g* 35 FEP 1239 (W.D. Pa. 1983) (qualified female applicant unlawfully excluded from employment as house parent in male teenage delinquency home where State Director requested and Civil Service Commission approved use of list restricted to qualified male applicants); Draper v. Smith Tool & Eng'g Co., 728 F.2d 256, 35 FEP 1402 (6th Cir. 1984) (no clear error in finding discrimination where employer had never employed a black in its 19-year history and failed to hire black job applicant who was qualified); Lewis v. Smith, 731 F.2d 1535, 34 FEP 1313 (11th Cir. 1984) (plaintiff's application was not reviewed because director would not hire female for investigator position; finding plaintiff was less qualified than male hires clearly erroneous when application records were destroyed and hiring officials have no recall of comparative qualifications); Ross v. City of Ft. Wayne, 590 F. Supp. 299, 35 FEP 1378 (N.D. Ind. 1983) (black applicant to police academy suffered disparate treatment where he was as well or better qualified than several candidates ultimately selected and other factors taken into account were unexplained); Morgan v. Department of the Treasury, 594 F. Supp. 476, 35 FEP 1541 (D.D.C. 1984), *aff'd without opinion,* 784 F.2d 1131 (D.C. Cir. 1986) (applicant did not suffer disparate treatment where those hired were as qualified as he, and employer did not intend to treat black applicants different from whites; where selection process was rational, statistics showing that first 30 applicants randomly selected would not have been white are not probative). *See infra,* note 11.

[10]*Compare* EEOC v. City of Linton, Ind., 623 F. Supp. 724, 40 FEP 607 (S.D. Ind. 1985) (state law prohibiting municipalities from hiring applicants over age 36 to regular police force not protected by BFOQ defense) *and* New York City Dep't of Personnel v. New York State Div. of Human Rights, 58 A.D.2d 787, 396 N.Y.S.2d 845, 39 FEP 927 (1977), *aff'd,* 44 N.Y.2d 904, 407 N.Y.S.2d 637, 379 N.E.2d 165 (1978) (New York City unlawfully discriminated against 54-year-old applicant when it refused to hire her as Parking Enforcement Agent; court rejected claim that age was a BFOQ, since restriction was eliminated on next exam) *and* Hahn v. City of Buffalo, 770 F.2d 12, 38 FEP 1069 (2d Cir. 1985) (statute making ineligible all police officer applicants over age 29 invalid under ADEA, which prohibits maximum age limits for hiring, as well as firing; court affirmed holding that age was not a BFOQ, since more than half of Buffalo police officers were over age 40 and a significant percentage of persons over age 40 could perform at level of average person in his or her twenties), *with* Fahn v. Cowlitz County, Wash., 93 Wash.2d 368, 610 P.2d 857, 39 FEP 387 (Sup. Ct. 1980) (sheriff's department entitled to show job-relatedness of height and weight requirements; existence of officers on force below minimum height did not automatically negate business necessity defense).

[11]*See generally* Chapter 6 (Subjective Criteria), particularly the discussion of the Supreme Court's recent decision in *Watson v. Fort Worth Bank & Trust Co.,* 487 U.S. —, 47 FEP 102 (1988), and the discussions and citations by the Ninth Circuit en banc in Atonio v. Wards Cove Packing Co., *supra* note 1.

*Decisions resolving these issues in favor of the defendant employer include:* Davis v. City of Dallas, 777 F.2d 205, 39 FEP 744 (5th Cir. 1985), *cert. denied,* 476 U.S. 1116, 40 FEP 1320 (1986) (court affirmed validity of educational and other hiring requirements for police officer positions because they were sufficiently job-related even though there was an adverse disparate impact); Gillespie v. Wisconsin, 771 F.2d 1035, 38 FEP 1487 (7th Cir. 1985), *cert. denied,* 474 U.S. 1083, 39 FEP 1424 (1986) (affirming district court's refusal to find disparate impact discrimination; district court properly found that essay tests and scored interviews measured abilities necessary to perform duties of personnel manager positions, e.g., to write standard English, interpersonal skills, decision making, ability to work under pressure, ability to prepare position descriptions, ability to establish priorities as in planning a recruiting trip; after extensive analysis of employer's test procedures, court rejected plaintiff's challenges to tests including argument that Uniform Guidelines express preference for criterion-related validity as opposed to content validity); Clay v. Hyatt Regency Hotel, 724 F.2d 721, 33 FEP 1364 (8th Cir. 1984) (although black applicant was denied position because bell captain found him headstrong, court found hotel's explanation that applicant was rejected because he would not fit into its organization was not pretextual when supported by statistics showing that substantial percentage of hotel's jobs were filled by blacks); Gay v. Waiters' & Dairy Lunchmen's Local 30, *supra* note 1, at 544–55; White v. Vathally, 570 F. Supp. 1431, 32 FEP 1611 (D. Mass. 1983), *aff'd,* 732 F.2d 1037, 34 FEP 1130 (1st Cir.), *cert. denied,* 469 U.S. 933, 36 FEP 112 (1984) (employer's articulated reasons for hiring a male rather than a female not pretextual because male had superior educational background, and consideration of this factor by employer was reasonable business decision); Jordan v. Tenpenny, 39 EPD ¶ 35,815 (M.D. Tenn. 1985) (employer established legitimate, nondiscriminatory reason for not hiring black, female applicant: negative references from past employers); Coleman v. St. Regis Corp., 39 FEP 479 (N.D. Ala. 1985) (court ruled that employer is entitled to establish legitimate, nondiscriminatory minimum qualifications for a position and that computer and accounting skills were reasonable requirements for this type of company); EEOC v. Sears Roebuck & Co., 628 F. Supp. 1264, 39 FEP 1672 (N.D. Ill. 1986), *aff'd,* 839 F.2d 302, 45 FEP 1257 (7th Cir. 1988) (use of highly subjective criteria for selection of commissioned sales personnel was not unlawful in absence of evidence of disparate impact on female applicants); EEOC Dec. 85-1, 36 FEP 1890 (1984) (Commission found prima facie case rebutted by statement to claimant that while athletic background was not necessary, it was helpful and all persons hired for position had prior athletic background).

*Decisions resolving those issues in favor of plaintiffs include:* Anderson v. City of Bessemer City, N.C., 470 U.S. 564, 37 FEP 396 (1985) (Fourth Circuit erred in denying plaintiff relief where district court's findings regarding petitioner's superior qualifications and bias of selection committee are sufficient to support inference plaintiff was denied position of recreational director on account of her sex); Fowler v. Blue Bell, 737 F.2d 1007, 35 FEP 752 (11th Cir. 1984) (where employer's reasons for rejection of employment application are based on purely subjective factors, defendant's burden is greater); Lewis v. Bloomsburg Mills, 773 F.2d 561, 567–70, 38 FEP 1692, 1698–1700 (4th Cir. 1985) (rejecting employer's defense that experience requirement sufficiently and legitimately explained selection rates reflecting disproportionate adverse impact on black females; employer's evidence was largely anecdotal testimony unsupported by statistical or other evidence of hiring decisions; plaintiff's evidence undercut claim that experience was required; hiring process was "manifestly subjective;"); Cox v. American Cast Iron Pipe Co., 784 F.2d 1546, 40 FEP 678 (11th Cir. 1986), *rev'g, vacating and remanding* 585 F. Supp. 1143, 36 FEP 1111 (N.D. Ala. 1984), *cert. denied,* 479 U.S. 883, 41 FEP 1712 (1986) (court concluded respondent company had policy of pervasive and overt work force sex segregation which was maintained through word-of-mouth hiring and system of subjective evaluation); Torres v. Wisconsin Dep't of Health & Social Servs., 639 F. Supp. 279, 40 FEP 1748 (E.D. Wis. 1986) (sex is not a BFOQ for correction officers; prior history of female inmates' physical and sexual abuse by men and lack of privacy arising from presence of male officers does not justify hiring only women); EEOC v. Rath Packing Co., *supra* note 3 (noting lack of objective criteria, court found hiring practices with discriminatory impact on women not justified by business necessity); Leftwich v. Harris-Stowe State College, 702 F.2d 686, 31 FEP 376 (8th Cir. 1983) (reservation of certain positions on college faculty for nontenured staff not shown necessary to achieve purported goal of increasing quality of faculty, where assertion that younger nontenured faculty would have new ideas apparently assumes that older tenured faculty members would cause college to "stagnate"); Minnesota v. Sports & Health Club dba St. Louis Park Sports & Health Club, 370 N.W.2d 844, 37 FEP 1463, 1470 (Minn. Sup. Ct. 1985) (employer's sincere religious beliefs did not justify refusal to hire "non-born again" Christians); Haskins v. Department of Health & Human Servs., 35 FEP 256 (W.D. Mo. 1984) (court held that employer's "recency factor," in which work experience more than 10 years old was not considered, disproportionately discriminated against female applicants, because women have greater tendency to leave work force for extended periods for purposes of child-rearing); Kilgo v. Bowman Transp., *supra* note 3 (remedy established for defendant's "flagrant and pernicious" use of prior over-the-road experience requirement, with adverse impact on women, and pattern and practice of disparate treatment of women applicants for over-the-road positions); Berkman v. City of New York, 626 F. Supp. 591, 43 FEP 305 (E.D.N.Y. 1985), *aff'd in relevant part,* 812 F.2d 52, 43 FEP 318 (2d Cir. 1987) (exam tested for important physical capacities but placed undue emphasis on speed and aerobic fitness; new scoring system to be developed with greater validity and least possible adverse impact on female applicants); Zalkins Peerless Wiping Co. v. Nebraska Equal Opportunity Comm'n, 217 Neb. 289, 348 N.W.2d 846, 39 FEP 46 (1984) (employment decisions based on subjective standards carry little weight in rebutting charges of discrimination; employer cannot shield its subjective hiring practice from scrutiny under Nebraska Fair Employment Practice Act by contending that it hires employees based on "gut reaction").

## B. Disparate Treatment

Courts continue to examine carefully the specific facts and circumstances of each case to determine if an applicant was subject to disparate treatment.[12]

---

[12]*Disparate treatment decisions for the plaintiff include:* Garza v. Brownsville Indep. School Dist., 31 FEP 396 (S.D. Tex. 1981), *rev'd and remanded as to remedy,* 700 F.2d 253, 31 FEP 403 (5th Cir. 1983) (employer determined in advance to hire a man and therefore paid little or no attention to plaintiff's background and qualifications); King v. Trans World Airlines, 738 F.2d 255, 35 FEP 102 (8th Cir. 1984) (female job applicant was asked about pregnancy, childbearing, and child care; no evidence male job applicants were asked same questions); EEOC v. Gaddis, 733 F.2d 1373, 34 FEP 1210 (10th Cir. 1984) (affirmed finding of intentional discrimination where district court found that employer's stated reasons for denying employment, that no vacancy existed and manager had no hiring authority, were pretextual); Joshi v. Florida State Univ. Health Center, 763 F.2d 1227, 38 FEP 38 (11th Cir.), *cert. denied,* 474 U.S. 948, 39 FEP 384 (1985) (where plaintiff was not even considered for the position, her qualifications vis-à-vis other applicants cannot be legitimate, nondiscriminatory reason for not hiring her); Easley v. Anheuser-Busch, 758 F.2d 251, 37 FEP 549 (8th Cir. 1985) (fact that plaintiff was tested almost nine months after she applied for position supports lower court's finding of intentional sex discrimination, where males were tested considerably earlier); Kilgo v. Bowman Transp., 789 F.2d 859, 40 FEP 1415 (11th Cir. 1986) (pattern and practice of disparate treatment found in failure to hire class of female truck drivers; not clearly erroneous for trial court to disregard applicant flow data in finding disparate impact, where posted over-the-road experience requirements and related practices deterred female applicants and some women were not allowed to file applications); Hahn v. City of Buffalo, *supra* note 10; Ross v. City of Ft. Wayne, *supra* note 9; Smith v. American Serv. Co. of Atlanta, 611 F. Supp. 321, 35 FEP 1552 (N.D. Ga. 1984) (employer's explanations for hiring decision were inconsistent with evidence); McDermott v. Lehman, 594 F. Supp. 1315, 36 FEP 531 (D. Me. 1984) (failure to complete formal application does not preclude plaintiff from establishing prima facie case, where he testified in deposition that Navy employee told him Navy was looking for younger engineer; plaintiff's testimony and other statements constituted direct evidence that Navy employee either rejected plaintiff because of his age or deterred him from applying because of his age); Griffin v. George B. Buck Consulting Actuaries, 551 F. Supp. 1385, 31 FEP 405 (S.D.N.Y. 1982) (black actuary established prima facie case; employer's general hiring statistics establishing employer does somewhat better than industry norm in hiring blacks do not rebut evidence that employer discriminated against particular individual); EEOC v. Riss Int'l Corp., 525 F. Supp. 1094, 35 FEP 416 (W.D. Mo. 1981) (10% ceiling on black employment constituted discrimination, even though based on mistaken view that racial "balance" was required to avoid reverse discrimination); Jackson v. City of Independence, Mo., 40 FEP 1466 (W.D. Mo. 1986) (plaintiff sought equitable relief under § 1983 and Title VII; jury verdict upheld her claim that she was denied employment three times as utility maintenance worker on basis of her sex; defendant, who conceded plaintiff was qualified for position, was ordered to employ her as utility maintenance worker, provide back pay, assign seniority benefits, and contribute to retirement plan); Parker v. Willis, Inc., of Carrabelle, 38 FEP 420 (N.D. Fla. 1980) (employer failed to rebut plaintiff's prima facie showing of race discrimination by arguing that they applied after hiring decision made, where employer interviewed and hired others after plaintiffs applied; employer failed to show those hired were better qualified than plaintiffs).

*Disparate treatment decisions for the defendant:* Jones v. Chubb/Pacific Indemnity Group, 35 FEP 1875 (C.D. Cal. 1983) (plaintiff failed to demonstrate he was qualified for position in face of employer's subjectively based evidence that he possessed poor verbal and written skills and lacked analytical skills); Cuddy v. Carmen, 762 F.2d 119, 37 FEP 1335 (D.C. Cir.), *cert. denied,* 474 U.S. 1034, 39 FEP 944 (1985) (testimony that best qualified applicant was hired supported finding that federal government did not discriminate against 65-year-old applicant); Morley v. County of Union, 35 FEP 1269 (D.N.J. 1984), *aff'd without opinion,* 760 F.2d 259, 41 FEP 64 (3d Cir. 1985) (plaintiff failed to prove employer's reasons for hiring younger person were pretextual, where younger applicant had experience, was familiar with government program that controlled job, and was more gregarious); Merwine v. State Insts. of Higher Learning Bd. of Trustees, 754 F.2d 631, 37 FEP 340 (5th Cir.), *cert. denied,* 474 U.S. —, 38 FEP 1727 (1985) (hiring committee's adherence to published minimum educational requirement not pretextual even though plaintiff's experience is equivalent, where no applicants lacking degree were considered; j.n.o.v. granted); Parker v. City of Indianapolis Bd. of School Comm'rs, 729 F.2d 524, 34 FEP 453 (7th Cir. 1984) (plaintiff failed to prove that hiring of male applicant because of his superior qualifications was pretext for discrimination); Grebin v. Sioux Falls Indep. School Dist. 49–5, 779 F.2d 18, 39 FEP 873 (8th Cir. 1985) (employer's reasons for hiring a man rather than a woman as English teacher were not pretextual in view of his greater work experience and outstanding qualifications; reliance on ability to coach as part of employment decision not sufficient to establish discrimination); Gilyard v. South Carolina Dep't of Youth Servs., 667 F. Supp. 266, 38 FEP 531 (D.S.C. 1985) (black school principal failed to establish prima facie case of race discrimination where his school was merged into second school whose white principal was retained; district had no obligation to place black principal in second school, where merger was not intended to effect integration); EEOC Dec. 86-5 (1985) (assignment of departmental secretary to place ice water pitchers on department chiefs' desks each day does not constitute sex discrimination; there were no male secretaries with whom to compare charging party and no other support functions had "female only" task assignments); Welborn v. Reynolds Metals Co., 629 F. Supp.

## C. Preemployment Inquiries

One court has observed that theoretically discriminatory questions that open an employment interview, even when used as "tension breakers" designed to relax the applicant, may be unlawful when they are directed to applicants who are unlikely to satisfy the employment criterion implied by the question.[13] However, in *Trapp v. State University College at Buffalo*,[14] the court determined that lying on the application was a good reason for refusal to hire plaintiff.

## IV. INITIAL JOB ASSIGNMENTS

Statistics continue to be the primary determinant in establishing claims of disparate treatment in initial job assignments.[15] Statistics alone, however, may not be sufficient to establish a prima facie case of discrimination where there is no showing that minorities assigned to the lower echelons were qualified for the more desirable positions.[16] The unexplained lack of transfers

---

1433, 40 FEP 1780 (N.D. Ala. 1986) (plaintiff failed to prove she was discriminated against where she was neither designated nor identified as an eligible female, as required by EEOC); Pridemore v. Rural Legal Aid Soc'y of W. Cent. Ohio, 625 F. Supp. 1180 (S.D. Ohio 1985) (plaintiff's discrimination claim rejected where plaintiff did not show his perceived handicap, cerebral palsy, was the basis for not being hired); Aleem aka Price v. United Parcel Serv., 39 FEP 594 (D. Ariz. 1985), aff'd, 815 F.2d 82 (9th Cir. 1987) (employer's reasons for not hiring black applicant not pretextual; applicant filled out applications inconsistently and failed to inform employer of prior knee injury).

[13]Thorne v. City of El Segundo, 726 F.2d 459, 33 FEP 441 (9th Cir. 1983), *cert. denied*, 469 U.S. 979, 36 FEP 234 (1984) (defendant considered female plaintiff's affair as a factor in decision not to hire her, but did not apply that factor equally to men); Bailey v. Southeastern Area Joint Apprenticeship Comm., 561 F. Supp. 895, 31 FEP 752 (N.D. W. Va. 1983) (questions at beginning of interview about military service unlawful when asked of women applicants).

[14]30 FEP 1499 (W.D.N.Y. 1983).

[15]*See generally* Chapter 36 (Proof). *See, e.g.*, Winfield v. St. Joe Paper Co., 38 EPD ¶ 35,580 (N.D. Fla. 1985) (unrebutted statistical evidence established overwhelming case of racial discrimination in employer's initial assignments of jobs); Bentley v. City of Thomaston, 32 FEP 1476 (M.D. Ga. 1983) (prima facie case of disparate treatment in hiring decisions, promotions, and pay established through statistics left unrebutted by defendant's affirmations of good faith in its hiring and promotion decisions); Veazie v. Greyhound Lines, 33 FEP 913 (E.D. La. 1983) (statistics alone may be sufficient, particularly where skill involved is one that many persons possess or can fairly readily acquire); United States v. New Jersey, 530 F. Supp. 328, 35 FEP 740 (D.N.J. 1981) (general population and labor force data appropriate for establishing prima facie case where employer hires unskilled applicants and trains them; employer's burden is to establish that applicant would not have been hired, even absent discrimination); Domingo v. New England Fish Co., 727 F.2d 1429, 34 FEP 584, *modified*, 742 F.2d 520, 37 FEP 1303 (9th Cir. 1984); Powell v. Georgia-Pacific Corp., 535 F. Supp. 713, 30 FEP 21 (W.D. Ark. 1980) (substantially greater percentage of blacks than whites assigned to more demanding and less desirable jobs); EEOC v. H.S. Camp & Sons, 542 F. Supp. 411, 33 FEP 330 (M.D. Fla. 1982) (blacks excluded entirely from certain departments). *But see* Anderson v. University of N. Iowa, 779 F.2d 441, 39 FEP 1379 (8th Cir. 1985) (statistics on composition of a work force may not be controlling with respect to individual hiring decisions); Wallace v. University of Mo., St. Louis, 624 F. Supp. 560 (E.D. Mo.), *aff'd without opinion*, 802 F.2d 465 (8th Cir. 1986) (statistics for school's overall hiring policies are of little worth where no discrimination is shown in particular department in which plaintiff is employed).

[16]Hill v. K-Mart Corp., 699 F.2d 776, 31 FEP 269 (5th Cir. 1983) (employee's statistical evidence failed to establish pattern or practice of intentional discrimination in compensation, hiring, placement, or promotion); Payne v. Travenol Laboratories, 673 F.2d 798, 28 FEP 1212 (5th Cir.), *cert. denied*, 459 U.S. 1038, 30 FEP 440 (1982) (no proof that blacks assigned to custodial jobs had requisite education for operative work); Moore v. Summa Corp., Hughes Helicopters Div., 708 F.2d 475, 32 FEP 97 (9th Cir. 1983) (assuming impact analysis applicable, statistical evidence of allegedly discriminatory job assignments and promotions inadequate where not supplemented with evidence that class members were qualified for upper-level skilled positions, or evidence that comparison with qualified labor pool showed adverse impact); EEOC v. Hartford Fire Ins. Co., 31 FEP 531 (D. Conn. 1983) (insurance company rebutted former female employee's claim by introducing evidence that it employed at least eight women as claims representatives during period former employee claimed field was closed to women); Falcon v. General Tel. Co. of the Sw., 611 F. Supp. 707, 39 FEP 1116 (N.D. Tex. 1985), *aff'd*, 815 F.2d 317, 43

to more desirable positions may support a finding of intentional discrimination in initial work assignments,[17] and evidence of discrimination in the assignment of specific tasks within a department or job category may be probative of a pattern and practice of discrimination in assigning jobs generally.[18] Furthermore, an employer may be found liable for disproportionately excluding members of a protected group from a particular job even where that job has not been shown to be more desirable than others.[19]

A claim of disparity in job assignments in only one segment or type of work within the employer's work force is cognizable under Title VII, even if the protected group generally fared as well as or better than the rest of the work force in overall job assignments. In *Williams v. New Orleans Steamship Association,*[20] the Fifth Circuit held that discrimination in assigning one particular type of longshore work was actionable even though there was no discrimination in the assignment of all other jobs. Thus, the practice of allocating grain work equally between the black union and white union was unlawful when the membership in the black local was three times greater than in the white local. The fact that the allocation rule was required by the contract negotiated between the employer and the union locals did not justify the intentional discrimination.

The Fourth Circuit, in a hiring and promotion case,[21] found that the county's system of granting preference to internal applicants for jobs was a valid seniority system under § 703(h) of Title VII. The court rejected the plaintiff's static work force statistical analysis as being unreliable, and questioned the underlying assumption that a work force hired in a completely nondiscriminatory way would mirror the general population, as a result of the vagaries of supply and demand in the labor market. The static work force analysis here was especially skewed by the inclusion of employees hired before the applicable date of Title VII. The court favored the county's use of applicant flow data in its statistics.

No recent developments have disturbed the line of decisions finding that applicant flow data are generally more convincing than work force/labor market comparisons and are preferred by the courts.[22]

---

FEP 1040 (5th Cir. 1987) (employer's applicant flow data showing it hired greater portion of Mexican-American applicants than white applicants found sufficient to rebut plaintiff's prima facie case of discrimination on account of national origin).

[17] EEOC v. H.S. Camp & Sons, *supra* note 15, at 446, 33 FEP at 355.

[18] *Id.* (blacks tended to receive more dangerous and undesirable jobs).

[19] Williams v. New Orleans S.S. Ass'n, 673 F.2d 742, 751, 28 FEP 1092, 1100 (5th Cir. 1982), *cert. denied,* 460 U.S. 1038, 31 FEP 368 (1983).

[20] Id.

[21] Allen v. Prince George's County, Md., 737 F.2d 1299, 38 FEP 1220 (4th Cir. 1984). *See* Moore v. Summa Corp., Hughes Helicopters Div., *supra* note 16. *See also* Shidaker v. Carlin, 782 F.2d 746, 39 FEP 1768 (7th Cir. 1986) (Seventh Circuit found that a female employee who was denied promotion made prima facie showing of disparate impact by evidencing that defendant promotes from within and that there is gross disparity between gender composition of relevant labor pool and composition of group occupying positions in question).

[22] In addition to Hazelwood School Dist. v. United States, 433 U.S. 299, 15 FEP 1 (1977), *see, e.g.,* Allen v. Prince George's County, Md., 737 F.2d 1299, 38 FEP 1220 (4th Cir. 1984); United States v. County of Fairfax, 629 F.2d 932, 23 FEP 485 (4th Cir. 1980), *cert. denied,* 449 U.S. 1078, 24 FEP 1154 (1981), *on remand,* 25 FEP 662 (E.D. Va. 1981); Reynolds v. Sheet Metal Workers Local 102, 498 F. Supp. 952, 965, 24 FEP 648 (D.D.C. 1980), *aff'd,* 702 F.2d 221, 25 FEP 837 (D.C. Cir. 1981).

CHAPTER 17

# PROMOTION

As women and minorities enter professional partnerships, the criteria for partnership selection have received increasing attention from an equal employment perspective, and the Supreme Court has declared, in *Hishon v. King & Spalding*,[1] that consideration for partnership can be a "term, condition or privilege of employment" which must not be based on factors prohibited by Title VII.

## I. Publicizing the Opening

Courts have continued to examine employer conduct such as efforts to make members of protected groups aware of job offerings,[2] use of impermissi-

---

[1]467 U.S. 69, 34 FEP 1406 (1984) (woman lawyer's complaint that law partnership discriminated when it failed to invite her to become partner states a claim that is cognizable under Title VII). *But see* Price Waterhouse v. Hopkins, 57 U.S.L.W. 4469, 49 FEP 954 (1989), *rev'g and remanding* 825 F.2d 458, 44 FEP 825 (D.C. Cir. 1987).

[2]Greer v. University of Ark. Bd. of Trustees, 544 F. Supp. 1085, 33 FEP 77 (E.D. Ark. 1982), *aff'd in pertinent part and vacated in part sub nom.* Behlar v. Smith, 719 F.2d 950, 33 FEP 92 (8th Cir. 1983), *cert. denied,* 466 U.S. 958, 34 FEP 1096 (1984) (female faculty member discriminated against when university appointed male to position prior to announcing vacancy and job announcements were tailored to fit qualifications of preselected male); Payne v. Travenol Laboratories, 673 F.2d 798, 28 FEP 1212 (5th Cir.), *cert. denied,* 459 U.S. 1038, 30 FEP 440 (1982) (failure to post job vacancies can only discourage applications by blacks to greater degree than it discourages whites who garner information through grapevine); Paxton v. Union Nat'l Bank, 688 F.2d 552, 29 FEP 1233 (8th Cir. 1982), *cert. denied,* 460 U.S. 1083, 31 FEP 824 (1983) (employer bank, which discriminated against blacks in its promotion practices, must post timely notices of all nonentry-level job vacancies and notices must contain reasonably specific job descriptions); Foster v. Arcata Assocs., 772 F.2d 1453, 38 FEP 1850 (9th Cir. 1985), *cert. denied,* 475 U.S. 1048, 40 FEP 272 (1986) (Title VII does not require employer to canvass its employees regarding their job preferences before filling vacancies); Davis v. Richmond, Fredericksburg & Potomac R.R., 593 F. Supp. 271, 35 FEP 1140 (E.D. Va. 1984), *aff'd in part, rev'd in part,* 803 F.2d 1323, 42 FEP 69 (4th Cir. 1986) (failure to notify employees of openings and reliance on word-of-mouth to fill them had disparate impact on female applicants for promotion); Hartman v. Wick, 600 F. Supp. 361, 36 FEP 622 (D.D.C. 1984) (prima facie case of disparate treatment established, despite plaintiff's failure to complete application for vacant position; position description withdrawn after she complained about it, and male employee had been preselected for vacancy); Rodgers v. Peninsular Steel Co., 542 F. Supp. 1215, 31 FEP 107 (N.D. Ohio 1982) (black employee's failure to demonstrate interest in promotion when vacancy arose does not preclude prima facie case, since employer filled job with white nonemployee without informing its own employees of vacancy); Lams v. General Waterworks Corp., 766 F.2d 386, 38 FEP 516 (8th Cir. 1985) (word-of-mouth recruitment for promotion openings perpetuated segregation of work force and violated Title VII); Box v. A&P Tea Co., 772 F.2d 1372, 38 FEP 1509, 1513 (7th Cir. 1985), *cert. denied,* 478 U.S. 1010, 41 FEP 271 (1986) (in promotion system in which jobs are not posted and candidates for promotion are "sought out by managers," plaintiff not required to prove she applied for job in question; "application" element of prima facie case satisfied by showing she would have applied for opening had she known of it). *But see* Brooks v. Ashtabula County Welfare Dep't, 717 F.2d 263, 32 FEP 1368 (6th Cir. 1983), *cert. denied,* 466 U.S. 907, 35 FEP 1120 (1984) (absence of written promotion policies, objective merit evaluations, and job vacancy postings, while important in evaluating defendant's motivation, do not operate under *Burdine* to nullify defendant's stated legitimate reason for not promoting plaintiff); Clay v. Consumer Programs, 576 F. Supp. 185, 35 FEP 1497 (E.D. Mo. 1983), *aff'd,* 745 F.2d 501, 35 FEP 1502 (8th Cir. 1984) (notice of supervisory positions does not have to be posted where policy is to post only nonmanagement positions).

ble criteria by supervisors in making promotion recommendations,[3] or the "chilling effect" of a discriminatory environment on minority applications for promotions.[4] Many courts have held that an employee's failure to apply for a promotion will not in itself preclude a prima facie case of discrimination.[5]

---

[3]*Compare* Payne v. Travenol Laboratories, *supra* note 2 (evidence supports finding that supervisor's recommendation, which was major factor in promotions, was delivered without guidance by any objective standards and operated to discriminate against blacks) *and* Paxton v. Union Nat'l Bank, *supra* note 2 (employer must develop specific, written job descriptions and supervisor's recommendation regarding promotion of employee must be written and in accordance with guidelines) *with* Brooks v. Ashtabula County Welfare Dep't, *supra* note 2 (in disparate treatment case, fact that supervisors made promotion decisions, even though there were no written promotion policies, no advertising of job vacancies, and no reliance upon objective merit evaluations, did not foreclose employer from offering legitimate reasons for not promoting plaintiff). *Contrast* Krulik v. New York City Bd. of Educ., 781 F.2d 15, 39 FEP 1448 (2d Cir. 1986) (supervisor's promotion of individuals with whom she prefers to work is not discrimination under §§ 1981 or 1983) *and* EEOC v. General Tel. Co. of the Nw., 40 FEP 1533 (W.D. Wash. 1985) (there were significant differences between men and women as to geographic mobility, willingness to work part-time or on-call, technical training, education, and experience; thus, sex was not factor in promotion decisions) *and* Mantolete v. Bolger, 767 F.2d 1416, 38 FEP 1081, *amended,* 38 FEP 1517 (9th Cir. 1985) (to exclude handicapped persons from applicant pool, employer must show reasonable probability of substantial harm, based upon individuals' work and medical history, and must show accommodations) *with* Hogan v. Pierce, 31 FEP 115 (D.D.C. 1983) (black supervisor's perception that black employee not humble enough to be promoted impermissible since "humility" not demanded of white employees) *and* City of Schenectady v. State Div. of Human Rights, 37 N.Y.2d 421, 373 N.Y.S.2d 59, 335 N.E.2d 290, 35 FEP 823 (Ct. App. 1975), *reargument denied,* 38 N.Y.2d 856, 382 N.Y.S.2d 1031, 345 N.E.2d 606 (Ct. App. 1976) (questions to female officer about husband's and son's attitudes regarding her work constituted substantial evidence of discrimination) *and* Patterson v. Masem, 774 F.2d 251, 39 FEP 1266 (8th Cir. 1985) (plaintiff's "perceived abrasiveness" and antagonism she allegedly induced in others not legitimate factors in failure to promote her, where they were results of her peers' racism or disagreement with her stand on desegregation). *See also* Police Officers Ass'n (San Francisco) v. City & County of San Francisco, 621 F. Supp. 1225, 40 FEP 1480 (N.D. Cal. 1985), *rev'd,* 812 F.2d 1125, 43 FEP 495 (9th Cir. 1987) (district court held city's rescoring promotion tests complied with Title VII consent decree; court of appeals held that exams were invalid, since they had adverse effect on minorities and women, and that rescoring exams to achieve racial balance was unlawful); Price Waterhouse v. Hopkins, *supra* note 1 (where partnership evaluations include substantial reliance on appraisals including sexual stereotypings, burden of persuasion shifts to employer to show legitimate factors would produce same result).

[4]Craik v. Minnesota State Univ. Bd., 731 F.2d 465, 34 FEP 649 (8th Cir. 1984) (subjective selection process, dominated by men, for chairpersons of departments permits inference that women were reluctant to run, causing underrepresentation among chairpersons); Gifford v. Atchison, Topeka & Santa Fe Ry., 685 F.2d 1149, 29 FEP 1345 (9th Cir. 1982) (former railroad employee's allegation that she failed to apply for promotion to wire chief, because to do so would have been futile in light of employer's promotion policies, is sufficient to make out prima facie case); Gray v. Walgreen Co., 33 FEP 835 (N.D. Ill. 1983) (plaintiff's deposition testimony that he was deterred from participating in on-the-job training opportunities and thus was not promoted because of "chill" of defendant's discriminatory practices sufficient to overcome defendant's motion for summary judgment); Powell v. Georgia-Pacific Corp., 535 F. Supp. 713, 30 FEP 21 (W.D. Ark. 1980) (employees' reluctance to become supervisors explained by past harassment of black supervisors and by improbability of advancement into management); Nieuwdorp v. Boorstin, 40 FEP 1282 (D.D.C. 1986) (court found defendant reverse discriminated against plaintiff by limiting vacancy to females and minorities, and ordered: (1) his personnel records be altered to show he was qualified to apply for the position but was prevented from doing so; (2) he be assigned to the position should he return to work; and (3) he be awarded expenses as prevailing party). *But see* Wright v. Olin Corp., 697 F.2d 1172, 30 FEP 889 (4th Cir. 1982), *vacated,* 767 F.2d 915, 40 FEP 192 (4th Cir. 1984) (no "direct" evidence of chilling atmosphere since no employee had ever filed charge with EEOC alleging he had been rejected from program on basis of race, although it was well-known fact that apprenticeship program had no minorities); Spight v. Tidwell Indus., 551 F. Supp. 123, 130, 30 FEP 1423, 1428 (N.D. Miss. 1982) (no showing that applying for promotion would have been "futile gesture" when company had black foreman in the past and plaintiff himself had been a lead man). *See also* Taylor v. Hudson Pulp & Paper Corp., 778 F.2d 1455, 48 FEP 282 (11th Cir. 1986), *cert. denied,* 484 U.S. 953, 48 FEP 384 (1987) (in dissenting opinion, Clark, C.J., states district court erred by finding no discrimination when no appellants requested transfer; court failed to consider significant relevant evidence that appellants believed they could not apply for "men's" jobs).

[5]Box v. A&P Tea Co., *supra* note 2; Hartman v. Wick, *supra* note 2; Rodgers v. Peninsular Steel Co., *supra* note 2. *But see* Jones v. Birdsong, 530 F. Supp. 221, 38 FEP 577 (N.D. Miss. 1980), *aff'd,* 679 F.2d 24, 38 FEP 590 (5th Cir. 1982), *cert. denied,* 459 U.S. 1202, 38 FEP 672 (1983) (plaintiff failed to establish prima facie case where plaintiff never applied for position despite knowing application procedures and asserted no credible reason for this failure).

## II. DISPARATE TREATMENT

It is well settled that normal Title VII standards, as well as an "intent" requirement,[6] apply to both Title VII and § 1981[7] disparate treatment promotion cases. While some courts have questioned the applicability of the traditional *McDonnell Douglas*[8] approach to promotion cases,[9] this concern has generally been resolved on the basis that the *McDonnell Douglas* test of

---

[6]United States Postal Serv. Bd. of Governors v. Aikens, 460 U.S. 711, 31 FEP 609 (1983); Bell v. Birmingham Linen Serv., 715 F.2d 1552, 32 FEP 1673 (11th Cir. 1983), *cert. denied*, 467 U.S. 1204, 34 FEP 1400 (1984) (mere statement of legitimate nondiscriminatory reason does not rebut direct testimony defendant acted with discriminatory intent; such testimony is rebutted through proof that same decision would have been reached absent illegal motive); Krodel v. Young, 748 F.2d 701, 36 FEP 468 (D.C. Cir. 1984), *cert. denied*, 474 U.S. 817, 38 FEP 1727 (1986) (agency's preselection of younger employee for promotion, while insufficient itself to support finding of age discrimination, is relevant to issue of discriminatory intent); Anderson v. City of Bessemer City, 470 U.S. 564, 37 FEP 396 (1985), *rev'g* 717 F.2d 149, 32 FEP 1586 (4th Cir. 1983) (district court did not clearly err in its factual findings that petitioner was more highly qualified than successful male candidate promoted from within, and that petitioner was denied employment because of her sex); Trout v. Lehman, 702 F.2d 1094, 31 FEP 286 (D.C. Cir. 1983), *vacated*, 465 U.S. 1056, 34 FEP 76 (1984); Wilmore v. City of Wilmington, 699 F.2d 667, 31 FEP 2 (3d Cir. 1983); Cuthbertson v. Biggers Bros., 702 F.2d 454, 32 FEP 1592 (4th Cir. 1983); EEOC v. Exxon Shipping Co. dba Exxon Co., U.S.A., 745 F.2d 967, 36 FEP 330 (5th Cir. 1984); Pegues v. Mississippi State Employment Serv., 699 F.2d 760, 31 FEP 257 (5th Cir.), *cert. denied*, 464 U.S. 991, 33 FEP 440 (1983); Verniero v. Air Force Academy School Dist. No. 20, 705 F.2d 388, 31 FEP 871 (10th Cir. 1983); Perryman v. Johnson Prods. Co., 698 F.2d 1138, 31 FEP 93 (11th Cir. 1983); Lincoln v. University Sys. of Ga. Bd. of Regents, 697 F.2d 928, 31 FEP 22 (11th Cir.), *cert. denied*, 464 U.S. 826, 32 FEP 1768 (1983); Metrocare v. Washington Metro. Area Transit Auth., 679 F.2d 922, 28 FEP 1585 (D.C. Cir. 1982); Valentino v. United States Postal Serv., 674 F.2d 56, 28 FEP 593 (D.C. Cir. 1982); Wilson v. Legal Assistance of N.D., 669 F.2d 562, 27 FEP 1567 (8th Cir. 1982); Harrell v. Northern Elec. Co., 672 F.2d 444, 28 FEP 911, *modified on reh'g*, 679 F.2d 31, 29 FEP 913 (5th Cir.), *cert. denied*, 459 U.S. 1037, 30 FEP 440 (1982); Bell v. Bolger, 535 F. Supp. 997, 29 FEP 116 (E.D. Mo. 1982), *aff'd*, 708 F.2d 1312, 32 FEP 32 (8th Cir. 1983); Cunningham v. Housing Auth. of the City of Opelousas dba Opelousas Hous. Auth., 764 F.2d 1097, 38 FEP 417 (5th Cir.), *cert. denied*, 474 U.S. 1007, 39 FEP 720 (1985); Foster v. Arcata Assocs., *supra* note 2; Price Waterhouse v. Hopkins, *surpa* note 1 and Chapter 1 (Overview).

[7]Hill v. K-Mart Corp., 699 F.2d 776, 31 FEP 269 (5th Cir. 1983); Metrocare v. Washington Metro. Area Transit Auth., *supra* note 6; Payne v. Travenol Laboratories, *supra* note 2; Pouncy v. Prudential Ins. Co. of Am., 668 F.2d 795, 28 FEP 121 (5th Cir. 1982); Cunningham v. Housing Auth. of the City of Opelousas dba Opelousas Hous. Auth., *supra* note 6; Patterson v. Masem, *supra* note 3 (same standards of proof of race discrimination under Title VII and § 1981).

[8]McDonnell Douglas Corp. v. Green, 411 U.S. 792, 5 FEP 965 (1973).

[9]Mason v. Continental Ill. Nat'l Bank, 704 F.2d 361, 31 FEP 629 (7th Cir. 1983); Jones v. Western Geophysical Co. of Am., 669 F.2d 280, 29 FEP 1117 (5th Cir. 1982). *But see* Uviedo v. Steves Sash & Door Co., 738 F.2d 1425, 35 FEP 906 (5th Cir. 1984), *cert. denied*, 474 U.S. 1054, 39 FEP 1200 (1986) (Mexican-American plaintiff met *McDonnell Douglas* test when employer filled position with white employee at salary requested by plaintiff when promotion was first offered to her); Stallworth v. Shuler, 35 FEP 770 (N.D. Fla. 1984) (black plaintiff met *McDonnell Douglas* test when he was denied promotion to administrative position in school district, where he had requisite education, experience, and seniority and white individuals hired for the positions did not); McAdoo v. Toll, 591 F. Supp. 1399, 35 FEP 833 (D. Md. 1984) (black plaintiff established prima facie case by showing state university rejected her for senior-level professorship and later filled the position with white employee by making it junior-level position); Monroe v. Burlington Indus., 784 F.2d 568, 40 FEP 273 (4th Cir. 1986) (plaintiff satisfied *McDonnell Douglas* where she applied for, was qualified for, and was rejected for position which remained open after her rejection); Diaz v. AT&T, 752 F.2d 1356, 36 FEP 1742 (9th Cir. 1985) (plaintiff established case under *McDonnell Douglas*, even though the individual promoted instead of plaintiff was member of same protected class). *See also* Garlington v. St. Anthony's Hosp. Ass'n dba Conway County Hosp., 792 F.2d 752, 40 FEP 1734 (8th Cir. 1986) (black, Baptist plaintiff established prima facie discrimination case as required by *McDonnell Douglas* test, but failed to prove he had been victim of intentional discrimination); Navarro v. Delco Elecs., 38 FEP 863 (C.D. Cal. 1983) (plaintiff did not show defendant's failure to promote him was discriminatory, where he did not show he was qualified for promotion sought); Mughal v. Chart House dba Burger King, 40 FEP 626 (N.D. Ill. 1986) (proof plaintiff was denied promotion because he failed nonrequired exam and had attempted to procure a copy of exam prior to test date, along with evidence he had engaged in sexual harassment, sufficient to rebut prima facie case of discrimination on basis of national origin); Lams v. General Waterworks Corp., *supra* note 2 (*McDonnell Douglas* formula of little use in Title VII action brought by employees who were never actually considered for vacancies); Bishopp v. District of Columbia, 602 F. Supp. 1401, 37 FEP 235 (D.D.C. 1985), *rev'd in part and vacated in part*, 788 F.2d 781, 40 FEP 903 (D.C. Cir. 1986) (appeals court found pretextual fire department's motives for promoting black employee over five white male plaintiffs who claimed discrimination and retaliatory and constructive discharge).

a prima facie case and prescribed order of proof, as modified by *Burdine*,[10] continues to apply but is not to be followed "mechanically."[11] It is equally well settled that this standard is the appropriate one in most contexts, with the possible exception of the disparate treatment or disparate impact class action.[12]

---

[10]Texas Dep't of Community Affairs v. Burdine, 450 U.S. 248, 25 FEP 113 (1981); Stacey v. Allied Stores Corp., 768 F.2d 402, 38 FEP 773 (D.C. Cir. 1985) (district court erred in granting j.n.o.v. where jury found pretextual employer's refusal to rehire employee terminated for age-neutral reasons into lower position); Lamphere v. Brown Univ., 613 F. Supp. 971, 38 FEP 871 (D.R.I. 1985) (refusal to promote woman not discriminatory where she had poor relationship with entire department; inability to get along with people legitimate reason for refusal to promote); Weber v. Department of Agriculture, 784 F.2d 313, 40 FEP 228 (8th Cir. 1986) (under *Burdine*, plaintiff bears ultimate burden of proving employer discriminated on prohibited basis). *See also* Monroe v. Burlington Indus., *supra* note 9; Bell v. Birmingham Linen Serv., *supra* note 6 (articulation of legitimate, nondiscriminatory reason does not rebut direct testimony that defendant acted with discriminatory intent); Ibrahim v. New York State Dep't of Health, 581 F. Supp. 228, 38 FEP 1059 (E.D.N.Y. 1984) (summary judgment inappropriate when considering employer's denial of pretext—credibility crucial and plaintiff should be permitted to probe motivation). *But see* King v. Palmer, 778 F.2d 878, 39 FEP 877 (D.C. Cir. 1985) (*Burdine* construed to hold plaintiff should prevail where she established prima facie case of discrimination and discredit defendant's rebuttal, though no direct evidence of discrimination offered); Steckl v. Motorola, 703 F.2d 392, 31 FEP 705 (9th Cir. 1983) (summary judgment granted where plaintiff produced evidence establishing prima facie case of age discrimination but did not produce "specific evidence" employer's proffered reason for denied promotion was pretextual).

[11]Casillas v. United States Navy, 735 F.2d 338, 343, 34 FEP 1493, 1496 (9th Cir. 1984) ("No formal trifurcation of trial is required. . . ."). *Compare* Brooks v. Ashtabula County Welfare Dep't, *supra* note 2 (trial court misapplied *Burdine* by requiring defendant to prove stated reason motivated it to act, rather than requiring plaintiff to prove stated reason pretextual) *with* Geisler v. Folsom, 735 F.2d 991, 34 FEP 1581 (6th Cir. 1984) (plaintiff made out prima facie case when she showed she applied for engineer position for which she met requirements, requirements were changed one week later, and she was never interviewed); Trout v. Lehman, *supra* note 6 (to establish prima facie case of sex discrimination in initial grade placements or promotions, plaintiffs are required to show only that it is more likely than not that employers failed to place or promote women properly because of discriminatory intent); Mortensen v. Callaway, 672 F.2d 822, 29 FEP 111 (10th Cir. 1982) (defendant showed legitimate, nondiscriminatory reason for promotion of female plaintiff who had established prima facie case); Jones v. Western Geophysical Co., *supra* note 9; Lams v. General Waterworks Corp., *supra* note 2 (district court's rigid adherence to *McDonnell Douglas* test in error where plaintiffs not considered for promotion because they were unaware of promotion opportunities, supervisor discouraged their applications, and employer had race-biased job classifications). *See also* United States Postal Serv. Bd. of Governors v. Aikens, *supra* note 6 (in order to establish prima facie case, plaintiff need not prove his qualifications are superior to those of person promoted); Kimbrough v. Secretary of Air Force, 764 F.2d 1279, 38 FEP 383 (9th Cir. 1985); Maddox v. Claytor, 764 F.2d 1539, 38 FEP 713 (11th Cir. 1985), *aff'g* 38 FEP 755 (M.D. Ga. 1983); Elam v. C&P Tel. Co., 609 F. Supp. 938, 38 FEP 969 (D.D.C. 1984) (*Burdine* prima facie case established for failure to transfer, but employer met burden by showing no lateral transfers had been permitted; plaintiff failed to establish prima facie case for denial of promotions where he failed to show specific promotion applied for and denied); Cox v. American Cast Iron Pipe Co., 784 F.2d 1546, 40 FEP 678 (11th Cir.), *cert. denied,* 479 U.S. 883, 41 FEP 1712 (1986) (*Burdine* standard held not applicable, where unlawful policy gave rise to presumption of discrimination and thus placed on employer burden of proving job decisions were not made pursuant to policy); Holmes v. Bevilacqua, 774 F.2d 636, 38 FEP 1831 (4th Cir. 1985) (*McDonnell Douglas* prima facie test met even though position filled—sufficient to show position remained in existence). *See also* Jackson v. RKO Bottlers of Toledo, 743 F.2d 370, 35 FEP 1318 (6th Cir. 1984), *cert. denied,* 478 U.S. — (1986).

[12]Jepsen v. Florida Bd. of Regents, 37 FEP 312 (N.D. Fla. 1982), *aff'd,* 754 F.2d 924, 37 FEP 326 (11th Cir. 1985) (female assistant professor not promoted to associate professor for 24 years established prima facie case by showing similarly qualified men were promoted and no women were promoted; combination of subjective criteria with disparate impact on protected group establishes prima facie case); Ward v. Arkansas State Police, 714 F.2d 62, 32 FEP 1434 (8th Cir. 1983); Cuthbertson v. Biggers Bros., *supra* note 6; Hawkins v. Anheuser-Busch, 697 F.2d 810, 30 FEP 1170 (8th Cir. 1983); Lincoln v. University Sys. of Ga. Bd. of Regents, *supra* note 6; Garner v. Boorstin, 690 F.2d 1034, 29 FEP 1762 (D.C. Cir. 1982); Freeman v. Lewis, 675 F.2d 398, 28 FEP 833 (D.C. Cir. 1982); Goff v. Continental Oil Co., 678 F.2d 593, 29 FEP 79 (5th Cir. 1982); White v. Washington Pub. Power Supply Sys., 692 F.2d 1286, 30 FEP 453 (9th Cir. 1982); Laborde v. University of Cal. Regents, 686 F.2d 715, 28 FEP 1183 (9th Cir.), *cert. denied,* 459 U.S. 1173, 36 FEP 1776 (1982); Farkas v. New York State Dep't of Health, 554 F. Supp. 24, 30 FEP 538 (N.D.N.Y. 1982), *aff'd without opinion,* 767 F.2d 907 (2d Cir.), *cert. denied,* 474 U.S. 1033 (1985); Leibovitch v. Administrator, Veterans Admin., 33 FEP 777 (D.D.C. 1982); Morgan v. Goldschmidt, 33 FEP 797 (D.D.C. 1980); Caravetta v. Goulding, 33 FEP 796 (D.D.C. 1980); Jackson v. RKO Bottlers of Toledo, Pepsi-Cola, Dr. Pepper Bottling Co. Div., 783 F.2d 50, 40 FEP 222 (6th Cir.), *cert. denied,* 478 U.S. 1006, 41 FEP 271 (1986); Mitchell v. Safeway Stores, 624 F. Supp. 932, 39 FEP 1213 (D. Kan. 1985); Farlow v. University of N.C., 624 F. Supp. 434, 39 FEP 1418 (M.D.N.C. 1985); Jones v. Mississippi Dep't of Corrections, 615 F. Supp. 456 (N.D. Miss. 1985); Downey v. Isaac, 622 F. Supp. 1125, 38 FEP 52 (D.D.C. 1985), *aff'd,* 794 F.2d 753 (D.C. Cir. 1986); Boykin v.

The Supreme Court has emphasized the need for less than mechanical application of the *McDonnell Douglas* standard in *United States Postal Service Board of Governors v. Aikens*, [13] where it cautioned the judiciary that in a disparate treatment case, once the case has been tried and all the evidence is in, the "ultimate question" is no different from that of any non-Civil Rights lawsuit—that is, "which side do you believe?"—and courts should not get "bogged down" in attempting to establish each step in the order of proof set out in *McDonnell Douglas* and *Burdine*.

Statistical evidence,[14] proof of past discrimination,[15] and the use of

---

Georgia-Pacific Corp., 706 F.2d 1384, 32 FEP 25 (5th Cir. 1983), *cert. denied*, 465 U.S. 1006, 33 FEP 1344 (1984) (to "combat" plaintiff's classwide statistics, defendant must either show statistics are flawed or provide nondiscriminatory explanation for these statistics; defendant cannot refute statistics by showing that "handful of minorities were promoted"); Page v. U.S. Indus., 726 F.2d 1038, 34 FEP 430 (5th Cir. 1984) (class discrimination due to promotional system based upon subjective selection criteria may be analyzed under either disparate treatment or disparate impact theory). *See also* Moore v. Summa Corp., Hughes Helicopters Div., 708 F.2d 475, 32 FEP 97 (9th Cir. 1983) (assuming, without deciding, that disparate impact analysis is appropriate in evaluating subjective promotion systems, black female employee failed to establish disparate impact when she presented no evidence of black women with appropriate skills who were available for promotion); EEOC v. Federal Reserve Bank of Richmond, 698 F.2d 633, 30 FEP 1137 (4th Cir. 1983); Perryman v. Johnson Prods. Co., 580 F. Supp. 1015 (N.D. Ga. 1983) (female plaintiffs in disparate treatment case established prima facie case of discrimination in hiring, firing, and promotion; defendant failed to establish legitimate, nondiscriminatory reason). Hill v. K-Mart Corp., *supra* note 7; Thompson v. Sawyer, 678 F.2d 257, 28 FEP 1614 (D.C. Cir. 1982); Bigby v. City of Chicago, 38 FEP 844 (N.D. Ill. 1984), *aff'd on other grounds*, 766 F.2d 1053, 38 FEP 853 (7th Cir. 1985), *cert. denied*, 474 U.S. 1056, 39 FEP 1200 (disparate impact is shown by black applicants' overall promotion rate of 52% of promotion rate for white applicants; 80% rule of Uniform Guidelines on Employee Selection Procedures tolerates significant disparate impact which should not be watered down by lax judicial application); Maddox v. Claytor, *supra* note 11 (utilizing *McDonnell Douglas* test for individual claims and disparate impact analysis for class claims regarding allegedly subjective promotion system); Griffin v. Carlin, 755 F.2d 1516, 37 FEP 741 (11th Cir. 1985).

[13]*Supra* note 6.

[14]Trout v. Lehman, *supra* note 6; EEOC v. Federal Reserve Bank of Richmond, *supra* note 12; Pegues v. Mississippi State Employment Serv., *supra* note 6; Hill v. K-Mart Corp., *supra* note 7; Thompson v. Sawyer, *supra* note 12; Payne v. Travenol Laboratories, 673 F.2d 798, 28 FEP 1212 (5th Cir.), *cert. denied*, 459 U.S. 1038, 30 FEP 440 (1982); Laborde v. University of Cal. Regents, *supra* note 12; Bell v. Bolger, *supra* note 6; Easley v. Anheuser-Busch, 758 F.2d 251, 37 FEP 549 (8th Cir. 1985) (statistics may be probative on issue of intent in individual claims of discrimination); Diaz v. AT&T, *supra* note 9 (statistics regarding employer's promotion practices as a whole are relevant, even though different managers made promotion decisions); Boykin v. Georgia-Pacific Corp., *supra* note 12. *But see* Molthan v. Temple Univ.-Commonwealth Sys. of Higher Educ., 778 F.2d 955, 39 FEP 816 (3d Cir. 1985) (general underrepresentation of women as full professors at state university did not establish prima facie case of sex discrimination in promotion, where there was simply a dispute over qualifications); Taylor v. Secretary of the Army, 583 F. Supp. 1503, 38 FEP 1408 (D. Md. 1984) (statistical evidence does not automatically make prima facie case on behalf of a single plaintiff; here, plaintiff did not prove he applied for open position or was qualified for any position which might have been available); Allen v. Isaac, 39 FEP 1142 (N.D. Ill. 1986) (successful class action by black Federal Deposit Insurance Corporation employees alleging promotion exam was discriminatory); Chang v. University of R.I., 606 F. Supp. 1161, 40 FEP 3 (D.R.I. 1985); Nash v. City of Houston Civic Center, 39 FEP 1503 (S.D. Tex. 1984); Anderson v. University of N. Iowa, 779 F.2d 441, 39 FEP 1379 (8th Cir. 1985) (statistics, although helpful, not controlling as to failure to promote); Mozee v. Jeffboat, Inc., 746 F.2d 365, 35 FEP 1810 (7th Cir. 1984) (probative value of statistics may be diminished where employer relies on subjective factors in making personnel decisions); Maddox v. Claytor, *supra* note 11 (statistics useful, but must use carefully chosen relevant labor market; disparities, which did not exceed standard deviation of 2–3, insufficient to establish discrimination); United States v. City of Chicago, 38 EPD ¶ 35,606 (N.D. Ill. 1984), *aff'd*, 796 F.2d 205, 41 FEP 378 (7th Cir. 1986) (80% Rule of Uniform Guidelines on Employee Selection Procedures used to invalidate test for promotions where black applicants' success rate only 18.1% of white, hispanic success rate 40% of white, and women's success rate 50% of white males'); Loiseau v. Department of Human Resources, 567 F. Supp. 1211, 39 FEP 289 (D. Or. 1983) (fact that state agency has not appointed one black as welfare assistant supervisor in 53 opportunities since 1976 is statistically significant, despite agency's failure to keep applicant data for 1976–1979 period, where expert is able to make reasonable estimates for the period by extrapolating from available data); Shidaker v. Carlin, 782 F.2d 746, 39 FEP 1768 (7th Cir. 1986), *vacated sub nom.* Tisch v. Shidaker, 481 U.S. 1001, 43 FEP 640 (1987), *remanded*, 833 F.2d 627, 56 USLW 2322 (7th Cir. 1987) (prima facie case of discrimination in promotions from within established where there is gross disparity between percentage of minority in upper- and lower-level positions).

[15]Adams v. Gaudet, 515 F. Supp. 1086, 30 FEP 1258 (W.D. La.), *aff'd without opinion, in part sub nom.* Adams v. Jefferson Davis Parish School Bd., 673 F.2d 1325, 30 FEP 1360 (5th Cir. 1982)

subjective criteria[16] are factors to be considered and may be sufficient to establish a prima facie case but may not be sufficient to carry plaintiff's ultimate burden of proof as to intentional discrimination. Nor may the presumption raised by the establishment of a prima facie case be a factor in meeting that burden once the employer has articulated a nondiscriminatory motive.[17]

---

(relying on *Lee v. Washington County Bd. of Educ.,* 625 F.2d 1235, 23 FEP 1472 (5th Cir. 1980)); *Wilmore v. City of Wilmington, supra* note 6 (fire department's exclusion of black employees from administrative jobs that could have contributed to their professional development had detrimental effect on promotion exam scores); *Maddox v. Claytor, supra* note 11 (proof of past discrimination relevant since it creates presumption that discrimination continued into relevant years); *Giles v. Ireland,* 742 F.2d 1366, 35 FEP 1718 (11th Cir. 1984) (given history of discrimination against blacks, and their concentration in low level positions, employer's no promotion policy, although not intended to discriminate, disproportionately hurt black employees more than white); *Winfield v. St. Joe Paper Co.,* 38 EPD ¶ 35,580 (N.D. Fla. 1985) (employer's maintenance of historically racially segregated lines of progression indicated by promotion statistics); *Stallworth v. Shuler,* 777 F.2d 1431, 39 FEP 983 (11th Cir. 1985) (black employee discriminated against in favor of less qualified white persons where: (1) school district was segregated until 1968; (2) there had never been a black administrator in the system; and (3) job requirements which a black employee met were lowered so that three otherwise unqualified whites could be appointed to administrative positions); *Wardwell v. Palm Beach County, Fla., School Bd.,* 786 F.2d 1554, 40 FEP 1006 (11th Cir. 1986) (case remanded with direction to reexamine board's reasons for not promoting appellant, reversing district court's findings of pattern of discrimination and constructive discharge).

[16]*Boykin v. Georgia-Pacific Corp., supra* note 12 (prima facie case established where rural lumber company made "no provision for informing employees of promotion opportunities, nor did it establish any objective bases for judging possible applicants"; plant manager's testimony reflected bias as to promotional preferences of black employees; and plaintiff showed gross statistical disparity in assignments of blacks and whites to unskilled positions and in subsequent promotions). *See also MacDonald v. Ferguson Reorganized School Dist. R-2,* 31 FEP 184 (8th Cir.), *cert. denied,* 464 U.S. 961 (1983); *Verniero v. Air Force Academy School Dist. No. 20, supra* note 6; *Monroe v. Burlington Indus., supra* note 9 (employer's explanation that plaintiff not promoted because of poor attendance was pretext for discrimination, where employer had no established standards for attendance and employees were not informed poor attendance could adversely affect their employment); *Crawford v. Western Elec. Co.,* 745 F.2d 1373, 36 FEP 1753 (11th Cir. 1984) (employer's "Index Review System," which allows supervisors to make wholly subjective evaluations of employees without simultaneously documenting their results, permits too much discretion and fails to rebut plaintiff's prima facie case); *King v. Palmer, supra* note 10 (supervisor's and a second nurse's involvement in sexual relationship justified district court's judgment in first nurse's favor for her Title VII action challenging promotion of second nurse); *Paxton v. Union Nat'l Bank,* 688 F.2d 552, 29 FEP 1233 (8th Cir. 1982), *cert. denied,* 460 U.S. 1083, 31 FEP 824 (1983) (fact that blacks had as much experience and education as whites undermines bank's contention that it promoted whites because they were better qualified); *McKenney v. Marsh,* 31 FEP 178 (D.D.C. 1983) (employer illegally refused to promote women instead of men with PhDs where there was no evidence PhD was of value to position, PhD was not mentioned in position description, and women offered wider range of experience and expertise than men); *Watson v. National Linen Serv.,* 686 F.2d 877, 30 FEP 107 (11th Cir. 1982) (district court's fact finding erroneous; circumstances of nonpromotion of black female plaintiff discriminatory). *But see Page v. U.S. Indus., supra* note 12 (promotions based on subjectively applied criteria, including experience and performance, not per se discriminatory; *Boykin* distinguished as involving "standardless" subjective system, "devoid of any objective bases for judging possible applicants"); *Estrada v. A. Siros Hardware, Inc.,* 39 FEP 597 (S.D. Tex. 1984) (employer did not violate Title VII when it hired man with more formal education and supervisory experience instead of promoting female employee to that position; subjective evaluations made in good faith and did not reflect sex discrimination); *Clay v. Consumer Programs,* 576 F. Supp. 185, 35 FEP 1497 (E.D. Mo. 1983), *aff'd,* 745 F.2d 501, 35 FEP 1502 (8th Cir. 1984) (posting only nonsupervisory positions not discriminatory); *Grant v. C&P Telephone Co. of Washington, D.C.,* 35 FEP 1397 (D.D.C. 1984); *Lasso v. Woodmen of the World Life Ins. Co.,* 741 F.2d 1241, 35 FEP 1417 (10th Cir. 1984), *cert. denied,* 471 U.S. 1099, 37 FEP 1216 (1985); *Mozee v. Jeffboat, Inc., supra* note 14 (subjective misjudgments do not necessarily create liability under Title VII); *Nieves v. Metropolitan Dade County, Fla.,* 598 F. Supp. 955, 36 FEP 1851 (S.D. Fla. 1984) (poor selection procedures do not violate Title VII absent discriminatory motive); *Namenwirth v. University of Wis. Sys., Bd. of Regents,* 769 F.2d 1235, 38 FEP 1155 (7th Cir. 1985), *cert. denied,* 474 U.S. 1061, 39 FEP 1200 (1986) (district court finding affirmed; university's defense that there was insufficient promise in plaintiff's work not pretextual).

[17]*Young v. Lehman,* 748 F.2d 194, 36 FEP 302 (4th Cir. 1984), *cert. denied,* 471 U.S. 1061, 37 FEP 848 (1985); *Cunningham v. Housing Auth. of the City of Opelousas dba Opelousas Hous. Auth.,* 764 F.2d 1097, 38 FEP 417 (5th Cir.), *cert. denied,* 474 U.S. 1007, 39 FEP 720 (1985) (plaintiff failed to prove intentional sex discrimination in authority's hiring of male executive director

At least one court has pointed out the lack of precedential value of cases in the promotion area[18] since virtually all of these cases turn on their individual facts.[19]

## III. EXPERIENCE REQUIREMENTS

Requirements based on length of service and level of experience,[20] as

---

where authority explained selection was reaffirmation of decision by three authority members to repay male for his political support of mayor); Mason v. Continental Ill. Nat'l Bank, *supra* note 9; Verniero v. Air Force Academy School Dist. No. 20, 705 F.2d 388, 31 FEP 871 (10th Cir. 1983); Watson v. National Linen Serv., *supra* note 16; Reid v. Fruehauf Corp., Fruehauf Div., 28 FEP 622 (N.D. Ga. 1982) (promotion of equally qualified white employee over black not discriminatory because employer gave nonpretextual explanation that white employee was better able to handle people and express himself clearly); Jones v. Konopnicki, 597 F. Supp. 235, 36 FEP 1590 (E.D. Mo. 1984) (Army rebutted black male's prima facie case by showing appointed black female and one white male employee had advanced degrees, black female employee made a more favorable impression during her interview, and other two selectees had experience); Jackson v. RKO Bottlers of Toledo, Pepsi-Cola, Dr. Pepper Bottling Co. Div., *supra* note 12 (prima facie case successfully rebutted by showing that candidate promoted more qualified than plaintiff, and plaintiff failed to prove promotion was pretextual); Eddins v. West Ga. Medical Center, 629 F. Supp. 753, 39 FEP 1492 (N.D. Ga. 1985) (employer's assertion plaintiff was not promoted because of poor attitude and inability to get along with supervisors rebutted plaintiff's prima facie case of race discrimination); Gilbert v. West Ga. Medical Center Auth., 629 F. Supp. 738, 39 FEP 1372 (N.D. Ga. 1985), *aff'd without opinion,* 784 F.2d 402 (11th Cir. 1986) (same); Bibbs v. Department of Agriculture, 778 F.2d 1318, 39 FEP 970 (8th Cir. 1985) (proof that race was discernible factor in decision not to promote plaintiff sufficient in mixed-motive context to establish liability under Title VII; plaintiff entitled to declaratory judgment in his favor and injunction prohibiting agency from future discrimination against him); Earvin v. Mississippi Employment Sec. Comm'n, 621 F. Supp. 760, 39 FEP 941 (S.D. Miss. 1985), *aff'd,* 795 F.2d 83, 41 FEP 1888 (5th Cir. 1986) (legitimate, nondiscriminatory reason articulated for five promotions, where each promoted white employee had same work responsibilities with change in title only). *But see* Trout v. Lehman, 702 F.2d 1094, 31 FEP 286 (D.C. Cir. 1983), *vacated,* 465 U.S. 1056, 34 FEP 76 (1984); McKenzie v. Sawyer, 684 F.2d 62, 29 FEP 633 (D.C. Cir. 1982) (once class discrimination has been established, presumption attaching to claims of individual class members must be rebutted by "clear and convincing evidence" from employer); Cox v. American Cast Iron Pipe Co., *supra* note 11 (class members need not prove either individual claims of sex discrimination or applications for jobs or promotions when sex discrimination was employer's standard operating procedure). *See also* Gold v. Gallaudet College, 630 F. Supp. 1176, 40 FEP 730 (D.D.C. 1986) (although one of her supervisors harbored religious animosity toward plaintiff, she was "an oversensitive employee who challenged the motivation behind even the most innocuous business decisions" and failed to establish sexual or religious discrimination).

[18]Valentino v. United States Postal Serv., 674 F.2d 56, 28 FEP 593 (D.C. Cir. 1982) (where there are special qualifications for position sought, proof must center on those qualifications).

[19]*E.g.,* Grano v. Department of Dev., City of Columbus, 699 F.2d 836, 31 FEP 1 (6th Cir. 1983) (subjective evaluation that plaintiff not qualified found not to be pretextual); Mortensen v. Callaway, *supra* note 11 (reasonable belief of decision maker that female was less qualified candidate prevailed); Metrocare v. Washington Metro. Area Transit Auth., 679 F.2d 922, 28 FEP 1585 (D.C. Cir. 1982) (later promotions and fair treatment do not preclude possibility plaintiff was earlier discriminated against); Patterson v. Greenwood School Dist. 50, 696 F.2d 293, 30 FEP 825 (4th Cir. 1982) (employer's proof that, absent discrimination, it would have selected different candidate precluded relief); Goff v. Continental Oil Co., *supra* note 12 (two of claimed jobs not available and plaintiff failed to prove he was qualified for third); Mitchell v. M.D. Anderson Hosp., 679 F.2d 88, 29 FEP 263 (5th Cir. 1982) ("suspicious circumstances"—reduced evaluations and termination—following application established pretext); Coble v. Hot Springs School Dist. No. 6, 682 F.2d 721, 29 FEP 201 (8th Cir. 1982) (repeated references to female candidate's family responsibilities established pretext); Jones v. Lumberjack Meats, 680 F.2d 98, 29 FEP 396 (11th Cir. 1982) (job not available within 180 days of filing EEOC charge); Woodard v. Lehman, 530 F. Supp. 139, 31 FEP 304 (D.S.C. 1982), *aff'd,* 717 F.2d 909, 32 FEP 1441 (4th Cir. 1983) (no vacancy at time of complaint and reasonable criteria used for later promotions).

[20]Walker v. Jefferson County Home, 726 F.2d 1554, 34 FEP 465 (11th Cir. 1984) (requirement of supervisory experience for promotion to position of housekeeping supervisor in nursing home had disparate impact on blacks; no business necessity proven); Payne v. Travenol Laboratories, *supra* note 14 (employer's consideration of length of service as criterion for advancement tended to perpetuate past discrimination in hiring; employer's erratic reliance upon length of service falls short of being bona fide seniority system); Jackson v. Seaboard Coast Line R.R., 678 F.2d 992, 1016–17, 29 FEP 442, 463 (11th Cir. 1982) (though facially neutral and neutrally applied, promotion system per-

well as bona fide seniority systems,[21] continue to be closely scrutinized by the courts.

## IV. SUBJECTIVE CRITERIA

Decisions scrutinizing so-called subjective criteria are tied closely to their facts. Courts have generally accepted the use of subjective criteria in promotions to upper-level or professional or other positions requiring specialized abilities where promotional judgments cannot readily be based on quantifiable data, and where the allegedly subjective selection decisions are not shown to have a substantial adverse impact on a protected group.[22] The practice is scrutinized much more closely, however, in blue-

petuated past discrimination by requiring specified number of hours in lower job before promotion when blacks had not been permitted in jobs until 1965). *But see* Meyer v. Lehman, 37 FEP 1565 (N.D. Cal. 1983), *aff'd,* 734 F.2d 21, 37 FEP 1816 (9th Cir. 1984), *cert. denied,* 469 U.S. 1208 (1985) (Navy did not violate Title VII by rejecting civilian female candidate for promotion to supervisory position due, in part, to her lack of supervisory experience); Moore v. Summa Corp., Hughes Helicopters Div., *supra* note 12 (employer's preference for outside hires of experienced applicants, instead of internal promotions, approved where special skills manifestly required); Hamm v. Board of Regents of Fla., 708 F.2d 647, 32 FEP 441 (11th Cir. 1983) (university entitled to laterally transfer plaintiff who did not possess requisite college degree and hire person who met degree requirements); EEOC v. Samsonite Corp., Luggage Div., 723 F.2d 748, 33 FEP 377 (10th Cir. 1983) (trial court erroneously found employer intentionally discriminated against black applicant for promotion where finding was reached without comparing his experience and qualifications with others, including person selected for position); Dreier v. Wilkes-Barre Area School Dist., 33 FEP 1334 (M.D. Pa. 1983) (court properly relied upon official's belief that a man was more qualified than woman plaintiff; and, in fact, he was more qualified because he had more lengthy administrative experience); Ridenour v. Lawson Co., 791 F.2d 52, 40 FEP 1455 (6th Cir. 1986) (legitimate, nondiscriminatory reasons for not promoting respondent were lack of experience and superior qualifications of younger individual ultimately employed); Jones v. Continental Corp., 785 F.2d 308, 40 FEP 1320 (6th Cir. 1986), *aff'g* 35 FEP 661 (M.D. Tenn. 1984) (white female, transferred to position which plaintiff claimed was promotion denied to her, had superior qualifications and more experience for that job); Berry v. University of Tex., 38 FEP 889 (W.D. Tex. 1977) (university did not violate Title VII because it based decision on fact that plaintiff did not have PhD or had not made significant progress toward it and had not published any scholarly works in her field); Downey v. Isaac, *supra* note 12 (prima facie case of sex discrimination in promotion rebutted by showing males chosen for promotions were more qualified than plaintiff by training and experience). *See also* Jackson v. RKO Bottlers of Toledo, Pepsi-Cola, Dr. Pepper Bottling Co. Div., *supra* note 12 (experience requirement held to be valid and not pretextual); Estrada v. A. Siros Hardware, Inc., *supra* note 16 (employer did not violate Title VII when it hired man with more formal education and supervisory experience instead of promoting female employee to that position; subjective evaluations made in good faith and did not reflect sex discrimination); Anderson v. University of N. Iowa, *supra* note 14 (scholarly achievement is clearly recognized as legitimate, nondiscriminatory reason for personnel decisions in academic setting); Karriem v. Oliver T. Carr Co., 38 FEP 882 (D.D.C. 1985) (employer did not discriminate against black Muslim security guard when it hired individual with superior qualifications for one supervisory position and other blacks and black Muslims were promoted); Unt v. Aerospace Corp., 765 F.2d 1440, 38 FEP 999 (9th Cir. 1985) (evidence supported finding that employer was justified in rejecting application for managerial positions where plaintiff lacked technical qualifications and communications skills necessary to be effective manager); Allen v. Prince George's County, Md., 737 F.2d 1299, 38 FEP 1220 (4th Cir. 1984) (Fourth Circuit found that county's system of granting preference in hiring and promotion to internal applicants was valid seniority system under § 703(h) of Title VII); Foster v. MCI Telecommunications Corp., 773 F.2d 1116, 39 FEP 698 (10th Cir. 1985) (plaintiff showed he was as well qualified for promotion as person who received it; court found defense pretextual); Burrows v. Chemed Corp. dba Vestal Laboratories, 743 F.2d 612, 35 FEP 1410 (8th Cir. 1984) (articulated reasons for hiring a male rather than a female not pretextual where male had research experience and where other women were accorded opportunities for advancement).

[21]*See* Firefighters Local 1784 v. Stotts, 467 U.S. 561, 34 FEP 1702 (1984) (with respect to layoffs, seniority system cannot be disregarded during financial emergency by court-ordered modification of consent decree to preserve percentage representation of minorities).

[22]Casillas v. United States Navy, 735 F.2d 338, 344–345, 34 FEP 1493, 1497 (9th Cir. 1984) ("Title VII is not a civil code of employment criteria * * * . [It] is the law's promise that employment

decisions will not be based on non-permissible discriminatory criteria, not that subjective criteria will be eliminated"); Moore v. Summa Corp., Hughes Helicopters Div., *supra* note 12 (affirming Rule 41(b) dismissal of plaintiff's class action that had challenged alleged impact on black females, by employer's promotion decisions, concededly based on "subjective evaluations of capability and experience"; adverse impact not statistically proven); Brooks v. Ashtabula County Welfare Dep't, 717 F.2d 263, 32 FEP 1368 (6th Cir. 1983), *cert. denied,* 466 U.S. 907, 35 FEP 1120 (1984) (refusal to promote because of plaintiff's abrasive personality and inappropriateness for supervisory position legitimate and not discriminatory); Cazalas v. Department of Justice, 569 F. Supp. 213, 36 FEP 1698 (E.D. La. 1983), *aff'd per curiam,* 731 F.2d 280, 36 FEP 1713 (5th Cir. 1984), *cert. denied,* 469 U.S. 1207, 37 FEP 64 (1985) (U.S. Attorney's Office rebutted any prima facie case that female Assistant U.S. Attorney might have established with regard to decision not to appoint her to supervisory position by presenting evidence of policies relative to operation of office and structure and assignment of work force as well as evidence of inadequacies in her performance); Royal v. Missouri Highway & Transp. Comm'n, 714 F.2d 867, 32 FEP 1389 (8th Cir. 1983) (affirming district court's finding that "[e]ach person promoted to the position plaintiff sought had higher qualifications by both subjective and objective measures"; district court had shown "proper sensitivity" to "subjective component" of the promotion process, in accord with Eighth Circuit mandate to give "particularly close scrutiny" to "articulated reason" for promotion decision "when the [employee] evaluation is in any degree subjective and when the evaluators themselves are not members of the protected minority"); Ellison v. C.P.C. Int'l, Best Foods Div., 598 F. Supp. 159, 36 FEP 643 (E.D. Ark. 1984) (mere existence of subjective factors in employment decision-making does not necessarily require inference that racial discrimination occurred); Harris v. Birmingham Bd. of Educ., 537 F. Supp. 716, 32 FEP 81 (N.D. Ala. 1982), *aff'd in part, rev'd and remanded in part,* 712 F.2d 1377, 32 FEP 1198 (11th Cir. 1983) (inability to get along with people legitimate and nondiscriminatory justification for refusal to promote); Lucero v. Continental Oil Co., 38 EPD ¶ 35,582 (S.D. Tex. 1985) (employer's use of both subjective and objective promotion and performance evaluations did not result in disparate treatment of plaintiff or disparate impact on female employees; plaintiff denied promotion because of inability to work amicably with co-workers); Reilly v. Califano, 537 F. Supp. 349, 29 FEP 1437 (N.D. Ill.), *aff'd,* 673 F.2d 1333, 30 FEP 120 (7th Cir. 1981), *cert. denied,* 456 U.S. 916, 30 FEP 120 (1982) (defendant rebutted prima facie case by female employee who was not promoted to management position by showing that, while she was competent, she lacked "strong," "outgoing" personality necessary for job); Pinckney v. County of Northampton, 512 F. Supp. 989, 27 FEP 528 (E.D. Pa. 1981), *aff'd,* 681 F.2d 808, 29 FEP 1472 (3d Cir. 1982) (personality is valid factor to consider in promotions to managerial jobs where ability to perform cannot be easily verified objectively and where job involves extensive contact with the public and other employees); MacDonald v. Ferguson Reorganized School Dist. R-2, *supra* note 16 (subjective criteria used to screen applicants for promotion to principal relevant and necessary); Lee v. Joseph T. Ryerson & Son, 36 FEP 449 (W.D.N.C.), *aff'd,* 745 F.2d 51, 37 FEP 1216 (4th Cir. 1984) (employer properly rebutted black employee's case by evidence of lack of responsibility, excessive absenteeism, and other unsatisfactory behavior); Ross v. Food Fair dba Pantry Pride Enters., 33 FEP 1449 (M.D. Fla. 1983) (Title VII does not prohibit basing promotional decisions on subjective, unwritten standards which include employee's past performance, attitude toward job, leadership ability, exposure to industry); Aikens v. Bolger, 33 FEP 1697 (D.D.C. 1984) (defendant did not violate Title VII by failing to promote plaintiff for perceived "lack of aggressiveness"); Allesberry v. Pennsylvania, 30 FEP 1634 (M.D. Pa. 1981) (subjective interview process resulting in nonpromotion of black administrator not pretextual because higher position required ability and competence difficult to measure by objective standards); Clark v. Lewis, 29 FEP 716 (D.D.C. 1982) (Federal Aviation Administration did not violate Title VII by refusing to promote female employee to GS-12 where refusal due to her poor attitude, resistance to supervision, and argumentativeness); Gold v. Gallaudet College, *supra* note 17 (although she was subject of religious animosity, plaintiff's case failed as she was "an oversensitive employee who challenged the motivation behind even the most innocuous business decisions"); Krulik v. New York City Bd. of Educ., 781 F.2d 15, 39 FEP 1448 (2d Cir. 1986) (court will not simply infer that an employer's subjective preferences are "inevitably influenced by race"); Maddox v. Claytor, 764 F.2d 1539, 38 FEP 713 (11th Cir. 1985) (where decisions based on subjective criteria are "as circumscribed by objective criteria and division of [decisional] authority as one could reasonably expect," no violation established); Robinson v. Lehman, 771 F.2d 772, 39 FEP 559 (3d Cir. 1985) (use of subjective criteria, such as qualifications, applied in same fashion to all applicants for promotion, does not violate Title VII); Allen v. Prince George's County, Md., *supra* note 20 (Fourth Circuit found that county's system of granting preference in hiring and promotion to internal applicants was valid seniority system under § 703(h) of Title VII); Nagel v. Avon Bd. of Educ., 575 F. Supp. 105, 39 FEP 602 (D. Conn. 1983) (screening committee's failure to recommend female candidate not based on gender; deficiencies in its procedure did not affect her differently from other candidates and, although committee relied in large part on subjective criteria regarding leadership capabilities, its evaluations were based on genuinely and sincerely held views and constituted reasonable, fair, and logical judgments). *But see* Shipes v. Trinity Indus., 40 FEP 1136 (E.D. Tex. 1985) (hiring and placement procedures subjective and discriminatory as to promotion, pay, layoffs, and termination for cause); United States v. City of Chicago, 38 EPD ¶ 35,606 (N.D. Ill. 1984), *aff'd,* 796 F.2d 205, 41 FEP 378 (7th Cir. 1986) (examination administered in compiling promotion eligibility roster had adverse impact on blacks, Hispanics, and women, and was not content-valid because not linked to specific job tasks or behavior); Winfield v. St. Joe Paper Co., *supra* note 15 (subjective criteria, combined with statistical evidence of disparities in hiring and initial job assignments and lines of progression, established discrimination); Patterson v. Masem, 774 F.2d 251, 39 FEP 1266 (8th Cir.

collar or low-level promotions.[23] Cases reflecting close scrutiny of an employer's supposedly subjective selection criteria often show selections made by nonminority supervisors with respect to lower-skilled positions, where the employer cannot articulate a specific basis for promotion decisions, and where the plaintiff shows gross statistical disparities in promotion rates.[24]

## V. STATISTICAL PROOF: THE QUALIFIED POTENTIAL APPLICANT POOL

Particularized statistics are recognized as more probative than generalized work force statistics in promotion cases, and the latter will usually be accorded little weight.[25]

---

1985) (evaluation of employee as abrasive and antagonistic not justification for nonpromotion where based on disagreement with employee's attitude toward desegregation and civil rights); Jackson v. Seaboard Coast Line R.R., 678 F.2d 992, 29 FEP 442 (11th Cir. 1982) (though facially neutral and neutrally applied, promotion system perpetuated past discrimination by requiring specified number of hours in lower job before promotion when blacks had not been permitted in jobs until 1965); Rollins v. Farris, 40 FEP 1495 (E.D. Ark. 1986), aff'd, 822 F.2d 1093 (8th Cir. 1987) (denial of tenure based on legitimate reason of poor status of plaintiff's department); Goldman v. Marsh, 31 EPD ¶ 33,605 (E.D. Ark. 1983) (army arsenal failed to justify disparate impact on blacks of its subjective selection procedures).

[23]E.g., Paxton v. Union Nat'l Bank, supra note 16 (subjective criteria used to fill first- and middle-level supervisory positions); Hawkins v. Bounds, 752 F.2d 500, 36 FEP 1285 (10th Cir. 1985) (subjective selection practice of "detailing" employees to higher-level promotions which negatively affected promotion of blacks beyond initial supervisory positions subject to close scrutiny); Carpenter v. Stephen F. Austin State Univ., 706 F.2d 608, 31 FEP 1758 (5th Cir. 1983) (class action alleged university "channelled" blacks and women into lower-paying positions and maintained discriminatory promotion practices; subjective promotion decisions by white supervisors were associated with "gross race and gender stratification"; Fifth Circuit remanded for determination whether subjective selection decisions reflected discriminatory intent pursuant to Pouncy v. Prudential Ins. Co. of Am., 668 F.2d 795, 28 FEP 121 (5th Cir. 1982)); Goldman v. Marsh, supra note 22 (army arsenal failed to justify disparate impact of its subjective selection procedures on black employees); Boykin v. Georgia-Pacific Corp., 706 F.2d 1384, 32 FEP 25 (5th Cir. 1983), cert. denied, 465 U.S. 1006, 33 FEP 1344 (1984); McKenzie v. Sawyer, supra note 17 (Government Printing Office discriminated against blacks and must make promotion selections based on length of service and performance instead of on supervisors' evaluations); Morrison v. Booth, 763 F.2d 1366, 38 FEP 145 (11th Cir. 1985) (bending promotion rule to help white employee and not black employee introduces subjectivity).

[24]Craik v. Minnesota State Univ. Bd., 731 F.2d 465, 34 FEP 649 (8th Cir. 1984) (subjective process for selection of chairpersons at university, dominated by men, requires "particularly close scrutiny" and permits conclusion of discrimination where only 3 of 71 chairpersons are women); Hill v. Seaboard Coastline R.R., 573 F. Supp. 1079, 33 FEP 1406 (M.D. Fla. 1983) (prima facie case, where those promoted appear to be less qualified, where promotion standards were not specific and entailed substantial reliance on subjective evaluations, and where respective candidates were not informed about promotion opportunities, about standards used to judge qualifications, or, if rejected, about reasons); Goldman v. Marsh, supra note 22 (defendant's promotion process, which relied largely upon subjective evaluations, violated Title VII where statistical underrepresentation of blacks existed and where defendant failed to show business necessity for subjective evaluations). See also Boykin v. Georgia-Pacific Corp., supra note 23; Bell v. Crakin Good Bakers, 777 F.2d 1497, 39 FEP 948 (11th Cir. 1985) (summary judgment improperly granted where statements made by supervisor before he attained that position were at least circumstantial evidence of discriminatory motive in denying promotion); Allen v. Isaac, supra note 14 (progress evaluations violated EEOC guidelines on employee selection procedures where evaluations were highly subjective and played significant role in determining promotions, and where blacks were shown to be less than half as likely as whites to pass evaluation).

[25]Goldman v. Marsh, supra note 22 (defendant's argument that general population statistics should be used in promotion case rejected because general policy was to promote from within, and proper labor pool was defendant's own work force); Casillas v. United States Navy, supra note 22; Gilbert v. City of Little Rock, 722 F.2d 1390, 33 FEP 557 (8th Cir. 1983), cert. denied, 466 U.S. 972, 34 FEP 1312 (1984), later proceeding, 799 F.2d 1210, 44 FEP 509 (8th Cir. 1986) (citing Paxton, court held general population statistics not probative where inference of discrimination arose from low number of blacks in higher levels of police force and where promotions are made from within); Woodard v. Lehman, 717 F.2d 909, 32 FEP 1441 (4th Cir. 1983) (comparison of racial composition of work force with general area population irrelevant); Lewis v. NLRB, 750 F.2d 1266, 36 FEP 1388 (5th Cir. 1985) (rejecting plaintiff's use of federal employer's work force statistics because, inter alia,

Adopting a standard derived from *EEOC v. Radiator Specialty Co.*, [26] the Ninth Circuit has defined, in *Moore v. Summa Corp., Hughes Helicopters Division*, [27] three possible allocations of burden to determine whether general population statistics or a qualified labor pool must be used to determine the disparate impact of promotion practices: (1) where "it is manifest as a matter of law that no special skills or qualifications are required for a job," the plaintiff may establish a prima facie case using general population statistics; (2) where "the need for special qualifications [is] manifest as a matter of law," the plaintiff is required to show a disparate impact "on the qualified labor market" to establish a prima facie case; and (3) where it is "not immediately obvious that a job requires any special qualification," it is the defendant's burden to establish that generalized population statistics "do not adequately reflect the pool of presumptively qualified individuals."[28]

---

such statistics took no account of employees' grade level or qualifications); Maddox v. Claytor, *supra* note 22. *See also* Coble v. Hot Springs School Dist. No. 6, *supra* note 19 (evidence that 21% of male teachers and less than 1% of female teachers are administrators has little probative value when statistics include those not qualified as administrators, rendering them overinclusive); Griffin v. Carlin, 755 F.2d 1516, 37 FEP 741 (11th Cir. 1985) (where promotions made almost exclusively from within and primary qualification for promotion was experience in craft work, craft work force was appropriate applicant pool); Wallace v. University of Mo., St. Louis, 624 F. Supp. 560 (E.D. Mo.), *aff'd without opinion*, 802 F.2d 465 (8th Cir. 1986) (statistics for school's overall hiring policies are of little value where discrimination does not exist in plaintiff's department); Cook v. Boorstin, 763 F.2d 1462, 37 FEP 1777 (D.C. Cir. 1985) (court of appeals vacated district court ruling and held that plaintiff intervenors could rely upon librarywide statistical evidence in presenting disparate treatment claims under Title VII and were not restricted to use of statistical evidence relating to particular job classifications); Diaz v. AT&T, 752 F.2d 1356, 36 FEP 1742 (9th Cir. 1985) (statistics regarding employer's promotion practices as a whole were relevant, even if plaintiff would not have been interested in jobs outside a particular area); *see also* Pace v. Southern Ry. Sys., 701 F.2d 1383, 31 FEP 710 (11th Cir. 1983), *cert. denied*, 464 U.S. 1018, 33 FEP 656 (1983), *reh'g denied*, 465 U.S. 1054 (1984) (statistics regarding promotions into a certain department significant only if compared with promotions into other of employer's departments or into comparable departments at other companies).

[26]610 F.2d 178, 21 FEP 351 (4th Cir. 1979), cited in the Second Edition on this issue in notes 255, 259, and 269 at pp. 1356, 1358, and 1360, respectively.

[27]708 F.2d 475, 32 FEP 97 (9th Cir. 1983).

[28]*See also* Chapter 36 (Proof). *Cf.* Boykin v. Georgia-Pacific Corp., *supra* note 23 (employer did not post vacancy notices; had no written procedures regarding filling of vacancies; delegated promotion decisions to foreman of department with vacancy, subject to superintendent's veto; and plaintiff showed significant statistical disparity in promotion rates from entry-level, unskilled "utility" position in lumber mill; distinguishing *Pouncy v. Prudential Ins. Co. of Am.*, *supra* note 23, Fifth Circuit held that data reflecting comparative promotion rates need not be standardized for qualifications "where unskilled persons are hired and then promoted on the basis of training received on the job"); Dalley v. Michigan Blue Cross/Blue Shield, 612 F. Supp. 1444, 38 FEP 301 (E.D. Mich. 1985) (in case where 4,300 women alleged sex discrimination in initial placement and promotion practices, comparing raw pay differentials between men and women inappropriate; skills, education, and experience factors were not interchangeable and job description included widely varying fields and professions); EEOC v. Sears, Roebuck & Co., 650 F.2d 14, 25 FEP 1338 (2d Cir. 1981) (EEOC's assumption that male and female applicants in pool are equally qualified for all commission sales positions with employer undermines validity of statistical studies, particularly since EEOC's report indicates female applicants in pool on average were younger, less educated, and less likely to have commission sales and experience than men). *See also* Regner v. City of Chicago, 601 F. Supp. 830, 36 FEP 1734 (N.D. Ill. 1985) (no significant disparity shown in promotion statistics since one additional promotion would have equalized the statistics); Stones v. Los Angeles Community College Dist., 572 F. Supp. 1072, 36 FEP 275 (C.D. Cal. 1983), *aff'd*, 796 F.2d 270, 41 FEP 710 (9th Cir. 1986) (statistical data indicating lower proportion of black deans in college district do not show officials' reasons for selecting nonblacks for dean position are pretextual, since statistical evidence is not highly probative on intentional discrimination under § 1981, and there is no evidence of systematic exclusion of black deans); EEOC v. Federal Reserve Bank of Richmond, 698 F.2d 633, 30 FEP 1137 (4th Cir. 1983) (statistical evidence fatally flawed by elimination of any employee, black or white, who after promotion may have quit or been fired; correct figure should be actual promotions made); Bigby v. City of Chicago, 38 FEP 844 (N.D. Ill. 1984), *aff'd*, 766 F.2d 1053, 38 FEP 853 (7th Cir. 1985), *cert. denied*, 474 U.S. 1056, 39 FEP 1200 (1986) (court found disparate impact, in that promotion rate for blacks was 52% of promotion rate for whites).

## VI. REMEDY

Various types of affirmative relief have been awarded to prevailing plaintiffs in Title VII promotion cases.[29] Some courts have held that, to obtain certain types of relief, a plaintiff must show that, but for illegal discrimination, he or she would have been promoted. As a remedy, the court ordered the immediate promotion of the 11 highest-ranked black police sergeants to lieutenant and ordered that subsequent promotions be made in accordance with the racial composition of the applicant pool. Classwide back pay was also awarded since it was impossible to determine which class members would have been promoted had the police department used job-related examination procedures.[30]

Courts continue to enjoin illegal promotion practices.[31] Courts are still

---

[29]*See* Blim v. Western Elec. Co., 731 F.2d 1473, 34 FEP 757 (10th Cir.), *cert. denied,* 469 U.S. 874, 36 FEP 816 (1984) (award of front pay to terminated employee previously denied promotion vacated and reinstatement and repromotion granted as preferred remedy); Pollard v. Grinstead, 741 F.2d 73, 35 FEP 891 (4th Cir. 1984) (Fourth Circuit upholds EEOC order that employer select one of two plaintiffs for position; selected plaintiff then awarded retroactive promotion and back pay); Dougherty v. Barry, 607 F. Supp. 1271, 37 FEP 1201 (D.D.C. 1985) (court denied promotion but ordered back pay for all eight reverse discrimination plaintiffs commensurate with Deputy Fire Chief salary level and any increased retirement benefits that would result from such adjustment); Leibovitch v. Administrator, Veterans Admin., 33 FEP 777 (D.D.C. 1982) (female employee denied administrative position entitled to retroactive promotion along with back pay, including appropriate within-grade step increases that have accrued along with retroactive back contribution to plaintiff's retirement); Roberts v. Fri, 29 FEP 1445 (D.D.C. 1980) (Department of Energy, which unlawfully failed to consider female employee for promotion, must provide her with vacancy notices for three years or until she is considered for 10 vacancies, give her special consideration for vacant jobs, and state specific reasons if she is rejected); League of United Latin Am. Citizens Monterey Chapter 2055 v. City of Salinas Fire Dep't, 654 F.2d 557, 27 FEP 409 (9th Cir. 1981) (fire department employee denied promotion entitled to retroactive promotion and back pay as well as 7% interest on back pay); Brewer v. Muscle Shoals Bd. of Educ., 790 F.2d 1515, 40 FEP 1580 (11th Cir. 1986) (court upheld EEOC presettlement agreement requiring school board to appoint black teacher to next available administrative vacancy for which he was qualified); Campbell v. Tennessee Valley Auth., 613 F. Supp. 611, 38 FEP 779 (E.D. Tenn. 1985) (mandamus denied in ADEA suit where plaintiff given second opportunity to compete for promotion with no discrimination); Segar v. Smith, 738 F.2d 1249, 35 FEP 31 (D.C. Cir. 1984), *cert. denied,* 471 U.S. 1115, 37 FEP 1312 (1985) (remedy requiring promotion goals, timetables, and front pay vacated as inappropriate; classwide back pay appropriate, but particular back pay awards need to be reformulated); Hill v. Seaboard Coast Line R.R., 767 F.2d 771, 39 FEP 1656 (11th Cir. 1985) (appeals court remanded district court's dismissal of five black plaintiffs' claim that nonpromotion based on race; damages to be divided among the five); Thomas v. Cooper Indus., 39 FEP 1826 (W.D.N.C. 1986) (plaintiff alleged constructive discharge and sex discrimination when less qualified male promoted to supervisory position over her and made her working conditions intolerable; reinstated and awarded back pay from date she would have been promoted).

[30]Lucas v. Ripley, 30 FEP 1630 (D.D.C. 1982) ("but for" test applied before retroactive promotion and back pay awarded); Lincoln v. University Sys. of Ga. Bd. of Regents, 697 F.2d 928, 31 FEP 22 (11th Cir.), *cert. denied,* 464 U.S. 826, 32 FEP 1768 (1983) ("but for" test required for plaintiff to prevail at all); Favors v. Ruckelshaus, 569 F. Supp. 363, 36 FEP 704 (N.D. Ga. 1983) (defendants' motion to dismiss granted on grounds that plaintiff would be unable to show age was substantial and motivating factor in denial of his promotion and that but for his age, plaintiff would have been promoted); Jones v. International Paper Co., 720 F.2d 496, 33 FEP 430 (8th Cir. 1983) (plaintiffs failed to prove they would have been selected for apprenticeship program but for test shown to have racially disparate impact). *But see* Bibbs v. Department of Agriculture, 778 F.2d 1318, 39 FEP 970 (8th Cir. 1985), *vacating* 749 F.2d 508, 36 FEP 713 (8th Cir. 1984) (defendant's showing that plaintiff would not have gotten job absent considerations of race does not extinguish liability under Title VII, it simply excludes remedy of reinstatement or back pay).

[31]Thompson v. Sawyer, 678 F.2d 257, 28 FEP 1614 (D.C. Cir. 1982) (in view of Government Printing Office's unwillingness to recognize discrimination apparent in conduct, lower court properly enjoined GPO from discriminating on basis of sex in providing training opportunities and in promotions); Bentley v. City of Thomaston, 32 FEP 1476 (M.D. Ga. 1983).

uncertain on the circumstances when quotas are appropriate to remedy discrimination in promotion.[32]

---

[32]*See* Firefighters Local 1784 v. Stotts, 467 U.S. 561, 34 FEP 1702 (1984) (facts of case involved court-ordered alteration of consent decree to override bona fide seniority system otherwise governing order of layoffs; rationale of decision suggests quotas for other than identifiable victims may be generally impermissible where there exists bona fide seniority system governing promotions). *Compare* Williams v. City of New Orleans, 543 F. Supp. 662, 29 FEP 30 (E.D. La.), *rev'd,* 694 F.2d 987, 30 FEP 1061 (5th Cir. 1982), *reh'g en banc ordered,* 31 FEP 464 (5th Cir. 1983), *aff'd en banc,* 729 F.2d 1554, 34 FEP 1009 (5th Cir. 1984), *appeal dismissed,* 763 F.2d 667 (5th Cir. 1985) (consent decree term requiring promotion of certain percentage of black police officers not approved because quota would fall most heavily on newer, nonblack recruits, because blacks represent smaller percentage in department than percentage of promotions called for, and because other agreed-upon provisions will eliminate discrimination with less adverse impact) *with* Segar v. Smith, 28 FEP 935 (D.D.C. 1982) (Drug Enforcement Administration must promote one black for every two white agents until black agents constitute 10% of agents at respective grade levels, or until five years after order date, whichever is sooner) *and* Chisholm v. United States Postal Serv., 665 F.2d 482, 499, 27 FEP 425 (4th Cir. 1981) (affirming trial court's quota remedy where an employer's racial discrimination was "egregious, purposive or blatant" and had persisted for a substantial period of time). *See also* Bratton v. City of Detroit, 704 F.2d 878, 31 FEP 465 (6th Cir.), *later proceeding,* 31 FEP 1520, *reh'g denied and opinion withdrawn in part,* 712 F.2d 222, 31 FEP 1795 (6th Cir. 1983), *cert. denied,* 464 U.S. 1040, 33 FEP 1084 (1984) (city's affirmative action plan, requiring alternate selection of black and white police sergeants until blacks make up 50% of lieutenant rank, reasonable); Firefighters Local 93 v. City of Cleveland, 478 U.S. 501, 41 FEP 139 (1986) (consent decree upholds agreement between city and union providing for race-conscious promotion plan, even though plan may benefit individuals who were not actual victims of prior discrimination); Paradise v. Prescott, 767 F.2d 1514, 38 FEP 1094 (11th Cir. 1985), *aff'd sub nom.* United States v. Paradise, 480 U.S. 149, 43 FEP 1 (1987) (consent decree enforced requiring promotion of one black trooper for every white trooper promoted to same rank until 25% of that rank is black). *See also* Williams v. Vukovich, 720 F.2d 909, 33 FEP 238 (6th Cir. 1983) (citing *Connecticut v. Teal,* 457 U.S. 440, 29 FEP 1 (1982), court held minority promotion quotas contained in proposed consent decree insufficient to mitigate discrimination suffered by individual plaintiffs).

## CHAPTER 18

# DISCHARGE

## II. PROOF

### A. The Order and Allocation of Proof in the Individual Disparate Treatment Case

The courts apply the order and allocation of proof principles established in *McDonnell Douglas Corp. v. Green*[1] and *Texas Department of Community Affairs v. Burdine*[2] to discharge cases.[3] However, some courts have noted that the analysis is not appropriate in all situations.[4] Moreover, the courts recognize that the order and allocation of proof is simply an analytical framework that does not require the compartmentalized production of evidence in support of each party's position.[5]

### B. The Plaintiff's Prima Facie Case

The four-part *McDonnell Douglas* test is most often used by courts in determining whether the plaintiff has established a prima facie case of discriminatory discharge.[6] Such a showing, however, is not the only means of

---

[1]411 U.S. 792, 5 FEP 965 (1973).

[2]450 U.S. 248, 25 FEP 113 (1981).

[3]*E.g.,* Sylvester v. Callon Energy Servs., 781 F.2d 520, 39 FEP 1660 (5th Cir. 1986); Wilkins v. Eaton Corp., 790 F.2d 515, 40 FEP 1349 (6th Cir. 1986); Box v. A&P Tea Co., 772 F.2d 1372, 38 FEP 1509 (7th Cir. 1985), *cert. denied,* 478 U.S. 1010, 41 FEP 271 (1986); Kauffman v. Sidereal Corp., 695 F.2d 343, 28 FEP 1605 (9th Cir. 1982); Chaline v. KCOH, 693 F.2d 477, 30 FEP 834 (5th Cir. 1982); Burrus v. United Tel. Co. of Kan., 683 F.2d 339, 29 FEP 663 (10th Cir.), *cert. denied,* 459 U.S. 1071, 30 FEP 592 (1982); DeLesstine v. Fort Wayne State Hosp. & Training Center, 682 F.2d 130, 29 FEP 193 (7th Cir.), *cert. denied,* 459 U.S. 1017, 30 FEP 224 (1982); Perry v. Prudential Ins. Co. of Am., 29 FEP 1837 (S.D. Tex. 1982).

[4]*Compare* Price Waterhouse v. Hopkins, 57 U.S.L.W. 4469, 49 FEP 954 (1989), *rev'g and remanding* 825 F.2d 458, 44 FEP 825 (D.C. Cir. 1987), discussed *supra* Chapter 1 (Overview) *with e.g.,* Hayes v. Shelby Memorial Hosp., 726 F.2d 1543, 34 FEP 444 (11th Cir. 1984) (discharge of pregnant female under fetal protection policy is discrimination *per se,* thus not within *McDonnell Douglas* analysis); Knighton v. Laurens County School Dist., 721 F.2d 976, 33 FEP 299 (4th Cir. 1983) (shifting burden of persuasion to defendant in § 1981 action appropriate when either intentional segregating action or recent history of discrimination exists; defendant must then prove by clear and convincing evidence that plaintiff not victim of discrimination); Williams v. Southwestern Bell Tel. Co., 718 F.2d 715, 33 FEP 297 (5th Cir. 1983) (*McDonnell Douglas* analysis inappropriate for case fully tried on the merits; since presumption of discrimination drops from case when employer articulates legitimate, nondiscriminatory reason, trial court must simply decide which party's explanation is more persuasive); Perryman v. Johnson Prods. Co., 698 F.2d 1138, 31 FEP 93 (11th Cir. 1983) (*McDonnell Douglas* analysis not rigidly adhered to in class actions).

[5]*E.g.,* Ekanem v. Health & Hosp. Corp. of Marion County, 724 F.2d 563, 33 FEP 1497 (7th Cir. 1983), *cert. denied,* 469 U.S. 821, 35 FEP 1607 (1984) (proper to grant defendant's motion to dismiss under Fed. R. Civ. P. 41(b) at close of plaintiff's case in chief if defendant's legitimate, nondiscriminatory reasons articulated and pretext not shown; plaintiff not entitled to additional opportunity to produce evidence of pretext); Gordon v. National R.R. Passenger Corp., 564 F. Supp. 199, 34 FEP 315 (E.D. Pa. 1983) (*McDonnell Douglas* provides useful analytical framework, but does not require that evidence be produced in compartmentalized form).

[6]Lewis v. Federal Prison Indus., 786 F.2d 1537, 40 FEP 998 (11th Cir. 1986); Wheeler v. Snyder Buick, Inc., 794 F.2d 1228, 41 FEP 341 (7th Cir. 1986); Bellissimo v. Westinghouse Elec. Corp., 764

establishing a prima facie case of unlawful termination. For example, the Fifth Circuit has held that a plaintiff ostensibly discharged for violation of a work rule can establish a prima facie case of discrimination, even where his replacement was a member of his same protected group, by showing that a person not belonging to the protected group was retained under apparently similar circumstances.[7] The Ninth Circuit, relying on statistical evidence offered by the plaintiff to prove that she was unlawfully denied tenure, noted that while the statistical data may not have been directly probative of any of the four specific elements set forth in the *McDonnell Douglas* test, the data tended to establish that it was "more likely than not" that the defendant's decision to deny tenure had been based on sex.[8] Similarly, where a plaintiff introduces evidence of direct discrimination sufficient to establish a discriminatory motive, reliance on the four-part test developed for circumstantial evidence is unnecessary.[9] The *McDonnell Douglas* test has also been modified where the plaintiff has not been replaced[10] or the plaintiff is not a member of a "protected class."[11]

---

F.2d 175, 37 FEP 1862 (3d Cir. 1985), *cert. denied,* 475 U.S. 1035, 40 FEP 192 (1986); LaGrant v. Gulf & W. Mfg. Co., 748 F.2d 1087, 36 FEP 465 (6th Cir. 1984); Nix v. WLCY Radio/Rahall Communications, 738 F.2d 1181, 35 FEP 1101 (11th Cir. 1984); Crawford v. Northeastern Okla. State Univ., 713 F.2d 586, 32 FEP 681 (10th Cir. 1983); Walker v. IBM Corp., 698 F.2d 959, 30 FEP 1840 (8th Cir. 1983); Vaughn v. Pool Co. of Tex., Pool Offshore Co. Div., 683 F.2d 922, 29 FEP 1017 (5th Cir. 1982). *Compare* Proctor v. Consolidated Freightways Corp. of Del., 795 F.2d 1472, 41 FEP 704 (9th Cir. 1986) (prima facie case of religious discrimination requires showing that (1) plaintiff had bona fide religious belief; (2) plaintiff informed his employer of his religious views and they were in conflict with his responsibilities as an employee; and (3) plaintiff was discharged because of his observance of that belief). *But see* Mills v. Ford Motor Co., 800 F.2d 635, 41 FEP 1397 (6th Cir. 1986) (prima facie proof depends on factual situation and rigid application of *McDonnell Douglas* criteria should be avoided; plaintiff need only show that her discharge raised an inference of discrimination); Barnes v. Yellow Freight Sys., 778 F.2d 1096, 39 FEP 1050 (5th Cir. 1985) (four-part test inappropriate where issue is whether supervisor of one race treats employees of same race more favorably under essentially identical circumstances).

[7]EEOC v. Brown & Root, 688 F.2d 338, 30 FEP 11 (5th Cir. 1982); Davin v. Delta Air Lines, 678 F.2d 567, 30 FEP 14 (5th Cir. 1982); Wise v. Mead Corp., 614 F. Supp. 1131, 38 FEP 1056 (M.D. Ga. 1985); *see also* Nix v. WLCY Radio/Rahall Communications, *supra* note 6.

[8]Lynn v. Regents of Univ. of Cal., 656 F.2d 1337, 28 FEP 410 (9th Cir. 1981), *cert. denied,* 459 U.S. 823 (1982). *See also* Babrocky v. Jewel Food Co., 773 F.2d 857, 38 FEP 1667 (7th Cir. 1985) (plaintiff's prima facie case can be established through statistical evidence alone); Spaulding v. University of Wash., 740 F.2d 686, 35 FEP 217 (9th Cir.), *cert. denied,* 469 U.S. 1036, 36 FEP 464 (1984) (statistics constitute an accepted form of circumstantial evidence of discrimination); Talley v. United States Postal Serv., 720 F.2d 505, 33 FEP 361 (8th Cir. 1983), *cert. denied,* 466 U.S. 952, 37 FEP 592 (1984) (statistical disparities accompanied by evidence that plaintiff treated differently from similarly situated employees held sufficient). *But see* Palmer v. United States, 794 F.2d 534, 41 FEP 559 (9th Cir. 1986) (to establish prima facie case of age discrimination, statistics must show "stark pattern" of discrimination unexplainable on grounds other than age); Carmichael v. Birmingham Saw Works, 738 F.2d 1126, 35 FEP 791 (11th Cir. 1984) (although statistics alone may create prima facie case of classwide discrimination, statistics alone cannot make a case of individual disparate treatment; individual must point to some specific instance of discrimination).

[9]Fields v. Clark Univ., 817 F.2d 931, 43 FEP 1247 (1st Cir. 1987); Wilson v. City of Aliceville, 779 F.2d 631, 39 FEP 1290 (11th Cir. 1986); Blalock v. Metals Trades, 775 F.2d 703, 39 FEP 140 (6th Cir. 1985); Thompkins v. Morris Brown College, 752 F.2d 558, 37 FEP 24 (11th Cir. 1985); Perryman v. Johnson Prods. Co., *supra* note 4.

[10]Beaven v. Kentucky, 783 F.2d 672, 40 FEP 264 (6th Cir. 1986) (where defendant did not seek applications for vacated position, prima facie case can be established by showing nonminorities were more favorably treated); Matthews v. Allis-Chalmers, 769 F.2d 1215, 1217, 38 FEP 1118, 1120 (7th Cir. 1985) (fourth prima facie element has no role in reduction-in-force case since, when employer reduces his work force, he hires no one to replace the one let go); Hughes v. Chesapeake & Potomac Tel. Co., 583 F. Supp. 66, 33 FEP 1651 (D.D.C. 1983) (when defendant fails to replace plaintiff, she must show that nonminority employees with comparable records were not treated similarly); Leite v. Kennecott Copper Corp., 558 F. Supp. 1170, 31 FEP 390 (D. Mass.), *aff'd without opinion,* 720 F.2d 658, 33 FEP 1520 (1st Cir. 1983) (plaintiff need not show he was replaced when he was discharged ostensibly because of reduction in force); Ryan v. Raytheon Data Sys. Co., 601 F. Supp. 243, 39 FEP 1398 (D. Mass. 1985) (prima facie case established by showing that plaintiff's "function" was continued by others even though her position was not filled after her termination).

[11]Legrand v. University of Ark. at Pine Bluff Trustees, 821 F.2d 478, 44 FEP 60 (8th Cir. 1987) (plaintiff need not show that he is member of minority group in order to establish prima facie case);

Proof of each element necessarily differs from case to case, but some general rules have evolved governing the type of proof necessary to establish a plaintiff's prima facie case. For example, although a plaintiff must show disparate treatment from that afforded similarly situated employees, "similarly situated" does not always require that the jobs of the plaintiff and of those treated more favorably be identical.[12] Also, in determining whether a plaintiff has proven qualifications for the job, some courts have limited their inquiry to whether the plaintiff met the employer's performance criteria.[13] Where the plaintiff is not performing to the legitimate satisfaction of the employer, courts have found that the plaintiff has failed to make out a prima facie case.[14] In addition, the Sixth Circuit has held that the mere termination of a competent employee when an employer is making cutbacks due to economic necessity is insufficient to establish a prima facie case.[15] The plaintiff in such reorganization cases must come forward with additional direct, circumstantial, or statistical evidence that an impermissible motive was a factor in his termination.[16] However, it is not necessary for the plaintiff to

---

Rivette v. United States Postal Serv., 625 F. Supp. 768, 39 FEP 1388 (E.D. Mich. 1986) (prima facie case of reverse discrimination is established upon showing by plaintiff that there exist sufficient background facts supporting suspicion that defendant is the unusual employer who discriminates against majority); Bishopp v. District of Columbia, 602 F. Supp. 1401, 37 FEP 235 (D.D.C. 1985), rev'd in part, vacated in part, 788 F.2d 781, 40 FEP 903 (D.C. Cir. 1986) (qualified plaintiff establishes discriminatory rejection from employment despite majority status by showing employer discriminates against majority); Turgeon v. Howard Univ., 571 F. Supp. 679, 32 FEP 925 (D.D.C. 1983) (in reverse discrimination claim, proof that plaintiff suffered racially discriminatory treatment is adequate substitute for proof that plaintiff belongs to protected class).

[12]Compare Hager v. Western Sizzlin Steak House, 537 F. Supp. 1016, 31 FEP 888 (S.D. Ga. 1982) (plaintiff waitress and male restaurant manager "similarly situated" when both had been promised they could return to their former jobs after helping to open new restaurant) with Moore v. Devine, 767 F.2d 1541, 38 FEP 1196 (11th Cir. 1985), modified, 780 F.2d 1559, 39 FEP 1644 (11th Cir. 1986) (plaintiff's position and position of labor relations officer were not "similarly situated" where latter was more complex and required greater exercise of discretion) and Talley v. United States Postal Serv., 33 FEP 233 (E.D. Mo. 1982), aff'd, 720 F.2d 505, 33 FEP 361 (8th Cir. 1983), cert. denied, 466 U.S. 952, 37 FEP 592 (1984) (temporary casual employee not similarly situated to permanent employees, although all had same duties).

[13]Scott v. Sears, Roebuck & Co., 798 F.2d 210, 41 FEP 805 (7th Cir. 1986) (plaintiff failed to establish prima facie case because she was unable to show she was qualified where plaintiff only capable of performing two brake jobs a day while other mechanics could perform as many as three a day); Mason v. Pierce, 774 F.2d 825, 39 FEP 21 (7th Cir. 1985) (because plaintiff's work suffered from high error rate and significant backlog, she was not qualified for position); Holloway v. Bolger, 41 FEP 353 (D.N.J. 1986) (plaintiff not qualified where he was absent from work, allegedly for medical reasons, for all but 16 hours during 37 months preceding his discharge); Franklin v. Greenwood Mills Mktg. Co., 33 FEP 1847 (S.D.N.Y. 1983) (testimony by customers that plaintiff was good salesman did not show he was qualified, since customer's and employer's expectations can legitimately differ); Gillard v. Sears, Roebuck & Co., 32 FEP 1274 (E.D. Pa. 1983) (plaintiff admitted poor production and failed to substantiate allegation that it was due to conditions created by defendant); Howard v. Miller Brewing Co., 31 FEP 850 (N.D.N.Y. 1983) (fact that plaintiff placed on probation for unsatisfactory performance proved he was not qualified for job).

[14]Dale v. Chicago Tribune Co., 797 F.2d 458, 41 FEP 714 (7th Cir. 1986), cert. denied, 479 U.S. 1066, 42 FEP 1536 (1987); Agarwal v. University of Minn. Regents, 788 F.2d 504, 40 FEP 937 (8th Cir. 1986); Mason v. Pierce, supra note 13; Oglesby v. Coca-Cola Bottling Co. of Chicago/Wis., 620 F. Supp. 1336, 39 FEP 327 (N.D. Ill. 1985); Bell v. Fremar Corp., 36 FEP 547 (D.D.C. 1984); Silvas v. Dow Chem. Co., 36 FEP 105 (S.D. Tex. 1984); Jacobs v. United States Postal Serv., 587 F. Supp. 384, 35 FEP 1515 (W.D. La. 1984), aff'd without opinion, 759 F.2d 20, 37 FEP 1072 (5th Cir. 1985); Everett v. Communications Satellite Corp., 33 FEP 793 (D.D.C. 1983); Sack v. Kimberly-Clark Corp., 33 FEP 624 (E.D. Wis. 1982).

[15]LaGrant v. Gulf & W. Mfg. Co., supra note 6; see also Holley v. Sanyo Mfg., 771 F.2d 1161 n.1, 38 FEP 1317, 1319 n.1 (8th Cir. 1985) (Age Discrimination in Employment Act does not require that every plaintiff in protected age group be allowed a trial simply because he was discharged during reduction in force).

[16]LaGrant v. Gulf & W. Mfg. Co., supra note 6 (plaintiff did not establish prima facie case because he came forward with nothing other than his subjective determination that he was better qualified than retained employee); see also Bechold v. IGW Sys., 817 F.2d 1282, 43 FEP 1512 (7th Cir. 1987); Barnes v. Southwest Forest Indus., 814 F.2d 607, 43 FEP 197 (11th Cir. 1987); Holt v. Gamewell Corp., 797 F.2d 36, 41 FEP 585 (1st Cir. 1986) (requirements for prima facie case reviewed and found lacking under

anticipate and refute an employer's legitimate, nondiscriminatory reason in order to establish his prima facie case.[17]

## C. The Employer's Legitimate, Nondiscriminatory Reason, and the Plaintiff's Burden to Show Pretext

When the plaintiff has established a prima facie case of discrimination, the defendant must be afforded the opportunity to articulate legitimate, nondiscriminatory reasons for its actions regardless of the type of evidence produced by the plaintiff.[18] The defendant's burden is only to articulate valid reasons for its actions. It need not prove either that it was actually motivated by proper justification[19] or that other employees treated more favorably than the plaintiff were not similarly situated.[20]

Any nondiscriminatory reason, regardless of the employer's wisdom in acting on it, will fulfill the defendant's burden of production.[21] However, normally the reasons articulated by the employer are not entitled to any heightened judicial deference when the totality of the evidence is considered.[22]

Once the defendant employer articulates a legitimate, nondiscriminatory reason for discharge, the plaintiff has the burden of proving that this reason was a mere pretext for discrimination. Such pretext can be established by direct evidence of discrimination,[23] comparative evi-

---

both disparate treatment and disparate impact analyses); Holley v. Sanyo Mfg., *supra* note 15; Matthews v. Allis-Chalmers, *supra* note 10.

[17]Crimm v. Missouri Pac. R.R., 750 F.2d 703, 36 FEP 883 (8th Cir. 1984) (district court erred in instructing jury that employee was required to prove compliance with employer's rules and regulations in order to establish prima facie case).

[18]*E.g.,* Iodice v. Southeastern Packing & Gaskets, 572 F. Supp. 1370, 33 FEP 275 (N.D. Ga. 1983) (defendant entitled to articulate reasons in spite of fact that plaintiff produced letter signed by defendant's vice president stating she was discharged because of pregnancy).

[19]Farmer v. Colorado & S. Ry., 723 F.2d 766, 33 FEP 955 (10th Cir. 1983); Snyder v. Washington Hosp. Center, 36 FEP 445 (D.D.C. 1984).

[20]Tate v. Weyerhaeuser Co., 723 F.2d 598, 33 FEP 666 (8th Cir. 1983), *cert. denied,* 469 U.S. 847, 38 FEP 358 (1984).

[21]*E.g.,* Tye v. Polaris Joint Vocational School Dist. Bd. of Educ., 811 F.2d 315, 43 FEP 34 (6th Cir. 1987) (even an untrue reason satisfies employer's intermediate burden under *Burdine*); Wilkins v. Eaton Corp., 790 F.2d 515, 40 FEP 1349 (6th Cir. 1986) (pilot discharged for refusing to use flight checklist of questionable value); Patkus v. Sangamon-Cass Consortium, 769 F.2d 1251, 38 FEP 1272 (7th Cir. 1985) (insubordination by employee even though no defiance of direct order); Bellissimo v. Westinghouse Elec. Corp., 764 F.2d 175, 37 FEP 1862 (3d Cir. 1985), *cert. denied,* 475 U.S. 1035, 40 FEP 192 (1986) (plaintiff's inability to get along with supervisor); Conner v. Fort Gordon Bus Co., 761 F.2d 1495, 37 FEP 1574 (11th Cir. 1985) (subjective standard of unreasonable endangerment of passengers and property); MacPherson v. Texas Dep't of Water Resources, 734 F.2d 1103, 35 FEP 213 (5th Cir. 1984) (sending an anonymous critique of a departmental memo to her supervisor); Jones v. Los Angeles Community College Dist., 702 F.2d 203, 31 FEP 717 (9th Cir. 1983) (employer's belief in truth of charges that female police officer misused sick leave and engaged in unsatisfactory service); Sack v. Kimberly-Clark Corp., *supra* note 14 (dissatisfaction with plaintiff's performance); Mason v. Continental Ins. Co., 32 FEP 578 (N.D. Ala. 1983) (employer's policy of allowing only 120 days per year for disability leave, regardless of nature of disability, legitimate reason for discharging pregnant employee who exceeded total).

[22]Williams v. Caterpillar Tractor Co., 770 F.2d 47, 38 FEP 985 (6th Cir. 1985); Lincoln v. University Sys. of Ga. Bd. of Regents, 697 F.2d 928, 31 FEP 22 (11th Cir.), *cert. denied,* 464 U.S. 826, 32 FEP 1768 (1983). *But see* Pirone v. Home Ins. Co., 559 F. Supp. 306, 31 FEP 311 (S.D.N.Y.), *aff'd without opinion,* 742 F.2d 1430, 37 FEP 280 (2d Cir. 1983) (deference to employer's reason based on credibility determination).

[23]Wheeler v. Snyder Buick, Inc., 794 F.2d 1228, 41 FEP 341 (7th Cir. 1986) (supervisor's comments including: firing the "dirty slut working as a car salesman," car sales being "man's field," and there being "no damn room in the new car business for a woman" are direct evidence of discriminatory motive and establish pretext); Morris v. Bianchini, 43 FEP 674 (E.D. Va. 1987), *aff'd,* 838 F.2d 467 (4th Cir. 1988) (pretext shown where female plaintiff was told of company policy not to hire women in particular position); Jackson v. Wakulla Springs & Lodge, 33 FEP 1301 (N.D. Fla. 1983) (new supervisor's demonstrable racial hatred, coupled with his quick termination of plaintiffs for petty infractions, showed pretext); Weatherspoon v. Andrews & Co., 32 FEP 1226 (D. Colo. 1983) (witness' testimony of racial slurs directed at, and physical abuse of, plaintiff proved pretext).

dence,[24] statistical evidence,[25] or a combination of the three.[26] In addition, some circuit courts have held that disproof of the employer's justification is alone sufficient to demonstrate pretext for discrimination.[27] Other courts have held, however, that no inference of discrimination is created where the evidence of pretext shows that the real reason for discharge was nondiscriminatory[28] or that the proffered reason, although incorrect, was believed by the employer in good faith to be correct.[29]

The reasonableness or wisdom of the employer's reason for discharge is not the issue. Even an unwise or arbitrary policy may be applied in an evenhanded, nondiscriminatory manner.[30] Conversely, an employer's genuine and reasonable explanation may have been used to exclude only members of a protected class.[31]

Plaintiffs often rely on comparative evidence by arguing that the employer retained similarly situated employees who were not members of the protected class.[32] For example, where the employer's legitimate reason stems

---

[24]Muldrew v. Anheuser-Busch, 554 F. Supp. 808, 34 FEP 60 (E.D. Mo. 1982), aff'd, 728 F.2d 989, 34 FEP 93 (8th Cir. 1984) (application of policy different from written policy proved pretext).

[25]Box v. A&P Tea Co., 772 F.2d 1372, 38 FEP 1509 (7th Cir. 1985), cert. denied, 478 U.S. 1010, 41 FEP 271 (1986) (statistical evidence offered was probative of promotion policy but not relevant to discharge); Sweat v. Miller Brewing Co., 708 F.2d 655, 32 FEP 384 (11th Cir. 1983) (statistical evidence may be relevant to show pretext); Carlton v. Interfaith Medical Center, 612 F. Supp. 118, 39 FEP 1477, 119 LRRM 3314 (E.D.N.Y. 1985) (statistical evidence failed to show any discrimination); Madreperla v. Williard Co., 606 F. Supp. 874, 38 FEP 336 (E.D. Pa. 1985) (statistical and circumstantial evidence sufficient to create issue whether age was determinative factor); Adams v. Grant-Holloday Nursing Home, 28 FEP 579 (D.D.C. 1982) (no direct, comparative, or statistical evidence).

[26]Reeves v. General Foods Corp., 682 F.2d 515, 29 FEP 779 (5th Cir. 1982).

[27]Thornbrough v. Columbus & Greenville R.R., 760 F.2d 633, 37 FEP 1414 (5th Cir. 1985) (by disproving employer's purported legitimate reason, plaintiff reinstitutes presumption created by prima facie case: in the absence of legitimate reasons for employer's decision, employer presumably was motivated by discriminatory reasons); Duffy v. Wheeling Pittsburgh Steel Corp., 738 F.2d 1393, 35 FEP 246 (3d Cir.), cert. denied, 469 U.S. 1087, 36 FEP 712 (1984) (once plaintiff establishes prima facie case, it is not necessary to prove actual discriminatory intent, only to demonstrate the pretextual nature of the proffered justification); Maxfield v. Sinclair Int'l, 36 FEP 87 (E.D. Pa. 1984), aff'd, 766 F.2d 788, 38 FEP 442 (3d Cir. 1985), cert. denied, 474 U.S. 1057, 39 FEP 1200 (1986) (same). See also Tye v. Polaris Joint Vocational School Dist. Bd. of Educ., supra note 21 (employer cannot successfully defend its decision without stated reason or reasonable inquiry; plaintiff demonstrates pretext by disproving all of defendant's proffered reasons). But see Askin v. Firestone Tire & Rubber Co., 600 F. Supp. 751, 36 FEP 1487 (E.D. Ky. 1985), aff'd without opinion, 785 F.2d 307, 40 FEP 984 (6th Cir. 1986) (when plaintiff proves employer's articulated reasons are pretext merely for some arbitrary or oppressive motive, rather than discriminatory motive, plaintiff cannot fall back on prima facie case without introducing specific evidence of discrimination).

[28]Confer v. SKF Indus., 40 FEP 1721 (W.D. Pa. 1986) (evidence that age claimant was harassed by management following injury which forced him to perform light duty work may suggest stated reason for discharge (falsifying report) is pretext, but such evidence does not show pretext for discrimination); O'Loughlin v. Procon, Inc., 627 F. Supp. 675, 40 FEP 977 (E.D. Tex.), aff'd, 808 F.2d 54 (5th Cir. 1986) (employer's reason for discharge, though purposely mischaracterized, animated by business necessity and had nothing to do with race).

[29]Bechold v. IGW Sys., 817 F.2d 1282, 43 FEP 1512 (7th Cir. 1987) (honestly held belief that employee was unqualified, even if erroneous, may be nondiscriminatory reason for discharge); Graham v. Jacksonville Coach Co., 568 F. Supp. 1575, 39 FEP 492 (M.D. Fla. 1983) (fact that employer may have been wrong about its nondiscriminatory reason irrelevant if decision was not in fact based on racial animus); Davis v. Greensboro News Co., 39 FEP 535 (M.D.N.C. 1985) (court's inquiry is not whether employer's reasons are correct but instead whether employer believed them to be correct).

[30]Smith v. Monsanto Chem. Co., 770 F.2d 719, 38 FEP 1141 (8th Cir. 1985), cert. denied, 475 U.S. 1050, 40 FEP 272 (1986).

[31]Namenwirth v. University of Wis. Sys. Bd. of Regents, 769 F.2d 1235, 38 FEP 1155 (7th Cir. 1985), cert. denied, 474 U.S. 1061, 39 FEP 1200 (1986).

[32]Duchon v. Cajon Co., 791 F.2d 43, 40 FEP 1432 (6th Cir. 1986); Barnes v. Yellow Freight Sys., 778 F.2d 1096, 39 FEP 1050 (5th Cir. 1985); Boner v. Little Rock Municipal Water Works Bd. of Comm'rs, 674 F.2d 693, 28 FEP 767 (8th Cir. 1982); Montgomery v. Yellow Freight Sys., 671 F.2d 412, 28 FEP 831 (10th Cir. 1982); Wright v. Southwest Bank, 648 F.2d 266, 28 FEP 1040 (5th Cir. 1981); Wise v. Mead Corp., 614 F. Supp. 1131, 38 FEP 1056 (M.D. Ga. 1985). But see Bluebeard's Castle Hotel v. Virgin Islands Dep't of Labor, 786 F.2d 168, 40 FEP 603 (3d Cir. 1986) (more than fact that another employee was not discharged for arguably similar conduct necessary to show intentional discrimination).

from a specific incident (e.g., insubordination, violation of a work rule), the plaintiff may attempt to rebut the legitimacy of this reason by showing that other employees guilty of comparable conduct were not discharged.[33]

The Seventh Circuit has observed that evidence indicating that the employer failed to conduct a thorough investigation, including the failure to obtain information from individuals with material knowledge, prior to the decision to terminate is relevant to the issue of whether the employer's articulated nondiscriminatory reasons for the discharge are a pretext.[34] The Sixth Circuit has held that an issue of pretext can be raised by evidence that the reason given for discharge was inconsistent with the employer's previous statements or actions.[35]

Only strong circumstantial evidence will suffice to carry the plaintiff's burden.[36] The plaintiff's subjective perception of discrimination is inadequate to prove pretext.[37]

According to the Eleventh Circuit, where the plaintiff establishes his prima facie case by direct testimony that the defendant acted with discriminatory intent, the defendant cannot rebut by articulating legitimate, nondiscriminatory reasons. Rather, the defendant can rebut this showing only by proving that the same decision would have been reached even absent the discriminatory factor.[38] However, the Eighth Circuit found it

---

[33]Abasiekong v. City of Shelby, 744 F.2d 1055, 35 FEP 1636 (4th Cir. 1984); Garner v. St. Louis Sw. Ry., 676 F.2d 1223, 28 FEP 1469 (8th Cir. 1982); Anderson v. Savage Laboratories, 675 F.2d 1221, 28 FEP 1473 (11th Cir. 1982); Meyer v. California & Hawaiian Sugar Co., 662 F.2d 637, 27 FEP 1175 (9th Cir. 1981).

[34]Christie v. Foremost Ins. Co., 785 F.2d 584, 40 FEP 508 (7th Cir. 1986); DeLesstine v. Fort Wayne State Hosp. & Training Center, 682 F.2d 130, 29 FEP 193 (7th Cir.), cert. denied, 459 U.S. 1017, 30 FEP 224 (1982); Cooper v. City of N. Olmsted, Ohio, 37 FEP 90 (N.D. Ohio 1985).

[35]Duchon v. Cajon Co., supra note 32 (pretext raised by fact that no warning given employee, that reason given to state agency varied from that given employee, as well as by failure to fully investigate plaintiff's version of events leading to discharge); Williams v. Caterpillar Tractor Co., 770 F.2d 47, 38 FEP 985 (6th Cir. 1985) (jury entitled to infer pretext from evidence that events relied upon to support discharge were not consistent with previously manifested management concerns).

[36]Griffin v. City of Omaha, 785 F.2d 620, 40 FEP 385 (8th Cir. 1986) (evidence sufficient to show firearms proficiency standard pretext for termination); Andre v. Bendix Corp., 774 F.2d 786, 38 FEP 1819 (7th Cir. 1985) (only hostility between employee and supervisor shown); Foster v. MCI Telecommunications Corp., 773 F.2d 1116, 39 FEP 698 (10th Cir. 1985) (low evaluation of subjective job abilities by accused racist inconsistent with objective criteria; pretext shown); Parker v. Federal Nat'l Mortgage Ass'n, 741 F.2d 975, 35 FEP 893 (7th Cir. 1984) (ambiguous comment on performance review does not raise reasonable inference of discriminatory motive); Williamson v. Owens-Illinois, 589 F. Supp. 1051, 34 FEP 1656 (N.D. Ohio 1984), aff'd, rev'd in part without opinion, 782 F.2d 1044 (6th Cir. 1985) (fact that employer articulated several reasons rather than one for discharge inadequate to show pretext); Hughes v. Chesapeake & Potomac Tel. Co., 583 F. Supp. 66, 33 FEP 1651 (D.D.C. 1983) (supervisor's different social interaction with white and black employees insufficient proof of pretext); French v. Mead Corp., 33 FEP 635 (S.D. Ohio 1983), aff'd without opinion, 758 F.2d 652, 37 FEP 1408 (6th Cir.), cert. denied, 474 U.S. 820, 38 FEP 1727 (1985) (lack of official policy covering plaintiff's situation inadequate to show pretext); Humphries v. Tenneco Retail Serv. Co., 31 FEP 855 (N.D. Ga. 1983) (immediate supervisor's sexist bias not proof of pretext when discharge based on disproportionately large cash shortage at store managed by plaintiff).

[37]Elliott v. Group Medical & Surgical Serv., 714 F.2d 556, 32 FEP 1451 (5th Cir. 1983), cert. denied, 467 U.S. 1215, 34 FEP 1472 (1984) (trier of fact not free to disregard articulated reason without countervailing evidence it was not real reason). But see Yarbrough v. Tower Oldsmobile, 789 F.2d 508, 40 FEP 1035 (7th Cir. 1986) (jury entitled to disregard articulated reason of defendant where reason relies on incident which is credibly denied by plaintiff; court notes jury instruction allowing plaintiff to prevail by showing proffered reason unworthy of belief was not objected to).

[38]Maddox v. Grandview Care Center, 780 F.2d 987, 39 FEP 1456 (11th Cir. 1986); Buckley v. Hospital Corp. of Am., 758 F.2d 1525, 37 FEP 1082 (11th Cir. 1985); Dybczak v. Tuskegee Inst., 737 F.2d 1524, 35 FEP 813 (11th Cir. 1984), cert. denied, 469 U.S. 1211, 37 FEP 64 (1985); Lee v. Russell County Bd. of Educ., 684 F.2d 769, 29 FEP 1508 (11th Cir. 1982); accord Blalock v. Metal Trades, 775 F.2d 703, 39 FEP 140 (6th Cir. 1985). See also Price Waterhouse v. Hopkins, supra note 4 and supra Chapter 1 (Overview).

inherently inconsistent to conclude that, although race was a discernible factor, the same decision would have been made absent racial considerations.[39]

## III. THE CLASS ACTION CASE

Whether or not a discharged employee is, under Rule 23, an adequate representative to bring an across-the-board class action continues to be an issue.[40]

## V. CONSTRUCTIVE DISCHARGE

Although most courts have held that constructive discharge allegations must be evaluated under an objective, rather than subjective, standard, the circuits remain divided as to the showing of intent to discriminate necessary to prove constructive discharge under Title VII.[41] Several courts only require that the plaintiff prove that the employer made working conditions so intolerable that a reasonable person would have been forced to resign.[42] Others follow the stricter view that a plaintiff must prove that the employer either intended to force the resignation or took deliberate actions, thereby subjecting the employee to discriminatory practices which made working conditions

---

[39]Bibbs v. Department of Agriculture, 778 F.2d 1318, 39 FEP 970 (8th Cir. 1985) (en banc) (with respect to liability determination under Title VII, once race is shown to be causative factor in employment decision, it is clearly erroneous to find that racial considerations did not affect outcome of decision; with respect to remedy, however, retroactive promotion and back pay may not be awarded if defendant proves by preponderance of the evidence that same decision not to promote plaintiff would have been made absent discrimination).

[40]See, e.g., Ladele v. Consolidated Rail Corp., 95 F.R.D. 198, 29 FEP 1547 (E.D. Pa. 1982) (class certification denied); see also Chapter 34 (Class Actions).

[41]See, e.g., Howard v. Marsh, 616 F. Supp. 1116 (E.D. Mo. 1985), aff'd, 808 F.2d 841 (8th Cir. 1986), cert. denied, 484 U.S. — (1987) (disagreement among circuits as to intent requirement, citing this treatise).

[42]Garner v. Wal-Mart Stores, 807 F.2d 1536, 42 FEP 1141 (11th Cir. 1987) (resigning one day after discriminatory demotion to "floater" not reasonable response); Jett v. Dallas Indep. School Dist., 798 F.2d 748, 41 FEP 1076 (5th Cir. 1986) (demotion from head to freshman football coach not sufficient under "objective" test); Derr v. Gulf Oil Corp., 796 F.2d 340, 41 FEP 166 (10th Cir. 1986) (adopting an objective standard of whether conditions intolerable to a reasonable person; employer's subjective intent irrelevant; employer held to have intended reasonably foreseeable consequences); Wardwell v. Palm Beach County, Fla., School Bd., 786 F.2d 1554, 40 FEP 1006 (11th Cir. 1986) (working conditions not proved to be intolerable); Williams v. Caterpillar Tractor Co., supra note 35 (employee constructively discharged when demoted from Class 10 job, disability benefits clerk, to Class 2 job, mail clerk); Goss v. Exxon Office Sys. Co., 747 F.2d 885, 36 FEP 344 (3d Cir. 1984) (acts of discrimination based on sex and pregnancy made working conditions for employee so intolerable as to constitute constructive discharge); Satterwhite v. Smith, 744 F.2d 1380, 36 FEP 148 (9th Cir. 1984) (black employee constructively discharged when less qualified white employees regularly promoted ahead of plaintiff); Nolan v. Cleland, 686 F.2d 806, 29 FEP 1732 (9th Cir. 1982) (history of discrimination provides sufficient aggravating factors that may have made plaintiff's job intolerable); Held v. Gulf Oil Co., 684 F.2d 427, 29 FEP 837 (6th Cir. 1982) (employee constructively discharged where employer subjected her to various forms of discriminatory treatment); Taylor v. Jones, 653 F.2d 1193, 28 FEP 1024 (8th Cir. 1981) (black employee was forced to resign from National Guard because of opprobrious racial atmosphere); Price Waterhouse v. Hopkins, 57 U.S.L.W. 4469, 49 FEP 954 (1989), rev'g and remanding 825 F.2d 458, 44 FEP 825 (D.C. Cir. 1987) (denial of partnership reasonably viewed by employee as career-ending action); Bailey v. Binyon, 583 F. Supp. 923, 36 FEP 1236 (N.D. Ill. 1984) (racial epithets caused intolerable working conditions); EEOC v. Hay Assocs., 545 F. Supp. 1064, 29 FEP 994 (E.D. Pa. 1982) (employee constructively discharged where supervisor subjected her to intolerable working conditions because of her sex); Robson v. Eva's Super Mkt., 538 F. Supp. 857, 30 FEP 1212 (N.D. Ohio 1982) (plaintiff stated cognizable claim of constructive discharge due to sexual harassment).

intolerable.[43] In either case, evidence of purposeful discrimination alone does not suffice to prove constructive discharge; rather, the employee must also present evidence of aggravating factors.[44] Consequently, the following have been held insufficient, in and of themselves, to establish constructive discharge: failure to promote,[45] a poor performance rating or evaluation,[46] a discriminatory raise or bonus,[47] or increasing an employee's workload[48] or territory.[49] Constructive discharges have been found where an employee resigned after being told she would be terminated if she did not resign[50] or her workweek was reduced by two-thirds.[51] Some courts have found constructive discharge where an inexperienced male was promoted over the female plaintiff,[52] she was denied admission to partnership,[53] or plaintiff was demoted even without a reduction in salary.[54]

The EEOC has endorsed a standard for proving constructive dis-

---

[43]Hervey v. City of Little Rock, 787 F.2d 1223, 40 FEP 928 (8th Cir. 1986) (plaintiff failed to prove that employer deliberately rendered employee's working conditions intolerable and that actions of employer were intended to force employee to quit); Bishopp v. District of Columbia, 788 F.2d 781, 40 FEP 903 (D.C. Cir. 1986) (white males claimed constructive discharge by not being promoted to position of assistant fire chief); Bristow v. Daily Press, 770 F.2d 1251, 38 FEP 1145 (4th Cir. 1985), *cert. denied,* 475 U.S. 1082, 40 FEP 608 (1986) (plaintiff must show deliberate employer action creating intolerable working conditions); Henry v. Lennox Indus., 768 F.2d 746, 42 FEP 771 (6th Cir. 1985) (court must inquire into intent of employer and the reasonably foreseeable impact of employer's conduct on employee); Craft v. Metromedia, 766 F.2d 1205, 38 FEP 404 (8th Cir. 1985), *cert. denied,* 475 U.S. 1058, 40 FEP 272 (1986) (employee must present evidence that employer specifically intended to force employee to resign); Martin v. Citibank, N.A., 762 F.2d 212, 37 FEP 1580 (2d Cir. 1985) (plaintiff must show that employer "deliberately" made working conditions sufficiently intolerable to force resignation); Downey v. Isaac, 622 F. Supp. 1125, 38 FEP 52 (D.D.C. 1985), *aff'd,* 794 F.2d 753 (D.C. Cir. 1986) (in order to establish prima facie case of constructive discharge plaintiff must establish that employer "deliberately" established intolerable working conditions which forced resignation); EEOC v. Federal Reserve Bank of Richmond, 698 F.2d 633, 30 FEP 1137 (4th Cir. 1983), *rev'd on other grounds sub nom.* Cooper v. Federal Reserve Bank of Richmond, 476 U.S. 867, 35 FEP 1 (1984) (no constructive discharge absent evidence that employer sought to force employee to resign); Sparrow v. Piedmont Health Sys. Agency, 593 F. Supp. 1107, 38 FEP 1621 (M.D.N.C. 1984) (employer's actions must be intended as effort to force employee to quit); Gan v. Kepro Circuit Sys., 28 FEP 639 (E.D. Mo. 1982) (employee not constructively discharged where she welcomed and encouraged alleged sexually harassing conduct).

[44]Yates v. Avco Corp., 819 F.2d 630, 43 FEP 1595 (6th Cir. 1987); Bishopp v. District of Columbia, *supra* note 43; Henry v. Lennox Indus., *supra* note 43; Cockrell v. Boise Cascade Corp., 781 F.2d 173, 39 FEP 1201 (10th Cir. 1986); Satterwhite v. Smith, *supra* note 42; Geisler v. Folsom, 735 F.2d 991, 34 FEP 1581 (6th Cir. 1984); Price Waterhouse v. Hopkins, *supra* note 42. *See also* Lincoln v. University Sys. of Ga. Bd. of Regents, 697 F.2d 928, 31 FEP 22 (11th Cir.), *cert. denied,* 464 U.S. 826, 32 FEP 1768 (1983); Nolan v. Cleland, *supra* note 42; EEOC v. Hay Assocs., *supra* note 42.

[45]EEOC v. Federal Reserve Bank of Richmond, *supra* note 43; Wardwell v. Palm Beach County, Fla., School Bd., *supra* note 42.

[46]Caslin v. General Elec. Co., 696 F.2d 45, 30 FEP 971 (6th Cir. 1982); Junior v. Texaco, 688 F.2d 377, 29 FEP 1696 (5th Cir. 1982).

[47]Alston v. Blue Cross & Blue Shield of Greater N.Y., 37 FEP 1792 (E.D.N.Y. 1985); Scott v. Oce Indus., 536 F. Supp. 141, 36 FEP 1226 (N.D. Ill. 1982).

[48]Wardwell v. Palm Beach County, Fla., School Bd., *supra* note 42.

[49]Bristow v. Daily Press, *supra* note 43.

[50]Burney v. City of Pawtucket, 559 F. Supp. 1089, 34 FEP 1274 (granting injunctive relief), *later proceeding,* 34 FEP 1287 (granting temporary restraining order on another claim), *order vacated,* 563 F. Supp. 1088, 34 FEP 1290 (D.R.I. 1983), *aff'd and remanded for determination of attorney's fees,* 728 F.2d 547, 34 FEP 1295 (1st Cir. 1984).

[51]Thurber v. Jack Reilly's, Inc., 521 F. Supp. 238, 32 FEP 1508 (D. Mass. 1981), *aff'd on other grounds,* 717 F.2d 633, 32 FEP 1511 (1st Cir. 1983), *cert. denied,* 466 U.S. 904, 34 FEP 544 (1984).

[52]Henry v. Lennox Indus., *supra* note 43 (employer promoted male with no experience over plaintiff, who had performed duties of the position over several years, and requested that she train her new supervisor).

[53]Hopkins v. Price Waterhouse, 618 F. Supp. 1109, 38 FEP 1630 (D.D.C. 1985), *aff'd in part, rev'd and remanded in part,* 825 F.2d 458, 44 FEP 825 (D.C. Cir. 1987).

[54]Real v. Continental Group, 627 F. Supp. 434, 39 FEP 1530 (N.D. Cal. 1986) (demotions sufficiently intolerable even though no decrease in salary); *see also* Cockrell v. Boise Cascade, *supra* note 44 (employee assumed demotions would include drop in salary, and employer failed to advise him of contrary).

charge that requires a charging party to prove only that the employer made working conditions so intolerable that a reasonable person would have been forced to resign.[55] Under the EEOC's objective test, the charging party must establish (1) that a reasonable person in the charging party's position would have found the working conditions intolerable; (2) that conduct which constituted a Title VII violation against the charging party created the intolerable working conditions; and (3) that the charging party's involuntary resignation resulted from the intolerable working conditions.[56] The Commission expressly declined to "require a showing that the intolerable working conditions were imposed deliberately by the employer or that the employer imposed them with the actual intention of having the employee resign."[57]

---

[55]EEOC Dec. 84-1, 33 FEP 1887, 1892 (1983).
[56]*Id., see also* EEOC Dec. 86-6, 40 FEP 1890 (1986).
[57]*Supra* note 55.

CHAPTER 19

# UNIONS

## I. A Union's Liability for Its Own Discrimination

### A. Liability of a Union in Its Role as an Employer

If a union is sued as an employer, rather than as a labor organization, the union must meet the Title VII definition of "employer" in terms of the number of employees. Union directors are not employees for this purpose unless a traditional employer-employee relationship exists between them and the union.[1]

### B. Liability of a Union in Its Role as a Union

#### 1. Membership, Referrals, and Officers

Where evidence reflected that a union created an atmosphere that discouraged minorities from seeking referral, and where the union maintained a "standardless" method of referral, the Second Circuit has affirmed a district court finding that the union was liable for discriminatory referral practices even though the impact of discriminatory practices was demonstrated by a statistical disparity based on a small sample.[2]

Where a recalcitrant craft union engaged in long-standing and egregious race discrimination in membership admission and referrals, the Supreme Court upheld a preferential 29 percent nonwhite membership goal, in addition to other relief, even where the goal favored persons who were not actual victims of the discrimination found to exist.[3]

#### 2. Duty of Fair Representation

A union may be held primarily liable for that part of an employee's damages caused by the union's breach of its duty of fair representation.[4]

---

[1]Chavero v. Transit Union Local 241, 787 F.2d 1154, 40 FEP 766 (7th Cir. 1986) (holding that members of union's executive board were not employees even though they received salaries, had some grievance handling and collective bargaining responsibilities, and oversaw operation of union; court found they did not report to anyone and did not perform as employees within traditional employer-employee relationship). See Sciss v. Metal Polishers Local 8A, 562 F. Supp. 293, 33 FEP 1333 (S.D.N.Y. 1983) (welfare and pension fund that employed only four persons not an employer under Title VII and not agent of union).

[2]Ingram v. Madison Square Garden Center, 709 F.2d 807, 32 FEP 641, 644 (2d Cir.), cert. denied, 464 U.S. 937, 33 FEP 48 (1983) (Local 3 of Electrical Workers, IBEW, had referred 10 minority members of 66 total referrals (15%) compared with 25–27% minority work force representation in two relevant SMSAs; referral of seven additional minority members would have increased minority referral percentage to 26%; district court had also found that efforts of minority class members to secure laborers' positions "were deliberately frustrated by union personnel" who "gave evasive answers * * * or just generally gave the runaround to class members").

[3]Sheet Metal Workers Local 28 v. EEOC, 478 U.S. 421, 41 FEP 107 (1986) (affirming imposition of broad relief, including appointment of an administrator to supervise compliance with Court's order).

[4]Bowen v. United States Postal Serv., 459 U.S. 212, 112 LRRM 2281 (1983) (damages increased by failure of union to take grievance to arbitration).

These damages may include attorneys' fees, court costs, and other expenses incidental to the plaintiff's effort to recover against the employer.[5] The limitations period applicable to a fair representation suit in court against a union is the six-month period specified in § 10(b) of the NLRA.[6]

A union's efforts to promote lawful affirmative action for the benefit of women and minority members has been held not to violate the duty of fair representation owed to white and male union members.[7] In fact, a union's failure to take "every reasonable step" to combat discriminatory policies of the employer has been held to violate Title VII.[8]

One court has held that federal labor laws preempted a claim brought under a state antidiscrimination law that a union violated its duty of fair representation to handicapped individuals.[9]

## 3. Handling of Grievances

In two disparate treatment cases under § 1981, one of which was also brought under Title VII, the requisite discriminatory intent was not found, and the courts dismissed claims that the union discriminatorily failed to process a grievance.[10]

## II. JOINT UNION-EMPLOYER LIABILITY

### A. A Union's Joint Liability for Discrimination Caused by the Provisions of Collective Bargaining Agreement

The courts continue to hold unions jointly liable with employers under Title VII, § 1981 and § 1983 for discrimination caused by provisions of a collective bargaining agreement.[11] The Fifth Circuit, applying the "efforts"

---

[5]Peterson v. Carpenters, Lehigh Valley Dist. Council, 676 F.2d 81, 36 FEP 1131 (3d Cir. 1982).

[6]DelCostello v. Teamsters, 462 U.S. 151, 113 LRRM 2737 (1983) (limitations period of § 10(b) also applies to employee's breach of collective bargaining agreement action against employer).

[7]Breschard v. Directors Guild, 34 FEP 1045 (C.D. Cal. 1984).

[8]Howard v. Molders Local 106, 779 F.2d 1546, 39 FEP 1413 (11th Cir.), cert. denied, 476 U.S. 1174, 40 FEP 1873 (1986). (union's failure to take "every reasonable step" to oppose use of nonvalidated promotion test which had adverse impact on black employees rendered it liable under Title VII, citing Terrell v. United States Pipe & Foundry Co., 644 F.2d 1112, 1120, 25 FEP 1262 (5th Cir. 1981), reh'g denied, 655 F.2d 235 (5th Cir. 1982)).

[9]Maynard v. Revere Copper Prods., 773 F.2d 733, 38 FEP 1729 (6th Cir. 1985) (employee's claim union violated state antidiscrimination act by failing to help procure light duty work for injured employee held preempted by § 301 of Labor Management Relations Act).

[10]Tate v. Weyerhaeuser Co., 723 F.2d 598, 607, 33 FEP 666, 673 (8th Cir. 1983), cert. denied, 469 U.S. 847, 38 FEP 358 (1984) (absent evidence of discriminatory intent, "the union need only articulate a legitimate, nondiscriminatory reason for its actions. Unions are not required to pursue nonmeritorious grievances"); Goodwin v. Be-Mac Transp., 567 F. Supp. 296, 32 FEP 1178 (E.D. Mo. 1983), aff'd without opinion, 732 F.2d 160, 35 FEP 472 (8th Cir. 1984) (union not liable under § 1981 where no discriminatory intent shown and no evidence that union processed grievances of white employees any differently from that of plaintiff).

[11]Philbrook v. Ansonia Bd. of Educ., 757 F.2d 476, 37 FEP 404 (2d Cir. 1985), aff'd and remanded, 479 U.S. 60, 42 FEP 359 (1986) (union and employer may be jointly liable for failure to accommodate plaintiff's religion because union may not have aggressively sought liberalization of leave policy even though union did not object to employer's accommodation or either of plaintiff's proposed accommodations); McDaniel v. Essex Int'l, 696 F.2d 34, 30 FEP 831 (6th Cir. 1982) (employer and union jointly liable for failure to accommodate plaintiff's religion; undue hardship does not exist even though accommodation by employer would have resulted in litigation with union); Sears v. Atchison, Topeka & Santa Fe Ry., 749 F.2d 1451, 36 FEP 783 (10th Cir. 1984), cert. denied, 471 U.S. 1099, 37 FEP 1216 (1985) (union liable for additional monetary loss over and above that provided by employer's settlement without regard to relative fault); Jackson v. Seaboard Coast Line R.R., 678 F.2d 992, 29 FEP 442 (11th Cir. 1982) (union liable on either disparate impact or disparate treatment theory for discriminatory promotion

test, ruled that the union may satisfy the legal requirements of taking all reasonable steps to oppose a discriminatory practice and be absolved from liability even if it stopped short of striking over the matter.[12]

The Second Circuit has held that a union becomes independently liable for violation of the ADEA when it assists the employer in discriminating against employees by joining as a party to a collective bargaining agreement binding the employer to a discriminatory practice. However, the remedial scheme of the ADEA was held to preclude an award of damages against a union.[13]

The religious accommodation cases present difficult problems for unions. Some courts uphold a union's right to bargain for scheduling provisions favorable to most employees and to enforce the agreement even if this prevents accommodating the religious beliefs of a particular employee.[14] However, the Second Circuit has held that a union may be liable where the paid leave provisions in a collective bargaining agreement were not sufficient to freely accommodate the plaintiff, and the plaintiff asserted that the union had not aggressively sought a more liberal policy.[15]

Where a union was sued on a theory of successor liability, one court defined a successor union's duty to be the elimination within a reasonable time of any discriminatory provisions of the contract entered into by its predecessor.[16]

## B. A Union's Liability for Inducing Employer Discrimination

Where a union was found to have joined the employer in age discrimination in a collective bargaining agreement, one court concluded that the union had violated § 623(c)(3) of the ADEA.[17]

---

system contained in collective bargaining agreement); Lyon v. Temple Univ., 543 F. Supp. 1372, 30 FEP 1030 (E.D. Pa. 1982) (union could be liable under § 1983 for affirmative action provisions of collective bargaining agreement allegedly discriminatory to males). *Cf.* Scarlett v. Seaboard Coast Line R.R., 676 F.2d 1043, 29 FEP 433 (5th Cir. 1982) (railroad and union jointly liable for disregarding and discriminatorily applying contractual seniority system).

[12]Waker v. Republic Steel Corp., 675 F.2d 91, 28 FEP 1201 (5th Cir. 1982).

[13]Air Line Pilots v. Trans World Airlines, 713 F.2d 940, 32 FEP 1185 (2d Cir. 1983), *aff'd in part, rev'd in part on other grounds, sub nom.* Trans World Airlines v. Thurston, 469 U.S. 111, 36 FEP 977 (1985) (Supreme Court declined to consider question of whether a union may be liable for monetary damages under ADEA as issue was not raised by proper party; *id.* at n. 14). *Cf.* Neuman v. Northwest Airlines, 28 FEP 1488 (N.D. Ill. 1982) (union may not be held liable under ADEA); Richardson v. Alaska Airlines, 750 F.2d 763, 36 FEP 986 (9th Cir. 1984) (award of attorneys' fees under ADEA may only be made against employer).

[14]Dickson v. Longshoremen, ILA, Local 40, 38 FEP 1253 (D. Or. 1985) (duty to accommodate religious beliefs does not require employer and union to violate collective bargaining agreement to detriment of other employees as long as parties are willing to make possible adjustments that do not create undue hardship); EEOC v. Caribe Hilton Int'l, 597 F. Supp 1007, 36 FEP 420 (D.P.R. 1984) (union not required to ignore contractual provision of four-day week where plaintiff cannot meet his scheduled work shift because of religious beliefs since accommodating plaintiff would be detrimental to other employees); McDonald v. McDonnell Douglas Corp., 35 FEP 1661 (N.D. Okla. 1984) (union not liable for failure to accommodate plaintiff where it was agreeable to any voluntary accommodation which would not require waiver or violation of seniority provisions or other contract rights of other employees).

[15]Philbrook v. Ansonia Bd. of Educ., *supra* note 11.

[16]Wust v. Northwest Airlines, 29 FEP 1435 (W.D. Wash. 1979).

[17]29 U.S.C. § 623(c)(3). *See* Air Line Pilots v. Trans World Airlines, *supra* note 13.

## C. A Union's Joint Liability for Acquiescing in Employer Discrimination Not Based on Provisions of Collective Bargaining Agreement

The Supreme Court has held that a union may be jointly liable for an employer's discrimination based on its policy of not grieving racial discrimination under a contract which prohibited such discrimination, even if the union's policy was not motivated by racial animus. However, the Court specifically declined to decide whether "mere passivity" in the face of employer discrimination could result in union liability.[18]

Lower courts have discussed in varying contexts the extent of a union's duty to oppose an employer's purportedly discriminatory practices.[19]

## E. Liability of Regional and International Unions

The Ninth Circuit has refused to find a local union to be the agent of the international union in one case, and has also refused to find that the local and international unions were a single "employer."[20]

## F. Contribution, Joinder, Realignment, and Cross-Claim

Relying on the rationale of *Northeast Airlines v. Transport Workers,*[21] courts have held that a defendant cannot counterclaim for contribution in a Title VII action,[22] that contribution is not available even where liability is established jointly under Title VII and § 1981, and that there is no common law right of contribution under § 1981.[23]

The Second Circuit has ruled that a provision included in a collective bargaining agreement by which the union agreed to hold the employer

---

[18]Goodman v. Lukens Steel Co., 482 U.S. 656, 44 FEP 1 (1987) (affirming holding that union was jointly liable under Title VII and § 1981 for employer's discrimination based on its policy of not including racial discrimination claims in grievances that alleged other violations of collective bargaining agreement and of not filing grievances that involved racial harassment in violation of contract provision prohibiting racial discrimination).

[19]Dominguez v. Bartenders Local 64, 674 F.2d 732, 28 FEP 797 (8th Cir. 1982) (union has no liability where employee did nothing to advise union of employer's allegedly discriminatory practices and her numerous grievances included no suggestion of discrimination); Parker v. Baltimore & Ohio R.R., 555 F. Supp. 1182, 30 FEP 1791 (D.D.C. 1983) (union liability to white male employee cannot be premised on union's failure to act to defeat employer's affirmative action plan which was not on its face or in practice unduly hostile to white male employees. *But see* Howard v. Molders Local 106, 779 F.2d 1546, 39 FEP 1413 (11th Cir.), *cert. denied,* 476 U.S. 1174, 40 FEP 1873 (1986), where the union was liable for the employer's nonintentional discrimination where, apparently, there was no complaint to the union that the challenged test had a disparate impact on black employees.

[20]Childs v. Electrical Workers, IBEW, Local 18, 719 F.2d 1379, 32 FEP 275 (9th Cir. 1983).

[21]451 U.S. 77, 25 FEP 737 (1981).

[22]State, County & Municipal Employees v. City of New York, 599 F. Supp. 916, 36 FEP 900 (S.D.N.Y. 1984) (dismissing counterclaim for contribution in Title VII action).

[23]Anderson v. Electrical Workers, IBEW, Local 3, 582 F. Supp. 627, 34 FEP 517 (S.D.N.Y.), *aff'd,* 751 F.2d 546, 36 FEP 1249 (2d Cir. 1984) (granting employer summary judgment in union's contribution claim in joint Title VII and § 1981 action because *Northwest Airlines* prohibits contribution whenever Title VII is one of the bases of liability and, alternatively, holding there is no common law right of contribution for liability established under § 1981 because the party seeking contribution is an intentional tort-feasor). *Cf.* Sears v. Atchison, Topeka & Santa Fe Ry., 749 F.2d 1451, 36 FEP 783 (10th Cir. 1984), *cert. denied,* 471 U.S. 1099, 37 FEP 1216 (1985) (union that, along with employer, discriminated against black employees by segregating jobs was required to pay back pay to all persons denied payment under settlement agreement between employees and employer, because union's violation of Title VII was characterized as a "separate wrong" from that of employer and to hold otherwise would discourage settlement).

harmless for judgments and expenses involving claims of sex discrimination is void as against public policy. The court declined to rule on whether a contractual contribution clause for sharing, rather than shifting, liability would be enforceable.[24]

## III. Union Challenges to Employer Affirmative Action Efforts or Employer Actions Taken Pursuant to Court or Government Directives

In *W. R. Grace & Co. v. Rubber Workers Local 759*,[25] the Supreme Court concluded that it is not contrary to public policy to enforce an arbitration award imposing back pay liability for breach of a labor contract against an employer who assumed and elected to satisfy inconsistent obligations of an EEOC conciliation agreement. The Court stated that "[a]bsent a judicial determination, the Commission, not to mention the Company, cannot alter the collective bargaining agreement without the Union's consent."[26] In this case, there had been a separate judicial proceeding which had ultimately determined that the seniority provisions of the collective bargaining agreement, which conflicted with the terms of the conciliation agreement, were lawful. The Court found it unnecessary to decide whether public policy would be violated by an arbitration award for breach of seniority provisions ultimately found to be illegal.

In *Firefighters Local 1784 v. Stotts*,[27] the Supreme Court permitted a union to challenge the application of a consent decree by an employer to vary the seniority order of a layoff where layoffs had not been covered by the underlying consent decree and neither the union nor nonminority employees had been parties to the original action. Subsequent lower court decisions have resisted attempts at broadening *Stotts* beyond its narrow fact pattern, generally holding *Stotts* does not apply where there has been a finding of discrimination or where the seniority system is not bona fide.[28] In *Firefighters*

---

[24]Stamford Bd. of Educ. v. Stamford Educ. Ass'n, 697 F.2d 70, 30 FEP 1379 (2d Cir. 1982). *See* Anderson v. Electrical Workers, IBEW, Local 3, *supra* note 23 (employer not liable to union for indemnification or contribution for judgment against union that had discriminatory referral policy); Gray v. City of Kansas City, Kan., 603 F. Supp. 872, 37 FEP 418 (D. Kan. 1985) (union not liable to City employer for contribution for claims under § 1981 or § 1983).

[25]461 U.S. 757, 31 FEP 1409 (1983).

[26]*Id.* at 771, 31 FEP at 1414.

[27]467 U.S. 561, 34 FEP 1702 (1984). *See also* discussion in Chapter 3 (Seniority), Section III, and Chapter 31 (EEOC Litigation), Section X. *See also* EEOC v. Safeway Stores, 714 F.2d 567, 576–80, 32 FEP 1465, 1472–75 (5th Cir. 1983), *cert. denied,* 467 U.S. 1204, 34 FEP 1400 (1984) (district court improperly enforced terms of EEOC consent decree that provided for retroactive seniority to four individual plaintiffs, where such terms conflicted with seniority provisions of collective bargaining agreement and where union neither consented to decree nor had opportunity to participate in adjudication on merits of discrimination claims).

[28]*See, e.g.,* Massachusetts Ass'n of Afro-American Police v. Boston Police Dep't, 780 F.2d 5, 39 FEP 1048 (1st Cir. 1985), *cert. denied,* 478 U.S. 1020, 41 FEP 272 (1986); EEOC v. Sheet Metal Workers Local 638, 753 F.2d 1172, 36 FEP 1466 (2d Cir. 1985), *aff'd sub nom.* Sheet Metal Workers Local 28 v. EEOC, 478 U.S. 421, 41 FEP 107 (1986) (*infra* note 30); United States v. City of Cincinnati, 771 F.2d 161, 38 FEP 1402 (6th Cir. 1985); Devereaux v. Geary, 765 F.2d 268, 38 FEP 23 (1st Cir. 1985), *aff'g* 596 F. Supp. 1481, 36 FEP 415 (D. Mass. 1984), *cert. denied,* 471 U.S. 1115, 41 FEP 272 (1986); Pennsylvania v. Operating Eng'rs Local 542, 770 F.2d 1068, 38 FEP 673 (3d Cir. 1985), *cert. denied,* 474 U.S. 1060, 39 FEP 1200 (1986); Diaz v. AT&T, 752 F.2d 1356, 36 FEP 1742 (9th Cir. 1985); Turner v. Orr, 759 F.2d 817, 37 FEP 1186 (11th Cir. 1985), *cert. denied,* 478 U.S. 1020, 41 FEP 272 (1986); Kromnick v. Philadelphia School Dist., 739 F.2d 894, 35 FEP 538 (3d Cir. 1984), *cert. denied,* 469 U.S.

*Local 93 v. City of Cleveland,* [29] the Court distinguished *Stotts* and held, over a union's challenge, that a court may enforce a consent decree between an employer and minority employees which provides race-conscious relief to persons who are not actual victims of discrimination, even if the remedial measures set forth in the decree exceed the scope of relief the court itself could have imposed by way of judgment following trial.[30]

---

1107, 36 FEP 976 (1985); Firefighters Local 1590 (Wilmington) v. City of Wilmington, 632 F. Supp. 1177, 40 FEP 1078 (D. Del. 1986); Youngblood v. Dalzell, 625 F. Supp. 30, 38 FEP 814 (S.D. Ohio 1985), *aff'd,* 804 F.2d 360, 42 FEP 415 (6th Cir. 1986), *cert. denied,* 480 U.S. 935, 43 FEP 560 (1987).
    [29]478 U.S. 501, 41 FEP 139 (1986).
    [30]*See also* Sheet Metal Workers Local 28 v. EEOC, 478 U.S. 421, 41 FEP 107 (1986) (courts may, in limited, appropriate cases, provide relief under Title VII that benefits individuals who were not actual victims of defendant's discriminatory practices).

CHAPTER 20

# EMPLOYMENT AGENCIES

## I. STATUTORY PROVISIONS

"Employment agency" means any person *regularly* undertaking with or without compensation to procure employees for an employer or to procure for employees opportunities to work for an employer, and includes an agent of such person.[1] While "regularly" may mean "on rare occasions," the procurement must be for an employer covered by Title VII.[2]

## II. DEFINITION OF EMPLOYMENT AGENCY

The EEOC has ruled that a university placement office which assists students and alumni in job searches through consultation services, preparation of résumés, and the arrangement of interviews with prospective employers is an employment agency within the meaning of Title VII.[3] Likewise, an entity that undertakes recruitment of staff for a hospital owned by a foreign government is an employment agency within the meaning of Title VII, since the hospital is a "person" for purposes of § 701(a) of the Act.[4]

## III. DISPARATE TREATMENT

### C. Discriminatory Referrals

A court of appeals has held that, where a female applicant was summarily rejected, her lack of qualifications is not relevant to the plaintiff's prima facie case or to the defendant's articulation of a reason for rejection. Once discrimination has been shown, the defendant has the burden of proving that an applicant would not have been referred or hired absent discrimination.[5]

In *Pegues v. Mississippi State Employment Service,*[6] the Fifth Circuit

---

[1]42 U.S.C. § 2000e(c) (emphasis added).

[2]Lavrov v. NCR Corp., 600 F. Supp. 923, 35 FEP 988 (S.D. Ohio 1984) (where employer's foreign subsidiary was not employer within meaning of Title VII, employer was not liable as employment agency under Title VII for expatriation of workers to foreign subsidiary at subsidiary's request).

[3]EEOC Dec. 84-2, 33 FEP 1983 (1983).

[4]EEOC July 85-12, 38 FEP 1880 (1985).

[5]*Compare* Ostroff v. Employment Exch., 683 F.2d 302, 29 FEP 683 (9th Cir. 1982) *with* Alaniz v. California Processors, 785 F.2d 1412, 1418, 40 FEP 768 (9th Cir. 1986).

[6]699 F.2d 760, 31 FEP 257 (5th Cir. 1983), *rev'g in part on other grounds* 22 FEP 389 (N.D. Miss. 1978), *cert. denied,* 464 U.S. 991, 33 FEP 440 (1983). *See* Regner v. City of Chicago, 789 F.2d 534, 539, 40 FEP 1027 (7th Cir. 1986).

reviewed various practices involved in a race and sex class action alleging discrimination by the state employment service against blacks and females under both the disparate treatment and disparate impact theories. While rejecting much of the statistical analysis and other evidence relied upon by the plaintiffs, the court did find sufficient evidence of unlawful sex preferences and race-based referrals to support a finding of liability.

## CHAPTER 21

# THE CIVIL RIGHTS ACTS OF 1866 AND 1871

## II. SCOPE AND COVERAGE OF CIVIL RIGHTS ACT OF 1866, 42 U.S.C. § 1981*

### A. Statutory Authority

The decisions continue to be split on whether the express exemptions and exclusions from Title VII implicitly limit the scope of § 1981.[1] The Eleventh Circuit has joined the majority of other circuits in holding that the § 703(h) seniority system exemption applies to § 1981 actions.[2]

### C. Applicability of § 1981 to State and Federal Discrimination

Where state governmental entities enjoy sovereign immunity under the Eleventh Amendment, state officials may be sued in their individual capacities for individual acts violating § 1981.[3]

While municipalities are not immune from suit under § 1981, the Su-

---

*As this chapter went to press, the Supreme Court indicated it might reconsider the applicability of § 1981 to private acts of racial discrimination. In *Patterson v. McLean Credit Union,* 485 U.S. _____, 46 FEP 979 (1988), the Supreme Court requested the parties to brief and argue the following question: "Whether or not the interpretation of 42 U.S.C. § 1981 adopted by this Court in *Runyon v. McCrary,* 427 U.S. 160 (1976), should be reconsidered?" *Runyon* applied § 1981 to acts of racial discrimination in private-school admission policies.

[1] Adams v. McDougal, 695 F.2d 104, 30 FEP 1123 (5th Cir. 1983) (appointed deputy sheriff is subject to protection of § 1981); Hudson v. Charlotte Country Club, 535 F. Supp. 313, 28 FEP 1208 (W.D.N.C. 1982) (suits against private membership clubs barred by Title VII also barred under § 1981). *Compare* Johnson v. Railway Express Agency, 421 U.S. 454, 10 FEP 817 (1975) (emphasizing separate and independent character of suits under Title VII and § 1981) *with* New York City Transit Auth. v. Beazer, 440 U.S. 568, 583–84 n.24, 19 FEP 149, 155 (1979) ("Although the exact applicability of § 1981 has not been decided by this Court, it seems clear that it affords no greater substantive protection than Title VII"). *See also* Chapter 3 (Seniority) at p. 26.

[2] Freeman v. Motor Convoy, 700 F.2d 1339, 31 FEP 517 (11th Cir. 1983). *Accord* Spain v. Republic Steel Corp., 35 FEP 1234 (N.D. Ohio 1983). *See also* Chapter 3 (Seniority).

[3] *See* Daisernia v. New York, 582 F. Supp. 792, 795–96, 34 FEP 626, 631–32 (N.D.N.Y. 1984) (§ 1981 does not abrogate sovereign immunity of State of New York or its agencies); Foulks v. Ohio Dep't of Rehabilitation & Correction, 713 F.2d 1229, 1231, 32 FEP 829, 831–32 (6th Cir. 1983) (state officials, however, can be sued under § 1981 in their individual capacities for individual acts violating § 1981); Culler v. South Carolina Dep't of Social Servs., 33 FEP 1590, 1595 (D.S.C. 1984) (state officials may be sued as individuals under § 1981, but may be immune from liability if acted in good faith); Lowe v. City of Monrovia, 775 F.2d 998, 39 FEP 350, 360 (9th Cir. 1985), *amended,* 784 F.2d 1407, 41 FEP 931 (9th Cir. 1986) (government officials entitled to qualified immunity only if a reasonable person would not have been aware that actions at issue violated well-established statutory or constitutional rights, based on objective reasonableness and not subjective good faith); Gladden v. Barry, 558 F. Supp. 676, 40 FEP 409, 411 (D.D.C. 1983) (city official must have personal involvement, and not be sued merely on a respondeat superior theory). *But see* Jones v. Singer Career Sys., 584 F. Supp. 1253, 1256–57, 34 FEP 1685, 1686–87 (E.D. Ark. 1984) (appeals referee of Arkansas Employment Security Division absolutely immune from suit under § 1981 when performing official duty of ruling on benefit claims) *and* Freeman v. Michigan, 808 F.2d 1174, 42 FEP 1090 (6th Cir. 1987) (an action for injunctive relief may be brought against state officials under § 1981 despite sovereign immunity defense). *See infra* note 18 and accompanying text.

preme Court and Fifth Circuit have held that liability must be based on official municipal policy, and not on the doctrine of respondeat superior.[4]

## D. Applicability of § 1981 to Racial Discrimination

The Fifth and Eleventh circuits have held that discrimination based on interracial marriage or association is by definition racial discrimination, regardless of a specific allegation of race discrimination toward the plaintiff.[5]

## F. Applicability of § 1981 to Other Bases of Discrimination

Prior to the Supreme Court's decisions in *St. Francis College v. Al-Khazraji*[6] and *Shaare Tefila Congregation v. Cobb*,[7] attempts to extend the reach of § 1981 beyond discrimination based on race or lineage had met with mixed success.[8] However, in *Al-Khazraji* as regards Arabs and in *Shaare Tefila Congregation* as regards Jews, the Court held that § 1981 and § 1982 were intended to protect identifiable classes of persons who are subject to intentional discrimination solely because of their ancestry or ethnic characteristics.[9]

The circuits disagree on whether § 1981 is applicable to claims of harassment or retaliation.[10] One trial court has held that white persons who oppose racial discrimination toward blacks in the workplace have standing to sue.[11]

---

[4]Pembaur v. City of Cincinnati, 475 U.S. 469 (1986) (discussed *infra,* Section III.D); Jett v. Dallas Indep. School Dist., 798 F.2d 748, 41 FEP 1076, 1086–87 (5th Cir. 1986) (constructive discharge claim); Hamilton v. Rodgers, 783 F.2d 1306, 40 FEP 453 (5th Cir. 1986) (action involving alleged "persistent widespread practice" of racial harassment and retaliation).

[5]Parr v. Woodmen of the World Life Ins. Co., 791 F.2d 888, 41 FEP 22, 25–26 (11th Cir. 1986) (claim stated under § 1981); Alizadeh v. Safeway Stores, 802 F.2d 111, 42 FEP 226 (5th Cir. 1986) (claimed discharge because of marriage to nonwhite states claim under § 1981).

[6]481 U.S. 604, 43 FEP 1305 (1987).

[7]481 U.S. 615, 43 FEP 1309 (1987).

[8]Anooya v. Hilton Hotels Corp., 733 F.2d 48, 49–50, 34 FEP 1529, 1530–31 (7th Cir. 1984) (alleged discrimination due to Iraqi background solely based on national origin, and accordingly fails to state cause of action under § 1981); Jatoi v. Hurst-Euless-Bedford Hosp. Auth., 807 F.2d 1214, 42 FEP 1235, *opinion modified on reh'g,* 819 F.2d 545 (5th Cir. 1987), *cert. denied,* 484 U.S. ____, 45 FEP 1256 (1988) (East Indian is member of group perceived as "racial" and states § 1981 claim); Chaiffetz v. Robertson Research Holding, Ltd., 798 F.2d 731, 41 FEP 1097, 1100 (5th Cir. 1986) (§ 1981 does not encompass claim based solely on national origin).

[9]The Supreme Court's analysis in *St. Francis College v. Al-Khazraji, supra* note 6, rested expressly on 42 U.S.C. § 1981. *In Shaare Tefila Congregation v. Cobb, supra* note 7, the Court held that 42 U.S.C. § 1982 "forbids both official and private discriminatory interference with property rights," and that these protections extend to Jews as one of the "identifiable classes of persons who are subjected to intentional discrimination solely because of their ancestry or ethnic characteristics." *Id.,* 43 FEP at 1310 (citing and relying upon the Court's § 1981 analysis in *Al-Khazraji, supra* note 6).

[10]Goff v. Continental Oil Co., 678 F.2d 593, 29 FEP 79 (5th Cir. 1982) (§ 1981 applicable to claim over retaliation because of plaintiff's opposition to racial discrimination); Benson v. Little Rock Hilton Inn, 742 F.2d 414, 35 FEP 1362 (8th Cir. 1984) (court rejects black employee's retaliation claim arising out of filing § 1981 suit while recognizing claim may be brought on proper facts; members of court disagree over use of "opposition conduct" characterization and application of "reasonable belief" standard); Nazaire v. Trans World Airlines, 807 F.2d 1372, 42 FEP 882 (7th Cir. 1986), *cert. denied,* 481 U.S. 1039, 44 FEP 1048 (1987) (it is well settled that racial harassment may be basis of an independent claim of violation of § 1981, as well as Title VII). *But see* Patterson v. McLean Credit Union, 805 F.2d 1143, 42 FEP 662 (4th Cir. 1986), *reargument ordered,* 485 U.S. ____, 46 FEP 979 (1988) ("standing alone, racial harassment does not abridge right to 'make' and 'enforce' contracts"); Tafoya v. Adams, 816 F.2d 555, 43 FEP 929 (10th Cir.), *cert. denied,* 484 U.S. ____, 44 FEP 1672 (1987) (§ 1981 retaliation claim would not be entertained where Mexican-Americans alleged they were discharged for filing EEOC charge, absent allegations of racial discrimination).

[11]Smithberg v. Merico, Inc. dba Rod's Foods Prods., 575 F. Supp. 80, 38 FEP 1868, 1870 (C.D. Cal. 1983). *See* Wilkey v. Pyramid Constr. Co., 619 F. Supp. 1453, 39 FEP 25, 27–28 (D. Conn. 1985).

## III. Scope and Coverage of Civil Rights Act of 1871, 42 U.S.C. § 1983

### B. The State Action Requirement and Private Discrimination

A university was subject to suit under § 1983 where the state had statutorily accepted responsibility for the institution.[12] However, even substantial state funding and regulation have been held not to convert the conduct of hospitals or utilities into state action for purposes of § 1983.[13]

### D. Applicability of § 1983 to State and Local Governments

Government officials may be sued in both their official and individual capacities.[14] In *Brandon v. Holt,*[15] the Supreme Court held that a § 1983 action against a public official in his official capacity imposes liability on the entity he represents, absent sovereign immunity, provided the entity has received notice and has had an opportunity to respond. In *Pembaur v. City of Cincinnati,*[16] the Supreme Court held that not every decision by municipal officers automatically subjects the municipality to § 1983 liability: "Municipal liability attaches only where the decisionmaker possesses final authority to establish municipal policy with respect to the action ordered."[17] The qualified immunity that protects a public servant from personal liability when acting individually and in good faith was not available to the entity as a defense. The doctrines of "good faith" or "qualified immunity" cause differences of opinion among certain circuits.[18]

---

[12]Krynicky v. University of Pittsburgh, 742 F.2d 94, 35 FEP 1133 (3d Cir. 1984), *cert. denied,* 471 U.S. 1015, 37 FEP 784 (1985).

[13]Mendez v. Belton, 739 F.2d 15, 35 FEP 625 (1st Cir. 1984) (§ 1983 not applicable to highly regulated private, nonprofit hospital that received Medicare and Medicaid funds); Beverly v. Douglas, 591 F. Supp. 1321, 35 FEP 1860 (S.D.N.Y. 1984) (sufficient nexus between private teaching hospital and state not shown even though hospital received significant public funding and was subject to governmental regulations; personnel decision of the hospital not compelled or influenced by any state or federal regulation); Stoutt v. Southern Bell Tel. & Tel. Co., 598 F. Supp. 1000, 36 FEP 1778 (S.D. Fla. 1984) (that defendant's operations are subject to state regulation and it is granted quasi-monopoly status does not transform company's conduct into state action).

[14]*See* Kentucky v. Graham, 473 U.S. 159 (1985) (Court summarizes distinctions between official-capacity actions and individual-capacity actions).

[15]469 U.S. 464 (1985).

[16]475 U.S. 469 (1986).

[17]*Id.* at _____.

[18]*Compare* Forrester v. White, 792 F.2d 647, 40 FEP 1633 (7th Cir. 1986) *with* McMillian v. Svetanoff, 793 F.2d 149, 40 FEP 1737 (7th Cir.), *cert. denied,* 479 U.S. 985, 43 FEP 80 (1986) (different results reached in case of judge firing probation officer and in case of termination of court reporter). *See* Jett v. Dallas Indep. School Dist., 798 F.2d 748, 41 FEP 1076 (5th Cir. 1986) (school district not liable under § 1983 for racially discriminatory transfer of white head coach, based solely on black principal's recommendation, where there was no jury finding that superintendant's decision was racially motivated or that superintendant knew or believed that principal's recommendation was racially motivated; black principal properly held individually liable); Kolar v. County of Sangamon, Ill., 756 F.2d 564, 37 FEP 298 (7th Cir. 1985) (local government's immunity from punitive damages waived by state law); Goodwin v. St. Louis County Circuit Court, 729 F.2d 541, 34 FEP 347 (qualified immunity unavailable to judge sued under § 1983 in his individual capacity for alleged sex discrimination in removal of female lawyer as juvenile hearing officer), *later proceedings,* 741 F.2d 1087, 35 FEP 1017 (8th Cir. 1984), *cert. denied,* 469 U.S. 828, 35 FEP 1608 (1984) *and* 469 U.S. 1216, 37 FEP 64 (1985) (affirming Title VII finding of sex discrimination entered by district court after earlier remand of that claim); Stathos v. Bowden, 728 F.2d 15, 34 FEP 142 (1st Cir. 1984) (if law clearly established, defense of good-faith immunity should normally fail, absent extraordinary circumstances); Wilhelm v. Continental Title Co., 720 F.2d 1173, 33 FEP 385 (10th Cir. 1983), *cert. denied,* 465 U.S. 1103, 34 FEP 416 (1984) (state civil rights commission director performed functions analogous to prosecutor, who is absolutely immune from suits for damages).

### E. Bases of Discrimination Under § 1983

The Seventh Circuit has joined the Second and Fifth circuits in holding that a plaintiff cannot bring an action under § 1983, based upon alleged violations of Title VII, against a person who could not be sued directly under Title VII, because § 1983 cannot "enlarge the relief available to one bringing an action for a violation of Title VII," and cannot cause a "substantive enlargement" of Title VII.[19] One court has held that § 1983 is not available to remedy age discrimination in employment.[20] The question whether § 1983 will support a private suit for violation of § 504 of the Rehabilitation Act requires further consideration in light of *Consolidated Rail Corp. v. Darrone.* [21] There, the Supreme Court held that § 504 created a private right of action for plaintiffs alleging injury because of discrimination against the handicapped by a recipient of federal financial assistance. Section 1983 does provide a remedy for an adverse employment decision motivated by an employee's exercise of First Amendment rights in protesting alleged discrimination.[22]

The Eighth Circuit has held that a disparate impact claim may not be asserted under § 1983.[23]

## IV. SCOPE AND COVERAGE OF CIVIL RIGHTS ACT OF 1871, 42 U.S.C. §§ 1985 AND 1986

### C. The Requirement of "Two or More Persons"

The emerging general rule continues to be that a single act of discrimination by a single entity does not constitute a § 1985(3) conspiracy, but

---

[19]Huebschen v. Wisconsin Dep't of Health & Social Servs., 716 F.2d 1167, 32 FEP 1582 (7th Cir. 1983) (does not reach question whether Congress intended Title VII to be exclusive remedy for employment discrimination by sexual harassment). *See* Hervey v. City of Little Rock, 787 F.2d 1223, 40 FEP 928 (8th Cir. 1986) (time-barred sex discrimination claim); Greenwood v. Ross, 778 F.2d 448, 40 FEP 435 (8th Cir. 1985) (however, claim of retaliatory discharge based on first amendment may be asserted); Day v. Wayne County Bd. of Auditors, 749 F.2d 1199, 36 FEP 743 (6th Cir. 1984) (claimant who was retaliated against in violation of Title VII does not have § 1983 claim; Title VII only remedy); Rivera v. City of Wichita Falls, 665 F.2d 531, 27 FEP 1352 (5th Cir. 1982); Carrion v. Yeshiva Univ., 535 F.2d 722, 729, 13 FEP 1521, 1527 (2d Cir. 1976); Talley v. City of De Soto, 37 FEP 375 (N.D. Tex. 1985) (if defendant not amenable to suit under Title VII, suit under § 1983 cannot be maintained); Torres v. Wisconsin Dep't of Health & Social Servs., 592 F. Supp. 922, 35 FEP 1041 (E.D. Wis. 1984) (rights guaranteed by Title VII may not be enforced through § 1983).

[20]McCroan v. Bailey, 543 F. Supp. 1201, 29 FEP 1533 (S.D. Ga. 1982) (§ 1983 does not encompass rights secured under ADEA, which provides its own exclusive remedy).

[21]465 U.S. 624, 34 FEP 79 (1984). *See* Meyerson v. Arizona, 709 F.2d 1235, 31 FEP 1183 (9th Cir. 1983), *vacated and remanded,* 465 U.S. 1095, 34 FEP 416 (1984), *on remand,* 740 F.2d 684, 35 FEP 127 (9th Cir. 1984) (violation of § 503 of Rehabilitation Act may not be basis of claim under § 1983); Norcross v. Sneed, 573 F. Supp. 533, 33 FEP 679 (W.D. Ark. 1983), *aff'd,* 755 F.2d 113, 37 FEP 77 (8th Cir. 1985) (action may not be maintained under § 1983 to remedy violation of § 504 of Rehabilitation Act where rejected job applicant did not prevail in private action under § 504); M. v. Alvin Indep. School Dist., 532 F. Supp. 460 (S.D. Tex. 1982) (rights created by § 504 of Rehabilitation Act cannot be asserted within remedial framework of § 1983); Brown v. County of Genesee, 37 FEP 1595 (W.D. Mich. 1985) (same).

[22]Dougherty v. Barry, 604 F. Supp. 1424, 37 FEP 1169 (D.D.C. 1985) (firefighter's First Amendment rights violated where employer denied promotion based on participation in a rally protesting employer's racial discrimination).

[23]Foster v. Wyrick, 823 F.2d 218, 44 FEP 313 (8th Cir. 1987) (since by definition claim of disparate impact does not involve intentional discrimination, such claims arise only under Title VII, and that remedy is exclusive). Title VII has also been held the exclusive remedy for alleged discrimination against a federal employee, and suit under § 1983 has been rejected. Owens v. United States, 822 F.2d 408, 44 FEP 247 (3d Cir. 1987).

recent cases reflect some judicial acceptance of factual variations as a basis for such a claim.[24]

### E. Bases of Discrimination Under §§ 1985 and 1986

Following the reasoning of *Great American Federal Savings & Loan Association v. Novotny*, [25] courts have held that §§ 1985 and 1986 cannot be used to enforce rights created by statutes which contain their own enforcement provisions.[26]

In *Carpenters Local 610 v. Scott*, [27] the Supreme Court confirmed that, absent state action, an alleged conspiracy to interfere with rights constitutionally protected only against state encroachment, such as First Amendment rights, is not a violation of § 1985(3).[28] The Court further held that § 1985(3) does not reach conspiracies motivated by commercial or economic animus, but it declined to determine whether § 1985(3) reaches conspiracies motivated by other than racial bias.

Since *Scott*, the Tenth Circuit has held that a § 1985 action for discrimination by a private employer requires invidious class-based animus against those classes with which Congress was concerned when it passed § 1985, and that this does not encompass handicapped persons.[29]

---

[24]Cross v. General Motors Corp., 721 F.2d 1152, 40 FEP 418 (8th Cir. 1983), *cert. denied*, 466 U.S. 980 (1984) (single act of discrimination by single entity does not constitute § 1985(3) conspiracy even if two or more agents participated; corporation and its agents are single person); Stathos v. Bowden, *supra* note 18 (sex discrimination conspiracy claim under § 1985(3) against municipal lighting commission and several commissioners for sex discrimination in pay not a single act of discrimination by single business entity); Novak v. World Bank, 703 F.2d 1305, 32 FEP 424 (D.C. Cir. 1983) (suit by former employee against World Bank, local bank, and agents asserted conspiracy between more than one entity; thus plaintiff not precluded from bringing action for age discrimination); Chambers v. Omaha Girls Club, 629 F. Supp. 925, 40 FEP 362 (D. Neb. 1986), *aff'd*, 834 F.2d 697, 45 FEP 698 (8th Cir. 1987) (a corporation cannot generally conspire with itself; as long as officers and employees acted within scope of their employment and without personal reasons, defendants did not engage in intracorporate conspiracy); Givan v. Greyhound Lines, 616 F. Supp. 1223, 39 FEP 123 (S.D. Ohio 1985) (corporation and individually named employees who acted within scope of their employment cannot be sued under 42 U.S.C. § 1985(3) as they comprise a single legal entity not capable of entering a conspiracy). *See* Thompson v. Machinists, 580 F. Supp. 662, 35 FEP 845 (D.D.C. 1984) (union and its officers alleged to have engaged in § 1985(3) conspiracy in regard to plaintiff's employment); Smith v. Private Indus. Council of Westmoreland & Fayette Counties, 622 F. Supp. 160, 39 FEP 702 (W.D. Pa. 1985) (conspiracy between corporation and its officers can be actionable under § 1985(3)).

[25]442 U.S. 366, 19 FEP 1482 (1979).

[26]Davis v. Devereux Found., 644 F. Supp. 482, 40 FEP 1560 (E.D. Pa. 1986) (claims within scope of Title VII preclude redress under 42 U.S.C. § 1985(3)); Lyon v. Temple Univ., 543 F. Supp. 1372, 30 FEP 1030 (E.D. Pa. 1982) (conspiracy to deprive plaintiff of rights under Equal Pay Act cannot be basis for claims under §§ 1985(3) and 1986); Hudson v. Teamsters Local 957, 536 F. Supp. 1138, 30 FEP 990 (S.D. Ohio 1982) (claims under 42 U.S.C. § 1981 but not under § 301 of LMRA may be enforced under § 1985(3)).

[27]463 U.S. 825, 113 LRRM 3145 (1983).

[28]*Cf.* Skadegaard v. Farrell, 578 F. Supp. 1209, 33 FEP 1528 (D.N.J. 1984) (state action requirement satisfied where sexual harassment suit brought against public official, whether or not actions officially authorized; plaintiff cannot assert violation of Title VII through § 1985(3), but may assert violations of independent rights, such as those provided under Equal Protection Clause of Fourteenth Amendment) *and* Eggleston v. Prince Edward Volunteer Rescue Squad, 569 F. Supp. 1344, 1352 (E.D. Va. 1983), *aff'd mem.*, 742 F.2d 1448 (4th Cir. 1984) ("Section 1985(3) protects against conspiracies to deprive persons of equal protection because of some discrete, insular, or immutable characteristic they possess such as race, national origin, or sex").

[29]Wilhelm v. Continental Title Co., 720 F.2d 1173, 33 FEP 385 (10th Cir. 1983), *cert. denied*, 465 U.S. 1103, 34 FEP 416 (1984); D'Amato v. Wisconsin Gas Co., 760 F.2d 1474, 37 FEP 1092 (7th Cir. 1985) (employment discrimination on basis of handicap outside scope of 42 U.S.C. § 1985(3); permitting handicap discrimination claim under § 1985(3) would intrude impermissibly on statutory scheme of both § 503 of Rehabilitation Act and § 1985(3)).

## V. LITIGATION, PROOF, PROCEDURE, AND REMEDIES

### A. Jurisdiction

#### 1. Actions Brought in Federal Court

For venue purposes, one court has held that where Title VII and § 1981 claims are joined, the Title VII claim should be considered the principal cause of action and its narrower venue provisions should control.[30]

### B. Statute of Limitations

The Supreme Court held in *Wilson v. Garcia*[31] that § 1983 claims are best characterized as personal injury actions for determining which state statute of limitations applies. In *Goodman v. Lukens Steel Co.,*[32] the Supreme Court extended this reasoning to cover claims under § 1981, resolving a split between certain circuits.[33] The majority of circuit courts have applied *Wilson* retroactively.[34]

Prior to *Goodman,* state limitations periods borrowed for suits under §§ 1981, 1985, and 1986 included those governing actions for lost wages,[35] actions on unwritten employment contracts,[36] and actions against state officers.[37]

---

[30]Hayes v. RCA Serv. Co., 546 F. Supp. 661, 31 FEP 246 (D.D.C. 1982).

[31]471 U.S. 261 (1986). A year earlier in *Burnett v. Grattan,* 468 U.S. 42, 35 FEP 15 (1984), the Supreme Court held in a §§ 1981, 1983, 1985, and 1986 action that the state residual three-year statute applied, not the state six-month period for filing administrative agency claims. As this Supplement went to press, the Supreme Court ruled in *Owens v. Okure,* _____ U.S. _____, 57 USLW 4065 (1989) that where state law provides multiple statutes of limitations for personal injury actions, the state's general or residual personal injury statute should be applied to § 1983 claims. *See also* Knoll v. Springfield Township School Dist., 699 F.2d 137, 30 FEP 1383 (3d Cir. 1983), *vacated and remanded,* 471 U.S. 288, 37 FEP 816 (1985), *on remand,* 763 F.2d 584, 37 FEP 1812 (3d Cir. 1985) (involving newly-enacted state six-month limitations period for action against government officials); Jones v. Preuit & Mauldin, 763 F.2d 1250 (11th Cir. 1985) (Alabama's six-year statute of limitations provided by Alabama Code § 6-2-34(i) should govern actions under § 1983); Wegrzyn v. Illinois Dep't of Children & Family Servs., 627 F. Supp. 636, 39 FEP 1760 (C.D. Ill. 1986) (Illinois' two-year statute of limitations for personal injury actions is appropriate for limitations period for actions under § 1983).

[32]777 F.2d 113, 39 FEP 658 (3d Cir. 1985), *aff'd,* 482 U.S. 656, 44 FEP 1 (1987).

[33]Nazaire v. Trans World Airlines, 807 F.2d 1372, 42 FEP 882 (7th Cir. 1986), *cert. denied,* 481 U.S. 1039, 44 FEP 1048 (1987) (Seventh Circuit applies Illinois longer contract action limitations period); Banks v. Chesapeake & Potomac Tel. Co., 802 F.2d 1416, 41 FEP 1125 (D.C. Cir. 1986) (contract statute of limitations not applicable); Weaver v. Gross, 40 FEP 1069 (D.D.C. 1986) (District of Columbia's three-year statute of limitations applies to action under 42 U.S.C. § 1981); Hess v. United Tel. Co. of Ohio, 40 FEP 1487 (N.D. Ohio 1986) (Ohio's one-year statute of limitations, which is applicable to actions under 42 U.S.C. § 1983, also applies to § 1981 actions).

[34]*See* Williams v. City of Atlanta, 794 F.2d 624 (11th Cir. 1986); Jones v. Bechtel, 788 F.2d 571, 40 FEP 1067 (9th Cir. 1986); Rivera v. Green, 775 F.2d 1381 (9th Cir. 1985), *cert. denied,* 475 U.S. 1128 (1986); Wycoff v. Menke, 773 F.2d 983 (8th Cir. 1985), *cert. denied,* 475 U.S. 1028 (1986); Mulligan v. Hazard, 777 F.2d 340 (6th Cir. 1985), *cert. denied,* 476 U.S. 1174, 90 L.Ed.2d 988 (1986); Smith v. City of Pittsburgh,764 F.2d 188, 119 LRRM 3118 (3d Cir. 1985), *cert. denied,* 474 U.S. 950 (1985). *Contra* Jackson v. City of Bloomfield, 731 F.2d 652 (10th Cir. 1984); Saldivar v. Cadena, 622 F. Supp. 949, 39 FEP 836 (W.D. Wis. 1985); Breen v. City of Scottsdale, 39 FEP 778 (D. Ariz. 1985); Hampson v. Thornton Fractional Township High School Dist. 215, Bd. of Educ., 41 FEP 606 (N.D. Ill. 1986).

[35]Whatley v. Department of Educ., 673 F.2d 873, 29 FEP 428 (5th Cir. 1982); Brown v. Delta Air Lines, 522 F. Supp. 1218, 30 FEP 38 (S.D. Tex. 1980), *aff'd mem.,* 673 F.2d 1325, 30 FEP 120 (5th Cir. 1982).

[36]White v. United Parcel Serv., 692 F.2d 1, 30 FEP 1135 (5th Cir. 1982), *cert. denied,* 464 U.S. 860, 32 FEP 1672 (1983).

[37]Brown v. St. Louis Police Dep't, 532 F. Supp. 518, 30 FEP 17 (E.D. Mo.), *aff'd on other grounds,* 691 F.2d 393, 30 FEP 18 (8th Cir. 1982), *cert. denied,* 461 U.S. 908 (1983); Knoll v. Springfield Township School Dist., *supra* note 31.

The Supreme Court ruled, in a § 1983 action, that state tolling rules should be borrowed along with the state limitations period, so long as the result does not offend federal policy.[38] The Ninth Circuit determined that the federal, rather than the state, continuing violation rule should be applied in a § 1981 action.[39] The Fifth and Eighth circuits have applied state tolling or savings rules in recent decisions.[40]

## E. Remedies

Under the standard of the Supreme Court in *Smith v. Wade*,[41] punitive damages may be recovered in a § 1983 action when "the defendant's conduct is shown to be motivated by evil motive or intent, or when it involves reckless or callous indifference to the federally protected rights of others." The Eighth Circuit has applied this standard to an employment case in confirming an award of punitive damages.[42]

While local government entities are subject to § 1981, two courts have held they are immune from punitive damages.[43]

Although injury to reputation, standing alone, does not provide a basis for an action under § 1983, persons who sustain such injury in connection with a termination of employment may claim a deprivation of liberty actionable under § 1983.[44]

In *Harris v. Richards Manufacturing Co.*,[45] the Sixth Circuit overruled its decision in *EEOC v. Detroit Edison Co.*,[46] limiting damages recoverable in a § 1981 action.

## F. Jury Trial

Courts continue to address various questions regarding the right to a jury trial in employment cases under § 1981, reaching differing conclusions

---

[38]Chardon v. Fumero Soto, 462 U.S. 650 (1983); *see* Berry v. E.I. du Pont de Nemours & Co., 625 F. Supp. 1364, 39 FEP 1295 (D. Del. 1985).
[39]Chung v. Pomona Valley Community Hosp., 667 F.2d 788, 28 FEP 30 (9th Cir. 1982). *Cf.* Nazaire v. Trans World Airlines, *supra* note 33.
[40]Griffen v. Big Spring Indep. School Dist., 706 F.2d 645, 31 FEP 1750 (5th Cir.), *cert. denied,* 464 U.S. 1008, 33 FEP 552 (1983) (Texas "wrong court" tolling statute applies to § 1983 claim); Garrison v. International Paper Co., 714 F.2d 757, 32 FEP 1278 (8th Cir. 1983) (state law savings clause, which allows one year to refile after dismissal without prejudice, applies to § 1981 action).
[41]461 U.S. 30, 45 (1983).
[42]Goodwin v. St. Louis County Circuit Court, 729 F.2d 541, 34 FEP 347, *later proceeding,* 741 F.2d 1087, 35 FEP 1017 (8th Cir. 1984), *cert. denied,* 469 U.S. 828, 35 FEP 1608 (1984) *and* 469 U.S. 1216, 37 FEP 64 (1985) (also holds award of actual damages not prerequisite to award of punitive damages); Garza v. City of Omaha, 814 F.2d 553, 43 FEP 572 (8th Cir. 1987) (punitive damages recovered where defendant exhibits oppression, malice, gross negligence, willful misconduct, or reckless disregard for plaintiff's civil rights). *Cf.* EEOC v. Gaddis, 733 F.2d 1373, 34 FEP 1210 (10th Cir. 1984) ("malicious, willful and in gross disregard of [the charging party's] rights"); Thompson v. Machinists, 580 F. Supp. 662, 35 FEP 845 (D.D.C. 1984).
[43]Poolaw v. City of Anadarko, Okla., 738 F.2d 364, 35 FEP 107 (10th Cir. 1984), *cert. denied,* 469 U.S. 1108, 36 FEP 976 (1985); Zewde v. Elgin Community College, 601 F. Supp. 1237, 37 FEP 895 (N.D. Ill. 1984).
[44]Campbell v. Pierce County, Ga., 741 F.2d 1342, 117 LRRM 3163 (11th Cir. 1984), *cert. denied,* 470 U.S. 1052, 118 LRRM 2968 (1985).
[45]675 F.2d 811, 28 FEP 1343 (6th Cir. 1982) (in joint Title VII and § 1981 action, all equitable and legal relief afforded by § 1981 is available).
[46]515 F.2d 301, 10 FEP 239 (6th Cir. 1975), *vacated and remanded on other grounds sub nom.* Utility Workers v. EEOC, 431 U.S. 951, 14 FEP 1686 (1977).

depending on the remedy to be considered: reinstatement, back pay, or compensatory or punitive damages.[47]

## G. Res Judicata

In *Migra v. Warren City School District Board of Education,* [48] the Supreme Court remanded the issue of the preclusive effect under 28 U.S.C. § 1738 of earlier state litigation where the §§ 1983 and 1985 claims could have been raised, but were not. The Court held the issue was to be decided by reference to state law.[49] The Court has also held that an adverse arbitration award did not bar a § 1983 action, that 28 U.S.C. § 1738 does not apply to arbitration awards, and that *Alexander v. Gardner-Denver Co.* [50] was controlling.[51]

Applying the principles of *Migra* and *Kremer v. Chemical Construction Corp.,* [52] courts have held that the decision of a state court reviewing an administrative determination has *res judicata* effect and bars a subsequent action under §§ 1981, 1983, or 1985.[53] In *University of Tennessee v. Elliott,* [54] the Supreme Court extended the holding of *Migra* to unreviewed agency

---

[47]*Cf.* Thomas v. Menley & James Laboratories, 34 FEP 71 (N.D. Ga. 1984) (claim for compensatory and punitive damages entitles plaintiff to jury trial in § 1981 suit; claim for reinstatement and back pay does not go to jury); Powell v. Pennsylvania Hous. Fin. Agency, 563 F. Supp. 419, 31 FEP 1595 (M.D. Pa. 1983) (back pay claim is legal relief to be decided by jury where plaintiff seeks instatement rather than reinstatement); Mitchell v. Alex Foods, Inc., 572 F. Supp. 825, 33 FEP 75 (N.D. Ga. 1983) (back pay is equitable remedy even though plaintiff does not seek reinstatement); Daisernia v. New York, 582 F. Supp. 792, 34 FEP 626 (N.D.N.Y. 1984) (jury trial denied in §§ 1981 and 1983 action against state and state officials because all remedies except reinstatement barred by Eleventh Amendment). *Compare* Setser v. Novak Inv. Co., 638 F.2d 1137, 24 FEP 1793 (8th Cir.), *cert. denied,* 454 U.S. 1064 (1981) (plaintiff entitled to jury trial on legal claims for compensatory damages and back pay under § 1981) *and* Thomas v. Resort Health Related Facility, 539 F. Supp. 630, 31 FEP 65 (E.D.N.Y. 1982) (same) *with* Earlie v. Jacobs, 745 F.2d 342, 38 FEP 729 (5th Cir. 1984) (no right to jury trial in § 1981 case, since plaintiff sought equitable relief of reinstatement, punitive damage claim was unsupported, and compensatory damage claim did not alter nature of basic claim); Sullivan v. School Bd. of Pinellas County, 773 F.2d 1182, 39 FEP 53 (11th Cir. 1985) (reinstatement, back pay, and reimbursement for other lost professional benefits viewed as equitable relief whether sought under 42 U.S.C. § 1983 or under Title VII and therefore jury trial denied); Williams v. Owens-Illinois, 665 F.2d 918, 929, 27 FEP 1273, 1281 (9th Cir.), *cert. denied,* 459 U.S. 971 (1982) (in § 1981 action, back pay properly viewed as either equitable remedy or legal remedy incidental to equitable cause of action and therefore not sufficient to create right to jury trial).

[48]465 U.S. 75, 33 FEP 1345 (1984).

[49]*Cf.* Foulks v. Ohio Dep't of Rehabilitation & Correction, 713 F.2d 1229, 32 FEP 829 (6th Cir. 1983) (plaintiff's state human rights and state court actions against employer do not preclude § 1981 action against supervisors); Novak v. World Bank, 703 F.2d 1305, 32 FEP 424 (D.C. Cir. 1983) (*res judicata* does not bar § 1985 action against alleged conspirator who was not party to original discrimination suit); Nilsen v. City of Moss Point, 701 F.2d 556, 31 FEP 612 (5th Cir. 1983) (dismissal of Title VII action for untimeliness bars subsequent § 1983 claim); Poe v. John Deere Co., 695 F.2d 1103, 30 FEP 827 (8th Cir. 1982) (determination of § 1981 action bars subsequent action asserting state law claims).

[50]415 U.S. 36, 7 FEP 81 (1974). *See* Second Edition at p. 1075.

[51]McDonald v. City of West Branch, Mich., 466 U.S. 284, 115 LRRM 3646 (1984).

[52]456 U.S. 461, 28 FEP 1412 (1982) (28 U.S.C. § 1738 mandates full faith and credit be given in Title VII action to prior state court determination on plaintiff's appeal of adverse administrative ruling).

[53]Brown v. St. Louis Police Dep't, 691 F.2d 393, 30 FEP 18 (8th Cir. 1982), *cert. denied,* 461 U.S. 908 (1983) (giving *res judicata* effect to court's affirmance of state board's determination that good cause existed for plaintiff's termination); Lee v. City of Peoria, 685 F.2d 196, 29 FEP 892 (7th Cir. 1982) (same); Davis v. United States Steel Corp., United States Steel Supply Div., 688 F.2d 166, 29 FEP 1202 (3d Cir. 1982), *cert. denied,* 460 U.S. 1014, 31 FEP 64 (1983) (giving *res judicata* effect to court's reversal of agency determination); Capers v. Long Island R.R., 31 FEP 668 (S.D.N.Y. 1983), *later proceeding,* 34 FEP 892 (S.D.N.Y. 1984) (same); Takahashi v. Lincoln Union School Dist., Bd. of Trustees, 783 F.2d 848, 40 FEP 267 (9th Cir.), *cert. denied,* 476 U.S. 1182, 40 FEP 873 (1986); Pillow v. Schoemehl, 620 F. Supp. 360, 39 FEP 438 (E.D. Mo. 1985), *aff'd,* 802 F.2d 462 (8th Cir. 1986); Stitzer v. University of P.R., 617 F. Supp. 1246, 38 FEP 1419 (D.P.R. 1985).

[54]478 U.S. 788, 41 FEP 177 (1986).

findings and held that "when a state agency acting in a judicial capacity * * * resolves disputed issues of fact properly before it which the parties have had an adequate opportunity to litigate, federal courts must give the agency's factfinding the same preclusive effect to which it would be entitled in the State's courts."[55] Two courts had reached the same conclusion prior to *Elliott*,[56] while the Fourth and Eleventh circuits had taken the contrary view.[57]

Jury determinations of factual issues under § 1981 and § 1983 may bar contrary rulings by the court on the equitable issues or on companion Title VII issues under the doctrines of collateral estoppel or estoppel by judgment.[58]

---

[55]*Id.*, 41 FEP at 181. *See* Duggan v. East Chicago Heights School Dist. 169, Cook County, Ill., Bd. of Educ., 40 FEP 1208 (N.D. Ill. 1986).

[56]Buckhalter v. Pepsi-Cola Gen. Bottlers, 768 F.2d 842, 38 FEP 682 (7th Cir. 1985); Parker v. National Corp. for Hous. Partnerships, 619 F. Supp. 1061, 38 FEP 1265 (D.D.C. 1985).

[57]Moore v. Bonner, 695 F.2d 799, 30 FEP 817 (4th Cir. 1982), *cert. denied*, 474 U.S. 827 (1985) (refusing to give estoppel effect to unreviewed agency determination); Stafford v. Muscogee County Bd. of Educ., 688 F.2d 1383, 29 FEP 1773 (11th Cir. 1982) (same). After *Elliott*, *see* DeCintio v. Westchester County Medical Center, 821 F.2d 111, 44 FEP 33 (2d Cir.), *cert. denied*, 484 U.S. _____, 45 FEP 520 (1987) (§ 1981 and § 1983 claims, but not Title VII claims, barred by state agency decision); Buckhalter v. Pepsi-Cola Gen. Bottlers, 820 F.2d 892, 43 FEP 1615 (7th Cir. 1987) (same); Abramson v. Council Bluffs Community School Dist., 808 F.2d 1307, 42 FEP 163 (8th Cir. 1986) (Title VII action is not precluded, but § 1983 action may be precluded); Barber v. American Sec. Bank, 655 F. Supp. 775, 43 FEP 335 (D.C.D.C. 1987) (collateral estoppel bars § 1981 and Title VII action where state agency, acting in judicial capacity, found facts adverse to claimant).

[58]Garza v. City of Omaha, 814 F.2d 553, 43 FEP 572, n. 41 (8th Cir. 1987) (jury verdict in § 1983 action in favor of plaintiff controls Title VII determination); King v. Emerson Elec. Co., Alco Controls Div., 746 F.2d 1331, 1332 n.2, 38 FEP 1666, 1667 n.2 (8th Cir. 1984) ("The factual question of discrimination vel. non. is, of course, common to both the § 1981 and Title VII claims. A jury verdict on this issue in the context of a § 1981 claim is normally conclusive on the same issue in the Title VII context as well"); Goodwin v. St. Louis County Circuit Court, 729 F.2d 541, 549 n.11, 34 FEP 347 (8th Cir. 1984) ("Ordinarily, when § 1983 and Title VII claims are tried jointly, the § 1983 theory to the jury and the Title VII theory to the court, a jury verdict on the issue of discrimination would collaterally estop the parties with respect to that issue on the Title VII claim."); Brooks v. Carnation Pet Food Co., 38 FEP 1663 (W.D. Mo. 1985) (special jury verdicts in § 1981 action preclude contrary finding on identical Title VII issues). *Cf.* Hussein v. Oshkosh Motor Truck Co., 816 F.2d 348, 43 FEP 857 (7th Cir. 1987) (where court improperly dismissed § 1981 claim, Title VII adverse determination no bar to claimant on remand). *See also* discussion in Chapter 30 (Litigation Procedure), Section IV. C.

## CHAPTER 22

# NATIONAL LABOR RELATIONS ACT

## II. REMEDIES AGAINST UNIONS

### C. Challenges to Certification

The Sixth Circuit denied enforcement of the NLRB's order to bargain when it found that a union representative shortly before a representation election, had made racial statements that had exacerbated racial tensions and interfered with employees' freedom of choice.[1] The Second Circuit, however, upheld the NLRB's order directing an employer to bargain where racial statements made by employees were found not to be deliberately inflammatory.[2]

## III. EMPLOYER DISCRIMINATION

### A. General Employment Discrimination

In *Vought Corp.-MLRS Systems Division*[3] the Board, with the later approval of the Eighth Circuit, reaffirmed its long line of decisions holding that concerted efforts by employees to alleviate racially discriminatory employment conditions constitute protected activity under the LMRA.

---

[1] NLRB v. Eurodrive, 724 F.2d 556, 33 FEP 1361, 115 LRRM 2361 (6th Cir. 1984) (relying upon Sewell Mfg. Co., 138 NLRB 66, 50 LRRM 1532 (1962)). *See also* NLRB v. Katz, 701 F.2d 703, 705–08, 31 FEP 319, 112 LRRM 3024, 3026–30 (7th Cir. 1983) (Catholic priest had made remarks at union meeting about employer being Jewish and rich while employees were poor; other ethnic and religious references were made during organizing campaign; court denied enforcement of Board's order); YKK (U.S.A.), 269 NLRB 82, 115 LRRM 1186 (1984) (NLRB set aside decertification election that union won, in part because union made appeals to racial prejudice on matters unrelated to election issues, relying on *Sewell, supra,* and *NLRB v. Silverman's Men's Wear,* 656 F.2d 53, 26 FEP 876, 107 LRRM 3273 (3d Cir. 1981)).

[2] NLRB v. Utell Int'l, 750 F.2d 177, 36 FEP 897, 118 LRRM 2006 (2d Cir. 1984) (distinguishing *NLRB v. Eurodrive, supra* note 1, on its facts). *See also* Arlington Hotel Co. v. NLRB, 712 F.2d 333, 337–38, 113 LRRM 3381, 3385–86 (8th Cir. 1983) (remarks by city official, although having racial overtones, did not impermissibly inject race into representation election campaign); Del Rey Tortilleria, 272 NLRB 1106, 117 LRRM 1449 (1984), *enf'd,* 787 F.2d 1118, 122 LRRM 2111 (7th Cir. 1986) (union organizer did not inject inflammatory ethnic or racial issues into election campaign by making statements that employer tipped off immigration authorities about undocumented aliens at its plants; organizer's statement was opinion and an "arguable comment" on a public event); Vitek Elecs., 268 NLRB 522, 115 LRRM 1075 (1984), *enf'd in part,* 763 F.2d 561, 119 LRRM 2699 (3d Cir. 1985) (union did not interfere with election when pro-union black employee made derogatory racial remarks to an anti-union black employee in presence of others, since such conduct was not intended to inflame racial feelings of employees; also, black union representative's letter to employees did not intimidate employees or appeal to racial prejudice, and therefore did not interfere with election).

[3] 273 NLRB 1290, 118 LRRM 1271 (1984), *aff'd,* 788 F.2d 1378, 122 LRRM 2168 (8th Cir. 1986) (employer violated §§ 8(a)(3) and (1) when it disciplined employee for spreading a rumor to three or four black employees that a white employee might be promoted over a black and suggesting that they take issue up at next meeting blacks had with management; in communicating the rumor employee's remarks related to group action concerning possible racial discrimination).

## B. Discharge of Minority Strikers Protesting Alleged Discrimination

The Board and courts have continued to find § 8(a)(1) violations in an employer's discharge of a group of employees for their concerted protest of discrimination[4] or of an individual employee for legal action taken to assert a statutory right growing out of the employment relationship.[5]

## C. Employer's Duty to Bargain and Furnish Union With Information on Composition of Work Force

In *Minnesota Mining & Manufacturing Co.,*[6] the Board reaffirmed its position that only certain statistics contained in the work force analysis portion of an employer's affirmative action plan are presumptively relevant to collective bargaining. However, in *Safeway Stores v. NLRB,*[7] the Tenth Circuit agreed with the Board's finding that the union had met its burden of establishing the relevance of a requested list of complaints and charges against the employer.

In *Black Grievance Committee v. NLRB,*[8] the Third Circuit was faced with the employer's refusal to grant similar grievance procedure privileges to a black dominated minority union as it accorded a larger independent union (which had not been recognized or certified under the Act). It set aside the Board's order dismissing an unfair labor practice complaint, holding that the Board erred in not recognizing that the protection of § 7 goes beyond selection of an exclusive bargaining representative and includes the right to be free from interference from any organizational activity.

---

[4]NLRB v. Downslope Indus., 676 F.2d 1114, 110 LRRM 2261 (6th Cir. 1982), *enf'g in part* 246 NLRB 948, 103 LRRM 1041 (1979) (discharge of group of nonsupervisory employees and one supervisor for concerted protest of sexual harassment violated § 8(a)(1)).

[5]NLRB v. Magnetics Int'l, 699 F.2d 806, 112 LRRM 2658, 30 FEP 1524 (6th Cir. 1983), *enf'g* 254 NLRB 520, 106 LRRM 1133 (1981) (discharge of employee in part for her union activity and prosecution of sex discrimination action constituted unfair labor practice); Country Club of Little Rock, 260 NLRB 1112, 109 LRRM 1301 (1982) (discharge of employee for filing EEOC charge and discussing charge with news media violated § 8(a)(1)). *But see* Meyers Indus., 268 NLRB 493, 115 LRRM 1025 (1984), *rev'd sub nom.* Prill v. NLRB, 755 F.2d 941, 118 LRRM 2649 (D.C. Cir.), *cert. denied,* 474 U.S. 971, 120 LRRM 3392 (1985), *decision pending on remand,* 281 NLRB No. 118, 123 LRRM 1137 (1986) (discharge of employee for his individual actions not violation of § 8(a)(1) as found not concerted).

[6]261 NLRB 27, 109 LRRM 1345 (1982), *enf'd sub nom.* Oil Workers Local 6-418 v. NLRB, 711 F.2d 348, 113 LRRM 3163 (D.C. Cir. 1983) (to obtain other portions of plan, union must demonstrate relevance).

[7]691 F.2d 953, 111 LRRM 2745 (10th Cir. 1982) (employer required to provide union with list of complaints; information concerning members, distribution, and status of employees in protected classes; work force analysis; and copies of actual complaints with complainants' names deleted).

[8]749 F.2d 1072, 117 LRRM 3389, 3393 (3d Cir. 1984), *cert. denied,* 472 U.S. 1008, 119 LRRM 2696 (1985) ("Because of the novelty of the issue before us, we are careful to delineate the scope of our decision. We are not holding that an employer violates section 8(a)(1) merely when it refuses to listen to or accord special status to the grievances of a minority labor organization, even if that refusal will affect the ability of that organization to attract members. Rather, we are holding that when an employer accords one non-majority employee group privileged status over another non-majority group, and thus encourages membership in the former while discouraging it in the latter, he unlawfully interferes with the section 7 rights of employees to band together in the group of their choice, even though neither organization seeks section 9(a) exclusive representative status.").

CHAPTER 23

# RELATED CAUSES OF ACTION

## I. INTRODUCTION

Federal and state equal employment claims are frequently supplemented in civil litigation by state common law claims on related allegations. Although the rapidly growing doctrines of wrongful discharge most obviously encourage claims where employment is terminated,[1] material claims also may include traditional tort allegations such as infliction of emotional distress, defamation, fraud, interference with contractual relations or prospective business advantage, or other theories of intentional or negligent torts.[2]

---

[1]Employment termination may not be a prerequisite to "wrongful discharge" claims under all circumstances in all jurisdictions. *See* Garcia v. Rockwell Int'l Corp., 187 Cal.App.3d 1556, 232 Cal. Rptr. 490 (1986) (alleged retaliatory six month suspension of "whistle-blower" survives motion for summary judgment).

[2]Gould, *Stemming the Wrongful Discharge Tide: A Case for Arbitration,* 13 EMPLOYEE REL. L.J. 404 (1988); Baxter, *Wrongful Termination Developments: Where Are We Going in So-called Employment-At-Will States?,* in 33d Annual Institute on Labor Law Developments, Southwestern Legal Foundation, Oct. 1986 (1987); Putz and Klippen, *Commercial Bad Faith: Attorney Fees—Not Tort Liability—Is the Remedy for "Stonewalling,"* 21 U.S.F. L. REV. 419 (1987); Gould, *The Idea of the Job as Property in Contemporary America: The Legal and Collective Bargaining Framework,* 1986 B.Y.U. L. REV. 885; Comment, *Employment-At-Will—Employers May Not Discharge At-Will Employees for Reasons That Violate Public Policy,* ARIZ. ST. L.J. 161 (1986); Mauk, *Wrongful Discharge: The Erosion of 100 Years of Employer Privilege,* 21 IDAHO L. REV. 201 (1985); Comment, *Reconstructing Breach of the Implied Covenant of Good Faith and Fair Dealing as a Tort,* 73 CALIF. L. REV. 1291 (1985); Note, *"Contort": Tortious Breach of the Implied Covenant of Good Faith and Fair Dealing in Noninsurance, Commercial Contracts—Its Existence and Desirability,* 60 NOTRE DAME L. REV. 510 (1985); Cathcart and Kruse, *The New American Law of Wrongful Termination,* INT. BUS. LAW. 73 (Feb. 1984); Lopatka, *The Emerging Law of Wrongful Discharge—A Quadrennial Assessment of the Labor Law Issue of the 80's,* 40 BUS. LAW. 1 (1984); Epstein, *In Defense of the Contract At Will,* 51 U. CHI. L. REV. 947 (1984); Rohwer, *Terminable-At-Will Employment: New Theories for Job Security,* 15 PAC. L.J. 759 (1984); Note, *Protecting Employees At Will Against Wrongful Discharge: The Public Policy Exception,* 96 HARV. L. REV. 1931 (1983); Hermann and Sor, *Property Rights in One's Job: The Case for Limiting Employment-At-Will,* 24 ARIZ. L. REV. 763 (1982); Miller and Estes, *Recent Judicial Limitations on the Right to Discharge: A California Trilogy,* 16 U.C. DAVIS L. REV. 65 (1982); Murg and Scharman, *Employment At Will: Do the Exceptions Overwhelm the Rule?,* 23 B.C.L. REV. 329 (1982); Pierce, Mann, and Roberts, *Employee Termination At Will: A Principled Approach,* 28 VILL. L. REV. 1 (1982); Summers, *The General Duty of Good Faith—Its Recognition and Conceptualization,* 67 CORNELL L. REV. 810 (1982); Note, *The Development of Exceptions to At-Will Employment: A Review of the Case Law From Management's Viewpoint,* 51 U. CIN. L. REV. 616 (1982); Note, *Limiting the Right to Terminate At Will—Have the Courts Forgotten the Employer?,* 35 VAND. L. REV. 201 (1982); De Guiseppe, *The Effect of Employee Rights to Job Security and Fringe Benefits,* 10 FORDHAM URB. L.J. 1 (1981); Note, *Defining Public Policy Torts in At-Will Dismissals,* 34 STAN. L. REV. 153 (1981); Burton, *Breach of Contract and the Common Law Duty to Perform in Good Faith,* 94 HARV. L. REV. 369 (1980); Note, *Protecting At Will Employees Against Wrongful Discharge: The Duty to Terminate Only in Good Faith,* 93 HARV. L. REV. 1816 (1980); Note, *Implied Contract Rights to Job Security,* 26 STAN. L. REV. 335 (1974); Blades, *Employment At-Will vs. Individual Freedom: On Limiting the Abusive Exercise of Employer Power,* 67 COLUM. L. REV. 1404 (1967); Blumrosen, *Settlement of Disputes Concerning the Exercise of Employer Disciplinary Power: United States Report,* 18 RUTGERS L. REV. 428 (1964). For recent overviews, *see* EMPLOYMENT-AT-WILL: A 1989 STATE-BY-STATE SURVEY (Cathcart and Dichter, eds.), A Report of the Litigation Section, Employment and Labor Relations Law Committee and the Labor and Employment Section, Committee on Employee Rights and Responsibilities in the Workplace, American Bar Association, available from the National Employment Law Inst., 444 Magnolia Ave., Suite 200, Larkspur, CA 94939;

## II. Procedural Problems in Combining Common Law and Federal Statutory Claims

### A. Pendent Jurisdiction

Federal courts continue to differ on whether to permit a plaintiff to add state common law claims to a federal cause of action.[3]

### B. Preemption

Defendants frequently attempt to limit state law claims by preemption doctrines derived from federal or state law.[4] Title VII generally is not preemptive. For example, a Florida state court held that a female employee's tort claims for battery and intentional infliction of emotional distress, which arose from a "fondling" episode by her supervisor, were not preempted by Title VII.[5] By contrast, federal labor law may be preemptive. For example,

---

Pepe and Dunham, Avoiding and Defending Wrongful Discharge Claims (1987); McCarthy, Punitive Damages in Wrongful Discharge Cases (1985).

[3]The leading pendent jurisdiction decision is still *Mine Workers v. Gibbs,* 383 U.S. 715, 61 LRRM 2561 (1966) (allowing pendent claims). For a list of courts allowing and courts rejecting pendent claims, see Appendix A (hereinafter referred to as App. A) to this Chapter.

[4]*Compare, e.g.,* Allis-Chalmers v. Lueck, 471 U.S. 202, 118 LRRM 3345 (1985) *and* Olguin v. Inspiration Consol. Copper Co., 740 F.2d 1468, 117 LRRM 2073 (9th Cir. 1984) (state law claims preempted by LMRA § 301) *with* Lingle v. Magic Chef, Norge Div., 486 U.S. ____, 46 FEP 1553 (1988) *and* Garibaldi v. Lucky Food Stores, 726 F.2d 1367, 1372–73, 115 LRRM 3089 (9th Cir. 1984), *cert. denied,* 471 U.S. 1099, 119 LRRM 2248 (1985) (no preemption of state law claims under § 301). *See infra* note 5 and accompanying text; *see also* Inglis v. Feinerman, 701 F.2d 97, 98, 114 LRRM 3481 (9th Cir. 1983), *cert. denied,* 464 U.S. 1040, 115 LRRM 2248 (1984) (wrongful discharge claim of bank officer preempted by Federal Home Loan Bank Act which grants power to "dismiss at pleasure such officers, employees and agents"); Oglesby v. RCA Corp., 752 F.2d 272, 118 LRRM 2203 (7th Cir. 1985), *cert. denied,* ____ U.S. ____ (1986) (wrongful discharge action properly removed even though employee did not claim right to recover under collective bargaining agreement; contended that he was fired because he refused to perform a job in violation of OSHA); Snow v. Bechtel Constr., 647 F. Supp. 1514, 123 LRRM 3245 (C.D. Cal. 1986) (claim that discharge from nuclear power plant was for whistleblowing preempted by both Atomic Energy Act of 1954 and § 301); Green v. Hughes Aircraft Co., 630 F. Supp. 423, 119 LRRM 3610 (S.D. Cal. 1985) (federal law preempts state court action for defamation by union-contract-covered employee accused of theft who was subsequently reinstated with back pay); Johnson v. Trans World Airlines, 149 Cal.App.3d 518, 196 Cal. Rptr. 896 (1983) (ERISA preempts plaintiff's claim his termination was to deprive him of benefits which would have accrued six months later; fraud and bad-faith actions precluded despite earlier contrary California cases); Ambro v. American Nat'l Bank & Trust Co. of Mich., 152 Mich. App. 613, 394 N.W.2d 46, 1 IER 1204 (1986) (National Bank Act preempts state court wrongful discharge action but there is no comparable provision in National Bank Holding Company Act); Berry v. American Fed. Sav., 730 P.2d 905, 1 IER 1203 (Colo. Ct. App. 1986) (state wrongful discharge action preempted by Federal Home Loan Bank Board regulation); Householder v. Kensington Mfg. Co., 360 Pa. Super. 290, 520 A.2d 461, 45 FEP 1594 (1987) (employee's common law wrongful discharge claim for dismissal due to health problems preempted by Pennsylvania Human Relations Act). *See also infra* notes 5, 6, and 9.

[5]Brown v. Winn-Dixie Montgomery, 427 So.2d 1065 (Fla. Dist. Ct. App. 1983); *see also* Caterpillar, Inc. v. Williams, 482 U.S. 386, 125 LRRM 2521, 2 IER 193 (1987) (claims bearing no relationship to collective bargaining agreement beyond fact they are asserted by an individual covered by such an agreement are not preempted by § 301); Rice v. United Ins. Co. of Am., 465 So.2d 1100, 36 FEP 1641 (Ala. 1984) (Title VII does not subsume former employee's state claim against employer for intentional infliction of emotional distress, where Title VII does not offer compensation for any physical or psychic damage that may have resulted from employer's outrageous acts); Tellez v. Pacific Gas & Elec. Co., 817 F.2d 536, 125 LRRM 2481, 2 IER 310 (9th Cir.), *cert. denied,* 484 U.S. ____, 126 LRRM 2696, 2 IER 960 (1987) (Ninth Circuit allowed state common law causes of action for defamation, intentional and negligent infliction of emotional distress to proceed, ruling that they were separate from and distinct from collective bargaining agreement); Otto v. Department of Health & Human Servs., 781 F.2d 754, 39 FEP 1754 (9th Cir. 1986) (Title VII does not bar claims for constitutional violations or tortious conduct); Wolk v. Saks Fifth Ave., 728 F.2d 221, 34 FEP 193, 115 LRRM 3064 (3d Cir. 1984) (woman discharged because of sexual discrimination can sue only under antidiscrimination laws, and cannot bring wrongful discharge tort cause of action); Trigg v. Fort Wayne Community Schools, 766 F.2d 299, 38 FEP 361 (7th Cir. 1985) (public employees may bypass Title VII and sue public employer under Fourteenth

if resolution of the employee's complaint requires an interpretation of a collective bargaining agreement governing the plaintiff's employment, tort actions for wrongful discharge and infliction of emotional distress are generally preempted by the Railway Labor Act or the National Labor Relations Act.[6]

---

Amendment through § 1983 suit); Cummings v. National R.R. Passenger Corp. (Amtrak), 514 Pa. 230, 523 A.2d 338, 126 LRRM 2654 (E.D. Pa. 1986), *cert. denied,* 484 U.S. _____, 2 IER 1022 (1987) (employee's state law claims for breach of individual employment contracts were peripheral to NLRA, deeply rooted in local law, and not preempted by federal legislation).

[6]As this Supplement went to press, application of these preemption doctrines under federal labor law continued to generate uncertainty and substantial appellate litigation. In *Lingle v. Magic Chef, Norge Div., supra* note 4, the Supreme Court held that § 301, Labor-Management Relations Act (LMRA), does not preempt a cause of action under state law for retaliatory discharge for filing workers' compensation claims, even where the plaintiff was employed within a bargaining unit subject to a collective bargaining agreement prohibiting discharge without just cause; the Court held unanimously that § 301 preempts state law claims only if interpretation of the collective bargaining agreement is necessary to determine the claim, and that no preemption occurs where interpretation of the state law claim can be resolved without contract interpretation. The ultimate reach of *Lingle* is unclear. *See, e.g.,* Dougherty v. Parsec, Inc., 486 U.S. _____, 128 LRRM 2568, 3 IER 544 (1988), *vacating and remanding* 824 F.2d 1477, 125 LRRM 3226, 2 IER 808 (6th Cir. 1987) (Sixth Circuit decision remanded for reconsideration in light of *Lingle, supra;* Sixth Circuit had held that state law claim for tortious interference with contract must have been based on collective bargaining agreement as the contract allegedly interfered with, and that collective bargaining agreement must be interpreted exclusively under federal law). Even before *Lingle, supra,* preemption issues were causing difficulty in employment litigation. *See, e.g.,* Alpha Beta, Inc. v. California Superior Court (Nahm), 236 Cal. Rptr. 403 (1987) (en banc) (California Supreme Court dismissed review as improvidently granted and transferred action to intermediate court of appeal for reconsideration in light of *De Tomaso v. Pan Am. Airways,* 43 Cal.3d 517, 528, 529, 235 Cal. Rptr. 292 (1986), *cert. denied,* 484 U.S. _____, 2 IER 896 (1987), *Truex v. Garrett Freight Lines,* 784 F.2d 1347, 121 LRRM 3065 (9th Cir. 1986), *Allis-Chalmers v. Lueck, supra* note 4 and *Friday v. Hughes Aircraft Co.,* 188 Cal.App.3d 117, 236 Cal. Rptr. 291 (1986)).

Leading pre-*Lingle* decisions on the preemption of state law employment claims under federal law include the following:

*State law claims preempted:* Allis-Chalmers Corp. v. Lueck, *supra* (LMRA § 301 preempts tort claim by employee covered by collective bargaining agreement because agreement contained grievance-arbitration procedure); Olguin v. Inspiration Consol. Copper Co., *supra* note 4 (LMRA § 301 preempts state law claims by employee covered by collective bargaining agreement; removal and subsequent dismissal upheld; public policy allegedly violated by purported wrongful discharge was based on federal statute and not state interest); Truex v. Garrett Freight Lines, *supra* (state law claims of harassment and intentional infliction of emotional distress preempted by LMRA § 301; action also barred by failure to exhaust contractual remedies); Taylor v. St. Regis Paper Co., 530 F. Supp. 546, 115 LRRM 2922 (C.D. Cal. 1983) (claim of wrongful discharge in violation of implied covenant of good faith and fair dealing preempted by LMRA § 301; state court claims are incidents of federal claims for breach of collective bargaining agreement arising from plaintiff's allegedly wrongful termination, and do not allege independent tortious conduct); Seid v. Pacific Bell, 121 LRRM 2349 (S.D. Cal. 1985) (claims of negligence, defamation, and intentional infliction preempted by LMRA § 301); Snow v. Bechtel Constr., *supra* note 4 (claim that discharge from nuclear power plant was for whistleblowing preempted both by Atomic Energy Act of 1954 and LMRA § 301); Basset v. Attebery, 180 Cal.App.3d 288, 225 Cal. Rptr. 399 (1986) (LMRA § 301 preempts former supervisor's claim of wrongful discharge in violation of public policy); Friday v. Hughes Aircraft Co., *supra* (LMRA § 301 preempts state law claim for intentional infliction of emotional distress, as inextricably intertwined with terms of collective bargaining agreement).

*State law claims not preempted:* Lingle v. Magic Chef, Norge Div., *supra;* Caterpillar, Inc. v. Williams, *supra* note 5 (complaint asserting breach of individual employment contracts made between employees and employer while employees were supervisors not preempted by LMRA § 301, though employees were members of collective bargaining unit at time of termination); Belknap, Inc. v. Hale, 463 U.S. 491, 113 LRRM 3057 (1983) (state court action for breach of contract and misrepresentation against employer by former employees not preempted by §§ 7 and 8, National Labor Relations Act (NLRA), where plaintiffs alleged that they had been hired to replace striking employees and had been promised "permanent" employment but were discharged when strike ended in order to permit reinstatement of strikers); Garibaldi v. Lucky Food Stores, *supra* note 4 (former employee's claim for discharge in violation of public policy not preempted by LMRA § 301; plaintiff alleged he was discharged for reporting to local health authorities that his employer had ordered him to deliver spoiled milk in violation of state statute; state has strong interest in enforcing health regulations, and could use private court action to enforcement without interfering with federal labor policy); Bloom v. General Truck Drivers Local 952, 783 F.2d 1356, 121 LRRM 3008 (9th Cir. 1986) (Labor-Management Reporting and Disclosure Act does not preempt claim of former employee of union for discharge in violation of public policy); Mungo v. UTA French Airlines, 166 Cal.App.3d 327, 212 Cal. Rptr. 369 (1985) (court of appeals reversed trial court's ruling that it lacked jurisdiction on basis of Railway Labor Act; plaintiffs were not members of union or subject to collective bargaining agreement); Seritis v. Hotel & Restaurant Employees Local 28,

## C. Federal Court Acceptance of State Court Determinations

The Supreme Court has held that a state court determination of an equal employment claim will govern later federal litigation of the same issue, based on 28 U.S.C. § 1738, which requires that "judicial proceedings * * * shall have the same full faith and credit in every court within the United States * * * as they have by law or usage in the courts of [the] state * * * from which they are taken."[7] This does not necessarily preclude federal claims on issues taken only as far as an administrative decision at the state level.[8]

---

167 Cal.App.3d 78, 213 Cal. Rptr. 588, 37 FEP 1501 (1985), *cert. denied,* 474 U.S. 1060, 121 LRRM 2208 (1986) (action not preempted by LMRA because torts involved were abusive or outrageous, under *Farmer v. Carpenters Local* 25, 430 U.S. 290, 94 LRRM 2759 (1977)); Pemberton v. Bethlehem Steel Corp., *infra* Appendix C (hereinafter referred to as App. C) (tort action for intentional infliction of emotional distress and invasion of privacy not preempted by NLRA §§ 7 and 8).

[7]Kremer v. Chemical Constr. Corp., 456 U.S. 461, 28 FEP 1412 (1982) (preclusive effect given to state court decision upholding state administrative agency's rejection of employment discrimination claim as meritless where plaintiff was able to raise claims, present evidence, rebut employer's evidence, request issuance of administrative subpoena, and had a right to judicial review); *see also* Whitfield v. City of Knoxville, 756 F.2d 455, 37 FEP 288 (6th Cir. 1985) (doctrine of *res judicata* applies to ADEA action brought following state proceedings); Unger v. Consolidated Foods Corp., 693 F.2d 703, 30 FEP 441 (7th Cir. 1982), *cert. denied,* 460 U.S. 1102, 31 FEP 904 (1983) (*Kremer* applied retroactively); Davis v. United States Steel Corp., United States Steel Supply Div., 688 F.2d 166, 29 FEP 1202 (3d Cir. 1982) (en banc), *cert. denied,* 460 U.S. 1014, 31 FEP 64 (1983) (state court decision overturning decision of Pittsburgh Commission on Human Relations precludes subsequent § 1981 action); Capers v. Long Island R.R., 31 FEP 668 (S.D.N.Y. 1983) (*Kremer* applied in action in which employer initiated state court review); Trujillo v. County of Santa Clara, 766 F.2d 1368, 38 FEP 1008 (9th Cir. 1985) (same); Rotert v. Jefferson Fed. Sav. & Loan Ass'n, 623 F. Supp. 1114, 39 FEP 1070 (D. Conn. 1985) (state administrative and judicial findings collaterally estopped plaintiff from pursuing action in federal court); Harding v. Ramsay, Scarlett & Co., 599 F. Supp. 180, 36 FEP 717 (D. Md. 1984) (same); Hirst v. California, 770 F.2d 776, 38 FEP 1496 (9th Cir. 1985) (doctrine of collateral estoppel, not *res judicata,* bars plaintiff from relitigating under Title VII issues decided earlier in state court). *But see* Patzer v. University of Wis. Bd. of Regents, 763 F.2d 851, 37 FEP 1847 (7th Cir. 1985) (plaintiff prevailed before state administrative agency and state court; subsequent Title VII claim for back pay not barred where state law did not provide for back pay at time of state court action).

[8]Moore v. Bonner, 695 F.2d 799, 30 FEP 817 (4th Cir. 1982), *cert. denied,* 474 U.S. 827 (1985) (rejecting "administrative collateral estoppel"; state administrative agency's decision against public employer, not appealed to state court, does not bind federal court determining same issues); Clinton v. Georgia Ports Auth., 37 FEP 593 (S.D. Ga. 1985); Jainchill v. New York State Human Rights Appeal Bd., 83 A.D.2d 665, 442 N.Y.S.2d 595, 35 FEP 1403 (1981); Parker v. Danville Metal Stamping Co., 603 F. Supp. 182, 37 FEP 250 (C.D. Ill. 1985); Shaffer v. National Can Corp., 35 FEP 840 (E.D. Pa. 1984); Heath v. John Morrell & Co., 768 F.2d 245, 38 FEP 700 (8th Cir. 1985) (district court erred in giving preclusive effect, in action under § 1981 and Title VII, to state department of labor denial of plaintiff's claim for unemployment benefits); Reedy v. Florida Dep't of Educ., 605 F. Supp. 172, 37 FEP 754 (N.D. Fla. 1985) (unappealed decision by state human relations commission in favor of employer did not preclude claimant from bringing Title VII action). *But see* Elliott v. University of Tenn., 478 U.S. 788, 41 FEP 177 (1986) (28 U.S.C. § 1738 by its terms applies only to judgments and records of state courts, and because it "antedates the development of administrative agencies it clearly does not represent a congressional determination that the decisions of state administrative agencies should not be given preclusive effect."); *see also* Snow v. Nevada Dep't of Prisons, 543 F. Supp. 752, 29 FEP 742 (D. Nev. 1982) (Title VII claim not barred, but §§ 1983 and 1985 matters are, where previously decided by administrative agency, where there was opportunity to litigate, and where agency acted in judicial capacity); Ryan v. New York Tel. Co., 62 N.Y.2d 494, 501–2, 478 N.Y.S.2d 823, 467 N.E.2d 487 (1984) (claims barred under theory of collateral estoppel due to prior administrative hearing before state unemployment insurance appeal board where "opportunity for a full and fair hearing [has] been satisfied"); Rolfe v. Arizona, 578 F. Supp. 1467, 37 FEP 276 (D. Ariz. 1983) (state personnel board's findings, reviewed by state court, preclude subsequent action where defendant had full and fair opportunity to litigate); Zywicki v. Versa Technology, Moxness Prods. Div., 610 F. Supp. 50, 37 FEP 710 (E.D. Wis. 1985) (failure to seek state court review of state agency finding bars Title VII action); Buckhalter v. Pepsi-Cola Gen. Bottlers, 768 F.2d 842, 38 FEP 682 (7th Cir. 1985), *cert. granted and judgment vacated,* _____ U.S. _____, 41 FEP 272 *and* 41 FEP 496 (1986) (§ 1981 and Title VII claims barred by doctrine of *res judicata,* where state agency acting in judicial capacity had dismissed claims); Parker v. National Corp. for Hous. Partnerships, *infra* Appendix B (D.C.) (hereinafter referred to as App. B) (doctrine of *res judicata* bars claims under § 1981, Title VII and District of Columbia Human Rights Act following D.C. Commission on Human Rights' dismissal of those claims).

## D. Exclusivity of State Statutory Remedy or Required Exhaustion of Administrative Remedies

Some courts have dismissed tort and contract claims based on employment discrimination allegations because state statutory remedies were found adequate and exclusive.[9] State and federal actions have also been dismissed on the basis of the claimant's failure to exhaust administrative remedies.[10]

---

[9]This issue has been extensively litigated in California with varying results. *Compare, e.g.,* Strauss v. A.L. Randall Co., 144 Cal.App.3d 514, 194 Cal. Rptr. 520, 37 FEP 1531 (1983) (California statutory remedy for age discrimination in employment under state fair employment act exclusive, precluding common law claim for discharge contrary to public policy), Ficalora v. Lockheed Corp., 193 Cal.App.3d 489, 238 Cal. Rptr. 360 (1987) (accord; no *Tameny* public policy discharge claim required for discharge allegedly in retaliation for challenging employer's discriminatory practices) *and* Robinson v. Hewlett-Packard Corp., 183 Cal.App.3d 1108, 228 Cal. Rptr. 591 (1986) (same; alleged racial comments of supervisor) *with* Froyd v. Cook, 681 F. Supp. 669 (E.D. Cal. 1988) (applying California law; holding California fair employment act restricted exclusivity of its remedies to age discrimination claims and that independent public policy claim can be brought under common law for sex discrimination) *and* Rojo v. Kliger, 205 Cal.App.3d 646, 252 Cal. Rptr. 605 (1988) (rehearing ordered) (relying on *Froyd v. Cook, supra,* holding wrongful termination claim for sexual harassment may be stated independent of California fair employment act). *See also* Gay Law Students Ass'n v. Pacific Tel. & Tel. Co., 24 Cal.3d 458, 490, 156 Cal. Rptr. 14, 34 (1979) (California fair employment act "in no sense declaratory of preexisting common law doctrine" but created new rights not previously found at common law). For decisions in other jurisdictions addressing the exclusivity of state statutory remedies for common law tort or contract claims, *see, e.g.,* Zywicki v. Versa Technology, Moxness Prods. Div., *supra* note 8 (sexual harassment); Wolk v. Saks Fifth Ave., *supra* note 5 (same); Hooten v. Pennsylvania College of Optometry, 601 F. Supp. 1151, 36 FEP 1826 (E.D. Pa. 1984) (same); Flynn v. New England Tel. Co., 615 F. Supp. 1205, 41 FEP 1755 (D. Mass. 1985) (same); Mahoney v. Crocker Nat'l Bank, *infra* App. A (same); Watkinson v. Great Atl. & Pac. Tea Co., 585 F. Supp. 879, 36 FEP 224 (E.D. Pa. 1984) (same); Hunnewell v. Manufacturers Hanover Trust Co., 628 F. Supp. 759, 44 FEP 1097 (S.D.N.Y. 1986) (same); Hudson v. Moore Business Forms, 609 F. Supp. 467, 37 FEP 1672 (N.D. Cal. 1985) (sex discrimination); *see also* Combs v. C.A.R.E., 617 F. Supp. 1011, 39 FEP 1086 (E.D. Ark. 1985) (where plaintiff's EEOC charge and EEOC's determination letter treated only discrimination, and where plaintiff abandoned additional issues in her deposition, she may not litigate those additional issues). *But see* DeRamo v. Consolidated Rail Corp., 607 F. Supp. 100, 38 FEP 860 (E.D. Pa. 1985) (age discrimination); Holien v. Sears, Roebuck & Co., 66 Or. App. 911, 677 P.2d 704, *aff'd,* 298 Or. 76, 689 P.2d 1292, 36 FEP 137 (1984); Hentzel v. Singer Co., 138 Cal.App.3d 290, 188 Cal. Rptr. 159, 115 LRRM 4036 (1982) (where statutory remedy is provided for enforcement of preexisting common law right, newer statutory remedy will be considered only cumulative); Kremer v. Chemical Constr. Corp., *supra* note 7; Odriozola v. Superior Cosmetic Distrib. Corp. (P.R. S.Ct. June 28, 1985, J.T.S. 51) (claims under Puerto Rico Civil Rights Act not precluded by Puerto Rico Workers' Compensation Act).

[10]Bertrand v. Quincy Mkt. Cold Storage & Warehouse Co., 728 F.2d 568, 115 LRRM 3215 (1st Cir. 1984) (federal LMRA preempts state tort and contract claims); Olguin v. Inspiration Consol. Copper Co., *supra* note 4 (same); McQuitty v. General Dynamics Corp., 204 N.J. Super. 514, 499 A.2d 526 (App. Div. 1985) (same); Smith v. United States Postal Serv., 742 F.2d 257, 35 FEP 1304 (6th Cir. 1984) (handicapped postal employee must exhaust administrative remedies before proceeding to federal court and seeking judicial remedies under Rehabilitation Act of 1973); Clark v. United States Postal Serv., 592 F. Supp. 631, 35 FEP 1408 (D.D.C. 1984) (same); Popkins v. Zagel, 611 F. Supp. 809, 39 FEP 611 (C.D. Ill. 1985) (plaintiff's age discrimination claims brought under Federally Assisted Programs Act dismissed where plaintiff failed to exhaust administrative remedies provided therein); Blank v. Donovan, 780 F.2d 808, 39 FEP 1425 (9th Cir. 1986) (action properly dismissed for failure to exhaust administrative remedies under Title VII); Tombollo v. Dunn dba Sioux Falls Rent-A-Car (Hertz), *infra* App. B (S.D.) (plaintiff required to exhaust available administrative remedies by appealing state commissioner's decision); Melley v. Gillette Corp., 397 Mass. 1004, 491 N.E.2d 252, 41 FEP 1322 (1986) (plaintiff could not bypass state administrative remedies applicable to age discrimination claim); *see also* Ramos v. Flagship Int'l, 612 F. Supp. 148, 38 FEP 400 (E.D.N.Y. 1985) (failure of some members of proposed class to exhaust their administrative remedies under Title VII is not bar to their participation in the action as long as some members have exhausted remedies); Truex v. Garrett Freight Lines, *supra* note 6 (state law tort claims of harassment and intentional infliction of emotional distress based on allegations that employer issued unjustified warning letters, altered work assignments, and generally sought to terminate collective bargaining contract-covered employees preempted; employees also barred from bringing Taft-Hartley action because of failure to exhaust contractual remedies); Spratley v. Winchell Donut House, 188 Cal.App.3d 1408, 234 Cal. Rptr. 121 (1987) ("[T]he existence of an injury not compensable under workers' compensation does not without more abrogate the Workers' Compensation Act's exclusive remedy provisions. * * * A failure of workers' compensation law to include an element of damages recoverable at common law is a legislative, not a judicial

## III. EMERGING CONTRACT AND TORT CAUSES OF ACTION WHICH LIMIT THE "EMPLOYMENT-AT-WILL" DOCTRINE

Employees have pursued both contract and tort theories in attacking the at-will doctrine, and the doctrine itself continues to receive widely varying treatment in state courts.[11] Generally, courts have focused on three situations to limit the discretion of an employer to terminate its employees at will. First, terminations allegedly in breach of express or implied-in-fact contractual obligations;[12] second, discharges in breach of an implied-in-law covenant of good faith and fair dealing,[13] which in some jurisdictions may give rise to tort

---

problem"); Perez v. Western-Southern Life Ins. Co., 43 FEP 1811 (E.D. Mich. 1987) (suit under Michigan Civil Rights Act barred even though statute provides three-year cause of action; court found contractual agreement between employer and employee limiting the period for filing claim over termination to six months is reasonable). *But see* Smith v. McClammy, 740 F.2d 925, 35 FEP 1316 (11th Cir. 1984) (exhaustion of state administrative remedies is not prerequisite to instituting action under § 1983); Martinez v. Automobile Workers Local 1373, 772 F.2d 348, 38 FEP 1361 (7th Cir. 1985) (same for action under Title VII; filing charge with EEOC satisfactory).

[11]*See* App. B, *infra,* for a sampling of approaches recently taken by state courts considering challenges to the at-will doctrine. For a cumulative state-by-state analysis of representative decisions bearing on employment at will through 1988, *see* EMPLOYMENT-AT-WILL: A 1989 STATE-BY-STATE SURVEY (Cathcart and Dichter, eds.), *supra* note 1. *See also* Bakaly and Grossman, MODERN LAW OF EMPLOYMENT CONTRACTS: FORMATION, OPERATION AND REMEDIES FOR BREACH (1984).

[12]Judicial acceptance of liability on an implied contract is not new. *See, e.g.,* Wood v. Lucy, Lady Duff-Gordon, 222 N.Y.88, 118 N.E.214 (1917) (Cardozo, J.):

The agreement of employment is signed by both parties. The defendant insists, however, that it lacks the elements of a contract. She says that the plaintiff does not bind himself to anything. It is true that he does not promise in so many words that he will use reasonable efforts to place the defendant's endorsements and market her designs. We think, however, that such a promise is fairly to be implied. The law has outgrown its primitive stage of formalism when the precise word was the sovereign talisman, and every slip was fatal. It takes a broader view today. A promise may be lacking, and yet the whole writing may be "instinct with an obligation," imperfectly expressed. [citations omitted] If that is so, there is a contract.

*Id.* For recent application and extension of this doctrine in employment cases, *see, e.g.,* Weiner v. McGraw-Hill, *infra* App. B (N.Y.) (contract claim based on published employee manual); Toussaint v. Blue Cross & Blue Shield of Mich., 408 Mich. 579, 292 N.W.2d 880, 115 LRRM 4708 (1980) (policy statements and oral statements during hiring interview); Pugh v. See's Candies (I), *infra* App. B (Cal.) (held, jury could find implied-in-fact contract where "the employer's conduct gave rise to an implied promise that it would not act arbitrarily in dealing with its employees," based on facts including "the duration of [the plaintiff's] employment, the commendations and promotions he received, the apparent lack of any direct criticism of his work, the assurances he was given, and the employer's acknowledged policies, all reflecting 'the totality of the parties' relationship.' " Id. at 329, 171 Cal. Rptr. at 927); Foley v. Interactive Data Corp., 47 Cal. 3d 654, 254 Cal. Rptr. 211, 3 IER 1729 (Cal. S.Ct. 1988) and *infra* App. B (Cal.) (recognizing implied covenant to discharge "for good cause only" on allegations of employment for six years and nine months, "repeated oral assurances of job security and consistent promotions, salary increases and bonuses" during employment term "contributing to [plaintiff's] reasonable expectation that he would not be discharged except for good cause," 3 IER at 1740; trier of fact "can infer an agreement to limit the grounds for termination based on the employee's reasonable reliance on the company's personnel manual or policies." *Id.;* separate consideration also alleged, based on noncompetition and trade secrecy agreement.)

[13]*See* Monge v. Beebe Rubber Co., 114 N.H. 130, 316 A.2d 549, 115 LRRM 4755 (1974) (implied-in-law covenant of good faith incorporated in all employment-at-will contracts; plaintiff female press machine operator found by jury to have been discharged because of her refusal to date her foreman; "[w]e hold that a termination by the employer of a contract of employment-at-will which is motivated by bad faith or malice or based on retaliation is not in the best interest of the economic system or the public good and constitutes a breach of the employment contract," *id.,* 316 A.2d at 551) (limited to public policy discharge situations in *Howard v. Dorr Woolen Co., infra* note 30); Fortune v. National Cash Register Co., 373 Mass. 96, 364 N.E.2d 1251, 115 LRRM 4658 (1977) (implied-in-law covenant of good faith incorporated in employment contract between company and commission salesman; held, "NCR's written contract contains an implied covenant of good faith and fair dealing, and a termination not made in good faith constitutes a breach of the contract * * * ." *Id.,* 364 N.E.2d at 1255–56); Cleary v. American Airlines, *infra* App. B (Cal.) (implied-in-law covenant of good faith and fair dealing adopted as alternative basis for wrongful employment termination action; disapproved in part in *Foley v. Interactive Data Corp., see infra* note 14).

damages;[14] and third, discharges in violation of fundamental public policy,[15] which may also give rise to tort damages.[16] Together, the varying judicial responses to these three situations substantially cover the developing law of wrongful discharge.

## A. Contract Theory

### 1. Breach of Express or Implied Contract

Generally, plaintiffs appear successful in many state forums in contentions that employer policies or statements can form a contractual basis for restricting the discretion of employers to terminate employment. The majority of states[17] and several federal jurisdictions[18] have so held. Developing case law encourages an analysis of substance rather than form. Cases differ on whether an employer's representations and other conduct may restrict the employer's discretion to terminate employment even in those circumstances where the employment application form signed by the employee expressly

---

[14]*Cleary v. American Airlines, infra* App. B (Cal.), "and its progeny * * * are disapproved to the extent that they permit a cause of action seeking tort remedies for breach of the implied covenant." *Foley v. Interactive Data Corp., supra* note 12, 3 IER at 1751 n.42. Leading cases supporting a tort action for "bad faith discharge" had also included *Khanna v. Microdata Corp., infra* App. B (Cal.), and *Koehrer v. California Superior Court (Oak Riverside Jurupa, Ltd.), infra* App. B (Cal.), both disapproved by the California Supreme Court when that court rejected tort liability for breaches of implied covenants in employment cases, in *Foley, supra.* Decisions appearing to sustain or reject tort damages for breach of an implied covenant or addressing application of the covenant itself in the context of employment relationships in various jurisdictions are collected and summarized by the California Supreme Court in *Foley, id.,* 3 IER at 1743 n.26. *See also* Murphy v. American Home Prods. Corp., 58 N.Y.2d 293, 461 N.Y.S.2d 232, 448 N.E.2d 86, 31 FEP 782 (1983) (rejecting tort claims for employment terminations absent legislative action).

[15]*See, e.g.,* Foley v. Interactive Data Corp., *supra* note 12; Tameny v. Atlantic Richfield Co., *infra* App. B (Cal.); Monge v. Beebe Rubber Co., *supra* note 13; Howard v. Dorr Woolen Co., *infra* note 30; Fortune v. National Cash Register Co., *supra* note 13. There is a question whether the alleged public policy must be based on a constitutional provision or statute. In arguing this issue, plaintiffs and defendants will refer to such cases as *Tameny v. Atlantic Richfield Co., infra* App. B (Cal.) (plaintiff allegedly discharged for refusing to commit a criminal act); *Foley v. Interactive Data Corp., supra* (reaffirming *Tameny* action for discharge contrary to public policy "since otherwise the threat of discharge could be used to coerce employees into committing crimes, concealing wrongdoing, or taking other action harmful to the public weal," 3 IER at 1731; reviewing controversy over question whether constitutional or statutory basis for public policy must be shown; declining to reach question in instant case; noting *Tameny* had insisted that public policy basis for cause of action must be a "firmly established," 27 Cal.3d at 172, "fundamental," *id.* at 176, and "substantial," *id.* at 177, policy, *see* Foley, *id.* at n.11, and that cases from other jurisdictions similarly require "clearly mandated public policy[;]" citing *Palmateer v. International Harvester Co.,* 421 N.E.2d 876, 878, 115 LRRM 4165 (Ill. 1981); *Parnar v. Americana Hotels, infra* App. B (Haw.), 652 P.2d at 630–31; *Thompson v. St. Regis Paper Co.,* 102 Wash. 2d 219, 685 P.2d 1081, 1088–89, 116 LRRM 3142 (Wash. 1984); *Adler v. American Standard Corp.,* 230 Md. 615, 432 A.2d 464, 472–73, 115 LRRM 4130 (Md. App. 1981). In *Foley,* the California Supreme Court adopted a public/private distinction for determining the adequacy of the public policy allegations in employment termination tort claims: "[w]e must inquire whether the discharge is against public policy and affects a duty which inures to the benefit of the public at large rather than to a particular employer or employee." 3 IER at 1733. In *Foley,* the plaintiff alleged that he was discharged from employment by the subsidiary of a bank, purportedly because he had disclosed to his former supervisor his knowledge that his current supervisor was under investigation for his suspected embezzlement from his former bank employer. The California Supreme Court held this did not sufficiently allege a fundamental public policy purportedly breached by the plaintiff's discharge. *See also infra* notes 43 and 44 and accompanying text.

[16]*See* Foley v. Interactive Data Corp., *supra* note 12, 3 IER at 1743 n.26 and *supra* notes 14 and 15.

[17]*See* articles cited *supra* note 11; *see also* App. B, *infra.*

[18]Enis v. Continental Ill. Nat'l Bank & Trust Co., *infra* App. B (Ill.) (district court properly held that handbook is a contract only if it is part of preexisting employment contract or is specific modification of at-will employment relationship); Leahy v. Federal Express Corp., *infra* App. B (N.Y.); Salanger v. USAir, *infra* App. B (N.Y.).

disclaims any restrictions on discharge.[19] Several courts have held that oral promises or representations may also restrict the employer's right to discharge at will.[20]

Notwithstanding these developments, courts in some states have under some circumstances denied contract status to employee manuals or other equivalent policy statements.[21] A Pennsylvania Superior Court withdrew its 1984 decision, which recognized a contract claim for breach of an employee manual provision, and held that unless the manual contains, "expressly or by clear implication," a just cause provision, then there is nothing to take the case "out of the settled employee-at-will rule."[22]

---

[19]*Compare* Novosel v. Sears, Roebuck & Co., 495 F. Supp. 344, 117 LRRM 2702 (E.D. Mich. 1980) (statement in employment application signed by employee that employment could be terminated at any time, with or without cause, precluded contract claim) *with* Kochis v. Sears, Roebuck & Co., No. CA-2175, slip op. (Richland County Ct. App. Feb. 23, 1984) (surrounding circumstances indicate some agreement had been reached whereby plaintiff would not be discharged without just cause) *and* Tiranno v. Sears, Roebuck & Co., 99 A.D.2d 675, 472 N.Y.S.2d 49, 120 LRRM 2112 (1984) (despite express disclaimer in application form, triable issue of fact existed as to whether there was written contract based on provisions in company personnel manual which provided that "[t]he Company may terminate an individual's employment at any time that his/her work * * * does not measure up to Company standards"). *See also* Schipani v. Ford Motor Co., 102 Mich. App. 606, 302 N.W.2d 307, 30 FEP 361 (1981) (employee alleged other written and oral assurances creating an implied contract, notwithstanding receipt of a letter from employer purportedly establishing employment at will); Stone v. Mission Bay Mortgage Co., 99 Nev. 802, 672 P.2d 629, 116 LRRM 2917 (1983) (alleged oral agreement may supersede at-will language in employment applications).

[20]Foley v. Interactive Data Corp., *supra* note 12 and *infra* App. B (Cal.) (rejecting statute of frauds defense to allegations that employer's statements, conduct, and personnel policies during six years and nine months employment gave rise to contract not to discharge plaintiff without good cause); Scott v. Lane, *infra* App. B (Ala.) (offer of permanent employment to induce employee to leave current job may be sufficient consideration to prevent contract from being terminable at will); Peters v. Alabama Power Co., *infra* App. B (Ala.) (oral contract providing for termination only "for cause" precludes summary judgment based on at-will defense); Murphree v. Alabama Farm Bureau Ins. Co., 449 So.2d 1218, 115 LRRM 3682 (Ala. 1984), *appeal after remand sub nom.* Stover v. Alabama Farm Bureau Ins. Co., 467 So.2d 251, 120 LRRM 2868 (Ala. 1985) (summary judgment improperly granted in first proceeding, because evidence that valuable consideration had been given by plaintiff in connection with employment, precluded employment-at-will status; summary judgment properly granted after remand on alternative ground that employer's agent allegedly making contract for permanent employment was without authority to do so); Ohanian v. Avis Rent-A-Car Sys., 779 F.2d 101, 121 LRRM 2169 (2d Cir. 1985) (oral promise of lifetime employment terminable only for good cause is not barred by statute of frauds, and is not so indefinite as to be unenforceable); Gray v. California Superior Court (Cipher Data Prods.), *infra* App. B (Cal.) (oral representation of job security sufficient to state contract claim). *But see* Toshiba Am. v. Simmons, 104 A.D.2d 649, 480 N.Y.S.2d 28 (2d Dep't 1984) (oral representation that employer would try to work out problems with employees did not alter at-will rule); Barrett v. Foresters, 625 F.2d 73 (5th Cir. 1980) (under Georgia law, promise of job for life at certain income levels unenforceable and could not form basis for fraud); Eller v. Houston's Restaurants, 117 LRRM 2651 (D.D.C. 1984) (employee of less than one year, who signed application specifically stating that employment was at-will, successfully alleged verbal promises and implications from employee handbook that she would not be terminated unless performance unsatisfactory; factors relied upon by court to deny summary judgment present in most employment relationships). *See also supra* note 19.

[21]Enis v. Continental Ill. Nat'l Bank & Trust Co. (Ill.), McCluskey v. Unicare Health Facility (Ala.), White v. Chelsea Indus. (Ala.), Heideck v. Kent Gen. Hosp. (Del.), Muller v. Stromberg Carlson Corp. (Fla.), Mead Johnson & Co. v. Oppenheimer (Ind.), Griffin v. Housing Auth. of Durham (N.C.), Woolley v. Hoffman-LaRoche (N.J.), Ruch v. Strawbridge & Clothier (Pa.), Wells v. Thomas (Pa.), Reynolds Mfg. Co. v. Mendoza (Tex.), Vallone v. Agip Petroleum Co. (Tex.), Parker v. United Airlines (Wash.), Bringle v. Methodist Hosp. (Tenn.), Graves v. Anchor Wire Corp. of Tenn. (Tenn.), all *infra* App. B; *see also* Brumbaugh v. Ralston Purina Co., 656 F. Supp. 582, 2 IER 877 (S.D. Iowa 1987) (Iowa law would treat employer's manual as gratuitous, unilateral expressions of employer's position, which is not bargained for, lacks consideration, and does not become part of employment contract); Fleming v. Kids & Kin Head Start, 71 Or. App. 718, 693 P.2d 1363 (1985) (employer in its handbook can reserve right to determine whether just cause exists, so long as it acts in good faith).

[22]Banas v. Matthews Int'l Corp., 348 Pa. Super. 464, 502 A.2d 637, 121 LRRM 2515 (1985), *withdrawing* 116 LRRM 3110 (1984); *see also* Walker v. Consumer's Power Co., 824 F.2d 499 (6th Cir. 1987), *cert. denied*, 484 U.S. _____ (1988) (federal court reversed jury verdict in favor of employee on breach of contract suit because employer's general assurances regarding promotions commensurate with employee's contribution did not create enforceable promise under Michigan law); Martin v. Capital Cities Media, *infra* App. B (Pa.).

## 2. Promissory Estoppel

In addition to alleging breach of an express or implied contract, plaintiffs in some states may assert reasonable and detrimental reliance on the employer's promises.[23]

## B. Tort Theories

### 1. Generally

As this Supplement went to press, the California Supreme Court had just issued its long-awaited decision in *Foley v. Interactive Data Corp.,*[24] which became upon publication the leading California decision on wrongful discharge issues. *Foley* reaffirms the existence of a tort cause of action for employment termination in contravention of fundamental public policy,[25] but rejects tort liability for violations of an implied covenant of good faith and fair dealing in employment contracts.[26] Several other states have also permitted common law tort claims arising from employment termination. However, the precise contours of these tort doctrines are still unclear in several jurisdictions, and New York, California, and certain other states have explicitly refused to recognize a general tort claim for wrongful discharge of an at-will employee.[27] Appendix B to this Chapter provides representative citations from the several states.

### 2. Breach of Implied Covenant of Good Faith and Fair Dealing

The California Supreme Court has now recognized contract claims for breach of an implied covenant of good faith and fair dealing, but has rejected a tort cause of action for such an alleged breach unless "fundamental public

---

[23]*See Rest. (2d) Contracts,* § 90: "A promise which the promisor should reasonably expect to induce action or forbearance on the part of the promisee or a third person and which does induce such action or forbearance is binding if injustice can be avoided only by enforcement of the promise. The remedy granted for breach may be limited as justice requires." *See also* Grouse v. Group Health Plan, 306 N.W.2d 114, 115 LRRM 4438 (Minn. 1981) (employee who resigned one job in reliance upon being hired into another position was entitled to damages where offer of second position was later withdrawn); Pepsi-Cola Gen. Bottlers v. Woods, *infra* App. B (Ind.) (at-will doctrine applies, but cause of action successfully stated for promissory estoppel, since plaintiff quit former job upon promise of employment). *But see* Rose v. Allied Dev. Co., *infra* App. B (Utah) (employer's approval of employee's plans and schedule to work and attend school did not create contractual obligation; employee's school enrollment, payment of tuition, and purchase of books insufficient for recovery on promissory estoppel theory).

[24]88 DAILY J. D.A.R. 16079, 3 IER 1729 (Cal. S.Ct. 1988). *See also supra* note 12 and *infra* App. B (Cal.).

[25]*Id. See also* Tameny v. Atlantic Richfield Co., and other cases cited *infra* App. B (Cal.); Crosier v. United Parcel Serv., *infra* App. B (Cal.) (25-year employee dismissed for violating unwritten rule proscribing sexual relationships between management and nonmanagement employees grounded on policies against sexual harassment, and for lying about conduct; did not show discharge breached covenant of good faith and fair dealing).

[26]*See supra* notes 12 through 15 and accompanying text, and *infra* App. B (Cal.).

[27]Murphy v. American Home Prods. Corp., 58 N.Y.2d 293, 461 N.Y.S.2d 232, 448 N.E.2d 86, 31 FEP 782 (1983); Foley v. Interactive Data Corp., *supra* note 24; *see* O'Connor v. Eastman Kodak Co. (N.Y.), Patrowich v. Chemical Bank (N.Y.), Sabetay v. Sterling Drug (N.Y.), Leahy v. Federal Express Corp. (N.Y.), Salanger v. US Air (N.Y.), all *infra* App. B; *see also* Kelly v. Mississippi Valley Gas Co., 397 So.2d 874, 115 LRRM 4631 (Miss. 1981) (court refused to create remedy for retaliatory discharge where legislature declined to, and refused to adopt public policy exception to at-will doctrine); Maus v. National Living Centers, *infra* App. B (Tex.) (tort of wrongful discharge on public policy grounds not recognized, even though state statute requires nursing home employees to report cases of abuse or neglect, and employer discharged at-will nurse's aide for making complaints about nursing home).

policy" has allegedly been violated by the discharge.[28] Other states appear to recognize tort liability for breaches of an implied covenant of good faith and fair dealing in only scattered decisions.[29]

In *Howard v. Dorr Woolen Co.,*[30] the New Hampshire Supreme Court limited the application of *Monge v. Beebe Rubber Co.*[31] to public policy discharge situations "where an employee is discharged because he performed an act that public policy would encourage, or refused to do that which public policy would condemn."[32] In *Murphy v. American Home Products Corp.,*[33] the New York Court of Appeals held that in the absence of an express provision such as in an employer's handbook, no obligation of good faith is implied that would impair an employer's right to terminate employment at will.

## 3. Public Policy

Tort liability may be imposed upon proof that an employee's termination violates an identifiable public policy, usually defined by statute, because the employee was discharged for doing what public policy requires or encourages, or opposing what public policy prohibits, or because the discharge itself was contrary to law. In *Foley v. Interactive Data Corp.*[34] the California Supreme Court reaffirmed tort liability for employment terminations contrary to "fundamental" public policy, where the discharge is "against public policy and affects a duty which inures to the benefit of the public at large rather than to a particular employer or employee."[35] The court expressly left open the question "whether a tort action alleging a breach of public policy * * * may be based only on policies derived from a statute or constitutional provision or whether nonlegislative sources may provide the basis for such

---

[28]*See* Foley v. Interactive Data Corp., *supra* note 24 at 16089 and *supra* note 12. The California Supreme Court expressly left open "questions concerning the measure of damages in a wrongful discharge action based on breach of contract." *Id.* at 16091 n.24.

[29]*Id.* at 16091 n.26 (authorities collected and summarized by California Supreme Court). *See supra* note 12 and accompanying text.

[30]120 N.H. 295, 414 A.2d 1273, 29 FEP 1397 (1980), *clarified in* Bergeron v. Travelers Ins. Co., 125 N.H. 107, 480 A.2d 42, 116 LRRM 3222 (1984).

[31]114 N.H. 130, 316 A.2d 549, 115 LRRM 4755 (1974).

[32]120 N.H. at 297, 29 FEP at 1398; *see also* Cloutier v. Great Atl. & Pac. Tea Co., *infra* App. B (N.H.) (*Monge* and *Howard* give rise to two-part test for wrongful discharge: (1) employer must have been motivated by bad faith, malice, or retaliation; and (2) employee must have been discharged because he performed an act that public policy would encourage, or refused to do that which public policy would condemn, regardless of whether there exists statutory expression of public policy); Scott v. Sears, Roebuck & Co., *infra* App. B (Ill.).

[33]*Supra* note 27; *see also* Wakefield v. Northern Telecom, 769 F.2d 109, 120 LRRM 2080 (2d Cir. 1985) ("Wakefield I"), *later proceedings on appeal following remand,* 813 F.2d 535 (2d Cir. 1987) ("Wakefield II") (alleged discharge to avoid sales commission payment; covenant of good faith and fair dealing should not be implied to modify employer's right to discharge at will; employee must prove entitlement to sales commissions under terms of applicable commission agreements, or that discharge was substantially motivated by desire to avoid payment of commission to which employee was "virtually certain to become vested," *id.,* 769 F. 2d at 113; in later proceedings on appeal after remand, summary judgment for defendant employer reversed because of circumstantial evidence, obtained in discovery, regarding employer's motivation and contents of applicable sales commission plan); Burdette v. Mepco/Electra, 673 F. Supp. 1012, 43 FEP 1224, 2 IER 214 (S.D. Cal. 1987) (need for firmwide reduction in force constituted good cause as a matter of law; covenant claim dismissed since four-year tenure is too short); Wexler v. Newsweek, 109 A.D.2d 714, 487 N.Y.S.2d 330 (N.Y. App. Div. 1985) (court will not imply covenant of good faith and fair dealing into an employment relationship).

[34]*Supra* note 24. *See supra* note 12 and accompanying text.

[35]3 IER at 1733. *See also supra* notes 12 through 15 and accompanying text, and *infra* notes 43 and 44.

a claim."[36] In a "public policy discharge" case where public policy is grounded on a statute, the employee may allegedly have been discharged for refusing to violate a criminal or other statute[37] or for exercising a statutory right, such as filing a workers' compensation claim.[38] The discharge itself may allegedly violate a statutory prohibition,[39] or may have been for reporting alleged violations of law to government agencies.[40] Tort liability based

---

[36]*Id.,* 3 IER at 1733 and 1734 n.11. *See also supra* notes 12 through 15 and accompanying text, and *infra* notes 43 and 44.

[37]Kalman v. Grand Union Co., *infra* App. B (N.J.) (discharge of registered pharmacist, allegedly resulting from refusal to close pharmacy on holiday, would conflict with statutory and ethical sources of public policy; dismissal reversed and case remanded for proof of alleged facts at trial); Tameny v. Atlantic Richfield Co., *infra* App. B. (Cal.) (discharge allegedly for refusal to fix gasoline prices); Phipps v. Clark Oil & Ref. Corp., 408 N.W.2d 569, 2 IER 341 (Minn. 1987) (Minnesota Supreme Court recognized public policy exception to employment at will when employee is discharged for refusing to participate in activity that the employee, in good faith, believes violates state or federal law or rule or regulation adopted pursuant to law); Merkel v. Scovill, Inc., 570 F. Supp. 133, 38 FEP 1020 (S.D. Ohio 1983) (Ohio Supreme Court would recognize public policy exception where employee is discharged for refusal to commit perjury had proof been presented that employer knew it was asking employee to do so). *See* Ostrofe v. H.S. Crocker Co., 740 F.2d 739, 117 LRRM 2105 (9th Cir. 1984), *cert. denied,* 469 U.S. 1200, 120 LRRM 3576 (1985) (discharged management employee may sue under antitrust laws, alleging he was discharged and blacklisted because of refusal to participate in an antitrust conspiracy).

[38]Rawson v. Sears, Roebuck & Co., *infra* App. B (Colo.) (plaintiff did not allege he was discharged for exercising "specifically enacted right or duty"; case was tried under state age discrimination theory; plaintiff awarded compensatory and punitive damages of $19,096,495.01; judgment later reversed by Tenth Circuit as preempted by Colorado penal statute imposing a fine from $100 to $250 upon employers who discharge employees solely because of age; Tenth Circuit held Colorado statute provided neither express nor implied private action); Meyer v. Byron Jackson, Inc., 161 Cal. App.3d 402, 207 Cal. Rptr. 663 (1984) (§ 132a is the exclusive remedy available to a claim of discharge because of filing a workers' compensation claim; punitive damage award in § 132a claim affirmed; malice includes a conscious disregard of the rights of others, and could be inferred from employer's opposition to filing workers' compensation claims; one could reasonably conclude that employer's actions were in retaliation for plaintiff's successful pursuit of a workers' compensation claim); Portillo v. G.T. Price Prods., 131 Cal.App.3d 285, 290, 182 Cal. Rptr. 291, 115 LRRM 4235 (1982) (same); Hollywood Refrigeration Sales Co. v. California Superior Court, 164 Cal.App.3d 754, 210 Cal. Rptr. 619 (1985) (workers' compensation settlement was *res judicata* and barred recovery based on claims of work-related intentional and negligent infliction of emotional distress); Young v. Libbey-Owens Ford Co., 168 Cal.App.3d 1037, 214 Cal. Rptr. 400 (1985) (on same facts, opposite conclusion to *Hollywood Refrigeration:* employee who recovered under workers' compensation for harassment entitled to bring common law action).

[39]Discharges in violation of equal employment statutes represent a subcategory of such claims. *See, e.g.,* Slohoda v. United Parcel Serv., 193 N.J. Super. 586, 475 A.2d 618 (App. Div. 1984) ("Slohoda I"), *appeal after remand,* 207 N.J. Super. 145, 504 A.2d 53 (App. Div.) *certification denied,* 104 N.J. 400, 517 A.2d 403 (1986) ("Slohoda II") (employee alleged he was discharged because he was a married man who had sexual relationship with fellow employee who is a woman other than his wife; held, in *Slohoda I,* that UPS violated New Jersey's statutory prohibition against marital status discrimination if UPS discharge policy is "based in significant part on an employee's marital status"; in *Slohoda II,* plaintiff raised material factual issues in prima facie case that precluded summary judgment). *See also* Garibaldi v. Lucky Food Stores, 726 F.2d 1367, 115 LRRM 3089 (9th Cir. 1984), *cert. denied,* 471 U.S. 1099, 119 LRRM 2248 (1985) (employee allegedly discharged for reporting shipment of purportedly spoiled milk violating health laws); Meyers v. Prudential-Bache Secs., *infra* App. B (Ill.) (court refused to dismiss plaintiff's claim for retaliatory discharge, reasoning that Illinois public policy favoring "citizen crime-fighters" applies to all unlawful activities occurring in Illinois, including violations of federal securities laws; plaintiff's claim for breach of an implied contract sustained, where employment manual imposed obligations on employer and employee).

[40]*See, e.g.,* Garibaldi v. Lucky Food Stores, *supra* note 29 (applying California law, discharge for reporting to health authorities instruction to deliver spoiled milk in violation of health code); Wolcowicz v. Intercraft Indus. Corp., 133 Ill.App.3d 157, 478 N.E.2d 1039 (1st Dist. 1985) (after plaintiff suffered heart attack and back injury, defendant convinced him to sign severance agreement; court held this was retaliatory discharge, since defendant intended, in violation of public policy, to deter plaintiff from filing for workers' compensation); Petrik v. Monarch Printing Corp., 143 Ill.App.3d 1, 493 N.E.2d 616, 1 IER 1460 (1st Dist. 1986) (court dismissed plaintiff's suit for retaliatory discharge, finding that what really was at issue was internal dispute over accounting methods, which did not affect citizens of the state collectively so as to support claim for retaliatory discharge in violation of public policy); Barr v. Kelso-Burnett Co., 106 Ill.2d 520, 478 N.E.2d 1354, 120 LRRM 3401 (1985) (plaintiffs alleged they were terminated in retaliation for exercising right to free speech; constitutional guarantee of free speech is against abridgment only by government, not private employers; also, no clear public policy mandates inclusion of right of free speech into employer-employee relationship); Hentzel v. Singer, 138 Cal.App.3d 290, 188 Cal. Rptr. 159, 115 LRRM 4036 (1982) (discharge for complaints protected by California OSHA

on public policy claims may be precluded, however, where the statute which is the source of the public policy provides a remedy,[41] or where a collective bargaining agreement preempts civil litigation.[42]

Some courts have declared or implied that other nonstatutory bases for public policy would be acceptable.[43] A few courts have addressed the question whether an employee's ethical or political concerns are grounds for assertion of a violation of public policy.[44]

---

about cigarette smoke in workplace was violation of public policy); Moffett v. Gene B. Glick Co., *infra* App. B. (Ind.) (discharge in retaliation for filing racial harassment charge with EEOC violated public policy); Fitzgerald v. Norwest Corp., *infra* App. B (Minn.) (state court of appeals found equal employment/affirmative action policy in handbook sufficient to form contractual basis for nondiscrimination claims, in addition to statutory rights). *But see* Gould v. Campbell's Ambulance Serv., 111 Ill.2d 54, 488 N.E.2d 993, 122 LRRM 2672 (1986) (municipal ordinance plaintiffs reported violations of was *not* clearly mandated public policy); Thomas v. Zamberletti, 134 Ill.App.3d 387, 480 N.E.2d 869 (4th Dist. 1985) (no clearly mandated public policy for seeking and receiving medical treatment); Powers v. Delnor Hosp., 135 Ill. App. 317, 481 N.E.2d 968 (2d Dist. 1985) (lying in employer's internal records is not against public policy); Burgess v. Chicago Sun-Times, 132 Ill.App.3d 181, 476 N.E.2d 1284 (1st Dist. 1985) (defendant's refusal to reassign plaintiff to less stressful route was not violation of public policy or extreme and outrageous conduct). *Cf.* Gray v. California Superior Court (Cipher Data Prods.), *infra* App. B (Cal.) (all California "public policy discharge" cases rest on alleged or proven violations of public policy embodied in statute); Slohoda v. United Parcel Serv., *supra* note 39 (employee claimed he was discharged because he was married man who had sexual liaison with woman other than his wife; violation of public policy as manifested in N.J. Stat. Ann. 10:5–12, which proscribes discharge based on marital status).

   *For representative statutory proscriptions, see: Florida:* Human Rights Act, Fla. Stat. Ann. § 23,167 (West 1982) (prohibiting discharge because of race, color, religion, sex, national origin, age, handicap, or marital status; also prohibits discriminating against employee because employee has made a charge, testified, assisted, or participated in any manner in any investigation, proceeding, or hearing under the act); *Missouri:* Mo. Ann. Stat. § 287.780 (1978) (prohibiting retaliation for having exercised workers' compensation rights) (*see* Arie v. Intertherm, Inc., 648 S.W.2d 142, 118 LRRM 3436 (Mo. Ct. App. 1983) (setting forth elements of cause of action)); *New York:* N.Y. Exec. Law Ann. § 296 (McKinney 1982) (prohibiting discharge based on age, race, creed, color, national origin, sex, disability, or marital status, and prohibiting retaliatory termination for any employee because he has opposed forbidden practices, or testified, assisted, or filed complaint under Human Rights Law); *Oklahoma:* Okla. Stat. tit. 85 § 5 (1985) (prohibits retaliation against employee who has filed workers' compensation claim) (*see* Webb v. Dayton Tire & Rubber Co., 697 P.2d 519 (Okla. 1985) (punitive damages awarded for intentional violation of workers' compensation retaliation prohibition)); *Texas:* Tex. Stat. Ann. art. 5196 (Vernon 1971) (prohibits blacklisting discharged employee and requires employer to give written reasons for discharge within 10 days), Tex. Hum. Res. Code Ann. § 121.003 (Vernon 1982) (prohibiting discharge because of handicap) (*see* Carnation Co. v. Borner, 610 S.W.2d 450 (Tex. 1980) (punitive damages are appropriate where plaintiff proves that employer intentionally violated Texas Stat. Ann. art. 8307c (Vernon 1986), which prohibits retaliation for employee's filing workers' compensation claim)); *Washington:* Wash. Rev. Code Ann. § 49.60.180 (Supp. 1983) (prohibiting discharge based on age, sex, marital status, race, creed, color, national origin, or presence of any sensory, mental, or physical handicap), Wash. Rev. Code § 49.60.210 (1962) (prohibiting retaliatory termination for an employee's filing a discrimination claim).

   [41]*See supra* notes 4-6, 38; Flynn v. New England Tel. Co., 615 F. Supp. 1205, 41 FEP 1755 (D. Mass. 1985) (no "public policy" exception to at-will rule for discharge motivated by age discrimination because state's policy against age discrimination is already protected by "comprehensive legislative scheme"); Strauss v. A.L. Randall Co., 144 Cal.App.3d 514, 194 Cal. Rptr. 520, 37 FEP 1531 (1983) (state law claim for discharge against public policy precluded because state statute prohibiting age discrimination provides exclusive remedy); Phillips v. McDermott, Inc., Babcock & Wilcox, Tubular Prods. Div., 349 Pa. Super. 351, 503 A.2d 36, 121 LRRM 2695 (1986).

   [42]*See* Basset v. Attebery, 180 Cal.App.3d 288, 225 Cal. Rptr. 399 (1986) (NLRA preempts former supervisor's claim of wrongful discharge in violation of public policy); *see also* Lingle v. Magic Chef, Norge Div., 486 U.S. _____, 46 FEP 1553 (1988); Allis-Chalmers Corp. v. Lueck, 471 U.S. 202, 118 LRRM 3345 (1985); Sklios v. Teamsters Local 70, 503 F. Supp. 123, 115 LRRM 3133 (N.D. Cal. 1980). *But see* Garibaldi v. Lucky Food Stores, *supra* note 29, 726 F.2d at 1372–73; Bloom v. General Truck Drivers Local 952, 783 F.2d 1356, 121 LRRM 3008 (9th Cir. 1986). *See also supra* note 6.

   [43]*See* discussion of this issue *supra* notes 15 and 16 and *infra* note 44, and accompanying text, and in *Foley v. Interactive Data Corp.,* 88 DAILY J. D.A.R. 16079, 16080–82, 3 IER 1729, 1731–34 (Cal. S.Ct. 1988) and accompanying notes. *See also* Sheets v. Teddy's Frosted Foods, *infra* App. B (Conn.) (dictum); Cloutier v. Great Atl. & Pac. Tea Co., *infra* App. B (N.H.) (dictum); Hentzel v. Singer, *supra* note 40 (dictum); Holien v. Sears, Roebuck & Co., 298 Or. 76, 689 P.2d 1292, 36 FEP 137 (1984) (dictum); Schmidt v. Yardney Elec. Corp., 4 Conn. App. 69, 492 A.2d 512 (1985) (dictum).

   [44]Novosel v. Nationwide Ins. Co., *infra* App. B (Pa.) (discharge of insurance company claims manager for refusal to participate actively in employer's lobbying campaign against pending no-fault insurance bill fell within Pennsylvania's public policy exception to at-will rule); Dabbs v. Cardiopulmonary Mgmt. Servs., 188 Cal.App.3d 1437, 234 Cal. Rptr. 129, 2 IER 205 (1987) (employee walked off job protesting working conditions at hospital and was terminated; general public policy claim not based

## IV. OTHER COMMON LAW TORT THEORIES

Plaintiffs have significantly expanded the range of common law tort theories for alleging employment claims. These theories receive varying treatment in different jurisdictions but a representative catalog would include those that follow.

### A. Intentional Infliction of Emotional Distress

In the absence of physical injury, courts continue to require proof of extreme, outrageous conduct as a basis for a claim that an employer has intentionally inflicted emotional distress.[45] In *Murphy v. American Home Products Corp.,*[46] the New York Court of Appeals held the plaintiff could not subvert the at-will contract rule by casting his wrongful discharge cause of action as a tort of intentional infliction of emotional distress. The California Supreme Court in *Cole v. Fair Oaks Fire Protection District*[47] recently reaffirmed that where the employer's actions are part of the normal employment

---

on statute can provide basis for public policy tort); Pierce v. Ortho Pharmaceutical Corp., 84 N.J. 58, 417 A.2d 505, 115 LRRM 3044 (1980) (refusal to perform drug-related research based on asserted ethical concerns not adequately grounded on public policy). *See also supra* notes 15 and 43.

[45]For representative cases reflecting circumstances in which courts have addressed the question whether employer's conduct was sufficiently extreme and outrageous to permit claim for infliction of emotional distress, *see, e.g., infra* App. C and the following cases:

  *Claim for infliction of emotional distress allowed:* Luna v. City & County of Denver, Smith v. Montgomery Ward & Co., Monge v. California Superior Court (Crown Gibralter Graphic Center), Stewart v. Thomas, Milton v. Illinois Bell Tel. Co., New York v. Holiday Inns, Wolber v. Service Corp. Int'l, Bell v. Crakin Good Bakeries, Grubb v. W.A. Foote Memorial Hosp., Garza v. Brownsville Indep. School Dist., Stallworth v. Shuler, Berndt v. Kaiser Aluminum & Chem. Sales, all *infra* App. C; Rulon-Miller v. IBM Corp., *infra* App. B (Cal.) (after supervisor stated employee could decide between a continued personal relationship and continued employment in a management position, supervisor then removed employee from management position without waiting for response, basing action on alleged conflict of interest without factual basis, stating "I'm making the decision for you," and discharging her when she protested; employee's privacy rights infringed); *see also* Hart v. National Mortgage & Land Co., 189 Cal.App.3d 1420, 235 Cal. Rptr. 68 (1987) (alleged physical sexual harassment of male employee by male supervisor not subject to exclusive workers' compensation remedy).

  *Claim for infliction of emotional distress not allowed:* Balark v. Ethicon, Inc., Harris v. Arkansas Book Co., Givens v. Hixson, Meredith v. C.E. Walther, Inc., Hubbard v. United Press Int'l, Gates v. Life of Mont. Ins. Co., Forde v. Royal's, Carrillo v. Illinois Bell Tel. Co., Elliott v. Employer's Reinsurance Corp., Beidler v. W.R. Grace, Inc., Gibson v. Hummel, Northrup v. Farmland Indus., Morris v. Hartford Courant Co., Pemberton v. Bethlehem Steel Corp., Leese v. Baltimore County, Avallone v. Wilmington Medical Center, Oakley v. St. Joseph's Hosp., all *infra* App. C; *see also* Cole v. Fair Oaks Fire Protection Dist., 43 Cal.3d 148, 233 Cal. Rptr. 308, 792 P.2d 743, 1 IER 1644 (1987) (plaintiff alleged his supervisor, an assistant fire chief, harassed him during labor negotiations, retaliated by setting up new personnel procedure, required appearance before supervisory "kangaroo" panel on false dishonesty claims, publicly demoted him, and assigned menial duties; plaintiff alleged this caused totally disabling cerebral vascular accident; court held workers' compensation remedy exclusive because alleged misconduct of employer was comprised of "actions which are a normal part of the employment relationship."); Spratley v. Winchell Donut House, 188 Cal.App.3d 1408, 234 Cal. Rptr. 121 (1987) (plaintiff's tort claim for injury by intruder, following purportedly fraudulent representation by employer that workplace was safe, relegated exclusively to workers' compensation remedy under *Cole, supra;* plaintiff had alleged "no conduct by the employer outside the role of employer").

[46]58 N.Y.2d 293, 303, 461 N.Y.S.2d 232, 448 N.E.2d 86, 31 FEP 782, 785 (1983).

[47]*Supra* note 45 (when misconduct attributed to employer is action which is normal part of employment relationship, employee suffering emotional distress causing disability may not avoid exclusive remedy provisions of workers' compensation code); *see also supra* notes 37–38 and 40; Burgess v. Chicago Sun-Times, *supra* note 40; Hansen v. Harrah's, 100 Nev. 60, 675 P.2d 394, 115 LRRM 3024 (1984) (retaliatory discharge actionable in tort); Harless v. First Nat'l Bank in Fairmont, *infra* App. B (W. Va.); Valenzuela v. California, No. D003617 (Cal. Ct. App. 1987) (public employee's remedy for wrongful termination lies exclusively within civil service system); Meyer v. Byron Jackson, Inc., *supra* note 38 (although current version of California Labor Code provides remedy for discharge in retaliation for filing workers' compensation claim, code provision in effect at time of plaintiff's discharge did not so provide and thus plaintiff's civil action was not barred).

relationship, an employee's claims for injury will be exclusively subject to the provisions of the state's workers' compensation statute.

## B. Defamation

Defamation claims arise in a variety of employment contexts. These may include, for example, postemployment referrals or statements made in predischarge investigations or postdischarge explanations to co-workers. By statute or common law rule, courts generally recognize varying privileges or other limitations shielding a defendant employer's conduct in differing degrees depending on the facts alleged or proven by a plaintiff.[48] Actionable defamation must express supposed fact, not opinion. Statements are absolutely privileged if truthful, and generally are protected by a qualified privilege if communicated without malice between persons with a legitimate interest in the subject matter. A New York court found a qualified privilege applicable to a statement made by a plaintiff's supervisor to a shop steward, and overheard by other employees, that the plaintiff was a thief.[49]

Other communications covered by a qualified privilege include a letter from an employer's attorney to a plaintiff's attorney explaining reasons for termination;[50] a communication to a prospective employer that the plaintiff had negligently caused an accident;[51] a discussion with a co-worker in response to the co-worker's inquiry about the reasons for discharge;[52] and a communication with an unemployment insurance agency which rendered the plaintiff ineligible for unemployment benefits.[53]

Statements by a former employer in an employment verification questionnaire that a former employee had "questionable loyalty and ethics" were held to be libel *per se.*[54]

---

[48]*See* Deaile v. General Tel. Co. of Cal., 40 Cal.App.3d 841, 115 Cal. Rptr. 582 (1974) (statements to other employees, fairly explaining basis of discharge, defensible as protected by qualified privilege in absence of malice); Stearns v. Ohio Sav. Ass'n, *infra* App. B (Ohio) (former employee's allegation that employer sent written notice of reasons for termination to other employees, and did so maliciously, avoids qualified privilege and states claim for defamation). *But see* Stevens v. Tillman, 568 F. Supp. 289, 36 FEP 1232 (N.D. Ill. 1983) (defendants' motion to dismiss denied where statements at official Board of Education meeting found not absolutely or conditionally privileged because plaintiff, a public school principal, was not public figure or official).

[49]Thompson v. Maimonides Medical Center, 86 A.D.2d 867, 447 N.Y.S.2d 308 (App. Div. 1982).

[50]Willis v. Demopolis Nursing Home, 336 So.2d 1117 (Ala. 1976).

[51]Brown v. Chem Haulers, 402 So.2d 887 (Ala. 1981).

[52]Jones v. J.C. Penney Co., 164 Ga. App. 432, 297 S.E.2d 339 (1982) (employer disclosure to another employee that plaintiff had been discharged for selling narcotics was privileged since employee had worked directly with plaintiff daily, was close friend of plaintiff, and disclosure was in direct response to employee's inquiry and outside presence of others); Deaile v. General Tel. Co. of Cal., *supra* note 48 (similar analysis and result).

[53]Chamberlin v. 101 Realty, 626 F. Supp. 865 (D.N.H. 1985) (information provided by former employer regarding employee's discharge may not form basis of action for defamation).

[54]Tedeschi v. Smith Barney, Harris Upham & Co., 548 F. Supp. 1172 (S.D.N.Y. 1982), *related proceeding,* 579 F. Supp. 657 (S.D.N.Y. 1984), *aff'd,* 757 F.2d 465 (2d Cir.), *cert. denied,* 474 U.S. 850 (1985) (upholding $10,000 award for attorney's fees for employer against former employee, after dismissal of former employee's claims that employer had abused process and otherwise injured former employee's claims); Leese v. Baltimore County, *infra* App. C (statement in personnel file that employee of six years failed to demonstrate managerial ability is libel *per quod;* grant of motion to dismiss improper); *see also* Saunders v. Van Pelt, 497 A.2d 1121 (Me. 1985) (former employer's statement to parents of plaintiff's potential client, regarding plaintiff's alleged incompetence, held to be slander *per se*); Thompson v. Lynch, 39 FEP 882 (W.D. Va. 1985) (governmental officials immune from defamation claims based upon utterances made pursuant to their official duties even where allegedly defamatory remarks are not tied to any specified duty within speaker's job description); Lewis v. Equitable Life Assurance Soc'y, 389

California and Pennsylvania courts have ruled that the conditional privilege may be overcome by showing that the employer acted negligently.[55]

## C. Misrepresentation

Some plaintiffs have alleged intentional or negligent misrepresentation on a theory that the employer made false statements intentionally or without reasonable care to determine their accuracy.[56]

## D. Interference With Contractual Relations

Courts continue to require evidence establishing that the alleged interference is by a third party, and is intentional and without justification.[57]

A New York court held that a cause of action for interference with contract property rights was stated by a former employee who claimed that a former employer had "blacklisted" him throughout the industry.[58]

## E. Negligence

In Michigan, a new potential theory for recovery has emerged—the tort of negligent evaluation. In *Schipani v. Ford Motor Co.* [59] the Michigan Court

---

N.W.2d 876, 1 IER 1269 (Minn. 1986) (publication requirement for defamation may be satisfied by facts showing plaintiff was compelled to publish defamatory statement to third person if it was foreseeable to defendant that plaintiff would be so compelled; this has been referred to as "self-publication").

[55]Banas v. Matthews Int'l Corp., 348 Pa. Super. 464, 502 A.2d 637, 121 LRRM 2515 (1985); Manguso v. Oceanside Unified School Dist., 153 Cal.App.3d 574, 200 Cal. Rptr. 535 (1984) (administrator's letter to former teacher's confidential file allegedly impugning her job performance protected by qualified privilege which plaintiff failed to overcome by showing of malice).

[56]Hamlen v. Fairchild Indus., *infra* App. B (Fla.) (allegation of fraudulent misrepresentation of permanent job, coupled with nonintent to perform, was actionable); Tyco Indus. v. California Superior Court, *infra* App. B (Cal.).

[57]Empire Gas of Ardmore v. Hardy, 487 So.2d 244 (Ala. 1985), *cert. denied,* 476 U.S. 1116 (1986) (former employer liable for its interference with plaintiff's attempts to obtain employment, since noncompetition clause had been signed as result of misrepresentations); Dawson v. Radewicz, 63 N.C. App. 731, 306 S.E.2d 171 (1983) (defendant liable only if not party to contract and has no legitimate interest in subject matter of employment contract); Wells v. Thomas, *infra* App. B (Pa.), at 434–35 (individual defendants were "managerial employees acting in their official capacities," and therefore no cause of action was stated because there was no "third person" who induced corporate employer to breach its employment contract with plaintiff); Hudson v. Moore Business Forms, 609 F. Supp. 467, 37 FEP 1672 (N.D. Cal. 1985); *accord* George A. Fuller Co. v. Chicago College of Osteopathic Medicine, 719 F.2d 1326 (7th Cir. 1983) (no showing that privilege of corporate officers to act on behalf of their corporation using their business judgment and discretion was violated because officers acted detrimentally to corporation and outside scope of corporate policy); Covell v. Spengler, 141 Mich. App. 76, 366 N.W.2d 76 (1985) (cause of action may lie against corporate officials for tortious interference with employment relationship of at-will employee where plaintiff sufficiently alleges that corporate officials were acting in their own personal interests); Stevens v. Tillman, *supra* note 48 (defendants' motion to dismiss denied because traditional elements of tort sufficiently pleaded); Powers v. Delnor Hosp., 135 Ill. App. 317, 481 N.E.2d 968 (2d Dist. 1985) (plaintiff stated cause of action for contract interference, but not wrongful discharge, where supervisor gave false reason to hospital for plaintiff's discharge); Toney v. Casey's Gen. Stores, 372 N.W.2d 220, 120 LRRM 2249 (Iowa 1985) (tortious interference with an employment contract can occur in at-will employment); Appley v. Lock, 396 Mass. 540, 487 N.E.2d 501 (1986) (tortious interference with employment cannot occur between employer and employee).

[58]Burba v. Rochester Gas & Elec. Corp., 90 A.D.2d 984, 456 N.Y.S.2d 578 (App. Div. 1982); *see also* Sherman v. St. Barnabas Hosp., 535 F. Supp. 564, 115 LRRM 5133 (S.D.N.Y. 1982) (plaintiff had cause of action against union for interference with contractual relations where union pressured employer into terminating plaintiff).

[59]102 Mich. App. 606, 302 N.W.2d 307, 30 FEP 361 (1981); *see also* Rouse v. Pepsi-Cola Metro. Bottling Co., 642 F. Supp. 34 (E.D. Mich. 1985) (court denied plaintiff's claims of contractual right to continued employment based on performance appraisal forms and employer's negligent performance of its contractual duties). The *Schipani* holding has drawn heavy criticism, and in 1987 the Michigan Supreme Court stated that *Schipani's* "recognition of the tort of negligent evaluation should be limited

of Appeals held that because the employer had undertaken to evaluate the plaintiff, it had a duty to perform the evaluations in a fair and reasonable manner. However, the court noted that if the plaintiff was an at-will employee, his allegations of negligence would not state a claim for relief.

In *Chamberlain v. Bissell, Inc.,* [60] a federal district court applied this concept under Michigan law in awarding damages for lost wages and mental distress to a terminated executive who was found not to have been wrongfully discharged. Relying on the employer's written policy regarding evaluations, the court found that the employer had a duty to inform the employee that discharge was a possible consequence if his performance did not improve. [61] Because this is a tort action sounding in negligence, the theories of contributory and comparative negligence were held applicable. A negligence claim has also been recognized by the New Jersey Supreme Court in *DiCosala v. Kay,* [62] where a plaintiff was permitted to plead a claim for negligent hiring. There, the plaintiff alleged that the defendants had negligently hired the uncle of one of the plaintiffs as a camp employee even though the camp was reportedly aware that the uncle possessed and used guns, and the plaintiff boy was thereafter shot with one of his uncle's guns by a camp counselor. A similar claim was allowed by a Minnesota appellate court in *Ponticas v. K.M.S. Inv.,* [63] where an apartment tenant had been raped by an apartment manager hired after allegedly insufficient reference checks that, if made with reasonable care, purportedly should have revealed the risks of hiring the apartment manager.

## V. APPLICABILITY OF WORKERS' COMPENSATION LAWS

Courts continue to reach varying results on the question whether emotional distress suffered during employment occurred in the course of employment, and therefore must be remedied exclusively through state workers' compensation statutes, or was caused by outrageous conduct outside the normal incidents of the employment relationship. [64]

---

to the particular facts of that case." Sankar v. Detroit Bd. of Educ., 160 Mich. App. 470, 409 N.W.2d 213 (1987); *see also* Loftis v. G.T. Prods., 167 Mich. App. 787, 423 N.W.2d 358, 3 IER 641 (1988); Dahlman v. Oakland Univ., 172 Mich. App. 502, 432 N.W. 2d 304, 3 IER 1765 (1988); Grant v. Michigan Osteopathic Medical Center, 172 Mich. App. 536, 432 N.W.2d 313, 48 FEP 1201 (1988).

[60]547 F. Supp. 1067, 30 FEP 347 (W.D. Mich. 1982).

[61]*Id.* at 1082, 30 FEP at 359. *But see* Tiranno v. Sears, Roebuck & Co., 99 A.D.2d 675, 472 N.Y.S.2d 49, 120 LRRM 2112 (1984) (fact-finder must objectively determine whether employee's performance measured up to employer's standards); Reid v. Sears, Roebuck & Co., *infra* App. B (Mich.) (where contract is terminable at will there could be no duty to evaluate before discharge); Struble v. Lacks Indus., 157 Mich. App. 169, 403 N.W.2d 71 (1986) (breach of employment contract does not give rise to action sounding in negligence when breach of duty is distinguishable from breach of contract); Gach v. National Educ. Corp., No. 84-1792 (E.D. Mich. 1985) (unpublished slip op.) (no tort action would lie where only source of duty to evaluate comes from contract of employment).

[62]91 N.J. 159, 450 A.2d 508 (1982).

[63]331 N.W.2d 907 (Minn. 1983). *See also* Green and Reibstein, *Negligent Hiring, Fraud, Defamation, and Other Emerging Areas of Employer Liability: A BNA Special Report* (Washington: Bureau of National Affairs 1988).

[64]Russell v. United Parcel Serv., 666 F.2d 1188 (8th Cir. 1981) (emotional distress suffered during employment relationship must be remedied via workers' compensation statute, and not via judicial action); Hood v. Trans World Airlines, 648 S.W.2d 167 (E.D. Mo. 1983); Flynn v. New England Tel. Co., 615 F. Supp. 1205, 41 FEP 1755 (D. Mass. 1985) (employee claims for intentional or negligent infliction of emotional distress barred by workers' compensation law). *But see* Brown v. Winn-Dixie Montgomery, 427 So.2d 1065 (Fla. Dist. Ct. App. 1983) (claims of emotional distress not barred by

The Georgia Court of Appeals held that an employee's claim for damages from alleged verbal and physical sexual abuse by her supervisor while on duty was neither covered nor barred by the state's Workers' Compensation Act.[65]

## VI. FEDERAL FUND WITHHOLDING AND REGULATORY AGENCY REMEDIES

The EEOC and the Department of Justice have issued regulations governing complaints of employment discrimination brought pursuant to Title VI and Title IX.[66]

The Supreme Court held in *Guardians Association of New York City Police Department v. Civil Service Commission,*[67] by separate opinions of a majority of the Justices, that monetary relief is not available in a private action under Title VI in the absence of proof of intentional discrimination.

The Supreme Court, in *Grove City College v. Bell,*[68] held that Title IX coverage is triggered because some college's students receive federal grants to pay for their education, notwithstanding the fact that the funds are paid directly to the students rather than to the college. The Court further held, however, that Title IX coverage only protects those who benefit from the

workers' compensation law, since intentional torts not compensable in Florida); Boscaglia v. Michigan Bell Tel. Co., 420 Mich. 308, 362 N.W.2d 642, 43 FEP 1155 (1984) (exclusive remedy provisions of Workers' Compensation Act did not constitute bar for physical, mental, or emotional injuries, if those injuries are compensable under state's FEP act); Mills v. Jefferson Bank E., 559 F. Supp. 34, 35 FEP 1384 (D. Colo. 1983) (claim for recovery of damages based primarily on mental suffering and humiliation under 42 U.S.C. § 1981 is not barred by state workers' compensation law). *See also* Galante v. Sandoz, Inc., 192 N.J. Super. 403, 470 A.2d 45, 115 LRRM 3370, *aff'd,* 196 N.J. Super. 568, 483 A.2d 829 (1984), *appeal dismissed,* 103 N.J. 492, 511 A.2d 665 (1986) (employee failed to establish prima facie case of retaliatory discharge since his claim for workers' compensation benefits did not enter into decision to terminate him and since employer's absence control policy, which did not excuse employees recuperating from work-related injuries, was not contrary to public policy surrounding workers' compensation law); Clifford v. Cactus Drilling Corp., 419 Mich. 356, 353 N.W.2d 469 (1984) (discharge of employee pursuant to absenteeism policy even if such absences are related to previously compensated injury, did not state cause of action for retaliation in violation of state public policy); Cole v. Fair Oaks Fire Protection Dist., 43 Cal.3d 148, 233 Cal. Rptr. 308, 1 IER 1644 (1987) (workers' compensation procedures exclusive where claim based on conduct normally occurring in workplace); Young v. Libbey-Owens Ford Co., 168 Cal.App.3d 1037, 214 Cal. Rptr. 400 (1985) (intentional torts, including intentional infliction of emotional distress, outside scope of California workers' compensation system); Hollywood Refrigeration Sales Co. v. California Superior Court, 164 Cal.App.3d 754, 210 Cal. Rptr. 619 (1985) (workers' compensation settlement and barred recovery based on claims of work-related intentional and negligent infliction of emotional distress); Meyer v. Byron Jackson, Inc., 161 Cal.App.3d 402, 207 Cal. Rptr. 663 (1984) (§ 132a is the exclusive remedy available to a claim of discharge because of filing a workers' compensation claim; punitive damage award in § 132a claim affirmed; malice includes a conscious disregard of the rights of others, and could be inferred from employer's opposition to filing workers' compensation claims; one could reasonably conclude that employer's actions were in retaliation for plaintiff's successful pursuit of a workers' compensation claim); Portillo v. G.T. Price Prods., 131 Cal.App.3d 285, 290, 182 Cal. Rptr. 291, 115 LRRM 4235 (1982) (same).

[65]Murphy v. ARA Servs., 164 Ga. App. 859, 298 S.E.2d 528 (1982); *see also* Luna v. City & County of Denver, *infra* Apps. A & C (claim for intentional infliction of emotional distress neither covered nor barred by Workers' Compensation Act, because Act covers only "personal injuries," which does not include those consisting primarily of mental suffering).

[66]48 FED. REG. 3570 *et seq.* (1983).

[67]463 U.S. 582, 32 FEP 250 (1983); *see* Bushey v. New York State Civil Serv. Comm'n, 571 F. Supp. 1562, 34 FEP 1050 (N.D.N.Y. 1983), *rev'd on other grounds,* 733 F.2d 220, 34 FEP 1065 (2d Cir. 1984), *cert. denied,* 469 U.S. 1117, 36 FEP 1166 (1985) (applying *Guardians* standard; monetary damages not allowed); Meyer v. Byron Jackson, Inc., *supra* note 64; Portillo v. G.T. Price Prods., *supra* note 64 (same); Hollywood Refrigeration Sales Co. v. California Superior Court, *supra* note 64; Young v. Libbey-Owens-Ford Co., *supra* note 64.

[68]465 U.S. 555 (1984).

federally aided program.[69] The effect of the *Grove City* decision subsequently was reversed by congressional action over a Presidential veto.[70]

Another issue concerns the damages available to a Title IX plaintiff. In *Lieberman v. University of Chicago,*[71] the District Court for the Northern District of Illinois held that money damages are not available under Title IX and denied the plaintiff damages of moving expenses, loss of consortium, and mental suffering.

An action to compel the FCC to issue rules under § 504 of the Rehabilitation Act of 1973 was dismissed because the court held that broadcast licenses are not a form of federal financial assistance.[72]

## VII. Unemployment Compensation

In North Carolina, an employee can receive unemployment compensation if he quits a job because of his employer's racial discrimination.[73]

---

[69]*Id.* at 574–75; *see also* Consolidated Rail Corp. v. Darrone, 465 U.S. 624, 34 FEP 79 (1984) (ban on discrimination in § 504 of Rehabilitation Act of 1973 is limited to specific program or activities receiving federal financial assistance); Tudyman v. United Airlines, 608 F. Supp. 739, 38 FEP 732 (N.D. Cal. 1984) (summary judgment appropriate for employer in action under § 504 if employer receives no federal financial assistance or if federal assistance is provided for function, activity, or purpose entirely unrelated to plaintiff or in which plaintiff is not involved).

[70]Civil Rights Restoration Act of 1987, Pub. L. No. 100-259, 102 Stat. 28 (1988).

[71]No. 79-C-3533, slip op. (N.D. Ill. Sept. 21, 1980), *aff'd,* 660 F.2d 1185 (7th Cir. 1981), *cert. denied,* 456 U.S. 937 (1982); *accord* Longoria v. Harris, 554 F. Supp. 102, 38 FEP 738 (S.D. Tex. 1982) (remedy under § 504 of Rehabilitation Act of 1973 is limited to injunctive and declaratory relief; money damages, reinstatement with seniority, and return of lost pension benefits not available).

[72]California Ass'n of the Physically Handicapped v. Federal Communications Comm'n, 721 F.2d 667, 33 FEP 802 (9th Cir. 1983), *cert. denied,* 469 U.S. 832, 35 FEP 1608 (1984).

[73]Tastee Freeze Cafeteria v. Watson, 64 N.C. App. 562, 307 S.E.2d 800 (1983); *see also* Cal. Unemployment Ins. Code § 1256.2; Rotert v. Jefferson Fed. Sav. & Loan Ass'n, 623 F. Supp. 1114, 39 FEP 1070 (D. Conn. 1985) (employee who resigned when employer told her she would be transferred collaterally estopped from asserting constructive discharge in violation of ADEA; claim for unemployment benefits rejected by both state court and agency, who found her transfer not disadvantageous enough to justify resignation); Sanchez v. California Unemployment Ins. Appeals Bd. (Tribal Am. Consol. Corp.), 36 Cal.3d 575, 205 Cal. Rptr. 501, 685 P.2d 61, 117 LRRM 3203 (1984) (employee eligible for unemployment insurance if in face of continuing harassment and threatened dismissal for whistleblowing she quits).

# APPENDIX A

## COURTS ALLOWING AND REJECTING PENDENT CLAIMS

*Federal courts allowing pendent claims:* EEOC v. City of Highland Park, 32 EPD ¶ 33,947 (E.D. Mich. 1983) (in ADEA action, complaint amended to include pendent cause of action under state civil rights act); Mahoney v. Crocker Nat'l Bank (Cal.), 571 F. Supp. 287, 32 FEP 1482 (N.D. Cal. 1983) (pendent state claims in ADEA action allowed; various state common law claims preempted by state age discrimination in employment statute); Luna v. City & County of Denver, 537 F. Supp. 798, 31 FEP 1357 (D. Colo. 1982) (intentional infliction of emotional distress claim arose from "nucleus of operative fact" common with claims under Title VII, 42 U.S.C. § 1981, and 42 U.S.C. § 1983); Rio v. Presbyterian Hosp. in New York, 561 F. Supp. 325, 31 FEP 1344 (S.D.N.Y. 1983) (abusive discharge claim permitted as pendent claim to ADEA claim to extent it is "identical" to ADEA claim, except for possibly differing scope of remedy); New York v. Holiday Inns, 35 FEP 1308 (W.D.N.Y. 1984) (pendent claim for intentional infliction of emotional distress not dismissed, even though it might require proof of elements beyond parameters of plaintiffs' Title VII and ADEA claims, since underlying facts were same); Frykberg v. State Farm Mut. Auto. Ins. Co., 557 F. Supp. 517, 32 FEP 575 (W.D.N.C. 1983) (claim for intentional infliction of emotional distress heard in context of Title VII sexual harassment claim); Goodman v. Community College Dist. 524 Bd. of Trustees, 511 F. Supp. 602, 27 FEP 1762 (N.D. Ill. 1981) (state contract claims appended to Title VII and ADEA claims); Palazon v. KFC Nat'l Mgmt. Co., 28 FEP 458 (N.D. Ill. 1981) (defamation claim pendent to Title VII national origin claim); Van Atta v. Kal-Aero, 555 F. Supp. 912, 32 FEP 1627 (W.D. Mich. 1983) (exercising pendent jurisdiction over claim which presented unsettled issues of state law); Langland v. Vanderbilt Univ., 589 F. Supp. 995, 36 FEP 200 (M.D. Tenn. 1984), *aff'd mem.,* 772 F.2d 907, 42 FEP 163 (6th Cir. 1985) (female professor's Title VII claim and state law claim for breach of contract arose out of " 'a common nucleus of operative fact' "); Keenan v. Foley Co., 35 FEP 937 (E.D. Wis. 1984) (claim for intentional infliction of emotional distress dismissed without prejudice, to permit plaintiff to replead; if facts alleged overlap his ADEA claim, court would exercise pendent jurisdiction); Taylor v. Levine, 37 FEP 331 (E.D. N.Y. 1985) (supervisor not dismissed as a defendant since he was proper party under pendent state claim brought under state's human rights act); Blessing v. County of Lancaster, 609 F. Supp. 485, 37 FEP 1721 (E.D. Pa. 1985) (claim for intentional infliction of emotional distress linked to Title VII claim for sexual harassment); Jones v. Cassens Transp., 617 F. Supp. 869, 39 FEP 1341 (E.D. Mich. 1985) (court permitted pendent state claim, even after Title VII claim dismissed on appeal, because claim had been tried); Mathews v. Puerto Rico Maritime Mgmt. Co., 613 F. Supp. 316, 39 FEP 1084 (S.D.N.Y. 1985) (court noted possible application of pendent jurisdiction, but did not exercise it); Wolf v. J.I. Case Co., 617 F. Supp. 858, 38 FEP 1647 (E.D. Wis. 1985) (court exercised pendent jurisdiction); Studint v. LaSalle Ice Cream Co., 623 F. Supp. 232, 39 FEP 1055 (E.D.N.Y. 1985) (court exercised pendent jurisdiction over claims of breach of contract, wrongful termination, intentional infliction of emotional distress, harassment, and fraud, but not over equitable and extraordinary remedies of claims regarding accounting, dissolution, and receivership); Wimberly v. Shoney's, 38 FEP 932 (S.D. Ga. 1985) (court distinguished *Owen Equip. & Erection Co. v. Kroger,* 437 U.S. 365 (1978) and *Aldinger v. Howard,* 427 U.S. 1

(1976), on grounds that these cases were limited to federal court jurisdiction over parties and not claims; court stated that refusal to exercise pendent jurisdiction would require substantially duplicative proceedings in state and federal court); Ibrahim v. New York State Dep't of Health, 581 F. Supp. 228, 38 FEP 1059 (E.D.N.Y. 1984) (but rejected pendent state claim where parallel federal claim dismissed); Collins v. Pfizer, Inc., 39 FEP 1316 (D. Conn. 1985) (court asserted jurisdiction over state claims for wrongful discharge and negligent infliction of emotional distress in Title VII suit); Savage v. Holiday Inn Corp., 603 F. Supp. 311, 37 FEP 328 (D. Nev. 1985) (remedies sought under pendent state law claims not barred because relief available under federal law also sought); Medina v. Spotnail, Inc., 591 F. Supp. 190, 40 FEP 1393 (N.D. Ill. 1984) (no predomination of state issues or novel issues of state law, and no jury confusion because facts similar for all claims); Davis v. United States Steel Corp., 779 F.2d 209, 39 FEP 955 (4th Cir. 1985) (state law claims for wrongful discharge, assault and battery, and intentional infliction of emotional distress could be addressed along with Title VII claim in federal court); Zichy v. City of Philadelphia, 476 F. Supp. 708, 36 FEP 1637 (E.D. Pa. 1979) (plaintiffs entitled to recovery under Title VII, state claims do not constitute body of case, and state courts have eliminated most doubt as to state laws).

*Federal courts rejecting pendent claims:* Wilhelm v. Continental Title Co., 720 F.2d 1173, 33 FEP 385 (10th Cir. 1983), *cert. denied,* 465 U.S. 1103, 34 FEP 416 (1984) (affirming dismissal of private action for handicap discrimination owing to failure to state claim on which relief could be granted, and affirming dismissal of pendent state claim); Bouchet v. National Urban League, 730 F.2d 799, 34 FEP 545 (D.C. Cir. 1984) ("the pendent claims might well become the predominant element of the lawsuit"); Curtis v. Continental Ill. Nat'l Bank, 568 F. Supp. 740, 32 FEP 1540 (N.D. Ill. 1983) (state law claims for unspecified intentional tort dismissed as merely amplifying Title VII claims; other state law claims for employment discrimination based on state constitution dismissed where unsupported by state precedent and because "such complicated and important issues of state law are best left for the state courts," and where plaintiff's state claim would likely be barred by exclusivity of state equal employment statutory procedures she failed to exhaust); Tate v. Pepsi-Cola Metro. Bottling Co., 32 EPD ¶ 33,951 (E.D. Wis. 1983), *aff'd mem.,* 35 EPD ¶ 34,697 (7th Cir. 1984) (state wrongful discharge claim dismissed on ground plaintiff's discharge did not violate clear mandate of public policy); Shestina v. Cotter & Co., 32 FEP 674 (N.D. Ohio 1983) (to assert pendent jurisdiction "would not promote judicial economy, convenience or fairness to all the litigants"); Lazic v. University of Pa., 513 F. Supp. 761, 29 FEP 1652 (E.D. Pa. 1981) (court declined to consider claim for tortious interference with contract in Title VII action because claim would involve issues unclear under state law); Carrillo v. Illinois Bell Tel. Co., 538 F. Supp. 793, 31 FEP 572 (N.D. Ill. 1982) (state claim of discriminatory discharge denied consideration where not clear whether it stated cause of action under state law); Marchetti v. Atlas Powder Co., 520 F. Supp. 271, 28 FEP 563 (E.D. Pa. 1981) (claims involved different legal and factual issues, and penalties for willful violation of ADEA were "akin" to damages for state claim for intentional infliction of emotional distress); Lettich v. Kenway, 590 F. Supp. 1225, 35 FEP 1289 (D. Mass. 1984) (state law claims involve complex issues of law reaching far beyond ADEA, creating "likelihood of jury confusion"; ADEA is an exclusive remedy, rendering court powerless to award relief under other legal theories); Ritter v. Colorado Interstate Gas Co., 593 F. Supp. 1279, 39 FEP 1364 (D. Colo. 1984) (no state court had previously recognized causes of action alleged by plaintiff); Davis v. Devereux Found., 644 F. Supp. 482, 40 FEP 1560 (E.D. Pa. 1986) (additional issues would delay progress of entire case and preclude assignment of case to master for expedited review); Brooms v. Regal Tube Co., 40 FEP 1766 (N.D. Ill. 1986) (intentional infliction of emotional distress claim would complicate Title VII claim); Torowski v. United Parcel Serv., 40 FEP 1472 (N.D. Ohio 1986) (court dismissed state age discrimination claim where federal claim dismissed before trial); Arnell v. Pan Am. World Airways, 611 F. Supp. 908, 38 FEP 1451 (S.D.N.Y. 1985) (court dismissed state claims which raised issues and involved proof that differed from federal claims); Shirley v. Brown & Williamson Tobacco Co., 608 F. Supp. 78, 44 FEP 218 (E.D. Tenn. 1984) (consideration of state claim would widen scope of recovery beyond limits of federal statute); Baer v. R&F Coal Co., 782 F.2d 600, 39 FEP 1764 (6th Cir. 1986) (court affirmed denial of leave to amend complaint to add state age discrimination claim where federal claim under ADEA had already been dismissed, even though plaintiff's motion for reconsideration was still pending); Mason v. Richmond Motor Co., 625 F. Supp. 883, 39 FEP 1359 (E.D. Va. 1986), aff'd, 825 F.2d 407 (1987) (more than loose factual connection is necessary before court should assert jurisdiction over pendent state claims); Anderson v. Wisconsin Gas Co., 619 F. Supp. 635, 39 FEP 1394 (E.D. Wis. 1985) (wrongful discharge and emotional distress declined, where defendant won summary judgment on Title VII claim); Garcia v. Kroger Co. dba Kroger Family Center, 40 FEP 1319 (S.D. Tex. 1985) (pendent state claims unknown to court; plaintiff granted leave to file amended complaint deleting them); Duva v. Bridgeport Textron, 632 F. Supp. 880, 40 FEP 1388 (E.D. Pa. 1985) (state tort claims (1) involved evidence not related to Title VII claims, (2) called for relief unavailable under Title VII, (3) required resolution of unsettled state law, and (4) named individuals not respondents to EEOC charge); Zabkowicz v. Dart Indus., West Bend Co. Div., 789 F.2d 540, 40 FEP 1171 (7th Cir. 1986) (pendent tort claims against co-workers rejected because parties stipulated to sever those claims from Title VII action); Wescott v. Wackenhut Corp., 581 F. Supp. 9, 38 FEP 983 (S.D. Cal. 1983) (state claims dismissed because scope of remedies for them would predominate federal claims; also, court intimated that asserting jurisdiction would be inconsistent with congressional intent); Frye v. Pioneer Logging Mach., 555 F. Supp. 730, 38 FEP 926 (D.S.C. 1983) (same); Haroldson v. Hospitality Sys. dba Fafaels, 596 F. Supp. 1460, 38 FEP 931 (D. Colo. 1984) (same); Durso v. John Wanamaker, 38 FEP 1127 (E.D. Pa. 1985) (state statute might permit greater relief than Title VII; unsettled nature of state law alternative reason not to assert pendent jurisdiction); Redenbaugh v. Valero Energy Corp., 603 F. Supp. 138, 38 FEP 1495 (W.D. Tex. 1985) (addition of state claims with their corresponding proofs of damages would expand issues and frustrate express intent of Congress to expedite Title VII claims); Chavez v. Guaranty Bank & Trust Co., 607 F. Supp. 484, 39 FEP 1371 (D. Colo. 1985) (same); Pfeiffer v. William Wrigley Jr. Co., 139 Ill. App.3d 320, 484 N.E.2d 1187, 39 FEP 246 (1985) (state law action not barred by federal district court's dismissal of ADEA action, even though it constituted final judgment on merits, since same evidence would not sustain both actions; federal court could not assert jurisdiction over state law claim).

# APPENDIX B

## AT-WILL DOCTRINE: SAMPLING OF JUDICIAL APPROACHES ADOPTED BY STATE COURTS

*Alabama:* Johnson v. Gary dba B&N Steakhouse, 443 So.2d 924, 116 LRRM 3405 (Ala. 1983) (court's adherence to employment-at-will doctrine reaffirmed; as to plaintiff's claim of tortious interference with efforts to receive unemployment compensation benefits, Ala. Code § 25-4-96 (1975) provides exclusive remedy for determinations regarding unemployment compensation); Scott v. Lane, 409 So.2d 791, 115 LRRM 4233 (Ala. 1982) (relinquishment of former job for promise of permanent employment may be sufficient consideration to preclude employment-at-will); Peters v. Alabama Power Co., 440 So.2d 1028, 114 LRRM 3482 (Ala. 1983) (oral contract providing for termination only "for cause" precludes summary judgment for defendant based upon at-will defense); Bates v. Jim Walter Resources, 418 So.2d 903, 115 LRRM 4027 (Ala. 1982) (since offer of employment contained no term or duration, contract was terminable at will even though employee gave up old job—equitable estoppel rejected); Jordan v. Mallard Exploration, 423 So.2d 896 (Ala. 1982) (employer not liable for damages to terminated permanent employee where employer closed operations); Willis v. Ideal Basic Indus., 484 So.2d 444 (Ala. 1986) (where plaintiff *accused* of sexual harassment did not identify any particular public policy issue, court rejected his plea for narrow public policy exception to at-will doctrine); Barton v. Alabama Elec. Coop., 487 So.2d 884 (Ala. 1986) (complaint properly dismissed because wrongful termination claim barred by at-will doctrine); McCluskey v. Unicare Health Facility, 484 So.2d 398 (Ala. 1986) (neither employee handbook nor alleged oral representations regarding it create contract limiting employment at will; plaintiff unsuccessfully cited *Peters*); White v. Chelsea Indus., 425 So.2d 1090 (Ala. 1983) (employee handbook does not create implied contract in derogation of at-will employment).

*Alaska:* Mitford v. de Lasala, 666 P.2d 1000, 115 LRRM 4254 (Alaska 1983) (plaintiff has cause of action for breach of implied covenant of good faith and fair dealing where, under his employment contract, he was a profit sharer and corporation fired him to prevent his collecting his share of profits); Knight v. American Guard & Alert, 714 P.2d 788 (Alaska 1986) (plaintiff has causes of action for termination in violation of public policy, breach of implied covenant of good faith and fair dealing, and termination not based on good or just cause); Schneider v. Pay 'N' Save Corp., 723 P.2d 619 (Alaska 1986) (handbook constitutes part of employment agreement).

*Arizona:* Leikvold v. Valley View Hosp., 141 Ariz. 544, 688 P.2d 170, 116 LRRM 2193 (1984) (employer's representations in personnel manual can be incorporated into employment contract and thus limit employer's ability to terminate at will); Wagenseller v. Scottsdale Memorial Hosp., 147 Ariz. 370, 710 P.2d 1025, 119 LRRM 3166 (1985) ("[A]n employer may fire for a good cause or for no cause. He may not fire for bad cause—that which violates public policy"); Vermillion v. AAA Pro Moving & Storage, 146 Ariz. 215, 704 P.2d 1360, 119 LRRM 2337 (1985).

*Arkansas:* Jackson v. Kinark Corp. dba Camelot Hotel, 282 Ark. 5, 669 S.W.2d 898, 117 LRRM 3374 (1984) (without deciding, court indicated that employee handbook may give rise to employment contract for indefinite term); Gaulden v. Emerson Elec. Co., 284 Ark. 149, 680 S.W.2d 92, 117 LRRM 3375 (1984) (court "will reexamine the [at-will] doctrine when presented with a case in which the contract of employment provides for discharge only for cause and the employee is discharged arbitrarily or in bad faith"); Harris v. Arkansas Book Co., 287 Ark. 353, 700 S.W.2d 41, 121 LRRM 2117 (1985) (if contract of employment was for more than one year, it must be reduced to writing, and since there was none, employment was at-will).

    *California:* Foley v. Interactive Data Corp., 47 Cal.3d 654, 254 Cal. Rptr. 211, 3 IER 1729 (Cal. S.Ct. 1988) (reaffirms tort cause of action for discharge contrary to fundamental public policy declared in *Tameny v. Atlantic Richfield Co., infra,* 3 IER at 1731–34; leaves open question whether constitutional or statutory basis must be shown for public policy in cause of action for discharge contrary to public policy, *id.* at 1733; holds cause of action for discharge contrary to public policy not sufficiently alleged in instant case, *id.* at 1734; recognizes causes of action for discharge contrary to implied-in-fact contract for nonarbitrary treatment as declared in *Pugh v. See's Candies, infra,* where factors including reasonable reliance on employment practices are alleged, *id.* at 1737–41, and for discharge in violation of covenant of good faith and fair dealing, *id.* at 1741–51 rejects statute of frauds defense to claim under implied or oral agreement to discharge only for cause, *id.* at 1735–37; holds that remedies for breach of implied covenant shall be limited to contract measures, *id.* at 1749; leaves open extent of contract remedy, *id.* at 1741 n.24, and question whether court's decision applies only prospectively, *id.* at 1752 n.43; disapproves wholly or partly several prior California decisions including *Koehrer v. California Superior Court, infra, Khanna v. Microdata Corp., infra,* and tort recovery analysis in *Cleary v. American Airlines, infra*) (see *supra* discussion in text); Tameny v. Atlantic Richfield Co., 27 Cal.3d 167, 164 Cal. Rptr. 839, 610 P.2d 1330, 115 LRRM 3119 (1980) (tort damages recoverable for discharge contrary to public policy, based on discharge allegedly for employee's refusal to comply with purported order to violate antitrust laws by fixing retail gasoline prices); Cleary v. American Airlines, 111 Cal.App.3d 443, 168 Cal. Rptr. 722, 115 LRRM 3030 (1980) (employee's long service and existence of unilateral grievance procedure supported implied covenant of good faith and fair dealing which would be violated by discharge allegedly for union organizing activities); Pugh v. See's Candies, 116 Cal.App.3d 311, 329, 171 Cal. Rptr. 917, 927, 115 LRRM 4002 (1981) (Pugh I) *and* 250 Cal. Rptr. 195, 3 IER 945 (1988) (Pugh II) (*Pugh II* affirmed trial court judgment for defendant on implied covenant claim recognized in *Pugh I; Pugh I* acknowledged implied-in-fact contract for nonarbitrary treatment, based on facts including "the duration of [the plaintiff's] employment, the commendations and promotions he received, the apparent lack of any direct criticism of his work, the assurances he was given, and the employer's acknowledged policies, all reflecting 'the totality of the parties' relationship' "; *Pugh II* held, *inter alia,* that specific acts of misconduct by plaintiff were relevant and admissible to show plaintiff's character or personality in the workplace, which was in issue where plaintiff held a managerial position and his "ability to work well with the president of the company and with other administrative staff was crucial to its success," *id,* 250 Cal. Rptr. at 204; "[i]n any free enterprise system, an employer must have wide latitude in making independent, good-faith judgments about high-ranking employees without the threat of a jury second-guessing its business judgment," *id.* at 213; "measuring the effective performance of such an employee involves consideration of many intangible attributes such as personality, initiative, ability to function as part of the management team and to motivate subordinates, and the ability to conceptualize and effectuate management style and goals." *Id.;* decision also contains discussion of "bad-faith discharge" actions under *Koehrer v. California Superior Court, infra,* which must be reconsidered in light of California Supreme Court decision in *Foley v. Interactive Data Corp., supra*); Hillsman v. Sutter Community Hosps. of Sacramento, 153 Cal.App.3d 743, 200 Cal. Rptr. 605, 119 LRRM 2645 (1984) (statement in offer letter that employee "looked forward to a long, pleasant, and mutually satisfactory relationship" was simply touch of personal warmth and did not constitute promise to terminate only for cause); Newfield v. Insurance Co. of the W., 156 Cal.App.3d 440, 203 Cal. Rptr.

9, 119 LRRM 2517 (1984) (promise of "permanent" employment, standing alone, not sufficient to create promise not to terminate without just cause); Shapiro v. Wells Fargo Realty Advisors, 152 Cal.App.3d 467, 199 Cal. Rptr. 613, 119 LRRM 2520 (1984) (employee of 3½ years failed to plead existence of either long service or breach of personnel policies, two prerequisites for establishing implied-in-law covenant of good faith and fair dealing); Brandt v. Lockheed Missiles & Space Co., 154 Cal.App.3d 1124, 201 Cal. Rptr. 746 (1984) (trial court award to plaintiffs reversed; implied covenant of good faith and fair dealing cannot be construed to supersede express terms of contract which provide company is *not* obligated to grant special invention award); Crosier v. United Parcel Serv., 150 Cal.App.3d 1132, 198 Cal. Rptr. 361, 115 LRRM 3585 (1983) (employer's business interests and employee's interest in maintaining his employment must be balanced in determining what constitutes "good cause"; summary judgment for defendant upheld where employee was dismissed for violating nonfraternization policy); Rulon-Miller v. IBM Corp., 162 Cal.App.3d 241, 208 Cal. Rptr. 524, *modified,* 162 Cal.App.3d 11816, 117 LRRM 3309 (1984) (covenant of good faith and fair dealing requires employer to treat like cases alike and to follow company rules and regulations adopted for employee's protection); Tyco Indus. v. California Superior Court, 164 Cal.App.3d 148, 211 Cal. Rptr. 540 (1985) (cause of action exists for discharge which is contrary to public policy under Labor Code § 970—employers may not coerce employees to relocate by misrepresenting terms of employment; plaintiff's case dismissed for failure to substantiate such cause); Clutterham v. Coachmen Indus., 169 Cal.App.3d 1223, 215 Cal. Rptr. 795 (1985) (even an implied promise of continued employment is only a promise not to terminate without "some good reason"); Khanna v. Microdata Corp., 170 Cal.App.3d 250, 215 Cal. Rptr. 860, 120 LRRM 2152 (1985) (covenant of good faith and fair dealing is breached whenever employer engages in "bad faith" action extraneous to employment contract with intent to frustrate employee's enjoyment of contract rights; analysis of bad-faith discharge claim must be reconsidered in light of *Foley v. Interactive Data Corp., supra,* in which this decision was disapproved); Gray v. California Superior Court (Cipher Data Prods.), 181 Cal.App.3d 813, 226 Cal. Rptr. 570 (1986) (when employer violates its own internal policy, breach of covenant of good faith and fair dealing occurs, but violation of public policy does not); Koehrer v. California Superior Court (Oak Riverside Jurupa, Ltd.), 181 Cal.App.3d 1155, 226 Cal. Rptr. 820 (1986) (plaintiffs have cause of action for breach of covenant of good faith and fair dealing where they had complied with terms of employment agreement and were discharged without cause; citing *Khanna* and *Seaman's Direct Buying Serv. v. Standard Oil Co. of Cal.,* 36 Cal.3d 752, 206 Cal. Rptr. 354, 686 P.2d 1158 (1984); analysis of bad-faith discharge claim must be reconsidered in light of *Foley v. Interactive Data Corp., supra,* in which this decision was disapproved); Gianaculus v. Trans World Airlines, 761 F.2d 1391, 119 LRRM 3246 (9th Cir. 1985) (statement in employment application that employment may be terminated "at any time without advance notice and without liability" construed as express contract for employment at will; court refused to construe provisions of personnel manual so as to contradict express contract and found that economic layoff did not violate duty of good faith and fair dealing); Burton v. Security Pac. Nat'l Bank, 197 Cal.App.3d 972, 243 Cal. Rptr. 277 (1988) (summary judgment proper where plaintiff relied solely on conjecture and speculation to support his claim that employer's stated reason was pretext for some other impermissible reason; even if former employee had not engaged in misconduct as charged by employer, implied covenant of good faith is not breached where employer believed in good faith and with probable cause that charge was true).

    *Colorado:* Rawson v. Sears, Roebuck & Co., 530 F. Supp. 776, 31 FEP 1350, 119 LRRM 2670 (D. Colo. 1982), *later proceedings,* 554 F. Supp. 327, 31 FEP 1354 (D. Colo. 1983), 585 F. Supp. 1393, 35 FEP 113 (D. Colo. 1984), 615 F. Supp. 1546, 1553, 38 FEP 1392, 1398 (D. Colo. 1985), *rev'd,* 822 F.2d 908, 44 FEP 191 (10th Cir. 1987), *cert. denied,* —U.S.—, 45 FEP 1080 *and* 45 FEP 1256 (1988) (complaint alleged defendant had earlier promised plaintiff "would have a job * * * until his retirement" and, stated claim in promissory estoppel but Colorado held not to recognize "wrongful discharge" claim absent express agreement as to length of employment; jury verdict of $19,096,495.01 for plaintiff after trial of Colorado state law claim for age discrimination; Tenth Circuit reversed, on grounds age claim preempted by exclusive remedy in Colorado statute imposing fine from $100 to $250 for discharging employees solely because of age).

*Connecticut:* Magnan v. Anaconda Indus., 193 Conn. 558, 479 A.2d 281, 117 LRRM 2163 (1984) (employee cannot maintain cause of action in contract for breach of implied covenant of good faith and fair dealing based wholly upon discharge without just cause); Kilbride v. Dushkin Publishing Group, 186 Conn. 718, 443 A.2d 922, 115 LRRM 4927 (1982) (claim of employees that manager procured their discharge desiring to employ them in his own secretly planned competing business held, by trial court, not within narrow public policy exception to employment-at-will doctrine; appeal dismissed on procedural grounds); Sheets v. Teddy's Frosted Foods, 179 Conn. 471, 427 A.2d 385, 115 LRRM 4626 (1980) (expressly limits circumstances under which employee may successfully challenge dismissal to those discharges which involve impropriety derived from violation of important public policy); D'Ulisse-Cupo v. Board of Directors, Notre Dame High School, 6 Conn. App. 153, 503 A.2d 1192, *cert. granted,* 199 Conn. 806, 508 A.2d 32 (1986) (plaintiff stated cause of action in promissory estoppel where employer made implied promise to fire only for cause); Finley v. Aetna Life & Casualty Co., 5 Conn. 802, 501 A.2d 1213 (1985), *rev'd and remanded,* 202 Conn. 190, 520 A.2d 208 (1987) (although general verdict for defendant must be sustained under procedural circumstances of this case, trial court erred in instructing jury (1) that statute of frauds barred consideration of employer's oral representations in determining whether employment contract existed, and (2) that employment contract could not be found solely from an employment manual; employers can avoid jury trial of existence of contract based on employment manual by avoiding language suggesting contractual purpose and by including disclaimers of intention to contract); Cook v. Alexander & Alexander of Conn., 40 Conn. Supp. 246, 488 A.2d 1295 (Conn. Super. Ct. 1985) (unpaid bonuses and vesting rights constitute unpaid wages under Connecticut statute; since statute represents public policy against withholding wages, plaintiff "sufficiently alleged a wrongful discharge within the contemplation of *Sheets*"; court also followed *Magnan, supra,* where implied covenant of good faith and fair dealing was breached when "the challenged discharge is allegedly related to the withholding of wages"); Sivell v. Conwed Corp., 605 F. Supp. 1265 (D. Conn. 1985) (court denied motion to dismiss plaintiff's state law claims that handbook created implied-in-fact contract); Saller v. GAB Business Servs., Civil Action No. N-84-237 (D. Conn. Apr. 25, 1985) (plaintiff claimed handbook provisions for equal employment opportunities free of sexual discrimination had been breached; court concluded plaintiff had viable state law claim if pleaded as breach of express or implied-in-fact contract, instead of breach of covenant of good faith and fair dealing); Lincoln v. Sterling Drug Co., 622 F. Supp. 66 (D. Conn. 1985) (once employer issues handbook without appropriate disclaimers against employee reliance, it cannot later selectively alter its provisions; court denied defendant's motion to dismiss claim for breach of implied contract).

*Delaware:* Heideck v. Kent Gen. Hosp., 446 A.2d 1095, 115 LRRM 4203 (Del. 1982) (booklet constituting "unilateral expression of [employer's] policies and procedures * * * issued for the guidance and benefit of employees" does not grant employee specific term of employment altering at-will status); Reiver v. Murdoch & Walsh, P.A., 625 F. Supp. 998, 118 LRRM 2238 (D. Del. 1985) (adheres to at-will rule); Avallone v. Wilmington Medical Center, 553 F. Supp. 931, 115 LRRM 4941 (D. Del. 1982) (employee handbooks do not alter at-will rule).

*Florida:* Forde v. Royal's, 537 F. Supp. 1173, 31 FEP 213 (S.D. Fla. 1982) (since "it is well-settled under Florida law that employment agreements are terminable at the will of either the employer or the employee unless the agreement contains a definite term of employment," employee failed to state common law claim on which relief could be granted by alleging discharge for refusal to submit to supervisor's sexual advances); Muller v. Stromberg Carlson Corp., 427 So.2d 266, 115 LRRM 3447 (Fla. Dist. Ct. App. 1983) ("Florida law does not reflect those views which appear to be based upon perception of social or economic policies thought to be beneficial"; the "settled law in Florida [is] that an employment contract which is indefinite as to term of employment is terminable at the will of either party without cause"; policy statements do not give rise to enforceable contracts); Lewis v. Compton, 416 So.2d 1219, *petition denied,* 416 So.2d 1219 (Fla. Dist. Ct. App.), *review denied,* 424 So.2d 760 (Fla. 1982) (as "an employee who could be terminated at-will, his subsequent discharge, even if wrongful, will not serve as a basis for either compensatory or punitive damages"); Hamlen v. Fairchild Indus., 413 So.2d 800 (Fla. Dist. Ct. App. 1982) (allegation of fraudulent misrepresentation of permanent job, coupled with no intent to perform, was actionable); Roy Jorgensen Assocs. v. Deschenes, 449 So.2d 1188, 115 LRRM 4917 (Fla. Dist. Ct. App. 1982) (letter confirming offer of employment and stating "on or about October 31 you will be assigned to our * * * project in the capacity of * * * for a period of 28 months" held merely language of expectation and not contract for specific term).

*Georgia:* Gunn v. Hawaiian Airlines, 162 Ga. App. 474, 291 S.E.2d 779, 115 LRRM 4203 (1982) (terminated probationary employee did not have tort or breach of contract action against employer based on implicit good-faith or public policy requirement); Hall v. Answering Serv., 161 Ga. App. 874, 289 S.E.2d 533, 115 LRRM 4677 (1982) (suit for wrongful discharge properly dismissed since employment was terminable at will).

*Hawaii:* Parnar v. Americana Hotels, 65 Haw. 370, 652 P.2d 625, 115 LRRM 4817 (1982) (allegation that employee was discharged in order to prevent her testimony before grand jury sufficient to state cause of action for retaliatory discharge under public policy exception to employment-at-will doctrine).

*Illinois:* Smith v. World Book-Childcraft Int'l, 31 FEP 457 (N.D. Ill. 1982) (employer's summary judgment motion denied where terminated employee alleged he was not given clear warning of action taken by employer or opportunity for remediation which he alleged was given to other employees whose managerial skills were said to be deficient); Meyers v. Prudential-Bache Secs., No. 85-C-7977, slip op. (N.D. Ill. Dec. 16, 1985) (claim for breach of implied contract sustained, where employment manual imposed obligations on both employee and employer). *But see* Scott v. Sears, Roebuck & Co., 605 F. Supp. 1047, 37 FEP 878 (N.D. Ill. 1985), *aff'd,* 798 F.2d 210, 41 FEP 805 (7th Cir. 1986) (no implied covenant of good faith and fair dealing in at-will employment); Enis v. Continental Ill. Nat'l Bank & Trust Co. of Chicago, 582 F. Supp. 876, 116 LRRM 2047 (N.D. Ill. 1984), *aff'd,* 795 F.2d 39, 1 IER 499 (7th Cir. 1986) (Posner, J.) (applying Illinois law, Seventh Circuit holds employer did not violate conditions in employment manual "even if, as we greatly doubt, those conditions are enforceable under the law of Illinois." *Id.,* 795 F.2d at 42; "* * * purpose of an employment manual is to explain the rules of employment to the employee—not to confer tenure, or arm the employee with grounds for suing the employer if the latter fails to follow the rules in the manual to the letter." *Id.* at 40)

*Indiana:* Morgan Drive Away v. Brant, 479 N.E.2d 1336 (Ind. Ct. App. 1985), *rev'd,* 489 N.E.2d 933, 122 LRRM 2130 (Ind. 1986) (termination for filing small claims action against employer does not violate public policy; at-will doctrine is "public policy of this state"); Hamblen v. Danner's, 478 N.E.2d 926, 119 LRRM 3470 (Ind. Ct. App. 1985) (at-will doctrine reaffirmed; termination for refusal to take polygraph examination not violation of public policy); Rice v. Grant County Bd. of Comm'rs, 472 N.E.2d 213, 118 LRRM 2822 (Ind. Ct. App. 1984) (at-will status is not affirmative defense that employer must raise); Mead Johnson & Co. v. Oppenheimer, 458 N.E.2d 668, 115 LRRM 3684 (Ind. Ct. App. 1984) (discharge for cutting off thumbs of pair of work gloves upheld since at-will employee could be discharged for any reason or no reason; company handbook immaterial absent enforceable employment agreement for definite duration); Eby v. Borg-Warner,

York Div., 455 N.E.2d 623 (Ind. Ct. App. 1983) (summary judgment for employer on promissory estoppel theory reversed); Pepsi-Cola Gen. Bottlers v. Woods, 440 N.E.2d 696, 115 LRRM 4450 (Ind. Ct. App. 1982) (at-will employee stated cause of action for promissory estoppel when plaintiff quit former job upon promise of employment); Moffett v. Gene B. Glick Co., 621 F. Supp. 244, 41 FEP 671 (N.D. Ind. 1985) (at-will employee's claim for wrongful discharge sustained where employee was discharged in retaliation for filing charge of racial harassment); Rollins v. American State Bank, 487 N.E.2d 842 (Ind. Ct. App. 1986) (continued employment, even though at will, constituted consideration to support noncompetition agreement); Ewing v. Pulaski Memorial Hosp. Bd. of Trustees, 486 N.E.2d 1094 (Ind. Ct. App. 1985) (rate of pay does not establish employment duration); Streckfus v. Gardenside Terrace Coop., 504 N.E.2d 273 (Ind. 1987) (Indiana Supreme Court declines to abandon general rule of construction presuming employment contracts for indefinite term are terminable at will of either party; assuming arguendo that parties intended to require "sufficient reason" for termination and approval by board of directors, summary judgment was properly granted to employer because board was informed of information upon which decision could be made).

*Kentucky:* Firestone Textile Co. v. Meadows, 666 S.W.2d 730 (Ky. 1983) (public policy exceptions to at-will rule recognized when discharge violates employee's constitutionally or statutorily protected right); McCarthy v. KFC Corp., 607 F. Supp. 343 (W.D. Ky. 1985) (state will recognize tort of outrage and will award damages for emotional distress in connection with discharge); Shah v. American Synthetic Rubber Corp., 655 S.W.2d 489, 114 LRRM 3343 (Ky. 1983) (oral contract to terminate only "for cause," in accordance with employer's personnel policies, was enforceable).

*Maine:* Wyman v. Osteopathic Hosp. of Me., 493 A.2d 330, 119 LRRM 3438 (1985) (employer could properly dismiss plaintiff for any good cause, as permitted in employee handbook).

*Massachusetts:* Gram v. Liberty Mut. Ins. Co., 384 Mass. 659, 429 N.E.2d 21, 115 LRRM 4152 (1981), *appeal after remand,* 391 Mass. 333, 461 N.E.2d 796, 118 LRRM 2401 (1984) (absence of good cause not necessarily absence of good faith) (reversing and remanding $325,000 jury verdict for plaintiff, on grounds that damages improperly included factors not relevant to recovery by at-will employee of clearly identifiable future compensation, reflective of past services).

*Michigan: See* Section IV.E in text. *See also* Ford v. Blue Cross/Blue Shield, 50 Mich. App. 462 (Mich. Ct. App. 1986) (policy providing for predischarge hearing does not alter express at-will status); Reid v. Sears, Roebuck & Co., 790 F.2d 453, 122 LRRM 2153 (6th Cir. 1986) (providing list of disciplinary rules does not negate express at-will relationship); Kay v. United Technologies Corp., 757 F.2d 100, 118 LRRM 3335 (6th Cir. 1985) (existence of evaluation procedure not sufficient to establish just-cause contract).

*Minnesota:* Pine River State Bank v. Mettille, 333 N.W.2d 622, 115 LRRM 4493 (Minn. 1983) (employee handbook constituted binding contract of employment); Fitzgerald v. Norwest Corp., 382 N.W.2d 290 (Minn. Ct. App. 1986) (state court of appeals found equal employment/affirmative action policy in handbook sufficient in addition to statutory rights to form contractual basis for nondiscrimination).

*Mississippi:* Shaw v. Burchfield, 481 So.2d 247, 254 (Miss. 1985) ("Were this a case where no employment contract established expressly the ground rules for termination and where the employer was calling upon the state to furnish the law which authorized termination, we might well be charged to reconsider the at will termination rule.").

*Missouri:* Amaan v. City of Eureka, Mo., 615 S.W.2d 414, 115 LRRM 4584 (Mo.) (en banc), *cert. denied,* 454 U.S. 1084, 115 LRRM 5195 (1981) (upholding at-will doctrine).

*Montana:* Gates v. Life of Mont. Ins. Co., 196 Mont. 178, 668 P.2d 213, 115 LRRM 4350 (1983), *appeal after remand,* 638 P.2d 1063, 118 LRRM 2071 (Mont.

1982) (while employee handbook distributed two years after hiring does not become part of employee's contract, covenant of good faith and fair dealing is implied in employment contracts and breach of covenant is tort for which punitive damages can be recovered) (reversing j.n.o.v. and holding that jury should determine whether fraud, oppression, or malice existed as basis for punitive damages).

*Nebraska:* Alford v. Life Savers, 210 Neb. 441, 315 N.W.2d 260, 115 LRRM 4066 (1982) (relying on at-will doctrine and noting that employee did not allege right to continued employment, court upheld dismissal of action where employee alleged employer discharged him without cause and was negligent in failing to investigate discharge and properly control employee's supervisor); Serafin v. City of Lexington, Neb., 547 F. Supp. 1118, 115 LRRM 5151 (D. Neb. 1982), *aff'd,* 716 F.2d 909 (8th Cir. 1983) (public employer's manual created mutual expectation that employment would continue unless cause for discharge was given, thus giving rise to constitutionally protected property interest in continued employment); Morris v. Lutheran Medical Center, 215 Neb. 677, 340 N.W.2d 388, 115 LRRM 4966 (1983) (implied contract based on written termination and grievance procedures); Jeffers v. Bishop Clarkson Memorial Hosp., 222 Neb. 829, 387 N.W.2d 692, 1 IER 621 (1986).

*Nevada:* Southwest Gas Corp. v. Ahmad, 99 Nev. 594, 668 P.2d 261, 114 LRRM 2633 (1983) (although discharge justified, employee entitled to damages for breach of oral employment contract when he was discharged without notice where handbook specifically required notice).

*New Hampshire:* Cloutier v. Great Atl. & Pac. Tea Co., 121 N.H. 915, 436 A.2d 1140, 115 LRRM 4329 (1981) (trial court's denial of employer's motion for directed verdict upheld; employee had met two-part test for wrongful discharge: (1) employer was motivated by bad faith, malice, or retaliation; and (2) employee was discharged because he performed act that public policy would encourage, or refused to do something that public policy would condemn, regardless of whether there exists statutory expression of public policy; existence of "public policy" is an appropriate jury question).

*New Jersey:* Cappiello v. Ragen Precision Indus., 192 N.J. Super. 523, 471 A.2d 432, 115 LRRM 3410 (App. Div. 1984) (commission salesman proved wrongful discharge and was entitled to punitive damages when he showed employer's representatives fired him in order to expropriate his right to accrued commissions); Kalman v. Grand Union Co., 183 N.J. Super. 153, 443 A.2d 728, 115 LRRM 4803 (1982) (trial court's grant of summary judgment reversed; if pharmacist's discharge resulted from reasons alleged, it conflicted with statutory and regulatory scheme and with pharmacists' professional code of ethics); Woolley v. Hoffman-LaRoche, 99 N.J. 284, 491 A.2d 1257, 119 LRRM 2380 (1985) (cause of action for breach of contract based upon implied promise that employees will be fired only for cause contained in provisions of employer's personnel manual; manual did not include an express disclaimer); Guidice v. Drew Chem. Co., 210 N.J. Super. 32, 509 A.2d 200, 1 IER 1465, *cert. denied,* 104 N.J. 465, 517 A.2d 449, 1 IER 1800 (1986) (App. Div. 1986) (discharged employee may maintain cause of action for wrongful discharge on theory of breach of implied contract of employment allegedly arising out of policy statements, manuals, memoranda, and past practices of employer).

*New York: Compare* Weiner v. McGraw-Hill, 57 N.Y.2d 458, 457 N.Y.S.2d 193, 443 N.E.2d 441, 118 LRRM 2689 (1982) (recognizing breach of contract action based on oral statements and employee handbook) *and* Gorrill v. Icelandair/Flugleidir, 761 F.2d 847, 119 LRRM 2505 (2d Cir. 1985) ("Operations Manual," which provided seniority would be sole factor in discharges during reductions in force and job elimination, limited employer's ability to discharge at will) *with* Murphy v. American Home Prods. Corp., 58 N.Y.2d 293, 461 N.Y.S.2d 232, 448 N.E.2d 86, 31 FEP 782 (1983) (tort cause of action for wrongful discharge, absent constitutional or statutory prohibitions or express agreement, rejected; issue should be resolved by legislature), O'Connor v. Eastman Kodak Co., 65 N.Y.2d 724, 492 N.Y.S.2d 9, 481 N.E.2d 549, 119 LRRM 3415 (1985) (absent express agreement, employer has right to terminate at-will employee at any time, for any or no reason; popular perception of employer as "womb to tomb" did not limit at-will employment), Sabetay v. Sterling Drug, 114 A.D.2d 6, 497 N.Y.S.2d 655 121 LRRM 2716 (1986) (not every statement regarding termination contained in personnel manual creates binding contract—there must be express statement that an employee will not be terminated without just cause), Patrowich v. Chemical Bank, 98 A.D.2d 318, 470 N.Y.S.2d 599, aff'd, 63 N.Y.2d 541, 483 N.Y.S.2d 659, 473 N.E.2d 11 (1984) (employment manual does not alter at-will rule where it contains no provision requiring termination only for good cause), Leahy v. Federal Express Corp., 609 F. Supp. 668 (E.D.N.Y. 1985) (even if employer "violated the spirit and letter" of its employment manual and personnel procedures, plaintiff's claim for breach of contract is legally insufficient where there is no evidence of any "express limitation" on employer's right to terminate its employees at will), Salanger v. US Air, 560 F. Supp. 202, 115 LRRM 4545 (N.D.N.Y. 1983) (denying summary judgment), 611 F. Supp. 427, 119 LRRM 2213 (N.D.N.Y. 1985) (findings of fact and conclusions of law after trial) (finding analysis of contractual restrictions on discharge in *Weiner v. McGraw-Hill, supra,* inapplicable because defendant had not limited its authority to terminate plaintiff's employment as required in *Murphy v. American Home Prods. Corp., supra*); Oakley v. St. Joseph's Hosp., 116 A.D.2d 911, 498 N.Y.S.2d 218 (3d Dep't 1986) (employer's handbook, which imposed only supervisory guidelines, did not create contract to discharge only for good cause) *and* Carlton v. Interfaith Medical Center, 612 F. Supp. 118, 39 FEP 1477, 119 LRRM 3314 (E.D.N.Y. 1985) (plaintiff's claim under *Weiner* must fail where she was not induced to forego other employment in reliance on assurances of job security, and alleged representations of job security were not contained in any employee handbook or manual).

*North Carolina:* Griffin v. Housing Auth. of Durham, 62 N.C. App. 556, 303 S.E.2d 200, 119 LRRM 2107 (1983) (unless employment contract expressly incorporates employer's personnel policies, employer need not follow those policies in dismissing at-will employee).

*Ohio:* Hedrick v. Center for Comprehensive Alcoholism Treatment, 7 Ohio App.3d 211, 454 N.E.2d 1343 (1982) (claims of breach of employment contract and promissory estoppel state cause of action where based upon employee handbook and policy statements regarding disciplinary and grievance procedures); Ackman v. Ohio Knife Co., 589 F. Supp. 768, 41 FEP 1006 (S.D. Ohio 1984) (employer's promise that employees would retain seniority rights if they accepted jobs as foremen states cause of action for promissory estoppel, avoiding at-will defense); Stearns v. Ohio Sav. Ass'n, 15 Ohio App.3d 18, 472 N.E.2d 372 (1984) (employee's affidavit that he relied on promise of stipulated annual salary and hiring responsibility in leaving other employment and accepting position avoided at-will defense and precluded summary judgment in favor of employer); Helle v. Landmark, Inc., 15 Ohio App.3d 1, 472 N.E.2d 765, 118 LRRM 2325 (1984) (at-will doctrine is no defense to claim for severance benefits based on oral assurances of severance pay under prior company policy if employees remained until office closed; such assurances controlled over disclaimer in employment manual regarding employer's ability to change benefits and created enforceable unilateral contract); Chambers v. Terex, No. 45377 (Cuyahoga County 1983) (unreported) (jury verdict of $10,000 upheld on claim of invasion of right to privacy when employee was discharged for falsification on employment application regarding convictions for criminal offense; malice not an element of tort of invasion of privacy); Walden v. General Mills Restaurant Group, No. C-840298 (Hamilton County 1986) (unreported) (claim for retaliatory discharge by employee who refused to take polygraph dismissed because Ohio does not recognize such public policy exception); Edwards v. Nationwide Mut. Ins. Co., No. 83-CA-65 (Greene County 1983) (unreported) (no tort exceptions to at-will doctrine, despite contentions of malice and bad faith in discharging employee); Dadas v. Prescott, Ball & Turben, 529 F. Supp. 203, 34 FEP 74, 115 LRRM 3073 (N.D. Ohio 1981) (no cause of action for wrongful discharge based on sex discrimination because employee failed to exhaust adequate statutory remedy; no cause of action for wrongful discharge based on public policy); Smith v. Cline, 23 Ohio App.3d 146

(1985) (court reversed summary judgment for employer because employee was obstructed by employer in discovering facts to show actual malice in his defamation claim); King v. Hospital Care Corp., No. 1-85-1 (Allen County 1986) (unreported) (claim of breach of implied covenant of good faith and fair dealing dismissed because Ohio does not recognize such a cause of action); Mers v. Dispatch Printing Co., 19 Ohio St.3d 100, 483 N.E.2d 150, 120 LRRM 3299 (1985), *on appeal after remand,* 39 Ohio App.3d 99, 529 N.E.2d 958, 3 IER 1566 (1988) (no exception to at-will doctrine for malicious acts by employer or for requirement to act in good faith; remanded because oral representations and employee handbook raised question of employment contract; on appeal after remand, held, whether just cause required for discharge, and, if so, whether just cause existed were both jury issues); Jones v. East Center for Community Mental Health, 19 Ohio App.3d 19, 482 N.E.2d 969 (1984) (summary judgment for employer because employee handbook did not create implied contract due to lack of consideration and mutuality of obligation); Phung v. Waste Mgmt., 23 Ohio St.3d 100, 491 N.E.2d 1114, 122 LRRM 2163 (1986) (no public policy exception to at-will doctrine for employee discharged for protesting to employer that employer was violating unspecified "legal and societal obligations"; at-will employee who is discharged for reporting to his employer that it is conducting its business in violation of law does not have a cause of action against employer for wrongful discharge; no cause of action for "whistle blowing" exists in Ohio, and courts should defer employment matters involving public policy to legislature).

*Oklahoma:* Singh v. Cities Serv. Oil Co., 554 P.2d 1367 (Okla. 1986) (absent contract of employment for specific duration, employment is at-will); Vinyard v. King, 728 F.2d 428, 115 LRRM 3563 (10th Cir. 1984) (applying Oklahoma law, affirmed holding that personnel handbooks may bind employer contractually).

*Pennsylvania: See* Section IV.A in text and notes 21–22. Banas v. Matthews Int'l Corp., 116 LRRM 3110 (Pa. Super. Ct. 1984), *withdrawn,* 348 Pa. Super. 464, 502 A.2d 637, 121 LRRM 2515 (1985); Novosel v. Nationwide Ins. Co., 721 F.2d 894, 114 LRRM 3105, *reh'g denied,* 115 LRRM 2426 (3d Cir. 1983) (discharged employee may sue employer under Pennsylvania law on theory of implied contract based on employer's "custom, practice, or policy"); Shipkowski v. United States Steel Corp., 585 F. Supp. 66, 116 LRRM 3166 (E.D. Pa. 1983) (denying motion to dismiss complaint because alleged modification of at-will employment by defendant's "course of conduct" was jury issue); Karr v. Township of Lower Merion, 582 F. Supp. 410, 34 FEP 1557 (E.D. Pa. 1983) (employer's "course of conduct" could evidence "just cause" requirement for discharge); *cf.* Richardson v. Charles Cole Memorial Hosp., 320 Pa. Super. 106, 466 A.2d 1084, 115 LRRM 2218 (1983) (unilaterally published personnel policies did not give contractual right to continued indefinite employment assuming satisfactory performance); Ruch v. Strawbridge & Clothier, 567 F. Supp. 1078, 115 LRRM 2044 (E.D. Pa. 1983) (personnel policy manual not contract under Pennsylvania law); Wells v. Thomas, 569 F. Supp. 426 (E.D. Pa. 1983) (summary judgment for employer appropriate absent clear indication by employer that published personnel policies were to be integral part of contractual structure and absent evidence that plaintiff relied on employer's policies); Rossi v. Pennsylvania State Univ., 340 Pa. Super. 39, 489 A.2d 828 (1985) (discharge of at-will employee as result of employee's disagreement with superiors' management of department does not violate clearly stated public policy, and summary judgment for employer was appropriate); Cisco v. United Parcel Serv., 328 Pa. Super. 300, 476 A.2d 1340, 116 LRRM 2514 (1984) (discharge of employee accused of theft and trespassing in connection with employment and refusal to rehire even after acquittal was not wrongful, even though it contravened public policy, where employer's business was to enter onto premises of others; protection of employer's reputation "plausible and legitimate" reason for discharge); Martin v. Capital Cities Media, 354 Pa. Super. 199, 511 A.2d 830, 122 LRRM 3321 (1986) (unilaterally promulgated employee handbook stating that employees will not be discharged without just cause does not constitute binding contract, despite fact that employer told employees handbook controlled employment relationship); Darlington v. General Elec., 350 Pa. Super. 183, 504 A.2d 306 (1986) (neither employee handbook nor alleged vague employer representation during hiring process created contract right to just-cause prerequisite to discharge; no public policy exception to at-will rule where statutory remedy exists).

*Rhode Island:* Rotondo v. Seaboard Foundry, 440 A.2d 751, 115 LRRM 4916 (R.I. 1981) (promise to render personal services for indefinite duration is terminable at will of either party); L.T. Huddon, Inc. v. Swarovski Am. Ltd., 510 A.2d 158, 1 IER 842 (R.I. 1986) (employment agreement for indefinite time period terminable at will by either party) (dictum); Bader v. Alpine Ski Shop, 505 A.2d 1162 (R.I. 1986) (where employment contract for indefinite period showed no intent to last forever, contract was terminable at will by either party).

*South Carolina:* Todd v. South Carolina Farm Bureau Mut. Ins. Co., 276 S.C. 284, 278 S.E.2d 607, 115 LRRM 4899 (S.C. 1981), *appeal after remand,* 283 S.C. 155, 321 S.E.2d 602, 118 LRRM 2931 (1984), *writ granted in part,* 285 S.C. 84, 328 S.E.2d 479, *decision quashed as to issue reviewed,* 287 S.C. 190, 336 S.E.2d 472, 122 LRRM 3077 (1985) (reaffirming traditional at-will doctrine) (reversing trial verdict for plaintiff, and holding employer's conduct not outrageous, not interference with contractual relations, and not in breach of public policy even assuming such claim legally cognizable; on review, held, evidence supported jury's finding that independent contractor, and investigative agency retained by insurance agent's employers to investigate arson, intentionally interfered with agent's employment contract; jury verdict on that issue reinstated).

*South Dakota:* Goodwyn v. Sencore, Inc., 389 F. Supp. 824, 115 LRRM 4832 (D.S.D. 1975) (employee hired at annual salary was hired for term of one year; burden of proving cause for discharge upon employer). The state legislature adopted the rule of *Goodwyn* in enacting S.D.C.L. ¶ 60-1-3 and ¶ 60-1-4. The South Dakota Supreme Court has yet to interpret the statutes. *See* Ruple v. Weinaug, 328 N.W.2d 857 (S.D. 1983); Tombollo v. Dunn dba Sioux Falls Rent-A-Car (Hertz), 342 N.W.2d 23, 115 LRRM 2827 (S.D. 1984) (plaintiff's wrongful discharge claim dismissed where plaintiff did not have employment contract and she failed to refer to any employer handbook or procedure for disciplining or terminating employees).

*Tennessee:* Whittaker v. Care-More, 621 S.W.2d 395, 115 LRRM 3367 (Tenn. 1981) (no public policy exception to traditional at-will rule of employment); Graves v. Anchor Wire Corp. of Tenn., 692 S.W.2d 420, 118 LRRM 2750 (Tenn. App. 1985) (employee handbooks do not create implied contract to limit at-will employment; contract for employment for indefinite term can be terminated by other party at any time without cause); Watson v. Cleveland Chair Co., slip op. (Tenn. App. 1985) (cause of action for retaliatory discharge arises when at-will employee is terminated solely for refusing to participate in, continue to participate in, or remain silent about illegal activities); Leatherwood v. United Parcel Serv., 708 S.W.2d 396 (Tenn. App. 1985) (employees discharged for filing workers' compensation claims have cause of action for retaliatory discharge); Bringle v. Methodist Hosp., 701 S.W.2d 622 (Tenn. App. 1985).

*Texas:* Sabine Pilot Serv. v. Hauck, 687 S.W.2d 733, 119 LRRM 2187 (Tex. 1985) (cause of action for wrongful termination is stated where employee alleges that discharge was result of refusal to carry out employer's request to commit illegal act having criminal penalties); Vallone v. Agip Petroleum Co., 705 S.W.2d 757 (Tex. App. 1986) (unless expressly stated, handbooks do not create contractual rights); *accord* Reynolds Mfg. Co. v. Mendoza, 644 S.W.2d 536 (Tex. Ct. App. 1982) (no contractual limit on employer's right to discharge without notice, where handbook called for oral and written warnings). *But see* Tex. Rev. Civ. Stat. Ann. art. 8307(c) (Supp. 1982) (prohibiting employer from discharging or discriminating against employee who proceeds under Texas Workers' Compensation Act).

*Utah:* Rose v. Allied Dev. Co., 719 P.2d 83, 1 IER 834 (Utah 1986) (traditional rule of employment-at-will "in the absence of some further express or implied stipulation as to the duration of the employment or of a good consideration in addition to the services contracted to be rendered").

*Vermont:* Sherman v. Rutland Hosp., 146 Vt. 204, 500 A.2d 230, 121 LRRM 3401 (1985) (indefinite period of employment does not preclude claim for wrongful discharge based on defendant's failure to follow personnel manual); Larose v. Agway, Inc., 147 Vt. 1, 508 A.2d 1364, 121 LRRM 3404 (1986) (plaintiff did not present evidence he relied on personnel manual upon entering or remaining in employment; thus, no contract); Ball v. Barre Elec. Supply Co., 146 Vt. 245, 499 A.2d 786 (1985) (plaintiff received favorable jury verdict in wrongful discharge claim and was awarded damages for breach of contract, lost wages, and intentional infliction of emotional distress, and punitive damages); Benoir v. Ethan Allen, Inc., 147 Vt. 268, 514 A.2d 716 (1986) (appeals court affirmed ruling that plaintiff was not at will, since policies and practices concerning termination were in handbook, which jury found constituted part of a binding contract; employees reviewed handbook during orientation, again within 30 days of employment, and then signed it and it became part of personnel file).

*Washington:* Parker v. United Airlines, 32 Wash. App. 722, 649 P.2d 181 (1982) (employee manual which listed grounds for termination and employer statement that employee "will be treated fairly" did not limit employer's right to terminate employment at will).

*West Virginia:* Harless v. First Nat'l Bank in Fairmont, 169 W.Va. 673, 289 S.E.2d 692, 117 LRRM 2792 (1982) (damages for emotional distress may be recovered as part of compensatory damages for retaliatory discharge in violation of public policy).

*Wisconsin:* Holloway v. K-Mart Corp., 113 Wis.2d 143, 334 N.W.2d 570, 118 LRRM 2582 (Ct. App. 1983) (court refuses to create bad faith exception to at-will doctrine).

*Wyoming:* Lukens v. Goit, 430 P.2d 607, 115 LRRM 4828 (Wyo. 1967) (where employee is hired at-will, both employer and employee may terminate employment relationship at any time without incurring further obligations); Mobil Coal Producing v. Parks, 704 P.2d 702, 1 IER 1341 (Wyo. 1985) (handbook provision for progressive discipline may create contractual rights for an otherwise at-will employee).

*District of Columbia:* Ivy v. Army Times Publishing Co., 428 A.2d 831, 115 LRRM 4549 (D.C. Ct. App. 1981) (en banc) (public policy exception to at-will doctrine rejected where employer required employee to testify in administrative proceeding brought against employer, then terminated employee who truthfully testified against interests of employer); Sullivan v. Heritage Found., 399 A.2d 856, 115 LRRM 4621 (D.C. Ct. App. 1979) (absent facts and circumstances indicating employment agreement is for specific term, employment contract providing for annual rate of compensation but making no provision as to duration of employment is indefinite employment contract and therefore terminable at will); Parker v. National Corp. for Hous. Partnerships, 619 F. Supp. 1061, 38 FEP 1265 (D.D.C. 1985) (District of Columbia does not recognize public policy exception to at-will doctrine; no federal cause of action for breach of implied covenant of good faith and fair dealing); Hodge v. Evans Fin. Corp., 823 F.2d 559, 2 IER 395 (D.C. Cir. 1987), *superseding* 778 F.2d 794, 121 LRRM 2088, 1 IER 1814 (D.C. Cir. 1985) (oral contract for permanent employment not unenforceable under statute of frauds).

# Appendix C

## Intentional Infliction of Emotional Distress

Luna v. City & County of Denver, 537 F. Supp. 798, 31 FEP 1357 (D. Colo. 1982) (long and detailed pattern of conduct combined with allegations of racial motivation for conduct stated claim for intentional infliction of emotional distress); *see* Balark v. Ethicon, Inc., 575 F. Supp. 1227 (N.D. Ill. 1983) (claim for intentional infliction of emotional distress may not be based on retaliatory discharge after plaintiff exercised legal rights by filing criminal complaint against his superior); Harris v. Arkansas Book Co., 287 Ark. 353, 700 S.W.2d 41, 121 LRRM 2117 (1985) (discharge of long-time employee at will and alleged breach of vague assurances not intentional infliction of emotional distress; there must be clear-cut proof that conduct has been "so outrageous in character, and so extreme in degree, as to go beyond all possible bounds of decency, and to be regarded as atrocious, and utterly intolerable in a civilized community"); Givens v. Hixson, 275 Ark. 370, 631 S.W.2d 263, 264 (1982) (only allegedly outrageous conduct was that employer was angry when discharge occurred; "merely describing conduct as outrageous does not make it so"; conduct must be so outrageous and extreme as to exceed bounds of decency, and be "regarded as atrocious, and utterly intolerable to civilized community"); Meredith v. C.E. Walther, Inc., 422 So.2d 761, 115 LRRM 4341 (Ala. 1982) (failure to inform of impending termination does not state cause of action); Hubbard v. United Press Int'l, 330 N.W.2d 428, 31 FEP 139 (Minn. 1983) (employment discipline and written and verbal criticism of job performance, even if intended to harass, not sufficient); Gates v. Life of Mont. Ins. Co., 196 Mont. 178, 668 P.2d 213, 115 LRRM 4350 (1983) (conduct which made plaintiff "rather disturbed" insufficient to state cause of action); Forde v. Royal's, 537 F. Supp. 1173, 31 FEP 213 (S.D. Fla. 1982) (allegation of sexual harassment does not state cause of action for intentional infliction of emotional distress absent allegation of physical injury or some other type of tortious conduct); Carrillo v. Illinois Bell Tel. Co., 538 F. Supp. 793, 31 FEP 572 (N.D. Ill. 1982) (discharge of at-will employee not conduct that would give rise to action for intentional infliction of emotional distress); Elliott v. Employer's Reinsurance Corp., 534 F. Supp. 690, 28 FEP 1058 (D. Kan. 1981) (failure to pay female equally does not state claim for tortious outrage); Beidler v. W.R. Grace, Inc., 641 F. Supp. 1013, 115 LRRM 4619 (E.D. Pa. 1978), *aff'd,* 609 F.2d 500, 115 LRRM 4621 (3d Cir. 1979) (exclusion of plaintiff from meetings, circulation of rumors that plaintiff would be replaced, and other annoyances did not state cause of action for emotional distress); Gibson v. Hummel, 688 S.W.2d 4, 118 LRRM 2943 (Mo. App. 1985) (employer's administration of mandatory polygraph did not establish prima facie case of outrage or intentional infliction of emotional distress); Northrup v. Farmland Indus., 372 N.W.2d 193 (Iowa 1985) (discharge of plant superintendent for alcoholism not outrageous conduct); Morris v. Hartford Courant Co., 200 Conn. 676, 513 A.2d 66 (1986) (claim that defendant falsely accused plaintiff of being involved in criminal activity insufficient to establish emotional distress absent showing that "defendant should have realized that its conduct involved an unreasonable risk of causing emotional distress and that that distress, if it were caused, might result in illness or bodily harm"); Pemberton v. Bethlehem Steel Corp., 66 Md. App. 133, 502 A.2d 1101, 123 LRRM 3015, *cert. denied,* 306 Md. 289, 508 A.2d 488 (Md.), _____ U.S. _____, 123 LRRM 3128 (1986) (distribution of truthful information regarding criminal conviction of union official, surveillance of official, and

sending of truthful information regarding extramarital affairs to his wife not sufficiently outrageous to support claim for intentional infliction of emotional distress);
Leese v. Baltimore County, 64 Md. App. 442, 497 A.2d 159, *cert. denied,* 305 Md.
106, 501 A.2d 845 (1985) (denial of promotion and firing do not amount to "major
outrage" of personal dignity necessary to support claim of intentional infliction of
emotional distress); Avallone v. Wilmington Medical Center, 553 F. Supp. 931, 115
LRRM 4941 (D. Del. 1982) (no cause of action for intentional or negligent infliction
of emotional distress where employer's conduct in forcing plaintiff to resign was not
outrageous); Oakley v. St. Joseph's Hosp., 116 A.D.2d 911, 498 N.Y.S.2d 218 (3d
Dep't 1986) (employer's inquiry concerning plaintiff's intention to retire is not
outrageous conduct); Amos v. Corporation of Presiding Bishop, Church of Jesus
Christ of Latter-Day Saints, 594 F. Supp. 791, 117 LRRM 2744 (D. Utah 1984)
(employer's inquiry of allegedly highly personal nature to determine employees'
satisfaction of Mormon Church "worthiness requirement" did not rise to level of
actionable outrageous or intolerable conduct). *Compare* Smith v. Montgomery
Ward & Co., 567 F. Supp. 1331, 32 FEP 995 (D. Colo. 1983) (whether adverse
employment action constitutes tortious outrageous conduct will be decided by "the
conscience of the community—the jury") *with* Rawson v. Sears, Roebuck & Co., 530
F. Supp. 776, 778–81, 31 FEP 1350, 1351–53, and *supra* App. B. (Colo.) (D. Colo.
1982) (defendant's discharging plaintiff without allowing him to "resign with dignity" not sufficiently outrageous to state claim for intentional infliction of emotional
distress) *and* Wells v. Thomas, 569 F. Supp. 426, 433–34 (E.D. Pa. 1983) (transferring plaintiff to newly created job with no meaningful responsibilities, depriving
plaintiff of private office and secretary, removing one of plaintiff's telephone lines,
giving plaintiff first poor performance review in 25 years, failing to award plaintiff
regular annual salary increase, and termination of plaintiff's employment, though
"intentional and highly inappropriate," not sufficiently outrageous to state claim for
intentional infliction of emotional distress). *But see* Monge v. California Superior
Court (Crown Gibraltar Graphic Center, 176 Cal.App.3d 503, 222 Cal. Rptr. 64
(1986) (supervisor complained to employer on behalf of employee after employer
allegedly flashed obscene message on computer screen used by employee; employee
and her supervisor were both thereafter discharged; held, both stated claims for
infliction of emotional distress); Miller v. Fairchild Indus., 797 F.2d 727, 41 FEP
809 (9th Cir. 1986) (former employees' claims of bad-faith negotiation of settlement
agreement regarding discrimination charge and of retaliatory discharge sufficiently
"outrageous" to withstand employer's motion for summary judgment); Stewart v.
Thomas, 538 F. Supp. 891, 30 FEP 1609 (D.D.C. 1982) (plaintiff's allegations of
blatant offensive sexual harassment presents prima facie case of intentional infliction
of emotional distress); Milton v. Illinois Bell Tel. Co., 101 Ill.App.3d 75, 427 N.E.2d
829, 115 LRRM 4428 (1981) (claim for infliction of emotional distress may be based
on retaliatory discharge for revealing or refusing to engage in unlawful conduct);
New York v. Holiday Inns, 35 FEP 1308 (W.D.N.Y. 1984) (defendants knowingly
and intentionally subjected plaintiff to personal harassment, intimidation, abuse, and
embarrassment; defendant's acts were so outrageous and extreme as to offend public
conscience); Wolber v. Service Corp. Int'l, 40 EPD ¶ 42,359 (D. Nev. 1985) (relief
under state workers' compensation law does not preclude claim for damages for
intentional infliction of emotional distress); Bell v. Crakin Good Bakers, 777 F.2d
1497, 39 FEP 948 (11th Cir. 1985) (summary judgment dismissing claim of intentional infliction of emotional distress reversed, where evidence showed employee's
supervisor had initiated a program to "get tough" in order to get rid of employee
and showed that employee's physical and mental health were both seriously impaired by supervisor's conduct); Grubb v. W.A. Foote Memorial Hosp., 533 F.
Supp. 671, 31 FEP 511 (E.D. Mich. 1981) (unlawfully discharged black employee
awarded $25,000 in damages for mental anguish and emotional distress where
supervisor belittled him, told him that black man had no place supervising white
women, failed to tell him for long period of time that his position was being eliminated after decision was known by other workers who reported it to him, eliminated

his office while he was overseeing work elsewhere, told him that "he was through," and caused him great anxiety and humiliation); Garza v. Brownsville Indep. School Dist., 31 FEP 396 (S.D. Tex. 1981), *rev'd and remanded as to denial of reinstatement only,* 700 F.2d 253, 31 FEP 403 (5th Cir. 1983) (individual unlawfully denied employment because of sex entitled to back pay and $6,000 in compensatory damages for mental anguish, humiliation, and travel expenses caused by deprivation of her constitutional rights); Stallworth v. Shuler, 777 F.2d 1431, 39 FEP 983 (11th Cir. 1985) (Court of Appeals upheld award of $100,000 in compensatory damages for emotional distress in action in which plaintiff prevailed on claim of unlawful race discrimination in violation of 42 U.S.C. § 1981 and § 1983); Berndt v. Kaiser Aluminum & Chem. Sales, 40 EPD ¶ 42,483 (E.D. Pa. 1985) (plaintiff successful in age discrimination claim entitled to award of prejudgment interest with no deduction of unemployment benefits).

## CHAPTER 24

# REVERSE DISCRIMINATION AND AFFIRMATIVE ACTION

## II. Reverse Discrimination Outside the Context of Affirmative Action

There have been several recent decisions relating to discrimination against individual whites. *Rucker v. Higher Educational Aids Board*[1] held that Title VII is violated if a black employee is fired because he opposed the efforts of his supervisors to discriminate on racial and sexual grounds against a white employee. Another district court supported a white man's claim for retaliatory discharge in *Spence v. Auto Workers Local 1250.*[2] The court found that the white employee was fired for opposing discriminatory actions directed toward a black fellow employee. The plaintiff was thus entitled to reinstatement, back pay, and attorneys' fees.[3]

*Chaline v. KCOH*[4] was a successful action under 42 U.S.C. § 1981 by the white production manager of a black-oriented radio station who claimed he was discharged and replaced by a black because he was white. The court of appeals affirmed the district court's decision holding arguments pretextual that the plaintiff's voice was not proper for a black-oriented station and he was not sensitive to the listening tastes of a black audience.

In *Planells v. Howard University,*[5] the district court ruled that Howard University violated Title VII by discharging a white Spanish language professor who was equally or better qualified than other professors in the same department. The court rejected the university's argument that, as a predominantly black institution, it could take race into consideration in faculty recruitment and promotion. Similarly, in *Turgeon v. Howard University,*[6] a different judge in the same district sustained a jury verdict awarding $50,000 to a fired white female French professor at Howard University. The court rejected the university's argument that black colleges historically have taken race into consideration in selection, retention, and tenure of faculty. The court held that the university had failed to raise the argument during the trial and that the evidence was furthermore sufficient to provide a reasonable basis for the jury's verdict.[7]

---

[1]669 F.2d 1179, 1181, 27 FEP 1553 (7th Cir. 1982). *But see* Jones v. Lyng, 669 F. Supp. 1108, 42 FEP 587 (D.D.C. 1986) (although male employee opposed sexual harassment of women employees, employer established legitimate nondiscriminatory reason for transferring man and removing most of his duties).

[2]595 F. Supp. 6, 35 FEP 1666 (N.D. Ohio 1984).

[3]*Id.* at 14, 35 FEP at 1671.

[4]693 F.2d 477, 30 FEP 834 (5th Cir. 1982).

[5]32 FEP 336 (D.D.C. 1983), *later proceeding,* 34 FEP 66 (D.D.C. 1984).

[6]32 FEP 335 (D.D.C. 1983).

[7]*But see* Dybczak v. Tuskegee Inst., 737 F.2d 1524, 35 FEP 813 (11th Cir. 1984), *cert. denied,* 469 U.S. 1211, 37 FEP 64 (1985) (evidence that predominantly black institute placed importance on black

## III. REVERSE DISCRIMINATION IN THE AFFIRMATIVE ACTION CONTEXT

In six significant decisions since the publication of the Second Edition* —*Firefighters Local 1784 v. Stotts,* [8] *Firefighters Local 93 v. City of Cleveland,* [9] *Wygant v. Jackson Board of Education,* [10] *Sheet Metal Workers Local 28 v. EEOC,* [11] *United States v. Paradise,* [12] and *Johnson v. Transportation Agency, Santa Clara County* [13]—the Supreme Court has clarified several critical issues concerning the propriety of affirmative action plans and orders left unresolved by *Regents of the University of California v. Bakke,* [14] *Steelworkers v. Weber,* [15] and *Fullilove v. Klutznick.* [16] While these new decisions have produced numerous opinions and indicate deep divisions within the Court, they are generally supportive of voluntary affirmative action,[17] at least where the interests of specific incumbents are not substantially affected.[18] The Court has also made clear that § 706(g)[19] has no application to voluntary affirmative action, including court-approved consent decrees, and does not always limit court-ordered affirmative action to identified victims of discrimination.

The effect of § 706(g) on affirmative action was placed in doubt by the Court's initial decision of this period in *Stotts.* [20] There, by a 6-to-3 vote,[21] the Court set aside a lower court order that had amended a Title VII consent

---

role models on faculty and expressed concern about increasing black faculty applicants was insufficient to prove intent to discriminate against white dean not retained or reappointed).

*In addition, just as this Supplement went to press the Supreme Court issued its opinion in *City of Richmond v. J.A. Croson Co.,* 488 U.S. _____, 57 USLW 4132 (1989). The Court held in *Croson* that a city's minority set-aside program must be supported by a factual predicate demonstrating a compelling governmental interest justifying the plan. This factual predicate must be specific to the industry, the affected class, and the public entity involved. *Id.,* 57 USLW at 4140.

[8]467 U.S. 561, 34 FEP 1702 (1984).
[9]478 U.S. 501, 41 FEP 139 (1986).
[10]476 U.S. 267, 40 FEP 1321 (1986).
[11]478 U.S. 421, 41 FEP 107 (1986).
[12]480 U.S. 149, 43 FEP 1 (1987).
[13]480 U.S. 616, 43 FEP 411 (1987).
[14]438 U.S. 265, 17 FEP 1000 (1978). *See* Second Edition at p. 787.
[15]443 U.S. 193, 20 FEP 1 (1979). *See* Second Edition at p. 820.
[16]448 U.S. 448 (1980). *See* Second Edition at p. 841.

[17]Commentators differ on the effect of the Court's recent affirmative action decisions. *Compare* Sullivan, *Comment: Sins of Discrimination: Last Term's Affirmative Action Cases,* 100 HARV. L. REV. 78 (1986) (arguing that recent cases have provided neither decisive victories nor defeats to proponents or opponents of affirmative action) *with* Schwartz, *The 1986 and 1987 Affirmative Action Cases: It's All Over But the Shouting,* 86 MICH. L. REV. 524 (1987) (arguing that most affirmative action questions have now been resolved in favor of such programs).

[18]The United States took a role in three of these cases, as amicus curiae in *Firefighters Local 1784 v. Stotts, supra* note 8, and *Firefighters Local 93 v. City of Cleveland, supra* note 9, and as a party in *United States v. Paradise, supra* note 12. In *Firefighters Local 93,* the Solicitor General's brief was filed only on behalf of the Attorney General and the federal government as an employer; the EEOC did not join the brief. 41 FEP at 147.

[19]The relevant part of § 706(g) provides:
"No order of the court shall require the admission or reinstatement of an individual as a member of a union, or the hiring, reinstatement, or promotion of an individual as an employee, or the payment to him of any back pay, if such individual was refused admission, suspended, or expelled, or was refused employment or advancement or was suspended or discharged for any reason other than discrimination on account of race, color, religion, sex, or national origin or in violation of section 2000e-3(a) of this title."
42 U.S.C. 2000e-5(g).

[20]Firefighters Local 1784 v. Stotts, 476 U.S. 561, 34 FEP 1702 (1984).

[21]Justice White authored the majority opinion for himself, Chief Justice Burger, and Justices Powell, Rehnquist, and O'Connor. Justice O'Connor also filed a separate opinion, stating her understanding of the Court's holding. Justice Blackmun dissented for himself and Justices Brennan and Marshall.

decree.[22] The district court had ordered the Memphis Fire Department to suspend its "last-hired, first-fired" seniority system during a layoff in order to preserve the percentage of black firefighters employed in the department. The district court had perceived such layoffs as otherwise eroding employment gains of blacks hired under two earlier Title VII consent decrees. The Sixth Circuit had found the Memphis seniority system to be bona fide under § 703(h) but had nonetheless upheld the district court's order modifying it. The Sixth Circuit also affirmed the district court's finding that the layoff was not discriminatorily motivated and was necessitated by legitimate economic reasons. The Supreme Court reversed, directing that the original consent decree be left unchanged, even though the effect of layoffs in reverse seniority order would be to reduce the percentage of blacks in affected positions.

The decree at issue had been entered by the district court based on the agreement of the parties to settle suits charging the city's fire department with hiring and promotion discrimination against blacks in violation of Title VII of the 1964 Civil Rights Act, as well as 42 U.S.C. §§ 1981 and 1983. The consent decree was entered by the district court in April 1980 without any finding of discrimination. The decree required promotions and back pay for certain named individuals and also established numerical goals for hiring and promotions of blacks. Specifically, the decree established:

  (a)  a long-term goal of increasing black representation in each job classification in the department to approximately that of the surrounding county's labor force;

  (b)  an interim goal of filling 50 percent of the job vacancies in the department each year with qualified blacks; and

  (c)  a requirement that the department attempt to ensure that 20 percent of promotions in each job classification would go to blacks.

The decree made no reference to layoffs, nor did it award any competitive seniority. The decree provided that the district court retained jurisdiction "for such further orders as may be necessary or appropriate to effectuate the purposes of this decree."[23]

In May 1981, the city announced a general reduction in force because of budget deficits. Layoffs were to be based on the "last-hired, first-fired" principle, pursuant to the collective bargaining agreement governing those laid off. The black firefighters petitioned the district court to prevent the layoffs of blacks. For the first time, the firefighters union intervened in the case. After a hearing, the district court ordered the city to suspend the seniority system of its collective bargaining agreement with the union where layoffs under that system would otherwise decrease the percentage of blacks in certain classifications. A modified layoff plan was then developed and approved by the court. Under the modified plan, some nonminority employees with more seniority than minority employees were laid off or demoted.

On appeal, the Sixth Circuit upheld the district court's order, but con-

---

[22]Stotts v. Memphis Fire Dep't, 679 F.2d 541, 28 FEP 1491 (6th Cir. 1982). The procedural history is summarized in the Supreme Court's majority opinion, 467 U.S. 561, 565–68, 34 FEP 1702, 1705–6 (1984). The 1980 decree is set forth in the Sixth Circuit opinion, 679 F.2d at 573–79, 28 FEP at 1518–22 (Appendix).

[23]679 F.2d at 578, 28 FEP at 1521, quoted by the Court majority, 467 U.S. at 565–66, 34 FEP at 1705.

cluded, contrary to the district court, that the city's "last-hired, first-fired" policy was a bona fide seniority system under § 703(h). Both the city and the union sought review by the Supreme Court.

Writing for the Court majority, Justice White defined the central issue as "whether the district court exceeded its powers in entering an injunction requiring white employees to be laid off, when the otherwise applicable seniority system would have called for the layoff of black employees with less seniority."[24] The Court found support for the district court's order neither in the original decree nor in the court's inherent power.

The majority's opinion rested on both § 703(h) and § 706(g):

> "The difficulty with this approach [regarding inherent powers] is that it overstates the authority of the trial court to disregard a seniority system in fashioning a remedy after a plaintiff has successfully proved that an employer has followed a pattern or practice having a discriminatory effect on black applicants or employees. If individual members of a plaintiff class demonstrate that they have been actual victims of the discriminatory practice, they may be awarded competitive seniority and given their rightful place on the seniority roster. This much is clear from *Franks v. Bowman Transportation Co.* * * * and *Teamsters v. United States* * * *. *Teamsters,* however, also made clear that mere membership in the disadvantaged class is insufficient to warrant a seniority award; each individual must prove that the discriminatory practice has had an impact on him * * *. Even when an individual shows that the discriminatory practice had an impact on him, he is not automatically entitled to have a non-minority employee laid off to make room for him. He may have to wait until a vacancy occurs, and if there are non-minority employees on layoff, the Court must balance the equities in determining who is entitled to the job. *Teamsters* * * *. See also *Ford Motor Co. v. EEOC* * * *. Here, there was no finding that any of the blacks protected from layoff had been a victim of discrimination and no award of competitive seniority to any of them. Nor had the parties in formulating the consent decree purported to identify any specific employee entitled to particular relief other than those listed in the exhibits attached to the decree. It therefore seems to us that in light of *Teamsters,* the Court of Appeals imposed on the parties as an adjunct of settlement something that could not have been ordered had the case gone to trial and the plaintiffs proved that a pattern or practice of discrimination existed.
>
> "Our ruling in *Teamsters* that a court can award competitive seniority only when the beneficiary of the award has actually been a victim of illegal discrimination is consistent with the policy behind § 706(g) of Title VII, which affects the remedies available in Title VII litigation. That policy, which is to provide make-whole relief only to those who have been actual victims of illegal discrimination, was repeatedly expressed by the sponsors of the Act during the congressional debates."[25]

Based on this reference, the Civil Rights Division of the U.S. Department of Justice then interpreted *Stotts* as declaring that the federal courts have no power under Title VII to order the hiring, retention, reinstatement, or promotion of members of an ethnic, racial, or sex-based group except with respect to individuals who have suffered actual employment discrimination.[26]

---

[24]Id., 34 FEP at 1708.

[25]467 U.S. at 578–80, 34 FEP at 1711 (citations and footnotes omitted).

[26]The Department of Justice took the position that consent decrees in Title VII cases pending against 51 public employers were contrary to *Stotts*. See NAACP v. Meese, 615 F. Supp. 200, 202 n.5, 38 FEP 324, 326 (D.D.C. 1985). However, this broad reading of *Stotts* had been rejected by many lower federal

Later decisions of the 1986 and 1987 term clarified the role of § 706(g) and made clear that *Stotts* is much more narrowly limited to its facts. *Firefighters Local 93*[27] and *Johnson*[28] establish that § 706(g) does not limit voluntary affirmative action. *Firefighters Local 93*[29] also determined that, for purposes of § 706(g), a court-approved consent decree is to be considered a voluntary agreement and not a court order.[30]

Less is certain about the effect of § 706(g) on court-ordered preferences, because the two cases in which the Court held that affirmative action need not be limited to actual victims of prior discrimination, *Sheet Metal Workers*[31] and *Paradise,*[32] are characterized by egregious facts.[33] Whether other circumstances might justify court-ordered affirmative action is a question that remains open.[34]

Taken together, the decisions of the 1986 and 1987 terms defined an analytical framework for distinguishing unlawful reverse discrimination from legitimate affirmative action. All affirmative action must rest on a minimum factual predicate. The necessary showing will vary depending on whether the action is voluntary or court-ordered, and on whether the challenge is brought under Title VII or the Constitution. For voluntary action, neither private nor public employers must show prior discrimination. Indeed, the Court held that the factual predicate for voluntary action under Title VII is less than that required for a prima facie case, though the Court suggested that the Constitution imposes a higher standard than the statute and may require a prima facie showing.

Affirmative action must also be reasonable in scope. The goals must be calculated with some precision based on the actual requirements of the job and the qualifications of available candidates. The impact of affirmative action on nonprotected group members must also be acceptable. Thus, the Court upheld promotion and hiring goals where the impact on nonprotected group members was viewed as "diffuse," but rejected voluntary and court-ordered plans that subordinated seniority protection from layoff of specific incumbents.

Finally, these decisions made clear that the burden of proof rests with those challenging an affirmative action plan. This burden extends to proof of the availability of alternative means which would have less impact on nonprotected group members.

---

courts by the time it was rejected in the decision discussed below. *See, e.g.,* Sheet Metal Workers Local 28 v. EEOC, 478 U.S. 421, 475, 41 FEP 107, 128 n.47 (1986) (listing cases that rejected a broad reading of *Stotts*).

[27]Firefighters Local 93 v. City of Cleveland, 478 U.S. 501, 41 FEP 139 (1986).

[28]Johnson v. Transportation Agency, Santa Clara County, 480 U.S. 616, 43 FEP 411 (1987).

[29]*Supra* note 27.

[30]In an October 6, 1987, memorandum to EEOC Regional Attorneys, EEOC General Counsel Charles A. Shanor discussed the implications of the recent Supreme Court decisions for EEOC consent decrees, and outlined the considerations which should be analyzed in consent decrees containing goals and timetables. The memorandum is set out in full as Appendix A to this chapter and is cited where appropriate as "EEOC General Counsel Memorandum, October 6, 1987, *infra* at _____."

[31]Sheet Metal Workers Local 28 v. EEOC, 478 U.S. 421, 41 FEP 107 (1986).

[32]United States v. Paradise, 480 U.S. 149, 43 FEP 1 (1987).

[33]Sheet Metal Workers Local 28 v. EEOC, *supra* note 31, and United States v. Paradise, *supra* note 32.

[34]"Whether there might be other circumstances that justify the use of court-ordered affirmative action is a matter that we need not decide here." *Supra* note 31, 41 FEP at 129.

## D. The Necessary Factual Predicate

### 1. Voluntary Affirmative Action Plans

a. *Under Title VII.* Although the Court in *Weber*[35] upheld a voluntary affirmative action plan under Title VII, it did not specify with any precision the necessary factual predicate for such a plan. The Court noted that the Kaiser plan had been adopted "to eliminate traditional patterns of discrimination" and held that the plan at issue "falls within the area of discretion left by Title VII to the private sector voluntarily to adopt affirmative action plans designed to eliminate conspicuous racial imbalance in traditionally segregated job categories." Beyond that, the Court did not define these terms nor provide a standard to measure "traditional patterns" or "conspicuous racial imbalance."

In *Firefighters Local 93 v. City of Cleveland,*[36] the Court reaffirmed the principles of the *Weber* decision, and held that § 706(g) did not apply to a consent decree. While the decision removed a potential impediment to affirmative action, its narrow focus left the necessary factual predicate for voluntary action unresolved.

In *Local 93,* an organization of black and Hispanic firefighters, the Vanguards of Cleveland, brought a class action in 1980 against the city for discrimination on grounds of race and national origin in hiring, assignment, and promotion. The city had lost similar cases in the past,[37] and in response to the Vanguards' action it began negotiations for settlement. The petitioner labor union, representing most of the city's firefighters, was permitted to intervene as a party-plaintiff. Over the objections of the union, the city and the Vanguards negotiated a consent decree which was approved by the court.[38] The decree was to remain in place for four years and would create a number of openings for promotion, to be based on an examination and divided evenly between minorities and nonminorities.[39]

A panel for the Court of Appeals for the Sixth Circuit affirmed, with one judge dissenting, holding that *Stotts* was inapplicable because that case involved an injunction over the objection of that city, while *Firefighters Local 93*[40] involved a consent decree to which the city had agreed.[41] The union sought certiorari.

Justice Brennan, writing for a six-member majority,[42] stated as the sole

---

[35]Steelworkers v. Weber, 443 U.S. 193, 209, 20 FEP 1, 7–8 (1979).

[36]*Supra* note 27.

[37]Cleveland had lost a suit brought by black police officers in 1972. Shield Club v. City of Cleveland, 370 F. Supp. 251, 5 FEP 566 (N.D. Ohio 1972). The court fixed minority hiring goals and enjoined certain hiring and promotion practices. *Id.* In 1975, similar litigation brought by black firefighters resulted in a consent decree establishing hiring quotas. Headen v. City of Cleveland, No. C73-330 (N.D. Ohio, Apr. 25, 1975). Although referenced in *Firefighters Local 93,* these findings of past discrimination played no part in the decision because of the manner in whih the issue was framed on appeal.

[38]Firefighters Local 93 v. City of Cleveland, 478 U.S. 501, 509-12, 41 FEP 139, 142–44 (1986). The union asserted no legal claims against the City or the Vanguards and the decree imposed no legal duties on the union. *Id.*

[39]*Id.,* 41 FEP at 144.

[40]Firefighters Local 93 v. City of Cleveland, 478 U.S. 501, 41 FEP 139 (1986).

[41]Vanguards of Cleveland v. City of Cleveland, 753 F.2d 479, 36 FEP 1431 (6th Cir. 1985).

[42]Justice Brennan was joined by Justices Marshall, Blackmun, Powell, Stevens, and O'Connor. Justice O'Connor filed a concurring opinion. Justice White dissented. Justice Rehnquist filed a dissenting opinion, joined by Chief Justice Burger.

issue before the Court, "whether § 706(g) of Title VII of the Civil Rights Act of 1964, as amended, 42 U.S.C. § 2000e-5(g), precludes the entry of a consent decree which provides relief that may benefit individuals who were not the actual victims of the defendant's discriminatory practices."[43] Finding the legislative objective embodied in § 706(g) to be the protection of "management prerogatives, and union freedoms"[44] and finding those prerogatives and freedoms not implicated by a voluntary decision to enter a consent decree, the Court held § 706(g) inapplicable to such decrees.[45] The Court did not, however, address the issue of the factual predicate required to support a consent decree: "Nor need we decide * * * what showing the employee would be required to make concerning possible prior discrimination on its part against minorities in order to defeat a challenge by nonminority employees based on §703."[46]

In his dissent, Justice White expressed his view that racial preferences may be ordered or adopted voluntarily only as a remedy for an employer's prior discriminatory practices. He wrote, "The Court's opinion pays scant attention to this necessary predicate for race conscious practices * * * ."[47]

In her concurring opinion, however, Justice O'Connor emphasized the narrowness of the holding:

> "It is clear, then, that the Court's opinion does not hold or otherwise suggest that there is no 'necessary predicate for race conscious practices * * * ' when those practices are embodied in a voluntary settlement or in a consent decree rather than ordered by the court over the objection of an employer or union. If *Weber* indicates that an employer's or union's 'prior discriminatory conduct' is the necessary 'predicate for a temporary remedy favoring black employees' * * * the Court's opinion leaves that requirement wholly undisturbed."[48]

The factual predicate issue, left unresolved by *Weber* and not addressed by the majority in *Firefighters Local 93,* was clarified during the 1987 term—at least by a five justice majority including Justice Powell—in *Johnson v. Transportation Agency, Santa Clara County.*[49] There, a voluntary affirmative action plan for the Santa Clara County, California, Transportation Agency had been adopted by the County Transit District Board of Supervisors in December 1978.[50] The plan provided that the sex of a qualified applicant might be considered as one of a number of factors in making promotions within traditionally segregated job categories in which women had been "significantly underrepresented."[51]

Although no specific number of positions was set aside for women or

[43]*Supra* note 40, 41 FEP at 141. The relevant part of § 706(g) is quoted *supra* at note 19.
[44]*Id.,* 41 FEP at 148, quoting H.R. Rep. No. 914, 88th Cong., 2d Sess., pt. 2 at 29 (1963).
[45]The Court noted that EEOC guidelines "plainly contemplate the use of consent decrees as an appropriate form of voluntary affirmative action," and held that "absent some contrary indication, there is no reason to think that voluntary, race-conscious affirmative action such as was held permissible in *Weber* is rendered impermissible by Title VII simply because it is incorporated into a consent decree." *Id.,* 41 FEP at 147.
[46]*Id.,* 41 FEP at 146 n.8.
[47]*Id.,* 41 FEP at 153.
[48]*Id.,* 41 FEP at 152.
[49]480 U.S. 616, 43 FEP 411 (1987).
[50]*Id.,* 43 FEP at 414.
[51]*Id.*

minorities, the Agency's plan intended to achieve a yearly improvement in hiring, training, and promotion of women and minorities in classifications in which they were underrepresented and, as a long-term goal, "to attain a work force whose composition reflected the proportion of minorities and women in the area labor force."[52]

Observing that underrepresentation existed in five of the seven job categories, the plan attributed this underrepresentation to societal causes. The plan noted that women "had not traditionally been employed in these positions, and * * * they had not been strongly motivated to seek training or employment in them 'because of the limited opportunities that have existed in the past for them to work in such classifications.' "[53]

A promotional vacancy occurred for the position of road dispatcher, a job classified by the EEOC as a skilled craft worker. Of the 238 skilled craft worker positions, none was held by a woman.[54] Twelve employees applied for the promotion, nine were deemed qualified, and seven were certified as eligible on the basis of scoring at a two-person interview.[55] At that interview, Paul Johnson tied for second by scoring 75, and Diane Joyce ranked next with a score of 73.[56] After a second interview before three supervisors, Mr. Johnson was recommended for promotion.[57] The County's affirmative action office, previously contacted by Diane Joyce, recommended that the Agency director promote her.[58] Any of the seven applicants certified eligible could have been selected, and the director chose Ms. Joyce.[59]

Mr. Johnson then brought a discrimination action under Title VII.[60] Finding that the plan was not temporary and hence did not meet the *Weber* standard, the district court found the plan invalid.[61] The Ninth Circuit reversed, holding that the plan was temporary in the sense that its express purpose was to attain, not maintain, a balanced work force, and that "[i]mplicit in the plan is the intent to stop taking sex into account once the long-range percentage goals are attained."[62]

Justice Brennan wrote the majority opinion in *Johnson,*[63] upholding the Agency's affirmative action plan. The Court found a sufficient predicate for the plan based on the underrepresentation of women in traditionally male jobs, notwithstanding the Agency's disavowal of prior discrimination. *Johnson* resolved a number of important issues concerning the lawfulness of voluntary affirmative action under Title VII:[64]

---

[52]*Id.*
[53]*Id.*
[54]*Id.*
[55]*Id.,* 43 FEP at 415.
[56]*Id.*
[57]*Id.*
[58]*Id.*
[59]*Id.*
[60]*Id.,* 43 FEP at 416.
[61]*Id.*
[62]770 F.2d 752, 756–57, 36 FEP 725, 729–30 (9th Cir. 1984).
[63]Johnson v. Transportation Agency, Santa Clara County, 480 U.S. 616, 43 FEP 411 (1987). His opinion was joined by Justices Marshall, Blackmun, Powell, and Stevens. Justice Stevens filed a concurring opinion, and Justice O'Connor filed an opinion concurring in the judgment. Justice White filed a dissenting opinion, as did Justice Scalia, joined by Chief Justice Rehnquist and Justice White.
[64]The Court observed:
"No constitutional issue was either raised or addressed in the litigation below. . . . We therefore decide in this case only the issue of the prohibitory scope of Title VII. Of course, where the issue is properly

(a)   The statutory standard is the same for both private and public employers;[65]

(b)   Sex-based preferences are to be judged by the same standards as race-based preferences;[66]

(c)   A statistical showing of a "manifest imbalance" disfavoring minorities or women in traditionally segregated job categories is sufficient to support affirmative action;[67]

(d)   According to five Justices, including Justice Powell, a "manifest imbalance" need not rise to the level of a prima facie case in order to be sufficient to support affirmative action;[68]

(e)   The employer need not admit prior discrimination, and the imbalance may have been caused by societal factors beyond its control.[69]

While the exact requirements for an imbalance to be considered "manifest" were not articulated by the Court, it did suggest that measurement of an imbalance must account for the skills required for particular jobs:

> "In determining whether an imbalance exists that would justify taking sex or race into account, a comparison of the percentage of minorities or women in the employer's work force with the percentage in the area labor market or general population is appropriate in analyzing jobs that require no special expertise * * * or training programs designed to provide expertise * * * . Where a job requires special training, however, the comparison should be with those in the labor force who possess the relevant qualifications."[70]

The *Johnson* decision is also important for its holdings concerning the permissible scope of affirmative action and the allocation of the bur-

---

raised, public employers must justify the adoption and implementation of a voluntary affirmative action plan under the Equal Protection Clause."
*Id.,* 43 FEP at 414 n.2.

[65]*Id.,* 43 FEP at 416–17 n.6.

[66]*Id.,* 43 FEP at 419 n.13.

[67]*Id.,* 43 FEP at 418.

[68]*Id.,* 43 FEP at 419. Justice O'Connor would have required a prima facie violation of Title VII as a minimal factual predicate for the affirmative action plan in *Johnson.* Her view and the departure of Justice Powell, who was part of the *Johnson* majority not requiring such a showing, have focused attention on Justice Kennedy with respect to this issue.

[69]*Id.,* 43 FEP at 418, 414.

[70]*Id.,* 43 FEP at 418. Based on *Johnson* and *Wygant v. Jackson Bd. of Educ.,* 476 U.S. 267, 40 FEP 1321 (1986), the Supreme Court vacated *Janowiak v. City of S. Bend,* 750 F.2d 557, 36 FEP 737 (7th Cir. 1984), *vacated,* 481 U.S. 1001, 43 FEP 640 (1987) (city could not adopt affirmative action program based solely on numerical disparity between minorities in community and minorities in fire and police departments). *See also* Higgins v. City of Vallejo, 823 F.2d 351, 44 FEP 676 (9th Cir. 1987) (in promotion case, city's affirmative action program found narrowly tailored and justified by "manifest imbalance" in work force); Hammon v. Barry, 826 F.2d 73, 44 FEP 869 (D.C. Cir. 1987) (post-*Johnson* decision addressing hiring provisions of District of Columbia's affirmative action plan; panel majority distinguished showing of "manifest imbalance" in *Johnson,* where women were "egregiously underrepresented" in the job category in question, in that "*none* of the 238 positions was occupied by a woman," *id.,* 44 FEP at 872 (emphasis in original), from statistical showing of 75.5% average annual post-1981 black hires in the D.C. fire department compared with percentage of blacks in either of the two applicant pools utilized by district court (74.53% in 1980 and 64.60% in 1984); one panel majority member, Starr, J., condemned D.C. affirmative action plan under Title VII, while other panel majority member, Silberman, J., reached same conclusion under both Title VII and the Constitution; Mikva, J., dissented on grounds *Johnson* requires public employer only to show manifest statistical imbalance under Title VII to support remedial affirmative action plan, and that applicant flow analysis showed underrepresentation of blacks among those hired from properly measured applicant pool, all reflecting continued effects of historical discrimination against blacks in District of Columbia). *See also infra* note 88.

den of proof in reverse discrimination cases, subjects which are discussed below.[71]

b. *Under the Constitution.* During the 1986 term, the Supreme Court addressed the factual predicate for affirmative action required by the Constitution in *Wygant v. Jackson Board of Education.*[72] However, the current effect of that decision is not clear since no opinion commanded a majority on this issue and because Justices Burger and Powell, who joined the plurality opinion, are no longer with the Court.[73]

*Wygant* arose from a challenge to the layoff of more senior whites to retain black teachers, in accordance with the terms of a collective bargaining agreement. In 1972, to address racial tensions in the community and the schools, the Board of Education of Jackson, Michigan, and the Jackson Education Association, its union, had agreed to modify the layoff provision in their collective bargaining agreement.[74] The new provision would adhere to seniority "except that at no time will there be a greater percentage of minority personnel laid off than the current percentage of minority personnel employed at the time of the layoff."[75] *Wygant* thus presented a collectively bargained seniority override with the same purpose and effect as the court-ordered override in *Stotts.* When layoffs were actually undertaken in 1974, rather than follow the modified provision, the Board retained tenured nonminority teachers and laid off probationary minority teachers.[76]

Following a successful state court challenge to the 1974 layoffs by the union and two minority teachers, the Board adhered to the modified layoff provision in two later layoffs. As a result, it laid off tenured nonminority teachers and retained minority teachers with less seniority.[77] The laid-off nonminority teachers sued in federal court, which dismissed all of the plaintiffs' claims.[78] The Court of Appeals for the Sixth Circuit affirmed, holding that under the Equal Protection Clause, racial preferences were acceptable as an attempt to remedy societal discrimination by providing role models for children.[79]

The Supreme Court reversed. A plurality opinion, authored by Justice Powell, held that to undertake an affirmative action program, a public employer must have "convincing evidence that remedial action is warranted. That is, it must have sufficient evidence to justify the conclusion that there had been prior discrimination."[80] The plurality found that neither past "societal discrimination," nor the perceived need to establish role models for minority students provided a sufficient basis for a racial preference in lay-

---

[71]*See* Sections E & F, *infra.*
[72]*Supra* note 70.
[73]Chief Justice Burger and Justice Powell. *See also* Hammon v. Barry, *supra* note 70 (one judge in panel majority condemned hiring provisions of District of Columbia affirmative action plan under Constitution as well as Title VII).
[74]*Supra* note 70, 40 FEP at 1322.
[75]*Id.*
[76]*Id.,* 40 FEP at 1322–23.
[77]*Id.,* 40 FEP at 1323.
[78]*Id.*
[79]Wygant v. Jackson Bd. of Educ., 746 F.2d 1152, 36 FEP 153 (6th Cir. 1984).
[80]*Supra* note 70, 40 FEP at 1325.

offs.[81] Exactly what this convincing or sufficient evidence must be remained undefined by the plurality opinion.

The concurring opinion of Justice O'Connor "agree[s] with the Court that a contemporaneous or antecedent finding of past discrimination by a court or other competent body is not a constitutional prerequisite to a public employer's voluntary agreement to an affirmative action plan."[82] She stated:

> "The imposition of a requirement that public employers make findings that they have engaged in illegal discrimination before they engage in affirmative action programs would severely undermine public employers' incentive to meet voluntarily their civil rights obligations."[83]

What is necessary according to the concurrence is that "the public employer must have a firm basis for determining that affirmative action is warranted";[84] evidence of statistical disparity "sufficient to support a prima facie Title VII pattern or practice claim" would provide such a firm basis.[85]

Justice White, who supplied the swing vote for reversal, concurred only in the judgment. While he viewed the bases for affirmative action asserted by the Board inadequate,[86] he did not elaborate, and appeared to base his view primarily on the impact of the layoff on nonminorities.[87]

As a result of the three opinions supporting its outcome, *Wygant* suggests, but does not hold, that public employers must be prepared to demonstrate at least a prima facie case of discrimination as a predicate for affirmative action challenged under the Constitution. A substantial majority in *Wygant* supported the proposition that a prior or contemporaneous finding of discrimination is not necessary.[88]

---

[81]*Id.*, 40 FEP at 1324–25. *Compare* Johnson v. Transportation Agency, Santa Clara County, 480 U.S. 616, 43 FEP 411, 414 (1987), discussed in text accompanying *supra* note 49 (agency's affirmative action plan attributed underrepresentation to societal causes rather than discrimination), J.A. Croson Co. v. City of Richmond, 822 F.2d 1355 (4th Cir. 1987), *aff'd*, 488 U.S. _____, 57 USLW 4132 (1989) (city's minority business utilization plan found invalid as not narrowly tailored and as based on mere assumptions of historical discrimination) *and* J. Edinger & Son v. City of Louisville, 802 F.2d 213, 55 USLW 2221 (6th Cir. 1986) (societal discrimination, without more, found insufficient basis for ordinance favoring minority businesses) *with* Associated Gen. Contractors of Cal. v. City & County of San Francisco, 813 F.2d 922 (9th Cir. 1987) (ordinance provision giving preference to minority-owned business found not narrowly tailored, and provisions giving preference to female-owned businesses found facially valid as substantially related to goal of compensating women for disparate treatment suffered in business community) *and* H.K. Porter Co. v. Metropolitan Dade County, 825 F.2d 324 (11th Cir. 1987) (per curiam), *cert. petition filed* (affirmative action program requiring 5% participation by minority businesses upheld as narrowly tailored, temporary, and justified by compelling interest in eradicating continued effects of past discrimination).

[82]40 FEP at 1330.

[83]*Id.*

[84]*Id.*, 40 FEP at 1331.

[85]*Id.*

[86]*Id.*, 40 FEP at 1332.

[87]*Id.*, 40 FEP at 1332–33. The dissent of Justices Marshall, Brennan, and Blackmun would have upheld the layoff plan and stated that "[t]he Court is correct to recognize, as it does today, that formal findings of past discrimination are not a necessary predicate to the adoption of affirmative-action policies, and that the scope of such policies need not be limited to remedying specific instances of identifiable discrimination." *Id.*, 40 FEP at 1337. Justice Stevens' dissent focused on the validity of the role model rationale as a basis for the collective bargaining agreement. *Id.*, 40 FEP at 1340.

[88]*See* Justice O'Connor's concurring opinion. *Id.*, 40 FEP at 1330. In *Johnson v. Transportation Agency, Santa Clara County,* 480 U.S. 616, 43 FEP 411 (1987), the Court held that a manifest imbalance need not be sufficient to support a prima facie case and stated that "we do not regard as identical the constraints of Title VII and the federal constitution on voluntarily adopted affirmative action plans." *Id.*, 43 FEP at 419. *Compare* Ledoux v. District of Columbia, 820 F.2d 1293, 43 FEP 1880, *reh'g granted in part en banc,* 833 F.2d 386 (D.C. Cir. 1987), *reh'g order vacated en banc,* 841 F.2d 400 (D.C. Cir. 1988) (in challenge to police department's affirmative action plan, plaintiffs failed to prove plan was invalid under Title VII; remanded to determine plan's validity under the Constitution based on whether

## 2. Court-Ordered Affirmative Action Plans

The Supreme Court has upheld two cases of court-ordered affirmative action involving challenges under both Title VII and the Constitution in *Sheet Metal Workers Local 28 v. EEOC*[89] and *United States v. Paradise.*[90] These cases evidence a much higher standard of justification than has been true for cases dealing with voluntary affirmative action. However, because each presented such an extreme example of historic discrimination, their usefulness for defining the minimum factual predicate for court-ordered affirmative action is limited.

### Sheet Metal Workers

In *Sheet Metal Workers,*[91] the Court primarily considered whether § 706(g) of Title VII limited affirmative action to identified victims of past discrimination. Necessarily, the Court considered the validity of the U.S. Department of Justice's interpretation of the Court's prior decision in *Stotts.*[92] Based on a record showing the union's "pervasive and egregious discrimination" and its "egregious violation of Title VII,"[93] the Court held that affirmative relief that extended to individuals who were not themselves victims of discrimination was a permissible and appropriate remedy. The Court also rejected the argument that the remedy was an unconstitutional deprivation of majority workers' rights, finding that the relief ordered was narrowly tailored to accomplish a compelling governmental interest.[94]

State and federal administrative and court rulings dating from 1964 had concluded that Local 28 had discriminated against blacks and Hispanics by excluding them from membership. When the district court, in 1975, found that the union had violated Title VII, it ordered them to establish a 29 percent nonwhite membership goal. An affirmative action plan developed by a court-appointed administrator was approved by the district court and affirmed on appeal. After agreeing to extend the timetable for achieving the goal, the district court twice found the union in civil contempt of its orders. The Supreme Court's decision was based on an order of the district court, affirmed on appeal, ordering the union to pay a fine, to be used to support affirmative action, and to meet a 29.23 percent nonwhite membership goal by 1987.

In affirming, the Second Circuit distinguished *Sheet Metal Workers* from *Stotts* in three respects. First, the *Sheet Metal Workers* case did not involve a bona fide seniority plan; second, *Stotts* focused on "make-whole

---

department had "strong basis" for belief that plan was necessary to remedy effects of past discrimination) *with* Hammon v. Barry, 813 F.2d 412, 43 FEP 89, *reh'g granted in part en banc,* 833 F.2d 367 (D.C. Cir. 1987), *reh'g order vacated en banc,* 841 F.2d 426, 46 FEP 760 (D.C. Cir.), *cert. denied,* 486 U.S. _____, 46 FEP 1552 (1988) (fire department's affirmative action plan, adopted wihout evidence of recent discriminatory hiring practices sufficient to justify race-conscious hiring, and not narrowly tailored to achieve remedial purposes; plan thus violates both Title VII and equal protection component of due process clause).

[89]478 U.S. 421, 41 FEP 107 (1986).
[90]480 U.S. 149, 43 FEP 1 (1987).
[91]Sheet Metal Workers Local 28 v. EEOC, *supra* note 89.
[92]Firefighters Local 1784 v. Stotts, 467 U.S. 561, 34 FEP 1702 (1984). *See* discussion *supra* note 25.
[93]Sheet Metal Workers Local 28 v. EEOC, *supra* note 89, 41 FEP at 129, 131.
[94]*Id.,* 41 FEP at 130–31.

relief" and not prospective relief; and third, although *Stotts* had no predicate of intentional discrimination, *Sheet Metal Workers* did.[95]

The principal issue presented by the petitioners on certiorari was whether remedies under § 706(g) of Title VII could extend to persons who were not identified as victims of discrimination.[96] Several lesser issues were also presented.[97] The Solicitor General supported the petitioners' position.

*Sheet Metal Workers* produced five opinions with Justice Brennan writing the opinion for a four-member plurality.[98] A clear majority agreed that § 706(g) does not always limit affirmative relief to actual victims of discrimination.[99] However, the specific order in *Sheet Metal Workers* was approved by only a bare majority.[100]

The same bare majority held that the Court's order was constitutional against a claim that the goal denied nonminorities equal protection on the basis of race. Justice Brennan's plurality opinion concluded that the district court's order met the most rigorous formulation of the constitutional standard since it was "narrowly tailored to further the Government's compelling interest in remedying past discrimination."[101] The plurality distinguished *Wygant* on the basis that the case lacked a "proper showing of prior discrimination that would justify the use of remedial classifications," while *Sheet Metal Workers* involved repeated judicial findings of "egregious violations of Title VII."[102] Justice Powell agreed with the plurality's constitutional holding in a separate opinion.[103]

The decision made clear that court-ordered affirmative relief must be a remedy for past discrimination.[104] In fact, the plurality suggests that past

---

[95]EEOC v. Sheet Metal Workers Local 638, 753 F.2d 1172, 1186, 36 FEP 1466, 1477 (2d Cir. 1985).
[96]Sheet Metal Workers Local 28 v. EEOC, *supra* note 89, 41 FEP at 114.
[97]The plurality also rejected claims that the district court relied on incorrect statistical evidence; that the court's contempt remedies were criminal and imposed without due process; that the appointment of an administrator interfered with the union's right to self-governance; and that the membership goal and the fund were unconstitutional. *Id.* Justice O'Connor, in dissent, would have struck down the membership goal and the fund on statutory grounds. *Id.,* 41 FEP at 138. Justice White, also dissenting, would have found the goal and the contempt remedy excessive. *Id.*
[98]Justice Brennan was joined by Justices Marshall, Blackmun, and Stevens.
[99]In a separate concurrence, Justice Powell stated: "I * * * agree that § 706(g) does not limit a court in all cases to granting relief only to actual victims of discrimination." *Id.,* 41 FEP at 132. Justice White, in his dissent, wrote: "I agree that § 706(g) does not bar relief to nonvictims in all circumstances." *Id.,* 41 FEP at 138. Justice O'Connor wrote separately, concurring in part and dissenting in part. She wrote: "It is now clear, however, that a majority of the Court believes that the last sentence of § 706(g) does not in all circumstances prohibit a court in a Title VII employment discrimination case from ordering relief that may confer some racial preferences with regard to employment in favor of nonvictims of discrimination." *Id.,* 41 FEP at 134. She maintained that the membership goal and fund order constituted racial quotas and were impermissible when § 706(g) is read in light of § 706(j) of Title VII. *Id.* Justice Rehnquist, joined by Chief Justice Burger, dissented, writing "that § 706(g) forbids a court from ordering racial preferences that effectively displace nonminorities except to minority individuals who have been the actual victims of a particular employer's racial discrimination." *Id.,* 41 FEP at 139.
[100]This holding was supported only by the plurality and Justice Powell. In his dissent, Justice White found the order of the district court to be a "strict racial quota, * * * excessive under § 706(g) absent findings that those benefitting from the relief had been victims of discriminatory practices by the union." *Id.,* 41 FEP at 138.
[101]*Id.,* 41 FEP at 130–31.
[102]*Id.,* 41 FEP at 131.
[103]*Id.,* 41 FEP at 132. Justice Powell found that "without a doubt" the record supported finding a compelling governmental interest. He observed: "It would be difficult to find defendants more determined to discriminate against minorities." Most of his separate opinion supported his conclusion that the remedy was "narrowly tailored" to remedy that discrimination. *Id.*
[104]*Id.,* 41 FEP at 116.

discrimination sufficient to warrant court-ordered affirmation action must be of a marked degree:

> "In the majority of Title VII cases, the court will not have to impose affirmative action as a remedy for past discrimination, but need only order the employer or union to cease engaging in discriminatory practices and award make-whole relief to the individuals victimized by those practices. However, in some cases, affirmative action may be necessary in order effectively to enforce Title VII. * * * [A] court may have to resort to race-conscious affirmative action when confronted with an employer or labor union that has engaged in persistent or egregious discrimination. Or, such relief may be necessary to dissipate the lingering effects of pervasive discrimination. Whether there might be other circumstances that justify the use of court-ordered affirmative action is a matter that we need not decide here."[105]

### *Paradise*

*United States v. Paradise*[106] involved an interim promotion plan fashioned by a district court to remedy long-standing racial discrimination by the Alabama state police force. Like *Sheet Metal Workers, Paradise* involved discrimination maintained in the face of previous remedial court orders.[107] In the Supreme Court, the United States argued that the district court's promotion order violated the Equal Protection Clause of the Fourteenth Amendment.

In 1972, the District Court for the Middle District of Alabama found that the Alabama Department of Public Safety had never hired a black state trooper, and ordered the Department to hire one black trooper for each white trooper hired until 25 percent of the state police force was black.[108] In 1977, the plaintiffs sought relief with respect to the Department's promotion practices, and, in 1979, the Court approved a partial consent decree in which the Department agreed to develop a fair promotion procedure within one year.[109] A second consent decree concerning promotion policies was approved by the Court in 1981.[110]

In 1983 the plaintiffs sought enforcement of the two consent decrees. Faced with the lack of nondiscriminatory promotion procedures, and the immediate need of the Department to make promotions, the district court entered an interim promotion order. Assuming qualified black candidates were available, promotions were to be made on a one-for-one basis pending development of promotion policies which did not have an adverse impact on blacks. The interim order applied to any rank which was less than 25 percent black. The following month the Department promoted eight blacks and eight whites to corporal. Four months later, the interim order was lifted for

---

[105]*Id.,* 41 FEP at 128–29.
[106]480 U.S. 149, 43 FEP 1 (1987).
[107]*Id.,* 43 FEP at 2–7.
[108]NAACP v. Allen, 340 F. Supp. 703, 4 FEP 318 (M.D. Ala. 1972), *aff'd,* 493 F.2d 614, 7 FEP 873 (5th Cir. 1974). In 1974, the district court reaffirmed the hiring order and enjoined further attempts by the department to deny full relief to the plaintiffs by restricted hirings. Paradise v. Dothard, Civil Action No. 3561-N (M.D. Ala., Aug. 5, 1975).
[109]*Supra* note 106, 43 FEP at 3.
[110]*Id.,* 43 FEP at 4.

promotions to corporal when the Department submitted new procedures for promotions to that rank.[111]

As in *Sheet Metal Workers,* Justice Brennan authored a plurality opinion in a 5–4 decision upholding the court's order.[112] The plurality again held that the order in question met even the "strict scrutiny" constitutional test, finding it to be " 'narrowly tailored' to serve a 'compelling governmental purpose.' "[113] After recounting the "tortuous course of [the] litigation in some detail,"[114] the plurality concluded: "the pervasive, systematic, and obstinate discriminatory conduct of the Department created a profound need and a firm justification for the race-conscious relief ordered by the District Court."[115] Emphasizing the flexible and temporary nature of the order, Justice Brennan also found it narrowly tailored to achieve the district court's objective of eliminating the effects of "long term, open, and pervasive" discrimination and ensuring expeditious compliance with the earlier consent decrees.[116]

Justice O'Connor began the principal dissenting opinion[117] by agreeing with the majority that "the District Court unquestionably had the authority to fashion a remedy designed to end the Department's egregious history of discrimination."[118] She concluded, however, that the order was not "manifestly necessary"[119] to achieve the court's objectives, but rather served an *"in terrorem* purpose."[120]

Whether less egregious or persistent factual predicates would justify court-imposed affirmative action plans remains to be seen. In these cases, the Court emphasized not only the flagrant nature of the predicate but also the care with which the remedy must be framed, important requirements that will be discussed below.

### E. The Scope of Affirmative Action Plans

The Court's recent decisions make clear that, even where the necessary predicate for affirmative action has been established, the scope of that action is limited by the rights of individuals adversely affected. This is because, under both Title VII and the Fourteenth Amendment, they are equally entitled to protection from employment discrimination.

Section 703 of Title VII protects nonminorities and males from employment discrimination, as the Court reiterated in *Firefighters Local 93.*[121] In the Title VII cases, this consideration is articulated in terms of whether a

---

[111]*Id.,* 43 FEP at 6. In October 1984, the interim order was lifted for promotion to sergeant based on new procedures.

[112]Justice Brennan was joined by Justices Marshall, Blackmun, and Powell. Justice Powell filed a concurring opinion, and Justice Stevens filed an opinion concurring in the judgment.

[113]*Id.,* 43 FEP at 7.

[114]*Id.,* 43 FEP at 2.

[115]*Id.,* 43 FEP at 7.

[116]*Id.,* 43 FEP at 9.

[117]Justice O'Connor was joined by Chief Justice Rehnquist and Justice Scalia. Justice White filed a dissenting statement, "[a]greeing with much of what Justice O'Connor has written in this case." *Id.,* 43 FEP at 21.

[118]*Id.,* 43 FEP at 19.

[119]*Id.*

[120]*Id.,* 43 FEP at 20.

[121]Firefighters Local 93 v. City of Cleveland, 478 U.S. 501, 41 FEP 139, 146 n.8 (1986).

particular action "unnecessarily trammeled the rights of [nonminority or] male employees or created an absolute bar to their [employment or] advancement."[122]

Considering a constitutional claim, the plurality in *Wygant* recognized "that the level of scrutiny does not change merely because the challenged classification operates against a group that historically has not been subject to governmental discrimination."[123] In the constitutional context, the issue is framed as whether "the means chosen by the State to effectuate its purpose" is " 'narrowly tailored to the achievement of that goal.' "[124] In either setting the practical considerations are similar.

A basic requirement, which relates to the old distinction between "goals" and "quotas," is that the extent of necessary affirmative action must be determined with reasonable precision. Thus, the Court in *Johnson* emphasized that the plan there called for supervisors to consider the number of qualified women available for particular job categories, rather than general work force availability.[125] The Court cautioned:

"[H]ad the Plan simply calculated imbalances in all categories according to the proportion of women in the area labor pool, and then directed that hiring be governed solely by those figures, its validity fairly could be called into question. This is because analysis of a more specialized labor pool normally is necessary in determining underrepresentation in some positions. If a plan failed to take distinctions in qualifications into account in providing guidance for actual employment decisions, it would dictate mere blind hiring by the numbers, for it would hold supervisors to achievement of a particular percentage of minority employment or membership * * * regardless of circumstances such as economic conditions or the number of qualified minority applicants * * * ."[126]

None of the affirmative action plans or orders approved to date has involved a total exclusion of nonminority or male opportunities, and the absence of such an exclusion has been often noted by the Court as evidence of permissible scope.[127] In *Johnson* the Court noted that the plan set aside

---

[122]Johnson v. Transportation Agency, Santa Clara County, 480 U.S. 616, 43 FEP 411, 421 (1987).
[123]Wygant v. Jackson Bd. of Educ., 476 U.S. 267, 40 FEP 1321, 1324 (1986) (citing Mississippi Univ. for Women v. Hogan, 458 U.S. 718, 724 n.9 (1982)).
[124]*Id.,* 40 FEP at 1324. *See* Britton v. South Bend Community School Corp., 819 F.2d 766, 43 FEP 1483 (7th Cir.), *cert. denied,* 484 U.S. _____, 45 FEP 648 (1987) (in layoff case, collective bargaining provision found not narrowly tailored because it created absolute preference for blacks).
[125]Goals in EEOC consent decrees are to be based on expert analysis of the labor market availability of the benefited group for the position in question. EEOC General Counsel Memorandum, October 6, 1987, *infra* at 344.
[126]Johnson v. Transportation Agency, Santa Clara County, 480 U.S. 616, 43 FEP 411, 420 (1987). In *United States v. Paradise,* 480 U.S. 149, 43 FEP 1 (1987), the plurality considered and rejected the Government's contention that the one-for-one interim order was inconsistent with the 25% black availability in the relevant labor pool. Justice Brennan concluded that the goal remained 25%, and that the accelerated 50% interim order was justified, if not mandated, by the extreme facts of that case. *Id.,* 43 FEP at 12–13. Justice O'Connor's disagreement on this point was a principal basis for the dissent:
"The one-for-one promotion quota used in this case far exceeded the percentage of blacks in the trooper force, and there is no evidence in the record that such an extreme quota was necessary to eradicate the effects of the Department's delay. . . . If strict scrutiny is to have any meaning . . . a promotion goal must have a closer relationship to the percentage of blacks eligible for promotions."
*Id.,* 43 FEP at 20.
EEOC consent decree goals, "[e]xcept in extraordinary circumstances," are to be set "at, rather than above, current labor market availability." EEOC General Counsel Memorandum, *supra* note 125.
[127]*See* Johnson v. Transportation Agency, Santa Clara County, *supra* note 122; United States v. Paradise, *supra* note 126, 43 FEP at 13; Sheet Metal Workers Local 28 v. EEOC, 478 U.S. 421, 479, 41 FEP 107, 130 (1986).

no positions for women and required no quotas, but "merely authorizes that consideration be given to affirmative action concerns when evaluating qualified applicants."[128] The fact that affirmative action benefits are available only to qualified minorities or women has been noted as a supporting feature in a number of the cases.[129]

Limitations on the duration as well as the scope of preferences are also suggested by the Court's decisions. As the Court stated in *Paradise:* "In determining whether race-conscious remedies are appropriate, we look to several factors, including * * * the flexibility and duration of relief * * * ."[130] In *Sheet Metal Workers,* the Court noted that "both the membership goal and the Fund order are temporary measures."[131] Preferential selection of union members was scheduled to end when the percentage of minority members approximated the minority percentage in the local labor force, and the Fund would terminate when the membership goal was achieved.[132] As the Court recognized in *Johnson,* an explicit termination point is more important where a specific numerical goal is established: "Express assurance that a program is only temporary may be necessary if the program actually sets aside positions according to specific numbers."[133] The Agency Plan approved in *Johnson* had no express end date; however, it contained no specific set-asides of jobs for women.

In addition to being of reasonable scope and duration, affirmative action plans, court-ordered or voluntary, must be designed to attain, not maintain, balanced work forces. The Court in *Sheet Metal Workers* held: "The District Court's orders * * * operate 'as a temporary tool for remedying past discrimination without attempting to 'maintain' a previously achieved balance.' "[134] Similarly, in *Johnson,* the Court noted that "the Agency's Plan was intended to *attain* a balanced work force, not to maintain one."[135] The Agency was viewed as having taken "a moderate, gradual approach" to affirmative action: "Given this fact, as well as the Agency's express commitment to 'attain' a balanced work force, there is ample assurance that the Agency does not seek to use its Plan to maintain a permanent racial and sexual balance."[136] Significantly, in the two cases where the avowed purpose of the preference

---

[128]Johnson v. Transportation Agency, Santa Clara County, *supra* note 122. Thus the Agency's plan resembled the Harvard Plan which was noted with approval in *Bakke.* Regents of the Univ. of Cal. v. Bakke, 438 U.S. 265, 316–19, 17 FEP 1000, 1020–21 (1978).

[129]Johnson v. Transportation Agency, Santa Clara County, *supra* note 122; United States v. Paradise, *supra* note 126, 43 FEP at 13; Sheet Metal Workers Local 28 v. EEOC, 478 U.S. 421, 439, 41 FEP 107, 117 (1986). The limitation of affirmative action to qualified beneficiaries is to be expressly stated in EEOC consent decrees. EEOC General Counsel Memorandum, October 6, 1987, *infra* at 344. Moreover, lack of qualified minority or female candidates is a valid excuse for a failure to meet consent decree goals. *Id.* at 4.

[130]United States v. Paradise, *supra* note 126, 43 FEP at 9.

[131]Sheet Metal Workers Local 28 v. EEOC, *supra* note 127.

[132]*Id.*

[133]Johnson v. Transportation Agency, Santa Clara County, 480 U.S. 616, 43 FEP 411, 421 (1987). EEOC consent decrees are to provide for timetables appropriate to eliminate the pattern of discrimination and "clearly state its termination date." EEOC General Counsel Memorandum, October 6, 1987, *infra* at 344. This period should not normally exceed three years without providing for readjustment of the goals to allow for changes in labor market availability. *Id.* at n.10.

[134]Sheet Metal Workers Local 28 v. EEOC, *supra* note 127 (quoting Steelworkers v. Weber, 443 U.S. 193, 216, 20 FEP 1, 10 (1979) (Blackmun, J., concurring)).

[135]Johnson v. Transportation Agency, Santa Clara County, *supra* note 133.

[136]*Id. See also* United States v. Paradise, *supra* note 126, 43 FEP at 12, 13.

at issue was the maintenance of prior affirmative action gains, *Stotts* and *Wygant,* the plans were rejected.

The permissible scope of affirmative action is also affected by the type of employment decision involved. Both of the 1986 and 1987 term decisions which invalidated affirmative action plans, *Stotts* and *Wygant,* involved plans which modified incumbent employees' protection from layoff. As Justice Powell wrote for the plurality in *Wygant:*

> "In cases involving valid *hiring* goals, the burden to be borne by innocent individuals is diffused to a considerable extent among society generally. Though hiring goals may burden some innocent individuals, they simply do not impose the same kind of injury that layoffs impose. Denial of a future employment opportunity is not as intrusive as loss of an existing job."[137]

Promotional goals may be regarded as relatively diffuse in impact, hence more similar to hiring goals than to layoffs. In *Paradise,* the Court held that the promotion plan at issue "only postpones the promotions of qualified whites. Consequently, like a hiring goal, it 'impose[s] a diffuse burden, * * * foreclosing only one of several opportunities.' "[138] In *Johnson,* the Court observed that petitioner "retained his employment with the Agency * * * and remained eligible for other promotions."[139]

However, Justice Powell, concurring in *Sheet Metal Workers,* has warned that labels such as layoffs, hirings, and promotions may mislead:

> "[I]t is too simplistic to conclude from the combined holdings in *Wygant* and this case that hiring goals withstand constitutional muster whereas layoff goals and fixed quotas do not. There may be cases, for example, where a hiring goal in a particularly specialized area of employment would have the same pernicious effect as the layoff goal in *Wygant.* The proper constitutional inquiry focuses on the effect, if any, and the diffuseness of the burden imposed on innocent nonminorities, not on the label applied to the particular employment plan at issue."[140]

The EEOC's General Counsel has directed Regional Attorneys to consider using goals and timetables in consent decrees "only in the absence of effective relief which has less impact on third parties."[141] He has also stated that "it will often be prudent to ask the Court, prior to seeking judicial approval for a consent decree containing goals, to hold a fairness hearing in order to afford all affected individuals—both beneficiaries and potentially adversely affected individuals—an opportunity to comment on the proposed remedy."[142] He has also stated that "[e]xcept in extraordinary circumstances, goals should be set at, rather than above, current labor market availability as measured by census work force data or nondiscriminatory applicant flow."[143]

---

[137]Wygant v. Jackson Bd. of Educ., 476 U.S. 267, 282-83, 40 FEP 1321, 1327 (1986).

[138]United States v. Paradise, 480 U.S. 149, 183, 43 FEP 1, 14 (1987) (quoting Wygant v. Jackson Bd. of Educ., *supra* note 137).

[139]Johnson v. Transportation Agency, Santa Clara County, *supra* note 133. Indeed, Mr. Johnson was promoted to a similar position in 1983. *Id.* at n.15.

[140]Sheet Metal Workers Local 28 v. EEOC, 478 U.S. 421, 488 n.3, 41 FEP 107, 134 n.3 (1986).

[141]EEOC General Counsel Memorandum, October 6, 1987, *infra* at 345.

[142]EEOC General Counsel Memorandum, October 6, 1987, *infra* at 345. The hearing should follow reasonable notice to affected individuals. *Id., infra* at 346.

[143]*Id.,infra* at 344.

## F. Burden of Proof

The Supreme Court's recent affirmative action cases have established that the allocation of the burden of proof is the same under the Constitution and Title VII. In *Johnson,* the Court noted that the petitioner bore the burden of establishing the affirmative action plan's invalidity.[144] The Court stated:

> "Only last term in *Wygant v. Jackson Board of Education* * * * we held that '[t]he ultimate burden remains with the employees to demonstrate the unconstitutionality of an affirmative-action program,' and we see no basis for a different rule regarding a plan's alleged violation of Title VII."[145]

The Court further noted that the analytical framework of *McDonnell Douglas*[146] was applicable. First, the plaintiff must establish a prima facie case that race or sex has been taken into account in an employment matter, and then the burden shifts to the employer to provide a "nondiscriminatory rationale" for its action: "The existence of an affirmative action plan provides such a rationale."[147] The burden then shifts back to the plaintiff to show pretext or the invalidity of the plan,[148] and the employer will ordinarily present supporting evidence for its plan.[149] The Court concluded:

> "That does not mean, however, as the petitioner suggests, that reliance on an affirmative action plan is to be treated as an affirmative defense requiring the employer to carry the burden of proving the validity of the plan. The burden of proving its invalidity remains on the plaintiff."[150]

---

[144] Johnson v. Transportation Agency, Santa Clara County, 480 U.S. 616, 43 FEP 411, 416 (1987).

[145] *Id.* (citation omitted).

[146] McDonnell Douglas Corp. v. Green, 411 U.S. 792, 5 FEP 965 (1973).

[147] Johnson v. Transportation Agency, Santa Clara County, *supra* note 144.

[148] Since *Albermarle Paper Co. v. Moody,* 422 U.S. 405, 10 FEP 1181 (1975), it has been established that the burden of establishing the availability of an alternative practice with less adverse impact rests with the plaintiff. *Id.* at 425. In a reverse discrimination case, the plaintiff has a similar burden, that of establishing that the practice at issue is not narrowly tailored. In *Wygant v. Jackson Bd. of Educ.,* 476 U.S. 267, 40 FEP 1321 (1986), the plurality stated:

> "The term 'narrowly tailored,' so frequently used in our cases, has acquired a secondary meaning. More specifically, as commentators have indicated, the term may be used to require consideration whether lawful alternative and less restrictive means could have been used."

*Id.,* 40 FEP at 1326 n.6. A plaintiff bears the burden of showing that an affirmative action plan is not narrowly tailored. *Id.,* 40 FEP at 1331–32 (O'Connor, J., concurring).

[149] Johnson v. Transportation Agency, Santa Clara County, *supra* note 144.

[150] *Id.*

APPENDIX A

EEOC GENERAL COUNSEL MEMORANDUM

October 6, 1987

MEMORANDUM

TO        :  Regional Attorneys
FROM      :  Charles A. Shanor
             General Counsel
SUBJECT   :  Goals and Timetables Provisions in Proposed Title VII Consent
             Decrees

Goals and timetables, in appropriate cases, may be used in EEOC consent decrees to enforce compliance with Title VII of the Civil Rights Act of 1964, as amended.[1] Because field legal units have raised several recurring questions concerning goals and timetables, this memorandum identifies and discusses the considerations which should be analyzed in consent decrees containing goals and timetables.[2]

A. Factual Predicate

The Supreme Court has held that carefully tailored goals and timetables may be incorporated in Title VII consent decrees.[3] Thus, employers may establish voluntary affirmative action plans which include goals and timetables without litigation and without prima facie evidence of Title VII violations.[4] The Office of General Counsel will, however, require such evidence before approving goals and timetables provisions in proposed EEOC Title VII consent decrees[5] because the initial finding of discrimination in the Letter of Determination and the initial suit authorization was based on the presence of at least prima facie evidence of a Title VII violation. Accordingly, comparable evidence justifying the use of goals and timetables should be made part of the proposed consent decree and should take the form of a joint stipulation of uncontested facts.

In determining whether sufficient evidence supports the inclusion of goals and

---

[1] Goals and timetables are characterized by their express use of a Title VII basis—race, sex, religion, or national origin—upon which discrimination is prohibited.

[2] All proposed Title VII consent decrees must be presented to the General Counsel or Associate General Counsel, Trial Services, for review.

[3] Local No. 93, International Association of Firefighters v. City of Cleveland, 106 S.Ct. 3063, 3073 (1986).

[4] See Johnson v. Transportation Agency, Santa Clara County, California, 107 S.Ct. 1442 (1987); United Steelworkers v. Weber, 443 U.S. 193 (1979); Guidelines on Affirmative Action Appropriate under Title VII of the Civil Rights Act of 1964, as amended, 44 FR 4422 (January 19, 1979), 29 C.F.R. Part 1608 (1986).

[5] Absent unusual circumstances found acceptable to the General Counsel or Associate General Counsel, Trial Services, voluntary goals and timetables should be entered into by EEOC field units only in consent decrees, not in settlements accompanied by joint notices of dismissal.

344 EDL FIVE-YEAR CUMULATIVE SUPPLEMENT CH. 24

timetables in proposed consent decrees, expert analysis should be employed.[6] This analysis should determine the appropriate labor market availability figure for the position or positions in question and should be part of the retained documentation in the case file.[7] Also, to preclude subsequent questions concerning the accuracy or validity of the availability figures included in the proposed consent decree, proposed consent decrees should explicitly state that the availability figures were based on and verified by expert analysis.

## B. Magnitude

Except in extraordinary circumstances, goals should be set at, rather than above, current labor market availability as measured by census work force data or nondiscriminatory applicant flow. Thus, a short term goal should generally be set at the same level as a long term goal.

Short term goals at levels higher than labor market availability have been sanctioned in egregious cases of overt job discrimination.[8] If such entrenched patterns or practices of overt discrimination exist, accelerated relief (and the concomitant increased impact on third parties) should be justified separately.

## C. Duration

Consent decree timetables should cover the approximate period necessary to disestablish the pattern of discrimination indicated by the evidence of Title VII's violation.[9] The goal should clearly state its termination date,[10] which will usually be on or prior to the expiration of the court's jurisdiction over the consent decree.[11]

## D. Beneficiary Qualifications

Employers are only required to select qualified individuals.[12] Thus, EEOC consent decrees should state that the employer has no obligation to select unqualified individuals.

Consent decrees containing goals and timetables should also make clear that failure to attain a goal will be excused if the employer proves by persuasive and specific evidence that it was unable to recruit or promote qualified minority or female applicants or employees.[13]

---

[6]As a matter of course, unless external experts have already performed such analysis, field legal units should rely upon internal experts in the Research and Analytic Services Division of the Office of General Counsel.

[7]Such goals and timetables will thus be appropriately tied to expected future applicant flow statistics. To help ensure such applicant flow, separate outreach measures should be included in the decree to encourage applications by members of the group expected to benefit from the goals and timetables provisions.

[8]*Cf.* United States v. Paradise, 107 S.Ct. 1053, 1071 (1987) (acceleration required by defendants' past delay and resistance to non-discriminatory procedures).

[9]*See* Johnson v. Transportation Agency, Santa Clara County, *supra,* 107 S.Ct. at 1456; United Steelworkers v. Weber, *supra,* 443 U.S. at 208.

[10]Because labor market availability changes over time, a goal should not normally be set for a period in excess of three years without readjustment of the goal to comport with such changing availability.

[11]For example, a termination provision might specify that the goal would become inapplicable when a non-discriminatory selection procedure is devised. *Cf.* United States v. Paradise, *supra,* 107 S.Ct. at 1063.

[12]*E.g.,* Johnson v. Transportation Agency, Santa Clara County, *supra;* LeDoux v. District of Columbia, 820 F.2d 1293, 1301 (D.C. Cir. 1987).

[13]Johnson v. Transportation Agency, *supra,* 107 S.Ct. at 1455, approved use of sex as a "plus factor" in deciding between two promotional candidates who were both well-qualified. The Court emphasized that under the plan at issue in *Johnson "no* persons are automatically excluded from consideration; *all* are able to have their qualifications weighed against those of other applicants." *Ibid.* (emphasis in original). EEOC decrees likewise should be structured

## E. Make Whole and Alternative Relief

In light of the Commission's Policy Statement on Remedies and Relief For Individual Cases of Unlawful Discrimination and the central make whole purpose of Title VII,[14] goals and timetables relief should not be substituted for make whole relief, including back pay, for specific victims of discrimination.[15]

Goals and timetables should be considered only in the absence of effective relief which has less impact on third parties. For example, it may be unnecessary to impose numerical hiring goals where the decree specifies a particular process for identifying individual victims, making them whole, and implementing prospective selection systems which are nondiscriminatory. Moreover, where there will be relatively few employment decisions by a particular employer, a race or sex conscious goal may serve no practical purpose when EEOC can effectively monitor individual employment decisions by reviewing such employment records.

## F. Monitoring and Enforcing Compliance

Consent decrees containing goals and timetables should be structured to facilitate enforcement by EEOC. Such decrees must provide for regular and detailed reports to EEOC in a format which will minimize EEOC's expenditure of resources on monitoring activities.

In addition, because enforcement disputes may arise over whether or not a respondent has complied in "good faith" with the goals set out in a consent decree,[16] the phrase "good faith" should be defined objectively in terms of activities to be performed. Consent decrees should also provide that the respondent bears the burden of showing by persuasive and specific evidence why goals have not been met.

These monitoring and enforcement provisions are based on two practical considerations. First, the respondent, not EEOC, is in the best position to ascertain and disclose all the facts surrounding its employment decisions. Second, without such provisions, EEOC will expend resources unnecessarily in discovering and presenting the facts needed to secure compliance with goal provisions in consent decrees.

## G. Fairness Hearings

In view of judicial sensitivity to the interests of beneficiaries and third parties who may be affected by the inclusion of goals in proposed consent decrees, it will often be prudent to ask the Court, prior to seeking judicial approval for a consent decree containing goals, to hold a fairness hearing in order to afford all affected individuals—both beneficiaries and potentially adversely affected individuals—an opportunity to comment on the proposed remedy.[17] Such a hearing should be sought

---

so that an employer considers all relevant aspects of each qualified candidate so that no candidates are isolated from competition. If sex, race, or national origin is only used as a "plus factor", EEOC can ensure that the decree does not unnecessarily trammel the rights of majority employees or create an absolute bar to their advancement. *Cf.* 107 S.Ct. at 1455. *See also* n.15 *infra.*

[14]The Policy Statement requires that Commission personnel seek prompt and complete relief for individual discriminatees, including nondiscriminatory placement and full backpay. Daily Labor Report No. 25 (Feb. 6, 1985). Cases supporting Title VII's make whole purpose include Teamsters v. United States, 431 U.S. 324, 364–365 (1977); Franks v. Bowman Transportation Co., 424 U.S. 409, 444 1976); Albemarle Paper Co. v. Moody, 422 U.S. 405, 421 (1975).

[15]Since goals and timetables involve no immediate monetary cost, employers in some circumstances may attempt to substitute this form of relief for relief which entails a monetary outlay.

[16]A principal difference between an impermissible quota and permissible goal is that the latter provides a good faith defense to its non-attainment. *Cf.* Johnson v. Transportation Agency, Santa Clara County, *supra,* 107 S.Ct. at 1455.

[17]Similar prudential concerns may arise when other remedies, such as retroactive seniority, are involved. The General Counsel may provide further guidance concerning fairness

where the consent decree establishes promotion goals, for example, because it can be expected that at least some incumbent employees will have promotion expectations which may be perceived as being adversely affected by the establishment of promotion goals.[18] Practical and effective notice of such fairness hearings should be given. For example, notice to incumbent employees may usually be effectuated through posting at the facility. Notice to applicants or potential applicants may be effectuated through letters, newspaper advertisements, and the like.[19]

---

hearings generally following the Supreme Court disposition of Marino v. Ortiz, 806 F.2d 1144 (2d Cir. 1986), *cert. granted,* 107 S.Ct. 3182 (1987), and Hispanic Society of the New York City Police Department, Inc. v. Police Department of New York, 806 F.2d 1147 (2d Cir. 1986), *cert. granted,* 107 S.Ct. 3182 (1987).

[18]Such a hearing will less frequently be necessary before judicial approval of proposed hiring goals is sought because the expectations of individuals not in the particular employer's workforce are not as firm as the promotion expectations of incumbent employees. *Cf.* United States v. Paradise, *supra,* 107 S.Ct. 1053 (1987). Wygant v. Jackson Board of Education, 476 U.S. 267 (1986), and Firefighters' Local 1784 v. Stotts, 467 U.S. 561 (1984), demonstrate that race-based layoff goals are seldom, if ever, appropriate.

[19]*See, e.g.,* Settlement Agreement in EEOC v. Libbey-Owens Ford Co., Article IV (notice through regional T.V. Guide magazines).

## Chapter 25

# EXECUTIVE ORDERS

## I. PROVISIONS OF EXECUTIVE ORDER 11246 AND APPLICABLE RULES AND REGULATIONS

### A. General Provisions and Overview

Executive Order 11246[1] has not been revised substantively since 1967, and its implementing regulations have not been amended since 1980. This surface quiet masks a depth of controversy about the scope and substance of the Executive Order and its regulations. The OFCCP proposed regulations to amend a number of significant features of the administration of the Executive Order in August of 1981.[2] The proposals were attacked by some as excessively relaxing agency oversight of contractor obligations and by others for failing to provide a sufficient response to serious problems in program administration. The significance of these proposed amendments has been undercut by the fact that they have been lingering without final action since the initial proposal.

On the policy level, there were major efforts during the Reagan Administration to revoke or substantially alter affirmative action requirements of the Executive Order so as to delete the mandate for "goals" which has been its cornerstone. The controversy reached its height in August 1985 when a proposed modification to the Executive Order that would have barred goals and timetables surfaced.[3] Support for the retention of goals came from many employer organizations, as well as civil rights groups, with the result that

---

[1] 3 C.F.R. 339 (1964–1965 Compilation), reprinted in 42 U.S.C. § 2000e note, issued on September 24, 1965, as amended by Executive Order 11375, 32 FED. REG. 14303 (Oct. 13, 1967). In 1978, Executive Order 12086 consolidated within OFCCP the enforcement and implementation functions previously performed by 11 different contracting agencies. 43 FED. REG. 46501 (Oct. 5, 1978). As set forth in the main text, the affirmative action obligations of contractors concerning veterans are beyond the scope of this Chapter. Nonetheless, contractors should be aware that the Department of Labor promulgated final regulations on March 4, 1987, requiring the submission of annual reports on veteran employees and new hires similar to the current EEO-1 reports. See 41 C.F.R. § 61-250 (1987).

[2] The proposals included: (1) raising the threshold requirements for affirmative action requirements under the Executive Order from 50 or more employees and a federal contract of $50,000 or more to 250 employees and a contract of $1,000,000 or more; (2) defining underutilization so that no underutilization would exist if minority and female representation in a job group is 80 percent or more of availability; (3) permitting contractors having 250 or more employees but fewer than 500 employees to use abbreviated affirmative action plans; (4) permitting contractors to have one affirmative action plan for various establishments located within the same "chain of command"; (5) eliminating preaward reviews; and (6) exempting contractors from compliance reviews for up to five years if the contractor participates in an approved training program. See 45 FED. REG. 42968, LAB. REL. REP. FEP MANUAL (BNA) at 401:4001 (BNA, Aug. 25, 1981).

[3] The proposal stated that "no government contractor shall be determined to have violated this order due to a failure to adopt or attain any statistical measures." Goals would be permitted only if "they are not used and do not operate to discriminate or grant a preference to any person on account of race, color, sex, religion or national origin." "New Version of E.O. 11246 Revision Permits Goals That Don't Discriminate," 199 DAILY LAB. REP. A-3 (BNA, Oct. 15, 1985).

retention received strong bipartisan support in Congress.[4] After much debate, efforts to modify the Executive Order were suspended pending further definition by the Supreme Court of the appropriate contours of affirmative action programs.[5]

As discussed more extensively in Chapter 24 (Reverse Discrimination and Affirmative Action), the Supreme Court has in fact provided guidelines on the permissible scope of goal-oriented affirmative action programs that benefit protected group members who have not been shown to be the victims of prior discrimination. These Supreme Court decisions have not yet focused directly on the validity of the affirmative action programs mandated by Executive Order 11246. However, there is clear legal support for the use of affirmative action programs in appropriate circumstances. Whether those circumstances reach the affirmative action programs mandated by the Executive Order is still ill-defined. The salient fact is that the Executive Order— and its affirmative action requirements—remain intact and continue to be an important focus of attention in equal employment opportunity law.

In addition, there was controversy about the level of enforcement under the Reagan Administration. Some who are highly critical of what they describe as underenforcement cite statistics showing, for example, a diminished level of back pay awards and debarment proceedings.[6] Defenders of the program point out that the number of compliance reviews has increased, and suggest that the efficiency and responsiveness of the bureaucracy has improved.[7] Certainly, the relationship between OFCCP and the business community appears to be less adversarial.[8] In turn, this improved relationship has probably contributed to employers' widespread support in the face of attacks to revoke or dramatically revise the Executive Order. Further, various commentators have asserted that the Executive Order has been an effective vehicle for improving job opportunities for protected groups.[9]

---

[4]For instance, more than two-thirds of the Republican-controlled Senate publicly expressed support for the current Executive Order. "Talks on Affirmative Action Order for Federal Contractors Still Continuing," 243 DAILY LAB. REP. A-1 (BNA, Dec. 18, 1985).

[5]See "White House to Delay Order on Affirmative Action Until Supreme Court Acts," 243 DAILY LAB. REP. A-14 (BNA, Aug. 28, 1986).

[6]The House Education and Labor Committee found that "the number of persons receiving back pay as a remedy for past discrimination has decreased from 4,336 in Fiscal Year 1980 to 499 in FY 1986, an 88 percent reduction. The aggregate amount of back pay obtained by OFCCP for discriminatees has also declined, from $9,253,861 to $1,911,145, a decrease of nearly 80 percent." The House Committee also found that cases referred to the Secretary of Labor for enforcement action decreased from 269 cases in 1980 to 22 cases in fiscal year 1986, and that actions initiated and/or completed to debar noncomplying contractors decreased from 5 in fiscal year 1980 to 1 in 1981 and none in 1982 through 1984. See House Comm. on Education and Labor, 100th Cong., 1st Sess., Investigation of the Civil Rights Enforcement Activities of the Office of Federal Contract Compliance Programs, U.S. Department of Labor, pp. 3–5. (Comm. Print 1987).

[7]The Under Secretary of Labor asserted that in FY 1980, "OFCCP completed 2,632 compliance reviews. In FY 1981 and 1982, that number rose to over 3,000, in FY 1983, to over 4,000; and has been above 5,000 ever since." See "Statements on Proposed Changes in Executive Order 11246 Before House Judiciary Subcommittee on Civil and Constitutional Rights: Statement of Deputy Under Secretary of Labor Meisinger on OFCCP Enforcement Before House Labor Subcommittee on Employment Opportunities," 107 DAILY LAB. REP. E-1, E-2 (BNA, June 5, 1987).

[8]The United States Chamber of Commerce has asserted that, under the Reagan Administration, there have been "substantial improvements" to the "antagonistic and inflexible" actions by OFCCP officials. See "Statement of Vincent J. Apruzzese on Behalf of the United States Chamber of Commerce on Proposed Changes in Executive Order 11246 Before House Judiciary Committee Subcommittee on Civil and Constitutional Rights," DAILY LAB. REP. E-3 (BNA, Nov. 8, 1985).

[9]The Executive Order covers more than 30 million workers. See House Comm. on Education and Labor report, supra note 6, at pp. 1–2. Numerous studies have concluded that the Executive Order has

What is perhaps most ironic is that after years of controversy during the Carter Administration, the Reagan Administration did not make major changes in the regulations implementing Executive Order 11246. Judging from that, one might assume that the Executive Order program has witnessed few substantive changes in administration. That assumption, however, would not be entirely correct. Instead, many important changes, both procedural and substantive, have been effected through policy directives or other, less formal administrative actions. Further, a number of court and Department of Labor decisions have resolved some difficult problems and have created new ones.

## 1. Policy Directives

In 1979, the Carter Administration issued a *Federal Contract Compliance Manual* (the *Manual*) which contained interpretative guidance on substantive issues, as well as instructions on the mechanics of administration, including compliance reviews and enforcement actions. At the time, the *Manual* constituted a compilation of past and new policy directives. Although it did not revise the *Manual*, the Reagan Administration has issued policy directives addressing both substantive and procedural issues, many of which supplant prior positions.

To alleviate the obvious problems posed by an obsolete *Manual*, OFCCP is in the process of issuing an entire new edition of the *Manual* that will provide the revisions necessary for more uniform and predictable enforcement.[10] Until the new *Manual* is available in its entirety, employers and their counsel should carefully determine the status of pertinent provisions.

Some of the more significant procedural and substantive revisions to policy directives include the following:

*Procedural Orders.* A review of the orders concerning administrative procedures discloses a number of important trends. For example, several directives reflect a policy of delegating substantial authority to regional and area offices. Some observers had suggested that the insistence on national office review significantly slowed Executive Order proceedings and discouraged aggressive compliance reviews. The current trend is clearly to encourage the exercise of discretion in the field.

OFCCP has delegated authority to sign most conciliation agreements to Regional Directors (RDs) (previously titled Assistant Regional Administrators). Formerly, most proposed conciliation agreements were forwarded to the national office for review before they became effective. OFCCP now

---

increased employment for minorities and women and may very well be one of the most successful federal programs to effectuate equal employment opportunity. For instance, a National Bureau of Economic Research study concluded that between 1974 and 1980, the proportion of blacks and white females "increased significantly faster in contractor establishments subject to affirmative action than in non-contractor establishments." 47 FED. CONTRACTS REP. 1092 (BNA, June 15, 1987). A 1983 study by the OFCCP, *see* Seymour, *Why Executive Order 11246 Should Be Preserved,* 11 EMPLOYEE REL. L.J. 568, 572 (1985), and 1981 Department of Labor Studies, *see* duRivage, *The OFCCP Under the Reagan Administration: Affirmative Action in Retreat,* 36 LAB. L.J. 360, 363 (June 1985), reached similar conclusions.

[10]*See* "Statement of Deputy Under Secretary of Labor Meisinger on OFCCP Enforcement Before House Labor Subcommittee on Employment Opportunities," *supra* note 7; "New OFCCP Director Charts Course for Improving Agency's Operations," 72 DAILY LAB. REP. A-11 (BNA, Apr. 14, 1988).

permits the execution of conciliation agreements by RDs without review except in specified circumstances.[11] In another order, OFCCP authorized the RDs to forward enforcement recommendations to the regional solicitor. Previously, OFCCP field officers had been required to forward such enforcement recommendations to the national office. The new directive authorizes an RD forward administrative enforcement recommendations to the regional solicitor without prior national office review except in cases where novel issues are raised.[12]

With this increased delegation of authority to the field, time delays occasioned by national office review and coordination have been reduced. Compliance review activity appears to be increasing, as is the number of conciliation agreements and letters of commitment. From a contractor's perspective, the principal concern is whether such decentralization will lead to inconsistent and uneven administration of the program.

Another trend reflected in the orders is an effort to ensure more uniform procedures in the handling of investigations. In one directive, OFCCP stated that management representatives, including attorneys, can be present during OFCCP's interviews of management and supervisory employees.[13] At the urging of the American Bar Association's Equal Employment Opportunity Committee, OFCCP established procedures to ensure that an attorney or other representative designated by the contractor or complainant is the agency's point of contact.[14]

In another order, OFCCP formalized the practice of providing contractors with predetermination notices in the event of an initial determination of pattern-or-practice discrimination.[15] In the past, contractors were often not provided with the evidence alleged to show potential discrimination and thus could not respond in advance of OFCCP's initial determination of liability. Contractors had long criticized the failure to provide such notice or a discussion of the evidence allegedly supporting potential discrimination claims. According to the order, the predetermination notice will describe the alleged discrimination, describe the supporting evidence, and offer the contractor an opportunity to respond in writing by a set date.

*Substantive Policy Directives.* A number of OFCCP's orders in the 1980s reflect substantive interpretations of the regulations. Some of these orders modify or reverse controversial interpretations developed under the Carter Administration. For example, OFCCP has eliminated the so-called "95 percent rule" contained in the *Manual.* Under that rule, compliance in attainment of prior goals was measured by determining whether 95 percent of the goal had been met. The 95 percent standard was regarded by many as arbitrary and insufficiently related to the regulatory obligation to apply

---

[11]Executive Order 650c10 (Jan. 13, 1988) permits the ARA (now RD) to execute the conciliation agreement except when the agreement concerns employment discrimination of a class of 50 or more persons, $100,000 or more in back pay settlements, or novel issues.

[12]Executive Order 650c9 (Feb. 24, 1987).

[13]Executive Order 630a (Mar. 1, 1983).

[14]Executive Order 660b18 (Oct. 18, 1984).

[15]Executive Order 640a3 (Jan. 22, 1987).

"good-faith" efforts toward goal attainment. Instead of a strict statistical standard, the new order highlights the obligation of contractors to make "good-faith" efforts to meet the stated goal.[16]

In a second order, OFCCP resolved the long-standing controversy as to whether regulations that call for "consideration" of availability factors require that each factor actually be given weight in a utilization analysis. The order states that only those factors relevant to actual availability in the particular job group need be used. The order further clarifies the point that a contractor may consider additional availability factors applicable to a particular industry.[17]

Another theme reflected in the recent policy directives is the effort to ensure continued consistency and harmony between the Executive Order and Title VII. OFCCP has issued a number of orders that have this very purpose in mind. For purposes of Executive Order enforcement, OFCCP has specifically adopted two major Title VII discrimination theories—"disparate treatment" and "disparate impact."[18] It has also rescinded a prior order detailing the elements of a discrimination case and instead has expressly adopted current Title VII principles.[19] OFCCP has also issued an order defining "continuing violation" in a manner consistent with the prevailing Title VII interpretations.[20] Finally, OFCCP has permitted back pay formula relief in cases where such approaches would be used in Title VII class actions.[21]

Finally, OFCCP has provided new guidance for determining underutilization. Since 1971, when Revised Order 4 was promulgated, OFCCP's regulations for preparing affirmative action programs have defined underutilization "as having fewer minorities or women in a particular job group than would *reasonably be expected* by their availability."[22] In 1974, in Technical Guidance Memorandum (TGM) 1, the OFCCP interpreted this definition as meaning that underutilization occurs whenever there exists *any difference* between the availability of minorities or women for a job group and the number of such persons employed in the job group. Employers frequently challenged this interpretation as being contrary to the agency's regulations. However, the "any difference" standard for underutilization remained in effect as OFCCP policy until 1981, when TGM 1 was vacated by the trial court in *Firestone Synthetic Rubber & Latex Co. v. Marshall,*[23] on the grounds that it constituted a substantive change in the OFCCP regulations

---

[16]Executive Order 660a2 (Mar. 1, 1983).
[17]Executive Order 660k5 (Sept. 8, 1986).
[18]Executive Order 640a5 (Feb. 23, 1987).
[19]Executive Order 640a2 (Jan. 20, 1987).
[20]Executive Order 640a4 (Jan. 21, 1987).
[21]*Supra* note 18; Executive Order 660c7 (Jan. 15, 1987). The number of cases involving back pay and the total amount of back pay secured by OFCCP was smaller under the Reagan Administration than under the Carter Administration. Given the controversial nature of back pay and the possible arguments against the validity of back pay awards under the Executive Order, there had been some questions as to whether the Reagan Administration was willing to apply this monetary remedy. The cited directives establish beyond question that back pay continues to be regarded by OFCCP as a remedy for asserted discrimination. These recent orders assert the existence of this remedy under the Executive Order and adopt the standards under Title VII for assessing liability and calculating damages.
[22]41 C.F.R. § 60-2.11(b) (1978) (emphasis added).
[23]507 F. Supp. 1330, 24 FEP 1699 (E.D. Tex. 1981).

that had not been subject to required notice and comment rulemaking procedures.

After *Firestone,* the issue of defining underutilization and setting goals, so critical to the entire affirmative action program process, has been addressed through informal instruction from the national office—a process critically referred to as "podium policy."[24] OFCCP officials have permitted contractors to identify underutilization using either a two-standard-deviations analysis or the so-called "80-percent rule."[25] How underutilization is to be determined is at the crux of the entire affirmative action program process and, as such, is essential information for contractors and those vested with enforcement responsibility.[26]

## D. Advice for Contractors in Dealing With Compliance Reviews

The advice previously provided on handling compliance reviews remains essentially unchanged and appropriate under current circumstances. There are additional concerns that should be kept in mind, however. Under Executive Order regulations, if a contractor wishes to contest a demand by OFCCP, current procedures call for the successive steps of negotiation,[27] issuance of a show-cause notice,[28] and finally an enforcement or sanctions proceeding.[29] If the administrative proceedings conclude with a determination adverse to the contractor, the Secretary of Labor may impose remedies or sanctions, including debarment, as may be appropriate.[30] It is true that debarment is not regarded as punitive,[31] but the fact remains that contesting OFCCP positions through administrative proceedings subjects a contractor to the possibility of debarment.

Accordingly, when an employer confronts a demand by OFCCP that it regards as incorrect, unreasonable, or unauthorized, it is faced with a dilemma of considerable proportions. If the contractor acquiesces in OFCCP's demands, it may irreparably compromise its position. On the other

---

[24]*See* House Comm. on Education and Labor, 100th Cong., 1st Sess., Investigation of the Civil Rights Enforcement Activities of the Office of Federal Contract Compliance Programs, U.S. Department of Labor, pp. 6–7 (Comm. Print 1987). Since 1981, podium policy-making has been the most frequently used means of disseminating policies to OFCCP field offices. The Report called this form of policy-making "questionable" and stated that podium policies "have been used apparently to avoid the public censure which would have resulted if such policies, inconsistent with the current OFCCP regulations and judicial decisions on equal employment opportunity (EEO) law, had been reduced to writing." *Id.* Perhaps in response to the concerns about the enforceability of "podium policy," OFCCP issued 18 policy directives in the period covering September 1986 through April 1987. *See Hearings Before Subcommittee on Employment Opportunities of the Committee on Education and Labor, Oversight Hearing on Office of Federal Contract Compliance Programs* (June 3 and 4, 1987) at 78.

[25]House Comm. on Education and Labor Report, *supra* note 24, at pp. 81–83. Another example of so-called "podium policy" is the position that ultimate goals are no longer required—only annual goals for the current affirmative action plans are necessary. *Id.* at 78.

[26]OFCCP officials state that all Assistant Regional Administrators are aware of this policy, which they claim is consistent with actual agency practice since *Firestone, Synthetic Rubber & Latex Co. v. Marshall, supra* note 23. *See, e.g.,* House Comm. on Education and Labor Report, *supra* note 24, at pp. 81–83.

[27]41 C.F.R. § 60-1.24(c)(2) (1978), 41 C.F.R. § 60-2.2 (1978).

[28]41 C.F.R. § 60-1.28 (1978), 41 C.F.R. § 60-2.2(c)(3) (1978).

[29]41 C.F.R. § 60-1.26 (1980), 41 C.F.R. § 60-2.2(c)(2)–(3) (1978).

[30]41 C.F.R. § 60-1.27 (1978).

[31]*See* Section I.E.2, *infra.*

hand, if it resists, it does so at peril of debarment. Some contractors have sought relief in federal court, seeking declaratory injunctive relief. Unfortunately, the courts have rejected this approach, relying on the doctrine of exhaustion of administrative remedies.[32]

One approach that contractors may have overlooked is the so-called protest procedure.[33] Under this procedure, the contractor could accept OFCCP's demand (either in the form of a conciliation agreement, letter of commitment, or inclusion of requested changes in the affirmative action program) and then file a protest pursuant to the regulations. This procedure forecloses OFCCP from initiating a sanction proceeding and reserves to the contractor the right to contest the demands of the government.

The protest procedure is, however, by no means a complete solution to the contractor's quandary. In the first place, the regulations regarding the protest procedure require that the contractor comply with its commitments pending resolution of the protest. In many cases, unless OFCCP agrees to stay implementation of its demands, the procedure is simply not practical. A related problem is that there is no defined time limit[34] within which the protest determination must be made. Thus, it is unlikely that the contractor can compel a prompt resolution of the issues. The protest procedure has been little used, and it is difficult to assess its practical effectiveness in the abstract.

### E. Enforcement Procedures and Sanctions for Noncompliance

#### 1. Administrative Enforcement

OFCCP's administrative tools for enforcing the Executive Order have remained largely unchanged.[35] OFCCP continues to rely heavily on its power to negotiate conciliation agreements and consent decrees as a method of resolving administrative complaints.[36] Using this tool, OFCCP has secured

---

[32]The filing of a preenforcement action has occasionally been successful. *See* Liberty Mut. Ins. Co. v. Friedman, 639 F.2d 164, 24 FEP 1168 (4th Cir. 1981). Further, it would appear that a strong argument could be made that the exhaustion doctrine ought not apply when the validity of the underlying regulations is in question, or where the contractor exposes itself to severe sanctions merely for contesting the Department's position.

[33]41 C.F.R. § 60-1.24(c)(4) (1978).

[34]The Administrative Procedures Act, 5 U.S.C. § 706(1), authorizes a court to "compel agency action unlawfully withheld or unreasonably delayed." In determining whether an agency's "foot-dragging" constitutes unreasonable delay, a court may consider the following factors: (1) the length of time that has elapsed since the agency came under the duty to act, (2) the prospect of early completion, (3) the reasonableness of the delay "in the context of the statute," and (4) the extent to which the delay may be undermining the statutory scheme. Cutler v. Hayes, 818 F.2d 879, 897–98 (D.C. Cir. 1987). *See also* Thompson v. Department of Labor, 813 F.2d 48, 52 (3d Cir. 1987) (district court has statutory duty to determine whether OFCCP unreasonably delayed resolution of employee's Rehabilitation Act complaint against alleged federal contractor).

[35]Nonetheless, although the regulations provide an expedited hearing procedure to dispose of uncomplicated issues, 41 C.F.R. § 60-30.31 *et seq.* (1979), Secretary Donovan criticized the use of such procedures in *OFCCP v. Safeco Ins. Co. of Am.,* No. 83-OFC-7 (July 31, 1984) (Final Decision), finding the short adjudicatory time frames involved inappropriate for the type of novel and complex issues presented by that case. *Id.* at n.1. However, in *Department of Labor v. Bruce Church, Inc.,* No. 87-OFC-7 (June 30, 1987) (Final Decision), Secretary Brock affirmed an ALJ's recommended debarment order under the expedited review procedures, noting that the case presented a settled question of law under *OFCCP v. Star Mach. Co.,* No. 83-OFCCP-4 (Sept. 21, 1983) (Final Decision), 189 DAILY LAB. REP. A-1, E-1 (BNA, Sept. 28, 1983). (For a discussion of *Star Machinery, see* Section II.B, *infra*).

[36]41 C.F.R. § 60-30.13 (1978).

substantial monetary and nonmonetary relief from contractors for the benefit of alleged victims of discrimination.[37] The terms of such agreements and decrees vary widely, however, with respect to such enforcement provisions as duration and the scope of subsequent enforcement proceedings.[38] The importance to an employer of limiting the scope of OFCCP's subsequent enforcement powers under such a decree was graphically demonstrated in the Title VII context in *EEOC v. CW Transport, Inc.,*[39] in which a court concluded that laches was the employer's only potential defense to a 1986 enforcement action concerning a 1974 consent decree that contained no express expiration date.

## 2. Debarment

Debarment remains the most severe sanction available to OFCCP to compel compliance with the Executive Order. Recently, debarment cases have often arisen in situations where the contractor denies that it is covered by the Executive Order and, accordingly, refuses to prepare an affirmative action plan[40] or to cooperate with OFCCP compliance review efforts.[41] In *Department of Labor v. Bruce Church, Inc.,*[42] the Secretary reaffirmed *immediate* debarment as an appropriate remedy against a contractor for refusal to prepare a written affirmative action program. The Secretary invoked the court's declaration in *Uniroyal v. Marshall*[43] that "[e]ffective enforcement * * * depends, first, on access to the employment, personnel, and similar records of the contractors; and second, on the availability of meaningful sanctions when such access is denied."

Despite this hard-line stance, the courts and to some extent the Department of Labor have been inclined to provide recalcitrant contractors with a second opportunity to comply before ordering debarment. In *First Alabama Bank of Montgomery v. Donovan,*[44] the Eleventh Circuit modified a

---

[37]*See, e.g.,* OFCCP v. Firstier Bank, No. 87-OFC-29 (Oct. 19, 1987) (Final Decision) (back pay of $105,000 to 5 individuals and preferential hiring); OFCCP v. Florida Nat'l Bank, No. 85-OFC-6 (July 29, 1987) (Final Decision) (back pay of $49,500 and favorable references); Department of Labor v. John H. Hampshire, Inc., No. 85-OFC-4 (May 22, 1986) (Final Decision) (good-faith efforts to achieve construction craft goals and undertake recruitment efforts); Department of Labor v. University of Ark., No. 84-OFC-4 (Dec. 17, 1984) (Final Decision) (back pay and submission of affirmative action plan).

[38]*Compare* OFCCP v. Florida Nat'l Bank, *supra* note 37, at ¶ 22 (no expiration date, but issues in enforcement proceeding limited to issues raised in motion) *with* Department of Labor v. John H. Hampshire, Inc., *supra* note 37, at ¶¶ 10–11 (effective for only two years, but OFCCP maintains that enforcement proceeding may consider entire scope of company's alleged noncompliance from which the decree resulted).

[39]658 F. Supp. 1278, 1296, 43 FEP 782, 797 (W.D. Wis. 1987).

[40]*See, e.g.,* Department of Labor v. Coldwell Banker & Co., No. 78-OFCCP-12 (Aug. 14, 1987) (Final Decision) (respondent claimed it was not a subcontractor and refused to submit AAP); Department of Labor v. Interco, Inc., No. 86-OFC-2 (Mar. 10, 1987) (Recommended Decision) (respondent claimed its autonomous divisions were not subject to Executive Order and refused to submit AAP).

[41]*See, e.g.,* OFCCP v. University of N.C., No. 84-OFC-20 (Dec. 12, 1986) (Recommended Decision) (university claimed its noncontracting divisions were not subject to Executive Order and refused to provide OFCCP access to books, records, accounts, and premises); OFCCP v. Monongahela R.R., No. 85-OFC-2 (Apr. 2, 1986) (Recommended Decision) (employer claimed it was not a subcontractor under § 503 of Rehabilitation Act and refused OFCCP access to its establishment).

[42]*Supra* note 35.

[43]482 F. Supp. 364, 375, 20 FEP 437, 444 (D.D.C. 1979). *See also* OFCCP v. Chicago Messenger Serv., No. 87-OFC-8 (Aug. 28, 1987) (Recommended Decision) (immediate debarment recommended for failure to develop written AAP and failure to respond to OFCCP's Administrative Complaint); Department of Labor v. William B. Reily & Co., No. 85-OFC-5 (May 28, 1985) (Final Decision) (same).

[44]692 F.2d 714, 30 FEP 448 (11th Cir. 1982).

district court's immediate debarment order to permit First Alabama to rectify its refusal to cooperate with OFCCP's compliance review. The court of appeals explained: "[T]he purpose of debarment is limited to encouraging compliance and is not intended for use as punishment for non-compliance."[45] Similarly, in *OFCCP v. Priester Construction Co.,*[46] Secretary Donovan rejected OFCCP's argument for mandatory debarment of contractors who violate the Executive Order, noting the "harsh and anticonciliatory nature" of such an approach. The Secretary found immediate debarment particularly inappropriate where, as in *Priester,* the defendant's compliance deficiencies were primarily the result of a lack of understanding of its obligations.

### 3. Judicial Enforcement

In *United States v. Whitney National Bank of New Orleans,*[47] the court reaffirmed the Justice Department's authority to bring suit to enforce the provisions of the Executive Order. Moreover, the court held that the Executive Order lawfully imposes a back pay obligation on government contractors found to be guilty of discriminatory employment practices.

## II. VALIDITY OF THE EXECUTIVE ORDER AND ACTIONS PURSUANT THERETO

### A. Validity of the Executive Order and Implementing Regulations[48]

Courts continue to uphold the validity of the Executive Order.[49] In *Utley v. Varian Associates,*[50] the Ninth Circuit reiterated that the principle of separation of powers requires that an executive order be "rooted" in an appropriate grant of authority. Authority for Executive Order 11246 has variously been found in the procurement laws (*e.g.,* 40 U.S.C. § 486(a)), the civil rights laws (*e.g.,* Title of VII of the Civil Rights Act of 1964, 42 U.S.C. § 2000e *et seq.*), and the Constitution.[51]

Although the precise authority for the Executive Order remains uncertain, a due process challenge to the Executive Order was summarily rejected by the Eleventh Circuit in *First Alabama Bank of Montgomery v. Donovan.*[52] In that case, the bank had challenged the Executive Order's administrative

---

[45]*Id.* at 722, 30 FEP at 453. *See generally* Department of Labor v. Coldwell Banker & Co., *supra* note 40 (30 days to comply); OFCCP v. Monongahela R.R., *supra* note 41 (same).

[46]No. 78-OFCCP-11 (Feb. 22, 1983) (Final Decision) at pp. 14–16, 54 DAILY LAB. REP. A-1 (BNA, Mar. 18, 1983).

[47]671 F. Supp. 441, 45 FEP 983 (E.D. La. 1987). *See also* United States v. Commercial Lovelace Motor Freight, 31 FEP 499, 502 (S.D. Ohio 1983).

[48]The validity of the Executive Order's affirmative action requirement is discussed at Section II.D, *infra.*

[49]In *OFCCP v. National Bank of Commerce of San Antonio,* No. 77-OFCCP-2 (Under Secretary of Labor Ford B. Ford, Acting Secretary of Labor, Dec. 11, 1984) (Final Decision), 241 DAILY LAB. REP. A-1 (BNA, Dec. 11, 1984), the Secretary held that, in contrast to the courts, an *administrative agency* is neither competent nor authorized to decide the constitutionality of the Executive Order and its regulations.

[50]811 F.2d 1279, 1285 n.4, 43 FEP 191, 194 n.4 (9th Cir.), *cert. denied,* 484 U.S. _____, 44 FEP 1672 (1987).

[51]Eatmon v. Bristol Steel & Iron Works, 769 F.2d 1503, 1516, 38 FEP 1364, 1374 (11th Cir. 1985) (citing Contractors Ass'n of E. Pa. v. Secretary of Labor, 442 F.2d 159, 170, 3 FEP 395, 402 (3d Cir.), *cert. denied,* 404 U.S. 854, 3 FEP 1030 (1971)).

[52]*Supra* note 44, at 722 n.17, 30 FEP at 453 n.17.

procedures that permit quasi-judicial hearings to be conducted by administrative law judges who are employed by the same agency that initiates the review.

However, in *United States v. New Orleans Public Service (NOPSI)*, [53] the Fifth Circuit imposed certain limits on OFCCP's authority to enter a contractor's premises to examine its facility and records. That case is discussed below. [54]

## B. Coverage Provisions of the Executive Order

In a number of its administrative decisions, OFCCP has set out a broad interpretation of the Executive Order's coverage provisions. One recent administrative proceeding tested perhaps the most important principle underlying the broad scope of the Executive Order. The Executive Order and its implementing regulations have long embraced the concept that a single government contract or subcontract means that all establishments of the company are covered, whether or not they are involved in performance of the contract or subcontract. [55] Thus, the simple rule is that once a contractor is awarded a covered contract or subcontract, the obligations under the Executive Order apply to the entire organization. [56]

In an administrative case, *Department of Labor v. Interco, Inc.,* [57] Interco refused the Department of Labor access to its Devon Apparel Division for a compliance review and refused to develop an affirmative action program. Interco argued that the Devon Apparel Division was independently operated and totally separate from the division that performed government contracts. The company maintained that the Supreme Court's decision in *Grove City* [58] mandated that the Executive Order be limited solely to regulation of contract performance. The Administrative Law Judge (ALJ) held that Interco violated the Executive Order by not implementing an affirmative action program for all of its corporate establishments. The ALJ found *Grove City* inapplicable, since Title IX is by its terms limited to programs, whereas there is no similar restriction in the Executive Order. [59]

The decision did not address perhaps a more complicated issue underly-

---

[53]723 F.2d 422, 33 FEP 1489, *reh'g denied,* 734 F.2d 226, 34 FEP 1801 (5th Cir. 1984) (per curiam), *cert. denied,* 469 U.S. 1180, 37 FEP 63 (1985). The court of appeals likened this case to "a vampire in the night . . . [that] refuses to die." *Id.,* 734 F.2d at 227, 34 FEP at 1801.

[54]*See* Section IV.A, *infra.*

[55]Executive Order 11246, § 204.

[56]The regulations do include a procedure under which a contractor may request exemption for facilities entirely separate from the contracting organization. 41 C.F.R. § 60-1.5(b)(2) (1978). This is an exemption rarely requested and rarely granted.

[57]No. 86-OFC-2 (Mar. 10, 1987) (Recommended Decision).

[58]Grove City College v. Bell, 465 U.S. 555 (1984). In *Grove City,* the Supreme Court held that Title IX's regulations purporting to cover the entire operation of an entity were inconsistent with the specific text of the statute. 20 U.S.C. § 1681, *et seq.*

[59]*See* OFCCP v. University of N.C., No. 84-OFC-20 (May 1, 1986) (Final Order) (ALJ holds that branches of state university that do not have federal contracts are nonetheless subject to requirements of Executive Order, because they are part of single multi-campus system). *See also* Department of Labor v. St. Regis Corp., No. 78-OFCCP-1 (Dec. 28, 1984) (Recommended Decision). In *St. Regis,* the ALJ also held that contracts for the *purchase* of goods from the government are as much covered by the Executive Order as are contracts for the sale of goods or services. The ALJ noted that the regulatory definition of a government contract refers to "*any* agreement between a contracting agency and a person." *Id.* at p. 119.

ing this entire area—namely, whether the Supreme Court's decision in *Chrysler Corp. v. Brown,*[60] rather than *Grove City,* should be the true focal point for testing the validity of the OFCCP's scope position. As discussed previously, the *Chrysler* case suggests that regulations issued under the Executive Order must bear a reasonable nexus to an underlying statutory authority. However, there remains no consensus about the underlying statutory authority for the Executive Order. The authority most often cited is the federal procurement laws.[61] If that is the authority upon which the corporation wide coverage principle is based, there would be some uncertainty about the nexus between the government contracts to be performed and regulations purporting to cover establishments that have nothing to do with such contracts. Obviously, finding a nexus would be far less difficult if the supporting authority for the Executive Order were determined to be the Constitution or Title VII. This continues to be an undefined, murky area of Executive Order legal development.[62]

Another important administrative decision, *OFCCP v. Loffland Brothers Co.,*[63] reflects one of the few occasions that a contractor prevailed on an argument that it was not covered by Executive Order 11246. The government asserted three bases of coverage: (1) that Loffland was a continuing government contractor because it held prime contracts in the past and was likely to hold them in the future; (2) that Loffland was a subcontractor because it drilled for major oil companies that refined oil and sold their products to the government; and (3) that Loffland was a subcontractor because it had contracts with major oil companies to drill on land leased from the government.

The ALJ adopted only the first of these theories. On review, Secretary Donovan rejected the ALJ decision as contrary to OFCCP regulations. The Secretary held that although a past contractor remains subject to the enforcement provisions of the Executive Order for any violations that occurred during the life of the contract, the contractor does not remain subject to the substantive affirmative action obligations of the Executive Order, even if the company is likely to hold future contracts. Thus, because the alleged causes of action arose after Loffland no longer held any prime contracts with the government, Loffland could not be considered a contractor for purposes of the Executive Order.

The government's subcontractor theories proved equally unavailing. The Secretary first rejected evidence that showed only that Loffland had drilling contracts with oil companies that, in turn, had contracts to supply fuel to government agencies. The Secretary held that such evidence was insufficient to prove OFCCP jurisdiction, in the absence of evidence actually tracing the oil that Loffland drilled directly, or by way of storage facilities,

---

[60]441 U.S. 281, 19 FEP 475 (1979).

[61]*See* Section II.A, *supra.*

[62]It should be noted that *Department of Labor v. Interco, Inc., supra* note 57, does not address the issue of whether separate corporations that are affiliated in various ways are to be considered as one entity subject to the Executive Order. The law in this area has remained unchanged.

[63]No. OEO 75-1 (Apr. 16, 1984) (Final Decision). This case was originally filed by the Office of Equal Opportunity of the Department of the Interior in 1975. It was transferred to OFCCP in accordance with the consolidation of the Executive Order 11246 program during the Carter Administration.

to the government.[64] Lastly, the Secretary rejected OFCCP's contention that Loffland was covered by the Executive Order because it had contracts with oil companies to drill wells on land leased from the government. The Secretary held that because the lessees had no contractual obligation to perform any drilling on the leased land, the drilling contracts between Loffland and the federal leaseholders were not "necessary" to the performance of the leaseholders' government contracts.[65] The reach of a "subcontract," subjecting a company to coverage, remains uncertain and the subject of litigation.[66]

Finally, in a series of administrative decisions, the Secretary of Labor has provided guidance on the application of the $50,000 affirmative action program threshold to Blanket Purchase Agreements and surety contracts. In *OFCCP v. Star Machinery Co.,*[67] Secretary Donovan held that a Blanket Purchase Agreement is a single contract within the meaning of the regulations and that the value of the contract for purposes of satisfying the $50,000 threshold is measured by aggregating all orders that the parties "reasonably anticipate" will be placed during the year. In so holding, the Secretary reversed the ALJ's decision and adopted a liberal interpretation of such contracts, despite the fact that the government was not obligated to make any purchases under the Agreement. The Secretary made clear, however, that with respect to other types of contracts, the regulations do not generally contemplate aggregation to reach the $50,000 threshold.[68]

In contrast, in *OFCCP v. Safeco Insurance Co.,*[69] Secretary Donovan rejected an ALJ's expansive interpretation of surety contracts, and held that

---

[64]The Secretary stated that if OFCCP had been able to show that Loffland's oil was commingled in storage facilities from which oil products were subsequently sold to the government, then Loffland would be a subcontractor whose services were "necessary to the performance of Government contracts under 41 CFR § 60-1.3(w)." It is unclear whether the Secretary would have required actual proof that oil from wells that Loffland drilled was intermingled with the oil sold to the government, or just that some oil from the facilities made its way to the government. In *OFCCP v. Monongahela R.R.,* No. 85-OFC-2 (Apr. 2, 1986) (Recommended Decision), the ALJ held that once the railroad's coal could be traced from the subcontractor through Detroit Edison to the government, the railroad was subject to the Executive Order, regardless of the minuscule contribution made by the subcontractor to the fulfillment of Detroit Edison's contract and regardless of whether Detroit Edison's contract with the government required its electricity to be made using coal, as opposed to some other fuel source.

[65]By contrast, in *Department of Labor v. Coldwell Banker & Co.,* No. 78-OFCCP-12 (Aug. 14, 1987) (Final Decision), Secretary Brock had little trouble determining that Coldwell was a subcontractor by virtue of its property management agreements with owners of commercial property that was leased to the government. Coldwell contended that it did not assume any of the owner's contractual duties toward the governmental tenants to provide heat, electricity, water, janitorial, and related services, but simply acted as the owner's agent in engaging subcontractors to perform those obligations. The Secretary rejected this argument, noting that if the owner had managed the buildings itself, it would have had to carry out the very functions Coldwell performed.

The Secretary also held that the regulations that require contractors to develop a written affirmative action program for "each" establishment, should not be interpreted literally. Rather, several facilities should be permitted to be grouped where there is central authority for employment and personnel decisions and the facilities are in the same labor market or recruiting area. *Id.* at 11.

[66]*See supra* notes 64–65.

[67]No. 83-OFCCP-4 (Sept. 21, 1983) (Final Decision), 189 DAILY LAB. REP. A-1, E-1 (BNA, Sept. 28, 1983). There are actually two thresholds under the Executive Order. The first, the basic threshold, subjects an employer to Executive Order coverage if it has more than $10,000 in federal contracts or subcontracts in one year. 41 C.F.R. § 60-1.5 (1978). If this threshold is satisfied, the contractor must include the equal opportunity clause in its contracts and is subject to complaint investigations and OFCCP audits. The second threshold subjects a nonconstruction contractor or subcontractor with 50 or more employees and a single contract of at least $50,000 to the additional obligation of developing and monitoring a written affirmative action program. 41 C.F.R. § 60-2.1(a) (1978).

[68]*See also* Department of Labor v. Bruce Church, Inc., No. 87-OFC-7 (June 30, 1987) (Final Decision); OFCCP v. Fulton Corp., No. 87-OFC-2 (July 23, 1987) (Final Decision).

[69]No. 83-OFC-7 (July 31, 1984) (Final Decision).

Safeco was not a government contractor. The Secretary held that the value of Safeco's government contract for purposes of determining whether the threshold requirement had been met was governed by the bond premium, not the penal amount of the bond.[70] The ALJ had held that the penal amount of the bond was the appropriate measure of value, since that amount reflects the surety's potential obligation to the government if the surety is required to complete a construction project upon the default of the prime contractor. The ALJ likened the situation to *Star Machinery,*[71] in which the Secretary had held that the contract's value was measured by "reasonably antici-pate[d]" orders. The Secretary found the ALJ's reasoning faulty. He concluded that the mere possibility that a contractor might default "does not rise to the level of predictability for reaching the AAP threshold dollar amount which might justify basing the dollar amount of the alleged subcontract on the penal sum of the bond."[72]

## C. Validity of "Affected Class" Provisions—The Back Pay Remedy

The authority of OFCCP and the courts to order back pay under the Executive Order remains uncertain. Despite continuing objections by government contractors, however, the courts have generally approved back pay awards.[73] Moreover, as set forth above, the Department of Labor has reaffirmed the appropriateness of the back pay remedy and has ordered substantial back pay awards in a number of administrative proceedings.[74] OFCCP's recent directive regarding back pay clarifies the agency's position that back pay may be awarded for violations that occur within two years prior to the time the contractor is notified of a compliance review.[75]

---

[70]Since neither of the projects on which OFCCP sought to base its jurisdiction involved bonds which, individually or cumulatively, bore a premium of more than $50,000, the Secretary found it unnecessary to decide whether payment and performance bond premiums should be aggregated to reach the threshold amount. Such an aggregation would constitute a marked expansion of the holding in *OFCCP v. Star Machinery, supra* note 67.

[71]OFCCP v. Star Mach. Co., *supra* note 67.

[72]Department of Labor v. Safeco, *supra* note 69, at 6. Because he held that the threshold amount had not been reached, the Secretary did not reach the issue of whether a surety contract constitutes a subcontract under the Executive Order.

[73]United States v. Whitney Nat'l Bank of New Orleans, 671 F. Supp. 441, 442, 45 FEP 983, 984 (E.D. La. 1987) ("Executive Order 11246 lawfully imposes a back pay obligation on government contractors allegedly guilty of discriminatory employment practices"); United States v. Commercial Lovelace Motor Freight, 31 FEP 499, 502 (S.D. Ohio 1983) (court refuses to dismiss plaintiff's back pay claim on summary judgment). With respect to back pay and front pay awards in actions enforcing conciliation agreements, *see* discussion of *Eatmon v. Bristol Steel & Iron Works,* 769 F.2d 1503, 38 FEP 1364 (11th Cir. 1985), Section III.B, *infra.*

[74]*See* discussion, Section I.A–C, *supra. See also* Department of Labor v. St. Regis Corp., No. 78-OFCCP-1 (Dec. 28, 1984) (Recommended Decision); United States v. Whitney Nat'l Bank of New Orleans, *supra* note 73 ($1.3 million award).

[75]Executive Order 640a5 (Feb. 23, 1987). There is a suggestion in several Recommended Decisions that back pay may be sought for violations prior to the two-year period if a continuing violation exists. Department of Labor v. St. Regis Corp., *supra* note 74, at pp. 131–32; Department of Labor v. Harris Trust & Sav. Bank, No. 78-OFCCP-2 (Dec. 22, 1986) (Recommended Decision) at pp. 10–11. This view is inconsistent with the later position expressed by the Department of Labor in Executive Order 640a5, and thus should not be considered authoritative. Those Recommended Decisions also provide, however, that the two-year period should be shortened to exclude any period covered by a compliance review which has been either approved by the Department of Labor or not acted upon within 45 days as required by regulation. *See* Department of Labor v. St. Regis Corp., *supra* note 74, at p. 131; Department of Labor v. Harris Trust & Sav. Bank, *supra,* at 10.

## D. Conflicts Between the Executive Order and Title VII

There have been several important Supreme Court decisions delineating the permissible contours of affirmative action programs under Title VII.[76] However, to date the Supreme Court has not explicitly addressed whether there is a conflict between the Executive Order's affirmative action requirements and Title VII.[77] As a consequence, the Supreme Court has not addressed whether the Executive Order's requirement of affirmative action "goals"[78] for minorities and women "underutilized" in comparison to their "availability" in the labor market satisfies the *Johnson v. Transportation Agency, Santa Clara County,* [79] "manifest imbalance" test. Nor has the Supreme Court addressed whether an affirmative action plan required by the Executive Order is "voluntarily" submitted by a contractor.[80]

Despite the lack of controlling Supreme Court precedent, lower courts generally have upheld affirmative action plans adopted in response to the requirements of the Executive Order against reverse discrimination claims. Two district courts, citing *Steelworkers v. Weber,* [81] have upheld affirmative action plans that were implemented to remedy past discrimination and were found not to "trammel" unnecessarily the interests of white employees.[82] The reported cases are relatively sparse and lack clear direction. In short, the precise interplay between the Executive Order's affirmative action requirements and Title VII remains unclear.

In a different vein, the Department of Labor ruled in *In re University of Texas at Austin* [83] that a judicial finding of no discrimination in an individual Title VII action bars a subsequent administrative proceeding under the Executive Order. Finding that the doctrines of *res judicata* and collateral estoppel prevent relitigation by OFCCP, Secretary Brock explained:

> "Although the legal bases for relief in the court case and the ALJ hearing were different (primarily Title VII in the court case, and the Order and Regulations in the ALJ hearing), the principal cause of action—sex discrimination in

---

[76]*See* discussion in Chapter 24 (Reverse Discrimination and Affirmative Action).

[77]In *Steelworkers v. Weber,* 443 U.S. 193, 209 n.9, 20 FEP 1, 8 n.9 (1979), the Supreme Court found it unnecessary to consider the contention that the affirmative action plan "represented an attempt to comply with Exec. Order. No. 11246." However, the Supreme Court has noted that in 1972 Congress "defeated resoundingly" Senator Ervin's amendment to extend to Executive Order 11246 the prohibition of § 703(j) of Title VII against requiring employers to engage in preferential hiring. Sheet Metal Workers Local 28 v. EEOC, 478 U.S. 421, 41 FEP 107, 126 (1986).

[78]In *Sheet Metal Workers Local 28 v. EEOC,* 478 U.S. 421, 41 FEP 107 (1986), Justice Powell warned that it is too simplistic to conclude that "hiring goals withstand constitutional muster whereas layoff goals and fixed quotas do not." He stated the proper constitutional inquiry does not focus on the "label" that has been applied to the plan. *Id.,* 41 FEP at 134 n.3 (Powell, J., concurring).

[79]480 U.S. 616, 43 FEP 411 (1987).

[80]Lower courts have not been persuaded by arguments that compliance with the Executive Order is not voluntary. *See, e.g.,* Tangren v. Wackenhut Servs., 480 F. Supp. 539, 21 FEP 570 (D. Nev. 1979), *aff'd,* 658 F.2d 705, 26 FEP 1647 (9th Cir. 1981), *cert. denied,* 456 U.S. 916, 28 FEP 712 (1982); McLaughlin v. Great Lakes Dredge & Dock Co., 495 F. Supp. 857, 23 FEP 1295 (N.D. Ohio 1980).

[81]*Supra* note 77.

[82]Smith v. Harvey, 648 F. Supp. 1103, 1115, 42 FEP 796, 805 (M.D. Fla. 1986); Parker v. Baltimore & Ohio R.R., 641 F. Supp. 1227, 1233, 41 FEP 761, 766 (D.D.C. 1986). *See also* OFCCP v. National Bank of Commerce of San Antonio, No. 77-OFCCP-2 (Dec. 11, 1984) (Final Decision), 241 DAILY LAB. REP. A-1 (BNA, Dec. 11, 1984) (affirmative action goals and timetables required by Executive Order do not conflict with Title VII). *Cf.* Ende v. Regency Univs. Bd. of Regents, 757 F.2d 176, 37 FEP 575 (7th Cir. 1985) (university's adjustment of female faculty salaries did not violate male faculty members' Equal Pay Act rights).

[83]38 FEP 886 (1985).

employment—was the same in both cases, arising out of the same facts and occurrences between the same parties. * * *"[84]

This case is significant because it confirms the Department of Labor's intention to apply the same substantive standards under the Executive Order as apply in Title VII actions.[85] A Title VII action's preclusive effect, however, likely will be limited to situations where the OFCCP allegations are substantially identical to those in the Title VII case.[86]

## III. JUDICIAL ACTION UNDER THE EXECUTIVE ORDER

### B. Private Right of Action

Courts continue to hold that the Executive Order does not provide a private right of action, reasoning[87] that the Executive Order contains no reference to a private right of action and there is no history indicating that such a right of action was contemplated. Indeed, according to the uniform view, a private right of action would undermine the conciliation and administrative enforcement mechanism contemplated by the Executive Order.[88] Complainants also have been unsuccessful bringing suit against OFCCP to force it to act on asserted claims. These cases hold that in circumstances where an investigation is not initiated by the OFCCP, nor any agreement reached between the federal contractor and OFCCP, the aggrieved employee has no independent cause of action under Executive Order 11246 against the federal contractor or OFCCP.[89] In short, there is no private right of action against the contractor. Although theoretically a mandamus action following *Alameda County*[90] is possible against the Department of Labor, courts have been most reluctant to intervene.

Nevertheless, there has been an important development that may well occasion significant expansion of the courts' involvement in Executive Order matters. In *Eatmon v. Bristol Steel & Iron Works,*[91] plaintiffs, 14 former employees and 1 former applicant, had been named in a conciliation agreement between a contractor and OFCCP. The agreement called for payment

---

[84]*Id.,* 38 FEP at 888.

[85]*See* discussion of recent policy directives, at Section I.A-C, *supra.*

[86]*See* Department of Labor v. Coldwell Banker & Co., No. 78-OFCCP-12 (Aug. 14, 1987) (Final Decision) (prior consent decree would have to cover all aspects of affirmative action dealt with in Executive Order to relieve contractor of its duties under the Order).

[87]Pecorella v. Oak Orchard Community Health Center, 559 F. Supp. 147, 31 FEP 1036 (W.D.N.Y. 1982), *aff'd mem.,* 722 F.2d 728, 33 FEP 1696 (2d Cir. 1983); McPartland v. American Broadcasting Cos., 623 F. Supp. 1334, 1339–40, 42 FEP 286, 289 (S.D.N.Y. 1985); Bey v. Schneider Sheet Metal, 603 F. Supp. 450, 452 n.1, 38 FEP 1139, 1140 n.1 (W.D. Pa. 1985).

[88]Utley v. Varian Assocs., 811 F.2d 1279, 1284–86, 43 FEP 191, 194–96 (9th Cir.), *cert. denied,* 484 U.S. ____, 44 FEP 1672 (1987).

[89]*See* Utley v. Varian Assocs., *supra* note 88; Solomon v. National Office-Office of Fed. Contract Compliance Programs, 627 F. Supp. 222, 39 FEP 968 (N.D. Tex. 1985). In Utley v. Varian Assocs., plaintiff alleged a violation of the Executive Order as a basis for a state unfair labor practice claim. The court rejected this approach as an unpersuasive manipulation to circumvent the rule proscribing private rights of action under the Executive Order.

[90]Legal Aid Soc'y of Alameda County v. Brennan, 608 F.2d 1319, 1331, 21 FEP 605, 611 (9th Cir. 1979), *cert. denied,* 447 U.S. 921, 22 FEP 1382 (1980) ("Judicial review is available to ensure that compliance officials perform their non-discretionary duty to refrain from approving plans that do not contain the [goals and timetable] elements mandated by the regulations.").

[91]769 F.2d 1503, 1505, 38 FEP 1364, 1366 (11th Cir. 1985).

of about $4,000 for each named affected class member along with a commit-
ment to "provide 'front pay' to compensate the affected class for economic
losses that they will continue to suffer * * * [until] they * * * attain their
rightful place." The contractor provided some, but not all, the back pay
provided for in the agreement, deciding on its own that it could make
deductions for the interim earnings of the class. The beneficiaries had signed
a release form and the contractor had hired them as employees, but without
retroactive seniority; the contractor had then laid them off because of their
lack of seniority.[92]

The court of appeals held that plaintiffs could enforce the conciliation
agreement on a third-party beneficiary theory, irrespective of the signed
releases. The court found the employer liable for back pay and "front pay."
"Front pay" was defined to include amounts relating to delays in gaining
employment, delays in reaching the pay rate they would have achieved
absent discrimination, and damages stemming from the premature layoff
because they had not been provided the appropriate seniority date. The broad
reach of the remedies approved by the court of appeals, including attorney's
fees, establishes in vivid terms the potential reach of third-party beneficiary
suits.

The importance of *Eatmon* cannot be overstated. Conciliation agreements are a common mode for completing compliance reviews. Under the
regulations, conciliation agreements are to be used to resolve serious deficiencies.[93] Though denying allegations of any significant problem, companies
often prefer to sign a conciliation agreement, thereby quickly concluding the
complex review process. *Eatmon* now raises new concerns. Is the third-party
beneficiary principle limited to those cases where individuals are named in
the conciliation agreement? Is it perhaps broad enough to include a particular class (*e.g.,* applicants or the pool of potential candidates for promotion)?
If *Eatmon* permits a third-party beneficiary claim by those not specifically
named, then the conciliation agreement process will necessarily become far
more significant and the possibility of subsequent court actions will be dramatically increased.

Another Eleventh Circuit case adds an interesting twist to *Eatmon.*
In *Terry v. Northrop Worldwide Aircraft Services,*[94] the court first confirmed the principle of *Eatmon,* but ruled that the particular conciliation
agreement could not be enforced by its beneficiary. After the signing of
the conciliation agreement, the contractor invoked the regulations' protest
procedures,[95] which enable a contractor to challenge demands made by
OFCCP without subjecting itself to a sanctions proceeding. Under this
procedure, the contractor must accept the terms asserted by OFCCP, implement those terms, and at the same time contest the terms in an admin-

---

[92]769 F.2d 1503, 1506, 38 FEP 1364, 1367 (11th Cir. 1985). In the release form, plaintiffs promised,
*inter alia,* not to institute a lawsuit or charge under Title VII. This fact led the court to rule that it also
had jurisdiction to enforce the agreement as a Title VII conciliation agreement.
[93]41 C.F.R. § 60-1.33(a) (1979).
[94]786 F.2d 1558, 40 FEP 985 (11th Cir. 1986).
[95]41 C.F.R. § 60-1.24(c)(4) (1978).

istrative procedure. In *Terry,* OFCCP had agreed to stay the requirement that the company implement the conciliation agreement pending resolution of the protest. The court accordingly ruled that OFCCP was not in a position to enforce a conciliation agreement during the pendency of the protest proceeding. This being the case, third-party beneficiaries likewise could not enforce the agreement.

There are a number of interesting questions arising from *Terry.* The protest procedure usually requires the contractor to comply during the pendency of the protest. An initial question is whether third-party beneficiaries could enforce the contract during the pendency of the protest in the absence of a stay. Persuasive arguments could be made that while the validity of the positions underlying the conciliation agreement are still to be tested in administrative proceedings, it is premature for state or federal courts to entertain third-party beneficiary claims. For the time being, contractors concerned about the possible third-party actions arising from a conciliation agreement might well consider use of the protest procedure.

## IV. DISCLOSURE OF INFORMATION

### A. Access of OFCCP to Contractor Data

Applying the standards of the Supreme Court's *Barlow's*[96] decision, the courts have limited OFCCP authority to search for information on an employer's premises. In *NOPSI,*[97] the Fifth Circuit held that the Fourth Amendment requires OFCCP to obtain a judicially issued search warrant or its equivalent before conducting a nonconsensual on-site inspection of a contractor's facility and employment records. The court of appeals held that three elements are essential to justify the reasonableness of a proposed search: (1) the search must be authorized by statute; (2) the search must be properly limited in scope; and (3) the search must have been initiated pursuant to either (a) specific evidence of an existing violation, (b) a showing that "reasonable legislative or administrative standards for conducting the inspection [are] satisfied with respect to" the establishment to be searched, or (c) a showing that the search is "pursuant to an administrative plan containing specific neutral criteria." Where these standards are not met, a contractor may refuse to provide the OFCCP access to information.[98]

Following the Supreme Court's decision in *Donovan v. Lone Steer,*[99] the Fifth Circuit has continued to apply the *Barlow's*[100] standards to determine whether the OFCCP reasonably selected a particular contractor for investigation and reasonably requested access to particular information, including

---

[96]Marshall v. Barlow's, Inc., 436 U.S. 307 (1978).

[97]United States v. New Orleans Pub. Serv., 723 F.2d 422, 426, 33 FEP 1489, 1491, *reh'g denied,* 734 F.2d 226, 34 FEP 1801 (5th Cir. 1984), *cert. denied,* 469 U.S. 1180, 37 FEP 63 (1985); First Ala. Bank of Montgomery v. Donovan, 692 F.2d 714, 721–22, 30 FEP 448, 452 (11th Cir. 1982).

[98]United States v. New Orleans Pub. Serv., *supra* note 97.

[99]464 U.S. 408, 26 WH 933 (1984).

[100]*Supra* note 96.

documents. In its earlier *NOPSI*[101] decision, the Fifth Circuit had held that OFCCP violated the Fourth Amendment when it selected NOPSI for a compliance review, because there was no evidence that the selection had been based on neutral criteria instead of on the unbridled discretion of the compliance official.[102]

On petition for rehearing, the Fifth Circuit panel reviewed its earlier *NOPSI* ruling in light of the Supreme Court's *Lone Steer*[103] decision. The government relied on *Lone Steer* and argued that the *Barlow's* standards should not have been applied to its investigation of NOPSI because the OFCCP sought only access to documents. The Fifth Circuit disagreed, observing that the government admitted it had sought to enter NOPSI's premises to examine the requested documents. The court concluded that entry by OFCCP representatives would invade the corporation's privacy and could disrupt the workplace, could result in significant administrative and monetary costs, and would permit the OFCCP representatives to examine documents in nonpublic areas and possibly discover plain view evidence against the firm.[104]

It is important to note, however, that the court of appeals did not terminate OFCCP's audit of NOPSI. Rather, the court presented OFCCP with the option of seeking an administrative warrant to conduct an on-site inspection of NOPSI's facilities and records, or requesting that NOPSI produce its records off-site. Thus, although it rejected the theory that companies automatically consent to on-site searches when they become government contractors, the Fifth Circuit's *NOPSI* decision is likely to be of little practical impact on contractors in limiting the scope of compliance reviews, other than identifying areas of concern and a possible option to produce documents offsite.

## B. Disclosure of Information to Third Parties

Affirmative action programs submitted to the government become "agency records" subject to the Freedom of Information Act (FOIA). Asserting a claim of confidential commercial information and the risk of competitive injury, contractors have resisted disclosure primarily through the vehicle of "reverse" FOIA cases. Recent developments clarify the applicable legal standards, but do little to allay the concerns of the contractor community.

In *CNA Financial Corp. v. Donovan,*[105] the D.C. Circuit Court of Appeals found that OFCCP could properly release information that the contractor contended was confidential and would cause substantial competitive harm if released. Brought as a reverse-FOIA case, *CNA* dealt with the

---

[101] *Supra* note 97.
[102] *Id.*
[103] United States v. New Orleans Pub. Serv., 734 F.2d 226, 34 FEP 1801 (5th Cir. 1984), *cert. denied,* 469 U.S. 1180, 37 FEP 63 (1985).
[104] *Id.,* 734 F.2d at 228, 34 FEP at 1802.
[105] 830 F.2d 1132, 44 FEP 1648 (D.C. Cir. 1987), *cert. denied,* 485 U.S. _____, 46 FEP 504 (1988).

difficult issue of defining the relationship between the Trade Secrets Act[106] and FOIA, particularly Exemptions 3 and 4.[107]

The D.C. Circuit found that the Trade Secrets Act was not the type of statute contemplated by FOIA Exemption 3.[108] However, the court determined that the Trade Secrets Act was virtually coextensive with Exemption 4 of FOIA, since both dealt with the same potential competitive harm resulting from the release of material to a third party. The effect of this overlap was significant—a finding that requested material falls within Exemption 4 would be tantamount to a determination that it could not be released under the Trade Secrets Act.

The court of appeals then reviewed the procedures and standards used by OFCCP for determining whether disclosure of CNA's affirmative action programs would cause competitive injury.[109] As to the procedures, the court determined that OFCCP need not provide an evidentiary hearing to the contractor to provide evidence concerning the possible competitive damage the release of the information could cause. As to the substance of the case, the court concluded that OFCCP's decision to release the data was based on a reasonable analysis of the likely competitive impact and, accordingly, was not arbitrary, capricious, or an abuse of discretion.[110]

The teaching of CNA is that contractors will have a difficult time effectively preventing OFCCP from disclosing affirmative action program materials. It is true that the particular affirmative action materials involved in CNA were quite old, which made CNA's effort to demonstrate competitive injury even more challenging. Nevertheless, the decision certainly reflects considerable deference to OFCCP procedures and decision-making on the issue of competitive injury. In these circumstances, it would seem prudent for companies to mark clearly those portions of the affirmative action program deemed commercially sensitive and to explain in some persuasive fashion why such data for this industry ought not to be released if there were an FOIA request. Asserting a position at the time of submission may appear

---

[106]The Trade Secrets Act, 18 U.S.C. § 1905 (1982), provides that any governmental employee who "publishes, divulges, discloses, or makes known in any manner or to any extent not authorized by law any information coming to him [or her] in the course of his [or her] employment or official duties * * *" which "concerns or relates to the trade secrets, processes, operations, style of work, or apparatus, or the identity, confidential statistical data, amount or source of any income, profits, losses, or expenditures of any person, firm, partnership, corporation, or association * * * shall be fined not more than $1,000, or imprisioned not more than one year, or both * * *."

[107]5 U.S.C. § 552(b)(3)–(4) (1982). Exemption 3 exempts from disclosure material specifically withheld from disclosure by another statute. It requires that the matters be withheld from the public by leaving no discretion on the issue, or by establishing particular criteria for withholding or referring to particular types of matters to be withheld. Exemption 4 exempts from disclosure trade secrets and commercial or financial information that is privileged and confidential.

[108]The court of appeals so ruled because the Trade Secrets Act did not provide any direction or guidance to an agency concerning whether or not officially collected commercial and financial information could be released.

[109]The criteria for determining whether financial or commercial information should be released has been consistently held to be whether the material is likely to cause substantial harm to the competitive position of the person from whom the information was obtained. See National Parks & Conservation Ass'n v. Morton, 498 F.2d 765, 770, (D.C. Cir. 1974).

[110]CNA Fin. Corp. v. Donovan, supra note 105, 803 F.2d at 1152–56, 44 FEP 1663–66.

more persuasive than any after-the-fact rationalization following an FOIA request.[111]

Courts continue to reach varying results regarding contractors' claims that the self-critical analysis privilege prevents the pretrial discovery in Title VII cases of affirmative action plans required by the Executive Order. The different results stem from courts reaching different outcomes in the clash between two important interests: (1) confidentiality that assures fairness to persons who have been required by law to engage in self-evaluation and creates an effective incentive for candid and unconstrained self-evaluation;[112] and (2) full disclosure[113] that is advanced by permitting the discovery.[114]

Courts deciding to apply the privilege have restricted its application to purely evaluative (subjective) materials and have ordered the disclosure of nonevaluative facts such as statistics.[115] Even if discovery of a defendant's self-critical analysis evaluation is denied at the pretrial stage, the Seventh Circuit has ruled that the contractor waives the privilege if it voluntarily offers the affirmative action policy at trial as a manifestation of nondiscrimination.[116]

In a separate development of interest, the Secretary of Labor applied the Federal Rules of Civil Procedure to an enforcement proceeding under Executive Order 11246. The Secretary held that the work product doctrine in Rule 26(b)(3) did not cover a contractor's statistical studies prepared by retained experts. He did hold, however, that a study prepared in anticipation of litigation, and not just pursuant to a contractor's affirmative action obligations, was protected from discovery under Rule 26(b)(4)(B). With respect to the latter study, the Secretary held that the contractor should not have been required to turn over such a study during a hearing on the contractor's compliance with the Executive Order.[117]

---

[111]The procedural issues were largely resolved in National Org. for Women, Washington D.C. Chapter v. Social Sec. Admin. (NOW), 736 F.2d 727, 34 FEP 1514 (D.C. Cir. 1984). In the NOW case, the court of appeals concluded that a reverse discrimination plaintiff is not entitled to a de novo review of an agency's FOIA decision. Such a procedure is appropriate only when the fact-finding procedures of the agency are inadequate. The decision in the NOW case specifically upheld the procedures used by OFCCP in reverse FOIA actions, procedures which were largely replicated in the CNA case, supra note 110.

[112]See Coates v. Johnson & Johnson, 756 F.2d 524, 552, 37 FEP 467, 489 (7th Cir. 1985) (citing O'Connor v. Chrysler Corp., 86 F.R.D. 211, 218, 26 FEP 459, 464 (D. Mass. 1980)); Granger v. National R.R. Passenger Corp., 116 F.R.D. 507, 509 (E.D. Pa. 1987). This rationale has been challenged. See Witten v. A.H. Smith & Co., 100 F.R.D. 446, 452–54, 33 FEP 1238, 1242–44 (D. Md. 1984), aff'd mem., 785 F.2d 306, 46 FEP 1222 (4th Cir. 1986); Hardy v. New York News, 114 F.R.D. 633, 641, 46 FEP 1199 (S.D.N.Y. 1987).

[113]Some courts that have permitted discovery of such plans have issued a protective order to maintain confidentiality. See Coates v. Johnson & Johnson, 756 F.2d 524, 551, 37 FEP 467, 489 (7th Cir. 1985); Witten v. A.H. Smith & Co., 100 F.R.D. 446, 450, 33 FEP 1238, 1241–42 (D. Md. 1984), aff'd mem., 785 F.2d 306, 46 FEP 1222 (4th Cir. 1986).

[114]Compare Coates v. Johnson & Johnson, supra note 113 ("prevailing" view is that self-critical portions of affirmative action plans are privileged) with Witten v. A.H. Smith & Co., 100 F.R.D. 446, 454, 33 FEP 1238, 1244 (D. Md. 1984), aff'd mem., 785 F.2d 306, 46 FEP 1222 (4th Cir. 1986) (need for all evidence to ascertain intent of the parties, particularly in employment discrimination cases, significantly outweighs countervailing interest).

[115]See Hardy v. New York News, supra note 112. Cf. Jackson v. Harvard Univ., 111 F.R.D. 472, 474 (D. Mass. 1986) (sex discrimination plaintiff entitled to objective statistical information and additional facts contained in subjective material but not found in objective data). The court may conduct an in camera inspection rather than permit the contractor to delete portions of the plan containing self-critical analysis. O'Connor v. Chrysler Corp., supra note 112.

[116]Coates v. Johnson & Johnson, supra note 112.

[117]Department of Labor v. Harris Trust & Sav. Bank, No. 78-OFCCP-2 (Dec. 22, 1986) (Recommended Decision).

## CHAPTER 26

# EEOC ADMINISTRATIVE PROCESS

## I. GENERAL ADMINISTRATIVE POWERS

### A. The EEOC

In August 1982, the EEOC headquarters organization was consolidated from 14 into 10 administrative units. The district offices thereafter reported to one of three Regional Directors, who in turn reported to the Director of the Office of Program Operations, which absorbed the former Office of Systemic Programs. The position of Executive Director was abolished and each of the 10 headquarters offices now report directly to the Chairman and the Commissioners.[1]

In June 1987, the three Regional Programs were consolidated into two Field Management Programs. The district offices now report to one of two Field Management Program Directors, who in turn report to the Director of the Office of Program Operations.[2] Also in June 1987, the Commission established a new Determinations Review Program, the function of which is to review charging parties' requests for review of "no cause" letters of determination issued by field office directors. The Determinations Review Program, which also reports to the Director of the Office of Program Operations, recommends "reasonable cause" determinations or issues final "no cause" determinations when field office letters of determination are sustained upon review; remands charge files to the field offices for further information or investigation; forwards recommendations to reverse field office letters of determination to the Director of the Office of Program Operations for decision; and issues final no cause determinations when requests for review are withdrawn.[3]

Effective July 1, 1979, the enforcement of the Equal Pay Act (EPA) and the Age Discrimination in Employment Act (ADEA) was transferred from the Department of Labor to the EEOC under the authority of the Reorganization Act of 1977.[4] However, the decision of the Supreme Court in *Immigration & Naturalization Service v. Chadha*[5] holding unconstitutional the legislative veto provision of the Immigration and Naturalization Act cast doubt upon the legality of this transfer from the Department of Labor to the EEOC. This led in turn to numerous challenges to the

---

[1]EEOC Order No. 110 (Aug. 17, 1982), 159 DAILY LAB. REP. A-3, D-1 (BNA, Aug. 17, 1982).
[2]EEOC Order No. 110, Organization, Mission, and Functions (June 10, 1987).
[3]Id. The procedural regulations implementing this program are found at 52 FED. REG. 26957 (July 17, 1987), to be codified at 29 C.F.R. § 1601.19(a). *See also* discussion *infra* at p. 374 and notes 57–59.
[4]Reorg. Plan No. 1 of 1978, *reprinted in* 1978 U.S. CODE CONG. & AD. NEWS 9799, issued pursuant to the Reorganization Act of 1977, 5 U.S.C. §§ 901 *et seq.* (1982).
[5]462 U.S. 919, 51 USLW 4907 (1983).

EEOC's right to process charges or litigate cases under the EPA and the ADEA. Although most courts found the transfer valid, despite the offending legislative veto provision in the Reorganization Act of 1977,[6] a Second Circuit decision declared the transfer unconstitutional under *Chadha.*[7] However, the Second Circuit stayed the effect of that decision until December 31, 1984, to permit corrective action by Congress,[8] which enacted Public Law 98-532, ratifying the transfer provision[9] and ending this controversy.

In 1986, the EEOC adopted new programs to serve both employers and employees. The Commission announced a toll free telephone number, 800-USA-EEOC, that provides bilingual information and allows individuals to file charges with the nearest EEOC field office. In addition, the Commission implemented the Expanded Presence Program, to provide service to individuals in high density population areas not previously served by EEOC, and the Voluntary Assistance Program, to provide education and technical assistance to small and midsize employers.

On July 14, 1986, the Commission issued a policy statement regarding Investigative Compliance which provides for an expedited subpoena process, a bypass of the subpoena process in certain circumstances, and a finding of adverse inference against respondents in cases where an employer's refusal to supply information deemed relevant to a charge of discrimination would otherwise lead to investigative delays unacceptable to the Commission.[10] One anticipated effect of the "adverse inference" rule is that the EEOC may issue cause determinations—admissible at trial in the Fifth, Ninth, and Eleventh circuits[11]—and commence Title VII actions based on limited evidence where employers are found to have improperly resisted administrative discovery.

---

[6]*E.g.,* EEOC v. Hernando Bank, 724 F.2d 1188, 34 FEP 15 (5th Cir. 1984) (EPA—unconstitutional legislative veto provision is severable); EEOC v. Pennsylvania, 596 F. Supp. 1333, 36 FEP 234 (M.D. Pa. 1984) (ADEA—severable); EEOC v. New York, 590 F. Supp. 37, 34 FEP 379 (N.D.N.Y. 1984) (same); EEOC v. Radio Montgomery, 588 F. Supp. 567, 34 FEP 378 (W.D. Va. 1984) (EPA—severable and subsequently ratified by Congress); EEOC v. Chrysler Corp., 595 F. Supp. 344, 33 FEP 1838 (E.D. Mich. 1984) (ADEA—not severable, but *Chadha* not to be applied retroactively); Muller Optical v. EEOC, 574 F. Supp. 946, 33 FEP 420 (W.D. Tenn. 1983), *aff'd,* 743 F.2d 380, 35 FEP 1147 (6th Cir. 1984) (ADEA—severable); EEOC v. City of Memphis, 581 F. Supp. 179, 33 FEP 1089 (W.D. Tenn. 1983) (ADEA—severable and transfer subsequently ratified); EEOC v. Cudahy Foods Co., 588 F. Supp. 13, 33 FEP 1836 (W.D. Wash. 1983) (ADEA—severable).

   *Contra* EEOC v. Westinghouse Elec. Corp., 576 F. Supp. 1530, 33 FEP 1232 (W.D. Pa.), *appeal dismissed,* 469 U.S. 806, 35 FEP 1608 (1984) (EPA); EEOC v. Pan Am. World Airways, 576 F. Supp. 1530, 33 FEP 1232 (S.D.N.Y. 1984) (ADEA—transfer potentially invalid and EEOC subpoena enforcement denied); EEOC v. Allstate Ins. Co., 570 F. Supp. 1224, 32 FEP 1337 (S.D. Miss. 1983), *appeal dismissed,* 467 U.S. 1232, 34 FEP 1785 (1984) (EPA). *Cf.* EEOC v. Chrysler Corp., 34 FEP 1862 (N.D. Ga. 1984), *aff'd on other grounds,* 759 F.2d 1523, 37 FEP 1244 (11th Cir. 1985) (ADEA—issue of legislative veto moot where it was never exercised).

[7]EEOC v. CBS, 743 F.2d 969, 35 FEP 1127 (2d Cir.), *rev'g* 34 FEP 257 (S.D.N.Y.), *motion denied,* 748 F.2d 124, 36 FEP 575 (2d Cir. 1984).

[8]*Id.,* 743 F.2d at 976, 35 FEP at 1133; *see also* EEOC v. Allstate Ins. Co., 467 U.S. 1232, 34 FEP 1785 (1984), *dismissing for want of jurisdiction appeal from* 570 F. Supp. 1224, 32 FEP 1337 (S.D. Miss. 1983).

[9]*See* EEOC v. CBS, *supra* note 7.

[10]EEOC Compliance Manual, BNA p. N:3181.

[11]*See* Second Edition at p. 977 and *infra,* notes 100–101 and accompanying text.

## B. Rule-Making Powers[12]

The EEOC has often followed the notice and comment process of the Administrative Procedure Act (APA) in exercising its authority under § 713 of Title VII to promulgate procedural regulations, interpretations, and opinions.[13] EEOC interpretations have been invalidated where they conflict with the statute.[14] However, the Fourth Circuit has found that the EEOC's regulations governing disclosure of information obtained in investigations are procedural and by definition are not governed by the procedures for notice and comment prescribed by the APA.[15]

The EEOC issued new regulations effective August 20, 1986, regarding Interpretations of the Equal Pay Act[16] and cautioned that these replace the regulations issued earlier by the Department of Labor, on which employers may no longer rely.[17] These regulations require employers to provide equal benefits to employees of both sexes[18] and expressly provide that a wage differential based on claimed differences between the average cost of employing workers of one sex as a group and the average cost of employing workers of the opposite sex as a group is discriminatory and does not qualify as a differential based on any "factor other than sex.[19]

The Commission also made minor changes in EEOC filing requirements for federal employees' charges of discrimination in 1986.[20]

## C. EEOC Posting Requirements

Applying precedent developed under the ADEA, the First Circuit concluded that a failure to post the statutorily required Title VII notice may, in some circumstances, extend the time period for filing a charge with the EEOC.[21]

---

[12]Title VII restricts the rule-making power of the Commission to procedural regulations. 42 U.S.C. § 2000e-12(a). *See, e.g.,* General Elec. Co. v. Gilbert, 429 U.S. 125, 141, 13 FEP 1657 (1976); Associated Dry Goods Corp. v. EEOC, 720 F.2d 804, 33 FEP 181 (4th Cir. 1983). Proposed EEOC regulations relating to ADEA have been finalized and, as amended effective April 1, 1984, are contained at 29 C.F.R. § 1926 *et seq.* (1984). Procedural regulations promulgated under the ADEA, and regulations jointly issued by the EEOC and the Department of Justice for processing charges filed with federal funding agencies, are discussed in Section II, *infra.* Substantive guidelines issued by the EEOC are discussed in the chapters relating to each subject matter area.

[13]*E.g.,* 44 FED. REG. 13278–81 (1979) as to appendix to 29 C.F.R. pt. 1604 (Questions and Answers on Pregnancy Discrimination Act); 42 FED. REG. 42022 *et seq.* (1977) as to 42 C.F.R. § 1601.22 (confidentiality of charge and other information); *see also* Emerson Elec. Co. v. Schlesinger, 609 F.2d 898, 904, 21 FEP 475, 497 (8th Cir. 1979) (suggesting advisability of such a procedure).

[14]Quinn v. New York State Elec. & Gas Corp., 569 F. Supp. 655, 32 FEP 1070 (N.D.N.Y. 1983) (EEOC interpretation that apprenticeship programs are exempt from ADEA inconsistent with language and purpose of Act).

[15]Associated Dry Goods Corp. v. EEOC, 720 F.2d 804, 812, 33 FEP 181, 186–87 (4th Cir. 1983), *rev'g* 543 F. Supp. 950, 29 FEP 526 (E.D. Va. 1982), *on remand from* 449 U.S. 590, 24 FEP 1356 (1981). The court found that the EEOC's rules and regulations necessarily fall within the exemption to Administrative Procedure Act compliance found at 5 U.S.C. § 553(b)(3)(A) (1984). The disclosure rules were 29 C.F.R. § 1610.17(d) and §§ 83.3(a) and 83.5 of the EEOC COMPLIANCE MANUAL, BNA pp. 83:0001–0002 (Mar. 1979). EEOC regulations are hereinafter referred to only by section numbers (*e.g.,* 29 C.F.R. § 1601.74 is referred to as § 1601.74).

[16]29 C.F.R. § 1620, 51 FED. REG. 29819 (1986).

[17]29 C.F.R. § 800.

[18]29 C.F.R. § 1620.11, 51 FED. REG. 29819 (1986).

[19]29 C.F.R. § 1620.13, 51 FED. REG. 29819 (1986).

[20]29 C.F.R. § 1613.806, 51 FED. REG. 22519 (1986).

[21]Earnhardt v. Puerto Rico, 691 F.2d 69, 30 FEP 65 (1st Cir. 1982). *But cf.* Kazanzas v. Walt Disney World Co., 704 F.2d 1527, 1529–32, 31 FEP 1590, 1592–93 (11th Cir.), *cert. denied,* 464 U.S. 982, 33

## D. Records and Reports

Effective April 1, 1986, the EEOC reduced reporting requirements for labor organizations subject to Title VII.[22] Such organizations must file their EEOC-3 Reports biannually instead of annually.[23] Recordkeeping provisions governing labor organizations remain unchanged.[24]

## II. THE EEOC COMPLIANCE PROCESS

The EEOC has issued final procedural regulations under the ADEA for processing and investigating charges, referring charges to state agencies, and issuing opinions.[25] It also has revised and augmented its compliance procedures for ADEA, EPA, and combined charges.[26] In addition, the EEOC and the Department of Justice have jointly published rules[27] for processing complaints that allege employment discrimination in violation of Title VI of the Civil Rights Act of 1964, Title IX of the Education Amendments of 1972, and the State and Local Fiscal Assistance Act of 1972, as amended. Under these rules, the EEOC should process individual complaints that allege only employment discrimination, while the fund-granting agency will normally retain complaints alleging a pattern and practice of employment discrimination or discrimination in practices in addition to employment.

The EEOC's rapid charge processing system, which was instituted in 1979 to address a backlog of nearly 100,000 pending charges, has been modified by the Commission.[28] While rapid charge processing was effective in eliminating the backlog, the program came under criticism both for encouraging frivolous complaints because of the opportunity for quick settlement, and for glossing over cases with litigation potential.

Under a resolution adopted December 6, 1983, the Commission shifted from a presumption in favor of rapid charge processing to case-by-case decisions on appropriate methods for resolving charges, and eliminated the practice of allowing a charging party to decide whether his or her charge would go through rapid charge processing or extended investigation.[29]

---

FEP 280 (1983) (ADEA limitations period not tolled by failure to post notice); Downey v. Firestone Tire & Rubber Co., 35 FEP 30 (D.D.C. 1984), aff'd in relevant part, 762 F.2d 137, 37 FEP 1072 (D.C. Cir. 1985) (ADEA limitations period not tolled by failure to post notice where complainant was represented by counsel during limitations period). See Chapter 28 (Timeliness).

[22]29 C.F.R. § 1602.22, 51 FED. REG. 11017 (1986).

[23]Id.

[24]29 C.F.R. § 1602.27.

[25]48 FED REG. 138 (1982); 29 C.F.R. §§ 1626.1–1626.19; see also supra note 12.

[26]See EEOC COMPLIANCE MANUAL §§ 1-93 (Oct. 1987).

[27]48 FED. REG. 3574 (1983); 29 C.F.R. §§ 1691.1–1691.13.

[28]Although the EEOC's procedures for processing age and equal pay charges generally are similar to those applied under Title VII, they are not identical. See, e.g., EEOC v. Home of Economy, 712 F.2d 356, 32 FEP 599 (8th Cir. 1983) (EEOC may file suit under EPA without first attempting conciliation; EEOC's power to investigate and bring suit under EPA is same as that of Department of Labor prior to 1979 transfer of authority).

[29]239 DAILY LAB. REP., A-5, D-1 (BNA, Dec. 12, 1983). See infra notes 50–51 and accompanying text.

## A. The Intake of a Charge

EEOC regulations do not permit the agency to reject for "lack of jurisdiction" a charge which validly alleges a violation of Title VII.[30] The EEOC's proposed regulation governing time limits under the ADEA became final as of January 3, 1983.[31] The regulation provides that charges will not be rejected as untimely unless barred by the statute of limitations contained in § 6 of the Portal-to-Portal Act of 1947.

## D. Deferral and Contracts With State and Local Agencies

The EEOC's regulations concerning designation of § 706 agencies were amended in November 1982, as was the regulation concerning § 706 Agency Notification.[32] Similarly, regulations concerning the referral and processing of ADEA charges have been revised.[33]

## E. Service of the Charge[34]

The impact of the Commission's failure to effectuate timely service of a charge has been considered chiefly in the context of suits brought by the EEOC.[35] A failure by the Commission to give notice of a charge or to attempt conciliation does not deprive the court of jurisdiction on a suit filed by the affected employees.[36]

## H. Negotiated Settlement Prior to Determination

The question whether the EEOC may bring an action in federal district court to enforce a predetermination settlement (PDS) agreement still has not

---

[30]McKee v. McDonnell Douglas Technical Servs. Co., 700 F.2d 260, 263–64, 31 FEP 383, 385, *reh'g denied and opinion amended on other grounds,* 705 F.2d 776, 31 FEP 1672 (5th Cir. 1983); *see also* Jennings v. Postal Workers Local 8, 672 F.2d 712, 714, 28 FEP 514, 517 (8th Cir. 1982). *But see* Bennett v. Russ Berrie & Co., 564 F. Supp. 1576, 32 FEP 225 (N.D. Ind. 1983) (letter from employee's attorney to EEOC and state FEP agency does not constitute Title VII charge; EEOC did not accept or treat letter as charge, process or investigate it, make attempt to conciliate the matter, or give employer notice of charge). An unverified EEOC intake questionnaire is not a "charge." Proffit v. Keycom Elec. Publishing, 625 F. Supp. 400, 39 FEP 884 (N.D. Ill. 1985), *reh'g denied,* 625 F. Supp. 400, 409, 40 FEP 1 (N.D. Ill. 1986). *Contra* Casavantes v. California State Univ., Sacramento, 732 F.2d 1441, 34 FEP 1336 (9th Cir. 1984) (intake questionnaire is a sufficient charge).
[31]29 C.F.R. § 1626.7(a), 48 FED. REG. 140 (1983).
[32]29 C.F.R. §§ 1601.70 and 1601.71, 47 FED. REG. 53733 (1982); §§ 1601.72 and 1601.73 are now reserved for future use. 29 C.F.R. § 1601.74, listing § 706 agencies, was amended March 14, 1983. 48 FED. REG. 10645 (1983).
[33]*See* 29 C.F.R. §§ 1626.9 and 1626.10.
[34]Notice of the charge need contain only that information required to be included in the charge itself under 29 C.F.R. § 1601.12(a)(3). EEOC v. Shell Oil Co., 466 U.S. 54, 81, 34 FEP 709, 719 (1984). *But see id.* at 82, 34 FEP at 726 (O'Connor, J., dissenting) (sufficiency of charge should be determined from face of charge; commissioner's good faith presumed); EEOC v. K-Mart Corp., 796 F.2d 139, 41 FEP 371 (6th Cir. 1986).
[35]EEOC v. Burlington N., 644 F.2d 717, 25 FEP 499 (8th Cir. 1981) (Commission's failure to serve employer notice of charge within 10 days not absolute bar to enforcement; if delay not willful or in bad faith, court must evaluate evidence of prejudice presented by defendant). *But see* EEOC v. Firestone Tire & Rubber Co., 626 F. Supp. 90, 39 FEP 583 (M.D. Ga. 1985) (33-month delay in service of charge constitutes evidence of laches).
[36]Brewster v. Shockley, 554 F. Supp. 365, 30 FEP 1390 (W.D. Va. 1983); Bey v. Schneider Sheet Metal, 596 F. Supp. 319, 38 FEP 1135 (W.D. Pa. 1984) (issuance of right-to-sue letter 27 days after receipt of charge does not deprive court of jurisdiction; fact that EEOC failed to investigate or conciliate does not prevent issuance of right to sue).

been finally resolved. The essential controversy is whether there must be an independent investigation and determination of reasonable cause prior to an EEOC lawsuit to enforce the PDS agreement.[37]

Other circuits appear not inclined to follow the Ninth Circuit's refusal in *EEOC v. Pierce Packing Co.* [38] to enforce a PDS agreement. In *EEOC v. Henry Beck Co.,* [39] the Fourth Circuit, noting that "pre-determination settlements (PDS) are no less effective in facilitating the Commission's essential role as a mediator than conciliation agreements," distinguished *Pierce Packing* on its facts, and held that jurisdiction to enforce a PDS agreement was implicit in § 706(f)(3) and 28 U.S.C. §§ 1337 and 1343.[40] In *EEOC v. Safeway Stores,* [41] the Fifth Circuit likewise distinguished *Pierce Packing.* The court noted that a refusal to exercise its jurisdiction to enforce conciliation agreements would undermine the statutory scheme incorporated in Title VII favoring voluntary settlement of disputes.[42]

The decision in *Safeway Stores,* however, calls into question whether the EEOC can settle fully claims involving bargaining-unit employees at the PDS stage. The Fifth Circuit, relying upon *W.R. Grace & Co. v. Rubber Workers Local 759,* [43] held that, absent union agreement, awards of individual, retroactive seniority could be made only after a finding of discrimination. Thus, the court declined to enforce that portion of the *Safeway* conciliation agreement calling for such awards.[44] There is also a question whether courts have jurisdiction under Title VII over an individual plaintiff's suit to enforce a settlement or conciliation agreement. In these cases some courts have considered whether the lapse or absence of a right-to-sue letter precludes the suit.[45] However, the Eleventh Circuit has twice held, under analo-

---

[37]*Compare* EEOC v. Pierce Packing Co., 669 F.2d 605, 28 FEP 393 (9th Cir. 1982) (necessary Title VII procedural prerequisites of independent investigation and reasonable cause determination not met) *with* EEOC v. Cleveland State Univ., 28 FEP 441 (N.D. Ohio 1982) (because of importance of conciliation, EEOC may enforce predetermination settlement agreement notwithstanding absence of reasonable cause determination). *But cf.* EEOC v. Liberty Trucking Co., 695 F.2d 1038, 30 FEP 884 (7th Cir. 1982) (federal district courts have jurisdiction under Title VII over EEOC suits to enforce postdetermination conciliation agreements); Eatmon v. Bristol Steel & Iron Works, 769 F.2d 1503, 38 FEP 1364 (11th Cir. 1985) (recognizing private right of action under Title VII to enforce conciliation agreement where individual plaintiffs had released Title VII claims in return for employer's compliance with OFCCP conciliation agreement).

[38]*Supra* note 37.

[39]729 F.2d 301, 34 FEP 373 (4th Cir. 1984).

[40]The court in *EEOC v. Henry Beck Co., supra* note 39, sought to distinguish *Pierce Packing, supra* note 37, by suggesting that the Commission in *Pierce* had sought to go beyond specific performance of the PDS agreement by filing a court complaint alleging that the employer had violated Title VII in its employment practices, without satisfying the jurisdictional prerequisites of 42 U.S.C. § 2000e-5(f)(1). However, the Fourth Circuit's wording broadly declares that "where an employer allegedly breaches a predetermination settlement agreement after voluntarily entering into it, and the Commission seeks enforcement of that agreement only, without attempting to litigate the underlying unfair employment practice charge, the suit is brought directly under Title VII, and the United States District Courts have jurisdiction under § 706(f)(3)." 729 F.2d at 305–6, 34 FEP at 376.

[41]714 F.2d 567, 32 FEP 1465 (5th Cir. 1983), *cert. denied,* 467 U.S. 1204, 34 FEP 1400 (1984).

[42]The *Safeway* court, *supra* note 41, declined to adopt the Seventh Circuit's position in *EEOC v. Liberty Trucking Co., supra* note 37, that state courts lacked the authority to hear suits to enforce PDS agreements. 714 F.2d at 572, 32 FEP at 1468–70.

[43]461 U.S. 757, 31 FEP 1409 (1983).

[44]In *Firefighters Local 93 v. City of Cleveland,* 478 U.S. 501, 41 FEP 139 (1986), the Supreme Court held (in the context of a consent decree) that enforcement of a settlement which altered a collectively bargained seniority system could not be interfered with by a nonconsenting union. The union was limited to an action for damages against the employer.

[45]*Compare* Perdue v. Roy Stone Transfer Corp., 690 F.2d 1091, 29 FEP 1673 (4th Cir. 1982) (right-to-sue letter not prerequisite to action for breach of predetermination settlement) *with* Parsons v. Yellow Freight Sys., 741 F.2d 871, 35 FEP 1121 (6th Cir. 1984) (private enforcement of EEOC settlement

gous circumstances dealing with an OFCCP conciliation agreement, that the question must be treated under principles of third-party beneficiary contract law and that employees may state federal claims for enforcement of an OFCCP conciliation agreement that has become enforceable as between the OFCCP and the employer.[46]

## J. The EEOC's Revised Charged-Handling Procedures—Additional Features

The EEOC adopted revised compliance procedures in April 1984. Once the intake process has been concluded, the case will be assigned to an enforcement unit.[47] Rapid processing will be reserved for charges (1) which clearly appear to be individual claims of harm and disparate treatment; (2) where the investigation to be made is clearly limited in scope, evidentiary requirements are straightforward, and the case involves a small group of potentially aggrieved persons or a single individual; or (3) on which the law is settled, or which will require minimal assistance of an attorney during the investigation.[48]

Extended processing will be given those charges where (1) the issues are necessarily classwide or affect a significant number of potentially aggrieved persons; (2) the allegations correspond to issues identified as priorities in EEOC litigation plans, or may require substantial investigative resources and continuing legal assistance; (3) several apparently meritorious charges on the same factual and legal bases have been filed against the respondent; (4) the allegations are without precedent in a Commission decision, and a decision on the issue can be made only after a full investigation; (5) the respondent has evidenced a past recalcitrance; or (6) the allegations involve the operation of a collective bargaining agreement requiring participation of the union in the administrative process. Other charges receiving extended processing will be Commissioner charges; classwide concurrent Title VII and EPA charges; pattern-or-practice ADEA and EPA complaints and directed investigations; and third-party charges filed under Title VII or the ADEA, or concurrently under Title VII and either the ADEA or EPA.[49]

### 1. The Fact-Finding Conference

A fact-finding conference is a processing option which may be used to investigate individual harm and limited class disparate treatment cases.[50] A

---

agreement must be premised upon filing of new charge and receipt of right-to-sue letter *and* Weills v. Caterpillar Tractor Co., 553 F. Supp. 640, 31 FEP 210 (N.D. Cal. 1982) (Title VII suit must be brought within 90 days of receipt of right-to-sue letter and federal question jurisdiction over breach of settlement suit could not be based on other Title VII provisions).

[46]Eatmon v. Bristol Steel & Iron Works, *supra* note 37 (third-party action to enforce OFCCP conciliation agreement is "brought under" Title VII where employees had released Title VII claims in return for employer's compliance with OFCCP conciliation agreement; Title VII charges need not be filed); Terry v. Northrop Worldwide Aviation Servs., 786 F.2d 1558, 40 FEP 985 (11th Cir. 1986).

[47]EEOC Compliance Manual, § 2.8. BNA pp. 2:0009–2:0011. The former rapid charge processing unit and extended compliance unit have been consolidated and are now designated generically as "enforcement units." EEOC Order No. 110, Organization, Mission, and Functions (June 10, 1987).

[48]EEOC Compliance Manual, § 2.8(b)(1), BNA pp. 2:0009–2:0010.

[49]EEOC Compliance Manual, § 2.8(b)(2), BNA p. 2:0010.

[50]EEOC Compliance Manual, § 14.7.

conference will generally not be held: where the alleged discrimination derives from an acknowledged or documented policy; in Commissioner charge cases; where a charge is filed on behalf of an aggrieved individual, where the aggrieved individual requests that his or her identity remain confidential; and in ADEA and EPA complaint cases.[51] The conference is "primarily an investigative forum intended to further define the issues, determine which elements are undisputed, clarify disputed issues and evidence, and determine what other evidence may be necessary," or to assist the parties in reaching a settlement.[52]

### 3. The New "Reasonable Cause" Standard

On September 11, 1984, the EEOC adopted a new statement of enforcement policy further refining its "litigation worthy" standard for "reasonable cause" determinations. In doing so, it noted that it was under a duty to achieve a "degree of certainty and predictability in enforcement which will more directly carry out [its] law enforcement responsibility."[53]

To meet this goal, the new policy provided that the Commission itself would review for litigation all "reasonable cause" determinations.[54] The policy reiterated that legal staff in each district office was to have input into the determination, and that the District Director is responsible for making the determination.[55]

The new policy also differs from its predecessor in that it sets forth specifically the questions the Regional Attorney is to answer in advising the District Director whether the evidence supports a "reasonable cause" determination. That question is whether "it is more likely than not" that there has been discrimination, a question to be assessed by determining first whether a prima facie case exists, and then by analyzing any evidence of pretext if the respondent has put forward a "viable defense."[56]

On December 15, 1986, the Commission supplemented its standard on "reasonable cause" with a new system, modeled on NLRB procedures, which provides for an appeal of matters in which there has been a finding of "no reasonable cause" to the agency's Office of Program Operations. Unusual cases may be appealed directly to the Commission itself.[57] The new appeal procedure became effective August 1, 1987. Charging parties may seek review of a "no cause" finding within 14 days of its issuance.[58] The review procedure shall not apply to charges processed by § 706 agencies under contract with the Commission.[59]

---

[51]EEOC COMPLIANCE MANUAL, § 14.9(c).
[52]EEOC COMPLIANCE MANUAL, § 14.9(b), BNA pp. 14:0003–14:0004.
[53]EEOC "Statement of Enforcement Policy," September 11, 1984, p. 1, 177 DAILY LAB. REP., D-1 (BNA, Sept. 17, 1984).
[54]Id. at 2. This policy was also made applicable to letters of violation. Id. at 1–3.
[55]Id. at 3.
[56]241 DAILY LAB. REP. p. A–4 (BNA, Dec. 16, 1986).
[57]29 C.F.R. § 1601.19(a)(3).
[58]29 C.F.R. § 1601.19(a)(4).
[59]Supra note 53 at 4.

## III. EEOC INVESTIGATION AND SUBPOENA POWERS

### C. Standards in Enforcement of Subpoena

The existence of a charge that meets the requirements of § 706(b) of Title VII is a jurisdictional prerequisite to enforcement of a subpoena issued by the EEOC.[60] Thus, the threshold question in determining whether a subpoena can be enforced is the extent to which § 706(b) and 29 C.F.R. § 1601.12(a)(3) require the inclusion of detailed information in the underlying charge. In *EEOC v. Shell Oil Co.,*[61] the Supreme Court held that for purposes of subpoena enforcement a Commissioner's pattern-and-practice charge need only

> "identify the groups of persons that [the Commissioner] has reason to believe have been discriminated against, the categories of employment positions from which they have been excluded, the methods by which the discrimination may have been effected, and the periods of time in which [the Commissioner] suspects the discrimination to have been practiced."[62]

Neither the charge nor the notice thereof need contain specific statistical data substantiating the allegations.

Because the Court found that the EEOC had complied with the charge and notice requirements of Title VII and its implementing regulations in *Shell Oil,* it did not reach the question whether inadequate notice is a legitimate defense to a subpoena enforcement action brought by the Agency.[63] Also unresolved is the question of the scope of discovery which may be undertaken in opposing subpoena enforcement.[64]

Documents requested by the EEOC during the investigative process may be subject to claims of privilege. At least in the academic context, this may include a claim of privilege to protect the peer review process.[65]

EEOC subpoenas have been enforced over the following objections by employers: the charge was filed outside the statute of limitations;[66] the EEOC deviated from the provisions of its Compliance Manual;[67] the investigation

---

[60]EEOC v. Shell Oil Co., 466 U.S. 54, 34 FEP 709 (1984) (citing, *inter alia,* EEOC v. K-Mart Corp., 694 F.2d 1055, 1061, 30 FEP 788, 794 (6th Cir. 1982)); EEOC v. Ocean City Police Dep't, 820 F.2d 1378, 44 FEP 97 (4th Cir. 1987) (en banc) (subpoena will not be enforced when underlying charge is untimely on its face). While the enforcement of an administrative subpoena must be premised upon the existence of a valid charge, the district court need not find that the charge is verifiable or well founded. EEOC v. Shell Oil Co., *supra,* at 72 n.26, 34 FEP at 718. *See also* EEOC v. Children's Hosp. Medical Center of N. Cal., 719 F.2d 1426, 33 FEP 461 (9th Cir. 1983) (subpoena enforced even though enforcement of underlying claims might have been barred by prior consent decree).

[61]*Supra* note 60.

[62]*Id.* at 73, 34 FEP at 716.

[63]*See* 29 C.F.R. § 1613.1201(a)(3); *see also* opinion of O'Connor, J., concurring in part and dissenting in part, 466 U.S. at 82, 34 FEP at 722.

[64]Generally, the employer may not engage in discovery on the merits of the underlying charge or depose a Commissioner concerning the facts surrounding its issuance. In re EEOC, 709 F.2d 392, 32 FEP 361 (5th Cir. 1983); Food Town Stores v. EEOC, 708 F.2d 920, 31 FEP 1327 (4th Cir. 1983), *cert. denied,* 465 U.S. 1005, 33 FEP 1344 (1984); EEOC v. K-Mart Corp., 694 F.2d 1055, 30 FEP 788 (6th Cir. 1981).

[65]*Compare* EEOC v. University of Notre Dame du Lac, 715 F.2d 331, 32 FEP 1057 (7th Cir. 1983) (peer review documents entitled to qualified privilege subject to *in camera* review and particularized showing of need by EEOC) *with* EEOC v. Franklin & Marshall College, 775 F.2d 110, 39 FEP 211 (3d Cir. 1985), *cert. denied,* 476 U.S. 1163, 40 FEP 1617 (1986) (no academic privilege shields peer review documents from access by EEOC).

[66]EEOC v. United States Steel Corp., 534 F. Supp. 416, 417–18, 28 FEP 592, 593 (S.D. W. Va. 1982). *But see* EEOC v. Ocean City Police Dep't, *supra* note 60.

[67]Sunbeam Appliance Co. v. Kelly, 532 F. Supp. 96, 99–100, 28 FEP 180, 182–83 (N.D. Ill. 1982).

was precluded by *res judicata* or collateral estoppel doctrines;[68] the EEOC failed to defer the charges to the § 706 agency: [69] the information sought was confidential;[70] the subpoena was unduly burdensome;[71] the subpoena required the employer to compile data;[72] the EEOC acted in bad faith;[73] the information sought was irrelevant;[74] the underlying charge was untimely;[75] and the EEOC has no authority to issue a subpoena in an ADEA action.[76] Courts have refused to stay enforcement of an EEOC subpoena under the automatic stay provisions of the Bankruptcy Code, holding that EEOC administrative proceedings are exempt from those provisions.[77]

### D. EEOC Informal Investigative and Determination Process

#### 5. Nonalleged Violations

The EEOC has replaced § 25.3(b) of its Compliance Manual with a new § 25.7.[78] The new § 25.7 changes the procedure for addressing nonalleged violations uncovered by the EOS during the course of his or her investigation. Under the old procedure, the Equal Opportunity Specialist (EOS) reported such violations to the District Director who could then initiate preparation of a Commissioner charge to address them. The EEOC's new procedure permits the supervisor of the EOS to authorize expansion of the original investigation to include nonalleged violations discovered in the course of that review.

### E. The Conciliation Process

On August 27, 1987, EEOC adopted a legislative regulation and administrative exemption under § 9 of the ADEA and 29 C.F.R. § 1627.15,[79] allowing for waivers and releases of private rights under the ADEA without EEOC participation or "supervision." This exemption to the provisions of

---

[68]New Orleans S.S. Ass'n v. EEOC, 680 F.2d 23, 25–26, 29 FEP 398, 400 (5th Cir. 1982).

[69]EEOC v. Maryland Cup Corp., 785 F.2d 471, 40 FEP 475 (4th Cir.), *cert. denied*, 479 U.S. 815, 41 FEP 1711 (1986); EEOC v. Laborers Local 75, 30 FEP 1339, 1339–40 (N.D. Ill. 1982).

[70]EEOC v. Bay Shipbuilding Corp., 668 F.2d 304, 312, 27 FEP 1377, 1384 (7th Cir. 1981) (criminal penalties of Title VII protect employer from disclosure by EEOC employees); EEOC v. Maryland Cup Corp., *supra* note 69; EEOC v. Laborers Local 75, *supra* note 69 (but court would entertain motion for protective order). *Contra* EEOC v. University of Notre Dame du Lac, *supra* note 65.

[71]EEOC v. Maryland Cup Corp., *supra* note 69 (broad interpretation of EEOC subpoena power; company required to compile lists, conduct internal investigation, and, if necessary, interview its employees to obtain data); EEOC v. Bay Shipbuilding Corp., 668 F.2d 304, 313, 27 FEP 1377, 1385 (7th Cir. 1981); EEOC v. Pan Am. World Airways, 31 FEP 1136, 1139 (S.D.N.Y. 1983) (ADEA).

[72]EEOC v. Bay Shipbuilding Corp., *supra* note 70; Sunbeam Applicance Co. v. Kelly, 532 F. Supp. 96, 101, 28 FEP 180, 185 (N.D. Ill. 1982).

[73]EEOC v. Michael Constr. Co., 706 F.2d 244, 250–52, 31 FEP 1081, 1085–86 (8th Cir. 1983), *cert. denied*, 464 U.S. 1038, 33 FEP 1084 (1984) (employer charged EEOC with issuing subpoena to force settlement); *see also* EEOC v. K-Mart Corp., 694 F.2d 1055, 1066–67, 30 FEP 788, 797–98 (6th Cir. 1982).

[74]New Orleans S.S. Ass'n v. EEOC, 680 F.2d 23, 26, 29 FEP 398, 401 (5th Cir. 1982); EEOC v. Elrod, 674 F.2d 601, 613, 28 FEP 607 (7th Cir. 1982).

[75]EEOC v. Roadway Express, 750 F.2d 40, 42, 36 FEP 867 (6th Cir. 1984) (subpoena enforcement stage is not the appropriate time to decide timeliness of underlying charge).

[76]EEOC v. Peat, Marwick, Mitchell & Co., 589 F. Supp. 534, 38 FEP 1843 (E.D. Mo. 1984), *aff'd*, 775 F.2d 928, 38 FEP 1846 (8th Cir. 1985), *cert. denied*, 475 U.S. 1046, 40 FEP 272 (1986).

[77]EEOC v. Sambo's Restaurant, 34 FEP 1451 (S.D. Tex. 1982); AM Int'l v. EEOC, 34 FEP 1535 (Bankr. N.D. Ill. 1982).

[78]BNA p. 25:0003.

[79]*See* 52 FED. Reg. 32293 (Aug. 27, 1987).

§ 7 of the ADEA would permit waivers or releases of claims under the ADEA without EEOC supervision or approval if such waivers or releases meet standards set forth in the regulation. Pursuant to this regulation, private waivers of ADEA rights must (1) express a knowing and voluntary waiver in clear written form, (2) include encouragement to consult with a lawyer, and (3) allow a reasonable opportunity for consideration before the waiver is made. In addition, private waivers accepted as valid under the EEOC's regulation must not provide for the release of prospective rights or claims, and must not be in exchange for consideration that includes employment benefits to which the employee is already entitled. No waiver or release shall affect the EEOC's rights and responsibilities to enforce the ADEA, nor shall a waiver be used to justify interfering with an employee's protected rights to file a charge or participate in an EEOC investigation. Implementation of this regulation, however, has been blocked by Congress.[80]

The Eleventh Circuit has held that conciliation agreements executed under Title VII are enforceable contracts.[81]

## F. Right-to-Sue Letters

Receipt of the right-to-sue letter triggers commencement of the 90-day period for filing suit under Title VII. While that period may be equitably tolled, there must be some affirmative factor which justifies that tolling.[82] Mere absence of prejudice to the defendant is insufficient.[83]

Counsel's receipt of the notice of right to sue may be imputed to his or her client for the purpose of commencing Title VII's 90-day filing period.[84]

## IV. CONFIDENTIALITY, ACCESS, AND ADMISSIBILITY OF THE EEOC DETERMINATION, INVESTIGATION, AND UNDERLYING DOCUMENTS

### A. Confidentiality—Statutory Framework

In *Associated Dry Goods Corp. v. EEOC*[85] the Fourth Circuit reversed the district court[86] and approved the EEOC's procedural regulations permitting a charging party to have access to the investigative file after 180 days from the filing of the charge. The Fourth Circuit specifically upheld the

---

[80]Congress suspended implementation of the EEOC's proposed rule in fiscal years 1988 and 1989 by language in appropriations bills. *See* Pub. L. No. 100-202, 101 Stat. 1329-31 (1987). Legislation to ban most unsupervised age waivers was pending as this Supplement went to press. *See* S.54, 101st Cong., 1st Sess. (1989), introduced by Sen. Metzenbaum (R-Ohio) on January 25, 1989.

[81]Eatmon v. Bristol Steel & Iron Works, 769 F.2d 1503, 38 FEP 1364 (11th Cir. 1985).

[82]*Compare* Baldwin County Welcome Center v. Brown, 466 U.S. 147, 34 FEP 929 (1984) (filing of notice of right to sue insufficient to toll running of filing period); Millard v. La Pointe's Fashion Store, 736 F.2d 501, 35 FEP 830 (9th Cir. 1984) (oral request for appointment of counsel insufficient to toll filing period) *and* Banks v. Teletype Corp., 563 F. Supp. 1358, 35 FEP 465 (E.D. Ark. 1983) (pending motion to intervene in another action insufficient to toll filing period) *with* Mahroom v. Defense Language Inst., 732 F.2d 1439, 34 FEP 1334 (9th Cir. 1984) (filing request for appointment of counsel, EEOC decision, and notice of right to sue sufficient to toll filing period) *and* Lewis v. Mobile County School Bd., 34 FEP 1223 (S.D. Ala. 1984) (magistrate's decision; plaintiff's filing in federal court of notice of right to sue, EEOC charge, and EEOC determination operated as "filing of complaint" under Fed. R. Civ. P. 8 sufficient to defeat statute of limitations defense).

[83]Baldwin County Welcome Center v. Brown, *supra* note 82.

[84]Josiah-Faeduwor v. Communications Satellite Corp., 785 F.2d 344, 40 FEP 442 (D.C. Cir. 1986).

[85]720 F.2d 804, 33 FEP 181 (4th Cir. 1983).

[86]543 F. Supp. 950, 29 FEP 526 (E.D. Va. 1982).

validity of the provisions of § 1610.17(d), as well as § 83.3(a) and portions of § 83.5 of the EEOC Compliance Manual[87] and found these rules and procedures not to be "unfair or discriminatory."[88]

Confidentiality provisions are now contained in EEOC procedural regulations on the ADEA.[89]

Federal appellate courts have continued to review Freedom of Information Act exemptions, reaffirming and extending prior decisions. In *Federal Trade Commission v. Grolier,*[90] the Supreme Court reviewed the fifth exemption, § 552(b)(7)(E), allowing agencies to withhold certain inter-agency and intra-agency letters and memoranda, and held that privileges incorporated by Exemption 5 are those " 'which the Government enjoys under the relevant statutory and case law in the pretrial discovery context' * * * (emphasis added)." The Court stated that the test under Exemption 5 is whether "the documents would be 'routinely' or 'normally' disclosed upon a showing of relevance."[91]

## B. Access to EEOC Investigative Files

### 1. Title VII Files

In *EEOC v. Associated Dry Goods,*[92] on remand from the Supreme Court, the district court had upheld § 1601.22 of the EEOC's rules regarding access to files as an "interpretative" rule, but invalidated § 1610.17(d) as well as § 83.3(a) and portions of § 83.5 of the Compliance Manual; this decision was reversed by the Fourth Circuit, which upheld all the EEOC's challenged disclosure rules.[93]

### 3. What the EEOC May and Must Remove From the File Prior to Disclosure to a Party

In *J.P. Stevens & Co. v. Perry,*[94] the Fourth Circuit rejected the EEOC's contention that all investigatory records of an ongoing proceeding are ex-

---

[87]Sec. 1610.17(d) is the EEOC regulation which establishes procedures for making Commission records available to the public. The rules for disclosure are set forth in § 83 of the EEOC Compliance Manual, BNA pp. 83:0001–83:0005.

[88]*Supra* note 85, at 811, 33 FEP at 186.

[89]ADEA Procedural Regulations, 29 C.F.R. § 1626.4, provides in relevant part: "The identity of complainant, confidential witness, or aggrieved person on whose behalf a charge was filed will ordinarily not be discussed without prior written consent, unless necessary in a court proceeding."

[90]462 U.S. 19, 26–27 (1983) (*quoting* Renegotiating Bd. v. Grumman Aircraft Eng'g Corp., 421 U.S. 168, 184 (1975)).

[91]462 U.S. 19, 20; *see also* United States v. Weber Aircraft Corp., 465 U.S. 792 (1984) (claim of privilege under Exemption 5, other than executive or attorney-client privilege, must be viewed with caution; however, legislative history of Exemption 5 does not provide comprehensive or exclusive list of privileges).

[92]449 U.S. 590, 24 FEP 1356 (1981).

[93]*Supra* note 86. As to disclosure by the EEOC of material to charging parties, the Supreme Court had held on the point under its review "charging parties [are not included] within 'the internal public' to whom [disclosure] was illegal" under 2000e-5(b), *supra* note 92, at 598, but that charging parties have no reason to know the content of any other employee's charge and should be considered a member of the public as to such other charges. *Id.* at 603. The Court had remanded for determination of other challenges to the EEOC's disclosure rules. The Fourth Circuit's ultimate decision on appeal from its remand to the district court rejected challenges to the EEOC's disclosure rules that had been based on the argument that they are substantive and prohibited outright by 42 U.S.C. § 2000e-12(12)(a), or alternatively were invalid because they were not issued in compliance with the notice and comment provision of the Administrative Procedure Act, 42 U.S.C. § 551, 5 U.S.C. § 553. *Supra* note 85, at 807–8, 33 FEP at 182–83. *See supra* note 15 and accompanying text.

[94]710 F.2d 136, 32 FEP 40 (4th Cir. 1983).

empt from disclosure under § 552a(b)(7) of the Freedom of Information Act,[95] but ruled that the exemption does apply to records which, if prematurely disclosed, would

> "(1) create a 'chilling effect' on potential witnesses and dry up sources of information, particularly those of charging parties and their attorneys; (2) hamper the free flow of ideas between Commission employees and supervisors or with other governmental agencies; (3) hinder [the EEOC's] ability to shape and control investigations; and (4) make more difficult the future investigation of charges and enforcement thereof."[96]

A court has held that a charging party in a Title VII action has a right to materials documenting the EEOC's conciliation efforts in her case.[97] According to one court, a draft of a proposed charge is part of the EEOC's deliberative process and is exempt from disclosure pursuant to § 522(a)(5) of the Freedom of Information Act, but the EEOC's inadvertent disclosure of the draft's contents removes "the mantle of confidentiality" and is a waiver of the agency's right to rely on the exemption.[98]

### 4. Disclosure of Age and Equal Pay Files

Effective July 29, 1985, EEOC amended its regulations enforcing the Equal Pay Act to ensure that the confidentiality policy under the EPA is consistent with that under Title VII and the ADEA.[99]

### C. Admissibility Into Evidence of EEOC Findings

Admission of EEOC letters of determination into evidence continues to be a matter of trial court discretion in most circuits.[100] The Fifth, Ninth, and Eleventh circuits remain the only circuits holding that EEOC letters of determination must be admitted into evidence if offered.[101]

### D. Federal Employees' EEO Procedures

EEOC regulations provide that the identity of an aggrieved Federal employee shall not be revealed without his or her authorization prior to the filing of a formal complaint.[102] The National Labor Relations Board held,

---

[95]5 U.S.C. § 522a(b)(7) (1982).

[96]710 F.2d at 143, 32 FEP at 45.

[97]Greene v. Thalhimer's Dep't Store, 93 F.R.D. 657, 28 FEP 918 (E.D. Va. 1982) (documents not covered by common-law executive privilege; however, decision prohibited charging party from using documents in any subsequent proceeding without written consent of persons concerned, and limited disclosure to charging party and her attorney).

[98]Dresser Indus. Valve Operations v. EEOC, 28 FEP 1819 (W.D. La. 1982).

[99]50 FED. REG. 30699–30701 (1985), amending 29 C.F.R. § 1620.19(c).

[100]Coleman v. City of Omaha, 714 F.2d 804, 807 n.4, 33 FEP 1462, 1463 n.4 (8th Cir. 1983); Whatley v. Skaggs Cos., 707 F.2d 1129, 31 FEP 1202 (10th Cir.), cert. denied, 464 U.S. 938, 33 FEP 48 (1983) (admission of investigative report harmless error where report corroborated by trial testimony); Strickland v. American Can Co., 575 F. Supp. 1111, 34 FEP 542 (N.D. Ga. 1983) (reasonable cause letter admitted); see also Michail v. Fluor Mining & Metals, 180 Cal.App.3d 284, 225 Cal. Rptr. 403, 40 FEP 1207 (1986) (trial court conducting jury trial under state Fair Employment and Housing Act properly excluded EEOC's reasonable cause determination on same claim where court held that prejudicial effect would outweigh probative value).

[101]See Second Edition at p. 977.

[102]29 C.F.R. § 1613.213.

however, that the purpose of this provision is to protect the employee from management, not to limit union participation at the precomplaint stage.[103]

## V. ADVICE TO RESPONDENTS ON RESPONDING TO A CHARGE OF EMPLOYMENT DISCRIMINATION

### C. Settlement Options

In making an unconditional offer of employment calculated to toll the accrual of back pay, the employer should be certain that the job offer is equivalent to the job previously denied.[104]

---

[103]*See* United States Postal Serv., 281 NLRB No. 138, 123 LRRM 1209 *and* 281 NLRB No. 139, 123 LRRM 1213 (1986) (when there are both grievances under union contract and an informal complaint under Title VII, union representatives may not be denied opportunity to participate in conciliation process by employer's invocation of EEOC's regulation concerning confidentiality of aggrieved party's identity).

[104]*See* Brady v. Thurston Motor Lines, 753 F.2d 1269, 36 FEP 1805 (4th Cir. 1985); EEOC v. Exxon Corp. dba Exxon Co., U.S.A., 583 F. Supp. 632, 36 FEP 306 (S.D. Tex.), *aff'd sub nom.* EEOC v. Exxon Shipping Co., 745 F.2d 967, 36 FEP 330 (5th Cir. 1984) (position offered was not substantially equivalent where it paid same salary as position denied, but was not consonant with claimant's particular skills, background, and experience); Cowen v. Standard Brands, 572 F. Supp. 1576, 33 FEP 53 (N.D. Ala. 1983) (unequivocal offer to Birmingham, Ala., employee of comparable job in Pittsburgh, Pa., at same pay, where defendant established preexisting right and practice to transfer salespersons, cut off back pay claims).

## CHAPTER 27

# TITLE VII COVERAGE

## II. A CHARGE OF DISCRIMINATION WITH THE EEOC: SUBSTANTIVE AND FORMAL ELEMENTS

### B. Formal Requirements

The courts continue to hold that the formal elements of a charge set forth in § 706(b), 42 U.S.C. § 2000e-5(b), are conditions precedent but not "jurisdictional prerequisites" to a Title VII individual suit,[1] and to take into consideration whether the EEOC accepted[2] and acted on the purported charge in determining whether it suffices as a basis for a suit.[3] Courts also continue to apply flexibly the requirements of what must be filed under Title VII with emphasis on whether substantial notice of alleged violations has been provided.[4] More stringent standards may be required for Commissioner charges.[5]

In *EEOC v. Shell Oil Co.,*[6] the Supreme Court held that the existence of a charge that meets the requirements set forth in § 706(b) is a "jurisdictional prerequisite" to judicial enforcement of a subpoena issued by the EEOC.[7] The Court also held that a Commissioner's charge satisfies § 706(b) if it identifies "the groups of persons [the Commissioner] has reason to

---

[1] *See* Liberles v. County of Cook, 709 F.2d 1122, 1125, 31 FEP 1537, 1538 (7th Cir. 1983) (failure to name heads of government entities in charge no bar to suit); Price v. Southwestern Bell Tel. Co., 687 F.2d 74, 77–79, 29 FEP 1584, 1586–87 (5th Cir. 1982) (verification of charge only a condition precedent); Waiters v. Robert Bosch Corp., 683 F.2d 89, 92, 29 FEP 401, 403 (4th Cir. 1982) (affidavit of charging party that omitted employer's address constitutes valid charge).

[2] Once a charge is filed, the issue of coverage must be challenged in the complaint process; it may not be raised by collateral attack. Ohio Civil Rights Comm. v. Dayton Christian Schools, 477 U.S. 619, 41 FEP 78 (1986).

[3] *See* Price v. Southwestern Bell Tel. Co., *supra* note 1 (EEOC's processing of charge presented issue of fact as to whether verification had been waived by EEOC and whether intake form sufficed as timely charge); Bennett v. Russ Berrie & Co., 564 F. Supp. 1576, 32 FEP 225 (N.D. Ind. 1983) (lack of oath did not defeat validity of letter from counsel as Title VII charge, but failure of EEOC to treat it as charge and to investigate or attempt to conciliate it did). *But see* EEOC v. Ocean City Police Dep't, 820 F.2d 1378, 44 FEP 97 (4th Cir. 1987) (en banc) (EEOC subpoena will not be enforced where underlying charge was accepted by EEOC but was untimely on its face).

[4] *See, e.g.,* Casavantes v. California State Univ., 732 F.2d 1441, 1442, 34 FEP 1336, 1338 (9th Cir. 1984) (former employee satisfied charge-filing requirement when he completed and filed Intake Questionnaire with EEOC); EEOC v. Charleston Elec. Joint Apprenticeship Training Comm. (JATC), 35 FEP 1007, 1008 (S.D. W. Va. 1984) (letter to EEOC that identified offending party, that described practice that forms basis of claim, and that was subsequently verified was sufficient to constitute charge). *But cf.* Rizzo v. WGN Continental Broadcasting Co., 601 F. Supp. 132, 135, 37 FEP 586, 588 (N.D. Ill. 1985) (absence of any reference in former employee's original EEOC charge, based solely on age, to facts indicating that employer discriminated against her on basis of her sex precluded her from litigating sex discrimination claim contained in amended charge, filed six months later, when amended charge was not like or reasonably related to original charge).

[5] EEOC v. K-Mart Corp., 694 F.2d 1055, 1064, 30 FEP 788, 796 (6th Cir. 1982) (compliance with § 706(b) and 29 C.F.R. § 1601.12(a)(3) must be evident on face of charge).

[6] 466 U.S. 54, 34 FEP 709 (1984).

[7] *Id.* at 65, 34 FEP at 715.

believe have been discriminated against, the categories of employment positions from which they have been excluded, the methods by which the discrimination may have been effected, and the period of time in which [the Commissioner] suspects the alleged discrimination to have been practiced."[8] The same information must be provided to the employer by the Commission within 10 days of the filing of the charge.[9]

## III. CHARGING PARTIES

### B. Charges Filed by Allegedly Aggrieved Individuals Who Are Members of the Protected Group in Question

Courts continue to hold that when challenging hiring and promotion decisions, a plaintiff's actual qualifications are not relevant to the preliminary issue of standing. In *Avagliano v. Sumitomo Shoji America,*[10] a class of current and former clerical employees alleged that they were denied promotions because of their sex and national origin. The company asserted that the plaintiffs lacked standing to maintain their suit as they were not, in fact, qualified for positions from which they were allegedly excluded. In holding that the plaintiffs possessed the requisite standing, the court stated that it is the "nature of the injury *asserted* that is relevant to the determination of whether plaintiffs have shown the requisite personal stake and concrete adverseness."[11]

In *Northeast Airlines v. Transport Workers,*[12] the Supreme Court stated in dictum that there may be circumstances in which an employer may be a "person aggrieved" by discriminatory union conduct.[13] However, according to a recent district court decision,[14] a defendant-employer does not have standing to assert a counterclaim under § 703(c) against a plaintiff-union when (1) the employer did not file an EEOC charge against the union and (2) its counterclaim merely alleged that the union " 'caused or attempted to cause defendants to discriminate against plaintiffs * * * .' "[15] Under such an allegation the only persons aggrieved are the plaintiff-employees.[16]

---

[8]*Id.* at 73, 34 FEP at 718. Reversing the Eighth Circuit, the Court concluded that the Commissioner's charge at issue satisfied the foregoing standards. The charge identified blacks and women as the victims of the employer's putative discriminatory practices, and specified six occupational categories to which blacks had been denied equal access and seven categories to which women had been denied equal access. The charge also alleged that the employer had engaged in discrimination in the areas of "recruitment, hiring, selection, job assignment, training, testing, promotion, and terms and conditions of employment." Finally, the charge stated that the employer had engaged in these illegal practices since at least the effective date of Title VII. *Id.*

[9]*Id.* at 81, 34 FEP at 721. The Court concluded this notice requirement was met because the employer was provided with a copy of the Commissioner's charge within 10 days after it was filed. *Id.* at 81, 34 FEP at 722.

[10]103 F.R.D. 562, 38 FEP 561 (S.D.N.Y. 1984).

[11]*Id.* at 571, 38 FEP at 566 (emphasis by the court).

[12]451 U.S. 77, 25 FEP 737 (1981).

[13]*Id.* at 90, 25 FEP at 742.

[14]State, County & Mun. Employees v. City of New York, 599 F. Supp. 916, 36 FEP 900 (S.D.N.Y. 1984).

[15]*Id.* at 921, 36 FEP at 904.

[16]*Id.*

## C. Allegedly Aggrieved Individuals Who Are Not Members of the Protected Group in Question

Courts continue to hold that certain persons are not sufficiently "aggrieved" to challenge an employer's allegedly discriminatory employment practices. A person who did not possess a particular employment requirement at the time he applied for a position, but who achieved that qualification prior to the commencement of suit, retains his standing to challenge the requirement in question: abatement of the individual injury does not destroy standing.[17] However, the failure to meet a given prerequisite at the time of application does preclude one from representing a class of persons actually aggrieved by the employer's requirements.[18]

The Sixth Circuit has tightened Title VII's standing requirements by holding that a class of plaintiffs who had never been employed by the defendant class of employers lacked standing to challenge the employers' allegedly discriminatory pregnancy leave policies.[19] Furthermore, the presence of their union as an additional party plaintiff was insufficient to confer upon them standing as a class of aggrieved persons.[20]

Courts have accorded standing to white employees who claim that racial discrimination against blacks causes injury to the white employees' right to work in an environment unaffected by racial discrimination.[21] A court rejected, however, the Title VII and EPA wage discrimination claims of a male plaintiff who alleged that a female was paid less than he, reasoning that the male plaintiff was the "wrong person to complain" and was not within the "zone of interest" protected by the statutes.[22]

One court has held that a person is not aggrieved and may not complain under Title VII about the effects of discrimination suffered by his or her spouse at the hands of the spouse's employer.[23] However, the Eleventh Circuit has joined those courts that have held a person may be aggrieved where he or she is discriminated against by his or her own employer because he or she is involved in an interracial relationship.[24]

---

[17]Walls v. Mississippi State Dep't of Pub. Welfare, 730 F.2d 306, 34 FEP 1114 (5th Cir. 1984), rev'g 542 F. Supp. 281, 309, 31 FEP 1795, 1818 (N.D. Miss. 1982).

[18]Payne v. Travenol Laboratories, 565 F.2d 895, 16 FEP 387 (5th Cir.), cert. denied, 439 U.S. 835 (1978). See also Griffin v. Dugger, 823 F.2d 1476, 44 FEP 938 (11th Cir. 1987), cert. denied, 486 U.S. _____, 46 FEP 1264 (1988).

[19]Thompson v. Romeo Community Schools Bd. of Educ., 709 F.2d 1200, 1204–05, 32 FEP 527, 530–31 (6th Cir. 1983).

[20]Id. at 1205–06, 32 FEP at 531.

[21]Stewart v. Hannon, 675 F.2d 846, 28 FEP 1268 (7th Cir. 1982) (white female assistant principal could challenge examination that allegedly discriminates against nonwhites); EEOC v. T.I.M.E.-D.C. Freight, 659 F.2d 690, 27 FEP 10 (5th Cir. 1981) (white truck drivers are "persons aggrieved" by discrimination against black truck drivers; they have right to working environment free of racial discrimination).

[22]Pecorella v. Oak Orchard Community Health Center, 559 F. Supp. 147, 31 FEP 1036 (W.D.N.Y. 1982), aff'd, 722 F.2d 728, 33 FEP 1696 (2d Cir. 1983); see also Patee v. Pacific Nw. Bell Tel. Co., 803 F.2d 476, 42 FEP 298 (9th Cir. 1986) (male employees do not have standing to raise claim that their salary is deflated because they are assigned to a predominantly female job). These cases, like most of those discussed in this Chapter, involve an issue of standing to maintain a lawsuit, not who may file a Title VII charge. It must be remembered that the standard which governs standing to maintain a suit in court may be more stringent than that which governs who may file a complaint with an administrative agency. See Section III.E, infra. Under some circumstances, the EEOC is authorized to investigate discrimination on its own initiative, even where no one outside the agency has filed a charge.

[23]Feng v. Sandrik, 636 F. Supp. 77, 41 FEP 922 (N.D. Ill. 1986).

[24]Parr v. Woodmen of the World Life Ins. Co., 791 F.2d 888, 41 FEP 22 (11th Cir. 1986) (reviewing conflicting decisions of other courts and adopting what court described as the EEOC's "consistently held" position).

## D. Charges Filed by an Organization as "Aggrieved Persons"

Courts have addressed, with differing results, the question whether an organization has standing to assert its own claim when it alleges direct injury to itself through, for example, loss of membership or diminished financial support, because of discriminatory actions against its members.[25]

## E. Charges Filed on Behalf of Persons Aggrieved

The precise circumstances under which a state, exercising its *parens patriae* authority, can maintain a Title VII suit on behalf of its citizens remains unclear. In *Alfred L. Snapp & Son v. Puerto Rico,*[26] the Supreme Court held that, in order to have standing, a state must assert an injury to a "quasi-sovereign" interest[27] and a substantial segment of the population, rather than an identifiable group of individuals, must be injured. The Court further held that the indirect effects of alleged injuries should be considered in determining whether a sufficiently large segment of the population was allegedly injured, and that the "articulation of such interests is a matter for case-by-case development."[28] In *New York v. Holiday Inns,*[29] New York's Attorney General brought a suit alleging discriminatory employment practices under Title VII, ADEA, and state law. Finding *Snapp* distinguishable, the district court held that the Attorney General did not have *parens patriae* authority to maintain the action as he failed to allege an injury to "a substantial segment of New York's population."[30] The court also denied the Attorney General standing on the ground that the individually named plaintiffs could receive complete relief for the entire class through their private suit.[31]

Unions appear more successful in establishing standing to appear in at least some types of Title VII actions on their members' behalf. For example, a union may intervene and appeal the entry of a consent decree that incorporates a race-conscious affirmative action plan.[32] The court ruled that the decree proved "*some* detriment" to nonminority firefighters and that the union was therefore sufficiently aggrieved by the decree to have standing to challenge it on behalf of its nonminority members.[33] Under the Sixth Cir-

---

[25]*Compare* NAACP, Detroit Branch v. Detroit Police Officers Ass'n, 525 F. Supp. 1215, 1218–19, 27 FEP 329, 330–31 (E.D. Mich. 1981) (standing requirements met in action under Title VI *and* §§ 1981, 1983, and 1985) *with* Black Faculty Ass'n of Mesa College v. San Diego Community College Dist., 664 F.2d 1153, 1156–57, 27 FEP 1037, 1039–40 (9th Cir. 1981) (no standing under § 1981) *and* Lucky v. Board of Regents, 34 FEP 986 (S.D. Fla. 1981) (no standing under §§ 1981 and 1983).

[26]458 U.S. 592 (1982); *see also* Abrams v. 11 Cornwell Co., 695 F.2d 34 (2d Cir. 1982), *modified on other grounds,* 718 F.2d 22 (2d Cir. 1983) (en banc) (*parens patriae* standing also requires finding that individuals could not obtain complete relief through private suit).

[27]Alfred L. Snapp & Son v. Puerto Rico, *supra* note 26, at 601.

[28]*Id.* at 607.

[29]35 FEP 1308 (W.D.N.Y. 1984).

[30]*Id.* at 1310 (allegations that "countless other employees *may* be subjected to defendants' discriminatory practice" not enough).

[31]*Id.* at 1311.

[32]Vanguards of Cleveland v. City of Cleveland, 753 F.2d 479, 36 FEP 1431 (6th Cir. 1985), *aff'd sub nom.* Firefighters Local 93 v. City of Cleveland, 478 U.S. 501, 41 FEP 139 (1986); *see also* NAACP, Detroit Branch v. Detroit Police Officers Ass'n, *supra* note 25 (standing requirement satisfied); Liberles v. County of Cook, 709 F.2d 1122, 31 FEP 1537 (7th Cir. 1983) (union president allowed to file charge on behalf of union members).

[33]753 F.2d at 484, 36 FEP at 1435 (emphasis by the court).

cuit's analysis, a union's standing depends on a showing of detriment to some or all of its members, without regard to whether the challenged preference is moderate or the detriment is slight, or the adversely affected interests are legally protected.[34]

Organizations representing minority individuals may not intervene in actions brought by the EEOC because they lack organizational (as opposed to representational) standing.[35]

### F. Commissioner's Charges

The Supreme Court has outlined what information must be contained within a pattern-and-practice charge filed by an EEOC Commissioner pursuant to 42 U.S.C. § 2000e–5. In *EEOC v. Shell Oil Co.,*[36] the Court held that the EEOC's own regulation[37] requiring that each charge contain a "clear and concise statement of the facts, including the pertinent dates, constituting the alleged unlawful employment practices" is binding on the Commission as well as private complainants. Insofar as is possible, the Commissioner should identify the groups of persons that he or she has reason to believe have been discriminated against, the categories of employment positions from which they have been excluded, the methods by which they have been excluded, the methods by which the discrimination may have been effected, and the periods of time in which he or she suspects the discrimination to have been practiced.[38]

One court has held that the right of intervention in a § 706 suit "may only be invoked [pursuant to Federal Rule of Civil Procedure 24(a)(1)] if (1) the proposed intervenor has an interest in the action sufficient to establish standing under Article III * * * and (2) the action was commenced by the EEOC in response to a charge filed either (a) by the proposed intervenor or (b) by another private party having a nearly identical claim to the claim raised by the proposed intervenor."[39]

## IV. Respondents

### A. Employer

*1. Definition*

*a. Who May Be Counted as "Employees."* Shareholders in a professional corporation engaged in the practice of law are not "employees," and therefore cannot be counted toward the requirement of having at least 15 employees for 20 weeks.[40] The courts continue to apply the "economic realities" and

---

[34]*Id.*

[35]EEOC v. Nevada Resort Ass'n, 792 F.2d 882, 41 FEP 7 (9th Cir. 1986).

[36]466 U.S. 54, 34 FEP 709 (1984).

[37]29 C.F.R. § 1601.12(a)(13) (1983).

[38]466 U.S. at 73, 34 FEP at 716, 718. *See* discussion of *Shell Oil* in Section II.B, *supra.*

[39]Spirt v. Teachers Ins. & Annuity Ass'n, 93 F.R.D. 627, 641–42, 28 FEP 489, 501 (S.D.N.Y. 1982) (intervention denied under Fed. R. Civ. P. 24(a)(1) and (2), and (b)(2)).

[40]EEOC v. Dowd & Dowd, Ltd., 736 F.2d 1177, 34 FEP 1815 (7th Cir. 1984); *see also* Hishon v. King & Spalding, 467 U.S. 69, 34 FEP 1406, 1411 (1984) (Powell, J., concurring) (relationship between

"right of control" tests when deciding whether an individual is an employee or an independent contractor.[41]

*b. How the Counting Is Done.* The courts continue to count regular part-time employees toward the 15-employee requirement.[42]

*c. "Personal Staff" Exemption.* Section 701(f) exempts from the definition of "employee" any person elected to public office "or any person chosen by such officer to be on such officer's personal staff." In *Teneyuca v. Bexar County,* [43] the Fifth Circuit found that an Assistant District Attorney position satisfied the personal staff exemption. The court considered six significant factors in making its determination: (1) the official's power of appointment, (2) the putative employee's personal accountability to the official, (3) whether the putative employee represents the official in the eyes of the public, (4) the official's control over the position, (5) the level of the position in the organization, and (6) the "actual intimacy" between the putative employee and the official.[44]

## 2. Requirement of Employment Setting for Coverage Under Title VII

Once the employment setting is established, advancement to a "non-employee" level may be governed by Title VII.

In *Hishon v. King & Spalding,* [45] the Supreme Court reversed the dismissal of a Title VII complaint alleging that consideration for partnership was one of the plaintiff's "terms, conditions, or privileges of employment" as an associate with King & Spalding and that the firm had rejected her for partnership because of her sex.[46] The Court held that "a benefit that is part and parcel of the employment relationship may not be doled out in a discriminatory fashion,"[47] and that the plaintiff was entitled to prove that

---

law partners not an employment relationship within meaning of Title VII); Wheeler v. Main Hurdman, 825 F.2d 257, 44 FEP 707 (10th Cir.), *cert. denied,* 484 U.S. _____, 45 FEP 776 (1987) (partner in brokerage firm is not an employee). *But see* Caruso v. Peat, Marwick, Mitchell & Co., 664 F. Supp. 144, 44 FEP 544 (S.D.N.Y. 1987) (partner in accounting firm is an employee under economic realities test).

[41]Dixon v. Burman, 593 F. Supp. 6, 32 FEP 1107 (N.D. Ind. 1983), *aff'd mem.,* 742 F.2d 1459, 37 FEP 1816 (7th Cir. 1984); Mares v. Marsh, 777 F.2d 1066, 40 FEP 858 (5th Cir. 1985); Chavero v. Transit Union Local 241, 787 F.2d 1154, 40 FEP 766 (7th Cir. 1986) (members of local union executive board who do not perform traditional employee duties are not employees within meaning of Title VII); Broussard v. L.H. Bossier, Inc., 789 F.2d 1158, 40 FEP 1362 (5th Cir. 1986). *See also* Shrock v. Altru Nurses Registry, 38 FEP 1709 (N.D. Ill. 1985), *aff'd in part, vacated and remanded in part,* 810 F.2d 658, 42 FEP 1393 (7th Cir. 1987) (complaint dismissed, in portion of decision affirmed by Seventh Circuit, because defendant nurses registry not an employer and not an employment agency since it did not employ the jurisdictional minimum under Title VII and did not refer nurses to Title VII employers; order denying attorneys' fees under Title VII vacated and remanded for determination whether attorneys' fees awardable as Rule 11 sanction); Wheeler v. Main Hurdman, *supra* note 40.

[42]Thurber v. Jack Reilly's, Inc., 717 F.2d 633, 32 FEP 1511 (1st Cir. 1983), *cert. denied,* 466 U.S. 904, 34 FEP 544 (1984); Lynn v. JER Corp., 573 F. Supp. 17, 33 FEP 541 (M.D. Tenn. 1983).

[43]767 F.2d 148, 38 FEP 989 (5th Cir. 1985).

[44]*Compare* Bostick v. Rappleyea, 629 F. Supp. 1328, 38 FEP 658 (N.D.N.Y. 1985) (budget analyst for state legislative committee held to be employee where she was neither in policy-making position nor an immediate advisor to a committee member; Congress intended exemption to be narrowly construed) *with* Clark v. Tarrant County, Tex., 608 F. Supp. 209, 38 FEP 396 (N.D. Tex. 1985), *aff'd in part,* 798 F.2d 736, 41 FEP 1238, *reh'g denied,* 802 F.2d 455 (5th Cir. 1986) (probation officers held subject to personal staff exemption where they were not protected by civil service rules and provided direct advice to elected judges).

[45]467 U.S. 69, 34 FEP 1406 (1984), *rev'g* 678 F.2d 1022, 29 FEP 51 (11th Cir. 1982), *aff'g* 24 FEP 1303 (N.D. Ga. 1980).

[46]*Id.,* 467 U.S. at 74, 34 FEP at 1409.

[47]*Id.,* 467 U.S. at 75, 34 FEP at 1410.

partnership consideration was either a contractual right or a privilege of her employment as an associate—and thus subject to Title VII prohibitions against employment discrimination.[48]

In another decision involving restrictions on advancement from employee status, the Ninth Circuit held in *Bonilla v. Oakland Scavenger Co.*[49] that Title VII covered a shareholder preference plan that limited eligibility to purchase shares to employees of Italian ancestry. In that case, the employer then gave employee-shareholders preference in job assignments.

In other cases involving employment setting issues, a franchise arrangement[50] and a student for whom employment opportunities were an incidental benefit[51] were held to be outside the reach of Title VII.

Where courts continue to rely on the distinction between an employee and an independent contractor to determine the scope of Title VII coverage, the line between the two remains an issue.[52] However, in *Gomez v. Alexian Brothers Hospital of San Jose,*[53] the Ninth Circuit rejected that distinction, and extended Title VII coverage where the defendant controls access to employment opportunities.

Once the employment relationship is established, all its aspects, including the allocation of noncompensatory opportunities or benefits, must be conducted in a nondiscriminatory fashion.[54] One court has recently recognized a Title VII complaint from a former employee whose complaints had their genesis in the employment relationship.[55]

### 3. Determining Who Is the "Employer"

*a. "Single Employer" Theory.* Courts continue to apply tests developed by the National Labor Relations Board in assessing whether two entities

---

[48]*Id.,* 467 U.S. at 73–76, 34 FEP at 1409–11.

[49]697 F.2d 1297, 31 FEP 50 (9th Cir. 1982), *cert. denied,* 467 U.S. 1251, 34 FEP 1800 (1984).

[50]Miss Greater New York City Scholarship Pageant v. Miss N.Y. State Scholarship Pageant, 526 F. Supp. 806, 27 FEP 1270 (S.D.N.Y. 1981).

[51]Pollack v. Rice Univ., 28 FEP 1273 (S.D. Tex.), *aff'd mem.,* 690 F.2d 903, 29 FEP 1846 (5th Cir. 1982), *cert. denied,* 459 U.S. 1175, 30 FEP 1256 (1983).

[52]Broussard v. L.H. Bossier, Inc., 789 F.2d 1158, 40 FEP 1362 (5th Cir. 1986); Armbruster v. Quinn, 711 F.2d 1332, 32 FEP 369, 375–77 (6th Cir. 1983), *rev'g and remanding* 498 F. Supp. 858, 23 FEP 1801 (E.D. Mich. 1980) (economic realities of relationship with employer must be examined) (noted in the Second Edition at p. 997, n.104); Hickey v. Arkla Indus., 699 F.2d 748, 31 FEP 238 (5th Cir. 1983) (since standards for employee status not met under more liberal "economic realities" test, court did not decide whether to adopt it over "right of control" test); Cobb v. Sun Papers, 673 F.2d 337, 28 FEP 837 (11th Cir.), *cert. denied,* 459 U.S. 874, 29 FEP 1560 (1982) (court rejected "economic realities" test and adopted common-law agency test, which should take into account economic realities of the relationship viewed in light of common-law principles of agency and employer's right of control); Brown v. American Family Life Assurance Co., 28 FEP 1384 (C.D. Cal. 1982) (insurance sales manager; right of control test applied).

[53]698 F.2d 1019, 30 FEP 1705 (9th Cir. 1983) (Hispanic plaintiff could contest alleged discriminatory denial to his company of contract under which he would serve as director of hospital emergency room because denial of contract interfered with his opportunity to be employed by his company as director); *accord* Doe v. St. Joseph's Hosp. of Fort Wayne, 788 F.2d 411, 40 FEP 820 (7th Cir. 1986) (physician denied staff privileges may sue under Title VII); Pao v. Holy Redeemer Hosp., 547 F. Supp. 484, 31 FEP 580 (E.D. Pa. 1982) (hospital's denial of admitting privileges to ophthalmologist actionable under Title VII; doctor deprived of access to prospective patients who are ultimate employers). *But see* Darks v. City of Cincinnati, 745 F.2d 1040, 36 FEP 27 (6th Cir. 1984) (city's role in licensing dance halls does not create employer/employee relationship with dance hall operators; they are independent contractors).

[54]Abrams v. Baylor College of Medicine, 581 F. Supp. 1570, 34 FEP 229 (S.D. Tex. 1984) (opportunities for foreign travel and overseas work assignments are covered components of employment relationship).

[55]Bilka v. Pepe's, Inc., 601 F. Supp. 1254, 38 FEP 1655 (N.D. Ill. 1985) (terminated employee may bring action challenging former employer's actions with respect to negative job references).

constitute a "single employer" for purposes of determining Title VII coverage and liability.[56]

b. *"Joint Employer" Theory.* There is disagreement whether an insurance provider that contracts to provide benefits for employees is liable under Title VII as a joint employer or agent of the employer for alleged discrimination in the benefit plans.[57] The Supreme Court held in *Norris v. Arizona Governing Committee*[58] that the employer is liable for the discriminatory benefit plan where it selected the insurer, but the answer is not clear in situations where the provider and terms of the plan are dictated by state law.[59] One court refused to hold that a city government was the joint employer with the city library board of a library employee where the city's only control over employment matters was its authority to approve the library's bottom-line budget request.[60] A member of the state national guard has been held to be a member of the U.S. armed forces rather than a state employee entitled to protection under Title VII.[61]

c. *The "Agent" Theory.* One court has held that "agency" liability under Title VII cannot be imposed on a nonsupervisory employee who was merely a senior co-worker with training responsibilities and a few additional privileges.[62] In *Rogero v. Noone,*[63] the Eleventh Circuit held that a county tax collector could not be sued as the agent of a county unless the county was also joined as a party.

d. *Special Application of Integrated-Enterprise Theory to Employer Associations.* In *York v. Tennessee Crushed Stone Association,*[64] an age discrimination case, the Sixth Circuit refused to impose liability under the "integrated

---

[56]*Compare* EEOC v. Wooster Brush Co. Employees Relief Ass'n, 727 F.2d 566, 33 FEP 1823 (6th Cir. 1984) (employer and employee's relief association distinct legal entities, not single employer, for purposes of Title VII) *with* Lynn v. JER Corp., 573 F. Supp. 17, 33 FEP 541 (M.D. Tenn. 1983) (subsidiary and parent so closely intertwined that both may be named as defendants although only subsidiary named in charge). *See also* Armbruster v. Quinn, *supra* note 52 (single employer found applying NLRB standards); Trevino v. Celanese Corp., 701 F.2d 397, 33 FEP 1324 (5th Cir. 1983) (conflicting testimony precludes summary judgment on joint employer issue); Massey v. Emergency Assistance, 580 F. Supp. 937, 33 FEP 1864 (W.D. Mo. 1983), *aff'd,* 724 F.2d 690, 34 FEP 1397 (8th Cir.), *cert. denied,* 469 U.S. 930, 36 FEP 112 (1984) (contractual relationship between two entities does not create single employer).

[57]*Compare* Peters v. Wayne State Univ., 691 F.2d 235, 238, 29 FEP 1753, 1754–55 (6th Cir. 1982), *vacated and remanded in light of Norris v. Arizona Governing Comm.,* 463 U.S. 1223, 32 FEP 359 (1983) (insurance company not bound by Title VII simply because it provides services to Title VII employer when employer exercises no control over it, although employer has liability for discriminatory practices of insurer it selected) *and* Barone v. Hackett, 28 FEP 1765 (D.R.I. 1982) (state, which mandated terms of income maintenance benefits for temporary disabilities, not joint employer of plaintiff and not agent of employer; private employer not liable for discriminatory benefit plan it did not select, but which was imposed by state law) *with* Spirt v. Teachers Ins. & Annuity Ass'n, 691 F.2d 1054, 1063, 29 FEP 1599, 1603 (2d Cir. 1982), *vacated and remanded in light of Norris v. Arizona Governing Comm.,* 463 U.S. 1223, 32 FEP 359 (1983) (insurers which exist solely for purpose of enabling university to delegate authority to provide employees with retirement benefits so "closely intertwined" with university that they must be deemed an employer, where employee participation in insurance program mandatory and university assisted in administration of benefit program).

[58]463 U.S. 1073, 1086–91, 32 FEP 233, 239–41 (1983) (opinion of Justice Marshall, Part III, joined by Justices Brennan, White, Stevens, and O'Connor).

[59]*See* Barone v. Hackett, *supra* note 57; EEOC v. Sanders Chevrolet, 36 FEP 348 (D.N.M. 1984) (insurance company providing disability benefits is not employer's agent for purposes of Title VII).

[60]Oaks v. City of Fairhope, Ala., 515 F. Supp. 1004, 1035–37, 28 FEP 74, 97–98 (S.D. Ala. 1981).

[61]Stinson v. Hornsby, 821 F.2d 1537, 44 FEP 594 (11th Cir. 1987).

[62]Guyette v. Stauffer Chem. Co., 27 FEP 483, 484–85 (D.N.J. 1981).

[63]704 F.2d 518, 31 FEP 969 (11th Cir. 1983).

[64]684 F.2d 360, 29 FEP 735 (6th Cir. 1982).

enterprise" theory on a trade association that had only two employees, holding that the association was not sufficiently integrated with its member companies, since the association was a separate legal entity and there was no centralized control of labor relations.

## B. Unions and Apprenticeship Programs

The courts have recognized that, when unions are sued in their capacity as employers, they must have the requisite number of employees as a predicate to Title VII coverage.[65] In *Childs v. Electrical Workers, IBEW, Local 18,*[66] the Ninth Circuit concluded that a local union with fewer than 15 employees was not a single employing entity with its international. The court made this assessment by applying a four-factor test used in other cases to determine whether a corporation and its subsidiary were separate or single employing entities:[67] (1) interrelation of operations, (2) common management, (3) centralized control of labor relations, and (4) common financial control.[68] A union's pension and welfare fund is an employing entity independent of the union it serves.[69] This is because the fund's fiduciary duty is owed to both the union members and the employer.[70]

One court has held that labor organizations representing state and local government employees were not brought within the purview of Title VII by § 701(h), which extended coverage to state and local governments.[71] Reasoning that § 701(h) was enacted pursuant to the Fourteenth Amendment and therefore "cannot * * * be used as a means of bootstrapping within reach of Title VII private entities such as labor organizations which merely represent * * * employees of governmental entities,"[72] the court required proof that either the union itself or the governments employing the employees it represented were engaged in an industry affecting commerce.

## V. CERTAIN EXEMPTIONS AND EXCLUSIONS

### A. Bona Fide Private Membership Clubs

Prior to 1986, the EEOC took the position that the membership of an organization must consist of individual persons in order to qualify for Title VII's exemption for bona fide private membership clubs,[73] and, additionally,

---

[65]*See* Chavero v. Transit Union Local 241, 787 F.2d 1154, 40 FEP 766 (7th Cir. 1986); Phelps v. Molders Local 63, 25 FEP 1164 (D. Minn. 1981). *But see* EEOC Dec. 71-57, 3 FEP 95 (1970).

[66]719 F.2d 1379, 32 FEP 275 (9th Cir. 1983) (applying traditional NLRB tests, court found local conducted own labor relations, hired and fired employees, elected own officials, and maintained separate treasury).

[67]*Id.* at 1382, 32 FEP at 277.

[68]*Id.*

[69]Sciss v. Metal Polishers Local 8A, 562 F. Supp. 293, 295, 33 FEP 1333, 1334 (S.D.N.Y. 1983) (pension and welfare fund with four employees not assimilated into union and held not covered by Title VII; court did not reach plaintiff's "strained" argument that unions are not covered by 15-employee statutory minimum applicable to employers).

[70]*Id.* at 294–95, 33 FEP at 1334.

[71]EEOC v. California Teachers Ass'n, 534 F. Supp. 209, 27 FEP 1337 (N.D. Cal. 1982).

[72]*Id.* at 217, 27 FEP at 1340–44.

[73]EEOC Dec. 85-1, 36 FEP 1890, 1891 (1984) (a voluntary, tax-exempt, unincorporated association of educational institutions and athletic organizations involved in administration of amateur athletic

that the lack of eligibility or exclusivity standards, the failure to accord the membership control over the club's operation, and the failure to limit access to the club's facilities to members were all factors which would defeat a claim of exemption.[74] On July 22, 1986, the Commission issued Policy Statement N-915, modifying this view.[75] The Commission now states that it will consider an organization a bona fide private club if, in addition to being tax-exempt under § 501(c) of the Internal Revenue Code, it: (1) is a club in the ordinary sense of the word, (2) is private, and (3) requires meaningful conditions of limited membership.[76] Although reaffirming that the exemption is a narrow one and that tax-exempt status alone is insufficient to qualify the organization for exempt status under Title VII, the Commission indicates that its modified test will allow greater latitude in considering the evidence regarding the character of an organization claiming to be a bona fide membership club.[77]

There is some conflict between the courts concerning the question whether the Title VII exemption for bona fide private clubs applies in actions brought under § 1981.[78]

## B. Exemption of Elected Officials, Policy-Making Appointees, and Their Advisors

A hearing officer and a staff attorney in state court,[79] the staff director for a city human rights board,[80] an assistant fire chief,[81] the general counsel to an elected board of education,[82] a legislative budget analyst,[83] and a deputy sheriff appointed under state law[84] have been held to be "employees" covered by Title VII. While declining to adopt a *per se* rule on deputy sheriffs, the Fourth Circuit has three times held particular deputy sheriffs not within the

---

programs was ineligible for exemption because it was not "an association of *persons* for * * * the promotion of some common object").

[74]New York v. Ocean Club, 602 F. Supp. 489 (E.D.N.Y. 1984).

[75]EEOC COMPLIANCE MANUAL, Policy Statement N-915, BNA pp. N:3171–3173 (July 1986).

[76]*Id.*

[77]*Id.* The Commission states that its revised test more closely resembles that set forth in *Quijano v. University Fed. Credit Union,* 617 F.2d 129, 22 FEP 1307 (5th Cir. 1980).

[78]*Compare* Hudson v. Charlotte Country Club, 535 F. Supp. 313, 28 FEP 1208 (W.D.N.C. 1982) (Title VII exemption supersedes and limits § 1981) *and* Kemerer v. Davis, 520 F. Supp. 256, 26 FEP 1652 (E.D. Mich. 1981) *with* Guesby v. Kennedy, 580 F. Supp. 1280, 34 FEP 1215 (D. Kan. 1984) (Title VII private club exemption does not apply to claim of race discrimination in employment under § 1981; *Hudson* and *Kemerer* disapproved) *and* Konicki v. Piedmont Driving Club, 44 FEP 486 (N.D. Ga. 1987).

[79]Goodwin v. St. Louis County Circuit Court, 729 F.2d 541, 34 FEP 347 (8th Cir.), *cert. denied,* 469 U.S. 828, 35 FEP 1608 (1984) (hearing officer, who exercised independent judgment in making recommendations for disposition of cases, had few personal contacts with Juvenile Court Judge); Marafino v. St. Louis County Circuit Court, 537 F. Supp. 206, 29 FEP 621 (E.D. Mo. 1982), *aff'd,* 707 F.2d 1005, 31 FEP 1536 (8th Cir. 1983) (staff attorney not "immediate" or "first line" advisor and lacked high level of personal accountability).

[80]Anderson v. City of Albuquerque, 690 F.2d 796, 29 FEP 1689 (10th Cir. 1982) (staff director implements rather than formulates policy).

[81]Bishopp v. District of Columbia, 35 FEP 1889 (D.D.C. 1984), *later proceeding,* 602 F. Supp. 1401, 37 FEP 235 (D.D.C. 1985), *rev'd in part and vacated in part,* 788 F.2d 781, 40 FEP 903 (D.C. Cir. 1986) (assistant fire chief, appointed by mayor, does not serve on high policy-making level and does not function as advisor with respect to the constitutional or legal powers of mayoralty).

[82]Murray v. District of Columbia Bd. of Educ., 31 FEP 988 (D.D.C. 1983) (general counsel not close political and legal advisor to board members).

[83]Bostick v. Rappleyea, 629 F. Supp. 1328, 38 FEP 658 (N.D.N.Y. 1985).

[84]Curl v. Reavis, 740 F.2d 1323, 35 FEP 930 (4th Cir. 1984).

"personal staff" exemption from Title VII coverage.[85] A probation officer,[86] an assistant district attorney,[87] and a congressional shorthand reporter[88] have been found not to be covered employees.

In applying the identical exemption language under the ADEA, a jail guard has been found to be a covered employee,[89] while an assistant state's attorney has been found not to be covered.[90]

## D. Coverage of Foreign Corporations

In *Sumitomo Shoji America v. Avagliano,*[91] the Supreme Court held that a U.S.-incorporated subsidiary of a Japanese corporation was not a "company of Japan" that could directly invoke treaty protection to exempt itself from Title VII coverage. It has not been determined whether companies covered by the Japanese Treaty are exempt from Title VII prohibitions or whether the subsidiary may have standing to assert treaty rights of its parent company as a Title VII defense.

The World Bank was held exempt from Title VII coverage despite a broad waiver of immunity in the Bank's articles of agreement.[92] The waiver was found to apply only to external activities, *i.e.,* those relations to countries and persons "to whom the Bank would have to subject itself to suit in order to achieve its chartered objectives."[93] There is no waiver of immunity from employee lawsuits because such a waiver "is not necessary for the Bank to perform its functions * * *," and therefore, "this immunity is preserved by the members' failure expressly to waive it."[94] Absent an express waiver, the

---

[85]Curl v. Reavis, *supra* note 84 (plaintiff deputy sheriff not within Title VII coverage exemption; court refuses to make *per se* rule; deputy, appointed and serving at the pleasure of elected sheriff, had primarily clerical duties, did not make policy, was not an immediate advisor to sheriff, and could not be said to be on his personal staff, held position created and compensated by county under state laws, never had "highly intimate and sensitive" working relationship with sheriff such as was intended by Congress as basis for narrow exemption from Title VII coverage); Brewster v. Barnes, 788 F.2d 985 (4th Cir. 1986) (corrections officer not exempt from coverage under Title VII exemption or essentially identical exemption under Equal Pay Act; corrections officer was deputy sheriff who was appointed by elected sheriff but served chiefly as correctional officer, did not make policy decisions and, after assuming corrections officer position, did not maintain intimate, high-level relationship with sheriff); United States v. Gregory, 818 F.2d 1114, 46 FEP 1743 (4th Cir.), *cert. denied,* 484 U.S. _____, 47 FEP 96 (1987) (no evidence road deputies advise sheriff respecting policy decisions or proper exercise of power, road deputies not high in chain of command, "do not occupy highly intimate and sensitive status vis-a-vis the sheriff," 818 F.2d at 1117, and not within "personal staff" exemption from Title VII under 42 U.S.C. § 2000e(f); small size of staff and service at sheriff's pleasure not relevant).

[86]Clark v. Tarrant County, Tex., 608 F. Supp. 209, 38 FEP 396 (N.D. Tex. 1985), *aff'd in part,* 798 F.2d 736, 41 FEP 1238, *reh'g denied,* 802 F.2d 455 (5th Cir. 1986) (probation officer, appointed and supervised by elected judge, is on his personal staff where close working relationship exists and officer serves as immediate advisor in exercise of judicial powers).

[87]Teneyuca v. Bexar County, 767 F.2d 148, 38 FEP 989 (5th Cir. 1985).

[88]Browning v. Clerk, House of Representatives, 789 F.2d 923, 40 FEP 992 (D.C. Cir.), *cert. denied,* 479 U.S. 996, 42 FEP 560 (1986) (Congress' exemption from suit under Title VII is not limited to employees with direct input into legislative process; it extends to employees directly involved in the functioning of the process).

[89]Galvan v. Bexar County, Tex., 785 F.2d 1298, 40 FEP 710, *reh'g denied,* 790 F.2d 890 (5th Cir. 1986) (jail guard, one of 500 employees in sheriff's office, performed routine tasks).

[90]EEOC v. Reno, 758 F.2d 581, 37 FEP 985 (11th Cir. 1985) (prohibitions of the ADEA are *in haec verba* from Title VII; assistant state attorney has powers and duties coextensive with appointing state attorney, serves on a policy-making level and as an advisor in exercise of constitutional and legal powers of office of state attorney).

[91]457 U.S. 176, 28 FEP 1753 (1982).

[92]Mendaro v. World Bank, 717 F.2d 610, 32 FEP 1688 (D.C. Cir. 1983).

[93]*Id.* at 615, 32 FEP at 1691.

[94]*Id.* at 615, 32 FEP at 1691–2.

United Nations is exempt from Title VII coverage under the terms of the International Organization Immunities Act[95] and the United Nations Convention.[96]

An Ohio District Court dismissed a Title VII action alleging that a foreign subsidiary of a U.S. corporation refused to offer extraterritorial employment to a U.S. citizen because of her sex,[97] holding that Title VII could not be applied to the foreign subsidiary in its extraterritorial employment activities.

The EEOC has decided that exemption under the Foreign Services Immunity Act (FSIA),[98] depends principally upon whether the entity is immune from the jurisdiction of state and federal courts.[99] A foreign government or purportedly government-related respondent contesting EEOC jurisdiction on the basis of claimed FSIA immunity for activities of a noncommercial nature would be required "to prove the non-applicability of the specified exemptions contained in Sections 1605–1607 of the FSIA."[100] Refusal to provide such proof to the EEOC would be litigable in subpoena enforcement proceedings.

## F. Security Clearance Exclusion

In *Moliero v. Federal Bureau of Investigation,*[101] the defendant did not hire the plaintiff as a special agent because he had close relatives who resided in a country (Cuba) whose government is hostile to the United States. The court rejected a disparate impact theory based on national origin, and upheld an absolute state secrets privilege which resulted in dismissal of the action.[102]

---

[95]22 U.S.C. §§ 288–288i.

[96]Boimah v. United Nations Gen. Assembly, 664 F. Supp. 69, 44 FEP 688 (S.D.N.Y. 1987).

[97]Lavrov v. NCR Corp., 591 F. Supp. 102, 35 FEP 988 (S.D. Ohio 1984).

[98]28 U.S.C. § 1602 *et seq.*

[99]EEOC Dec. 85-11, 38 FEP 1876 (July 11, 1985). An anomalous aspect of this decision suggests that certain classes of employees (*i.e.,* clerical employees) may not be subject to the FSIA exemption even though the employing entity is exempt and, therefore, not subject to enforcement proceedings.

[100]*Id.* at 1880.

[101]36 FEP 582 (D.D.C. 1983), *aff'd,* 749 F.2d 815, 36 FEP 586 (D.C. Cir. 1984).

[102]*See also* Northrop Corp. v. McDonnell Douglas Corp., 751 F.2d 395, 406–07 (D.C. Cir. 1984) ("*Molerio* held that when the *reason* for the FBI's decision not to hire an applicant was itself a state secret, all documents that would disclose the reason for that decision are not subject to discovery and need not be actually examined. To the extent that the documents discuss the state secret (the reason for the non-hire decision), they would be privileged; to the extent that they do not discuss the reason for the non-hire decision (which was the subject of the suit), they are irrelevant and not subject to discovery." (Emphasis by the court)).

## CHAPTER 28

# TIMELINESS

## II. TIMELINESS OF FILING THE EEOC CHARGE

### B. Deferral to State or Local 706 Agency

#### 1. Statutory Authority

Both the Second and Third circuits have held that, unlike Title VII, the ADEA does not require resort to a state agency before filing a charge with the EEOC.[1] The rationale for these decisions is that the ADEA only requires that a lawsuit not be filed until 60 days after state proceedings have been instituted, and that so long as state procedures are invoked at least 60 days prior to expiration of the appropriate statute of limitations (*i.e.*, two or three years), further agency proceedings are unnecessary.

#### 2. Validity of EEOC Deferral Procedure

Courts continue to reject arguments that would require charging parties to file separately before the EEOC and deferral agencies where the EEOC is required by regulation to defer the charge.[2]

#### 3. The Circumstances Under Which Prior Resort to State or Local Agency Is Required

*a. State Law Must Authorize Appropriate Agency to Prosecute Claim of Discrimination.* Where state agency jurisdiction excludes employers covered by federal law, the agency cannot serve as a deferral agency.[3]

#### 4. Deferral Mistakes by Charging Parties; Cure of Such Mistakes

An Illinois resident employed in Illinois was not allowed to file suit on the basis of a charge filed before the New York rather than the Illinois agency.[4]

---

[1]Seredinski v. Litton Sys., Clifton Precision Prods. Co. Div., 776 F.2d 56, 39 FEP 248 (3d Cir. 1985); Reinhard v. Fairfield Maxwell, Ltd., 707 F.2d 697, 31 FEP 1438 (2d Cir. 1983); *accord* Nogar v. Henry F. Teichmann, Inc., 640 F. Supp. 365 (W.D. Pa. 1985), *aff'd mem.*, 800 F.2d 1137, 44 FEP 448 (3d Cir. 1986); Silverstein v. United Men's Store, No. 85-2838, slip op. (E.D. Pa. Oct. 25, 1985).

[2]Shaffer v. National Can Corp., 565 F. Supp. 909, 34 FEP 172 (E.D. Pa. 1983); Marsh v. WMAR TV, 32 FEP 806 (D. Md. 1982). *But see* Kocian v. Getty Ref. & Mktg. Co., 707 F.2d 748, 31 FEP 1211 (3d Cir.), *cert. denied,* 464 U.S. 852, 32 FEP 1672 (1983) (where EEOC neither required to nor did defer charge to state agency, 300-day period unavailable).

[3]Keitz v. Lever Bros., 563 F. Supp. 230, 31 FEP 1230 (N.D. Ind. 1983) (ADEA case).

[4]Lyda v. American Broadcasting Cos., 587 F. Supp. 670, 34 FEP 1151 (S.D.N.Y. 1984). *See also* Cornett v. AVCO Fin. Servs., One, 792 F.2d 447, 40 FEP 1763 (4th Cir. 1986) (failure to file before appropriate state agency bars age claim); Kocian v. Getty Ref. & Mktg Co., *supra* note 2 (charging party's failure to initiate state proceedings bars suit where EEOC does not itself defer charge because state statute of limitations has run). *But see* Williams v. Warehouse Mkts., 637 F. Supp. 724 (D. Nev. 1986).

## 5. Availability of 300-Day Filing Period for EEOC Charges

In response to *Mohasco Corp. v. Silver,*[5] the EEOC has entered into "Worksharing Agreements" with certain deferral agencies,[6] providing that the deferral agency will waive its 60-day exclusive processing period whenever a charge is filed more than 240 days after the discriminatory act, while reserving its right to take action subsequent to the waiver.[7]

The Supreme Court, in *EEOC v. Commercial Office Products Co.,*[8] resolved the question of whether or not a deferral agency effectively 'terminates' its proceedings prior to the expiration of the 300-day statute of limitations when it waives its exclusive 60-day period for the initial processing of a discrimination charge so that the EEOC may immediately deem the charge filed.[9] The Supreme Court accepted the EEOC's interpretation that a waiver pursuant to a work-sharing agreement should be deemed such a termination.[10]

The Supreme Court, in *Commercial Office Products,* also resolved the issue of whether or not the 300-day filing period is available to claimants who failed to file a state charge within the state limitations period.[11] The Court held that the 300-day filing period was available, holding that 'state time limits for filing discrimination claims do not determine the applicable federal time limit.'[12] This validated the EEOC practice of accepting untimely state filings as sufficient if the 300-day limit is met.[13]

Courts continue to hold that the statute is satisfied where the local deferral agency waives its jurisdiction at the charging party's request.[14]

## 6. Effect of State Action or Inaction on Title VII Rights

In *University of Tennessee v. Elliott,*[15] the Supreme Court elaborated on the rule originally announced in *Kremer v. Chemical Construction Corp.*[16] and held that an unappealed state administrative agency ruling barred a race discrimination claim under 42 U.S.C. § 1981 and § 1983. Congress, by requiring that the EEOC should give "substantial weight" to final findings and orders of state agencies,[17] suspended normal application of full faith and

---

[5]447 U.S. 807, 23 FEP 1 (1980).

[6]*See* EEOC regulations at 29 C.F.R. § 1601.13(c) (1982).

[7]29 C.F.R. § 1601.13(a) (1982) provides that charges which are apparently untimely under the state or local statute of limitations will be deemed timely under § 706(e) if received by the EEOC within 300 days from the date of the alleged violation.

[8]486 U.S. _____, 46 FEP 1265 (1988).

[9]The issue was critical because the Supreme Court in *Mohasco* determined that a charge filed between the 240th and 300th day will be deemed timely filed with the EEOC only if the state agency "terminates" its proceedings prior to the expiration of the 300-day filing period. 447 U.S. at 814 n.16.

[10]46 FEP at 1268–70.

[11]46 FEP at 1271.

[12]46 FEP at 1271.

[13]29 C.F.R. § 1601.13(a)(3). *Cf.* 29 C.F.R. § 1601.13(a)(2) (300-day limit not available when charge filed with local agency without jurisdiction).

[14]Langston v. Long Island R.R., 33 FEP 1814 (E.D.N.Y. 1982); Lusardi v. Xerox Corp., 99 F.R.D. 89, 33 FEP 1143 (D.N.J. 1983), *appeal dismissed,* 747 F.2d 174, 36 FEP 258 (3d Cir. 1984) (ADEA case). *But see* Fick v. Canterbury Coal Co., 568 F. Supp. 927, 32 FEP 1305 (W.D. Pa. 1983) (where EEOC refers charge to § 706 agency, which then refers charge back to EEOC 328 days after incident of discrimination, charge held untimely).

[15]478 U.S. 788, 41 FEP 177 (1986).

[16]456 U.S. 461, 28 FEP 1412, *reh'g denied,* 458 U.S. 1133 (1982).

[17]Sec. 706(b), 42 U.S.C. § 2000e-5(h).

credit principles. No such intent was evidenced in the Reconstruction Era statutes, and thus an unappealed state agency ruling could be considered *res judicata* if it has preclusive effect under state law.

*Elliott,* which has been applied broadly,[18] calls into question lower court rulings that allow unappealed state agency determinations to bar a Title VII claim.[19] The proper rule, after *Elliott,* would appear to be that unappealed state agency rulings do not *per se* bar Title VII claims.[20] *Kremer* would continue to apply where a state agency proceeding is appealed to a state court, provided the plaintiff has had a full and fair opportunity to litigate the issue under state law.[21]

## C. When Discrimination Has Occurred

### 1. Individual Acts

The Supreme Court's decisions in *Delaware State College v. Ricks*[22] and *Chardon v. Fernandez,*[23] emphasizing the date the employee is notified of the employment decision, continue to be the leading authorities for identifying the occurrence from which the charge-filing period should be calculated.[24]

---

[18]*See* Chapter 29 (Election and Exhaustion of Remedies).

[19]*See, e.g.,* Buckhalter v. Pepsi-Cola Gen. Bottlers, 768 F.2d 842, 38 FEP 682 (7th Cir. 1985), *vacated and remanded,* 478 U.S. 1017, 41 FEP 272 (1986); Parker v. National Corp. for Hous. Partnerships, 619 F. Supp. 1061, 38 FEP 1265 (D.D.C. 1985); Zywicki v. Versa Technology, Moxness Prods. Div., 610 F. Supp. 50, 37 FEP 710 (E.D. Wis. 1985), *rev'd mem.,* 801 F.2d 1343, 43 FEP 1648 (7th Cir. 1986).

[20]Abramson v. Council Bluffs Community School Dist., 808 F.2d 1307, 42 FEP 163 (8th Cir. 1986); Bottini v. Sadore Mgmt. Corp., 764 F.2d 116, 38 FEP 5 (2d Cir. 1985); Moore v. Bonner, 695 F.2d 799, 30 FEP 817 (4th Cir. 1982), *cert. denied,* 474 U.S. 827 (1985); Snow v. Nevada Dep't of Prisons, 543 F. Supp. 752, 29 FEP 742 (D. Nev. 1982). *Kremer* has been applied even where the employer or a state agency, rather than the plaintiff, has appealed the state agency determination. *See* Trujillo v. County of Santa Clara, 766 F.2d 1368, 38 FEP 1008, *opinion withdrawn and opinion replaced,* 775 F.2d 1359, 44 FEP 954 (9th Cir. 1985) (employer appeal); Hickman v. Electronic Keyboarding Co., 741 F.2d 230, 35 FEP 1281 (8th Cir. 1984) (agency appeal on employee's behalf). *See also* Reedy v. Florida Dep't of Educ., 605 F. Supp. 172, 37 FEP 754 (N.D. Fla. 1985); Parker v. Danville Metal Stamping Co., 603 F. Supp. 182, 37 FEP 250 (C.D. Ill. 1985); Jones v. Progress Lighting Corp., 595 F. Supp. 1031, 36 FEP 25 (E.D. Pa. 1984).

[21]*See, e.g.,* Hirst v. California, 770 F.2d 776, 38 FEP 1496 (9th Cir. 1985); Burney v. Polk Community College, 728 F.2d 1374, 34 FEP 727 (11th Cir. 1984); Davis v. United States Steel Corp., United States Steel Supply Div., 688 F.2d 166, 29 FEP 1202 (3d Cir. 1982), *cert. denied,* 460 U.S. 1014, 31 FEP 64 (1983); Unger v. Consolidated Foods Corp., 693 F.2d 703, 30 FEP 441 (7th Cir. 1982), *cert. denied,* 460 U.S. 1102, 31 FEP 904 (1983); Lee v. City of Peoria, 685 F.2d 196, 29 FEP 892 (7th Cir. 1982); Brown v. St. Louis Police Dep't, 691 F.2d 393, 30 FEP 18 (8th Cir. 1982), *cert. denied,* 461 U.S. 908 (1983). *Kremer* has been applied only where the issue of discrimination was or could have been litigated; *compare* Kirk v. Bremen Community High School Dist. 228, Cook County, Ill., Bd. of Education, 811 F.2d 347, 42 FEP 1473 (7th Cir. 1987) (significant differences in underlying issues) *and* Jones v. City of Alton, 757 F.2d 878, 37 FEP 523 (7th Cir. 1985) (no *res judicata* where plaintiff precluded from making record on discrimination issue) *with* Carpenter v. Reed, 728 F.2d 1302, 34 FEP 942 (10th Cir. 1984) (*res judicata* applies if plaintiff could have raised issue). *See also* Heath v. John Morrell & Co., 768 F.2d 245, 38 FEP 700 (8th Cir. 1985). *See generally* Chapter 29 (Election and Exhaustion of Remedies), at Section III.B.

[22]449 U.S. 250, 24 FEP 827 (1980).

[23]454 U.S. 6, 27 FEP 57 (1981).

[24]*See, e.g.,* Merrill v. Southern Methodist Univ., 806 F.2d 600, 42 FEP 1045 (5th Cir. 1986) (180-day period begins to run when plaintiff receives notice, not when she first apprehends possibility of discrimination); Cervantes v. IMCO-Halliburton Servs., 724 F.2d 511, 34 FEP 13, *reh'g denied,* 728 F.2d 255, 34 FEP 1403 (5th Cir. 1984) (filing period begins to run on date employee notified he had been terminated and would not be rehired, not on earlier date when he suffered temporarily disabling injury); Price v. Litton Business Sys., 694 F.2d 963, 965, 30 FEP 803, 804–05 (4th Cir. 1982) (limitation period triggered on date employee learned of impending termination date rather than actual termination date); *see also* Cameron v. United States Trust Co. of N.Y., 754 F.2d 109, 37 FEP 254 (2d Cir. 1985) (filing period begins upon termination of employment, not date when severance benefits cease); EEOC v. Westinghouse Elec. Corp., 646 F. Supp. 555, 42 FEP 324 (D.N.J. 1986), *dismissed,* 651 F. Supp. 1172, 42 FEP 1203 (D.N.J.

There continues to be some debate regarding when an employee obtains sufficient facts to warrant the filing of an action.[25] Some courts have relied upon this rationale to allow an individual to challenge employment decisions outside the normal charge-filing period where the charge was prompted by different treatment of similarly situated individuals occurring within 180/300 days prior to the filing of the charge.[26]

## 2. Continuing Violations

The confusion surrounding the "continuing violation" concept[27] was exacerbated by the Supreme Court ruling in *Bazemore v. Friday*,[28] in which the Court held that an employer was required to rectify a salary structure that perpetuated pre-Act differentials between black and white employees. The Fourth Circuit had concluded, based upon *Hazelwood*[29] and *Evans*,[30] that so long as an employer acted evenhandedly after the effective date of the statute, pre-Act disparities were merely of historical significance. The Supreme Court, deeming this error "too obvious to warrant extended discussion,"[31] held that a salary system perpetuating pre-Act disparities constituted present discrimination because "[e]ach week's pay check that delivers less to

---

1987) (cause of action accrues at time of plant closing not expiration of severance benefits); Cole v. CBS, 634 F. Supp. 1558, 42 FEP 127 (S.D.N.Y. 1986) (employer's notice not so equivocal as to excuse failure to file). *But see* EEOC v. Westinghouse Elec. Corp., 725 F.2d 211, 218–19, 33 FEP 945, 949–50 (3d Cir. 1983), *amended,* 33 FEP 1816 (3d Cir.), *cert. denied,* 469 U.S. 820, 35 FEP 1607 (1984) (in ADEA case, court holds that *Ricks* applies only to discrete isolated acts, and is inapplicable to complaint involving several related acts); Elliott v. Group Medical & Surgical Serv., 714 F.2d 556, 563, 32 FEP 1451, 1456 (5th Cir. 1983), *cert. denied,* 467 U.S. 1215, 34 FEP 1472 (1984) (in ADEA case, court refused to apply *Ricks* and *Chardon* retroactively); Smith v. Fred W. Albrecht Grocery Co., 31 FEP 1848 (N.D. Ohio 1983) (*Ricks* applies to one isolated incident); Leite v. Kennecott Copper Corp., 558 F. Supp. 1170, 31 FEP 390, 392–93 (D. Mass), *aff'd mem.,* 720 F.2d 658, 33 FEP 1520 (1st Cir. 1983) (question of whether "unofficial" notice of impending termination sufficient to trigger limitation period); Zises v. Prudential Ins. Co., 30 FEP 1218, 1221 (D. Mass. 1982) (holding *Ricks* inapplicable to constructive discharge cases); Carpenter v. University of Wis. Sys. Bd. of Regents, 529 F. Supp. 525, 532, 27 FEP 1569, 1574 (W.D. Wis. 1982), *aff'd on other grounds,* 728 F.2d 911, 34 FEP 248 (7th Cir. 1984) (distinguishing *Ricks* because initial and ultimate decision to deny tenure was temporarily reversed during appeal procedure).

[25]*Compare* Vaught v. R.R. Donnelley & Sons Co., 745 F.2d 407, 410–12, 35 FEP 1820 (7th Cir. 1984) (duty to file charge arises when claimant possesses knowledge of facts sufficient to establish prima facie case) *and* Monnig v. Kennecott Corp., 603 F. Supp. 1035, 1038, 37 FEP 193 (D. Conn. 1985) ("To constitute a notice of termination, a specific date on which employment will be discontinued must be stated.") *with* Janowiak v. City of S. Bend, 750 F.2d 557, 560, 36 FEP 737 (7th Cir. 1984), *vacated on other grounds,* 481 U.S. 1001, 43 FEP 640 (1987) (claimant will be excused from learning of alleged unlawful conduct only by "circumstances beyond his control") *and* Mull v. Arco Durethene Plastics, 599 F. Supp. 158, 161–62, 36 FEP 1052, 1056–58 (N.D. Ill. 1984), *aff'd,* 784 F.2d 284, 40 FEP 311 (7th Cir. 1986) (oral notice sufficient even though employer's regular practice was to give written notice and oral notice couched in terms of termination or transfer).

[26]*E.g.,* Perez v. Laredo Junior College, 706 F.2d 731 (5th Cir. 1983), *cert. denied,* 464 U.S. 1042 (1984) (although college professor's claims of salary discrimination under 42 U.S.C. §§ 1981 and 1983 untimely as to time his salary was established, plaintiff could pursue salary issue where he alleged other similarly situated individuals given raises within time limitations); Ortiz v. Chicago Transit Auth., 639 F. Supp. 310, 41 FEP 350 (N.D. Ill. 1986), *summary judgment granted,* 43 FEP 348 (N.D. Ill. 1987) (statute begins to run when similarly situated employee allowed to return to work); Reid v. University of Mich., 612 F. Supp. 320, 38 FEP 491 (E.D. Mich. 1985) (salary issue); Coleman v. Apex Acquisition, Clark Oil & Ref. Co. Div., 568 F. Supp. 1035, 36 FEP 758 (E.D. Wis. 1983) (charge alleging denial of promotion timely where younger white employee promoted during 300-day period). *Compare* Glass v. Petro-Tex Chem. Corp., 757 F.2d 1554, 37 FEP 972 (5th Cir. 1985) (failure to apprehend discrimination in prior promotion allows timely complaint) *with* Merrill v. Southern Methodist Univ., *supra* note 24 (rejecting timeliness argument premised upon subjective appreciation of possibility of discrimination).

[27]Glass v. Petro-Tex Chemical Corp., *supra* note 26, at 1560 (citing other cases).

[28]478 U.S. 385, 41 FEP 92 (1986).

[29]Hazelwood School Dist. v. United States, 433 U.S. 299, 15 FEP 1 (1977).

[30]United Airlines v. Evans, 431 U.S. 553, 14 FEP 1510 (1977).

[31]41 FEP at 97.

a black than to a similarly situated white is a wrong actionable under Title VII, regardless of the fact that this pattern was begun prior to the effective date of Title VII."[32] The Court distinguished *Hazelwood* and *Evans* as cases involving post-Act conduct that was in no way a continuation of pre-Act patterns of discrimination.[33]

It is not clear whether *Bazemore v. Friday* has applicability beyond the wage disparity factual situation. The case would not seem to call into question prior rulings refusing to allow reliance on the continuing violation doctrine to revive stale individual claims.[34] The case would not seem to affect court holdings indicating that a discharge is not a continuing violation.[35] The case leaves open the debate as to whether or not the continuing violation theory applies to acts such as a failure to promote pursuant to a promotion system or otherwise.[36]

*a. A Series of Acts With One Independent Discriminatory Act Occurring Within the Charge-Filing Period.* These cases, difficult to reconcile, continue to fall into three categories: (1) under special circumstances, the plaintiff may be allowed to litigate prior acts by alleging one act within the charge-filing period and advancing a continuing violation theory;[37] (2) the plaintiff is allowed only to litigate the act within the charge-filing period;[38] and (3) the plaintiff is allowed to litigate prior acts if it is shown that those acts are related to the act occurring within the charge-filing period.[39]

---

[32]*Id.*

[33]41 FEP at 97 n. 6.

[34]Hill v. AT&T Technologies, 731 F.2d 175, 34 FEP 620 (4th Cir. 1984) (continuing violation doctrine not talismanic or shibboleth term to revive stale claims); Woodard v. Lehman, 717 F.2d 909, 32 FEP 1441 (4th Cir. 1983) (continuing violation theory rejected where plaintiff failed to assert specific instance of discriminatory denial of promotion within filing period).

[35]Most courts hold that a discharge is not a continuing violation. Hill v. AT&T Technologies, *supra* note 34; Berry v. Louisiana State Univ. Bd. of Supervisors, 715 F.2d 971, 32 FEP 1567 (5th Cir. 1983), *aff'd,* 783 F.2d 1270, 42 FEP 917, *reh'g denied en banc,* 788 F.2d 1562 (5th Cir.), *cert. denied,* 479 U.S. 868, 44 FEP 848 (1986); Welty v. SF&G dba Mercury, 605 F. Supp. 1548, 37 FEP 926 (N.D. Ala. 1985); Kinniry v. Aetna Ins. Co., 35 FEP 1474 (D. Conn. 1984); Castillo v. City of Phoenix, 33 FEP 1597 (D. Ariz. 1983); Quillen v. United States Postal Serv., 564 F. Supp. 314, 32 FEP 1631 (E.D. Mich. 1983). *But cf.* EEOC v. Chicago Miniature Lamp Works, 640 F. Supp. 1291, 41 FEP 911 (N.D. Ill. 1986) (illegal hiring policy may constitute continuing violation).

[36]*Compare* Glass v. Petro-Tex Chem. Corp., *supra* note 26 (failure to promote is continuing violation); Cajigas v. Banco de Ponce, 741 F.2d 464, 35 FEP 758 (1st Cir. 1984) (same), Trevino v. Celanese Corp., 701 F.2d 397, 402, 33 FEP 1324, 1328, *reh'g denied,* 707 F.2d 515 (5th Cir. 1983) (same) *and* Coleman v. Apex Acquisition, Clark Oil & Ref. Co. Div., *supra* note 26 (charge alleging denial of promotion timely where younger white employee promoted during 300-day period) *with* Jones v. City of Somerville, 735 F.2d 5, 34 FEP 1577 (1st Cir. 1984) (promotion denial not continuing violation), Woodard v. Lehman, *supra* note 34 (continuing violation theory rejected where plaintiff failed to assert specific instance of discriminatory denial of promotion within filing period), Ross v. Food Fair dba Pantry Pride Enters., 33 FEP 1449 (M.D. Fla. 1983) (no continuing violation where plaintiff knew of his last rejection for more than two years prior to filing his charge and no other similarly situated employee promoted ahead of plaintiff) *and* Soble v. University of Md., 572 F. Supp. 1509, 33 FEP 611 (D. Md. 1983) (series of denials of promotion not continuing violation).

[37]*E.g.,* Hall v. Ledex, Inc., 669 F.2d 397, 398, 30 FEP 82, 82–83 (6th Cir. 1982); Mamos v. School Comm. of Wakefield, 553 F. Supp. 989, 993, 30 FEP 1051, 1053 (D. Mass. 1983).

[38]*E.g.,* Pao v. Holy Redeemer Hosp., 547 F. Supp. 484, 493–94 n.4, 31 FEP 580, 585–86 (E.D. Pa. 1982) (plaintiff allowed to litigate the one refusal-to-hire within charge-filing period); Donaldson v. Cafritz Co., 30 FEP 436, 437 (D.D.C. 1981) (plaintiff could litigate only those incidents within charge-filing period).

[39]E.g., Glass v. Petro-Tex Chem. Corp., 757 F.2d 1554, 37 FEP 972 (5th Cir. 1985); Berry v. Louisiana State Univ. Bd. of Supervisors, *supra* note 35 (establishing conceptual framework for application of doctrine); Held v. Gulf Oil Co., 684 F.2d 427, 430, 29 FEP 837, 839–40 (6th Cir. 1982) (*Evans* does not bar litigation of related incidents outside charge-filing period); Caston v. Duke Univ., 34 FEP 102 (M.D.N.C. 1983); Smith v. Fred W. Albrecht Grocery Co., 31 FEP 1848 (N.D. Ohio 1983) (transfer and subsequent retaliatory reduction in hours sufficiently related to allow litigation of all allegations);

*b. Maintenance of a System or Policy Which Discriminates.* Formal rules and policies remain the most widely recognized type of continuing violation[40] when the plaintiff can show that the rule or policy was in effect during the charge-filing period.[41] Questions have arisen as to whether the implementation date of a policy or some other event should be used to trigger the charge-filing period.[42] Whether informal practices rise to the level of a system or policy continues to be discussed on a case-by-case basis.[43]

### 3. The Present Effects of Past Discrimination

Claims of the "present effects of past discrimination" have been summarily rejected,[44] as have arguments that an employer's failure to remedy prior discrimination is actionable as a continuing violation.[45]

### D. Tolling of Time to File Charge With EEOC

### 1. The Nature of Tolling

Some courts allow plaintiffs who have not timely filed to rely upon the properly submitted charge of another similarly situated employee.[46] Citing

---

Donaldson v. Cafritz Co., *supra* note 38 (recognizing that plaintiff could have contended that time-barred incidents were related to actionable incident).

[40]*E.g.,* Gifford v. Atchison, Topeka & Santa Fe Ry., 685 F.2d 1149, 1153–55, 34 FEP 240, 243–44 (9th Cir. 1982) (terms of collective bargaining agreement); Boyd v. Madison County Mut. Ins. Co., 653 F.2d 1173, 1176–77, 28 FEP 54, 56 (7th Cir. 1981) (per curiam), *cert. denied,* 454 U.S. 1146, 28 FEP 117 (1982) (bonus policy). *But see* O'Malley v. GTE Serv. Corp., 758 F.2d 818, 37 FEP 697 (2d Cir. 1985) ("facially proper" employment policy is not a continuing violation); Zangrillo v. Fashion Inst. of Technology, 601 F. Supp. 1346, 37 FEP 162 (S.D.N.Y.), *aff'd mem.,* 788 F.2d 2, 40 FEP 1617 (2d Cir. 1985).

[41]Abrams v. Baylor College of Medicine, 805 F.2d 528, 42 FEP 806 (5th Cir. 1986) (continuation of illegal policy during the 180-day period); EEOC v. Westinghouse Elec. Corp., 725 F.2d 211, 33 FEP 945 (3d Cir. 1983), *amended,* 33 FEP 1816 (3d Cir.), *cert. denied,* 469 U.S. 820, 35 FEP 1607 (1984) (continuing discriminatory policy found in formal rule regarding eligibility for layoff income and benefits in event of plant shutdown); Serpe v. Four-Phase Sys., 718 F.2d 935, 33 FEP 178 (9th Cir. 1983) (existence of systematic refusal to transfer is question of fact for district court on remand). *But see* Domingo v. New England Fish Co., 727 F.2d 1429, 34 FEP 584, *modified,* 742 F.2d 520, 37 FEP 1303 (9th Cir. 1984) (even where hiring system constitutes continuing violation, individuals must show injury within 300 days prior to charge in order to recover; contrary holding would read limitations period out of statute); EEOC v. Chrysler Corp., 683 F.2d 146, 149–50, 29 FEP 371, 374–75 (6th Cir. 1982) (abandoned mandatory maternity leave policy); Valentino v. United States Postal Serv., 674 F.2d 56, 65–66, 28 FEP 593, 599–600 (D.C. Cir. 1982) (promotion system had changed).

[42]*Compare* Simmons v. South Carolina State Ports Auth., 694 F.2d 63, 64–65, 30 FEP 457, 458–59 (4th Cir. 1982) (charge-filing period for attack against pension policy began when employees entered pension system rather than when pension claims made) *and* Castillo v. City of Phoenix, *supra* note 35 (series of discharges not deemed sufficiently related to be continuing violation) *with* Abrams v. Baylor College of Medicine, *supra* note 41 (informal exclusion of Jewish physicians from surgical teams sent to Saudi Arabia continuing violation), Coleman v. Apex Acquisition, Clark Oil & Ref. Co. Div., 568 F. Supp. 1035, 36 FEP 758 (E.D. Wis. 1983) (covert policy of ridding company of black managers) *and* EEOC v. Home Ins. Co., 553 F. Supp. 704, 30 FEP 841, 845–46 (S.D.N.Y. 1982) (date of termination rather than date notified of unlawful mandatory retirement policy triggered charge-filing period).

[43]*Compare* Slevin v. Safeguard Business Sys., 31 FEP 193, 195 (N.D. Ill. 1982) (plaintiff's demotion not part of overall promotion policy) *with* Rivas v. State Bd. for Community Colleges & Occupational Educ., 517 F. Supp. 467, 470–71, 27 FEP 715, 717 (D. Colo. 1981) (failure to promote allegations sufficient to allow plaintiff to prove policy at trial).

[44]*E.g.,* Scott v. Pacific Maritime Ass'n, 695 F.2d 1199, 30 FEP 1517, 1520–22 (9th Cir. 1983); Scarlett v. Seaboard Coast Line R.R., 676 F.2d 1043, 1049–50, 29 FEP 433, 439 (5th Cir. 1982); Hartwell v. Pennsylvania, 568 F. Supp. 793, 34 FEP 830 (W.D. Pa. 1983); Ka Nam Kuan v. City of Chicago, 563 F. Supp. 255, 32 FEP 566 (N.D. Ill. 1983) (denial of promotion based on earlier unfavorable performance rating does not revive ability to challenge performance evaluation on continuing violation theory).

[45]Golletti v. Arco Polymers, 32 FEP 1796 (W.D. Pa. 1983), *vacated and remanded memo,* 762 F.2d 993, 41 FEP 64 (3d Cir. 1985).

[46]Snell v. Suffolk County, N.Y., 782 F.2d 1094, 39 FEP 1590 (2d Cir. 1986) (adopting "single filing rule"); Gray v. Phillips Petroleum Co., 638 F. Supp. 789, 41 FEP 440 (D. Kan. 1986) (allowing one

*Zipes v. Trans World Airlines,* [47] some courts have held that Title VII actions brought by federal employees are subject to equitable tolling, notwithstanding the doctrine of sovereign immunity. [48]

## 2. Resort to Another Forum

Following *Electrical Workers, IUE, Local 790 v. Robbins & Meyers,* [49] courts continue to hold that the pendency of a grievance or the pursuit of another independent remedy does not suspend the 180/300-day limitation period. [50] The Eleventh Circuit has affirmed that, notwithstanding a joint filing agreement between the agencies, an ADEA charge filed with the OFCCP, which lacks jurisdiction over age discrimination matters, does not constitute proper filing with the EEOC. [51]

## 3. Charging Parties Who Have Been Misled

The Second, Fourth, Fifth, and Eleventh circuits recently confirmed that equitable tolling generally will be allowed only when the plaintiff has been actively misled by the employer or misinformed by the EEOC or a responsible state fair employment agency. [52] Cases continue to indicate that courts are extremely reluctant to exercise their equitable discretion where the plaintiff has retained counsel during the filing period, even when the attorney has misinformed his client. [53] Some decisions hold that under certain conditions an employer's failure to post ADEA informational notices will toll the

---

named plaintiff who had timely filed to satisfy 180-day limitation for all plaintiffs, even though charge did not allege discrimination against other employees).

[47] 455 U.S. 385, 28 FEP 1, *reh'g denied,* 456 U.S. 940 (1982).

[48] Royall v. United States Postal Serv., 624 F. Supp. 211, 41 FEP 311 (E.D.N.Y. 1985) (Congress intended to give federal employees same rights and remedies as private employees); Grier v. Carlin, 620 F. Supp. 1364, 39 FEP 497 (W.D.N.C. 1985) (same); Neves v. Kolaski, 602 F. Supp. 645, 37 FEP 110 (D.R.I. 1985) (illogical to argue that single statutory provision confers lesser degree of jurisdiction merely because it is brought against federal employer). *But see* Dimetry v. Department of the Army, 637 F. Supp. 269, 40 FEP 1192 (E.D.N.C. 1985) (time limits for filing Title VII suit against federal employer may not be tolled absent clear waiver of sovereign immunity).

[49] 429 U.S. 229, 13 FEP 1813 (1976).

[50] Vaught v. R.R. Donnelley & Sons Co., 745 F.2d 407, 35 FEP 1820 (7th Cir. 1984) (resort to informal grievance procedure does not stop running of limitations period); Dyer v. Jefferson Parish, La., 619 F. Supp. 284, 38 FEP 698 (E.D. La. 1985) (no tolling during period plaintiff appealed dismissal to county personnel board).

[51] Meckes v. Reynolds Metals Co., 604 F. Supp. 598, 37 FEP 1269 (N.D. Ala.), *aff'd,* 776 F.2d 1055, *reh'g denied,* 779 F.2d 60 (11th Cir. 1985) (en banc) (filing claim with OFCCP ineffective as to ADEA action).

[52] Dillman v. Combustion Eng'g, 784 F.2d 57, 39 FEP 1750 (2d Cir. 1986) (equitable modification invoked only where plaintiff is ignorant of cause of action or delayed filing charge due to employer concealment or misconduct); Felty v. Graves-Humphreys Co. (I), 785 F.2d 516, 40 FEP 447 (4th Cir. 1986) (employer who allegedly coerced plaintiff to delay filing EEOC charge is not entitled to summary judgment on grounds charge was untimely); Pruet Prod. Co. v. Ayles, 784 F.2d 1275, 40 FEP 619 (5th Cir. 1986) (tolling not allowed where no misrepresentation or concealment caused plaintiff to miss filing deadline); Manning v. Carlin, 786 F.2d 1108, 40 FEP 959 (11th Cir. 1986) (equitable tolling allowed only if defendant concealed facts supporting cause of action, plaintiff was misled by defendant as to nature of his rights, or action is pending in state court); James v. Miller-Wohl Co., 35 FEP 1846 (W.D.N.Y. 1984) (tolling permitted where unrepresented plaintiff was misled by responsible FEP agency).

[53] Williams v. Whirlpool Corp., 41 FEP 383 (W.D. Ark. 1986) (equitable tolling not appropriate where plaintiff had counsel during charge filing period); Welty v. S.F.&G. dba Mercury, 605 F. Supp. 1548, 37 FEP 926 (N.D. Ala. 1985) (doctrine of equitable tolling not available if plaintiff's attorney improperly advised her about time limits). *But see* Burton v. United States Postal Serv., 612 F. Supp. 1057, 38 FEP 1591 (N.D. Ohio 1985) (tolling permitted where attorney abandoned client and left town without informing him that he had not mailed charge).

filing period for the ignorant putative charging party.[54] Courts disagree about whether a plaintiff's mental or physical incapacity permits equitable tolling. The First Circuit and also some lower courts have determined that mental or physical incapacity by itself is inadequate to justify tolling the charge-filing requirement.[55] But one court has decided that the limitation period may be tolled during the time a plaintiff is adjudged mentally incompetent or is institutionalized under a diagnosis of mental incapacity.[56]

## III. TIMELINESS OF FILING SUIT

### A. Time of Issuing Notice of Right to Sue

#### 1. General Considerations

Several courts have held that receipt of a right-to-sue notice is a condition precedent rather than a jurisdictional prerequisite, and have modified the requirement for equitable reasons.[57] The Ninth Circuit has allowed an action to proceed where timely filed on a second right-to-sue letter, issued after the EEOC had rescinded its first right-to-sue notice. The rescission had occurred within 90 days of the issuance of the first notice.[58] The Ninth Circuit clarified this decision by holding that unless the EEOC intends to withdraw its earlier reasonable cause determination and withdraw a previously issued right-to-sue notice, issuance of a second right-to-sue notice on the same charge is invalid.[59]

---

[54]McClinton v. Alabama By-Products Corp., 574 F. Supp. 43, 35 FEP 1517 (N.D. Ala. 1983), aff'd, 743 F.2d 1483, 35 FEP 1893 (11th Cir. 1984) (employer's failure to post notices tolls filing period until employee acquires general knowledge of his rights, but he need not be notified about specific 180-day limit); Bomberger v. Consolidated Coal Co., 623 F. Supp. 89, 39 FEP 908 (W.D. Pa. 1985) (failure of employer to post notices will toll filing period at least until plaintiff seeks out counsel or acquires knowledge of his ADEA rights); Klausing v. Whirlpool Corp., 623 F. Supp. 156, 38 FEP 667 (S.D. Ohio 1985), appeal dismissed, 785 F.2d 309, 40 FEP 984 (6th Cir. 1986) (failure to display informational posters tolls limitation period at least until plaintiff acquires actual knowledge of 180-day time requirement).

[55]Cano v. United States Postal Serv., 755 F.2d 221, 37 FEP 209 (1st Cir. 1985) (plaintiff's illness does not require tolling, as it did not affect her attorney's knowledge of appropriate legal remedies); Kerver v. Exxon Prod. Research Co., 40 FEP 1567 (S.D. Tex. 1986), aff'd, 810 F.2d 196 (5th Cir. 1987) (limitation period not tolled due to plaintiff's psychological impairment resulting from job loss); Steward v. Holiday Inn, 609 F. Supp. 1468, 40 FEP 191 (E.D. La. 1985) (physical and mental incapacity is not an additional tolling category).

[56]Bassett v. Sterling Drug, 578 F. Supp. 1244, 35 FEP 382 (S.D. Ohio 1984), appeal dismissed, 770 F.2d 165, 40 FEP 1617 (6th Cir. 1985) (mental incompetence is compelling reason to toll filing period).

[57]E.g., Josiah-Faeduwor v. Communications Satellite Corp., 785 F.2d 344, 40 FEP 442 (D.C. Cir. 1986) (refusing to modify where right-to-sue received by plaintiff's counsel); Fouche v. Jekyll Island-State Park Auth., 713 F.2d 1518, 33 FEP 303 (11th Cir. 1983) (where charging party attempts to obtain right-to-sue notice, but Attorney General refused to issue such notice, issuance may be waived); Lugo v. City of Charlotte, 577 F. Supp. 988, 33 FEP 1354 (W.D.N.C. 1984) (failure to obtain right-to-sue notice from Attorney General rather than EEOC no barrier to suit); Gillum v. District of Columbia Pub. Schools, 32 FEP 231 (D.D.C. 1983) (lawsuit allowed to proceed without right-to-sue notice); Black v. Brown Univ., 555 F. Supp. 880, 31 FEP 659 (D.R.I. 1983) (reliance upon right-to-sue notice issued by state agency permissible if plaintiff takes steps to obtain proper notice from EEOC).

[58]Lute v. Singer Co., Kearfott Div., 678 F.2d 844, 28 FEP 1700 (9th Cir. 1982), reh'g denied and amended, en banc, 696 F.2d 1266, 34 FEP 1372 (9th Cir. 1983).

[59]Mahroom v. Defense Language Inst., 732 F.2d 1439, 34 FEP 1334 (9th Cir. 1984). Accord Lo v. Pan Am. World Airways, 787 F.2d 827, 45 FEP 26 (2d Cir. 1986). But see Brown v. Continental Can Co., 765 F.2d 810, 38 FEP 695 (9th Cir. 1985) (plaintiff may litigate like or related claims, even though such claims were subject of previous right-to-sue notice); Dougherty v. Barry, 34 FEP 339 (D.D.C. 1984) (suit on second right-to-sue notice allowed when state claim pending at all times).

### 3. Premature Issuance of Right-to-Sue Letters Within 180 Days and Premature Filing of Suit

Some courts have permitted actions premised upon a right-to-sue letter prematurely issued by the EEOC.[60]

The Fourth Circuit has held that a plaintiff need only be entitled to receive a notice of right to sue in order to commence an action.[61] As in other settings, courts have not held plaintiffs responsible for the EEOC's failures and have permitted plaintiffs who unsuccessfully sought a right-to-sue letter to proceed.[62] Some courts hold that receipt of a right-to-sue letter after filing but before trial has satisfied the requirement,[63] but a plaintiff's failure to obtain a right-to-sue notice before, during, or after trial requires dismissal.[64]

### 4. Preliminary Relief Before Filing EEOC Charge or Before Receiving Right-to-Sue Letter

Several recent decisions state that preliminary relief prior to receipt of a right-to-sue letter is within the court's equitable jurisdiction,[65] and at least one court has refused to limit preliminary relief to retaliation cases.[66] However, most courts refuse to grant preliminary relief upon failure to demonstrate irreparable injury.[67]

---

[60]Brown v. Puget Sound Elec. Apprenticeship & Training Trust, 732 F.2d 726, 34 FEP 1201 (9th Cir. 1984), *cert. denied,* 469 U.S. 1108, 36 FEP 976 (1985). *But see* Mills v. Jefferson Bank E., 559 F. Supp. 34, 35 FEP 1384 (D. Colo. 1983) (court lacks jurisdiction of Title VII action filed on basis of right-to-sue notice that EEOC issued prior to 180-day period).

[61]Moore v. City of Charlotte, 754 F.2d 1100, 36 FEP 1582 (4th Cir.), *cert. denied,* 472 U.S. 1021, 37 FEP 1816 (1985); Perdue v. Roy Stone Transfer Corp., 690 F.2d 1091, 29 FEP 1673 (4th Cir. 1982); *see also* Bradford v. General Tel. Co. of Mich., 618 F. Supp. 390, 44 FEP 80, 121 LRRM 2106 (W.D. Mich. 1985).

[62]Kahn v. Pepsi Cola Bottling Group, 526 F. Supp. 1268, 27 FEP 770 (E.D.N.Y. 1981).

[63]Gooding v. Warner-Lambert Co., 744 F.2d 354, 35 FEP 1707 (3d Cir. 1984); Wrighten v. Metropolitan Hosps., 726 F.2d 1346, 33 FEP 1714 (9th Cir. 1984); Williams v. Washington Metro. Area Transit Auth., 721 F.2d 1412, 33 FEP 581 (D.C. Cir. 1983); Pinkard v. Pullman-Standard, 678 F.2d 1211, 1215–19, 29 FEP 216, 218–22, *reh'g denied,* 685 F.2d 1383 (5th Cir. 1982), *cert. denied,* 459 U.S. 1105, 30 FEP 1048 (1983); Soble v. University of Md., 572 F. Supp. 1509, 33 FEP 611 (D. Md. 1983).

[64]Lambert v. Georgia-Pacific Corp., 38 FEP 745 (S.D. Ga. 1985).

[65]Bailey v. Delta Air Lines, 722 F.2d 942, 33 FEP 713 (1st Cir. 1983) (refusing to hold that preliminary relief only available at EEOC's behest); Holt v. Continental Group, 708 F.2d 87, 31 FEP 1468 (2d Cir. 1983), *cert. denied,* 465 U.S. 1030, 33 FEP 1884 (1984); Sheehan v. Purolator Courier Corp., 676 F.2d 877, 28 FEP 202 (2d Cir. 1981), *aff'd,* 839 F.2d 99 (2d Cir. 1988); Guerrero v. Reeves Bros., 562 F. Supp. 603, 33 FEP 1021 (W.D.N.C. 1983); Winfrey v. Philadelphia Child Guidance Clinic, 32 FEP 1054 (E.D. Pa. 1983).

[66]Irizarry v. New York City Hous. Auth., 575 F. Supp. 571, 33 FEP 1025 (S.D.N.Y. 1983).

[67]Moteles v. University of Pa., 730 F.2d 913, 34 FEP 424 (3d Cir.), *cert. denied,* 469 U.S. 855, 35 FEP 1800 (1984) (involuntary transfer to different shift not irreparable injury; court may consider whether charging party truncated EEOC procedures as factor in determining whether to grant injunctive relief); Bailey v. Delta Air Lines, *supra* note 65 (business reorganization resulting in transfers and layoffs not irreparable harm; nature of injury must be sufficient to warrant disruption of normal administrative processes); Holt v. Continental Group, *supra* note 65 (financial distress or inability to find employment generally not irreparable injury; case remanded to allow lower court to determine whether impact on other employees of retaliation claim supports preliminary relief); Berman v. New York City Ballet, 616 F. Supp. 555, 38 FEP 1286 (S.D.N.Y. 1985).

## C. Filing Timely Complaint Within 90 Days of Receipt of Statutory Notice

### 1. Ninety Days Runs From Receipt of Notice

Courts have continued to hold that the 90-day suit-filing period runs from the plaintiff's receipt of notice, rejecting defense efforts to start the suit-filing period on the date of the notice[68] or plaintiff's efforts to add three days where the notice was sent by mail.[69] Courts apply the constructive receipt doctrine with circumspection, barring lawsuits only where the fault can fairly be attributed to the plaintiff.[70]

In determining whether or not an attorney's receipt of a right-to-sue notice would trigger the running of the suit-filing period, courts have considered such factors as the scope and extent of the attorney-client relationship, whether the charging party has authorized the representative to accept the right-to-sue notice, and whether and when the representative personally received the right-to-sue notice.[71]

## D. Complying With 90-Day Suit-Filing Period

### 1. Equitable Considerations in Extending Suit-Filing Period

In *Baldwin County Welcome Center v. Brown,* [72] the Supreme Court held that a failure to file a complaint within 90 days of receipt of a right-to-sue notice barred suit. The Court refused to hold that the filing of the right-to-sue

---

[68]Motley v. Bell Tel. Co., 562 F. Supp. 497, 32 FEP 1050 (E.D. Pa. 1983); Weatherspoon v. Andrews & Co., 32 FEP 1226 (D. Colo. 1983). *See also* Davis v. Buffalo Psychiatric Center, 613 F. Supp. 462, 37 FEP 69, *vacated in part and reconsideration denied,* 623 F. Supp. 19, 39 FEP 1814 (W.D.N.Y. 1985) (date of receipt excluded from 90-day period).

[69]Norris v. Florida Dep't of Health & Rehabilitative Servs., 730 F.2d 682, 35 FEP 1505 (11th Cir. 1984); Suarez v. Little Havana Activities & Nutrition Centers of Dade County, 721 F.2d 338, 33 FEP 806 (11th Cir. 1983); *see also* Robinson v. City of Fairfield, 750 F.2d 1507, 37 FEP 106 (11th Cir. 1985) (trial court presumption as to mailing date not clearly erroneous). Where the notice was not sent by mail, there is no basis for addition of three days. Mosel v. Hills Dep't Store, 789 F.2d 251, 40 FEP 1049 (3d Cir. 1986).

[70]*E.g.,* Hunter v. Stephenson Roofing, 790 F.2d 472, 40 FEP 1193 (6th Cir. 1986) (90 days begins to run 5 days after notice mailed, in case where plaintiff fails to inform EEOC of new address and notice received by former roommate); Josiah-Faeduwor v. Communications Satellite Corp., 785 F.2d 344, 40 FEP 442 (D.C. Cir. 1986) (90-day period begins when notice received by plaintiff's counsel, where plaintiff has informed EEOC of counsel and counsel requested right-to-sue notice); Espinoza v. Missouri Pac. R.R., 754 F.2d 1247, 37 FEP 415 (5th Cir. 1985) (plaintiff's absence from city on date notice received does not excuse untimely filing); St. Louis v. Alverno College, 744 F.2d 1314, 35 FEP 1715 (7th Cir. 1984) (plaintiff's failure to notify EEOC of change of address justifies application of constructive receipt doctrine); Law v. Hercules, Inc., 713 F.2d 691, 32 FEP 1291 (11th Cir. 1983) (constructive receipt applied when notice received by plaintiff's son); Trinkle v. Bell Litho, 627 F. Supp. 764, 41 FEP 357 (N.D. Ill. 1986) (absent wrongdoing by plaintiff, 90 days runs from actual receipt); Pole v. Citibank, N.A., 556 F. Supp. 822, 31 FEP 751 (S.D.N.Y. 1983) (suit allowed 11 months after EEOC unable to deliver notice because plaintiff had moved but continued to go to prior address to pick up mail); Croffut v. United Parcel Serv., 575 F. Supp. 1264, 33 FEP 1245 (E.D. Mo. 1984) (constructive receipt rejected where plaintiff's wife signed for notice, was in accident and hospitalized, and plaintiff did not see notice until three days later).

[71]Jones v. Madison Serv. Corp., 744 F.2d 1309, 35 FEP 1711 (7th Cir. 1984) (discussing prerequisites for application of constructive receipt doctrine); Harper v. Burgess, 701 F.2d 29, 31 FEP 450 (4th Cir. 1983) (where attorney requests and receives right-to-sue letter, constructive receipt doctrine applicable); Ahia v. Hawaii Protective Ass'n, 606 F. Supp. 847, 38 FEP 59 (D. Hawaii 1984) (constructive receipt rejected where plaintiff seeks notice from attorney); Decker v. Anheuser-Busch, 558 F. Supp. 445, 31 FEP 446 (M.D. Fla. 1983), *on remand from* 670 F.2d 506, 28 FEP 559 (5th Cir. 1982) (en banc) (constructive receipt rejected where notice served on plaintiff's attorney); Thomas v. KATV Channel 7, 692 F.2d 548, 30 FEP 231 (8th Cir. 1982), *cert. denied,* 460 U.S. 1039, 31 FEP 368 (1983) (90 days runs from receipt by charging party).

[72]466 U.S. 147, 34 FEP 929 (1984).

notice within 90 days tolled the suit-filing period, where the plaintiff failed to file an appropriate form for appointment of counsel until 96 days after the right-to-sue letter had issued. Although the Court acknowledged that equitable tolling might be appropriate in some cases,[73] it held that no reason supporting equitable tolling had been presented to it.[74]

While *Baldwin County*'s holding that the filing of a right-to-sue notice does not satisfy the statute overrules a number of cases, it is not clear whether the decision would preclude equitable tolling.[75] However, where the plaintiff either fails to execute an affidavit proving that he was misled,[76] or is in a position to know his or her rights,[77] tolling will not be allowed.[78] Prior to *Baldwin County* courts had allowed tolling where plaintiffs submitted complaints to the clerk's office within 90 days, even though the clerk had filed the pleadings after the time limit.[79] The impact of *Baldwin County* on these decisions is unclear.

## 2. Filing Petition for Appointment of Counsel

*Baldwin County* apparently overrules cases holding that the filing of a request for counsel in and of itself satisfies the filing requirement.[80] However, the decision leaves open whether or not filing a motion for the appointment of counsel would toll the statute.[81]

---

[73]The Court noted that tolling might be appropriate where the plaintiff had received inadequate notice; where a motion for appointment of counsel was pending; where the court had led the plaintiff to believe that further action was unnecessary; or where the defendant had misled the plaintiff.

[74]The Court specifically rejected plaintiff's argument that the defendant had not been prejudiced, holding that absence of prejudice becomes relevant only when the plaintiff has presented a reason for invoking the court's equitable powers in the first instance. 466 U.S. at 152, 34 FEP at 931. *Accord* Valenzuela v. Kraft, Inc., 801 F.2d 1170, 41 FEP 1849 (9th Cir. 1986), *amended,* 815 F.2d 570, 41 FEP 1849 (9th Cir. 1987) (where plaintiff improperly files Title VII claim in state court, tolling allowed in part because employer placed on notice); Davis v. Sears, Roebuck & Co., 708 F.2d 862, 31 FEP 1525 (1st Cir. 1983) (that defendant suffered no harm from late filing not grounds for equitable tolling).

[75]Gonzalez-Aller Balseyro v. GTE Lenkurt, 702 F.2d 857, 31 FEP 502 (10th Cir. 1983) (where court clerk informed *pro se* plaintiff that filing right-to-sue letter satisfied statute, tolling required). *But see* Millard v. La Pointe's Fashion Store, 736 F.2d 501, 35 FEP 830 (9th Cir. 1984) (merely speaking to clerk does not constitute filing). *See also* pre-*Baldwin County* cases, *infra* note 79.

[76]Johnson v. Al Tech Specialty Steel Corp., 731 F.2d 143, 34 FEP 861 (2d Cir. 1984).

[77]Goddard v. Department of Health & Human Servs., 32 FEP 587 (D.D.C. 1983) (plaintiff employed by EEOC at time right-to-sue notice issued); Miller v. IT&T Corp., 755 F.2d 20, 37 FEP 8 (2d Cir.), *cert. denied,* 474 U.S. 851, 38 FEP 1728 (1985) (attorney knew of rights; no basis for tolling).

[78]*See also* St. Louis v. Alverno College, *supra* note 70; Jones v. Madison Serv. Corp., *supra* note 71 (tolling refused where plaintiff awaiting favorable Supreme Court ruling in another case); Davis v. Sears, Roebuck & Co., *supra* note 74 (tolling refused where plaintiff relied erroneously on distance between her hometown and court).

[79]Suarez v. Little Havana Activities & Nutrition Centers of Dade County, *supra* note 69 (statute tolled where complaint mailed to court in same city on 88th day of period); Loya v. Desert Sands Unified School Dist., 721 F.2d 279, 33 FEP 739 (9th Cir. 1983) (complaint filed although clerk refused to accept because plaintiff used wrong size paper); Quiles v. O'Hare Hilton, 572 F. Supp. 866, 33 FEP 399 (N.D. Ill. 1983) (complaint timely filed on 89th day, although clerk did not file complaint until 94th day).

[80]*See, e.g.,* Judkins v. Beech Aircraft Corp., 723 F.2d 818, 33 FEP 1527, *modified,* 745 F.2d 1330, 36 FEP 367 (11th Cir. 1984); Firle v. Mississippi State Dep't of Educ., 762 F.2d 487, 37 FEP 1817 (5th Cir. 1985) (filing request for appointment of counsel and notice of right-to-sue letter insufficient to be deemed filing).

[81]Lower court cases discussing related issues include Brown v. J.I. Case Co., 756 F.2d 48, 36 FEP 1399 (7th Cir. 1985) (limiting *Baldwin-Wallace* result to cases where plaintiff engages in some form of "inequitable conduct"); Ruiz v. Shelby County Sheriff's Dep't, 725 F.2d 388, 33 FEP 1225 (6th Cir.), *cert. denied,* 469 U.S. 1016, 36 FEP 320 (1984); Neal v. Machinists Local Lodge 2386, 722 F.2d 247, 33 FEP 1229 (5th Cir. 1984). *See also* Mahroom v. Defense Language Inst., 732 F.2d 1439, 34 FEP 1334 (9th Cir. 1984) (filing of letter stating plaintiff seeking counsel, accompanied by right-to-sue notice and EEOC determination, constituted filing); Rice v. Hamilton AFB Commissary, 720 F.2d 1082, 33 FEP

The Supreme Court has held that at least in some circumstances the suit-filing period is tolled for putative class members during the period of time from the filing of the complaint to the denial of class certification.[82]

## E. State Statutes of Limitations and Laches

The Third Circuit raised, but did not rule on, the possibility that the laches defense is not available as a matter of law in actions brought by the federal sovereign, including Title VII actions brought by the EEOC on behalf of others.[83]

In a number of private Title VII actions, the courts have found inadequate factual support for a laches defense, particularly where the plaintiff is proceeding *pro se*.[84] The courts have often focused on requiring proof of actual prejudice to the defendant.[85]

The Eleventh Circuit, however, barred an EEOC court action where five years and eight months elapsed between receipt of the charge and filing suit, and the defendant established unavailability of witnesses and records crucial to its defenses.[86] The analysis remains essentially factual. The Ninth Circuit has denied summary judgment to an employer and a union, sued by a former employee more than nine years after she had filed her EEOC charge, where her attorney's affidavit reflected that he had made repeated efforts to monitor the progress of the charge and that the EEOC had informed him on several occasions that it intended to file suit.[87]

---

468 (9th Cir. 1983) (employee filed complaint by submitting request for counsel, letter stating claim, and copies of administrative decisions).

[82]Crown, Cork & Seal Co. v. Parker, 462 U.S. 345, 31 FEP 1697 (1983).

[83]EEOC v. Great Atl. & Pac. Tea Co., 735 F.2d 69, 80, 34 FEP 1412, 1419–20 (3d Cir.), *cert. dismissed,* 469 U.S. 925 (1984) (court also suggested that district court's authority to protect defendants from prejudice occasioned by delay dealt only with back pay, not maintenance of suit). *But see, e.g.,* cases cited in note 86, *infra.*

[84]Brown v. Continental Can Co., 765 F.2d 810, 38 FEP 695 (9th Cir. 1985) (*pro se* plaintiff not responsible for EEOC's mistakes in processing case; defendant was on notice to preserve records needed for defense); Holsey v. Armour & Co., 743 F.2d 199, 35 FEP 1064 (4th Cir. 1984), *cert. denied,* 470 U.S. 1028, 37 FEP 192 (1985) (plaintiff awaited end of four-year EEOC administrative process); Rozen v. District of Columbia, 702 F.2d 1202, 31 FEP 618 (D.C. Cir. 1983) ("resort to technicalities" is "particularly inappropriate" where legislation is "dependent for its enforcement on laymen"). *See also* Howard v. Roadway Express, 726 F.2d 1529, 1523–33, 34 FEP 341, 344–45 (11th Cir. 1984) (five-year EEOC delay in issuing right-to-sue notice does not bar subsequent private action); Bishopp v. District of Columbia, 602 F. Supp. 1401, 37 FEP 235 (D.D.C. 1985), *rev'd in part and vacated in part,* 788 F.2d 781, 40 FEP 903 (D.C. Cir. 1986) (plaintiffs were unaware of right to initiate lawsuit prior to conclusion of EEOC investigation); Gillum v. District of Columbia Pub. Schools, 32 FEP 231 (D.D.C. 1983) (*pro se* plaintiff not charged with EEOC's mistakes in processing case).

[85]Patzer v. University of Wis. Bd. of Regents, 577 F. Supp. 1553, 1557, 37 FEP 1019, 1022 (W.D. Wis. 1984), *rev'd and remanded,* 763 F.2d 851, 37 FEP 1847 (7th Cir. 1985) (former managers still available to testify; no prejudice despite passage of 11 years, where "detailed recollection" of facts not needed); Jones v. Milwaukee County, 574 F. Supp. 500, 503, 33 FEP 400, 402 (E.D. Wis. 1983) ("no indication" that passage of two years' time obscured facts or rendered witnesses or records unavailable).

[86]EEOC v. Dresser Indus., 668 F.2d 1199, 29 FEP 249 (11th Cir. 1982); *see also* Jeffries v. Chicago Transit Auth., 770 F.2d 676, 38 FEP 1282 (7th Cir. 1985), *cert. denied,* 475 U.S. 1050, 40 FEP 272 (1986) (significant prejudice to defendant justifies bar to suit); EEOC v. Firestone Tire & Rubber Co., 626 F. Supp. 90, 39 FEP 583 (M.D. Ga. 1985) (EEOC precluded from bringing class action five years after filing of individual charges where there was significant prejudice to defendant). *But see* EEOC v. K-Mart Corp., 694 F.2d 1055, 30 FEP 788 (6th Cir. 1982) (no laches found since there was no proof of lack of diligence by the EEOC or prejudice to employer).

[87]Gifford v. Atchison, Topeka & Santa Fe Ry., 685 F.2d 1149, 34 FEP 240 (9th Cir. 1982). *See also* Sunbeam Appliance Co. v. Kelly, 532 F. Supp. 96, 28 FEP 180 (N.D. Ill. 1982) (doctrine of laches did not prevent enforcement of EEOC's subpoena).

Courts continue to deny the applicability of state statutes of limitations in Title VII actions for a variety of reasons.[88]

---

[88]Watson v. Republic Airlines, 553 F. Supp. 939, 944 n.5, 33 FEP 475, 477 (N.D. Ga. 1982) (private plaintiff who never filed charge with EEOC may not rely on 20-year state statute of limitations in Title VII court action for reinstatement and accrued seniority). *See also* EEOC v. Great Atl. & Pac. Tea Co., *supra* note 83 ("no statute of limitations applies" to EEOC action for injunctive relief and back pay).

## CHAPTER 29

# ELECTION AND EXHAUSTION OF REMEDIES

## II. Duty to Exhaust Other Rights

In *Patsy v. Board of Regents of Florida*,[1] the Supreme Court held that plaintiffs who sue in federal court under § 1983 are not required first to exhaust the state administrative remedies available to them. Courts continue to hold that there is no requirement to exhaust administrative remedies under § 1981.[2] Likewise, plaintiffs alleging violation of Title VII need not exhaust contractual grievance procedures.[3] In addition, the Court of Appeals for the District of Columbia Circuit has held that, unlike Title VII, the Equal Pay Act imposes no requirement that federal employees exhaust administrative remedies before seeking judicial review of their claims.[4]

Two recent circuit court decisions have considered administrative exhaustion requirements in public sector suits. The Eleventh Circuit has held that a U.S. Postal Service employee who filed an administrative complaint in 1971 under the then-existing third-party complaint procedure adequately exhausted remedies before commencing a class action, where the regulations at the time the administrative complaint was filed provided no clear means by which class claims could be raised at the administrative level and where the third-party complaint satisfied the purposes underlying the exhaustion requirement.[5] The Tenth Circuit held that enactment of § 505(a)(1) of the Rehabilitation Act of 1973,[6] making applicable "remedies, procedures, and rights" set forth in § 717 of the Civil Rights Act of 1964,[7] evidenced congressional intent to require exhaustion of administrative remedies before an Air Force employee could sue under the Rehabilitation Act.[8]

---

[1]457 U.S. 496, 29 FEP 12 (1982); *see also* Maryland National Capital Park & Planning Comm'n v. Crawford, 59 Md. App. 276, 475 A.2d 494, 34 FEP 1731 (1984), *aff'd,* 307 Md.1, 511 A.2d 1079 (1986) (state administrative remedies need not be exhausted before suit under § 1983 in state court); True v. New York State Dep't of Correctional Servs., 613 F. Supp. 27, 36 FEP 1048 (W.D.N.Y. 1984) (state administrative remedies need not be exhausted and Title VII procedures need not be instituted before § 1983 action in federal court).

[2]Lilly v. Harris-Teeter Supermkt., 720 F.2d 326, 33 FEP 195 (4th Cir. 1983), *cert. denied,* 466 U.S. 951, 34 FEP 1096 (1984); Holt v. Continental Group, 708 F.2d 87, 31 FEP 1468 (2d Cir. 1983), *cert. denied,* 465 U.S. 1030, 33 FEP 1884 (1984).

[3]Knorr v. ARCO Medical Supply Corp., Abbey Richmond Div., 571 F. Supp. 799, 32 FEP 1885 (S.D.N.Y. 1983) (contractual grievance-arbitration procedures not mandatory); Cummings v. Walsh Constr. Co., 561 F. Supp. 872, 31 FEP 930 (S.D. Ga. 1983) (no duty to exhaust employer's own internal grievance procedure).

[4]Ososky v. Wick, 704 F.2d 1264, 31 FEP 777 (D.C. Cir. 1983).

[5]Griffin v. Carlin, 755 F.2d 1516, 37 FEP 741 (11th Cir. 1985).

[6]29 U.S.C. § 794(a)(1).

[7]42 U.S.C. § 2000e-16.

[8]Johnson v. Orr, 747 F.2d 1352, 36 FEP 515 (10th Cir. 1984).

## III. EFFECT OF PRIOR RESORT TO OTHER FORUMS

### A. Resort to Arbitration

In *McDonald v. City of West Branch, Michigan,*[9] the Supreme Court ruled that a prior arbitration award, pursuant to a collective bargaining agreement, does not preclude a claim under § 1983. Similarly, the Sixth and Eighth circuits have held an arbitration award does not preclude a subsequent § 1981 action,[10] and the Seventh Circuit has held that an arbitrator's decision does not preclude an ADEA action.[11]

Litigation continues concerning the weight to accord an arbitrator's findings in a subsequent discrimination lawsuit. In *Becton v. Detroit Terminal of Consolidated Freightways,*[12] the Sixth Circuit rejected the lower court's decision that it was "conclusively bound" by an arbitration decision, but held that "an arbitration decision in favor of the employer is sufficient to carry the employer's burden of *articulating* 'some legitimate, non-discriminatory reason for the employee's rejection' " under the *McDonnell Douglas*[13] analysis.[14] Arbitral awards that allegedly conflict with Title VII conciliation agreements, public policy, or discrimination law are subject to attack in suits to vacate or enforce the award,[15] as well as in discrimination suits.

Where a black female and a white female were discharged for fighting, and an arbitration award reinstated the white but upheld the black's discharge, a district court ruled the black could not sue the employer for implementing the award under Title VII or § 1981. In balancing the federal policy promoting labor peace through use of arbitration and the "equally important" right to a trial *de novo* under Title VII, the court distinguished the case from *Gardner-Denver*[16] because the act complained of was the implementation of the award—not the discharge which was the subject of the award—whereas in *Gardner-Denver* the same act was the subject of both proceedings.[17]

---

[9] 466 U.S. 284, 115 LRRM 3646 (1984).

[10] Rodgers v. General Motors Corp., Fisher Body Div., 739 F.2d 1102, 35 FEP 349 (6th Cir. 1984), *cert. denied,* 470 U.S. 1054, 37 FEP 376 (1985); Wilmington v. J.I. Case Co., 793 F.2d 909, 40 FEP 1833 (8th Cir. 1986).

[11] Johnson v. University of Wis.-Milwaukee, 783 F.2d 59, 39 FEP 1822 (7th Cir. 1986).

[12] 687 F.2d 140, 29 FEP 1078 (6th Cir. 1982), *cert. denied,* 460 U.S. 1040, 31 FEP 368 (1983). The lower court's decision is cited at p. 1084 n.23 of the Second Edition.

[13] McDonnell Douglas Corp. v. Green, 411 U.S. 792, 5 FEP 965 (1973).

[14] 687 F.2d at 142, 29 FEP at 1080 (emphasis by the court). *But see* Wilmington v. J.I. Case Co., *supra* note 10 (no abuse of discretion not to instruct jury that arbitrator's finding of just cause for discharge satisfied employer's burden to articulate legitimate, nondiscriminatory reason).

[15] *See* W.R. Grace & Co. v. Rubber Workers Local 759, 461 U.S. 757, 31 FEP 1409 (1983) (arbitrator's back pay award to employees laid off contrary to seniority provisions of collective bargaining agreement, but in conformity with conciliation agreement between employer and the EEOC, did not "inappropriately affect" public policy encouraging voluntary compliance with Title VII); General Contractor's Ass'n of N.Y. v. Teamsters Local 282, 28 FEP 1203 (S.D.N.Y. 1982) (arbitrator's award vacated on ground, *inter alia,* that it would conflict with Title VII and Executive Order 11246).

[16] Alexander v. Gardner-Denver Co., 415 U.S. 36, 7 FEP 81 (1974).

[17] Wynn v. North Am. Sys., 608 F. Supp. 30, 34 FEP 1869 (N.D. Ohio 1984).

## B. *Res Judicata*

Under the Supreme Court's decision in *Kremer v. Chemical Construction Corp.,* [18] a state court's review of a state administrative decision must be given full faith and credit by the federal court in a subsequent Title VII suit, including dismissal of the Title VII suit if precluded by *res judicata* or collateral estoppel rules.[19] The Court had held earlier in *Allen v. McCurry* [20] that collateral estoppel precludes the relitigation in § 1983 actions of issues previously decided by a state court, but had declined to rule on whether *res judicata* also barred the litigation in a § 1983 action of claims a plaintiff could have raised, but did not, in a prior state proceeding against the same adverse party.[21] Since *Kremer* a number of federal courts have applied *res judicata* and collateral estoppel rules in holding that state court review will bar subsequent actions under §§ 1981, 1983, and 1985,[22] including those where the discrimination claims or alleged violations of federal rights were not raised in the state proceeding.[23] The Supreme Court held in *Migra v. Warren City School District Board of Education* [24] that a plaintiff is barred by *res judicata* from raising in a federal lawsuit §§ 1983 and 1985 claims that she failed to raise in a prior state court action for breach of her employment contract. As in *Kremer,* preclusive effect is determined by state law.[25]

---

[18]456 U.S. 461, 28 FEP 1412 (1982). *Kremer* has been given retrospective effect in *Unger v. Consolidated Foods Corp.,* 693 F.2d 703, 707, 30 FEP 441, 444–48 (7th Cir. 1982), *cert. denied,* 460 U.S. 1102, 31 FEP 904 (1983). *Cf.* McDonald v. City of West Branch, Mich., *supra* note 9 (arbitrator's decision that there was just cause for discharge does not preclude § 1983 action).

[19]*See* Hirst v. California, 758 F.2d 417, 37 FEP 982 (9th Cir. 1985) (state court decision affirming state personnel board decision given *res judicata* effect); Wakeen v. Hoffman House, 724 F.2d 1238, 33 FEP 1476 (7th Cir. 1983), *amended,* 33 FEP 1816 (1984) (applying *Kremer* in Title VII context); Burney v. Polk Community College, 728 F.2d 1374, 34 FEP 727 (11th Cir. 1984) (Title VII claim barred by state court affirmance of community college board of trustees decision); Rolfe v. Arizona, 578 F. Supp. 1467, 37 FEP 276 (D. Ariz. 1983) (Title VII claim barred by prior state court affirmance of personnel board findings); Cooper v. Oak Park School Dist., 624 F. Supp. 515, 39 FEP 1227 (E.D. Mich. 1986) (Title VII claim barred by state court affirmance of tenure commission finding of just cause for discharge). *But see* Reynolds v. New York State Dep't of Correctional Servs., 568 F. Supp. 747, 32 FEP 1103 (S.D.N.Y. 1983) (refusing to apply *Kremer* where federal and state laws, though facially similar, may lead to different results); Calderon Rosado v. General Elec. Circuit Breakers, 805 F.2d 1085, 42 FEP 579 (1st Cir. 1986) (no *res judicata* effect resulting from state court dismissal with prejudice where employer agreed to permit federal litigation as condition of dismissal).

[20]449 U.S. 90 (1980).

[21]*Id.* at 97 n.10.

[22]*See, e.g.,* Carpenter v. Reed, 757 F.2d 218 (10th Cir. 1985) (§ 1981 action barred by state court affirmance of prior personnel board decision); Lee v. City of Peoria, 685 F.2d 196, 29 FEP 892 (7th Cir. 1982); Davis v. United States Steel Corp., United States Steel Supply Div., 688 F.2d 166, 29 FEP 1202 (3d Cir. 1982), *cert. denied,* 460 U.S. 1014, 31 FEP 64 (1983); Capers v. Long Island R.R., 34 FEP 892 (S.D.N.Y. 1984) (§ 1983 claim barred by state court judgment reversing state FEP agency's ruling for former employee, even though constitutional claim not raised in state proceeding).

[23]*See, e.g.,* Bolling v. City & County of Denver, 790 F.2d 67, 40 FEP 1274 (10th Cir. 1986) (§§ 1981 and 1983 claims barred by state court's affirmance of civil service board decision, even though discrimination claim not raised); Brown v. St. Louis Police Dep't, 691 F.2d 393, 30 FEP 18 (8th Cir. 1982), *cert. denied,* 461 U.S. 908 (1983) (prior state court proceeding appealing discharge of black police officer barred §§ 1981, 1983, and 1985 claims, even though race discrimination issue had not been raised in state proceeding). *But see* Foulks v. Ohio Dep't of Rehabilitation & Correction, 713 F.2d 1229, 32 FEP 829 (6th Cir. 1983) (neither *res judicata* nor collateral estoppel bars § 1981 suit against supervisors who could not have been sued in prior state proceedings because under state FEP statute they were not employers subject to suit).

[24]465 U.S. 75, 33 FEP 1345 (1984).

[25]In *Marrese v. American Academy of Orthopaedic Surgeons,* 470 U.S. 373, 53 USLW 4265 (1985), the Court extended the analysis of *Kremer* and held that state preclusion law binds federal courts even with respect to certain statutory claims such as antitrust or (perhaps) Title VII actions over which state courts have no jurisdiction. *But cf.* Betances v. Quiros, 603 F. Supp. 201, 205 (D.P.R. 1985) (state law of *res judicata* inapplicable where plaintiff invokes federal question jurisdiction under §§ 1983 and

Title VII suits have also been barred by *res judicata*[26] and controlled by collateral estoppel[27] even though the prior state court proceedings did not involve discrimination claims.[28] However, a decision by the state court that does not reach the merits of the underlying claim does not preclude a subsequent action because the doctrine of *res judicata* does not apply in these circumstances.[29] Whether it is the plaintiff or defendant who pursues state court review of the administrative decisions has been immaterial for purposes of *res judicata*.[30] However, a prior state court judgment in plaintiff's favor

---

1985(3)). *Compare* Al-Khazraji v. St. Francis College, 784 F.2d 505, 40 FEP 397 (3d Cir. 1986), *aff'd*, 481 U.S. 604, 43 FEP 1305 (1987) (no preclusive effect to state court dismissal for want of prosecution) *with* Parker v. National Corp. for Hous. Partnerships, 619 F. Supp. 1061, 38 FEP 1265 (D.D.C. 1985) (District of Columbia law gives preclusive effect to dismissal for want of prosecution).

[26]Hirst v. California, *supra* note 19; Soto v. Lee Filters Div., 35 FEP 1603 (D.N.J. 1984) (Title VII claim barred by prior state court dismissal of wrongful discharge claim); Clayton v. City of Chicago, No. 81-C4998 (N.D. Ill. June 28, 1982) (barred by dismissal of previous mandamus action brought under state statute and constitution).

[27]Rotert v. Jefferson Fed. Sav. & Loan Ass'n, 623 F. Supp. 1114, 39 FEP 1070 (D. Conn. 1985) (state court affirmance of unemployment compensation decision operated as collateral estoppel on constructive discharge issue); Knox v. Cornell Univ., 30 FEP 433 (N.D.N.Y. 1982) (state court affirmance of unemployment compensation agency decision denying benefits to claimant because of discharge for misconduct collaterally estops relitigation of reason for discharge in subsequent Title VII action). *Contra* Cooper v. City of N. Olmstead, 795 F.2d 1265, 41 FEP 425 (6th Cir. 1986) (no estoppel of Title VII or § 1981 claim created where state court affirmed adverse ruling in unemployment compensation proceeding); Hill v. Coca-Cola Bottling Co. of N.Y., 786 F.2d 550, 40 FEP 639 (2d Cir. 1986) (just cause determination in unemployment compensation proceedings does not necessarily negate discrimination claims under Title VII and § 1981, particularly absent fair opportunity to litigate discrimination claim); Harding v. Ramsay, Scarlett & Co., 599 F. Supp. 180, 36 FEP 717 (D. Md. 1984) (state court affirmance of unemployment compensation decision no bar since discrimination issue was not litigated); Rawson v. Sears, Roebuck & Co., 554 F. Supp. 327, 31 FEP 1354 (D. Colo. 1983), and *supra* Chapter 23 App. B (Colo.) (no collateral estoppel where state court affirmance of unemployment compensation agency decision did not focus on discrimination issue); Goldsmith v. E.I. du Pont de Nemours & Co., 32 FEP 1879, *later proceeding on merits,* 571 F. Supp. 235, 39 FEP 108 (D. Del. 1983) (prior state court affirmance of unemployment compensation agency decision no bar to Title VII and § 1981 claims).

[28]*But see* Ross v. Communications Satellite Corp., 759 F.2d 355, 362, 37 FEP 797 (4th Cir. 1985) (judicially affirmed findings of Maryland unemployment insurance agency not accorded preclusive effect in Title VII case because Maryland law would deny issue preclusion where issue arose in second proceeding under substantially different statute).

[29]Polk v. Yellow Freight Sys., 801 F.2d 190, 41 FEP 1279 (6th Cir. 1986) (court decision affirming adverse ruling by state employment security commission does not preclude Title VII claim where employment security commission could not provide remedy for discrimination); Jones v. City of Alton, 757 F.2d 878, 37 FEP 523 (7th Cir. 1985) (state court affirmance of Civil Service Commission discharge decision did not bar Title VII or § 1983 claims because plaintiff lacked full and fair opportunity to litigate issues); Ross v. Communications Satellite Corp., *supra* note 28 (state court affirmance of unemployment compensation findings has no preclusive effect under Maryland law); Whitfield v. City of Knoxville, 756 F.2d 455, 37 FEP 288 (6th Cir. 1985) (ADEA claim not barred because could not raise in prior state proceeding); Patzer v. University of Wis. Bd. of Regents, 763 F.2d 851, 37 FEP 1847 (7th Cir. 1985) (state court dismissal for lack of personal jurisdiction did not constitute judgment on merits); Grann v. City of Madison, 738 F.2d 786, 35 FEP 296 (7th Cir.), *cert. denied,* 469 U.S. 918, 35 FEP 1800 (1984) (no privity of parties); Clinton v. Georgia Ports Auth., 37 FEP 593 (S.D. Ga. 1985) (*res judicata* not applicable where state court dismissal pertained to procedural untimeliness issues); Griffin v. George B. Buck Consulting Actuaries, 551 F. Supp. 1385, 1386 n.2, 31 FEP 405, 406 (S.D.N.Y. 1982) (state court's refusal to set aside state agency dismissal of claim for failure to file timely notice of appeal did not constitute judicial review of merits); *cf.* New Orleans S.S. Ass'n v. EEOC, 680 F.2d 23, 29 FEP 398 (5th Cir. 1982) (neither *res judicata* nor collateral estoppel bars EEOC investigation of issues similar to but not same as those addressed in earlier litigation). *But see* Santos v. Todd Pac. Shipyards Corp., 585 F. Supp. 482, 35 FEP 681 (C.D. Cal. 1984) (state court judgment on statute of limitations issue is final judgment entitled to *res judicata* effect).

[30]*See* Trujillo v. County of Santa Clara, 775 F.2d 1359, 44 FEP 954 (9th Cir. 1985) (*res judicata* applicable although it was employer who appealed state administrative decision to state court); Hickman v. Electronic Keyboarding Co., 741 F.2d 230, 35 FEP 1281 (8th Cir. 1984) (although state agency, not employee, was party in state court's action, employee was in privity and hence bound by decision); Davis v. United States Steel Corp., United States Steel Supply Div., *supra* note 22, 688 F.2d at 170, 29 FEP at 1205–06 (§ 1981 action); Capers v. Long Island R.R., 31 FEP 668 (S.D.N.Y. 1983) (Title VII claim barred though employee-initiated state court review); Gonsalves v. Alpine Country Club, 727 F.2d 27, 33 FEP 1817 (1st Cir. 1984) (Title VII action).

may not bar his subsequent Title VII action if such an application of *res judicata* would defeat the purposes of Title VII.[31]

Since *Kremer* and *Migra,* a number of federal courts have applied the doctrines of *res judicata* and collateral estoppel in holding that state court review will bar subsequent actions under §§ 1981, 1983, and 1985,[32] including those situations where the claims of discrimination or a violation of federal rights were not raised in the state proceeding.[33] Similarly, a federal court has held that an ADEA action can be barred by an earlier state court proceeding, so long as the plaintiff has in fact been given the opportunity to raise the claim in the state forum.[34]

Although *Kremer* states that "unreviewed administrative determinations by state agencies * * * should not preclude [federal court] review even if such a decision were to be afforded preclusive effect in a State's own courts,"[35] several recent federal court opinions have interpreted this rule as applying only to those administrative determinations which render only investigative decisions or are purely administrative, as opposed to those in which the agency acted in a judicial capacity.[36] In *University of Tennessee v. Elliott,*[37] the Supreme Court concluded that Congress did not intend unreviewed state administrative proceedings to have preclusive effect in Title VII actions. According to the Court in *Elliott,* however, where the state agency acted in a judicial capacity to resolve issues properly before it, and the parties were afforded an adequate opportunity to litigate their claims, a federal court hearing an action premised upon §§ 1981, 1983, or 1985 must give the agency's determination the same preclusive effect to which it would be entitled in state court.[38] Whether a

---

[31]Patzer v. University of Wis. Bd. of Regents, *supra* note 29. *But see* Trujillo v. County of Santa Clara, *supra* note 30.

[32]*See, e.g.,* Gorin v. Osborne, 756 F.2d 834 (11th Cir. 1985); Santos v. Todd Pac. Shipyards Corp., *supra* note 29.

[33]*See, e.g.,* Casagrande v. Agoritsas, 748 F.2d 47, 49 (1st Cir. 1984) (double costs assessed against employee-appellant in part because of "obvious similarity" between state claims and subsequent § 1983 action); Brown v. St. Louis Police Dep't, *supra* note 23. *But cf.* Carpenter v. Reed, 757 F.2d 218 (10th Cir. 1985) (Title VII and § 1981 claims accorded preclusive effect only if plaintiff was required by state law to raise discrimination claims, and only if state administrative agency had authority to hear them); Barnell v. Paine Webber Jackson & Curtis, 614 F. Supp. 373, 44 FEP 563 (S.D.N.Y. 1985) (*res judicata* and collateral estoppel do not preclude complainant from asserting that Title VII charge-filing period should be tolled, even though she failed to make that claim in state court, where state law did not permit equitable tolling).

[34]Whitfield v. City of Knoxville, *supra* note 29.

[35]Kremer v. Chemical Constr. Corp., 456 U.S. 461, 470 n.7, 28 FEP 1412, 1416 (1982).

[36]Heath v. John Morrell & Co., 768 F.2d 245, 38 FEP 700 (8th Cir. 1985); Jones v. Progress Lighting Corp., 595 F. Supp. 1031, 36 FEP 25 (E.D. Pa. 1984); Parker v. Danville Metal Stamping Co., 603 F. Supp. 182, 37 FEP 250 (C.D. Ill. 1985); Reedy v. Florida Dep't of Educ., 605 F. Supp. 172, 37 FEP 754 (N.D. Fla. 1985); *see also* Zywicki v. Versa Technology Moxness Prods. Co. Div., 610 F. Supp. 50, 37 FEP 710 (E.D. Wis. 1985), *rev'd and remanded,* 801 F.2d 1343, 43 FEP 1648 (7th Cir. 1986).

[37]478 U.S. 788, 41 FEP 177 (1986).

[38]*See also* Buckhalter v. Pepsi-Cola Gen. Bottlers, 820 F.2d 892, 43 FEP 1615 (7th Cir. 1987) (unreviewed decision of human rights commission not entitled to preclusive effect in Title VII action, but *res judicata* with respect to § 1983 claim); Brown v. J.I. Case, 813 F.2d 848, 43 FEP 355 (7th Cir.), *cert. denied,* 484 U.S. 912 (1987) (state court decision overturning state administrative agency's finding of racial discrimination is *res judicata* with respect to subsequent Title VII action); Yancy v. McDevitt, 802 F.2d 1025, 46 FEP 260 (8th Cir. 1986) (school board termination proceeding later upheld by arbitrator had preclusive effect on subsequent § 1981, § 1983 action); Abramson v. Council Bluffs Community School Dist., 808 F.2d 1307, 42 FEP 163 (8th Cir. 1986); Scroggins v. Kansas, 802 F.2d 1289 (10th Cir. 1986) (state civil service decision, which was judicially affirmed, upholding employee's termination was not preclusive on Title VII or § 1983 action where employee was not afforded full and fair opportunity to litigate discrimination claim). For pre-*Elliott* cases, *compare* Griffen v. Big Spring Indep. School Dist., 706 F.2d 645, 31 FEP 1750 (5th Cir.), *cert. denied,* 464 U.S. 1008, 33 FEP 552 (1983)

similar preclusive rule applies in ADEA cases remains an open question.[39]

A prior federal action may prevent the plaintiff from obtaining a remedy under new theories in a subsequent federal suit. In *Nilsen v. City of Moss Point,*[40] *res judicata* precluded a plaintiff from maintaining an action under § 1983 after the plaintiff's earlier lawsuits, mounting the same challenge under Title VII, had been dismissed as untimely.[41]

Where a single action presents claims under both Title VII and §§ 1981 or 1983, a jury verdict on the §§ 1981/1983 claim will be *res judicata* on the nonjury Title VII issues.[42] Similarly, a jury finding on pendent state claims estops the court from making a contrary ruling on companion nonjury federal claims.[43] Where the court erroneously dismisses jury claims, the estoppel effect of an adverse ruling on related nonjury issues upon the subsequently reinstated jury claims is unclear.[44]

The extent to which the partial settlement of a Title VII claim will bar

---

(state board of education decision does not bar federal action under § 1983 where there is reason to doubt quality and fairness of the board's procedures; state court action for review of school board's decision had been dismissed for lack of jurisdiction) *and* Moore v. Bonner, 695 F.2d 799, 30 FEP 817 (4th Cir. 1982), *cert. denied,* 474 U.S. 827 (1985) (adverse state administrative decision does not bar subsequent federal action under §§ 1981, 1983, and 1985) *with* Snow v. Nevada Dep't of Prisons, 543 F. Supp. 752, 29 FEP 742 (D. Nev. 1982) (plaintiff not barred from pursuing Title VII claim in federal court, but is estopped from relitigating under §§ 1983 and 1985 issues previously decided by administrative agency where there was adequate opportunity to litigate and where agency was acting in judicial capacity). *Cf.* McDonald v. City of West Branch, Mich., 466 U.S. 284, 115 LRRM 3646 (1984) (a federal court may not accord preclusive effect to unappealed arbitration award in a § 1983 case); Patsy v. Board of Regents of Fla., 457 U.S. 496, 514, 29 FEP 12, 20 (1982) (dicta that if exhaustion of state administrative remedies were required prior to § 1983 action, further litigation would be necessary to determine *res judicata* and collateral estoppel effect of particular administrative determinations); Parker v. National Corp. for Hous. Partnerships, 619 F. Supp. 1061, 38 FEP 1265 (D.D.C. 1985) (§ 1981 action barred where claims were dismissed for lack of prosecution). *But cf.* Stafford v. Muscogee County Bd. of Educ., 688 F.2d 1383, 29 FEP 1773 (11th Cir. 1982) (unsuccessful pursuit of HEW administrative procedure under Title VI does not preclude race bias complainant from proceeding in federal court under Title VII or § 1981, since HEW proceeding is narrower in scope and not a competent forum for Title VII and § 1981 claims).

[39]*Compare* Duggan v. East Chicago Heights School Dist. 169, Cook County, Ill., Bd. of Educ., 40 FEP 1208 (N.D. Ill. 1986) (ADEA claim barred by prior state school hearing) *with* Johnson v. University of Wis.-Milwaukee, 783 F.2d 59, 39 FEP 1822 (7th Cir. 1986) (unemployment appeal agency decision not entitled to *res judicata* effect in ADEA action because issues of misconduct and age discrimination are different), Mack v. South Bay Beer Distribs. dba Bay Beer Distribs., 798 F.2d 1279, 41 FEP 1224 (9th Cir. 1986) (unemployment compensation hearing not preclusive of ADEA claim) *and* Kendall v. C.F. Indus., 624 F. Supp. 1102, 40 FEP 1658 (N.D. Ill. 1986) (misconduct issues in unemployment hearing were different from ADEA issues).

[40]701 F.2d 556, 561, 31 FEP 612, 614 (5th Cir. 1983) (en banc); *see also* Fleming v. Travenol Laboratories, 707 F.2d 829, 31 FEP 1219 (5th Cir. 1983) (Title VII suit for alleged sex discrimination barred by previous unsuccessful action under § 1983 and Fourteenth Amendment for alleged racial discrimination); Poe v. John Deere Co., 695 F.2d 1103, 30 FEP 827 (8th Cir. 1982) (*res judicata* bars tort claims in second federal diversity lawsuit filed after plaintiff was denied leave to add tort claims to her earlier § 1981 complaint); Kalodner v. Philadelphia School Dist. Bd. of Educ., 558 F. Supp. 1124, 34 FEP 302 (E.D. Pa. 1983) (Title VII suit barred by prior class action judgment based on Fourteenth Amendment); Talley v. City of De Soto, 37 FEP 375 (N.D. Tex. 1985) (action under § 1983 precluded by prior Title VII action dismissed on jurisdictional grounds).

[41]*See* Miller v. United States Postal Serv., 825 F.2d 62, 44 FEP 1049 (5th Cir. 1987) (adverse judgment in Title VII action is *res judicata* on subsequent claim of handicap discrimination under § 501, even where Title VII action was dismissed as untimely, where § 501 claim could have been raised in original proceeding).

[42]Ward v. Texas Employment Comm'n, 823 F.2d 907, 44 FEP 849 (5th Cir. 1987); Garza v. City of Omaha, 814 F.2d 553, 43 FEP 572 (8th Cir. 1987).

[43]Kitchen v. Chippewa Valley Schools, 825 F.2d 1004, 44 FEP 663 (6th Cir. 1987).

[44]*Compare* Ritter v. Mount St. Mary's College, 814 F.2d 986, 43 FEP 654 (4th Cir.), *cert. denied,* 484 U.S. _____, 45 FEP 200 (1987) (findings of fact in Title VII bench trial collaterally estop relitigation of those facts to a jury on EPA and ADEA counts even where jury claims were wrongly dismissed and should have been tried at same time as Title VII count) *with* Hussein v. Oshkosh Motor Truck Co., 816 F.2d 348, 43 FEP 857 (7th Cir. 1987) (adverse ruling on Title VII claim does not estop litigation of wrongly dismissed § 1981 claim; permitting estoppel in these circumstances would deprive plaintiff of Seventh Amendment jury trial right).

subsequent attempts to obtain additional relief was raised in *Jordan v. County of Los Angeles.*[45] The named plaintiff in a class action settled his individual back pay claim after the district court denied his motion for class certification, but the settlement failed to provide for the plaintiff's release of claims for injunctive relief. The plaintiff subsequently appealed the denial of class certification and the Ninth Circuit held that the settlement did not bar him from representing a class of plaintiffs seeking injunctive relief.[46] Although a private consent decree may not necessarily operate as *res judicata* to preclude a subsequent EEOC investigation,[47] a class action settlement may resolve, and therefore bar, the claim of an individual who received notice of the settlement and did not opt out.[48]

The offensive use of collateral estoppel was denied in *Davis v. West Community Hospital*[49] because the parties opposing estoppel had not had a fair opportunity to litigate the issues.

*Res judicata* principles also have been applied by the Department of Labor. In *In re University of Texas at Austin,*[50] the Secretary of Labor concluded that an investigation by OFCCP under Executive Order 11246 was precluded by a prior ruling of nondiscrimination in a Title VII action brought by the complainant.

## C. Tolling

Consistent with the Supreme Court's holding that prior resort to contractual grievance procedures will not toll Title VII or § 1981 time limits, it has been held that the use of arbitration procedures under a collective bargaining agreement by federal employees does not toll the running of the 30-day limitations period for federal employees to file administrative complaints with their agencies (the latter being a prerequisite for a Title VII suit by federal employees).[51]

---

[45]669 F.2d 1311, 28 FEP 518 (9th Cir.), *vacated on other grounds,* 459 U.S. 810, 29 FEP 1560 (1982), *on remand,* 713 F.2d 503, 33 FEP 1435, *amended,* 726 F.2d 1366, 36 FEP 1592 (9th Cir. 1984); *cf.* Freeman v. Motor Convoy, 700 F.2d 1339, 31 FEP 517 (11th Cir. 1983) (conciliation agreement based on Title VII claim bars § 1981 claim though not explicitly mentioned in conciliation agreement).

[46]669 F.2d at 1317–18 & n.3, 28 FEP at 552.

[47]*See* EEOC v. Children's Hosp. Medical Center of N. Cal., 719 F.2d 1426, 33 FEP 461 (9th Cir. 1983) (court avoiding resolution of "difficult question" of preclusive effect of consent decree on claims arising after entry of decree).

[48]King v. South Cent. Bell Tel. & Tel. Co., 790 F.2d 524, 40 FEP 1355 (6th Cir. 1986); Johnson v. American Airlines, 157 Cal. App.3d 427, 203 Cal. Rptr. 638, 38 FEP 1017 (1984). *But cf.* Cooper v. Federal Reserve Bank of Richmond, 467 U.S. 867, 35 FEP 1 (1984) (although adverse class decision on merits bars further litigation of class claims, individual claims are not barred).

[49]786 F.2d 677, 40 FEP 800 (5th Cir. 1986).

[50]38 FEP 886 (1985).

[51]Sales v. Bolger, 35 FEP 1803 (E.D. Mo. 1983).

## CHAPTER 30

# LITIGATION PROCEDURE

## I. EFFECT OF DEFICIENCIES IN EEOC ADMINISTRATIVE PROCESS ON CHARGING PARTY'S RIGHT TO SUE

Courts continue generally to hold that the EEOC's failure to comply with procedural requirements does not bar a Title VII suit by the charging party.[1] Courts are reluctant to penalize a charging party for mistakes made

---

[1] *EEOC errors in charge filing do not bar action:* McKee v. McDonnell Douglas Technical Servs. Co., 700 F.2d 260, 31 FEP 383, *amended,* 705 F.2d 776, 31 FEP 1672 (5th Cir. 1983) (dismissed for failure to file charge improper where charging party made every effort to file but EEOC refused to accept claim); Larsen v. Jewel Cos., 34 FEP 640 (N.D. Ill. 1983) (summary judgment inappropriate on claims not included in EEOC charges where question of fact exists whether charging parties informed EEOC of additional claims and EEOC refused to include same in charges).

*EEOC failure to defer charge does not bar action:* Carter v. Smith Food King, 765 F.2d 916, 120 LRRM 2479 (9th Cir. 1985) (plaintiff not required to exhaust administrative remedies and may rely on EEOC's interpretation of statute); Williams v. Owens-Illinois, 665 F.2d 918, 27 FEP 1273, *modified and reh'g denied,* 28 FEP 1820 (9th Cir.), *cert. denied,* 459 U.S. 971, 30 FEP 56 (1982) (plaintiffs should not be prejudiced by EEOC's failure to follow its own policy of deferring to state agency); Deyo v. City of Deer Park, 664 F.2d 518, 27 FEP 1348 (5th Cir. 1981) (EEOC's erroneous prosecution of case during state agency deferral period will not bar action).

*EEOC failure to serve charge on respondent does not bar action:* Waiters v. Robert Bosch Corp., 683 F.2d 89, 29 FEP 401 (4th Cir. 1982) (EEOC failure to notify employer of charge does not bar action). *But see* EEOC v. AirGuide Corp., 29 FEP 236 (S.D. Fla. 1978) (employer so prejudiced by EEOC failure to notify of charge that dismissal with prejudice is warranted).

*EEOC failure to investigate does not bar action:* Oglesby v. Coca-Cola Bottling Co. of Chicago/ Wis., 620 F. Supp. 1336, 39 FEP 327 (N.D. Ill. 1985) (court rejected defendant's argument that EEOC's failure to investigate necessitated dismissal of ADEA charge); Ferguson v. E.I. du Pont de Nemours & Co., 560 F. Supp. 1172, 31 FEP 795 (D. Del. 1983) (claim not precluded because of EEOC's failure to investigate).

*EEOC failure to conciliate does not bar action:* Sedlacek v. Hach, 752 F.2d 333, 36 FEP 1253 (8th Cir. 1985) (EEOC's failure to attempt conciliation cannot affect complainant's substantive rights); EEOC v. Hernando Bank, 724 F.2d 1188, 34 FEP 15 (5th Cir. 1984) (conciliation is not a precondition to filing of suit to enforce substantive provisions to Equal Pay Act; inadequate conciliation efforts do not bar judicial proceedings); EEOC v. Home of Economy, 712 F.2d 356, 32 FEP 599 (8th Cir. 1983) (EEOC not required to conciliate before bringing Equal Pay Act proceeding); EEOC v. Colgate-Palmolive Co., 34 FEP 1551 (S.D.N.Y. 1983) (failure of EEOC to conciliate does not warrant dismissal); Donaldson v. Cafritz Co., 30 FEP 436 (D.D.C. 1981) (EEOC failure to attempt conciliation does not justify dismissal of ADEA action).

*Charge not under oath does not bar action:* Casavantes v. California State Univ., 732 F.2d 1441, 34 FEP 1336 (9th Cir. 1984) (plaintiff's filing of an Intake Questionnaire sufficient "charge" to initiate administrative process); Price v. Southwestern Bell Tel. Co., 687 F.2d 74, 29 FEP 1584 (5th Cir. 1982) (verification of charge is not jurisdictional prerequisite to maintaining Title VII action); Watson v. Gulf & W. Indus., 650 F.2d 990, 26 FEP 1180 (9th Cir. 1981) (employee is not responsible for such EEOC failures as permitting claimant to mail it an unnotarized charge).

*EEOC failure to issue notice of right to sue when charging party entitled to it does not bar action:* Baldwin County Welcome Center v. Brown, 466 U.S. 147, 34 FEP 929, *reh'g denied,* 467 U.S. 1231 (1984), *on remand,* 740 F.2d 833 (11th Cir. 1984); Antoine v. United States Postal Serv., 781 F.2d 433, 39 FEP 1613 (5th Cir. 1986) (applied *Brown* retroactively to dismiss because Federal Rules of Civil Procedure 3 and 8 were not met by papers filed); Firle v. Mississippi State Dep't of Educ., 762 F.2d 487, 37 FEP 1817 (5th Cir. 1985) (*Brown* followed; plaintiff's right-to-sue notice and request for appointment of counsel was not adequate pleading; amended complaint did not relate back); Moore v. City of Charlotte, 754 F.2d 1100, 36 FEP 1582 (4th Cir.), *cert. denied,* 472 U.S. 1021, 37 FEP 1816 (1985) (EEOC rather than U.S. Attorney General issued right-to-sue notice); Gooding v. Warner-Lambert Co., 744 F.2d 354, 35 FEP 1707 (3d Cir. 1984) (issuance of right-to-sue notice not jurisdictional); Perdue v. Roy Stone Transfer Corp., 690 F.2d 1091, 1093, 29

by the EEOC, and generally will not dismiss pending actions unless the charging party is responsible for the procedural problem.[2] An employer who is prejudiced by failure to receive timely notice of a charge, however, may claim that the doctrine of laches requires dismissal.[3] A charging party has no right of action under Title VII or the U.S. Constitution against the EEOC for its administrative failings.[4]

---

FEP 1673, 1674–75 (4th Cir. 1982) ("it is entitlement to a 'right to sue' notice, rather than its actual issuance or receipt, which is a prerequisite to the jurisdiction of the federal courts"); Bradford v. General Tel. Co. of Mich., 618 F. Supp. 390, 44 FEP 80, 121 LRRM 2106 (W.D. Mich. 1985) (entitlement not possession of right-to-sue notice is prerequisite to jurisdiction); State, County & Municipal Employees Dist. Council 47 v. Bradley, 619 F. Supp. 381, 39 FEP 1565 (E.D. Pa. 1985), *vacated,* 795 F.2d 310, 41 FEP 273 (3d Cir. 1986) (absolute failure to file charge with EEOC necessitates dismissal of Title VII claim); Bishopp v. District of Columbia, 602 F. Supp. 1401, 37 FEP 235 (D.D.C. 1985), *rev'd in part and vacated in part,* 788 F.2d 781, 40 FEP 903 (D.C. Cir. 1986) (*Rozen* followed; action not barred by laches where delay not unreasonable and defendants did not show prejudice); Rozen v. District of Columbia, 702 F.2d 1202, 31 FEP 618 (D.C. Cir. 1983) (*pro se* complainant not precluded from suit where EEOC delayed issuance of right-to-sue notice for 21 months after reasonable cause determination); Pole v. Citibank, N.A., 556 F. Supp. 822, 31 FEP 751 (S.D.N.Y. 1983) (plaintiff not precluded from suing where EEOC delivered notice to prior address); *cf.* Espinoza v. Missouri Pac. R.R., 754 F.2d 1247, 37 FEP 415 (5th Cir. 1985) (case dismissed because notice given to plaintiff's spouse despite plaintiff's absence from home); St. Louis v. Alverno College, 744 F.2d 1314, 35 FEP 1715 (7th Cir. 1984) (plaintiff failed to tell EEOC of change of address, therefore 90-day filing limit began to run when notice was delivered to his most recent address known to the EEOC); Pinkard v. Pullman-Standard, 678 F.2d 1211, 29 FEP 216, *reh'g denied,* 685 F.2d 1383 (5th Cir. 1982), *cert. denied,* 459 U.S. 1105, 30 FEP 1048 (1983) (subsequent receipt of right-to-sue notice cures any defect caused by suing before obtaining notice). *But see* Mills v. Jefferson Bank E., 559 F. Supp. 34, 35 FEP 1384 (D. Colo. 1983) (premature issuance of right-to-sue notice invalid and case dismissed). As discussed in Chapter 28 (Timeliness), issuance of a right-to-sue notice during litigation generally resolves a motion to dismiss based upon failure to obtain a notice prior to suit.

  *Agency failure to follow certain procedures does not bar action:* Waiters v. Robert Bosch Corp., *supra* (employee's affidavit constitutes charge even though it lacks employer's address as required by EEOC regulation); *cf.* Logan v. Zimmerman Brush Co., 455 U.S. 422, 28 FEP 9 (1982) (charging party denied constitutionally protected property right by state court's dismissal of action for state FEP agency's neglect to hold settlement conference within period provided by state law).

  [2]Solomon v. Hardison, 746 F.2d 699, 36 FEP 261 (11th Cir. 1984) (right-to-sue request waived); Bihler v. Singer Co., 710 F.2d 96, 32 FEP 66 (3d Cir. 1983) (while court's jurisdiction not dependent upon EEOC having taken action on charge, charge itself must notify agency of claim; where charge does not do so, dismissal for failure to exhaust proper); Edwards v. Department of the Army, 708 F.2d 1344, 32 FEP 658 (8th Cir. 1983) (failure to supply allegations of individual harm upon request of EEOC results in defective charge and dismissal); Hrivnak v. First of Mich. Corp., 617 F. Supp. 990, 39 FEP 1339 (E.D. Mich. 1985) (case dismissed for plaintiff's failure to pursue administrative remedies); Wasilchuk v. Harvey's Wagon Wheel, 610 F. Supp. 206, 39 FEP 237 (D. Nev. 1985) (EEOC's oversight in filling out Notice of Dismissal of Charge did not preclude jurisdiction); McLemore v. Interstate Motor Freight Sys., 33 FEP 1384 (N.D. Ala. 1984) (suit dismissed because charging party found in part responsible for eight-year administrative delay at agency level); Bennett v. Russ Berrie & Co., 564 F. Supp. 1576, 32 FEP 225 (N.D. Ind. 1983) (dismissal for failure to file charge, even though attorney filed letter with EEOC outlining claim).

  [3]*See, e.g.,* Jeffries v. Chicago Transit Auth., 770 F.2d 676, 38 FEP 1282 (7th Cir. 1985), *cert. denied,* 475 U.S. 1050, 40 FEP 272 (1986) (ten-year administrative delay bars suit where complainant did nothing to force conclusion of EEOC processing); EEOC v. Bethlehem Steel Corp., 765 F.2d 427, 38 FEP 345 (4th Cir. 1985) (reversed laches ruling because no prejudice shown); EEOC v. Firestone Tire & Rubber Co., 626 F. Supp. 90, 39 FEP 583 (M.D. Ga. 1985) (EEOC's unreasonable five-year delay in filing complaint prejudiced defendant company; case dismissed on laches ground); EEOC v. Martin Processing, 533 F. Supp. 227, 28 FEP 1825 (W.D. Va. 1982) (laches applied to bar suit where employer disputed receiving notice of charge).

  [4]Gillis v. Department of Health & Human Servs., 759 F.2d 565, 53 USLW 2554 (6th Cir. 1985); Ward v. EEOC, 719 F.2d 311, 33 FEP 294 (9th Cir. 1983), *cert. denied,* 466 U.S. 953, 34 FEP 1096 (1984) (charging party may not sue EEOC for negligent processing of charge); McCottrell v. EEOC, 726 F.2d 350, 33 FEP 1880 (7th Cir. 1984) (Title VII provides no cause of action against EEOC to challenge its processing of charge); Feldstein v. EEOC, 547 F. Supp. 97, 29 FEP 1394 (D. Mass. 1982) (no explicit or implied right of action against EEOC exists under Title VII, Administrative Procedure Act, or U.S. Constitution); Chastain v. Western Elec. Co., 27 FEP 77 (N.D. Cal. 1981) (EEOC not proper party to suit for its failure to notify plaintiffs of their exclusion from class); *see also* Polk v. Kramarsky, 711 F.2d

## II. SUIT AGAINST PARTIES NOT NAMED IN EEOC CHARGE

### A. Introduction

Courts continue to apply different standards in determining whether suit is permissible against a party not formally named as a respondent in the charge of discrimination. On the one hand, the Fifth and Eleventh circuits, following the lead of the Ninth Circuit in *Kaplan v. Stage Employees, IATSE,*[5] have adopted the *Sanchez*[6] rule and permit suit against an unnamed party where the party's involvement is likely to have been revealed in the course of the EEOC investigation which could reasonably have been expected to grow out of the charge.[7] By contrast, the approach applied in the Fourth Circuit appears to be more stringent and to require that the party be named somewhere in the body of the charge.[8] The Sixth[9] and Eighth[10] circuits

---

505, 37 FEP 1150 (2d Cir.), *cert. denied,* 464 U.S. 1000 (1983) (EEOC deferred to state agency which improperly held claim for seven years; because federal claims survived, no right of action accrued against state agency).

[5]525 F.2d 1354, 1358–59, 11 FEP 872, 876 (9th Cir. 1975); *see also* Wrighten v. Metropolitan Hosps., 726 F.2d 1346, 1352–53, 33 FEP 1714, 1718–19 (9th Cir. 1984) (management company providing supervisory personnel for hospital housekeeping department could be sued by discharged hospital employee even though not named in charge where it was involved in discriminatory acts); Chung v. Pomona Valley Community Hosp., 667 F.2d 788, 792, 28 FEP 30, 33 (9th Cir. 1982) (physician supervisors who denied plaintiff promotion could have anticipated being sued); *cf.* Cooper v. United States Postal Serv., 740 F.2d 714, 35 FEP 364 (9th Cir. 1984), *cert. denied,* 471 U.S. 1022, 37 FEP 951 (1985) (naming Postal Service rather than Postmaster General was fatal).

[6]Sanchez v. Standard Brands, 431 F.2d 455, 2 FEP 788, 796 *and* 2 FEP 912 (5th Cir. 1970).

[7]Walls v. Mississippi State Dep't of Pub. Welfare, 730 F.2d 306, 317–18, 34 FEP 1114, 1122–23 (5th Cir. 1984), *on remand,* 624 F. Supp. 46, 41 FEP 1206 (N.D. Miss. 1985) (black applicant's claims could include challenge to state examinations even though failed to name state Merit System Council, which administers tests, in EEOC charge, because charge could be read to encompass claim against entire state system); Hamm v. Board of Regents of Fla., 708 F.2d 647, 649–50, 32 FEP 441, 442–43, *reh'g denied,* 715 F.2d 580 (11th Cir. 1983) (complaint dismissed against two state agencies not named in or on charge because unclear whether scope of EEOC investigation which could reasonably grow out of charge would have included them).

[8]Dickey v. Greene, 603 F. Supp. 102, 105, 36 FEP 905, 907 (E.D.N.C. 1984), *on remand from* 710 F.2d 1003, 31 FEP 1528 (4th Cir. 1983), *modified,* 729 F.2d 957, 34 FEP 336 (4th Cir. 1984) (en banc) (state agency executives not named as respondents or in body of charge dismissed but executive named only in body of charge not dismissed); *see also* Acampora v. Boise Cascade Corp., 635 F. Supp. 66, 70–72, 40 FEP 1468, 1471–72 (D.N.J. 1986) (suit against manager named in body of charge but not designated as a respondent held permissible); Arenas v. Ladish Co., 619 F. Supp. 1304, 1306–8, 39 FEP 740, 741–42 (E.D. Wis. 1985) (same); Pauls v. Elaine Revell, Inc., 571 F. Supp. 1018, 1020–21, 33 FEP 1182, 1183–84 (N.D. Ill. 1983) (claimant permitted to sue president and chairman of defendant company where they were sufficiently named in charge which focused on their activity); Small v. Bethlehem Steel Corp., 33 FEP 414, 417 (D. Md. 1983) (foreman named in body of charge could anticipate being sued because he was also acting as agent of corporate interests); Barone v. Hackett, 602 F. Supp. 481, 484, 40 FEP 961, 963 (D.R.I. 1984) (suit against state allowed where named in Intake Questionnaire even though not named in charge drafted by EEOC official). *But see* Curtis v. Continental Ill. Nat'l Bank, 568 F. Supp. 740, 743–44, 32 FEP 1540, 1542 (N.D. Ill. 1983) (unnamed supervisor not subject to suit where he did not appear in EEOC investigation and had no opportunity to resolve employee's discrimination claims).

[9]Romain v. Kurek, 772 F.2d 281, 283, 38 FEP 1599, 1599–1600 (6th Cir. 1985) (summary judgment reversed because genuine issue of fact had been raised whether there was a clear identity of interest between restaurant and purported co-owner); Jones v. Teamsters Local 299, 748 F.2d 1083, 1086, 36 FEP 569, 570–71 (6th Cir. 1984) (unnamed union dismissed because its interests were not similar to those of named employer).

[10]Greenwood v. Ross, 778 F.2d 448, 450–52, 40 FEP 435, 437–38 (8th Cir. 1985) (sufficient identity of interest between university named in charge and unnamed chancellor, athletic director, and Board of Trustees); Sedlacek v. Hach, *supra* note 1, at 335–36, 36 FEP at 1254–55 (named and unnamed parties were found to be a "single employer" for Title VII jurisdictional purposes and hence to have substantial identity).

have joined the Third,[11] Seventh,[12] and Tenth[13] circuits in taking a middle ground and look principally at whether the named and unnamed parties have an "identity of interests."

## B. Circumstances in Which Joinder of Unnamed Party Has Been Permitted

### 1. Where Injustice Would Otherwise Result to Plaintiff and Defendant Named in EEOC Charge: Joinder Pursuant to Rule 19 and Court's Equitable Powers

The Seventh Circuit reversed a dismissal under Rule 19 which was based on the plaintiff's failure to name an indispensable party.[14] The district court had ruled that since the indispensable party had not been named in the EEOC charge, joinder of the party was not feasible. The court of appeals reversed, relying on the Supreme Court's ruling in *Zipes v. Trans World Airlines*[15] that a timely charge with the EEOC is not jurisdictional and is subject to equitable considerations. It then concluded that the failure to name a party is similarly not jurisdictional and remanded for a determination, by a balancing of equitable considerations, whether the remedial purposes of Title VII are best served by permitting suit against the indispensable party.[16]

### 2. Parties Necessary Only for Purposes of Modifying Seniority Provisions of Collective Bargaining Agreements: Joinder Pursuant to Rule 19

The Supreme Court has held that a party not guilty of discrimination may not be subjected to injunctive relief which requires it to share the financial costs of implementing a remedial decree and further requires compliance with goals necessary to eradicate discrimination.[17] However, upon an appropriate evidentiary showing, a party may be retained in a lawsuit and

---

[11]Goodman v. Lukens Steel Co., 777 F.2d 113, 127–28, 39 FEP 658, 669 (3d Cir. 1985), *aff'd,* 482 U.S. _____, 44 FEP 1 (1987) (statute of limitations for unnamed local union cannot be based on state agency charges naming only employer but can be based on later filed EEOC charges naming international and another local); Glus v. G.C. Murphy Co., 629 F.2d 248, 251–52, 23 FEP 86, 87–88 (3d Cir. 1980), *vacated and remanded on other grounds sub nom.* Retail, Wholesale & Dep't Store Union v. G.C. Murphy Co., 451 U.S. 935, 25 FEP 847, *aff'd in relevant part on remand,* 654 F.2d 944, 944, 36 FEP 101, 102 (1981).

[12]Eggleston v. Plumbers Local 130, 657 F.2d 890, 904–8, 26 FEP 1192, 1202–6 (7th Cir. 1981), *cert. denied,* 455 U.S. 1017, 28 FEP 584 (1982) (substantial similarity of interests between named local union and unnamed joint apprenticeship committee); see also Tillman v. City of Milwaukee, 715 F.2d 354, 359–60, 32 FEP 1287, 1291 (7th Cir. 1983) (naming party in EEOC charge is not jurisdictional prerequisite to suit and is subject to balancing of equitable considerations).

[13]Gonzalez-Aller Balseyro v. GTE Lenkurt, 702 F.2d 857, 859–60, 31 FEP 502, 504 (10th Cir. 1983) (remanded for determination whether unnamed parent corporation and named subsidiary have sufficient identity of interests); Romero v. Union Pac. R.R., 615 F.2d 1303, 1311, 22 FEP 338, 344–45 (10th Cir. 1980) (remanded for district court to apply factors in *Glus v. G.C. Murphy Co., supra* note 11, to suit against railroad employee and union general chairman where only railroad union named in charges).

[14]Tillman v. City of Milwaukee, *supra* note 12.

[15]455 U.S. 385, 393, 28 FEP 1, 4, *reh'g denied,* 456 U.S. 940 (1982).

[16]*See also* Jackson v. Seaboard Coast Line R.R., 678 F.2d 992, 1009–10 n.24, 29 FEP 442, 457 n.24 (11th Cir. 1982).

[17]General Bldg. Contractors Ass'n v. Pennsylvania, 458 U.S. 375, 399, 29 FEP 139, 150–52 (1982).

subjected to "minor and ancillary" provisions of an injunctive order necessary to grant complete relief.[18]

### 3. Where There Is Agency Relationship or Substantial Identity Between Named Party and Unnamed Defendant

There are two lines of cases involving the relationship between defendants named in the EEOC charge and unnamed defendants: cases where the defendants are considered substantially identical and cases where the named and unnamed parties have a substantial identity of interests. The first line of cases focuses on whether the two parties are so interrelated that they should be considered a single entity. For instance, a partnership and a corporation, found to be a "single employer" for Title VII jurisdictional purposes, have been held to have a substantial identity permitting suit against both entities even though only the partnership had been named in the charge.[19] Where substantial identity exists, the named party is often considered the alter ego[20] or agent[21] of the unnamed party and both may be sued.

A substantial identity of interests is a broader concept and has been found to exist, in particularly fact-sensitive decisions, in a variety of relationships, including a parent corporation and its subsidiary,[22] an employer and its supervisory employees,[23] a local union and its international,[24] a local union

---

[18]*Id.*, 458 U.S. at 399, 29 FEP at 150–51; *see also* Zipes v. Trans World Airlines, *supra* note 15 (Court reaffirmed its holding in *Teamsters v. United States,* 431 U.S. 324, 14 FEP 1514 (1977), that a union not guilty of discrimination should remain in lawsuit so full relief can be awarded).

[19]Sedlacek v. Hach, 752 F.2d 333, 335–36, 36 FEP 1253, 1254–55 (8th Cir. 1985) (corporation and partnership with which it had subsidiary relationship found to be single employer due to common management and ownership).

[20]Davis v. Buffalo Psychiatric Center, 613 F. Supp. 462, 466, 37 FEP 69, 71–72, *vacated in part,* 623 F. Supp. 19, 39 FEP 1814 (W.D.N.Y. 1985) (citing A. Larson, *Employment Discrimination* §49.42 (1983), for proposition that an unnamed party may be considered "alter ego" of named party if it ws partially responsible for acts of discrimination or exercised sufficient control over discriminating party).

[21]Brewster v. Shockley, 554 F. Supp. 365, 368–70, 30 FEP 1390, 1392–94 (W.D. Va. 1983) (named county Board of Supervisors and Sheriff acted in agency relationship with state board in carrying out alleged discriminatory acts); *cf.* Darnell v. City of Jasper, Ala., 730 F.2d 653, 655–56, 37 FEP 1315, 1316–17 (11th Cir. 1984) (remedy could run against local civil service commission even though not named in charge or lawsuit).

[22]Watson v. Fuller Brush Co., 570 F. Supp. 1299, 1301–2, 33 FEP 585, 587–88 (W.D. Mich. 1983) (employee of subsidiary could sue parent corporation not named in charge where interests of two corporations similar and parent's interest protected by subsidiary); Lynn v. JER Corp., 573 F. Supp. 17, 19–20, 33 FEP 541, 542–43 (M.D. Tenn. 1983) (unnamed subsidiary could be sued even though only parent corporation named in EEOC charge where interests of two identical and subsidiary had actual notice of charge); Jacobson v. American Home Prods. Corp., 36 FEP 559, 562 (N.D. Ill. 1982) (same). *But see* Clouser v. Copperweld Steel Co., 38 FEP 1807, 1808 (N.D. Ohio 1985) (mere existence of parent-subsidiary relationship not sufficient to establish clear identity of interests); Medina v. Spotnail, Inc., 591 F. Supp. 190, 193, 40 FEP 1393, 1394 (N.D. Ill. 1984) (parent corporation not named in charge dismissed where it did not receive actual notice of the charge); Evans v. Meadow Steel Prods., 579 F. Supp. 1391, 1393, 35 FEP 1191, 1192–93 (N.D. Ga. 1984) (claims dismissed against parent company that received notice of charge only because it was acting as subsidiary's representative); *see also* Gonzalez-Aller Balseyro v. GTE Lenkurt, *supra* note 13 (question of fact whether parent and subsidiary have identity of interests).

[23]Greenwood v. Ross, 778 F.2d 448, 450–52, 40 FEP 435, 437–38 (8th Cir. 1985) (identity of interest between university and both chancellor and athletic director); Vermett v. Hough, 606 F. Supp. 732, 738–39, 37 FEP 1624, 1628–29 (W.D. Mich. 1984) (interests of individual officials and police officers substantially similar to those of state police department named in charge, hence no prejudice because their interests would or could have been protected by department in EEOC proceedings). *But see* Duva v. Bridgeport Textron, 632 F. Supp. 880, 882–83, 40 FEP 1388, 1390 (E.D. Pa. 1985) (supervisors' interests substantially similar to those of employer but suffered actual prejudice by being denied opportunity to conciliate).

[24]Goodman v. Lukens Steel Co., 777 F.2d 113, 39 FEP 658 (3d Cir. 1985), *aff'd,* 482 U.S. 656, 44 FEP 1 (1987).

and a joint apprenticeship committee,[25] an independent contractor and its principal client,[26] and a local state agency and a state department.[27] Conversely, it has been recognized that there is no identity of interests between an employer and a union.[28]

### 4. Where Named Party Has Since Been Acquired or Merged With or Succeeded by Different Entity

Additional Circuits have adopted the approach of the Sixth Circuit in *EEOC v. MacMillan Bloedel Containers,*[29] applying NLRB doctrines of successor liability to determine exposure of unnamed successor employers to suit.[30] The test involves a balancing of interests,[31] however, and notice of the existing charge may be critical.[32] The rule has been held inapplicable to purchasers at judicial sales in bankruptcy.[33]

## C. Necessary and Indispensable Parties

### 1. Necessary Parties

A local governmental agency not named in an EEOC charge may be a necessary party because of its regulatory power over a defendant employer,[34] or its participation in the employment process.[35]

### 2. Indispensable Parties

Courts have continued to hold that a suit should not be dismissed under Rule 19 if meaningful relief could be granted despite the absence of certain parties.[36]

---

[25]Tillman v. City of Milwaukee, 715 F.2d 354, 32 FEP 1287 (7th Cir. 1983).

[26]Norwood v. Dale Maintenance Sys., 33 FEP 1730, 1732–33 (N.D. Ill. 1983) (employee of maintenance company could sue building operator not named in EEOC charge where contractor knew of charge and imposed on maintenance company policy that was at issue).

[27]Davis v. Buffalo Psychiatric Center, *supra* note 20 (psychiatric center has identity of interest with state office of civil service which formulated and had control over personnel policies as well as state department and its predecessor department which administered the center).

[28]Jones v. Teamsters Local 299, 748 F.2d 1083, 36 FEP 569 (6th Cir. 1984); *see also* General Bldg. Contractors Ass'n v. Pennsylvania, 458 U.S. 375, 29 FEP 139 (1982) (holding that unions running hiring hall are not agents of employers and that employers have no duty to see that unions do not discriminate).

[29]503 F.2d 1086, 1094, 8 FEP 897, 902–3 (6th Cir. 1974).

[30]Bates v. Pacific Maritime Ass'n, 744 F.2d 705, 35 FEP 1806 (9th Cir. 1984); In re National Airlines, 700 F.2d 695, 698, 31 FEP 369, 372 (11th Cir.), *cert. denied,* 464 U.S. 933, 33 FEP 48 (1983); Trujillo v. Longhorn Mfg. Co., 694 F.2d 221, 224–25, 30 FEP 737, 739–40 (10th Cir. 1982); Dominguez v. Bartenders Local 64, 674 F.2d 732, 733–34, 28 FEP 797, 797–98 (8th Cir. 1982); *see also* Kolosky v. Anchor Hocking Corp., 585 F. Supp. 746, 748–50, 33 FEP 1185, 1187–88 (W.D. Pa. 1983) (purchaser of facility where discrimination occurred could be joined as defendant to allow complete prospective injunctive relief).

[31]In re National Airlines, *supra* note 30 (on balance, prejudice to successor prohibits carryover of obligation to obey injunction order).

[32]*Compare* Trujillo v. Longhorn Mfg. Co., *supra* note 30 (no undue hardship results because successor had knowledge of EEOC charge) *with* Dominguez v. Bartenders Local 64, *supra* note 30 (no liability where successor acquired employer company at foreclosure sale and had no knowledge of discrimination charge).

[33]In re New England Fish Co., 19 B.R. 323, 34 FEP 496 (Bankr. W.D. Wash. 1982).

[34]Baranek v. Kelly, 630 F. Supp. 1107, 40 FEP 779 (D. Mass. 1986) (injunction necessary to compel regulatory changes to prevent future discrimination by employers).

[35]Lilly v. City of Beckley, W. Va., 615 F. Supp. 137, 40 FEP 1213 (S.D. W. Va. 1985), *aff'd,* 797 F.2d 191, 41 FEP 772 (4th Cir. 1986) (police commission which tested applicants is a necessary party to hiring discrimination suit even though not employer).

[36]Liberles v. County of Cook, 709 F.2d 1122, 31 FEP 1537 (7th Cir. 1983) (federal government not indispensable party in Title VII lawsuit against local governments because federal government presence

## D. Joinder of One Defendant by Another

In several cases, local governments sued under Title VII were held not entitled to contribution from the United States, and thus it would appear that joinder of the federal government as a joint tort-feasor would generally be improper.[37] A referral union has been held not to have a right of contribution or indemnity against an employer to whom it referred workers.[38] While courts continue to hold that joinder for purposes of obtaining contribution is improper under *Northeast Airlines v. Transport Workers*,[39] some decisions hold that joinder among defendants to secure other "complete and final relief" is possible where the joined defendant has an interest in the litigation.[40]

## III. SCOPE OF EEOC CHARGE AS LIMITING SCOPE OF TITLE VII LAWSUIT

### B. Application of *Sanchez* Doctrine

#### 1. Basic Rationale

The relationship between the EEOC charge and the subsequent lawsuit has become increasingly important in class actions in which the EEOC charge relates to individual treatment and the lawsuit alleges broad, class-wide discrimination. Similar issues arise when new individuals who have not filed their own EEOC charges have sought to intervene as class members or serve as class representatives. Most cases continue to fall between the view of the Fifth Circuit in *Vuyanich v. Republic National Bank of Dallas*[41]—that regardless of the scope of the EEOC charge, nonfiling litigants may not expand the scope of the litigation beyond that properly presented by the filing named plaintiffs[42]—and that of the Fourth Circuit in *Lilly v. Harris-Teeter*

---

not required for full relief and no right of contribution against federal government); Smith v. Carpenters, 685 F.2d 164, 33 FEP 380 (6th Cir. 1982); EEOC v. Sanders Chevrolet, 36 FEP 348 (D.N.M. 1984) (insurance company not indispensable); Crowder v. Fieldcrest Mills, 569 F. Supp. 825, 36 FEP 394 (M.D.N.C. 1983) (same).

[37]Walls v. Mississippi State Dep't of Pub. Welfare, 730 F.2d 306, 34 FEP 1114 (5th Cir. 1984), *on remand*, 624 F. Supp. 46, 41 FEP 1206 (N.D. Miss. 1985) (right of contribution barred by sovereign immunity); Liberles v. County of Cook, *supra* note 36 (contribution denied pursuant to *Northeast Airlines v. Transport Workers*, 451 U.S. 77, 25 FEP 737 (1981), court refused to decide claims for indemnification under other federal statutes).

[38]Anderson v. Electrical Workers, IBEW, Local 3, 582 F. Supp. 627, 34 FEP 517 (S.D.N.Y.), *aff'd*, 751 F.2d 546, 36 FEP 1249 (2d Cir. 1984) (union's claim that it acted as employer's agent refused relying on *General Bldg. Contractors Ass'n v. Pennsylvania*, *supra* note 28; *Northeast Airlines v. Transport Workers*, *supra* note 37, barred contribution under both Title VII and 42 U.S.C. § 1981; union, as intentional tort-feasor, not entitled to contribution or indemnity).

[39]*Supra* note 37.

[40]*See, e.g.*, Forsberg v. Pacific N. Bell Tel. Co., 622 F. Supp. 1147 (D. Or. 1985) (where relief could alter collective bargaining agreement, joinder of union proper); McCooe v. Town of Manchester, Conn. 101 F.R.D. 339, 35 FEP 463 (D. Conn. 1984) (union has interest in litigation where collective bargaining agreement forms some basis of plaintiff's action).

[41]723 F.2d 1195, 33 FEP 1521 (5th Cir.), *cert. denied*, 469 U.S. 1073, 36 FEP 568 (1984).

[42]*See, e.g.*, Hill v. AT&T Technologies, 731 F.2d 175, 34 FEP 620 (4th Cir. 1984) (discrimination claims of present and former employees not sufficiently related to hiring claims of rejected applicant); Ezell v. Mobile Hous. Bd., 709 F.2d 1376, 32 FEP 594 (11th Cir. 1983) (insufficient factual identity between claims); Ekanem v. Health & Hosp. Corp. of Marion County, Ind., 724 F.2d 563, 33 FEP 1497 (7th Cir. 1983), *modified*, 33 FEP 1883 (7th Cir.), *cert. denied*, 469 U.S. 821, 35 FEP 1607 (1984) (class claims of race discrimination not like or related to individual claims of retaliation); Hopper v. Timex Corp., 595 F. Supp. 668, 35 FEP 1858 (E.D. Ark. 1984) (individual plaintiff's EEOC charge insufficient

*Supermarket*[43]—that exhaustion is not required of nonfiling parties' claims where the failure to successfully conciliate separate and distinct exhausted claims by the named plaintiffs "foreshadows an inevitable lack of success in conciliating" the nonexhausted claims.[44]

### 2. Issues Rooted in Same Basis of Discrimination

While several courts continue to apply a liberal rule allowing litigation of virtually any claim raising the same type of discrimination as alleged in the EEOC charge,[45] the Ninth Circuit and several other lower courts continue to take a far narrower view, focusing on the precise claims and theories presented in the charge.[46] The courts usually base their narrow or expansive view on whether or not the claims before the EEOC could reasonably have been expected to include or lead to investigation of the additional claims in the complaint.

---

to serve as jurisdictional basis for subsequent ADEA class action); Valente v. Moore Business Forms, 596 F. Supp. 1280, 39 FEP 541 (D. Vt. 1984) (broad-based allegations and alleged continuing violations may not be presented when EEOC charge was limited to specific instances against one individual).

[43]720 F.2d 326, 33 FEP 195 (4th Cir. 1983), *cert. denied,* 466 U.S. 951, 34 FEP 1096 (1984).

[44]*See, e.g.,* Snell v. Suffolk County, N.Y., 782 F.2d 1094, 39 FEP 1590 (2d Cir. 1986) (black and Hispanic corrections officers who did not file EEOC charges properly were allowed to join in Title VII action brought by other officers who had filed charges); Harris v. Amoco Prod. Co., 768 F.2d 669, 38 FEP 1226 (5th Cir. 1985), *cert. denied,* 475 U.S. 1011, 40 FEP 192 (1986) (EEOC may intervene even though named plaintiff's claims have been settled and EEOC has never independently satisfied prerequisites to Commission lawsuit); Cook v. Boorstin, 763 F.2d 1462, 37 FEP 1777 (D.C. Cir. 1985) (substantial identity between claims of filing plaintiffs and nonfiling intervenors); EEOC v. Keco Indus., 748 F.2d 1097, 36 FEP 511 (6th Cir. 1984) (EEOC may sue employer for alleged classwide discrimination against all of its female employees, even though charge was filed by woman in her name only); Hartman v. Wick, 600 F. Supp. 361, 36 FEP 622 (D.D.C. 1984) (court will hear claims of all women who have opposed U.S. Information Agency's discriminatory practices and not just claims of those women who have filed charge).

[45]Babrocky v. Jewel Food Co., 773 F.2d 857, 38 FEP 1667 (7th Cir. 1985), *on remand,* 645 F. Supp. 1396, 42 FEP 92 (N.D. Ind. 1986) (sex segregation charge sufficient to allow suit challenging hiring, firing, transfer, and promotion practices); Davis v. Buffalo Psychiatric Center, 613 F. Supp. 462, 37 FEP 69, *vacated in part,* 623 F. Supp. 19, 39 FEP 1814 (W.D.N.Y. 1985) (employee whose EEOC charge alleged discrimination in promotion and assignments may litigate claims regarding transfers, assignments, and denial of performance advancement); Borumka v. Rocky Mountain Hosp. & Medical Serv. dba Blue Cross/Blue Shield of Colo., 599 F. Supp. 857, 37 FEP 685 (D. Colo. 1984) (employee may bring ADEA action for retaliation even though her EEOC charge does not use term "retaliation"); Scott v. City of Overland Park, 595 F. Supp. 520, 41 FEP 1211 (D. Kan. 1984) (retaliation and denial of training claims litigated even though not mentioned in failure to promote charge); Waiters v. Parsons, 729 F.2d 233, 34 FEP 178 (3d Cir. 1984) (discharge and retaliation claims).

[46]Lowe v. City of Monrovia, 775 F.2d 998, 39 FEP 350 (9th Cir. 1985), *amended,* 784 F.2d 1407, 41 FEP 931 (9th Cir. 1986) (sex claim dismissed where charge alleged denial of job was due to race); Brown v. Puget Sound Elec. Apprenticeship & Training Trust, 732 F.2d 726, 34 FEP 1201 (9th Cir. 1984), *cert. denied,* 469 U.S. 1108, 36 FEP 976 (1985) (claims of intentional mistreatment on the basis of age and sex could not be raised where charge was limited to disparate impact claims); Hampson v. Thornton Fractional Township High School Dist. 215 Bd. of Educ., 41 FEP 606 (N.D. Ill. 1986) (failure to promote claim not allowed where charge limited to employer's failure to rehire); Combs v. C.A.R.E., 617 F. Supp. 1011, 39 FEP 1086 (E.D. Ark. 1985) (where charge alleged only discrimination in discharge former employee not allowed to litigate claims of discrimination in promotion, wages, placement, or other policies); Proffit v. Keycom Elec. Publishing, 625 F. Supp. 400, 39 FEP 884 (N.D. Ill. 1985), *reconsideration denied,* 625 F. Supp. 409, 40 FEP 1 (N.D. Ill. 1986) (black former employee whose EEOC charge focused solely on discrimination in employer's promotion policies may not challenge employer's allegedly discriminatory refusal to send her to trade show); Calcote v. Jacobsen Mfg. Co., 35 FEP 1581 (S.D. Miss. 1984) (individual who alleged discriminatory demotion and discharge in EEOC charge may not litigate claims of discrimination in failure to promote and in compensation, terms, and conditions of employment); Willis v. Merck & Co., 36 FEP 39 (W.D. Va. 1984), *aff'd,* 762 F.2d 1001, 37 FEP 1216 (4th Cir. 1985) (claims of discrimination in compensation, terms, conditions, and privileges of employment not allowed where EEOC charge expressly limited to discharge); Pickney v. American Dist. Tel. Co., 568 F. Supp. 687, 32 FEP 1232 (E.D. Ark. 1983) (complainant's specific charge alleging discriminatory discharge precludes litigation of promotion and training complaints).

### 3. Incidents Occurring Subsequent to the Filing of the EEOC Charge

The Second Circuit has held that district courts may assume jurisdiction over a claim reasonably related to a charge filed with the EEOC, including incidents occurring after the filing of the EEOC claim,[47] but the courts may not assume jurisdiction when the subsequent claim is not reasonably related to the filed charge.[48] There remains disagreement among courts where a claim of retaliatory discharge is sought to be raised on the basis of an earlier charge.[49]

### 4. Suit Alleging Different Basis of Discrimination Than That Specified in Charge

Courts continue to disagree whether a lawsuit may embrace a different basis of discrimination than that alleged in the charge, with most decisions turning on the relationship between the facts underlying the claims.[50]

## IV. RES JUDICATA AND RELATED PROBLEMS

### A. Previous Title VII Suit Dismissed for Failure to Comply With Procedural Requirement

There is a significant split in authority regarding the right of parties who have not filed EEOC charges to enter into existing litigation and rely upon the charges of persons who have been held improper class representatives

---

[47]Almendral v. New York State Office of Mental Health, 743 F.2d 963, 34 FEP 1680 (2d Cir. 1984) (lower court's failure to consider post-charge allegations was error); *see also* Domingo v. New England Fish Co., 727 F.2d 1429, 34 FEP 584, *modified,* 742 F.2d 520, 37 FEP 1303 (9th Cir. 1984) (error not to grant relief for acts occurring after trial); EEOC v. West Co., 40 FEP 1024 (E.D. Pa. 1986) (additional acts of retaliation by employer litigated though not mentioned in charge).

[48]Stewart v. Immigration & Naturalization Serv., 762 F.2d 193, 37 FEP 1357 (2d Cir. 1985) (suspension claim based on gun incident subsequent to charge not "reasonably related" to earlier claims of discrimination with respect to promotions and upgrading); Zangrillo v. Fashion Inst. of Technology, 601 F. Supp. 1346, 37 FEP 162 (S.D.N.Y.), *aff'd without opinion,* 788 F.2d 2, 40 FEP 1617 (2d Cir. 1985) (EEOC charge filed January 7, 1977, cannot support action for alleged discriminatory act occurring on February 1, 1977).

[49]*Compare* Winters v. Prudential-Bache Secs., 608 F. Supp. 751, 37 FEP 1685 (N.D. Ill. 1984) (claims of constructive discharge not allowed where charge only alleged discrimination in salary increase) *and* Warren v. Halstead Indus., 33 FEP 1416 (M.D.N.C. 1983), *dismissed,* 613 F. Supp. 499, 41 FEP 1658 (M.D.N.C. 1985), *aff'd in part and rev'd in part,* 802 F.2d 746, 41 FEP 1665 (4th Cir. 1986), *aff'd,* 835 F.2d 535, 45 FEP 1381 (4th Cir.), *cert. denied,* 487 U.S. _____ (1988) (refusing to allow litigation of retaliatory discharge) *with* Molthan v. Temple Univ.-Commonwealth Sys. of Higher Educ., 778 F.2d 955, 39 FEP 816 (3d Cir. 1985), Howze v. Jones & Laughlin Steel Corp., 750 F.2d 1208, 36 FEP 1026 (3d Cir. 1984) *and* Jeter v. Boswell, 554 F. Supp. 946, 33 FEP 1410 (N.D. W. Va. 1983) (all three allowing litigation of retaliation claims). Where the original claim alleges retaliation, a post-charge occurrence alleged to be in furtherance of the prior pattern may be litigated. Waiters v. Parsons, *supra* note 45.

[50]*Compare* Castro v. United States, 775 F.2d 399, 39 FEP 162 (1st Cir. 1985) (claim of national origin discrimination dismissed where only age discrimination issue was raised in complaint with FDIC's equal employment office), Ekanem v. Health & Hosp. Corp. of Marion County, Ind., *supra* note 42 (retaliation charge will not support race discrimination suit) *and* Miller v. Smith, 584 F. Supp. 149, 36 FEP 96 (D.D.C. 1984) (U.S. Marshals Service employee whose administrative complaint alleged only sex discrimination may not sue for racial discrimination) *with* Galvan v. Bexar County, Tex., 785 F.2d 1298, 40 FEP 710, *reh'g denied en banc,* 790 F.2d 890 (5th Cir. 1986) (age discrimination claim allowed where EEOC misinterpreted claim as one of national origin), Keller v. Association of Am. Medical Colleges, 644 F. Supp. 459, 41 FEP 577 (D.D.C. 1985), *aff'd,* 802 F.2d 1483, 42 FEP 464 (D.C. Cir. 1986) (racial discrimination claim allowed where EEOC charge alleged only national origin discrimination) *and* Obradovich v. Federal Reserve Bank of New York, 569 F. Supp. 785, 34 FEP 1803 (S.D.N.Y. 1983) (claims of religious discrimination could be raised even though charge related to national origin).

under Rule 23.[51] However, it appears clear that where the claims of the filing party are no longer before the court—either because the party never filed suit or because the claims were previously dismissed on procedural grounds—a nonfiling party cannot rely upon those charges to satisfy exhaustion requirements.[52]

Courts have explained further the conditions under which they will allow persons who have not filed EEOC charges to join in the non-class-action of an individual who did file a charge,[53] and some appear to have relaxed somewhat the necessity that the EEOC charge be "identical" to the issue being litigated.[54] The Fifth Circuit has explained further,[55] and refused to extend,[56] its decision in *Truvillion v. King's Daughters Hospital.*[57]

## C. Relief for Claims Previously Litigated Under a Different Statute

The preclusive effect of a state court judgment in a subsequent federal lawsuit generally is determined in accordance with the Full Faith and Credit Clause of the Constitution.[58] The Supreme Court held in *Kremer v. Chemical Construction Corp.*[59] that where a state court proceeding conforms to minimum due process requirements, a state judicial determination that would bind the parties in that state's courts will also bind the parties in federal

---

[51]*See* Section III.B.1, *supra,* and cases there cited.

[52]*See* Hill v. AT&T Technologies, *supra* note 42 (claims never filed); Wakeen v. Hoffman House, 724 F.2d 1238, 33 FEP 1476 (7th Cir. 1983), *amended,* 33 FEP 1816 (1984) (claims previously dismissed); Kizas v. Webster, 707 F.2d 524, 31 FEP 905 (D.C. Cir. 1983), *cert. denied,* 464 U.S. 1042, 33 FEP 1084 (1984) (claims never filed). *But see* Harris v. Amoco Prod. Co., *supra* note 44 (EEOC allowed to intervene even though claims of named plaintiffs have been settled); Falcon v. General Tel. Co. of the Sw., 611 F. Supp. 707, 39 FEP 1116 (N.D. Tex. 1985), *aff'd,* 815 F.2d 317, 43 FEP 1040 (5th Cir. 1987) (recognizing that under *Vuyanich* it would be improper to allow intervenors to present claims not within scope of original named plaintiff's claims, court allows exception in light of Fifth Circuit's earlier "like or related" ruling in case, which is *res judicata*).

[53]Payne v. Travenol Laboratories, 673 F.2d 798, 28 FEP 1212 (5th Cir.), *cert. denied,* 459 U.S. 1038, 30 FEP 440 (1982) (nonfiling persons can litigate under umbrella of EEOC charge filed by appropriate class representative if those nonfiling individuals could have filed timely charge when class representative filed); Hood v. New Jersey Dep't of Civil Serv., 680 F.2d 955, 29 FEP 65 (3d Cir.), *cert. denied,* 458 U.S. 1122, 29 FEP 200 (1982) (employee who filed otherwise untimely EEOC charge may not rely on filing of another person's charge to justify tolling of 180-day period within which he was required to file his own charge, where other person's charge was itself untimely); Scarlett v. Seaboard Coast Line R.R., 676 F.2d 1043, 29 FEP 433 (5th Cir. 1982) (untimeliness of charging party's EEOC charge precludes other employees, who sought to rely on his charge to satisfy Title VII's procedural requirements, from litigating their Title VII claims); Allen v. United States Steel Corp., 665 F.2d 689, 27 FEP 1293 (5th Cir. 1982) (employee "A" who did not file timely EEOC charges cannot rely on employee "B"'s charge that was not timely as to that person's own claims, even though that charge would be timely as to employee "A"'s claim).

[54]*Compare* Dalton v. Employment Sec. Comm'n, 671 F.2d 835, 28 FEP 178 (4th Cir.), *cert. denied,* 459 U.S. 862, 29 FEP 1560 (1982) (individual who did not file charge with EEOC after he was allegedly discriminated against in hiring may not rely on charge filed by another person who alleged discriminatory treatment in employment, since claims were not substantially identical) *with* Jackson v. Seaboard Coast Line R.R., 678 F.2d 992, 29 FEP 442 (11th Cir. 1982) (employees who did not file charge with EEOC were properly permitted to join Title VII action brought by employee who filed timely charge, where claims of all of these employees arose out of similar discriminatory treatment in same time frame).

[55]New Orleans S.S. Ass'n v. EEOC, 680 F.2d 23, 29 FEP 398 (5th Cir. 1982) (EEOC may challenge a transaction which was subject of prior judicial scrutiny in a private law suit, if subsequent action seeks different relief).

[56]Nilsen v. City of Moss Point, 674 F.2d 379, 28 FEP 1325 (5th Cir. 1982), *on reh'g,* 701 F.2d 556, 31 FEP 612 (5th Cir. 1983) (timely filing requirements are not merely conditions to reaching merits, and failure to fulfill them will bar subsequent action, giving filing requirements operational effect, for *res judicata* purposes, of statute of limitations).

[57]614 F.2d 520, 22 FEP 554 (5th Cir. 1980).

[58]U.S. Const. art. IV, § 1; *see also* 28 U.S.C. § 1738.

[59]456 U.S. 461, 28 FEP 1412 (1982).

court, as to issues which were or could have been resolved in the prior state court proceedings.

In *Migra v. Warren City School District Board of Education,*[60] the Supreme Court expanded upon its holding in *Kremer* by according preclusive effect to a state court judgment as to the federal claims that could have been, but were not, litigated in the state court. In *Migra,* the Court held that no federal policy underlying 42 U.S.C. § 1983 required an exception to the normal principles of "full faith and credit," and that where the law of the state provided broad preclusionary effect to a prior judgment, the same rule would be applied under federal civil rights statutes.

Relying on both *Kremer* and *Migra,* the Supreme Court in *Marrese v. American Academy of Orthopaedic Surgeons*[61] held that 28 U.S.C. § 1738 requires a federal court to look first to state law in determining the preclusive effects of a prior state court judgment, regardless of whether the federal claim could have been raised in the prior state proceedings. However, in *McDonald v. City of West Branch, Michigan,*[62] the Supreme Court refused to extend its *Kremer* decision to arbitration awards, holding that an arbitration award did not preclude a subsequent lawsuit under 42 U.S.C. § 1983.

Lower courts, while generally following *Kremer,*[63] have articulated two exceptions to issue preclusion. Prior state proceedings will not bar a subsequent federal suit where (1) the state administrative proceedings were substantially inadequate;[64] or (2) the underlying purpose of the federal and state statutes differ in substance,[65] indicating that in some instances a divergence in statutory schemes may undercut issue preclusion.[66]

There is a split among the circuits on whether a prior unreviewed administrative agency decision will preclude a subsequent Title VII action in federal court.[67] The Eleventh Circuit in *Stafford v. Muscogee County Board*

---

[60]465 U.S. 75, 33 FEP 1345 (1984).

[61]470 U.S. 373, 53 USLW 4265 (1985).

[62]466 U.S. 284, 115 LRRM 3646 (1984).

[63]*See* Hirst v. California, 758 F.2d 417, 37 FEP 982 (9th Cir. 1985) (Title VII suit barred by prior state court judgment); Gorin v. Osborne, 756 F.2d 834 (11th Cir. 1985) (same); Gonsalves v. Alpine Country Club, 727 F.2d 27, 33 FEP 1817 (1st Cir. 1984) (same); Carpenter v. Reed, 728 F.2d 1302, 34 FEP 942 (10th Cir. 1984) (same); Burney v. Polk Community College, 34 FEP 727 (11th Cir. 1984) (same); Wakeen v. Hoffman House, 724 F.2d 1238, 33 FEP 1476 (7th Cir. 1983) (same).

[64]Bottini v. Sadore Mgmt. Corp., 764 F.2d 116, 38 FEP 5 (2d Cir. 1985) (state court's narrow scope of arbitration award review deprived it of power to entertain Title VII action); Jones v. City of Alton, 757 F.2d 878, 37 FEP 523 (7th Cir. 1985) (plaintiff prevented from presenting evidence of racial discrimination at state agency proceedings); Griffen v. Big Spring Indep. School Dist., 706 F.2d 645, 31 FEP 1750 (5th Cir.), *cert. denied,* 464 U.S. 1008, 33 FEP 552 (1983) (state board reversal of trial examiner's credibility findings without stated reason, *ex parte* contacts by employer, and adoption of employer's findings warranted disregard for state ruling).

[65]Ross v. Communications Satellite Corp., 759 F.2d 355, 37 FEP 797 (4th Cir. 1985) (Title VII and state unemployment statute have different enforcement procedures and purposes); Patzer v. University of Wis. Bd. of Regents, 763 F.2d 851, 37 FEP 1847 (7th Cir. 1985) (Title VII action sought supplemental remedies not available under state statute).

[66]*See also* Whitfield v. City of Knoxville, 567 F. Supp. 1344, 32 FEP 1052 (E.D. Tenn. 1983), *aff'd,* 756 F.2d 455, 37 FEP 288 (6th Cir. 1985) (prior adjudication no barrier in ADEA case where statutes and issues not identical). *But see* Wakeen v. Hoffman, *supra* note 63 (plaintiff should have argued difference between federal and state standards in state proceedings).

[67]*Compare* Elliott v. University of Tenn., 766 F.2d 982, 38 FEP 522 (6th Cir. 1985) (Title VII action not barred following unreviewed state administrative decision, even though state agency that rendered decision was authorized to grant full relief and provide litigants with elaborate judicial process) *with* Buckhalter v. Pepsi-Cola Gen. Bottlers, 768 F.2d 842, 38 FEP 682 (7th Cir. 1985), *vacated,* 478 U.S. 1017, 41 FEP 272 (1986) (Title VII action barred following unreviewed state human rights commission's decision, where proceeding was conducted in same manner as trial in state court).

*of Education*[68] held that the doctrine of *res judicata* did not bar claims brought under Title VII and 42 U.S.C. § 1981 where the plaintiff's previous claim of racial discrimination under Title VI of the Civil Rights Act of 1964 had been heard and rejected by the U.S. Department of Health, Education and Welfare, Office of Civil Rights (HEW). The court found that there was no demonstration that HEW was a competent forum in which to litigate Title VII or § 1981 claims.[69]

### D. Relief for Claims Which Have Previously Been Involved in Title VII Action by the Government

In *Cooper v. Federal Reserve Bank of Richmond,*[70] the Supreme Court held that an adverse judgment on the merits of a Title VII action brought by the EEOC and several private intervenors barred further litigation of class claims in a subsequent lawsuit brought under 42 U.S.C. § 1981. The Court held that basic principles of *res judicata* (merger and bar or claim preclusion) and collateral estoppel (issue preclusion) apply to employment claims and prevent class members from bringing another pattern-or-practice suit covering the same time period, or from relitigating in any other lawsuits whether the employer engaged in a pattern or practice of discrimination during the relevant time period.

However, the Court distinguished class claims from individual claims, and held that subsequent individual lawsuits were not necessarily precluded by a prior adverse determination of class issues. The Court held that individual disparate treatment claims were conceptually and legally distinct from classwide pattern-or-practice claims, and that while a prior judgment in favor of the employer on class issues would be relevant in determining whether the employer's reason for treatment of an individual was a pretext, an adverse judgment did not bar a later individual lawsuit filed by a class member.

Prior to the Supreme Court's decision in *Cooper,* an en banc panel of the Fourth Circuit held that the filing of an action by the EEOC under § 706(f)(1) and the entry of a consent decree in that action precluded private individuals who had not intervened in the EEOC action from initiating their own Title VII actions.[71] However, in dicta, the court stated that if an EEOC action concludes on technical grounds without a judgment on the merits, then the EEOC may issue right-to-sue letters to the private individuals.[72]

---

[68] 688 F.2d 1383, 29 FEP 1773 (11th Cir. 1982).

[69] *Compare* Barrentine v. Arkansas-Best Freight Sys., 450 U.S. 728, 24 WH 1284 (1981) (arbitrator's finding on wage claim not binding on subsequent FLSA proceeding); Moore v. Bonner, 695 F.2d 799, 30 FEP 817 (4th Cir. 1982), *cert. denied,* 474 U.S. 827 (1985) (reversing district court finding of "administrative collateral estoppel" in federal action under §§ 1981, 1983, and 1985, which district court based on state administrative finding against public employer defendant); Nilsen v. City of Moss Point, 674 F.2d 379, 28 FEP 1325 (5th Cir. 1982), *on reh'g,* 701 F.2d 556, 31 FEP 612 (5th Cir. 1983) (all theories of remedy or recovery must be joined in civil rights action arising out of same transaction; subsequent suits by plaintiff seeking to assert different litigation theories based on same operative facts may be dismissed).

[70] 467 U.S. 867, 35 FEP 1 (1984); *see also* Johnson v. American Airlines, 157 Cal.App.3d 427, 203 Cal. Rptr. 638, 38 FEP 1017 (1984) (individual class member's state court action barred by resolution of federal class action, in which employee chose not to participate).

[71] Adams v. Procter & Gamble Mfg. Co., 697 F.2d 582, 30 FEP 1228 (4th Cir. 1983) (en banc) (per curiam), *cert. denied,* 465 U.S. 1041 (1984).

[72] *Id.,* 697 F.2d at 583, 30 FEP at 1229.

## V. MOOTNESS

In nonemployment cases, courts have shown increasing willingness to dismiss for mootness on the ground of the voluntary cessation of the alleged illegal conduct by the defendant.[73] This trend has not been followed as strictly in employment cases. In *Firefighters Local 1784 v. Stotts,* [74] the firefighters' union in Memphis challenged the district court's order enjoining the City of Memphis from following its "last hired, first fired" seniority system. As a result of this injunction and pursuant to a modified consent decree, white firefighters were laid off or demoted before black firefighters with less seniority. One month after their demotion or layoff, however, the white firefighters were restored to their previous positions.

The Court held the controversy was not moot for three reasons. First, the terms of the district court's injunction remained in force and, unless set aside, would apply in the event of future layoffs. Second, the modified consent decree, providing that layoffs were not to reduce the percentage of blacks employed by the fire department, remained in effect. Finally, the Court ruled that unless the injunction and consent decree were vacated, the displaced white firefighters could not properly make a claim for back pay.[75]

The Supreme Court also has ruled that the death of a plaintiff claiming handicap discrimination under § 504 of the Rehabilitation Act does not moot the claim because the plaintiff's estate could recover back pay.[76]

In *Fletcher v. Adult Training Center,* [77] the district court narrowly construed *County of Los Angeles v. Davis*[78] and distinguished *Cramer v. Virginia Commonwealth University*[79] in holding that a Title VII claim for race discrimination was not mooted, even though the claim for damages had been dismissed. The court ruled that there was some possibility that the alleged offending supervisor would be rehired and that injunctive relief would effectively prevent present and future supervisors from engaging in discriminatory activities.[80]

---

[73]*E.g.,* Iron Arrow Honor Soc'y v. Heckler, 464 U.S. 67 (1983), *on remand,* 722 F.2d 213 (5th Cir. 1984) (no reasonable likelihood that challenged conduct would recur); Lewis v. Louisiana State Bar Ass'n, 792 F.2d 493 (5th Cir. 1986) (no reasonable expectation that challenged conduct would recur and interim events completely eradicated effects of alleged violation); Lindquist v. Idaho State Bd. of Corrections, 776 F.2d 851 (9th Cir. 1985) (prison's decision to move library to more spacious quarters mooted inmates' claim that prison failed to provide adequate library facilities).

[74]467 U.S. 561, 34 FEP 1702 (1984).

[75]*See also* Firefighters Local 718 (Boston) v. NAACP, Boston Chapter, 749 F.2d 102, 36 FEP 771 (1st Cir. 1984), *cert. denied,* 471 U.S. 1075, 37 FEP 952 (1985). On remand from the Supreme Court for reconsideration in light of the *Stotts* decision, the First Circuit distinguished *Stotts* and reaffirmed its earlier holding that a supervening state statute mandating reinstatement of laid-off firefighters and policemen mooted a claim seeking modification of a consent decree that prohibited the city from reducing the percentages of minorities employed as firefighters and policemen when such employees were laid off; *cf.* EEOC Dec. 86-7, 40 FEP 1892 (Apr. 18, 1986) (citing *Stotts,* Commission held that charging party's release from prison after filing charge does not moot charge because, if it is determined that employment relationship existed between prison and charging party, a reasonable cause finding could entitle charging party to relief under Title VII).

[76]Consolidated Rail Corp. v. Darrone, 465 U.S. 624, 34 FEP 79 (1984).

[77]34 FEP 1035 (D.N.J. 1984).

[78]440 U.S. 625, 19 FEP 282 (1979).

[79]486 F. Supp. 187, 22 FEP 315 (E.D. Va. 1980).

[80]*See also* McKinney v. Dole, 765 F.2d 1129, 38 FEP 364 (D.C. Cir. 1985) (sexual harassment claim not moot, even though only declaratory and injunctive relief available, since claim for injunctive relief would remain viable if plaintiff prevailed on retaliation claim and obtained reinstatement and plaintiff might be entitled to attorney's fees if she prevailed on either claim); Ezell v. Mobile Hous. Bd., 709 F.2d 1376, 32 FEP 594 (11th Cir. 1983) (an unsuccessful job applicant's death moots her Title VII claim for

## VI. VENUE

Venue in employment discrimination actions under Title VII will be governed by the specific venue provisions of the statute and not by the general venue provisions of 28 U.S.C. § 1931.[81]

Venue is usually established in the judicial district where the alleged unlawful employment practice took place.[82] Several recent cases have considered the approach to be used in determining where the alleged unlawful employment practice took place.[83] Under these cases, the "event of overriding operative significance" is controlling for venue purposes.[84] Generally, the "decision to hire, fire or deny employment * * *" will be considered to be such an event. The fact that a position was advertised in a particular state or that correspondence concerning an application was mailed to or from that state is not, by itself, enough to lay venue in that state.[85]

Where a parent corporation exercises control over the development and enforcement of the personnel policies and practices of its subsidiary corporations, venue will lie in the state where the parent corporation is located.[86]

In *Sconion v. Thomas,*[87] the plaintiff sought to establish venue in the district where the defendant had sent plaintiff's employment records "for her perusal."[88] Venue was held to be improper on the grounds that:

> "[T]he fact that a portion of her employment record may have been sent to this district * * * does not mean that the records were 'transferred' for purposes of the venue statute. To so hold would mean that a Title VII complainant may bring a discrimination action in any district in the United States."[89]

### A. Pendent Venue

In *Rodriguez v. Chandler*[90] the court, applying the doctrine of "pendent venue," denied a motion to dismiss for improper venue §§ 1981 and 1983 claims that were factually related to a claim subject to proper venue under Title VII, stating:

---

injunctive and declaratory relief, but does not moot her entire claim since her estate could secure some monetary relief). *But see* Backus v. Baptist Medical Center, 671 F.2d 1100, 28 FEP 221 (8th Cir. 1982) (claim of discrimination in job assignment moot where plaintiff left hospital's employ and sought only declaratory and injunctive relief).

[81]*See* Thurmon v. Martin Marietta Data Sys., 596 F. Supp. 367, 36 FEP 249 (M.D. Pa. 1984) (citing Stebbins v. State Farm Mut. Auto. Ins. Co., 413 F.2d 1100, 1102, 1 FEP 745 (D.C. Cir.), *cert. denied,* 396 U.S. 895, 2 FEP 388 (1969) ("the venue of the right of action here in suit was limited by the statute which created the right").

[82]Other choices are the judicial district where the employment records relevant to such practices are maintained and administered, the judicial district where the person would have worked but for the alleged unlawful employment practice, and, if the respondent is not found in any of those judicial districts, in the district where the respondent has its principal offices. *See* Wright v. Newport News Shipbuilding, slip op. No. 83-C-7935 (N.D. Ill. 1984).

[83]Hill v. Secretary of Dep't of Health & Human Servs., 39 FEP 607 (D.D.C. 1985); Wright v. Newport News Shipbuilding, *supra* note 82; Donnell v. National Guard Bureau, 568 F. Supp. 93, 32 FEP 589 (D.D.C. 1983).

[84]Wright v. Newport News Shipbuilding, *supra* note 82.

[85]*Id.*

[86]Hoffman v. United Telecommunications, 575 F. Supp. 1463, 1484, 35 FEP 1215 (D. Kan. 1983).

[87]603 F. Supp. 66, 36 FEP 618, 620 (D.D.C. 1984).

[88]*Id.,* 36 FEP at 620.

[89]*Id.*

[90]641 F. Supp. 1292, 41 FEP 1038 (S.D.N.Y. 1986), *aff'd,* 841 F.2d 1117 (2d Cir. 1988).

"Pendent venue has often been used in cases in which venue over one claim is already established under a specialized venue statute. [footnote omitted] To separate plaintiff's § 1983 and § 1981 claims from his factually related Title VII claims would result in inefficiency, waste of judicial resources, and a possibility of inconsistent judgments, and would deter Title VII plaintiffs with related claims from freely exercising the special statewide choice of venue granted them by Congress."[91]

## VII. Jury Trial

The Supreme Court has expressed approval of the consensus view that there is no right to a jury trial under Title VII, "[b]ecause the Act expressly authorizes only equitable remedies."[92]

When a claim affording legal remedies such as compensatory and punitive damages is joined with a claim under Title VII,[93] jury trial is available on all factual issues determining the legal claim.[94] Whether a jury trial is available on all issues pertaining to back pay, including entitlement and amount, depends upon the characterization of the remedy as "equitable"[95] or "legal."[96] The right to (re)instatement or "front pay" in lieu thereof would appear to be equitable and properly resolved by the court.

---

[91]*Id.*, 41 FEP at 1046.

[92]Great Am. Fed. Sav. & Loan Ass'n v. Novotny, 442 U.S. 366, 375, 19 FEP 1482, 1485 (1979); *see* Lehman v. Nakshian, 453 U.S. 156, 164, 26 FEP 65, 68 (1981) (ADEA action against U.S. Government, "of course * * * there is no right to trial by jury in cases arising under Title VII"). Recent cases squarely so holding include *Moll v. Parkside Livonia Credit Union,* 525 F. Supp. 786, 793–94, 30 FEP 1236, 1241–42 (E.D. Mich. 1981).

[93]Generally, these are claims under 42 U.S.C. §§ 1981, 1983, or pendent state law claims. *See generally* Chapter 21 (The Civil Rights Acts Of 1866 and 1871) and Chapter 23 (Related Causes of Action).

[94]As to the legal claim, jury trial is available on both the factual issues pertaining to liability and the amount of recovery. As to the Title VII claim, jury trial is available only on the common issues of fact, while the facts related solely to the Title VII claim, as well as the appropriate equitable remedy, are issues for the court. Thomas v. Resort Health Related Facility, 539 F. Supp. 630, 634, 31 FEP 65, 67 (E.D.N.Y. 1982) (Title VII and § 1981); Powell v. Pennsylvania Hous. Fin. Agency, 563 F. Supp. 419, 420, 31 FEP 1595, 1596 (M.D. Pa. 1983) (Title VII and §§ 1981 and 1983; whether legal claim is "substantial" and will, therefore, support jury demand, should be determined under Rule 56, Fed. R. Civ. P.).

[95]Courts characterizing back pay as an "equitable" remedy (or as a legal remedy incidental to equitable relief) deny jury trial. Williams v. Owens-Illinois, 665 F.2d 918, 929, 27 FEP 1273, 1281 (9th Cir.), *cert. denied,* 459 U.S. 971, 30 FEP 56 (1982) (back pay "properly viewed as either equitable or as a legal remedy incidental to an equitable cause of action").

[96]Courts characterizing back pay as a "legal" remedy grant jury trial on all related factual issues. Thomas v. Resort Health Related Facility, *supra* note 94; Powell v. Pennsylvania Hous. Fin. Agency, *supra* note 94.

CHAPTER 31

# EEOC LITIGATION

## I. INTRODUCTION

The EEOC's authority to enforce the ADEA and Equal Pay Act pursuant to the 1979 Presidential Reorganization Plan was questioned as a result of the Supreme Court's decision in *Immigration & Naturalization Service v. Chadha.*[1] In *Chadha* the Supreme Court held unconstitutional the legislative veto provision of the Immigration and Naturalization Act.[2] Following *Chadha,* a number of respondents around the country challenged the EEOC's right to litigate cases under the ADEA or the Equal Pay Act, while the EEOC maintained that its authority was unaffected by that decision. The EEOC's authority to enforce the ADEA and the Equal Pay Act remained in doubt, with the Fifth and Sixth circuits upholding the EEOC's authority and the district courts dividing,[3] until Congress passed Public Law No. 98-532.[4] Public Law No. 98-532, effective October 19, 1984, retroactively ratified and affirmed as law all reorganization plans implemented prior to the date of its enactment. Since its passage, courts have summarily held that Public Law No. 98-532 sufficiently removed any questions regarding the EEOC's enforcement authority.[5]

---

[1]462 U.S. 919, 51 USLW 4907 (1983).

[2]*Id.*

[3]EEOC v. Hernando Bank, 724 F.2d 1188, 34 FEP 15 (5th Cir. 1984) (in Equal Pay Act case, legislative veto provisions of statute found unconstitutional but severable from remaining provisions of Act); Muller Optical Co. v. EEOC, 574 F. Supp. 946, 33 FEP 420 (W.D. Tenn. 1983), *aff'd,* 743 F.2d 380, 35 FEP 1147 (6th Cir. 1984) (legislative veto provision does not deprive EEOC of authority to investigate ADEA charge because veto was not exercised, veto provision is severable from other provisions of Act, and Congress ratified Reorganization Plan by appropriating money for EEOC); EEOC v. Chrysler Corp., 595 F. Supp. 344, 33 FEP 1838 (E.D. Mich. 1984) (in ADEA case, Chadha decision not applied retroactively); EEOC v. Allstate Ins. Co., 570 F. Supp. 1224, 32 FEP 1337 (S.D. Miss. 1983), *appeal dismissed,* 467 U.S. 1232, 34 FEP 1785 (1984) (legislative veto provision not severable; congressional appropriation of funds insufficient to constitute ratification; Chadha applied retroactively).

[4]98 Stat. 2705.

[5]Santos v. Stanley Home Prods., 36 FEP 319 (D. Mass. 1984) (Pub. L. No. 98-532 conclusively established EEOC's authority to carry out ADEA functions); Barrett v. Suffolk Transp. Servs., 600 F. Supp. 81, 37 FEP 725 (E.D.N.Y. 1984) (recent federal law removes any questions posed by *Chadha* and its progeny regarding EEOC's jurisdictional authority); EEOC v. First Citizens Bank of Billings, 758 F.2d 397, 45 FEP 1337 (9th Cir.), *cert. denied,* 474 U.S. 902 (1985) (Pub. L. No. 98-532 makes it clear EEOC not only has authority to bring future Equal Pay Act actions, but has retroactive authority as well on any previous actions it brought); EEOC v. Westinghouse Elec. Corp., 765 F.2d 389, 45 FEP 1342 (3d Cir. 1985) (no manifest injustice nor violation of due process by retroactive application of Pub. L. No. 98-532); *see* EEOC v. CBS, Inc., 748 F.2d 124, 36 FEP 575 (2d Cir. 1984) (court indicated that Pub. L. No. 98-532 ratified reorganization plan).

## II. ADMINISTRATIVE PREREQUISITES TO SUIT

### A. Administrative Prerequisites to Suit Under § 706 and the ADEA

#### 1. A Timely Charge

The Supreme Court addressed the validity of a Commissioner's charge under 29 C.F.R. § 1601.12(a)(3)[6] in *EEOC v. Shell Oil Co.,*[7] holding that, at least in a pattern-or-practice case, a Commissioner should

> "identify the groups of persons that he has reason to believe have been discriminated against, the categories of employment positions from which they have been excluded, the methods by which discrimination may have been effected and the periods of time in which he suspects the discrimination to have been practiced."[8]

#### 2. Notice of the Charge

The Supreme Court held in *EEOC v. Shell Oil Co.*[9] that § 706(b) requires the Commission, within 10 days of the filing of a charge, to reveal to the employer all of the information that must be included in the charge itself.

#### 3. Investigation

The EEOC has been relieved of any obligation to undertake a separate investigation of each type of alleged employment discrimination that forms

---

[6]Sec. 1601.12(a) (1986) provides: "Each charge should contain * * * (3) A clear and concise statement of the facts, including pertinent dates, constituting the alleged unlawful employment practices * * * ."
[7]466 U.S. 54, 34 FEP 709 (1984).
[8]*Id.* at 73, 34 FEP at 718. The Court determined that the charge in *Shell Oil* met these standards, where it (1) identified blacks and women as the victims of discrimination; (2) specified six occupational categories to which blacks, and seven to which women, had been denied equal access; (3) alleged that the employer had discriminated in "recruitment, hiring, selection, job assignment, training, testing, promotion, and terms and conditions of employment;" and (4) charged the employer with discriminatory practices since at least the effective date of the Civil Rights Act. *Id.* Justice O'Connor, whose opinion concurring in part and dissenting in part was joined by three other Justices, agreed that the charge in *Shell Oil* was sufficient, but only because 29 C.F.R. § 1601.12(b) provides that the charge need not contain a detailed description of the circumstances of discrimination: "Notwithstanding the provisions of paragraph (a) of this section, a charge is sufficient when the Commission receives from the person making the charge a written statement sufficiently precise to identify the parties, and to describe generally the action or practices complained of." *Id.* at 83–85, 34 FEP at 722–23. The majority suggested, without resolving the issue, that § 1601.12(b) might apply only to charges filed by laymen, and not one filed, as was the one in *Shell Oil,* by the Commissioner. *Id.* at 74 n.28, 34 FEP at 718.
[9]*Supra* note 7, at 81, 34 FEP at 721–22 (1984). Justice O'Connor, joined by three other Justices, disagreed, concluding that § 706(b) "expressly requires more in the notice of charge than in the charge itself. A charge need only allege an unlawful employment practice and 'contain such information and be in such form as the Commission requires.' " *Id.* at 86, 34 FEP at 724. As indicated, *supra* note 8, Justice O'Connor viewed the applicable regulations as requiring only a general description of the employer's discriminatory practices in the charge. In contrast, she continued, a "notice of charge * * * must 'includ(e) the date, place and circumstances of the alleged unlawful employment practice.' " *Id.* She concluded that service on the employer of the "brief, formal, and wholly uninformative 'charge,' " described *supra* note 8, "did not comport with the language and purposes of [706(b)'s] notice requirement." *Id.* at 89, 34 FEP at 725. *Cf.* EEOC v. Bethlehem Steel Corp., 765 F.2d 427, 38 FEP 345 (4th Cir. 1985) (Notice of Charge, which was worded similarly to the one in *Shell Oil* and which requested company information covering 1976 through 1980 sufficiently notified employer of circumstances of alleged discrimination); EEOC v. Michael Constr. Co., 706 F.2d 244, 249–50, 31 FEP 1081, 1084–85 (8th Cir. 1983), *cert. denied,* 464 U.S. 1038, 33 FEP 1084 (1984) (statutory requirement that notice of EEOC charge include statement of "circumstances of the alleged unlawful employment practice" does not require recitation of specific incidents of dissimilar treatment in notice); EEOC v. AirGuide Corp., 29 FEP 236, 241 (S.D. Fla. 1978) (EEOC's failure to notify employer of charge until almost one year after its filing substantially prejudiced employer and warranted dismissal of suit).

the basis of a complaint;[10] has been allowed to expand target locations in litigation from the site identified in the reasonable cause determination where the challenged practices were the same;[11] and has been insulated from suits challenging its investigation and processing of a charge.[12]

Courts have restrained attempts by defendants to restrict EEOC's ability to investigate charges by claiming inadequate notice,[13] excessive delays,[14] undue burden,[15] and insufficiency of EEOC's investigation.[16] Courts have also supported the EEOC's administrative use of discovery tools such as subpoenas[17] and interrogatories,[18] granted a preliminary injunction to prevent an employer from impeding EEOC's investigation,[19] and ruled that the automatic stay provisions of the Bankruptcy Code do not prevent an EEOC investigation.[20] EEOC also has adopted a policy statement asserting that an employer's unjustified refusal to provide relevant information in an EEOC investigation will allow the EEOC to adopt inferences on open factual issues adverse to the employer, as a basis for a reasonable cause determination and a Commission decision to litigate a charge in federal court.[21]

---

[10]EEOC v. Nestle Co., 29 FEP 491 (E.D. Cal. 1982) (EEOC adequately investigated alleged "white collar" sex discrimination); EEOC v. Westinghouse Elec. Corp., 632 F. Supp. 343, 40 FEP 643 (E.D. Pa. 1986) (EEOC does not have to conduct exhaustive investigation of all charges before it can file ADEA action).

[11]Lucky Stores v. EEOC, 714 F.2d 911, 32 FEP 1281 (9th Cir. 1983) (EEOC may challenge employer's practices not only at warehouse named in reasonable cause determination but also at two other warehouses where same alleged discrimination occurred, because employer had adequate notice during investigation of issue being litigated).

[12]McCottrell v. EEOC, 726 F.2d 350, 33 FEP 1880 (7th Cir. 1984) (employee has no right to challenge EEOC determination of no reasonable cause; only remedy is private suit in district court, where employee is entitled to *de novo* review).

[13]EEOC v. Shell Oil Co., *supra* note 7, at 75, 34 FEP at 719 (Congress did not envision the notice requirement as substantive constraint on EEOC's investigative authority); Mississippi Chem. Corp. v. EEOC, 786 F.2d 1013, 1017–18, 40 FEP 609, 611–12 (11th Cir. 1986).

[14]EEOC v. Great Atl. & Pac. Tea Co., 735 F.2d 69, 34 FEP 1412 (3d Cir.), *cert. dismissed,* 469 U.S. 925 (1984) (31 months between end of employer's resistance to investigation and EEOC's determination of reasonable cause was not excessive).

[15]EEOC v. Maryland Cup Corp., 785 F.2d 471, 477, 40 FEP 475, 478 (4th Cir.), *cert. denied,* 479 U.S. 815, 41 FEP 1711 (1986). (EEOC subpoena of relevant and material information is enforceable, and employer is not entitled to reimbursement for reproduction costs, unless employer demonstrates that producing documents would seriously disrupt its normal business operations; employer's conclusory allegations that it needs constant access to all documents and that it fears EEOC will lose the documents are insufficient).

[16]EEOC v. Keco Indus., 748 F.2d 1097, 36 FEP 511 (6th Cir. 1984) (lower court erred by inquiring into sufficiency of EEOC investigation of charge and by allowing employer to challenge sufficiency of EEOC's investigation); EEOC v. New York News, Nos. 81 Civ. 337, 82 Civ. 1147, 82 Civ. 3662, 84 Civ. 6133 (S.D.N.Y. July 26, 1985).

[17]State Farm Mut. Auto. Ins. Co. v. EEOC, 34 FEP 1072 (N.D. Cal. 1981), *aff'd in part and vacated in part without opinion,* 707 F.2d 519 (9th Cir. 1983) (EEOC may issue subpoena prior to preliminary determination by EEOC as to whether it has jurisdiction over employer); EEOC v. Quadrant Club, 35 FEP 195 (N.D. Tex. 1984) (EEOC is entitled to enforcement of subpoena seeking information about employer's recruitment and hiring practices where information sought is relevant to charge of age discrimination); EEOC v. W.A. Krueger Co., 35 EPD ¶ 34,772 (E.D. Wis. 1984) (EEOC charge which failed to specify dates of alleged discriminatory acts other than to assert violations throughout entire period of Act was proper and did not invalidate subpoena issued by Commission); EEOC v. Peat, Marwick, Mitchell & Co., 775 F.2d 928, 38 FEP 1846 (8th Cir. 1985), *cert. denied,* 475 U.S. 1046, 40 FEP 272 (1986) (EEOC has authority to issue *subpoena duces tecum* in age discrimination action).

[18]EEOC v. State Farm Mut. Auto. Ins. Co., 34 FEP 1073 (N.D. Cal. 1982) (employers can be required to compile lists and answer interrogatories under EEOC subpoena).

[19]EEOC v. United States Steel Corp., 583 F. Supp. 1357, 34 FEP 973 (W.D. Pa. 1984) (EEOC granted preliminary injunction where employer's action hindered and impeded EEOC's investigation and administrative processes).

[20]AM Int'l v. EEOC, 34 FEP 1535 (Bankr. N.D. Ill. 1982) (automatic stay provisions of Bankruptcy Code do not preclude EEOC from investigating charge against employer that has filed petition under Chapter XI of Code).

[21]EEOC Compliance Manual, BNA p. N:3181.

## 4. Reasonable Cause Determination

The EEOC may not litigate all of its discrimination claims in a suit unless there is direct evidence that each claim was the subject of a reasonable cause determination.[22]

Two courts have ruled that a party to a settlement agreement may seek its enforcement in federal district court, even though the EEOC has not issued a reasonable cause determination. The plaintiff, however, is limited to enforcing the agreement and may not litigate the underlying charge.[23]

## 5. Conciliation

Courts continue to rule that an attempt by the EEOC to conciliate is a jurisdictional prerequisite to filing suit,[24] but that a good-faith effort is all that is required.[25] One court has held that this obligation requires that the employer "be told how to achieve compliance."[26] Another has ruled that the EEOC's conciliation effort must follow its determination of reasonable cause.[27] If conciliation is insufficient, a stay pending further conciliation is preferred over dismissal of the action.[28]

---

[22]Wright v. Olin Corp., 697 F.2d 1172, 30 FEP 889 (4th Cir. 1982), *vacated without opinion,* 767 F.2d 915, 40 FEP 192 (4th Cir. 1984) (EEOC may not rely on vague and conclusory stipulation that it complied with "administrative and procedural requirements of Title VII material to this action and with all conditions precedent to bringing this action").

[23]EEOC v. Henry Beck Co., 729 F.2d 301, 34 FEP 373 (4th Cir. 1984) (employee, employer, and EEOC entered into settlement agreement after employee filed charge with EEOC but before EEOC issued reasonable cause determination; as Title VII encourages voluntary compliance, action by EEOC to enforce agreement is "brought under" Title VII, and district court therefore has jurisdiction); Eatmon v. Bristol Steel & Iron Works, 769 F.2d 1503, 38 FEP 1364 (11th Cir. 1985) (employees, who never filed charges with EEOC, executed releases, accepting benefits under conciliation agreement between employer and Office of Federal Contract Compliance Programs of Department of Labor and releasing claims of employment discrimination; employees' action to enforce releases is "brought under" Title VII, and district court therefore had jurisdiction).

[24]EEOC v. Blue Ox Restaurant, 40 EPD ¶ 36,325 (N.D. Ill. 1984).

[25]EEOC v. Keco Indus., *supra* note 16 (EEOC is under no duty to attempt further conciliation with employer after employer rejects good-faith conciliation effort; form and substance of conciliation are within discretion of EEOC; court should determine only whether attempt was satisfactory); EEOC v. Riss Int'l Corp., 525 F. Supp. 1094, 35 FEP 416 (W.D. Mo. 1981) (conciliation efforts on employee's charge were adequate, where EEOC did not consider conciliation efforts unsuccessful until employer stated that it would provide no further information and where employer made it clear that it would not be likely to conciliate on any terms); EEOC v. St. Louis-San Francisco Ry., 35 FEP 86 (N.D. Okla. 1980), *appeal dismissed,* 651 F.2d 718, 35 FEP 90 (10th Cir. 1981), *rev'd,* 743 F.2d 739, 35 FEP 1163 (10th Cir. 1984) (EEOC did not fail to attempt conciliation, even though its efforts fell far short of exhaustive efforts in that it made stringent demands on employer and did not change its position as to its offers); EEOC v. KDM School Bus Co., 612 F. Supp. 369, 38 FEP 602 (S.D.N.Y. 1985) (EEOC's letter to employer school district was adequate conciliation, under standard of "reasonableness and responsiveness * * * under all the circumstances," where EEOC's action challenged state mandatory retirement regulation that school district had no discretion to disregard, and school district's only response to letter was request that EEOC reverse its decision).

[26]EEOC v. Westinghouse Elec. Corp., 632 F. Supp. 343, 360, 40 FEP 643, 654 (E.D. Pa. 1986) ("Specifically, the employer should be informed (1) of the ways compliance may be achieved, (2) that affected employees may receive 'make whole' remedies, (3) that the Commission may institute legal action, and (4) that the employer may respond to the Commission's allegations").

[27]EEOC v. New York News, Nos. 81 Civ. 337, 82 Civ. 1147, 82 Civ. 3662, 84 Civ. 6133 (S.D.N.Y. July 26, 1985) (reasonable cause determination is significant because that is first time employer is put on actual notice of sufficiency of charges).

[28]EEOC v. Prudential Fed. Sav. & Loan Ass'n, 763 F.2d 1166, 1169, 37 FEP 1691, 1693 (10th Cir.), *cert. denied,* 474 U.S. 946, 39 FEP 384 (1985) ("when the EEOC initially makes a sufficient albeit limited effort to conciliate, the minimal jurisdictional requirement of the [ADEA] is satisfied * * * . Once this initial effort is made, 'if the district court finds that further conciliation efforts are required the proper course is to stay proceedings until such informal conciliation can be concluded.' " (citing Marshall v. Sun Oil Co., 592 F.2d 563, 566, 18 FEP 1632, 1634 (10th Cir.), *cert. denied,* 444 U.S. 826, 20 FEP 1473 (1979)); EEOC v. New York News, *supra* note 27 (under Title VII, if conciliation is insufficient, the

The Fifth and Eighth circuits have allowed the EEOC to sue under the Equal Pay Act without prior conciliation efforts.[29]

## III. INTERNAL PROCESS OF THE EEOC

### B. Organization of the Office of the General Counsel

*1. Structure*

In 1985 the EEOC Office of the General Counsel (OGC) was reorganized as a result of a realignment of the functions of Systemic Programs.[30] The OGC manages and conducts all EEOC enforcement litigation through three services: Trial Services, which conducts enforcement litigation in the district courts, except for those systemic cases assigned by the General Counsel to Systemic Litigation Services for litigation from EEOC headquarters;[31] Appellate Services, which handles appeals and also amicus presentations in the courts; and Systemic Litigation Services, which conducts pattern-or-practice litigation.[32] The litigation functions of Trial Services are carried out by the legal units in each district office.[33] Since the 1982 reorganization of the EEOC, the services of internal counsel to the Commission are performed by the independent Office of Legal Counsel which reports directly to the Commissioners.[34]

*2. Processing Original Suit Under § 706(f)(1)*

The EEOC does not file an original suit under § 706(f)(1) until the administrative processes have been completed. Attorneys in each district office are required to review reasonable cause determinations before they are issued.[35] In 1985, in an effort to obtain credibility and increase the rate of conciliation success, the EEOC adopted the policy that a reasonable cause determination should be tantamount to a "determination that the case is 'worthy of litigation.' "[36] The number of "no cause" findings has thereafter

---

proper procedure is to stay proceeding pending further conciliation rather than dismissal of action); EEOC v. State Employees' Credit Union, 36 EPD ¶ 35,046 (E.D.N.C. 1985) (under ADEA motion to dismiss EEOC suit on ground that conciliation was adequate failed; affidavits showed that Commission tried extensively to reach mutually agreeable resolution).

[29]EEOC v. Hernando Bank, 724 F.2d 1188, 34 FEP 15 (5th Cir. 1984); EEOC v. Home of Economy, 712 F.2d 356, 32 FEP 599 (8th Cir. 1983).

[30]EEOC Order No. 110, as amended (Aug. 18, 1985).

[31]Trial Services performs the same functions as did the former Trial Division, OGC. *Id.* at ch. III, § IV, B.

[32]*Supra* note 30, at ch. III, § IV, D.

[33]*Id.* at ch. III, § IV, B.

[34]Prior to 1982 the house counsel function was performed by the OGC legal counsel division. "EEOC Order No. 110, as amended (Aug. 17, 1982)," 159 DAILY LAB. REP. A-3, D-1-3 (BNA) (Aug. 17, 1982).

[35]EEOC COMPLIANCE MANUAL § 40.2 (May 1985), EEOC GENERAL COUNSEL MANUAL ch. 2, § 1-A, BNA p. 1110:0002 (July 1980).

[36]On May 5, 1985, the Commission adopted the following definition on the Reasonable Cause Standard:

"a determination of reasonable cause is a determination that it is more likely than not that the charging party(ies) and/or member of a class were discriminated against because of a basis prohibited by the statutes enforced by EEOC. The likelihood that discrimination occurred is assessed based upon evidence that establishes, under the appropriate legal theory, a *prima facie* case. If the respondent has provided a viable defense, evidence of pretext must also be assessed."

EEOC COMPLIANCE MANUAL § 40.2 (May 1985).

increased, producing a reduced volume of "reasonable cause" cases deemed litigation-worthy. Notwithstanding this downturn in "reasonable cause" cases, the number of suits filed by the EEOC has increased substantially as a percentage of those filed in the period before that policy change.[37]

In 1984, in response to criticisms that it was not making the best use of its litigation authority,[38] the EEOC adopted an enforcement policy that every case in which reasonable cause is found, but where the conciliation efforts fail, will be forwarded to the Commission for litigation consideration.[39]

Whenever conciliation fails,[40] an attorney in the district office prepares a litigation presentation memorandum either in favor of or against litigation together with a proposed complaint, and forwards the presentation memorandum along with the file to the District Director.[41] The District Director prepares a written concurrence with, or dissent from, the attorney's recommendation and transmits the proposed litigation to the OGC in Washington, D.C., for presentation to the Commission.[42] The OGC then presents the proposed litigation to the Commission together with its advice on the merits of the case.[43] If the Commission authorizes the litigation, the OGC notifies the regional attorney, who files the suit.[44]

In February 1985 the EEOC adopted a new policy statement which provides that the Commission will seek full, corrective, remedial, and preventative relief in all suits involving individual claims of discrimination, including those brought under § 706(f)(1).[45]

---

[37]The reduction in "cause" findings evidently resulted from a reduction in the depth of investigation which was a byproduct of both an expansion in the EEOC workload and an effort to reduce a backlog of charges and dispose of charges rapidly. Oversight Hearings on the Federal Enforcement of Equal Opportunity Laws Before House Subcomm. on Employment Opportunities of the Committee on Education and Labor, 98th Cong., 1st Sess. 4 (1983) ("1983 Oversight Hearings") at 155–56. The EEOC experienced a backlog of unresolved cases as early as 1971. *Id.* at 5. The growing backlog gave rise, in the mid- and late-1970s, to various programs to dispose of charges more rapidly. However, the EEOC workload expanded before the effect of these programs was felt. *Id.* at 8–9. Effective 1979, the Presidential Reorganization Plan No. 1 of 1978, 43 Fed. Reg. 19807 (May 9, 1978), transferred to the EEOC enforcement responsibilities under the Age Discrimination in Employment Act of 1967, as amended, 29 U.S.C. §§ 621, 623, 625, and 626–634, and the Equal Pay Act of 1963, as amended, 29 U.S.C. § 206(d). Despite the attendant increases in its caseload and the dramatic rise in the number of ADEA claims filed, the EEOC staff did not experience a commensurate increase in numbers. *Id.* at 102.

[38]*E.g.*, 1983 Oversight Hearings at 3, 15, 118, 122; *see also* "Statements During EEOC Oversight Hearings Conducted by House Labor Subcommittee on Employment Opportunities," 208 Daily Lab. Rep. A-1-3, D-1-14 (BNA) (Oct. 26, 1983).

[39]"EEOC Directive on Enforcement Policy," 177 Daily Lab. Rep. A-4, D-1-2 (BNA) (Sept. 12, 1984) (policy removes from district office and OGC the discretion to determine which cases will be forwarded to the Commission for litigation approval).

[40]Unlike Title VII and the ADEA, the EPA does not impose a conciliation obligation on the Commission. The EEOC, however, has chosen to follow the Title VII model with regard to conciliation in EPA cases. EEOC Compliance Manual § 40.5(g) (July 1985).

[41]EEOC Compliance Manual § 66.5(a) (July 1986).

[42]*Id.,* § 66.5(b), (specifying the documents which will be forwarded to OGC and presented to Commission).

[43]*Id.,* § 66.5(d).

[44]*Id.,* § 66.5(e). Concurrently, the district office will notify the charging party, or ADEA/EPA complainant that: (1) suit was approved; and, (2) via written notice, she/he has a right to intervene in the lawsuit. The requirement for written notice applies to actions pursuant to Title VII and not to suits based on EPA or ADEA. EEOC Compliance Manual § 66.8 (July 1985).

[45]The EEOC adopted a policy statement on remedies and relief for individual cases to secure predictable enforcement, which calls for all remedies sought in court, or agreed on in settlement, to contain five elements: (1) signing or posting of notice that addresses various elements of compliance; (2) taking corrective action to avoid repetition; (3) offering immediate and unconditional "nondiscriminatory placement" and making the alleged discriminate "whole" until that occurs; (4) providing net back pay with interest; and (5) agreeing, or being ordered to cease the specific practices involved. "EEOC Remedies Policy," 25 Daily Lab. Rep. A-4-5, E-1-2 (BNA) (Feb. 6, 1985).

### 4. Processing Actions for Preliminary Relief

In appropriate ADEA cases, the EEOC continues its policy of seeking preliminary relief under Rule 65 of the Federal Rules of Civil Procedure. These actions are limited, however, by the need to satisfy the pre-suit conciliation requirements of ADEA § 7(b).[46]

### 5. Processing Pattern-or-Practice Suits Under § 707[47]

Responsibility for conducting pattern-or-practice litigation was placed in the OGC when the EEOC reorganized in 1982.[48] Systemic Litigation Services[49] conducts pattern-or-practice systemic suits approved by the Commission for litigation from EEOC headquarters in Washington, D.C.[50] Trial Services, through the legal units in the district offices, is responsible for conducting all those pattern-or-practice suits not approved by the Commission for litigation by Systemic Litigation Services.[51] Developing procedures and policies for pattern-or-practice investigations, ensuring that systemic "reasonable cause" decisions meet appropriate legal standards, and coordinating pattern-or-practice cases between the district offices and Systemic Litigation Services are delegated to the Systemic Investigations and Individual Compliance Programs.[52]

## IV. EEOC SUITS IN THE NATURE OF CLASS ACTIONS; NO NECESSITY FOR COMPLIANCE WITH RULE 23

In at least one case a district court held that *General Telephone Co. of the Northwest v. EEOC*[53] does not require retrospective decertification of a class in a pending EEOC suit. However, the court did decertify the class with respect to the remaining proceedings.[54] The Sixth Circuit has indicated that *General Telephone* is not applicable to a private action in which the EEOC intervenes.[55] Consequently, the presence of the EEOC in a suit may not relieve a private plaintiff from meeting the requirements of Rule 23. At least one district court disagrees with the Sixth Circuit, however.[56] In the Fifth

---

[46]EEOC COMPLIANCE MANUAL § 13.7(b), BNA pp. 13:0003–13:0004 (Sept. 1985).

[47]Reorganization Plan No. 1 of 1978 transferred the Commission's § 707 investigatory authority over state and local governments to the Attorney General of the United States. *See* 1978 U.S. CODE CONG. & AD. NEWS at 9800. The EEOC retained the authority to investigate charges filed against government entities under § 706. EEOC v. Savannah & Chatham County Bd. of Pub. Educ., 643 F. Supp. 134, 40 FEP 1654 (S.D. Ga. 1986).

[48]*See* "Statements of EEOC Chairman on Reorganization of Commission and EEOC Charts Summarizing New Structure," 159 DAILY LAB. REP. A-2, D-1-4 (BNA) (Aug. 17, 1982).

[49]In 1985, the OGC was reorganized to include Systemic Litigation Services, which was made responsible for the enforcement functions formerly conducted by the Litigation Enforcement Division of Systemic Programs. EEOC Order No. 110, as amended (Aug. 18, 1985).

[50]EEOC Order No. 110, as amended (Aug. 18, 1985) ch. II, § IV, B.

[51]*Id.*, ch. VII, § IV, B.

[52]*Id.* Systemic Investigations also recommends the issuance of Systemic Commissioner's charges alleging pattern-or-practice violations. *Id.*, § IV, D.

[53]446 U.S. 318, 22 FEP 1196 (1980).

[54]EEOC v. H.S. Camp & Sons, 542 F. Supp. 411, 33 FEP 330 (M.D. Fla. 1982).

[55]Horn v. Eltra Corp., 686 F.2d 439, 441 n.1, 29 FEP 1266, 1276 (6th Cir. 1982) (EEOC appeal from revocation of permission to intervene was moot because of settlement and dismissal of private plaintiff's Title VII action).

[56]Fields v. Beech Aircraft Corp., 95 F.R.D. 1, 6, 38 FEP 1239, 1243 (D. Kan. 1981), *reh'g granted and modified,* 39 FEP 582 (D. Kan. 1982) (presence of EEOC as intervenor made issue of class

Circuit the EEOC can proceed with its own suit on behalf of the public interest even though it joined the litigation as an intervenor and the private plaintiffs subsequently settled with the defendant before the case was certified as a class action.[57] The Tenth Circuit extended *General Telephone* without qualification to an EEOC intervention.[58]

In addition, the EEOC is exempt from Rule 23 when it is pursuing an action under the ADEA,[59] as well as when bringing an Equal Pay Act suit under § 7 of the FLSA.[60]

## V. STATUTES OF LIMITATIONS AND LACHES

### B. Laches

The Third Circuit has questioned whether laches can ever be applied against the EEOC,[61] because the EEOC is a governmental agency against which the defense of laches does not apply absent statutory authority.[62] The court noted that the reference in *Occidental Life Insurance Co. v. EEOC*[63] to a district court's power to afford protection from prejudice arising from delays in prosecution "may well speak" only to the discretion respecting back pay liability and not to other forms of prospective equitable relief.[64]

Some courts have refused to find prejudice to the defendant employer because of the notice given by the EEOC at the time of the charge[65] and the record-keeping requirements under EEOC regulations.[66]

---

certification academic because EEOC could seek classwide relief without comporting with Rule 23) (altering certified class in light of *General Tel. Co. of the Sw. v. Falcon*, 457 U.S. 147, 28 FEP 1745 (1982)).

[57]Harris v. Amoco Prod. Co., 768 F.2d 669, 38 FEP 1226 (5th Cir. 1985), *cert. denied*, 475 U.S. 1011, 40 FEP 192 (1986) (EEOC is advocate of public interest and can litigate its suit in intervention even though: private plaintiffs' case was not certified pursuant to Rule 23; private plaintiffs settled with defendants and ceased litigation; and EEOC previously had not met § 706(f)(1) jurisdictional requisites—investigation, decision, and conciliation—for independent government suit; *see also* Fields v. Beech Aircraft Corp., *supra* note 56.

[58]United Telecommunications v. Saffels, 741 F.2d 312, 313–14, 35 FEP 1232, 1232–33 (10th Cir. 1984), *cert. denied*, 470 U.S. 1060, 37 FEP 376 (1985) (employer not entitled to writ of mandamus requiring district court to make EEOC, an intervenor, satisfy Rule 23 before seeking classwide relief because Rule 23 does not apply to EEOC in an intervention any more so than when it files suit in its own name).

[59]EEOC v. Chrysler Corp., 546 F. Supp. 73, 29 FEP 1385 (E.D. Mich. 1982), *aff'd*, 733 F.2d 1183, 34 FEP 1401 (6th Cir. 1984) (EEOC suit enforcing the ADEA under § 16(c) is not subject to either Rule 23 or "opt-in" provisions of § 16(c); individual claimants do not have to consent to being joined as party plaintiffs in order to be represented by EEOC).

[60]Donovan v. University of Tex., at El Paso, 643 F.2d 1201, 25 FEP 1050 (5th Cir. 1981) (suit by Secretary of Labor prior to transfer of authority to EEOC); *see also* Dunlop v. Pan Am. World Airways, 672 F.2d 1044, 1049 n.6, 28 FEP 290, 293–94 (2d Cir. 1982) (settlement between Secretary of Labor and defendant did not have to comply with Rule 23(e)'s requirements regarding settlement).

[61]EEOC v. Great Atl. & Pac. Tea Co., 735 F.2d 69, 34 FEP 1412 (3d Cir.), *cert. dismissed*, 469 U.S. 925 (1984) (issue not decided; nine and one-half years between filing of charge and filing of complaint not inordinate delay considering complexity of case, difficulty of discovery, and absence of prejudice to employer).

[62]*Id.*, 735 F.2d at 84, 34 FEP at 1419. The court did not address whether the Administrative Procedure Act, 5 U.S.C. § 706 (1966), may provide the necessary statutory authority. *See* EEOC v. May & Co., 572 F. Supp. 536, 543 (N.D. Ga. 1983).

[63]432 U.S. 355, 14 FEP 1718 (1977), reproduced in the Second Edition at p. 1155.

[64]*Supra* note 61, 735 F.2d at 80, 34 FEP at 1419–20.

[65]EEOC v. May & Co., *supra* note 62, at 543.

[66]29 C.F.R. § 1602.14 (1983); *see* EEOC v. Great Atl. & Pac. Tea. Co., *supra* note 61, 735 F.2d at 84, 34 FEP at 1423 ("any records unavailable by virtue of A&P's failure to comply with the record-preservation requirements of 29 CFR § 1602.14 (1983) would not, of course, qualify as establishing prejudice"); EEOC v. Bethlehem Steel Corp., 765 F.2d 427, 38 FEP 345 (4th Cir. 1985) (respon-

## VI. Scope of the Litigation

### A. Additional Defendants

Courts continue to hold that a party not specifically named in the charge may be named as a defendant in a suit brought by the EEOC if the party the EEOC seeks to sue was an agent of the party who was named in the charge[67] or had adequate notice during the investigation.[68]

### B. Expansion of Basis and Issue

Courts continue to decide whether substantive issues raised in litigation are sufficiently "like or related" to issues raised in the charge to permit the EEOC to litigate them.[69] Some courts allow expansion of the civil action to issues and facts found in a reasonable investigation of the charge.[70]

### C. Geographic Scope

The expansion of EEOC litigation to other facilities of the employer may be allowed where the facts demonstrate a substantial interrelationship between the employment practices of the facilities.[71]

---

dent fails to show prejudice in subpoena enforcement proceeding where subpoena sought only production of documents and since company could produce documents it still possessed there could be no prejudice).

[67]EEOC v. Charleston Elec. Joint Apprenticeship Training Comm. (JATC), 587 F. Supp. 528, 35 FEP 473 (S.D. W. Va. 1984) (denial of summary judgment to union and contractor who were not named in charge and alleged they were separate legal entities from named apprenticeship committee (JATC); factual questions existed as to whether the union or the contractor could be considered agent of JATC for purposes of the suit; whether they had received notification of alleged violation; and they had an opportunity to participate in conciliation process sufficient to justify bringing them into the suit).

[68]EEOC v. Blue Ox Restaurant, No. 82-C-1985, slip op. at 2–4, 8 (N.D. Ill. Feb. 18, 1986) (on motion to reconsider, court found that failure to use defendant's registered corporate name, did not void judgment, as restaurant was equivalent of corporation, and individual owner-defendants were on notice that corporation was being sued; court adopted EEOC proposed findings that one owner-defendant's sale of his stock did not prevent his being named as a defendant, as owner or manager). *See supra* Chapter 30, Section II.

[69]EEOC v. Keco Indus., 748 F.2d 1097, 36 FEP 511 (6th Cir. 1984) (contrary to holding in *EEOC v. Malinckrodt, Inc.,* 22 FEP 311 (E.D. Mo. 1980), cited at note 115 of p. 1163, 2d ed., the Sixth Circuit reversed summary judgment which had been granted to defendants and allowed the EEOC to broaden scope of litigation from individual plaintiff to entire class of discriminatees because the EEOC had issued reasonable cause determination and had attempted conciliation of class-based claim and because class-based claim could reasonably be expected to grow out of the individual complaint of discrimination).

[70]*See* EEOC v. West Co., 40 FEP 1024, 1026 (E.D. Pa. 1986) (individual permitted to intervene in Title VII allegations and to expand scope of retaliation claims as claims could reasonably have been expected to be investigated by EEOC; individual not permitted to expand scope to include state law tort, contract and statutory claims); *see also* EEOC v. Chicago Miniature Lamp Works, 640 F. Supp. 1291, 41 FEP 911, 916 n.10 (N.D. Ill. 1986) (court reaffirmed expansion of issues to include recruitment and hiring, under "reasonable investigation" test; court noted as relevant to beginning of back pay liability, that defendant may have been put on notice of scope of investigation by EEOC letter and questionnaire to which defendant "did not respond by providing information going beyond the scope of" the charge). *But see* Harris v. Amoco Prod. Co., 768 F.2d 669, 675, 38 FEP 1226 (5th Cir. 1985), *cert. denied,* 475 U.S. 1011, 40 FEP 192 (1986) (EEOC as intervenor permitted to maintain suit after settlement by private plaintiffs but its use of discovery material was limited by scope of complaint.

[71]EEOC v. Westinghouse Elec. Corp., 632 F. Supp. 343, 356, 40 FEP 643, 657 (E.D. Pa. 1986) (expansion in second amended ADEA complaint properly related back, as targeted severance pay plan was in effect nationwide; Title VII principles apply).

## VII. RIGHT OF EEOC TO SUE WHERE PRIVATE SUIT IS FILED FIRST

### A. The EEOC's Right to File Suit in Addition to Private Suit

There continues to be a split in authority as to whether later-filed EEOC suits preempt pending private ADEA suits. The Fourth Circuit, in dicta, suggests pending private suits are "suspended" by an EEOC action.[72] The Second[73] and Eleventh[74] circuits have held to the contrary.

### C. Permissive Intervention by EEOC in a Pending Action

Contrary to the evident rationale of a prior Sixth Circuit decision,[75] the Fifth Circuit has held that when the EEOC is allowed to be a permissive intervenor its action may survive even when the claims of the original plaintiffs are settled.[76] However, the Ninth Circuit has held that, if the EEOC continues its suit, it can no longer seek back pay for the employee who has settled.[77]

### 2. Factors Considered

Factors considered when deciding whether to grant the EEOC's motion to intervene include timeliness and the impact of intervention in causing further delay or prejudice to the parties.[78]

## VIII. PRELIMINARY RELIEF

### A. Statutory Authority

The EEOC continues to obtain preliminary relief in appropriate cases.[79]

---

[72]Vance v. Whirlpool Corp., 707 F.2d 483, 488, 31 FEP 1115, 1118, *supplemental opinion,* 716 F.2d 1010, 32 FEP 1391 (4th Cir. 1983), *cert. denied,* 465 U.S. 1102, 34 FEP 416 and 467 U.S. 1226, 34 FEP 1560 (1984).

[73]Burns v. Equitable Life Assurance Soc'y, 696 F.2d 21, 30 FEP 873 (2d Cir. 1982), *cert. denied,* 464 U.S. 933, 33 FEP 48 (1983).

[74]EEOC v. Eastern Airlines, 736 F.2d 635, 35 FEP 503 (11th Cir. 1984); Castle v. Sangamo Weston, Inc., 744 F.2d 1464, 36 FEP 113 (11th Cir. 1984), *rev'g* 31 FEP 324 (M.D. Fla. 1983).

[75]Horn v. Eltra Corp., 686 F.2d 439, 29 FEP 1266 (6th Cir. 1982) (EEOC appealed revocation of order granting permissive intervention; appeal held moot after charging party's Title VII action was settled; EEOC had not issued "reasonable cause" determination or engaged in conciliation).

[76]Harris v. Amoco Prod. Co., 768 F.2d 669, 38 FEP 1226 (5th Cir. 1985), *cert. denied,* 475 U.S. 1011, 40 FEP 192 (1986) (EEOC should not have been dismissed after private plaintiffs settled as matter of law, but may maintain suit subject to court's sound discretion; *Horn v. Eltra Corp., supra* note 75, distinguished because in part dependent on finding of mootness).

[77]EEOC v. Goodyear Aerospace Corp., 813 F.2d 1539, 43 FEP 875 (9th Cir. 1987).

[78]Spirt v. Teachers Ins. & Annuity Ass'n, 93 F.R.D. 627, 28 FEP 489 (S.D.N.Y.), *aff'd in part and rev'd in part on other grounds,* 691 F.2d 1054, 29 FEP 1599 (2d Cir. 1982), *cert. granted and opinion vacated on other grounds,* 463 U.S. 1223, 32 FEP 359 (1983), *cert. denied,* 469 U.S. 881, 35 FEP 1688 (1984); (intervention granted in part only); Molthan v. Temple Univ.-Commonwealth Sys. of Higher Educ., 93 F.R.D. 585, 28 FEP 430 (E.D. Pa. 1982), *aff'd,* 778 F.2d 955, 39 FEP 816 (3d Cir. 1985) (intervention denied).

[79]EEOC v. United States Steel Corp., 583 F. Supp. 1357, 34 FEP 973 (W.D. Pa. 1984) (preliminary injunction issued after temporary restraining order granted); EEOC v. Pacific Sw. Airlines, 587 F. Supp. 686, 34 FEP 1430 (N.D. Cal. 1984). *Cf.* EEOC v. Target Stores, 36 FEP 543 (D. Minn. 1984) (preliminary injunction request denied).

## C. Standards for Relief

The courts remain split over what showing is necessary to support issuance of preliminary relief to the EEOC under Title VII.[80] However, in cases brought under the ADEA, courts thus far have required a showing of irreparable injury.[81]

## IX. DISCOVERY AGAINST THE EEOC

While courts treat the EEOC as just another litigant for discovery purposes with respect to relevant facts in its possession, courts generally refuse to permit discovery of EEOC procedure against the EEOC itself or its employees unless there is a substantial showing of an "abuse of process."[82] However, in one ADEA case[83] a district court accepted the EEOC's claim of informer's privilege as it pertained to identities of witnesses, but rejected the claim of privilege as to information regarding witnesses already identified, based on the employer's need for adequate trial preparation. In addition, although the court denied the EEOC's assertion of work product privilege as to investigative files, it required an *in camera* inspection of the documents to protect against disclosure of the investigator's mental impressions.

In an action to enforce an EEOC subpoena issued as part of an investigation of a Commissioner's charge, the Sixth Circuit vacated a district court's discovery order requiring the EEOC to produce a former Commissioner and certain current employees for depositions.[84]

In reviewing an application for attorney's fees, an Alabama district court took into consideration the EEOC's unresponsiveness in the discovery process, reaching the conclusion that the prevailing defendant was entitled to attorney's fees.[85]

---

[80]EEOC v. United States Steel Corp., *supra* note 79 (applying irreparable injury standard to claim for preliminary relief pending completion of administrative proceedings under provisions of § 706(f)(2) of Title VII); EEOC v. Target Stores, *supra* note 79 (EEOC could not satisfy standard for relief under either *EEOC v. Pacific Press Publishing Ass'n,* 535 F.2d 1182, 12 FEP 1312 (9th Cir. 1976) or *EEOC v. Anchor Hocking Corp.,* 666 F.2d 1037, 27 FEP 809 (6th Cir. 1981).

[81]EEOC v. Chrysler Corp., 738 F.2d 167, 41 FEP 1011 (6th Cir. 1984); EEOC v. New Jersey, 620 F. Supp. 977, 39 FEP 516 (D.N.J. 1985), *aff'd without opinion,* 815 F.2d 694, 43 FEP 653 *and* 43 FEP 1647 (3d Cir. 1987); EEOC v. City of Bowling Green, Ky., 607 F. Supp. 524, 37 FEP 963 (W.D. Ky. 1985); EEOC v. United States Steel Corp., *supra* note 79.

[82]Food Town Stores v. EEOC, 708 F.2d 920, 31 FEP 1327 (4th Cir. 1983), *cert. denied,* 465 U.S. 1005, 33 FEP 1344 (1984); EEOC v. St. Regis Paper Co.-Kraft Div., 717 F.2d 1302, 32 FEP 1849 (9th Cir. 1983); In re EEOC, 709 F.2d 392, 32 FEP 361 (5th Cir. 1983) (statement of charging party's spouse that she had friends who could get Commissioner to make sure company "paid," followed by issuance of broad-based Commissioner's charge, insufficient to raise substantial question of abuse of process).

[83]EEOC v. Consolidated Edison Co. of N.Y., 37 FEP 1660 (S.D.N.Y. 1981), *motion denied,* 557 F. Supp. 468, 37 FEP 1666 (S.D.N.Y. 1983).

[84]EEOC v. K-Mart Corp., 694 F.2d 1055, 30 FEP 788 (6th Cir. 1982) (district court directed former EEOC Commissioner and other EEOC employees to submit to depositions in subpoena enforcement proceeding based on Commissioner's charge; Sixth Circuit held there was no proper basis for discovery directed toward circumstances surrounding issuance of charge; validity of charge must be determined from its face); *see also* EEOC v. Roadway Express, 580 F. Supp. 1063, 35 FEP 842 (W.D. Tenn.), *aff'd,* 750 F.2d 40, 36 FEP 867 (6th Cir. 1984) (district court refused to allow deposition of EEOC District Director in subpoena enforcement proceeding; court held that allegations of bad faith must be buttressed by specific facts and put in issue good faith of the agency, and not just agent handling the matter).

[85]EEOC v. Shoney's, Inc., 542 F. Supp. 332, 35 FEP 386 (N.D. Ala. 1982).

## X. DECREE ENFORCEMENT

Federal courts have jurisdiction to hear actions where the EEOC alleges a respondent breached a settlement agreement, and, in appropriate cases, to issue an order specifically enforcing the agreement.[86]

Courts have held that the EEOC may sue to enforce a voluntary conciliation agreement.[87] However, there is a split as to whether the EEOC can sue to enforce a predetermination settlement agreement absent a reasonable cause determination,[88] and one district court has decided that the EEOC could not sue for enforcement of a settlement agreement allegedly breached by the employer, where the settlement agreement was not incorporated in the court order approving it.[89]

The Ninth Circuit has held, en banc, that a consent decree which establishes a procedure for dealing with post-consent-decree claims of discrimination cannot strip the EEOC of jurisdiction to issue a subpoena and investigate charges filed by employees who are members of a class governed by the decree.[90]

## XI. EEOC LIABILITY FOR ATTORNEY'S FEES AND COSTS

When justified by the record courts have continued to award prevailing defendants attorney's fees from the EEOC.[91]

---

[86]EEOC v. Safeway Stores, 714 F.2d 567, 32 FEP 1465 (5th Cir. 1983), *cert. denied,* 467 U.S. 1204, 34 FEP 1400 (1984).

[87]EEOC v. Liberty Trucking Co., 695 F.2d 1038, 30 FEP 884 (7th Cir. 1982) (although Title VII did not explicitly provide EEOC with authority to seek enforcement of conciliation agreements in federal courts, Congress intended to provide EEOC with federal forum to enforce conciliation agreements).

[88]*Compare* EEOC v. Pierce Packing Co., 669 F.2d 605, 28 FEP 393 (9th Cir. 1982) (EEOC cannot sue to enforce settlement agreement entered into prior to reasonable cause determination and good-faith attempts at conciliation) *with* EEOC v. Henry Beck Co., 729 F.2d 301, 34 FEP 373 (4th Cir. 1984), *rev'g* 34 FEP 370 (D. Md. 1982) (EEOC may enforce predetermination settlement reached without reasonable cause determination, but may not sue on underlying charge); EEOC v. Liberty Trucking Co., *supra* note 87, at 1044 n.72, 30 FEP at 889 (dictum) (finding of reasonable cause not a prerequisite to EEOC suit to enforce voluntary settlement agreement).

[89]EEOC v. University of Notre Dame du Lac, 629 F. Supp. 837, 39 FEP 1265 (N.D. Ind. 1985) (class action settlement not incorporated in approval order, and therefore was in the nature of a contract, not a consent decree).

[90]EEOC v. Children's Hosp. Medical Center of N. Cal., 719 F.2d 1426, 33 FEP 461 (9th Cir. 1983) (en banc), *rev'g* 695 F.2d 412, 30 FEP 961 (9th Cir. 1982).

[91]*See* Chapter 39 (Attorney's Fees).

## CHAPTER 32

# JUSTICE DEPARTMENT LITIGATION

## II. DEPARTMENT OF JUSTICE POST-1972 PUBLIC SECTOR TITLE VII SUITS

### B. Department of Justice Authority Under § 706

There has been some confusion as to whether the EEOC or the Attorney General is the proper party to issue a right-to-sue letter in cases involving state and local government employers. Where there has not been a dismissal of a charge, the Attorney General, and not the EEOC, is the proper issuer of a right-to-sue letter for claims involving state and local governmental entities, and issuance of a right-to-sue letter by the EEOC will not trigger an individual's obligation to bring suit within 90 days.[1] The EEOC nevertheless retains authority to investigate governmental entities under § 706.[2]

The EEOC guidelines concerning issuance of right-to-sue letters in cases involving state and local governments[3] provide that the EEOC shall issue a right-to-sue letter where there has been a dismissal of a charge. At least two courts have declared the regulations invalid in this respect, finding that Congress, by the clear language of § 706(f)(1), intended the Attorney General to issue all such letters,[4] while another court has specifically found the EEOC regulations to be valid.[5] Despite this uncertainty, courts have generally given effect to an EEOC right-to-sue letter to avoid frustrating an individual's right to proceed.[6] The Justice Department apparently has taken the position on at least one occasion that the EEOC may properly issue a

---

[1]Hendrix v. Memorial Hosp. of Galveston County, 776 F.2d 1255, 39 FEP 609 (5th Cir. 1985) (period for filing suit after receipt of right-to-sue letter from EEOC not commenced in suit brought by governmental employee until notice is received from Attorney General).

[2]EEOC v. Savannah & Chatham County Bd. of Pub. Educ., 643 F. Supp. 134, 40 FEP 1654 (S.D. Ga. 1986).

[3]29 C.F.R. § 1601-28(b) and (d).

[4]Woods v. Missouri Dep't of Mental Health, Kansas City Regional Diagnostic Center, 581 F. Supp. 437, 35 FEP 1587 (W.D. Mo. 1984) (finding right-to-sue letter should have issued from Attorney General, but waiving this requirement under equities of the case); Ying Shen v. Oklahoma State Dep't of Health, 647 F. Supp. 189 (W.D. Okla. 1985) (regulatory language permitting EEOC to issue right-to-sue letter is in conflict with statute and is without effect).

[5]Flint v. California, 594 F. Supp. 443, 35 FEP 1582 (E.D. Cal. 1984) (if petitioner obtains EEOC right-to-sue letter, § 706(f)(1) can be ignored).

[6]Dillard v. Rumph, 584 F. Supp. 1266, 35 FEP 656 (N.D. Ga. 1984) (§ 706(f)(1) requirement of issuance of right-to-sue letter from Attorney General waived when EEOC right-to-sue letter failed to mention any need to obtain such letter from Attorney General); Solomon v. Hardison, 746 F.2d 699, 36 FEP 261 (11th Cir. 1984) (requirements of § 706(f)(1) waived when petitioner "conclusively demonstrated" inability to comply); *see also* Moore v. City of Charlotte, 754 F.2d 1100, 36 FEP 1582 (4th Cir.), *cert. denied,* 472 U.S. 1021, 37 FEP 1816 (1985). *But see* Thames v. Oklahoma Historical Soc'y, 646 F. Supp. 13 (W.D. Okla. 1985), *aff'd,* 809 F.2d 699 (10th Cir. 1987) (suit under Title VII could not be brought against governmental agency without Right-to-Sue Notice from Office of Attorney General rather than EEOC); Ying Shen v. Oklahoma Dep't of Health, *supra* note 4.

right-to-sue letter where a charge against a state or local governmental entity has been dismissed by the EEOC.[7]

## C. Department of Justice Suits Under § 707

Since June 1, 1982, courts have consistently held that, pursuant to the Presidential Reorganization Plan of 1979, the EEOC assumed enforcement functions with respect to federal employee discrimination claims.[8] The Justice Department continues to bring pattern-or-practice suits on behalf of state and local government employees without referral from the EEOC.[9]

## III. Jᴜʀɪsᴅɪᴄᴛɪᴏɴᴀʟ Pʀᴇʀᴇǫᴜɪsɪᴛᴇs ᴛᴏ Dᴇᴘᴀʀᴛᴍᴇɴᴛ ᴏꜰ Jᴜsᴛɪᴄᴇ Lɪᴛɪɢᴀᴛɪᴏɴ

### B. Under § 707

Two district courts have decided that the Department of Justice need not adhere to the administrative requirements of § 707.[10] In both cases, the courts held that a "reasonable cause" determination is the only prerequisite imposed upon Department of Justice litigation.

## V. Dᴇᴘᴀʀᴛᴍᴇɴᴛ ᴏꜰ Jᴜsᴛɪᴄᴇ Jᴜʀɪsᴅɪᴄᴛɪᴏɴ Uɴᴅᴇʀ Oᴛʜᴇʀ Sᴛᴀᴛᴜᴛᴇs

### A. Crime Control Act

One district court has held that the Justice Department is not required to exhaust the administrative remedies available under the Crime Control Act before commencing suit to remedy discrimination.[11]

### B. Revenue Sharing Act

The Consolidated Budget Reconciliation Act of 1985 (COBRA)[12] repealed the Revenue Sharing Act effective October 18, 1986. Actions to enforce the nondiscrimination requirements of the Revenue Sharing Act may, however, still be brought to remedy unlawful acts of discrimination in programs funded with revenue sharing funds.[13]

---

[7]Solomon v. Hardison, *supra* note 6.

[8]*See, e.g.,* EEOC v. Wyoming, 460 U.S. 226, 31 FEP 74 (1983); Thomas v. KATV Channel 7, 692 F.2d 548, 30 FEP 231 (8th Cir. 1982), *cert. denied,* 460 U.S. 1039, 31 FEP 368 (1983); Stember v. Borough of Baldwin, 31 FEP 690 (W.D. Pa. 1983).

[9]*See, e.g.,* Hammon v. Barry, 606 F. Supp. 1082, 37 FEP 609 (D.D.C. 1985), *rev'd on other grounds,* 813 F.2d 412, 43 FEP 89, *petition for reh'g denied,* 826 F.2d 73, 44 FEP 869 (D.C. Cir. 1987) (majority recognizes Title VII pattern-or-practice suit by United States under 42 U.S.C. § 2000e-6; one member of majority panel, Silberman, J., and dissenter, Mikva, J., would recognize pattern-or-practice suits claiming that employment practices violate both Title VII and constitutional prohibitions against employment discrimination); United States v. Pasadena Indep. School Dist., 43 FEP 1319 (S.D. Tex. 1987).

[10]United States v. New Jersey, 473 F. Supp. 1199, 20 FEP 819 (D.N.J. 1979); United States v. City of Yonkers, 592 F. Supp. 570, 40 FEP 941 (S.D.N.Y. 1984).

[11]United States v. City of Yonkers, *supra* note 10.

[12]Pub. L. No. 99-272, 100 Stat. 327.

[13]*Id.,* § 14001(a).

The Treasury Department and the Justice Department have entered into a working arrangement to provide for the processing of complaints. All complaints received by the Treasury Department after September 30, 1987 will be referred to the Civil Rights Division of the Department of Justice.[14]

## C. Immigration Reform and Control Act

Section 274B of the Immigration Reform and Control Act of 1986 (IRCA)[15] amends the Immigration and Nationality Act[16] to prohibit discrimination (other than against an unauthorized alien) because of national origin, or in the case of a citizen or intending citizen, because of his or her citizenship status. These provisions of IRCA will be enforced by a Special Counsel for Immigration-Related Unfair Employment Practices within the Justice Department. Employers with fewer than four employees are not covered by these provisions, and charges of national origin discrimination may not be prosecuted under this section where they are covered by Title VII. Thus, charges of national origin discrimination involving employers with at least 15 employees during 20 of the preceding 52 weeks would continue to be filed with the EEOC.[17]

---

[14]Inter-agency Civil Rights Agreement on Revenue Sharing, 52 Fed. Reg. 16323 (1987).
[15]Pub. L. No. 99-272. *See supra* Chapter 10 (National Origin).
[16]8 U.S.C. § 1101 *et seq.* (Supp V 1987).
[17]EEOC Policy Statement on the Relationship of Title VII to IRCA (Feb. 1987), 401 Fair Employment Practices Manual 445. *See* Chapter 10 (National Origin) for a discussion of the Immigration Reform and Control Act of 1986, including the role of the Justice Department.

## CHAPTER 33

# FEDERAL EMPLOYEE LITIGATION

## II. ADMINISTRATIVE ENFORCEMENT

### A. General Procedure

Courts still follow the well-established rule requiring federal employees[1] to exhaust available administrative remedies before pursuing a Title VII[2] or a Rehabilitation Act[3] claim.

Regulations require that an employee initiate an administrative complaint with the agency within 30 days of the alleged violation.[4] Some courts have held the 30-day filing rule may be waived or tolled on the basis of equitable considerations.[5] Other courts have rejected equitable tolling of the 30-day filing rule.[6] A federal employee is required only to give the EEOC 30

---

[1]Not all potential employees of federal executive agencies come within the scope of Title VII. In *Mares v. Marsh,* 777 F.2d 1066, 40 FEP 858 (5th Cir. 1985), the court determined that grocery baggers at the U.S. Army Commissary were not federal employees within the meaning of Title VII. Likewise, officers of the U.S. Public Health Service Commissioned Corps were held not "members of military departments" entitled to protection. Salazar v. Heckler, 787 F.2d 527, 40 FEP 721 (10th Cir. 1986). *But see* Hill v. Berkman, 635 F. Supp. 1228, 40 FEP 1444 (E.D.N.Y. 1986) ("members of military departments" extends to members of uniformed military). In *Stinson v. Hornsby,* 821 F.2d 1537, 44 FEP 594 (11th Cir. 1987), a member of the National Guard was found to be "military personnel" for purposes of Title VII.

[2]*See, e.g.,* Kizas v. Webster, 707 F.2d 524, 31 FEP 905 (D.C. Cir. 1983), *cert. denied,* 464 U.S. 1042, 33 FEP 1084 (1984) (federal employees covered under Title VII must formally file with agency charged with discrimination to exhaust administrative remedies); Edwards v. Department of the Army, 708 F.2d 1344, 32 FEP 658 (8th Cir. 1983) (complainant failed to exhaust administrative remedies where specific allegation of discrimination personal to complainant not presented); Limongelli v. Postmaster Gen. of the U.S., 707 F.2d 368, 31 FEP 1554 (9th Cir. 1983) (employee failed to exhaust with respect to one part of suit involving alleged retaliation); Quillen v. United States Postal Serv., 564 F. Supp. 314, 32 FEP 1631 (E.D. Mich. 1983) (employee failed to exhaust administrative remedies by not filing formal complaint with EEOC within 15 days of final interview).

[3]Morgan v. United States Postal Serv., 798 F.2d 1162, 41 FEP 959 (8th Cir. 1986), *cert. denied,* 480 U.S. 948, 43 FEP 560 (1987); Johnson v. Orr, 747 F.2d 1352, 36 FEP 515 (10th Cir. 1984); McGuinness v. United States Postal Serv., 744 F.2d 1318, 35 FEP 1762 (7th Cir. 1984). *See also* cases cited at note 42, *infra.*

[4]29 C.F.R. § 1613.214(a) (1987).

[5]Arnold v. United States, 816 F.2d 1306, 43 FEP 1256 (9th Cir. 1987); Henderson v. Veterans Admin., 790 F.2d 436, 40 FEP 1524 (5th Cir. 1986) (time limit waived where agency made initial finding that complaint was timely); Royall v. United States Postal Serv., 624 F. Supp. 211, 41 FEP 311 (E.D.N.Y. 1985) (failure to file formal complaint within 15 days with EEO counselor excused under doctrine of equitable tolling); Miller v. Marsh, 766 F.2d 490, 38 FEP 805 (11th Cir. 1985) (employee entitled to equitable tolling of requirement to file suit within 30 days where employee misled by Agency into pursuing other channels at expense of her federal court remedy); Burton v. United States Postal Serv., 612 F. Supp. 1057, 38 FEP 1591 (N.D. Ohio 1985) (former employee entitled to equitable tolling of filing period due to abandonment by his attorney); Wolfolk v. Rivera, 729 F.2d 1114, 34 FEP 468 (7th Cir. 1984) (time limit waived because complainant lacked knowledge of discriminatory facts until month after incident).

[6]Koucky v. Department of the Navy, 820 F.2d 300, 44 FEP 156 (9th Cir. 1987) (rejects argument that 30-day limit is not jurisdictional and should be subject to equitable tolling); King v. Dole, 782 F.2d 274, 40 FEP 624 (D.C. Cir.), *cert. denied,* 479 U.S. 856, 43 FEP 640 (1986) (30-day filing period not subject to equitable tolling); McKinney v. Dole, 765 F.2d 1129, 38 FEP 364 (D.C. Cir. 1985) (30-day period not tolled; plaintiff unaware of time limits); Dimetry v. Department of the Army, 637 F. Supp. 269, 40 FEP 1192 (E.D.N.C. 1985) (doctrine of equitable tolling not applicable in action against the federal government).

days' notice, however, of his intent to sue before he can file suit under the ADEA.[7]

## C. Individual Charges Appealed to the MSPB

Under the voluntary expedited appeals procedure, employees may also request that their petitions be processed under appeal arbitration.[8] If the regional director grants the request, an arbitrator with special training will be selected. The procedure is informal; there is no discovery, and decisions are final but not precedential.[9] If a petition for review is accepted, the 30-day period for filing under Title VII does not begin to run until the initial decision of the presiding official becomes the final decision of the Merit Systems Review Board.[10]

## D. Class Charges

When determining whether a class charge satisfies the requirements of numerosity, commonality, typicality, and adequacy of representation, an agency should take into account the employee's difficulties in obtaining access to pertinent information about the class.[11]

## E. Employees Covered by Bargaining Agreements

Even though the right of federal employees and their unions[12] to raise discrimination claims through negotiated grievance procedures has existed since 1978, it was a somewhat amorphous right until 1983 because there were no regulations pertaining solely to discrimination claims raised under collective bargaining agreements. Compelled by the legal requirement that it entertain appeals with respect to issues of discrimination raised in conjunction with agreement grievances,[13] the EEOC amended its

---

[7]Tkac v. Veterans Admin., 610 F. Supp. 1075, 37 FEP 840 (W.D. Mich. 1985).

[8]5 C.F.R. § 1201.200–1201.22 (1987).

[9]*Id.*

[10]Ballard v. Tennessee Valley Auth., 768 F.2d 756, 38 FEP 904 (6th Cir. 1985) ("decision of the Board" as specified in § 7702(a)(3), which begins running of limitations period for seeking judicial review of Board decision in a mixed case, is final decision of the Board); *accord* Tolliver v. Deniro, 790 F.2d 1394, 40 FEP 1646 (9th Cir. 1986) (initial decision of MSPB presiding official becomes "final action by the Board" 35 days after decision for purpose of judicial review); Cansler v. Tennessee Valley Auth., 774 F.2d 433, 39 FEP 68 (11th Cir. 1985) (citing and relying on *Ballard, supra,* holds that 30-day period to appeal to federal district court from MSPB decision in mixed case runs from date on which Board's decision becomes final rather than from date on which employee receives decision); Sousa v. NLRB, 817 F.2d 10, 43 FEP 1057 (2d Cir. 1987) (30-day period did not begin to run when certified notice was placed in employee's post box, but five days later when he actually received notice by claiming certified letter at post office); Koucky v. Department of the Navy, *supra* note 6 (receipt of decision by employee's attorney begins running of 30-day period). There is a split of authority as to whether the 30-day period is extended when the thirtieth day falls on a weekend or legal holiday. *Compare* Arnold v. United States, *supra* note 5 (where thirtieth day falls on Saturday, filing on following Monday is timely) *with* Hilliard v. United States Postal Serv., 814 F.2d 325, 43 FEP 600 (6th Cir. 1987) (since 30-day period is jurisdictional, it is not subject to expansion pursuant to Rule 6(a) of Federal Rules of Civil Procedure).

[11]Wade v. Secretary of the Army, 796 F.2d 1369, 41 FEP 1691 (11th Cir. 1986) (reviewing court should consider plaintiff's limited access to information where agency claims employee failed to provide sufficient information about class requirements).

[12]A suspected violation of an employee's rights may be raised by the union representing the employee. 5 U.S.C. § 7103(a)(9)(B) (1983).

[13]5 U.S.C. § 7121(d) (1983); *see* Jones v. Department of Health & Human Servs., 622 F. Supp. 829, 39 FEP 1860 (N.D. Ill. 1985) (federal district court lacks jurisdiction over Title VII action that former

regulations[14] to include administrative procedures for appeals[15] by a federal employee of decisions issued by (1) the agency, (2) a grievance arbitrator,[16] or (3) the Federal Labor Relations Authority (FLRA) or "exceptions" to the arbitrator's award.[17] As is the case with appeals from the agency EEO procedure, an appeal to the EEOC is decided by the Commission's Office of Review and Appeals.[18]

The regulations that govern judicial review of an agency-processed discrimination complaint under § 717(c) of Title VII also govern claims of discrimination litigated administratively pursuant to negotiated grievance systems. The employee grievant may file in the appropriate district court within 30 calendar days after receiving notice of the final decision of the agency, or of the Office of Review and Appeals if the matter is appealed to the EEOC.[19] Federal employees may proceed to court after 180 calendar days from the filing of a grievance with their agency or an appeal with the EEOC, if there has been no decision by either since the time of filing.[20] It seems likely that the "receipt of notice of final action" taken by an agency will also establish the time parameters for applications for judicial review of the last act of an agency in a discrimination grievance. However, neither Title VII nor the 1983 regulations address specifically the right to judicial review of decisions issued by arbitrators or the FLRA.[21] The right to appeal from these decisions, and the time limits for filing, are issues that will have to be decided by the courts or made the subject of future regulations.[22]

---

employee brought more than 30 days after grievance filed under collective bargaining contract was denied because, by electing to file grievance, he was foreclosed from being able to file administrative complaint).

[14]29 C.F.R. § 1613.231 et seq. (1987). The EEOC has proposed a revised rule so that § 1613.231 conforms with the procedure for appeals of matters under § 1613.217(b), noncompliance with settlement agreement, and failure to implement final agency decision. 51 FED. REG. 29482, 29490 (1986) (proposed Aug. 18, 1986).

[15]The amendments apply to all federal workers, except those of the U.S. Postal Service, who are not covered by 5 U.S.C. § 7121.

[16]The employee's grievance can go to arbitration only if the agency or the union invokes arbitration. 5 U.S.C. § 7121(b)(C) (1983). Should the union choose not to proceed to arbitration, the employee's remedy would be to appeal the agency's final decision to the EEOC. 29 C.F.R. § 1613.231 (1986). If an employee believes the union's decision not to invoke arbitration was influenced by discrimination, a separate charge could be filed against the union pursuant to § 703(c). Cf. Jennings v. Postal Workers Local 8, 672 F.2d 712, 28 FEP 514 (8th Cir. 1982) (union representing federal employees may be held liable for employment discrimination under civil rights statute guaranteeing equal rights under the law). The EEOC has proposed a rule revision stating that a complainant may appeal to the EEOC on issues of employment discrimination raised in a negotiated grievance procedure where the agency's negotiated labor-management agreement permits such issues to be raised. 51 FED. REG. 29482, 29490 (1986) (proposed Aug. 18, 1986).

[17]The appeal must be filed within 20 calendar days after (1) the receipt of the agency's decision on the grievance and the expiration of the time during which the union and the agency may move the matter to the next stage of the grievance process, i.e., arbitration; (2) receipt of an arbitrator's award; or (3) receipt of the decision of the FLRA. 29 C.F.R. § 1613.233(b) (1987).

[18]29 C.F.R. § 1613.232 (1987). There has been a change of mailing address for appeals, petitions, and requests for reconsideration submitted to the EEOC Office of Review and Appeals and for the filing requirements of § 1613.414. 51 FED. REG. 22519 (1986) (codified at 29 C.F.R. §§ 1613.232, 1613.414, and 1613.806 (1987)).

[19]29 C.F.R. § 1613.281(a) and (c) (1987), respectively.

[20]29 C.F.R. § 1613.281(b) and (d) (1987), respectively.

[21]Although the Civil Service Reform Act expressly precludes from judicial review "Exceptions to Award" decisions (5 U.S.C. § 7123(a)(1) (1983)), presumably the discrimination claims raised in a grievance appealed to the FLRA can be taken to a district court for de novo consideration. Cf. Chandler v. Roudebush, 425 U.S. 840, 12 FEP 1368, 1377 (1976) (federal government employees who bring Title VII actions have some right to trial de novo as private employees in view of § 717 of Title VII and legislative history of 1972 amendments).

[22]See supra note 14.

## F. Retaliation and Reprisal

Federal employees who allege they have been subject to coercion or reprisal in connection with the filing of a discrimination complaint may, where the prior complaint from which the allegation derives is in process at the agency or before a hearing examiner, partially expedite the processing of their reprisal allegation by having the claim consolidated with the original complaint; the two will thereafter be processed together.[23] Consolidation is at the discretion of the agency or the Complaints Examiner and will be considered only if the employee requests consolidation within 30 calendar days after the reprisal action occurs, or becomes effective,[24] if it is a personnel action.[25]

## III. LITIGATION PROCEDURE

### A. Class Complaints

In cases arising since 1978, when the EEOC promulgated regulations[26] for the administrative processing of federal employee class complaints,[27] courts have held the failure of plaintiffs to exhaust administrative class remedies is fatal to Rule 23 certification of a class action.[28] Although some

---

[23]29 C.F.R. § 1613.262(b) (1986). The EEOC has proposed a rule revision so that § 1613.262(b) conforms clearly to § 704 of Title VII. 51 FED. REG. 29482, 29491 (1986) (proposed Aug. 18, 1986). *See* Lawson v. McPherson, 39 FEP 719 (D.D.C. 1985) (employee's failure to seek EEO counseling before amending complaint in pending Title VII action to include termination of his position after action filed does not require dismissal of reprisal claim as such claim is inextricably related to pending action). *But see* Mason v. Pierce, 774 F.2d 825, 39 FEP 21 (7th Cir. 1985) (employee who failed to seek recourse for alleged retaliation through EEO officer and then through EEOC may not litigate claim of retaliatory discharge as violation of rights under First Amendment).

[24]29 C.F.R. § 1613.262(b) (1987).

[25]Another avenue for immediate relief open to the federal employee is to seek to enjoin the alleged retaliatory act of the agency. The employee may find it more difficult to prevail than would a nonfederal employee. The Second, Fifth, Sixth, and Ninth circuits have completely adopted the ruling of *Sampson v. Murray*, 415 U.S. 61 (1974), which necessitates federal employees to show, in addition to the traditional requisites for preliminary relief, that they will suffer not simply irreparable injury, but extraordinary harm that outweighs the government's interest in unfettered internal regulations. Stewart v. Immigration & Naturalization Serv., 762 F.2d 193, 37 FEP 1357 (2d Cir. 1985) (irreparable harm and extraordinary circumstances not established to merit injunctive relief by claims that suspension degraded complainant, caused his family to suffer undue hardship, and prevented him from adequately providing for family, and where there is no showing that suspension caused others to refrain from exercising their rights); Hartikka v. United States, 754 F.2d 1516 (9th Cir. 1985) (preliminary injunction denied where assertions of lost income, lost retirement and relocation pay, and damage to reputation from stigma of less than honorable discharge were insufficient to support finding of irreparable injury). The application of the rule is not uniform, however. *Compare* Government Employees, AFGE v. Office of Personnel Mgmt., 618 F. Supp. 1254 (D.D.C. 1985), *aff'd without opinion,* 782 F.2d 278 (D.C. Cir. 1986) (preliminary injunctive relief denied where irreparable injury was lacking) *with* Government Employees, AFGE, Local 51 v. Secretary of the Treasury, 40 FEP 395 (N.D. Cal. 1986) (employees entitled to preliminary injunction, where, among other things, irreparable harm may be presumed from likelihood that violation of Rehabilitation Act has occurred or is threatened and employees have sufficiently stated prima facie case to support probable success on merits, especially considering serious harm that is threatened in event injunctive relief denied). *See also* Fischer v. Dole, 624 F. Supp. 468 (D. Mass. 1985) (preliminary injunction denied as proposed transfer to new city which would disrupt employee's friendships and social life would not irreparably harm employee). *But see* Garcia v. Lawn, 805 F.2d 1400, 42 FEP 873 (9th Cir. 1986) (preliminary injunction granted where employee transferred to new city, as such retaliation causes irreparable harm by chilling exercise of Title VII rights by others).

[26]29 C.F.R. §§ 1613.601–.643 (1981).

[27]*See generally* Barrett v. Civil Serv. Comm'n, 69 F.R.D. 544, 553, 11 FEP 1089, 1095–96 (D.D.C. 1975) (ordering Civil Service Commission to modify regulations and provide for consideration, processing, and resolution of class claims advanced through individual complaint).

[28]Wade v. Secretary of the Army, 796 F.2d 1369, 41 FEP 1691 (11th Cir. 1986); Williams v. United States Postal Serv., 33 FEP 533, 534–35 (N.D. Ga. 1983) (employees' failure to exhaust class administra-

courts view the exhaustion requirements as jurisdictional prerequisites,[29] most have viewed the administrative class complaint procedures as limitation schemes subject to waiver, estoppel, or equitable modification, and have granted certification where the employer agency had an opportunity to investigate and remedy the issues.[30]

## B. Trial *de Novo*

When reviewing a Merit System Protection Board decision adverse to the complaining employee in a case containing discrimination claims as well as charges of procedural violations (a mixed case), the district court conducts a trial *de novo* on the discrimination claims but conducts only a review on the record of the other personnel matters.[31]

Trial *de novo* is not available to the federal government in cases where the EEOC issues a decision in favor of the federal employee.[32] An employee may seek from the appropriate district court an order enforcing a favorable EEOC ruling without risking *de novo* review.[33]

Trial *de novo* from a decision adverse to the complaining employee has also been held available in handicap cases.[34]

## C. Class Actions

Since class actions brought by federal employees are subject to the same standards as are Rule 23 actions,[35] the case law developed to date generally must be reviewed in light of the rigorous reading of Rule 23(a) enunciated

---

tive remedies precludes class action since administrative charges contained specific allegations of discrimination and did not allege pattern or practice of class discrimination); *see also* Moore v. Orr, 33 FEP 523 (D. Colo. 1982); Patton v. Brown, 95 F.R.D. 205, 33 FEP 529 (E.D. Pa. 1982).

[29]*E.g.,* Lewis v. Smith, 731 F.2d 1535, 34 FEP 1313 (11th Cir. 1984).

[30]In *McIntosh v. Weinberger,* 617 F. Supp. 107, 34 FEP 911 (E.D. Mo. 1984), *aff'd in part,* 810 F.2d 1411, 45 FEP 398 (8th Cir. 1987) the court denied certification, finding that none of the five named plaintiffs had pursued class remedies and that the agency had therefore never had an opportunity to address the classwide allegations. 34 FEP at 913. *See also* Kizas v. Webster, 707 F.2d 524, 547, 31 FEP 905, 919 (D.C. Cir. 1983), *cert. denied,* 464 U.S. 1042, 33 FEP 1084 (1984) (class exhaustion requirement not met where named plaintiffs, none of whom filed administrative class charges, tried to join similarly situated individual who did exhaust available remedies). For an example of equitable modification or tolling, *see* Wade v. Secretary of the Army, *supra* note 28 (rejecting defendant's argument that plaintiff failed to exhaust and holding that employee is required only to make good-faith effort to provide available information); Brown v. Marsh, 777 F.2d 8, 39 FEP 505 (D.C. Cir. 1985) (burden of showing nonexhaustion placed on agency raising defense; agency found to have waived exhaustion defense); Fitzwater v. Veterans Admin., 90 F.R.D. 435, 26 FEP 177 (S.D. Ohio 1981) (adherence to EEOC class complaint regulations not required as condition precedent to federal jurisdiction where charges sufficiently apprise agency of alleged pattern of discrimination involving similarly situated employees); *see also* Griffin v. Carlin, 755 F.2d 1516, 37 FEP 741 (11th Cir. 1985) (use of old third-party complaint procedure in 1971 satisfied purpose of exhaustion requirement, when no other administrative class claim procedure was available).

[31]Romain v. Shear, 799 F.2d 1416, 43 FEP 264 (9th Cir. 1986), *cert. denied,* 481 U.S. 1050, 43 FEP 1896 (1987); Rana v. United States, 812 F.2d 887, 43 FEP 161 (4th Cir. 1987). The MSPB administrative record is admissible as evidence in the *de novo* trial. *Id.* An employee cannot get a trial *de novo* by merely making bare allegations of discrimination. Hill v. Department of the Air Force, 796 F.2d 1469, 41 FEP 528 (Fed. Cir. 1986) (employee must allege nonfrivolous discrimination claim sufficient to support minimum prima facie case).

[32]Moore v. Devine, 780 F.2d 1559, 39 FEP 1644 (11th Cir. 1986), *clarifying* 767 F.2d 1541, 38 FEP 1196 (11th Cir. 1985) (dictum; agency bound by EEOC decision and not entitled to seek *de novo* review).

[33]Haskins v. Department of the Army, 808 F.2d 1192, 42 FEP 1120 (6th Cir.), *cert. denied,* 484 U.S. _____, 44 FEP 1672 (1987).

[34]Shirey v. Devine, 670 F.2d 1188, 27 FEP 1148 (D.C. Cir. 1982).

[35]One court has now ruled that if the federal employee seeks only review of the final agency action (as opposed to a trial *de novo*) then he does not have to independently meet the requirements of Rule 23. Hansen v. Webster, 41 FEP 214 (D.D.C. 1986).

in *General Telephone Co. of the Southwest v. Falcon.* [36] This general trend toward strict interpretation of Rule 23(a) is demonstrated in *Lucas v. Ripley.* [37] The scope of the class need not, however, be limited to employees identically situated to the named plaintiff.[38] The settlement of class actions, especially those certified under Rule 23(b)(2), continues to pose troublesome questions.[39]

## D. Exclusivity of Remedy

While the courts have continued to hold that § 717 of Title VII provides the exclusive judicial remedy for claims of discrimination in federal employment,[40] recent cases indicate there are circumstances under which the alleged discriminatory conduct can justify additional relief under theories other than discrimination.[41]

---

[36]457 U.S. 147, 28 FEP 1745 (1982), *aff'd,* 815 F.2d 317, 43 FEP 1040 (5th Cir. 1987). *See generally* Chapter 34 (Class Actions).

[37]30 FEP 1630 (D.D.C. 1982) (class certification denied where plaintiff presented only general statistical data; showing of typicality required submission of specific evidence and identification of specific policies adversely affecting class); *see also* Gilchrist v. Bolger, 733 F.2d 1551, 35 FEP 81 (11th Cir. 1984) (class certification denied for lack of numerosity); Sperling v. Donovan, 104 F.R.D. 4, 35 FEP 983 (D.D.C. 1984) (overzealous definition of class raises doubts as to adequacy of representation; accountant class not certified absent showing of typicality).

[38]McKenzie v. Sawyer, 684 F.2d 62, 29 FEP 633 (D.C. Cir. 1982) (certification of class encompassing both journeymen and supervisors affirmed where single policy at root of their promotion discrimination claims). *But see* Gilchrist v. Bolger, *supra* note 37, affirming elimination of applicants and supervisors from class and denying certification for lack of numerosity.

[39]Bachman v. Miller, 559 F. Supp. 150, 30 FEP 125 (D.D.C. 1982) (publication in newspapers of general circulation adequate notice of settlement and sufficient to bind class).

[40]Owens v. United States, 822 F.2d 408, 44 FEP 247 (3d Cir. 1987); Arnold v. United States, 816 F.2d 1306, 43 FEP 1256 (9th Cir. 1987); Germane v. Heckler, 804 F.2d 366, 42 FEP 1053 (7th Cir. 1986); McGuinness v. United States Postal Serv., 744 F.2d 1318, 35 FEP 1762 (7th Cir. 1984); Thompson v. Sawyer, 678 F.2d 257, 28 FEP 1614 (D.C. Cir. 1982); Neves v. Kolaski, 602 F. Supp. 645, 37 FEP 110 (D.R.I. 1985); Sanders v. General Servs. Admin., 529 F. Supp. 551, 31 FEP 1634 (N.D. Ill. 1982), *aff'd,* 707 F.2d 969, 32 FEP 627 (7th Cir. 1983); Tankha v. Costle, 536 F. Supp. 480, 28 FEP 1192 (N.D. Ill. 1982); Templeton v. Veterans Admin., 540 F. Supp. 695, 31 FEP 900 (S.D.N.Y. 1982); Talavera v. United States, 34 FEP 534 (E.D. Wis. 1982); McCray v. Alexander, 29 FEP 653 (D. Colo. 1982), *aff'd,* 38 EPD ¶ 35,509 (10th Cir. 1985).

[41]McKenna v. Weinberger, 729 F.2d 783, 791, 34 FEP 509, 516 (D.C. Cir. 1984) (district court erred by dismissing separate claim under Administrative Procedure Act for failure to follow agency's own rules); Lage v. Thomas, 585 F. Supp. 403, 40 FEP 1013 (N.D. Tex. 1984) (court refuses to dismiss pendent common-law assault claim based on § 717 exclusivity); Quillen v. United States Postal Serv., 564 F. Supp. 314, 321, 32 FEP 1631, 1637 (E.D. Mich. 1983) (assault and battery claim not dismissed because it does not constitute cause of action for employment discrimination); Perry v. Boorstin, 29 FEP 1227 (D.D.C. 1982) (plaintiff able to withstand motion to dismiss one discrimination-related claim because in addition to his Title VII claims, which he failed to timely pursue, he raised Fifth Amendment due process claim concerning decision agency had made earlier to delegate responsibility to investigate internal complaints of employment discrimination to private entities); Weiss v. Marsh, 543 F. Supp. 1115, 40 FEP 129 (M.D. Ala. 1981) (Equal Pay Act claim not pre-empted by § 717); Stewart v. Thomas, 538 F. Supp 891, 30 FEP 1609 (D.D.C. 1982) (plaintiff alleged she was subjected to verbal and physical sexual harassment and sex discrimination violative of Title VII and also charged supervisor individually with common-law torts of assault, battery, and intentional infliction of emotional distress). *But see* Ethnic Employees of the Library of Congress v. Boorstin, 751 F.2d 1405, 36 FEP 1216 (D.C. Cir. 1985) (Title VII exclusive, organization of employees cannot recast Title VII claims as constitutional claims, but constitutional claims not covered by Title VII are not barred and are remanded); Ray v. Nimmo, 704 F.2d 1480, 31 FEP 1310 (11th Cir. 1983) (per curiam) (claim that defendant violated plaintiff's due process rights by not following its own regulations or affirmative action plan was distinct from claim of discrimination, but nevertheless subject to dismissal if plaintiff was federal employee who must submit such claims through separate administrative remedies); Nolan v. Cleland, 686 F.2d 806, 29 FEP 1732 (9th Cir. 1982) (plaintiff's separate due process claim alleging she was forced to resign because of employer's deceit, coercion, and duress, which constituted taking of property, dismissed on basis that Title VII provides exclusive judicial remedy for claims of discrimination in federal employment); Grenci v. United States, 36 FEP 1044 (W.D. Pa. 1984) (Title VII preempts § 1983 claim, and Fifth Amendment claim to extent founded on allegations of discrimination); Valentine v. Drug Enforcement Admin., 544 F. Supp. 830, 34 FEP 535 (N.D. Ill. 1982)

## E. Exhaustion and Timeliness

Courts continue to require exhaustion of administrative remedies as a condition precedent to suit under Title VII,[42] the ADEA, and the Rehabilitation Act.[43] Equitable modifications of administrative prerequisites have been permitted where the failure to comply was attributable to the agency,[44] or where the complainant proceeded promptly after learning of the discrimination.[45] Courts will not, however, permit suits by federal employees who are amply aware of the final agency action.[46]

A split in authority has developed over whether the 30-day time limit

---

(claim that lack of notice of affirmative action plan deprived plaintiff of due process under Fifth Amendment found to be duplicate of his Title VII claim, which provided exclusive judicial remedy). *And see* Postal Workers, San Francisco Local v. Postmaster Gen., 35 FEP 1484 (N.D. Cal. 1984), *rev'd and remanded on other grounds,* 781 F.2d 772, 39 FEP 1847 (9th Cir. 1986) (district court ruled that Title VII does not preempt First Amendment freedom of religion claims; Ninth Circuit treats appeal as Title VII case, without discussion of First Amendment issues, and reverses and remands for district court determination whether accommodation to religious belief proposed by Postal Service reasonably preserved plaintiff's employment status; Postal Service employee plaintiffs, objecting to participation in selective service registration, proposed that draft registrants be directed to other post office windows for registration; Postal Service proposed that plaintiffs be reassigned to other positions).

[42]Ethnic Employees of the Library of Congress v. Boorstin, *supra* note 41 (failure to file administrative complaint bars Title VII claims; organization cannot evade rigorous administrative exhaustion requirements); Curry v. United States Post Office, 599 F. Supp. 506, 37 FEP 373 (E.D. Mich. 1984) (failure to file with EEOC bars Rehabilitation Act claim, Title VII claim).

[43]Gardner v. Morris, 752 F.2d 1271, 1278, 36 FEP 1272, 1276 (8th Cir. 1985); *accord* Boyd v. United States Postal Serv., 752 F.2d 410, 36 FEP 1417 (9th Cir. 1985); Johnson v. Orr, 747 F.2d 1352, 36 FEP 515 (10th Cir. 1984) (failure to exhaust administrative remedies bars Rehabilitation Act claim, despite inclusion in Merit Systems Protection Board complaints because MSPB correctly found it lacked jurisdiction); McGuinness v. United States Postal Serv., *supra* note 40; Smith v. United States Postal Serv., 742 F.2d 257, 262, 35 FEP 1304 (6th Cir. 1984); Clark v. United States Postal Serv., 592 F. Supp. 631, 35 FEP 1408 (D.D.C. 1984); Curry v. United States Post Office, *supra* note 42.

[44]Wade v. Secretary of the Army, 796 F.2d 1369, 41 FEP 1691 (11th Cir. 1986) (defendant's interference excused exhaustion requirement and suit in district court permitted even though defendant never ruled on merits of complaint); Allen v. Smith, 36 FEP 1245 (D.D.C. 1985) (failure to exhaust informal administrative complaint procedure excused, defendant failed to refer complaint to counselor or notify plaintiff of its rejection of complaint; 1983 complaint should have been processed as a new matter, *i.e.,* a violation of 1981 settlement agreement).

[45]Jarrell v. United States Postal Serv., 753 F.2d 1088, 36 FEP 1169 (D.C. Cir. 1985) (30-day limit equitably tolled by EEOC officer's assurances that officer was attempting to have information expunged and because government excised objectionable information from response to plaintiff's FOIA request preventing his awareness of information which is basis of complaint); Allen v. Bolger, 597 F. Supp. 482, 36 FEP 701 (D. Kan. 1984) (limit tolled, plaintiff filed in 1981 within one week of learning of discrimination, although acts occurred in 1977); *see also* Wolfolk v. Rivera, 729 F.2d 1114, 34 FEP 468 (7th Cir. 1984) (filing of administrative complaint within 20 days of learning of racially discriminatory pay is timely, even though filing was 13 months after hire; falls within rule's exception of "circumstances beyond his control").

[46]Scott v. St. Paul Postal Serv., 720 F.2d 524, 33 FEP 544 (8th Cir. 1983) (per curiam), *cert. denied,* 465 U.S. 1083, 34 FEP 192 (1984) (action dismissed owing to failure of *pro se* plaintiff to file for 51 days after receipt of final agency action which included notice of options); Obi v. Lehman, 35 FEP 1823 (E.D. Pa. 1984) (acting "on advice of previous counsel" does not excuse failure to exhaust, where plaintiff withdrew appeals from MSPB; Boyd v. United States Postal Serv., 32 FEP 1217 (W.D. Wash. 1983), *aff'd,* 752 F.2d 410, 36 FEP 1417 (9th Cir. 1985) (failure to raise Rehabilitation Act charge for more than two and one-half months unexcused where time requirement for filing was noted on workplace bulletin boards and explained by EEO counselor, and where letter denying requested reinstatement characterized decision as "final"); Goddard v. Department of Health & Human Servs., 32 FEP 587 (D.D.C. 1983) (court dismissed civil action filed within 30 days of EEOC decision denying request to reopen charge, where employee's rights were adequately explained and employee failed to take any action for two years after receiving agency's "final" determination); Jackson v. United States Postal Serv., 33 FEP 1381, 1383 (D.D.C. 1983) (court dismissed action filed two and one-half years after EEOC's final decision where plaintiff received explicit notice concerning administrative procedural rights); Smith v. Department of Hous. & Urban Dev., 568 F. Supp. 1175, 32 FEP 1538 (N.D. Ill. 1983), *aff'd without opinion,* 746 F.2d 1483 (7th Cir. 1984) (summary judgment allowed for failure to exhaust where plaintiff, told repeatedly of his rights and directed to see EEO counselor, filed suit without seeking counseling before filing charge).

for filing suit in federal court is jurisdictional,[47] or is subject to equitable tolling.[48] Courts have also differed on whether to permit amendments under Fed. R. Civ. P. 15(c) to relate back to the original complaint, where the amendment is made to cure the failure to name as a party and serve the head of the government agency.[49]

Courts have also differed on the effect of requesting administrative reconsideration of an EEOC decision. Several courts have held that a request to reconsider tolls the 30-day limit.[50] Other courts have held that a request to reconsider does not extend the time for filing a complaint.[51] The Tenth Circuit has held the limit equitably tolled because of the ambiguity of the EEOC notice as to the expiration of the right to sue.[52]

---

[47]Hilliard v. United States Postal Serv., 814 F.2d 325, 43 FEP 600 (6th Cir. 1987); Hymen v. Merit Sys. Protection Bd., 799 F.2d 1421, 43 FEP 271 (9th Cir. 1986), *cert. denied,* 481 U.S. 1019, 44 FEP 1048 (1987); Cooper v. United States Postal Serv., 740 F.2d 714, 35 FEP 364 (9th Cir. 1984), *cert. denied,* 471 U.S. 1022, 37 FEP 951 (1985) (30-day limit is jurisdictional, strictly applied, and not subject to equitable tolling; Fed.R.Civ. P. 15(c) leave to amend cannot relate back to cure failure to serve Postmaster General and Attorney General within 30-day limit) (White, J., dissenting); Lofton v. Heckler, 781 F.2d 1390, 39 FEP 1806 (9th Cir. 1986); Harris v. Brock, 642 F. Supp. 1134, 41 FEP 1561 (N.D. Ill. 1986), *aff'd,* 835 F.2d 1190, 45 FEP 931 (7th Cir. 1987) (30-day period jurisdictional, not subject to equitable tolling); King v. Dole, 595 F. Supp. 1140, 36 FEP 11 (D.D.C. 1984), *aff'd,* 782 F.2d 274, 40 FEP 624 (D.C. Cir.), *cert. denied,* 479 U.S. 856, 43 FEP 640 (1986) (request for judicial review of MSPB decision must be made within 30 days, 5 U.S.C. § 7703(b)(2)). *See also* cases cited *supra* notes 5 and 6.

Even those courts that agree to the jurisdictional nature of the 30-day limit disagree on the effect of filing suit the following business day when the 30th day falls on a weekend or holiday. *Compare* Hilliard v. United States Postal Serv., *supra* (untimely) *with* Arnold v. United States, *supra* note 40 (timely).

[48]Hornsby v. United States Postal Serv., 787 F.2d 87, 40 FEP 615 (3d Cir. 1986) (time limits in Title VII are in nature of statute of limitations and subject to equitable tolling); Cano v. United States Postal Serv., 755 F.2d 221, 37 FEP 209 (1st Cir. 1985) (assuming subject to tolling, plaintiff held not entitled to tolling due to illness because consulted an attorney); Bright v. Butler, 37 FEP 782 (D.D.C. 1985) (dictum; plaintiff failed to prove timely filing and did not request equitable tolling); Neves v. Kolaski, *supra* note 40 (dictum; plaintiff held aware of time limits after filing two timely complaints; three new complaints untimely and not continuing violations); *cf.* Anderson v. Block, 807 F.2d 145, 42 FEP 982 (8th Cir. 1986) (employee subjected to repeated incidents of discrimination need not file new administrative complaint with each incident if events not timely complained of are "alike or reasonably related" to charges timely brought).

[49]*Compare* Romain v. Shear, 799 F.2d 1416, 43 FEP 264 (9th Cir. 1986), *cert. denied,* 481 U.S. 1050, 43 FEP 1896 (1987), Koucky v. Department of the Navy, 820 F.2d 300, 44 FEP 156 (9th Cir. 1987), Lofton v. Heckler, *supra* note 47, Cooper v. United States Postal Serv., *supra* note 47 *and* Hale v. United States Postal Serv., 663 F. Supp. 7, 41 FEP 1601 (N.D. Ill. 1986), *aff'd,* 826 F.2d 1067, 48 FEP 551 (7th Cir. 1987) (not allowing inclusion of party under Rule 15(c)) *with* Jarrell v. United States Postal Serv., *supra* note 45, Allen v. Bolger, *supra* note 45 *and* Gonzales v. Secretary of the Air Force, 824 F.2d 392, 44 FEP 971 (5th Cir. 1987), *cert. denied,* 485 U.S. _____, 46 FEP 504 (1988) (amendment to properly name Secretary of the Air Force would have related back had improper defendant, Department of the Air Force, been timely served; since service on Department not accomplished within required time period, court refuses to impute notice to Secretary and dismisses suit).

[50]Donaldson v. Tennessee Valley Auth., 759 F.2d 535, 37 FEP 869 (6th Cir. 1985); Nordell v. Heckler, 749 F.2d 47, 48, 36 FEP 695 (D.C. Cir. 1984) (request for reconsideration within 30 days extends 30-day deadline for filing suit).

[51]Paetz v. United States, 795 F.2d 1533, 41 FEP 1682, *reh'g denied en banc,* 804 F.2d 681 (11th Cir. 1986); Dorsey v. Bolger, 581 F. Supp. 43, 35 FEP 459 (E.D. Pa. 1984) (30-day limit not tolled by request for reconsideration); Hanger v. United States Postal Serv., 34 FEP 1399 (M.D. Fla. 1984) (action dismissed as untimely; failed to file within 30 days of EEOC initial decision, although filed within 30 days of EEOC refusal to reconsider).

[52]Martinez v. Orr, 738 F.2d 1107, 35 FEP 367 (10th Cir. 1984) (30-day limit equitably tolled where EEOC notice of final decision ambiguous as to expiration of right to sue, misleading, and lulling employee into inaction; however, pendency of request to EEOC to reconsider does not in itself toll 30-day limit).

## F. Scope of Relief

The Supreme Court held in *Library of Congress v. Shaw*[53] that the language of § 706 (k) of Title VII[54] does not waive the federal government's immunity from interest[55] on an attorney's fee award. The Supreme Court also reaffirmed in *Loeffler v. Frank*[56] the general immunity of the United States against interest judgments except where a waiver of sovereign immunity can fairly be inferred, as with the United States Postal Service. Congress subsequently passed legislation expressly permitting the award of interest on back pay for federal employees.[57]

## G. Attorney's Fees

Attorney's fees and costs may be available to plaintiffs prevailing against the government under the ADEA, at least in judicial proceedings.[58]

---

[53]478 U.S. 310, 41 FEP 85 (1986).

[54]Sec. 706 (k), 42 U.S.C. § 2000e-5(k), provides:

"In any action or proceeding under this title the court, in its discretion, may allow the prevailing party, other than the [EEOC] or the United States, a reasonable attorney's fee as part of the costs, and the [EEOC] and the United States shall be liable for costs the same as a private person."

(Emphasis added)

[55]The Court found no reason to differentiate between interest and an adjustment for delay in payment, since both serve the same function of compensating for belated receipt of money. *Id.,* 41 FEP at 90.

[56]486 U.S. _____, 46 FEP 1659 (1988), *rev'g and remanding sub nom.* Loeffler v. Tisch, 806 F.2d 817, 42 FEP 792 (8th Cir. 1986). *See also infra* Chapter 38, note 98 and accompanying text.

[57]Pub. L. No. 100-202, § 623, 101 Stat. 1329-428 (100th Cong., 1st Sess.) (1987).

[58]*Compare* Krodel v. Young, 576 F. Supp. 390, 33 FEP 701 (D.D.C. 1983), *aff'd,* 748 F.2d 701, 36 FEP 468 (D.C. Cir. 1984), *cert. denied,* 474 U.S. 817, 38 FEP 1727 (1985) (unless fees and costs can be awarded, courts could not return successful ADEA litigants to economic position occupied prior to discriminatory conduct) *and* Sterling v. Lehman, 574 F. Supp. 415, 40 FEP 707 (N.D. Cal. 1983) ("award of attorneys' fees for plaintiff's judicial proceedings is necessary to effectuate purpose of ADEA") *with* Kennedy v. Whitehurst, 690 F.2d 951, 29 FEP 1373 (D.C. Cir. 1982) (attorney's fees not available for obtaining relief solely at administrative level, because § 15(c) of ADEA does not explicitly authorize such an award; judicial actions "clearly play a role distinct from administrative proceedings" (dictum) in ADEA enforcement).

## CHAPTER 34

# CLASS ACTIONS

## I. THE APPLICATION OF RULE 23 TO TITLE VII CLASS ACTIONS

### C. The Supreme Court's *Rodriguez* and *Falcon* Decisions and Their Impact on Title VII Class Actions

In *General Telephone Co. of the Southwest v. Falcon,*[1] the Supreme Court reiterated the *Rodriguez*[2] rule that classes, particularly "across-the-board" classes, are not to be certified on the basis of presumptions in Title VII cases. Instead, actual compliance with the requirements of Rule 23 must be demonstrated, with specific facts presented which identify the questions of law and fact common to the class, and which show that the plaintiff's claims are typical of those of the class.[3] The same principles apply to other employment class actions.[4]

After *Falcon,* courts have recognized that rigorous Rule 23 scrutiny proves fatal to many proposed "across-the-board" class actions.[5] Nonethe-

---

[1]457 U.S. 147, 28 FEP 1745 (1982).

[2]East Tex. Motor Freight Sys. v. Rodriguez, 431 U.S. 395, 14 FEP 1505 (1977).

[3]The Supreme Court quickly illustrated the scope of *Falcon* when it vacated three appellate decisions in light of *Falcon.* Eckerd Drugs v. Brown, 457 U.S. 1128, 28 FEP 1840 (1982), *vacating and remanding* 663 F.2d 1268, 27 FEP 137 (4th Cir. 1981) (Fourth Circuit had allowed discharged employees to represent a class claiming general workplace discrimination); Jordan v. County of Los Angeles, 459 U.S. 810, 29 FEP 1560 (1982), *vacating and remanding* 669 F.2d 1311, 28 FEP 518 (9th Cir. 1982) (Ninth Circuit had allowed certification of a class of future, present, and past job applicants who had arrest records, marijuana conviction records, or juvenile offense records); University of Houston v. Wilkins, 459 U.S. 809, 29 FEP 1559 (1982), *vacating and remanding* 654 F.2d 388, 26 FEP 1230 (5th Cir. 1981) (Fifth Circuit had upheld certification of a class of past, present, and future employees in different job classifications).

[4]*See, e.g.,* Vuyanich v. Republic Nat'l Bank of Dallas, 723 F.2d 1195, 1199, 33 FEP 1521, 1523 (5th Cir.), *cert. denied,* 469 U.S. 1073, 36 FEP 568 (1984) (applying *Falcon's* admonition of strict adherence to Rule 23 requirements to alleged class action under Title VII); Penk v. Oregon State Bd. of Higher Educ., 99 F.R.D. 511, 513, 37 FEP 922 (D. Or. 1983) ("the requirements of Fed. R. Civ. P. 23 must be adhered to as strictly in employment discrimination cases as in other types of cases").

[5]*See, e.g.,* Adams v. Bethlehem Steel Corp., 736 F.2d 992, 994–95, 38 FEP 1042, 1043 (4th Cir. 1984), *aff'd sub nom.* Davis v. Bethlehem Steel, 769 F.2d 210, 38 FEP 1054 (4th Cir.), *cert. denied,* 474 U.S. 1021, 39 FEP 808 (1985) (across-the-board certification denied where plaintiffs failed to specify their individual claims and where no nexus between those claims and the 37 challenged practices was shown); Gilchrist v. Bolger, 733 F.2d 1551, 1554–55, 35 FEP 81, 84 (11th Cir. 1984) (affirmed trial court's denial of certification where nonsupervisory employee sought to represent class containing supervisory employees and applicants); Walker v. Jim Dandy Co., 747 F.2d 1360, 1364–65, 36 FEP 928, 931 (11th Cir. 1984) (denying across-the-board treatment where no sufficient basis shown in complaint to permit person with sex discrimination hiring claim to represent applicants and employees with claims relating to recruitment, job assignment, transfer, and promotion); Redditt v. Mississippi Extended Care Centers, 718 F.2d 1381, 1387, 33 FEP 286, 290 (5th Cir. 1983) ("*Falcon* * * * prohibits plaintiff, who alleges only discrimination in discharge, from mounting an across-the-board attack on defendant's employment practices"); Wilkins v. University of Houston, 695 F.2d 134, 135, 31 FEP 318, 318 (5th Cir. 1983) (after Supreme Court remand) ("*Falcon* tightens the requirements for class certification in Title VII cases such as this * * * casting cold water on the former liberal application of our 'across-the-board' rule by enjoining careful attention to the prerequisites of Rule 23(a)"); Freeman v. Motor Convoy, 700 F.2d 1339, 1347, 31 FEP 517, 523 (11th Cir. 1983) (holding that across-the-board rule is "now defunct" and finding that plaintiff failed to make sufficient factual showing); Falcon v. General Tel. Co. of the Sw., 611 F. Supp. 707, 39 FEP 1116, 1117–23 (N.D. Tex. 1985), *on remand from* 686 F.2d 261, 29 FEP 1442 (5th Cir. 1982) (promotion claimant cannot maintain class action on behalf of hiring claimants: "certifications in dis-

less, courts have also recognized that *Falcon* does not wholly foreclose the possibility that an across-the-board class action might be properly certified in appropriate circumstances.[6] Indeed, the Supreme Court indicated as much in footnote 15 to its opinion in *Falcon* stating, in part, that "[s]ignificant proof that an employer operated under a general policy of discrimination conceivably could justify a class of both applicants and employees if the discrimination manifested itself in hiring and promotion practices in the same general fashion, such as through entirely subjective decision-making processes."[7]

Several courts have applied and interpreted footnote 15 in determining the propriety of certifying an across-the-board class action. The typical case involves allegations that all of the challenged decisions (only some of which affected the named plaintiffs) are made through a subjective process, in which a group of white and/or male supervisors exercises total or near total discretion in a discriminatory fashion.[8] Where plaintiffs are able to support these allegations sufficiently, some courts have certified[9] across-the-board

crimination cases are to be *drastically* curtailed"); Tuber v. Continental Grain Co., 36 FEP 933, 938–40 (S.D.N.Y. 1984) (certification of nationwide across-the-board class denied where plaintiff made no specific presentation of commonality between her claims and those of the class); Sperling v. Donovan, 104 F.R.D. 4, 6–7, 35 FEP 983, 985 (D.D.C. 1984) (named plaintiffs holding accounting jobs not permitted to represent all employees spanning 71 job categories where no typicality was affirmatively shown by plaintiffs).

[6]*See, e.g.,* Eastland v. Tennessee Valley Auth., 704 F.2d 613, 618, 31 FEP 1578, 1581, *amended and reh'g denied,* 714 F.2d 1066, 34 FEP 283 (11th Cir. 1983), *cert. denied,* 465 U.S. 1066, 34 FEP 415 (1984) ("The Supreme Court * * * cautioned against the overzealous application of the 'across-the-board' approach"); Jordan v. County of Los Angeles, 713 F.2d 503, 504, 33 FEP 1435, 1436, *amended,* 726 F.2d 1366, 36 FEP 1592 (9th Cir. 1984) (after Supreme Court remand) (*"Falcon* does not prohibit 'across-the-board' class formation in every instance"); Vuyanich v. Republic Nat'l Bank of Dallas, 723 F.2d 1195, 1198, 33 FEP 1521, 1522 (5th Cir.), *cert denied,* 469 U.S. 1073, 36 FEP 568 (1984) ("[T]he across-the-board theory is appropriate only in limited instances"); Lilly v. Harris-Teeter Supermkt., 720 F.2d 326, 333, 33 FEP 195, 201 (4th Cir. 1983), *cert. denied,* 466 U.S. 951, 34 FEP 1096 (1984) (whether across-the-board class is certifiable depends upon particular facts of named plaintiffs' claims and claims of putative class); Sheehan v. Purolator, 103 F.R.D. 641, 647, 36 FEP 1452, 1458 (E.D.N.Y. 1984), *aff'd,* 839 F.2d 99 (2d Cir. 1988) (although certification was denied here, court stated that *Falcon* does not establish a *per se* rule "that disparate treatment Title VII cases should never be certified as class actions").

[7]457 U.S. at 159 n.15, 28 FEP at 1750 n.15; *see also* Vuyanich v. Republic Nat'l Bank of Dallas, 723 F.2d 1195, 33 FEP 1521, *reh'g denied,* 736 F.2d 160, 163, 35 FEP 345, 347 (5th Cir.), *cert. denied,* 469 U.S. 1073, 36 FEP 568 (1984) (dissenting from denial of rehearing en banc) (referring to footnote 15 as *"Falcon's* reservation for broad class certification"); Sheehan v. Purolator, *supra* note 6.

[8]Richardson v. Byrd, 709 F.2d 1016, 1020, 32 FEP 603, 605–6 (5th Cir.), *cert. denied,* 464 U.S. 1009, 33 FEP 552 (1983) (although plaintiff had only transfer claim, she could represent sex discrimination claims of both employees and applicants because decisions of defendant's mostly male supervisors were entirely subjective); Carpenter v. Stephen F. Austin State Univ., 706 F.2d 608, 617, 31 FEP 1758, 1765 (5th Cir. 1983) (black former hourly employees allowed to represent both hourly and salaried clerical employees because all were allegedly affected by same subjective decision-making practices and all would rely upon same set of supporting statistics); Jordan v. Swindall, 105 F.R.D. 45, 48, 42 FEP 947 (M.D. Ala. 1985) (law enforcement employees seeking promotion only to specified jobs allowed to represent broader promotion claims where they contended that subjective decision-making by promotion panel and mayor affected all promotions); Johnson v. Montgomery County Sheriff's Dep't, 99 F.R.D. 562, 566, 33 FEP 1844, 1847 (M.D. Ala. 1983) (employee permitted to represent applicants because evidence reflected "an overarching subjective decisionmaking process affecting both applicants and employees"); Brown v. Eckerd Drugs, 564 F. Supp. 1440, 1445–46, 36 FEP 1543, 1547–48 (W.D.N.C. 1983) (named plaintiffs with demotion and discharge claims could represent class with promotion and transfer claims because all decisions were made by virtually all-white supervisory staff vested with unfettered discretion); *cf.* Goodman v. Lukens Steel Co., 777 F.2d 113, 39 FEP 658 (3d Cir. 1985), *aff'd,* 482 U.S. 656, 44 FEP 1 (1981) (although no "general policy" of discrimination as contemplated by *Falcon* footnote 15 was found, "across-the-board" pattern-and-practice class action approved with different representatives raising numerous differing claims).

[9]*Id.* Some courts have not been satisfied with mere allegations or proof of subjectivity, and have essentially held that subjectivity alone does not bind a class together unless it is exercised by the same person or group of persons with respect to each challenged facet of employment. *See* Holsey v. Armour & Co., 743 F.2d 199, 215–17, 35 FEP 1064, 1078 (4th Cir. 1984), *cert. denied,* 470 U.S. 1028, 37 FEP

classes. Thus, when (1) numerous different employment decisions are made by a group of persons demographically different from the plaintiff class and having totally unfettered discretion, and (2) the foregoing proof is coupled with statistics showing that the plaintiff class is significantly disfavored by these discretionary decisions, some courts allow across-the-board classes challenging a range of decisions.[10]

Success in certifying an across-the-board class in a subjectivity case after *Falcon* appears to turn in part on the pervasiveness of subjectivity or discretion in the defendant's decision-making.[11] In cases that do not involve subjectivity, it remains true that where a single practice or policy can affect both hiring and promotions, employees who were not promoted have been allowed to represent unsuccessful applicants.[12]

## II. The "Nexus" Requirements of Rule 23(a): Commonality, Typicality, and Adequacy of Representation

### A. Nexus Between Claims Asserted

In *Falcon,* the Supreme Court reemphasized that for a class action to be maintained, a close nexus between the named plaintiff's individual claims and the claims of the class must be shown.[13] This evaluation is particularly important where the plaintiff seeks to be certified as the representative for

---

192 (1985) (reversing district court's certification of hiring and promotion class under footnote 15, where plaintiff did not show that hiring and promotion decisions were made by identical superiors); Rossini v. Ogilvy & Mather, 597 F. Supp. 1120, 1130–32, 41 FEP 861 (S.D.N.Y. 1984) (permitting certification across classifications on salary claims where all salaries are set by small committee with relatively constant membership and where same set of challenged subjective factors were generally used to set all salaries). The courts in *Holsey* and *Rossini* both relied on the footnote to the concurring opinion in *Falcon,* 457 U.S. at 162, 28 FEP at 1752, in which Chief Justice Burger pointed out (but did not explain the significance of) plaintiff Falcon's failure to show that the hiring and promotion decisions at issue in *Falcon* were made by the same person. The focus on the identity of the decision-makers is apparently a result of courts' recognition that it is the bias of the decision-maker that is critical, not the subjectivity of the decision. Apparently, these courts have concluded that class treatment may be warranted in subjectivity cases where the bias of a common decision-maker or decision-making body is at issue, but unwarranted where the bias of a diverse array of decision-makers would have to be adjudicated independently for each decision at issue.

[10]*Supra* notes 8 and 9.

[11]*See, e.g.,* Vuyanich v. Republic Nat'l Bank, of Dallas, 723 F.2d 1195, 1199–1200, 33 FEP 1521, 1523 (5th Cir.), *reh'g denied,* 736 F.2d 160, 162–63, 35 FEP 345, 347 (5th Cir.), *cert. denied,* 469 U.S. 1073, 36 FEP 568 (1984) (defendant's reliance "on two objective inputs—education and experience—in its necessarily subjective hiring process * * * precludes [plaintiffs'] reliance on [the] 'general policy of discrimination' exception" embodied in footnote 15 of *Falcon*) (five members dissenting from denial of rehearing and criticizing panel's reading of footnote 15); Lilly v. Harris-Teeter Supermkt., 720 F.2d 326, 334, 33 FEP 195, 201 (4th Cir. 1983), *cert. denied,* 466 U.S. 951, 34 FEP 1096 (1984) (where termination decisions were within unfettered discretion of white supervisory force and promotion decisions were subject to some objective criteria, the two types of decisions were not equivalent practices, even though plaintiffs alleged that objective promotion criteria were subjectively and disparately applied).

[12]*See, e.g.,* Johnson v. Montgomery County Sheriff's Dep't, 99 F.R.D. 562, 565–66, 33 FEP 1844, 1846–47 (M.D. Ala. 1983) (defendant's policy limiting number of female employees assigned to jail to six and promoting females only when new female jail employee was hired adversely affected both female employees and applicants, thus allowing employee to represent applicants); *cf.* Avagliano v. Sumitomo Shoji Am., 103 F.R.D. 562, 579, 38 FEP 561, 572–73 (S.D.N.Y. 1984) (nationwide class of all past, present, and future female employees certified where challenge was to an apparently admitted, centrally administered policy of preference for Japanese nationals); *see also* General Tel. Co. of the Sw. v. Falcon, *supra* note 7.

[13]457 U.S. 147, 160, 28 FEP 1745, 1751 (1982).

several groups who allegedly experienced different types of discriminatory practices.[14]

## 1. Adverse Impact Claims

*Falcon*'s reemphasis of the nexus requirements presumably applies to all employment discrimination class actions. The nexus requirements are easily satisfied (and thus have "little effect") in a true disparate impact case, where the named plaintiff has been excluded from an employment opportunity because of his or her failure to satisfy a neutral, discrete, and objective selection criterion and where the individual seeks to represent a class of persons likewise excluded at a significantly disproportionate rate from the same opportunity by the same criterion.[15] *Falcon* may not be so readily satisfied, however, where subjective practices are challenged under an adverse impact theory, or where the validity of an objective practice may differ depending upon the job at issue.

## 2. Disparate Treatment Claims

Following *Falcon,* most courts have denied certification of "across-the-board" disparate treatment claims,[16] refusing to allow persons claiming disparate treatment in one aspect of employment to represent persons allegedly affected by disparate treatment in other aspects. Specifically, courts have

---

[14]Walker v. Jim Dandy Co., *supra* note 5 (no basis shown to allow applicant with hiring claim to represent class with claims concerning recruiting, job assignments, transfers, and promotions); Adams v. Bethlehem Steel Corp., *supra* note 5 (named plaintiffs affected by limited set of practices cannot supply nexus between claims by alleging that they are also disturbed by "mere existence" of other practices); Giles v. Ireland, 742 F.2d 1366, 1372–73, 35 FEP 1718, 1721–22 (11th Cir. 1984) (excluding orderlies from mental health worker class where orderlies not affected by main claims of discrimination in pay and promotion); Wheeler v. City of Columbus, Miss., 703 F.2d 853, 32 FEP 651 (5th Cir. 1983) (class certification denied; individual claims were based on theory of disparate treatment, while class claims were based on theory of adverse impact); Sperling v. Donovan, 104 F.R.D. 4, 8–9, 35 FEP 983, 987 (D.D.C. 1984) (two alleged instances of discriminatory awards do not support across-the-board attack on defendant's employment practices); Rossini v. Ogilvy & Mather, 597 F. Supp. 1120, 1135, 1139, 41 FEP 861 (S.D.N.Y. 1984) (plaintiff with transfer claim challenging barriers not permitted to litigate promotion and training claims where she was not affected by training practices and where promotion claims challenged performance measurement, not alleged barriers); *cf.* Holsey v. Armour & Co., 743 F.2d 199, 217, 35 FEP 1064, 1079 (4th Cir. 1984), *cert. denied,* 470 U.S. 1028, 37 FEP 192 (1985) (where one or more named plaintiffs were affected by each promotion and retaliation practice challenged, certification as to those claims permitted); Griffin v. Carlin, 755 F.2d 1516, 1531–32, 37 FEP 741, 753–54 (11th Cir. 1985) (where 22 named plaintiffs were affected by diverse array of practices, certification of class of past, present, and future black employees upheld).

[15]Nation v. Winn-Dixie Stores, 95 F.R.D. 82, 86, 29 FEP 756, 761 (N.D. Ga. 1982) (*Falcon* has "little, if any, effect on the certification of so-called [true] disparate impact cases"); *accord* Sheehan v. Purolator, 103 F.R.D. 641, 36 FEP 1452, 1456–57 (E.D.N.Y. 1984), *aff'd,* 839 F.2d 99 (2d Cir. 1988); *cf.* Davidson v. United States Steel Corp., 104 F.R.D. 1, 3–4, 35 FEP 995, 997 (W.D. Pa. 1984) (plaintiff excluded from job opportunity because of test failure cannot represent class where no other person similarly excluded has been identified).

[16]*See, e.g.,* cases cited at note 5, *supra; see also, e.g.,* De la Fuente v. Chicago Tribune Co., No. 84-C-4596 (N.D. Ill. July 24, 1985) (under *Falcon*'s rigorous analysis, allegation of pervasive subjective decision-making insufficient; must offer significant proof that other members of putative class have suffered similar injury); Hawkins v. Fulton County, 95 F.R.D. 88, 92, 29 FEP 762, 765 (N.D. Ga. 1982) (plaintiff's "across-the-board" claims did not meet "stringent" *Falcon* guidelines); Meyers v. Ace Hardware, 95 F.R.D. 145, 35 FEP 310 (N.D. Ohio 1982) (across-the-board class action not permitted since plaintiffs failed to meet Rule 23(a) requirements specified by *Falcon*). *But cf.* Cox v. American Cast Iron Pipe Co., 784 F.2d 1546, 1557–58, 40 FEP 678, 687–88 (11th Cir.), *cert. denied,* 479 U.S. 883, 41 FEP 1712 (1986) (certification of class encompassing training, promotion, and compensation discriminatees is not an "exceptional combination" precluded by *Falcon* in this pattern-and-practice disparate treatment case arising from subjective decision-making); Sheehan v. Purolator, *supra* note 6 (no *per se* rule against disparate treatment class actions).

held that present employees could not represent unsuccessful applicants,[17] terminated employees could not represent rejected applicants,[18] and an employee who never sought a promotion could not represent employees denied promotions.[19] As indicated earlier, however, some courts have held that *Falcon* does not preclude across-the-board class actions involving disparate treatment claims where there is significant proof that the various alleged incidents of disparate treatment are the products of defendant's general policy of discrimination.[20]

Courts continue to rule that certain disparate treatment claims are so individualized that no class treatment is appropriate.[21] Moreover, the individual aspects of the named plaintiff's claims may be relevant in another respect. The constitutional principle of standing may impose an additional limitation beyond the requisites of Rule 23(a) on a named plaintiff's ability to represent absent class members whose claims are of a different type from his own.[22] Unlike the nexus required by Rule 23(a), which sometimes permits, for example, persons with hiring claims to represent persons with promotion claims, at least one court has held that persons with disparate

---

[17]Holsey v. Armour & Co., *supra* note 9 (employee not permitted to represent applicants where identity of decision-makers not proved); Freeman v. Motor Convoy, 700 F.2d 1339, 31 FEP 517 (11th Cir. 1983) (rejected applicants not included in class represented by incumbent employees); Minority Police Officers Ass'n of S. Bend v. City of S. Bend, 555 F. Supp. 921, 32 FEP 398 (N.D. Ind.), *aff'd in relevant part,* 721 F.2d 197, 33 FEP 433 (7th Cir. 1983) (named plaintiff employees could not represent unsuccessful applicants). *But cf.* Wester v. Special School Dist. No. 1, 35 FEP 199, 202–3 (D. Minn. 1984) (employees seeking promotion to administrator could represent applicants for teaching positions).

[18]O'Neal v. Riceland Foods, 684 F.2d 577, 29 FEP 956 (8th Cir. 1982); Ladele v. Consolidated Rail Corp., 95 F.R.D. 198, 29 FEP 1547 (E.D. Pa. 1982); *cf.* Batesville Casket Co. EEO Litigation, 35 FEP 1560, 1564 (D.D.C. 1984) (discharged employees not permitted to represent present and future employees because of potential for divergent interests).

[19]Warren v. ITT World Communications, 95 F.R.D. 425, 428–29, 31 FEP 1054, 1057 (S.D.N.Y. 1982); *cf.* Rossini v. Ogilvy & Mather, 597 F. Supp. 1120, 1135, 41 FEP 861 (S.D.N.Y. 1984) (plaintiff's failure to allege promotion claim not necessarily fatal to her efforts to represent promotion class, but promotion class not certified here because transfer claim and promotion claims are not similar). *But cf.* Craik v. Minnesota State Univ. Bd., 731 F.2d 465, 480, 34 FEP 649, 660 n.18 (8th Cir. 1984) (non-promotee permitted to represent class complaining of promotions and salary differentials where, unlike promotion and hiring, promotion and salary are related practices).

[20]*Supra* note 8; *see also* Carpenter v. Stephen F. Austin State Univ., 706 F.2d 608, 31 FEP 1758 (5th Cir. 1983) (allowed broad class action based on claim that blacks and females were overrepresented in lower-paid clerical and custodial positions, although they were not underrepresented in higher-paid groups); Bustamonte v. Property Mgmt. Sys., 38 EPD ¶ 35,391 at 39,671 (S.D. Tex. 1985) (former president's statement at staff meeting that no women were to be promoted constitutes preliminary showing of "across-the-board" policy); Meyer v. Macmillan Publishing Co., 95 F.R.D. 411, 415, 34 FEP 1650, 1653 (S.D.N.Y. 1982) (plaintiff employees could represent applicants since adequate showing was made of "significant proof [of] * * * general policy of discrimination"); Shannon v. Hess Oil Virgin Islands Corp., 96 F.R.D. 236, 242, 34 FEP 1299, 1304 (D.V.I. 1982) (rejected applicants could not be summarily disqualified as representatives of employees without first being given opportunity to offer "significant proof" of general policy of discrimination).

[21]Berggren v. Sunbeam Corp., 108 F.R.D. 410, 411, 39 FEP 953 (N.D. Ill. 1985) (promotion and compensation claims of female employees would necessarily depend on variety of factors peculiar to individual); Batesville Casket Co. EEO Litigation, 35 FEP 1560, 1563 (D.D.C. 1984) (class treatment not appropriate in view of plaintiff's individualized discharge claims); Gray v. Walgreen Co., 33 FEP 835, 837 (N.D. Ill. 1983) (where plaintiff's individual claims of discrimination involve number of incidents at four different locations with four different supervisors, claims too individualized to permit class treatment); Rowe v. Prudential Property & Casualty Ins. Co., 37 FEP 762, 766 (N.D. Ga. 1983) (where statistical proof was lacking and existence of common promotion claims could only be proved by individualized proof, "[t]he particular uniqueness of the factual basis for each claim in a promotion case would not advance 'the efficiency and economy of the [class action] procedure' "). *But cf.* Holsey v. Armour & Co., 743 F.2d 199, 215–17, 35 FEP 1064, 1078–79 (4th Cir. 1984), *cert. denied,* 470 U.S. 1028, 37 FEP 192 (1985) (retaliation and harrassment claims were susceptible to class treatment where plaintiffs proved general practice of retaliation and where class action device would be destroyed if separate retaliation claims were required).

[22]Vuyanich v. Republic Nat'l Bank of Dallas, 723 F.2d 1195, 1200, 33 FEP 1521, 1524 (5th Cir.), *cert. denied,* 469 U.S. 1073, 36 FEP 568 (1984).

treatment hiring or termination claims only have standing to represent persons with the same exact type of claims.[23]

## B. Nexus Between Job Classifications

The trend is to deny certification of a class containing several distinct job classifications, unless the representative's claim concerning his classification is typical of the claims of persons holding different classifications.[24]

## C. Nexus Between Organizational Units or Geographical Facilities

In the absence of evidence of some form of centralized decision-making authority, courts in most disparate treatment cases continue to find that a plaintiff employed in one organizational unit or geographical facility cannot demonstrate the nexus required to represent a companywide class.[25]

---

[23]*Id.* ("Because Johnson and Vuyanich can allege injuries only as a result of the Bank's hiring and termination practices, respectively, they lack standing to assert class claims arising from the bank's other employment practices—compensation, promotion, placement, and maternity practices."); *see also* Hill v. AT&T Technologies, 731 F.2d 175, 177–78, 34 FEP 620, 621 n.4, 622 n.5 (4th Cir. 1984) (indicating that Fourth Circuit may hereafter follow *Vuyanich's* standing rule). *But cf.* Wester v. Special School Dist. No. 1, 35 FEP 199, 202 (D. Minn. 1984) (standing contentions are more properly treated under Rule 23(a), and standing is satisfied so long as there is any injury in fact).

[24]*Classes excluding certain classifications:* Giles v. Ireland, *supra* note 14 (orderlies excluded from mental health worker class where orderlies not affected by salary and promotion claims raised by named plaintiffs); Walker v. Jim Dandy Co., 747 F.2d 1360, 1365, 36 FEP 928, 931–33 (11th Cir. 1984) (applicants for supervisory positions not permitted to represent applicants for plant level, nonsupervisory jobs); Sperling v. Donovan, 104 F.R.D. 4, 6–7, 35 FEP 983, 985 (D.D.C. 1984) (employees holding accounting jobs not permitted to represent employees in 71 job classifications where no typicality shown; in dicta court states that it is generally true that supervisory and nonsupervisory employees may not be placed in same class); Bell v. J. Ray McDermott & Co., 30 EPD ¶ 33,310 (E.D. La. 1982) (blue-collar workers could not also represent white-collar workers, since administrative and professional workers did not suffer the same discrimination); Ladele v. Consolidated Rail Corp., *supra* note 18, at 204, 29 FEP at 1552 (black former nonunion white-collar employee may not represent black union members; claims not typical); Nation v. Winn-Dixie Stores, 95 F.R.D. 82, 86, 29 FEP 756, 760 (N.D. Ga. 1982) (black clerks challenging promotional practices to manager cannot represent part-time clerks, cashiers, bookkeepers, assistant managers; claims not typical).

*Classes with several distinct job classifications:* Holsey v. Armour & Co., *supra* note 14 (persons seeking promotions to sales representative and to supervisor included when at least one of named plaintiffs sought promotion to each classification); Carpenter v. Stephen F. Austin State Univ., *supra* note 20 (certifying class of salaried clerical and hourly custodial employees in initial assignment, pay, and promotion case); Paxton v. Union Nat'l Bank, 688 F.2d 552, 561, 29 FEP 1233, 1242 (8th Cir. 1982), *cert. denied,* 460 U.S. 1083, 31 FEP 824 (1983) ("Typicality is not defeated because of * * * the differing qualifications of the plaintiffs and class members"); McKenzie v. Sawyer, 684 F.2d 62, 74, 29 FEP 633, 641 (D.C. Cir. 1982) (class composed of blacks seeking advancement to journeyman and those seeking promotions beyond journeyman level; subject to similar employment practices); Rossini v. Ogilvy & Mather, 597 F. Supp. 1120, 1130–32, 41 FEP 861 (S.D.N.Y. 1984) (permitting certification across professional and managerial classifications on salary claims); Kuenz v. Goodyear Tire & Rubber Co., 104 F.R.D. 474, 476–78, 37 FEP 124, 125–26 (E.D. Mo. 1985) (without citing *Falcon,* court certified nationwide class of past, present, and future female retail employees); Osmer v. Aerospace Corp., 30 FEP 204 (C.D. Cal. 1982) (class of technical and professional women certified; typical claims).

[25]*Compare* Bazemore v. Friday, 478 U.S. 385, 41 FEP 92 (1986) (per curiam) (affirming decision not to certify statewide class of defendant counties, but vacating refusal to certify class of Extension Service employees in action challenging hiring and pay decisions where plaintiffs showed that hiring and pay decisions in counties were made in conjunction with state Extension Service, a defendant common to all plaintiffs' claims), Kilgo v. Bowman Transp., 789 F.2d 859, 875–78, 40 FEP 1415, 1427–30 (11th Cir. 1986) (certifying class of all female plaintiffs from nationwide facilities adversely impacted by one-year experience requirement and class of disparate treatment plaintiffs whose applications at various terminals would have been processed through a centralized terminal) *and* Avagliano v. Sumitomo Shoji Am., 103 F.R.D. 562, 38 FEP 561 (S.D.N.Y. 1984) (nationwide class of female employees certified challenging centrally administered policy of preference for Japanese nationals) *with* Williams v. New Orleans Pub. Serv., 30 FEP 1127 (E.D. La. 1982) (previously defined systemwide class embracing 16 departments redefined and limited to one department in which plaintiffs have worked) *and* Ladele v. Consolidated Rail Corp., *supra* note 18 (plaintiff's failure to offer evidence of central administration,

## III. SPECIAL ISSUES PERTAINING TO ADEQUACY OF REPRESENTATION

The failure of the representative party's counsel to prosecute vigorously, or counsel's generally poor performance, is a sufficient basis upon which to deny class certification.[26] In addition, concerns about the quality of the named plaintiff's claims may result in a denial of class certification in order to spare the class from being bound by wide-ranging negative rulings.[27]

A class representative may not head a class which includes persons whose interests substantially conflict with his own.[28] The class representative's interests must be co-extensive with those of remaining class members with respect to the types of claims asserted or the jobs involved.[29]

The class may be decertified where the individual claims are dismissed,

---

statistical patterns, or other similar instances of discrimination precludes certification of nationwide class).

[26]Key v. Gillette Co., 782 F.2d 5, 7 (1st Cir. 1986) (decertification upheld where counsel displayed inadequacy by using seriously flawed expert testimony and by intentionally failing to introduce evidence explaining regression analysis used by plaintiffs expert); Hervey v. City of Little Rock, 787 F.2d 1223, 1226–30, 40 FEP 928, 930–33 (8th Cir. 1986) (antagonism between counsel for subclasses, inadequacy of expert statistical testimony, and excessive introduction of irrelevant testimony raised issue of adequacy and justified decertification); Lusted v. San Antonio Indep. School Dist., 741 F.2d 817, 820–21 (5th Cir. 1984) (denial of certification upheld where plaintiff moved for certification for first time after trial and decision, and complaint contained no class allegations); Davis v. Buffalo Psychiatric Center, 613 F. Supp. 462, 37 FEP 69, 70 (W.D.N.Y. 1985) (certification motion denied where untimely under local rules); Dunn v. Midwest Buslines, 94 F.R.D. 170, 28 FEP 1653 (E.D. Ark. 1982) (plaintiff's counsel's inability to state proper class action complaint, errors in brief, and his deposition conduct contribute to denial of class certification); Quintanilla v. Scientific-Atlanta, 28 FEP 1178 (N.D. Tex. 1982), *appeal dismissed,* 33 EPD ¶ 34,050 (5th Cir. 1983), *cert. denied,* 464 U.S. 1069 (1984) (failure to comply with local rules relating to form of class action complaint and time for submission of motion to certify); Mayes v. Crown Cent. Petroleum Corp., 29 FEP 873, 875 (S.D. Tex. 1980) (dilatory prosecution due to plaintiff's counsel's heavy class action case load); *cf.* Sperling v. Donovan, 104 F.R.D. 4, 5, 35 FEP 983, 984 n.1 (D.D.C. 1984) (request to certify extremely broad class, later voluntarily scaled down, reflects adversely on adequacy of representation and on sincerity of effort to vindicate classwide wrongs). *But see* Slanina v. William Penn Parking Corp., 106 F.R.D. 419, 34 FEP 1426, 1427 (W.D. Pa. 1984) (failure to seek certification within time period set by local rule not fatal when further discovery was necessary).

[27]Gilchrist v. Bolger, 733 F.2d 1551, 1556, 35 FEP 81, 86 n.4 (11th Cir. 1984) (affirmed denial of certification in part because "[a]ny adverse consequences of denying class certification may well have been outweighed by the negative *res judicata* effects of certifying a class action with [a poor class representative]"); Keeton v. Hayes Int'l Corp., 106 F.R.D. 366, 369–71 (N.D. Ala. 1985) (plaintiff's adequacy questioned where she failed to vigorously prosecute her EEOC charge and allowed it to sit for five years); *see also* discussion of *Cooper v. Federal Reserve Bank of Richmond,* 467 U.S. 867, 35 FEP 1 (1984), at Section IVB, *infra.*

[28]Batesville Casket Co. EEO Litigation, *supra* note 18 (former employees not permitted to represent present and future employees where potential for divergent interests too great); Keeton v. Hayes Int'l Corp., *supra* note 27 (named plaintiff's adequacy questioned where class of females sought, but plaintiff complained of better treatment received by some female class members); Sheehan v. Purolator, 103 F.R.D. 641, 36 FEP 1452, 1461–64 (E.D.N.Y. 1984), *aff'd,* 839 F.2d 99 (2d Cir. 1988) (high level exempt employee cannot represent low level exempt employees because of conflicting interests; employee responsible for promotion decisions cannot represent employees seeking promotions); Payne v. Travenol Laboratories, 673 F.2d 798, 810, 28 FEP 1212, 1220 (5th Cir.), *cert. denied,* 459 U.S. 1038, 30 FEP 440 (1982); Byrd v. Prudential Ins. Co. of Am., 30 FEP 304, 305 (S.D. Tex. 1982) (one of the tests for adequate representation is whether any antagonism exists between interests of plaintiffs and those of remainder of the class). *But cf.* Wester v. Special School Dist. No. 1, 35 FEP 199, 203 (D. Minn. 1984) (mere suggestions of antagonistic interests without proof does not require denial of certification of class of administrators and teachers).

[29]Anderson v. City of Albuquerque, 690 F.2d 796, 799, 29 FEP 1689, 1691 (10th Cir. 1982) (plaintiff's voluntary termination irrelevant to her ability to represent adequately the class because she remained applicant for city employment who could be affected by alleged discriminatory employment practices); Powell v. Georgia-Pacific Corp., 535 F. Supp. 713, 30 FEP 21 (W.D. Ark. 1980) (present and former employees employed in defendant's plywood and paper mills were inadequate representatives of any persons who might constitute class of rejected applicants for clerical, sales, or upper-management positions).

no class representatives with valid claims remain, and no evidence of class-wide discrimination has been submitted.[30] But where class bias has been found, the failure of the representatives' individual claims does not require decertification.[31] In some such instances, courts have appointed a new class representative.[32]

When a plaintiff appeals a district court's denial of class certification and also appeals the district court's subsequent finding of no individual discrimination against a plaintiff, one appellate court held that, if it affirms the district court's ruling on the plaintiff's individual claim, then the plaintiff can no longer challenge the district court's denial of class certification, even if the plaintiff appeared to be a proper class representative at the time certification was denied.[33]

## IV. NUMEROSITY AND MANAGEABILITY

### A. Numerosity

Questions continue to arise about the propriety of counting certain groups of persons for purposes of satisfying the numerosity requirement.[34]

### B. Manageability

The Supreme Court's decision in *Cooper v. Federal Reserve Bank of Richmond*[35] adds another consideration to the assessment of the manageability of the disparate treatment class action. In *Cooper,* the Supreme Court held that a ruling in favor of the defendant in a disparate treatment class

---

[30]O'Brien v. Sky Chefs, 670 F.2d 864, 869, 28 FEP 661, 666, *as amended,* 28 FEP 1690, 1694 (9th Cir. 1982).

[31]Scott v. City of Anniston, Ala., 682 F.2d 1353, 29 FEP 932 (11th Cir. 1982) (class should not be decertified after class prevails but individual named plaintiff does not).

[32]Carpenter v. Stephen F. Austin State Univ., 706 F.2d 608, 31 FEP 1758 (5th Cir. 1983) (if after class has been properly certified and its claims heard, representatives are found to be inadequate during course of litigating class claims or during bifurcated hearing with respect to individual claims, appropriate step is appointment of new representatives from existing class, not decertification); *see also* Simmons v. Brown, 611 F.2d 65, 26 FEP 447 (4th Cir. 1979) (where denial of class certification reversed, but class representatives' individual claims denied and not appealed, class action suit will be retained on court docket for reasonable time to allow new class representative to come forward).

[33]Everitt v. City of Marshall, 703 F.2d 207, 210–12, 31 FEP 985, 987–88 (5th Cir.), *cert. denied,* 464 U.S. 894, 32 FEP 1768 (1983); *see also* Walker v. Jim Dandy Co., 747 F.2d 1360, 1364, 36 FEP 928, 932 (11th Cir. 1984) (affirming denial of class certification where individual claim adjudicated as meritless).

[34]Holsey v. Armour & Co., 743 F.2d 199, 35 FEP 1064, 1079 (4th Cir. 1984), *cert. denied,* 470 U.S. 1028, 37 FEP 192 (1985) (distinguishing Kelley v. Norfolk & W. Ry., 584 F.2d 34, 18 FEP 359 (4th Cir. 1978) (per curiam), cited at p. 1243 note 90 of *Second Edition,* court rejected attempts to determine numerosity by looking only at number of available promotions, indicating that it is number of persons possibly affected that controls); Firefighters Local 1590 (Wilmington) v. City of Wilmington, 109 F.R.D. 89, 91–92, 40 FEP 1073, 1075–76 (D. Del. 1985) (class includes not just individuals with "probable chance" for promotion and thus actually subject to challenged discriminatory ranking, but all "adversely affected" by restructured ranking system without regard to chances); Batesville Casket Co. EEO Litigation, 35 FEP 1560, 1563 n.3 (D.D.C. 1984) (future employees cannot be counted; geographic dispersion of 11 salespersons does not satisfy numerosity requirement); Slanina v. William Penn Parking Corp., 106 F.R.D. 419, 34 FEP 1426, 1428–29 (W.D. Pa. 1984) (certifying class of 25, indicating that numerosity requirement is not to be strictly applied where equitable relief is sought and class members fear reprisal if joined).

[35]*Supra* note 27 (ruling against pattern-or-practice claims of disparate treatment class does not preclude members of class from subsequently pursuing their individual claims of disparate treatment).

action does not preclude individual class members from subsequently pursuing their individual claims, even when such class members testified on the merits of the class claims.[36] The Supreme Court indicated that whether the claims of these individual class member witnesses should be adjudicated along with the individual claims of the named plaintiffs in the same case is a question of judicial administration for district courts to decide.[37]

## V. INQUIRY INTO THE MERITS—PROHIBITED, PERMITTED, OR REQUIRED?

While it remains unresolved whether and to what extent a court will inquire into the merits at the class certification stage,[38] it appears that a majority of courts either permit or require such inquiry, at least insofar as it is necessary to determine whether the requirements of Rule 23 have been satisfied.[39]

Most courts consider affidavits,[40] statistics,[41] discovery responses,[42] similar allegations by other employees,[43] and hearsay testimony[44] as evidence competent to establish compliance with Rule 23.

---

[36]467 U.S. at 880, 35 FEP at 6. The class members are bound by the finding of no classwide discrimination, but that does not preclude individual claims.

[37]*Id.* at 881, 35 FEP at 7.

[38]*Compare* Lilly v. Harris-Teeter Supermkt., 720 F.2d 326, 332–33, 33 FEP 195, 200 (4th Cir. 1983), *cert. denied,* 466 U.S. 951, 34 FEP 1096 (1984) (certification not concerned with apparent merit of claims, no proof of any statistical disparity required, and allegations that class was affected by a common practice (unbridled discretion) sufficient) *with* Harris v. Marsh, 100 F.R.D. 315, 45 FEP 1037 (E.D.N.C. 1983) (*Falcon* requires court to conduct extensive factual analysis to see whether Rule 23 has been satisfied, and plaintiff must demonstrate typicality either through persuasive statistical showing or relevant anecdotal evidence or both); *see also* Moore v. Summa Corp., Hughes Helicopter Div., 708 F.2d 475, 32 FEP 97 (9th Cir. 1983) (while some inquiry into substance of case may be necessary, it is improper to decide merits); Anderson v. City of Albuquerque, 690 F.2d 796, 799, 29 FEP 1689, 1691–92 (10th Cir. 1982) (court must determine whether there are extant common questions of law or fact based on evidence submitted at hearing; error to evaluate merits of claim); Ladele v. Consolidated Rail Corp., 95 F.R.D. 198, 200, 29 FEP 1547, 1549 (E.D. Pa. 1982) (plaintiff need not establish case on merits, but must present factual information for court to evaluate propriety of class action); Warren v. ITT World Communications, 95 F.R.D. 425, 31 FEP 1054 (S.D.N.Y. 1982) (plaintiff's motion for class certification denied where plaintiff could not provide specific factual support for assertion of class determination).

[39]Love v. Turlington, 733 F.2d 1562 (11th Cir. 1984) (while trial court may not properly reach merits in determining whether class certification is warranted, this rule should not be invoked to limit trial court's examination of factors necessary to a reasoned determination of whether plaintiff has met Rule 23 requirements); Nelson v. United States Steel Corp., 709 F.2d 675, 679–80, 32 FEP 838, 841–42 (11th Cir. 1983) (while advance adjudication of merits is not permitted, neither is presumed satisfaction of requisites of Rule 23; because evidence relating to commonality is intertwined with merits, some merits evidence must be offered; plaintiff must prove commonality with more than allegations, but less than is required to establish prima facie case of discrimination); Redditt v. Mississippi Extended Care Centers, 718 F.2d 1381, 33 FEP 286 (5th Cir. 1983) (proof of liability by preponderance of evidence is not a requisite for certification and cannot be demanded); Sperling v. Donovan, 104 F.R.D. 4, 35 FEP 983 (D.D.C. 1984) (mere allegation of classwide discrimination insufficient; plaintiffs must present competent evidence applicable to the class); Sheehan v. Purolator, 103 F.R.D. 641, 36 FEP 1452 (E.D.N.Y. 1984), *aff'd,* 839 F.2d 99 (2d Cir. 1988) (plaintiffs must produce affidavits or other evidence to establish the existence of aggrieved class).

[40]State, County & Mun. Employees v. City of New York, 599 F. Supp. 916, 36 FEP 900 (S.D.N.Y. 1984); Sheehan v. Purolator, *supra* note 39; Meyer v. Macmillan Publishing Co., 95 F.R.D. 411, 414–15, 34 FEP 1650, 1652 (S.D.N.Y. 1982).

[41]Holsey v. Armour & Co., *supra* note 34; Salinas v. Roadway Express, 735 F.2d 1574, 35 FEP 533 (5th Cir. 1984); Nation v. Winn-Dixie Stores, 95 F.R.D. 82, 88, 29 FEP 756, 762 (N.D. Ga. 1982).

[42]Evans v. United States Pipe & Foundry Co., 696 F.2d 925, 929–30, 33 FEP 1620, 1621 (11th Cir. 1983).

[43]Ladele v. Consolidated Rail Corp., *supra* note 38.

[44]Paxton v. Union Nat'l Bank, 688 F.2d 552, 562, 29 FEP 1233, 1242 (8th Cir. 1982), *cert. denied,* 460 U.S. 1083, 31 FEP 824 (1983).

## VI. THE CLASS DETERMINATION HEARING

The discretion of a district court to deny class certification without a requested hearing is extremely limited,[45] although the decision whether to excuse noncompliance with local rules on moving for class certification is within the discretion of the trial court.[46]

While matters pertaining to discovery usually are committed to the discretion of the trial judge, unduly limited pre-class determination discovery may constitute reversible error.[47]

## VII. RULE 23(B) REQUIREMENTS

The courts continue to favor the use of (b)(2) classes in Title VII cases and to base their certifications upon findings: (1) that the employer is accused of acting or refusing to act on grounds generally applicable to the class, and (2) that injunctive relief, if appropriate, would apply to the class as a whole.[48]

At least one court has strongly suggested that where atypical back pay claims are asserted, the absent members of a Rule 23(b)(2) class ought to be treated as members of a Rule 23(b)(3) class and afforded the associated opportunity to opt out once the case reaches Stage II.[49]

Recent decisions have adhered to the Supreme Court's ruling in *Falcon* that Rule 23(a) and (b) requirements should not be construed more liberally in Title VII cases than in other actions.[50]

---

[45]Morrison v. Booth, 730 F.2d 642, 34 FEP 1142 (11th Cir. 1984), *reh'g denied,* 742 F.2d 1328, *appeal after remand, on other issues,* 763 F.2d 1366, 38 FEP 145, *reh'g denied,* 770 F.2d 1084 (11th Cir. 1985) (held, even though plaintiffs had not complied with court's order to move for class certification and request hearing, and even though several hearings ordered by court had been cancelled because of plaintiffs' problem in retaining counsel, district court erred in denying class certification without hearing; on remand, court directed plaintiffs to submit evidence in support of class certification, considered evidence submitted thereafter and later at trial, and denied motion for class certification and dismissed class allegations; class ruling not at issue on appeal after remand).

[46]*See, e.g.,* Slanina v. William Penn Parking Corp., 106 F.R.D. 419, 34 FEP 1426 (W.D. Pa. 1984) (noncompliance with local rules excused because plaintiff satisfied Rule 23(c)(1) requirements); Davis v. Buffalo Psychiatric Center, 613 F. Supp. 462, 37 FEP 69, *vacated in part,* 623 F. Supp. 19, 39 FEP 1814 (W.D.N.Y. 1985) (class certification denied because of failure by plaintiff to move for certification within 60 days after filing complaint as required by local rule).

[47]Duke v. University of Tex. at El Paso, 729 F.2d 994, 34 FEP 982 (5th Cir.), *cert. denied,* 469 U.S. 982, 36 FEP 234 (1984) (court held that limited discovery constituted reversible error).

[48]Giles v. Ireland, 742 F.2d 1366, 35 FEP 1718 (11th Cir. 1984) (23(b)(2) particularly applicable to claim of unlawful discrimination against a class); Chisholm v. United States Postal Serv., 665 F.2d 482, 492, 27 FEP 425, 433 (4th Cir. 1981) (evidence of systemic discrimination against blacks in promotion opportunities satisfies (b)(2)'s requirements and presence of back pay claims does not make (b)(2) certification improper); Batesville Casket Co. EEO Litigation, 35 FEP 1560 (D.D.C. 1984) (recognizing 23(b)(2) as appropriate certification mechanism, but denying class certification because 23(a) requirements not satisfied); Osmer v. Aerospace Corp., 30 FEP 204, 208–9 (C.D. Cal. 1982) (a broad (b)(2) class was appropriate because injunctive relief requested would not have to be individually crafted); Kraszewski v. State Farm Gen. Ins. Co., 27 FEP 27, 32 (N.D. Cal. 1981) (class action seeking declaratory, injunctive, and monetary relief may be maintained under (b)(2) if evidence does not indicate that claims for monetary relief are paramount).

[49]Holmes v. Continental Can Co., 706 F.2d 1144, 31 FEP 1707 (11th Cir. 1983) ("the presence in a lawsuit of a significant number of atypical claims not common to the class activates a requirement that absent class members be given an opportunity to opt out of a Title VII lawsuit or a settlement * * * . Because the monetary relief stage of this particular Title VII case is functionally more similar to a (b)(3) class than to a (b)(2) class, the opt out protection of (b)(3) must be applied.").

[50]Batesville Casket Co. EEO Litigation, *supra* note 48, at 1562 (plaintiff seeking class certification under Rule 23(b) must satisfy 23(b) requirements; strict application); Gilchrist v. Bolger, 733 F.2d 1551, 35 FEP 81 (11th Cir. 1984) (Title VII actions must meet Rule 23(a) prerequisites just as any other class action).

## VIII. Organizations as Class Representatives

It remains unsettled whether an organization, such as a labor union or civil rights organization, may bring a class action as named representative.[51]

Following the Supreme Court's ruling in *General Telephone Co. of the Northwest v. EEOC*[52] the Tenth Circuit has held that Rule 23 does not apply to the EEOC when it intervenes as plaintiff any more than when it brings a direct action.[53]

## IX. Jurisdictional Requirements and Limitations Period for Class Members

A class may encompass individuals who have not satisfied Title VII's statutory prerequisites for suit.[54] Class membership will, however, be restricted to those who could have filed a timely charge when the named plaintiff did,[55] unless the discrimination is continuing.[56] The scope of the class action is limited by the scope of the EEOC charge, and there must be a close congruity of the claims of the class and its representative.[57] The class, however, is not always limited to allegations covered in the representative's charge or even allegations investigated by the EEOC, but in some cases may also embrace ancillary matters which "could reasonably be expected to grow out of" the EEOC charge.[58]

Although there is still some authority for the general proposition that an intervenor need not satisfy the statutory prerequisites of Title VII in order to represent a class, the Fifth and Eleventh circuits have held that a class representative must have been in a position to pursue his or her own Title VII action with respect to the represented claims.[59] When an intervenor, who

---

[51]Miller v. Smith, 584 F. Supp. 149, 153, 36 FEP 96, 98 (D.D.C. 1984) (court noted question of standing under Title VII of National Black Deputy United States Marshal's Organization to bring civil action as named plaintiff).

[52]446 U.S. 318, 22 FEP 1196 (1980).

[53]United Telecommunications v. Saffels, 741 F.2d 312, 35 FEP 1232 (10th Cir. 1984), *cert. denied,* 470 U.S. 1060, 37 FEP 376 (1985).

[54]Ulloa v. City of Philadelphia, 95 F.R.D. 109, 113–14, 34 FEP 906, 908 (E.D. Pa. 1982).

[55]*Id.*

[56]Leach v. Standard Register Co., 94 F.R.D. 621, 625, 34 FEP 1777, 1780 (W.D. Ark. 1982) (where continuing violations are alleged, charge may be filed at any time by present employee, and only employees barred from class are those who left employ of defendant more than 180 days prior to filing of the charges); *see also* Avagliano v. Sumitomo Shoji Am., 103 F.R.D. 562, 578, 38 FEP 561, 572 (S.D.N.Y. 1984) (where continuing violations are alleged in a deferral state, those persons who challenged the defendant's policies "which continued to affect them as of 300 days prior to the first filing of a complaint with the EEOC are members of the class * * * [and those] who terminated their employment prior to the 300 day cutoff may not join the class.").

[57]Fellows v. Universal Restaurants, 701 F.2d 447, 31 FEP 483 (5th Cir.), *cert. denied,* 464 U.S. 828, 32 FEP 1672 (1983) (EEOC charge which alleged discharge and pay discrimination due to sex could be construed as supporting a class action); Evans v. United States Pipe & Foundry Co., 696 F.2d 925, 929, 33 FEP 1620, 1622–23 (11th Cir. 1983) (a class can contain only those individuals whose claims are "like or related" to those included in plaintiff's charge or in EEOC's "substantive inquiry").

[58]Fellows v. Universal Restaurants, *supra* note 57, at 450–51, 31 FEP at 486 (a class should not be denied because EEOC charge and investigation did not cover class allegations: "a cause of action for Title VII employment discrimination may be based, not only upon the specific complaints made by the employee's initial EEOC charge, but also upon any kind of discrimination like or related to the charge's allegations, limited by the scope of the EEOC investigation that could reasonably be expected to grow out of the initial charges of discrimination").

[59]Ulloa v. City of Philadelphia, 95 F.R.D. 109, 113 n.3, 34 FEP 906, 908 (E.D. Pa. 1982) ("all class representatives need not meet the jurisdictional filing requirements of Title VII"); *But see* Salinas v. Roadway Express, 735 F.2d 1574, 1579, 35 FEP 533, 537 (5th Cir. 1984) (intervention denied where

has not individually satisfied the requisites of Title VII, seeks to intervene to represent the claims which the named plaintiffs cannot represent because of *Falcon,* the courts disagree on whether the intervenor can satisfy Title VII by relying upon the EEOC charges and other actions of the named plaintiffs.[60] However, a class member who never filed any EEOC charge may not intervene to take over as the sole representative where the named class representative is dismissed for failing to meet the jurisdictional prerequisites to suit.[61] An individual seeking to intervene as class representative must make his application for intervention prior to a ruling on class certification.[62] Intervention may be permitted for the purpose of appealing denial of a class action when the original-named plaintiffs have settled.[63]

At least one court has suggested that the scope of a Title VII class action is circumscribed by the scope of the claims which the named plaintiffs, who individually satisfied the requisites of Title VII, have standing to raise; as a corollary, no one has standing to challenge a practice which did not affect him personally.[64]

The filing of a class action tolls the applicable statute of limitations and permits all members of the putative class to file individual actions or to intervene if class certification is denied, "provided, of course, that those actions are instituted within the time that remains on the limitations period."[65] The filing of a class action normally tolls the statute of limitations for a member of a certified class until he exercises his right to opt out of the class.[66] While putative class members who file individual actions after

---

intervenor's individual action had been dismissed on timeliness grounds; court held "to qualify as a named plaintiff, * * * [an individual] must have been in a position to pursue his own Title VII action."); Griffin v. Dugger, 823 F.2d 1476, 44 FEP 938 (11th Cir. 1987), *vacating order certifying class sub nom.* Griffin v. Wainwright, 34 FEP 1859 (N.D. Fla. 1982), *cert. denied,* 486 U.S. _____, 46 FEP 1264 (1988) (major Eleventh Circuit class certification decision with extensive discussion of *General Tel. Co. of the Sw. v. Falcon,* 457 U.S. 147, 28 FEP 1745 (1982) and impact of *Falcon* on prior Fifth Circuit across-the-board class certifications; held, three named plaintiffs could not represent class of black correctional officer applicants with testing claims, because two plaintiffs had not been denied employment opportunities by test results and third plaintiff who failed test had not filed timely charge; "single filing" rule encompasses only claims for which charge filer has standing and for which class members seek relief).

[60]*Compare* Vuyanich v. Republic Nat'l Bank of Dallas, 723 F.2d 1195, 1201, 31 FEP 1521, 1524 (5th Cir.), *cert. denied,* 469 U.S. 1073, 36 FEP 568 (1984) (named plaintiffs could only represent hiring and termination claims, and intervenors could not bring their transfer, promotion, compensation, classification, and assignment claims in reliance upon named plaintiffs' EEOC charges because named plaintiffs have no standing to assert such claims) *with* Lilly v. Harris-Teeter Supermkt., 720 F.2d 326, 334–35, 33 FEP 195, 201–2 (4th Cir. 1983), *cert. denied,* 466 U.S. 951, 34 FEP 1096 (1984) (after court found that named plaintiffs could not represent promotion claims, court allowed intervenors to rely upon named plaintiffs' EEOC charges to bring their promotion claims because named plaintiffs' charges mentioned promotion and because there had been no indication that employer would conciliate any claims filed with the EEOC, thus rendering filing by intervenors purposeless); *see also* Hill v. AT&T Technologies, 731 F.2d 175, 34 FEP 620 (4th Cir. 1984) (intervenor's hiring claim barred at time named plaintiffs filed their EEOC charges and intervenor could not rely upon earlier filed EEOC charges of nonparties where nonparties were employees and lacked standing to raise hiring claims and where their EEOC charges, in any event, only complained of discrimination in summer, not permanent, hiring). *And see* Griffin v. Dugger, *supra* note 59.

[61]Wakeen v. Hoffman House, 724 F.2d 1238, 33 FEP 1476 (7th Cir. 1983), *amended,* 33 FEP 1816 (1984) (named class representative's claim dismissed in its entirety because of *res judicata*).

[62]Walker v. Jim Dandy Co., 747 F.2d 1360, 36 FEP 928 (11th Cir. 1984).

[63]Williams v. City of New Orleans, 543 F. Supp. 662, 678 n.19, 29 FEP 30, 43 (E.D. La. 1982), *aff'd en banc,* 729 F.2d 1554, 34 FEP 1009 (5th Cir. 1984).

[64]Vuyanich v. Republic Nat'l Bank of Dallas, *supra* note 60.

[65]Crown Cork & Seal Co. v. Parker, 462 U.S. 345, 354, 31 FEP 1697, 1700 (1983) ("[o]nce the statute of limitations has been tolled, it remains tolled for all members of the putative class until class certification is denied. At that point, class members may choose to file their own suits or to intervene as plaintiffs in the pending action.").

[66]Tosti v. City of Los Angeles, 754 F.2d 1485, 37 FEP 348 (9th Cir. 1985).

denial of class certification benefit from the tolling of the limitations period, they do not so benefit if they subsequently file class actions.[67]

The extent of the necessary identity between claims of putative class members and the allegations of the tolling charge has not been conclusively established.[68] When the timeliness of a federal cause of action is controlled by a state statute of limitations, state law will also control the effect of tolling occasioned by the filing of a federal class action, unless state law in that respect is inconsistent with federal law.[69] If, after certification is denied and tolling ends, state law provides for a complete renewal of the state statute of limitations and does not require that unnamed class members file suit within the time which remained on the original limitations period before tolling began, such a state law is not inconsistent with federal law.[70]

## XI. Settlement

Class actions may be settled only with the approval of the district court under Rule 23(e), in order to protect absent class members whose interests may not have been given due regard by the negotiating parties.[71] The typical procedure involves a determination that the settlement is the result of good faith, arms-length negotiations, and notice to class members and others who may be affected by the settlement of their right to submit written objections and attend a fairness hearing.[72]

Although Rule 23(e) is silent on the standard by which a proposed settlement is to be evaluated, the universally applied measure is whether the settlement is fundamentally fair, adequate, and reasonable.[73] In assessing the

---

[67]Smith v. Flagship Int'l, 609 F. Supp. 58, 64, 36 FEP 1682, 1686 (N.D. Tex. 1985) ("even if there were conflicting suggestions * * * that the tolling rule should apply to future class actions, this court would be disinclined to give them much weight. The rule advanced by [the named plaintiff] would allow the attorney for a class to revive the class claims upon denial of certification by simply refiling a new class action using a different putative class member as representative.").

[68]Crown Cork & Seal Co. v. Parker, 462 U.S. 345, 355, 31 FEP 1697, 1701 (in his concurring opinion, Mr. Justice Powell cautioned that "when a plaintiff invokes American Pipe in support of a separate lawsuit, the district court should take care to ensure that the suit raises claims that 'concern the same evidence, memories, and witnesses as the subject matter of the original class suit,' so that 'the defendant will not be prejudiced' (citation omitted). Claims as to which the defendant was not fairly placed on notice by the class suit are not protected under American Pipe and are barred by the statute of limitations.").

[69]Chardon v. Fumero Soto, 462 U.S. 650 (1983) (suit under 42 U.S.C. § 1983, governed by Puerto Rico statute of limitations; while not an employment discrimination case, its ruling could affect discrimination cases filed under 42 U.S.C. § 1981).

[70]Id.; see also American Pipe & Constr. Co. v. Utah, 414 U.S. 538 (1974) (in case controlled by federal limitations period, after certification was denied and tolling ceased, class members required to intervene within time remaining on original period before tolling began).

[71]Officers for Justice v. Civil Serv. Comm'n, 688 F.2d 615, 29 FEP 1473 (9th Cir. 1982), cert. denied, 459 U.S. 1217, 34 FEP 1096 (1983); Collins v. Thompson, 679 F.2d 168 (9th Cir. 1982).

[72]Stotts v. Memphis Fire Dep't, 679 F.2d 541, 28 FEP 1491 (6th Cir. 1982), rev'd on other grounds sub nom. Firefighters Local 1784 v. Stotts, 467 U.S. 561, 34 FEP 1702 (1984); Officers for Justice v. Civil Serv. Comm'n, supra note 71; Sweet v. General Tire & Rubber Co., 28 FEP 804 (N.D. Ohio 1982); see also Williams v. City of New Orleans, 729 F.2d 1554, 34 FEP 1009 (5th Cir. 1984) (en banc) (in approving settlement involving consent decree, court should examine it carefully to ascertain not only that it is a fair settlement but also that it does not put the court's sanction on and power behind decree that violates Constitution, statute, or jurisprudence).

[73]EEOC v. Hiram Walker & Sons, 768 F.2d 884, 38 FEP 820 (7th Cir. 1985), cert. denied, 478 U.S. 1004, 41 FEP 271 (1986); Parker v. Anderson, 667 F.2d 1204, 28 FEP 788 (5th Cir.), cert. denied, 459 U.S. 828 (1982); Franks v. Kroger Co., 670 F.2d 71, 27 FEP 1433 (6th Cir. 1982) (settlement agree-

adequacy and fairness of a proposed class settlement, courts continue to recognize that the probability of plaintiff's success on the merits is often the most important factor to consider.[74] One court has said that the relative importance to be attached to any particular factor will depend on the unique facts and circumstances of each case.[75] The fact that substantial numbers of class members, including named plaintiffs, object to the proposed settlement need not necessarily result in the court's rejection of the settlement.[76]

The distribution of settlement proceeds among class members is subject to the same fairness scrutiny as the settlement agreement itself, and proponents of a preferential allocation scheme bear a heavy burden of proof.[77] The opinion of class counsel as to the merits of the various claims is not sufficient by itself to justify approval of a preferential distribution scheme.[78]

Denial of approval of a class action settlement is an appealable order, as is approval.[79] The standard of appellate review is whether there is a strong showing of clear abuse of discretion by the district court.[80]

Following the *Stotts*[81] decision, challenges were raised to affirmative action plans resulting from Title VII class actions on the ground that such plans are not limited to benefiting the actual victims of discrimination. Most courts thus far have rejected such challenges,[82] and have upheld settlement agreements which include affirmative action plans, endorsing the view that *Stotts* is of limited application.[83]

---

ment that provides specific benefits to class representatives and their attorney approved where agreement has effect of creating presumption of discrimination against class members who then seek individual relief).

[74]Kirkland v. New York State Dep't of Correctional Servs., 711 F.2d 1117, 32 FEP 509 (2d Cir. 1983), *cert. denied,* 465 U.S. 1005, 33 FEP 1344 (1984); Dekro v. Stern Bros., 571 F. Supp. 97, 100 (W.D. Mo. 1983); Morales v. Turman, 569 F. Supp. 332, 337–38 (E.D. Tex. 1983); Parker v. Anderson, *supra* note 73.

[75]Officers for Justice v. Civil Serv. Comm'n, *supra* note 71.

[76]Parker v. Anderson, *supra* note 73 (10 out of 11 named plaintiffs, as well as several unnamed class members, objected); Elliott v. Sperry Rand Corp., 680 F.2d 1225, 29 FEP 1281 (8th Cir. 1982) (790 class members out of 3,000 objected); League of Martin v. City of Milwaukee, 588 F. Supp. 1004, 42 FEP 562 (E.D. Wis. 1984) (over 50% of class objected to all or part of agreement).

[77]Holmes v. Continental Can Co., 706 F.2d 1144, 1148, 31 FEP 1707 (11th Cir. 1983); *see also* Plummer v. Chemical Bank, 97 F.R.D. 486, 33 FEP 547 (S.D.N.Y. 1983) (proposed consent decree not approved where no apparent reason for providing named plaintiffs with immediate cash payments and guaranteed future benefits, while relief for class members contingent on future promotion or success under grievance procedure).

[78]Holmes v. Continental Can Co., 706 F.2d 1144, 1150, 31 FEP 1707, 1712 (11th Cir. 1983) (allocation of half of back pay to eight named plaintiffs not justified).

[79]Williams v. City of New Orleans, *supra* note 72.

[80]*Id.; see* Officers for Justice v. Civil Serv. Comm'n, *supra* note 71; *see also* Ficalora v. Lockheed Cal. Co., 751 F.2d 995, 36 FEP 1172 (9th Cir. 1985) (settlement approval vacated and remanded where district court did not inquire into named plaintiff's objections concerning class attorney's conflict of interest and overreaching).

[81]Firefighters Local 1784 v. Stotts, 467 U.S. 561, 34 FEP 1702 (1984).

[82]*See, e.g.,* Williams v. City of New Orleans, *supra* note 72, at 1557, 34 FEP at 1011 ("According to the government's argument, the last sentence of § 706(g) of Title VII proscribes the use of any remedy which is not limited to actual victims of past discrimination * * *. We cannot accept this *per se* rule; the statute does not so require.").

[83]Vanguards of Cleveland v. City of Cleveland, 753 F.2d 479, 36 FEP 1431 (6th Cir. 1985), *aff'd sub nom.* Firefighters Local 93 v. City of Cleveland, 478 U.S. 501, 41 FEP 139 (1986); Turner v. Orr, 722 F.2d 661, 33 FEP 1105 (11th Cir. 1984), *aff'd,* 759 F.2d 817, 37 FEP 1186 (11th Cir. 1985), *cert. denied,* 478 U.S. 1020, 41 FEP 272 (1986); NAACP, Boston Chapter v. Beecher, 749 F.2d 102, 36 FEP 771 (1st Cir. 1984), *cert. denied,* 471 U.S. 1075, 37 FEP 952 (1985); Massachussetts Ass'n of Afro-American Police v. Boston Police Dep't, 106 F.R.D. 80, 37 FEP 1569 (D. Mass.), *aff'd,* 780 F.2d 5, 39 FEP 1048 (1st Cir. 1985), *cert. denied,* 478 U.S. 1020, 41 FEP 272 (1986); *see also* Chapter 37 (Injunctive and Affirmative Relief) and Chapter 24 (Reverse Discrimination and Affirmative Action).

## XII. Appeals

A plaintiff whose individual claim has been rejected at the trial level may nevertheless appeal the interlocutory denial of class certification at the same time the individual determination is appealed.[84] The Fifth Circuit has held that a court of appeals has jurisdiction to consider a class certification definition where the definition has, by exclusion, led to the denial of injunctive relief.[85]

On appeal from the denial of class certification and the trial on the merits of the individual claims, the appellate court will consider the full record upon which class denial was premised, not just the record before the court at the certification hearing.[86] Thus, affirmance of a finding of no individual discrimination may prove fatal to the class certification claim because the individual will have no nexus with or membership in the proposed class.[87] One court has stated that the Supreme Court's decision in *Coopers & Lybrand v. Livesay,*[88] which holds that a denial of class certification is not subject to interlocutory appeal as a "collateral order," also means that a denial of class certification is not subject to interlocutory appeal as a final judgment on a separate claim, even if so certified by the district court under Fed. R. Civ. P. 54(b).[89]

---

[84]Anderson v. City of Albuquerque, 690 F.2d 796, 29 FEP 1689 (10th Cir. 1982).

[85]Payne v. Travenol Laboratories, 673 F.2d 798, 28 FEP 1212 (5th Cir.), *cert. denied,* 459 U.S. 1038, 30 FEP 440 (1982).

[86]Everitt v. City of Marshall, 703 F.2d 207, 31 FEP 985, 987 (5th Cir.), *cert. denied,* 464 U.S. 894, 32 FEP 1768 (1983).

[87]*Id.*

[88]437 U.S. 463 (1978).

[89]Minority Police Officers Ass'n of S. Bend v. City of S. Bend, Ind., 721 F.2d 197, 201, 33 FEP 433, 436 (7th Cir. 1983).

## CHAPTER 35

# DISCOVERY

## III. LIMITATIONS ON DISCOVERY

### A. Discovery Sought by Plaintiff

Failure to cooperate in discovery has resulted in sanctions against defendants.[1]

### 1. Privileged Materials

Discovery by a plaintiff of the critical self-analysis parts of plans remains an unsettled area,[2] as does the academic freedom privilege asserted in faculty tenure cases relating to discovery of individual faculty members' votes.[3]

---

[1]Easley v. Anheuser-Busch, 758 F.2d 251, 37 FEP 549 (8th Cir. 1985) (trial judge did not abuse discretion by excluding testimony of expert witness not properly disclosed during discovery); Johnson v. Smith dba Diversified Contract Servs., 630 F. Supp. 1, 40 FEP 1044 (N.D. Cal. 1986) (plaintiff awarded attorney's fees for excessive length of deposition and for interrogatories propounded to harass plaintiff); EEOC v. A.E. Staley Mfg. Co., 38 FEP 1803 (N.D. Ill. 1985) (attorney's fees and costs assessed from defendant's counsel's willful delay in complying with EEOC subpoena court had ordered enforced); Shipes v. Trinity Indus., 40 FEP 1136, 1145 (E.D. Tex. 1985) (counsel ordered to pay plaintiff's attorney's fees and costs associated with repeated failure to comply with discovery orders); Fautek v. Montgomery Ward & Co., 96 F.R.D. 141, 42 FEP 1395, 1398–99 (N.D. Ill. 1982) (santctions against employer for giving plaintiff's counsel misinformation about system of computerizing records and interpretive codes).

[2]Coates v. Johnson & Johnson, 756 F.2d 524, 37 FEP 467 (7th Cir. 1985) (recognizing prevailing view that self-critical portion of affirmative action plan is privileged, but qualified, and can be waived if used by defendant to prove nondiscrimination); cf., Witten v. A.H. Smith & Co., 100 F.R.D. 446, 33 FEP 1238, later proceedings on other issues, 104 F.R.D. 398, 36 FEP 268 and 36 FEP 271 (D. Md. 1984), aff'd 785 F.2d 306, 46 FEP 1222 (4th Cir. 1986) (evaluative portions of affirmative action plans not exempt from discovery under critical self-analysis privilege where no showing that evaluative portions were expected to be privileged when prepared or that disclosure would significantly diminish voluntary cooperation by employer with federal government); In re Burlington N., 679 F.2d 762, 29 FEP 565 (8th Cir. 1982) (employer not entitled to writ of mandamus compelling district court to vacate order which required personnel director to answer deposition questions about goals and timetable development in self-analysis section of affirmative action plan); Hoffman v. United Telecommunications, 36 EPD ¶ 35,158 at 37,221 (D. Kan. 1985) (self-evaluation analysis privileged; objective data discoverable); Mister v. Illinois Cent. Gulf R.R., 42 FEP 1710, 1714–15 (S.D. Ill. 1982) (affirmative action plans and EEO-1 forms covered by privilege of self-critical analysis, but only with respect to subjective self-evaluative statements therein); Zahorik v. Cornell Univ., 98 F.R.D. 27, 31 FEP 1366 (N.D.N.Y. 1983), aff'd on other grounds, 729 F.2d 85, 34 FEP 165 (2d Cir. 1984) (ordering full disclosure of affirmative action plans, including critical self-analysis); Penk v. Oregon State Bd. of Higher Educ., 99 F.R.D. 506, 37 FEP 918 (D. Or. 1982) (self-critical analyses privileged; objective data discoverable); Resnick v. American Dental Ass'n, 95 F.R.D. 372, 31 FEP 1359 (N.D. Ill. 1982) (critical self-analysis privilege does not justify refusal to produce personnel practices study prepared by management consulting firm, nor minutes and documents of defendant's ad hoc committee on employee relations; work-product doctrine inapplicable even though work initiated with advice of counsel); Banks v. Lockheed-Georgia Co., 53 F.R.D. 283, 285, 4 FEP 117 (N.D. Ga. 1971) (privilege of critical self-analysis precludes discovery of written opinions and conclusions of team members who studied company's problems and progress in affirmative action; ultimate report of team to government agency and underlying factual and statistical information must be produced).

[3]EEOC v. Franklin & Marshall College, 775 F.2d 110, 39 FEP 211 (3d Cir. 1985), cert. denied, 476 U.S. 1163, 40 FEP 1617 (1986) (denying any privilege and refusing to undertake any balancing test weighing competing factors before ordering disclosure); EEOC v. University of Notre Dame du Lac, 715 F.2d 331, 32 FEP 1057 (7th Cir. 1983) (personnel files subject to discovery, but university entitled to keep identity of reviewing peers confidential by redacting files); Gray v. New York City Bd. of Higher Educ., 692 F.2d 901, 30 FEP 297 (2d Cir. 1982) (instructor denied tenure without being given reasons

Courts have also addressed other general privilege claims[4] and have developed procedures for preserving confidentiality while permitting appropriate discovery.[5]

## 2. Burdensome or Irrelevant Discovery

The relevancy of requests for information is evaluated on a case-by-case basis.[6] In order to determine the relevant time period for which information must be made available, courts have used a reasonableness approach.[7] The appropriate time period for discoverable information may be expanded where the plaintiff was a member of a certified class at the time he filed his EEOC charge.[8] When the information sought concerns departments, units,

---

entitled to discover votes of two members of tenure committee; qualified privilege against discovery of academic peer review will be recognized if unsuccessful candidate is given a meaningful written statement of reasons for rejection); Rollins v. Farris, 108 F.R.D. 714, 39 FEP 1102 (E.D. Ark. 1985) (adopting *Franklin & Marshall College* rule; information discoverable if claims arise out of act occurring in tenure committee deliberations); Zaustinsky v. University of Cal., 96 F.R.D. 622, 30 FEP 1535 (N.D. Cal. 1983), *aff'd without opinion,* 782 F.2d 1055 (9th Cir. 1985) (discovery of peer review evaluation preliminarily denied with proviso that plaintiff be given a written statement of reasons for decision denying tenure, including detailed summary of the substance of confidential documents; further production would then be weighed by the court).

[4]Trevino v. Celanese Corp., 701 F.2d 397, 33 FEP 1324 (5th Cir. 1983) (overturning broad protective order which denied discovery into management structure and policies of employer); Price v. Erie County, N.Y., 40 FEP 115, 116–18 (W.D.N.Y. 1986) (files of county law department regarding its investigation of plaintiff and others held privileged in action against county); EEOC v. Fox Point-Bayside School Dist., 31 EPD ¶ 33,609 (E.D. Wis. 1983) (attorney-client privilege no bar to discovery where individual board members sought and considered attorney's counsel on teacher's termination); Greene v. Thalhimer's Dep't Store, 93 F.R.D. 657, 28 FEP 918 (E.D. Va. 1982) (plaintiff entitled to discover conciliation documents on condition that she not use materials as evidence without consent of persons concerned).

[5]Rossini v. Ogilvy & Mather, 798 F.2d 590, 601, 42 FEP 1615, 1622–23 (2d Cir. 1986) (affirming order restricting personnel file access to plaintiff's counsel); EEOC v. University of Notre Dame du Lac, *supra* note 3; Sanders v. Shell Oil Co., 678 F.2d 614, 29 FEP 98 (5th Cir. 1982) (court ordered stolen documents sealed pending ruling on relevancy and need for confidentiality); Davis v. Burlington Indus., 34 FEP 917 (N.D. Ga. 1983) (protective order entered prohibiting plaintiff from disseminating confidential commercial data and placing data under seal); Schafer v. Parkview Memorial Hosp., 593 F. Supp. 61, 35 FEP 1489 (N.D. Ind. 1984) (ordering disclosure of peer review committee meeting minutes after balancing competing factors and finding that plaintiff's need for discovery outweighed reasons underlying statutory privilege).

[6]*See* Sweat v. Miller Brewing Co., 708 F.2d 655, 32 FEP 384 (11th Cir. 1983) (statistical information concerning employer's general policies and practices may be relevant to establish pretext and thus discoverable even in individual discrimination case); O'Neal v. Riceland Foods, 684 F.2d 577, 29 FEP 956 (8th Cir. 1982) (employer not required to answer interrogatories pertaining to hiring because partial summary judgment had previously determined that hiring was not an issue in the case); Helt v. Metropolitan Dist. Comm'n, 113 F.R.D. 7, 12, 42 FEP 1561, 1565 (D. Conn. 1986) (in suit alleging sex discrimination in retirement benefits, not all documents interpreting or requesting interpretation of plan are relevant); Allen v. Colgate-Palmolive Co., 539 F. Supp. 57, 27 FEP 1408 (S.D.N.Y. 1981) (defendant compelled to produce all evaluations prepared by supervisor which contain same discriminatory phrase as the one contained in the plaintiff's).

[7]*See, e.g.,* Robbins v. Camden City Bd. of Educ., 105 F.R.D. 49, 62–63 (D.N.J. 1985) (general discovery limited to three-year period of employment and two-year periods preceding and succeeding employment); EEOC v. Kelly-Springfield Tire Co., 38 FEP 194, 197 (E.D.N.C. 1985) (period two years prior to alleged acts reasonable); EEOC v. Delaware State Police, 618 F. Supp. 451, 453, 39 FEP 81, 82 (D. Del. 1985) (enforcing EEOC subpoena for information three years prior to ADEA charge over objection that EEOC must show willfulness before discovering earlier than two years); Williams v. United Parcel Serv., 34 FEP 1655 (N.D. Ohio 1982) (interrogatory answers and production of documents limited to period beginning one year prior to earliest alleged act of discrimination); Nash v. City of Oakwood, Ohio, 90 F.R.D. 633, 28 FEP 279 (S.D. Ohio 1981) (plaintiffs entitled to discovery for five-year period before filing of charge, but not from 1968; restriction "not etched in stone" and could be modified upon a proper showing); Ford v. University of Notre Dame du Lac, 29 FEP 1710 (N.D. Ind. 1980) (plaintiff not entitled to discovery predating applicability of Title VII to employer in 1972).

[8]Edwards v. Boeing Vertol Co., 717 F.2d 761, 32 FEP 1696 (3d Cir. 1983), *vacated on other grounds in light of* Cooper v. Federal Reserve Bank of Richmond, 468 U.S. 1201, 35 FEP 96 (1984) (district court erred in limiting discovery to acts occurring within 180 days of date plaintiff filed EEOC charge where he had been member of certified class at time he filed charge).

or businesses other than the one in which the plaintiff is employed, courts have reached differing conclusions as to the relevant geographic and functional areas.[9]

Computerized information is discoverable, if otherwise relevant, although there remain issues as to the form in which such information should be produced.[10] Assessment of the expenses associated with producing computer-generated information is determined by balancing the relative cost to the parties against the need for the information.[11]

Several courts are of the view that discovery as to the merits in class actions cannot proceed until after class certification; however, sufficient discovery is allowed in order to determine the class action issue and the proper scope of any class.[12]

A number of other issues relating to the scope of discovery have also been addressed.[13]

---

[9]*Compare* Witten v. A.H. Smith & Co., 785 F.2d 306, 46 FEP 1222 (4th Cir. 1986) (court did not abuse discretion in limiting discovery to three facilities under same umbrella as plaintiff's where plaintiff did not conduct discovery in three facilities made available), Hendrix v. Safeway Stores, 39 FEP 118 (W.D. Mo. 1985) (discovery limited to division where plaintiff employed, not nationwide divisions) *and* Prouty v. National R.R. Passenger Corp., 99 F.R.D. 545 (D.D.C. 1983) (in individual action, court limited discovery to department in which plaintiff worked) *with* Duke v. University of Tex. at El Paso, 729 F.2d 994, 34 FEP 982 (5th Cir.), *cert. denied,* 469 U.S. 982, 36 FEP 234 (1984) (promotional and pay records of other departments of university are discoverable prior to class action certification hearing), Owens v. Bethlehem Mines Corp., 108 F.R.D. 207, 213, 39 FEP 782, 789 (S.D. W. Va. 1985) (permitting companywide discovery to obtain pattern-or-practice evidence), Brown v. Marriott Corp., 33 FEP 550 (N.D. Ga. 1983) (plaintiff in promotion case entitled to discover promotion practices in hotels other than where employed because transfers to other hotels did occur) *and* Whalen v. McLean Trucking Co., 37 FEP 835 (N.D. Ga. 1983) (plaintiff entitled to discover age discrimination claims without regard to any geographical restriction).

[10]*Compare* Bills v. Kennecott Corp., 108 F.R.D. 459, 40 FEP 1182, 1184–85 (D. Utah 1985) (computerized information discoverable; form may vary) *and* Penk v. Oregon State Bd. of Higher Educ., 99 F.R.D. 504, 37 FEP 916 (D. Or. 1982) (computer tapes discoverable) *with* Williams v. Owens-Illinois, 665 F.2d 918, 27 FEP 1273 (9th Cir.), *cert. denied,* 459 U.S. 971, 30 FEP 56 (1982) (district court upheld in its refusal to order employer to surrender computer tapes, as all information sought on tapes was contained on wage cards previously discovered) *and* Zahorik v. Cornell Univ., *supra* note 2 (plaintiffs not entitled to free access to defendant's computer which contains confidential information irrelevant to their claims; instead, plaintiffs ordered to reformulate and narrow requests).

[11]Bills v. Kennecott Corp., *supra* note 10 (balancing cost to defendant, relatively greater cost to plaintiff, and benefit of requested information to both parties, defendant not entitled to recover expense of production); Penk v. Oregon State Bd. of Higher Educ., *supra* note 10 (costs shared equally).

[12]Mantolete v. Bolger, 767 F.2d 1416, 1425, 38 FEP 1081, 1088, *amended,* 38 FEP 1517 (9th Cir. 1985) (affirming trial court's refusal to permit class discovery unless plaintiff makes prima facie showing that Rule 23 requirements satisfied or that discovery likely to substantiate class allegations); Washington v. Brown & Williamson Tobacco Corp., 106 F.R.D. 592, 594, 41 FEP 1746, 1747 (M.D. Ga. 1985) (denying motion to compel discovery on class issues where evidence shows no possibility plaintiffs able to show requisite nexus with proposed class members); Zahorik v. Cornell Univ., *supra* note 2 (plaintiffs whose prior motion for class certification was denied without prejudice may engage in broad discovery relating to class claims); Hawkins v. Fulton County, 95 F.R.D. 88, 29 FEP 762 (N.D. Ga. 1982) (class-related discovery is permissible even though no class has been certified); Pittman v. E.I. du Pont de Nemours & Co., 552 F.2d 149, 29 FEP 876 (5th Cir. 1977) (certain amount of discovery is essential in order to determine existence and scope of class, but interrogatories as propounded here were overly broad and burdensome); Nash v. City of Oakwood, *supra* note 7 (discovery limited to determining maintainability of cause of action as class); *cf.* Vivone v. Acme Mkts, 105 F.R.D. 65, 66, 37 FEP 561, 563 (E.D. Pa. 1985) (plaintiffs in ADEA "class action" may discover names, addresses, and other information on potential class members, both for pattern-or-practice and class notice purposes).

[13]Harris v. Amoco Prod. Co., 768 F.2d 669, 683–85, 38 FEP 1226, 1237–38 (5th Cir. 1985), *cert. denied,* 475 U.S. 1011, 40 FEP 192 (1986) (though permitting broad discovery, district court did not abuse discretion in issuing protective order limiting intervenor (EEOC) to use of information only in instant action); Massa v. Eaton Corp., 109 F.R.D. 312, 314–15, 39 FEP 1211, 1213 (W.D. Mich. 1985) (protective order prohibiting *ex parte* communication with managerial employees, making evidence from such sources inadmissible); Sears v. Atchison, Topeka & Santa Fe Ry., 30 FEP 1084 (D. Kan. 1982), *aff'd on other grounds,* 749 F.2d 1451, 36 FEP 783 (10th Cir. 1984), *cert. denied,* 471 U.S. 1099, 37 FEP 1216 (1985) (plaintiff not entitled to discover identity and location of defendant's assets since no judgment had been entered and defendant was entitled to assumption that it would pay

## B. Discovery Sought by the Defendant

In actions filed by the EEOC on behalf of a class, defendants are entitled to appropriate discovery, although protective orders have been granted with respect to certain information.[14] Absent a showing of abuse of process by the EEOC, discovery sought by defendants resisting enforcement of an EEOC subpoena[15] or seeking to ascertain the underlying basis of a charge[16] is severely circumscribed.

Plaintiff's failure to cooperate in discovery has prompted sanctions,[17] including the sanction of dismissal where a plaintiff totally or recurringly refuses to participate in the discovery process.[18] The sanction of dismissal, however, is inappropriate where less drastic measures would suffice.[19]

---

any judgment rendered); Catherman v. Reynolds Metal Co., 28 FEP 668 (N.D. Ga. 1980) (plaintiff entitled to disclosure of names of other persons in employer's electrical division who have filed age discrimination complaints).

[14]EEOC v. Troy State Univ., 693 F.2d 1353, 30 FEP 929 (11th Cir. 1982), cert. denied, 463 U.S. 1207, 32 FEP 120 (1983) (although lower court's dismissal of EEOC suit for failure to comply with discovery order not warranted, case was remanded with EEOC agreement to produce all exhibits and data in Department of Labor file); EEOC v. Howard Univ., 31 FEP 1263 (D.D.C. 1983) (employer allowed to depose without restrictions witnesses upon whose testimony EEOC intended to rely in support of its motion for preliminary injunction, although protective order granted to prohibit questioning about whether deponents had given statement to EEOC or whether they had cooperated with EEOC's investigation of other charges); EEOC v. Colgate-Palmolive Co., 34 FEP 1551 (S.D.N.Y. 1983) (defendant not entitled to discovery as to whether EEOC's conciliation efforts made in good faith where EEOC agents made it clear that proposals were subject to approval of Commission).

[15]In re EEOC, 709 F.2d 392, 32 FEP 361 (5th Cir. 1983) (EEOC Commissioner required to submit to deposition with respect to reasons for issuance of charge only when charged party presents meaningful evidence that EEOC is attempting to abuse its investigative authority); EEOC v. St. Regis Paper Co.-Kraft Div., 717 F.2d 1302, 32 FEP 1849 (9th Cir. 1983) (discovery against EEOC should be allowed only where exceptional circumstances show abuse of process by EEOC). But see EEOC v. Neches Butane Prods. Co., 31 FEP 1097 (E.D. Tex. 1981), appeal dismissed, 704 F.2d 144, 31 FEP 1099 (5th Cir. 1983) (permitting deposition of EEOC official upon "substantial showing" of issue as to whether Commission abused process).

[16]EEOC v. K-Mart Corp., 694 F.2d 1055, 30 FEP 788 (6th Cir. 1982) (vacating order which required EEOC officials to submit to depositions on facts and circumstances surrounding decision to issue charge; court held that such discovery would divert EEOC from its primary purpose of determining whether Title VII was violated); Valley Indus. Servs. v. EEOC, 570 F. Supp. 902, 32 FEP 482 (N.D. Cal. 1983) (employer denied discovery as to validity of allegations of charge where he had not made requisite substantial showing of abuse of process and discovery would interfere with investigative process).

[17]Gray v. Frito-Lay, 35 FEP 598 (S.D. Miss. 1982) (plaintiff's failure to appear for deposition and to answer interrogatories is evidence of bad faith justifying award of attorneys' fees to employer).

[18]Tolliver v. Northrop Corp., 786 F.2d 316, 40 FEP 470 (7th Cir. 1986) (dismissal and refusal to reinstate suit not an abuse of discretion); Bluitt v. Atlantic Richfield Co., Arco Chem. Co. Div., 777 F.2d 188 (5th Cir. 1985) (plaintiff's willful disregard of discovery orders justified dismissal); Batson v. Neal Spelce Assocs., 765 F.2d 511, 516, 38 FEP 867, 870 (5th Cir. 1985), aff'd, 805 F.2d 546, 550–51, 42 FEP 817, 820–21 (5th Cir. 1986) (affirming dismissal with prejudice and $30,000 attorneys' fee award for plaintiff's failure to comply with discovery order); Cross v. General Motors Corp., 721 F.2d 1152, 40 FEP 418 (8th Cir. 1983), cert. denied, 466 U.S. 980 (1984) (district court properly dismissed race discrimination suit without prejudice where plaintiff refused to comply with discovery); Ford v. American Broadcasting Co., 101 F.R.D. 664 (S.D.N.Y. 1983), aff'd without opinion, 742 F.2d 1434 (2d Cir.), cert. denied, 469 U.S. 830 (1984) (dismissal ordered for plaintiffs' failure to comply with discovery requested and for concealment of evidence).

[19]Cox v. American Cast Iron Pipe Co., 784 F.2d 1546, 1555–57, 40 FEP 678, 685–86 (11th Cir.), cert. denied, 479 U.S. 883, 41 FEP 1712 (1986) (dismissal from suit of class members who failed to respond to interrogatories without finding of willfulness or bad faith was an abuse of discretion); Batson v. Neal Spelce Assocs., 765 F.2d 511, 38 FEP 867 (5th Cir. 1985), aff'd, 805 F.2d 546, 42 FEP 817 (5th Cir. 1986) (remanding to district court, which granted sanction of dismissal, to determine whether less drastic sanction would equally serve Rule 37's purposes); Jones v. Smith, 99 F.R.D. 4 (M.D. Pa. 1983), aff'd without opinion, 734 F.2d 6 (3d Cir. 1984) (plaintiff's failure to comply with discovery orders warrants imposition of sanctions, but plaintiff receives one last chance before imposition of dismissal sanction).

## 1. Privileged Materials

Defendants have typically been successful in obtaining information for which a privilege is asserted. Thus, where the plaintiff's emotional state is placed in issue, plaintiff may not assert a privilege to avoid discovery of medical records of the plaintiff's psychotherapist.[20] Documents sent to the EEOC with respect to a prior charge filed by the plaintiff may be discovered by a defendant.[21] Discovery of information contained in questionnaires sent by class members to the named plaintiffs' attorney is not precluded by the attorney-client privilege or work-product doctrine.[22] Conciliation materials may be discovered by the defendant.[23] Except in limited circumstances,[24] discovery of the identity of governmental informers is not permitted.[25]

## 2. Burdensome or Irrelevant Discovery

Discovery as to the basis for the named plaintiff's allegations regarding class claims has been utilized by courts in ruling on class certification motions.[26]

---

[20]Koster v. Chase Manhattan Bank, 35 EPD ¶ 34,770 (S.D.N.Y. 1984), *later proceedings on other issues,* 609 F. Supp. 1191, 41 FEP 1379 (S.D.N.Y. 1985) (state law physician-patient privilege unavailable under federal common law when plaintiff's physical well-being at issue); Zabkowicz v. Dart Indus., West Bend Co. Div., 585 F. Supp. 635, 35 FEP 209 (E.D. Wis. 1984) (where plaintiffs allegedly suffered emotional distress arising from defendant's sexual harassment, defendant entitled to have psychiatrist examine both husband and wife); *cf.* Sczesnik v. McDonald's Corp., 40 FEP 1794, 1795–96 (N.D. Ill. 1986) (not deciding whether patient-psychotherapist privilege existed, since waived at deposition after defense counsel pointed out allegations in complaint of "emotional difficulties"); Jennings v. D.H.L. Airlines, 101 F.R.D. 549, 34 FEP 1423 (N.D. Ill. 1984) (psychotherapist-patient privilege precludes discovery of plaintiff's psychotherapist for purpose of proving that plaintiff's complaints of sexual harassment were caused by emotional problems; court noted that plaintiff did not claim her psychological well-being was affected by harassment).

[21]Travers v. Travenol Laboratories, 94 F.R.D. 92, 33 FEP 1457 (N.D. Ill. 1982), *aff'd without opinion,* 723 F.2d 66 (7th Cir. 1983), *cert. denied,* 465 U.S. 1028 (1984) (defendant entitled to obtain from plaintiff's former counsel documents relating to discrimination charge which plaintiff had filed against her prior employer; privilege, if any, waived when documents sent to EEOC).

[22]Penk v. Oregon State Bd. of Higher Educ., 99 F.R.D. 511, 516–17 (D. Or. 1983) (work-product doctrine abrogated by showing that information on class members' claims necessary; information not protected by attorney-client privilege since class members are neither parties nor clients of plaintiffs' counsel).

[23]Greene v. Thalhimer's Dep't Store, 93 F.R.D. 657, 28 FEP 918 (E.D. Va. 1982) (employer entitled to access to conciliation materials which court had ordered EEOC to make available to plaintiff).

[24]EEOC v. Consolidated Edison Co. of N.Y., 37 FEP 1660 (S.D.N.Y. 1981) (allowing limited discovery of documents by or concerning 163 persons known to defendant, but declining as to other "informers" represented by EEOC).

[25]Donovan v. Forbes, 614 F. Supp. 124, 126, 27 WH 669, 670 (D. Vt. 1985) (employer not entitled to discover names of employee-informers or employee questionnaires, despite meritorious reasons for disclosure; other sources available); Donovan v. First Fed. Sav. & Loan Ass'n, 26 WH 108 (S.D. Iowa 1982) (employer's claim of need for information as to source for Labor Department investigation because it feared harassment from former employees held insufficient to overcome government's assertion of informer's privilege); Donovan v. Fasgo, Inc., 25 WH 332 (E.D. Pa. 1981) (institution of equal pay action did not waive government's privilege to withhold informer's identity).

[26]Quintanilla v. Scientific-Atlanta, 28 FEP 1178 (N.D. Tex. 1982), *appeal dismissed,* 33 EPD ¶ 34,050 (5th Cir. 1983), *cert. denied,* 464 U.S. 1069 (1984) (plaintiff's answers to interrogatories that he had "no knowledge" of other putative class members' claims held basis for denying certification); Dunn v. Midwest Buslines, 94 F.R.D. 170, 28 FEP 1653 (E.D. Ark. 1982) (plaintiff inadequate representative in part due to lack of knowledge as to forms of discrimination allegedly suffered by other class members); Sessum v. Houston Community College, 94 F.R.D. 316, 32 FEP 1172 (S.D. Tex. 1982) (deposition demonstrated "highly individualized" nature of plaintiff's claims and her failure to satisfy commonality and representation requirements of Rule 23).

Discovery of fee arrangements between the class representatives and their attorneys has also been permitted.[27]

Discovery into plaintiff's unrelated past sexual conduct is not permitted in a sexual harassment case.[28] However, a plaintiff's sexual fantasies and sexually provocative speech or dress are relevant in determining whether sexual advances were in fact unwelcome.[29]

---

[27]Trader v. Fiat Distribs., 30 FEP 1567 (D. Del. 1981) (discovery as to nature of fee arrangement between class plaintiffs and their attorneys permitted as relevant to issue of adequacy of representation; discovery of plaintiffs' financial resources not permitted without specific evidence to indicate "class action may founder for lack of funds," where plaintiffs' counsel have agreed to advance costs).

[28]Priest v. Rotary dba Fireside Motel & Coffee Shoppe, 98 F.R.D. 755, 32 FEP 1064 (N.D. Cal. 1983) (evidence of prior sexual activity not admissible to prove propensity to engage in such conduct and not discoverable because victims of sexual harassment would be discouraged from prosecuting Title VII lawsuits).

[29]Meritor Sav. Bank v. Vinson, 477 U.S. 57, 40 FEP 1822, 1827–28 (1986).

CHAPTER 36

# PROOF

## I. OVERVIEW

As described in the Second Edition, there are four theories of proving discrimination: disparate treatment, adverse impact, perpetuation in the present of the effects of past discrimination, and failure to make reasonable accommodation. Disparate treatment and adverse impact are the two principal theories of discrimination. Significant developments with respect to these two theories that have occurred during the period covered by this Supplement are addressed within this Chapter.

In disparate treatment cases, the courts continue generally to apply the analysis developed in *McDonnell Douglas Corp. v. Green*[1] and *Texas Department of Community Affairs v. Burdine*[2] to determine whether a plaintiff has sustained his burden of proof. However, in *United States Postal Service Board of Governors v. Aikens,*[3] the Supreme Court emphasized that consideration of this analytical framework should not cause district courts to lose sight of the ultimate issue: whether the plaintiff sustained his burden of proving that the defendant intentionally discriminated against him.

Courts do not rigidly apply the *McDonnell Douglas* test, but fashion its elements to the facts of a particular case. For example, prima facie case requirements have been adapted for religious discrimination cases,[4] discipline cases,[5] and cases involving an academic setting.[6] Of course, the *McDonnell Douglas* test is inapplicable when a plaintiff presents direct evidence of discrimination which is sufficient in itself to sustain the plaintiff's burden.[7] Also, plaintiffs will argue that the *McDonnell Douglas-Burdine* framework is inapplicable where a pattern and practice of disparate treatment is demonstrated.[8]

---

[1]411 U.S. 792, 5 FEP 965 (1973).

[2]450 U.S. 248, 25 FEP 113 (1981).

[3]460 U.S. 711, 31 FEP 609 (1983).

[4]*See* Turpen v. Missouri-Kansas-Texas R.R., 736 F.2d 1022, 1026, 35 FEP 492, 495 (5th Cir. 1984) (plaintiff must show (1) he has bona fide religious belief that conflicts with employment requirement, (2) he informed employer of belief, and (3) he was disciplined for failure to comply with requirement); *see also* Philbrook v. Ansonia Bd. of Educ., 757 F.2d 476, 481, 37 FEP 404, 409 (2d Cir. 1985), *aff'd and remanded,* 479 U.S. 60, 42 FEP 359 (1986) (adopting *Turpen* test).

[5]*See* Moore v. City of Charlotte, 754 F.2d 1100, 1105–6, 36 FEP 1582, 1585 (4th Cir.), *cert. denied,* 472 U.S. 1021, 37 FEP 1816 (1985) (plaintiff must show (1) that he engaged in prohibited conduct similar to that of person of another race, color, sex, religion, or national origin, and (2) plaintiff's discipline was more severe than that of others).

[6]*See* Carlile v. South Routt School Dist. Re-3J, 739 F.2d 1496, 1500, 35 FEP 689, 691 (10th Cir. 1984) (plaintiff required to show (1) membership in protected class, (2) qualified for rank sought, (3) denied tenure or reappointment, and (4) others with similar qualifications reappointed or granted tenure).

[7]Trans World Airlines v. Thurston, 469 U.S. 111, 121, 36 FEP 977, 982 (1985); Thompkins v. Morris Brown College, 752 F.2d 558, 563, 37 FEP 24, 28 (11th Cir. 1985). *See* Price Waterhouse v. Hopkins, _____ U.S. _____, 49 FEP 954 and *supra* Chapter 1 (Overview), notes 90–91 and text.

[8]Cox v. American Cast Iron Pipe Co., 784 F.2d 1546, 1559, 40 FEP 678 (11th Cir.), *cert. denied,* 479 U.S. 883, 41 FEP 1712 (1986) (holding that district court erred in allowing defendant to defend by

Statistics continue to play an important part in both class disparate treatment and adverse impact actions.[9] Statistics alone, if sufficiently persuasive, may create a prima facie case of classwide discrimination, but normally cannot alone make a case of individual disparate treatment.[10] Plaintiff's statistical evidence need not account for every factor in order to establish a prima facie case.[11] However, where the defendant rebuts with statistics which plaintiff claims are contaminated by a potentially biased factor, the burden is on the plaintiff to show that the factor is indeed biased.[12]

The single most significant development involves application of the adverse impact theory to employment decisions based upon subjective criteria. In *Watson v. Fort Worth Bank & Trust Co.,*[13] the Supreme Court ended a decade-old debate over whether the adverse impact as well as the disparate treatment theory may properly be applied to employment decisions based upon subjective criteria. The Court unanimously agreed that subjective decisions could be challenged by means of adverse impact analysis.[14] An obvious consequence of the *Watson* decision is that a plaintiff need not prove discriminatory intent in order to successfully challenge subjective criteria.[15] But what must a plaintiff prove? This question was not answered by *Watson.* Indeed, *Watson* raised, but left unresolved, a number of issues concerning evidentiary standards and allocation of the burden of proof.[16] As evidenced by *Watson,* the Court is sharply divided on these issues.

## II. PROOF IN THE DISPARATE TREATMENT CASE

### A. The Individual Disparate Treatment Case

The order and allocation of proof adopted by the Supreme Court in *McDonnell Douglas,* and restated by the Court in *Furnco,*[17] *Burdine,*[18] *Aik-*

---

"articulations," as per *Burdine;* once a pattern and practice is proven, burden shifts to defendant to show by "clear and convincing evidence" that job decisions were not in pursuit of policy); *see also* Riordan v. Kempiners, 831 F.2d 690, 44 FEP 1355, 1360 (7th Cir. 1987) (holding it error to exclude statistical proof in an individual case and stating that "as far as [they] know" no court had ever held that such evidence could be excluded). The relevance of evidence reflecting patterns of discrimination in an individual case also is noted in *McDonnell Douglas v. Green, supra* note 1, at 805.

[9]*See generally* Mozee v. Jeffboat, Inc., 746 F.2d 365, 35 FEP 1810 (7th Cir. 1984); Segar v. Smith, 738 F.2d 1249, 35 FEP 31 (D.C. Cir. 1984), *cert. denied,* 471 U.S. 1115, 37 FEP 1312 (1985).

[10]Carmichael v. Birmingham Saw Works, 738 F.2d 1126, 1131, 35 FEP 791, 795 (11th Cir. 1984).

[11]Bazemore v. Friday, 478 U.S. 385, 41 FEP 92 (1986).

[12]Coates v. Johnson & Johnson, 756 F.2d 524, 544, 37 FEP 467, 482 (7th Cir. 1985).

[13]487 U.S. _____, 47 FEP 102 (1988).

[14]*Id.,* 47 FEP at 107. The case was decided by eight members of the Court. Justice Kennedy did not participate.

[15]*See* Griggs v. Duke Power Co., 401 U.S. 424, 3 FEP 175 (1971).

[16]Justice O'Connor, joined by Justices Rehnquist, White, and Scalia, concluded that extension of the reach of the adverse impact theory "calls for a fresh and somewhat closer examination of the constraints that operate to keep that analysis within its proper bounds." Watson v. Fort Worth Bank & Trust Co., *supra* note 13, 47 FEP at 108. As stated by the plurality:

"[W]e do not believe that each verbal formulation used in prior opinions to describe the evidentiary standards in disparate impact cases is automatically applicable in light of today's decision * * *. Congress expressly provided that Title VII not be read to require preferential treatment or numerical quotas. 42 U.S.C. § 2000e-2(j). This congressional mandate requires in our view that a decision to extend the reach of disparate impact theory be accompanied by safeguards against the result that Congress clearly said it did not intend."

*Id.* at n.2. Justice Kennedy did not participate. *See supra* Chapter 1, note 21.

[17]Furnco Constr. Corp. v. Waters, 438 U.S. 567, 17 FEP 1062 (1978).

[18]Texas Dep't of Community Affairs v. Burdine, 450 U.S. 248, 25 FEP 113 (1981).

*ens,* [19] and *Cooper,* [20] has been continually applied to individual actions alleging disparate treatment in hiring,[21] discharge,[22] discipline,[23] promotion,[24] transfer,[25] retaliation,[26] demotion,[27] and other related matters.[28] However, the

---

[19]United States Postal Serv. Bd. of Governors v. Aikens, 460 U.S. 711, 31 FEP 609 (1983).

[20]Cooper v. Federal Reserve Bank of Richmond, 467 U.S. 867, 35 FEP 1 (1984).

[21]Lowe v. City of Monrovia, 775 F.2d 998, 39 FEP 350 (9th Cir. 1985), *modified,* 784 F.2d 1407, 41 FEP 931 (9th Cir. 1986) (plaintiff who was not hired established prima facie case of sex and race discrimination but failed to persuade court on motion for summary judgment that defendant's reasons for not hiring her were pretextual); Cunningham v. Housing Auth. of the City of Opelousas dba Opelousas Hous. Auth., 764 F.2d 1097, 38 FEP 417 (5th Cir.), *cert. denied,* 474 U.S. 1007, 39 FEP 720 (1985) (defendant rebutted plaintiff's prima facie case by establishing that hiring of successful applicant was politically motivated); Cuddy v. Carmen, 762 F.2d 119, 37 FEP 1335 (D.C. Cir.), *cert. denied,* 474 U.S. 1034, 39 FEP 944 (1985) (plaintiff who was not hired established prima facie case of age discrimination but failed to persuade court that defendant's reasons for rejecting him were discriminatory where successful applicant appeared to be better qualified); Easley v. Anheuser-Busch, 572 F. Supp. 402, 34 FEP 380 (E.D. Mo. 1983), *aff'd in relevant part and rev'd on other grounds,* 758 F.2d 251, 37 FEP 549 (8th Cir. 1985) (defendant's reason for not hiring applicant was not legitimate in light of evidence suggesting racially discriminatory decision).

[22]Bluebeard's Castle Hotel v. Virgin Islands Dep't of Labor, 786 F.2d 168, 40 FEP 603 (3d Cir. 1986) (evidence did not sustain allegations that white male was discriminated against on basis of race and national origin where he was discharged after argument with manager); Beaven v. Kentucky, 783 F.2d 672, 40 FEP 264 (6th Cir. 1986) (plaintiff who was discharged established prima facie case of race discrimination even though there was no evidence that employer attempted to replace him); Baz v. Walters, 782 F.2d 701, 40 FEP 173 (7th Cir. 1986) (discharged government hospital chaplain established prima facie case of religious discrimination but failed to carry his burden of persuasion where defendants presented evidence that chaplain had failed to conform to hospital's patient-care philosophy); Loeffler v. Carlin, 780 F.2d 1365, 39 FEP 1089 (8th Cir. 1985), *aff'd on reh'g en banc sub nom.* Loeffler v. Tisch, 806 F.2d 817, 42 FEP 792 (8th Cir. 1986), *rev'd and remanded on other grounds sub nom.* Loeffler v. Frank, 486 U.S. _____, 46 FEP 1659 (1988) (male Postal Service employee successfully established that employer's reasons for discharging him were pretextual and his discharge constituted sex discrimination).

[23]Duchon v. Cajon Co., 791 F.2d 43, 40 FEP 1432 (6th Cir. 1986) (discharged employee established prima facie case of sex discrimination, even though she was replaced by another female, where employee alleged that her discharge was disparate discipline for her involvement in personal affair with another employee); Alires v. Amoco Prod. Co., 774 F.2d 409, 38 FEP 1731 (10th Cir. 1985) (plaintiff's discharge due to his refusal to follow order and not due to discrimination); Martin v. Citibank, N.A., 762 F.2d 212, 37 FEP 1580, 1 IER 929 (2d Cir. 1985) (plaintiff did not persuade court that defendant's action was discriminatory where defendant had good cause to require polygraph exam as part of an investigation of missing funds).

[24]Holmes v. Bevilacqua, 794 F.2d 142, 41 FEP 43 (4th Cir. 1986) (unsuccessful black applicant failed to establish prima facie case of discrimination where he did not present any evidence regarding employer's decision to promote qualified white applicant and not to promote plaintiff); Stallworth v. Shuler, 777 F.2d 1431, 39 FEP 983 (11th Cir. 1985) (black school employee established prima facie case of racial discrimination where she was consistently overlooked for promotion to administrative positions in favor of less qualified white employees); Dance v. Ripley, 776 F.2d 370, 39 FEP 466 (1st Cir. 1985) (plaintiff did not carry her burden of persuasion in case alleging that she had been rejected for promotion because of race discrimination).

[25]Goodwin v. St. Louis County Circuit Court, 729 F.2d 541, 34 FEP 347 (8th Cir. 1984), *cert. denied,* 469 U.S. 1216, 37 FEP 64 (1985) (defendant's explanation for transferring female hearing officer while retaining male hearing officer was pretextual).

[26]Davis v. Lambert of Ark., 781 F.2d 658, 39 FEP 1410 (8th Cir. 1986) (employer did not retaliate against black employee by refusing to recall her from layoff until her discrimination suit was over where employer in good faith believed it would be improper to discuss reemployment in view of imminent trial date); Mitchell v. Baldridge, 759 F.2d 80, 37 FEP 689 (D.C. Cir. 1985) (plaintiff must have opportunity to rebut defendant's purported nondiscriminatory reasons after establishing prima facie case of reprisal and discrimination).

[27]Allen v. Montgomery County, Ala., 788 F.2d 1485, 40 FEP 1278 (11th Cir. 1986) (trial court improperly excluded black female employee's proffered evidence of racial discrimination prior to her demotion in determining whether plaintiff had met burden of persuasion); Williams v. Caterpillar Tractor Co., 770 F.2d 47, 38 FEP 985 (6th Cir. 1985) (employee was constructively discharged by being demoted, because of her age, from job with rating of class 10 to job with rating of class 2); Moore v. City of Charlotte, 754 F.2d 1100, 36 FEP 1582 (4th Cir.), *cert. denied,* 472 U.S. 1021, 37 FEP 1816 (1985) (police officer did not establish prima facie case of discrimination where no evidence existed showing similarly situated white officers had not been demoted).

[28]Griffin v. City of Omaha, 785 F.2d 620, 40 FEP 385, *reh'g denied en banc,* 40 EPD ¶36,151 (8th Cir. 1986) (training); Maddox v. Grandview Care Center, 780 F.2d 987, 39 FEP 1456 (11th Cir. 1986) (maternity leave); Barber v. Boilermakers Dist. Lodge 57, 778 F.2d 750, 39 FEP 1092 (11th Cir. 1985), *on remand,* 651 F. Supp. 265, 42 FEP 1521 (N.D. Ala. 1986) (union referrals); Murray v. Thistledown Racing Club, 770 F.2d 63, 38 FEP 1065 (6th Cir. 1985) (reverse discrimination in constructive discharge case); McDaniel v. Temple Indep. School Dist., 770 F.2d 1340, 38 FEP 1567 (5th Cir. 1985) (evaluation,

order and allocation of proof specified in *McDonnell Douglas* does not apply if the plaintiff proves by direct evidence that the defendant acted with a discriminatory motive.[29] Plaintiffs will challenge the applicability of the *McDonnell Douglas-Burdine* framework where the plaintiff proves a pattern or practice of discrimination.[30]

## 1. The Prima Facie Case

Recent decisions continue to hold that the elements of a prima facie case are flexible and should be tailored, on a case-by-case basis, to differing factual circumstances.[31] The central inquiry in evaluating whether the plaintiff has met his initial burden is whether the circumstantial evidence presented is sufficient to create an inference (*i.e.,* a rebuttable presumption) that the basis for an employment-related decision was an illegal criterion.[32] Some courts further recognize that in some factual situations the plaintiff may create a rebuttable presumption without literally meeting all four elements of a prima facie case announced in *McDonnell Douglas.*[33]

---

promotion, retaliation, and discharge); Namenwirth v. University of Wis. Sys. Bd. of Regents, 769 F.2d 1235, 38 FEP 1155 (7th Cir. 1985), *cert. denied,* 474 U.S. 1061, 39 FEP 1200 (1986) (tenure).

[29]Trans World Airlines v. Thurston, 469 U.S. 111, 36 FEP 977 (1985) (shifting burdens of proof set out in *McDonnell Douglas* are designed for use when direct evidence of discrimination is unavailable; when direct evidence is presented, *McDonnell Douglas* test is inapplicable); McCarthney v. Griffin-Spalding County Bd. of Educ., 791 F.2d 1549, 41 FEP 245, 248 (11th Cir. 1986) (where "defendants establish an absolute defense to a direct showing of discriminatory motive, they cannot be held liable under *McDonnell Douglas,* which relies on the use of circumstantial evidence to prove discriminatory intent"); Buckley v. Hospital Corp. of Am., 758 F.2d 1525, 37 FEP 1082 (11th Cir. 1985) (where plaintiff presents direct evidence of age discrimination, burden on defendant is higher than under *McDonnell Douglas*). *See also supra* note 7.

[30]*Supra* note 8.

[31]Legrand v. University of Ark. at Pine Bluff Trustees, 821 F.2d 478, 44 FEP 60 (8th Cir. 1987) (qualifications for purposes of prima facie case relate only to objective qualifications; plaintiffs discharged because of employer's subjective belief that they were "unreliable" have established prima facie case by showing objective qualifications as electricians); Jasany v. United States Postal Serv., 755 F.2d 1244, 37 FEP 210 (6th Cir. 1985) (reverse discrimination plaintiff must show background facts supporting claim that defendant is unusual employer discriminating against majority); La Montagne v. American Convenience Prods., 750 F.2d 1405, 36 FEP 913 (7th Cir. 1984) (ADEA discharge case; plaintiff must show satisfaction of legitimate employer expectations rather than mere qualifications); Agarwal v. University of Minn. Regents, 788 F.2d 504, 40 FEP 937 (8th Cir. 1986) (same); Blackwell v. Sun Elec. Corp., 696 F.2d 1176, 30 FEP 1177 (6th Cir. 1983) (modifying four-part *McDonnell Douglas* test for prima facie case to fit discharge allegation); Cockrham v. South Cent. Bell Tel. Co., 695 F.2d 143, 30 FEP 1788 (5th Cir. 1983) (black employee's evidence that he was discharged for reasons for which white employees were not establishes prima facie case); Walker v. Ford Motor Co., 684 F.2d 1355, 29 FEP 1259 (11th Cir. 1982) (listing elements to establish prima facie case of retaliatory discharge); Ostroff v. Employment Exch., 683 F.2d 302, 29 FEP 683 (9th Cir. 1982) (plaintiff's qualifications irrelevant where employer falsely informed her that position had been filled before any inquiry was made concerning her qualifications); Henson v. City of Dundee, 682 F.2d 897, 29 FEP 787 (11th Cir. 1982) (outlining elements of prima facie case of sexual harassment).

[32]Byrd v. Roadway Express, 687 F.2d 85, 29 FEP 1588 (5th Cir. 1982) (purpose of prima facie test is to identify actions taken by employer from which discrimination can be inferred); Halsell v. Kimberly-Clark Corp., 683 F.2d 285, 29 FEP 1185 (8th Cir. 1982), *cert. denied,* 459 U.S. 1205, 30 FEP 1856 (1983) (to establish prima facie case plaintiff must produce evidence supporting inference of discrimination).

[33]Meiri v. Dacon, 759 F.2d 989, 37 FEP 756 (2d Cir.), *cert. denied,* 474 U.S. 829, 38 FEP 1728 (1985) (plaintiff as part of prima facie case need not show she was replaced; the fact that position was not filled is irrelevant since employer sought to fill it; the fact that she was not replaced weakens but does not eliminate inference of discrimination); Geisler v. Folsom, 735 F.2d 991, 34 FEP 1581 (6th Cir. 1984) (employee did not need to prove she possessed requisite qualifications for vacant position where qualifications changed abruptly after she applied and employer never contacted her); Robinson v. Arkansas State Highway & Transp. Comm'n, 698 F.2d 957, 30 FEP 1711 (8th Cir. 1983) (plaintiff held qualified for position for purposes of prima facie case since position as advertised did not include shorthand requirement); Lerma v. Bolger, 689 F.2d 589, 29 FEP 1828 (5th Cir. 1982) (prima facie case established although plaintiff did not literally meet fourth requirement of *McDonnell Douglas* test); Byrd v. Roadway Express, *supra* note 32 (plaintiff can establish prima facie case of racially motivated discharge even if plaintiff

Most recent decisions concerning the sufficiency of evidence presented for establishing a rebuttable presumption turn on whether one or more of these elements has been proven.[34] Plaintiffs contend there is no reason for the plaintiff to present evidence creating an inference of discrimination when the plaintiff presents sufficient direct evidence of discriminatory motive.[35] Statistics[36] and the opinions of others in the plaintiff's field have also been successfully employed by plaintiffs to establish a rebuttable presumption. On the other hand, a plaintiff will fail to establish a prima facie case when the evidence consists of nothing more than a claim of being in a protected group,[37] of simply feeling discriminated against,[38] or of having been discouraged from applying by an employee of the defendant.[39]

Direct evidence of discrimination may take such forms as an employer's policy which on its face calls for consideration of a prohibited factor,[40] or

replaced by individual of his own race); Gifford v. Atchison, Topeka & Santa Fe Ry., 685 F.2d 1149, 34 FEP 240 (9th Cir. 1982) (prima facie case established even though plaintiff did not apply for position where application would have been futile); Fugate v. Allied Corp., 582 F. Supp. 780, 34 FEP 1745 (N.D. Ill. 1984) (employee who lost job during reorganization not required to prove application for position he was qualified to assume); Abrams v. Baylor College of Medicine, 581 F. Supp. 1570, 34 FEP 229 (S.D. Tex. 1984), *aff'd in part and rev'd in part,* 805 F.2d 528, 42 FEP 806 (5th Cir. 1986) (failure to make application for position not fatal where effort would be futile in face of overt discrimination and fact that no formal application procedure existed); Donovan v. Georgia Sw. College, 580 F. Supp. 859, 39 FEP 1637 (M.D. Ga. 1984), *aff'd in part and remanded in part sub nom.* Brock v. Georgia Sw. College, 765 F.2d 1026, 43 FEP 1525 (11th Cir. 1985) (where plaintiff was demoted as result of his wife's complaints about employer's discriminatory practices, plaintiff established prima facie case without being member of protected class).

[34]Ferguson v. Veterans Admin., 723 F.2d 871, 33 FEP 1525 (11th Cir.), *cert. denied,* 469 U.S. 1072, 36 FEP 568 (1984) (plaintiff failed to establish prima facie case of hiring discrimination when she did not meet educational qualifications for librarian position); Felton v. California State Univs. & Colleges Trustees, 708 F.2d 1507, 32 FEP 135 (9th Cir. 1983) (defendant's burden to rebut prima facie case is one of production, not persuasion); Marafino v. St. Louis County Circuit Court, 707 F.2d 1005, 31 FEP 1536 (8th Cir. 1983) (plaintiff failed to prove that defendant's reason for not hiring her was pretextual); Lee v. National Can Corp., 699 F.2d 932, 31 FEP 13 (7th Cir.), *cert. denied,* 464 U.S. 845, 32 FEP 1672 (1983) (black applicant failed to establish he was qualified for job); Cuddy v. Carmen, 694 F.2d 853, 30 FEP 600 (D.C. Cir. 1982), *cert. denied,* 474 U.S. 1034, 39 FEP 944 (1985) (plaintiff not as familiar with employer's operations as persons selected); Lerma v. Bolger, *supra* note 33 (person selected over Mexican-American applicant was "known factor," having previously worked for employer).

[35]Trans World Airlines v. Thurston, *supra* note 29, 36 FEP at 982; Thompkins v. Morris Brown College, 752 F.2d 558, 563, 37 FEP 24, 28 (11th Cir. 1985); Perryman v. Johnson Prods. Co., 698 F.2d 1138, 31 FEP 93 (11th Cir. 1983); Hardin v. Stynchcomb, 691 F.2d 1364, 30 FEP 624 (11th Cir. 1982).

[36]Carmichael v. Birmingham Saw Works, 738 F.2d 1126, 35 FEP 791 (11th Cir. 1984) (statistics may be used to support prima facie case, but cannot suffice alone; some direct injury to plaintiff required); Minority Employees at NASA v. Beggs, 723 F.2d 958, 34 FEP 63 (D.C. Cir. 1983) (plaintiff may use statistical evidence to establish prima facie case of race discrimination in individual case); Gilbert v. City of Little Rock, 722 F.2d 1390, 33 FEP 557 (8th Cir. 1983), *cert. denied,* 466 U.S. 972, 34 FEP 1312 (1984), *rev'd,* 799 F.2d 1210, 44 FEP 509 (8th Cir. 1986) (internal statistics, but not general labor force statistics, were probative of promotion discrimination claim).

[37]Zahorik v. Cornell Univ., 729 F.2d 85, 34 FEP 165 (2d Cir. 1984) (prima facie case established by showing that significant portion of departmental faculty, referrants, or other scholars in field hold favorable view on plaintiff's tenure qualifications).

[38]*See, e.g.,* Holley v. Sanyo Mfg., 771 F.2d 1161, 1168, 38 FEP 1317 (8th Cir. 1985) (in ADEA force reduction, plaintiff's subjective determination he was better qualified not sufficient to establish prima facie case).

[39]Clark v. Atchison, Topeka & Santa Fe Ry., 731 F.2d 698, 34 FEP 1148 (10th Cir. 1984) (plaintiff's race is not itself qualification or reason for promotion); EEOC v. F&D Distrib., 728 F.2d 1281, 34 FEP 253 (10th Cir. 1984) (company not liable for employee's comments discouraging plaintiff from applying, where employee had no authority to refuse, and did not refuse, to give plaintiff an application).

[40]Trans World Airlines v. Thurston, 469 U.S. 111, 36 FEP 977 (1985) (only pilots disqualified due to age not allowed to bump flight engineers); Smallwood v. United Airlines, 728 F.2d 614, 34 FEP 217 (4th Cir.), *cert. denied,* 469 U.S. 832, 35 FEP 1608 (1984) (applications for flight officer positions not processed if applicant over 35); Maddox v. Grandview Care Center, 607 F. Supp. 1404, 37 FEP 1263 (M.D. Ga. 1985), *aff'd,* 780 F.2d 987, 39 FEP 1456 (11th Cir. 1986) (maternity leave limited to three months; leave for other disabilities indefinite).

statements by relevant managers demonstrating bias.[41] A panel of the Eleventh Circuit has held that when the plaintiff introduces statements showing a selecting manager's bias, the statements establish that a prohibited factor was a substantial motivating factor in the challenged decision.[42] This holding has been the subject of criticism within the Eleventh Circuit.[43]

The Supreme Court emphasized in *United States Postal Service Board of Governors v. Aikens,*[44] involving the analytical framework of proof announced in *McDonnell Douglas,* that district courts should not lose sight of the ultimate issue in a discrimination case.[45] Where the defendant has responded to plaintiff's evidence of discrimination, the Court stated that instead of focusing on whether the plaintiff established a prima facie case, the district court should consider the ultimate issue and determine whether the plaintiff sustained his burden of proving that the defendant intentionally discriminated against him.[46]

The Fourth Circuit in *Holmes v. Bevilacqua*[47] relied upon *Aikens* to conclude that an applicant must demonstrate that the position sought remained open after his rejection in order to establish a prima facie case, absent "other evidence" of discriminatory intent.[48] In contrast, the Ninth Circuit has concluded that a claimant need not demonstrate that any discrete period of time elapsed between his rejection for a position and the hiring of an equally or less qualified individual.[49]

The Eleventh Circuit in *Carmichael v. Birmingham Saw Works*[50] extended the oft-cited principle of *Rowe v. General Motors Corp.*[51] by holding

---

[41]Miles v. M.N.C. Corp. 750 F.2d 867, 36 FEP 1289 (11th Cir. 1985) (racial slur about work abilities of blacks); Buckley v. Hospital Corp. of Am., 758 F.2d 1525, 1527–28, 37 FEP 1082 (11th Cir. 1985) (statements by hospital administrator to plaintiff that she had lost her temper "due to her advanced age," that hospital needed new blood, and that he wanted to attract younger doctors and nurses); Thompkins v. Morris Brown College, 752 F.2d 558, 561, 37 FEP 24 (11th Cir. 1985) (college president told plaintiff that there was no reason for a woman to have second job and that her class schedule was different from those of male faculty members because the men had families and needs she did not have); Bell v. Birmingham Linen Serv., 715 F.2d 1552, 1557, 32 FEP 1673 (11th Cir. 1983), *cert. denied,* 467 U.S. 1204, 34 FEP 1400 (1984) (production manager told female applicant that he would not give her a job in washroom because if she got it, every woman in the plant would want to work in washroom); Bailey v. Binyon, 583 F. Supp. 923, 36 FEP 1236 (N.D. Ill. 1984) (use of racial epithets coupled with harassment constitutes unlawful, unequal treatment); Jackson v. Wakulla Springs & Lodge, 33 FEP 1301 (N.D. Fla. 1983) (use of racial slurs by person responsible for termination of plaintiffs).

[42]Miles v. M.N.C. Corp., *supra* note 41; Perryman v. Johnson Prods. Co., *supra* note 35; Lee v. Russell County Bd. of Educ., 684 F.2d 769, 29 FEP 1508 (11th Cir. 1982).

[43]Spanier v. Morrison's Mgmt. Servs., 611 F. Supp. 642, 38 FEP 177 (N.D. Ala. 1985), *aff'd in part and rev'd in part,* 822 F.2d 975, 44 FEP 628 (11th Cir. 1987) (mode of analysis enables plaintiff completely to avoid causation issue, shifting risk of nonpersuasion to defendant).

[44]460 U.S. 711, 31 FEP 609 (1983).

[45]*Id.* at 715, 31 FEP at 611.

[46]*Id.* Whether the district court bases its ruling on the absence of a prima facie case or the ultimate issue of discriminatory motivation is significant with respect to the standard of review. The issue of motivation is a question of fact subject to the clearly erroneous standard, *Pullman-Standard v. Swint,* 456 U.S. 273, 28 FEP 1073 (1982), while the issue whether a prima facie case has been established is a question of law, subject to *de novo* review. Carmichael v. Birmingham Saw Works, *supra* note 36, at 1130, 35 FEP at 794; Gay v. Waiters' & Dairy Lunchmen's Local 30, 694 F.2d 531, 540, 30 FEP 605, 612 (9th Cir. 1982).

[47]794 F.2d 142, 146, 41 FEP 43, 47 (4th Cir. 1986).

[48]*Id.*

[49]Williams v. Edward Apffels Coffee Co., 792 F.2d 1482, 41 FEP 396 (9th Cir. 1986).

[50]738 F.2d 1126, 35 FEP 791 (11th Cir. 1984).

[51]457 F.2d 348, 4 FEP 445 (5th Cir. 1972) (subjective evaluation procedures "are a ready mechanism for discrimination"); *see also* Watson v. National Linen Serv., 686 F.2d 877, 881, 30 FEP 107, 110 (11th

that a plaintiff establishes a prima facie case of discriminatory refusal to promote if the evidence shows adverse impact upon the plaintiff's protected group and that the employer failed to establish a formal system for announcing job openings and conducted "informal review procedures."[52] The Eleventh Circuit further held that, in the absence of a formal system announcing job openings, the employer has a legal "duty to consider all those who might reasonably be interested, as well as those who have learned of the job opening and expressed an interest."[53] Similarly, the Seventh Circuit, in *Box v. A&P Tea Co.,*[54] held that when employees do not apply to be promoted, but are sought out by management, the plaintiff need not actually apply but may establish a prima facie case by showing application would have been made if plaintiff had known of the opening. These decisions go beyond the well-established rules that no application need be made where it would be futile or where the employer has discouraged application by protected group members.[55]

## 2. Defendant's Burden of Going Forward

In *Aikens,*[56] the Supreme Court emphasized that the *McDonnell Douglas-Burdine* order of proof was established only as a sensible way to aid in the litigation of disparate treatment cases, because Title VII makes an employer's state of mind an issue of fact.[57] The *Aikens* Court held that once a defendant produces evidence of a nondiscriminatory reason for less favorable treatment of a plaintiff, whether or not the plaintiff has properly satisfied his preliminary burden of proof, the establishment of a prima facie case "is no longer relevant."[58] The trial court's analysis at that point proceeds to a determination of the ultimate factual issue in the case: Did the employer intentionally discriminate against the plaintiff?[59]

To rebut a plaintiff's prima facie case based upon circumstantial evidence inferring intent, the employer need only articulate a legitimate, nondiscriminatory reason for its actions.[60] Reasons which employers have articulated to rebut a plaintiff's prima facie case successfully include

---

Cir. 1982) (per curiam) (failure to establish reasonably objective standards for hiring was discriminatory practice).

[52]Carmichael v. Birmingham Saw Works, *supra* note 50, at 1133, 35 FEP at 796.

[53]*Id.*

[54]772 F.2d 1372, 38 FEP 1509 (7th Cir. 1985), *cert. denied,* 478 U.S. 1010, 41 FEP 271 (1986) (plaintiff failed to show she would have applied had she known of opening). Interestingly, the court in *Box* did not cite *Rowe v. General Motors Corp., supra* note 51.

[55]*E.g.,* Easley v. Empire, Inc., 757 F.2d 923, 37 FEP 542 (8th Cir. 1985) (plaintiff was told men do not like to answer to women, therefore her failure to apply in writing per company policy excused); Holsey v. Armour & Co., 743 F.2d 199, 35 FEP 1064 (4th Cir. 1984), *cert. denied,* 470 U.S. 1028, 37 FEP 192 (1985) (employer had no black employees in sales and told black employee that customers would not buy from them, therefore, application unnecessary).

[56]United States Postal Serv. Bd. of Governors v. Aikens, 460 U.S. 711, 31 FEP 609 (1983).

[57]*Id.* at 715, 31 FEP at 611.

[58]*Id.*

[59]*Id; see also* Benzies v. Illinois Dep't of Mental Health & Developmental Disabilities, 810 F.2d 146, 42 FEP 1537 (7th Cir.), *cert. denied,* 483 U.S. 1006, 43 FEP 1896 (1987) (once a disparate treatment case has been tried, the issue is whether plaintiff established that employer's use of criterion forbidden by statute caused discrimination).

[60]The employer's burden will be greater if the plaintiff adduces direct evidence of discrimination, *supra* notes 7 and 26, or evidence of a pattern and practice of discrimination, *supra* note 8.

lesser comparative qualifications,[61] inability to get along with fellow employees,[62] lack of reliability,[63] misconduct,[64] failure to take a polygraph examination,[65] lack of friendship with the employer,[66] poor responses in oral interviews,[67] unsatisfactory performance on psychological tests,[68] and age.[69] An employer can also rebut by showing that its less favorable treatment accords with the dictates of union contracts[70] or the employer's knowledge of the favored employees' work.[71] Still, such a reason will succeed in rebutting the prima facie case only if it creates an issue of fact as to the charges against

---

[61]Cuthbertson v. Biggers Bros., 702 F.2d 454, 461, 32 FEP 1592, 1596 (4th Cir. 1983) (failure to promote based on lack of either two years of college or two years of sales/management experience); Grano v. City of Columbus, Dep't of Dev., 699 F.2d 836, 838, 31 FEP 1, 2 (6th Cir. 1983) (per curiam) (employer's subjective employment evaluations sufficient to rebut); Perryman v. Johnson Prods. Co., 698 F.2d 1138, 1144, 31 FEP 93, 98 (11th Cir. 1983) (lack of experience among other factors); Robinson v. Arkansas State Highway & Transp. Comm'n, 698 F.2d 957, 958, 30 FEP 1711, 1712 (8th Cir. 1983) (lack of shorthand skills); Jefferies v. Harris County Community Action Ass'n, 693 F.2d 589, 590, 31 FEP 992, 993 (5th Cir. 1982) (per curiam) (promotion of better qualified candidate); Laborde v. University of Cal. Regents, 686 F.2d 715, 718, 28 FEP 1183, 1185 (9th Cir.), cert. denied, 459 U.S. 1173, 36 FEP 1776 (1982) (failure to meet university's scholarship and research standards); Valentino v. United States Postal Serv., 674 F.2d 56, 64, 28 FEP 593, 598 (D.C. Cir. 1982) (lack of experience); Hervey v. City of Little Rock, 599 F. Supp. 1524, 40 FEP 912 (E.D. Ark. 1984), aff'd, 787 F.2d 1223, 40 FEP 928 (8th Cir. 1986) (same); Williams v. New Orleans S.S. Ass'n, 673 F.2d 742, 754, 28 FEP 1092, 1103 (5th Cir. 1982), cert. denied, 460 U.S. 1038, 31 FEP 368 (1983) (less seniority and skills); Mortensen v. Callaway, 672 F.2d 822, 824, 29 FEP 111, 112 (10th Cir. 1982) (less qualified and less probability of success).

[62]Burrus v. United Tel. Co. of Kan., 683 F.2d 339, 343, 29 FEP 663, 666 (10th Cir.), cert. denied, 459 U.S. 1071, 30 FEP 592 (1982) (inability to get along with others); Jones v. Lumberjack Meats, 680 F.2d 98, 101, 29 FEP 396, 398 (11th Cir. 1982) (poor relations with fellow employees).

[63]Coble v. Hot Springs School Dist. No. 6, 682 F.2d 721, 726, 29 FEP 201, 205 (8th Cir. 1982) (concern about employee's availability).

[64]Meiri v. Dacon, 759 F.2d 989, 37 FEP 756 (2d Cir.), cert. denied, 474 U.S. 829, 38 FEP 1728 (1985) (prima facie case rebutted based on plaintiff's admitted significant job deficiencies); Jones v. Los Angeles Community College Dist., 702 F.2d 203, 205, 31 FEP 717, 718 (9th Cir. 1983) (misuse of sick leave and other unfavorable charges in plaintiff's record); Yarbrough v. Tower Oldsmobile, 789 F.2d 508, 40 FEP 1035 (7th Cir. 1986) (refusal to complete work assignment); Wells v. Gotfredson Motor Co., 709 F.2d 493, 31 FEP 496, 498 (8th Cir. 1983) (employee visited front office too often); Lee v. National Can Corp., 699 F.2d 932, 937, 31 FEP 13, 16 (7th Cir.), cert. denied, 464 U.S. 845, 32 FEP 1672 (1983) (dicta: falsified job application); Jefferies v. Harris County Community Action Ass'n, 693 F.2d 589, 591, 31 FEP 992, 993 (5th Cir. 1982) (per curiam) (discharge for distributing confidential personnel records); Jones v. Lumberjack Meats, supra note 62 (carrying tear gas pistol); Montgomery v. Yellow Freight Sys., 671 F.2d 412, 413, 28 FEP 831, 832 (10th Cir. 1982) (sleeping on job); Holloway v. Bolger, 41 FEP 353 (D.N.J. 1986) (excessive absenteeism and refusal to cooperate); Garner v. St. Louis Sw. Ry., 676 F.2d 1223, 28 FEP 1469 (8th Cir. 1982) (employee arrested for rape on company property even though criminal charges later dropped).

[65]Brown v. Tennessee, 693 F.2d 600, 605, 30 FEP 459, 463 (6th Cir. 1982) (employee refused to take polygraph test administered in response to theft).

[66]Lamphere v. Brown Univ., 685 F.2d 743, 750 n.2, 29 FEP 701, 706 (1st Cir. 1982), later proceeding, 613 F. Supp. 971, 38 FEP 871 (D.R.I. 1985), vacated, 798 F.2d 532, 41 FEP 828 (1st Cir. 1986) (per curiam) (granting less-qualified male higher salary than female employee-plaintiff as a result of friendship meets defendant-employer's Burdine burden).

[67]Milton v. Weinberger, 696 F.2d 94, 100, 30 FEP 1, 5 (D.C. Cir. 1982) (failure to answer questions concerning candidate's "management concept" allowed as a defense but court stated the defense was "troubling" and that "the record suggests that Milton's interview performance may have been cited for the first time at trial as a post hoc rationalization of her promotion denial").

[68]Perryman v. Johnson Prods. Co., 698 F.2d 1138, 1144–45, 31 FEP 93, 98 (11th Cir. 1983) (employee's psychological reports were unfavorable).

[69]Stewart v. CPC Int'l, 679 F.2d 117, 122, 33 FEP 1680 (7th Cir. 1982) (plaintiff's age exceeded maximum for acceptance into apprenticeship program and thus constituted legitimate nondiscriminatory reason in defense of Title VII race discrimination claim).

[70]Jackson v. Seaboard Coast Line R.R., 678 F.2d 992, 1018, 29 FEP 442, 465 (11th Cir. 1982) (promotion requirements contained in contract negotiated with union).

[71]Sims v. Cleland, 813 F.2d 790, 43 FEP 362 (6th Cir. 1987) (finding that one of employer's two reasons is false does not necessarily require rejection of remaining reason; employer indicated preference for younger male attorney since female allegedly unqualified to handle medical malpractice cases and younger attorney better on hard work and dedication; rejection of medical malpractice reason did not impugn the alternative nondiscriminatory reason); Waters v. Furnco Constr. Corp., 688 F.2d 39, 40, 29 FEP 1256, 1257 (7th Cir. 1982) (employer used list of employees with whom he had worked in past).

the employer.[72] Courts have continued to require that, under *Burdine,* the defendant articulate its nondiscriminatory reason for the challenged action with some specificity in order to afford the plaintiff a full and fair opportunity to demonstrate pretext.[73]

Some courts have held that the employer does not meet its burden of articulating a legitimate, nondiscriminatory reason when the articulated reason does not contradict the prima facie case,[74] is too vague,[75] or simply is not legitimate or job-related.[76] Evidence concerning the plaintiff's performance in a time frame other than that at issue has been held insufficient,[77] as have been internally inconsistent reasons articulated in multiple denials.[78]

---

[72]Curry v. Oklahoma Gas & Elec. Co., 730 F.2d 598, 34 FEP 559 (10th Cir. 1984) (creating an issue of fact as to reason for discharge is sufficient to rebut prima facie case, even where basis of prima facie case is evidence contrary to articulated reason); George v. Farmers Elec. Coop., 715 F.2d 175, 32 FEP 1801 (5th Cir. 1983) (issue of fact not created where employer's reason for firing wife, rather than husband, under anti-nepotism policy was that husband, being a man, was "head of the household"); Williams v. Edward Apffels Coffee Co., 792 F.2d 1482, 41 FEP 396 (9th Cir. 1986) (employer's evidence must raise genuine issue of fact as to whether it discriminated against plaintiff); *see also* Mantolete v. Bolger, 767 F.2d 1416, 38 FEP 1081 (9th Cir. 1985) (issue was whether postal service could introduce evidence of physical condition of which it was not aware at time of rejection; evidence admitted on basis of a flexible test, holding that evidence was relevant to rebut applicant's claim that she was qualified for the position, but was not admissible to enlarge basis upon which employer made the decision; if trier of fact finds evidence insufficient to rule that applicant was not qualified for the position, the evidence has no further relevance and cannot be used to justify applicant's rejection).

[73]*E.g.,* Miles v. M.N.C. Corp., 750 F.2d 867, 36 FEP 1289 (11th Cir. 1985) (vague, subjective reasons "do not allow a reasonable opportunity for rebuttal"); Crawford v. Western Elec. Co., 745 F.2d 1373, 36 FEP 1753 (11th Cir. 1984) (defendant must produce credible testimony of person supervising or evaluating plaintiff during relevant time period); White v. Vathally, 732 F.2d 1037, 1040, 34 FEP 1130, 1132 (1st Cir.), *cert. denied,* 469 U.S. 933, 36 FEP 112 (1984) (employer's explanation must be clear and specific rather than passing reference to some deficiency in plaintiff's qualifications); Sweeney v. State Univ. of N.Y. Research Found., 711 F.2d 1179, 1185, 32 FEP 378, 382 (2d Cir. 1983) (employer's need to utilize plaintiff in her current position, rather than transferring her, constitutes legitimate, nondiscriminatory reason for employment decision); Grano v. City of Columbus, Dep't of Dev., 699 F.2d 836, 837, 31 FEP 1, 2 (6th Cir. 1983) (subjective employment qualifications not illegal *per se* and can constitute valid, nondiscriminatory reason for employment decision).

[74]Williams v. City of Montgomery, 742 F.2d 586, 37 FEP 52 (11th Cir. 1984), *cert. denied,* 471 U.S. 1005, 37 FEP 592 (1985) (employer's statement it fired black firefighter due to his felony conviction was insufficient to establish legitimate, nondiscriminatory justification where basis of prima facie case was white firefighter's reinstatement after felony convictions); George v. Farmers Elec. Coop., *supra* note 72.

[75]Cox v. American Cast Iron Pipe Co., 784 F.2d 1546, 40 FEP 678 (11th Cir.), *cert. denied,* 479 U.S. 883, 41 FEP 1712 (1986); Nation v. Winn-Dixie Stores, 567 F. Supp. 997, 32 FEP 493, *modified,* 570 F. Supp. 1473, 32 FEP 1602 (N.D. Ga. 1983) (statement that white person possessed qualifications of good attitude and taking pride in his work was not comparative statement; meaning of terms too vague to articulate clear reason for denying black employee equal training opportunities); *cf.* McKenna v. Weinberger, 729 F.2d 783, 34 FEP 509 (D.C. Cir. 1984) (prima facie case rebutted by evidence that plaintiff denied promotion due to her asserted abrasiveness and difficulty in working with fellow analysts); Altschuler v. Walters, 34 FEP 522 (E.D. Pa. 1983) (statements that man was more worthy of encouragement and that his subspecialty was more common in department were enough to rebut prima facie case).

[76]Firefighters for Racial Equality v. Bach, 731 F.2d 664, 34 FEP 1005 (10th Cir. 1984) (court must determine whether promotion practices in question were part of bona fide seniority system); Abrams v. Baylor College of Medicine, 581 F. Supp. 1570, 34 FEP 229 (S.D. Tex. 1984), *aff'd in part and rev'd in part,* 805 F.2d 528, 42 FEP 806 (5th Cir. 1986) (unilateral decision to exclude Jewish doctors from program in Saudi Arabia not justified by business necessity); Easley v. Anheuser-Busch, 572 F. Supp. 402, 34 FEP 380 (E.D. Mo. 1983), *aff'd in relevant part,* 758 F.2d 251, 37 FEP 549 (8th Cir. 1985) (employer must establish validity of pre-employment test); Cox v. American Cast Iron Pipe Co., *supra* note 75 (employer's reason, although flattering, was patronizing and sexually biased, and therefore, not legitimate).

[77]Crawford v. Western Elec. Co., *supra* note 73.

[78]Paxton v. Union Nat'l Bank, 688 F.2d 552, 566, 29 FEP 1233 (8th Cir. 1982), *cert. denied,* 460 U.S. 1083, 31 FEP 824 (1983) ("Where the bank did attempt to offer specific nondiscriminatory reasons, the explanations were often inconsistent. If a black person had more education than the white person receiving a promotion, the bank claimed that it made its selection on the basis of experience. Conversely, if a black employee had more experience than the white promoted the bank claimed that education was the key to performing that job. And if the black employee had more experience and a better education,

Neither will the employer always succeed by producing evidence that a person in the same protected class as the plaintiff filled the position in question.[79] In some contexts these reasons may fail even to satisfy the employers' light burden of rebuttal.[80] When an employer fails to meet such a burden, a court may conclude that discrimination is established as a matter of law.[81]

The employer must articulate the actual reason for the challenged employment decision. As stated by the Fifth Circuit, the factfinder is concerned with "what an employer's actual motive was; hypothetical or *post hoc* theories really have no place in a Title VII suit."[82] In *Eastland v. Tennessee Valley Authority,*[83] the trial court held the hiring decision justified because the qualifications of the person chosen were superior to those of the plaintiff. The Eleventh Circuit reversed, noting that because the selecting supervisor had not in fact compared the qualifications of plaintiff and the person selected at the time the selection was made, the company could not urge such a justification after the fact.[84]

The employer may also be required, where possible, to produce the actual decision maker. In *Monroe v. Burlington Industries,*[85] the Fourth Circuit refused to allow the actual decision makers to escape scrutiny by articulating their defense through the testimony of a newly hired personnel officer who sought to explain the decision based exclusively on a review of the applicants' personnel files.

To rebut a plaintiff's prima facie case based upon substantial *direct evidence,* an employer bears a heavier burden and generally must either refute that evidence or demonstrate the absence of a causal connection between the biased individual and the adverse decision.[86] Plaintiffs will argue that an employer must rebut direct evidence of maintenance of a discriminatory policy with "clear and convincing evidence that job decisions made when the discriminatory policy was in force were not made in pursuit of that policy."[87]

---

the bank often simply stated that the white employee was better qualified without giving a reason for the decision.").

[79]Howard v. Roadway Express, 726 F.2d 1529, 34 FEP 341 (11th Cir. 1984) (hiring black 11 months after rejecting black plaintiff's application does not establish that no discrimination existed); Ratliff v. Governor's Highway Safety Program, 791 F.2d 394, 40 FEP 1729 (5th Cir. 1986) (hiring black after allegedly discriminating against another black); Giannotti v. Foundry Cafe, 582 F. Supp. 503, 34 FEP 1753 (D. Conn. 1984) (goes to weight of evidence, not to legal sufficiency).

[80]Rowe v. Cleveland Pneumatic Co., Numerical Control, 690 F.2d 88, 96, 29 FEP 1682, 1688 (6th Cir. 1982) (per curiam) (employer's assertion that those to whom employment decision had been delegated did not want plaintiff, without expressing reason, will not satisfy burden to rebut).

[81]See Gerdom v. Continental Airlines, 692 F.2d 602, 609, 30 FEP 235, 241 (9th Cir. 1982), *cert. denied,* 460 U.S. 1074 (1983) (employer unsuccessfully asserted that weight restrictions on female flight attendants alone, to keep them attractive, was necessary to keep airline competitive).

[82]EEOC v. West Bros. Dep't Store, Mansfield, La., 805 F.2d 1171, 1172, 42 FEP 916 (5th Cir. 1986).

[83]704 F.2d 613, 31 FEP 1578 (11th Cir. 1983).

[84]*Id.* at 626.

[85]784 F.2d 568, 572, 40 FEP 273 (4th Cir. 1986) ("otherwise employers could avoid liability under Title VII by insulating the ultimate personnel decision-maker").

[86]Miles v. M.N.C. Corp., 750 F.2d 867, 36 FEP 1289 (11th Cir. 1985).

[87]Cox v. American Cast Iron Pipe Co., 784 F.2d 1546, 40 FEP 678, 688 (11th Cir.), *cert. denied,* 479 U.S. 883, 41 FEP 1712 (1986) (principles developed in pattern-and-practice class action applied in nonclass context). *But see* Price Waterhouse v. Hopkins, *supra* note 7.

### 3. Plaintiff's Proof of "Pretext"

The Supreme Court's decision in *Aikens*[88] confirms that the *McDonnell Douglas-Burdine* line of cases does not prescribe a trifurcated trial on issues of proof in employment discrimination cases.[89] Instead, the cases simply set forth an appropriate method for analyzing the relevant evidence before the court.[90]

When an employer articulates legitimate, nondiscriminatory reasons for an employee's discharge or other adverse employment decision, a plaintiff must be afforded an opportunity to prove that the stated reasons were merely a pretext for discrimination.[91] Regardless of the shifting burdens, the ultimate burden of persuasion always remains with the plaintiff.[92]

The plaintiff may satisfy his burden by proving by a preponderance of the evidence that the defendant's articulated reasons were pretextual.[93] One way this is done is for the plaintiff to introduce substantial and sufficient direct evidence of discrimination.[94]

In proving pretext, the plaintiff is not required to show that an illegal consideration such as age, race, or sex was the sole factor in the employer's decision, but rather need only show that the illegal consideration resulted in

---

[88]United States Postal Serv. Bd. of Governors v. Aikens, 460 U.S. 711, 31 FEP 609 (1983).

[89]*See* Barber v. Boilermakers Dist. Lodge 57, 778 F.2d 750, 755 n.6, 39 FEP 1092, 1095 n.6 (11th Cir. 1985) (although *McDonnell Douglas-Burdine* line of cases is analyzed in three phases, there is no requirement that evidence be introduced in compartmentalized form).

[90]*See, e.g.,* Monroe v. Burlington Indus., 784 F.2d 568, 570, 40 FEP 273, 274 (4th Cir. 1986) (these cases contain correct format for receiving and analyzing evidence in employment discrimination cases under Title VII); Foster v. Arcata Assocs., 772 F.2d 1453, 1458, 38 FEP 1850, 1853 (9th Cir. 1985), *cert. denied,* 475 U.S. 1048, 40 FEP 272 (1986) (these cases set forth basic allocation of burdens and order of proof for Title VII cases alleging disparate treatment).

[91]Griffin v. City of Omaha, 785 F.2d 620, 625, 40 FEP 385, 388, *reh'g denied en banc,* 40 EPD ¶36,151 (8th Cir. 1986) (once initial burdens are met, plaintiff is afforded opportunity to show that employer's justifications for decision are mere pretext); Yarbrough v. Tower Oldsmobile, 789 F.2d 508, 511, 40 FEP 1035, 1037 (7th Cir. 1986) (after presumption of discrimination drops from case, plaintiff bears burden of persuading trier of fact that explanation offered by defendant is pretextual); Jackson v. RKO Bottlers of Toledo Pepsi-Cola, Dr. Pepper Bottling Co. Div., 783 F.2d 50, 54, 40 FEP 222, 225 (6th Cir.), *cert. denied,* 478 U.S. 1006, 41 FEP 271 (1986) (plaintiff has opportunity to prove that defendant's legitimate reasons were mere pretext).

[92]Wilmington v. J.I. Case Co., 793 F.2d 909, 914, 40 FEP 1833, 1838 (8th Cir. 1986) (plaintiff has ultimate burden of proving that employer's articulated reason was pretext for discrimination); O'Connor v. Peru State College, 781 F.2d 632, 638, 39 FEP 1241, 1246 (8th Cir. 1986) (plaintiff retains ultimate burden of proving discrimination); Sylvester v. Callon Energy Servs., 781 F.2d 520, 523, 39 FEP 1660, 1663, *reh'g denied en banc,* 786 F.2d 1162 (5th Cir. 1986) (same).

[93]Holden v. Owens-Illinois, 793 F.2d 745, 753, 41 FEP 49, 56 (6th Cir.), *cert. denied,* 479 U.S. 1008, 42 FEP 1536 (1986) (plaintiff must prove by preponderance of evidence that legitimate reasons of employer were pretext); Davis v. Lambert of Ark., 781 F.2d 658, 660, 39 FEP 1410, 1411 (8th Cir. 1986) (plaintiff has opportunity to prove by preponderance of evidence that legitimate reasons offered were pretext to cover discriminatory motive); Foster v. MCI Telecommunications Corp., 773 F.2d 1116, 1118, 39 FEP 698, 700 (10th Cir. 1985) (once defendant articulates legitimate nondiscriminatory explanation, plaintiff must prove by preponderance of evidence that defendant's stated reason was not true motivation but mere pretext); Robinson v. Lehman, 771 F.2d 772, 777 n.13, 39 FEP 559, 563 n.13 (3d Cir. 1985) (plaintiff must have opportunity to prove by preponderance of evidence that legitimate reasons offered by defendant were not its true reasons but were pretext for discrimination).

[94]*See* Ratliff v. Governor's Highway Safety Program, 791 F.2d 394, 401, 40 FEP 1729, 1733 (5th Cir. 1986) (plaintiff may succeed directly by persuading court that discriminatory reason more likely motivated employer or indirectly by showing that employer's proffered explanation is unworthy of credence); Sylvester v. Callon Energy Servs., *supra* note 92; Andre v. Bendix Corp., 774 F.2d 786, 792, 38 FEP 1819, 1824 (7th Cir. 1985).

a different decision.[95] Generally, it must be shown that age, race, or sex was a "but for" factor in the decision.[96]

Evidence that may be relevant in showing pretext includes facts about the employer's general policy and practice with respect to employment of the protected group.[97] Comparative evidence and statistics can be used to show pretext.[98]

Some courts have concluded that the legitimacy of an employer's articulated reason for an employment decision is subject to particularly close scrutiny when the decision is based on subjective criteria or standards.[99]

---

[95]Benzies v. Illinois Dep't of Mental Health & Developmental Disabilities, 810 F.2d 146, 42 FEP 1537 (7th Cir.), cert. denied, 483 U.S. 1006, 43 FEP 1896 (1987) (rejection of employer's legitimate, nondiscriminatory reason is strong evidence of discriminatory intent, but court may still conclude that neither proffered explanation nor discrimination accounts for adverse decision); Fields v. Clark Univ., 817 F.2d 931, 43 FEP 1247 (1st Cir. 1987) (lower court erred in finding discrimination with respect to tenure denial because of its finding that decision was "impermissibly infected" with discrimination; university is entitled to a determination as to whether plaintiff established that she would have been granted tenure absent discrimination); Smith v. Papp Clinic, P.A., 808 F.2d 1449, 42 FEP 1553 (11th Cir. 1987) (jury properly instructed that discharge is not based on race if employer honestly believed that employee had violated company policy even if employer was mistaken); Schuler v. Chronicle Broadcasting Co. dba KRON-TV, 793 F.2d 1010, 42 FEP 1699 (9th Cir. 1986) ("To withstand an employer's motion for summary judgment in a discrimination suit, the employee must do more than establish a prima facie case and deny the credibility of the employer's witnesses, Steckl v. Motorola, 703 F.2d 392 [, 31 FEP 705] (9th Cir. 1983). The plaintiff must also offer specific and significantly probative evidence that the employer's alleged purpose is a pretext for discrimination."); Johnson v. University of Wis.-Milwaukee, 783 F.2d 59, 39 FEP 1822 (7th Cir. 1986) (while plaintiff's showing that proffered reason is false frequently leads to conclusion that discrimination was real reason, in this case the "bad" real reason nevertheless did not establish age discrimination); Bellissimo v. Westinghouse Elec. Corp., 764 F.2d 175, 179 n.1, 37 FEP 1862, 1864 n.1 (3d Cir. 1985), cert. denied, 475 U.S. 1035, 40 FEP 192 (1986) ("but for" test does not require plaintiff to prove that discriminatory reason was the determinative factor, but only that it was a determinative factor) (emphasis in opinion). But see Bibbs v. Block, 778 F.2d 1318, 1324, 39 FEP 970, 975 (8th Cir. 1985) (en banc) (where plaintiff proves that race is discernible factor, that is sufficient in mixed-motive context to establish intentional discrimination and liability under Title VII). Cf. Price Waterhouse v. Hopkins, supra note 7.

[96]McQuillen v. Wisconsin Educ. Ass'n Council, 830 F.2d 659, 664, 44 FEP 1566 (7th Cir. 1987), cert. denied, 485 U.S. _____, 46 FEP 292 (1988) ("employee must establish that the discriminatory motivation was a determining factor in the challenged employment decision in that the employee would have received the job absent the discriminatory motivation"); Goostree v. Tennessee, 796 F.2d 854, 42 FEP 1154 (6th Cir. 1986), cert. denied, 480 U.S. 918, 43 FEP 160 (1987) (proper to reject jury instruction requested by plaintiff that liability would be established if "sex was a factor"; sex must be a "but for" factor); Molthan v. Temple Univ.-Commonwealth Sys. of Higher Educ., 778 F.2d 955, 961, 39 FEP 816, 820–21 (3d Cir. 1985) (discrimination must be a "but for" cause of decision); Bellissimo v. Westinghouse Elec. Corp., 764 F.2d 175, 179, 37 FEP 1862, 1864 (3d Cir. 1985), cert. denied, 475 U.S. 1035, 40 FEP 192 (1986) (plaintiff must show that his status was "but for" reason for treatment accorded); Blalock v. Metals Trades, 775 F.2d 703, 709, 39 FEP 140 (6th Cir. 1985) ("this 'but for' causation is satisfied when the plaintiff establishes that the defendant's discriminatory intent more likely than not was the basis of the adverse employment action.").

[97]Ratliff v. Governor's Highway Safety Program, 791 F.2d 394, 402, 40 FEP 1729, 1734 (5th Cir. 1986) (employer's past discriminatory policy and practice may well illustrate that employer's asserted reasons for disparate treatment are pretext for intentional discrimination); Patterson v. Masem, 774 F.2d 251, 255, 39 FEP 1266, 1269 (8th Cir. 1985) (defendant's general policy and practice with respect to minority employment may be evidence that reasons offered for an individual employment decision are pretextual).

[98]Lowe v. City of Monrovia, 775 F.2d 998, 1008, 39 FEP 350 (9th Cir. 1985), modified, 784 F.2d 1407, 41 FEP 931, 938 (9th Cir. 1986) (disparate treatment plaintiff may rely on relevant statistical evidence to show that defendant's articulated nondiscriminatory reason for employment decision is pretextual); Box v. A&P Tea Co., 772 F.2d 1372, 1379, 38 FEP 1509, 1515 (7th Cir. 1985), cert. denied, 478 U.S. 1010, 41 FEP 271 (1986) (plaintiff may submit probative statistical evidence to show that employer's proffered reason for employment decision was pretext for discrimination).

[99]O'Connor v. Peru State College, 781 F.2d 632, 637–38, 39 FEP 1241, 1246 (8th Cir. 1986) (employer's asserted reliance on subjective factors particularly is to be closely scrutinized for discriminatory abuse); Henry v. Lennox Indus., 768 F.2d 746, 751, 42 FEP 771 (6th Cir. 1985) (legitimacy of articulated reason for employment decision is subject to particularly close scrutiny where evaluation is subjective and evaluators themselves are not members of protected minority); Love v. Alamance County Bd. of Educ., 757 F.2d 1504, 1506, 37 FEP 633, 636 (4th Cir. 1985) (subjective criteria for selection procedures should be subject to strict scrutiny).

However, a contrary conclusion was advanced by the plurality of the Supreme Court in *Watson v. Fort Worth Bank & Trust Co.,* [100] which stated that subjective employment decisions may be easier to justify in terms of legitimate business purposes. [101]

## B. The Disparate Treatment Class Action

*Cooper v. Federal Reserve Bank of Richmond* [102] reaffirms that proof of isolated discriminatory acts is insufficient to establish a prima facie case of a pattern and practice of discrimination. [103] Moreover, while statistics alone may be used to establish discriminatory intent where they show a "gross disparity" in the treatment of workers based upon discriminatory factors, [104] the courts now acknowledge that statistical evidence is rarely sufficient by itself. [105] Plaintiffs therefore frequently seek to establish a pattern and practice of discriminatory intent by combining statistics with nonstatistical factors. [106]

The focus on statistics has led to extensive discussion of the relevance and adequacy of the statistical evidence used to prove discriminatory treatment. In the area of discriminatory failure to hire, the cases indicate that appropriate comparison groups could consist of individuals actually applying for a particular position or individuals in the relevant labor pool who possess the qualifications for the positions at issue. [107] While both such groups can be relevant, a comparison with actual applicants is generally more probative than a comparison with the larger qualified labor market. [108] When employing the actual applicant pool as a comparison group, the courts

---

[100] 487 U.S. _____, 47 FEP 102, 111 (1988).

[101] *Id.* "In evaluating claims that discretionary employment practices are insufficiently related to legitimate business purposes, it must be borne in mind that 'courts are generally less competent than employers to restructure business practices, and unless mandated to do so by Congress they should not attempt it.' [citations omitted]." 47 FEP at 111.

[102] 467 U.S. 867, 35 FEP 1 (1984).

[103] *Id.* at 876, 35 FEP at 4–5 (citing Teamsters v. United States, 431 U.S. 324, 336, 14 FEP 1514, 1519 (1977)); *see* Chang v. University of R.I., 606 F. Supp. 1161, 40 FEP 3 (D.R.I. 1985) (plaintiff must do more than establish occurrence of isolated, sporadic acts of discriminatory behavior); Page v. U.S. Indus., 726 F.2d 1038, 1045, 34 FEP 430, 434 (5th Cir. 1984) (same).

[104] Lewis v. NLRB, 750 F.2d 1266, 1271, 36 FEP 1388, 1392 (5th Cir. 1985) (court may infer racial discrimination from gross statistical disparities); *see also* Page v. U.S. Indus., 726 F.2d 1038, 1046, 34 FEP 430, 435 (5th Cir. 1984). *But see* Segar v. Smith, 738 F.2d 1249, 1278, 35 FEP 31, 51 (D.C. Cir. 1984), *cert. denied,* 471 U.S. 1115, 37 FEP 1312 (1985). (where statistics are finely tuned "gross disparities need not be shown to permit an inference of discrimination").

[105] State, County & Mun. Employees v. Washington, 770 F.2d 1401, 1407, 38 FEP 1353, 1359 (9th Cir. 1985); Gay v. Waiters' & Dairy Lunchmen's Local 30, 694 F.2d 531, 552, 30 FEP 605, 621 (9th Cir. 1982); *see also* Spaulding v. University of Wash., 740 F.2d 686, 703, 35 FEP 217, 228 (9th Cir.), *cert. denied,* 469 U.S. 1036, 36 FEP 464 (1984).

[106] Smith v. Western Elec. Co., 770 F.2d 520, 38 FEP 1605 (5th Cir. 1985); Maddox v. Claytor, 764 F.2d 1539, 1556–57, 38 FEP 713, 728 (11th Cir. 1985); Lewis v. NLRB, *supra* note 104 (court "may examine the history of the employer's practices, anecdotal evidence of class members, and the degree of opportunity to treat employees unfairly in the appraisal process" to determine issue of discriminatory intent); *see also* Page v. U.S. Indus., *supra* note 104 (if statistical disparity alone is insufficient, it may be combined "with historical, individual, or circumstantial evidence" to establish prima facie case; Spaulding v. University of Washington, *supra* note 105 (statistics are most useful when supplemented with specific instances of discrimination).

[107] *See, e.g.,* Payne v. Travenol Laboratories, 673 F.2d 798, 823–24, 28 FEP 1212, 1232 (5th Cir.), *cert. denied,* 459 U.S. 1038, 30 FEP 440 (1982); EEOC v. H.S. Camp & Sons, 542 F. Supp. 411, 442–43, 33 FEP 330, 352–53 (M.D. Fla. 1982).

[108] EEOC v. H.S. Camp & Sons, *supra* note 107; *accord* Payne v. Travenol Laboratories, *supra* note 107; Williams v. Owens-Illinois, 665 F.2d 918, 927, 27 FEP 1273, 1279 (9th Cir.), *cert. denied,* 459 U.S. 971, 30 FEP 56 (1982).

should consider the applicants' qualifications.[109] An applicant pool that excludes potentially eligible individuals, whom the employer eliminated at some stage in the screening process, may be inappropriate.[110] However, when courts consider labor market data, there has been some controversy concerning the definition of the relevant pool. At least one court has held that the pool should include all individuals the employer could easily train for the positions at issue, unless the employer can show a need for specific specialized skills.[111]

In addition to questions regarding the relevance of comparison groups, disparate treatment class actions also raise questions concerning the adequacy of statistical data.[112] For example, statistical inferences of disparate treatment may not be valid if the sample size is too small.[113] Such inferences may or may not be proper where the evidence groups data into a single sample instead of presenting it as year-by-year samples.[114] Courts have questioned inferences of disparate treatment based on less than three standard deviations between the representation of the plaintiff class and the comparison group.[115] Including data from years prior to the statute of limitations for

[109]See, e.g., United States v. Massachusetts Maritime Academy, 762 F.2d 142, 154–55 (1st Cir. 1985) (finding that Academy intentionally discriminated against women was supported by evaluation of qualifications of applicants, showing that significant number of women who were rejected had better academic records than men who were accepted); Domingo v. New England Fish Co., 727 F.2d 1429, 1436, 34 FEP 584, 591, modified, 742 F.2d 520, 37 FEP 1303 (9th Cir. 1984) (court recognizes necessity of considering qualifications of applicant pool "because without that information, no inference of discrimination may be drawn; lack of minority representation in work force might simply be due to a lack of qualified applicants"); Piva v. Xerox Corp., 654 F.2d 591, 596, 26 FEP 1267, 1271 (9th Cir. 1981).

[110]Griffin v. Carlin, 755 F.2d 1516, 1526, 37 FEP 741, 749 (11th Cir. 1985) (lower court erred when it disregarded statistics based upon entire applicant pool and held instead that appropriate pool consisted of those on supervisory register who had already been screened by agency).

[111]Lilly v. Harris-Teeter Supermkt., 545 F. Supp. 686, 709, 33 FEP 98, 116 (W.D.N.C. 1982), aff'd in part, rev'd in part and vacated in part, 720 F.2d 326, 33 FEP 195 (4th Cir. 1983), cert. denied, 466 U.S. 951, 34 FEP 1096 (1984) (defendant failed to justify its limitation of labor force to a special market); see also Miles v. M.N.C. Corp., 750 F.2d 867, 872, 36 FEP 1289, 1293 (11th Cir. 1985) (pool of Alabama employment service referral list not too broad since "there were no specific qualifications or criteria for employment" at defendant corporation); De Medina v. Reinhardt, 686 F.2d 997, 1003, 29 FEP 1084, 1088 (D.C. Cir. 1982) (validity of statistical data does not depend upon comparison group having every conceivable qualification required for positions at issue); O'Brien v. Sky Chefs, 670 F.2d 864, 867, 28 FEP 661, 663–64, amended, 28 FEP 1690 (9th Cir. 1982) (comparison with general labor pool is more probative when position involves skills which may be learned easily by most members of labor pool). But see Valentino v. United States Postal Serv., 674 F.2d 56, 67–69, 28 FEP 593, 601–2 (D.C. Cir. 1982) (when job qualifications involved are ones relatively few possess or can acquire, statistical data not focusing on those qualifications is of little value); EEOC v. H.S. Camp & Sons, supra note 107 (failure to limit applicant pool to those who possess necessary qualifications lessens value of resulting statistical analysis).

[112]See Spaulding v. University of Wash., supra note 105 (statistics must be relied upon with caution; they are "inherently slippery," and weight given them depends upon "proper supportive facts and the absence of variables").

[113]EEOC v. H.S. Camp & Sons, supra note 107 (where statistical evidence is based on small sample size, statistical evidence must be supplemented with additional proof); EEOC v. American Nat'l Bank, 680 F.2d 965, 966–70, 30 FEP 906, 907–10 (4th Cir.), cert. denied, 459 U.S. 923, 30 FEP 960 (1982) (Widener, J., dissenting) (failure to take into account small sample size was error). But see Valentino v. United States Postal Serv., 674 F.2d 56, 72–73, 28 FEP 593, 606 (D.C. Cir. 1982) (court stated that a small sample is not useless per se, especially if disparity shown is egregious); Spight v. Tidwell Indus., 551 F. Supp. 123, 133, 30 FEP 1423, 1431 (N.D. Miss. 1982) (a sample of 58 promotions is not so small as to lack probative force).

[114]Compare Coates v. Johnson & Johnson, 756 F.2d 524, 540–42, 37 FEP 467, 479–81 (7th Cir. 1985) (pooling into single sample may be appropriate if sample size is small, but is inappropriate if an expert can show that pooling would distort statistical results) with Capaci v. Katz & Besthoff, 711 F.2d 647, 32 FEP 961 (5th Cir. 1983), cert. denied, 466 U.S. 927, 34 FEP 696 (1984) (samples need not be analyzed in year-by-year samples) and Lilly v. Harris-Teeter Supermkt., 720 F.2d 326, 33 FEP 195, 203 n.17 (4th Cir. 1983), cert. denied, 466 U.S. 951, 34 FEP 1096 (1984) ("highly preferable to examine the statistical data for the time period in combined form, rather than year by year").

[115]Gay v. Waiters' and Dairy Lunchmen's Local 30, 694 F.2d 531, 551, 30 FEP 605, 621 (9th Cir. 1982) ("courts should be 'extremely cautious' of drawing any inferences from standard deviations in the

the class action will render the statistical analysis ineffectual.[116] At least one court also held that it is proper to disregard statistics concerning disciplinary action merely because each disciplinary action is based upon separate factual situations.[117]

In those cases where the statistical data are analytically deficient or otherwise inadequate as proof of discriminatory intent, courts have relied upon supplemental nonstatistical evidence to find improper motive. Testimony of specific instances of discrimination against plaintiff class members, for example, has buttressed class action claims.[118] A history of discrimination practiced by the employer may also bolster a statistical showing of disparate impact.[119] For example, the undisputed existence of discrimination prior to the enactment of Title VII has been relied upon to support a finding of discriminatory intent.[120] In addition, an employer's use of a subjective employment decision-making process, both in making it more difficult to discern the qualifications necessary for obtaining an employment position and in providing a convenient opportunity and cover for unlawful discrimination, has been held to strengthen a statistically based claim of classwide discrimination.[121]

In the assessment of statistical proof, plaintiffs can be expected to argue that an inappropriately high standard of proof should not be required. One court noted: "A plaintiff in a Title VII suit need not prove discrimination

---

range of 1 to 3"); *see also* EEOC v. American Nat'l Bank, 680 F.2d 965, 966–73, 30 FEP 906, 907–13 (4th Cir.) (Widener, J., dissenting), *cert. denied,* 459 U.S. 923, 30 FEP 960 (1982) (probity questioned where standard deviation for relevant period ranged from 1.38 to 3.81); EEOC v. H.S. Camp & Sons, 542 F. Supp. 411, 442, 33 FEP 330, 352 (M.D. Fla. 1982) (statistical disparity greater than 3 standard deviations has been held to constitute gross disparity).

[116]Smith v. Western Elec. Co., *supra* note 106, at 526, 38 FEP at 1609–10.

[117]Mozee v. Jeffboat, Inc., 746 F.2d 365, 35 FEP 1810 (7th Cir. 1984). *But see* Wilmington v. J.I. Case Co., 793 F.2d 909, 40 FEP 1833 (8th Cir. 1986) (expert's finding of statistical significance comparing percentage of black and white terminations).

[118]*E.g.,* Payne v. Travenol Laboratories, 673 F.2d 798, 817, 819, 28 FEP 1212, 1226, 1228 (5th Cir.), *cert. denied,* 459 U.S. 1038, 30 FEP 440 (1982).

[119]Lewis v. NLRB, 750 F.2d 1266, 1277, 36 FEP 1388, 1396 (5th Cir. 1985); *see also* United States v. Massachusetts Maritime Academy, 762 F.2d 142, 157 (1st Cir. 1985) (evidence of persistent past discrimination in recruitment and admission of women into maritime academy entitled court to infer that defendant could easily revert to earlier discriminatory practices; therefore an injunction permanently enjoining any repeat discriminatory conduct was proper). While data on employment practices that occurred prior to the liability period do have some probative value, such data are less valuable than data focusing on practices after the liability cut-off date. Coates v. Johnson & Johnson, 756 F.2d 524, 540, 37 FEP 467, 479 (7th Cir. 1985); *see also* Trout v. Lehman, 702 F.2d 1094, 1104, 31 FEP 286, 294 (D.C. Cir. 1983), *vacated and remanded on other grounds,* 465 U.S. 1056, 34 FEP 76 (1984) ("[s]tatistics tuned to the proper time period are more probative than statistics not so tuned").

[120]Payne v. Travenol Laboratories, 673 F.2d 798, 816–17, 819, 28 FEP 1212, 1212, 1225–26, 1228 (5th Cir.), *cert. denied,* 459 U.S. 1038, 30 FEP 440 (1982) (evidence that work force was all white except for custodial positions prior to passage of Title VII in 1964 coalesced with other evidence to establish prima facie case of disparate treatment); Van Aken v. Young, 541 F. Supp. 448, 457, 28 FEP 1669, 1675–76 (E.D. Mich. 1982), *aff'd,* 750 F.2d 43, 36 FEP 777 (6th Cir. 1984) (pre-Act discrimination is probative where employment decision-making process has undergone little change since passage of the Act). However, the probative value of such pre-Act evidence should normally wane with time, especially if the selection factors and decision-makers have changed.

[121]EEOC v. H.S. Camp & Sons, 542 F. Supp. 411, 447, 33 FEP 330, 356 (M.D. Fla. 1982) (evidence of lack of written standards for qualifications, undue emphasis on supervisor recommendations, and no system of promotion opportunities supported inference of discrimination); Lilly v. Harris-Teeter Supermkt., 545 F. Supp. 686, 708, 33 FEP 98, 116 (W.D.N.C. 1982); *see also* Payne v. Travenol Laboratories, 673 F.2d 798, 819 n.29, 28 FEP 1212, 1228 n.29, (5th Cir.), *cert. denied,* 459 U.S. 1038, 30 FEP 440 (1982); O'Brien v. Sky Chefs, 670 F.2d 864, 28 FEP 661, *amended,* 28 FEP 1690 (9th Cir. 1982); *cf.* Watson v. Fort Worth Bank & Trust Co., *supra* notes 100 and 101; Smith v. Western Elec. Co., 770 F.2d 520, 528, 38 FEP 1605, 1611 (5th Cir. 1985) ("[a]n opportunity to discriminate, standing alone, will not establish discriminatory impact or treatment").

with scientific certainty; rather, his or her burden is to prove discrimination by a preponderance of the evidence."[122]

The defendant can rebut the plaintiff's prima facie showing of a pattern and practice of discrimination in two ways.[123] First, the defendant can show that the plaintiff's statistics are inaccurate or insignificant.[124] For example, the employer can show that the disparity between the number of minorities employed in its work force and the number in the general labor force results from pre-Title VII discrimination.[125] But the employer should do more than simply raise theoretical objections to the data or the statistical analysis; the defendant should demonstrate how the errors affect the result.[126] Second, the defendant can provide a nondiscriminatory explanation for the apparently discriminatory result.[127] Usually the strength of the evidence necessary to meet the rebuttal burden will be higher in the class action pattern-or-practice case than in the individual disparate treatment case.[128] Once the defendant offers a factor that changes the result of the plaintiff's analysis, the plaintiff then bears the burden of persuading the factfinder that the explanatory factor is biased, inaccurate, or "otherwise unworthy of credence."[129]

Once the court has found that an employer engaged in a pattern or practice of discrimination, it presumes that discrimination existed on a class-wide basis.[130] Thus, each claimant need not prove the employer's discriminatory intent at the remedy phase of the litigation.[131] Instead, the employer carries the burden to overcome the inference of unlawful discrimination against each individual class member.[132] In this regard, the Eleventh Circuit has held that the burden on the defendant is proof by "clear and convincing evidence."[133]

---

[122]Bazemore v. Friday, 478 U.S. 385, 41 FEP 92, 99 (1986). *Bazemore* also extends the rationale of *United Postal Service Board of Governors v. Aikens,* 460 U.S. 711, 31 FEP 609 (1983), to a pattern-or-practice class action and further concludes: "[A]s long as the court may fairly conclude, in light of all the evidence, that it is more likely than not that impermissible discrimination exists, the plaintiff is entitled to prevail." 41 FEP at 99.

[123]Payne v. Travenol Laboratories, 673 F.2d 798, 817, 28 FEP 1212, 1226 (5th Cir.), *cert. denied,* 459 U.S. 1038, 30 FEP 440 (1982).

[124]*Id.; see also* Watson v. Fort Worth Bank & Trust Co., 487 U.S. _____, 47 FEP 102, 109–10 (1988), and cases cited therein; Bazemore v. Friday, 478 U.S. 385, 41 FEP 92, 98–100 (1986) (Brennan, J., concurring); Lewis v. Bloomsburg Mills, 773 F.2d 561, 38 FEP 1692 (4th Cir. 1985); Spaulding v. University of Wash., 740 F.2d 686, 703, 35 FEP 217, 228 (9th Cir.), *cert. denied,* 469 U.S. 1036, 36 FEP 464 (1984); Segar v. Smith, 738 F.2d 1249, 1268, 35 FEP 31, 42–43 (D.C. Cir. 1984), *cert. denied,* 471 U.S. 1115, 37 FEP 1312 (1985) (defendants will often refute plaintiffs' evidence of disparity with alternative statistical analysis); White v. Washington Pub. Power Supply Sys., 692 F.2d 1286, 1289, 30 FEP 453, 455 (9th Cir. 1982).

[125]Payne v. Travenol Laboratories, *supra* note 123.

[126]Capaci v. Katz & Besthoff, 711 F.2d 647, 653–54, 32 FEP 961 (5th Cir. 1983), *cert. denied,* 466 U.S. 927, 34 FEP 696 (1984); *see also* Bazemore v. Friday, 478 U.S. 385, n.14, 41 FEP 92, 100 (1986).

[127]*Id.; see also* Paxton v. Union Nat'l Bank, 688 F.2d 552, 567, 29 FEP 1233, 1246 (8th Cir. 1982), *cert. denied,* 460 U.S. 1083, 31 FEP 824 (1983) (introduction of employment records listing reasons why each employee was discharged held sufficient to rebut plaintiff's prima facie case).

[128]Rossini v. Ogilvy & Mather, 597 F. Supp. 1120, 1159, 41 FEP 861, 895 (S.D.N.Y. 1984); *see also* Segar v. Smith, 738 F.2d 1249, 1268–70, 35 FEP 31, 43 (D.C. Cir. 1984), *cert. denied,* 471 U.S. 1115, 37 FEP 1312 (1985). If the employer identifies a factor that alters the results of plaintiff's analysis, plaintiff may argue that the defendant must prove the business necessity of this factor. Griffin v. Carlin, 755 F.2d 1516, 37 FEP 741, 749–50 (11th Cir. 1985).

[129]Coates v. Johnson & Johnson, 756 F.2d 524, 542–45, 37 FEP 467, 481–83 (7th Cir. 1985).

[130]Craik v. Minnesota State Univ. Bd., 731 F.2d 465, 470, 34 FEP 649, 653 (8th Cir. 1984).

[131]EEOC v. American Nat'l Bank, 652 F.2d 1176, 1201, 26 FEP 472, 490 (4th Cir. 1981), *cert. denied,* 459 U.S. 923, 30 FEP 960 (1982); *see also* Taylor v. Teletype Corp., 550 F. Supp. 781, 785–87, 34 FEP 1385, 1388–90 (E.D. Ark. 1982).

[132]McKenzie v. Sawyer, 684 F.2d 62, 75–78, 29 FEP 633, 643–45 (D.C. Cir. 1982).

[133]Cox v. American Cast Iron Pipe Co., 784 F.2d 1546, 1559, 40 FEP 678, 688 (11th Cir.), *cert. denied,* 479 U.S. 883, 41 FEP 1712 (1986). *Cf.* Price Waterhouse v. Hopkins, *supra* note 7.

## III. PROOF IN THE ADVERSE IMPACT CASE

Many courts continue to analyze the evidence in a Title VII case under both the disparate treatment and adverse impact theories of proof,[134] with the not infrequent result that a plaintiff is able to make out a case under one but not both theories.[135] In some instances courts have applied disparate treatment and adverse impact analyses to different claims of discrimination within the same suit.[136] On other occasions courts have confused the two methods of proof, erroneously applying the disparate treatment model when adverse impact analysis was proper.[137] The differences in these models of proof also have been discussed in the context of an ADEA case.[138] Although the adverse impact model may be used to prove both individual[139] and class[140] claims, the plaintiff must establish a causal connection between the observed adverse impact and the practice being challenged.[141]

Further delineating the boundaries of the adverse impact theory, a number of courts had refused to extend it to decision-making processes that depended upon subjective criteria or discretion.[142] These courts reasoned that

---

[134]Segar v. Smith, *supra* note 124; Page v. U.S. Indus., 726 F.2d 1038, 34 FEP 430 (5th Cir. 1984); Robinson v. Polaroid Corp., 732 F.2d 1010, 34 FEP 1134 (1st Cir. 1984); Walker v. Jefferson County Home, 726 F.2d 1554, 34 FEP 465 (11th Cir. 1984); Talley v. United States Postal Serv., 720 F.2d 505, 33 FEP 361 (8th Cir. 1983), *cert. denied,* 466 U.S. 952, 37 FEP 592 (1984); Zahorik v. Cornell Univ., 729 F.2d 85, 34 FEP 165 (2d Cir. 1984); Wright v. Olin Corp., 697 F.2d 1172, 30 FEP 889 (4th Cir. 1982); Bonilla v. Oakland Scavenger Co., 697 F.2d 1297, 31 FEP 50 (9th Cir. 1982), *cert. denied,* 467 U.S. 1251, 34 FEP 800 (1984); *see also* Wang v. Hoffman, 694 F.2d 1146, 30 FEP 703 (9th Cir. 1982) (in a questionably reasoned case the Ninth Circuit held that an adverse impact claim could be established without plaintiff submitting any statistics); Peters v. Lieuallen, 693 F.2d 966, 30 FEP 706 (9th Cir. 1982), *aff'd,* 746 F.2d 1390, 36 FEP 524 (9th Cir. 1984) (case analyzed both as disparate treatment and adverse impact claim).

[135]*E.g.,* EEOC v. Federal Reserve Bank of Richmond, 698 F.2d 633, 30 FEP 1137 (4th Cir. 1983), *rev'd sub nom.* Cooper v. Federal Reserve Bank of Richmond, 467 U.S. 867, 35 FEP 1 (1984); Rowe v. Cleveland Pneumatic Co., Numerical Control, 690 F.2d 88, 29 FEP 1682 (6th Cir. 1982); Wheeler v. City of Columbus, Miss., 686 F.2d 1144, 29 FEP 1699 (5th Cir. 1982); Foster v. MCI Telecommunications Corp., 555 F. Supp. 330, 30 FEP 1493 (D. Colo. 1983), *aff'd,* 773 F.2d 1116, 39 FEP 698 (10th Cir. 1985); *see also* EEOC v. Borden's, 724 F.2d 1390, 33 FEP 1708 (9th Cir. 1984) (ADEA case where both adverse impact and disparate treatment claims prevailed).

[136]*E.g.,* Segar v. Smith, *supra* note 128; Wright v. Olin Corp., *supra* note 134; Pina v. City of E. Providence, 492 F. Supp. 1240, 31 FEP 230 (D. R.I. 1980).

[137]Nash v. Consolidated City of Jacksonville, Duval County, Fla., 763 F.2d 1393, 38 FEP 151 (11th Cir. 1985); EEOC v. St. Louis-San Francisco Ry., 743 F.2d 739, 35 FEP 1163 (10th Cir. 1984).

[138]Allison v. Western Union Tel. Co., 680 F.2d 1318, 29 FEP 393 (11th Cir. 1982); Heward v. Western Elec. Co., 35 FEP 807 (10th Cir. 1984); Yartzoff v. Oregon Employment Div., Dep't of Human Resources, 745 F.2d 557, 36 FEP 16 (9th Cir. 1984); *see also* Blum v. Witco Chem. Corp., 829 F.2d 367, 372, 46 FEP 306 (3d Cir. 1987) ("Statistical evidence is an appropriate method for establishing disparate impact as indirect evidence of age discrimination"); Palmer v. United States, 794 F.2d 534, 536, 41 FEP 559 (9th Cir. 1986) ("A plaintiff alleging discrimination under the ADEA may proceed under either of two theories: disparate treatment or disparate impact."). *But see generally,* Stacy, "A Case Against Extending the Adverse Impact Doctrine to ADEA," 10 EMPLOYEE REL. L.J. 437 (1984).

[139]Zuniga v. Kleberg County Hosp., Kingsville, Tex., 692 F.2d 986, 30 FEP 650 (5th Cir. 1982).

[140]*E.g.,* Gay v. Waiters' & Dairy Lunchmen's Local 30, 694 F.2d 531, 30 FEP 605 (9th Cir. 1982); Kouba v. Allstate Ins. Co., 691 F.2d 873, 30 FEP 57 (9th Cir. 1982).

[141]Watson v. Fort Worth Bank & Trust, *supra* note 24; Johnson v. Allyn & Bacon, 731 F.2d 64, 34 FEP 804 (1st Cir.), *cert. denied,* 469 U.S. 1018, 36 FEP 320 (1984); Yartzoff v. Oregon Employment Div., Dep't of Human Resources, *supra* note 138; Peters v. Lieuallen, 746 F.2d 1390, 36 FEP 524 (9th Cir. 1984).

[142]EEOC v. Inland Marine Indus., 729 F.2d 1229, 34 FEP 881 (9th Cir.), *cert. denied,* 469 U.S. 855, *reh'g denied,* 469 U.S. 1029 (1984) (treating black employees differently pursuant to subjective wage-setting system properly analyzed under disparate treatment theory); Vuyanich v. Republic Nat'l Bank of Dallas, 723 F.2d 1195, 33 FEP 1521 (5th Cir.), *cert. denied,* 469 U.S. 1073, 36 FEP 568 (1984) (broad scale statistical attack on combination of subjective and objective employment practices properly analyzed under disparate treatment theory); Carroll v. Sears, Roebuck & Co., 708 F.2d 183, 32 FEP 286 (5th Cir. 1983); Pegues v. Mississippi State Employment Serv., 699 F.2d 760, 31 FEP 257 (5th Cir.), *cert. denied,* 464 U.S. 991, 33 FEP 440 (1983); Cunningham v. Housing Auth. of the City of Opelousas dba Opelousas Hous. Auth., 764 F.2d 1097, 38 FEP 417 (5th Cir.), *cert. denied,* 474 U.S. 1007, 39 FEP 720 (1985);

subjective decision-making policies are not "facially neutral" and, therefore, do not fit the adverse impact model as defined by the Supreme Court in *Teamsters v. United States.*[143] Other courts maintained that the adverse impact model is a valid method for analyzing subjectively based employment selection decisions.[144] This conflict among the circuits has now been resolved by the Supreme Court's decision in *Watson v. Fort Worth Bank & Trust Co.*[145]

The eight Justices participating in the *Watson* decision unanimously agreed that adverse impact analysis can be applied to subjective criteria, for the reasons set forth by Justice O'Connor in her opinion. First, according to Justice O'Connor, if adverse impact analysis were limited to objective, standardized selection practices, that analysis might effectively be abolished since an employer could insulate itself from liability under *Griggs*[146] and its progeny simply by combining objective practices with subjective components and refusing to make objective factors determinative.[147] Second, Justice O'Connor reasoned, adverse impact analysis is based on the principle that a facially neutral practice, adopted without discriminatory intent, may nevertheless have effects that are "indistinguishable from intentionally discriminatory practices."[148] This principle, Justice O'Connor stated, is no less applicable to subjective criteria. Simply because no inference of discriminatory intent can be drawn from the customary and reasonable practice in some businesses of leaving promotion decisions to the unchecked discretion of the lower level

---

Carpenter v. Stephen F. Austin State Univ., 706 F.2d 608, 31 FEP 1758 (5th Cir. 1983); Talley v. United States Postal Serv., *supra* note 134; Heward v. Western Elec. Co., *supra* note 138; *see* Pope v. City of Hickory, N.C., 679 F.2d 20, 22, 29 FEP 405, 406 (4th Cir. 1982) (discriminatory discipline and discharge case citing *Pouncy v. Prudential Ins. Co. of Am.,* 668 F.2d 795, 800, 28 FEP 121, 125 (5th Cir. 1982), for proposition that adverse impact model is not appropriate for across-the-board-attack on defendant's employment practice; model applies only where employer "has instituted a specific procedure" which is connected to "class based imbalance in the work force"); Sheehan v. Purolator Courier Corp., 103 F.R.D. 641, 36 FEP 1452 (E.D.N.Y. 1984), *aff'd,* 839 F.2d 99 (2d Cir. 1988) (plaintiffs alleged discrimination in promotion, training, transfer, and compensation which involved subjective rather than objective criteria; therefore, adverse impact analysis improper); Caston v. Duke Univ., 34 FEP 102 (M.D.N.C. 1983) (adverse impact theory only applies to specific, objective employment procedures or criteria which allegedly have discriminatory effects); Nation v. Winn-Dixie Stores, 567 F. Supp. 997, 32 FEP 493 (N.D. Ga. 1983) (same); EEOC v. Sears, Roebuck & Co., 628 F. Supp. 1264, 39 FEP 1672 *and* 39 FEP 1745 (N.D. Ill. 1986), *aff'd,* 839 F.2d 302, 45 FEP 1257 (7th Cir. 1988) (adverse impact theory inapplicable to defendant's highly subjective selection process); *see also* State, County & Mun. Employees v. Washington, 770 F.2d 1401, 38 FEP 1353 (9th Cir. 1985) (adverse impact analysis confined to cases which challenge specific, clearly delineated employment practice applied at a single point in job selection process); Eastland v. Tennessee Valley Auth., 704 F.2d 613, 31 FEP 1578 (11th Cir. 1983), *cert. denied,* 465 U.S. 1066, 34 FEP 415 (1984) (application of adverse impact theory to subjective employment promotion procedures is "troublesome").

[143]431 U.S. 324, 335 n.15, 14 FEP 1514, 1519 (1977). *But cf.* Page v. U.S. Indus., *supra* note 134 (holding subjective promotion system may be facially neutral).

[144]Atonio v. Wards Cove Packing Co., 810 F.2d 1477, 43 FEP 130 (9th Cir. 1987) (en banc), *cert. granted,* 487 U.S. _____ (1988) (resolving conflict in circuit, holds disparate impact analysis may be applied to subjective employment practices; challenged practices included use of separate hiring channels for cannery workers than those for higher paying jobs, word-of-mouth recruitment, nepotism, prehire policies favoring prior hires, and lack of objective job qualifications, as well as housing and eating facilities segregated between whites and nonwhites; "We now hold that disparate impact analysis may be applied to challenge subjective employment practices or criteria provided the plaintiffs have proved a causal connection between those practices and the demonstrated impact on members of a protected class"); Griffin v. Carlin, 755 F.2d 1516, 37 FEP 741 (11th Cir. 1985) (exclusion of subjective practices from scope of adverse impact analysis will encourage employees to use subjective rather than objective selection criteria; adverse impact model is applicable to all selection procedures, whether objective or subjective); Hill v. Seaboard Coast Line R.R., 767 F.2d 771, 39 FEP 1656 (11th Cir. 1985).

[145]487 U.S. _____, 47 FEP 102 (1988).

[146]Griggs v. Duke Power Co., 401 U.S. 424, 3 FEP 175 (1971).

[147]47 FEP at 107.

[148]*Id.*

supervisors most familiar with the jobs and candidates, it does not follow that supervisors always act without discriminatory intent.[149]

In urging a result different from that reached in *Watson,* one of the Bank's principal arguments was that subjective selection practices would be so impossibly difficult to defend under adverse impact analysis that employers would be forced to adopt numerical quotas in order to avoid liability, thus violating Title VII's express provision that it not be read to require preferential treatment or numerical quotas.[150] While this argument did not persuade the Court to limit the adverse impact theory to objective practices and procedures,[151] it did cause Justice O'Connor, joined by Justices Rehnquist, White, and Scalia, to conclude that the Court's decision to extend the reach of the adverse impact theory "calls for a fresh and somewhat closer examination of the constraints that operate to keep that analysis within its proper bounds."[152] The plurality opinion then articulated the following "evidentiary guidelines" for the lower courts in analyzing adverse impact challenges to subjective criteria.

First, Justice O'Connor noted that to establish a prima facie case of adverse impact, a plaintiff must show more than statistical disparities in the employer's work force. The plaintiff must identify the specific employment practice being challenged as discriminatory. Justice O'Connor recognized that this task may be more difficult when the challenge is not to standardized tests or objective criteria, but to subjective selection criteria or circumstances where an employer combines subjective criteria with objective standards. Nevertheless, Justice O'Connor concluded, the plaintiff is responsible for "isolating" and "identifying" the specific employment practices allegedly responsible for any observed statistical disparities.[153] According to Justice O'Connor's opinion, it is not enough for the plaintiff to identify specific employment practices and show statistical work force disparities. Causation must be proved; "that is, the plaintiff must offer statistical evidence of a kind and degree sufficient to show that the practice in question has caused the exclusion of applicants for jobs or promotions because of their membership in a protected group."[154] The plurality declined, however, to attempt to determine what constitutes "sufficient" statistical proof, preferring instead, "at least at this stage," a case-by-case determination.[155]

Second, Justice O'Connor identified as a restraint on application of

---

[149]*Id.*

[150]42 U.S.C. § 2000e-2(j).

[151]In response to the Bank's argument, the plurality noted:

"that today's extension of [the adverse impact] theory into the context of subjective selection practices could increase the risk that employers will be given incentives to adopt quotas or engage in preferential treatment."

47 FEP at 108.

"[T]he inevitable focus on statistics in [adverse] impact cases could put undue pressure on employers to adopt inappropriate prophylactic measures. It is completely unrealistic to assume that unlawful discrimination is the sole cause of people failing to gravitate to jobs and employers in accord with the laws of chance. [citations omitted] It would be equally unrealistic to suppose that employers can eliminate, or discover and explain, the myriad of innocent causes that may lead to statistical imbalances in the composition of their work forces."

*Id.*

[152]47 FEP at 108.

[153]47 FEP at 109.

[154]*Id.*

[155]47 FEP at 109 n.3.

adverse impact theory the nature of the "business necessity" or "job related-ness" defense. In the plurality's opinion,

> "[a]lthough we have said that an employer has "the burden of showing that any given requirement must have a manifest relationship to the employment in question," *Griggs* [*v. Duke Power Co., supra* note 146, 401 at 432], such a formulation should not be interpreted as implying that the ultimate burden of proof can be shifted to the defendant. On the contrary, the ultimate burden of proving that discrimination against a protected group has been caused by a specific employment practice remains with the plaintiff at all times."[156]

In response to a prima facie case of adverse impact, the defendant "has the burden of producing evidence that its employment practices are based on legitimate business reasons."[157] Justice O'Connor observed that even when defending standardized or objective tests, a defendant need not introduce formal "validation studies" showing that particular criteria predict actual on-the-job performance. Rather, the "manifest relationship" test may be satisfied by proof that legitimate goals are "significantly served by" the practice at issue.[158] In the case of subjective or discretionary employment decisions, Justice O'Connor noted an employer may often find it easier than in the case of standardized tests to produce evidence of a "manifest relation-ship." For example, the Justice cited jobs involving managerial responsibili-ties as requiring personal qualities that have never been considered amenable to standardized testing. She further observed that in evaluating claims that discretionary practices are not sufficiently related to legitimate business goals, the courts must bear in mind they are generally less competent than employers to restructure business practices.[159]

Justice Blackmun, joined by Justices Brennan and Marshall, strongly disagreed with what he labeled as Justice O'Connor's mischaracterization of the nature of the burdens and evidentiary standards applicable to an adverse impact analysis of subjective employment practices. According to Justice Blackmun, Justice O'Connor's views on the allocation of burdens of proof and production that apply in an adverse impact case are "flatly contradicted" by Supreme Court precedent.[160] As read by Justice Blackmun, prior Supreme Court cases make clear that a plaintiff who successfully establishes a prima facie case of adverse impact shifts the burden of proof, not production, to establish that the employment practice in question is a business necessity.

Justice Blackmun further took issue with the plurality's "implication that the defendant may satisfy this burden simply by 'producing evidence that its employment practices are based on legitimate business reasons.' "[161] According to Justice Blackmun, it is "simply not enough" to offer some

---

[156] 47 FEP at 110.

[157] *Id.* When a defendant meets its burden of producing evidence of legitimate business reasons, the plaintiff must show, according to Justice O'Connor, that other tests or selection devices without a similarly undesirable racial effect would also serve the employer's legitimate interest. Factors such as the cost or other burdens of proposed alternative selection devices would be relevant at this stage of the proceeding, and these same factors would, Justice O'Connor stated, also be relevant in determining whether the challenged practice has operated as the functional equivalent of a pretext for discriminatory treatment.

[158] *Id.*

[159] 47 FEP at 111.

[160] *Id.*

[161] 47 FEP at 113.

legitimate, nondiscriminatory reason in an effort to legitimize a practice that has the effect of excluding a protected class at a significantly disproportionate rate. Justice Blackmun emphasized the word "necessity," noting that it went a long way toward establishing the limits of the defense—that is, to be justified as a business necessity, employment criteria must bear more than an indirect or minimal relationship to job performance; they must relate directly to a prospective employee's ability to perform the job effectively.[162]

Finally, Justice Blackmun expressed his concern over Justice O'Connor's projection that an employer may find it easier, in the case of subjective decisions, to satisfy the "manifest relationship" test. In Justice Blackmun's opinion, the less defined the particular criteria involved, or the system relied upon to assist these criteria, the more difficult it may be for a reviewing court to assess the connection between the selection process and job performance.[163]

Justice Stevens did not join either Justice O'Connor's or Justice Blackmun's opinions regarding burdens of proof and evidentiary standards in adverse impact cases. Justice Stevens declined to comment on these issues because, in his opinion, at this stage of the proceeding it is unwise to announce a "fresh" interpretation of prior cases applying disparate impact analysis to objective employment criteria.[164] Because of the many variables involved, Justice Stevens seems to favor a case-by-case approach, or more specifically resolution within a particular factual context, rather than a broad-based attempt to define the parameters of the extended adverse impact theory.

Whether Justice O'Connor's views are adopted as the majority view may well depend on Justice Kennedy. While his views as a Justice are unknown, he has authored a major Ninth Circuit decision holding that "[adverse] impact is confined to cases that challenge a specific, clearly delineated employment practice applied at a single point in the job selection process."[165]

Presumably, at least some of the questions raised by *Watson* will be addressed by the Supreme Court in *Wards Cove Packing Co.* v. *Atonio*.[166] The two questions on which the Supreme Court granted review in *Atonio* are:

1. Does statistical evidence that shows only a concentration of minorities in unskilled jobs fail, as a matter of law, to establish disparate impact in hiring for skilled jobs where the employer hires for skilled

---

[162]*Id.* Justice Blackmun reviewed various examples of how employers can link selection procedures and job performance:

> Courts have recognized that the results of studies, see *Davis v. City of Dallas,* 777 F.2d 205, 218–19 [, 39 FEP 744] (CA5 1985), *cert. denied,* 476 U.S. 1116, [40 FEP 1320] (1986) (nationwide studies and reports showing job-relatedness of college-degree requirement); the presentation of expert testimony, *id.* at 219–222, 224–225, (criminal justice scholars' testimony explaining job-relatedness of college-degree requirement and psychologist's testimony explaining job-relatedness of prohibition on recent marijuana use); and prior successful experience, *Zahorik v. Cornell University,* 729 F.2d 85, 96 [, 34 FEP 165] (CA2 1984) ("generations" of experience reflecting job-relatedness of decentralized decision-making structure based on peer judgments in academic setting), can all be used, under appropriate circumstances to establish business necessity.

47 FEP at 114 (footnote omitted).

[163]47 FEP at 115.

[164]47 FEP at 116.

[165]State, County & Mun. Employees v. Washington, 770 F.2d 1401, 1405, 38 FEP 1353 (9th Cir. 1985) (rejecting comparable worth liability under Title VII on disparate treatment and adverse impact analyses).

[166]810 F.2d 1477, 43 FEP 130 (9th Cir. 1987), *cert. granted* 487 U.S. _____ (1988).

jobs from outside its work force and does not promote from within or provide training for skilled jobs, and where minorities are not underrepresented in skilled jobs?

2. Did the Ninth Circuit err in allowing employees to challenge the cumulative effect of a wide range of alleged employment practices under the disparate impact model?

## A. The Order and Allocation of Proof

While most courts continue to use the *Griggs-Albemarle* tripartite order for allocation of proof in an adverse impact case,[167] several courts, following the lead of the Supreme Court in *Connecticut v. Teal,*[168] have recognized two different ways for the plaintiff to overcome the defendant's business necessity or job-relatedness defense (step three in the order of proof).[169] In *Teal,* the Court held that the plaintiff could prevail at the third step "if he shows that the employer was using the practice justified * * * at step 2 as a business necessity as a mere pretext for discrimination."[170] Courts have characterized the plaintiff's burden at the third stage as establishing either (1) that defendant could have achieved the same result as that obtained by the challenged practice by using a known available selection device or employment practice that produced a lesser adverse impact, or (2) that the employer's defense that the challenged practice was job-related or a "business necessity" is in reality a mere pretext for unlawful discrimination.[171]

## B. The Prima Facie Case

### 1. Plaintiff's Case in Chief

The adverse impact model requires that plaintiffs demonstrate the causal relationship between a specific, facially neutral employment practice[172] and the exclusion of disproportionate numbers of protected group

---

[167]Wright v. Olin Corp., 697 F.2d 1172, 1186, 30 FEP 889, 901 (4th Cir. 1982); Zuniga v. Kleberg County Hosp., Kingsville, Tex., 692 F.2d 986, 989, 30 FEP 650, 652 (5th Cir. 1982); Rowe v. Cleveland Pneumatic Co., Numerical Control, 690 F.2d 88, 93–94, 29 FEP 1682, 1686 (6th Cir. 1982); Shidaker v. Carlin, 782 F.2d 746, 39 FEP 1768 (7th Cir. 1986), *vacated sub nom.* Tisch v. Shidaker, 481 U.S. 1001, 43 FEP 640 (1987); Contreras v. City of Los Angeles, 656 F.2d 1267, 1271–72, 25 FEP 866, 868 (9th Cir. 1981), *cert. denied,* 455 U.S. 1021, 29 FEP 1559 (1982); Kilgo v. Bowman Transp., 789 F.2d 859, 40 FEP 1415 (11th Cir. 1986).

[168]457 U.S. 440, 29 FEP 1 (1982).

[169]Walker v. Jefferson County Home, 726 F.2d 1554, 34 FEP 465 (11th Cir. 1984); Moore v. Summa Corp., Hughes Helicopters Div., 708 F.2d 475, 481 n.4, 32 FEP 97, 101 (9th Cir. 1983); Pegues v. Mississippi State Employment Serv., 699 F.2d 760, 31 FEP 257 (5th Cir.), *cert. denied,* 464 U.S. 991, 33 FEP 440 (1983); Burney v. City of Pawtucket, 559 F. Supp. 1089, 34 FEP 1274, *vacated,* 563 F. Supp. 1088, 34 FEP 1290 (D.R.I. 1983), *aff'd and remanded,* 728 F.2d 547, 34 FEP 1295 (1st Cir. 1984).

[170]Connecticut v. Teal, 457 U.S. at 447.

[171]*Cf.* EEOC v. St. Louis-San Francisco Ry., 743 F.2d 739, 742, 35 FEP 1163, 1165 (10th Cir. 1984) (remanding where lower court "failed to consider whether EEOC had shown that alternative selection devices would have effectively served the company's legitimate interest"); Kilgo v. Bowman Transp., *supra* note 167 (plaintiff prevailed by showing that defendant's claim of business necessity was pretextual); Chambers v. Omaha Girls Club, 629 F. Supp. 925, 40 FEP 362 (D. Neb. 1986), *aff'd,* 834 F.2d 697, 45 FEP 698 (8th Cir. 1987) (plaintiff failed to establish that suggested less restrictive alternatives were feasible; defendant not required to present empirical data validating business necessity of challenged policy having adverse impact).

[172]*See* Section III, *supra,* "Proof in the Adverse Impact Case." *Craft v. Metromedia,* 766 F.2d 1205, 38 FEP 404 (8th Cir. 1985), *cert. denied,* 475 U.S. 1058, 40 FEP 272 (1986), illustrates how the approach of the parties can influence the court's selection of an analytical model. Craft sued on a disparate

members.[173] This demonstration need not be made with perfect accuracy,[174] only with reasonable precision by a preponderance of the evidence.[175] Courts continue to evaluate the nature and strength of plaintiff's case in chief along a conceptual continuum of statistical and anecdotal evidence.[176] The illustration of the asserted adverse impact by specific individual experiences is desirable.[177] Even where the statistical evidence appears at first significant, the failure to produce specific examples of impact may defeat the prima facie showing unless the statistical disparities are "gross."[178]

Regression analyses remain familiar and acceptable analytical tools.[179] The *Castaneda-Hazelwood*[180] threshold standard of two to three standard deviations from the mean generally serves as the starting point for an analysis of the likelihood that any observed disparity is attributable to chance or to unlawful discrimination.[181]

## 2. The Defendant's Rebuttal of the Plaintiff's Statistics

The plurality opinion in *Watson* contains a detailed discussion of statistical proof and the defendant's rebuttal of the plaintiff's statistics.[182] Signifi-

---

treatment (intentional discrimination) theory and argued there was direct evidence of unlawful intent. While the court used that analytical approach, it discounted Craft's evidence and her suggested inferences, holding (as if this were an adverse impact case) that defendant's "appearance standards were shaped only by neutral professional and technical considerations." *Id.*, 766 F.2d at 1211–16, 38 FEP at 409–12. *See also* Lewis v. Bloomsburg Mills, 773 F.2d 561, 571 n.16, 38 FEP 1692, 1700 (4th Cir. 1985) (impact or treatment analysis may result from strength of parties' proofs and responsive evidence).

[173]EEOC v. Rath Packing Co., 787 F.2d 318, 40 FEP 580 (8th Cir.), *cert. denied,* 479 U.S. 910, 41 FEP 1712 (1986) (no-spouse rule and subjective hiring practices); Lowe v. City of Monrovia, 775 F.2d 998, 39 FEP 350 (9th Cir. 1985) (lateral hiring and limited eligibility periods); Clady v. County of Los Angeles, 770 F.2d 1421, 38 FEP 1575 (9th Cir. 1985), *cert. denied,* 475 U.S. 1109, 40 FEP 792 (1986) (high school diploma and pre-employment testing); Andrews v. Bechtel Power Corp., 780 F.2d 124, 39 FEP 1033 (1st Cir. 1985), *cert. denied,* 476 U.S. 1172, 40 FEP 1873 (1986) (union hiring hall and pre-employment testing); Maddox v. Claytor, 764 F.2d 1539, 38 FEP 713 (11th Cir. 1985) (subjective promotion practices); *see* Lujan v. Franklin County Bd. of Educ., 766 F.2d 917, 38 FEP 9 (6th Cir. 1985) (school desegregation case analyzed as if it were an employment discrimination action; plaintiff failed to show that subjective criteria caused any adverse impact).

[174]Bazemore v. Friday, 478 U.S. 385, 41 FEP 92, 99 (1986) (a regression analysis that "includes less than 'all measurable variables' may serve to prove a plaintiff's case," since scientific accuracy is not required); *accord* Lewis v. Bloomsburg Mills, 773 F.2d 561, 576, 38 FEP 1692, 1703–4 (4th Cir. 1985) (no statistical analysis can prove "beyond question that race or gender discrimination has caused any demonstrated disparity"). In *Bloomsburg* the defendant improperly disposed of applicant flow data. Accordingly, plaintiff was permitted to use other data to show the available pool of new hire candidates.

[175]Bazemore v. Friday, *supra* note 174.

[176]As a practical matter plaintiffs will produce, and courts will require, some combination of statistical and anecdotal evidence. "Only in very limited instances may a court find discriminatory impact from non-statistical evidence." Shidaker v. Carlin, *supra* note 167, 782 F.2d at 750, 39 FEP at 1771, citing Dothard v. Rawlinson, 433 U.S. 321, 15 FEP 10 (1977).

[177]Kilgo v. Bowman Transp., *supra* note 167, at 872–73, 40 FEP at 1424–26 (proof of differential application of prior experience and intimidation of female applicants); Lowe v. City of Monrovia, *supra* note 173, at 1004 & n.3, 39 FEP at 354–55 (failure to make out prima facie case because insufficient statistical case not supplemented by other evidence); Smith v. Western Elec. Co., 770 F.2d 520, 527, 38 FEP 1605, 1611 (5th Cir. 1985) (inadequate statistical presentation augmented by proof of racial slurs, subjective assignments, and performance appraisals).

[178]Bunch v. Bullard, 795 F.2d 384, 395, 41 FEP 515, 524 (5th Cir. 1986) (simple statistics showing gross disparities, even on small sample, sufficient for prima facie case); Shidaker v. Carlin, 782 F.2d 746, 749–50, 39 FEP 1768, 1770–71 (7th Cir. 1986) ("gross disparity" in selection rates sufficient for prima facie showing); Lewis v. Bloomsburg Mills, 773 F.2d 561, 568–69, 38 FEP 1692, 1699 (4th Cir. 1985) (prima facie case made on statistics alone when probability was one in one thousand that disparity was chance occurrence).

[179]*See, e.g.,* Bazemore v. Friday, *supra* note 174.

[180]Castaneda v. Partida, 430 U.S. 482, 496 n.17 (1977); Hazelwood School Dist. v. United States, 433 U.S. 299, 308–9 n.14, 15 FEP 1, 5 (1977).

[181]*See* Section IV.F.1., *infra,* "Sufficiency of the Disparity," and the notes thereto.

[182]Watson v. Fort Worth Bank & Trust Co., 487 U.S. _____, 47 FEP 102 (1988).

cantly, the plurality (Justices O'Connor, Rehnquist, White, and Scalia), at least with respect to subjective criteria adverse impact cases, would require only that a defendant responding to a prima facie case produce evidence that its employment practices are based upon legitimate business reasons.[183] Justice Blackmun, joined by Justices Brennan and Marshall, disagreed sharply, asserting that if a plaintiff establishes a prima facie case of adverse impact, the defendant's burden is one of proof, not production.[184]

## C. Business Necessity and Job-Relatedness

Once a plaintiff establishes that a challenged employment practice has an adverse impact upon a protected class,[185] the burden shifts to the employer to justify that practice by showing a relationship to the employment in question.[186] However, unless the plaintiff proves that a challenged employment practice exerts a significantly disproportionate impact, no inquiry should be undertaken into its job-relatedness or validity.[187]

Employers cannot justify a discriminatory practice by inconsequential business considerations. Courts held before *Watson* that the employer must demonstrate that the practice has a "manifest relationship" to the employment in question,[188] that there is a genuine need to maintain the practice,[189] that the practice contributes to the safe or efficient operation of the busi-

---

[183]47 FEP at 110.

[184]47 FEP at 113. *Cf.* Price Waterhouse v. Hopkins, *supra* note 7.

[185]Bushey v. New York State Civil Serv. Comm'n, 733 F.2d 220, 34 FEP 1065 (2d Cir. 1984), *cert. denied,* 469 U.S. 1117, 36 FEP 1166 (1985) (job-related explanations which may rebut prima facie adverse impact case do not demonstrate that prima facie case has not been established in first instance).

[186]Hawkins v. Bounds, 752 F.2d 500, 502, 36 FEP 1285, 1288 (10th Cir. 1985); Levin v. Delta Air Lines, 730 F.2d 994, 34 FEP 1192 (5th Cir. 1984); Walker v. Jefferson County Home, 726 F.2d 1554, 34 FEP 465 (11th Cir. 1984); Massarsky v. General Motors Corp., 706 F.2d 111, 31 FEP 832 (3d Cir.), *cert. denied,* 464 U.S. 937, 33 FEP 48 (1983); Jones v. International Paper Co., 720 F.2d 496, 33 FEP 430 (8th Cir. 1983); Eastland v. Tennessee Valley Auth., 704 F.2d 613, 31 FEP 1578, *modified and reh'g denied,* 714 F.2d 1066, 34 FEP 283 (11th Cir. 1983), *cert. denied,* 465 U.S. 1066, 34 FEP 415 (1984); Hawkins v. Anheuser-Busch, 697 F.2d 810, 30 FEP 1170 (8th Cir. 1983); Jackson v. Seaboard Coast Line R.R., 678 F.2d 992, 1016, 29 FEP 442, 462–63 (11th Cir. 1982) (citing Robinson v. Lorillard Corp., 444 F.2d 791, 798, 3 FEP 653, 657–58 (4th Cir.), *cert. dismissed,* 404 U.S. 1006 (1971)); Zuniga v. Kleberg County Hosp., Kingsville, Tex., 692 F.2d 986, 30 FEP 650 (5th Cir. 1982); Wright v. Olin Corp., 697 F.2d 1172, 30 FEP 889 (4th Cir. 1982); Bonilla v. Oakland Scavenger Co., 697 F.2d 1297, 31 FEP 50 (9th Cir. 1982), *cert. denied,* 467 U.S. 1251, 34 FEP 1800 (1984) (preferences in wages, hours, and assignments to members of families of founders has adverse impact on blacks and Spanish-surnamed persons and not justified); *see also* Segar v. Smith, 738 F.2d 1249, 1271, 35 FEP 31, 45 (D.C. Cir. 1984), *cert. denied,* 471 U.S. 1115, 37 FEP 1312 (1985) (employer will not be forced to justify all of its employment practices—only job-relatedness of practice or practices identified as cause of the disparity); Bushey v. New York Civil Serv. Comm'n, *supra* note 185 (job-relatedness is never presumed); Kirkland v. New York State Dep't of Correctional Servs., 531 F.2d 5, 11 FEP 1253 (2d Cir. 1975) (judicial determination that policy or practice creating adverse impact is not job-related not required as basis for settlement).

[187]Pegues v. Mississippi State Employment Serv., 699 F.2d 760, 31 FEP 257 (5th Cir.), *cert. denied,* 464 U.S. 991, 33 FEP 440 (1983).

[188]EEOC v. St. Louis San Francisco Ry., 743 F.2d 739, 742, 35 FEP 1163, 1164 (10th Cir. 1984) (railroad's 5'7" height requirement has no manifest relation to position of switchman-brakeman); Walker v. Jefferson County Home, *supra* note 186 (prior supervisory experience did not have manifest relationship to supervisory position).

[189]EEOC v. Rath Packing Co., 787 F.2d 318, 40 FEP 580 (8th Cir.), *cert. denied,* 479 U.S. 910, 41 FEP 1712 (1986) (where employer was unable to identify criteria and qualifications that were considered in its hiring decisions employer could not establish that such criteria and qualifications were necessary to safety and efficiency of its operations); Hayes v. Shelby Memorial Hosp., 726 F.2d 1543, 34 FEP 444 (11th Cir. 1984) (potential liability is too contingent and too broad a factor to amount to business necessity; business necessity defense in fetal protection case is justified by genuine desire to promote health

ness,[190] or that the practice promotes more compelling social objectives.[191] When a job requires a small amount of skill and training, the employer has a "heavy burden" to demonstrate job-relatedness of the employment criteria which cause adverse impact.[192]

However, as described in Section III, *supra,* "Proof in the Adverse Impact Case," the business necessity test may now be less stringent than some courts previously indicated. According to the plurality in *Watson,* [193] a defendant responding to a prima facie case of adverse impact "has the burden of producing evidence that its employment practices are based on legitimate business reasons," and of proving that legitimate goals are "significantly served by" the practice at issue.

The courts continue to give general definitions of the business necessity defense and the job-relatedness standard in the context of specific fact situations. The scope of these decisions includes definitions of business necessity and/or job-relatedness in the context of subjective hiring and/or promotion criteria,[194] tenure decisions,[195] salary determin-

---

of employee offspring, not because of potential litigation costs); Easley v. Anheuser-Busch, 572 F. Supp. 402, 34 FEP 380 (E.D. Mo. 1983), *aff'd in relevant part,* 758 F.2d 251, 37 FEP 549 (8th Cir. 1985) (employer failed to demonstrate compelling need for employment test which had material adverse impact on black applicants).

[190]Liberles v. County of Cook, 709 F.2d 1122, 31 FEP 1537 (7th Cir. 1983); *see* Aguilera v. Cook County Police & Corrections Merit Bd., 760 F.2d 844, 846–47, 37 FEP 1140, 1142 (7th Cir.), *cert. denied,* 474 U.S. 907 (1985) (citing *Caviale v. Wisconsin Dep't of Health & Social Servs.,* 744 F.2d 1289, 1294, 35 FEP 1642, 1646–47 (7th Cir. 1984), and holding that "essential to safe and efficient" conduct of employer's business is a tolerant, rather than stringent standard interpreted by the Seventh Circuit to require "a reasonably tight fit between the challenged criterion and the actual demands of the job"); Levin v. Delta Air Lines, *supra* note 186 (policy of removing flight attendants from flight duty as soon as pregnancy discovered was justified by airline's commitment to safety); Hayes v. Shelby Memorial Hosp., *supra* note 189 (hospital's termination of pregnant x-ray technician without seriously considering rearranging her duties to minimize radiation exposure found discriminatory); Jackson v. Seaboard Coast Line R.R., *supra* note 186 (requirement that carmen helpers serve 8,320 hours before promotion not justified as necessary for safe and efficient operation).

[191]*See* Ellison v. C.P.C. Int'l, Best Foods Div., 598 F. Supp. 159, 170, 36 FEP 643, 648 (E.D. Ark. 1984) ("[w]ork teams created under employer's self-regulated work force system, which may result in some degree of disparate impact against minorities, will not be subjected to disparate impact analysis" because of "wider social objectives" of such employee-democracy systems).

[192]Walker v. Jefferson County Home, *supra* note 186 (defendant failed to meet rigorous standard of proving that requirement of supervisory experience for housekeeping department supervisor's job was job-related and business necessity).

[193]Watson v. Fort Worth Bank & Trust Co., 487 U.S. _____, 47 FEP 102, 110–11 (1988); *see also* *supra* note 16 and 157 and accompanying text.

[194]Hawkins v. Bounds, *supra* note 186 (practice of detailing current employees into temporarily vacant positions and then giving great weight to detailing experience for vacancies violated Title VII where adverse impact resulted) (citing Williams v. Colorado Springs School Dist. No. 11, 641 F.2d 835, 840–41, 25 FEP 256, 260 (10th Cir. 1981)); Caviale v. Wisconsin Dep't of Health & Social Servs., 744 F.2d 1289, 1294, 35 FEP 1642, 1647 (7th Cir. 1984) (Wisconsin's policy of limiting consideration of candidates to those who were in Career Executive Program, which resulted in adverse impact on women, was not found to be job-related); *see* Harrell v. Northern Elec. Co., 672 F.2d 444, 28 FEP 911, *modified,* 679 F.2d 31, 29 FEP 913 (5th Cir.), *cert. denied,* 459 U.S. 1037, 30 FEP 440 (1982) (rejecting employer's business justification that its all-white personnel could properly measure qualifications of black clerical applicants on basis of subjective criteria); *see also* Rowe v. Cleveland Pneumatic Co., Numerical Control, 690 F.2d 88, 29 FEP 1682 (6th Cir. 1982). The *Rowe* court acknowledged the heavy burden employers bear when subjective evaluations are the basis for rehire decisions; however, in this case the plaintiffs failed to establish a prima facie case of adverse impact discrimination, and therefore the court was not required to rule on whether the employer met its burden. The court further noted that if the plaintiff had succeeded in establishing a prima facie case of adverse impact, the record in the case would not have supported any finding that defendant's unique selection process with respect to former employees was job-related.

[195]Zahorik v. Cornell Univ., 729 F.2d 85, 34 FEP 165 (2d Cir. 1984) (university's selection criteria, which included consideration of accomplishments and skills in scholarship, based upon peer judgment, is job-related); Carpenter v. University of Wis. Sys. Bd. of Regents, 728 F.2d 911, 34 FEP 248 (7th Cir.

ations,[196] the employer's interest in providing positive role models,[197] maternity leave policies,[198] and fetal protection policies which may require dismissal or disability leave, or restrict the job assignments of pregnant employees.[199] However, cases continue to present courts with basic fact situations requiring the evaluation of college degree requirements,[200] assessment center ratings,[201] and prior related experience[202] as job-related criteria. Thus, both objective and subjective hiring and/or promotion criteria persist as subjects which courts will closely scrutinize if the employer bases its defense on business necessity.

## D. Suitable Alternatives With a Lesser Adverse Impact

Although most adverse impact cases are resolved at the first (prima facie case) or second (business necessity or job-relatedness) levels of proof, some cases do reach the third stage, that is, whether there are known available and suitable alternatives to the employer's business practice which would have a lesser adverse impact.[203] In such a case, the plaintiff has the burden to show that another available employment procedure, which does not produce a similar discriminatory impact, would satisfy the employer's legitimate needs.[204]

---

1984) (minimal level of competence, demonstration of reasonable likelihood of future growth, performance in teaching, research, and scholarly writing, and service to university and community are job-related tenure criteria).

[196]*See* Spaulding v. University of Wash., 740 F.2d 686, 708, 35 FEP 217, 232–33 (9th Cir.), *cert. denied,* 469 U.S. 1036, 36 FEP 464 (1984) (practice of employers relying on market to set salaries for different jobs is job-related).

[197]Chambers v. Omaha Girls Club, 629 F. Supp. 925, 40 FEP 362 (D. Neb. 1986), *aff'd,* 834 F.2d 697, 45 FEP 698 (8th Cir. 1987) (employer permitted to discharge pregnant, unmarried employee because employee was negative role model; court found a manifest relationship between employer's fundamental purpose to serve young girls and provide them with exposure to positive options in life and employer's pregnancy policy regarding unmarried females).

[198]EEOC v. Western Elec. Co., 28 FEP 1122 (M.D.N.C. 1982) (rejecting business necessity defense where employer guarantees reinstatement to employees who are on non-pregnancy-related disability leave but not to employees on maternity leave); Levin v. Delta Air Lines, 730 F.2d 994, 34 FEP 1192 (5th Cir. 1984) (upholding maternity disability leave policy for flight attendants as valid business necessity); Marafino v. St. Louis County Circuit Court, 537 F. Supp. 206, 29 FEP 621 (E.D. Mo. 1982), *aff'd,* 707 F.2d 1005, 31 FEP 1536 (8th Cir. 1983) (permitting defendant to deny plaintiff employment because her pregnancy and impending maternity leave would interfere with vital training period).

[199]Hayes v. Shelby Memorial Hosp., *supra* note 189, at 1554, 34 FEP at 453 (fetal protection policy that only applies to members of one sex violates Title VII unless employer shows (1) substantial risk of harm exists, (2) risk is borne only by members of one sex, and (3) employee fails to show that there are acceptable alternative policies that would have lesser impact on affected sex); Wright v. Olin Corp., *supra* note 186; *see also* Levin v. Delta Air Lines, *supra* note 198 (upholding forced maternity leave policy).

[200]Merwine v. State Inst. of Higher Learning Bd. of Trustees, 754 F.2d 631, 37 FEP 340 (5th Cir.), *cert. denied,* 474 U.S. 823, 38 FEP 1727 (1985) (employer's requirement that applicants for faculty librarian post hold master's degree had "manifest" relationship to the position and was justified as "business necessity"); Hawkins v. Anheuser-Busch, 697 F.2d 810, 30 FEP 1170 (8th Cir. 1983).

[201]Wilson v. Michigan Bell Tel. Co., 550 F. Supp. 1296, 30 FEP 427 (E.D. Mich. 1982).

[202]Lewis v. Bloomsburg Mills, 30 FEP 1715 (D.S.C. 1982), *rev'd in part, vacated in part and remanded,* 773 F.2d 561, 38 FEP 1692 (4th Cir. 1985).

[203]Hayes v. Shelby Memorial Hosp., 726 F.2d 1543, 34 FEP 444 (11th Cir. 1984) (hospital terminated x-ray technician upon learning of her pregnancy; assuming hospital's policy justified by business necessity, employee successfully showed that hospital failed to explore seriously other duties within hospital that employee could perform); *see also* Walker v. Jefferson County Home, 726 F.2d 1554, 34 FEP 465 (11th Cir. 1984) (if employer fails to show job-relatedness, court need not consider suitable alternatives).

[204]Page v. U.S. Indus., 726 F.2d 1038, 34 FEP 430 (5th Cir. 1984); Hawkins v. Anheuser-Busch, *supra* note 200; Hayes v. Shelby Memorial Hosp., *supra* note 203; Chambers v. Omaha Girls Club, *supra* note 197 (plaintiff's argument that there were less restrictive alternatives to employer's prohibition against single women being pregnant, such as transfers to no-contact positions or leaves of absence, was rejected); *see also* Zuniga v. Kleberg County Hosp., Kingsville, Tex., 692 F.2d 986, 992, 30 FEP 650, 654 (5th Cir.

## IV. USE OF STATISTICS

### A. Introduction

Although a plaintiff's prima facie case may under proper circumstances be established by statistics alone, statistical evidence, at least to the same extent as any other type of circumstantial evidence, is not to be accepted uncritically.[205] Courts continue to caution against the use of data which may have been "segmented and particularized and fashioned to obtain a desired result."[206]

In contrast, however, scientific certainty is not required of a Title VII plaintiff.[207] A regression analysis including less than all measurable variables may, depending upon the factual context of the case, satisfy plaintiff's initial burden. "Normally, failure to include variables will affect the analysis' probativeness, not its admissibility."[208]

### B. Types of Statistical Proof

#### 1. Pass/Fail Comparisons

Pass/fail comparisons of hiring rates and applicant flow are still useful statistical tools,[209] as long as the application process itself is free from discriminatory impact.[210]

---

1982). In *Zuniga* the plaintiff was forced to resign from her job in accordance with an unwritten termination policy for pregnant x-ray technicians. Although the hospital had a discretionary leave of absence policy applicable to all other employees which guaranteed them their jobs upon return to work, plaintiff was told her reemployment could not be guaranteed. Holding that the hospital's facially neutral rule had a discriminatory impact upon women, the court rejected out of hand the hospital's business necessity defense, namely, that firing her was necessary to protect the hospital from future tort liability for radiation injury to the fetus. The court found that the plaintiff had sustained her burden of establishing that the hospital's proffered defense was a pretext for discrimination because the employer had failed to utilize "an available, alternative, less discriminatory means of achieving its business purpose," such as affording the plaintiff a leave of absence during her pregnancy.

[205]EEOC v. Federal Reserve Bank of Richmond, 698 F.2d 633, 646–47, 30 FEP 1137, 1146 (4th Cir. 1983), *rev'd on other grounds sub nom.* Cooper v. Federal Reserve Bank of Richmond, 467 U.S. 867, 35 FEP 1 (1984). After casting a jaundiced eye upon the use of statistics generally, the court in *EEOC v. Federal Reserve Bank of Richmond* stated that "statistical evidence is circumstantial in character and its acceptability depends on the magnitude of the disparity it reflects, the relevance of its supporting data, and other circumstances in the case supportive of or in rebuttal of a hypothesis of discrimination. And, in reviewing statistical evidence and its supporting data, the Court must give consideration and evaluate fairly such conflicting opinions and hypotheses as may have been presented, tempering its conclusion with * * * 'a pinch of common sense.' " 698 F.2d at 646–47, 30 FEP at 1146 (quoting Otero v. Mesa County Valley School Dist. No. 51, 470 F. Supp. 326, 335, 19 FEP 1015 (D. Colo. 1979)).

[206]EEOC v. Western Elec. Co., 713 F.2d 1011, 1019, 32 FEP 708, 714 (4th Cir. 1983) (quoting *EEOC v. Datapoint Corp.*, 570 F.2d 1264, 1269, 17 FEP 281, 285 (5th Cir. 1978)).

[207]Bazemore v. Friday, 478 U.S. 385, 41 FEP 92, 99 (1986).

[208]*Id.*

[209]Falcon v. General Tel. Co. of the Sw., 611 F. Supp. 707, 39 FEP 1116 (N.D. Tex. 1985), *aff'd*, 815 F.2d 317, 43 FEP 1040 (5th Cir. 1987) (defendant successfully rebutted plaintiff's charge of race discrimination with applicant flow data showing it hired greater percentage of Mexican-American applicants than it did white applicants).

[210]EEOC v. Rath Packing Co., 787 F.2d 318, 40 FEP 580 (8th Cir.), *cert. denied*, 479 U.S. 910, 41 FEP 1712 (1986) (applicant flow data are significant indicator of employer's discriminatory practices only when those same discriminatory practices do not deter people from applying); Kilgo v. Bowman Transp., 789 F.2d 859, 40 FEP 1415 (11th Cir. 1986) (use of applicant flow data in sex discrimination case is inappropriate where company posted experience requirement which was likely to deter women from applying).

## 2. Population/Work Force Comparisons

When analyzing population/work force comparisons, courts are attuned to the importance of defining the appropriate labor force in terms of qualified individuals[211] who live in an area, either actual or representative, which is geographically accessible to the workplace.[212]

## 3. The Use of Regression Analysis

In *Bazemore v. Friday,*[213] the Supreme Court approved the use of multiple regression analysis in proving salary discrimination. In addition, the Court held that the regression analysis need not include all measurable variables thought to have an effect on salary level to be admissible. According to the Court, the omission of variables from a regression analysis affects the analysis' probativeness, not its admissibility. Whether a regression analysis will carry the plaintiff's ultimate burden of proof will depend on the factual context of each case in light of all the evidence presented by the parties.[214]

Multiple regression analysis is now widely used to establish or rebut a prima facie case of discrimination in hiring, compensation, promotion, and other employment decisions.[215] The courts generally require that a foundation for using the multiple regression analysis be established.[216] The cases demonstrate a continuing effort to scrutinize closely the factors selected or

---

[211]Gomez v. City of S. Bend, 605 F. Supp. 1173, 39 FEP 1625 (N.D. Ind. 1985) (qualifications of work force are essential factors when upper level jobs are at issue); Kraszewski v. State Farm Gen. Ins. Co., 38 FEP 197 (N.D. Cal. 1985) (relevant labor market to consider for insurance company trainees does not need to be controlled for personal characteristics, since there are none which would screen out more women than men and no special skills are required to become insurance company trainee); Minority Police Officers Ass'n of S. Bend v. City of S. Bend, Ind., 617 F. Supp. 1330, 42 FEP 503 (N.D. Ind. 1985), *aff'd,* 801 F.2d 964, 42 FEP 525 (7th Cir. 1986) (when determining correct comparison pool, only minimum objective qualifications, not subjective qualifications, are relevant); EEOC v. Rath Packing Co., *supra* note 210 (burden is on defendant to establish that positions in question require special qualifications which are not possessed or readily acquired by the general population).

[212]Castaneda v. Pickard, 781 F.2d 456, 40 FEP 154 (5th Cir. 1986) (inappropriate to define relevant labor market for district school teachers as "the nation" where majority of new teachers are recruited from five universities); Shidaker v. Carlin, 782 F.2d 746, 39 FEP 1768 (7th Cir. 1986), *vacated sub nom.* Tisch v. Shidaker, 481 U.S. 1001, 43 FEP 640 (1987) (for company which promotes from within, relevant labor pool for upper level positions is the group of employees from which promotees will be drawn; thus, large disparity between composition of upper and lower positions is sufficient to make prima facie case of disparate impact); EEOC v. Chicago Miniature Lamp Works, 622 F. Supp. 1281, 39 FEP 297 (N.D. Ill. 1985) (to determine whether relevant labor market for statistical analysis is Standard Metropolitan Statistical Area (SMSA) or smaller part thereof, factors to consider include location of employer within SMSA, accessibility of employer, commuting patterns, and sometimes employer's applicant flow).

[213]478 U.S. 385, 41 FEP 92 (1986).

[214]*Id. See also* Chapter 1, *supra* notes 23–24 and text.

[215]*E.g.,* EEOC v. Sears, Roebuck & Co., 628 F. Supp. 1264, 39 FEP 1672 (N.D. Ill. 1986), *aff'd,* 839 F.2d 302, 45 FEP 1257 (7th Cir. 1988) (defendant's multiple regression analysis accepted over that of plaintiff based on superior approach to selection of variables); Griffin v. Regency Univs. Bd. of Regents, 795 F.2d 1281, 41 FEP 228 (7th Cir. 1986) (plaintiff's multiple regression analysis rejected as insufficiently reliable to demonstrate sex discrimination in faculty promotions and salary); EEOC v. McCarthy, 768 F.2d 1, 38 FEP 536 (1st Cir. 1985) (plaintiff's multiple regression analysis accepted to demonstrate historical treatment of salaries as well as to determine trend of increasing disparity with years of employment despite fact that equation included personnel hired prior to statute of limitations date provided in Equal Pay Act for which recovery could be made).

[216]*E.g.,* Maddox v. Claytor, 764 F.2d 1539, 38 FEP 713 (11th Cir. 1985) (defendant's selection of variables including age, educational level, length of time on job, and time since last promotion found to be relevant on issue of promotion discrimination).

omitted in the regression analysis,[217] as well as the use of proxies for factors omitted.[218]

### 4. Other Kinds of Statistical Comparisons

Other statistics found probative include an employer's overall hiring practices, with respect to the filling of upper-level positions.[219] Cohort analyses have been used in promotion and pay cases, but these have been found by some courts to be less probative than other forms of analysis.[220]

## C. Sources of Statistics

### 1. Actual Applicant Flow Data

Actual applicant flow data continue to be considered reliable and are often used to measure adverse impact with respect to pass/fail statistical comparisons.[221] In a case where statistical figures indicated a heavy minority applicant flow, the Fifth Circuit noted the superiority of actual applicant flow statistics over census or other general labor market statistics.[222] Applicant flow statistics have also been relied on in fashioning remedies for proven discrimination (*e.g.,* to determine the number of positions which shall be offered to the protected group).[223] However, courts remain quick to discredit the validity of actual applicant flow data where the statistics are flawed by

---

[217]*E.g.,* Rossini v. Ogilvy & Mather, 615 F. Supp. 1520, 1534, 42 FEP 1595 (S.D.N.Y. 1985), *rev'd on other grounds,* 798 F.2d 590, 42 FEP 1615 (2d Cir. 1986) (defendant's regression analysis dealing with salary differences found to be more convincing than regression analysis done by plaintiff since it did not use independent variable of former salary, considering that prior salary could reflect sex-biased employment practices by some other employer).

[218]*Compare* Trout v. Lehman, 702 F.2d 1094, 31 FEP 286 (D.C. Cir. 1983), *vacated on other grounds,* 465 U.S. 1056, 34 FEP 76 (1984) (proxy accepted) *and* Melani v. Board of Higher Educ. of New York City, 561 F. Supp. 769, 31 FEP 648 (S.D.N.Y. 1983) (same) *with* Sobel v. Yeshiva Univ., 566 F. Supp. 1166, 32 FEP 154 (S.D.N.Y. 1983) (proxies rejected).

[219]Anderson v. City of Albuquerque, 690 F.2d 796, 29 FEP 1689 (10th Cir. 1982) (due to subjective evaluations).

[220]Trout v. Lehman, *supra* note 218 (rejecting employer's cohort analysis).

[221]Moore v. Summa Corp., Hughes Helicopter Div., 708 F.2d 475, 483, 32 FEP 97, 102 (9th Cir. 1983) ("disparate impact should always be measured against the actual pool of applicants or eligible employees unless there is a characteristic of the challenged selection device that makes use of the actual applicant pool of applicants or eligible employees inappropriate"); Markey v. Tenneco Oil Co., 707 F.2d 172, 174–75, 32 FEP 148, 149 (5th Cir. 1983) (applicant flow to be used as basis in determining labor market unless skewed by discriminatory recruiting practices); Payne v. Travenol Laboratories, 673 F.2d 798, 823–24, 28 FEP 1212, 1232, *reh'g denied,* 683 F.2d 417 (5th Cir.), *cert. denied,* 459 U.S. 1038, 30 FEP 440 (1982) (applicant flow superior to census or general labor market statistics); Rowe v. Cleveland Pneumatic Co., Numerical Control, 690 F.2d 88, 93, 29 FEP 1682, 1686–87 (6th Cir. 1982) (court stated applicant flow was an appropriate indication by which to judge composition of employer's work force); Green v. United States Steel Corp., 570 F. Supp. 254, 275, 46 FEP 670 (E.D. Pa. 1983), *aff'd in part, vacated and rev'd in part, and remanded sub nom.* Green v. USX Corp., 843 F.2d 1511, 46 FEP 720 (3d Cir. 1988) (applicant flow data are preferred over labor market data because they compare those who actually offered themselves for hire); Easley v. Anheuser-Busch, 572 F. Supp. 402, 34 FEP 380 (E.D. Mo. 1983), *aff'd in part and rev'd in part on other grounds,* 758 F.2d 251, 37 FEP 549 (8th Cir. 1985); *see also* Williams v. City of New Orleans, 729 F.2d 1554, 1562, 34 FEP 1009, 1015–16 (5th Cir. 1984) (en banc), *appeal dismissed,* 763 F.2d 667 (5th Cir. 1985).

[222]Payne v. Travenol Laboratories, *supra* note 221, (court refused to consider fact that proportion of minorities in employer's work force equaled or exceeded proportion of minorities in qualified population).

[223]Berkman v. City of New York (I), 705 F.2d 584, 595, 31 FEP 767 (2d Cir. 1983) (court relied on applicant flow data to determine number of firefighter positions which would be offered to qualified women applicants when it determined that available work force statistics were not accurate).

discriminatory, inadequate, or excessive recruiting practices,[224] or unreliable applicant records.[225] Likewise, a general perception that an employer's hiring practices are discriminatory may sufficiently skew the applicant data to serve as the basis for the rejection of the use of anemic applicant flow data comparisons.[226] The Ninth Circuit has stated that proof of the qualifications of members of the applicant pool may be necessary if the court is to draw an inference of discrimination from such statistics.[227]

## 2. Potential Applicant Flow Data

Potential applicant flow data continue to be used in pass/fail comparisons where actual applicant flow data are unavailable,[228] incomplete,[229] or contain flaws due to discriminatory recruiting practices.[230]

## 3. General Population Data

Most courts limit the use of general population data to situations where applicant flow or labor pool data are either unavailable[231] or flawed[232] and where individual job candidates would not be expected to be different from the general populace.[233] Comparisons to the general labor force are of little

---

[224]Moore v. Summa Corp., Hughes Helicopter Div., *supra* note 221; Green v. United States Steel Corp., *supra* note 221; United States v. North Carolina, 512 F. Supp. 968, 970, 28 FEP 566, 567 (E.D.N.C. 1981), *aff'd,* 679 F.2d 890, 30 FEP 824 (4th Cir. 1982), *cert. denied,* 459 U.S. 1103, 30 FEP 1048 (1983); Carroll v. Sears, Roebuck & Co., 514 F. Supp. 788, 30 FEP 1446 (W.D. La. 1981), *aff'd in part and rev'd in part on other grounds,* 708 F.2d 183, 32 FEP 286 (5th Cir. 1983) (employer's applicant flow affected by proximity of personnel office to state employment office and by company's substantial recruitment efforts).

[225]Wheeler v. City of Columbus, Miss., 686 F.2d 1144, 1152, 29 FEP 1699, 1705 (5th Cir. 1982) (citing the Second Edition).

[226]EEOC v. Rath Packing Co., 787 F.2d 318, 40 FEP 580 (8th Cir.), *cert. denied,* 479 U.S. 910, 41 FEP 1712 (1986) (applicant flow rejected where employer was one of few large employers in small community, and company's employment record was known to community).

[227]Domingo v. New England Fish Co., 727 F.2d 1429, 1436, 34 FEP 584, 591, *modified,* 742 F.2d 520, 37 FEP 1303 (9th Cir. 1984); *see also* Pegues v. Mississippi State Employment Serv., 699 F.2d 760, 766–68, 31 FEP 257, 261–63 (5th Cir.), *cert. denied,* 464 U.S. 991, 33 FEP 440 (1983). *But see* Harris v. Marsh, 100 F.R.D. 315, 322, 45 FEP 1037 (E.D.N.C. 1983) (applicant flow may support an inference if sample and disparity are significant).

[228]Lewis v. Bloomsburg Mills, 773 F.2d 561, 568, 38 FEP 1692, 1698 (4th Cir. 1985) (employer improperly disposed of applications for relevant period, therefore, census data were used to determine available pool of minority applicants).

[229]Kraszewski v. State Farm Gen. Ins. Co., 38 FEP 197, 259 (N.D. Cal. 1985) ("defendants' test-taker flow data was not complete in that records for all applicants were not maintained, particularly oral applications").

[230]EEOC v. Chicago Miniature Lamp Works, 622 F. Supp. 1281, 1289, 39 FEP 297, 302 (N.D. Ill. 1985); Kraszewski v. State Farm Gen. Ins. Co., 38 FEP 197, 259–60 (N.D. Cal. 1985).

[231]Green v. United States Steel Corp., *supra* note 221.

[232]Williams v. City of New Orleans, 729 F.2d 1554, 34 FEP 1009 (5th Cir. 1984) (en banc), *appeal dismissed,* 763 F.2d 667 (5th Cir. 1985) (comparison to general population statistics used for purpose of evaluating injunctive relief in consent decree where applicant flow is distorted by heavy recruiting of black applicants); Kilgo v. Bowman Transp., 570 F. Supp. 1509, 31 FEP 1451 (N.D. Ga. 1983) (where applicant flow data are distorted by recruiting and hiring practices, general population statistics used for truck driver position).

[233]Moore v. Summa Corp., Hughes Helicopter Div., 708 F.2d 475, 482, 492, 32 FEP 97, 102 (9th Cir. 1983) ("general population statistics are useful as a proxy for a pool of potential applicants, if ever, only where the challenged employer practice screens applicants for entry level jobs requiring little or no specialized skills"); Costa v. Markey, 706 F.2d 1, 31 FEP 1324 (1st Cir.), *cert. denied,* 464 U.S. 1017, 33 FEP 656 (1983) (general population statistics utilized to measure adverse impact of height and weight requirement on female applicants); O'Brien v. Sky Chefs, 670 F.2d 864, 867, 28 FEP 661, 663–64, *amended,* 28 FEP 1690 (9th Cir. 1982) (comparison with general labor pool is more probative when position involves skills which may be learned easily by most members of labor pool); Brown v. Frank Ix & Sons, 530 F. Supp. 1230, 28 FEP 682, 687 (W.D. Va. 1982); Walker v. North Ala. Elec. Coop., 29 FEP 1470 (N.D. Ala. 1982) (court assumed general population statistics relevant where job involved skills possessed by general population).

or no probative value where the job in question requires specific skills or abilities[234] or the policy is to fill a vacancy from within an employer's own work force.[235] However, one court has taken the position that where an employer has not established that the job in question requires any special qualifications not possessed or readily acquirable by the general population, general population statistics were an appropriate measure of the extent of the employer's discrimination.[236]

### 4. Qualified Labor Market Data

In those cases in which the general labor force does not reflect the available qualified labor pool, the courts continue to require that the labor market be refined to include only those qualified for the position.[237] To be included in the available labor market pool, it is not necessary that an individual be qualified in every way.[238] However, to account for qualifications, courts increasingly are resorting to multiple regression analyses and other statistical techniques.[239] Furthermore, many courts have recognized the need for flexibility where data regarding the qualified labor market are inaccessible.[240]

### 5. Employer's Work Force Data

In promotion cases, when the relevant labor market is the employer's work force, the statistics continue to be refined so as to include only those

---

[234]Casillas v. United States Navy, 735 F.2d 338, 345–46, 34 FEP 1493, 1497 (9th Cir. 1984); EEOC v. Western Elec. Co., 713 F.2d 1011, 1018, 32 FEP 708, 714 (4th Cir. 1983); Moore v. Summa Corp., Hughes Helicopter Div., *supra* note 233; O'Neal v. Riceland Foods, 684 F.2d 577, 580, 29 FEP 956, 958 (8th Cir. 1982) (general population statistics not indicative where clerical duties are involved); Paxton v. Union Nat'l Bank, 688 F.2d 552, 564, 29 FEP 1233, 1243–44 (8th Cir. 1982), *cert. denied,* 460 U.S. 1083, 31 FEP 824 (1983) (general population figures irrelevant in promotion cases where majority of above entry-level positions are filled from within employer's ranks).

[235]Gilbert v. City of Little Rock, 722 F.2d 1390, 1396, 33 FEP 557, 562 (8th Cir. 1983), *cert. denied,* 466 U.S. 972, 34 FEP 1312 (1984); Paxton v. Union Nat'l Bank, *supra* note 234.

[236]EEOC v. Rath Packing Co., *supra* note 226. The use of population rather than labor force data is questionable and will inappropriately inflate the data for any protected group with an above-average birth rate.

[237]Lamphere v. Brown Univ., 685 F.2d 743, 750, 29 FEP 701, 706 (1st Cir. 1982) (per curiam); Pegues v. Mississippi State Employment Serv., 699 F.2d 760, 793, 31 FEP 257, 267 (5th Cir.), *cert. denied,* 464 U.S. 991, 33 FEP 440 (1983) (comparison to general population valueless where qualifications must be considered because position requires examination of "work preferences, experience, education, and the state of the job market"); Coble v. Hot Springs School Dist. No. 6, 682 F.2d 721, 733, 29 FEP 201, 219 (8th Cir. 1982) (failure of statistics with respect to pay and promotion to consider education and experience factors undermines their probative value); Valentino v. United States Postal Serv., 674 F.2d 56, 67–69, 28 FEP 593, 601–2 (D.C. Cir. 1982) (when job qualifications involved are ones relatively few possess or can acquire, statistical data not focusing on those qualifications are of little value); EEOC v. H.S. Camp & Sons, 542 F. Supp. 411, 442–43, 33 FEP 330, 352–53 (M.D. Fla. 1982); Ladele v. Consolidated Rail Corp., 95 F.R.D. 198, 29 FEP 1547, 1552 (E.D. Pa. 1982).

[238]De Medina v. Reinhardt, 686 F.2d 997, 1010, 29 FEP 1084, 1091 (D.C. Cir. 1982) (citing Baldus and Cole, STATISTICAL PROOF OF DISCRIMINATION 120 (1980); the objective is to define "a population that closely *approximates* the characteristics of those who would be likely to apply and 'meet legitimate threshold qualification requirements.' " (emphasis supplied)); Kilgo v. Bowman Transp., *supra* note 232 (court examined several relevant labor pools in effort to determine whether defendant discriminated against female over-the-road drivers).

[239]McDowell v. Safeway Stores, 575 F. Supp. 1007, 33 FEP 1735 (E.D. Ark. 1983), *aff'd,* 753 F.2d 716, 36 FEP 1593 (8th Cir. 1985). *See also* Section IV.B.3, *supra.*

[240]O'Neal v. Riceland Foods, *supra* note 234 (where qualified labor market data with respect to clerical workers not given, court permitted use of percentage of blacks actively engaged in clerical work). *But see* Bryant v. International Schools Servs., 675 F.2d 562, 573, 28 FEP 726, 734 (3d Cir. 1982) (plaintiff failed to show adverse impact when no proof was made with respect to applicant pool or relevant labor market because it was unable to obtain such data since it had been destroyed or was unavailable as a result of turmoil in Iran).

employees who are qualified.[241] One court has held that once the work force statistics are so defined, a great disparity between the proportion of the protected class occupying the available pool and the upper-level position will permit a summary judgment in favor of the plaintiff.[242] Absent a refined statistical analysis of an employer's work force, however, courts have been reluctant to give much probative weight to proffered statistical comparisons.[243]

## D. Proper Geographic Scope of Statistics

The determination of the proper geographical boundaries of the relevant labor market is a factual issue for the trial court, reviewable only for clear error.[244] Typical factors utilized in the analysis include the location of the employer within a Standard Metropolitan Statistical Area (SMSA), the accessibility of the employer, alternative work opportunities, and commuting patterns.[245] In determining whether the relevant labor market for entry-level jobs is the entire SMSA or some lesser part, courts continue to reject the employer's applicant flow as a conclusive factor where the recruiting process used to generate the applicant flow is itself being challenged as discriminatory.[246]

A trial court did not commit clear error when it held that a school district's relevant labor market consisted of teachers graduating from five college campuses located in counties corresponding to two of the state education agency's regions.[247] Nor did a district court err in admitting *national* labor market statistics where the employer hired throughout an entire *region,* absent evidence that the regional figures differed substantially from the national figures.[248]

Where a retailer with nationwide stores was geographically and administratively decentralized, plaintiff erroneously performed its statistical

---

[241]Carpenter v. Stephen F. Austin State Univ., 706 F.2d 608, 626, 31 FEP 1758, 1773, *reh'g denied,* 712 F.2d 1416 (5th Cir. 1983); Gilbert v. City of Little Rock, *supra* note 235; Ekanem v. Health & Hosp. Corp. of Marion County, Ind., 724 F.2d 563, 33 FEP 1497 (7th Cir. 1983), *modified and reh'g denied,* 33 FEP 1883 (7th Cir.), *cert. denied,* 469 U.S. 821, 35 FEP 1607 (1984); Pouncy v. Prudential Ins. Co. of Am., 668 F.2d 795, 803, 28 FEP 121, 128 (5th Cir. 1982); Metrocare v. Washington Metro. Area Transit Auth., 679 F.2d 922, 930, 28 FEP 1585, 1592 (D.C. Cir. 1982); Novotny v. Great Am. Fed. Sav. & Loan Ass'n, 539 F. Supp. 437, 457, 28 FEP 1796, 1814 (W.D. Pa. 1982); Michigan State Univ. Faculty Ass'n v. Michigan State Univ., 93 F.R.D. 54, 29 FEP 413, 418 (W.D. Mich. 1981); Broadnax v. Missouri Pac. R.R., 27 FEP 669, 675 (E.D. Ark. 1978).

[242]McKenzie v. Sawyer, 684 F.2d 62, 73, 29 FEP 633, 640–41 (D.C. Cir. 1982).

[243]Maddox v. Claytor, 764 F.2d 1539, 38 FEP 713, 722 (11th Cir. 1985) (static "snapshots" comparisons of positions held by black and white employees not highly probative); Bibbs v. Block, 778 F.2d 1318, 39 FEP 970, 972 (8th Cir. 1985) (en banc) ("bottom line" statistics that work force was racially integrated does not insulate employer from individual claim of discrimination).

[244]Kilgo v. Bowman Transp., 570 F. Supp. 1509, 31 FEP 1451 (N.D. Ga. 1983); Castaneda v. Pickard, 781 F.2d 456, 464, 40 FEP 154, 160 (5th Cir. 1986); EEOC v. Chicago Miniature Lamp Works, 622 F. Supp. 1281, 1308, 39 FEP 297, 317 (N.D. Ill. 1985).

[245]EEOC v. Chicago Miniature Lamp Works, 622 F. Supp. 1281, 1289, 1308, 39 FEP 297, 301, 317 (N.D. Ill. 1985).

[246]EEOC v. Rath Packing Co., 787 F. Supp. 318, 337, 40 FEP 580, 596 (8th Cir.), *cert. denied,* 479 U.S. 910, 41 FEP 1712 (1986) (applicant flow inappropriate where employer's discriminatory employment record was known in community and deterred women from applying); EEOC v. Chicago Miniature Lamp Works, 622 F. Supp. 1281, 1289–90, 1309, 39 FEP 297, 301–2, 318 (N.D. Ill. 1985) (historical applicant flow data cannot be assumed automatically to constitute accurate picture of relevant labor market).

[247]Castaneda v. Pickard, 781 F.2d 456, 463–64, 40 FEP 154, 160–61 (5th Cir. 1986).

[248]Kilgo v. Bowman Transp., 789 F.2d 859, 870, 40 FEP 1415, 1423 (11th Cir. 1986).

analyses as though every applicant at one store was simultaneously an applicant at every other store.[249] According to the court, the preferable practice
would have been to analyze each of the nationwide retailer's territories
separately to control for differences between territories and variances within
territories.[250]

## E. The Proper Time-Frame for Statistics

While not flatly precluding earlier data, most courts continue to prefer
statistics that focus on employment decisions made during the relevant time
period, which generally is defined by the filing of the EEOC charge[251] or, in
a few remaining cases, by the effective date of Title VII for the employer.[252]

## F. The Proper Weight to Be Given Statistical Proof

Statistics may be used to establish[253] or rebut[254] a prima facie case, to
show that the defendant's articulated reasons are a pretext,[255] or to demonstrate intentional discrimination.[256] In order to have probative value the
statistics must be controlled for the appropriate labor pool[257] and must

[249]EEOC v. Sears, Roebuck & Co., 628 F. Supp. 1264, 1316, 39 FEP 1672, 1710 (N.D. Ill. 1986),
aff'd, 839 F.2d 302, 45 FEP 1257 (7th Cir. 1988).

[250]Id., 628 F. Supp. at 1344, 39 FEP at 1733–34 (compensation); cf. Regner v. City of Chicago, 789
F.2d 534, 538, 40 FEP 1027, 1030 (7th Cir. 1986) (district court erred in considering work force data
from main library and branch libraries together where promotions of minorities may have been concentrated in branch libraries).

[251]Compare Lewis v. Bloomsburg Mills, 773 F.2d 561, 568 n.12, 38 FEP 1692, 1699 n.12 (4th Cir.
1985) (pre-charge period data relevant "for the limited purpose of inferring from it the continuation of
the practice into the charge period") and Smith v. Western Elec. Co., 770 F.2d 520, 527–28, 38 FEP
1605, 1610–11 (5th Cir. 1985) (plaintiffs' promotion and termination statistics unpersuasive because based
primarily on facts that occurred outside liability period) with Coates v. Johnson & Johnson, 756 F.2d
524, 540, 37 FEP 467, 479 (7th Cir. 1985) (plaintiffs' statistical evidence which included data prior to
class-liability cut-off date not necessarily unreliable, though less probative than data focusing on practices
after liability cut-off date); cf. EEOC v. McCarthy, 768 F.2d 1, 4, 38 FEP 536, 539 (1st Cir. 1985) (Equal
Pay Act) (admitted statistical evidence relating to years outside statute of limitations period "was relevant
to historical treatment of salaries at the college, as well as helpful in determining the trend of increasing
disparity with years of employment"); Rossini v. Ogilvy & Mather, 615 F. Supp. 1520, 1522, 42 FEP
1595 (S.D.N.Y. 1985), rev'd on other grounds, 798 F.2d 590, 42 FEP 1615 (2d Cir. 1986) (studies of
salaries which included data prior to the limitation date are relevant background evidence and may also
be considered as part of a pattern and practice of discrimination).

[252]Compare Griffin v. Regency Univs. Bd. of Regents, 795 F.2d 1281, 1289–90, 41 FEP 228, 236–37
(7th Cir. 1986) (as Title VII did not become applicable to public employers until March 1972, district
court did not err in its preference for statistics that control for effects of pre-1972 decisions) with
Bazemore v. Friday, 478 U.S. 385, 41 FEP 92, 97 & n.6 (1986) (reiterating that pre-Act evidence may
constitute relevant background evidence where current practice is at issue).

[253]Cook v. Boorstin, 763 F.2d 1462, 37 FEP 1777 (D.C. Cir. 1985); Diaz v. AT&T, 752 F.2d 1356,
36 FEP 1742 (9th Cir. 1985); Griffin v. Carlin, 755 F.2d 1516, 37 FEP 741 (11th Cir. 1985). But see
Latinos Unidos de Chelsea en Accion v. Secretary of Hous. & Urban Dev., 799 F.2d 774, 41 FEP 838
(1st Cir. 1986) (mere employment statistics insufficient to establish prima facie case of adverse impact);
Jones v. General Tire & Rubber Co., 608 F. Supp. 1013, 39 FEP 1517 (W.D.N.C. 1985) ("In no case
should there be blind adherence to the position that mere statistical imbalance equals discrimination.");
EEOC v. Halls Motor Transit Co., 609 F. Supp. 852, 40 FEP 756 (W.D. Pa. 1985), vacated, 789 F.2d
1011, 40 FEP 1441 (3d Cir. 1986) (pattern-and-practice statistics will not shift burden in an individual
disparate treatment case).

[254]Ridenour v. Lawson Co., 791 F.2d 52, 40 FEP 1455 (6th Cir. 1986); Holley v. Sanyo Mfg., 771
F.2d 1161, 38 FEP 1317 (8th Cir. 1985).

[255]Cook v. Boorstin, supra note 253; Diaz v. AT&T, supra note 253.

[256]Miles v. M.N.C. Corp., 750 F.2d 867, 36 FEP 1289 (11th Cir. 1985).

[257]Atonio v. Wards Cove Packing Co., 768 F.2d 1120, 38 FEP 1170 (9th Cir. 1985), rev'd on other
grounds, 810 F.2d 1477, 43 FEP 130 (9th Cir. 1987) (en banc); Kilgo v. Bowman Transp. Co., 789 F.2d
859, 40 FEP 1415 (11th Cir. 1986) (error to disregard study which accounted for major factors but failed
to include some variables); Coates v. Johnson & Johnson, 756 F.2d 524, 37 FEP 467 (7th Cir. 1985)

account for major variable factors.[258] General labor force statistics may be sufficient where the employer has failed to identify the selection criteria used or to demonstrate common qualifications or skills,[259] while statistics tending to show discrimination in one area of employment normally are entitled to little or no weight in establishing discrimination in a different area.[260]

In classwide disparate treatment cases, a "gross" statistical disparity may satisfy the initial burden of creating an inference of intent.[261] Thus one court indicated that a "marked disproportion" is sufficient under an adverse impact theory.[262] Where protected groups are blatantly underrepresented in discrete job categories, some courts have found that straight percentage comparisons alone may be sufficient to constitute a prima facie case,[263] although in most cases courts likely will require a standard deviation analysis to demonstrate a statistically and legally significant disparity.[264] Plaintiffs' statistics must show a causal nexus between the challenged practice and resultant disparities to raise an inference of unlawful discrimination.[265]

## 1. Sufficiency of the Disparity

Following the *Hazelwood*[266] and *Castaneda*[267] cases, standard deviation analysis has become the predominant tool used in evaluating the legal

---

(plaintiff need not account for an allegedly biased factor in establishing prima facie case; however, if defendant offers rebuttal statistics accounting for it, plaintiff must prove that factor is biased and therefore not valid); EEOC v. Sears, Roebuck & Co., 628 F. Supp. 1264, 39 FEP 1672 (N.D. Ill. 1986), *aff'd,* 839 F.2d 302, 45 FEP 1257 (7th Cir. 1988); Chang v. University of R.I., 606 F. Supp. 1161, 40 FEP 3 (D.R.I. 1985).

[258]Bazemore v. Friday, 478 U.S. 385, 41 FEP 92 (1986); Latinos Unidos de Chelseaen Accion v. Secretary of Hous. & Urban Dev., *supra* note 253; Atonio v. Wards Cove Packing Co., *supra* note 257; Dalley v. Michigan Blue Cross/Blue Shield, 612 F. Supp. 1444, 38 FEP 301 (E.D. Mich. 1985).

[259]EEOC v. Rath Packing Co., 787 F.2d 318, 40 FEP 580 (8th Cir.), *cert. denied,* 479 U.S. 910, 41 FEP 1712 (1986); Miles v. M.N.C. Corp., *supra* note 256 (statistics showing white hiring rate far exceeded black were sufficient). However, for conflicting results on use of census data regarding impact of a high school diploma requirement see *Aguilera v. Cook County Police & Corrections Merit Bd.,* 760 F.2d 844, 37 FEP 1140 (7th Cir.), *cert. denied,* 474 U.S. 907 (1985) (census data showing one-half as many Hispanics as whites have diploma established prima facie case); Fudge v. City of Providence Fire Dep't, 766 F.2d 650, 38 FEP 648 (1st Cir. 1985) (rejecting census data because aliens included and not differentiated for age); Clady v. County of Los Angeles, 770 F.2d 1421, 38 FEP 1575 (9th Cir. 1985), *cert. denied,* 475 U.S. 1109, 40 FEP 792 (1986) (same).

[260]Powers v. Dole, 782 F.2d 689, 39 FEP 1774 (7th Cir. 1986) (proof of discriminatory training programs has no weight in allegations of discriminatory grievance procedure); Box v. A&P Tea Co., 772 F.2d 1372, 38 FEP 1509 (7th Cir. 1985), *cert. denied,* 478 U.S. 1010, 41 FEP 271 (1986) (management level incumbents versus discipline); Atkins v. City of Greensboro, N.C., 39 FEP 424 (M.D.N.C. 1985) (general discipline versus criminal investigation).

[261]Carroll v. Sears, Roebuck & Co., 708 F.2d 183, 32 FEP 286 (5th Cir. 1983); Lewis v. NLRB, 750 F.2d 1266, 1271, 36 FEP 1388, 1392 (5th Cir. 1985) (court may infer racial discrimination from gross statistical disparities). *But see* Segar v. Smith, 738 F.2d 1249, 35 FEP 31 (D.C. Cir. 1984), *cert. denied,* 471 U.S. 1115, 37 FEP 1312 (1985).

[262]Page v. United States Indus., 726 F.2d 1038, 34 FEP 430 (5th Cir. 1984) (underrepresentation of disfavored group which reflects "marked disproportion" is sufficient to establish prima facie impact case).

[263]*E.g.,* Liberles v. County of Cook, 709 F.2d 1122, 31 FEP 1537 (7th Cir. 1983) (81% of case aides were black and were paid less than, although performing same work as caseworkers, 81% of whom were white); Capaci v. Katz & Besthoff, 711 F.2d 647, 32 FEP 961 (5th Cir. 1983), *cert. denied,* 466 U.S. 927, 34 FEP 696 (1984) ("the inexorable zero" highly probative as signifying total exclusion of women); Hogan v. Pierce, 31 FEP 115, 125 (D.D.C. 1983) (sample of 18 promotions sufficient in light of "inexorable zero").

[264]EEOC v. Western Elec. Co., 713 F.2d 1011, 1018, 32 FEP 708, 714 (4th Cir. 1983) (standard deviation analysis must be applied before drawing conclusions from percentage comparisons).

[265]Carroll v. Sears, Roebuck & Co, *supra* note 261.

[266]Hazelwood School Dist. v. United States, 433 U.S. 299, 15 FEP 1 (1977).

[267]Castaneda v. Partida, 430 U.S. 482 (1977).

significance of statistical disparities,[268] although courts sometimes utilize the sometimes criticized "four-fifths" or "80-percent" rule.[269] In calculating standard deviations, while both the binomial distribution formula ("two-tailed" test) and the hypergeometric distribution formula ("one-tailed" test) statistical analyses have been accepted in employee selection cases, the former generally is preferable due to its neutrality as to the anticipated result.[270]

While most courts find a disparity in excess of three standard deviations sufficient to establish statistical significance and below two standard deviations generally insufficient,[271] the case law varies as to whether a disparity between two and three standard deviations is sufficient to establish statistical significance.[272] Courts appear to recognize that the use for which the statisti-

---

[268]EEOC v. Western Elec. Co., supra note 264 (Fourth Circuit requires standard deviation analysis before conclusion can be drawn from straight percentages); Capaci v. Katz & Besthoff, supra note 263, 711 F.2d at 652 n.2, 32 FEP at 964 (court noted that 2 and 3 standard deviation tests correspond to probabilities of 1 in 20 (.05) and 1 in 100 (.01)). See also notes 271–272 and accompanying text, infra.

[269]See, e.g., Bigby v. City of Chicago, 38 FEP 844 (N.D. Ill. 1984), aff'd, 766 F.2d 1053, 38 FEP 853 (7th Cir. 1985), cert. denied, 474 U.S. 1056, 39 FEP 1200 (1986); Easley v. Anheuser-Busch, 575 F. Supp. 402, 34 FEP 380 (E.D. Mo. 1983), aff'd in relevant part, 758 F.2d 251, 37 FEP 549 (8th Cir. 1985) (application of 80-percent rule). But see Fudge v. City of Providence Fire Dep't, supra note 259, at 659 n.10 (four-fifths rule not accurate test of discriminatory impact when sample is small); Clady v. County of Los Angeles, supra note 259 (80-percent test rejected; Uniform Guidelines do not have force of law).

[270]For a useful discussion of when each of these statistical distribution formulas is most appropriate see Lilly v. Harris Teeter Supermkt., 720 F.2d 326, 336 n.18, 33 FEP 195, 203 (4th Cir. 1983), cert. denied, 466 U.S. 951, 34 FEP 1096 (1984) and EEOC v. Federal Reserve Bank of Richmond, 698 F.2d 633, 647–48, 30 FEP 1137, 1146–47 (4th Cir. 1983), rev'd and remanded on other grounds sub nom. Cooper v. Federal Reserve Bank of Richmond, 467 U.S. 867, 35 FEP 1 (1984) (binomial distribution formula is statistically preferable to hypergeometric distribution when sample size is not small). See also Baldus and Cole, STATISTICAL PROOF OF DISCRIMINATION, 1982 CUMULATIVE SUPPLEMENT 82 (binomial test is appropriate when sample is at least 30); Pegues v. Mississippi State Employment Serv., 699 F.2d 760, 31 FEP 257 (5th Cir.), cert. denied, 464 U.S. 991, 33 FEP 440 (1983) ("two-tailed" test defective because did not account for relative qualifications and preferences of employees). But see Hartman v. Wick, 600 F. Supp. 361, 36 FEP 622 (D.D.C. 1984) (disparity unlikely to have occurred by chance where number of standard deviations exceeds 1.65).

[271]Compare Gay v. Waiters' & Dairy Lunchmen's Local 30, 694 F.2d 531, 30 FEP 605 (9th Cir. 1982) (2.46 standard deviation disparity not sufficiently gross to establish § 1981 proof; statistics showing that chance is not more likely explanation are not in themselves sufficient to demonstrate that race is more likely explanation) with Harrell v. Northern Elec. Co., 672 F.2d 444, 28 FEP 911, modified, 679 F.2d 31, 29 FEP 913 (5th Cir.), cert. denied, 459 U.S. 1037, 30 FEP 440 (1982) (standard deviation greater than 2.33 sufficient to show "highly statistically significant disparity") and Spight v. Tidwell Indus., 551 F. Supp. 123, 30 FEP 1423 (N.D. Miss. 1982) (standard deviation disparity of 2.29 sufficient). See generally EEOC v. Western Elec. Co., supra note 264 ("courts should be extremely cautious in drawing any conclusions from standard deviations in the range of 1 to 3"); Hill v. K-Mart Corp., 699 F.2d 776, 31 FEP 269 (5th Cir. 1983) (insufficient standard deviation to demonstrate significant disparities).

[272]In Kilgo v. Bowman Transp. Co., 789 F.2d 859, 40 FEP 1415 (11th Cir. 1986), the statistical disparities ranged from 1.92 to 5.3 standard deviations. The employer argued that Castaneda and Hazelwood established a per se rule that observed disparities must exceed 3 standard deviations to support an inference of discrimination. The court rejected this argument and noted that no "bright line" of a given number of standard deviations could be drawn. Disparities below 2–3 standard deviations could still be discriminatory, just as greater disparities might not foreclose chance as an explanation when the statistics are analyzed with all surrounding facts and circumstances. 789 F.2d at 871–73, 40 FEP at 1424–25. Accord Maddox v. Claytor, 764 F.2d 1539, 1551–56, 38 FEP 713, 722–28 (11th Cir. 1985) (standard deviation analysis measures random probability, but does not attribute disparity conclusively to chance or discrimination); Clady v. County of Los Angeles, 770 F.2d 1421, 1428–29, 38 FEP 1575 (9th Cir. 1985), cert. denied, 475 U.S. 1109, 40 FEP 792 (1986) (Ninth Circuit analyzes statistical disparities for significance in each case individually; the 2–3 standard deviation or 80-percent Uniform Guidelines rule should not be applied uncritically); EEOC v. Federal Reserve Bank of Richmond, 698 F.2d 633, 647–48, 30 FEP 1137, 1147 (4th Cir. 1983) (courts should be extremely cautious in drawing any conclusions of legal significance from standard deviations in range of 1 to 3 but statistical analysis with standard deviations of more than 3 could safely be used); EEOC v. American Nat'l Bank, 680 F.2d 965, 966–73, 30 FEP 906, 907–13 (4th Cir.) (Widener, J., dissenting), cert. denied, 459 U.S. 923, 30 FEP 960 (1982) (probity of statistical analysis is questionable when standard deviation disparity is less than 3).

cal proof is offered bears substantially on the level of statistical significance which will be required.

The uncertainty surrounding the sufficiency of statistical disparities is highlighted by the Supreme Court's discussion of statistical proof in *Watson*.[273]

> "We have emphasized the useful role that statistical methods can have in Title VII cases, but we have not suggested that any particular number of "standard deviations" can determine whether a plaintiff has made out a prima facie case in the complex area of employment discrimination. *See Hazelwood School Dist. v. United States,* 433 U.S. 299, 311, n. 17, 97 S.Ct. 2736, 2743, n. 17, 53 L.Ed.2d 768 (1977).
>
> "Nor has a consensus developed around any alternative mathematical standard. Instead, courts appear generally to have judged the "significance" or "substantiality" of numerical disparities on a case-by-case basis. *See Clady, supra,* at 1428–1429; B. Schlei & P. Grossman, Employment Discrimination Law 98-99, and n. 77 (2d ed. 1983); *id.* 18–19, and n. 33 (Supp. 1983–1985). At least at this stage of the law's development, we believe that such a case-by-case approach properly reflects our recognition that statistics "come in infinite variety and * * * their usefulness depends on all of the surrounding facts and circumstances." *Teamsters v. United States,* 431 U.S. 324, 340, 97 S.Ct. 1843, 1856–1857, 52 L.Ed.2d 396 (1977)."

## 2. Size of the Statistical Sample

Courts continue to gauge the reliability of inferences from statistics by the degree of disparity and the size of the data sample. Statistical evidence based on a small sample size has been rejected as unreliable.[274] In *Fudge v.*

---

[273]Watson v. Fort Worth Bank & Trust Co., 487 U.S. _____, 47 FEP 102, 109 & n.3 (1988). Although the referenced discussion is contained within the plurality opinion authored by Justice O'Connor, the partial concurrence of Justice Blackmun, joined by Justices Brennan and Marshall, contains a note approving of the "characterization of the plaintiff's burden of establishing that any disparity is significant." 47 FEP at 111 n.2.

[274]Matthews v. Trans World Airlines, 41 EPD ¶36,454 (S.D.N.Y. 1986) (flight attendant training class of 19, including 1 black male plaintiff; statistical evidence unreliable); Palmer v. United States, 794 F.2d 534, 41 FEP 559, 563 (9th Cir. 1986) (sample size too small to have any predictive value); Kim v. Commandant, Defense Language Inst., Foreign Language Center, 772 F.2d 521, 38 FEP 1710 (9th Cir. 1985) (sample of 12 clearly too small to support claim for adverse impact, even though there was only a 50% pass rate on challenged test); Gillespie v. Wisconsin, 771 F.2d 1035, 1044, 38 FEP 1487, 1494 (7th Cir. 1985), *cert. denied,* 474 U.S. 1083, 39 FEP 1424 (1986) ("the number of employees taking the pretest was so small that a correlation between the test scores and job performance would be statistically meaningless"); Moore v. Summa Corp., Hughes Helicopter Div., 708 F.2d 475, 32 FEP 97 (9th Cir. 1983) (evidence that only two black females received promotions in period in which three or four class members should have received promotions, based on work force representation, failed to establish discriminatory pattern where sample pool was small); Pace v. Southern Ry. Sys., 701 F.2d 1383, 31 FEP 710 (11th Cir.), *cert. denied,* 464 U.S. 1018, 33 FEP 656 (1983), *reh'g denied,* 465 U.S. 1054 (1984) (sample of 12 employees too small); Soria v. Ozinga Bros., 704 F.2d 990, 31 FEP 720 (7th Cir. 1983) (sample of 15 employees too small); Murray v. District of Columbia, 34 FEP 644 (D.D.C. 1983), *aff'd,* 740 F.2d 58, 37 FEP 784 (D.C. Cir. 1984) (evidence that 4 whites and 7 blacks were selected for interview from pool of 74 whites and 34 blacks was inadequate because of small sample size); Pirone v. Home Ins. Co., 559 F. Supp. 306, 31 FEP 311 (S.D.N.Y.), *aff'd,* 742 F.2d 1430, 37 FEP 280 (2d Cir. 1983) (data base of 16 to 18 too small); *see also* Zick v. Verson Allsteel Press Co., 644 F. Supp. 906, 41 FEP 1828 (N.D. Ill. 1986), *aff'd,* 819 F.2d 1143 (7th Cir. 1987); Jordan v. Tenpenny, 39 EPD ¶ 35,815 (M.D. Tenn. 1985); Smith v. Western Elec. Co., 770 F.2d 520, 38 FEP 1605 (5th Cir. 1985); EEOC v. American Nat'l Bank, 680 F.2d 965, 968, 30 FEP 906, 909 (4th Cir.), *cert. denied,* 459 U.S. 923, 30 FEP 960 (1982) (failure to take into account small sample size was error); Schutz v. Western Publishing Co., 609 F. Supp. 888, 37 FEP 1698 (N.D. Ill. 1985) (where company's reorganization affected 11 employees, and only 3 women and 2 men were terminated, sample too small to create any statistically reliable inference supporting adverse impact claim); Levy v.

*City of Providence Fire Department,*[275] the First Circuit emphasized that plaintiffs bear the burden of demonstrating that racial differentials in test results are statistically significant, that is, that there is a "low probability" that the results occurred by chance, with substantial consideration paid to the sample size.

If the statistical disparity is great, however, courts have found that even a marginal sample size may justify an inference of discrimination.[276] Other courts have placed heavy reliance on nonstatistical evidence where data sampling was questionable.[277]

## 3. The "Bottom Line" Concept

Courts have applied the *Connecticut v. Teal*[278] rationale and rejected a "bottom line" defense where a pass/fail barrier in the hiring process had a

---

Ellingwood, 36 FEP 634 (D.D.C. 1984) (in male GS-11 employee's claim of reverse gender discrimination in agency's promotion procedure, court held that sample of all GS-11 presiding officers was simply too small to permit any statistical or even percentage analysis of differential promotion rate; due to small sample size, court relied instead on a reasonable "common sense" evaluation of data and drew an inference negative to plaintiff from his own statistics); Haskell v. Kaman Corp., 743 F.2d 113, 35 FEP 941 (2d Cir. 1984) (in ADEA claim, court held that district court erred in allowing testimony on plaintiff's behalf of six former officers concerning circumstances surrounding their terminations and those of four others over 11-year period, because sample size too small to be statistically significant); Parker v. Federal Nat'l Mortgage Ass'n, 741 F.2d 975, 980–81, 35 FEP 893, 897 (7th Cir. 1984) (plaintiff was only Senior Loan Representative (SLR) terminated out of 12 employees in a reorganization of the Chicago office of defendant; plaintiff brought a claim under ADEA and presented evidence showing that of 12 employees at loan representative level, 3 out of the 4 terminated were in protected class; court held that small size of sample coupled with selective manner of plaintiff's categorization of data (6 of the 11 SLR's retained were members of protected class) resulted in a failure to make out reasonable inference of discriminatory motive). *But see* Osahar v. Carlin, 642 F. Supp. 448 (S.D. Fla. 1986).

[275]766 F.2d 650, 38 FEP 648 (1st Cir. 1985).

[276]Bunch v. Bullard, 795 F.2d 384, 395, 41 FEP 515, 524 (5th Cir. 1986) (black plaintiffs challenged police promotional exam; "the limited size of the population in question does not preclude us from recognizing a decisive pattern emerging from a history of experiences"); Wilmington v. J.I. Case Co., 793 F.2d 909, 40 FEP 1833 (8th Cir. 1986) (discharge case involving only 27 discharges; "gross disparity" in discharge rates of black and white employees); Ingram v. Madison Square Garden Center, 709 F.2d 807, 32 FEP 641 (2d Cir.), *cert. denied,* 464 U.S. 937, 33 FEP 48 (1983) (significant statistical disparity justified inference of discrimination in job referrals despite small sample size); Valentino v. United States Postal Serv., 674 F.2d 56, 72–73, 28 FEP 593, 606 (D.C. Cir. 1982) (while not ruling on sample size, court stated that small sample is not useless *per se,* especially if disparity shown is egregious); Goldstein v. Manhattan Indus., 758 F.2d 1435, 37 FEP 1217 (11th Cir.), *cert. denied,* 474 U.S. 1005, 39 FEP 720 (1985) (in ADEA claim plaintiff presented statistical evidence to show company's high turnover rate from 1976 to date of trial; court held that although statistical evidence regarding termination of three other employees age 40 or above was not sufficiently significant to establish discrimination prong of prima facie case, plaintiff had enough circumstantial evidence surrounding his own discharge to make out a claim); Segar v. Smith, 738 F.2d 1249, 35 FEP 31 (D.C. Cir. 1984), *cert. denied,* 471 U.S. 1115, 37 FEP 1312 (1985) (although statistical evidence presented by plaintiff class of black DEA agents with regard to racial differences in agents' promotion rates to GS-12 level among whites and blacks was not significant due to small sample size, anecdotal testimony regarding initial grade assignments, work assignments, discipline, supervisory evaluations, and general hostile atmosphere in the agency successfully buttressed statistical sample to create inference of racially motivated discrimination in GS-12 promotion procedure).

[277]Endres v. Helms, 617 F. Supp. 1260, 39 FEP 933 (D.D.C. 1985) (statistical evidence, though based on a small sample, showed adverse effects of reorganization plan on older workers); Walls v. Mississippi State Dept. of Pub. Welfare, 730 F.2d 306, 34 FEP 1114 (5th Cir. 1984) (court combined data with "historical and anectodal evidence to draw composite picture of bias"); Spight v. Tidwell Indus., *supra* note 271 (sample of 58 promotions sufficient when combined with: (1) evidence of specific instances of discrimination, and (2) promotion policy based predominantly on subjective criteria applied by all-white supervisory staff without written guidelines).

[278]457 U.S. 440, 29 FEP 1 (1982).

discriminatory impact upon a protected group as shown by its effect upon either a particular member[279] or the group as a whole.[280]

The First Circuit, sitting en banc, reversed an earlier panel decision applying *Teal* to a situation where a female was not selected for employment as a police officer because she failed to meet a minimum height requirement.[281] The full court, distinguishing *Teal*,[282] found that the height requirement could have no adverse impact on women where only women were in competition for the job since a female-only hiring list was used. Thus, the court concluded that the plaintiff had not made out a prima facie case of adverse impact.

Following a lengthy discussion, the district court in *Brunet v. City of Columbus*[283] refused to apply the *Teal* rationale to a multicomponent selection process for firefighters, reasoning that *Teal* is limited by its terms to pass/fail barriers.[284]

### 4. Conflicting Statistical Conclusions

Courts continue to recognize the potential for the manipulation of statistics in discrimination cases. As stated by the Ninth Circuit, "the court often admonishes that statistics are inherently slippery and the weight given to them depends on proper supportive facts and the absence of variables."[285] Statistical evidence can become so overwhelming that a district court will retain its own expert to assist it in understanding the "intricacies" of the

---

[279]Burney v. City of Pawtucket, 559 F. Supp. 1089, 34 FEP 1274 (D.R.I. 1983) (requisite physical training test in selection process for police officers had adverse impact on women where female was denied employment because she failed test; *de minimis* argument emphasizing limited role of physical test was summarily rejected).

[280]Moon v. Cook County Police & Corrections Merit Bd., No. 86-C-0466 (N.D. Ill. May 30, 1986) (racially balanced work force cannot immunize employer from liability for specific acts of discrimination); Carpenter v. Stephen F. Austin State Univ., 706 F.2d 608, 31 FEP 1758, *reh'g denied,* 712 F.2d 1416 (5th Cir. 1983) (data showing that 47% of whites and 28.4% of blacks received high school diplomas and composition of jobs requiring diplomas was 80% white presented prima facie case despite fact that large number of blacks survived selection device); Griffin v. Carlin, 755 F.2d 1516, 37 FEP 741 (11th Cir. 1985) (plaintiffs in class action against Postal Service charged that promotion procedure had a disparate impact on blacks; components of procedure being challenged were written test and subjective elements such as interviews and supervisory recommendations; citing *Connecticut v. Teal, supra* note 278, Eleventh Circuit reversed district court's dismissal of plaintiff's claim, holding that no bottom line defense may be raised by defendant with regard to either objective or *subjective* criteria which create barriers to employment).

[281]Costa v. Markey, 706 F.2d 1, 31 FEP 1324 (1st Cir. 1982), *cert. denied,* 464 U.S. 1017, 33 FEP 656 (1983).

[282]*Id.,* 706 F.2d at 3 n.1, 31 FEP at 1325. While the court acknowledged that "[b]oth cases involved a pass-fail hiring barrier that statistics demonstrated had a greater impact on members of the protected class than on non-members [and both] also involved an additional aspect of the hiring process that operated to remove the impact of that barrier," it found a crucial distinction in the fact that "the aspects of the process that operated to remove the overall impact of the barrier were at different ends of the process. [*Id.*] In Teal the initial discrimination was compensated for at the end; in Costa the separation of the hiring lists meant that there was no discrimination to begin with." *Id.*

[283]642 F. Supp. 1214, 1226, 42 FEP 1846, 1856 (S.D. Ohio 1986).

[284]*Id.* The court cited the Second Edition, at 1377–78, to conclude that a pass-fail barrier to further consideration in the selection process will probably not be applied in the "multi-component selection processes" where all candidates complete all components of the process before the selection is made. The *Brunet* court points out that the Second Circuit decision in *Teal* had held this and that the four justices in dissent had interpreted the majority opinion in this way.

[285]Atonio v. Wards Cove Packing Co., 768 F.2d 1120, 1128, 38 FEP 1170, 1176, *withdrawn en banc,* 787 F.2d 462 (9th Cir. 1985), *later proceeding,* 810 F.2d 1477, 43 FEP 130 (9th Cir. 1987) (en banc), *cert. granted,* 487 U.S. _____ (1988); Spaulding v. University of Wash., 740 F.2d 686, 35 FEP 217 (9th Cir.), *cert. denied,* 469 U.S. 1036, 36 FEP 464 (1984).

conflicting statistical evidence presented by the parties.[286] In another case, the experts reached diametrically opposed conclusions while using virtually the same data, which prompted the court to express an axiom regarding the use of statistics and the law as follows, "statisticians can manipulate numbers to such a degree that sustenance can be found for an otherwise unsupportable position."[287]

## V. NONSTATISTICAL PROOF

While statistical evidence continues to dominate adverse impact cases and disparate treatment class actions, nonstatistical evidence is also frequently presented to support or rebut plaintiffs' claims. As stated by some courts, "the testimonial evidence of specific acts of discrimination corroborates the statistics" and brings "the cold numbers convincingly to life."[288] For example, the testimony of individual employees describing discriminatory treatment[289] or the testimony of individual managers describing nondiscriminatory conduct[290] is often presented. Similarly, evidence of highly subjective selection systems,[291] specific exclusionary practices,[292] word-of-mouth

---

[286]Dalley v. Michigan Blue Cross/Blue Shield, 612 F. Supp. 1444, 1448 n.10, 38 FEP 301, 305 n.10 (E.D. Mich. 1985).

[287]Chang v. University of R.I., 606 F. Supp. 1161, 1206, 40 FEP 3, 39 (D.R.I. 1985); Smith v. Western Elec. Co., 770 F.2d 520, 527, 38 FEP 1605, 1610–11 (5th Cir. 1985) (district court justified in rejecting plaintiff's statistical evidence because of its own limitations rather than strengths of defendant's studies); EEOC v. Sears, Roebuck & Co., 628 F. Supp. 1264, 1305, 39 FEP 1672, 1701 (N.D. Ill. 1986), aff'd, 839 F.2d 302, 45 FEP 1257 (7th Cir. 1988) (erroneous assumptions rendered EEOC's statistical analysis virtually meaningless); EEOC v. Chicago Miniature Lamp Works, 622 F. Supp. 1281, 1302, 39 FEP 297, 313 (N.D. Ill. 1985) (plaintiff's expert "unfortunately lent weight to, and tended to legitimize, the canard that there are (in ascending order) 'liars, damned liars and statisticians' "); Coates v. Johnson & Johnson, 756 F.2d 524, 539, 37 FEP 467, 478 (7th Cir. 1985) (only consistency between two experts' testimony was their insistence that the other's study contained serious statistical flaws); Bazemore v. Friday, 751 F.2d 662, 676, 36 FEP 834, 846 (4th Cir. 1984), aff'd in part and vacated in part, 478 U.S. 385, 41 FEP 92 (1986) (statistics do not tell full story); Carroll v. Sears, Roebuck & Co., 708 F.2d 183, 195, 32 FEP 286, 295 (5th Cir. 1983) (Fifth Circuit instructed district courts to "accept what figures are available; allow for imperfections, skewing factors, and margins of error; and then take the figures for what they are worth"); see also EEOC v. IBM Corp., 583 F. Supp. 875, 906, 34 FEP 766, 789 (D. Md. 1984) (court concluded EEOC's statistics were completely unreliable); Robinson v. Polaroid Corp., 567 F. Supp. 192, 198, 32 FEP 621, 626 (D. Mass. 1983), aff'd, 732 F.2d 1010, 34 FEP 1134 (1st Cir. 1984) (court noted that expert witness replied, "it was not completely clear that BMDP did what he thought it did"); Murray v. District of Columbia, 34 FEP 644, 646 (D.D.C. 1983), aff'd, 740 F.2d 58, 37 FEP 784 (D.C. Cir. 1984) (expert witness admitted inadequacy of sample size and that statistical results were, therefore, highly unstable).

[288]Kraszewski v. State Farm Gen. Ins. Co., 38 FEP 197, 260 (N.D. Cal. 1985); see also Miles v. M.N.C. Corp., 750 F.2d 867, 873, 36 FEP 1289, 1294 (11th Cir. 1985) (individual claim assessed against statistical evidence); Mozee v. Jeffboat, Inc., 746 F.2d 365, 373, 35 FEP 1810, 1816 (7th Cir. 1984) (probative value of statistical evidence diminished by employer's genuine reliance on subjective factors); Blim v. Western Elec. Co., 731 F.2d 1473, 1477, 34 FEP 757, 760 (10th Cir.), cert. denied, 469 U.S. 874, 36 FEP 816 (1984) (whether evidence supports statistical conclusion is issue for jury).

[289]Smith v. Western Elec. Co., 770 F.2d 520, 527, 38 FEP 1605, 1611 (5th Cir. 1985) (plaintiff offered testimony of other black installers who complained of discrimination).

[290]EEOC v. Sears, Roebuck & Co., 628 F. Supp. 1264, 1306, 39 FEP 1672, 1702 (N.D. Ill. 1986), aff'd, 839 F.2d 302, 45 FEP 1257 (7th Cir. 1988) (defendant offered uncontradicted testimony of numerous managers regarding affirmative recruitment efforts which court found to be most credible and convincing).

[291]Lewis v. Bloomsburg Mills, 773 F.2d 561, 38 FEP 1692, corrected, 40 FEP 1615 (4th Cir. 1985); Smith v. Western Elec. Co., supra note 287; Grubb v. W.A. Foote Memorial Hosp., 741 F.2d 1486, 35 FEP 1048 (6th Cir. 1984), vacated, 759 F.2d 546, 37 FEP 867 (6th Cir.), cert. denied, 474 U.S. 946, 39 FEP 384 (1985).

[292]Miles v. M.N.C. Corp., supra note 288.

recruiting,[293] and past patterns of discrimination[294] have been used in combination with statistical evidence to establish a prima facie case.

Some courts have also considered evidence regarding the employer's general reputation and the frequency with which charges of discrimination are filed against the employer.[295] In addition, supplementary nonstatistical evidence may be pivotal in cases where the statistical sample or disparities are small and the statistical conclusions in conflict.[296]

The presence or absence of effective recruiting efforts and affirmative action plans has been used to support statistical evidence in adverse impact cases and disparate treatment class actions.[297]

---

[293]EEOC v. Chicago Miniature Lamp Works, 622 F. Supp. 1281, 1288, 39 FEP 297, 301 (N.D. Ill. 1985) (entry level recruitment primarily by word of mouth); Kraszewski v. State Farm Gen. Ins. Co., 38 FEP 197, 229 (N.D. Cal. 1985) (word of mouth recruiting restricted number of female recruits).

[294]Bazemore v. Friday, *supra* note 287 (present salary structure illegal if it continues pre-1965 discriminatory pay structure). *But see* Lewis v. NLRB, 750 F.2d 1266, 1277, 36 FEP 1388, 1396, *reh'g denied en banc,* 756 F.2d 882 (5th Cir. 1985) (court not only failed to find past pattern of discrimination, but instead found that "NLRB's affirmative action programs did not indicate an employer prone to discrimination, but instead one which vigorously pursued aggressive affirmative action efforts").

[295]Krodel v. Young, 748 F.2d 701, 709, 36 FEP 468, 474 (D.C. Cir. 1984), *cert. denied,* 474 U.S. 817, 38 FEP 1727 (1985), *later proceeding,* 624 F. Supp. 720, 41 FEP 170 (D.D.C. 1985).

[296]EEOC v. Sears, Roebuck & Co., *supra* note 287; Kraszewski v. State Farm Gen. Ins. Co., *supra* note 288; Smith v. Western Elec. Co., *supra* note 287; Coates v. Johnson & Johnson, *supra* note 287; Mozee v. Jeffboat, *supra* note 288; Meschino v. IT&T Corp., 563 F. Supp. 1066, 1073, 34 FEP 1634, 1638 (S.D.N.Y. 1983).

[297]Chang v. University of R.I., 606 F. Supp. 1161, 1183–84, 40 FEP 3, 20 (D.R.I. 1985) (blemished affirmative action efforts caused court to review other employment practices with heightened scrutiny); Coser v. Moore, 739 F.2d 746, 751, 40 FEP 195, 198 (2d Cir. 1984) (existence of comprehensive affirmative action plan is antithesis of pattern-and-practice discrimination); EEOC v. Sears, Roebuck & Co., *supra* note 290 (female sales recruiting was important priority in affirmative action plan); EEOC v. IBM Corp., *supra* note 287 (affirmative action program and open door policy found to support defendant's position); Craik v. Minnesota State Univ. Bd., 731 F.2d 465, 472–73, 34 FEP 649, 654–55, *later proceeding,* 738 F.2d 348, 35 FEP 243 (8th Cir. 1984) (failure to abide by affirmative action program, failure of affirmative action committee to meet regularly, and ignorance of administration and faculty concerning affirmative action supported plaintiff's contentions); Lewis v. NLRB, *supra* note 294.

CHAPTER 37

# INJUNCTIVE AND AFFIRMATIVE RELIEF

## I. Statutory Authority

The Supreme Court has determined that principles developed under the Labor Management Relations Act generally guide but do not bind courts in tailoring remedies under Title VII.[1] A specific finding of intentional discrimination is not necessary to obtain relief in disparate impact cases, but is necessary to obtain relief in disparate treatment cases.[2]

A district court may exercise its statutory remedial authority to eradicate the effects of unlawful discrimination and make the victims whole.[3] The Supreme Court, in *Sheet Metal Workers Local 28 v. EEOC,*[4] held that where a court is employing the first of these powers, to eradicate the effects of discrimination, the beneficiaries need not show that they themselves were the victims of past discrimination.[5] In the majority of Title VII cases, the court will not have to impose broad-based affirmative action as a remedy for past discrimination, but need only order the employer or union to cease engaging in discriminatory practices and award make-whole relief to the individuals victimized by those practices.[6] However, in some cases, affirmative action may be necessary in order to enforce effectively Title VII. A court may have to resort to affirmative relief when confronted with an employer or labor union that has engaged in persistent or egregious discrimination, or such relief may be necessary to dissipate the lingering effects of pervasive discrimination.[7] In cases where affirmative action is necessary, the court must tailor its order to fit the nature of the violation it seeks to correct.[8]

The Supreme Court emphasized the second type of remedial authority,

---

[1]Ford Motor Co. v. EEOC, 458 U.S. 219, 223–38, 29 FEP 121, 123–25 (1982).

[2]*Compare* Connecticut v. Teal, 457 U.S. 440, 452, 29 FEP 1, 6–7 (1982) ("A non-job-related test that has a disparate racial impact, and is used to 'limit' or 'classify' employees, is 'used to discriminate' within the meaning of Title VII, whether or not it was 'designed or intended' to have this effect and despite an employer's efforts to compensate for its discriminatory effect.") *with* Texas Dep't of Community Affairs v. Burdine, 450 U.S. 248, 256, 25 FEP 113, 116 (1981) (in disparate treatment case, plaintiff has "ultimate burden of persuading the court that she has been the victim of intentional discrimination. She may succeed in this either directly by persuading the court that a discriminatory reason more likely motivated the employer or indirectly by showing that the employer's proffered explanation is unworthy of credence"). *See also* Duffy v. Wheeling Pittsburgh Steel Corp., 738 F.2d 1393, 1396, 35 FEP 246, 247 (3d Cir.), *cert. denied,* 469 U.S. 1087, 36 FEP 712 (1984) (in disparate impact case, "a showing that a proffered justification is pretextual is itself *equivalent* to a finding that the employer intentionally discriminated."); Payne v. Travenol Laboratories, 673 F.2d 798, 815–16, 28 FEP 1212, 1223–25 (5th Cir.), *cert. denied,* 459 U.S. 1038, 30 FEP 440 (1982).

[3]Sheet Metal Workers Local 28 v. EEOC, 478 U.S. 421, 41 FEP 107, 127 (1986).

[4]478 U.S. 421, 41 FEP 107 (1986).

[5]*Id.,* 41 FEP at 116, 128.

[6]*Id.,* 41 FEP at 128–29.

[7]*Id.*

[8]*Id.*

to make the victims of past discrimination whole, in *Firefighters Local 1784 v. Stotts,*[9] holding that "make-whole relief" may be provided only to identifiable victims of illegal discrimination.[10] The Supreme Court ruled that a court must respect bona fide seniority systems during layoffs, even though the effect is to undo the results of a prior Title VII consent decree.

The Second Circuit, in an action brought under the Constitution, not Title VII, has held that a court has the power to override seniority systems that perpetuate racial discrimination.[11]

## II. ENJOINING PRACTICES FOUND UNLAWFUL

Courts continue to enjoin practices which violate Title VII and to order specific relief.[12] In cases presenting abundant evidence of consistent past discrimination, injunctive relief is mandatory absent clear and convincing

---

[9] 467 U.S. 561, 34 FEP 1702 (1984).

[10] *Id.* at 579–80, 34 FEP at 1711–12, *rev'g sub nom.* Stotts v. Memphis Fire Dep't, 679 F.2d 541, 28 FEP 1491 (6th Cir. 1982) (holding unlawful injunction to override seniority provisions during layoffs, designed to preserve racial balance in work force gained by Title VII consent decree); *see also* Vulcan Pioneers v. New Jersey Dep't of Civil Serv., 588 F. Supp. 732, 35 FEP 24 (D.N.J. 1984), *aff'd,* 770 F.2d 1077 (3d Cir. 1985) (court that had originally held that it had equitable power to override seniority provisions in order to effectuate affirmative action plan reverses itself in response to *Stotts*); United States v. City of Cincinnati, 35 FEP 676 (S.D. Ohio 1984), *aff'd in relevant part,* 771 F.2d 161, 38 FEP 1402 (6th Cir. 1985) (injunction barring layoffs of minority employees dissolved in light of *Stotts*). *But see* Kromnick v. Philadelphia School Dist., 739 F.2d 894, 35 FEP 538 (3d Cir. 1984), *cert. denied,* 469 U.S. 1107, 36 FEP 976 (1985) (*Stotts* does not bar transfer of teachers within system to achieve racial balance).

[11] Arthur v. Nyquist, 712 F.2d 816, 32 FEP 822 (2d Cir. 1983), *cert. denied,* 467 U.S. 1259, 34 FEP 1887 (1984) (because hiring minority teachers under school desegregation plan will vindicate constitutional rights of minority students, court has power to override seniority system that perpetuates racial discrimination); *see also* Paradise v. Prescott, 767 F.2d 1514, 1529, 38 FEP 1094, 1106 (11th Cir. 1985), *aff'd sub nom.* United States v. Paradise, 480 U.S. 149, 43 FEP 1 (1987). (*Stotts* distinguished, in part, as based on Title VII; claim based on Fourteenth Amendment).

[12] Zipes v. Trans World Airlines, 455 U.S. 385, 399–400, 28 FEP 1, 7 (1982) (retroactive class-based seniority relief awarded though contrary to collective bargaining agreement); Pennsylvania v. Operating Eng'rs Local 542, 807 F.2d 330, 42 FEP 836 (3d Cir. 1986) (injunction modifying collective bargaining agreement provisions regarding recalls and referrals, and ordering appointment of hiring hall monitor); Davis v. Richmond, Fredericksburg & Potomac R.R., 803 F.2d 1322, 42 FEP 69 (4th Cir. 1986) (retroactive seniority awarded where apprentice program, which was basis of promotions, was illegally discriminatory); Walters v. City of Atlanta, 803 F.2d 1135, 1148–50, 42 FEP 387, 397–99 (11th Cir. 1986) (injunction ordering hiring of unlawfully rejected white applicant even though innocent current holder of position would be "bumped"); Pecker v. Heckler, 801 F.2d 709, 711–13, 41 FEP 1485, 1487–88 (4th Cir. 1986) (plaintiff entitled to injunction prohibiting Title VII violations as well as promotion to position plaintiff would have attained absent discrimination); Bunch v. Bullard, 795 F.2d 384, 41 FEP 515 (5th Cir. 1986) (general injunctive relief ordering local police to pursue nondiscriminatory promotion policies); Brady v. Thurston Motor Lines, 726 F.2d 136, 146, 33 FEP 1370, 1380 (4th Cir.), *cert. denied,* 469 U.S. 827, 35 FEP 1608 (1984) (broad injunctive relief to remedy intentional racial discrimination); Criswell v. Western Airlines, 709 F.2d 544, 557–58, 32 FEP 1204, 1215–16 (9th Cir. 1983), *aff'd on other grounds,* 472 U.S. 400, 37 FEP 1829 (1985) (systemwide injunctive relief appropriate in age discrimination case even though suit not class action); Evans v. Harnett County Bd. of Educ., 684 F.2d 304, 306, 29 FEP 672, 673 (4th Cir. 1982) (injunction against practice of appointing whites as principals of formerly white schools and blacks as principals of formerly black schools); Norris v. Arizona Governing Comm., 671 F.2d 330, 335–36, 28 FEP 369, 373–74 (9th Cir. 1982), *aff'd in part and rev'd in part,* 463 U.S. 1073, 32 FEP 233 (1983) (injunction against carrying out provisions of deferred compensation plan through use of sex-segregated annuity tables); Berkman v. City of New York (I), 536 F. Supp. 177, 216, 28 FEP 856, 891 (E.D.N.Y. 1982), *aff'd,* 705 F.2d 584, 31 FEP 767 (2d Cir. 1983) (injunction prohibiting appointment based on physical portion of examination that discriminated against women); EEOC v. H.S. Camp & Sons, 542 F. Supp. 411, 448, 33 FEP 330, 360 (M.D. Fla. 1982) (injunction ordering desegregation of restrooms and departments); Toombs v. Greer-Smyrna, 529 F. Supp. 497, 504 n. 10, 28 FEP 444, 449 (M.D. Tenn. 1982), *aff'd,* 709 F.2d 1509, 33 FEP 376 (6th Cir. 1983) (injunction mandating reinstatement and restoration of bidding rights to teacher); Morgan v. Hertz Corp., 542 F. Supp. 123, 128, 27 FEP 990, 994 (W.D. Tenn. 1981), *aff'd on other grounds,* 725 F.2d 1070, 33 FEP 1237 (6th Cir. 1984) (injunction forbidding sexually indecent comments to female employees).

evidence that further noncompliance is unlikely.[13] Courts continue to issue injunctions requiring employers to reform discriminatory systems in the workplace.[14]

An injunction will be denied, however, where equitable relief is found to be unnecessary[15] or where the relief sought is beyond the scope of the complaint or the proof at trial.[16] An injunction may be denied if its enforcement will injure an innocent third party.[17] It also may be denied when such relief would unnecessarily interfere with a defendant's operations[18] or would significantly burden a party innocent of Title VII violations.[19]

---

[13]Cox v. American Cast Iron Pipe Co., 784 F.2d 1546, 1561, 40 FEP 678, 689–90 (11th Cir.), *cert. denied,* 479 U.S. 883, 41 FEP 1712 (1986) (female employees, if they proved their claim, were entitled to injunctive relief from disparate compensation schemes between male and female workers); Abrams v. Baylor College of Medicine, 581 F. Supp. 1570, 1580, 34 FEP 229, 237–38 (S.D. Tex. 1984), *aff'd in part and rev'd in part on other grounds,* 805 F.2d 528, 42 FEP 806 (5th Cir. 1986).

[14]Sheet Metal Workers Local 28 v. EEOC, 478 U.S. 421, 41 FEP 107 (1986) (defendant required to develop nondiscriminatory promotion and apprenticeship plans); Brady v. Thurston Motor Lines, *supra* note 13 (employer required to create nondiscriminatory working conditions by posting notices of employment, surveying minority employees as to interest, and providing detailed job descriptions); Carpenter v. Stephen F. Austin State Univ., 706 F.2d 608, 623–26, 31 FEP 1758, 1770–73, *reh'g denied,* 712 F.2d 1416 (5th Cir. 1983) (employer required to reevaluate standards for promotion and to adopt preferential promotion policies to remedy effects of past discrimination); United States v. Sheriff of Lancaster County, 561 F. Supp. 1005, 31 FEP 827 (E.D. Va. 1983) (sweeping decree reaches all details of hiring in sheriff's office); Paxton v. Union Nat'l Bank, 688 F.2d 552, 574, 29 FEP 1233, 1251–52 (8th Cir. 1982), *cert. denied,* 460 U.S. 1083, 31 FEP 824 (1983) (defendant ordered to develop nondiscriminatory promotion standards and methods).

[15]Hammon v. Barry, 813 F.2d 412, 43 FEP 89 (D.C. Cir. 1987) (injunction denied where structure of discrimination had long been dismantled); Payne v. Travenol Laboratories, 673 F.2d 798, 825, 28 FEP 1212, 1233–34, (5th Cir.), *cert. denied,* 459 U.S. 1038, 30 FEP 440 (1982) (injunction denied because employer's modification of hiring procedure removed its discriminatory character); Schiffman v. Cimarron Aircraft Corp., 615 F. Supp. 382, 387, 38 FEP 1245, 1248 (W.D. Okla. 1985) (injunction denied where plaintiff had retired from company; relief limited to back wages); Pree v. Stone & Webster Eng'g Corp., 607 F. Supp. 945, 950, 37 FEP 1277, 1281 (D. Nev. 1985) (injunction denied where plaintiff had retired from company); Goodwin v. St. Louis County Circuit Court, 555 F. Supp. 658, 663, 30 FEP 1375, 1379 (E.D. Mo. 1982), *vacated in part on other grounds,* 729 F.2d 541, 34 FEP 347 (8th Cir.), *cert. denied,* 469 U.S. 828, 35 FEP 1608 (1984) *and* 469 U.S. 1216, 37 FEP 64 (1985) (injunctive relief denied where position sought by plaintiff had been eliminated and where there was no evidence of continued discrimination); Ingram v. Madison Square Garden Center, 535 F. Supp. 1082, 1094, 32 FEP 548, 558 (S.D.N.Y. 1982), *aff'd as modified,* 709 F.2d 807, 32 FEP 641 (2d Cir.), *cert. denied,* 464 U.S. 937, 33 FEP 48 (1983) (cleaners not entitled to order limiting union's future role in laborer hiring and referral where union had ceased to play any role in hiring of laborers).

[16]Quinn v. New York State Elec. & Gas Corp., 621 F. Supp. 1086, 1092, 39 FEP 690, 694 (N.D.N.Y. 1985) (plaintiff seeking placement in training program denied relief, in part because he failed to prove he was denied entry to program and all that was shown was that he was denied opportunity to compete for admission); Marshall v. Edward J. Meyer Memorial Hosp., 32 FEP 1335 (W.D.N.Y. 1983), *aff'd sub nom.* EEOC v. County of Erie, 751 F.2d 79, 36 FEP 830 (2d Cir. 1984) (relief sought exceeded pleading and proof on Equal Pay Act claim).

[17]Sheet Metal Workers Local 28 v. EEOC, *supra* note 14, 41 FEP at 130 ("Finally, we think it significant that neither the membership goal nor the Fund order unnecessarily trammel the interests of white employees."). *Compare* Spagnuolo v. Whirlpool Corp., 717 F.2d 114, 120, 32 FEP 1382, 1386 (4th Cir. 1983) (grant of injunction under ADEA reversed because reinstatement would require displacement of innocent incumbent) *and* Romasanta v. United Airlines, 717 F.2d 1140, 1154–55, 32 FEP 1545, 1557 (7th Cir. 1983), *cert. denied,* 466 U.S. 944 *and* 471 U.S. 1065, 34 FEP 920 (1984) (retroactive seniority denied because of adverse impact on incumbents) *with* Garza v. Brownsville Indep. School Dist., 700 F.2d 253, 255, 31 FEP 403, 404 (5th Cir. 1983) (hiring preference ordered in spite of argument that it might injure other potential applicants).

[18]In re National Airlines, 700 F.2d 695, 699, 31 FEP 369, 372 (11th Cir.), *cert. denied,* 464 U.S. 933, 33 FEP 48 (1983) (injunctive relief against air carrier's maternity leave policy denied because injunction would work against carrier's efforts to consolidate its flight attendant system on routewide basis).

[19]General Bldg. Contractors Ass'n v. Pennsylvania, 458 U.S. 375, 397–402, 29 FEP 139, 150–51 (1982) (although union was found to have engaged in discriminatory conduct, absent finding of employer liability court cannot, under 42 U.S.C. § 1981, allocate a portion of costs to implement decree or grant affirmative relief, such as minority hiring quotas, against employer; however, under appropriate circumstances, employer could be subjected to ancillary injunctive orders necessary to grant complete relief from

An injunction should be limited to enjoining the specific conduct found to violate the law.[20]

## III. Relief for Identifiable Victims of Unlawful Employment Practices

Courts continue to order injunctive relief to remedy the effects of unlawful discrimination in a wide variety of circumstances.[21] Reinstatement continues to be the preferred remedy for wrongfully discharged employees,[22] often with retroactive seniority.[23] Reinstatement will be denied, however, where it is inappropriate,[24] will result in excessive friction or antagonism,[25]

---

union's discrimination); Walls v. Mississippi State Dep't of Pub. Welfare, 730 F.2d 306, 326, 34 FEP 1114, 1128–29 (5th Cir. 1984) (federal agencies innocent of Title VII violations may not be compelled to contribute to costs of implementing decree to remedy another party's Title VII violations).

[20]Davis v. Richmond, Fredericksburg & Potomac R.R., *supra* note 12 (portion of injunction directing defendant to refrain from "further violations of Title VII" struck down as too broad); EEOC v. Wooster Brush Co. Employees Relief Ass'n, 727 F.2d 566, 576–77, 33 FEP 1823, 1830–31 (6th Cir. 1984) (because district court found Title VII violation only as to denial of disability benefits for pregnancy, injunction was overboard in enjoining "discrimination against women" and would be limited to enjoining violations of Pregnancy Discrimination Act); *see also* Sheet Metal Workers Local 28 v. EEOC, *supra* note 14, 41 FEP at 128–29 ("the court should also take care to tailor its order to fit the nature of the violation it seeks to correct").

[21]Black Law Enforcement Officers Ass'n v. City of Akron, 824 F.2d 475, 481–82, 44 FEP 1477, 1482–83 (6th Cir.), *reh'g denied en banc,* _____ F.2d _____ (1987) (permanent promotions enjoined, but temporary promotions to police sergeant permitted in order to avoid harm to city); Jepsen v. Florida Bd. of Regents, 754 F.2d 924, 37 FEP 326 (11th Cir. 1985) (retroactive promotion to assistant professor affirmed; trial court has wide discretion in fashioning remedy); Curl v. Reavis, 740 F.2d 1323, 35 FEP 930 (4th Cir. 1984) (reinstatement to appropriate job level based upon experience; not entitled to higher position); Few v. Yellow Freight Sys., 40 EPD ¶ 36,374 (N.D. Ill. 1986) (reinstatement ordered within 48 hours); Gutierrez v. Municipal Court, County of Los Angeles, 41 FEP 1464 (C.D. Cal. 1985), *aff'd in pertinent part and rev'd and remanded in part,* 838 F.2d 1031 (9th Cir. 1988) (employer enjoined from instituting work rule requiring only English be spoken on the job); Cook v. United States, 36 FEP 1260, 1264 (D. Colo. 1983) (back pay with certificate of job readiness and 700-hour position at GS-7 level ordered in handicap case); Spirt v. Teachers Ins. & Annuity Ass'n, 735 F.2d 23, 34 FEP 1510 (2d Cir.), *cert. denied,* 469 U.S. 881, 35 FEP 1688 (1984) (enjoining use of gender-distinct mortality tables).

[22]Goldstein v. Manhattan Indus., 758 F.2d 1435, 37 FEP 1217 (11th Cir.), *cert. denied,* 474 U.S. 1005, 39 FEP 720 (1985) (reinstatement, not front pay, proper remedy where employer willing and conditions advantageous to claimant, even though claimant reluctant); *see also* McClure v. Mexia Indep. School Dist., 750 F.2d 396, 36 FEP 1402, *reh'g denied,* 755 F.2d 173 (5th Cir. 1985) (reinstatement as business manager where plaintiff previously had de facto exercised functions of position); Ford v. Nicks, 741 F.2d 858, 35 FEP 1080 (6th Cir. 1984), *cert. denied,* 469 U.S. 1216, 37 FEP 64 (1985); Dillon v. Coles, 746 F.2d 998, 36 FEP 159 (3d Cir. 1984) (affirmed reinstatement without front pay); Leftwich v. Harris-Stowe State College, 702 F.2d 686, 693, 31 FEP 376, 381 (8th Cir. 1983) (professor reinstated under ADEA but denied promotion); Armsey v. Nestle Co., 631 F. Supp. 717, 720, 41 FEP 983, 986 (S.D. Ohio 1985) (employee ordered reinstated to former position or similar position in different geographic area).

[23]EEOC v. Rath Packing Co., 787 F.2d 318, 355, 40 FEP 580, 595 (8th Cir.), *cert. denied,* 479 U.S. 910, 41 FEP 1712 (1986) (absent compelling reasons, failure to award retroactive seniority reversible error); *see* Leftwich v. Harris-Stowe State College, *supra* note 22; Dillon v. Coles, *supra* note 22. *But see* Romasanta v. United Airlines, *supra* note 17 (retroactive seniority denied because of adverse impact on incumbents); Ingram v. Madison Square Garden Center, *supra* note 15, 709 F.2d at 813, 32 FEP at 647.

[24]EEOC v. Financial Assurance, 624 F. Supp. 686, 692 (W.D. Mo. 1985) (given nature of relationship between executive secretary and employer, reinstatement inappropriate); Bitsounis v. Sheraton Hartford Corp., 33 FEP 894 (D. Conn. 1983) (no evidence that plaintiff still seeks her old position or that such position still exists); Kiel v. Goodyear Tire & Rubber Co., 575 F. Supp. 847, 849, 33 FEP 1122, 1123 (N.D. Ohio 1983), *aff'd without opinion,* 762 F.2d 1008 (6th Cir. 1985) (where there were other legitimate business reasons to discharge plaintiff other than age, reinstatement denied).

[25]Cassino v. Reichhold Chems., 817 F.2d 1338, 1347, 47 FEP 865 (9th Cir. 1987), *cert. denied,* 484 U.S. _____, 47 FEP 1776 (1988) (reinstatement not ordered where hostility developed between employer and employee during litigation); McIntosh v. Jones Truck Lines, 767 F.2d 433, 435, 38 FEP 710, 711 (8th Cir. 1985) (when hostility caused in part by plaintiff's attitude, reinstatement inappropriate).

or will cause an innocent incumbent to be displaced.[26] Where reinstatement may not be appropriate, courts offer limited "front pay" as an alternative, often in ADEA cases.[27]

A placement injunction will be denied if the position is abolished[28] or where the plaintiff would not have been placed in the position regardless of discrimination.[29]

Hiring[30] and promotion[31] preferences are used to place victims of discrimination on the employment roster.[32] Cases involving non-job-related

---

[26]Briseno v. Central Technical Community College Area, 739 F.2d 344, 37 FEP 57 (8th Cir. 1984); Romasanta v. United Airlines, *supra* note 17; Spagnuolo v. Whirlpool Corp., *supra* note 17; Carter v. Community Action Agency of Chambers, Tallapoosa & Coosa Counties, 625 F. Supp. 199, 39 FEP 1618 (M.D. Ala. 1985) (when successor innocent, reinstatement not ordered); Wangsness v. Watertown School Dist. 14-4, Codington County, S.D., 541 F. Supp. 332, 339, 29 FEP 375, 380–81 (D.S.D. 1982). *But see* Walters v. City of Atlanta, 803 F.2d 1135, 1148–50, 42 FEP 387, 397–99 (11th Cir. 1986) (where current occupant of unique position is direct beneficiary of repeated acts of discrimination against victim and where current occupant was aware of litigation prior to taking position, instatement of victim was appropriate despite "bumping").

[27]Cassino v. Reichhold Chems., *supra* note 25; Shore v. Federal Express Corp., 777 F.2d 1155, 1159, 39 FEP 809, 811–12 (6th Cir. 1985) (front pay available in Title VII cases under similar standards as in an ADEA claim; Maxfield v. Sinclair Int'l, 766 F.2d 788, 796, 38 FEP 442, 448–49 (3d Cir. 1985), *cert. denied,* 474 U.S. 1057, 39 FEP 1200 (1986) (in ADEA action front pay is an alternative remedy when reinstatement is unfeasible); Whittlesey v. Union Carbide Corp., 742 F.2d 724, 35 FEP 1089 (2d Cir. 1984) (front pay appropriate when there was no reasonable prospect of obtaining comparable employment). *But see* Wildman v. Lerner Stores Corp., 771 F.2d 605, 38 FEP 1377 (1st Cir. 1985) (front pay in lieu of reinstatement inappropriate when plaintiff received adequate compensatory and liquidated damages under state law); Bonura v. Chase Manhattan Bank, N.A., 629 F. Supp. 353, 43 FEP 163 (S.D.N.Y.), *aff'd,* 795 F.2d 276, 43 FEP 173 (2d Cir. 1986) (front pay inappropriate if plaintiff is able to obtain comparable alternative employment, or reinstatement is practicable, or calculation of front pay requires undue speculation). *See also* the discussion in Chapter 38 (Monetary Relief), Section III.C.

[28]Bhaya v. Westinghouse Elec. Corp., 624 F. Supp. 921, 922, 39 FEP 1556, 1558 (E.D. Pa. 1985), *vacated on other grounds,* 832 F.2d 258, 45 FEP 212 (3d Cir. 1987); Jatczak v. Ochburg, 540 F. Supp. 698, 705, 28 FEP 1773, 1779 (E.D. Mich. 1982).

[29]Fields v. Clark Univ., 817 F.2d 931, 43 FEP 1247 (1st Cir. 1987) (employer must show that decision to deny tenure would have been made absent discrimination); Bibbs v. Block, 778 F.2d 1318, 1324, 39 FEP 970, 975 (8th Cir. 1985) (employer must show by preponderance that other candidate would have been promoted absent discrimination); Patterson v. Greenwood School Dist. 50, 696 F.2d 293, 295, 30 FEP 825, 827 (4th Cir. 1982) (clear and convincing evidence demonstrated another applicant would have been promoted); *see* Muntin v. California Parks & Recreation Dep't, 671 F.2d 360, 363, 28 FEP 904, 906–7 (9th Cir. 1982). *But see* Haskins v. Department of the Army, 808 F.2d 1192, 42 FEP 1120 (6th Cir.), *cert. denied,* 484 U.S. _____, 44 FEP 1672 (1987) (analysis as to whether same decision would have been reached absent discrimination to be applied to determine whether Title VII liability exists rather than to fashion appropriate relief, declining to follow Bibbs v. Block, *supra*).

[30]Rivers v. Washington County Bd. of Educ., 770 F.2d 1010, 1012 (11th Cir. 1985) (applicant ordered placed in next available vacancy); Easley v. Anheuser-Busch, 758 F.2d 251, 37 FEP 549 (8th Cir. 1985) (successful Title VII litigants awarded wrongfully denied jobs); Darnell v. City of Jasper, Ala., 730 F.2d 653, 37 FEP 1315 (11th Cir. 1984) (hiring ordered, conditional on applicant injured by Title VII violation passing civil service exam); Garza v. Brownsville Indep. School Dist., 700 F.2d 253, 255, 31 FEP 403, 404 (5th Cir. 1983) (plaintiff to be hired for next available position comparable to one unlawfully denied her); Robinson v. City of Lake Station, 630 F. Supp. 1052, 1064 (N.D. Ind. 1986) (plaintiff to be hired into next available position and given seniority as of date of initial discrimination).

[31]Taylor v. Home Ins. Co., 777 F.2d 849, 860, 39 FEP 769, 777–78 (4th Cir. 1985), *cert. denied,* 476 U.S. 1142, 40 FEP 1512 (1986) (plaintiff ordered promoted to his choice of two positions as vacancies occur); Paxton v. Union Nat'l Bank, 688 F.2d 552, 574, 29 FEP 1233, 1252 (8th Cir. 1982), *cert. denied,* 460 U.S. 1083, 31 FEP 824 (1983) (plaintiff to be promoted to first vacancy for which she is qualified and receive rate of pay of position denied her to date of placement); Feher v. Department of Labor & Indus. Relations, 29 FEP 768, 769 (D. Haw. 1982) (plaintiff granted retroactive promotion). *Compare* Collins v. Robinson, 568 F. Supp. 1464, 115 LRRM 2621 (E.D. Ark. 1983), *aff'd,* 734 F.2d 1321 (8th Cir. 1984) (police officer reinstated with promotion) *with* Leftwich v. Harris-Stowe State College, *supra* note 22 (promotion to full professor denied reinstated plaintiff).

[32]Courts continue to place limits on the utilization of goals and timetables, finding they are not appropriate to remedy classwide discrimination where alternate effective methods could secure relief for victims without upsetting the legitimate expectations of individuals in the majority group. Segar v. Smith, 738 F.2d 1249, 35 FEP 31 (D.C. Cir. 1984), *cert. denied,* 471 U.S. 1115, 37 FEP 1312 (1985).

preemployment and prepromotion testing[33] and employer-imposed minimum educational standards[34] continue to result in injunctive relief. An employee who prevails in an antidiscrimination action is often entitled to have his personnel records purged.[35]

The Equal Employment Opportunity Commission issued a statement, approved on February 5, 1985, on Remedies and Relief for Individual Cases of Unlawful Discrimination.[36] This statement establishes a policy which is applicable where there is a basis for believing a violation of any laws the EEOC enforces has occurred. This policy provides for (1) notices to employees, (2) measures to prevent recurrences, (3) rightful placement of identified victims, (4) reimbursement of lost earnings of identified victims, and (5) measures to insure a cessation of the unlawful practice.

## IV. QUOTA HIRING AND PROMOTION ORDERS BENEFITING PERSONS OTHER THAN IDENTIFIABLE VICTIMS OF UNLAWFUL DISCRIMINATION

### A. Hiring and Union Membership Quotas

The Supreme Court decision in *Firefighters Local 1784 v. Stotts*[37] denies district courts the power under Title VII to override bona fide seniority provisions during layoffs, even in order to preserve progress made in integrating a racially imbalanced work force.[38] The Court reversed the Sixth Circuit ruling[39] that had enjoined the City of Memphis from following seniority provisions in laying off black members of the fire department, even though they were not identifiable victims of discrimination.

---

[33]Gilbert v. City of Little Rock, 799 F.2d 1210, 44 FEP 509 (8th Cir. 1986) (police department which had used discriminatory oral examination required to validate future oral examinations in compliance with EEOC guidelines); Easley v. Anheuser-Busch, *supra* note 30 (racially discriminatory preemployment test enjoined); Darnell v. City of Jasper, Ala., *supra* note 30 (employer ordered to administer preemployment test to applicant); Berkman v. City of New York (I), 705 F.2d 584, 595, 31 FEP 767, 774 (2d Cir. 1983) (discriminatory preemployment physical exam for firefighters enjoined); Brunet v. City of Columbus, 642 F. Supp. 1214, 42 FEP 1846 (S.D. Ohio 1986), *appeal dismissed,* 826 F.2d 1062, 44 FEP 1671 *and* 45 FEP 1080 (6th Cir. 1987), *cert. denied,* 485 U.S. ____ (1988). (non-content-valid discriminatory preemployment physical test banned, and employer enjoined from hiring on basis of test). *But see* Vanguard Justice Soc'y v. Hughes, 592 F. Supp. 245, 36 FEP 1494 (D. Md. 1984) (remedy limited to establishing valid promotional procedure and reevaluation of victims pursuant to new procedure).

[34]Carpenter v. Stephen F. Austin State Univ., 706 F.2d 608, 619, 31 FEP 1758, 1767, *reh'g denied,* 712 F.2d 1416 (5th Cir. 1983) (employer required to reevaluate educational standards for promotion and to adopt promotional policies to remedy effect of past discrimination).

[35]Rosemond v. Cooper Tire & Rubber Co., Cooper Indus. Prods. Div., 612 F. Supp. 1105, 1118, 43 FEP 518 (N.D. Ind. 1985) (employer required to expunge plaintiff's employment records, including performance appraisals, error log, and written memorandum in personnel files); Clemente v. United States, 568 F. Supp. 1150, 1163, 36 FEP 1716, 1726 (C.D. Cal. 1983), *vacated and reversed,* 766 F.2d 1358, 38 FEP 808 (9th Cir. 1985), *cert. denied,* 474 U.S. 1101, 39 FEP 1424 (1986); EEOC v. Domino's Pizza, 34 FEP 1075 (E.D. Mich. 1983); *see also* Ambrose v. United States Steel Corp., 39 FEP 30, 35 (N.D. Cal. 1985) (employer prohibited from disclosing to anyone that plaintiff had been involuntarily discharged).

[36]25 DAILY LAB. REP. E-1 (BNA, Feb. 6, 1985).

[37]467 U.S. 561, 34 FEP 1702 (1984).

[38]*See also* White v. Colgan Elec. Co., 781 F.2d 1214, 1271, 39 FEP 1599, 1601–2 (6th Cir. 1986) (consent decree which was silent as to seniority did not prevent employer from invoking inverse layoff procedure dictated by collective bargaining agreement); United States v. City of Cincinnati, 771 F.2d 161, 167, 38 FEP 1402, 1407 (6th Cir. 1985) (consent decree which did not mention layoffs could not be basis for injunction prohibiting city police department from following bona fide seniority system in effecting layoffs).

[39]Stotts v. Memphis Fire Dep't, 679 F.2d 541, 28 FEP 1491 (6th Cir. 1982).

*Stotts* does not, however, affect a court's power to order relief under a civil rights statute other than Title VII.[40] *Stotts* also does not have the effect of eliminating all remedial affirmative action under Title VII other than that which benefits specifically identifiable victims of past discrimination. Under Title VII, district courts still have the authority to impose remedial hiring[41] or union membership[42] goals and quotas which do not interfere with bona fide seniority systems. In *Sheet Metal Workers Local 28 v. EEOC,*[43] the Supreme Court affirmed this principle by holding that Title VII does not prohibit a court from ordering minority goals as preferential relief benefiting individuals who were not the actual victims of discrimination to remedy egregious discrimination where the relief is narrowly tailored to achieve the remedial goals.

Although courts have the authority to impose remedial quotas, and some have found them a useful tool for reforming a workplace formerly closed to women or minorities,[44] other courts remain hostile to the idea and have refused to impose hiring quotas.[45] While quota hiring from an identified pool may be proper,[46] quotas may be unnecessary if the employer is ordered to take other affirmative action to seek out women or minorities for positions at issue.[47]

## B. Promotion Quotas

The Supreme Court clarified the remedial authority of the federal courts in *United States v. Paradise,*[48] upholding a one-to-one promotion quota for Alabama state troopers against a challenge under the Equal Protection Clause of the Fourteenth Amendment. Emphasizing that the employer's egregious history of resistance to integration amply justified race-conscious relief, the Court nevertheless cautioned that such relief must be narrowly tailored to the legitimate purpose of eliminating past and present discrimina-

---

[40]Pennsylvania v. Operating Eng'rs Local 542, 807 F.2d 330, 42 FEP 836 (3d Cir. 1986) (distinguishing *Stotts* because wider relief may be available under § 1981 than under Title VII); Arthur v. Nyquist, 712 F.2d 816, 32 FEP 822 (2d Cir. 1983), *cert. denied,* 467 U.S. 1259, 34 FEP 1887 (1984) (employment quota may modify seniority system in order to attain racial balance in school system when it is imposed as part of school desegregation plan under constitutional standards rather than as Title VII remedy).

[41]United States v. City of Buffalo, 609 F. Supp 1252, 37 FEP 1729 (W.D.N.Y.), *aff'd sub nom.* United States v. NAACP, 779 F.2d 881, 39 FEP 1168 (2d Cir. 1985), *cert. denied,* 478 U.S. 1020, 41 FEP 272 (1986) (*Stotts* does not require modification of remedial hiring decree that offers prospective relief and does not conflict with seniority system).

[42]Pennsylvania v. Operating Eng'rs Local 542, *supra* note 40 (*Stotts* does not require modification of remedial injunction imposing minority referral goals on union hiring hall).

[43]478 U.S. 421, 41 FEP 107, 114–130 and n.47 (1986) (upholding union membership goal).

[44]Ingram v. Madison Square Garden Center, 535 F. Supp. 1082, 32 FEP 548 (S.D.N.Y. 1982), *aff'd as modified,* 709 F.2d 807, 32 FEP 641 (2d Cir.), *cert. denied,* 464 U.S. 937, 33 FEP 48 (1983).

[45]Kilgo v. Bowman Transp., 576 F. Supp. 600, 601, 40 FEP 1412, 1413 (N.D. Ga. 1984), *aff'd,* 789 F.2d 859, 40 FEP 1415 (11th Cir. 1986) ("Preferential treatment on the grounds of sex, by means of a quota, is destructive of self-respect and merely substitutes one form of discrimination for another"); United States v. Sheriff of Lancaster County, 561 F. Supp. 1005, 1011, 31 FEP 827, 832 (E.D. Va. 1983) ("Why not * * * disclaim quotas in any form and require extensive remedial recruitment * * * ?").

[46]Berkman v. City of New York (I), 705 F.2d 584, 596, 31 FEP 767, 775 (2d Cir. 1983); Association Against Discrimination in Employment v. City of Bridgeport, 710 F.2d 69, 75, 32 FEP 20, 25 (2d Cir. 1983).

[47]Williams v. Owens-Illinois, 665 F.2d 918, 931–32, 27 FEP 1273, 1283–84, *modified,* 28 FEP 1820 (9th Cir.), *cert. denied,* 459 U.S. 971, 30 FEP 56 (1982); United States v. Sheriff of Lancaster County, *supra* note 45.

[48]480 U.S. 149, 43 FEP 1 (1987).

tion.[49] The *Paradise* decision gave support to a series of lower court orders enforcing promotion goals where warranted by the facts. In *Williams v. City of New Orleans,*[50] for example, the Fifth Circuit, en banc, reaffirmed its position that the imposition of a quota to remedy past discrimination is not forbidden by Title VII even where it is not limited to actual victims of discrimination.

Refusing to uphold a three-to-one promotion quota in *Thompson v. Sawyer,*[51] the D.C. Circuit stated that quotas should be of short duration, be targeted specifically at mending the identified discrimination, avoid unnecessary infringement upon others' rights, and be implemented only after consideration is given to an alternate or supplemental method of relief.[52] The *Thompson* court refused to uphold this quota because it did not focus on unlawful practices and ignored concerns of others who might seek employment and could theoretically be shut out for as long as 50 years.[53]

In light of the Supreme Court's holding in *Steelworkers v. Weber,*[54] the courts are less reluctant to uphold the validity of quotas contained in voluntary consent decrees.[55] The Supreme Court distinguished relief awarded in consent decrees from relief that is court-ordered in *Firefighters Local 93 v. City of Cleveland.*[56] The Court held that Title VII does not bar voluntary agreements that provide race-conscious relief, even though a "court might be barred from ordering the same relief after a trial or, as in *Stotts,* in disputed proceedings to modify a decree entered upon consent."[57]

[49]*Id.,* 43 FEP at 9–15 (quota was narrowly tailored because it is limited only to qualified candidates, is temporary, and imposes no absolute bar to white advancement).

[50]729 F.2d 1554, 34 FEP 1009 (5th Cir. 1984) (en banc), *appeal dismissed,* 763 F.2d 667 (5th Cir. 1985); *see also* McKenzie v. Sawyer, 684 F.2d 62, 80, 29 FEP 633, 647 (D.C. Cir. 1982) (goals do not overreach their usefulness); Powell v. Georgia-Pacific Corp., 535 F. Supp. 713, 720, 30 FEP 21, 26 (W.D. Ark. 1980) (employer must recruit or qualify sufficient black maintenance employees to be representative of their availability in plant's work force); Clayton v. Children's Hosp. Medical Center, 30 FEP 996, 997 (N.D. Cal. 1979) (consent decree amended to permit magistrate to enforce decree's promotion quota for black professionals).

[51]678 F.2d 257, 28 FEP 1614 (D.C. Cir. 1982).

[52]*Id.* at 298, 28 FEP at 1646.

[53]*Id.* at 295, 28 FEP at 1646; *see also* Hammon v. Barry, 813 F.2d 412, 43 FEP 89 (D.C. Cir. 1987) (promotion provisions of fire department's affirmative action plan struck down because they unnecessarily trammeled upon rights of white firefighters who were in line for promotion); Segar v. Smith, 738 F.2d 1249, 35 FEP 31 (D.C. Cir. 1984), *cert. denied,* 471 U.S. 1115, 37 FEP 1312 (1985) (promotion goal ordered by district court was not appropriate because court did not consider whether less severe remedies might prove equally efficacious); Vanguard Justice Soc'y v. Hughes, 592 F. Supp. 245, 36 FEP 1494 (D. Md. 1984) (court refused to award quota-type relief in absence of significant prior discrimination); United States v. Virginia, 554 F. Supp. 268, 272, 30 FEP 1054, 1057, *reh'g,* 558 F. Supp. 99, 31 FEP 183 (E.D. Va. 1983) (Fourteenth Amendment equal protection guarantees override Title VII).

[54]443 U.S. 193, 20 FEP 1 (1979).

[55]Deveraux v. Geary, 765 F.2d 268, 38 FEP 23 (1st Cir. 1985), *cert. denied,* 471 U.S. 1115, 41 FEP 272 (1986) (Supreme Court's decision in *Stotts* does not render invalid voluntary consent decree which includes promotion goals); Turner v. Orr, 759 F.2d 817, 37 FEP 1186 (11th Cir. 1985), *cert. denied,* 478 U.S. 1020, 41 FEP 272 (1986) (Title VII does not bar voluntary affirmative action plan adopted in consent decree that does not conflict with seniority system and does not involve third-party rights); Block v. Revlon, 37 FEP 1327 (S.D.N.Y. 1985) (court upheld proposed consent decree containing placement and promotion goals which relate reasonably to racial composition of relevant work force); Youngblood v. Dalzell, 625 F. Supp. 30, 38 FEP 814 (S.D. Ohio 1985), *aff'd,* 804 F.2d 360, 42 FEP 415 (6th Cir. 1986), *cert. denied,* 480 U.S. 935, 43 FEP 560 (1987) (court interpreted consent decree to require affirmative action in promotions).

[56]478 U.S. 50, 41 FEP 139 (1986).

[57]*Id.,* 41 FEP at 151. *And compare* Johnson v. Transportation Agency, Santa Clara County, 480 U.S. 616, 43 FEP 411 (1987) (upholding public employer's voluntarily implemented affirmative action plan against Title VII challenge, utilizing analysis developed in *Weber*) *with* City of Richmond v. J.A. Croson Co., 488 U.S. _____, 57 U.S.L.W. 4132 (1989) (affirming city construction contracts on constitutional challenge, for failure to meet strict scrutiny standard).

## V. PRELIMINARY INJUNCTIONS

### A. Rule 65 Preliminary Relief

A consensus among those circuits deciding the issue concludes that preliminary injunctions are available under Federal Rule of Civil Procedure 65 in employment discrimination litigation before state remedies are exhausted and the EEOC issues a right-to-sue letter.[58] Some courts apply the traditional four-part test for a preliminary injunction,[59] while others customize or add special emphasis to the traditional analysis.[60] Where a litigant fails to make the necessary showing, relief will be denied.[61] Irreparable harm

---

[58]Aronberg v. Walters, 755 F.2d 1114, 1115, 45 FEP 522 (4th Cir. 1985) (where intent of Congress in enacting 1972 Amendments to Title VII extending its coverage to federal employment was to give those public employees same rights as private employees, federal employee was not required to exhaust administrative remedies to obtain injunctive relief to preserve status quo); Holt v. Continental Group, 708 F.2d 87, 31 FEP 1468 (2d Cir. 1983), cert. denied, 465 U.S. 1030, 33 FEP 1884 (1984); Bailey v. Delta Air Lines, 722 F.2d 942, 944, 33 FEP 713, 715 (1st Cir. 1983); Duke v. Langdon, 695 F.2d 1136, 1137, 30 FEP 1059, 1060 (9th Cir. 1983); Sheehan v. Purolator Courier Corp., 676 F.2d 877, 887, 28 FEP 202, 209 (2d Cir. 1981) (where court eventually will have jurisdiction of substantive claims and administrative tribunal has preliminary jurisdiction, court has incidental equity jurisdiction to grant temporary relief to preserve status quo); Berman v. New York City Ballet, 616 F. Supp. 555, 556, 38 FEP 1286, 1287 (S.D.N.Y. 1985) (court's jurisdiction not dependent upon EEOC's issuance of right-to-sue letter).

[59]Castro v. United States, 775 F.2d 399, 407–8, 39 FEP 162, 168 (1st Cir. 1985); Shaffer v. Globe Protection, 721 F.2d 1121, 1123, 33 FEP 450, 451 (7th Cir. 1983); United States v. Jefferson County, 720 F.2d 1511, 1519, 33 FEP 829, 831 (11th Cir. 1983); Golden v. Lutheran Family Servs. in N.C., 601 F. Supp. 383, 384, 39 FEP 1422, 1424 (W.D.N.C. 1984); EEOC v. Pennsylvania, 39 FEP 587, 589 (M.D. Pa. 1984); EEOC v. City of Bowling Green, Ky., 607 F. Supp. 524, 525, 37 FEP 963, 964 (W.D. Ky. 1985); Berman v. New York City Ballet, supra note 58; Bryan v. Chemical Bank, 617 F. Supp. 1070, 1071, 38 FEP 1809, 1809–10 (S.D.N.Y. 1985); Morrow v. Inmont Corp., 30 FEP 1019, 1024 (W.D.N.C. 1982).

[60]Duke v. Langdon, supra note 58 (applicant must demonstrate either probable success on merits and irreparable harm, or that serious questions are raised and balance of hardship tips sharply in his favor); York v. Alabama State Bd. of Educ., 581 F. Supp. 779, 787, 39 FEP 548, 554 (M.D. Ala. 1983) (since plaintiffs seek preliminary injunctive relief pursuant to Title VII, they are not required to make usual showing of irreparable harm as prerequisite to relief) (citing Middleton-Keirn v. Stone, 655 F.2d 609, 611, 26 FEP 1154, 1155–56 (5th Cir. 1981); United States v. Hayes Int'l Corp., 415 F.2d 1038, 1045, 2 FEP 67, 71 (5th Cir. 1969)); Ferrell v. Durham Technical Inst., 569 F. Supp. 16, 19, 33 FEP 855, 858 (M.D.N.C. 1983) (two most important factors are probable irreparable injury to plaintiff and likely harm to defendant).

[61]Compare Castro v. United States, supra note 59 (terminated employee's allegations of inability to find other employment and loss of credit insufficient to demonstrate irreparable damage), Stewart v. Immigration & Naturalization Serv., 762 F.2d 193, 199, 37 FEP 1357, 1361–62 (2d Cir. 1985) (damage to reputation and self-esteem coupled with financial hardship held insufficient to establish irreparable harm), O'Connor v. Peru State College, 728 F.2d 1001, 34 FEP 85 (8th Cir. 1984), aff'd, 781 F.2d 632, 39 FEP 1241 (8th Cir. 1986) (no showing of irreparable harm and balance of equities did not favor plaintiff), Shaffer v. Globe Protection, supra note 59 (no showing of irreparable injury), United States v. Jefferson County, supra note 59 (no showing of irreparable harm), EEOC v. New Jersey, 620 F. Supp. 977, 995–97, 39 FEP 516 (D.N.J. 1985), aff'd, 815 F.2d 694, 43 FEP 653 and 43 FEP 1647 (3d Cir. 1987) Johnson v. Orr, 617 F. Supp. 170, 177–78, 37 FEP 580, 586 (E.D. Cal. 1985), aff'd, 787 F.2d 597 (9th Cir. 1986) (no showing of likelihood of success or irreparable injury by officer who was separated from service after identifying herself as homosexual; she alleged violation of First Amendment of the Constitution), Berman v. New York City Ballet, 616 F. Supp. 555, 557–58, 38 FEP 1286, 1288 (S.D.N.Y. 1985) (damage to reputation, denial of promotion, and claim that court eventually deciding her claim would not be able to reinstate her in unique position, since position would then be filled, was held insufficient to establish irreparable harm), Akili v. Sise, 38 FEP 553, 556 (N.D.N.Y. 1984) (stigmatization, humiliation, and loss of human dignity attendant to discriminatory discharge insufficient to show irreparable harm), Bryan v. Chemical Bank, supra note 59 (no showing of irreparable injury; plaintiff ignored advice of employment counselors and chose not to seek employment outside his area of specialization for some time after his termination), Jones v. Monroe Community College, 38 FEP 645, 646–47 (W.D.N.Y. 1984), aff'd, 755 F.2d 914, 38 FEP 672 (2d Cir. 1985) (no showing of irreparable injury on grounds that unique nature of plaintiff's qualifications and current position would make it impossible to find similar employment in area and nonrenewal of her contract would impose financial hardship on her family), EEOC v. Dravo Corp., 36 FEP 1211, 1212 (W.D. Pa. 1984) (loss of wages due to discharge or suspension does not constitute irreparable harm), Guerrero v. Reeves Bros., 562 F. Supp. 603, 606–7,

is not presumed and is seldom found from the mere loss of a job, since that loss may ordinarily be remedied by damages if the litigant prevails.[62] An injunction may issue, however, if there is potential irreparable harm to the public interest.[63]

Where the applicable standard has been met, preliminary relief is granted to preserve the status quo.[64] Where the status quo has already been disturbed, the courts fashion preliminary relief to fit the particular circumstances.[65]

---

33 FEP 1021, 1024 (W.D.N.C. 1983) (no showing of irreparable harm or likelihood of success; court did not maintain jurisdiction over claim because right-to-sue letter would not issue for several months), Lebron v. Hotel & Restaurant Employees Local 6, 540 F. Supp. 1389, 1390, 29 FEP 1069, 1070 (S.D.N.Y. 1982) (injunction to stay arbitration denied; no irreparable injury and injunction could cause greater hardship to employer) *and* Batsche v. National Broadcasting Co., 28 EPD ¶ 32,568 (S.D.N.Y. 1982) (no proof of irreparable injury or likelihood of success on merits) *with* Golden v. Lutheran Family Servs. in N.C., *supra* note 59 (terminated black employee demonstrated likelihood of success and irreparable harm; he showed not only loss of wages and benefits but also loss of reputation that will make it difficult to find other employment), EEOC v. City of Bowling Green, Ky., 607 F. Supp. 524, 524–27, 37 FEP 963, 964–66 (W.D. Ky. 1985) (likelihood of success and irreparable harm established; EEOC showed that police officer forced to retire would suffer anxiety and emotional problems and also be unable to keep up with current matters in department, even though he could collect damages and be reinstated) *and* York v. Alabama State Bd. of Educ., *supra* note 60 (plaintiffs established irreparable harm in light of fact they would be removed from their professional environment and unable to advance their careers).

[62]Moteles v. University of Pa., 730 F.2d 913, 918, 34 FEP 424, 427 (3d Cir.), *cert. denied,* 469 U.S. 855, 35 FEP 1800 (1984) (involuntary transfer to less desirable shift); Duke v. Langdon, *supra* note 58; Shaffer v. Globe Protection, *supra* note 59; Cuesta v. New York Office of Court Admin., 571 F. Supp. 392, 393–94, 37 FEP 1411, 1412–14 (S.D.N.Y. 1983) (no showing of likelihood of success on merits or irreparable injury due to loss of job; court's remedial powers can repair any damages); Nelson v. Baldrige, 578 F. Supp. 320, 322, 33 FEP 1576, 1577 (W.D. Mo. 1984); *see also* Holt v. Continental Group, *supra* note 58 (retaliatory discharge may deter other employees from asserting rights under Act; this may constitute irreparable injury).

[63]EEOC v. City of Bowling Green, Ky., 607 F. Supp. 524, 527, 37 FEP 963, 965 (W.D. Ky. 1985) (ADEA shows there is public interest in keeping person on the job until age 70); Golden v. Lutheran Family Servs. in N.C., *supra* note 59 (reinstatement of terminated black employee would serve public interest as expressed in statutes against racially discriminatory treatment and retaliatory action); York v. Alabama State Bd. of Educ., 581 F. Supp. 779, 787, 39 FEP 548, 555 (M.D. Ala. 1983) (where there is strong evidence of artificial, arbitrary, and unnecessary barriers to employment caused by unlawful discrimination, public interest is served by granting temporary injunction); United States v. Jefferson County, *supra* note 59 ("this court * * * will presume irreparable harm in a Title VII case in which the employee has exhausted his administrative remedies") (dictum); Monroe v. United Airlines, 34 FEP 1610 (N.D. Ill. 1983) (ADEA's goals are served by enjoining employer from implementing mandatory retirement policy); Sebastian v. Texas Dep't of Corrections, 541 F. Supp. 970, 978–79, 30 FEP 1320, 1327 (S.D. Tex. 1982) (plaintiff reinstated in job upon court's determination that "irreparable harm * * * will be presumed from the very fact that the statute [Title VII] has been violated"). *But see* EEOC v. New Jersey, 620 F. Supp. 977, 997–98, 39 FEP 516, 534 (D.N.J. 1985), *aff'd,* 815 F.2d 694, 43 FEP 653 *and* 43 FEP 1647 (3d Cir. 1987) (public interest would be adversely affected if state would be enjoined from enforcing mandatory retirement policy, since retention of officers over age 55 would present risk of harm to them, their fellow officers, and the public).

[64]York v. Alabama State Bd. of Educ., *supra* note 60 (terminated teachers to be reinstated, thereby maintaining status quo); EEOC v. City of Bowling Green, Ky., *supra* note 59; Berman v. New York City Ballet, 616 F. Supp. 555, 556, 38 FEP 1286, 1288 (S.D.N.Y. 1985) (where plaintiff alleges significant retaliatory conduct on part of employer, court will grant injunctive relief to preserve status quo); Aguilar v. Baine Serv. Sys., 538 F. Supp. 581, 32 FEP 1834 (S.D.N.Y. 1982) (employees claiming retaliation are to remain employed while action is pending); Cassidy v. Virginia Carolina Veneer Corp., 538 F. Supp. 651, 33 FEP 1018 (W.D. Va. 1982).

[65]EEOC v. Chrysler Corp., 733 F.2d 1183, 34 FEP 1401, *reh'g denied,* 738 F.2d 167, 41 FEP 1011 (6th Cir. 1984) (forced retirees provided opportunity to be placed on layoff status in ADEA case); Golden v. Lutheran Family Servs. in N.C., *supra* note 59 (plaintiff reinstated in position to which he was demoted); Farkas v. New York State Dep't of Health, 554 F. Supp. 24, 29, 30 FEP 538, 541–42 (N.D.N.Y. 1982), *aff'd without opinion,* 767 F.2d 907 (2d Cir.), *cert. denied,* 474 U.S. 1033 (1985) (promotion withheld, salary increased pending final determination, and plaintiff directed to post bond to cover salary increase in event he is unsuccessful on merits); Sebastian v. Texas Dep't of Corrections, *supra* note 63 (restoration of vacation and holiday benefits used to prosecute claim for preliminary injunction).

## B. § 706(f)(2) Preliminary Relief

The courts continue to disagree on whether, under § 706(f)(2), the EEOC must meet the traditional test for preliminary relief by showing irreparable harm and likelihood of success, or whether a more relaxed standard is applicable.[66] Those courts which adhere to the traditional standard hold that the irreparable injury may be shown either as to the charging party or the EEOC.[67] Irreparable injury to the EEOC is established by showing that the failure to grant preliminary relief will discourage other employees from cooperating with the EEOC's investigation or from filing their own claims.[68]

## VI. Appropriateness of Injunctive Relief Where Unlawful Employment Practices Have Been Discontinued

Although a court will not enjoin behavior that is neither threatened nor imminent,[69] or which is "moot,"[70] the fact that an employer has changed or abandoned its discriminatory practice is not by itself sufficient to foreclose injunctive relief necessary to make whole a victim of discrimination.[71] Absent clear and convincing proof that no reasonable probability of further noncompliance exists, the normally discretionary grant of an injunction may be considered mandatory, even where the unlawful discrimination no longer exists.[72] However, injunctive relief may not be appropriate for an isolated

---

[66]*Compare* EEOC v. Anchor Hocking Corp., 666 F.2d 1037, 27 FEP 809, 814 (6th Cir. 1981) (traditional standard), EEOC v. Dravo Corp., *supra* note 61 (same), EEOC v. City of Bowling Green, Ky., *supra* note 59, EEOC v. New Jersey, *supra* note 61, EEOC v. Target Stores, 36 FEP 543 (D. Minn. 1984), EEOC v. Howard Univ., 32 FEP 331, 334 (D.D.C. 1983) *and* EEOC v. Bronson Methodist Hosp., 489 F. Supp. 1066, 27 FEP 884 (W.D. Mich. 1979) *with* EEOC v. Pacific Sw. Airlines, 587 F. Supp. 686, 34 FEP 1430 (N.D. Cal. 1984) (when EEOC requests preliminary injunction under § 706(f)(2), court should presume existence of irreparable injury) *and* EEOC v. Credit Consultants, 532 F. Supp. 11, 12, 28 FEP 71, 72 (N.D. Ohio 1981) (traditional standard should be relaxed when EEOC seeks preliminary relief under § 706(f)(2)).

[67]EEOC v. Target Stores, *supra* note 66; EEOC v. Howard Univ., *supra* note 66.

[68]*Compare* EEOC v. ABC Rentals, 39 EPD ¶ 35,835 (N.D. Tex. 1985) (temporary restraining order granted to restrain defendant from harassing employees and interfering with investigation), EEOC v. Target Stores, *supra* note 66 (preliminary injunction granted) *and* EEOC v. Atlantic Richfield Co., 30 FEP 551, 552 (C.D. Cal. 1979) (preliminary injunction granted) *with* EEOC v. Howard Univ., *supra* note 66 (preliminary relief denied because EEOC failed to establish that alleged retaliation discouraged employees from cooperating in its investigation) *and* EEOC v. Bronson Methodist Hosp., *supra* note 66 (preliminary relief denied because EEOC failed to establish that other employees are reluctant to pursue any Title VII claims because of employer's alleged retaliatory acts).

[69]Walls v. Mississippi State Dep't of Pub. Welfare, 730 F.2d 306, 325, 34 FEP 1114, 1128 (5th Cir. 1984) (vacating injunction against offending selection procedure discontinued 11 years prior to district court order).

[70]EEOC v. Goodyear Aerospace Corp., 813 F.2d 1539, 43 FEP 875 (9th Cir. 1987) (employer's settlement with employee renders EEOC's claim for back pay on behalf of employee moot, but does not moot action for classwide relief); *cf.* Garcia v. Lawn, 805 F.2d 1400, 42 FEP 873 (9th Cir. 1986) (if court can grant any effective relief in event it decides in employee's favor, matter is not moot).

[71]Garza v. Brownsville Indep. School Dist., 700 F.2d 253, 31 FEP 403 (5th Cir. 1983) (employer's elimination of hiring barrier not basis for denying injunctive relief including reinstatement or hiring preference); *cf.* Smith v. Flesh Co., 512 F. Supp. 46, 53, 35 FEP 448, 455 (E.D. Mo. 1981) (where reinstatement provided full remedy to complainant, no injunction against discriminatory practices where evidence did not show practices were ongoing).

[72]Cox v. American Cast Iron Pipe Co., 784 F.2d 1546, 1561, 40 FEP 678, 689–90 (11th Cir.), *cert. denied,* 479 U.S. 883, 41 FEP 1712 (1986) (where abundant evidence of past discrimination exists, injunctive relief mandatory absent clear and convincing proof of no reasonable probability of further noncompliance with law); Lewis v. Smith, 731 F.2d 1535, 1540, 34 FEP 1313, 1316 (11th Cir. 1984);

unlawful incident without evidence that an employer is likely to repeat the violation.[73]

Recent efforts at compliance and an improved statistical employment profile may not convince a court that discrimination has been eliminated and an injunction is unnecessary.[74] However, injunctive relief may not be necessary if modification of discriminatory performance requirements for an entry level job position removes its discriminatory character,[75] a remedy is no longer available because the facilities involved in litigation are no longer in operation,[76] or corrective measures to address past incidents of discrimination have been taken.[77] Additionally, an injunction will be vacated when it has served its purpose,[78] and the nondiscriminatory objective system established by the decree is redundant in light of other appropriate company personnel systems.[79]

# VII. Monitoring the Court Decree

A district court may retain jurisdiction over a matter to review compliance with its remedial order[80] and to assure that discriminatory practices are not continued.[81] Specific time limits may be set on the continuing exercise

---

In re National Airlines Inc., 700 F.2d 695, 697, 31 FEP 369, 370 (11th Cir.), *cert. denied,* 464 U.S. 933, 33 FEP 48 (1983); NAACP v. City of Evergreen, Ala., 693 F.2d 1367, 1370, 30 FEP 925, 927 (11th Cir. 1982) (even where court finds that discrimination no longer exists, court may still enjoin discontinued illegal conduct); Abrams v. Baylor College of Medicine, 581 F. Supp. 1570, 1580, 34 FEP 229, 237–38 (S.D. Tex. 1984), *aff'd in part and rev'd in part on other grounds,* 805 F.2d 528, 42 FEP 806 (5th Cir. 1986); *see also* Donovan v. Kaszycki & Sons Contractors, 599 F. Supp. 860, 872, 27 WH 35 (S.D.N.Y. 1984) (FLSA action sustaining injunction even though work completed and violation had ceased).

[73]EEOC v. Financial Assurance, 624 F. Supp. 686, 695 (W.D. Mo. 1985) (injunction not entered for isolated finding of unlawful discharge of executive secretary due to pregnancy).

[74]EEOC v. Cook Paint & Varnish Co., 35 FEP 437, 440 (W.D. Mo. 1981).

[75]Payne v. Travenol Laboratories, 673 F.2d 798, 825, 28 FEP 1212, 1233–34 (5th Cir.), *cert. denied,* 459 U.S. 1038, 30 FEP 440 (1982).

[76]Domingo v. New England Fish Co., 727 F.2d 1429, 1438, 34 FEP 584, 592, *modified,* 742 F.2d 520, 37 FEP 1303 (9th Cir. 1984) (injunctive relief not available where company with segregated eating facilities was no longer operating); *cf.* Nord v. United States Steel Corp., 758 F.2d 1462, 1473 n.11, 37 FEP 1232, 1248 (11th Cir. 1985) (suggesting availability of reinstatement at other offices of defendant, where location of plaintiff's previous employment was no longer operating; depending on treatment afforded comparably situated individuals when office was closed).

[77]Hammon v. Barry, 813 F.2d 412, 43 FEP 89 (D.C. Cir. 1987); Snow v. Nevada Dep't of Prisons, 582 F. Supp. 53, 65, 39 FEP 1133, 1141 (D. Nev. 1984) (no injunction warranted where prison administrators took corrective measures to address sex discrimination involving female correctional officers).

[78]Neely v. City of Grenada, 799 F.2d 203, 41 FEP 1853 (5th Cir. 1986).

[79]Stewart v. General Motors Corp., 756 F.2d 1285, 1289–94 (7th Cir. 1985) (affirming vacation of injunction containing promotional structure designed to replace employer's selective, unstructured procedure which had violated Title VII).

[80]Pennsylvania v. Operating Eng'rs Local 542, 807 F.2d 330, 42 FEP 836 (3d Cir. 1986) (district court extended injunctive decree for two years); Darnell v. City of Jasper, Ala., 730 F.2d 653, 37 FEP 1315 (11th Cir. 1984) (district court should retain jurisdiction after remand so that it may order plaintiff instated as police officer if he passes exam and meets other valid qualifications for position); Kilgo v. Bowman Transp., 576 F. Supp. 600, 40 FEP 1412 (N.D. Ga. 1984), *aff'd,* 789 F.2d 859, 40 FEP 1415 (11th Cir. 1986) (court retains jurisdiction over trucking company to consider hiring goals if company fails to make special effort to recruit women for over-the-road positions); Stallworth v. Shuler, 35 FEP 770, 776 (N.D. Fla. 1983), *aff'd,* 777 F.2d 1431, 39 FEP 983 (11th Cir. 1985) (court which found that school board and superintendent of schools discriminated against black teacher retained jurisdiction of action to assure compliance with court's remedial order); United States v. Sheriff of Lancaster County, 561 F. Supp. 1005, 31 FEP 827 (E.D. Va. 1983).

[81]Bigby v. City of Chicago, 38 FEP 844, 852–53 (N.D. Ill. 1984), *aff'd,* 766 F.2d 1053, 38 FEP 853 (7th Cir. 1985), *cert. denied,* 474 U.S. 1056, 39 FEP 1200 (1986) (court retains jurisdiction over future development of promotion tests to ensure defendants do not again embark on course of discriminatory conduct).

of jurisdiction.[82] A court may modify its order to accommodate changed circumstances,[83] and additional violations are not needed to trigger modification of remedies originally ordered.[84] Modifications may include establishing procedures for removal and replacement of members of the advisory body set up by the decree to monitor compliance with nondiscriminatory goals.[85] However, a court may be unwilling to amend its decree where injunctive provisions or reporting requirements are neither vague nor overbroad.[86]

A court generally will not subject nonliable parties to provisions of an injunction, such as reporting requirements,[87] but a court's injunctive power extends to nonparties that interfere with the court's orders.[88] Courts routinely order defendants to maintain and submit reports on their compliance progress, but the parties also may be permitted to establish their own monitoring procedures.[89] It is within a district court's discretion to appoint an administrator to supervise compliance with its orders where a defendant has an established record of resistance.[90]

---

[82]Stallworth v. Shuler, *supra* note 80 (five years); United States v. Sheriff of Lancaster County, *supra* note 80 (after four years, employer may move for dissolution of decree).

[83]Association Against Discrimination in Employment v. City of Bridgeport, 710 F.2d 69, 74, 32 FEP 20, 24 (2d Cir. 1983).

[84]EEOC v. Sheet Metal Workers Local 638, 753 F.2d 1172, 1185, 36 FEP 1466, 1476–77 (2d Cir. 1985), *aff'd sub nom.* Sheet Metal Workers Local 28 v. EEOC, 478 U.S. 421, 41 FEP 107 (1986).

[85]Keith v. Volpe, 784 F.2d 1457, 1460–61 (9th Cir. 1986) (when necessary procedural provisions are absent from consent decree, court has wide discretion to amend it to include such provisions).

[86]Shakman v. Democratic Org. of Cook County, 607 F. Supp. 1086, 1087 (N.D. Ill. 1985) (decree requirements prohibiting county political organization from giving political recommendations more weight than other relevant recommendations in hiring and further requiring reports on all politically recommended hiring not amended).

[87]General Bldg. Contractor's Ass'n v. Pennsylvania, 458 U.S. 375, 399–400, 29 FEP 139, 150–51 (1982) (quarterly reports improper without liability, but see Justice O'Connor's concurrence suggesting that such reports conceivably may be required to assure compliance by persons liable); Zipes v. Trans World Airlines, 455 U.S. 385, 399–400, 28 FEP 1, 7–8 (1982).

[88]Darnell v. City of Jasper, Ala., *supra* note 80 (district court should have ordered nonparty civil service board to administer exam to plaintiff).

[89]Berkman v. City of New York (I), 705 F.2d 584, 31 FEP 767 (2d Cir. 1983) (parties to agree on monitoring procedures; court retaining jurisdiction to resolve issue if agreement cannot be reached).

[90]Sheet Metal Workers Local 28 v. EEOC, 478 U.S. 421, 41 FEP 107 (1986) (administrator appointed by court to supervise union's establishment of affirmative action program).

CHAPTER 38

# MONETARY RELIEF

## I. STATUTORY AUTHORIZATION

In *Ford Motor Co. v. EEOC,* [1] the Supreme Court reaffirmed that back pay is a basic and integral remedy under § 706(g) of Title VII. The Court held that the back pay period was ended by the employer's bona fide, unconditional offer of reinstatement. [2]

Back pay as a remedy for intentional discrimination under § 504 of the Rehabilitation Act of 1973 was authorized by the Supreme Court in *Consolidated Rail Corp. v. Darrone.* [3]

Courts have also held that back pay may be granted as a remedy for discriminatory employment practices in violation of the Export Administration Act of 1979[4] and that a veteran denied reemployment in violation of the Vietnam Era Veterans' Readjustment Assistance Act of 1974 may be entitled to an award of back pay. [5] However, at least one court has held that no right to back pay arises under Title IX of the Education Act Amendments of 1972. [6]

## II. A DISCRIMINATEE'S GENERAL RIGHT TO BACK PAY

The strong presumption in favor of an award of back pay to victims of employment discrimination under Title VII, discussed by the Supreme Court in *Albemarle Paper Co. v. Moody,* [7] has been applied by some courts to constrain the authority for partial denial of back pay. [8] The *Albemarle* pre-

---

[1]458 U.S. 219, 29 FEP 121 (1982).

[2]*Id.* at 225–28, 39 FEP at 124–25, 130–31 ("absent special circumstances, the rejection of an employer's unconditional job offer ends the accrual of potential backpay liability."). *See also* Section III.B, *infra.*

[3]465 U.S. 624, 34 FEP 79 (1984).

[4]50 U.S.C. § 2401 *et seq.* (Supp. IV 1986); Abrams v. Baylor College of Medicine, 581 F. Supp. 1570, 1582, 34 FEP 229, 239 (S.D. Tex. 1984) (finding violation of Export Administration Act in exclusion of Jewish physician-employees from participating in program in Saudi Arabia, but denying award of back pay where it would duplicate award of back pay under Title VII).

[5]38 U.S.C. § 2021 *et seq.* (1982 and Supp. IV 1986); Hanna v. American Motors Corp., 724 F.2d 1300, 1305, 115 LRRM 2393, 2398 (7th Cir.), *cert. denied,* 467 U.S. 1241, 116 LRRM 2632 (1984); Carr v. RCA Rubber Co., 609 F. Supp. 526, 529, 118 LRRM 3249, 3251 (N.D. Ohio 1985) (back pay awarded only for period between honorable discharge and reemployment).

[6]20 U.S.C. § 1681 *et seq.* (1984); Storey v. University of Wis. Sys. Bd. of Regents, 604 F. Supp. 1200, 1205, 37 FEP 701, 704 (W.D. Wis. 1985).

[7]422 U.S. 405, 10 FEP 1181 (1975), reproduced in the Second Edition at p. 1419.

[8]Laffey v. Northwest Airlines, 567 F.2d 429, 13 FEP 1068 (D.C. Cir. 1976), *cert. denied,* 434 U.S. 1086, 16 FEP 998 (1978) (authority for partial denial of back pay "must be as narrowly construed as authority to totally deny; its exercise, therefore, must be supported by reasons faithful to the dual purpose attributed to the back pay remedy by the *Albemarle* court"); Nord v. United States Steel Corp., 758 F.2d 1462, 1473, 37 FEP 1232 (11th Cir. 1985) (reversible error to exclude four months from back pay period); EEOC v. Korn Indus., 662 F.2d 256, 262–64, 27 FEP 13 (4th Cir. 1981).

sumption in favor of back pay has been applied in actions for discrimination in employment on the basis of age under the ADEA.[9] The circumstances (other than a failure of mitigation) justifying a denial of back pay once discriminatory action has been established are rare.[10] However, plaintiff must be able to establish actual loss as a result of the discrimination to justify relief.[11] Upon a finding of discrimination, the burden of proof shifts to the employer to demonstrate that monetary relief is not proper.[12] The courts have been split as to whether the employer's burden is governed by "the preponderance of the evidence" or the "clear and convincing evidence" standard.[13]

---

[9]*See* Kneisley v. Hercules, Inc., 577 F. Supp. 726, 735, 33 FEP 1579, 1586 (D. Del. 1983) (identical objectives of ending discrimination and compensating injured victims underlie remedy of back pay under both Title VII and ADEA).

[10]*See, e.g.,* Alaniz v. California Processors, 785 F.2d 1412, 1416–17, 40 FEP 768, 771–72 (9th Cir. 1986) (employer immunized from liability for back pay where employer relied in good faith upon an order by state commission prohibiting employers from assigning female employees to any job requiring lifting of more than 25 pounds); Trujillo v. County of Santa Clara, 775 F.2d 1359, 1369–70, 44 FEP 954 (9th Cir. 1985) (plaintiff who had already received award of back pay under state law could not seek back pay remedy in federal court); Horn v. Windsor Mobile Homes, Duke Homes Div., 755 F.2d 599, 37 FEP 228 (7th Cir. 1985) (a special factor which could preclude back pay award is conflicting state legislation); Le Beau v. Libbey-Owens-Ford Co., 727 F.2d 141, 150, 33 FEP 1700, 1707 (7th Cir. 1984) (no back pay awarded where employer relied on conflicting Illinois Female Employment Act before that Act was declared unconstitutional). *But see* EEOC v. Rath Packing Co., 787 F.2d 318, 330, 40 FEP 580 (8th Cir.), *cert. denied,* 479 U.S. 910, 41 FEP 1712 (1986) (back pay should not be denied on basis of adverse economic consequences either to employer or to other employees, who were also majority stockholders in the corporation); Salinas v. Roadway Express, 735 F.2d 1574, 1578–79, 35 FEP 533, 536 (5th Cir. 1984) (difficulty in calculating precise amount of back pay does not defeat the right itself); Carpenter v. Stephen F. Austin State Univ., 706 F.2d 608, 631, 31 FEP 1758, 1779 (5th Cir. 1983) (neither fact that injunctive relief would prospectively correct discriminatory practices nor fact that back pay award might financially weaken state-financed employer justified denial of back pay); Kneisley v. Hercules, Inc., *supra* note 9 (employee's misconduct, unknown to employer at time of termination but just cause for termination, not an equitable bar to back pay under ADEA); Seep v. Commercial Motor Freight, 575 F. Supp. 1097, 1109, 45 FEP 203 (S.D. Ohio 1983) (that victims of discrimination had never applied for jobs and offered no proof that they would have been successful in bidding for jobs did not bar award of back pay).

[11]Smallwood v. United Airlines, 728 F.2d 614, 626, 34 FEP 217, 228 (4th Cir.), *cert. denied,* 469 U.S. 832, 35 FEP 1608 (1984) (proof that plaintiff would never have been hired by defendant barred award of back pay); Martinez v. El Paso County, 710 F.2d 1102, 1106, 32 FEP 747, 750 (5th Cir. 1983) (court not bound by pretrial stipulation as to amount of back pay where court found that even if plaintiff received desired transfer, he would have been laid off in three months); Patterson v. Greenwood School Dist. 50, 696 F.2d 293, 30 FEP 825 (4th Cir. 1982) (plaintiff established she was discriminated against in promotion process but was nevertheless not entitled to back pay where defendant employer showed she would not have been promoted even absent discrimination); Walker v. Ford Motor Co., 684 F.2d 1355, 29 FEP 1259 (11th Cir. 1982) (plaintiff in discharge case involving fixed-term contract failed to produce evidence that he would have continued working beyond fixed term; he was limited to back pay recovery to period for which he established economic loss); Ostroff v. Employment Exch., 683 F.2d 302, 29 FEP 683 (9th Cir. 1982) (defendant had burden of proving by clear and convincing evidence that plaintiff was not entitled to back pay because she would not have been hired even absent discrimination); Doughtery v. Barry, 607 F. Supp. 1271, 37 FEP 1201, 1215 (D.D.C. 1985) (where defendants could not show that any particular plaintiff would not have been promoted absent discrimination, award of back pay and annuity adjustment appropriate despite eight plaintiffs and only two promotions in question).

[12]Teamsters v. United States, 431 U.S. 324, 14 FEP 1514 (1977); *see also* Franks v. Bowman Transp. Co., 424 U.S. 747, 12 FEP 549 (1976) ("the burden will be upon the [defendant] to prove that individuals who [seek relief] were not in fact victims of previous hiring discrimination").

[13]*Compare* Muntin v. California Parks & Recreation Dep't, 738 F.2d 1054, 35 FEP 746 (9th Cir. 1984) (defendant can defeat Stage II presumption of entitlement to relief by demonstrating by "clear and convincing evidence" that plaintiff would not have been hired even absent proven discrimination), United States v. United States Steel Corp., 520 F.2d 1043, 1056, 11 FEP 553 (5th Cir. 1975), *cert. denied,* 429 U.S. 817, 13 FEP 962 (1976) (clear and convincing evidence), Stewart v. General Motors Corp., 542 F.2d 445, 453, 13 FEP 1035 (7th Cir. 1976), *cert denied,* 433 U.S. 919, 15 FEP 31 (1977) (in Stage II, burden shifts to defendant "to demonstrate by clear and convincing evidence that employee" would not have received job benefit in question because of factors "unrelated to discrimination"), Day v. Mathews, 530 F.2d 1083, 1085, 12 FEP 1131 (D.C. Cir. 1976) ("the employee must prevail unless the employer proves its case by 'clear and convincing evidence.' "), King v. Trans World Airlines, 738 F.2d 255, 259, 35 FEP 102 (8th Cir. 1984) (same) *and* Knighton v. Laurens County School Dist. No. 56, 721 F.2d 976, 33 FEP 299 (4th Cir. 1983) (Stage II burden in 42 U.S.C. § 1981 race discrimination case is clear and convincing

The Fifth Circuit has held that the federal government cannot be estopped from recovering back pay on behalf of victims of discrimination in actions brought under § 707(e) of Title VII[14] by the prior acts of government officers which may have led to the discriminatory practices.[15]

## III. THE PERIOD OF RECOVERY

### A. Commencement of the Back Pay Period

Although the back pay period for Title VII may not normally commence prior to the statute's effectiveness, the District of Columbia Circuit has held that in suits brought by federal government employees the back pay period can extend to two years prior to the filing of a charge, even though that period begins prior to the 1972 application of Title VII to federal employment.[16] The Seventh Circuit has refused to grant such pre-Act back pay to local government employees, however.[17]

In determining the amount of back pay due, some courts have held that illegal acts of discrimination occurring outside the two-year period preceding the charge may affect the amount awarded, even though recovery outside the period is not allowed.[18]

A plaintiff can recover back pay for a willful violation of the Equal Pay Act for up to three years prior to the filing of suit, and for up to two years prior to the filing of suit in nonwillful cases.[19] A plaintiff may recover back pay under both Title VII and the Equal Pay Act, but the award will be calculated so as to prevent any overlap or double award.[20]

### B. Termination of the Back Pay Period

The general rule regarding termination of the back pay period is that back pay will terminate whenever the victim of discrimination is no longer suffering the economic effects of discrimination. The right to back pay normally terminates on the date judgment is rendered[21] or the jury returns its

---

evidence) *with* Sledge v. J.P. Stevens & Co., 585 F.2d 625, 637, 18 FEP 261 (4th Cir. 1978), *cert. denied,* 440 U.S. 981, 19 FEP 467 (1979) (applying preponderance of evidence standard). *Cf.* Price Waterhouse v. Hopkins _____ U.S. _____, 49 FEP 954 (1989), and *supra* Chapter 1.

[14]42 U.S.C. § 2000e-6(e).

[15]Walls v. Mississippi State Dep't of Pub. Welfare, 730 F.2d 306, 324, 34 FEP 1114, 1129–30 (5th Cir. 1984) (reversing denial of retroactive relief).

[16]Thompson v. Sawyer, 678 F.2d 257, 288, 28 FEP 1614, 1642 (D.C. Cir. 1982).

[17]Liberles v. County of Cook, 709 F.2d 1122, 1137–38, 31 FEP 1537, 1550 (7th Cir. 1983) (Title VII's two-year back pay provision does not extend to actions of state and local governments prior to effective date of Act).

[18]Glass v. Petro-Tex Chem. Corp., 757 F.2d 1554, 1560, 37 FEP 972, 976 (5th Cir. 1985) (defendant's "continuing violation" supported back pay award commencing within statutory period); Thompson v. Sawyer, *supra* note 16; *see also* Powell v. Georgia-Pacific Corp., 535 F. Supp. 713, 725, 30 FEP 21, 30 (W.D. Ark. 1980) (defendant's "history of discriminatory practices, customs, and usages" justifies use of "outer parameter" (two years before filing of first charge) for commencement of class back pay period).

[19]29 U.S.C. § 255 (1985); Sinclair v. Automobile Club of Okla., 733 F.2d 726, 729, 34 FEP 1206, 1208 (10th Cir. 1984); EEOC v. Central Kan. Medical Center, 705 F.2d 1270, 1274, 31 FEP 1510, 1512 (10th Cir. 1983); Hudson v. Moore Business Forms, 609 F. Supp. 467, 471, 37 FEP 1672, 1674 (N.D. Cal. 1985); EEOC v. McCarthy, 578 F. Supp. 45, 49, 32 FEP 815, 822 (D. Mass. 1983), *aff'd,* 768 F.2d 1, 38 FEP 536 (1985).

[20]Putterman v. Knitgoods Workers Local 155, 33 EPD ¶ 33,964 (S.D.N.Y. 1983) (plaintiff awarded back pay under Title VII from date two years prior to filing of charge with EEOC up until commencement of relevant Equal Pay Act recovery period).

[21]*E.g.,* Anderson v. Group Hospitalization, 820 F.2d 465, 43 FEP 1840 (D.C. Cir. 1987); Nord v. United States Steel Corp., 758 F.2d 1462, 1472–73, 37 FEP 1232, 1239 (11th Cir. 1985); Wells v. North

verdict.[22] The back pay period will end sooner, however, if the plaintiff ceases to suffer the adverse economic effects of discrimination, as when plaintiff acquires a higher-paying job and his earnings exceed his losses.[23] The burden of proving such a prejudgment termination of the back pay period rests upon the employer.[24]

In *Ford Motor Co. v. EEOC,*[25] the Supreme Court held that "absent special circumstances" the claimant's rejection of an employer's unqualified job offer, supplemented by the right to continue to pursue full court-ordered compensation, terminates the back pay period even though the offer does not include either retroactive seniority or accrued back pay. The Court did not define what constitutes "special circumstances"; however, a claimant's reasons for not accepting the offer must be "exceptional."[26] In evaluating whether an offer terminates back pay, courts continue to look at the circumstances under which it was made, its terms, and the reasons why it was rejected.[27] Several courts have refused to give legal effect to unconditional

---

Carolina Bd. of Alcoholic Control, 714 F.2d 340, 46 FEP 1766 (4th Cir. 1983), *cert. denied,* 464 U.S. 1044, 47 FEP 96 (1984); Gathercole v. Global Assocs., 560 F. Supp. 642, 647, 31 FEP 736, 740 (N.D. Cal. 1983), *rev'd on other grounds,* 727 F.2d 1485, 34 FEP 502 (9th Cir.), *cert. denied,* 469 U.S. 1087, 36 FEP 712 (1984) (even though pilot's flight certificate expired prior to trial).

[22]Koyen v. Consolidated Edison Co. of N.Y., 560 F. Supp. 1161, 1164, 31 FEP 488, 490 (S.D.N.Y. 1983).

[23]*See, e.g.,* Di Salvo v. Chamber of Commerce of Greater Kansas City, 568 F.2d 593, 598, 20 FEP 825 (8th Cir. 1978); EEOC v. Riss Int'l Corp., 35 FEP 423 (W.D. Mo. 1982) (no back pay for period in which interim earnings exceed wages that would have been earned); Somers v. Aldine Indep. School Dist., 464 F. Supp. 900, 22 FEP 1097 (S.D. Tex. 1979), *aff'd,* 620 F.2d 298, 23 FEP 778 (5th Cir. 1980) (higher paying job ends back pay period). Where interim earnings exceed back pay only for some periods, however, the back pay period continues and any excess earnings are not deducted from total back pay liability. *E.g.,* United States v. Lee Way Motor Freight, 15 FEP 1385 (N.D. Okla. 1977), *aff'd in relevant part,* 625 F.2d 918, 20 FEP 1345 (10th Cir. 1979) (special master erred in deducting excess interim earnings from claimants' back pay awards); Leftwich v. Harris-Stowe State College, 702 F.2d 686, 31 FEP 376 (8th Cir. 1983) (district court erred in denying back pay to plaintiff whose total earnings exceeded total lost back pay; court should award back pay for two of three years where plaintiff's earnings less than lost income); Brady v. Thurston Motor Lines, 753 F.2d 1269, 36 FEP 1805 (4th Cir. 1985) (applying NLRB rule of calculating back pay on quarterly basis, with full difference awarded for those quarters in which back pay exceeds actual earnings).

[24]*See, e.g.,* Teamsters v. United States, 431 U.S. 324, 14 FEP 1514 (1977); Richardson v. Restaurant Mktg. Assocs., 527 F. Supp. 690, 697, 31 FEP 1562 (N.D. Cal. 1981).

[25]458 U.S. 219, 29 FEP 121 (1982).

[26]*Id.* at 238 n.27, 29 FEP at 130.

[27]*Compare* Shore v. Federal Express Corp., 777 F.2d 1155, 1158, 39 FEP 809, 811 (6th Cir. 1985) (refusal of reinstatement offer was reasonable where differences in responsibilities between claimant's former job and offered job rendered them incomparable), Dickerson v. Deluxe Check Printers, 703 F.2d 276, 281–82, 31 FEP 621, 624–25 (8th Cir. 1983) (claimant's refusal to accept offer of position she has no background or interest in does not end back pay period), Orzel v. City of Wauwatosa Fire Dep't, 697 F.2d 743, 757, 30 FEP 1070, 1080–81 (7th Cir.), *cert. denied,* 464 U.S. 992, 33 FEP 440 (1983) (claimant's refusal of offer conditioned on taking and passing physical arranged by employer, given prior questionable settlement conduct by employer, did not toll back pay period), Spagnuolo v. Whirlpool Corp., 548 F. Supp. 104, 108, 32 FEP 1372, 1375 (W.D.N.C. 1982), *aff'd in relevant part,* 717 F.2d 114, 117–18, 32 FEP 1382 (4th Cir. 1983) (*Ford Motor Co.* rule not applicable where employer failed to offer claimant original job or one substantially equivalent to it) *and* Loubrido v. Hull Dobbs Co. of P.R., 526 F. Supp. 1055, 1057–58, 30 FEP 1243, 1244 (D.P.R. 1981) (offer not bona fide where new job less prestigious, compensation system more speculative, and fringe benefits not substantially similar) *with* Giandonato v. Sybron Corp. dba Taylor Instrument Co., 804 F.2d 120, 42 FEP 219 (10th Cir. 1986) (salesman not justified in rejecting unconditional reinstatement offer because wife ill and because he did not want to work under manager who had criticized performance), Figgs v. Quick Fill Corp., 766 F.2d 901, 38 FEP 865 (5th Cir. 1985) (unconditional offer of reinstatement made one month after discharge tolls all back pay after offer rejected), Fiedler v. Indianhead Truck Line, 670 F.2d 806, 808–9, 28 FEP 849, 850 (8th Cir. 1982) (claimant's failure to accept reinstatement offer terminated back pay period notwithstanding subjective reasons for rejection; subjective reasons for rejection not relevant in evaluating reasonableness of refusal; however, rejection of offer had no effect on damages accrued from date of termination until expiration of offer), Patterson v. Youngstown Sheet & Tube Co., 659 F.2d 736, 740, 28 FEP 1434, 1437 (7th Cir.), *cert. denied,* 454 U.S. 1100, 28 FEP 1655 (1981) (back pay period ended when claimants were offered opportunity to become apprentices in jobs previously denied discriminatees) *and* Cowen v. Standard

offers of employment that were not explicit.[28] Rule 408 of the Federal Rules
of Evidence should not preclude testimony regarding offers of reinstatement
even though the offer involved settlement negotiations.[29] Appropriate pretrial guidance should limit evidence to the unconditional offer, stripped of
any concomitant settlement proposals.

The facts of each case play an important role in determining the termination date for an award of back pay. A claimant's disability[30] or decision
to attend school[31] does not necessarily terminate back pay. Courts continue
to terminate the back pay period when a corporation goes out of business,[32]
but a plant closure may not terminate the back pay period when the claimant
can establish he would have been retained by the company elsewhere, notwithstanding closure of that facility.[33]

A back pay award will normally terminate on the day the plaintiff would
have been laid off[34] or would have been discharged for a nondiscriminatory

---

Brands, 572 F. Supp. 1576, 33 FEP 53 (N.D. Ala. 1983) (offer of comparable position in other city
giving plaintiff one day to respond sufficient to terminate back pay liability).
[28]Kilgo v. Bowman Transp., 789 F.2d 859, 879, 40 FEP 1415, 1430 (11th Cir. 1986) (offer " 'to
submit an application' " for one of unknown number of openings which stated that claimant stood " 'good
chance' " of being hired if she were " 'minimally qualified' " does not amount to unconditional offer of
reinstatement); Rasimas v. Michigan Dep't of Mental Health, 714 F.2d 614, 625, 32 FEP 688, 696 (6th
Cir. 1983), cert. denied, 466 U.S. 950, 34 FEP 1096 (1984) (interview letter is not unconditional offer
of employment); Dickerson v. Deluxe Check Printers, supra note 27 (conflicting evidence of offer's
existence precludes legal determination and leaves jury questions). But see Davis v. Ingersoll Johnson
Steel Co., 628 F. Supp. 25, 28–29, 39 FEP 1197, 1199–1200 (S.D. Ind. 1985) (claimant's refusal of
reinstatement offer tolled accrual of back pay liability even though offer was vague as to which shift
claimant would work).
[29]Orzel v. City of Wauwatosa Fire Dep't, supra note 27; Thomas v. Resort Health Related Facility,
539 F. Supp. 630, 31 FEP 65 (E.D.N.Y. 1982) (defendant may establish unconditional offer of reinstatement despite fact claimant's counsel insisted discussions were "without prejudice"; otherwise plaintiff
would have too much control over litigation and subject employers to unnecessarily burdensome back
pay claims).
[30]Compare EEOC v. Riss Int'l Corp., supra note 23, at 425 (back pay period terminates when
claimant's disability renders him unavailable for employment) with Wells v. North Carolina Bd. of
Alcoholic Control, supra note 21 (back pay period not terminated on date plaintiff became disabled and
quit job because it could be reasonably inferred that plaintiff would not have been injured had he been
granted promotion denied him).
[31]Smith v. American Serv. Co. of Atlanta, 796 F.2d 1430, 1432, 41 FEP 802 (11th Cir. 1986) (decision
to attend school did not terminate back pay after plaintiff's reasonable efforts to mitigate); Nord v. United
States Steel Corp., 758 F.2d 1462, 1471, 37 FEP 1232, 1238 (11th Cir. 1985) (plaintiff's enrollment in
college does not foreclose availability for employment in light of continued search for full-time position);
Brady v. Thurston Motor Lines, supra note 23 at 1274, 36 FEP at 1809 (back pay period continues despite
plaintiff's enrollment in college where plaintiff continued to search for full-time employment and would
have quit school had position become available); Washington v. Kroger Co., 671 F.2d 1072, 1079, 29
FEP 1739, 1745–46 (8th Cir. 1982) (general rule reaffirmed); Ryan v. Raytheon Data Sys. Co., 601 F.
Supp. 243, 252–53, 39 FEP 1398, 1406 (D. Mass. 1985) (full-time attendance at night school does not
terminate back pay period where plaintiff remained available for daytime work). But cf. McDowell v.
Mississippi Power & Light, 641 F. Supp. 424, 430, 44 FEP 1088 (S.D. Miss. 1986) (tolling back pay
liability for period of claimant's enrollment in college during which time she had ceased looking for
employment).
[32]Haynes v. Miller, 669 F.2d 1125, 1127, 27 FEP 1611, 1613 (6th Cir. 1982) (corporation forced out
of business by IRS for nonpayment of income tax).
[33]Gibson v. Mohawk Rubber Co., 695 F.2d 1093, 1097–99, 30 FEP 859, 862–63 (8th Cir. 1982)
(whether plant closure will terminate back pay period is question of fact and claimant has burden of
proving he would have been transferred to another facility within company's operations); Bonura v. Chase
Manhattan Bank, N.A., 629 F. Supp. 353, 356, 43 FEP 163, 165 (S.D.N.Y.), aff'd, 795 F.2d 276, 43 FEP
173 (2d Cir. 1986) (sale of bank department in which claimants had worked did not toll back pay liability
where evidence indicated that claimants would have retained their positions after the sale or that
defendants would have retained them in another of its departments; cf. Jackson v. Shell Oil Co., 702 F.2d
197, 200–1, 31 FEP 686, 689–90 (9th Cir. 1983) (back pay period not terminated by claimant's refusal
to accept offer of employment by purchaser of plant where new job not substantially equivalent to old
position).
[34]Protos v. Volkswagen of Am., 615 F. Supp. 1513, 1519, 38 FEP 1292, 1297 (W.D. Pa. 1985), aff'd
in part and vacated in part, 797 F.2d 129, 41 FEP 598 (3d Cir.), cert. denied, 479 U.S. 972, 44 FEP 216
(1986); Lamb v. Smith Int'l, Drilco Div., 32 FEP 105, 107 (S.D. Tex. 1983); cf. Nash v. City of Houston
Civic Center, 805 F.2d 1030, 39 FEP 1512, 1515 (S.D. Tex. 1985) (tolling back pay liability on date

reason.[35] However, a court awarded an ADEA plaintiff back pay past the date on which the division in which he had worked was eliminated, since the plaintiff's successor continued employment with the defendant beyond that date.[36]

Courts generally hold that a back pay period terminates when the plaintiff obtains comparable employment,[37] and will not resume if the plaintiff voluntarily quits,[38] or is terminated for cause from,[39] a new, better paying position. The back pay period may also be terminated when the plaintiff ceases to look for alternative employment or fails to exert reasonable efforts in mitigation.[40] The burden of proving plaintiff's failure to fulfill this duty to mitigate rests upon the employer.[41]

claimant's position was eliminated in a reorganization, there being no evidence he was qualified for position under reorganization plan); Fitzgerald v. Green Valley Area Educ. Agency, 589 F. Supp. 1130, 1139, 39 FEP 899, 906 (S.D. Iowa 1984) (back pay period ended for bus driver on termination of school year for which he was unlawfully denied employment, as there was no evidence that position would have been available for succeeding school year).

[35]See Protos v. Volkswagen of Am., supra note 34; Nash v. City of Houston Civic Center, supra note 34; Fitzgerald v. Green Valley Area Educ. Agency, supra note 34; Lamb v. Smith Int'l, Drilco Div., supra note 34; Kiper v. Louisiana State Bd. of Elementary & Secondary Educ., 592 F. Supp. 1343, 1358, 38 FEP 1432, 1443 (E.D. La. 1984), aff'd, 778 F.2d 789, 40 FEP 984 (5th Cir. 1985) (back pay period ended for plaintiff discriminatorily denied temporary position when temporary position terminated).

[36]Hill v. Spiegel, Inc., 708 F.2d 233, 238, 31 FEP 1532, 1535 (6th Cir. 1983).

[37]See, e.g., Chescheir v. Liberty Mut. Ins. Co., 713 F.2d 1142, 1150, 32 FEP 1344, 1350 (5th Cir. 1983) (back pay period for plaintiffs discriminatorily denied opportunity to continue working and who attended law school terminated when they obtained legal employment, not when they graduated from law school); Smith v. American Serv. Co. of Atlanta, 38 FEP 377, 378 (N.D. Ga. 1985) (back pay liability for unlawfully rejected applicant for receptionist position ended when she accepted employment as cosmetologist); McIntosh v. Jones Truck Lines, 38 FEP 704, 709 (E.D. Ark. 1984) (trucking company's back pay liability ended when claimant ceased looking for comparable employment in freight business and accepted full-time teaching position).

[38]EEOC v. Domino's Pizza, 34 FEP 1075, 1076 (E.D. Mich. 1983) (period ended on date plaintiff obtained new employment and did not resume when plaintiff voluntarily quit better paying job); Griffin v. George B. Buck Consulting Actuaries, 566 F. Supp. 881, 32 FEP 1884 (S.D.N.Y. 1983) (period terminated on date plaintiff obtained new employment despite contention that he left new higher paying job shortly thereafter because of discriminatory experiences with defendant); EEOC v. Riss Int'l Corp., 35 FEP 423 (W.D. Mo. 1982) (voluntary quit because of personal preference tolls back pay period; however, voluntary quits do not end back pay period when justification is reasonable).

[39]EEOC v. Riss Int'l Corp. supra note 38 (subsequent discharge for cause tolls back pay period); Brady v. Thurston Motor Lines, 753 F.2d 1269, 36 FEP 1805 (4th Cir. 1985) (same; plaintiff must exercise reasonable diligence in maintaining subsequent employment). But see EEOC v. Stone Container Corp., 548 F. Supp. 1098, 1107 n.1, 30 FEP 134, 143 (W.D. Mo. 1982) (back pay period did not end when discriminate discharged for cause from subsequent employer).

[40]Compare Hunter v. Allis-Chalmers Corp., Engine Div., 797 F.2d 1417, 41 FEP 721, 729 (7th Cir. 1986) (very limited work and only 16 applications for employment over five years warrants reduction of back pay from five to three years); Ryan v. Raytheon Data Sys. Co., supra note 31 (back pay terminated when claimant moved from Massachusetts to Florida), Weatherspoon v. Andrews & Co., 32 FEP 1226, 1229 (D. Colo. 1983) (plaintiff failed to mitigate damages upon ceasing to seek alternative employment; back pay period terminates), Griffin v. George B. Buck Consulting Actuaries, supra note 38 (plaintiff no longer seeking employment not entitled to front pay), Coley v. Consolidated Rail Corp., 561 F. Supp. 645, 652, 34 FEP 129, 135 (E.D. Mich. 1982) (plaintiff's failure to seek employment terminates back pay period at point when plaintiff's inaction is no longer attributable to former supervisor's sexual harassment) and Hayes v. Shelby Memorial Hosp., 546 F. Supp. 259, 266–67, 29 FEP 1173, 1177–78 (N.D. Ala. 1982), aff'd on other grounds, 726 F.2d 1543, 34 FEP 444 (11th Cir. 1984) (back pay award reduced where claimant unreasonably assumed any effort to obtain employment would be futile because of her pregnancy) with Baggett v. Program Resources, 806 F.2d 178, 182, 42 FEP 648 (8th Cir. 1986) (discriminatee entitled to back pay if "good faith effort" to find work is made), Maxfield v. Sinclair Int'l, 766 F.2d 788, 796, 38 FEP 442, 449 (3d Cir. 1985), cert. denied, 474 U.S. 1057, 39 FEP 1200 (1986) (65-year-old claimant's failure to seek alternate employment was reasonable in view of his income from other sources), Nord v. United States Steel Corp., supra note 31 (abandonment of unsuccessful two-and-one-half year search for employment in order to establish own business does not terminate back pay period), Brady v. Thurston Motor Lines, supra note 39, at 1274, 36 FEP at 1809 (abandonment of search after one year to accept lower paying job does not terminate back pay period) and Thorkildson v. Insurance Co. of N. Am., 631 F. Supp. 372, 40 FEP 813 (D. Minn. 1986) (employee who was 61 years old at time of discharge did not fail to mitigate damages by voluntarily removing herself from labor market where company did not offer her reinstatement and she looked for work until her husband became ill).

[41]Jackson v. Shell Oil Co., 702 F.2d 197, 31 FEP 686 (9th Cir. 1983); Sprogis v. United Airlines, 517 F.2d 387, 10 FEP 1249 (7th Cir. 1975); EEOC v. Kallir, Phillips, Ross, Inc., 420 F. Supp. 919, 925,

If a plaintiff is discriminatorily denied consideration for a job, but the employer proves that, even if considered fairly, the plaintiff would not have been awarded the job for legitimate reasons, the plaintiff is not entitled to back pay.[42] Notwithstanding the employer's elimination of the discriminatory practice, however, many courts will continue the back pay period as long as the plaintiff suffers continuing economic harm as a result of the earlier discriminatory practice.[43]

In some circumstances a claimant may be entitled to back pay beyond the duration of a fixed-term employment relationship.[44] Some courts continue to terminate the back pay period based on the fact that it is speculative whether the claimant would have continued working for the defendant beyond a certain period.[45] As in the past, the effect on the back pay period of a discriminatee's rejection of employment[46] turns on the facts of the individual case.

---

13 FEP 1508 (S.D.N.Y. 1976), aff'd, 559 F.2d 1203, 15 FEP 1369 (2d Cir.), cert. denied, 434 U.S. 920, 15 FEP 1618 (1977).

[42]Smallwood v. United Airlines, 728 F.2d 614, 34 FEP 217 (4th Cir.), cert. denied, 469 U.S. 832, 35 FEP 1608 (1984) (employer refused to consider applicant because of age, but no remedy because employer established that even if plaintiff had been considered, he would not have been hired because of previous employment record); cf. Fadhl v. City & County of San Francisco, 741 F.2d 1163, 35 FEP 1291 (9th Cir. 1984) (discharged female trainee not entitled to back pay if City proves she was not qualified as police officer); Muntin v. California Parks & Recreation Dep't, 738 F.2d 1054, 1056–57, 35 FEP 746, 747 (9th Cir. 1984) (defendant must show by clear and convincing evidence that plaintiff would not have been hired absent proven discrimination).

[43]Parson v. Kaiser Aluminum & Chem. Corp., 727 F.2d 473, 478, 34 FEP 505, 508 (5th Cir.), cert. denied, 467 U.S. 1243, 34 FEP 1688 (1984) (award of back pay not terminated upon defendant's institution of nondiscriminatory selection procedures, or upon rejection of plaintiff's application under those new procedures, where effects of defendant's original failure to promote continued to be felt until plaintiff received promotion he was unlawfully denied); EEOC v. Monarch Mach. Tool Co., 737 F.2d 1444, 1451–53, 42 FEP 859 (6th Cir. 1980) (commencement of hiring of women does not ordinarily terminate back pay period for prior discriminatees absent special equitable considerations); see also EEOC v. Enterprise Ass'n of Steamfitters Local 638, 542 F.2d 579, 13 FEP 705 (2d Cir. 1976), cert. denied, 430 U.S. 911, 14 FEP 702 (1977) (reversible error to terminate back pay on date of court-ordered injunctive relief); United States v. Lee Way Motor Freight, 625 F.2d 918, 931–33, 20 FEP 1345 (10th Cir. 1979) (rejecting argument that back pay should terminate on date of preliminary injunction). But see George v. Farmers Elec. Coop., 715 F.2d 175, 32 FEP 1801 (5th Cir. 1983) (where employer amended its discriminatory antinepotism policy and under amended policy plaintiff would have been terminated, back pay period ends as of amendment to policy) and Bell v. Automobile Club of Mich., 34 FEP 3, 6 (E.D. Mich. 1983) (consent judgment properly terminates back pay period as of date of implementation of nondiscriminatory employment practices which reduce likelihood that applicant class members could establish subsequent discrimination).

[44]Walker v. Ford Motor Co., 684 F.2d 1355, 29 FEP 1259 (11th Cir. 1982) (rebuttable presumption that back pay period terminates at end of fixed-term contract); Wangsness v. Watertown School Dist. 14-4, Codington County, S.D., 541 F. Supp. 332, 339–40, 29 FEP 375, 381 (D.S.D. 1982) (back pay period not limited to claimant's fixed-term teaching contract).

[45]Haynes v. Miller, 669 F.2d 1125, 1127, 27 FEP 1611, 1613 (6th Cir. 1982) (claimant's back pay period of four months too speculative where employees had worked no more than two or three weeks); cf. EEOC v. Spokane Concrete Prods., 534 F. Supp. 518, 526, 28 FEP 423, 430 (E.D. Wash. 1982) (court terminated back pay period based on defendant's high employee turnover rate caused by physically demanding nature of position).

[46]Cf. Babrocky v. Jewel Food Co., 773 F.2d 857, 868, 38 FEP 1667, 1675 (7th Cir. 1985) (former employees' rejection of apprentice meatcutter positions might limit eventual damage award but it does not prove they had rejected meatcutter positions). Compare EEOC v. Exxon Shipping Co., 745 F.2d 967, 979–80, 36 FEP 330, 340 (5th Cir. 1984) (back pay period does not terminate upon plaintiff's rejection of position which would have required plaintiff to work every weekend) and O'Donnell v. Georgia Osteopathic Hosp., 574 F. Supp. 219, 221, 36 FEP 944, 947 (N.D. Ga. 1983), aff'd in part and rev'd in part on other grounds, 748 F.2d 1543, 36 FEP 953 (11th Cir. 1984) (rejection of offer of reinstatement to ADEA plaintiff does not terminate back pay period where harassment and deterioration of working conditions made reinstatement infeasible) with Rimedio v. Revlon, 528 F. Supp. 1380, 1390–91, 30 FEP 1205, 1212 (S.D. Ohio 1982) (claimant's entitlement to full back pay ended when she rejected similar employment because it paid $2,000 less than position with defendant; thereafter, only difference in pay was recoverable) and Davis v. Western-Southern Life Ins. Co., 34 FEP 97, 102 (N.D. Ohio 1984) (sexual harassment claimant's rejection of offer of reinstatement at different location terminates back pay period).

A back pay settlement arrived at between some, but not all, of the defendants does not terminate the back pay period with respect to the nonsettling defendants.[47] In an Equal Pay Act case the defendant's retroactive pay increase did not obviate its obligation to pay liquidated damages equal to the amount of the back pay ordered.[48]

## C. Front Pay

Front pay is an award of future lost earnings to make a victim of discrimination whole.[49] A majority of courts in appropriate cases continue to make awards of front pay in class actions and suits involving individual plaintiffs. In class action suits concerning promotion discrimination, front pay has been awarded where it was expected that a significant time would elapse before the discriminatees could assume their "rightful place" in the work force.[50] With regard to civil actions involving individual plaintiffs, front pay also has been deemed proper where, among other factors, there is no vacancy to which the plaintiff can be promoted immediately,[51] or where the court finds that reinstatement of a discharged plaintiff is neither appropriate nor feasible due to the likelihood of continuing antagonism or hostility between the plaintiff and the employer.[52] On the other hand, most courts still

---

[47]Ingram v. Madison Square Garden Center, 535 F. Supp. 1082, 32 FEP 548, 559 (S.D.N.Y. 1982), aff'd and modified on other grounds, 709 F.2d 807, 32 FEP 641 (2d Cir.), cert. denied, 464 U.S. 937, 33 FEP 48 (1983) (union liable for back pay notwithstanding back pay settlements by other employer defendants). See Chapter 19 (Unions) at Section II.F.

[48]Laffey v. Northwest Airlines, 582 F. Supp. 280, 283, 32 FEP 754, 756 (D.D.C. 1982), aff'd, 740 F.2d 1071, 1098–99, 35 FEP 508, 529–30 (D.C. Cir. 1984), cert. denied, 469 U.S. 1181, 36 FEP 1168 (1985).

[49]Cassino v. Reichhold Chems., 817 F.2d 1338, 1346, 47 FEP 865 (9th Cir. 1987), cert. denied, 484 U.S. ____, 47 FEP 1776 (1988).

[50]Chewning v. Seamans, 28 FEP 1735 (D.D.C. 1979) (class member entitled to front pay until he reaches rightful place of equivalent grade, or refuses promotion to same); Stamps v. Detroit Edison Co., 30 FEP 1805 (E.D. Mich. 1978) (class member entitled to front pay until he reaches rightful position or its equivalent, or refuses promotion to same or to any job in relevant job progression line); cf. Wattleton v. Ladish Co., 520 F. Supp. 1329, 29 FEP 1307 (E.D. Wis. 1981), aff'd sub nom. Wattleton v. Boilermakers Local 1509, 686 F.2d 586, 29 FEP 1389 (7th Cir. 1982), cert. denied, 459 U.S. 1208, 30 FEP 1856 (1983) (involving discriminatory union seniority systems and award of front pay until discriminatees obtain rightful place by being allowed to transfer between union jurisdictions without loss of carryover seniority); Thompson v. Sawyer, 678 F.2d 257, 293, 28 FEP 1614, 1644 (D.C. Cir. 1982) (court stated that front pay, while appropriate, should persist "only until the wrongs for which the plaintiffs are owed back pay have been righted" and suggested, in remanding the matter, that front pay should terminate instead at point where plaintiffs received 50% of total number of openings which had occurred, and had been filled by males, during actual period of discrimination); Segar v. Smith, 738 F.2d 1249, 1296, 35 FEP 31, 64 (D.C. Cir. 1984), cert. denied, 471 U.S. 1115, 37 FEP 1312 (1985) (lower court's order requiring employer to pay classwide front pay vacated because it was premised on existence of promotion goals and timetables which were also vacated, but court could impose new front pay order if appropriate).

[51]Briseno v. Central Technical Community College Area, 739 F.2d 344, 348, 37 FEP 57, 60 (8th Cir. 1984) (Mexican-American discriminatorily denied full-time position is entitled to front pay until assigned to that position or comparable one); Carter v. Community Action Agency of Chambers, Tallapoosa, & Coosa Counties, 625 F. Supp. 199, 207, 39 FEP 1618, 1624 (M.D. Ala. 1985) (unlawfully discharged employee to be awarded front pay if another, comparable position is not available); Parker v. Siemens-Allis, 601 F. Supp. 1377, 1389, 37 FEP 39, 50 (E.D. Ark. 1985) (female employee who was unlawfully terminated is entitled to reinstatement as foreman and if no such position exists, front pay until placed in comparable job); Velez v. Devine, 28 FEP 671 (D.D.C. 1982) (female employee discriminatorily denied promotion entitled to pay and benefits of position sought until actually promoted thereto, or to equivalent position).

[52]Cassino v. Reichhold Chems., supra note 49 (court may elect to award front pay if reinstatement is not feasible); Blum v. Witco Chem. Corp., 829 F.2d 367, 46 FEP 306 (3d Cir. 1987) (front pay is available as equitable remedy under ADEA when back pay and/or reinstatement do not fully compensate victim or are impractical); EEOC v. Prudential Fed. Sav. & Loan Ass'n, 763 F.2d 1166, 1173, 37 FEP 1691, 1696 (10th Cir.), cert. denied, 474 U.S. 946, 39 FEP 384 (1985) (front pay is proper in ADEA cases

prefer reinstatement of the discharged plaintiff rather than granting front pay.[53]

Front pay may be denied where the employer can prove that, for some other legitimate and nondiscriminatory reason, the plaintiff would no longer have been employed at the time of judgment, particularly where there has been a reduction in the employer's business, the employer has closed the facility,[54] or the plaintiff is no longer seeking employment.[55] The courts disagree regarding the requisite burden and degree of proof.[56]

While recognizing that front pay awards have been criticized as uncertain and speculative, a majority of courts in appropriate circumstances have approved finite front pay under the ADEA.[57] Periods of six months to two years are typical front pay awards, with the determination based on facts such as the plaintiff's skills, the job market, and the nature of the position at issue.[58] At least one court has ruled that lost pension benefits may be

---

when employer's hostility makes reinstatement inappropriate); Nord v. United States Steel Corp., 758 F.2d 1462, 37 FEP 1232 (11th Cir. 1985) (front pay is proper if court determines that, due to extraordinary circumstances, reinstatement is inappropriate); Whittlesey v. Union Carbide Corp., 742 F.2d 724, 35 FEP 1089 (2d Cir. 1984) (reinstatement inappropriate because of hostility generated by litigation); Goss v. Exxon Office Sys. Co., 747 F.2d 885, 889–90, 36 FEP 344, 347 (3d Cir. 1984) (likelihood of continuing disharmony between female plaintiff and employer in sensitive jobs); Fadhl v. City & County of San Francisco, *supra* note 42 (plaintiff awarded front pay if found otherwise qualified for permanent employment and if reinstatement not appropriate in light of antagonism between her and employer). *See* Chapter 14 (Age) at Section VI.C.

[53]Goldstein v. Manhattan Indus., 758 F.2d 1435, 1449, 37 FEP 1217, 1227 (11th Cir.), *cert. denied*, 474 U.S. 1005, 39 FEP 720 (1985) (reinstatement rather than front pay appropriate since employer was willing to reemploy discharged plaintiff in a job in which he could function effectively); (1985); Blim v. Western Elec. Co., 731 F.2d 1473, 34 FEP 757 (10th Cir.), *cert. denied*, 469 U.S. 874, 36 FEP 816 (1984) (without deciding whether court may award front pay under ADEA, court concluded front pay should be avoided whenever possible, and reinstatement proper because no hostility between parties).

[54]Dillon v. Coles, 746 F.2d 998, 1006, 36 FEP 159, 164–65 (3d Cir. 1984) (plaintiff denied front pay because of uncertainty of hiring date since employer closed its business and there were disputed issues as to plaintiff's competency and ability to get along with co-workers and supervisor); Fadhl v. City & County of San Francisco, 741 F.2d 1163, 35 FEP 1291 (9th Cir. 1984) (if employer can show that absent discrimination plaintiff would not have been hired, plaintiff may not be awarded back pay or front pay); Cerminara v. Allegheny Hous. Rehabilitation Corp., 37 FEP 998 (W.D. Pa. 1985) (front pay denied since employer no longer managed project and position filled by white employee with more seniority); Manuel v. International Harvester Co., 28 FEP 560 (N.D. Ill. 1981) (post-termination discovery of independent cause for termination may serve to cut off right to reinstatement or front pay; here defendant failed to prove plaintiff would have been terminated for independent cause). *But see* Davis v. Combustion Eng'g, 742 F.2d 916, 922–23, 35 FEP 975, 980 (6th Cir. 1984) (59-year-old plaintiff awarded six years' front pay notwithstanding potential layoff due to reduction in employer's work force).

[55]Griffin v. George B. Buck Consulting Actuaries, 566 F. Supp. 881, 32 FEP 1884 (S.D.N.Y. 1983) (front pay unavailable to unlawfully rejected job applicant no longer seeking employment). *But see* Maxfield v. Sinclair Int'l, 766 F.2d 788, 796, 38 FEP 442, 449 (3d Cir. 1985), *cert. denied*, 474 U.S. 1057, 39 FEP 1200 (1986) (front pay awarded notwithstanding 65-year-old employee's failure to seek employment).

[56]*See* Wildman v. Lerner Stores Corp., 771 F.2d 605, 38 FEP 1377 (1st Cir. 1985) (court makes "a definitive ruling" on front pay under ADEA and concludes that front pay is always speculative; numerous front pay cases reviewed); *see also supra* note 13.

[57]Dominic v. Consolidated Edison Co. of N.Y., 822 F.2d 1249, 44 FEP 268 (2d Cir. 1987) (amount of front pay under ADEA is equitable issue to be resolved by the court); Cassino v. Reichhold Chems., *supra* note 49; Whittlesey v. Union Carbide Corp., *supra* note 52; Davis v. Combustion Eng'g, *supra* note 54; EEOC v. Prudential Fed. Sav. & Loan Ass'n, *supra* note 52; Maxfield v. Sinclair Int'l, *supra* note 55. *But see* Wildman v. Lerner Stores Corp., *supra* note 56 (in what court characterized as "a definitive ruling" on front pay under ADEA, after discussing many other front pay cases, held front pay inappropriate, since plaintiff received liquidated damages and total judgment was high).

[58]*E.g.,* Toth v. American Greetings Corp., 40 FEP 1768, 1775 (N.D. Ohio 1985), *aff'd,* 811 F.2d 608 (6th Cir. 1986), *cert. denied,* 484 U.S. _____, (1987) (awarding six months' front pay); Hopkins v. City of Jonesboro, Ark., 578 F. Supp. 137, 39 FEP 1000, 1004 (E.D. Ark. 1983) (three months' front pay); Reeder-Baker v. Lincoln Nat'l Corp., 649 F. Supp. 647, 42 FEP 1567, 1581 (N.D. Ind. 1986) (two years wage differential as front pay); Snow v. Pillsbury Co., 650 F. Supp. 299, 42 FEP 1391, 1392 (D. Minn. 1986) (three years); Dominic v. Consolidated Edison Co of N.Y., 652 F. Supp. 815, 44 FEP 1865, 1870 (S.D.N.Y. 1986), *aff'd,* 822 F.2d 1249, 44 FEP 268 (2d Cir. 1987) (vacating jury award of $378,000

recoverable as front pay under the ADEA.[59] In addition, one court has held that an award of front pay is proper under the Rehabilitation Act of 1973.[60]

As a general rule, front pay should be calculated in the same manner as back pay, with the front pay pool constructed as a continuation of the back pay pool.[61] Expert testimony is not normally required to prove what the plaintiff would have received in future earnings, raises, and the like.[62]

## IV. EQUITABLE DEFENSES LIMITING THE PERIOD OF RECOVERY OF OR RIGHT TO BACK PAY

### A. Laches

The extent to which laches may bar all or part of a back pay claim continues to depend on the specific facts involved.[63]

### B. Good Faith

Courts continue to struggle with the application of a good-faith defense to back pay liability to employers who rely on state statutes.[64]

## V. CALCULATION OF INDIVIDUAL BACK PAY AWARD

### A. Elements of Back Pay Award

Courts continue to include many elements other than salary in calculating back pay awards. For example, lost sales commissions, raises, bonuses, cost-of-living increases, tips, medical insurance, pensions, overtime pay,

---

front pay—salary differential until age 70—and awarding $34,000—two years' salary differential); *see also* Eivins v. Adventist Health Sys. Eastern & Middle Am., 660 F. Supp. 1255, 43 FEP 1536, 1543 (D. Kan. 1987) (entering jury verdict of $180,000 in front pay to 57-year-old plaintiff). The longest reported front pay period is the six years awarded to a 59-year-old plaintiff in *Davis v. Combustion Eng'g, supra* note 54. This extended award appears peculiar to the facts of that case. *See also* Whittlesey v. Union Carbide Corp., *supra* note 52, 742 F.2d at 729 (affirming award to former chief labor counsel of four years' front pay in lieu of reinstatement, which would take him to then-permissible mandatory retirement age of 70).

[59]Blum v. Witco Chem. Corp., *supra* note 52.

[60]Crane v. Dole, 617 F. Supp. 156, 37 FEP 255, 261 (D.D.C. 1985) (handicapped former employee discriminatorily denied reemployment entitled to next vacancy and front pay until then).

[61]Thompson v. Sawyer, 678 F.2d 257, 28 FEP 1614 (D.C. Cir. 1982) (front pay formula must mirror back pay formula); Wattleton v. Ladish Co., 520 F. Supp. 1329, 29 FEP 1307 (E.D. Wis. 1981), *aff'd sub nom.* Wattleton v. Boilermakers Local 1509, 686 F.2d 586, 29 FEP 1389 (7th Cir. 1982), *cert. denied,* 459 U.S. 1208, 30 FEP 1856 (1983) (front pay to be calculated in manner similar to that utilized for back pay).

[62]Cassino v. Reichhold Chems., 817 F.2d 1338, 47 FEP 865 (9th Cir. 1987), *cert. denied,* 484 U.S. _____, 47 FEP 1776 (1988); Maxfield v. Sinclair Int'l, *supra* note 55.

[63]McLemore v. Interstate Motor Freight Sys., 33 FEP 1384 (N.D. Ala. 1984) (laches found based on eight-year delay, dimming of memories of key witnesses, and destruction of some records); Wangsness v. Watertown School Dist. 14-4, Codington County, S.D., 541 F. Supp. 332, 29 FEP 375 (D.S.D. 1982) (back pay period not suspended for five-year period case was pending before EEOC because plaintiff did not know he could request right-to-sue letter from EEOC and he did not retain attorney until after EEOC finally sent his right-to-sue letter); Thomas v. City of Evanston, 610 F. Supp. 422, 42 FEP 1795 (N.D. Ill. 1985).

[64]Alaniz v. California Processors, 785 F.2d 1412, 40 FEP 768 (9th Cir. 1986) (no back pay liability for failure to hire women in jobs requiring heavy lifting when state protective laws in effect); Le Beau v. Libbey-Owens-Ford Co., 727 F.2d 141, 149–50, 33 FEP 1700, 1707 (7th Cir. 1984) (good-faith defense sustained); Guardians Ass'n of New York City Police Dep't v. Civil Serv. Comm'n, 539 F. Supp. 627, 629, 32 FEP 648, 649 (S.D.N.Y. 1982) (reliance on state law rejected because law "not necessarily inconsistent with Title VII").

business vacations, profit-sharing plans, and job search expenses have been considered in determining a discriminatee's back pay award.[65] Courts remain split as to whether compensation for life, health, and other insurance coverage should be based upon the cost of the insurance to the employer, the out-of-pocket expenses of the plaintiff in obtaining substitute coverage, or the losses incurred which would have been covered by the insurance.[66] One court

[65]Gilchrist v. Jim Slemons Imports, 803 F.2d 1488, 42 FEP 314 (9th Cir. 1986) (former employee's last year of commission revenues used to estimate lost earnings); Kossman v. Calumet County, 800 F.2d 697, 41 FEP 1355 (7th Cir. 1986), cert. denied, 479 U.S. 1088, 43 FEP 80 (1987) (overtime benefits should be considered in back pay award); Cox v. American Cast Iron Pipe Co., 784 F.2d 1546, 40 FEP 678 (11th Cir.), cert. denied, 479 U.S. 883, 41 FEP 1712 (1986) (back pay award in Title VII case should take into account interest, overtime, shift differentials, vacations and sick pay, pension benefits, bonuses and interest, as well as straight salary, plus monetary considerations such as retroactive departmental seniority, and denial of job promotions and assignments based on sex); Goldstein v. Manhattan Indus., 758 F.2d 1435, 37 FEP 1217, reh'g denied, 765 F.2d 154 (11th Cir.), cert. denied, 474 U.S. 1005, 39 FEP 720 (1985) (lost sales commission); Sinclair v. Automobile Club of Okla., 733 F.2d 726, 729, 34 FEP 1206, 1207 (10th Cir. 1984) (salary differential plus raises and bonuses); EEOC v. Liggett & Myers, 690 F.2d 1072, 40 FEP 1285 (4th Cir. 1982), on remand, 32 EPD ¶ 33,875 (M.D.N.C. 1983) (female employee compensated for salary increases that comparable male employee would have received); EEOC v. House of Prime Rib, 31 FEP 981 (N.D. Cal. 1983), aff'd, 735 F.2d 1369, 35 FEP 736 (9th Cir. 1984), cert. denied, 469 U.S. 1209, 37 FEP 64 (1985) (bartenders entitled to tips as component of back pay award); cf. Airport Inn v. Nebraska Equal Opportunity Comm'n, 217 Neb. 852, 353 N.W.2d 727, 39 FEP 3 (1984) (bartender not entitled to collect tips he would have earned although tips are included in interim earnings); Kumar v. University of Mass. Bd. of Trustees, 34 FEP 1231 (D. Mass. 1984), rev'd on other grounds, 774 F.2d 1, 38 FEP 1734 (1st Cir. 1985), cert. denied, 475 U.S. 1097, 40 FEP 792 (1986) (cost-of-living increases, merit increases, additional 4% per year to reflect value of all fringe benefits); Merkel v. Scovill, Inc., 570 F. Supp. 141, 38 FEP 1026 (S.D. Ohio 1983), aff'd in part and rev'd in part, 787 F.2d 174, 40 FEP 1383, 122 LRRM 2399 (6th Cir.), cert. denied, 479 U.S. 990, 42 FEP 560 (1986) (pension plan contributions); Sears v. Atchison, Topeka & Santa Fe Ry., 30 FEP 1084 (D. Kan. 1982), aff'd, 749 F.2d 1451, 36 FEP 783 (10th Cir. 1984), cert. denied, 471 U.S. 1099, 37 FEP 1216 (1985) (spousal and supervisors' retirement benefits considered to be fringe benefits are included in back pay award, as is tax component which offsets tax disadvantage of receiving large back pay award in one year rather than spread over time); Nurses, ANA v. Illinois, 783 F.2d 716, 40 FEP 244 (7th Cir. 1986) (court to consider what wages in different jobs would have been but for bias before adjusting determined amount of back pay owed to state employees in female-dominated job classifications and could devise substitute remedy in lieu of comparable worth). But see Berndt v. Kaiser Aluminum & Chem. Sales, 604 F. Supp. 962, 38 FEP 182 (E.D. Pa. 1985), aff'd, 789 F.2d 253, 3d Cir. 1986) (no reimbursement of reasonable costs incurred on business trips which were not sales-related expenses); Ryan v. Raytheon Data Sys. Co., 601 F. Supp. 243, 39 FEP 1398 (D. Mass. 1985) (no evidence of pay increases to employee had she not been discharged defeats inclusion of pay increases in back pay award, nor would bonus or losses from alleged failure to exercise stock option be included).

[66]Kossman v. Calumet County, supra note 65 (cost of insurance coverage recoverable if alternative insurance coverage expenses were incurred); Berndt v. Kaiser Aluminum & Chem. Sales, supra note 65 (medical insurance coverage and unreimbursed medical expenses are recoverable but not average amount employer spent per employee in providing dental, vision, and life insurance coverage, as that would be punitive); cf. EEOC v. Rath Packing Co., 40 FEP 576 (S.D. Iowa 1984), aff'd in part and rev'd in part, 787 F.2d 318, 40 FEP 580 (8th Cir.), cert. denied, 479 U.S. 910, 41 FEP 1712 (1986) (value of dental, vision, and prescription benefits included in back pay award); Fariss v. Lynchburg Foundry, 769 F.2d 958, 38 FEP 992 (4th Cir. 1985) (proper measure of value of terminated employee's insurance benefits is amount that employer would have paid in premiums rather than proceeds of policy; if terminated employee obtains substitute insurance, make-whole concept permits full recovery of premiums for comparable individual policy); Blackwell v. Sun Elec. Corp., 696 F.2d 1176, 30 FEP 1177 (6th Cir. 1983) (plaintiff entitled to value of health benefits he would have received); Jackson v. City of Independence, Mo., 40 FEP 1466 (W.D. Mo. 1986) (city not required to pay past health insurance benefits for job applicant absent showing that she suffered damage from not receiving benefits from date she was denied employment to judgment date); Foster v. Excelsior Springs City Hosp. & Convalescent Center, 631 F. Supp. 174, 40 FEP 1616 (W.D. Mo. 1986) (if age discrimination is established, widow of former employee who died without life insurance may recover proceeds under life insurance policy as if he had died while still employed, rather than just premiums employer paid on that policy); EEOC v. Emerson Elec. Co., 39 FEP 1569 (E.D. Mo. 1986) (insurance benefits award is in nature of back pay; prejudgment interest based on state statutory interest rate is appropriate); Barone v. Hackett, 602 F. Supp. 481, 40 FEP 961 (D.R.I. 1984) (damages for denial of disability benefits program that treated pregnancy differently from other disabilities are recoverable); Spagnuolo v. Whirlpool Corp., 550 F. Supp. 432, 32 FEP 1377 (W.D.N.C. 1982), aff'd in part and rev'd in part, 717 F.2d 114, 32 FEP 1382 (4th Cir. 1983) (plaintiff not entitled to be compensated for lost value of insurance where he has not incurred any losses which would have been covered by insurance and has not incurred any out-of-pocket expenses to obtain replacement insurance coverage).

has held that whichever of these three methods yields the largest amount should be used.[67] Another court, in a Title VII action, included the difference in the quality of housing provided to white employees as opposed to non-whites as an element of a back pay award.[68] Plaintiffs under the ADEA have also received compensation to fully restore their Social Security benefits.[69]

## B. Deductions and Offsets

### 1. Interim Earnings

The courts continue to deduct actual interim earnings from the amount of back pay to be awarded.[70] Interim earnings include moonlighting earnings that could not have been earned if the victim had not suffered discrimination.[71] Interim earnings considered in calculating back pay awards are not limited to net taxable income and may include in-kind compensation for services rendered.[72]

---

[67]EEOC v. Pacific Press Publishing Ass'n, 35 FEP 322 (N.D. Cal. 1982). Particularly given the enactment of the Consolidated Omnibus Budget Reconciliation Act of 1985, Pub. L. No. 99-272, §§ 10,001–10,003, 100 Stat. 222 (1986), providing terminated employees with the opportunity to continue health insurance coverage at group rates for a period of time, this holding appears contrary to the plaintiff's duty to mitigate except in compelling economic circumstances.

[68]Domingo v. New England Fish Co., 727 F.2d 1429, 1446, 34 FEP 584, 599, *modified,* 742 F.2d 520, 37 FEP 1303 (9th Cir. 1984) (measurable differences in quality of housing is a wage differential because room and board provided to employees is part of compensation).

[69]Hawks v. Ingersoll Johnson Steel Co., 38 FEP 93 (S.D. Ind. 1984) (employee entitled to compensation for lower Social Security benefits resulting from his termination); *see also* Guthrie v. J.C. Penney Co., 803 F.2d 202, 42 FEP 185 (5th Cir. 1986) (social security benefits not deducted from back pay award); Maxfield v. Sinclair Int'l, 766 F.2d 788, 38 FEP 442 (3d Cir. 1985) (social security benefits from back pay award in ADEA case were not offset because court found no discernible differences between Social Security, unemployment, and pension benefits; award was not punitive even though employer's violation of ADEA was not willful). *But see* EEOC v. Wyoming Retirement Sys., 771 F.2d 1425, 38 FEP 1544 (10th Cir. 1985) (Social Security payments were properly deducted from back pay award to state employees because court concluded public treasury should not bear burden of providing windfall to employees).

[70]Horn v. Windsor Mobile Homes, Duke Homes Div., 755 F.2d 599, 37 FEP 228 (7th Cir. 1985) (earnings from babysitting, housecleaning, and sewing should be deducted from back pay award); Nord v. United States Steel Corp., 758 F.2d 1462, 37 FEP 1232 (11th Cir. 1985); Merkel v. Scovill, Inc., *supra* note 65 (interim earnings will be deducted from back pay award under ADEA because there is no justification for making plaintiff more than whole). *But see* Eatmon v. Bristol Steel & Iron Works, 769 F.2d 1503, 38 FEP 1364 (11th Cir. 1985) (employer not allowed to introduce parol evidence establishing parties' intent to deduct interim earnings from back pay awards where conciliation agreement regarding employer's back pay obligation was unambiguous); Wangsness v. Watertown School Dist. 14-4, Codington County, S.D., *supra* note 63. *See also* Cline v. Roadway Express, 689 F.2d 481, 29 FEP 1365 (4th Cir. 1982) (in ADEA case actual earnings from real estate career are commissions minus expenses, not capital gains from real estate sales).

[71]*Compare* Whatley v. Skaggs Cos., 707 F.2d 1129, 31 FEP 1202 (10th Cir.), *cert. denied,* 464 U.S. 938, 33 FEP 48 (1983) (prior position would have precluded moonlighting) *and* Nash v. City of Houston Civic Center, 805 F.2d 1030, 39 FEP 1512 (S.D. Tex. 1985), *aff'd in part and rev'd in part,* 800 F.2d 491, 41 FEP 1480 (5th Cir. 1986) (discriminatorily discharged employee's earnings from running own business are interim earnings to be deducted from back pay award) *with* Hawks v. Ingersoll Johnson Steel Co., *supra* note 69 (earnings from part-time job held before and after employee's discharge not deducted from back pay because income was received regardless of employee's employment status with company), Lilly v. City of Beckley, W. Va., 615 F. Supp. 137, 40 FEP 1213 (S.D. W. Va. 1985), *aff'd,* 797 F.2d 191, 41 FEP 772 (4th Cir. 1986) (applicant's earnings from secondary employment not offset from back pay award because he established such earnings could have been maintained had he been hired) *and* Behlar v. Smith, 719 F.2d 950, 33 FEP 92 (8th Cir. 1983), *cert. denied,* 466 U.S. 958, 34 FEP 1096 (1984) (amounts earned by plaintiff female faculty members during summer and in evenings during school term did not offset back pay award). *See also* Smith v. American Serv. Co. of Atlanta, 38 FEP 377 (N.D. Ga. 1985) (interim earnings should be increased by amount unlawfully rejected job applicant would have earned had she accepted job assignment from temporary employment agency).

[72]McCluney v. Joseph Schlitz Brewing Co., 540 F. Supp. 1100, 1103–4, 29 FEP 1294, 1297 (E.D. Wis. 1982), *aff'd,* 728 F.2d 924, 34 FEP 273 (7th Cir. 1984) (value of ownership interests in oil, coal, and gas exploration ventures received by plaintiff to be deducted from awardable back pay; value of

Interim earnings may include special compensation or stock received from the discriminating employer, if that compensation would not have been earned in the absence of discrimination.[73] In addition, back pay may be reduced by the amount of any employment-related expenses the plaintiff avoids by virtue of not being employed by defendant, such as travel and parking expenses.[74]

Courts have applied various approaches, including calculating back pay on a quarterly, yearly, or total period basis, to deal with situations where the interim earnings during some portion of the back pay period exceed the amounts that would have been earned in that period absent discrimination or where the total interim earnings exceed the amount of any possible back pay award.[75]

Courts continue to disagree on deducting unemployment compensation benefits from back pay awards.[76] Courts offer a variety of reasons for not

---

in-kind compensation at time received by discrimination victim, not value at time of trial, is amount to be deducted from back pay). *Compare* Scott v. Oce Indus., 536 F. Supp. 141, 36 FEP 1226 (N.D. Ill. 1982) (back pay award reduced by value of services performed for company in exchange for equity interest) *with* Nord v. United States Steel Corp., *supra* note 70 (back pay award not reduced by value of services performed in setting up spouse's business where business not earning money and no compensation received).

[73]Officers for Justice v. Civil Serv. Comm'n, 688 F.2d 615, 29 FEP 1473 (9th Cir. 1982), *cert. denied,* 459 U.S. 1217, 34 FEP 1096 (1983) ("hazard pay" received by policemen discriminatorily denied promotions to sergeant deducted from back pay award because policemen probably could not have earned both sergeant's pay and hazard pay); Cline v. Roadway Express, *supra* note 70 (value of company stock received on involuntary termination of employment may under some circumstances be deducted from back pay).

[74]Sabala v. Western Gillette, 516 F.2d 1251, 1265, 11 FEP 98 (5th Cir. 1975), *vacated and remanded on other grounds sub nom.* Teamsters Local 988 v. Sabala, 431 U.S. 951, 14 FEP 1686 (1977) (10% deducted for avoided employment-related expenses); Mitchell v. West Feliciana Parish School Bd., 507 F.2d 662, 666 n.7 (5th Cir. 1975) (plaintiff suffered no financial loss because lower travel expenses in commuting offset lower salary).

[75]Jennings v. Dumas Pub. School Dist., 763 F.2d 28 (8th Cir. 1985) (back pay award not reduced by enhanced earning capacity conferred by masters degree obtained after discriminatory discharge); Matthews v. A-1, 748 F.2d 975, 36 FEP 894 (5th Cir. 1984) (back pay that accrued while working at lower paying job not reduced by amounts earned at subsequently obtained higher paying job); Darnell v. City of Jasper, Ala., 730 F.2d 653, 657, 37 FEP 1315, 1318 (11th Cir. 1984) (adopts quarterly earnings formula); Leftwich v. Harris-Stowe State College, 702 F.2d 686, 31 FEP 376 (8th Cir. 1983) (awardable back pay calculated on year-to-year basis in age discrimination case); Sims v. Mme. Paulette Dry Cleaners, 638 F. Supp. 224, 41 FEP 193 (S.D.N.Y. 1986) (present earnings not interim earnings to be deducted from pay award); *see also supra* note 23.

[76]*Deduction Allowed:* Protos v. Volkswagen of Am., 615 F. Supp. 1513, 38 FEP 1292 (W.D. Pa. 1985), *aff'd in part and vacated in part,* 797 F.2d 129, 41 FEP 598 (3d Cir.), *cert. denied,* 479 U.S. 972, 44 FEP 216 (1986) (discharged employee should not recover compensation for unemployment benefits that she would have received during back pay period for temporary layoffs or higher rate of benefits she would have received had she been laid off in 1983 rather than 1980); Sims v. Mme. Paulette Dry Cleaners, *supra* note 75 (liquidated damages were allowed instead of unemployment compensation); Kossman v. Calumet County, 800 F.2d 697, 41 FEP 1355 (7th Cir. 1986), *cert. denied,* 479 U.S. 1088, 43 FEP 80 (1987); Merkel v. Scovill, Inc., 570 F. Supp. 141, 38 FEP 1026 (S.D. Ohio 1983), *aff'd in part and rev'd in part,* 787 F.2d 174, 40 FEP 1383, 122 LRRM 2399 (6th Cir.), *cert. denied,* 479 U.S. 990, 42 FEP 560 (1986); Townsend v. Gray Line Bus Co., 597 F. Supp. 1287, 36 FEP 577 (D. Mass. 1984), *aff'd,* 767 F.2d 11, 38 FEP 483 (1st Cir. 1985); *see also* Boomsma v. Greyhound Food Mgmt., 639 F. Supp. 1448, 41 FEP 1365 (W.D. Mich. 1986) (employee's failure to inform court of unemployment benefits he received bars back pay award for that period because wage loss could not be determined.

*Deduction Not Allowed:* Guthrie v. J.C. Penney Co., *supra* note 69; Hunter v. Allis-Chalmers Corp., Engine Div., 797 F.2d 1417, 41 FEP 721 (7th Cir. 1986) (decision by lower court not to deduct unemployment compensation benefits from back pay award upheld); Berndt v. Kaiser Aluminum & Chem. Sales, 604 F. Supp. 962, 38 FEP 182 (E.D. Pa. 1985), *aff'd,* 789 F.2d 253, 40 FEP 1252 (3d Cir. 1986) (unemployment compensation benefits not deducted in computing prejudgment interest on back pay award); Brown v. A.J. Gerrard Mfg. Co., 715 F.2d 1549, 32 FEP 1701 (11th Cir. 1983) (en banc) (unemployment compensation benefits, even if supported by tax on employers, may not be deducted as matter of law); Smith v. American Serv. Co. of Atlanta, *supra* note 71; EEOC v. United Airlines, 575 F. Supp. 309, 37 FEP 33 (N.D. Ill. 1983), *on remand,* 755 F.2d 94, 37 FEP 36 (7th Cir. 1985) (no offset where plaintiff required to repay unemployment benefits to state).

deducting unemployment benefits from a back pay award, including the belief that such credits constitute a "windfall" to the offending employer and recoupment of unemployment benefits by the state is a preferable method of remedying any possible unfairness between the plaintiff and the state.[77] On the other hand, some courts have offset unemployment benefits received against an award of back pay to avoid making the plaintiff "more than whole."[78] One logical distinction would be to deduct the award only when it has been charged against the defendant employer's account or experience rating.

Courts disagree on whether public assistance benefits,[79] Social Security benefits,[80] or taxes[81] should be deducted from back pay. Most courts hold that pension benefits are to be deducted from a back pay award.[82] Separation payments are deductible except where the employer fails to prove the amount of separation pay.[83] However, leave time accumulated by an employee prior

[77]Craig v. Y & Y Snacks, 721 F.2d 77, 33 FEP 187 (3d Cir. 1983); EEOC v. United Airlines, *supra* note 76. *But see* Dillon v. Coles, 746 F.2d 998, 1007, 36 FEP 159, 165 (3d Cir. 1984) (where state is defendant, it would be a waste of public funds to require state to institute separate recoupment action that it is authorized to bring).

[78]Protos v. Volkswagen of Am., *supra* note 76 (recovery of benefits would constitute duplicate recovery); Townsend v. Gray Line Bus Co., *supra* note 76 (no double recovery for plaintiff).

[79]*Deduction allowed:* Dillon v. Coles, *supra* note 77 (public assistance benefits deducted because state considers benefits a loan to be repaid). *Deduction not allowed:* Littlejohn v. Null Mfg. Co., 45 FEP 1882 (W.D.N.C. 1983), *aff'd,* 732 F.2d 150, 45 FEP 1889 (4th Cir.), *cert. denied,* 469 U.S. 900, 45 FEP 1888 (1984) (benefits under Aid to Families With Dependent Children Act); Lilly v. Harris-Teeter Supermkt., 545 F. Supp. 686, 33 FEP 98 (W.D.N.C. 1982), *aff'd in part and rev'd in part,* 720 F.2d 326, 33 FEP 195 (4th Cir. 1983), *cert. denied,* 466 U.S. 951, 34 FEP 1096 (1984) (welfare benefits).

[80]*Deduction allowed:* EEOC v. Wyoming Retirement Sys., 771 F.2d 1425, 38 FEP 1544 (10th Cir. 1985) (public treasury should not have burden of windfall to plaintiffs); Crosby v. New England Tel. & Tel. Co., 624 F. Supp. 487, 39 FEP 1271 (D. Mass. 1985). *Deduction not allowed:* Guthrie v. J.C. Penney Co., 803 F.2d 202, 42 FEP 185 (5th Cir. 1986); Maxfield v. Sinclair Int'l, 766 F.2d 788, 38 FEP 442 (3d Cir. 1985).

[81]*Deduction allowed:* Leonard v. City of Frankfort Elec. & Water Plant Bd., 752 F.2d 189, 36 FEP 1181 (6th Cir. 1985); Cross v. United States Postal Serv., 34 FEP 1442 (E.D. Mo. 1983), *aff'd,* 733 F.2d 1327, 34 FEP 1447 (8th Cir. 1984), *cert. denied,* 470 U.S. 1051, 37 FEP 376 (1985); Counts v. United States Postal Serv., 33 EPD ¶ 34,011 (N.D. Fla. 1983). *Deduction not allowed:* Rasimas v. Michigan Dep't of Mental Health, 714 F.2d 614, 32 FEP 688 (6th Cir. 1983), *cert. denied,* 466 U.S. 950, 34 FEP 1096 (1984); Curl v. Reavis, 608 F. Supp. 1265, 45 FEP 1846 (W.D.N.C. 1985). *Compare* Blim v. Western Elec. Co., 731 F.2d 1473, 34 FEP 757 (10th Cir.), *cert. denied,* 469 U.S. 874, 34 FEP 816 (1984) (damages not awarded for increased tax liability caused by back pay award) *with* Sears v. Atchison, Topeka & Santa Fe Ry., 749 F.2d 1451, 36 FEP 783 (10th Cir. 1984), *cert. denied,* 471 U.S. 1099, 37 FEP 1216 (1985) (back pay awards to class members increased to compensate for additional tax liability caused by receiving as much as 17 years' back pay).

[82]Guthrie v. J.C. Penney Co., *supra* note 80 (back pay award reduced by payments from employer's retirement fund; such benefits were not collateral in nature); Fariss v. Lynchburg Foundry, 769 F.2d 958, 38 FEP 992 (4th Cir. 1985) (lump sum pension benefits should be offset from ADEA damage claim); Merkel v. Scovill, Inc., *supra* note 76. *But see* Dreyer v. Atlantic Richfield Co., ARCO Chem. Co. Div., 801 F.2d 651, 41 FEP 1450 (3d Cir. 1986), *cert. denied,* 480 U.S. 906, 43 FEP 80 (1987) (court's failure to instruct jury to subtract from back pay award amounts received from early retirement program followed precedent disallowing reductions from ADEA back pay awards); Bhaya v. Westinghouse Elec. Corp., 624 F. Supp. 921, 39 FEP 1556 (E.D. Pa. 1985), *vacated by j.n.o.v.,* 1986 WL 15013 (E.D. Pa. December 30, 1986), *vacated on other grounds and remanded for reinstatement of jury verdict and consideration of motion for new trial,* 832 F.2d 258, 45 FEP 212 (3d Cir. 1987), *cert. denied,* 488 U.S. _____, 48 FEP 1088 (1989) (at 624 F. Supp. 921, 39 FEP 1556, damages following plaintiffs' ADEA verdict considered and pension benefits held not deductible from back pay award, 39 FEP at 1557 n.1, citing and relying on *McDowell v. Avtex Fibers,* 740 F.2d 214, 217–18, 35 FEP 371 (3d Cir. 1984), *vacated and remanded on other grounds,* 469 U.S. 1202, 37 FEP 64 (1985)).

[83]*Deduction allowed:* Berndt v. Kaiser Aluminum & Chem. Sales, *supra* note 76; Hawks v. Ingersoll Johnson Steel Co., 38 FEP 93 (S.D. Ind. 1984); Ryan v. Raytheon Data Sys., 601 F. Supp. 243, 39 FEP 1398 (D. Mass. 1985); Francoeur v. Corroon & Black Co., 552 F. Supp. 403, 34 FEP 323 (S.D.N.Y. 1982); Smith v. Flesh Co., 512 F. Supp. 46, 35 FEP 448 (E.D. Mo. 1981); *see also* Chang v. University of R.I., 606 F. Supp. 1161, 40 FEP 3 (D.R.I. 1985) (back pay awards reduced by voluntary payment made to correct discrimination). *Deduction not allowed:* Jacobson v. Pitman-Moore, 582 F. Supp. 169, 179, 34 FEP 1267, 1273 (D. Minn. 1984) (jury refusal to deduct severance pay from back pay award held justified by employer's unsuccessful attempt to prove by convoluted formula amount of severance provided).

to termination and paid to the employee upon termination is not deducted from an award of back pay.[84]

## 2. Amounts Earnable With Reasonable Diligence

A plaintiff is required to make reasonable efforts to mitigate back pay damages.[85] Failure to do so is an affirmative defense which must be pleaded. If the employer contests the plaintiff's compliance with this duty, the employer bears the burden of proving that a back pay award should be reduced for lack of reasonable diligence.[86] One court has described defendant's burden as consisting of two parts: (1) proof that the damage suffered by plaintiff could have been avoided, and (2) proof that plaintiff failed to exercise reasonable diligence in seeking an available position for which plaintiff was qualified.[87]

One court interpreted plaintiff's duty to mitigate as not requiring a plaintiff to apply for jobs outside the city in which he lived, but only that he apply for in-town positions.[88] However, another court held that an employer's offer, prior to the plaintiff's filing of an EEOC claim, of employment in a different city with no reduction in compensation was an absolute defense to the employee's claim for back pay.[89] The nature of the employer's business operations (local, regional, or national) may be significant in this regard.

The duty to mitigate damages may require that a plaintiff accept alternative employment that is "the substantial equivalent of the position from which the claimant was discriminatorily terminated."[90] The "substantial equivalent" test is met if the new employment affords the claimant similar promotion opportunities, compensation, job responsibilities, and working conditions and status.[91] Refusal of an unconditional offer of reinstatement to a substantially equivalent position constitutes a breach of the statutory obli-

---

[84]Coleman v. City of Omaha, 714 F.2d 804, 808 n.5, 33 FEP 1462, 1464 (8th Cir. 1983).

[85]See 42 U.S.C. § 2000e-5(g) (1982).

[86]Jackson v. Shell Oil Co., 702 F.2d 197, 31 FEP 686 (9th Cir. 1983); Di Salvo v. Chamber of Commerce of Greater Kansas City, 568 F.2d 593, 598, 20 FEP 825 (8th Cir. 1978); Sprogis v. United Airlines, 517 F.2d 387, 10 FEP 1249 (7th Cir. 1975); EEOC v. Kallir, Phillips, Ross, Inc., 420 F. Supp. 919, 925, 13 FEP 1508 (S.D.N.Y. 1976), aff'd, 559 F.2d 1203, 15 FEP 1369 (2d Cir.), cert. denied, 434 U.S. 920, 15 FEP 1618 (1977).

[87]Sias v. City Demonstration Agency, 588 F.2d 692, 18 FEP 981 (9th Cir. 1978).

[88]Coleman v. City of Omaha, supra note 84 (former deputy police chief not required to apply for police chief jobs in two small towns but failure to apply for position with local security company presents jury question).

[89]Cowen v. Standard Brands, 572 F. Supp. 1576, 1581, 33 FEP 53, 57 (N.D. Ala. 1983) (corporate employee should expect to be asked to move); see also supra notes 25–27.

[90]Rasimas v. Michigan Dep't of Mental Health, supra note 81, 714 F.2d at 624, 32 FEP at 695; Walters v. City of Atlanta, 803 F.2d 1135, 42 FEP 387 (11th Cir. 1986) (extensive efforts to obtain one particular position insufficient; plaintiff obligated to seek employment in other fields when not awarded position in own field).

[91]Wheeler v. Snyder Buick, Inc., 794 F.2d 1228, 41 FEP 341 (7th Cir. 1986) (duty to mitigate damages does not require discriminatee to stay in job in different business that pays substantially less money); Shore v. Federal Express Corp., 589 F. Supp. 662, 35 FEP 405 (W.D. Tenn. 1984), aff'd in part and remanded in part, 777 F.2d 1155, 39 FEP 809 (6th Cir. 1985) (jobs offered to and rejected by dischargee were not comparable to former position); see also EEOC v. Exxon Shipping Co., 745 F.2d 967, 36 FEP 330 (5th Cir. 1984) (employee not required to accept alternative employment with identical pay but requiring weekend work); Hawks v. Ingersoll Johnson Steel Co., supra note 83 (discharged managerial employee not obliged to accept inferior job); Thomas v. Cooper Indus., 627 F. Supp. 655, 39 FEP 1826 (W.D.N.C. 1986) (extraordinary expenses incurred by employee's acceptance of job with another company in effort to mitigate damages will be deducted in terms of assessing economic consequences of her new employment compared with management position unlawfully denied to her).

gation to mitigate damages.[92] A subsequent unconditional offer of employment arguably may partially mitigate a plaintiff's losses if it is objectively superior to his then-current employment, even though not fully comparable to plaintiff's last job with the defendant.

Plaintiff's reasonable pursuit of alternative employment is usually held to satisfy the duty to mitigate damages. The plaintiff is not required to be successful in his new employment.[93] One court ruled that a plaintiff failed to mitigate damages because her full-time "commitment as a first-year law student would necessarily preclude her from accepting employment equivalent to her former position."[94] Another full-time student did mitigate damages by simultaneously maintaining full-time employment.[95]

## C. Interest

Courts continue to exercise their discretion in awarding prejudgment interest in Title VII and § 1981 actions.[96] Until expressly authorized by

---

[92]Giandonato v. Sybron Corp. dba Taylor Instrument Co., 804 F.2d 120, 42 FEP 219 (10th Cir. 1986) (employee who rejected unconditional offer of reinstatement not entitled to back pay or reinstatement after date of offer). *But see* Cerminara v. Allegheny Hous. Rehabilitation Corp., 37 FEP 998 (W.D. Pa. 1985) (superintendent's refusal to accept janitor position was reasonable).

[93]Wheeler v. Synder Buick, Inc., *supra* note 91 (voluntary resignation from second job did not preclude discharged employee's entitlement to back pay because job positions were not comparable and her failure to secure work in new car field was excusable because of supervisor's threat to blackball her in the car business); Glass v. Petro-Tex Chem. Corp., 757 F.2d 1554, 37 FEP 972 (5th Cir. 1985) (employee exercised due diligence in seeking comparable employment by contracting with two employment agencies and submitting 26 job applications); Desira v. Consolidated Mktg., 41 FEP 494 (N.D. Ga. 1986) (employee made good-faith effort to obtain other jobs after discharge and was entitled to lost earnings and cost of insurance).

[94]Miller v. Marsh, 766 F.2d 490, 492, 38 FEP 805, 806 (11th Cir. 1985) (plaintiff not ready, willing, and available for employment). *But see* Smith v. American Serv. Co. of Atlanta, 796 F.2d 1430, 41 FEP 802 (11th Cir. 1986) (discriminatee's decision to become full-time cosmetology student did not constitute failure to mitigate damages because she had actively sought work without success); *cf.* Nord v. United States Steel Corp., 758 F.2d 1462, 37 FEP 1232 (11th Cir. 1985) (status as part-time student does not foreclose possibility of full-time employment).

[95]Brady v. Thurston Motor Lines, 753 F.2d 1269, 36 FEP 1805 (4th Cir. 1985) (even though employment was in lower paying job).

[96]United States v. Gregory, 818 F.2d 1114, 46 FEP 1743 (4th Cir. 1987); Hunter v. Allis-Chalmers Corp., Engine Div., 797 F.2d 1417, 41 FEP 721 (7th Cir. 1986) (award of back pay plus interest necessary to put former employee in monetary position he would have been in but for his discharge); Smith v. American Serv. Co. of Atlanta, *supra* note 94 (decision by lower court not to award prejudgment interest on back pay award remanded in light of LMRA practice); Butler v. Coral Volkswagen, 629 F. Supp. 1034, 41 FEP 432 (S.D. Fla. 1986) (prejudgment interest at rate of 12% compounded on quarterly basis); Priest v. Rotary dba Fireside Motel & Coffee Shoppe, 634 F. Supp. 571, 40 FEP 208 (N.D. Cal. 1986) (discharged waitress entitled to interest on back pay and compensatory damages award); Machakos v. Meese, 647 F. Supp. 1253, 42 FEP 259 (D.D.C. 1986), *aff'd,* 48 FEP 306 (D.C. Cir. 1988) (back pay award for discriminatee should include interest; interest issue not addressed on appeal); Walters v. City of Atlanta, *supra* note 90 (see prior proceeding: 610 F. Supp. 715, 42 FEP 369 (N.D. Ga. 1985)) (quarterly interest on back pay awarded in amount computed under IRS adjusted prime rate). *But see* EEOC v. Rath Packing Co., 787 F.2d 318, 40 FEP 580 (8th Cir.), *cert. denied,* 479 U.S. 910, 41 FEP 1712 (1986) (court did not abuse its discretion in denying prejudgment interest on EEOC's back pay award against employer in Chapter 11 reorganization; court weighed interests of discriminatees against financial impact of interest award); Bunch v. Bullard, 795 F.2d 384, 41 FEP 515 (5th Cir. 1986) (failure to appeal lower court's judgment precludes plaintiffs' attack on failure to award prejudgment interest on back pay award); Kossman v. Calumet County, 800 F.2d 697, 41 FEP 1355 (7th Cir. 1986), *cert. denied,* 479 U.S. 1088, 43 FEP 80 (1987) (interest award vacated because liquidated damages granted in ADEA action); Domingo v. New England Fish Co., 727 F.2d 1429, 1446, 34 FEP 584, 599, *modified,* 742 F.2d 520, 37 FEP 1303 (9th Cir. 1984) (district court did not abuse discretion in refusing to award interest where amount of back pay is not readily determinable and is based on subjective factors); Ingram v. Cox Communications fka Cox Broadcasting Corp., 611 F. Supp. 150, 38 FEP 1594 (N.D. Ga. 1985) (account executive not entitled to prejudgment interest on back pay award).

recent legislation, interest was generally unavailable in a Title VII action against the federal government because of the doctrine of sovereign immunity.[97] The Supreme Court, however, had expressly allowed prejudgment interest on a Title VII back pay claim against the Postal Service, under a waiver of sovereign immunity inferred by the Court from the Postal Reorganization Act.[98]

Under the Equal Pay Act and the ADEA some courts award prejudgment interest only in lieu of liquidated damages.[99]

Failure to follow procedural rules may result in denial of prejudgment interest.[100]

---

[97]*See* Pub. L. No. 100-202, § 623, Stat. 1329-428 (100th Cong., 1st Sess.) (1987). For pre-enactment holdings, *see, e.g.,* Library of Congress v. Shaw, 478 U.S. 310, 41 FEP 85 (1986); Thompson v. Kennickell, 797 F.2d 1015, 41 FEP 1435 (D.C. Cir. 1986), *cert. denied,* 480 U.S. 905, 43 FEP 80 (1987) (GPO employees); Krodel v. Young, 624 F. Supp. 720, 41 FEP 170 (D.D.C. 1985) (HHS employee; § 15(c) of ADEA does not constitute waiver of sovereign immunity). *But cf.* Nagy v. United States Postal Serv., 773 F.2d 1190, 39 FEP 1 (11th Cir. 1985) (interest is recoverable against USPS because Postal Reorganization Act's "sue and be sued" clause constitutes waiver of sovereign immunity which was not limited when Title VII was extended to USPS); Eastland v. Tennessee Valley Auth., 35 FEP 1640, 1641–42 (N.D. Ala. 1984) (prejudgment interest may be awarded against government corporation, engaging in commercial transactions on equal basis with private corporations, regardless of government corporation's authorization to sue or be sued in its own name).

[98]Loeffler v. Frank, 486 U.S. _____, 46 FEP 1659 (1986) (reaffirming general immunity of United States against interest judgments, while holding waiver inferred from sue-and-be-sued clause of 1970 Postal Reorganization Act, 39 U.S.C. § 401(1), and from congressional purpose that Postal Service be operated more like private business).

[99]*EPA Cases:* EEOC v. Liggett & Myers, 690 F.2d 1072, 40 FEP 1285 (4th Cir. 1982), *on remand,* 32 EPD ¶ 33,875 (M.D.N.C. 1983) (prejudgment interest awarded); Donovan v. Georgia Sw. College, 39 FEP 1634 (M.D. Ga. 1983), *vacated,* 580 F. Supp. 859, 39 FEP 1637 (M.D. Ga. 1984), *aff'd in part and remanded in part sub nom.* Brock v. Georgia Sw. College, 765 F.2d 1026, 43 FEP 1525 (11th Cir. 1985) (rate of prejudgment interest for back pay awards is based on state law rate for liquidated demands); Grimes v. Athens Newspaper, 604 F. Supp. 1166, 40 FEP 1792 (M.D. Ga. 1985); Laffey v. Northwest Airlines, 32 FEP 750 (D.D.C. 1981), *aff'd in part and rev'd in part,* 740 F.2d 1071, 35 FEP 508 (D.C. Cir. 1984), *cert. denied,* 469 U.S. 1181, 36 FEP 1168 (1985). The Fifth Circuit appears to bar awards of prejudgment interest in all cases based upon remedies in the Fair Labor Standards Act. Hill v. J.C. Penney Co., 688 F.2d 370, 29 FEP 1757 (5th Cir. 1982); Schulte v. Wilson Indus., 547 F. Supp. 324, 31 FEP 1373 (S.D. Tex. 1982). In enforcement actions by the EEOC, prejudgment interest awards have been approved. EEOC v. Whitin Mach. Works, 699 F.2d 688, 35 FEP 583 (4th Cir. 1983). *But see* EEOC v. Rath Packing Co., *supra* note 96 (prejudgment interest on back pay award improper because of employer's precarious financial status).

*ADEA Cases:* Kossman v. Calumet County, *supra* note 96 (interest award vacated in light of liquidated damage award so that retirees would not receive surplus compensation); Heiar v. Crawford County, 746 F.2d 1190, 1201–2, 35 FEP 1458, 1466–67 (7th Cir. 1984), *cert. denied,* 472 U.S. 1027, 37 FEP 1883 (1985) (if liquidated damages awarded, prejudgment interest would be duplicative; liquidated damages are compensatory rather than punitive); Blim v. Western Elec. Co., 731 F.2d 1473, 34 FEP 757 (10th Cir.), *cert. denied,* 469 U.S. 874, 36 FEP 816 (1984). *Contra* Criswell v. Western Airlines, 709 F.2d 544, 556–57, 32 FEP 1204, 1214 (9th Cir. 1983), *aff'd,* 472 U.S. 400, 37 FEP 1829 (1985) (awarding prejudgment interest on portion of damages representing actual loss but not on liquidated damages under ADEA); Lindsey v. American Cast Iron Pipe Co., 810 F.2d 1094, 43 FEP 143 (11th Cir. 1987) (because ADEA liquidated damages are punitive in nature, both prejudgment interest and liquidated damages may be awarded). Rose v. National Cash Register Corp., 703 F.2d 225, 230, 31 FEP 706, 710 (6th Cir.), *cert. denied,* 464 U.S. 939, 33 FEP 48 (1983) (plaintiff awarded liquidated damages under ADEA is not also entitled to award of prejudgment interest); *see also* Berndt v. Kaiser Aluminum & Chem. Sales, 604 F. Supp. 962, 38 FEP 182 (E.D. Pa. 1985), *aff'd,* 789 F.2d 253, 40 FEP 1252 (3d Cir. 1986) (discharge who was not entitled to liquidated damages received prejudgment interest on back pay award, including medical expenses and automobile cost reimbursements, but not on pension or profit-sharing benefits).

[100]Bunch v. Bullard, *supra* note 96 (failure to appeal lower court's judgment precludes nonpromoted employees from challenging award that did not include prejudgment interest); Goodman v. Heublein, Inc., 682 F.2d 44 (2d Cir. 1982) (prejudgment interest barred in ADEA action where prevailing plaintiff had not moved to alter or amend judgment under Fed. R. Civ. P. 59(a) following return of jury's verdict); Andre v. Bendix Corp., 38 FEP 1817 (N.D. Ind. 1984) (former employee who waited two years to file Title VII claim is not entitled to prejudgment interest because her failure to obtain right-to-sue notice and promptly file suit substantially increased employer's back pay liability). *But see* Sellers v. Delgado College, 781 F.2d 503, 39 FEP 1766 (5th Cir. 1986), *appeal after remand, judgment aff'd in part and vacated in part,* 46 FEP 464 (5th Cir. 1988) (former instructor held to have preserved her claim to interest and fringe benefits by giving *pro se* notice of appeal of back pay award; on appeal after remand, magistrate's denial of prejudgment interest held abuse of discretion).

The method of computing interest is left to the reasonable discretion of the court.[101]

## VI. Compensatory and Punitive Damages

Courts routinely deny requests for compensatory and punitive damages under Title VII.[102] However, where a Title VII claim is joined with a § 1981 or § 1983 claim, compensatory and punitive damages may be awarded on the latter claims.[103]

Punitive damages have been awarded under § 1983 even where only nominal actual damages were shown.[104] In a § 1981 action, one court has held that the employer may be vicariously liable for punitive damages where it ratifies or authorizes an individual's discriminatory acts or where the individual acts in a managerial capacity.[105] However, punitive damages have been denied where the evidence did not implicate an official company policy.[106] In another § 1981 action, the Seventh Circuit has held that a successor employer may be liable for the discriminatory acts of its predecessor, but would not be liable for any compensatory or punitive damage remedy.[107]

---

[101]Walters v. City of Atlanta, 803 F.2d 1135, 42 FEP 387 (11th Cir. 1986) (prejudgment interest on back pay award computed under IRS' adjusted prime interest rate; interest accrues on quarterly basis); Butler v. Coral Volkswagen, *supra* note 96; Ryan v. Raytheon Data Sys. Co., 601 F. Supp. 243, 39 FEP 1398 (D. Mass. 1985) (prejudgment interest calculated at 12% from date on which back pay and stock options were due to date of entry of judgment); Berndt v. Kaiser Aluminum & Chem. Sales, *supra* note 99 (discharged salesman entitled to 8% on prejudgment interest rather than his suggested rate of 11%, as he failed to show that he could have invested money at that rate); Amos v. Corporation of Presiding Bishop, Church of Jesus Christ of Latter-Day Saints, 618 F. Supp. 1013, 38 FEP 1779 (D. Utah 1985), *rev'd on other grounds,* 483 U.S. 327, 44 FEP 20 (1987) (prejudgment interest calculated per IRS' adjusted prime interest rate); Thomas v. Jack Marshall Foods, 37 FEP 1607, 1611 (N.D. Ala. 1983) (interest computed at prime rate used by NLRB if that information is timely provided to court, if not, prejudgment interest rate of state where court is located is used).

[102]Boddy v. Dean, 821 F.2d 346, 45 FEP 586 (6th Cir. 1987); Walker v. Ford Motor Co., 684 F.2d 1355, 29 FEP 1259 (11th Cir. 1982); Padway v. Palches, 665 F.2d 965, 27 FEP 1403 (9th Cir. 1982); Miller v. Butler Mfg. Co., Walker Div., 577 F. Supp. 948, 950, 33 FEP 1397, 1398 (S.D. W. Va. 1984); Desai v. Tompkins County Trust Co., 31 FEP 40, 45 (N.D.N.Y. 1983); Evans v. Meadow Steel Prods., 572 F. Supp. 250, 254, 35 FEP 1187, 1190 (N.D. Ga. 1983).

[103]Easley v. Anheuser-Busch, 572 F. Supp. 402, 415, 34 FEP 380, 390 (E.D. Mo. 1983), *aff'd in part and rev'd in part,* 758 F.2d 251, 37 FEP 549 (8th Cir. 1985) (in Title VII/§ 1981 action, damages for emotional distress awarded under § 1981; "damages for emotional harm are to be presumed where plaintiff establishes infringement of substantive constitutional rights"; specific proof of loss not necessary to support award and plaintiff's testimony may be sufficient) (compensatory damages only available under § 1981, hence can be upheld only on proof of intentional discrimination); Rowlett v. Anheuser-Busch, Inc., 832 F.2d 194, 44 FEP 1617 (1st Cir. 1987) (reducing punitive damages of $3 million on grounds "grossly excessive," to $300,000); Jackson v. Wakulla Springs & Lodge, 33 FEP 1301, 1315 (N.D. Fla. 1983) (in joint Title VII/§ 1981 action, compensatory and punitive damages awarded under § 1981); Jeter v. Boswell, 554 F. Supp. 946, 954, 33 FEP 1410, 1416 (N.D. W. Va. 1983) (granting motion to strike prayer for punitive damages under Title VII, but denying same for § 1981 claim); Sebastian v. Texas Dep't of Corrections, 558 F. Supp. 507, 509 (S.D. Tex. 1983) (awarding compensatory fine for damage to plaintiff's reputation, mental distress, and humiliation due to civil contempt resulting from defendant's failure to obey preliminary injunction in Title VII and § 1983 action); *cf.* Ambrose v. United States Steel Corp., 39 FEP 35 (N.D. Cal. 1985) (punitive damages awarded in action under California Constitution and Title VII).

[104]Goodwin v. St. Louis County Circuit Court, 729 F.2d 541, 548, 34 FEP 347, 353 (8th Cir. 1984) ($1.00 in actual damages and $1,000 in punitive damages awarded).

[105]Mitchell v. Keith, 752 F.2d 385, 36 FEP 1443 (9th Cir.), *cert. denied,* 472 U.S. 1028, 37 FEP 1883 (1985).

[106]Foster v. MCI Telecommunications Corp., 555 F. Supp. 330, 337, 30 FEP 1493, 1499 (D. Colo. 1983), *aff'd,* 773 F.2d 1116, 39 FEP 698 (10th Cir. 1985) (plaintiff established discrimination by individuals and was entitled to back pay, but failure to implicate company policy precluded punitive damage award).

[107]Musikiwamba v. ESSI, 760 F.2d 740, 37 FEP 821 (7th Cir. 1985).

Where plaintiff requests equitable relief (*e.g.*, reinstatement and back pay) and legal remedies (*e.g.*, compensatory and punitive damages), a right to a jury trial appears to exist for the legal relief issue, with the question of equitable relief left to the court.[108]

Liquidated damages may be awarded under the Equal Pay Act.[109] In order to avoid the imposition of liquidated damages, the burden is on the employer to show that it acted in good faith and had reasonable grounds for believing that it did not violate the Act.[110]

Punitive and compensatory damages may not be recovered under the ADEA.[111] Where an ADEA claim is joined with a state law claim which allows for compensatory damages, however, such damages may be awarded on the state law claim.[112]

In *Trans World Airlines v. Thurston,* [113] the Supreme Court upheld the Second Circuit's standard for assessing liquidated damages for willful violations of the ADEA. A violation is "willful" if "the employer * * * knew or showed reckless disregard for the matter of whether its conduct was prohibited by the ADEA."[114] However, the Court reversed the award of liquidated damages in this case because the employer acted "reasonably and in good faith" in determining whether its actions violated the ADEA.[115] At least one court has considered an employer's economic circumstances in determining whether the employer's conduct toward its employee constituted "willful" violation of the ADEA.[116] Moreover, some courts have held that, since liquidated damages are punitive in nature, a plaintiff must show outrageous conduct in addition to willfulness in order to obtain liquidated damages under the ADEA.[117] In addition, it has been held that liquidated damages

---

[108]Harris v. Richards Mfg. Co., 675 F.2d 811, 28 FEP 1343 (6th Cir. 1982) (employer entitled to jury trial on claims for legal relief under § 1981); Thomas v. Menley & James Laboratories, 34 FEP 71 (N.D. Ga. 1984). *But see* Earlie v. Jacobs, 745 F.2d 342, 38 FEP 729 (5th Cir. 1984) (unsupported claim for punitive damages does not entitle plaintiff to jury trial).

[109]29 U.S.C. § 216(b); Morgado v. Birmingham-Jefferson County Civil Defense Corps, 706 F.2d 1184, 1189, 32 FEP 12, 16 (11th Cir. 1983), *cert. denied,* 464 U.S. 1045, 33 FEP 1084 (1984); Laffey v. Northwest Airlines, 740 F.2d 1071, 35 FEP 508 (D.C. Cir. 1984), *cert. denied,* 469 U.S. 1181, 36 FEP 1168 (1985).

[110]Sinclair v. Automobile Club of Okla., 733 F.2d 726, 730, 34 FEP 1206, 1208 (10th Cir. 1984) (reversing denial of liquidated damages based on lack of good faith; defendant had no reasonable grounds for believing its conduct did not violate Act); Laffey v. Northwest Airlines, *supra* note 109.

[111]Perrell v. FinanceAmerica Corp., 726 F.2d 654, 33 FEP 1728 (10th Cir. 1984); Johnson v. Al Tech Specialties Steel Corp., 731 F.2d 143, 147, 34 FEP 861, 864–65 (2d Cir. 1984); Hill v. Spiegel, Inc., 708 F.2d 233, 235, 31 FEP 1532, 1533 (6th Cir. 1983); Fiedler v. Indianhead Truck Line, 670 F.2d 806, 28 FEP 849 (8th Cir. 1982).

[112]Merkel v. Scovill, Inc., 570 F. Supp. 141, 38 FEP 1026 (S.D. Ohio 1983), *aff'd in part and rev'd in part,* 787 F.2d 174, 40 FEP 1383, 122 LRRM 2399 (6th Cir.), *cert. denied,* 479 U.S. 990, 42 FEP 560 (1986). Where the court concludes that the evidence supporting the state law claim for exemplary damages would be prejudicial to the employer on the ADEA claim, the state law count may be dismissed without prejudice. Balmer v. Community House Ass'n, 572 F. Supp. 1048, 33 FEP 627 (E.D. Mich. 1983) (evidence supporting state law claim for exemplary damages would be prejudicial to ADEA claim); James v. KID Broadcasting Corp., 559 F. Supp. 1153, 38 FEP 439 (D. Utah 1983).

[113]469 U.S. 111, 36 FEP 977 (1985).

[114]*Id.,* 36 FEP at 984; *accord* Reynolds v. CLP Corp., 812 F.2d 671, 675, 43 FEP 504 (11th Cir. 1987) ("pretextual scheme" to demote and discharge employee may constitute reckless disregard for whether conduct violated the ADEA); Gilchrist v. Jim Slemons Imports, 803 F.2d 1488, 1495, 42 FEP 314 (9th Cir. 1986) (willfulness may be shown by circumstantial evidence, including statistical evidence and discriminatory statements).

[115]36 FEP at 985.

[116]Gilliam v. Armtex, Inc., 820 F.2d 1387, 1390, 44 FEP 113 (4th Cir. 1987).

[117]Dreyer v. Atlantic Richfield Co., ARCO Chem. Co. Div., 801 F.2d 651, 41 FEP 1450 (3d Cir. 1986), *cert. denied,* 480 U.S. 906, 43 FEP 80 (1987); McKenzie v. Sawyer, 684 F.2d 62, 29 FEP 633 (D.C. Cir. 1982); *cf.* Lindsey v. American Cast Iron Pipe Co., 810 F.2d 1094, 1099–1100, 43 FEP 143 (11th Cir. 1987) (declining to adopt *Dreyer* "outrageous" standard).

are not recoverable against the federal government.[118] In calculating the amount of liquidated damages, a majority of courts appear to exclude front pay from the calculation.[119] Since a jury trial right exists under the ADEA, most courts treat "willfulness" as a jury issue.[120]

## VII. Class Action Procedures for Entitlement to Back Pay

### A. Bifurcation

Federal courts in class action litigation generally continue to bifurcate proceedings into liability and relief stages.[121] The relief stage usually is fashioned in one of three models, which are listed in descending order of frequency: (1) a series of hearings to determine each individual's relief;[122] (2) a classwide formula recovery;[123] or, infrequently, (3) a hybrid approach which combines individual hearings and a classwide formula.[124] In *Segar v. Smith,* [125] the District of Columbia Circuit approved the district court's decision to use a "hybrid" method to determine back pay. In *Segar,* the district court found an extensive pattern of racial discrimination permeating the defendant's employment practices and ordered classwide relief. The court declined to set individual liability hearings for a portion of the class,

---

[118]Smith v. Office of Personnel Mgmt., 778 F.2d 258, 39 FEP 1851 (5th Cir. 1985), *cert. denied,* 476 U.S. 1105, 40 FEP 1048 (1986).

[119]*See, e.g.,* Bhaya v. Westinghouse Elec. Corp., 624 F. Supp. 921, 39 FEP 1556 (E.D. Pa. 1985), *vacated by j.n.o.v.,* 1986 WL 15013 (E.D. Pa. Dec. 30, 1986), *vacated on other grounds and remanded for reinstatement of jury verdict and consideration of motion for new trial,* 832 F.2d 258, 45 FEP 212 (3d Cir. 1987), *petition for cert. filed* (holding, at 624 F. Supp. at 924, 39 FEP at 1559, "that plaintiffs' front pay awards should not be doubled as liquidated damages"); front pay is not among "amounts owing" under ADEA §§ 216 and 626, but is awarded in lieu of reinstatement based on courts' authority under ADEA to order equitable remedies including reinstatement; hence front pay may not be treated as "amount[ ] owing" to be doubled in computing liquidated damages); O'Donnell v. Georgia Osteopathic Hosp., 574 F. Supp. 214, 30 FEP 195 (N.D. Ga. 1982), *aff'd in part and rev'd in part,* 748 F.2d 1543, 36 FEP 953 (11th Cir. 1984). *But see* Blim v. Western Elec. Co., 496 F. Supp. 818, 30 FEP 198 (W.D. Okla. 1980), *aff'd in part and rev'd in part,* 731 F.2d 1473, 34 FEP 757 (10th Cir.), *cert. denied,* 469 U.S. 874, 36 FEP 816 (1984) (court includes front pay in calculating liquidated damages without discussing the issue).

[120]*See, e.g.,* Mitroff v. Xomox Corp., 797 F.2d 271, 41 FEP 290, 296 (6th Cir. 1986) (trial court has no discretion to reduce or strike liquidated damages unless no evidence of "willfulness"); Armsey v. Nestle Co., 631 F. Supp. 717, 41 FEP 983 (S.D. Ohio 1985) (court not required to make independent evaluation of defendant's good faith prior to awarding liquidated damages pursuant to jury finding of "willfulness").

[121]Segar v. Smith, 28 FEP 935, 937 (D.D.C. 1982), *aff'd in relevant part,* 738 F.2d 1249, 35 FEP 31 (D.C. Cir. 1984), *cert. denied,* 471 U.S. 1115, 37 FEP 1312 (1985); *see also* Liberles v. County of Cook, 709 F.2d 1122, 31 FEP 1537 (7th Cir. 1983); *cf.* Pettway v. American Cast Iron Pipe Co., 681 F.2d 1259, 29 FEP 897 (11th Cir. 1982), *cert. denied,* 467 U.S. 1243, 34 FEP 1688 (1984) (district court's decision on whether to bifurcate proceedings was appealable order).

[122]Segar v. Smith, *supra* note 121 (court affirmed district court's order of individual hearings where feasible for black special agents with Federal Drug Enforcement Agency and ordered classwide relief in levels above GS-11 where reconstruction would result in mere guesswork); McKenzie v. Sawyer, *supra* note 117.

[123]*See, e.g.,* Pettway v. American Cast Iron Pipe Co., *supra* note 121; Hameed v. Iron Workers Local 396, 637 F.2d 506, 24 FEP 352 (8th Cir. 1980).

[124]Segar v. Smith, 738 F.2d 1249, 35 FEP 31 (D.C. Cir. 1984), *cert. denied,* 471 U.S. 1115, 37 FEP 1312 (1985) (individual hearings for claims of discrimination in promotion, evaluation, discipline, salary, and work assignment claims); Domingo v. New England Fish Co., 727 F.2d 1429, 34 FEP 584 (9th Cir. 1984) (individual hearings for discriminatory retaliation claims; classwide formula for recruitment, job allocation, and housing claims).

[125]*Supra* note 121.

finding that the pervasive pattern of discrimination made individual hearings "impossible."[126]

## B. Reference of Back Pay Claims to Special Master

The use of special masters in Title VII cases continues to be approved by the courts. Special masters are most commonly used in Stage II proceedings when individual back pay claims are addressed.[127] Costs for the special master may be taxed against the defendant.[128]

## VIII. CLASS ACTION STANDARDS OF PROOF FOR INDIVIDUAL BACK PAY ENTITLEMENT

Courts continue to prefer the use of evidentiary hearings to determine back pay for individual class members.[129] However, in the fifth separate appeal of *Pettway v. American Cast Iron Pipe Co.,*[130] the Eleventh Circuit ordered classwide, as opposed to individualized, relief where the reconstruction of class members' individual work histories would have been impractical. When classwide relief is required to ensure that the class is made whole for the discrimination suffered, the employers proven to have discriminated bear the risk that a few nonvictims may benefit from the relief.[131]

One district court awarded back pay to a subclass of applicants, those hired in 1980, based upon the discriminatory use of a pre-employment test in 1979, even though the subclass actually hired would probably not have been the same individuals hired absent the discriminatory test.[132]

Courts continue to find that once discriminatory practices are established, an individual class member need only prove that he applied for a position, or would have, if not for the discriminatory practice. The burden then shifts to the employer to prove the applicant was unqualified for the job or establish that there was some other nondiscriminatory reason why the plaintiff was not acceptable.[133] As with individual remedies cases, the courts

---

[126]*Id.* (ordering individual hearings for retaliation claims, but classwide formula for recruitment, job allocation, and housing claims).

[127]Chisholm v. United States Postal Serv., 665 F.2d 482, 498, 27 FEP 425, 438 (4th Cir. 1981); Wattleton v. Ladish Co., 520 F. Supp. 1329, 1350, 29 FEP 1307, 1324 (E.D. Wis. 1981), *aff'd sub nom.* Wattleton v. Boilermakers Local 1509, 686 F.2d 586, 29 FEP 1389 (7th Cir. 1982), *cert. denied,* 459 U.S. 1208, 30 FEP 1856 (1983); Kohne v. IMCO Container Co., 480 F. Supp. 1015, 1039, 21 FEP 535, 555 (W.D. Va. 1979); Kyriazi v. Western Elec. Co., 465 F. Supp. 1141, 1147, 26 FEP 398, 402–3 (D.N.J. 1979) (case so complex three special masters' experienced trial attorneys appointed).

[128]Kyriazi v. Western Elec. Co., *supra* note 127 (rate of compensation equal to what special master would receive in private practice).

[129]Guardians Ass'n of New York City Police Dep't v. Civil Serv. Comm'n, 539 F. Supp. 627, 32 FEP 648 (S.D.N.Y. 1982).

[130]*Supra* note 121.

[131]Dillon v. Coles, 746 F.2d 998, 36 FEP 159 (3d Cir. 1984) (analysis of different standards of proof employer must meet to avoid liability to individual class members where class discrimination shown); Domingo v. New England Fish Co., 727 F.2d 1429, 1445, 34 FEP 584, 598, *modified,* 742 F.2d 520, 37 FEP 1303 (9th Cir. 1984) (word-of-mouth recruiting and pervasive discrimination make it difficult to determine who would have been hired); Richardson v. Byrd, 709 F.2d 1016, 1021, 32 FEP 603, 606 (5th Cir.), *cert. denied,* 464 U.S. 1009, 33 FEP 552 (1983).

[132]Segar v. Smith, 28 FEP 935 (D.D.C. 1982), *aff'd in relevant part,* 738 F.2d 1249, 35 FEP 31 (D.C. Cir. 1984), *cert. denied,* 471 U.S. 1115, 37 FEP 1312 (1985).

[133]Domingo v. New England Fish Co., *supra* note 131; Richardson v. Byrd, *supra* note 131; *cf.* Turner v. Orr, 759 F.2d 817, 37 FEP 1186 (11th Cir. 1985), *cert. denied,* 478 U.S. 1020, 41 FEP 272

are split on whether this burden on the employer is governed by the "preponderance of the evidence" standard or the tougher "clear and convincing evidence" standard.[134] The trend has been toward the latter.

Appellate courts will review individual back pay awards in class actions. The framing of a remedial decree, however, is left largely in the hands of the district judge whose assessment of the situation is a factual judgment reviewable only for clear error.[135] In *Ingram v. Madison Square Garden,* [136] the court reduced the number of back pay awards to correspond to the statistical evidence presented by plaintiffs as to the number of minority members who would have been hired but for the discrimination; the court divided the awards among all class members so as to avoid granting a windfall to the plaintiffs at the expense of the employer, the union, and white employees.[137]

Decisions as to the proper distribution of back pay to class members, particularly in the face of objections by some members of the class, continue to turn on the evidence presented.[138]

## X. BACK PAY AGAINST STATE GOVERNMENT DEFENDANTS— EFFECT OF ELEVENTH AMENDMENT

The courts continue to interpret the Eleventh Amendment as prohibiting judgments against state governments under 42 U.S.C. §§ 1981 and 1983 which are paid out of public funds, but not prohibiting an award of damages against state officials sued in their individual capacities.[139] In *Davis v. Scherer,* [140] the Supreme Court held that a plaintiff may collect monetary damages against a state official acting in his individual capacity, but only if

---

(1986) (court affirmed district court's finding that special master who found that U.S. Air Force violated good-faith requirements of consent decree was authorized to order back pay and promotion to unsuccessful black applicant for supervisory position, even though master did not find that applicant would have been appointed to position "but for" violation; relief was being granted not for violation of Title VII, but for violation of consent judgment which was voluntarily entered into by the parties).

[134]*Cf. supra* note 13.

[135]Segar v. Smith, *supra* note 132.

[136]709 F.2d 807, 32 FEP 641 (2d Cir.), *cert. denied,* 464 U.S. 937, 33 FEP 48 (1983).

[137]*Id.,* 709 F.2d at 812, 32 FEP at 646. *But see* Kraszewski v. State Farm Gen. Ins. Co., 41 FEP 1088 (N.D. Cal. 1986) (rejecting employer's attempt to cap liability at 40% of male-filled vacancies, based on court's acceptance of 40% as appropriate estimate of female labor force availability; principle enunciated in *Connecticut v. Teal,* 457 U.S. 440, 29 FEP 1 (1982), "is clearly applicable to all stages of Title VII law").

[138]Holmes v. Continental Can Co., 706 F.2d 1144, 31 FEP 1707 (11th Cir. 1983) (court set aside award of one-half of settlement fund to eight named plaintiffs as "disproportionate and facially unfair" where only evidence supporting individual awards was counsel's opinion that settlement was fair and that the eight individuals had meritorious claims); Reed v. General Motors Corp., 703 F.2d 170, 174–75, 32 FEP 531, 535–36 (5th Cir. 1983) (court approved settlement over objections of 23 of 27 named plaintiffs and 40% of class members, noting that objections to fund allocation were by persons not economically harmed by discriminatory practices and whose sentiments did not represent class as a whole; "linchpin of an adequate settlement is adequacy of representation").

[139]Foulks v. Ohio Dep't of Rehabilitation & Correction, 713 F.2d 1229, 1232–33, 32 FEP 829, 831–32 (6th Cir. 1983) (§ 1981 suit); Lecompte v. University of Houston Sys., 535 F. Supp. 317, 29 FEP 1141 (S.D. Tex. 1982) (§ 1983 suit); *see* Daisernia v. New York, 582 F. Supp. 792, 34 FEP 626 (N.D.N.Y. 1984) (§ 1983 suit against individual state officials for reinstatement not barred); *see also* Atascadero State Hosp. v. Scanlon, 473 U.S. 234, 38 FEP 97 (1985) (Rehabilitation Act suit barred); Pennhurst State School & Hosp. v. Halderman, 465 U.S. 89 (1984) (suit for injunctive relief by citizen of state against state agency and officials alleging violation of state law as pendent claim in federal court barred); EEOC v. KDM School Bus Co., 612 F. Supp. 369, 38 FEP 602 (S.D.N.Y. 1985) (ADEA suit not barred); Schulte v. New York, 533 F. Supp. 31, 37 FEP 1438 (E.D.N.Y. 1981) (EPA suit not barred).

[140]468 U.S. 183 (1984).

the official knew or reasonably should have known that his actions would violate the plaintiff's clearly established constitutional or statutory rights. However, federal and state "officials become liable for damages only to the extent that there is a clear violation of the statutory rights that give rise to the cause of action for damages."[141]

---

[141] *Id.*

CHAPTER 39

# ATTORNEY'S FEES

## I. PREVAILING PLAINTIFF'S RIGHT TO ATTORNEY'S FEES

### A. Statutory Authorization

Attorney's fees may now also be awarded to plaintiffs who prevail in actions against the United States pursuant to the Equal Access to Justice Act,[1] which provides in part:

"Unless expressly prohibited by statute, a court may award reasonable fees and expenses of attorneys, * * * to the prevailing party in any civil action brought by or against the United States or any agency or any official of the United States acting in his or her official capacity in any court having jurisdiction of such action. The United States shall be liable for such fees and expenses to the same extent that any other party would be liable under the common law or under the terms of any statute which specifically provides for such an award."

### C. The General Rule for Prevailing Plaintiffs Under Title VII and the Civil Rights Attorney's Fees Awards Act of 1976

A plaintiff prevails in a discrimination suit upon gaining the opportunity to seek an employment position, whether or not he or she ultimately qualifies for it.[2]

Only the prevailing party, not the party's attorney, has standing to seek attorney's fees under 42 U.S.C. § 1988[3] or 42 U.S.C. § 2000e-5(k).[4] Nor is the plaintiff's law firm a prevailing party under Title VII with standing to file an application for award of attorney's fees.[5] In *North Carolina Department of Transportation v. Crest Street Community Council,*[6] the Supreme

---

[1]28 U.S.C. § 2412(b) (Supp. V 1987). A prevailing party may be awarded attorney's fees only if it establishes that "the position of the United States was not substantially justified." 28 U.S.C. § 2412(d)(1)(B).

[2]Burney v. City of Pawtucket, 728 F.2d 547, 549, 34 FEP 1295, 1297 (1st Cir. 1984); *see also* King v. Trans World Airlines, 738 F.2d 255, 35 FEP 102 (8th Cir. 1984) (plaintiff discriminated against in interview process is prevailing party though employer can demonstrate that plaintiff would not have been hired in any event); Cox v. American Cast Iron Pipe Co., 585 F. Supp. 1143, 36 FEP 1111 (N.D. Ala. 1984), *vacated in pertinent part, rev'd in part and remanded,* 784 F.2d 1546, 40 FEP 678 (11th Cir.), *cert. denied,* 479 U.S. 883, 41 FEP 1712 (1986) (plaintiffs in class action that did not receive individual awards still prevailing parties).

[3]Brown v. General Motors Corp., Chevrolet Div., 722 F.2d 1009, 1011, 33 FEP 417, 419 (2d Cir. 1983) (no standing for employee's former attorney to recover attorney's fees from defendant after plaintiff discharged attorney).

[4]Soliman v. Ebasco Servs., 822 F.2d 320, 44 FEP 278 (2d Cir. 1987), *cert. denied,* 484 U.S. ___ (1988); Keesee v. Orr, 816 F.2d 545, 43 FEP 952 (10th Cir. 1987) (attorney dismissed before settlement reached could not bring suit for fees since court without jurisdiction).

[5]Rainsbarger v. Columbia Glass & Window Co., 600 F. Supp. 299, 36 FEP 1303 (W.D. Mo. 1984).

[6]479 U.S. 6, 42 FEP 177, 180–81 (1986). Attorney's fees still may be awarded, however, for administrative proceedings to enforce the civil rights laws covered by § 1988 "when those proceedings are part of or followed by a lawsuit." *Id.,* 42 FEP at 180. "Under the plain language and legislative history

Court held that attorney's fees under § 1988 may only be awarded if a court action to enforce civil rights laws has been initiated; fees are not recoverable when compliance with civil rights laws has been achieved short of litigation. This same rule probably will also be applied to Title VII under the identical language of 42 U.S.C. § 2000e-5(k).

Although a "special circumstance" can result in the denial of attorney's fees to a prevailing plaintiff,[7] neither a defendant's good faith nor its prompt action in remedying the discrimination is such a circumstance.[8] The Tenth Circuit held that the existence of a contingent fee contract does not itself constitute "special circumstances" sufficient to deny attorney's fees to a prevailing plaintiff.[9]

The "bright prospects" standard of the Second and Ninth circuits, which denies attorney's fees in cases likely to bring substantial monetary relief,[10] has not been followed in other circuits, and is of dubious continuing vitality.

### E. Prevailing Plaintiffs in Suits Against Federal Government

In areas other than Title VII litigation, attorney's fees to prevailing plaintiffs in actions by or against the United States are authorized generally by the Equal Access to Justice Act.[11] While not limited specifically to employment-related cases, the Equal Access to Justice Act has been construed by courts in a manner similar to other attorney's fees provisions in such cases.[12]

Until expressly authorized by recent legislation, prejudgment interest on awards against the United States was barred by sovereign immunity, although attorney's fees were not.[13]

A plaintiff may prevail against the federal government, even if the government started to investigate the alleged violations prior to the initiation of the lawsuit, if the lawsuit "encouraged the federal government" to comply with the law.[14] However, when no relief is sought from the federal government, which was joined as a necessary party, prevailing plaintiff may not recover attorney's fees.[15]

---

of § 1988, however, only a court in an action to enforce one of the civil rights laws listed in § 1988 may award attorney's fees." *Id.,* 42 FEP at 181.

[7]*See* Martin v. Heckler, 773 F.2d 1145, 1149 (11th Cir. 1985) (en banc) and cases cited therein.

[8]Martin v. Heckler, 773 F.2d 1145 (11th Cir. 1985), *rev'g* 733 F.2d 1499 (11th Cir. 1984).

[9]Cooper v. Singer, 719 F.2d 1496, 114 LRRM 3667 (10th Cir. 1983).

[10]Sanchez v. Schwartz, 688 F.2d 503 (7th Cir. 1982); *see also* Benston v. United States Postal Serv., 36 EPD ¶ 35,023 (N.D. Ill. 1984) (even though plaintiff's EEOC claim was successful and employer ordered to implement changes, not clear that relief to employee would have been available without filing lawsuit). *But see* Kerr v. Quinn, 692 F.2d 875 (2d Cir. 1982) (fees allowed only because case not strong enough to assure easy retention of counsel in similar case).

[11]*Supra* note 1.

[12]Hoska v. Department of the Army, 694 F.2d 270 (D.C. Cir. 1982) (employee reinstated pursuant to Merit Systems Review Board decision entitled to fees); Fitzgerald v. Hampton, 545 F. Supp. 53 (D.D.C. 1982) (employee successfully reinstated entitled to fees because of government bad faith); *see* Goldhaber v. Foley, 698 F.2d 193 (3d Cir. 1983) (partial fees allowed for success on one of two counts; application under 1985 revisions to Equal Access to Justice Act questioned in *Russell v. National Mediation Bd.,* 775 F.2d 1284, 120 LRRM 3172 (5th Cir. 1985)).

[13]*See* Pub. L. No. 100-202, § 623, 101 Stat. 1329-428 (100th Cong., 1st Sess.) (1987). For earlier decisions, *see, e.g.,* Library of Congress v. Shaw, 478 U.S. 310, 41 FEP 85 (1986); Hall v. Bolger, 768 F.2d 1148, 38 FEP 1314 (9th Cir. 1985).

[14]Mendoza v. Blum, 560 F. Supp. 284, 288 (S.D.N.Y. 1983) (attorney's fees awarded under Equal Access to Justice Act).

[15]Walls v. Mississippi State Dep't of Pub. Welfare, 730 F.2d 306, 326, 34 FEP 1114, 1129–30 (5th Cir. 1984) (United States sued state agency and then was joined as necessary party by private plaintiff suing state agency in similar action).

In addition, prevailing plaintiffs can recover their attorney's fees from the federal government under the ADEA.[16] Some circuit courts have held that a plaintiff cannot recover attorney's fees from the federal government under the Equal Access to Justice Act in a suit that is analogous to a 42 U.S.C. § 1983 action against state officials.[17]

## F. Prevailing Plaintiffs Before Administrative Agencies

Although *New York Gas Light Club v. Carey*[18] authorizes courts to award attorney's fees for mandatory administrative proceedings related to Title VII claims,[19] the courts have disagreed over whether to allow fees for work done before an administrative agency under other equal employment and civil rights statutes.[20] Some courts have expanded *Carey* and awarded counsel fees for state court proceedings in non-Title VII cases.[21] Attorney's fees for work on administrative hearings prior to the filing of a formal complaint with the EEOC have been denied.[22]

In *Webb v. County Board of Education of Dyer County, Tenn.,*[23] the Supreme Court held that attorney's fees cannot be automatically recovered for pursuing state administrative remedies associated with actions under 42 U.S.C. § 1983 because these actions are an independent avenue of relief and state proceedings are not mandatory. These fees may be recoverable if the trial court finds that the state or administrative hearings or suits are related to the successful federal court action.[24]

---

[16]Lowenstein v. Baldrige, 38 FEP 466 (D.D.C. 1985); Sterling v. Lehman, 574 F. Supp. 415, 417, 40 FEP 707, 709 (N.D. Cal. 1983); *see also* Wood v. Regan, 622 F. Supp. 399, 38 FEP 1480 (E.D. Pa. 1985) (successful discrimination plaintiff in Merit Systems Protection Board procedure can file for attorney's fee under 5 U.S.C. § 7703; not required to file with the EEOC).

[17]Lauritzen v. Lehman, 736 F.2d 550 (9th Cir. 1984) (attorneys' fees not available); Premachandra v. Mitts, 753 F.2d 635, 638–41 (8th Cir. 1985) (en banc); *see also* Saxner v. Benson, 727 F.2d 669 (7th Cir. 1984), *aff'd sub nom.* Cleavinger v. Saxner, 474 U.S. 193, 54 USLW 4048 (1985).

[18]447 U.S. 54, 22 FEP 1642 (1980), reproduced at p. 1474 of the Second Edition.

[19]Curtis v. Bill Hanna Ford, Inc., 822 F.2d 549 (5th Cir. 1987) (court erred in denying fees for time spent on EEOC hearings).

[20]*Compare* Kennedy v. Whitehurst, 690 F.2d 951, 29 FEP 1373 (D.C. Cir. 1982) (ADEA does not authorize attorney's fees on behalf of federal employees at administrative level) *and* Mertz v. Marsh, 786 F.2d 1578, 40 FEP 1110 (11th Cir.), *cert. denied,* 479 U.S. 1008, 42 FEP 1536 (1986) (precomplaint processing of grievance is not a "proceeding" eligible for fees under Title VII) *with* Reichman v. Bonsignore, Brignati & Mazzotta, P.C., 818 F.2d 278, 43 FEP 1384 (2d Cir. 1987) (fees proper in ADEA suit), Bleakley v. Jekyll Island-State Park Auth., 536 F. Supp. 236, 29 FEP 1525 (S.D. Ga. 1982) (attorney's fees allowed for state FEP proceedings in ADEA, § 1983 case) *and* Webb v. Bacova Guild, Ltd., 631 F. Supp. 35 (W.D. Va. 1985) (consent decree in ADEA case constitutes "judgment"); *see also* Lowenstein v. Baldrige, *supra* note 16.

[21]Ciechon v. City of Chicago, 686 F.2d 511 (7th Cir. 1982) (court applies reasoning of *Carey* to § 1988 awards); Bartholomew v. Watson, 665 F.2d 910 (9th Cir. 1982) (district court action filed, then state court action pursued due to *Pullman* abstention doctrine; plaintiffs entitled to fees because state court proceedings essential to their claim). *But see* Cooper v. Williamson County Bd. of Educ., 820 F.2d 180 (6th Cir. 1987), *cert. denied,* 484 U.S. __ (1988) (fees for defending in state dismissal proceedings denied since not part of Title VII "scheme") (citing *Carey*); Brown v. Bathke, 588 F.2d 634 (8th Cir. 1978) (it is within trial court's discretion to award fees for proceedings before state court and state FEP agency), disapproved on other grounds by Hensley v. Eckerhart, 461 U.S. 424, 31 FEP 1169 (1983).

[22]Smith v. Heckler, 40 FEP 1112, (D.D.C. 1984), *vacated,* 776 F.2d 365, 40 FEP 1320 (D.C. Cir. 1985).

[23]471 U.S. 234, 37 FEP 785, 788 (1985). Prior to the Supreme Court's decision in *Webb*, the Second, Third, Fifth, Eighth, and Eleventh circuits had determined that when a plaintiff has been made whole in a state administrative proceeding for a § 1983 violation, he cannot then file in federal court for an award of attorney's fees under § 1988. Blow v. Lascaris, 668 F.2d 670 (2d Cir.), *cert. denied,* 459 U.S. 914 (1982); Latino Project v. City of Camden, 701 F.2d 262 (3d Cir. 1983); Redd v. Lambert, 674 F.2d 1032 (5th Cir. 1982); Horacek v. Thone, 710 F.2d 496 (8th Cir. 1983); Estes v. Tuscaloosa County, 696 F.2d 898 (11th Cir. 1983).

[24]471 U.S. at 243, 37 FEP at 788.

## G. Prevailing Plaintiffs Represented by Public Interest Law Firms

The Third Circuit has held that a contractual provision purportedly barring attorney's fees to legal service attorneys which would be payable by the state was contrary to public policy and hence unenforceable.[25]

## H. Prevailing Plaintiffs in Negotiated Settlements

Attorney's fees continue to be awarded in settlements, even if the plaintiff never proves discrimination, as long as the plaintiff obtains the result desired through litigation and has some legal basis for his claim.[26] Attorney's fees may be denied where a settlement agreement disposes of all claims and does not provide for attorney's fees.[27]

Courts will enforce a consent decree limiting attorney's fees unless there is an extraordinary change in circumstances.[28] Similarly, courts may exercise discretion to approve a waiver of attorney's fees agreed upon during simultaneous negotiations on attorney's fees and the merits.[29]

The court may consider the propriety of an attorney's fee agreement at a hearing on the settlement, and retains authority to approve or modify the agreed-upon attorney's fees.[30] Attorney's fees awarded to a party prevailing on a preliminary injunction have been approved by the First and Sixth circuits, even where the merits of the case were never finally resolved.[31] However, the ultimate loss of the case will preclude any interim award since the requisite prevailing party status no longer exists.[32]

## I. Interim Awards

The Fifth Circuit has held that interim awards of attorney's fees may be granted, in the absence of specific reasons for the denial of those fees,

---

[25]Shadis v. Beal, 685 F.2d 824 (3d Cir.), *cert. denied,* 459 U.S. 970 (1982).

[26]EEOC v. Madison Community Unit School Dist. 12, 818 F.2d 577, 43 FEP 1419 (7th Cir. 1987); Eatmon v. Bristol Steel & Iron Works, 769 F.2d 1503, 38 FEP 1364 (11th Cir. 1985); Jones v. Graphic Arts Local 4B, 595 F. Supp. 792, 36 FEP 18 (D.D.C. 1984); Echols v. Nimmo, 586 F. Supp. 467, 476, 34 FEP 1363, 1371 (W.D. Mich. 1984) (negotiated settlement).

[27]Moore v. National Ass'n of Sec. Dealers, 762 F.2d 1093, 37 FEP 1749 (D.C. Cir. 1985); Young v. Powell, 729 F.2d 563, 37 FEP 664 (8th Cir. 1984); Brown v. General Motors Corp., Chevrolet Div., 722 F.2d 1009, 33 FEP 417 (2d Cir. 1983); *see* Evans v. Jeff D., 475 U.S. 717, 40 FEP 860 (1986) (within discretion of district court to approve settlement under Rule 23 when counsel expressly waives fees as condition of settlement).

[28]*Compare* Rajender v. University of Minn., 730 F.2d 1110, 1118, 34 FEP 607, 614 (8th Cir. 1984) (court refused to modify consent agreement's $6,000 limit for trial of damages of individual claimants) *with* Bachman v. Miller, 567 F. Supp. 317, 319–20, 35 FEP 1493, 1495–96 (D.D.C. 1983) (stipulation to $3,000 limit voided owing to unforeseeable circumstances).

[29]Evans v. Jeff D. (approving waiver and simultaneous merits and fees negotiations), *supra* note 27.

[30]Moore v. City of Des Moines, 766 F.2d 343, 38 FEP 189 (8th Cir. 1985), *cert. denied,* 474 U.S. 1060, 39 FEP 1200 (1986); Parker v. Anderson, 667 F.2d 1204, 28 FEP 788 (5th Cir.), *cert. denied,* 459 U.S. 828, 29 FEP 1560 (1982).

[31]Coalition for Basic Human Needs v. King, 691 F.2d 597 (1st Cir. 1982) (attorney's fees pursuant to 42 U.S.C. § 1988 awarded for preliminary injunction approved where claims mooted before trial on merits); Louisville Black Police Officers Org. v. City of Louisville, 700 F.2d 268, 30 FEP 1505 (6th Cir. 1983) (fees awarded to Title VII plaintiffs whose claims were ultimately settled but who had won preliminary injunction).

[32]Frazier v. Northwest Miss. Regional Medical Center Bd. of Trustees, 777 F.2d 329, 39 FEP 872, *modifying* 765 F.2d 1278, 38 FEP 783 (5th Cir. 1985) (success in obtaining preliminary injunction cannot be considered separate from or unrelated to ultimate failure to prevail on merits).

when a plaintiff has prevailed on some of the issues in protracted litigation.[33]

## J. Prevailing Plaintiff's Right to Attorney's Fees for Time Spent on Fee Claim

The courts have continued to award a prevailing plaintiff fees for attorney's time spent in preparation of the fee claim itself.[34] However, this time sometimes is discounted when a new firm is hired to bring the claim.[35]

## L. Costs

Cost awards to a prevailing plaintiff continue to depend largely upon the circumstances of the particular case. The courts generally find that the prevailing plaintiff is not limited to statutory costs, but is entitled to those costs usually passed on to a client.[36] These costs can include such items as filing fees, witness fees, reproduction costs, and travel expenses.[37]

Courts will generally award the cost of experts only when the experts testify at trial.[38] Court rulings on the expense of legal assistants and computer research as a component of costs are not consistent.[39]

Although the EEOC cannot recover attorney's fees, the courts will award costs to the agency.[40]

---

[33]Carpenter v. Stephen F. Austin State Univ., 706 F.2d 608, 31 FEP 1758, 1779, *reh'g denied,* 712 F.2d 1416 (5th Cir. 1983); *see also* Kraszewski v. State Farm Gen. Ins. Co., 36 FEP 1371 (N.D. Cal. 1984) (plaintiffs entitled to fees for defendant's abuse of discovery).

[34]*See, e.g.,* Coulter v. Tennessee, 805 F.2d 146, 42 FEP 305 (6th Cir. 1986), *cert. denied,* 482 U.S. 914, 43 FEP 1896 (1987) (limiting, absent unusual circumstances, compensation for hours in preparing and litigating attorney's fee issue to 3% of time spent in the main case when issue is submitted without trial, and 5% of time spent on the main case when trial was necessary); Jones v. MacMillan Bloedel Containers, 685 F.2d 236, 29 FEP 939 (8th Cir. 1982). *Contra* EEOC v. Union Camp Corp., 536 F. Supp. 64, 27 FEP 1400 (W.D. Mich 1982) (court exercises discretion to deny award for time spent preparing fee claim).

[35]Hall v. City of Auburn, 567 F. Supp. 1222, 1227, 32 FEP 486, 490 (D. Me. 1983).

[36]Laffey v. Northwest Airlines, 746 F.2d 4, 35 FEP 1609 (D.C. Cir. 1984), *cert. denied,* 472 U.S. 1021, 37 FEP 1816 (1985); Freeman v. Dole, 36 FEP 686 (D.D.C. 1984). *But see* EEOC v. Sears, Roebuck & Co., 114 F.R.D. 615, 42 FEP 1358 (N.D. Ill. 1987) (holding, in part, that costs for pretrial transcripts recoverable, but only at statutory rate).

[37]Goss v. Exxon Office Sys. Co., 36 FEP 341 (E.D. Pa.), *aff'd,* 747 F.2d 885, 36 FEP 344 (3d Cir. 1984); Crawford Fitting Co. v. J.T. Gibbons, Inc., 482 U.S. 437, 43 FEP 1775 (1987); Gottlieb v. Tulane Univ., 809 F.2d 278, 45 FEP 67 (5th Cir. 1987) (expert's fees sought by prevailing party limited to amount authorized by 28 U.S.C. § 1821 absent contract or specific statutory authority to the contrary); *see also* Zabkowicz v. Dart Indus., West Bend Co., Div., 601 F. Supp. 139, 36 FEP 1540 (E.D. Wis. 1985), *rev'd in part on other grounds,* 789 F.2d 540, 40 FEP 1171 (7th Cir. 1986) (awaiting costs for filing fees, witness fees, service of process, transcript fees, travel expenses, preparation of materials for trial); Ryan v. Raytheon Data Sys. Co., 601 F. Supp 243, 39 FEP 1398 (D. Mass. 1985) (costs for counsel's travel and travel and lodging of plaintiff to trial); Henry v. Webermeier, 738 F.2d 188 (7th Cir. 1984) (housing discrimination case; § 1988 authorizes payment of reasonable out-of-pocket expenses).

[38]Jacobson v. Pitman-Moore, 34 FEP 1082, 1085–86 (D. Minn. 1984). *But see* Schmid v. Frosch, 609 F. Supp. 490, 36 FEP 1687 (D.D.C. 1985) (ADEA plaintiff who settled claim can apply for expert witness fee and demonstrate expert's role in obtaining substantial relief); Bruno v. Western Elec. Co., 618 F. Supp. 398, 38 FEP 1679 (D. Colo. 1985) (plaintiff entitled to expert witness fees even though experts did not testify when employer changed strategy).

[39]*Compare* Babb v. Sun Co., 562 F. Supp. 491, 494–95, 31 FEP 1340, 1343–44 (D. Minn. 1983) (computer-aided research is part of overhead; legal assistants' time is not cost item but may be awarded as attorney's fees) *with* Johnson v. University of Ala., Birmingham, Univ. College, 706 F.2d 1205, 1209, 31 FEP 1744, 1748 (11th Cir.), *cert. denied,* 464 U.S. 994, 33 FEP 440 (1983) (computer research costs may be recovered if reasonable), Roberts v. National Bank of Detroit, 556 F. Supp. 724, 39 FEP 221 (E.D. Mich. 1983), Grogg v. General Motors Corp., 612 F. Supp. 1375, 38 FEP 796 (S.D.N.Y. 1985) (fees granted for paralegals) *and* Abrams v. Baylor College of Medicine, 35 FEP 695 (S.D. Tex. 1984), *rev'd in part on other grounds,* 805 F.2d 528, 42 FEP 806 (5th Cir. 1986) (no fees for paralegals).

[40]Monroe v. United Airlines, 565 F. Supp. 274, 281, 34 FEP 1599, 1606 (N.D. Ill 1983).

## II. COMPUTATION OF ATTORNEY'S FEES FOR PREVAILING PLAINTIFFS

### A. General Principles

In *Hensley v. Eckerhart,*[41] a case involving attorney's fees under the Civil Rights Attorney's Fees Awards Act of 1976, 42 U.S.C. § 1988, the Supreme Court cited with approval the list of 12 factors set forth in *Johnson v. Georgia Highway Express.*[42] In *Hensley,* the Court's methodology for determining the appropriate attorney's fees was initially to calculate the number of hours reasonably spent on the litigation multiplied by a reasonable hourly rate (the "lodestar"); this figure may then be adjusted according to the *Johnson* criteria.[43]

Application of the *Johnson* criteria was again considered by the Supreme Court in *Blum v. Stenson.*[44] The Court cautioned against the cumulative application of those factors, noting that many of them are subsumed in the lodestar figure. The burden of proving an upward adjustment is on the fee applicant. The Court's analysis in *Hensley* and *Blum* closely parallels the analysis of the District of Columbia Circuit in *Copeland v. Marshall.*[45]

In a case involving the award of attorney's fees to a plaintiff who prevails on only a part of his claims, the Supreme Court held in *Hensley* that "the extent of a plaintiff's success is a crucial factor in determining the proper amount of an award of attorney's fees under 42 U.S.C. § 1988."[46]

Prior to *Blum,* most lower courts generally followed the "lodestar" method of computing attorney's fees for prevailing plaintiffs.[47] The Fifth and Eleventh circuits still rely primarily on the *Johnson* criteria, although they are giving increasing weight to the *Blum* decision.[48]

### B. Applying the General Criteria

#### 1. Extent of Success

In *Hensley v. Eckerhart,*[49] where attorney's fees were sought under 42 U.S.C. § 1988, the Supreme Court held that attorney's fees should be

---

[41]461 U.S. 424, 31 FEP 1169 (1983).

[42]488 F.2d 714, 7 FEP 1 (5th Cir. 1974). Discussed in the Second Edition at pages 1486–88.

[43]*Supra* note 41, at 434, 31 FEP at 1173.

[44]465 U.S. 886, 34 FEP 417 (1984).

[45]641 F.2d 880, 23 FEP 967 (D.C. Cir. 1980) (en banc), reproduced at p. 1488 of the Second Edition.

[46]*Supra* note 41, at 440, 31 FEP at 1175–76.

[47]National Ass'n of Concerned Veterans v. Secretary of Defense, 675 F.2d 1319, 28 FEP 1134 (D.C. Cir. 1982) (applying lodestar method from *Copeland v. Marshall, supra* note 45); Planells v. Howard Univ., 34 FEP 66 (D.D.C. 1984) (court relied almost exclusively on *Copeland* formulation to calculate lodestar); Sears v. Atchison, Topeka & Santa Fe Ry., 30 FEP 1084 (D. Kan. 1982), *aff'd,* 749 F.2d 1451, 36 FEP 783 (10th Cir. 1984), *cert. denied,* 471 U.S. 1099, 37 FEP 1216 (1985) (applied 12 *Johnson* criteria to raise or lower lodestar calculation).

[48]*Compare* Abrams v. Baylor College of Medicine, 805 F.2d 528, 42 FEP 806 (5th Cir. 1986) *and* Jones v. Central Soya Co., 748 F.2d 586, 589, 38 FEP 1386, 1388 (11th Cir. 1984) (*Blum* cited for proposition that lodestar is computed, then adjusted in light of other considerations) *with* Rivera v. City of Wichita Falls, 665 F.2d 531, 27 FEP 1352 (5th Cir. 1982) (pre-*Blum* ), Laje v. R.E. Thomason Gen. Hosp., 665 F.2d 724 (5th Cir. 1982) (same) *and* Yates v. Mobile County Personnel Bd., 719 F.2d 1530, 1534, 35 FEP 870, 872 (11th Cir. 1983) (same: "The discretion of the district court does not extend to modifying the *Johnson* formulation.").

[49]*Supra* note 41, at 440, 31 FEP at 1175–76.

awarded in an amount reasonable in relation to the results obtained. Lower courts have applied *Hensley* to reduce the total attorney's fees sought where plaintiff prevailed on some, but not all, issues.[50]

Although the results obtained are a crucial factor, there is no absolute requirement that fees in civil rights cases be proportionate to the damages award. In *City of Riverside v. Rivera,*[51] the Supreme Court held that, although the damage amount may be relevant, the correct standard is one of compensation for time reasonably expended.[52]

Some circuits have refused to apply a mechanical formula to reduce attorney's fees as a function of the number of issues on which the plaintiff won. If the issues are sufficiently related, the court will only disallow any repetitive or unrelated work.[53] When a reviewing court has disagreed with the lower court on the merits of a claim and altered the judgment below, the assessment of attorney's fees must be remanded to reflect the new outcome.[54]

The Supreme Court held in *Marek v. Chesny*[55] that Federal Rule of Civil Procedure 68 applies to attorney's fee awards under 42 U.S.C. § 1988. A defendant is not required to pay attorney's fees incurred after a valid offer of judgment is made under Rule 68 and rejected, when plaintiff recovers less than the offer.[56]

## 2. *"Lodestar" Components and Adjustments*

In *Blum v. Stenson,*[57] the Supreme Court recognized a presumption that the lodestar figure reflects a reasonable attorney's fee and that "in some cases of exceptional success an enhancement award may be justified." The Court found in that case that the novelty and complexity of the issues were fully reflected in allowed billable hours and that the quality of representation or the skill and experience of the attorney should be reflected in normal hourly

---

[50]Uviedo v. Steves Sash & Door Co., 753 F.2d 369, 37 FEP 82, *reh'g denied,* 760 F.2d 87, 37 FEP 1852 (5th Cir. 1985), *cert. denied,* 474 U.S. 1054, 39 FEP 1200 (1986); Craik v. Minnesota State Univ. Bd., 738 F.2d 348, 35 FEP 243 (8th Cir. 1984); King v. McCord, 707 F.2d 466, 35 FEP 831 (11th Cir. 1983) (court upheld award of 36.6% of plaintiff's attorney's fees based on percentage of case in which plaintiff prevailed); Richardson v. Byrd, 709 F.2d 1016, 1022, 32 FEP 603, 607–8 (5th Cir.), *cert. denied,* 464 U.S. 1009, 33 FEP 552 (1983) (case remanded to consider reduction for unsuccessful claims); Black Grievance Comm. v. Philadelphia Elec. Co., 802 F.2d 648, 41 FEP 1820 (3d Cir. 1986) (25% reduction for limited success), *vacated and remanded,* 483 U.S. __, 45 FEP 1895 (1987) (for consideration in light of Pennsylvania v. Delaware Valley Citizens' Council for Clean Air, 483 U.S. __, 45 FEP 1750 (1987)); *see* Afro-American Patrolmen's League v. City of Atlanta, 817 F.2d 719, 43 FEP 1589 (11th Cir. 1987) (failure to achieve all relief sought considered under *Johnson* factors, but does not rise to "special circumstance" to bar fee award) (*see supra* notes 7 & 8 and accompanying text).

[51]477 U.S. 561, 41 FEP 65 (1986).

[52]41 FEP at 69; *see also* Thorne v. City of El Segundo, 802 F.2d 1131, 46 FEP 1651, 3 IER 657 (9th Cir. 1986); Zabkowicz v. Dart Indus., West Bend Co. Div., 789 F.2d 540, 40 FEP 1171 (7th Cir. 1986) (total denial of fee may be an abuse of discretion).

[53]Fishman v. Clancy, 763 F.2d 485, 119 LRRM 3047 (1st Cir. 1985); Black Grievance Comm. v. Philadelphia Elec. Co., *supra* note 50.

[54]Walje v. City of Winchester, Ky., 773 F.2d 729, 120 LRRM 2714 (6th Cir. 1985); Holsey v. Armour & Co., 743 F.2d 199, 35 FEP 1064 (4th Cir. 1984), *cert. denied,* 470 U.S. 1028, 37 FEP 192 (1985); Domingo v. New England Fish Co., 727 F.2d 1429, 34 FEP 584, *modified,* 742 F.2d 520, 37 FEP 1303 (9th Cir. 1984).

[55]473 U.S. 1, 8, 38 FEP 124, 126 (1985).

[56]*Id.*

[57]465 U.S. 886, 897, 34 FEP 417, 421, 423 (1984), quoting Hensley v. Eckerhart, *supra* note 4. *See also* Coulter v. Tennessee, 805 F.2d 146, 149–50, 42 FEP 305 (6th Cir. 1986), *cert. denied,* 482 U.S. 914, 43 FEP 1896 (1987) (reducing lodestar fee rate to market rate because "fee awards should not exceed the market rates necessary to encourage competent lawyers to undertake the representation in question").

billing rates.[58] The burden is on the party requesting to justify an upward adjustment to the lodestar.[59]

The Supreme Court in *Blum* concluded that the record in that case did not support a "contingency" adjustment to the lodestar.[60] The circuit courts are still divided in their consideration of this factor. The District of Columbia Circuit has reversed a panel decision to hold that attorney's fees must be measured by market rates, not the discounted past *pro bono* billing rates of plaintiff's counsel.[61] The Seventh and District of Columbia circuits have suggested that the use of the contingency adjustment could subsidize unsuccessful lawsuits, contrary to the language of Title VII, which mandates attorney's fees only to prevailing parties.[62] The First Circuit has expressly disagreed with this concept.[63]

The Supreme Court addressed the issue again in *Pennsylvania v. Delaware Valley Citizens' Council for Clean Air*[64] and reversed an award of attorney's fees that had been adjusted upward because of the contingency factor. Relying heavily on the analysis of the District of Columbia Circuit,[65] the plurality and Justice O'Connor, concurring in part, concluded that a contingency adjustment is appropriate only when the relevant market compensates contingent-fee cases, as a class, differently than other cases, and when the plaintiff would have encountered "substantial difficulties in finding counsel in the local or other relevant market" because of the difficult nature of the case.[66] The Court also reversed the lower court's use of multipliers to reward exceptional success and restated its position in *Blum* that the lodestar is presumed to be the reasonable fee and should rarely be adjusted.[67]

The District of Columbia Circuit has supported an adjustment factor for delay in payment.[68] Although courts continue to reaffirm broad district

---

[58]465 U.S. 886, 897, 34 FEP 417, 422 (1984). *Compare* Curtis v. Bill Hanna Ford, Inc., 828 F.2d 549 (5th Cir. 1987) (court erred by lowering rate when nothing in record showed it was not customary rate) *and* Laffey v. Northwest Airlines, 746 F.2d 4, 35 FEP 1609 (D.C. Cir. 1984), *cert. denied,* 472 U.S. 1021, 37 FEP 1816 (1985) (customary billing rates are presumptively reasonable) *with* Lucero v. City of Trinidad, 815 F.2d 1384 (10th Cir. 1987) (customary hourly rate relevant but not conclusive), Maldonado v. Lehman, 811 F.2d 1341, 43 FEP 209 (9th Cir.), *cert. denied,* 484 U.S. __, 45 FEP 855 (1987) (not abuse of discretion for trial court to apply reasonable community standard in fixing rate) *and* Kyles v. Secretary of Agric., 604 F. Supp. 426, 37 FEP 12 (D.D.C. 1985) (court determined reasonable hourly rate).
[59]Blum v. Stenson, 465 U.S. 886, 901–2, 34 FEP 417, 421–22 (1984); *see also* Hall v. Bolger, 768 F.2d 1148, 38 FEP 1314 (9th Cir. 1985) (enhancement to fee reversed where district court failed to demonstrate that factors considered were not subsumed in initial lodestar calculation); Black Grievance Comm. v. Philadelphia Elec. Co., *supra* note 50 (after *Blum,* Third Circuit has adopted method of first adjusting lodestar for results obtained and then combining other adjustments as single factor).
[60]465 U.S. 886, 901 n.17, 34 FEP 417, 423 (1984).
[61]Save Our Cumberland Mountains v. Hodel, 857 F.2d 1516, 47 FEP 1363 (D.C. Cir. 1988) (en banc) (measuring fee award to plaintiff's counsel with mixed private and pro bono practice by market rates; overruling Laffey v. Northwest Airlines, *supra* note 58, to extent inconsistent). *See also* Murray v. Weinberger, 741 F.2d 1423, 35 FEP 1172 (D.C. Cir. 1984); Thompson v. Kennickell, 1989 U.S. Dist. LEXIS 3138 (D.D.C. 1989) (Richey, J.) ($1,732,700 fee award, at market rates with 100% enhancement to lodestar).
[62]McKinnon v. City of Berwyn, 750 F.2d 1383 (7th Cir. 1984) (§ 1988 civil rights case); Laffey v. Northwest Airlines, *supra* note 58; Murray v. Weinberger, *supra* note 61.
[63]Wildman v. Lerner Stores Corp., 771 F.2d 605, 38 FEP 1377 (1st Cir. 1985).
[64]483 U.S. 711, 45 FEP 1750 (1987).
[65]*See supra* note 61.
[66]45 FEP at 1758. Because no majority agreed on the rationale, the decision may offer limited guidance.
[67]45 FEP at 1757–58. For further discussion of this decision, *see In re Burlington N. Employment Practices Litig.,* 810 F.2d 601, 45 FEP 1705 (7th Cir. 1986), *cert. denied,* 484 U.S. __ (1987).
[68]National Ass'n of Concerned Veterans v. Secretary of Defense, 675 F.2d 1319, 28 FEP 1134 (D.C. Cir. 1982); Murray v. Weinberger, *supra* note 61 (circuit court reverses and remands district court decision granting adjustments, including those for delay of payment, for more specific discussion of

court discretion in fee awards and approving other adjustments to the lodestar,[69] the many decisions prior to *Blum* upholding upward adjustments to the lodestar must now be analyzed with care.[70]

## C. General Level of Awards

### 1. Public Interest Law Firms

Most courts now hold that a public interest law firm should receive the same rates and be eligible for an upward adjustment of the lodestar to the same extent as similarly situated private attorneys.[71]

### 2. Effect of Agreement Between Plaintiff and Counsel

The courts generally will not limit a party to a contingency agreement that yields less to a successful plaintiff than a statutory award of attorney's fees.[72] A fee agreement which provides the attorney with more than the court awarded as a reasonable fee may be declared void or may even result in no award or a nominal award.[73] Some circuits have limited the amount attorneys may recover to the statutory award regardless of other arrangements with the client.[74] Others have refused to treat the statutory award as a ceiling on the award of fees where there is a contingency fee agreement.[75] To avoid

---

entitlement to adjustments). *But cf.* Library of Congress v. Shaw, 478 U.S. 310, 41 FEP 85 (1986) (suggesting it may be inappropriate to award both an adjustment for delay and interest).

[69]Kyles v. Secretary of Agric., 604 F. Supp. 426, 37 FEP 12 (D.D.C. 1985) (upward adjustment at interest rate plaintiff paid to borrow money to pay her attorney during the case); Merkel v. Scovill, Inc., 590 F. Supp. 529, 40 FEP 1376 (S.D. Ohio, 1984) (upward adjustment of lodestar to make award reasonable).

[70]*See, e.g.,* Yates v. Mobile County Personnel Bd., 719 F.2d 1530, 35 FEP 870 (11th Cir. 1983) (payment adjusted 35% higher because of high level of skill, results, contingency, and delay in payment); Monroe v. United Airlines, 565 F. Supp 274, 34 FEP 1599 (N.D. Ill. 1983) (in long, thoughtful opinion, court added $75 hourly premium to $125 basic rate); Sears v. Atchison, Topeka & Santa Fe Ry., 30 FEP 1084 (D. Kan. 1982), *aff'd,* 749 F.2d 1451, 36 FEP 783 (10th Cir. 1984), *cert. denied,* 471 U.S. 1099, 37 FEP 1216 (1985) (lodestar enhanced by factor of .75 reflecting contingency and quality factors).

[71]Blum v. Stenson, 465 U.S. 886, 34 FEP 417 (1984); Domingo v. New England Fish Co., 727 F.2d 1429, 1447, 34 FEP 584, 599, *modified,* 742 F.2d 520, 37 FEP 1303 (9th Cir. 1984) (same rates as charged by comparable private counsel); Mammano v. Pittston Co., 792 F.2d 1242 (4th Cir. 1986) (fact that firm is public interest firm does not jeopardize its entitlement to fees); Minority Employees at NASA v. Frosch, 694 F.2d 846, 35 FEP 462 (D.C. Cir. 1982) (public interest law firm eligible for incentive award to same extent as similarly situated private attorneys); Louisville Black Police Officers Org. v. City of Louisville, 700 F.2d 268, 30 FEP 1505 (6th Cir. 1983) (attorney's fees awarded to public interest law firm at rates comparable to private attorneys). *But see* Greenspan v. Automobile Club of Mich., 536 F. Supp. 411, 28 FEP 988 (E.D. Mich. 1982) (reduced fees awarded to nonparty civil rights organization based upon salary costs to organization).

[72]Dominic v. Consolidated Edison Co. of N.Y., 822 F.2d 1249, 44 FEP 268 (2d Cir. 1987) (contingent fee does not limit award in ADEA case); Sisco v. J.S. Alberici Constr. Co., 733 F.2d 55, 57, 34 FEP 1306, 1308 (8th Cir. 1984) (contingent fee contract no limit to fee under Title VII or 42 U.S.C. § 1988); Sullivan v. Crown Paper Bd. Co., 719 F.2d 667, 670, 33 FEP 13, 15 (3d Cir. 1983) (ADEA case; attorney's fees based on greater of statutory fee or contingent fee); Cooper v. Singer, 719 F.2d 1496, 114 LRRM 3667 (10th Cir. 1983) (contingent fee contract does not limit statutory fee which prevailing plaintiff could recover under 42 U.S.C. § 1988); Sanchez v. Schwartz, 688 F.2d 503 (7th Cir. 1982) (contingent fee agreement did not serve as automatic ceiling on attorney's fee awarded pursuant to 42 U.S.C. § 1988).

[73]Rogers v. Fansteel, Inc., 533 F. Supp. 100, 31 FEP 415 (E.D. Mich. 1981) (contract providing for $2,500 retainer, one-third of money judgment, plus court-awarded fee held void).

[74]Cooper v. Singer, *supra* note 72 (award under § 1988 circumscribes amount attorney can recover); Wheatley v. Ford, 679 F.2d 1037 (2d Cir. 1982) (claim for services rendered in § 1983 nonemployment case under contingency fee arrangement deemed paid and satisfied by payment of statutory award).

[75]Kirchoff v. Flynn, 786 F.2d 320, 328 (7th Cir. 1986) (contingency fee arrangement in § 1983 nonemployment case is appropriate measure of attorney's fees if it represents market rate for services reasonably required to produce victory); Hamner v. Rios, 769 F.2d 1404, 1408–9 (9th Cir. 1985) (contingency fee arrangement in § 1983 nonemployment case should be enforced if reasonable); Sears v. Atchison, Topeka & Santa Fe Ry., 779 F.2d 1450, 1453–54, 39 FEP 1029, 1033 (10th Cir. 1985) (*Cooper*

a windfall, a statutory award may be applied toward the amount due under a contingency fee agreement.[76]

### 3. Procedure

In a decision involving two Freedom of Information Act cases and one Title VII case against the federal government, the District of Columbia Circuit promulgated exacting standards for documentation of fee applications, specificity in opposition to such applications, and discovery available on attorney's fee requests. In *National Association of Concerned Veterans v. Secretary of Defense,*[77] the District of Columbia Circuit held that (1) an attorney's fee applicant is required to provide specific evidence of the prevailing community rate for the type of work for which the award is sought, not generalized and conclusory "information and belief" affidavits from friendly attorneys; (2) the preferred practice for documenting the number of hours spent is to prepare detailed summaries based upon contemporaneous time records indicating the work performed by each attorney for whom fees are sought; (3) when seeking an adjustment to the lodestar figure, a fee applicant should clearly identify the specific circumstances of the case which support the requested adjustment to the lodestar; and (4) a party opposing a fee request is entitled to discovery of information it reasonably requires to appraise the reasonableness of the fee requested and in order that it may present any legitimate challenges to the application to the district court.[78] The court further held that the party opposing an attorney's fee application should be equally detailed in setting forth the specific basis for its opposition.[79]

Absent a local rule establishing time limits, a successful party may submit its request for attorney's fees or costs at any time that does not prejudice the opposing side.[80]

## III. A PREVAILING DEFENDANT'S RIGHT TO ATTORNEY'S FEES

Courts generally have continued to follow the Supreme Court's standard in *Christiansburg Garment Co. v. EEOC*[81] in awarding attorney's fees to

---

*v. Singer* applied prospectively only; attorney's fees awarded in accordance with contingency fee agreement); Pharr v. Housing Auth. of City of Prichard, Ala., 704 F.2d 1216, 1218 (11th Cir. 1983) (contingency fee contract represents client's and attorney's notions of reasonable fee and should be enforced if reasonable).

[76]Wilmington v. J.I. Case Co., 793 F.2d 909, 923, 40 FEP 1833, 1845 (8th Cir. 1986) (statutory award applied toward amount due attorneys under contingency fee agreement, not in addition to amount due under agreement).

[77]*Supra* note 68 (hereinafter "NACV").

[78]*Id.* at 1324–28, 28 FEP at 1138–42; *cf.* Pennsylvania v. Delaware Valley Citizens' Council for Clean Air, 483 U.S. 711, 45 FEP 1750 (1987) (upward adjustment to lodestar reversed because lower court did not make detailed findings concerning basis for adjustment); McClure v. Mexia Indep. School Dist., 750 F.2d 396, 36 FEP 1402 (5th Cir. 1985) (suggests use of procedure outlined in *NACV*); Murray v. Weinberger, 741 F.2d 1423, 35 FEP 1172 (D.C. Cir. 1984) (attorney's fees award reversed for failure to specifically discuss reasoning of the award); Davis v. Combustion Eng'g, 742 F.2d 916, 35 FEP 975 (6th Cir. 1984) (adjustment to award reversed because district court failed to explain its reasoning).

[79]675 F.2d at 1326, 28 FEP at 1139.

[80]Houghton v. McDonnell Douglas Corp., 716 F.2d 526 (8th Cir. 1983) (doctrine of laches found inapplicable to EEOC's recovery of costs request); Neidhardt v. D.H. Holmes Co., 701 F.2d 553, 31 FEP 626 (5th Cir. 1983), *on remand,* 583 F. Supp. 1271, 37 FEP 1588 (E.D. La. 1984); O'Donnell v. Georgia Osteopathic Hosp., 99 F.R.D. 576, 36 FEP 948 (N.D. Ga. 1983).

[81]434 U.S. 412, 16 FEP 502 (1978), reproduced at p. 1512 of the Second Edition.

prevailing defendants.[82] Some courts have applied a "bad-faith" standard in awards under the ADEA.[83] Although attorney's fees are denied to a defendant as a prevailing party at trial, a defendant still may obtain fees for abuse of discovery or a frivolous appeal.[84] A court may award fees to a prevailing defendant on appeal even when such fees have not been requested.[85] Although attorney's fees are normally assessed against the parties, courts may assess them against a plaintiff's attorney for prosecuting a vexatious case.[86]

---

[82]EEOC v. Caribe Hilton Int'l, 821 F.2d 74 (1st Cir. 1987) (EEOC acted unreasonably and without foundation in bringing case); Jackson v. Color Tile, Inc., 803 F.2d 201, 42 FEP 191 (5th Cir. 1986) (attorney's fees award to employer appropriate where action was frivolous, unreasonable, or without foundation, even though not brought in bad faith); Lane v. Sotheby Parke Bernet, 758 F.2d 71, 37 FEP 696 (2d Cir. 1985) (summary judgment granted to defendant but no attorney's fees award; remanded to district court to determine if defendant entitled to fees after discovery indicated plaintiff's case was meritless); Beard v. Annis, 730 F.2d 741, 745, 34 FEP 1139, 1142 (11th Cir. 1984) (attorney's fees awarded because lawsuit groundless, baseless, and frivolous); Charves v. Western Union Tel. Co., 711 F.2d 462 (1st Cir. 1983) (award of attorney's fees to defendant upheld where plaintiff not a credible witness); Bugg v. Industrial Workers, AIW, Local 507, 674 F.2d 595, 28 FEP 40 (7th Cir.), cert. denied, 459 U.S. 805, 32 FEP 1672 (1982) (attorney's fees awarded to defendant for work at trial and on appeal); Neidhart v. D.H. Holmes Co., supra note 80 (plaintiffs' claims frivolous and brought in bad faith; fee award to be paid by EEOC and plaintiffs); Peters v. Dart & Kraft, Ralph Wilson Plastics Div., 38 FEP 937 (N.D. Ill. 1985) ("complaint is groundless and totally meritless"); Parker v. Bell Helicopter Co., 35 EPD ¶ 34,733 (N.D. Tex. 1984) (plaintiff brought suit against employer and union; claims against union meritless); Rainsbarger v. Columbia Glass & Window Co., 600 F. Supp. 299, 36 FEP 1303 (W.D. Mo. 1984) (defendant not entitled to attorney's fee award after negotiated settlement); Steinberg v. St. Regis/Sheraton Hotel, 583 F. Supp. 421, 424–26, 34 FEP 745, 747–49 (S.D.N.Y. 1984) (attorney's fees assessed against two plaintiffs and plaintiffs' attorney in ADEA and Title VII suits which were meritless, frivolous, and vexatious); EEOC v. IPCO Hosp. Supply Co., 565 F. Supp. 134, 32 FEP 130 (S.D.N.Y. 1983) (attorney's fees awarded where "implausibility of employee's story should have been apparent on the agency's first encounter with her"); EEOC v. Shoney's, Inc., 542 F. Supp. 332, 35 FEP 386 (N.D. Ala. 1982) (court considered EEOC's unresponsiveness to discovery in awarding prevailing defendant attorney's fees); cf. Trevino v. Holly Sugar Corp., 811 F.2d 896, 43 FEP 280 (5th Cir. 1987) (denial of fees upheld where entire case not frivolous and defendants' counsel failed to ask trial court to analyze claims separately); Shrock v. Altru Nurses Registry, 810 F.2d 658, 42 FEP 1393 (7th Cir. 1987) (fees available as Rule 11 sanctions even though suit not "frivolous" in traditional sense); Thomas v. Metroflight dba Metro Airlines, 814 F.2d 1506, 43 FEP 703 (10th Cir. 1987) (error to assess fees against plaintiffs when nonfrivolous issue is one of first impression in circuit).

[83]Ford v. Temple Hosp., 790 F.2d 342 (3d Cir. 1986) (reversal of attorney's fee against plaintiff's attorney where no showing of willful bad faith on part of attorney); Morgan v. Union Metal Mfg. Co., 757 F.2d 792, 37 FEP 625 (6th Cir. 1985) (suit not initiated in bad faith, but continuing suit after discovery and settlement offer demonstrated bad faith); Cote v. James River Corp., 761 F.2d 60, 37 FEP 1243 (1st Cir. 1985) (defendant entitled to fees it incurred after plaintiff continued to prosecute her claim); Singer v. Uni-Marts, 37 FEP 1197 (W.D. Pa. 1985) (defendant not entitled to award; plaintiff did not pursue ADEA claim in bad faith); EEOC v. Federated Foods, 37 FEP 711 (N.D. Ill. 1985) (nonliability defendant not entitled to attorney's fees after its dismissal from case; was a party defendant pursuant to Federal Rules of Civil Procedure 19(a)(2)); Snyder v. Washington Hosp. Center, 36 FEP 445 (D.D.C. 1984) (defendant has not shown plaintiff brought case in bad faith).

[84]Reynolds v. Humko Prods., 756 F.2d 469, 37 FEP 294 (6th Cir. 1985) (award against plaintiff and/or attorney for frivolous appeal); Johnson v. Allyn & Bacon, 731 F.2d 64, 74, 34 FEP 804, 811 (1st Cir.), cert. denied, 469 U.S. 1018, 36 FEP 320 (1984) (defendant awarded recovery of double costs on appeal); EEOC v. Sanders Chevrolet, 36 FEP 348 (D.N.M. 1984) (EEOC liable for attorney's fees incurred by third party when EEOC tried to join it; EEOC's attempts to join third party ignored Federal Rules and case law); Crawford v. Government Employees, AFGE, 576 F. Supp. 812, 815, 41 FEP 412, 414 (D.D.C. 1983) (defendants awarded attorney's fees for plaintiff's abuse of discovery process).

[85]Bacon v. State, County & Mun. Employees Council 13, 795 F.2d 33, 42 FEP 1520 (7th Cir. 1986).

[86]Greene v. Union Mut. Life Ins. Co. of Am., 764 F.2d 19, 37 FEP 872 and 37 FEP 1856 (1st Cir. 1985) (plaintiff's attorney assessed costs of appeal caused by his own mistake); Hornbuckle v. ARCO Oil & Gas Co., 732 F.2d 1233, 1237 n.6, 34 FEP 1566, 1569 (5th Cir. 1984), aff'd, 770 F.2d 1321, 39 FEP 1426 (5th Cir. 1985), cert. denied, 474 U.S. 1016, 40 FEP 272 (1986) (district court ordered to determine whether sanction against attorney who refused to begin trial more appropriate than dismissing plaintiff's case); Hernandez v. New York Hosp., 37 FEP 1388 (S.D.N.Y. 1984) (attorney jointly and severally liable for attorney's fees award against plaintiff for pursuing meritless case); Kuzmins v. Employee Transfer Corp., 587 F. Supp. 536, 35 FEP 653 (N.D. Ohio 1984) (plaintiff's attorney ordered to pay $100 fine to defendant for filing frivolous claims); Rogers v. Kroger Co., 586 F. Supp. 597, 40 FEP 795 (S.D. Tex. 1984) ($10,000 award against plaintiff and attorney, plus separate penalties against attorney). Defendants may also pursue sanctions against plaintiff's attorneys pursuant to Rule 11 of the Federal Rules of Civil Procedure. Carvahlo v. MacArthur Corp., 615 F. Supp. 164, 37 FEP 1587 (S.D. Fla. 1985) (plaintiff's attorney assessed fees under Rule 11 for defendant's filings required to dismiss meritless claims); Love v. Kraft, Inc., 37 EPD ¶ 35,238 (N.D. Tex. 1985) (award against plaintiff's attorney under Rule 11 where

The calculation of fees is generally the same for defendants as plaintiffs.[87] However, some courts will consider the financial status of the plaintiff and reduce the fees[88] or even deny them entirely.[89] Costs may also be reduced for the same reason.[90]

Other aspects of attorney's fees available to plaintiffs may not be as available to defendants, such as interim relief. For example, a defendant's partial success on a summary judgment motion will not result in the award of attorney's fees.[91]

## IV. PREVAILING INTERVENOR'S RIGHT TO ATTORNEY'S FEES

Courts continue to exercise discretion in evaluating the rights of prevailing intervenors to attorney's fees.[92]

An intervening plaintiff who obtains modification of a consent decree may recover attorney's fees.[93] A would-be party was assessed attorney's fees after the court denied it the right to intervene in the appeal of a plaintiff's successful Title VII action.[94] Fees were not assessed, however,

---

[no indication of discrimination at all); Ring v. R.J. Reynolds Indus., 597 F. Supp. 1277, 119 LRRM 2693 (N.D. Ill. 1984), aff'd without opinion, 804 F.2d 143 (7th Cir. 1986) (in case brought under Illinois Human Rights Act, defendant entitled to sanctions against plaintiff's attorney for failure to make "reasonable inquiry" as to basis of claim).

[87]Arnold v. Burger King Corp., 719 F.2d 63, 67, 32 FEP 1769, 1772 (4th Cir. 1983), cert. denied, 469 U.S. 826, 35 FEP 1608 (1984); Brown v. Fairleigh Dickinson Univ., 560 F. Supp. 391 (D.N.J. 1983); Hunter v. Effingham County Bd. of Educ., 33 FEP 67, 73–75 (S.D. Ga. 1983) (attorney's fees awarded to defendant calculated under 12 factors in Johnson). A prevailing defendant may be entitled to costs and attorney's fees or just costs. See Matthews v. Allis-Chalmers, 769 F.2d 1215, 38 FEP 1118 (7th Cir. 1985) (successful ADEA defendant entitled to costs); Woodworkers Local 5-376 v. Champion Int'l Corp., 752 F.2d 163, 43 FEP 383 (5th Cir. 1985), aff'd sub nom. Crawford Fitting Co. v. J.T. Gibbons, Inc., 482 U.S. 437, 43 FEP 1775 (1987) (prevailing defendant in Title VII action not entitled to greater than statutory costs since case brought in good faith).

[88]Charves v. Western Union Tel. Co., supra note 82; Bateau v. Skelton, 36 EPD ¶ 35,110 (E.D. Mich. 1984) (plaintiff required to pay only 10% of award to corporate and individual defendants; corporate defendant paid all defense fees); Wilson v. Continental Mfg. Co., 599 F. Supp. 284 (E.D. Mo. 1984) (plaintiff ordered to pay part of attorney's fee award even if indigent, because failure to award fees may encourage frivolous suits); Piljan v. Michigan Dep't of Social Servs., 585 F. Supp. 1579, 41 FEP 1093 (E.D. Mich. 1984) (award reduced from $48,000 to $3,000 due to plaintiff's financial circumstances); Steinberg v. St. Regis/Sheraton Hotel, supra note 82; cf. National Org. for Women v. Bank of Cal., 680 F.2d 1291, 29 FEP 300 (9th Cir. 1982) (affirmed finding that plaintiffs could afford attorney's fees awarded to prevailing defendant).

[89]Manabat v. Columbus-Cuneo-Cabrini Medical Center, 34 FEP 254, 257 (N.D. Ill. 1984); Saunders v. Bechtel Civil & Minerals, 34 FEP 1759 (D.D.C. 1984) (defendant not entitled to award against pro se and judgment-proof plaintiff); Luna v. Machinists Local 36, 35 FEP 324 (W.D. Tex. 1982). Contra Durrett v. Jenkins Brickyard, 678 F.2d 911, 29 FEP 58 (11th Cir. 1982) (district court may not refuse to award defendant any attorneys' fees due to plaintiff's financial condition).

[90]Wrighten v. Metropolitan Hosps., 726 F.2d 1346, 1357, 33 FEP 1714, 1722 (9th Cir. 1984); Badillo v. Central Steel & Wire Co., 717 F.2d 1160, 1165, 32 FEP 1679, 1682–83 (7th Cir. 1983) (superseded by statute as stated in Zaldivar v. City of Los Angeles, 780 F.2d 823 (9th Cir. 1986)).

[91]Santiago v. Victim Servs. Agency of the Metro. Assistance Corp., 753 F.2d 219 (2d Cir. 1985) (defendant not entitled to attorneys' fees after plaintiff's request for injunctive relief denied); Howard v. Roadway Express, 726 F.2d 1529, 1536, 34 FEP 341, 347 (11th Cir. 1984).

[92]EEOC v. Exxon Corp. dba Exxon Co., U.S.A., 583 F. Supp. 632, 36 FEP 306 (S.D. Tex.), aff'd sub nom. EEOC v. Exxon Shipping Co., 745 F.2d 967, 36 FEP 330 (5th Cir. 1984) (attorney's fees awarded to plaintiff-intervenor in Title VII action filed by EEOC where complainant intervened and was successfully represented by her counsel).

[93]Miller v. Staats, 706 F.2d 336, 342, 31 FEP 976, 980 (D.C. Cir. 1983); Gautreaux v. Chicago Hous. Auth., 610 F. Supp. 29 (N.D. Ill. 1985); Plummer v. Chemical Bank, 592 F. Supp. 1168, 35 FEP 1546 (S.D.N.Y. 1984).

[94]Thompson v. Sawyer, 586 F. Supp. 635, 34 FEP 1327 (D.D.C. 1984), later proceeding sub nom. Thompson v. Kennickell, 797 F.2d 1015, 41 FEP 1435 (D.C. Cir. 1986), cert. denied, 480 U.S. 905, 43 FEP 80 (1987) (plaintiffs awarded $37,461 attorney's fees expended in defeating union's three attempts to intervene); see also Vulcan Soc'y of Westchester County v. Fire Dep't of White Plains, 533 F. Supp.

against an unsuccessful labor union intervenor in an age discrimination lawsuit.[95]

1054, 34 FEP 1691 (S.D.N.Y. 1982) (attorney's fees to prevailing plaintiff against defendant and intervenors allocated based upon relative responsibilities of defendant and intervenors in incurring those fees). *But see* Paradise v. Prescott, 626 F. Supp. 117, 39 FEP 1744 (M.D. Ala. 1985) (plaintiffs could not be awarded attorney's fees incurred in defeating defendant-intervenors since intervenors were "functionally plaintiffs," and plaintiffs failed to show that intervenors' claims were "frivolous," "unreasonable," or "without foundation").

[95]Richardson v. Alaska Airlines, 750 F.2d 763, 36 FEP 986 (9th Cir. 1984) (the ADEA does not provide recovery of attorney's fees from nonemployer).

## Chapter 40

# SETTLEMENT

## I. General Principles

### A. Settlement Is Encouraged

Although settlements are encouraged, a district court cannot summarily approve a consent decree. It must analyze the fairness of each provision with respect to the parties and any affected third parties.[1] The court must also consider whether the decree is consistent with Title VII.[2]

### B. Waiver of Rights Must Be Voluntary and Knowing

Courts will not enforce a settlement agreement where the executing party did not understand the agreement[3] or where there is evidence of fraud or duress.[4] Where the language of the waiver is clear and unambiguous, a court need not inquire into the voluntariness of the employee's consent absent a claim of fraud or duress.[5] Although once unclear, it now appears that an unsupervised waiver of an ADEA claim is enforceable under appropriate circumstances.[6]

---

[1]EEOC v. Hiram Walker & Sons, 768 F.2d 884, 38 FEP 820 (7th Cir. 1985), *cert. denied*, 478 U.S. 1004, 41 FEP 271 (1986) (affirming settlement approved as to class over objection of 39 intervening class members); Williams v. City of New Orleans, 729 F.2d 1554, 34 FEP 1009 (5th Cir. 1984) (en banc) (affirmed refusal to approve consent decree requiring one-to-one promotional quota).

[2]Fire Fighters Local 1784 v. Stotts, 467 U.S. 561, 34 FEP 1702 (1984) (consent decree should not have been modified to protect minority employees from layoff at expense of nonminority employees with greater seniority).

[3]Cross v. United States Postal Serv., 34 FEP 1442 (E.D. Mo. 1983), *aff'd on other grounds*, 733 F.2d 1327, 34 FEP 1447 (8th Cir. 1984), *cert. denied*, 470 U.S. 1051, 37 FEP 376 (1985) (court refused to enforce portion of settlement agreement where defendant failed to provide plaintiff with information material to that portion); EEOC v. United States Steel Corp., 583 F. Supp. 1357, 34 FEP 973 (W.D. Pa. 1984) (employer preliminarily enjoined from enforcing release contained within form employer required all individuals to execute as prerequisite to obtaining retirement benefits; no evidence that employees were represented by counsel or that release had been explained to them). *But see* Rogers v. General Elec. Corp. dba General Elec. Supply Co., 36 FEP 674 (W.D. Tex. 1984), *aff'd*, 781 F.2d 452, 39 FEP 1581 (5th Cir. 1986) (release signed to obtain benefits specified in EEOC conciliation agreement is binding despite contention that employee was forced to submit to the stipulation).

[4]Hand v. Dayton-Hudson, 775 F.2d 757, 39 FEP 269 (6th Cir. 1985) (plaintiff, an attorney, unilaterally altered a release to preserve his ADEA and employment contract claims and obtained employer's signature without disclosure of the changes); Robertson v. Hodel, 39 FEP 69 (D.D.C. 1985) (contention that plaintiff had 10 minutes to consider release and was promised, but not given, chance to confer with EEO officer precluded granting defendant's summary judgment motion on effectiveness of release).

[5]Pilon v. University of Minn. Regents, 710 F.2d 466, 32 FEP 508 (8th Cir. 1983) (general release was negotiated by parties and plaintiff was represented by counsel).

[6]Runyan v. National Cash Register Corp., 787 F.2d 1039, 40 FEP 807 (6th Cir.), (en banc), *cert. denied*, 479 U.S. 850, 41 FEP 1712 (1986) (release of ADEA claim by experienced labor lawyer valid despite lack of EEOC supervision); Lancaster v. Buerkle Buick Honda Co., 809 F.2d 539, 42 FEP 1472 (8th Cir.), *cert. denied*, 482 U.S. 928, 43 FEP 1896 (1987) (absence of counsel did not invalidate settlement agreement waiving ADEA claim where terms were plain and unambiguous); Moore v. McGraw Edison Co., 804 F.2d 1026, 42 FEP 229 (8th Cir. 1986). The Third and Fourth circuits have

## II. ADVICE CONCERNING THE TERMS OF THE SETTLEMENT

### A. The Individual Case

*1. Considerations for Defendants in Private Negotiated Settlements*

Although defendants in Title VII cases are advised always to incorporate in conciliation agreements or releases specific reference to other possible related claims under 42 U.S.C. § 1981, Executive Order 11246, or other federal or state statutes or common law theories, some courts have held that a conciliation agreement which is limited to a Title VII claim will bar claims raised under 42 U.S.C. § 1981, in view of the close relationship between the two statutes.[7]

A settlement agreement may specify the remedies available to plaintiff in the event the agreement is breached by defendant.[8]

*2. Considerations for Defendants in Conciliation Agreements*

Courts differ as to whether the federal courts have jurisdiction to entertain an action for breach of a predetermination settlement agreement.[9]

It has been held that a conciliation agreement waiving claims under Title VII will bar a plaintiff's sex discrimination claims under the Fifth and Fourteenth amendments.[10]

A consent decree with the EEOC is valid despite an intervenor's lack of consent.[11] The intervenor under certain circumstances may be allowed to

---

taken the same position in unpublished decisions. *See* Dorosiewicz v. Kayser-Roth Hosiery, 823 F.2d 546 (4th Cir. 1987); Sullivan v. Boron Oil Co., 831 F.2d 288, 8 EBC 2590 (3d Cir. 1987).

On July 30, 1987, the EEOC issued a final rule permitting individuals to waive their private rights under the ADEA without EEOC supervision if the waiver (1) is knowing and voluntary, (2) does not waive rights prospectively, and (3) is not given in exchange for benefits to which the employee is already entitled. A key element to the voluntariness of the waiver is that sufficent time is provided for reasonable deliberation and consultation with an attorney. 52 FED. REG. 32293 (1987) (to be codified at 29 C.F.R. § 1627.16) (effective Sept. 28, 1987). This EEOC rule was suspended for fiscal 1988 by a rider to an appropriations bill reported at 1987–88 Congressional Record-House at p. 12,534 (December 21, 1987). Suspension was continued for fiscal 1989. Legislation is pending which would prohibit most unsupervised waivers of age discrimination claims. *See* Age Discrimination in Employment Waiver Protection Act, S. 54 and H.R. 1432, 101st Cong., 1st Sess. (1989).

[7]Freeman v. Motor Convoy, 700 F.2d 1339, 31 FEP 517 (11th Cir. 1983) (agreement limited to Title VII also bars § 1981 action, as it is unlikely parties intended to limit release to Title VII); *see* Perez v. Maine, 760 F.2d 11, 47 FEP 1575 (1st Cir. 1985) (settlement agreement disposing of State discrimination claims barred federal claim even though release language ambiguous; employer intended to dispose of both claims and plaintiff failed to expressly preserve federal claim).

[8]Kirby v. Dole, 32 FEP 721 (N.D. Ga. 1983), *aff'd*, 736 F.2d 661, 35 FEP 347 (11th Cir. 1984) (plaintiff not permitted to seek specific enforcement of settlement agreement where agreement provided that remedy for breach by defendant was reinstatement of original complaint).

[9]*Compare* EEOC v. Henry Beck Co., 729 F.2d 301, 34 FEP 373 (4th Cir. 1984) (federal courts have jurisdiction under § 706(f)(3) to enforce predetermination settlement agreements without litigating underlying charge of discrimination) *and* EEOC v. Safeway Stores, 714 F.2d 567, 32 FEP 1465 (5th Cir. 1983), *cert. denied*, 467 U.S. 1204, 34 FEP 1400 (1984) (same) *with* EEOC v. Pierce Packing Co., 669 F.2d 605, 28 FEP 393 (9th Cir. 1982) (no jurisdiction over action for breach of predetermination settlement agreement without prior reasonable cause determination and good-faith efforts at conciliation) *and* Parsons v. Yellow Freight System, 741 F.2d 871, 35 FEP 1121 (6th Cir. 1984) (plaintiff may not sue to enforce settlement agreement negotiated during EEOC conciliation efforts without first filing EEOC charge and obtaining right-to-sue letter).

[10]Davis v. Devereux Found., 644 F. Supp. 482, 40 FEP 1560, 1562–63 (E.D. Pa. 1986) (plaintiff executed document releasing defendant " 'from all claims arising in any manner from the complaint' " in EEOC charge and " 'wav[ing] any actions she may have had or will have under local, state or federal laws regarding said complaint' ").

[11]Firefighters Local 93 v. City of Cleveland, 478 U.S. 501, 41 FEP 139 (1986) (intervenor may present evidence to have objections heard at hearing approving affirmative action consent decree, but may not block decree by withholding consent).

litigate underlying claims.[12] A consent decree has been held not to limit private action by a nonparticipant.[13]

## B. Class Actions

Courts evaluating a proposed class settlement will examine whether the settlement is fundamentally fair, adequate, and reasonable.[14] The Fourth Circuit has held that a consent decree with the EEOC will bar individual actions by charging parties who failed to exercise their right of intervention when the EEOC originally instituted its suit against the employer.[15] A consent decree cannot preclude complaints about future discrimination.[16] The Ninth Circuit has held that a consent decree which establishes a procedure for dealing with post-consent decree claims of discrimination cannot strip the EEOC of jurisdiction.[17]

## C. Attorney's Fees

A plaintiff's right to attorney's fees in a settled case is dependent upon the understandings reached in the settlement.[18] While courts in the past have discouraged defendants from seeking a waiver as a condition precedent to settlement, the Supreme Court held in *Evans v. Jeff D.*[19] that 42 U.S.C. § 1988 does not prohibit conditioning a settlement agreement on the waiver of attorney's fees, and reaffirmed that the merits of settlements and the amount of attorney's fees for plaintiffs' counsel may be negotiated simultaneously.[20]

---

[12]*Id.*, 41 FEP at 151–52.

[13]Tucker v. Electrical Workers, IBEW, Local 26, 761 F.2d 809, 811, 37 FEP 1323, 1326 (D.C. Cir. 1985) (plaintiff, a nonparticipant in consent decree, was not required to petition monitoring board established by the decree before seeking judicial relief for Title VII claims).

[14]*See* EEOC v. Hiram Walker & Sons, 768 F.2d 884, 889, 38 FEP 820 (7th Cir. 1985) *cert. denied,* 478 U.S. 1004, 41 FEP 271 (1986); Ficalora v. Lockheed Cal. Co., 751 F.2d 995, 997, 36 FEP 1172 (9th Cir. 1985) (before district court approved class settlement it should have considered in detail named class representative's objections of inadequacy and conflict of interest by counsel); *see also* Chapter 34 (Class Actions), Section XI.

[15]Adams v. Procter & Gamble Mfg. Co., 697 F.2d 582, 30 FEP 1228 (4th Cir. 1983) (en banc) (per curiam), *cert. denied,* 465 U.S. 1041 (1984) (employer successfully argued that EEOC is not empowered to issue right-to-sue notices after negotiating settlement and that employer would be unfairly subjected to individual suits after it had apparently disposed of all claims brought on behalf of all its employees; charging parties must intervene in EEOC suit and watch over negotiations in their behalf). The continued validity of this precedent is questionable, however. An underlying premise of the Fourth Circuit opinion was that if a charging party "wishes to participate in settlement negotiations or to have the right to reject any settlement agreement negotiated by the EEOC, he may fully protect himself by intervening." *Id.*, 697 F.2d at 583. But the Supreme Court held in *Firefighters Local 93 v. City of Cleveland, supra* note 11, that there is no such right to block an EEOC consent decree.

[16]Williams v. Vukovich, 720 F.2d 909, 33 FEP 238 (6th Cir. 1983) (consent decree containing waiver of right to complain about future discriminatory practices is illegal).

[17]EEOC v. Children's Hosp. Medical Center of N. Cal., 719 F.2d 1426, 33 FEP 461 (9th Cir. 1983) (en banc) (consent decree could be valid defense to EEOC court action affecting employer and class, but it did not deprive EEOC of investigatory authority).

[18]El Club del Barrio v. United Community Corps., 735 F.2d 98 (3d Cir. 1984) (attorney's fees under 42 U.S.C. § 1988); Johnston v. Jago, 691 F.2d 283 (6th Cir. 1982) (same); Echols v. Nimmo, 586 F. Supp. 467, 34 FEP 1363 (W.D. Mich. 1984) (Title VII); Wexler v. Thomas, 30 FEP 1370 (D.D.C. 1983) (Title VII; absence from settlement agreement of express provision awarding fees irrelevant to question of whether plaintiff had expressly waived right to apply for fees).

[19]475 U.S. 717, 40 FEP 860 (1986). The principle should apply under Title VII since 42 U.S.C. § 1988 was modeled after § 706(k) of Title VII.

[20]*Id.*, 40 FEP at 866–69 (nothing in Civil Rights Attorney's Fee Awards Act forbids a district court from approving proposed settlement in which plaintiff waives right to attorney's fees).

## III. Rule 68 Offers of Judgment

In *Marek v. Chesney*,[21] the Supreme Court held that a plaintiff who recovers something less than a defendant's offer pursuant to Rule 68 may not recover attorney's fees thereafter where the underlying statute (42 U.S.C. § 1988) defines recoverable "costs" to include attorney's fees.[22] Further, the Court held that a Rule 68 offer can be made in one lump sum including attorney's fees, costs, and damages.[23] The Court did not decide whether a defendant can recover its own post-offer attorney's fees,[24] or whether its decision would be extended to other statutes where "costs" are not specifically defined to include attorney's fees.[25]

Rule 68 does not permit the offer to be served upon the opposing party rather than their counsel of record, nor may briefs be sent to a represented party with the offer explaining the offeror's position or the reasonableness of the offer.[26]

Where a defendant is granted a summary judgment incorporating a partial confession of judgment on the same terms as the Rule 68 offer that the defendant had previously made, the defendant is not prevented from recovering the costs incurred after the offer was refused. The summary judgment in such a context is considered as taken against the defendant and as being favorable to the plaintiff.[27]

One court has held that where a Rule 68 offer included reasonable attorney's fees through the date of acceptance of the offer, the plaintiffs cannot later recover for fees incurred after acceptance which relate to litigating the amount of attorney's fees.[28] However, this would appear to be bad law. A plaintiff who accepts a Rule 68 offer should be in the same position as a plaintiff who went through a trial and prevailed to the same degree. The defendant would be free to make a new Rule 68 offer on the attorney's fee issue and, if the offer is not accepted, would not have to pay the plaintiff's attorney's fees incurred in litigating attorney's fees after the date of the offer if the ultimate award with respect to attorney's fees incurred prior to the offer did not exceed the amount set forth in the offer.

A Rule 68 offer will not bar a Title VII plaintiff from amending his complaint to include claims under 42 U.S.C. § 1981.[29] The plaintiff, however, will be subject to the operation of Rule 68 as to the Title VII claims in the original and amended complaint.[30]

---

[21]473 U.S. 1, 38 FEP 124 (1985).

[22]*Id.* at 7–8, 38 FEP at 127–28.

[23]*Id.* at 5–6, 38 FEP at 126–27.

[24]*See, e.g.,* Bitsounis v. Sheraton Hartford Corp., 33 FEP 898 (D. Conn. 1983) (term "costs" in Rule 68 includes only plaintiff's attorney's fees, so where plaintiff recovers less than offer he must bear all his attorney's fees incurred after offer).

[25]*But see* Justice Brennan's dissent in *Marek v. Chesney, supra* note 21, 38 FEP at 130–145.

[26]Pettway v. American Cast Iron Pipe Co., 681 F.2d 1259, 29 FEP 897 (11th Cir. 1982), *cert. denied,* 467 U.S. 1243, 34 FEP 1688 (1984) (trial court erred by granting order allowing service of offer of judgment on each member of class and allowing defendant to reflect on reasonableness of offer and its validity).

[27]Liberty Mut. Ins. Co. v. EEOC, 691 F.2d 438, 35 FEP 574 (9th Cir. 1982).

[28]Jones v. Federated Dep't Stores, 527 F. Supp. 912, 27 FEP 1678 (S.D. Ohio 1981).

[29]Ashby v. Butler County Memorial Hosp., 38 FEP 1589, 1590 (W.D. Pa. 1985) (plaintiff did not act in bad faith by amending complaint following Rule 68 offer of judgment).

[30]*Id.* at 1590 n.18.

# TABLE OF CASES

Cases are referenced to chapter and footnote number(s), e.g., 21: 13, 25 indicates the case is cited in Chapter 21, footnotes 13 and 25.

Barber v. American Sec. Bank, 655 F. Supp. 775, 43 FEP 335 (D.D.C. 1987)   21: 57

Barber v. Boilermakers Dist. Lodge 57, 778 F.2d 750, 39 FEP 1092 (11th Cir. 1985), *on remand*, 651 F. Supp. 265, 42 FEP 1521 (N.D. Ala. 1986)   9: 11; 36: 28, 89

Barkley v. Carraux, 533 F. Supp. 242, 28 FEP 544 (S.D. Tex. 1982)   14: 107

Barnell v. Paine Webber Jackson & Curtis, 614 F. Supp. 373, 44 FEP 563 (S.D.N.Y. 1985)   28: 21; 29: 33

Barnes v. Oody, 514 F. Supp. 23, 28 FEP 816 (E.D. Tenn. 1981)   12: 238

Barnes v. Southwest Forest Indus., 814 F.2d 607, 43 FEP 197 (11th Cir. 1987)   18: 16

Barnes v. Yellow Freight Sys., 778 F.2d 1096, 39 FEP 1050 (5th Cir. 1985)   2: 4; 18: 6, 32

Barone v. Hackett, 28 FEP 1765 (D.R.I. 1982)   27: 57, 59

—602 F. Supp. 481, 40 FEP 961 (D.R.I. 1984), *later proceeding sub nom.* United States v. Rhode Island Dep't of Employment Sec., 619 F. Supp. 509 (D.R.I. 1985)   12: 50, 135; 30: 8; 38: 66

Barr v. Kelso-Burnett Co., 106 Ill.2d 520, 478 N.E.2d 1354, 120 LRRM 3401 (1985)   23: 40, 47

Barrentine v. Arkansas-Best Freight Sys., 450 U.S. 728, 24 WH 1284 (1981), *later appeal*, 750 F.2d 47, 26 WH 1663 (8th Cir. 1984), *cert. denied*, 471 U.S. 1054, 27 WH 208 (1985)   21: 58; 30: 69

Barrett v. Civil Serv. Comm'n, 69 F.R.D. 544, 11 FEP 1089 (D.D.C. 1975)   33: 27

Barrett v. Foresters, 625 F.2d 73 (5th Cir. 1980)   23: 20

Barrett v. Omaha Nat'l Bank, 584 F. Supp. 22, 35 FEP 585 (D. Neb. 1983), *aff'd*, 726 F.2d 424, 35 FEP 593 (8th Cir. 1984)   12: 196; 15: 15, 84, 90

Barrett v. Suffolk Transp. Servs., 37 FEP 724, *reconsideration denied*, 600 F. Supp. 81, 37 FEP 725 (E.D.N.Y. 1984)   14: 33, 67, 219; 31: 5

Barreyro v. Garfinckel's, 34 FEP 1743 (D. Md. 1984), *appeal dismissed*, 758 F.2d 645, 37 FEP 1408 (4th Cir. 1985)   10: 1

Bartholomew v. Fischl, 782 F.2d 1148 (3d Cir. 1986)   15: 148

Bartholomew v. Watson, 665 F.2d 910 (9th Cir. 1982)   39: 21

Barton v. Alabama Elec. Coop., 487 So.2d 884 (Ala. 1986)   23: App. B

Basset v. Attebery, 180 Cal. App.3d 288, 225 Cal. Rptr. 399 (1986)   1: 165; 23: 4, 6, 41, 42

Bassett v. Sterling Drug, 578 F. Supp. 1244, 35 FEP 382 (S.D. Ohio 1984), *appeal dismissed*, 770 F.2d 165, 40 FEP 1617 (6th Cir. 1985)   14: 89, 93; 28: 56

Bateau v. Skelton, 36 EPD ¶35,110 (E.D. Mich. 1984)   39: 89

Bates v. Jim Walter Resources, 418 So.2d 903, 115 LRRM 4027 (Ala. 1982)   23: App. B

Bates v. Pacific Maritime Ass'n, 744 F.2d 705, 35 FEP 1806 (9th Cir. 1984)   30: 30

Batesville Casket Co. EEO Litigation, 35 FEP 1560 (D.D.C. 1984)   34: 18, 21, 28, 34, 48, 50

Batsche v. National Broadcasting Co., 28 EPD ¶32,568 (S.D.N.Y. 1982)   37: 61

Batson v. Neal Spelce Assocs., 765 F.2d 511, 38 FEP 867 (5th Cir. 1985), *aff'd*, 805 F.2d 546, 42 FEP 817 (5th Cir. 1986)   35: 18, 19

Battle v. Isaac, 624 F. Supp. 1109, 40 FEP 1664 (N.D. Ill. 1986)   15: 3

Batts v. NLT Corp., 34 EPD ¶34,444 (M.D. Tenn. 1984)   15: 61, 70, 102

Bauer v. Bailar, 647 F.2d 1037, 25 FEP 963 (10th Cir. 1981)   6: 13

Bay Beer Distribs., *see* Mack v. South Bay Beer Distribs.

Bay Shipbuilding Corp.; EEOC v., 668 F.2d 304, 27 FEP 1377 (7th Cir. 1981)   26: 70, 71, 72

Baylor Univ. Medical Center; United States v., 736 F.2d 1039 (5th Cir. 1984), *cert. denied*, 469 U.S. 1189 (1985)   8: 23, 76

Baz v. Walters, 782 F.2d 701, 40 FEP 173 (7th Cir. 1986)   7: 62; 36: 22

Bazemore v. Friday, 751 F.2d 662, 36 FEP 834 (4th Cir. 1984), *aff'd in part, vacated and remanded in part*, 478 U.S. 385, 41 FEP 92 (1986)   1: 9, 23, 24, 37, 86, 87, 140; 13: 51; 28: 28, 31, 32, 33; 34: 25; 36: 11, 122, 124, 126, 127, 174, 175, 179, 207, 208, 213, 214, 239, 252, 258, 287, 294

Beall v. Curtis, 603 F. Supp. 1563, 37 FEP 644 (M.D. Ga.), *aff'd without opinion*, 778 F.2d 791, 40 FEP 984

Bergeron v. Travelers Ins. Co.—*Contd.*
107, 480 A.2d 42, 116 LRRM 3222
(1984) 23: 30

Berggren v. Sunbeam Corp., 108 F.R.D.
410, 39 FEP 953 (N.D. Ill. 1985)
34: 21

Berke v. Ohio Dep't of Pub. Welfare, 30
FEP 387 (S.D. Ohio 1978), *aff'd*, 628
F.2d 980, 30 FEP 395 (6th Cir.
1980) 15: 105

Berkman v. City of New York (I), 536 F.
Supp. 177, 28 FEP 856 (E.D.N.Y.
1982), *aff'd*, 705 F.2d 584, 31 FEP 767
(2d Cir. 1983) 4: 22, 31, 35, 37, 74,
82, 88; 5: 13, 14; 12: 160; 36: 223;
37: 12, 33, 46, 89

—(II), 626 F. Supp. 591, 43 FEP 305
(E.D.N.Y. 1985), *aff'd in relevant part*,
812 F.2d 52, 43 FEP 318 (2d Cir.
1987) 5: 14; 16: 11

Berkowitz v. Allied Stores of Penn-Ohio,
541 F. Supp. 1209, 31 FEP 337 (E.D.
Pa. 1982) 14: 38, 141, 151, 152

Berman v. New York City Ballet, 616 F.
Supp. 555, 38 FEP 1286 (S.D.N.Y.
1985) 15: 120, 126; 28: 67; 37: 58,
59, 61, 64

Bernal v. Fainter, 467 U.S. 216
(1984) 10: 21

Bernard v. Gulf Oil Corp., 643 F. Supp.
1494 (E.D. Tex. 1986), *aff'd in part,
vacated and remanded in part*, 841 F.2d
547 (5th Cir. 1988) 1: 142; 3: 24;
4: 29, 69, 78

Berndt v. Kaiser Aluminum & Chem.
Sales, 604 F. Supp. 962, 38 FEP 182
(E.D. Pa. 1985), *aff'd*, 789 F.2d 253,
40 FEP 1252 (3d Cir. 1986) 14: 122,
288; 38: 65, 66, 76, 83, 99, 101

—40 EPD ¶42,483 (E.D. Pa.
1985) 23: 45, App. B, App. C

Berry v. American Fed. Sav., 730 P.2d
905, 1 IER 1203 (Colo. Ct. App.
1986) 23: 4, 41

Berry v. E.I. du Pont de Nemours & Co.,
625 F. Supp. 1364, 39 FEP 1295 (D.
Del. 1985) 21: 38

Berry v. Louisiana State Univ. Bd. of Supervisors, 715 F.2d 971, 32 FEP 1567
(5th Cir. 1983), *aff'd*, 783 F.2d 1270,
42 FEP 917, *reh'g denied en banc*, 788
F.2d 1562 (5th Cir.), *cert. denied*, 479
U.S. 868, 44 FEP 848 (1986) 13: 2;
28: 35

Berry v. University of Tex., 38 FEP 889
(W.D. Tex. 1977) 17: 20

Bertrand v. Quincy Mkt. Cold Storage &
Warehouse Co., 728 F.2d 568, 115
LRRM 3215 (1st Cir. 1984) 23: 10

Betances v. Quiros, 603 F. Supp. 201
(D.P.R. 1985) 28: 21; 29: 25

Bethlehem Steel Corp.; EEOC v., 765 F.2d
427, 38 FEP 345 (4th Cir. 1985) 30: 3;
31: 9, 66

Beverly v. Douglas, 591 F. Supp. 1321,
35 FEP 1860 (S.D.N.Y. 1984) 21: 13

Bey v. Bolger, 540 F. Supp. 910, 32 FEP
1652 (E.D. Pa. 1982) 8: 102, 106

Bey v. Schneider Sheet Metal, 596 F.
Supp. 319, 38 FEP 1135 (W.D. Pa.
1984), *summary judgment*, 603 F. Supp.
450, 38 FEP 1139 (W.D. Pa.
1985) 25: 87; 26: 12, 36

Bhandari v. First Nat'l Bank of Commerce, 829 F.2d 1343, 45 FEP 126 (5th
Cir. 1987) 1: 104; 10: 19

Bhatia v. Chevron U.S.A., 734 F.2d 1382,
34 FEP 1816 (9th Cir. 1984) 7: 59,
60

Bhaya v. Westinghouse Elec. Corp., 624
F. Supp. 921, 39 FEP 1556 (E.D. Pa.
1985), *vacated by j.n.o.v.*, 1986 WL
15013 (E.D. Pa. Dec. 30, 1986), *vacated on other grounds and remanded
for reinstatement of jury verdict and
consideration of motion for new trial*,
832 F.2d 258, 45 FEP 212 (3d Cir.
1987), *cert. denied*, 488 U.S. __, 48
FEP 1088 (1989) 37: 28; 38: 82, 119

Bibbs v. Department of Agriculture, 749
F.2d 508, 36 FEP 713 (8th Cir. 1984),
*vacated*, 778 F.2d 1318, 39 FEP 970
(8th Cir. 1985) 2: 22; 9: 14; 17: 17,
30; 18: 39; 36: 95, 243; 37: 29

Bigby v. City of Chicago, 38 FEP 844
(N.D. Ill. 1984), *aff'd*, 766 F.2d 1053,
38 FEP 853 (7th Cir. 1985), *cert. denied*, 474 U.S. 1056, 39 FEP 1200
(1986) 1: 31; 4: 4, 11; 17: 12, 28;
36: 181, 269; 37: 81

Bihler v. Singer Co., 710 F.2d 96, 32 FEP
66 (3d Cir. 1983) 30: 1

Bilka v. Pepe's, Inc., 601 F. Supp. 1254,
38 FEP 1655 (N.D. Ill. 1985) 15: 2;
27: 55

Billings v. Wichita State Univ., 557 F.
Supp. 1348, 39 FEP 489 (D. Kan.
1983) 13: 51

Bills v. Kennecott Corp., 108 F.R.D. 459,
40 FEP 1182 (D. Utah 1985) 35: 10,
11

Birmingham Reverse Discrimination Employment Litig., In re, 37 FEP 1 (N.D.
Ala. 1985) 4: 85, 86

Brown v. General Motors Corp.—*Contd.*
rolet Div., 722 F.2d 1009, 33 FEP 417
(2d Cir. 1983)    39: 3, 27

Brown v. J.I. Case Co., 756 F.2d 48, 36
FEP 1399 (7th Cir. 1985)    28: 81

—813 F.2d 848, 43 FEP 355 (7th Cir),
*cert. denied*, 484 U.S. 912 (1987)
28: 21; 29: 38

Brown v. Manufacturers Hanover Trust
Co., 602 F. Supp. 549, 36 FEP 1830
(S.D.N.Y. 1984)    15: 5

Brown v. Marriott Corp., 33 FEP 550
(N.D. Ga. 1983)    35: 9

Brown v. Marsh, 777 F.2d 8, 39 FEP 505
(D.C. Cir. 1985)    33: 30

Brown v. Parker-Hannifin Corp., 746 F.2d
1407, 36 FEP 127 (10th Cir. 1984)
10: 17

Brown v. Porcher, 502 F. Supp. 946
(D.S.C. 1980), *aff'd in relevant part*,
660 F.2d 1001 (4th Cir. 1981), *cert.
denied*, 459 U.S. 1150 (1983)    12: 50,
140

Brown v. Puget Sound Elec. Apprenticeship & Training Trust, 732 F.2d 726,
34 FEP 1201 (9th Cir. 1984), *cert. denied*, 469 U.S. 1108, 36 FEP 976
(1985)    12: 257, 258; 28: 60; 30: 46

Brown v. St. Louis Police Dep't, 532 F.
Supp. 518, 30 FEP 17 (E.D. Mo.), *aff'd*,
691 F.2d 393, 30 FEP 18 (8th Cir. 1982),
*cert. denied*, 461 U.S. 908, 48 FEP
1531 (1983)    21: 37, 53; 28: 21;
29: 23, 33

Brown v. Tennessee, 693 F.2d 600, 30
FEP 459 (6th Cir. 1982)    36: 65

Brown v. Winn-Dixie Montgomery, 427
So.2d 1065 (Fla. Dist. Ct. App.
1983)    23: 4, 5, 41, 64

Brown & Root; EEOC v., 688 F.2d 338,
30 FEP 11 (5th Cir. 1982)    18: 7

—725 F.2d 348, 34 FEP 73 (5th Cir.
1984)    14: 127

Browning v. Clerk, House of Represen-
tatives, 789 F.2d 923, 40 FEP 992 (D.C.
Cir.), *cert. denied*, 479 U.S. 996, 42
FEP 560 (1986)    27: 88

Brudne v. Amalgamated Trust & Sav.
Bank, 627 F. Supp. 458, 39 FEP 1607
(N.D. Ill. 1986)    14: 93

Brumbaugh v. Ralston Purina Co., 656 F.
Supp. 582, 2 IER 877 (S.D. Iowa
1987)    23: 21, App. B

Brunet v. City of Columbus, 642 F. Supp.
1214, 42 FEP 1846 (S.D. Ohio 1986),
*appeal dismissed mem.*, 826 F.2d 1062,
44 FEP 1671 *and* 45 FEP 1080 (6th

Cir. 1987), *cert. denied*, 485 U.S. __,
46 FEP 1080 (1988)    1: 129, 130, 133;
4: 6, 23, 29, 38, 42, 45, 48, 64, 78,
79, 84, 88; 5: 2, 4, 13, 14; 36: 283,
284; 37: 33

Bruno v. Western Elec. Co., 618 F. Supp.
398, 38 FEP 1679 (D. Colo.
1985)    14: 275; 39: 38

Bryan v. Chemical Bank, 617 F. Supp.
1070, 38 FEP 1809 (S.D.N.Y.
1985)    37: 59, 61

Bryant v. International Schools Servs., 675
F.2d 562, 28 FEP 726 (3d Cir.
1982)    36: 240

Buchanan v. Director, Employment Sec.
Div., 393 Mass. 329, 36 FEP 1884
(1984)    12: 50, 139

Buckhalter v. Pepsi-Cola Gen. Bottlers,
768 F.2d 842, 38 FEP 682 (7th Cir.
1985), *vacated*, 478 U.S. 1017, 41 FEP
272 *and* 41 FEP 496 (1986), *on remand*, 820 F.2d 892, 43 FEP 1615 (7th
Cir. 1987)    21: 56, 57, 58; 23: 8;
28: 19, 21; 29: 38; 30: 67

Buckley v. Hospital Corp. of Am., 758
F.2d 1525, 37 FEP 1082 (11th Cir.
1985)    18: 38; 36: 29, 41

Buffalo, City of; United States v., 609 F.
Supp. 1252, 37 FEP 1729 (W.D.N.Y.),
*aff'd sub nom.* United States v. NAACP,
779 F.2d 881, 39 FEP 1168 (2d Cir.
1985), *cert. denied*, 478 U.S. 1020, 41
FEP 272 (1986)    37: 41

Bugg v. Industrial Workers, AIW, Local
507, 674 F.2d 595, 28 FEP 40 (7th
Cir.), *cert. denied*, 459 U.S. 805, 32
FEP 1672 (1982)    39: 82

Bunch v. Bullard, 795 F.2d 384, 41 FEP
515 (5th Cir. 1986)    4: 5, 10, 28, 52;
6: 17; 36: 136, 139, 142, 228; 37: 178,
276; 38: 96, 100

Bundy v. Jackson, 641 F.2d 934, 24 FEP
1155 (D.C. Cir. 1981)    12: 213, 215

Burba v. Rochester Gas & Elec. Corp.,
90 A.D.2d 984, 456 N.Y.S.2d 578
(App. Div. 1982)    23: 58

Burdette v. Mepco/Electra, 673 F. Supp.
1012, 43 FEP 1224, 2 IER 214 (S.D.
Cal. 1987)    23: 33

Burger King, *see* Mughal v. Chart House

Burgess v. Chicago Sun-Times, 132
Ill.App.3d 181, 476 N.E.2d 1284 (1st
Dist. 1985)    23: 40, 47, App. B

Burlington N.; EEOC v., 644 F.2d 717,
25 FEP 499 (8th Cir. 1981)    26: 35

Burlington N.; In re, 679 F.2d 762, 29
FEP 565 (8th Cir. 1982)    35: 2

California Brewers Ass'n v. Bryant, 444 U.S. 598, 22 FEP 1 (1980)   1: 139; 3: 7

California Fed. Sav. & Loan Ass'n v. Guerra, 34 FEP 562 (C.D. Cal. 1984), rev'd, 758 F.2d 390, 37 FEP 849 (9th Cir. 1985), aff'd, 479 U.S. 272, 42 FEP 1073 (1987)   1: 79, 80; 12: 2, 6, 9, 10, 11, 12, 13, 15, 17, 18, 19, 20, 21, 22, 23, 24, 50, 124, 125, 130, 131, 132, 135, 138, 142

California Teachers Ass'n; EEOC v., 534 F. Supp. 209, 27 FEP 1337 (N.D. Cal. 1982)   27: 71, 72

Callaway v. Hafeman, 628 F. Supp. 1478 (W.D. Wis. 1986), aff'd, 832 F.2d 414, 45 FEP 154 (7th Cir. 1987)   15: 154

Calloway v. Westinghouse Elec. Corp., 642 F. Supp. 663, 41 FEP 1715 (M.D. Ga. 1986)   3: 8, 22

Calumet, County of; EEOC v., 686 F.2d 1249, 29 FEP 1020 (7th Cir. 1982)   14: 194

Camelot Hotel, see Jackson v. Kinark

Cameron v. United States Trust Co. of N.Y., 754 F.2d 109, 37 FEP 254 (2d Cir. 1985)   28: 24

Camp, H.S., & Sons; EEOC v., 542 F. Supp. 411, 33 FEP 330 (M.D. Fla. 1982)   6: 29; 16: 15, 17, 18; 31: 54; 36: 107, 108, 111, 113, 115, 121, 237; 37: 12

Campbell v. Connelie, 542 F. Supp. 275, 28 FEP 1726 (N.D.N.Y. 1982)   14: 193

Campbell v. Pierce County, Ga., 741 F.2d 1342, 117 LRRM 3163 (11th Cir. 1984), cert. denied, 470 U.S. 1052, 118 LRRM 2968 (1985)   21: 44

Campbell v. Tennessee Valley Auth., 613 F. Supp. 611, 38 FEP 779 (E.D. Tenn. 1985)   3: 26; 17: 29

Cancellier v. Federated Dep't Stores, 672 F.2d 1312, 28 FEP 1151 (9th Cir.), cert. denied, 459 U.S. 859, 31 FEP 704 (1982)   14: 134, 155, 222, 228, 250, 269, 275; 38: 52

Canino v. EEOC, 707 F.2d 468, 32 FEP 139 (11th Cir. 1983)   10: 1; 15: 86

Cano v. United States Postal Serv., 755 F.2d 221, 37 FEP 209 (1st Cir. 1985)   28: 55; 33: 48

Cansler v. Tennessee Valley Auth., 774 F.2d 433, 39 FEP 68 (11th Cir. 1985)   33: 10

Capaci v. Katz & Besthoff, 525 F. Supp.

317, 30 FEP 1541 (E.D. La. 1981), aff'd in part and rev'd in part, 711 F.2d 647, 32 FEP 961 (5th Cir. 1983), cert. denied, 466 U.S. 927, 34 FEP 696 (1984)   15: 101, 104; 36: 114, 126, 127, 181, 263, 268

Capers v. Long Island R.R., 31 FEP 668 (S.D.N.Y. 1983), later proceeding, 34 FEP 892 (S.D.N.Y. 1984)   21: 53; 23: 7; 28: 21; 29: 22, 30

Cappiello v. Ragen Precision Indus., 192 N.J. Super. 523, 471 A.2d 432, 115 LRRM 3410 (App. Div. 1984)   23: App. B

Caravetta v. Goulding, 33 FEP 796 (D.D.C. 1980)   14: 151, 152; 17: 12

Carbonell v. Louisiana Dep't of Health & Human Resources, 772 F.2d 185, 38 FEP 1792 (5th Cir. 1985)   10: 1

Caribe Hilton Int'l; EEOC v., 597 F. Supp. 1007, 36 FEP 420 (D.P.R. 1984)   7: 38; 19: 14

—821 F.2d 74 (1st Cir. 1987)   39: 82

Carino v. University of Okla. Bd. of Regents, 750 F.2d 815, 36 FEP 826 (10th Cir. 1984)   10: 1, 13, 15

Carlile v. South Routt School Dist. Re-3J, 739 F.2d 1496, 35 FEP 689 (10th Cir. 1984)   1: 7; 36: 6

Carlton v. Interfaith Medical Center, 612 F. Supp. 118, 39 FEP 1477, 119 LRRM 3314 (E.D.N.Y. 1985)   18: 25; 23: App. B

Carmichael v. Birmingham Saw Works, 738 F.2d 1126, 35 FEP 791 (11th Cir. 1984)   1: 10; 16: 1; 18: 8; 36: 10, 36, 46, 50, 52, 53

Carnation Co. v. Borner, 610 S.W.2d 450 (Tex. 1980)   23: 40, 47

Carney v. Martin Luther Home, Inc., 824 F.2d 643, 44 FEP 683 (8th Cir. 1987)   2: 12

Carosella v. United States Postal Serv., 816 F.2d 638, 43 FEP 845 (Fed. Cir. 1987)   12: 220, 223, 224, 234, 244

Carpenter v. Reed, 728 F.2d 1302, 34 FEP 942 (10th Cir. 1984), later proceeding, 757 F.2d 218 (10th Cir. 1985)   21: 58; 28: 21; 29: 22, 33; 30: 63

Carpenter v. Stephen F. Austin State Univ., 706 F.2d 608, 31 FEP 1758, reh'g denied, 712 F.2d 1416 (5th Cir. 1983)   5: 5; 6: 17; 12: 94, 95, 96; 17: 23; 34: 8, 10, 20, 24, 32; 36: 142, 172, 241, 280; 37: 14, 34; 38: 10; 39: 33

Cervantes v. IMCO-Halliburton Servs., 724 F.2d 511, 34 FEP 13, *reh'g denied*, 728 F.2d 255, 34 FEP 1403 (5th Cir. 1984)   28: 24

Chaiffetz v. Robertson Research Holding, Ltd., 798 F.2d 731, 41 FEP 1097 (5th Cir. 1986)   21: 8

Chaline v. KCOH, 693 F.2d 477, 30 FEP 834 (5th Cir. 1982)   9: 30; 18: 3; 24: 4

Chalk v. United States Dist. Court Cent. Dist. of Cal., 840 F.2d 701, 46 FEP 279 (9th Cir. 1988)   1: 115

Chamberlain v. Bissell, Inc., 547 F. Supp. 1067, 30 FEP 347 (W.D. Mich. 1982)   23: 60, 61, App. B

Chamberlin v. 101 Realty, 626 F. Supp. 865 (D.N.H. 1985)   12: 228; 23: 53

Chambers v. European Am. Bank & Trust Co., 601 F. Supp. 630, 36 FEP 1550 (E.D.N.Y. 1985)   14: 55, 89, 93

Chambers v. Omaha Girls Club, 629 F. Supp. 925, 40 FEP 362 (D. Neb. 1986), *aff'd*, 834 F.2d 697, 45 FEP 698 (8th Cir. 1987)   5: 4, 20; 12: 50, 58, 65, 66, 67, 68, 69, 121, 122, 149, 150; 21: 24; 36: 171, 197, 204

Chambers v. Terex, No. 45377 (Cuyahoga County 1983)   23: App. B

Champion Int'l Corp. v. Brown, 731 F.2d 1406, 34 FEP 1154 (9th Cir. 1984)   14: 307

Chandler v. Roudebush, 425 U.S. 840, 12 FEP 1368 (1976)   33: 21

Chang v. University of R.I., 606 F. Supp. 1161, 40 FEP 3 (D.R.I. 1985)   13: 124; 17: 14; 36: 103, 257, 287, 297; 38: 83

Chaplin v. Consolidated Edison Co. of New York, 579 F. Supp. 1470, 34 FEP 50 (S.D.N.Y. 1984)   8: 4

Chappell v. GTE Prods. Corp., 803 F.2d 261, 42 FEP 23 (6th Cir. 1986), *cert. denied*, 480 U.S. 919, 43 FEP 160 (1987)   14: 317

Chardon v. Fernandez, 454 U.S. 6, 27 FEP 57 (1981), *reh'g denied*, 454 U.S. 1166 (1982), *on remand*, 681 F.2d 42 (1st Cir. 1982), *aff'd sub nom.* Chardon v. Fumero Soto, 462 U.S. 650 (1983)   21: 38; 28: 23; 34: 69, 70

Charleston Elec. Joint Apprenticeship Training Comm. (JATC); EEOC v., 35 FEP 1007 (S.D. W. Va. 1984)   27: 4; 31: 67

Charves v. Western Union Tel. Co., 711 F.2d 462 (1st Cir. 1983)   39: 82, 88

Chastain v. Western Elec. Co., 27 FEP 77 (N.D. Cal. 1981)   30: 4

Chavero v. Transit Union Local 241, 787 F.2d 1154, 40 FEP 766 (7th Cir. 1986)   19: 1; 27: 41, 65

Chaves v. Thomas, 35 FEP 397 (D.D.C. 1984)   10: 1

Chavez v. Guaranty Bank & Trust Co., 607 F. Supp. 484, 39 FEP 1371 (D. Colo. 1985)   23: App. A

Chern v. Ogden Food Serv. Corp., 33 FEP 1547 (E.D. Pa. 1984)   14: 147, 250; 38: 52

Chescheir v. Liberty Mut. Ins. Co., 713 F.2d 1142, 32 FEP 1344 (5th Cir. 1983)   38: 2, 37

Chewning v. Seamans, 28 FEP 1735 (D.D.C. 1979)   38: 50

Chicago, City of; United States v., 38 EPD ¶35,606 (N.D. Ill. 1984), *aff'd*, 796 F.2d 205, 41 FEP 378 (7th Cir. 1986)   17: 14, 22

Chicago Miniature Lamp Works; EEOC v., 622 F. Supp. 1281, 39 FEP 297 (N.D. Ill. 1985), *determination of remedies*, 640 F. Supp. 1291, 41 FEP 911 (N.D. Ill. 1986)   16: 1; 28: 35; 31: 70; 36: 212, 230, 244, 245, 246, 287, 293

Children's Hosp. Medical Center of N. Cal.; EEOC v., 719 F.2d 1426, 33 FEP 461 (9th Cir. 1983), *rev'g* 695 F.2d 412, 30 FEP 961 (9th Cir. 1982)   19: 27; 26: 60; 28: 21; 29: 47; 31: 90; 40: 17

Childs v. Electrical Workers, IBEW, Local 18, 719 F.2d 1379, 32 FEP 275 (9th Cir. 1983)   19: 20; 27: 66, 67, 68

Chisholm v. United States Postal Serv., 665 F.2d 482, 27 FEP 425 (4th Cir. 1981)   17: 32; 34: 48; 38: 127

Choudhury v. Polytechnic Inst. of N.Y., 735 F.2d 38, 34 FEP 1572 (2d Cir. 1984)   15: 128

Christiansburg Garment Co. v. EEOC, 434 U.S. 412, 16 FEP 502 (1978)   13: 36; 39: 81

Christie v. Foremost Ins. Co., 785 F.2d 584, 40 FEP 508 (7th Cir. 1986)   14: 333; 18: 34

Chrysler Corp.; EEOC v., 683 F.2d 146, 29 FEP 371 (6th Cir. 1982)   28: 41

—546 F. Supp. 54, 29 FEP 284, *clarified*, 546 F. Supp. 73, 29 FEP 1385 (E.D. Mich. 1982), *aff'd*, 733 F.2d 1183, 34 FEP 1401, *petition for reh'g en banc denied*, 738 F.2d 167, 41 FEP 1011 (6th Cir. 1984)   14: 88, 106, 139, 225, 315, 322; 31: 59, 81; 37: 65

Clymore v. Far-Mar-Co., 706 F.2d 499, 42 FEP 439 (8th Cir. 1983) 13: 38, 57, 58

Coalition for Basic Human Needs v. King, 691 F.2d 597 (1st Cir. 1982) 39: 31

Coates v. Johnson & Johnson, 756 F.2d 524, 37 FEP 467 (7th Cir. 1985) 1: 11; 25: 112, 113, 114, 116; 35: 2; 36: 12, 114, 119, 129, 251, 257, 287, 296

Cobb v. Dufresne-Henry, 603 F. Supp. 1048, 37 FEP 1287 (D. Vt. 1985) 15: 116

Cobb v. Sun Papers, 673 F.2d 337, 28 FEP 837 (11th Cir.), *cert. denied*, 459 U.S. 874, 29 FEP 1560 (1982) 27: 52

Coble v. Hot Springs School Dist. No. 6, 682 F.2d 721, 29 FEP 201 (8th Cir. 1982) 17: 19, 25; 36: 63, 237

Coburn v. Pan Am. World Airways, 711 F.2d 339, 32 FEP 843 (D.C. Cir.), *cert. denied*, 464 U.S. 994, 33 FEP 440 (1983) 14: 155, 294, 323

Cocke v. Merrill Lynch & Co., 817 F.2d 1559, 43 FEP 1724 (11th Cir. 1987), *vacating and remanding* 41 FEP 308 (N.D. Ala. 1986) 14: 58, 309

Cockrell v. Boise Cascade Corp., 781 F.2d 173, 39 FEP 1201 (10th Cir. 1986) 14: 48, 309; 18: 44, 54

Cockrham v. South Cent. Bell Tel. Co., 695 F.2d 143, 30 FEP 1788 (5th Cir. 1983) 36: 31

Coe v. Yellow Freight Sys., 646 F.2d 407, 25 FEP 900 (10th Cir. 1981) 6: 13

Coffin v. South Carolina Dep't of Social Servs., 562 F. Supp. 579, 33 FEP 1267 (D.S.C. 1983) 14: 30

Cohen v. Fred Meyer, Inc., 686 F.2d 793, 29 FEP 1268 (9th Cir. 1982) 15: 105

Colbert v. City of Wichita, 33 FEP 218 (D. Kan. 1983) 15: 99

Colby v. Graniteville Co., 635 F. Supp. 381, 40 FEP 1513 (S.D.N.Y. 1986) 14: 20, 58, 309

Colby v. J.C. Penney Co., 811 F.2d 1119, 43 FEP 47 (7th Cir. 1987) 12: 111

Cole v. CBS, 634 F. Supp. 1558, 42 FEP 127 (S.D.N.Y. 1986) 28: 24

Cole v. Fair Oaks Fire Protection Dist., 43 Cal.3d 148, 233 Cal. Rptr. 308, 729 P.2d 743, 1 IER 1644 (1987) 23: 45, 47, 64, App. B

Coleman v. Apex Acquisition, Clark Oil & Ref. Co. Div., 568 F. Supp. 1035, 36 FEP 758 (E.D. Wis. 1983) 14: 60; 28: 26, 36, 42

Coleman v. City of Omaha, 714 F.2d 804, 33 FEP 1462 (8th Cir. 1983) 14: 234, 243, 274; 26: 11, 100; 38: 52, 84, 88

Coleman v. St. Regis Corp., 39 FEP 479 (N.D. Ala. 1985) 16: 11

Coley v. Consolidated Rail Corp., 561 F. Supp. 645, 34 FEP 129 (E.D. Mich. 1982) 38: 2, 40

Coley v. Potters Indus., 35 FEP 1015 (D.N.J. 1984) 9: 16

Colgate-Palmolive Co.; EEOC v., 34 FEP 1551 (S.D.N.Y. 1983) 14: 109; 30: 1; 35: 14

—586 F. Supp. 1341, 34 FEP 1749 (S.D.N.Y. 1984) 14: 108, 127

College-Town v. Massachusetts Comm'n Against Discrimination, 400 Mass. 156, 508 N.E.2d 587 (1987) 12: 188, 210

Collins v. Pfizer, Inc., 39 FEP 1316 (D. Conn. 1985) 23: App. A

Collins v. Robinson, 568 F. Supp. 1464, 115 LRRM 2621 (E.D. Ark. 1983), *aff'd*, 734 F.2d 1321 (8th Cir. 1984) 37: 31

Collins v. Thompson, 679 F.2d 168 (9th Cir. 1982) 34: 72; 40: 14

Colon-Sanchez v. Marsh, 733 F.2d 78, 34 FEP 1144 (10th Cir.), *cert. denied*, 469 U.S. 855, 35 FEP 1608 (1984) 10: 1

Colucci v. New York Times Co., 533 F. Supp. 1005, 32 FEP 1812 (S.D.N.Y. 1982) 15: 103

Combs v. C.A.R.E., 617 F. Supp. 1011, 39 FEP 1086 (E.D. Ark. 1985) 23: 4, 9; 30: 46

Commercial Lovelace Motor Freight; United States v., 31 FEP 499 (S.D. Ohio 1983) 25: 47, 73

Commercial Office Prods. Co.; EEOC v., 486 U.S. ___, 46 FEP 1265 (1988) 28: 8, 10, 11, 12

Communications Workers v. Donovan, 37 FEP 1362 (S.D.N.Y. 1985) 8: 13

Confer v. SKF Indus., 40 FEP 1721 (W.D. Pa. 1986) 18: 28

Connecticut v. Teal, 457 U.S. 440, 29 FEP 1 (1982) 1: 31; 4: 43, 98; 5: 3, 4; 17: 32; 36: 168, 170, 278, 280; 37: 2; 38: 137

Connecticut State Employees Ass'n v. Connecticut, 31 FEP 191 (D. Conn. 1983) 13: 137

Conner v. Fort Gordon Bus Co., 761 F.2d 1495, 37 FEP 1574 (11th Cir. 1985) 18: 21

Cote v. James River Corp., 761 F.2d 60, 37 FEP 1243 (1st Cir. 1985)   14: 282; 39: 83

Coulter v. Tennessee, 805 F.2d 146, 42 FEP 305 (6th Cir. 1986), *cert. denied*, 482 U.S. 914, 43 FEP 1896 (1987) 39: 34, 57

Country Club of Little Rock, 260 NLRB 1112, 109 LRRM 1301 (1982)   22: 5

Counts v. United States Postal Serv., 33 EPD ¶34,011 (N.D. Fla. 1983)   38: 81

County of, *see* name of county

Covell v. Spengler, 141 Mich. App. 76, 366 N.W.2d 76 (1985)   23: 57

Coventry v. United States Steel Corp., 34 FEP 971 (W.D. Pa. 1984)   14: 135

Covington v. Southern Ill. Univ., 816 F.2d 317, 43 FEP 839 (7th Cir.), *cert. denied*, 484 U.S. 848, 44 FEP 1672 (1987)   1: 87; 13: 95, 96, 97, 98

Cowen v. Standard Brands, 572 F. Supp. 1576, 33 FEP 53 (N.D. Ala. 1983) 14: 124, 149, 157, 169, 245; 26: 104; 38: 2, 27, 52, 89

Cox v. American Cast Iron Pipe Co., 585 F. Supp. 1143, 36 FEP 1111 (N.D. Ala. 1984), *vacated in part, rev'd in part and remanded*, 784 F.2d 1546, 40 FEP 678 (11th Cir.), *cert. denied*, 479 U.S. 883, 41 FEP 1712 (1986)   1: 5; 16: 1, 5, 11; 17: 11, 17; 34: 16; 35: 19; 36: 8, 30, 60, 75, 76, 87, 133; 37: 13, 72; 38: 65; 39: 2

Craft v. Metromedia, 766 F.2d 1205, 38 FEP 404 (8th Cir. 1985), *cert. denied*, 475 U.S. 1058, 40 FEP 272 (1986) 2: 12; 12: 157, 158; 18: 43; 36: 172

Craig v. Y&Y Snacks, 721 F.2d 77, 33 FEP 187 (3d Cir. 1983)   12: 32, 184, 217; 38: 77

Craik v. Minnesota State Univ. Bd., 731 F.2d 465, 34 FEP 649, *later proceeding*, 738 F.2d 348, 35 FEP 243 (8th Cir. 1984)   17: 4, 24; 36: 130, 297; 39: 50

Cramer v. Virginia Commonwealth Univ., 486 F. Supp. 187, 22 FEP 315 (E.D. Va. 1980)   30: 79

Crane v. Dole, 617 F. Supp. 156, 37 FEP 255 (D.D.C. 1985)   38: 60

Crawford v. Government Employees, AFGE, 576 F. Supp. 812, 41 FEP 412 (D.D.C. 1983)   39: 84

Crawford v. Northeastern Okla. State Univ., 713 F.2d 586, 32 FEP 681 (10th Cir. 1983)   18: 6

Crawford v. Western Elec. Co., 745 F.2d 1373, 36 FEP 1753 (11th Cir. 1984)   1: 5; 17: 16; 36: 73, 77

Crawford Fitting Co. v. J.T. Gibbons, Inc., *see* Woodworkers of Am. Local 5-376 v. Champion Int'l Corp.

Credit Consultants; EEOC v., 532 F. Supp. 11, 28 FEP 71 (N.D. Ohio 1981) 37: 66

Crimm v. Missouri Pac. R.R., 750 F.2d 703, 36 FEP 883 (8th Cir. 1984)   12: 32, 184, 220, 223, 224, 234, 244; 14: 171, 309; 18: 17

Criswell v. Western Airlines, 709 F.2d 544, 32 FEP 1204 (9th Cir. 1983), *aff'd*, 472 U.S. 400, 37 FEP 1829 (1985)   1: 58; 14: 52, 144, 161, 179, 181, 182, 183, 184, 186, 221, 277, 287; 37: 13, 99; 38: 99

Croffut v. United Parcel Serv., 575 F. Supp. 1264, 33 FEP 1245 (E.D. Mo. 1984)   28: 70

Crosby v. New England Tel. & Tel. Co., 624 F. Supp. 487, 39 FEP 1271 (D. Mass. 1985)   14: 246; 38: 52, 80

Crosier v. United Parcel Serv., 150 Cal.App.3d 1132, 198 Cal. Rptr. 361, 115 LRRM 3585 (1983)   23: 25, App. B

Crosland v. Charlotte Eye, Ear & Throat Hosp., 686 F.2d 208, 29 FEP 1178 (4th Cir. 1982)   14: 63, 151, 152, 192

Croson, J.A., Co. v. City of Richmond, 822 F.2d 1355 (4th Cir. 1987), *aff'd*, 488 U.S. ___, 57 U.S.L.W. 4132 (1989)   1: 48, 51, 52, 135; 24: *, 81; 37: 57

Cross v. General Motors Corp., 721 F.2d 1152, 40 FEP 418 (8th Cir. 1983), *cert. denied*, 466 U.S. 980 (1984)   21: 24; 35: 18

Cross v. United States Postal Serv., 34 FEP 1442 (E.D. Mo. 1983), *aff'd*, 733 F.2d 1327, 34 FEP 1447 (8th Cir. 1984), *cert. denied*, 470 U.S. 1051, 37 FEP 376 (1985)   38: 81; 40: 3

Croushorn v. University of Tenn. Bd. of Trustees, 518 F. Supp. 9, 30 FEP 168 (M.D. Tenn. 1980)   15: 10, 11, 20

Crowder v. Fieldcrest Mills, 569 F. Supp. 825, 36 FEP 394 (M.D.N.C. 1983) 12: 116; 30: 36

Crown, Cork & Seal Co. v. Parker, 462 U.S. 345, 31 FEP 1697 (1983)   28: 82; 34: 65, 68

Crown Zellerbach Corp.; EEOC v., 720 F.2d 1008, 32 FEP 809 (9th Cir. 1983)   15: 20, 29, 30

Danks v. City of Cincinnati, 745 F.2d 1040, 36 FEP 27 (6th Cir. 1984)  27: 53

Darlington v. General Elec., 350 Pa. Super. 183, 504 A.2d 306 (1986)  23: App. B

Darnell v. City of Jasper, Ala., 730 F.2d 653, 37 FEP 1315 (11th Cir. 1984)  30: 21; 37: 30, 33, 80, 88; 38: 75

Datapoint Corp.; EEOC v., 570 F.2d 1264, 17 FEP 281 (5th Cir. 1978)  36: 206

Daubert v. United States Postal Serv., 31 FEP 459 (D. Colo. 1982), aff'd, 733 F.2d 1367, 34 FEP 1260 (10th Cir. 1984)  8: 115; 14: 141

Davidson v. United States Steel Corp., 104 F.R.D. 1, 35 FEP 995 (W.D. Pa. 1984)  34: 15

Davin v. Delta Air Lines, 678 F.2d 567, 30 FEP 14 (5th Cir. 1982)  18: 7

Davis v. Bethlehem Steel Corp., see Adams v. Bethlehem Steel Corp.

Davis v. Buffalo Psychiatric Center, 613 F. Supp. 462, 37 FEP 69, vacated in part and reconsideration denied, 623 F. Supp. 19, 39 FEP 1814 (W.D.N.Y. 1985)  28: 68; 30: 20, 27, 45; 34: 26, 46

Davis v. Burlington Indus., 34 FEP 917 (N.D. Ga. 1983)  13: 52; 35: 5

Davis v. City of Dallas, 777 F.2d 205, 39 FEP 744 (5th Cir. 1985), cert. denied, 476 U.S. 1116, 40 FEP 1320 (1986)  5: 7, 17, 22; 16: 11

Davis v. Combustion Eng'g, 742 F.2d 916, 35 FEP 975 (6th Cir. 1984)  14: 141, 144, 151, 152, 250; 38: 52, 54, 58; 39: 78

Davis v. Devereux Found., 644 F. Supp. 482, 40 FEP 1560 (E.D. Pa. 1986)  21: 26; 23: App. A; 40: 10

Davis v. Devine, 736 F.2d 1108, 34 FEP 1807 (6th Cir.), cert. denied, 469 U.S. 1020, 36 FEP 320 (1984)  14: 81, 83

Davis v. Greensboro News Co., 39 FEP 535 (M.D.N.C. 1985)  18: 29

Davis v. Ingersoll Johnson Steel Co., 628 F. Supp. 25, 39 FEP 1197 (S.D. Ind. 1985)  38: 2, 28

Davis v. Lambert of Ark., 781 F.2d 658, 39 FEP 1410 (8th Cir. 1986)  15: 104; 36: 26, 60, 93

Davis v. Richmond, Fredericksburg & Potomac R.R., 593 F. Supp. 271, 35 FEP 1140 (E.D. Va. 1984), aff'd in part and rev'd in part, 803 F.2d 1322, 42 FEP 69 (4th Cir. 1986)  6: 36; 12: 62; 17: 2; 37: 13, 20

Davis v. Scherer, 468 U.S. 183 (1984)  38: 140, 141

Davis v. Sears, Roebuck & Co., 708 F.2d 862, 31 FEP 1525 (1st Cir. 1983)  28: 74, 78

Davis v. State Univ. of N.Y., 802 F.2d 638, 42 FEP 77 (2d Cir. 1986)  15: 32

Davis v. United States Steel Corp, 779 F.2d 209, 39 FEP 955 (4th Cir. 1985)  12: 174, 211; 23: App. A

Davis v. United States Steel Corp., United States Steel Supply Div., 688 F.2d 166, 29 FEP 1202 (3d Cir. 1982), cert. denied, 460 U.S. 1014, 31 FEP 64 (1983)  21: 53; 23: 7; 28: 21; 29: 22, 30

Davis v. West Community Hosp., 786 F.2d 677, 40 FEP 800 (5th Cir. 1986)  28: 21; 29: 49

Davis v. Western-Southern Life Ins. Co., 34 FEP 97 (N.D. Ohio 1984)  12: 32, 186, 210; 38: 2, 46

Dawson v. Radewicz, 63 N.C. App. 731, 306 S.E.2d 171 (1983)  23: 57

Day v. Mathews, 530 F.2d 1083, 12 FEP 1131 (D.C. Cir. 1976)  38: 13, 56, 134

Day v. Wayne County Bd. of Auditors, 749 F.2d 1199, 36 FEP 743 (6th Cir. 1984)  15: 132; 21: 19

Dayton Power & Light Co.; EEOC v., 605 F. Supp. 13, 35 FEP 401 (S.D. Ohio 1984)  13: 19; 14: 77

Dayton Tire & Rubber Co.; EEOC v., 573 F. Supp. 782, 33 FEP 318 (S.D. Ohio 1983)  13: 22

De la Fuente v. Chicago Tribune Co., #84-C-4596 (N.D. Ill. July 24, 1985)  34: 16

De la Torres v. United States Postal Serv., 781 F.2d 1134, 39 FEP 1795 (5th Cir. 1986)  8: 50, 91

De Medina v. Reinhardt, 686 F.2d 997, 29 FEP 1084 (D.C. Cir. 1982), on remand sub nom. Hartman v. Wick, 600 F. Supp. 361, 36 FEP 622 (D.D.C. 1984)  15: 88, 89; 17: 2, 5; 30: 44, 51; 36: 111, 181, 238, 268, 270

De Tomaso v. Pan Am. Airways, 43 Cal.3d 517, 235 Cal. Rptr. 292 (1986), cert. denied, 484 U.S. ___, 2 IER 896 (1987)  1: 165; 23: 4, 6, 41, 42

Deaile v. General Tel. Co. of Cal., 40 Cal.App.3d 841, 115 Cal. Rptr. 582 (1974)  23: 48, 52

Dean v. Civiletti, 29 FEP 881 (D.N.D. 1981), aff'd in part, vacated and re-

Durso v. John Wanamaker, 38 FEP 1127 (E.D. Pa. 1985)  23: App. A

Duva v. Bridgeport Textron, 632 F. Supp. 880, 40 FEP 1388 (E.D. Pa. 1985)  23: App. A; 30: 23

Dybczak v. Tuskegee Inst., 737 F.2d 1524, 35 FEP 813 (11th Cir. 1984), *cert. denied*, 469 U.S. 1211, 37 FEP 64 (1985)  18: 38; 24: 7

Dyer v. Jefferson Parish, La., 619 F. Supp. 284, 38 FEP 698 (E.D. La. 1985) 14: 97; 28: 50

## E

Earlie v. Jacobs, 745 F.2d 342, 38 FEP 729 (5th Cir. 1984)  21: 47; 38: 108

Earnhardt v. Puerto Rico, 691 F.2d 69, 30 FEP 65 (1st Cir. 1982), *on remand*, 582 F. Supp. 25, 34 FEP 1837 (D.P.R. 1983), *aff'd*, 744 F.2d 1, 35 FEP 1406 (1st Cir. 1984)  10: 1, 16; 23: 21

Earvin v. Mississippi Employment Sec. Comm'n, 621 F. Supp. 760, 39 FEP 941 (S.D. Miss. 1985), *aff'd*, 795 F.2d 83, 41 FEP 1888 (5th Cir. 1986)  17: 17

Easley v. Anheuser-Busch, 572 F. Supp. 402, 34 FEP 380 (E.D. Mo. 1983), *rev'd in relevant part and aff'd in part*, 758 F.2d 251, 37 FEP 549 (8th Cir. 1985)  1: 5, 26; 4: 12, 29, 31, 35, 37, 74, 90; 5: 3; 16: 12; 17: 14; 35: 1; 36: 21, 76, 181, 189, 221, 269; 37: 30, 33; 38: 103

Easley v. Empire, Inc., 757 F.2d 923, 37 FEP 542 (8th Cir. 1985)  36: 55

Easley v. Northern Shipping Co., 597 F. Supp. 954, 37 FEP 1055 (E.D. Pa. 1984)  9: 11

East Tex. Motor Freight Sys. v. Rodriguez, 431 U.S. 395, 14 FEP 1505 (1977)  34: 2

Eastern Airlines; EEOC v., 736 F.2d 635, 35 FEP 503 (11th Cir. 1984)  31: 74

Eastex, Inc. v. NLRB, 437 U.S. 556, 98 LRRM 2712 (1978)  15: 134

Eastland v. Tennessee Valley Auth., 704 F.2d 613, 31 FEP 1578, *amended and reh'g denied*, 714 F.2d 1066, 34 FEP 283 (11th Cir. 1983), *cert. denied*, 465 U.S. 1066, 34 FEP 415 (1984), *on remand*, 35 FEP 1640 (N.D. Ala. 1984)  1: 5; 34: 6; 36: 83, 84, 142, 172, 186; 37: 27; 38: 97

Eatmon v. Bristol Steel & Iron Works, 769 F.2d 1503, 38 FEP 1364 (11th Cir.

1985)  25: 51, 61, 73, 91, 92; 26: 12, 37, 46, 81; 31: 23; 38: 70; 39: 26

Eby v. Borg-Warner, York Div., 455 N.E.2d 623 (Ind. Ct. App. 1983) 23: App B

Echols v. Nimmo, 586 F. Supp. 467, 34 FEP 1363 (W.D. Mich. 1984)  39: 26; 40: 18

Eckerd Drugs v. Brown, 457 U.S. 1128, 28 FEP 1840 (1982), *vacating and remanding* 663 F.2d 1268, 27 FEP 137 (4th Cir. 1981), *on remand*, 564 F. Supp. 1440, 36 FEP 1543 (W.D.N.C. 1983)  34: 3, 8, 10, 20

Eddins v. West Ga. Medical Center, 629 F. Supp. 753, 39 FEP 1492 (N.D. Ga. 1985)  17: 17

Edinger, J., & Son v. City of Louisville, 802 F.2d 213, 55 USLW 2221 (6th Cir. 1986)  24: 81

Edmondson v. United States Steel Corp., 659 F.2d 582, 27 FEP 39 (5th Cir. 1981)  12: 74

Edwards v. Alabama Dep't of Corrections, 615 F. Supp. 804 (M.D. Ala. 1985)  12: 53

Edwards v. Boeing Vertol Co., 717 F.2d 761, 32 FEP 1696 (3d Cir. 1983), *vacated*, 468 U.S. 1201, 35 FEP 96 (1984)  35: 8

Edwards v. Department of the Army, 708 F.2d 1344, 32 FEP 658 (8th Cir. 1983)  30: 2; 33: 2

Edwards v. Nationwide Mut. Ins. Co., No. 83-CA-65 (Greene County 1983)  23: App. B

EEOC v., *see also* name of opposing party

EEOC, In re, 709 F.2d 392, 32 FEP 361 (5th Cir. 1983)  26: 64; 31: 82; 35: 15

Eggleston v. Plumbers Local 130, 657 F.2d 890, 26 FEP 1192 (7th Cir. 1981), *cert. denied*, 455 U.S. 1017, 28 FEP 584 (1982)  30: 12

Eggleston v. Prince Edward Volunteer Rescue Squad, 569 F. Supp. 1344 (E.D. Va. 1983), *aff'd mem.*, 742 F.2d 1448 (4th Cir. 1984)  21: 28

Eison v. City of Knoxville, 570 F. Supp. 11, 33 FEP 1141 (E.D. Tenn. 1983)  4: 22, 29, 63

Eivins v. Adventist Health Sys./Eastern & Middle Am., 660 F. Supp. 1255, 43 FEP 1536 (D. Kan. 1987)  38: 58

Ekanem v. Health & Hosp. Corp. of Marion County, Ind., 724 F.2d 563, 33 FEP 1497 (7th Cir. 1983), *modified*, 33 FEP 1883 (7th Cir.), *cert. denied*, 469 U.S.

## G

Gaddis; EEOC v., 733 F.2d 1373, 34 FEP 1210 (10th Cir. 1984)   16: 12; 21: 42

Gairola v. Virginia Dep't of Gen. Servs., 753 F.2d 1281, 36 FEP 1800 (4th Cir. 1985)   9: 11; 10: 1

Galante v. Sandoz, Inc., 192 N.J. Super. 403, 470 A.2d 45, 115 LRRM 3370, *aff'd*, 196 N.J. Super. 568, 483 A.2d 829 (1984), *appeal dismissed*, 103 N.J. 492, 511 A.2d 665 (1986)   23: 64

Galvan v. Bexar County, Tex., 785 F.2d 1298, 40 FEP 710, *reh'g denied*, 790 F.2d 890 (5th Cir. 1986)   14: 80, 82; 27: 89; 30: 50

Galvin v. Vermont, 598 F. Supp. 144, 36 FEP 1674 (D. Vt. 1984)   14: 67, 90, 93

Gan v. Kepro Circuit Sys., 28 FEP 639 (E.D. Mo. 1982)   12: 175; 18: 43

Gantlin v. West Virginia Pulp & Paper Co., 734 F.2d 980, 34 FEP 1316 (4th Cir. 1984), *aff'g* 526 F. Supp. 1356, 29 FEP 1406 (D.S.C. 1981)   1: 142; 3: 11, 18, 21, 22

Garcia v. Kroger Co. dba Kroger Family Center, 40 FEP 1319 (S.D. Tex. 1985)   23: App. A

Garcia v. Lawn, 805 F.2d 1400, 42 FEP 873 (9th Cir. 1986)   33: 25; 37: 70

Garcia v. Rockwell Int'l Corp., 187 Cal.App.3d 1556, 232 Cal. Rptr. 490 (1986)   23: 1

Gardner v. Morris, 752 F.2d 1271, 36 FEP 1272 (8th Cir. 1985)   8: 121; 33: 43

Garibaldi v. Lucky Food Stores, 726 F.2d 1367, 115 LRRM 3089 (9th Cir. 1984), *cert. denied*, 471 U.S. 1099, 119 LRRM 2248 (1985)   1: 165; 23: 4, 6, 39, 40, 41, 42, 47

Garlington v. St. Anthony's Hosp. Ass'n dba Conway County Hosp., 792 F.2d 752, 40 FEP 1734 (8th Cir. 1986)   17: 9

Garner v. Boorstin, 690 F.2d 1034, 29 FEP 1765 (D.C. Cir. 1982)   14: 141, 146, 309; 17: 12

Garner v. St. Louis Sw. Ry., 676 F.2d 1223, 28 FEP 1469 (8th Cir. 1982)   18: 33; 36: 64

Garner v. Wal-Mart Stores, 807 F.2d 1536, 42 FEP 1141 (11th Cir. 1987)   18: 42

Garrett v. Okaloosa County, Fla., 734 F.2d 621 (11th Cir. 1984)   12: 53

Garrett v. Phillips Mills, Inc., 721 F.2d 979, 33 FEP 487 (4th Cir. 1983)   14: 15

Garrison v. International Paper Co., 714

F.2d 757, 32 FEP 1278 (8th Cir. 1983)   21: 40

Garza v. Brownsville Indep. School Dist., 31 FEP 396 (S.D. Tex. 1981), *rev'd and remanded as to remedy*, 700 F.2d 253, 31 FEP 403 (5th Cir. 1983)   16: 12; 23: 45, App. B, App. C; 37: 17, 30, 71

Garza v. City of Omaha, 814 F.2d 553, 43 FEP 572 (8th Cir. 1987)   21: 42, 58; 28: 21; 29: 42

Garziano v. E.I. du Pont de Nemours & Co., 818 F.2d 380, 43 FEP 1790 (5th Cir. 1987)   12: 220, 223, 224, 236, 237, 238, 244

Gates v. Life of Mont. Ins. Co., 196 Mont. 178, 668 P.2d 213, 115 LRRM 4350 (1983), *appeal after remand*, 638 P.2d 1063, 118 LRRM 2071 (Mont. 1982)   23: 45, App. B, App. C

Gathercole v. Global Assocs., 560 F. Supp. 642, 31 FEP 736 (N.D. Cal. 1983), *rev'd*, 727 F.2d 1485, 34 FEP 502 (9th Cir.), *cert. denied*, 469 U.S. 1087, 36 FEP 712 (1984)   14: 186, 246; 38: 2, 21, 52

Gaulden v. Emerson Elec. Co., 284 Ark. 149, 680 S.W.2d 92, 117 LRRM 3375 (1984)   23: App. B

Gautreaux v. Chicago Hous. Auth., 610 F. Supp. 29 (N.D. Ill. 1985)   39: 93

Gavagan v. Danbury Civil Serv. Comm'n, 32 EPD ¶33,674 (D. Conn. 1983)   16: 8

Gay v. Waiters' & Dairy Lunchmen's Local 30, 694 F.2d 531, 30 FEP 605 (9th Cir. 1982)   16: 1, 11; 36: 46, 105, 115, 140, 172, 181, 268, 271

Gay Law Students Ass'n v. Pacific Tel. & Tel. Co., 24 Cal.3d 458, 156 Cal. Rptr. 14 (1979)   23: 4, 9

Gazder v. Air India, 574 F. Supp. 134, 33 FEP 427 (S.D.N.Y. 1983)   14: 43

Geisler v. Folsom, 735 F.2d 991, 34 FEP 1581 (6th Cir. 1984)   15: 90; 17: 11; 18: 44; 36: 33

Gelman v. Department of Educ., 544 F. Supp. 651, 29 FEP 926 (D. Colo. 1982)   8: 43, 76

General Bldg. Contractors Ass'n v. Pennsylvania, 458 U.S. 375, 29 FEP 139 (1982)   3: 4; 30: 17, 18, 28, 38; 37: 19, 87

General Contractors Ass'n of N.Y. v. Teamsters Local 282, 28 FEP 1203 (S.D.N.Y. 1982)   16: 6, 7; 29: 15

Gilyard—*Contd.*
    Servs., 667 F. Supp. 266, 38 FEP 531
    (D.S.C. 1985)   16: 12
Givan v. Greyhound Lines, 616 F. Supp.
    1223, 39 FEP 123 (S.D. Ohio
    1985)   21: 24
Givens v. Hixson, 275 Ark. 370, 631
    S.W.2d 263 (1982)   23: 45, App. B
Gladden v. Barry, 558 F. Supp. 676, 40
    FEP 409 (D.D.C. 1983)   21: 3
Glass v. Petro-Tex Chem. Corp., 757 F.2d
    1554, 37 FEP 972 (5th Cir.
    1985)   28: 26, 27, 36, 39; 38: 18, 93
Glenn v. General Motors Corp., 841 F.2d
    1567, 46 FEP 1331 (11th Cir.), *cert.
    denied*, 488 U.S. ___, 48 FEP 232
    (1988)   1: 87
Glus v. G.C. Murphy Co., 629 F.2d 248,
    23 FEP 86 (3d Cir. 1980), *vacated and
    remanded on other grounds sub nom.*
    Retail, Wholesale & Dep't Store Union
    v. G.C. Murphy Co., 451 U.S. 935,
    25 FEP 847, *aff'd in relevant part on
    remand*, 654 F.2d 944, 36 FEP 101
    (1981)   30: 11, 13
Goddard v. Department of Health & Hu-
    man Servs., 32 FEP 587 (D.D.C.
    1983)   28: 77; 33: 46
Goff v. Continental Oil Co., 678 F.2d
    593, 29 FEP 79 (5th Cir. 1982)
    15: 127; 17: 12, 19; 21: 10
Gold v. Gallaudet College, 630 F. Supp.
    1176, 40 FEP 730 (D.D.C. 1986)
    15: 117; 17: 17, 22
Golden v. Lutheran Family Servs. in N.C.,
    601 F. Supp. 383, 39 FEP 1422
    (W.D.N.C. 1984)   9: 30; 37: 59, 61,
    63, 65
Goldhaber v. Foley, 698 F.2d 193 (3d Cir.
    1983)   39: 12
Goldman v. Marsh, 31 EPD ¶33,605 (E.D.
    Ark. 1983)   17: 22, 23, 24, 25
Goldsmith v. E.I. du Pont de Nemours &
    Co., 32 FEP 1879, *later proceeding on
    merits*, 571 F. Supp. 235, 39 FEP 108
    (D. Del. 1983)   28: 21; 29: 27
Goldstein v. Manhattan Indus., 758 F.2d
    1435, 37 FEP 1217, *reh'g denied*, 765
    F.2d 154 (11th Cir.), *cert. denied*, 474
    U.S. 1005, 39 FEP 720 (1985)
    14: 141, 146, 147, 148, 228, 240, 250,
    309; 36: 276; 37: 22; 38: 52, 53, 65
Golletti v. Arco/Polymers, Inc., 32 FEP
    1796 (W.D. Pa. 1983), *vacated and re-
    manded mem.*, 762 F.2d 993, 41 FEP
    64 (3d Cir. 1985)   28: 45

—35 FEP 1325 (W.D. Pa. 1984)   14: 90,
    93
Golomb v. Prudential Ins. Co. of Am.,
    688 F.2d 547, 29 FEP 1491 (7th Cir.
    1982)   14: 141, 155
Gomez v. Alexian Bros. Hosp. of San
    Jose, 698 F.2d 1019, 30 FEP 1705 (9th
    Cir. 1983)   10: 11, 12; 27: 53
Gomez v. City of S. Bend, 605 F. Supp.
    1173, 39 FEP 1625 (N.D. Ind.
    1985)   36: 211
Gonsalves v. Alpine Country Club, 727
    F.2d 27, 33 FEP 1817 (1st Cir.
    1984)   21: 58; 28: 21; 29: 30; 30: 63
Gonzales v. Secretary of the Air Force,
    824 F.2d 392, 44 FEP 971 (5th Cir.
    1987), *cert. denied*, 485 U.S. ___, 46
    FEP 504 (1988)   33: 49
Gonzalez-Aller Balseyro v. GTE Lenkurt,
    702 F.2d 857, 31 FEP 502 (10th Cir.
    1983)   28: 75; 30: 13, 22
Gooding v. Warner-Lambert Co., 744 F.2d
    354, 35 FEP 1707 (3d Cir. 1984)
    28: 63; 30: 1
Goodman v. Community College Dist. 524
    Bd. of Trustees, 511 F. Supp. 602, 27
    FEP 1762 (N.D. Ill. 1981)   23: App.
    A
Goodman v. Heublein, 645 F.2d 127, 25
    FEP 645 (2d Cir. 1981), *later appeal*,
    682 F.2d 44 (2d Cir. 1982)   14: 84,
    141, 151, 152; 38: 100
Goodman v. Lukens Steel Co., 777 F.2d
    113, 39 FEP 658 (3d Cir. 1985), *aff'd*,
    482 U.S. 656, 44 FEP 1 (1987)   9: 18;
    19: 18; 21: 32; 30: 11, 24; 34: 8, 10,
    20
Goodrich v. Electrical Workers, IBEW,
    815 F.2d 1519, 43 FEP 727 (D.C. Cir.
    1987)   13: 59
Goodwin v. Be-Mac Transp., 567 F. Supp.
    296, 32 FEP 1178 (E.D. Mo. 1983),
    *aff'd without opinion*, 732 F.2d 160, 35
    FEP 472 (8th Cir. 1984)   19: 10
Goodwin v. St. Louis County Circuit Court,
    555 F. Supp. 658, 30 FEP 1375 (E.D.
    Mo. 1982), *vacated in part*, 729 F.2d
    541, 34 FEP 347, *later proceeding*, 741
    F.2d 1087, 35 FEP 1017 (8th Cir.),
    *cert. denied*, 469 U.S. 828, 35 FEP
    1608 (1984) *and* 469 U.S. 1216, 37
    FEP 64 (1985)   21: 3, 18, 42, 58;
    27: 79; 36: 25; 37: 15; 38: 104
Goodwyn v. Sencore, Inc., 389 F. Supp.
    824, 115 LRRM 4832 (D.S.D. 1975)
    23: App. B

Great Atl. & Pac. Tea Co.; EEOC v.—*Contd.*
*dismissed*, 469 U.S. 925 (1984)
28: 83, 88; 31: 14, 61, 62, 64, 66
—618 F. Supp. 115, 38 FEP 827 (N.D.
Ohio 1985)    14: 173, 301, 315
Grebin v. Sioux Falls Indep. School Dist.
49-5, 779 F.2d 18, 39 FEP 873 (8th
Cir. 1985)    16: 12
Green v. Edward J. Bettinger Co., 608 F.
Supp. 35, 36 FEP 452 (E.D. Pa. 1984),
*aff'd without opinion*, 791 F.2d 917, 41
FEP 1888 (3d Cir. 1986), *cert. denied*,
479 U.S. 1069 (1987)    16: 2
Green v. Hughes Aircraft Co., 630 F. Supp.
423, 119 LRRM 3610 (S.D. Cal.
1985)    23: 4, 41
Green v. United States Steel Corp., 570
F. Supp. 254, 46 FEP 670 (E.D. Pa.
1983), *aff'd in part, vacated and rev'd
in part and remanded sub nom.* Green
v. USX Corp., 843 F.2d 1511, 46 FEP
720 (3d Cir. 1988)    1: 26; 36: 221, 224,
231
Green County, Wis.; EEOC v., 618 F.
Supp. 91, 41 FEP 61 (W.D. Wis.
1985)    13: 122
Greene v. Thalhimer's Dep't Store, 93
F.R.D. 657, 28 FEP 918 (E.D. Va.
1982)    26: 97; 35: 4, 23
Greene v. Union Mut. Life Ins. Co. of
Am., 764 F.2d 19, 37 FEP 872 *and* 37
FEP 1856 (1st Cir. 1985)    39: 86
Greene v. Whirlpool Corp., 708 F.2d 128,
31 FEP 1779 (4th Cir. 1983), *cert. de-
nied*, 464 U.S. 1042, 33 FEP 1084
(1984)    14: 89, 93
Greenspan v. Automobile Club of Mich.,
536 F. Supp. 411, 28 FEP 988 (E.D.
Mich. 1982)    39: 71
Greenwood v. Ross, 778 F.2d 448, 40
FEP 435 (8th Cir. 1985)    15: 129, 132;
21: 19; 30: 10, 23
Greer v. University of Ark. Bd. of Trust-
ees, 544 F. Supp. 1085, 33 FEP 77
(E.D. Ark. 1982), *aff'd in pertinent part
and vacated in part sub nom.* Behlar v.
Smith, 719 F.2d 950, 33 FEP 92 (8th
Cir. 1983), *cert. denied*, 466 U.S. 958,
34 FEP 1096 (1984)    17: 2; 38: 71
Gregory; United States v., 582 F. Supp.
1319, 34 FEP 602 (W.D. Va. 1984),
*aff'd in part, rev'd and remanded in
part*, 818 F.2d 1114, 46 FEP 1743 (4th
Cir.), *cert. denied*, 484 U.S. ___, 47
FEP 96 (1987)    27: 85; 37: 27; 38: 96
Grenci v. United States, 36 FEP 1044
(W.D. Pa. 1984)    33: 41

Gresham v. Waffle House, 586 F. Supp.
1442, 35 FEP 763 (N.D. Ga.
1984)    9: 22; 15: 130
Grier v. Carlin, 620 F. Supp. 1364, 39
FEP 497 (W.D.N.C. 1985)    28: 48
Griffin v. Big Spring Indep. School Dist.,
706 F.2d 645, 31 FEP 1750 (5th Cir.),
*cert. denied*, 464 U.S. 1008, 33 FEP
552 (1983)    21: 40, 58; 28: 21; 29: 38;
30: 64
Griffin v. Carlin, 755 F.2d 1516, 37 FEP
741 (11th Cir. 1985)    6: 14; 17: 12,
25; 29: 5; 33: 30; 34: 14; 36: 110, 128,
144, 172, 253, 280
Griffin v. City of Omaha, 785 F.2d 620,
40 FEP 385, *reh'g denied en banc*, 40
EPD ¶36,151 (8th Cir. 1986)    18: 36;
36: 28, 91
Griffin v. Dugger, *see* Griffin v. Wainwright
Griffin v. George B. Buck Consulting Actuaries, 551 F. Supp. 1385, 31 FEP 405
(S.D.N.Y. 1982), *later proceedings*,
566 F. Supp. 881, 32 FEP 1884 *and*
573 F. Supp. 1134 (S.D.N.Y.
1983)    16: 12; 28: 21; 29: 29; 38: 2,
38, 40, 55
Griffin v. Housing Auth. of Durham, 62
N.C. App. 556, 303 S.E.2d 200, 119
LRRM 2107 (1983)    23: 21, App. B
Griffin v. Michigan Dep't of Corrections,
654 F. Supp. 690, 30 FEP 638 (E.D.
Mich. 1982)    12: 54; 15: 59
Griffin v. Regency Univs. Bd. of Regents, 795 F.2d 1281, 41 FEP 228 (7th
Cir. 1986)    1: 36, 140; 5: 3, 4; 6: 18;
15: 81, 102; 36: 215, 239, 252
Griffin v. Wainwright, 34 FEP 1859 (N.D.
Fla. 1982), *vacated sub nom.* Griffin
v. Dugger, 823 F.2d 1476, 44 FEP 938
(11th Cir. 1987), *cert. denied*, 486
U.S. ___, 46 FEP 1264 (1988)    27: 18;
34: 59, 60
Griggs v. Duke Power Co., 401 U.S. 424,
3 FEP 175 (1971)    1: 17; 4: 1, 20; 5: 1,
19; 12: 20, 255; 36: 15, 146, 172
Grigsby v. Reynolds Metals Co., 821 F.2d
590, 44 FEP 449 (11th Cir. 1987)
2: 23; 14: 318
Grimes v. Athens Newspaper, 604 F. Supp.
1166, 40 FEP 1792 (M.D. Ga. 1985)
37: 27; 38: 99
Grogg v. General Motors Corp., 612 F.
Supp. 1375, 38 FEP 796 (S.D.N.Y.
1985)    39: 39
Grossman v. Schwartz, No. CV-86-0209
(S.D.N.Y. 1986)    15: 153

Hamlen v. Fairchild Indus., 413 So.2d 800 (Fla. Dist. Ct. App. 1982)   23: 56, App. B

Hamm v. Board of Regents of Fla., 708 F.2d 647, 32 FEP 441, *reh'g denied*, 715 F.2d 580 (11th Cir. 1983)   10: 1; 15: 40; 17: 20; 30: 7

Hamm v. University of S. Fla., 35 FEP 1879 (M.D. Fla. 1984)   15: 108

Hammon v. Barry, 606 F. Supp. 1082, 37 FEP 609, *stay granted*, 37 FEP 1184 (D.D.C. 1985), *rev'd on other grounds*, 813 F.2d 412, 43 FEP 89, *petition for reh'g denied*, 826 F.2d 73, 44 FEP 869, *reh'g granted in part en banc*, 833 F.2d 367 (D.C. Cir. 1987), *reh'g order vacated en banc*, 841 F.2d 426, 46 FEP 760 (D.C. Cir.), *cert. denied*, 486 U.S. ___, 46 FEP 1552 (1988)   24: 70, 73, 88; 32: 9; 37: 15, 53, 77

Hamner v. Rios, 769 F.2d 1404 (9th Cir. 1985)   39: 75

Hampson v. Thornton Fractional Township High School Dist. 215 Bd. of Educ., 41 FEP 606 (N.D. Ill. 1986)   21: 34; 30: 46

Hand v. Dayton-Hudson, 775 F.2d 757, 39 FEP 269 (6th Cir. 1985)   40: 3

Hanger v. United States Postal Serv., 34 FEP 1399 (M.D. Fla. 1984)   33: 51

Hanna v. American Motors Corp., 724 F.2d 1300, 115 LRRM 2393 (7th Cir.), *cert. denied*, 467 U.S. 1241, 116 LRRM 2632 (1984)   38: 5

Hansen v. Continental Ill. Nat'l Bank & Trust, No. 83-C-8961 (N.D. Ill. 1986)   14: 318

Hansen v. Harrah's, 100 Nev. 60, 675 P.2d 394, 115 LRRM 3024 (1984)   23: 47, App. B

Hansen v. Webster, 41 FEP 214 (D.D.C. 1986)   33: 55

Harden v. Dayton Human Rehabilitation Center, 520 F. Supp. 769, 27 FEP 1575 (S.D. Ohio 1981), *aff'd*, 779 F.2d 50, 45 FEP 1895 (6th Cir. 1985)   12: 54

Hardin v. Stynchcomb, 691 F.2d 1364, 30 FEP 624 (11th Cir. 1982)   12: 53; 36: 35

Harding v. Ramsay, Scarlett & Co., 599 F. Supp. 180, 36 FEP 717 (D. Md. 1984)   23: 7; 28: 21; 29: 27

Hardy v. New York News, 114 F.R.D. 633, 46 FEP 1199 (S.D.N.Y. 1987)   25: 112, 115

Harless v. First Nat'l Bank in Fairmont,

246 S.E.2d 270, 115 LRRM 4380 (W. Va. 1978)   23: 47, App. B
—169 W. Va. 673, 289 S.E.2d 692, 117 LRRM 2792 (1982)   23: 36, App. B

Haroldson v. Hospitality Sys. dba Fafaels, 596 F. Supp. 1460, 38 FEP 931 (D. Colo. 1984)   23: App. A

Harper v. Burgess, 701 F.2d 29, 31 FEP 450 (4th Cir. 1983)   28: 71

Harrell v. Northern Elec. Co., 672 F.2d 444, 28 FEP 911, *modified on reh'g*, 679 F.2d 31, 29 FEP 913 (5th Cir.), *cert. denied*, 459 U.S. 1037, 30 FEP 440 (1982)   6: 22; 17: 6; 36: 181, 194, 268, 271

Harris v. Amoco Prod. Co., 768 F.2d 669, 38 FEP 1226 (5th Cir. 1985), *cert. denied*, 475 U.S. 1011, 40 FEP 192 (1986)   30: 44, 51, 52; 31: 57, 70, 76; 35: 13

Harris v. Arkansas Book Co., 287 Ark. 353, 700 S.W.2d 41, 121 LRRM 2117 (1985)   23: 45, App. B, App. C

Harris v. Birmingham Bd. of Educ., 537 F. Supp. 716, 32 FEP 81 (N.D. Ala. 1982), *aff'd in part, rev'd and remanded in part*, 712 F.2d 1377, 32 FEP 1198 (11th Cir. 1983)   2: 13; 6: 22, 29; 16: 1; 17: 22

Harris v. Brock, 642 F. Supp. 1134, 41 FEP 1561 (N.D. Ill. 1986), *aff'd*, 835 F.2d 1190, 45 FEP 931 (7th Cir. 1987)   33: 47

Harris v. Ford Motor Co., 651 F.2d 609, 28 FEP 537 (8th Cir. 1981)   6: 19

Harris v. Marsh, 100 F.R.D. 315, 45 FEP 1037 (E.D.N.C. 1983)   34: 38; 36: 227

Harris v. Richards Mfg. Co., 675 F.2d 811, 28 FEP 1343 (6th Cir. 1982)   21: 45; 38: 108

Harrison v. Reed Rubber Co., 603 F. Supp. 1456, 37 FEP 1544 (E.D. Mo. 1984)   12: 232

Hart v. National Mortgage & Land Co., 189 Cal.App.3d 1420, 235 Cal. Rptr. 68 (1987)   23: 45, App. B

Hartford Fire Ins. Co.; EEOC v., 31 FEP 531 (D. Conn. 1983)   16: 16

Hartikka v. United States, 754 F.2d 1516 (9th Cir. 1985)   33: 25

Hartman v. Wick, *see* De Medina v. Reinhardt

Hartwell v. Pennsylvania, 568 F. Supp. 793, 34 FEP 830 (W.D. Pa. 1983)   28: 44

Haskell v. Kaman Corp., 743 F.2d 113,

Henn v. National Geographic Soc'y, 819 F.2d 824, 43 FEP 1620 (7th Cir.), *cert. denied*, 484 U.S. ___, 45 FEP 520 (1987)   14: 294, 295, 296, 323

Henry v. Lennox Indus., 768 F.2d 746, 42 FEP 771 (6th Cir. 1985)   18: 43, 44, 52; 36: 99

Henry v. Webermeier, 738 F.2d 188 (7th Cir. 1984)   39: 37

Hensley v. Eckerhart, 461 U.S. 424, 31 FEP 1169 (1983)   13: 31, 32, 33, 34, 35; 39: 21, 41, 43, 46, 49, 57

Henson v. City of Dundee, 682 F.2d 897, 29 FEP 787 (11th Cir. 1982)   1: 74; 12: 27, 32, 164, 166, 174, 184, 186, 206, 210; 36: 31

Hentzel v. Singer Co., 138 Cal.App.3d 290, 188 Cal. Rptr. 159, 115 LRRM 4036 (1982)   23: 4, 9, 15, 16, 26, 35, 36, 40, 43, 44, 47

Herman v. National Broadcasting Co., 569 F. Supp. 282, 33 FEP 1278 (N.D. Ill. 1983), *aff'd in relevant part and rev'd in part*, 744 F.2d 604, 35 FEP 1653 (7th Cir. 1984), *cert. denied*, 470 U.S. 1028, 37 FEP 192 (1985)   14: 89, 93, 146, 151, 152, 155, 156, 309

Hernandez v. New York Hosp., 37 FEP 1388 (S.D.N.Y. 1984)   39: 86

Hernando Bank; EEOC v., 724 F.2d 1188, 34 FEP 15 (5th Cir. 1984)   13: 19, 21, 48, 49, 50; 14: 77; 26: 6; 30: 1; 31: 3, 29

Hervey v. City of Little Rock, 101 F.R.D. 45, 40 FEP 784 *and* 599 F. Supp. 1524, 40 FEP 912 (E.D. Ark. 1984), *aff'd*, 787 F.2d 1223, 40 FEP 928 (8th Cir. 1986)   9: 17; 18: 43; 21: 19; 34: 26; 36: 61

Hess v. United Tel. Co. of Ohio, 40 FEP 1487 (N.D. Ohio 1986)   21: 33

Heward v. Western Elec. Co., 35 FEP 807 (10th Cir. 1984)   6: 13; 14: 157, 159, 165, 309; 36: 138, 142, 172

Hickey v. Arkla Indus., 688 F.2d 1009, 29 FEP 1719 (5th Cir. 1982), *vacated without change in result and opinion replaced*, 699 F.2d 748, 31 FEP 238 (5th Cir. 1983)   14: 16; 27: 52

Hickman v. Electronic Keyboarding Co., 741 F.2d 230, 35 FEP 1281 (8th Cir. 1984)   28: 20, 21; 29: 30

Hickman v. Flood & Peterson Ins., 29 FEP 1467 (D. Colo. 1982), *aff'd*, 766 F.2d 422, 38 FEP 186 (10th Cir. 1985)   15: 56, 86

Higgins v. City of Vallejo, 823 F.2d 351,

44 FEP 676 (9th Cir. 1987)   24: 70

Highland Park, City of; EEOC v., 32 EPD ¶33,947 (E.D. Mich. 1983)   23: App A

Hill v. AT&T Technologies, 731 F.2d 175, 34 FEP 620 (4th Cir. 1984)   28: 34, 35; 30: 42, 51, 52; 34: 23, 60

Hill v. Berkman, 635 F. Supp. 1228, 40 FEP 1444 (E.D.N.Y. 1986)   12: 44, 45, 46; 33: 1

Hill v. Coca-Cola Bottling Co. of N.Y., 786 F.2d 550, 40 FEP 639 (2d Cir. 1986)   28: 21; 29: 27

Hill v. Department of the Air Force, 796 F.2d 1469, 41 FEP 528 (Fed. Cir. 1986)   33: 31

Hill v. J.C. Penney Co., 688 F.2d 370, 29 FEP 1757 (5th Cir. 1982)   13: 26, 41, 65; 37: 27; 38: 99

Hill v. K-Mart Corp., 699 F.2d 776, 31 FEP 269 (5th Cir. 1983)   6: 17; 9: 7; 16: 16; 17: 7, 12, 14; 36: 181, 268, 271

Hill v. Metropolitan Atlanta Rapid Transit Auth., 591 F. Supp. 125, 45 FEP 782 (N.D. Ga. 1984), *aff'd in part, rev'd and remanded in part*, 841 F.2d 1533, 46 FEP 930 (11th Cir. 1988)   1: 129; 4: 7, 8, 33

Hill v. Seaboard Coast Line R.R., 573 F. Supp. 1079, 33 FEP 1406 (M.D. Fla. 1983), *rev'd and remanded*, 767 F.2d 771, 39 FEP 1656 (11th Cir. 1985)   2: 3, 20; 6: 20; 17: 24, 29; 36: 144, 172

Hill v. Secretary of Dep't of Health & Human Servs., 39 FEP 607 (D.D.C. 1985)   30: 83

Hill v. Spiegel, 708 F.2d 233, 31 FEP 1532 (6th Cir. 1983)   38: 2, 36, 111

Hilliard v. United States Postal Serv., 814 F.2d 325, 43 FEP 600 (6th Cir. 1987)   33: 10, 47

Hillis v. Marsh, 40 EPD ¶36,462 (E.D. Tex. 1986)   6: 31

Hillsman v. Sutter Community Hosps. of Sacramento, 153 Cal.App.3d 743, 200 Cal. Rptr. 605, 119 LRRM 2645 (1984)   23: 25, App. B

Hingson v. Pacific Sw. Airlines, 743 F.2d 1408 (9th Cir. 1984)   8: 21, 76

Hirst v. California, 758 F.2d 417, 37 FEP 982 (9th Cir. 1985)   21: 58; 28: 21; 29: 19, 26; 30: 63

—770 F.2d 776, 38 FEP 1496 (9th Cir. 1985)   23: 7; 28: 21

Hishon v. King & Spalding, 467 U.S. 69, 34 FEP 1406 (1984), *rev'g and re-*

Jackson v. Shell Oil Co.—*Contd.*
31 FEP 686 (9th Cir. 1983) 38: 2, 33, 41, 86

Jackson v. United States Postal Serv., 33 FEP 1381 (D.D.C. 1983) 33: 46

Jackson v. Wakulla Springs & Lodge, 33 FEP 1301 (N.D. Fla. 1983) 18: 23; 36: 41; 38: 103

Jackson County; EEOC v., 33 FEP 963 (W.D. Mo. 1983) 14: 77

Jacobs v. College of William & Mary, 517 F. Supp. 791, 28 FEP 1105 (E.D. Va. 1980), *aff'd*, 661 F.2d 922, 28 FEP 1818 (4th Cir.), *cert. denied*, 454 U.S. 1033, 33 FEP 1696 (1981) 13: 69

Jacobs v. United States Postal Serv., 587 F. Supp. 374, 35 FEP 1515 (W.D. La. 1984) *aff'd without opinion*, 759 F.2d 20, 37 FEP 1072 (5th Cir. 1985) 18: 14

Jacobson v. American Home Prods. Corp., 36 FEP 559 (N.D. Ill. 1982) 15: 1, 136; 30: 22

Jacobson v. Delta Air Lines, 742 F.2d 1202 (9th Cir. 1984), *cert. dismissed*, 471 U.S. 1062 (1985) 8: 21, 22, 76

Jacobson v. Pitman-Moore, 573 F. Supp. 565, 33 FEP 49 (D. Minn. 1983), *later proceeding*, 34 FEP 1082, *motions for new trial and j.n.o.v. denied*, 582 F. Supp. 169, 34 FEP 1267 (D. Minn. 1984) 14: 234, 243; 38: 52, 83; 39: 38
—624 F. Supp. 937, 39 FEP 1274 (D. Minn. 1985), *aff'd*, 786 F.2d 1172, 41 FEP 928 (8th Cir. 1986) 14: 95

Jainchill v. New York State Human Rights Appeal Bd., 83 A.D.2d 665, 442 N.Y.S.2d 595, 35 FEP 1403 (1981) 23: 8

James v. KID Broadcasting Corp., 559 F. Supp. 1153, 38 FEP 439 (D. Utah 1983) 14: 269, 272, 287; 38: 112

James v. Miller-Wohl Co., 35 FEP 1846 (W.D.N.Y. 1984) 14: 68, 89, 93, 227, 268, 272; 28: 52

James v. Stockham Valves & Fittings Co., 559 F.2d 310, 15 FEP 827 (5th Cir. 1977), *cert. denied*, 434 U.S. 1034, 16 FEP 501 (1978) 1: 141; 3: 10, 20

Janesville, City of; EEOC v., 630 F.2d 1254, 24 FEP 1294 (7th Cir. 1980 14: 188

Janikowski v. Bendix Co., 603 F. Supp. 1284, 39 FEP 1482 (E.D. Mich. 1985), *aff'd*, 823 F.2d 945, 47 FEP 544 (6th Cir. 1987) 14: 55, 57

Janowiak v. City of S. Bend, 750 F.2d 557, 36 FEP 737 (7th Cir. 1984), *va-*

*cated*, 481 U.S. 1001, 43 FEP 640 (1987) 24: 70; 28: 25

Jarrell v. United States Postal Serv., 753 F.2d 1088, 36 FEP 1169 (D.C. Cir. 1985) 33: 45, 49

Jasany v. United States Postal Serv., 33 FEP 1115 (N.D. Ohio 1983), *aff'd*, 755 F.2d 1244, 37 FEP 210 (6th Cir. 1985) 1: 112, 113; 8: 46, 54, 55, 56, 87, 91, 96; 36: 31

Jatczak v. Ochburg, 540 F. Supp. 698, 28 FEP 1773 (E.D. Mich. 1982) 12: 58; 37: 28

Jatoi v. Hurst-Euless-Bedford Hosp. Auth., 807 F.2d 1214, 42 FEP 1235, *opinion modified on reh'g*, 819 F.2d 545 (5th Cir. 1987), *cert. denied*, 484 U.S. ___, 45 FEP 1256 (1988) 21: 8

Jayasinghe v. Bethlehem Steel Corp., 760 F.2d 132, 37 FEP 817 (7th Cir. 1985) 6: 26

Jefferies v. Harris County Community Action Ass'n, 693 F.2d 589, 31 FEP 992 (5th Cir. 1982) 36: 61, 64

Jeffers v. Bishop Clarkson Memorial Hosp., 222 Neb. 829, 387 N.W.2d 692, 1 IER 621 (1986) 23: App. B

Jefferson County; United States v., 720 F.2d 1511, 33 FEP 829 (11th Cir. 1983) 37: 59, 61, 63

Jeffries v. Chicago Transit Auth., 770 F.2d 676, 38 FEP 1282 (7th Cir. 1985), *cert. denied*, 475 U.S. 1050, 40 FEP 272 (1986) 28: 83, 86; 30: 3

Jehle v. Heckler, 603 F. Supp. 124, 37 FEP 1310 (D.D.C. 1985) 13: 47, 119

Jennings v. Alexander, 715 F.2d 1036 (6th Cir. 1983), *rev'd sub nom.* Alexander v. Choate, 469 U.S. 287, 53 USLW 4072 (1985) 8: 83, 112

Jennings v. D.H.L. Airlines, 101 F.R.D. 549, 34 FEP 1423 (N.D. Ill. 1984) 12: 174, 205; 35: 20

Jennings v. Dumas Pub. School Dist., 763 F.2d 28 (8th Cir. 1985) 38: 75

Jennings v. Postal Workers Local 8, 672 F.2d 712, 28 FEP 514 (8th Cir. 1982) 26: 12, 30; 33: 16

Jennings v. Tinley Park Community Consol. School Dist. 146, 796 F.2d 962, 41 FEP 497 (7th Cir. 1986), *cert. denied*, 481 U.S. 1017, 43 FEP 856 (1987) 15: 102

Jeppsen v. Wunnicke, 611 F. Supp. 78, 37 FEP 994 (D. Alaska 1985) 12: 188, 210

Jepsen v. Florida Bd. of Regents, 754 F.2d

Jones v. Central Soya Co., 748 F.2d 586, 38 FEP 1386 (11th Cir. 1984)   14: 276; 39: 48

Jones v. Chubb/Pacific Indemnity Group, 35 FEP 1875 (C.D. Cal. 1983)   16: 12

Jones v. City of Alton, 757 F.2d 878, 37 FEP 523 (7th Cir. 1985)   21: 58; 28: 21; 29: 29; 30: 64

Jones v. City of Somerville, 735 F.2d 5, 34 FEP 1577 (1st Cir. 1984)   28: 36

Jones v. Continental Corp., 785 F.2d 308, 40 FEP 1320 (6th Cir. 1986), aff'g 35 FEP 661 (M.D. Tenn. 1984)   17: 20

Jones v. Department of Health & Human Servs., 622 F. Supp. 829, 39 FEP 1860 (N.D. Ill. 1985)   33: 13

Jones v. East Center for Community Mental Health, 19 Ohio App.3d 19, 482 N.E.2d 969 (1984)   23: App. B

Jones v. Federated Dep't Stores, 527 F. Supp. 912, 27 FEP 1678 (S.D. Ohio 1981)   40: 28

Jones v. Flagship Int'l dba Sky Chefs, 793 F.2d 714, 41 FEP 358 (5th Cir. 1986), cert. denied, 479 U.S. 1065, 43 FEP 80 (1987)   15: 32

Jones v. General Tire & Rubber Co., 608 F. Supp. 1013, 39 FEP 1517 (W.D.N.C. 1985)   36: 253

Jones v. Graphic Arts Local 4B, 595 F. Supp. 792, 36 FEP 18 (D.D.C. 1984)   39: 26

Jones v. Hinds Gen. Hosp., 666 F. Supp. 933, 44 FEP 1076 (S.D. Miss. 1987)   12: 57

Jones v. International Paper Co., 720 F.2d 496, 33 FEP 430 (8th Cir. 1983)   4: 36; 17: 30; 36: 186

Jones v. J.C. Penney Co., 164 Ga. App. 432, 297 S.E.2d 339 (1982)   23: 52

Jones v. Konopnicki, 597 F. Supp. 235, 36, FEP 1590 (E.D. Mo. 1984)   17: 17

Jones v. Los Angeles Community College Dist., 702 F.2d 203, 31 FEP 717 (9th Cir. 1983)   18: 21; 36: 64

Jones v. Lumberjack Meats, 680 F.2d 98, 29 FEP 396 (11th Cir. 1982)   15: 110; 17: 19; 36: 62, 64

Jones v. Lyng, 669 F. Supp. 1108, 42 FEP 587 (D.D.C. 1986)   24: 1

Jones v. MacMillan Bloedel Containers, 685 F.2d 236, 29 FEP 939 (8th Cir. 1982)   39: 34

Jones v. Madison Serv. Corp., 744 F.2d 1309, 35 FEP 1711 (7th Cir. 1984)   28: 71, 78

Jones v. Memphis Light, Gas & Water Div., 642 F. Supp. 644, 41 FEP 1165 (W.D. Tenn. 1986)   3: 54

Jones v. Milwaukee County, 574 F. Supp. 500, 33 FEP 400 (E.D. Wis. 1983)   28: 85

Jones v. Mississippi Dep't of Corrections, 615 F. Supp. 456 (N.D. Miss. 1985)   17: 12

Jones v. Monroe Community College, 38 FEP 645 (W.D.N.Y. 1984), aff'd, 755 F.2d 914, 38 FEP 672 (2d Cir. 1985)   37: 61

Jones v. Premier Indus. Corp., 611 F. Supp. 142, 38 FEP 277 (N.D. Ga. 1985)   14: 92, 98

Jones v. Preuit & Mauldin, 763 F.2d 1250 (11th Cir. 1985)   21: 31

Jones v. Progress Lighting Corp., 595 F. Supp 1031, 36 FEP 25 (E.D. Pa. 1984)   28: 20, 21; 29: 36

Jones v. Singer Career Sys., 584 F. Supp. 1253, 34 FEP 1685 (E.D. Ark. 1984)   21: 3

Jones v. Smith, 99 F.R.D. 4 (M.D. Pa. 1983), aff'd without opinion, 734 F.2d 6 (3d Cir. 1984)   35: 19

Jones v. Teamsters Local 299, see Jones v. Cassens Transp.

Jones v. Western Geophysical Co. of Am., 669 F.2d 280, 29 FEP 1117 (5th Cir. 1982)   17: 9, 11

Jordan v. County of Los Angeles, 669 F.2d 1311, 28 FEP 518 (9th Cir.), vacated on other grounds, 459 U.S. 810, 29 FEP 1560 (1982), on remand, 713 F.2d 503, 33 FEP 1435, amended, 726 F.2d 1366, 36 FEP 1592 (9th Cir. 1984)   28: 21; 29: 45, 46; 34: 3, 6

Jordan v. Mallard Exploration, 423 So.2d 896 (Ala. 1982)   23: App. B

Jordan v. Swindall, 105 F.R.D. 45, 42 FEP 947 (M.D. Ala. 1985)   34: 8, 10, 20

Jordan v. Tenpenny, 39 EPD ¶35,815 (M.D. Tenn. 1985)   16: 11; 36: 274

Jordan v. Wilson, 649 F. Supp. 1038, 42 FEP 950 (M.D. Ala. 1986)   5: 3

Jorgensen, Roy, Assocs. v. Deschenes, 409 So.2d 1188, 115 LRRM 4917 (Fla. Dist. Ct. App. 1982)   23: App. B

Joshi v. Florida State Univ. Health Center, 763 F.2d 1227, 38 FEP 38 (11th Cir.), cert. denied, 474 U.S. 948, 39 FEP 384 (1985)   2: 4; 16: 12

Joshi v. Professional Health Servs., 606 F. Supp. 302, 43 FEP 1092 (D.D.C. 1985)   15: 110

Kellin v. ACF Indus.—*Contd.*
1982) 15: 87

Kellner v. General Refractories Co., 631 F. Supp. 939, 41 FEP 538 (N.D. Ind. 1986) 15: 86

Kelly v. Mississippi Valley Gas Co., 397 So.2d 874, 115 LRRM 4631 (Miss. 1981) 23: 27

Kelly v. Wauconda Park Dist., 801 F.2d 269, 41 FEP 1376 (7th Cir. 1986), *cert. denied*, 480 U.S. 940, 43 FEP 560 (1987) 14: 27

Kelly-Springfield Tire Co.; EEOC v., 38 FEP 194 (E.D.N.C. 1985) 35: 7

Kemerer v. Davis, 520 F. Supp. 256, 26 FEP 1652 (E.D. Mich. 1981) 27: 78

Kempe v. Prince Gardner, Inc., 569 F. Supp. 779, 36 FEP 969 (E.D. Mo. 1983) 14: 268, 270

Kendall v. Block, 821 F.2d 1142, 46 FEP 183 (5th Cir. 1987) 2: 12

Kendall v. C.F. Indus., 624 F. Supp. 1102, 40 FEP 1658 (N.D. Ill. 1986) 28: 21; 29: 39

Kendon of Dallas; EEOC v., 34 EPD ¶35,393 (E.D. Tex. 1984) 15: 109

Kennedy v. McDonald's Corp., 610 F. Supp. 203, 37 FEP 1813 (S.D. W. Va. 1985) 13: 12

Kennedy v. Whitehurst, 690 F.2d 951, 29 FEP 1373 (D.C. Cir. 1982) 14: 278; 33: 58; 39: 20

Kenny v. Valley County School Dists. No. 1 & 1A Bd. of Trustees, 563 F. Supp. 95, 31 FEP 1502 (D. Mont. 1983), *aff'd mem.*, 770 F.2d 170 (9th Cir. 1985) 14: 34

Kentucky v. Graham, 473 U.S. 159 (1985) 21: 14

Kern v. Dynalectron Corp., 577 F. Supp. 1196, 33 FEP 255 (N.D. Tex. 1983), *aff'd mem.*, 746 F.2d 810, 36 FEP 1716 (5th Cir. 1984) 7: 79, 80

Kerr v. Quinn, 692 F.2d 875 (2d Cir. 1982) 39: 10

Kerver v. Exxon Prod. Research Co., 40 FEP 1567 (S.D. Tex. 1986), *aff'd*, 810 F.2d 196 (5th Cir. 1987) 14: 94; 28: 55

Key v. Gillette Co., 104 F.R.D. 139 (D. Mass. 1985), *aff'd*, 782 F.2d 5 (1st Cir. 1986) 34: 26

Khanna v. Microdata Corp., 170 Cal.App.3d 250, 215 Cal. Rptr. 860, 120 LRRM 2152 (1985) 23: 14, 16, 25, 26, 35, 36, App. B

Keil v. Goodyear Tire & Rubber Co., 575 F. Supp. 847, 33 FEP 1122 (N.D. Ohio 1983), *aff'd without opinion*, 762 F.2d 1008 (6th Cir. 1985) 14: 155, 228; 37: 24

Kilbride v. Dushkin Publishing Group, 186 Conn. 718, 443 A.2d 922, 115 LRRM 4927 (1982) 23: App. B

Kilgo v. Bowman Transp., 570 F. Supp. 1509, 31 FEP 1451 (N.D. Ga. 1983), *modified*, 576 F. Supp. 600, 40 FEP 1412 (N.D. Ga. 1984), *aff'd*, 789 F.2d 859, 40 FEP 1415 (11th Cir. 1986) 1: 32; 5: 9; 16: 3, 8, 11, 12; 34: 25; 36: 167, 171, 177, 181, 210, 232, 238, 244, 248, 257, 268, 272; 37: 45, 80; 38: 2, 28

Kim v. Commandant, Defense Language Inst., Foreign Language Center, 772 F.2d 521, 38 FEP 1710 (9th Cir. 1985) 10: 2; 36: 274

Kimbrough v. Secretary of the Air Force, 764 F.2d 1279, 38 FEP 383 (9th Cir. 1985) 17: 11

King v. Dole, 595 F. Supp. 1140, 36 FEP 11 (D.D.C. 1984), *aff'd*, 782 F.2d 274, 40 FEP 624 (D.C. Cir.), *cert. denied*, 479 U.S. 856, 43 FEP 640 (1986) 33: 47

King v. Emerson Elec. Co., Alco Controls Div., 746 F.2d 1331, 38 FEP 1666 (8th Cir. 1984) 21: 58

King v. Hospital Care Corp., No. 1-85-1 (Allen County 1986) (unreported) 23: App. B

King v. McCord, 707 F.2d 466, 35 FEP 831 (11th Cir. 1983) 13: 35; 39: 51

King v. Palmer, 778 F.2d 878, 39 FEP 877 (D.C. Cir. 1985) 12: 180; 17: 10, 16

King v. Ralston Purina Co., 97 F.R.D. 477, 31 FEP 373, 115 LRRM 4951 (W.D.N.C. 1983) 14: 115

King v. Smith, 39 FEP 614 (E.D. Ark. 1985) 9: 25

King v. South Cent. Bell Tel. & Tel. Co., 790 F.2d 524, 40 FEP 1355 (6th Cir. 1986) 28: 21; 29: 48

King v. Trans World Airlines, 738 F.2d 255, 35 FEP 102 (8th Cir. 1984) 16: 12; 38: 13, 56, 134; 39: 2

Kinney Shoe Corp. v. Vorhes, 564 F.2d 859 (9th Cir. 1977) 14: 136

Kinniry v. Aetna Ins. Co., 35 FEP 1474 (D. Conn. 1984) 14: 56, 67, 90, 93; 28: 35

Kinoshita v. Canadian Pac. Airlines, 803 F.2d 471, 1 IER 971 (9th Cir. 1986) 5: 15

Koyen v. Consolidated Edison Co. of N.Y., 560 Supp. 1161, 31 FEP 488 (S.D.N.Y. 1983)   14: 243, 250, 278; 38: 2, 22, 52

Kraszewski v. State Farm Gen. Ins. Co., 27 FEP 27 (N.D. Cal. 1981)   34: 48 —36 FEP 1371 (N.D. Cal. 1984)   39: 33 —38 FEP 197 (N.D. Cal. 1985), *attorneys' fees awarded*, 41 FEP 1088 (N.D. Cal. 1986)   4: 6, 57, 83, 103; 6: 36; 16: 2, 8; 36: 211, 229, 230, 288, 293, 296; 38: 137

Kraus v. Canteen Serv. Co., 39 FEP 1377 (E.D. Mich. 1985)   14: 93

Kremer v. Chemical Constr. Corp., 456 U.S. 461, 28 FEP 1412, *reh'g denied*, 458 U.S. 1133 (1982)   1: 152; 21: 52, 58; 23: 4, 7, 9; 28: 16, 21; 29: 18, 35; 30: 59

Krieg v. Paul Revere Life Ins. Co., 718 F.2d 998, 33 FEP 594 (11th Cir. 1983), *cert. denied*, 466 U.S. 929, 34 FEP 696 (1984)   14: 148, 309

Kriegesmann v. Barry-Wehmiller Co., 739 F.2d 357, 35 FEP 651 (8th Cir.), *cert. denied*, 469 U.S. 1036, 36 FEP 464 (1984)   14: 55, 58, 89, 91, 93, 309

Krodel v. Department of Health & Human Servs., 33 FEP 689, *aff'd sub nom.* Krodel v. Young, 576 F. Supp. 390, 33 FEP 701 (D.D.C. 1983), *aff'd*, 748 F.2d 701, 36 FEP 468 (D.C. Cir. 1984), *cert. denied*, 474 U.S. 817, 38 FEP 1727 (1985), *later proceeding*, 624 F. Supp. 720, 41 FEP 170 (D.D.C. 1985)   14: 141, 148, 153, 155, 157, 309; 17: 6; 33: 58; 36: 295; 37: 27; 38: 97

Kroger Family Center, *see* Garcia v. Kroger Co.

Kromnick v. Philadelphia School Dist., 739 F.2d 894, 35 FEP 538 (3d Cir. 1984), *cert. denied*, 469 U.S. 1107, 36 FEP 976 (1985)   3: 46; 19: 27, 28; 37: 10

Krueger, W.A., Co.; EEOC v., 35 EPD ¶34,772 (E.D. Wis. 1984)   31: 17

Krulik v. New York City Bd. of Educ., 781 F.2d 15, 39 FEP 1448 (2d Cir. 1986)   17: 3, 22

Krynicky v. University of Pittsburgh, 742 F.2d 94, 35 FEP 1133 (3d Cir. 1984), *cert. denied*, 471 U.S. 1015, 37 FEP 784 (1985)   21: 12

Kuenz v. Goodyear Tire & Rubber Co., 104 F.R.D. 474, 37 FEP 124 (E.D. Mo. 1985)   34: 24

Kulick v. Tri-State Regional Planning Comm'n, 33 FEP 741 (S.D.N.Y. 1983)   14: 29

Kumar v. University of Mass. Bd. of Trustees, 566 F. Supp. 1299, 32 FEP 306 (D. Mass. 1983), *determination remedy*, 34 FEP 1231 (D. Mass. 1984), *rev'd on other grounds*, 774 F.2d 1, 38 FEP 1734 (1st Cir. 1985), *cert. denied*, 475 U.S. 1097, 40 FEP 792 (1986)   10: 1; 15: 78, 103; 38: 65

Kureshy v. City Univ. of N.Y., 561 F. Supp. 1098, 31 FEP 1264 (E.D.N.Y. 1983), *aff'd*, 742 F.2d 1431, 37 FEP 280 (2d Cir. 1984)   10: 14

Kuzmins v. Employee Transfer Corp., 587 F. Supp. 536, 35 FEP 653 (N.D. Ohio 1984)   39: 86

Kyles v. Secretary of Agric., 604 F. Supp. 426, 37 FEP 12 (D.D.C. 1985)   39: 58, 69

Kyriazi v. Western Elec. Co., 465 F. Supp. 1141, 26 FEP 398, *later opinion*, 476 F. Supp. 335, 26 FEP 413 (D.N.J. 1979), *aff'd*, 647 F.2d 388, 33 FEP 1147 (3d Cir. 1981)   38: 127, 128

## L

La Montagne v. American Convenience Prods., 750 F.2d 1405, 36 FEP 913 (7th Cir. 1984)   2: 16; 14: 141, 151, 152, 155; 36: 31

Laborde v. University of Cal. Regents, 686 F.2d 715, 28 FEP 1183 (9th Cir.), *cert. denied*, 459 U.S. 1173, 36 FEP 1776 (1982)   17: 12, 14; 36: 61

Laborers Local 75; EEOC v., 30 FEP 1339 (N.D. Ill. 1982)   26: 69, 70

Ladele v. Consolidated Rail Corp., 95 F.R.D. 198, 29 FEP 1547 (E.D. Pa. 1982)   18: 40; 34: 18, 24, 25, 38, 43; 36: 237

Laffey v. Northwest Airlines, 567 F.2d 429, 13 FEP 1068 (D.C. Cir. 1976), *cert. denied*, 434 U.S. 1086, 16 FEP 998 (1978)   13: 3; 38: 8 —572 F. Supp. 354, 32 FEP 770 (D.D.C. 1983), *aff'd in part and remanded in part*, 746 F.2d 4, 35 FEP 1609 (D.C. Cir. 1984), *cert. denied*, 472 U.S. 1021, 37 FEP 1816 (1985)   13: 31, 32; 39: 36, 58, 61, 62, 65 —32 FEP 750 (D.D.C. 1981) *and* 582 F. Supp. 280, 32 FEP 754 (D.D.C. 1982), *aff'd in part and dismissed in part*, 740 F.2d 1071, 35 FEP 508 (D.C. Cir.

Ledoux v. District of Columbia, 40 FEP 1258 (D.D.C. 1986), *aff'd in part and remanded in part*, 820 F.2d 1293, 43 FEP 1880, *reh'g granted in part en banc*, 833 F.2d 368 (D.C. Cir. 1987), *reh'g order vacated en banc*, 841 F.2d 400 (D.C. Cir. 1988)   24: 88

Lee v. City of Peoria, 685 F.2d 196, 29 FEP 892 (7th Cir. 1982)   21: 53; 28: 21; 29: 22

Lee v. Joseph T. Ryerson & Son, 36 FEP 449 (W.D.N.C.), *aff'd*, 745 F.2d 51, 37 FEP 1216 (4th Cir. 1984)   15: 104; 17: 22

Lee v. National Can Corp., 699 F.2d 932, 31 FEP 13 (7th Cir.), *cert. denied*, 464 U.S. 845, 32 FEP 1672 (1983)   36: 34, 64

Lee v. Russell County Bd. of Educ., 684 F.2d 769, 29 FEP 1508 (11th Cir. 1982)   15: 92; 18: 38; 36: 42

Lee v. Washington County Bd. of Educ., 625 F.2d 1235, 23 FEP 1472 (5th Cir. 1980)   17: 15

Lee Way Motor Freight; United States v., 15 FEP 1385 (N.D. Okla. 1977), *aff'd in relevant part*, 625 F.2d 918, 20 FEP 1345 (10th Cir. 1979)   38: 2, 23, 43, 75

Leese v. Baltimore County, 64 Md. App. 442, 497 A.2d 159, *cert. denied*, 305 Md. 106, 501 A.2d 845 (1985)   23: 45, 54, App. B, App. C

Leftwich v. Harris-Stowe State College, 702 F.2d 686, 31 FEP 376 (8th Cir. 1983)   14: 147, 162, 174, 175, 228, 235, 273, 274, 309; 16: 11; 37: 22, 23, 31; 38: 2, 23, 52, 75

Legal Aid Soc'y of Alameda County v. Brennan, 608 F.2d 1319, 21 FEP 605 (9th Cir. 1979), *cert. denied*, 447 U.S. 921, 22 FEP 1382 (1980)   25: 90

Legrand v. University of Ark. at Pine Bluff Trustees, 821 F.2d 478, 44 FEP 60 (8th Cir. 1987), *cert. denied*, 485 U.S. __, 46 FEP 1080 (1988)   2: 4, 6; 18: 11; 36: 31

Lehman v. Nakshian, 453 U.S. 156, 26 FEP 65 (1981)   14: 130, 266; 30: 92

Leibovitch v. Administrator, Veterans Admin., 33 FEP 777 (D.D.C. 1982)   14: 141, 151, 152, 267; 17: 12, 29

Leikvold v. Valley View Hosp., 141 Ariz. 544, 688 P.2d 170, 116 LRRM 2193 (1984)   23: App. B

Leite v. Kennecott Copper Corp., 558 F.

Supp. 1170, 31 FEP 390 (D. Mass.), *aff'd without opinion*, 720 F.2d 658, 33 FEP 1520 (1st Cir. 1983)   14: 55, 89, 93, 108, 141, 146, 309; 18: 10; 28: 24

Lemmo v. Willson, 583 F. Supp. 557, 34 FEP 1079 (D. Colo. 1984)   8: 17, 19, 36, 76, 77

Lemon v. Kurtzman, 403 U.S. 602 (1971)   7: 12

Leonard v. City of Columbus, 705 F.2d 1299, 31 FEP 1441 (11th Cir. 1983), *cert. denied*, 468 U.S. 1204, 35 FEP 213 (1984)   9: 21

Leonard v. City of Frankfort Elec. & Water Plant Bd., 752 F.2d 189, 36 FEP 1181 (6th Cir. 1985)   9: 14; 38: 81

Lerma v. Bolger, 689 F.2d 589, 29 FEP 1828 (5th Cir. 1982)   6: 24; 10: 1; 36: 33, 34

Lettich v. Kenway, 590 F. Supp. 1225, 35 FEP 1289 (D. Mass. 1984)   14: 110, 118, 269; 23: App. A

Leveen v. Stratford Hous. Auth., 629 F. Supp. 228, 42 FEP 1685 (D. Conn. 1986)   15: 110

Levin v. Delta Air Lines, 730 F.2d 994, 34 FEP 1192 (5th Cir. 1984), *aff'g* 34 FEP 1187 (S.D. Tex. 1982)   1: 15, 97; 12: 50, 52, 123, 148; 36: 186, 190, 198, 199

Levy v. Ellingwood, 36 FEP 634 (D.D.C. 1984)   36: 274

Lewan v. Department of the Navy, Military Sealift Command, Atlantic, 35 FEP 1009 (D.N.J. 1982)   14: 56

Lewis v. Bloomsburg Mills, 30 FEP 1715 (D.S.C. 1982), *aff'd, rev'd, remanded and vacated*, 773 F.2d 561, 38 FEP 1692, *corrected on other grounds*, 40 FEP 1615 (4th Cir. 1985)   6: 16, 20, 29; 16: 11; 36: 124, 172, 174, 178, 202, 228, 251, 291

Lewis v. Compton, 416 So.2d 1219 (Fla. Dist. Ct. App.), *review denied*, 424 So.2d 760 (Fla. 1982)   23: App. B

Lewis v. Equitable Life Assurance Soc'y, 389 N.W.2d 876, 1 IER 1269 (Minn. 1986)   23: 54

Lewis v. Federal Prison Indus., 786 F.2d 1537, 40 FEP 998 (11th Cir. 1986)   18: 6

Lewis v. General Elec. Co., 34 FEP 1756 (W.D. Ky. 1983)   14: 55

Lewis v. Louisiana State Bar Ass'n, 792 F.2d 493 (5th Cir. 1986)   30: 73

Lewis v. Mobile County School Bd., 34

Loiseau v. Department of Human Resources, 567 F. Supp. 1211, 39 FEP 289 (D. Or. 1983) 10: 1, 14; 15: 49, 100; 17: 14

Lombardo v. Columbia Dentoform Corp., 103 F.R.D. 630, 36 FEP 869 (S.D.N.Y. 1984) 14: 155

Long v. Florida, 805 F.2d 1542, 42 FEP 1058 (11th Cir. 1986), *cert. denied*, 484 U.S. ___, 44 FEP 1672 (1987) 12: 85, 86

Longnecker v. Ore Sorters (N. Am.), 634 F. Supp. 1077 (N.D. Ga. 1986) 10: 20

Longoria v. Harris, 554 F. Supp. 102, 38 FEP 738 (S.D. Tex. 1982) 23: 71

Longworth v. National Supermkts., 41 FEP 30 (E.D. Mo. 1986) 15: 80

Lopez v. Bulova Watch Co., 582 F. Supp 755, 34 FEP 575 (D.R.I. 1984) 14: 76

Lopez v. City of Austin, 710 F.2d 196, 32 FEP 601 (5th Cir. 1983) 15: 145

Los Angeles, County of; EEOC v., 706 F.2d 1039, 31 FEP 1474 (9th Cir. 1983), *cert. denied*, 464 U.S. 1073, 33 FEP 1224 (1984) 14: 52, 186

Los Angeles, County of v. Davis, 440 U.S. 625, 19 FEP 282 (1979) 30: 78

Los Angeles, Dep't of Water & Power, City of v. Manhart, 435 U.S. 702, 17 FEP 395 (1978) 1: 89; 12: 40, 78

Loubrido v. Hull Dobbs Co. of P.R., 526 F. Supp. 1055, 30 FEP 1243 (D.P.R. 1981) 38: 2, 27, 89

Louisville Black Police Officers Org. v. City of Louisville, 700 F.2d 268, 30 FEP 1505 (6th Cir. 1983) 39: 31, 71

Love v. Alamance County Bd. of Educ., 757 F.2d 1504, 37 FEP 633 (4th Cir. 1985) 36: 99

Love v. Kraft, Inc., 37 EPD ¶35,238 (N.D. Tex. 1985) 39: 86

Love v. Re/Max of Am., 738 F.2d 383, 35 FEP 565 (10th Cir. 1984) 15: 21, 102

Love v. Turlington, 733 F.2d 1562 (11th Cir. 1984) 34: 39

Lovelace v. Sherwin-Williams Co., 681 F.2d 230, 29 FEP 172 (4th Cir. 1982) 14: 132, 144, 146, 171, 309

Lowe v. City of Monrovia, 775 F.2d 998, 39 FEP 350 (9th Cir. 1985), *amended*, 784 F.2d 1407, 41 FEP 931 (9th Cir. 1986) 21: 3; 30: 46; 36: 21, 98, 173, 177

Lowenstein v. Baldrige, 38 FEP 466 (D.D.C. 1985) 39: 16, 20

Loya v. Desert Sands Unified School Dist.,

721 F.2d 279, 33 FEP 739 (9th Cir. 1983) 28: 79

Lucas v. Brown & Root, 736 F.2d 1202, 35 FEP 1855 (8th Cir. 1984) 12: 227

Lucas v. Ripley, 30 FEP 1630 (D.D.C. 1982) 17: 30; 33: 37

Lucero v. City of Trinidad, 815 F.2d 1384 (10th Cir. 1987) 39: 58

Lucero v. Continental Oil Co., 38 EPD ¶35,582 (S.D. Tex. 1985) 6: 31; 17: 22

Lucky v. Board of Regents, 34 FEP 986 (S.D. Fla. 1981) 27: 25

Lucky Stores v. EEOC, 714 F.2d 911, 32 FEP 1281 (9th Cir. 1983) 31: 11

Lugo v. City of Charlotte, 577 F. Supp. 988, 33 FEP 1354 (W.D.N.C. 1984) 28: 57

Lui v. Intercontinental Hotels Corp., 634 F. Supp. 684, 3 IER 761 (D. Haw. 1986) 12: 228, 232

Lujan v. Franklin County Bd. of Educ., 766 F.2d 917, 38 FEP 9 (6th Cir. 1985) 2: 13; 36: 173

Lukens v. Goit, 430 P.2d 607, 115 LRRM 4828 (Wyo. 1967) 23: App. B

Luna v. City & County of Denver, 537 F. Supp. 798, 31 FEP 1357 (D. Colo. 1982) 23: 45, 65, App. A, App. B, App. C

Luna v. Machinists Local 36, 35 FEP 324 (W.D. Tex. 1982) 39: 89

Lusardi v. Xerox Corp., 99 F.R.D. 89, 33 FEP 1143 (D.N.J. 1983), *appeal dismissed*, 747 F.2d 174, 36 FEP 258 (3d Cir. 1984) 14: 136; 28: 14

Lusted v. San Antonio Indep. School Dist., 741 F.2d 817 (5th Cir. 1984) 34: 26

Lute v. Singer Co., Kearfott Div., 678 F.2d 844, 28 FEP 1700 (9th Cir. 1982), *reh'g denied and amended*, 696 F.2d 1266, 34 FEP 1372 (9th Cir. 1983) 28: 58

Lyda v. American Broadcasting Cos., 587 F. Supp. 670, 34 FEP 1151 (S.D.N.Y. 1984) 28: 4

Lynn v. JER Corp., 573 F. Supp. 17, 33 FEP 541 (M.D. Tenn. 1983) 27: 42, 56; 30: 22

Lynn v. Regents of Univ. of Cal., 656 F.2d 1337, 28 FEP 410 (9th Cir. 1981), *cert. denied*, 459 U.S. 823, 29 FEP 1559 (1982) 18: 8

Lyon v. Temple Univ., 543 F. Supp. 1372, 30 FEP 1030 (E.D. Pa. 1982) 19: 11; 21: 26

**M**

M. v. Alvin Indep. School Dist., 532 F. Supp. 460 (S.D. Tex. 1982) 21: 21

M.D. Pneumatics, Inc.; EEOC v., 779 F.2d 21, 44 FEP 530 (8th Cir. 1985) 3: 55

MTC Gear Corp.; EEOC v., 595 F. Supp. 712, 36 FEP 1738 (N.D. Ill. 1984) 12: 50, 120

MacDonald v. Ferguson Reorganized School Dist. R-2, 711 F.2d 80, 31 FEP 184 (8th Cir.), *cert. denied*, 464 U.S. 961 (1983) 6: 26; 17: 16, 22

MacGill v. Johns Hopkins Univ., 33 FEP 1254 (D. Md. 1983) 14: 69, 250; 38: 52

Machakos v. Meese, 647 F. Supp. 1253, 42 FEP 259 (D.D.C. 1986), *aff'd*, 859 F.2d 1487, 48 FEP 306 (D.C. Cir. 1988) 37: 27; 38: 96

Machinists Lodge 751 v. Boeing Co., 833 F.2d 165, 45 FEP 791 (9th Cir. 1987) 1: 122

Mack v. South Bay Beer Distribs. dba Bay Beer Distribs., 798 F.2d 1279, 41 FEP 1224 (9th Cir. 1986) 28: 21; 29: 39

MacMillian Bloedel Containers; EEOC v., 503 F.2d 1086, 8 FEP 897 (6th Cir. 1974) 30: 29

Macpherson v. Texas Dep't of Water Resources, 734 F.2d 1103, 35 FEP 213 (5th Cir. 1984) 18: 21

Maddox v. Claytor, 764 F.2d 1539, 38 FEP 713 (11th Cir. 1985), *aff'g*, 38 FEP 755 (M.D. Ga. 1983) 6: 14, 30, 31, 35; 17: 11, 12, 14, 15, 22, 25; 36: 106, 173, 181, 216, 239, 243, 268, 272

Maddox v. Grandview Care Center, 607 F. Supp. 1404, 37 FEP 1263 (M.D. Ga. 1985), *aff'd*, 780 F.2d 987, 39 FEP 1456 (11th Cir. 1986) 12: 50, 126, 135; 18: 38; 36: 28, 40

Madison Community Unit School Dist. 12; EEOC v., 818 F.2d 577, 43 FEP 1419 (7th Cir. 1987) 39: 26

Madreperla v. Williard Co., 606 F. Supp. 874, 38 FEP 336 (E.D. Pa. 1985) 18: 25

Magnan v. Anaconda Indus., 193 Conn. 558, 479 A.2d 781, 117 LRRM 2163 (1984) 23: App. B

Magnetics Int'l; NLRB v., 699 F.2d 806, 112 LRRM 2658, 30 FEP 1524 (6th Cir. 1983), *enf'g* 254 NLRB 520, 106 LRRM 1133 (1981) 15: 133; 22: 5

Mahdavi v. Fair Employment Practice Comm'n, 67 Cal.App.3d 326, 136 Cal. Rptr. 421, 33 FEP 755 (Ct. App. 1977) 10: 20

Mahoney v. Croker Nat'l Bank (Cal.), 571 F. Supp. 287, 32 FEP 1482 (N.D. Cal. 1983) 23: 4, 9, App. A

Mahoney v. Trabucco, 738 F.2d 35, 35 FEP 97 (1st Cir.), *cert. denied*, 469 U.S. 1036, 36 FEP 464 (1984) 14: 188

Mahroom v. Defense Language Inst., 732 F.2d 1439, 34 FEP 1334 (9th Cir. 1984) 26: 82; 28: 59, 81

Maine Human Rights Comm'n v. Canadian Pac., Ltd., 458 A.2d 1225, 31 FEP 1028 (Me. Sup. Jud. Ct. 1983) 8: 102, 106

Maki v. New York State Comm'n of Educ., 568 F. Supp. 252, 32 FEP 630 (N.D.N.Y. 1983), *aff'd without opinion*, 742 F.2d 1437, 37 FEP 280 (2d Cir. 1984) 14: 186

Malave v. Bolger, 599 F. Supp. 221, 41 FEP 226 (D. Conn. 1984) 15: 1

Maldonado v. Lehman, 811 F.2d 1341, 43 FEP 209 (9th Cir.), *cert. denied*, 484 U.S. ___, 45 FEP 855 (1987) 39: 58

Malinckrodt, Inc.; EEOC v., 22 FEP 311 (E.D. Mo. 1980) 31: 69

Mammano v. Pittston Co., 792 F.2d 1242 (4th Cir. 1986) 39: 71

Mamos v. School Comm. of Wakefield, 553 F. Supp. 989, 30 FEP 1051 (D. Mass. 1983) 28: 37

Manabat v. Columbus-Cuneo-Cabrini Medical Center, 34 FEP 254 (N.D. Ill. 1984) 15: 104; 39: 89

Mandia v. ARCO Chem. Co., 618 F. Supp. 1248, 39 FEP 793 (W.D. Pa. 1985) 15: 8, 21

Manguso v. Oceanside Unified School Dist., 153 Cal.App.3d 574, 200 Cal. Rptr. 535 (1984) 23: 55

Mann v. Milgram Food Stores, 730 F.2d 1186, 34 FEP 735 (8th Cir. 1984) 7: 56

Mannikko v. Harrah's Reno, 630 F. Supp. 191, 3 IER 1225 (D. Nev. 1986) 15: 86, 104

Manning v. Carlin, 786 F.2d 1108, 40 FEP 959 (11th Cir. 1986) 28: 52

Mantolete v. Bolger, 767 F.2d 1416, 38 FEP 1081, *amended*, 38 FEP 1517 (9th Cir. 1985) 8: 98, 106; 17: 3; 35: 12; 36: 73

Manuel v. International Harvester Co., 28 FEP 560 (N.D. Ill. 1981) 38: 54

Manufacturers Hanover Trust Co. v. United States, 775 F.2d 459 (2d Cir. 1985), *rev'g* 576 F. Supp. 837 (S.D.N.Y. 1983), *cert. denied*, 475 U.S. 1095 (1986)   12: 92, 93

Marafino v. St. Louis County Circuit Court, 537 F. Supp. 206, 29 FEP 621 (E.D. Mo. 1982), *aff'd per curiam*, 707 F.2d 1005, 31 FEP 1536 (8th Cir. 1983)   12: 50, 127, 135; 27: 79; 36: 34, 198

Marchetti v. Atlas Powder Co., 520 F. Supp. 271, 28 FEP 563 (E.D. Pa. 1981)   23: App. A

Marcoux v. Maine, 35 FEP 553 (D. Me. 1984), *aff'd*, 797 F.2d 1100, 41 FEP 636 (1st Cir. 1986)   12: 97, 98, 99

Marek v. Chesny, 473 U.S. 1, 38 FEP 124 (1985)   1: 174, 177; 39: 55, 56; 40: 21, 22, 23, 25

Mares v. Marsh, 777 F.2d 1066, 40 FEP 858 (5th Cir. 1985)   10: 12; 27: 41; 33: 1

Maresca v. Cuomo, 64 N.Y.2d 242, 485 N.Y.S.2d 724, 475 N.E.2d 95, 45 FEP 1606 (1984), *appeal dismissed*, 474 U.S. 802, 45 FEP 1896 (1985)   14: 52

Maricopa County Community College Dist.; EEOC v., 736 F.2d 510, 35 FEP 234 (9th Cir. 1984)   13: 58, 113, 114

Markey v. Tenneco Oil Co., 707 F.2d 172, 32 FEP 148 (5th Cir. 1983)   1: 26; 16: 1; 36: 221

Markham v. Geller, 451 U.S. 945, 25 FEP 847 (1981)   14: 158, 309

Marrese v. American Academy of Orthopaedic Surgeons, 470 U.S. 373, 53 USLW 4265 (1985)   21: 58; 28: 21; 29: 25; 30: 61

Marsh v. WMAR TV, 32 FEP 806 (D. Md. 1982)   28: 2

Marshall v. Barlow's, Inc., 436 U.S. 307 (1978)   25: 96, 100

Marshall v. Central Kan. Medical Center, 29 FEP 1817 (D. Kan. 1981), *aff'd sub nom.* EEOC v. Central Kan. Medical Center, 705 F.2d 1270, 31 FEP 1510 (10th Cir. 1983)   13: 41; 38: 19

Marshall v. Edward J. Meyer Memorial Hosp., 32 FEP 1355 (W.D.N.Y. 1983); *aff'd sub nom.* EEOC v. County of Erie, 751 F.2d 79, 36 FEP 830 (2d Cir. 1984)   13: 45; 37: 16

Marshall v. Sun Oil Co., 592 F.2d 563, 18 FEP 1632 (10th Cir.), *cert. denied*, 444 U.S. 826, 20 FEP 1473 (1979)   31: 28

Martin v. Capital Cities Media, 354 Pa. Super. 199, 511 A.2d 830, 122 LRRM 3321 (1986)   23: 22, App. B

Martin v. Citibank, N.A., 762 F.2d 212, 37 FEP 1580, 1 IER 929 (2d Cir. 1985)   18: 43; 36: 23

Martin v. Heckler, 733 F.2d 1499 (11th Cir. 1984), *rev'd*, 773 F.2d 1145 (11th Cir. 1985)   39: 7, 8, 50

Martin v. Norbar, Inc., 537 F. Supp. 1260, 30 FEP 103 (S.D. Ohio 1982)   12: 195, 217

Martin Indus.; EEOC v., 581 F. Supp. 1029, 34 FEP 201 (N.D. Ala.), *appeal dismissed*, 469 U.S. 806, 35 FEP 1607 (1984)   13: 19; 14: 77

Martin Processing; EEOC v., 533 F. Supp. 227, 28 FEP 1825 (W.D. Va. 1982)   30: 3

Martinez v. Automobile Workers Local 1373, 772 F.2d 348, 38 FEP 1361 (7th Cir. 1985)   23: 10

Martinez v. El Paso County, 710 F.2d 1102, 32 FEP 747 (5th Cir. 1983) 38: 11

Martinez v. Orr, 738 F.2d 1107, 35 FEP 367 (10th Cir. 1984)   33: 52

Maryland Cup Corp.; EEOC v., 785 F.2d 471, 40 FEP 475 (4th Cir.), *cert. denied*, 479 U.S. 815, 41 FEP 1711 (1986)   26: 69, 70, 71; 31: 15

Maryland Nat'l Capital Park & Planning Comm'n v. Crawford, 59 Md. App. 276, 475 A.2d 494, 34 FEP 1731 (1984), *aff'd*, 307 Md. 1, 511 A.2d 1079 (1986)   29: 1

Mason v. Continental Ill. Nat'l Bank, 704 F.2d 361, 31 FEP 629 (7th Cir. 1983)   6: 26; 17: 9, 17

Mason v. Continental Ins. Co., 32 FEP 578 (N.D. Ala. 1983)   18: 21

Mason v. Pierce, 774 F.2d 825, 39 FEP 21 (7th Cir. 1985)   18: 13, 14; 33: 23

Mason v. Richmond Motor Co., 625 F. Supp. 883, 39 FEP 1359 (E.D. Va. 1986), *aff'd*, 825 F.2d 407 (1987) 23: App. A

Massa v. Eaton Corp., 109 F.R.D. 312, 39 FEP 1211 (W.D. Mich. 1985) 35: 13

Massachusetts Ass'n of Afro-American Police v. Boston Police Dep't, 106 F.R.D. 80, 37 FEP 1569 (D. Mass.), *aff'd*, 780 F.2d 5, 39 FEP 1048 (1st Cir. 1985), *cert. denied*, 478 U.S. 1020, 41 FEP 272 (1986)   19: 28; 34: 83; 40: 14

Massachusetts Maritime Academy; United

McDaniel v. Temple Indep. School Dist., 770 F.2d 1340, 38 FEP 1567 (5th Cir. 1985)   2: 10; 15: 117; 36: 28

McDermott v. Lehman, 594 F. Supp. 1315, 36 FEP 531 (D. Me. 1984)   16: 12

McDonald v. City of West Branch, Mich., 466 U.S. 284, 115 LRRM 3646 (1984)   1: 154; 21: 51, 58; 28: 21; 29: 9, 18, 38; 30: 62

McDonald v. McDonnell Douglas Corp., 35 FEP 1661 (N.D. Okla. 1984)   7: 38; 19: 14

McDonald v. Santa Fe Trail Transp. Co., 427 U.S. 273, 12 FEP 1577 (1976)   2: 15

McDonnell Douglas Corp. v. Green, 411 U.S. 792, 5 FEP 965 (1973)   1: 2; 2: 1; 4: 8; 10: 148; 12: 214; 14: 142; 15: 93; 17: 8; 18: 1; 24: 71, 146; 29: 13; 36: 1, 8, 30, 60

McDowell v. Avtex Fibers, 740 F.2d 214, 35 FEP 371 (3d Cir. 1984), *vacated on other grounds and remanded*, 469 U.S. 1202, 37 FEP 64 (1985)   14: 246; 38: 52

McDowell v. Mississippi Power & Light, 641 F. Supp. 424, 44 FEP 1088 (S.D. Miss. 1986)   38: 2, 31

McDowell v. Safeway Stores, 575 F. Supp. 1007, 33 FEP 1735 (E.D. Ark. 1983), *aff'd*, 753 F.2d 716, 36 FEP 1593 (8th Cir. 1985)   36: 239

McGraw v. Warren County Oil Co., 32 FEP 1798 (S.D. Iowa 1982), *aff'd per curiam*, 707 F.2d 990, 32 FEP 1801 (8th Cir. 1983)   14: 35, 36, 37

McGuinness v. United States Postal Serv., 744 F.2d 1318, 35 FEP 1762 (7th Cir. 1984)   33: 3, 40, 43

McIntosh v. Jones Truck Lines, 767 F.2d 433, 38 FEP 710 (8th Cir. 1985), *aff'g, vacating and modifying in part* 38 FEP 704 (E.D. Ark. 1984)   37: 25; 38: 2, 37

McIntosh v. Weinberger, 617 F. Supp. 107, 34 FEP 911 (E.D. Mo. 1984), *aff'd in part*, 810 F.2d 1411, 45 FEP 398 (8th Cir. 1987)   33: 30

McKee v. McDonnell Douglas Technical Servs. Co., 700 F.2d 260, 31 FEP 383, *amended*, 705 F.2d 776, 31 FEP 1672 (5th Cir. 1983)   26: 12, 30; 30: 1

McKelvy v. Metal Container Corp., 37 FEP 270 (M.D. Fla. 1984)   14: 67

McKenna v. Champion Int'l Corp., 747 F.2d 1211, 36 FEP 325 (8th Cir. 1984)   14: 136

McKenna v. Weinberger, 34 FEP 284

(D.D.C. 1983), *aff'd*, 729 F.2d 783, 34 FEP 509 (D.C. Cir. 1984)   1: 5; 15: 86, 117; 33: 41; 36: 75

McKenney v. Marsh, 31 FEP 178 (D.D.C. 1983)   5: 5; 17: 16

McKenzie v. Sawyer, 684 F.2d 62, 29 FEP 633 (D.C. Cir. 1982)   17: 17, 23; 33: 38; 34: 24; 36: 132, 242; 37: 50; 38: 117, 122

McKinney v. Dole, 765 F.2d 1129, 38 FEP 364 (D.C. Cir. 1985)   12: 178, 179; 14: 93; 15: 86; 30: 80; 33: 6, 47

McKinnon v. City of Berwyn, 750 F.2d 1383 (7th Cir. 1984)   39: 62

McLaughlin v. Great Lakes Dredge & Dock Co., 495 F. Supp. 857, 23 FEP 1295 (N.D. Ohio 1980)   25: 48, 80

McLemore v. Interstate Motor Freight Sys., 33 FEP 1384 (N.D. Ala. 1984)   30: 2; 38: 63

McMillan v. Rust College, 710 F.2d 1112, 32 FEP 939 (5th Cir. 1983)   15: 116

McMillian v. Svetanoff, 793 F.2d 149, 40 FEP 1737 (7th Cir.), *cert. denied*, 479 U.S. 985, 43 FEP 80 (1986)   21: 3, 18

McNeil v. Greyhound Lines, 31 FEP 1068 (S.D. Fla. 1983)   15: 102

McPartland v. American Broadcasting Cos., 623 F. Supp. 1334, 42 FEP 286 (S.D.N.Y. 1985)   25: 87

McQuillen v. Wisconsin Educ. Ass'n Council, 830 F.2d 659, 44 FEP 1566 (7th Cir. 1987), *cert. denied*, 485 U.S. ___, 46 FEP 292 (1988)   36: 96

McQuitty v. General Dynamics Corp., 204 N.J. Super. 514, 499 A.2d 526 (App. Div. 1985)   23: 10

McTighe v. Mechanics Local 19, 772 F.2d 210, 38 FEP 1477, 120 LRRM 2364 (6th Cir. 1985)   14: 103

Mead Foods; EEOC v., 466 F. Supp. 1, 29 FEP 677 (W.D. Okla. 1977)   15: 36

Mead Johnson & Co. v. Oppenheimer, 458 N.E.2d 668, 115 LRRM 3684 (Ind. Ct. App. 1984)   23: 21, App. B

Meckes v. Reynolds Metals Co., 604 F. Supp. 598, 37 FEP 1269 (N.D. Ala.), *aff'd mem.*, 776 F.2d 1055, *reh'g denied*, 779 F.2d 60 (11th Cir. 1985)   28: 51

Medina v. Spotnail, Inc., 591 F. Supp. 190, 40 FEP 1393 (N.D. Ill. 1984)   23: App. A; 30: 22

Meiri v. Dacon, 759 F.2d 989, 37 FEP 756 (2d Cir.), *cert. denied*, 474 U.S. 829, 38 FEP 1728 (1985)   36: 33, 64

Melani v. Board of Higher Educ. of New

Moore v. Bonner—*Contd.*
U.S. 827 (1985)    21: 57, 58; 23: 8;
28: 20, 21; 29: 38; 30: 69
Moore v. City of Charlotte, 754 F.2d 1100,
36 FEP 1582 (4th Cir.), *cert. denied*,
472 U.S. 1021, 37 FEP 1816
(1985)    1: 7; 28: 61; 30: 1; 32: 6; 36: 5,
27
Moore v. City of Des Moines, 766 F.2d
343, 38 FEP 189 (8th Cir. 1985), *cert.
denied*, 474 U.S. 1060, 39 FEP 1200
(1986)    39: 30
Moore v. Devine, 767 F.2d 1541, 38 FEP
1196 (11th Cir. 1985), *modified on other
grounds*, 780 F.2d 1559, 39 FEP 1644
(11th Cir. 1986)    2: 4; 18: 12; 33: 32
Moore v. Inmont Corp., 608 F. Supp.
919, 39 FEP 1382 (W.D.N.C.
1985)    9: 10
Moore v. McGraw Edison Co., 804 F.2d
1026, 42 FEP 229 (8th Cir.
1986)    14: 156; 40: 6
Moore v. National Ass'n of Sec. Dealers,
762 F.2d 1093, 37 FEP 1749 (D.C. Cir.
1985)    39: 27
Moore v. Orr, 33 FEP 523 (D. Colo.
1982)    33: 28
Moore v. Sears, Roebuck & Co., 683 F.2d
1321, 29 FEP 931 (11th Cir.
1982)    14: 171, 309
Moore v. Stage Employees, IATSE, Local 659, 29 FEP 542 (C.D. Cal.
1982)    3: 8; 12: 74
Moore v. Summa Corp., Hughes Helicopter Div., 708 F.2d 475, 32 FEP 97
(9th Cir. 1983)    1: 26, 28; 16: 16, 21;
17: 12, 20, 22, 27; 34: 38; 36: 169, 221,
224, 233, 234, 274
Morales v. Turman, 569 F. Supp. 332
(E.D. Tex. 1983)    34: 74; 40: 14
Morgado v. Birmingham-Jefferson County
Civil Defense Corps, 706 F.2d 1184,
32 FEP 12 (11th Cir. 1983), *cert. denied*, 464 U.S. 1045, 33 FEP 1084
(1984)    13: 35, 39, 64, 75; 38: 109
Morgan v. Department of the Treasury,
594 F. Supp. 476, 35 FEP 1541 (D.D.C.
1984), *aff'd without opinion*, 784 F.2d
1131 (D.C. Cir. 1986)    16: 9
Morgan v. Goldschmidt, 33 FEP 797
(D.D.C. 1980)    17: 12
Morgan v. Hertz Corp., 542 F. Supp. 123,
27 FEP 990 (W.D. Tenn. 1981), *aff'd
on other grounds*, 725 F.2d 1070, 33
FEP 1237 (6th Cir. 1984)    37: 12
Morgan v. Union Metal Mfg. Co., 757
F.2d 792, 37 FEP 625 (6th Cir.
1985)    14: 281; 39: 83

Morgan v. United States Postal Serv., 798
F.2d 1162, 41 FEP 959 (8th Cir. 1986),
*cert. denied*, 480 U.S. 948, 43 FEP 560
(1987)    33: 3
Morgan Drive Away v. Brant, 479 N.E.2d
1336 (Ind. Ct. App. 1985), *rev'd*, 489
N.E.2d 933, 122 LRRM 2130 (Ind.
1986)    23: App. B
Morley v. County of Union, 35 FEP 1269
(D.N.J. 1984), *aff'd without opinion*,
760 F.2d 259, 41 FEP 64 (3d Cir.
1985)    14: 141, 151, 152; 16: 12
Morris v. Bianchini, 43 FEP 674 (E.D.
Va. 1987), *aff'd*, 838 F.2d 467, 46 FEP
176 (4th Cir. 1988)    18: 23
Morris v. Hartford Courant Co., 200 Conn.
676, 513 A.2d 66 (1986)    23: 45, App.
B, App. C
Morris v. Kaiser Eng'rs, 14 Ohio St.3d
45, 471 N.E.2d 471, 36 FEP 807
(1984)    14: 68
Morris v. Lutheran Medical Center, 215
Neb. 677, 340 N.W.2d 388, 115 LRRM
4966 (1983)    23: App. B
Morris v. Russell, Burdsall & Ward Corp.,
577 F. Supp. 147, 38 FEP 1453 (N.D.
Ohio 1983)    14: 104
Morrison v. Booth, 730 F.2d 642, 34 FEP
1142 (11th Cir. 1984), *reh'g denied*,
742 F.2d 1328, *appeal after remand on
other issues*, 763 F.2d 1366, 38 FEP
145, *reh'g denied*, 770 F.2d 1084 (11th
Cir. 1985)    17: 23; 34: 45
Morrow v. Inmont Corp., 30 FEP 1019
(W.D.N.C. 1982)    37: 59
Mortensen v. Callaway, 672 F.2d 822, 29
FEP 111 (10th Cir. 1982)    17: 11, 19;
36: 61
Morvay v. Maghielse Tool & Die Co.,
708 F.2d 229, 31 FEP 1471 (6th Cir.),
*cert. denied*, 464 U.S. 1011, 33 FEP
552 (1983)    10: 1
Mosel v. Hills Dep't Store, 789 F.2d 251,
40 FEP 1049 (3d Cir. 1986)    28: 69
Moss v. Southern Ry., 41 FEP 553 (N.D.
Ga. 1986)    15: 71, 106
Moteles v. University of Pa., 730 F.2d
913, 34 FEP 424 (3d Cir.), *cert. de-
nied*, 469 U.S. 855, 35 FEP 1800
(1984)    12: 55; 28: 67; 37: 62
Motley v. Bell Tel. Co., 562 F. Supp.
497, 32 FEP 1050 (E.D. Pa. 1983)
28: 68
Mt. Healthy School Dist. Bd. of Educ. v.
Doyle, 429 U.S. 274 (1977)    2: 19;
14: 176
Mt. Lebanon, Pa., City of; EEOC v., 651
F. Supp. 1259, 42 FEP 1413 (W.D.

Owens v. United States—*Contd.*
    44 FEP 247 (3d Cir. 1987)   21: 23;
    33: 40


# P

Pace v. Southern Ry. Sys., 701 F.2d 1383,
    31 FEP 710 (11th Cir.), *cert. denied*,
    464 U.S. 1018, 33 FEP 656 (1983),
    *reh'g denied*, 465 U.S. 1054
    (1984)   14: 47, 141, 149; 17: 25;
    36: 274
Pacific Press Publishing Ass'n; EEOC v.,
    535 F.2d 1182, 12 FEP 1312 (9th Cir.
    1976)   31: 80
—676 F.2d 1272, 28 FEP 1596 (9th Cir.
    1982)   7: 11, 12; 13: 6
—35 FEP 322 (N.D. Cal. 1982)   38: 67
Pacific Sw. Airlines; EEOC v., 587 F.
    Supp. 686, 34 FEP 1430 (N.D. Cal.
    1984)   31: 79; 37: 66
Padway v. Palches, 665 F.2d 965, 27 FEP
    1403 (9th Cir. 1982)   38: 102
Paetz v. United States, 795 F.2d 1533,
    41 FEP 1682, *reh'g denied en banc*,
    804 F.2d 681 (11th Cir. 1986)   33: 51
Page v. U.S. Indus., 726 F.2d 1038, 34
    FEP 430 (5th Cir. 1984)   6: 7, 17, 30,
    35; 17: 12, 16; 36: 103, 104, 106, 134,
    143, 172, 204, 262
Palazon v. KFC Nat'l Mgmt. Co., 28 FEP
    458 (N.D. Ill. 1981)   23: App. A
Palmateer v. International Harvester Co.,
    421 N.E.2d 876, 115 LRRM 4165 (Ill.
    1981)   23: 15, 16, 26, 35, 36, 43, 44
Palmer v. General Servs. Admin., 787
    F.2d 300, 40 FEP 630 (8th Cir.
    1986)   14: 278
Palmer v. Reader's Digest Ass'n, 42 FEP
    209 (S.D.N.Y. 1986)   14: 137
Palmer v. United States, 794 F.2d 534,
    41 FEP 559 (9th Cir. 1986)   14: 147,
    149; 18: 8; 36: 138, 172, 274
Pan Am. World Airways; EEOC v., 31
    FEP 1136 (S.D.N.Y. 1983)   26: 71
—576 F. Supp. 1530, 33 FEP 1232
    (S.D.N.Y. 1984)   14: 77; 26: 6
—34 FEP 321 (N.D. Cal. 1984)   14: 77
Pantry Pride Enters., *see* Ross v. Food
    Fair
Pao v. Holy Redeemer Hosp., 547 F. Supp.
    484, 31 FEP 580 (E.D. Pa.
    1982)   27: 53; 28: 38
Paolillo v. Dresser Indus. (I), 813 F.2d
    583, 43 FEP 338 (2d Cir.
    1987)   14: 298, 299, 323

—(II), 821 F.2d 81, 44 FEP 71 (2d Cir.
    1987)   14: 297, 323
Paradise v. Dothard, Civil Action No.
    3561-N (M.D. Ala., Aug. 5,
    1975)   24: 108
Paradise v. Prescott, 767 F.2d 1514, 38
    FEP 1094 (11th Cir. 1985), *attorney's
    fees denied*, 626 F. Supp. 117, 39 FEP
    1744 (M.D. Ala. 1985), *aff'd sub nom.*
    United States v. Paradise, 480 U.S. 149,
    43 FEP 1 (1987)   1: 43, 49, 50, 148,
    153; 3: 35; 17: 32; 19: 27; 24: 12, 18,
    32, 33, 71, 90, 106, 107, 109, 110,
    111, 113, 114, 115, 116, 117, 118,
    119, 120, 126, 127, 129, 130, 136,
    138; 37: 11, 48, 49; 39: 94
Paralyzed Veterans of Am. v. Civil Aero-
    nautics Bd., 752 F.2d 694, 53 USLW
    2381 (D.C. Cir. 1985), *rev'd sub nom.*
    Department of Transp. v. Paralyzed
    Veterans of Am., 477 U.S. 597, 54
    USLW 4854 (1986)   8: 16, 20, 22, 76
Parker v. Anderson, 667 F.2d 1204, 28
    FEP 788 (5th Cir.), *cert. denied*, 459
    U.S. 828, 29 FEP 1560 (1982)   34: 73,
    74, 76; 39: 30; 40: 14
Parker v. Baltimore & Ohio R.R., 555 F.
    Supp. 1182, 30 FEP 1791 (D.D.C.
    1983)   19: 19
—641 F. Supp. 1227, 41 FEP 761 (D.D.C.
    1986)   25: 48, 82
Parker v. Bell Helicopter Co., 35 EPD
    ¶34,733 (N.D. Tex. 1984)   39: 82
Parker v. City of Indianapolis Bd. of School
    Comm'rs, 729 F.2d 524, 34 FEP 453
    (7th Cir. 1984)   16: 12
Parker v. Danville Metal Stamping Co.,
    603 F. Supp. 182, 37 FEP 250 (C.D.
    Ill. 1985)   23: 8; 28: 20, 21; 29: 36
Parker v. Federal Nat'l Mortgage Ass'n,
    567 F. Supp. 265, 33 FEP 1207 (N.D.
    Ill. 1983), *aff'd*, 741 F.2d 975, 35 FEP
    893 (7th Cir. 1984)   14: 149, 155, 156,
    302, 315, 335; 18: 36; 36: 274
Parker v. Mississippi State Dep't of Pub.
    Welfare, 811 F.2d 925, 43 FEP 243
    (5th Cir. 1987)   6: 35
Parker v. National Corp. for Hous. Part-
    nerships, 619 F. Supp. 1061, 38 FEP
    1265 (D.D.C. 1985)   21: 56; 23: 8,
    App. B; 28: 19, 21; 29: 25, 38
Parker v. Siemens-Allis, 601 F. Supp.
    1377, 37 FEP 39 (E.D. Ark.
    1985)   38: 51
Parker v. United Airlines, 32 Wash. App.
    722, 649 P.2d 181 (1982)   23: 21, App.
    B

Planells v. Howard Univ., 32 FEP 336 (D.D.C. 1983), *later proceeding*, 34 FEP 66 (D.D.C. 1984)   9: 30; 24: 5; 39: 48

Plemer v. Parsons-Gilbane, 713 F.2d 1127, 32 FEP 1351 (5th Cir. 1983)   13: 37

Plessey, Inc.; EEOC v., 34 FEP 500 (D. Kan. 1984)   14: 77

Plummer v. Chemical Bank, 97 F.R.D. 486, 33 FEP 547 (S.D.N.Y. 1983)   34: 77; 40: 14

—592 F. Supp. 1168, 35 FEP 1546 (S.D.N.Y. 1984)   39: 93

Poe v. John Deere Co., 695 F.2d 1103, 30 FEP 827 (8th Cir. 1982)   21: 49; 28: 21; 29: 40

Pole v. Citibank, N.A., 556 F. Supp. 822, 31 FEP 751 (S.D.N.Y. 1983)   28: 70; 30: 1

Police Officers Ass'n (San Francisco) v. City & County of San Francisco, 621 F. Supp. 1225, 40 FEP 1480 (N.D. Cal. 1985), *rev'd*, 812 F.2d 1125, 43 FEP 495 (9th Cir. 1987)   17: 3

Police Officers for Equal Rights v. City of Columbus, 644 F. Supp. 393, 42 FEP 1752 (S.D. Ohio 1985)   1: 129; 4: 23, 29, 31, 38

Polk v. Kramarsky, 711 F.2d 505, 37 FEP 1150 (2d Cir.), *cert. denied*, 464 U.S. 1000 (1983)   30: 4

Polk v. Yellow Freight Sys., 801 F.2d 190, 41 FEP 1279 (6th Cir. 1986)   28: 21; 29: 29

Pollack v. Rice Univ., 28 FEP 1273 (S.D. Tex.), *aff'd mem.*, 690 F.2d 903, 29 FEP 1846 (5th Cir. 1982), *cert. denied*, 459 U.S. 1175, 30 FEP 1256 (1983)   27: 51

Pollard v. Grinstead, 741 F.2d 73, 35 FEP 891 (4th Cir. 1984)   17: 29

Pollard v. Rea Magnet Wire Co., 824 F.2d 557, 44 FEP 1137 (7th Cir.), *cert. denied*, 484 U.S. ___, 45 FEP 648 (1987)   2: 6

Ponticas v. K.M.S. Invs., 331 N.W.2d 907 (Minn. 1983)   23: 63, App. B

Poolaw v. City of Anadarko, Okla., 738 F.2d 364, 35 FEP 107 (10th Cir. 1984), *cert denied*, 469 U.S. 1108, 36 FEP 976 (1985)   21: 43

Pope v. City of Hickory, N.C., 679 F.2d 20, 29 FEP 405 (4th Cir. 1982)   6: 16; 36: 142, 172

Popkins v. Zagel, 611 F. Supp. 809, 39 FEP 611 (C.D. Ill. 1985)   14: 103; 23: 10

Popko v. City of Clairton, 570 F. Supp. 446, 32 FEP 1414 (W.D. Pa. 1983)   14: 155, 168, 172, 309

Porter, H.K., Co. v. Metropolitan Dade County, 825 F.2d 324 (11th Cir. 1987)   24: 81

Portillo v. G.T. Price Prods., 131 Cal.App.3d 285, 182 Cal. Rptr. 291, 115 LRRM 4235 (1982)   23: 38, 47, 64, 67

Posey v. Skyline Corp., 702 F.2d 102, 31 FEP 274 (7th Cir.), *cert. denied*, 464 U.S. 960, 33 FEP 152 (1983)   14: 89, 93

Postal Workers, San Francisco Local v. Postmaster Gen., 35 FEP 1484 (N.D. Cal. 1984), *rev'd and remanded*, 781 F.2d 772, 39 FEP 1847 (9th Cir. 1986)   7: 33; 33: 41

Pouncy v. Prudential Ins. Co. of Am., 668 F.2d 795, 28 FEP 121 (5th Cir. 1982)   6: 17, 27; 17: 7, 23, 28; 36: 142, 172, 241

Powell v. Georgia-Pacific Corp., 535 F. Supp. 713, 30 FEP 21 (W.D. Ark. 1980)   16: 15; 17: 4; 34: 29; 37: 50; 38: 18

Powell v. Pennsylvania Hous. Fin. Agency, 563 F. Supp. 419, 31 FEP 1595 (M.D. Pa. 1983)   21: 47; 30: 94, 96

Power v. Barry County, Mich., 539 F. Supp. 721, 29 FEP 559 (W.D. Mich. 1982)   13: 128

Powers v. Delnor Hosp., 135 Ill. App. 317, 481 N.E.2d 968 (2d Dist. 1985)   23: 40, 47, 57

Powers v. Dole, 782 F.2d 689, 39 FEP 1774 (7th Cir. 1986)   36: 260

Pree v. Stone & Webster Eng'g Corp., 607 F. Supp. 945, 37 FEP 1277 (D. Nev. 1985)   37: 15

Premachandra v. Mitts, 753 F.2d 635 (8th Cir. 1985)   39: 17

Preston v. Heckler, 734 F.2d 1359 (9th Cir. 1984)   11: 6

Price, *see* Aleem v. United Parcel Serv.

Price v. Cannon Mills Co., 607 F. Supp. 1146, 39 FEP 708 (M.D.N.C. 1985)   15: 13, 101

Price v. Erie County, N.Y., 40 FEP 115 (W.D.N.Y. 1986)   35: 4

Price v. Litton Business Sys., 694 F.2d 963, 30 FEP 803 (4th Cir. 1982)   14: 55, 90, 93; 28: 24

Price v. Southwestern Bell Tel Co., 687 F.2d 74, 29 FEP 1584 (5th Cir. 1982)   27: 1, 3; 30: 1

Scott v. St. Paul Postal Serv., 720 F.2d
524, 33 FEP 544 (8th Cir. 1983), *cert
denied*, 465 U.S. 1083, 34 FEP 192
(1984)    33: 46
Scott v. Sears, Roebuck & Co., 605 F.
Supp. 1047, 37 FEP 878 (N.D. Ill.
1985), *aff'd*, 798 F.2d 210, 41 FEP 805
(7th Cir. 1986)    12: 170, 196; 18: 13;
23: 32, App. B
Scroggins v. Kansas, 802 F.2d 1289 (10th
Cir. 1986)    28: 21; 29: 38
Sczesnik v. McDonald's Corp., 40 FEP
1794 (N.D. Ill. 1986)    35: 20
Seaman's Direct Buying Serv. v. Standard Oil Co. of Cal., 36 Cal.3d 752, 206
Cal. Rptr. 354, 686 P.2d 1158
(1984)    23: 25, App. B
Sears v. Atchison, Topeka & Santa Fe
Ry., 30 FEP 1084 (D. Kan. 1982), *aff'd*,
749 F.2d 1451, 36 FEP 783 (10th Cir.
1984), *cert. denied*, 471 U.S. 1099, 37
FEP 1216 (1985)    19: 11, 23; 35: 13;
38: 2, 47, 65, 81; 39: 47, 70
—779 F.2d 1450, 39 FEP 1029 (10th Cir.
1985)    39: 75
Sears, Roebuck & Co.; EEOC v., 650
F.2d 14, 25 FEP 1338 (2d Cir. 1981)
17: 28
—628 F. Supp. 1264, 39 FEP 1672 *and*
39 FEP 1745 (N.D. Ill. 1986), *award
of attorney's fees and costs*, 114 F.R.D.
615, 42 FEP 1358 (N.D. Ill. 1987),
*aff'd*, 839 F.2d 302, 45 FEP 1257 (7th
Cir. 1988)    12: 257; 16: 11; 36: 142,
172, 215, 239, 249, 250, 257, 287,
290, 296, 297; 39: 36
Sebastian v. Texas Dep't of Corrections,
541 F. Supp. 970, 30 FEP 1320 (S.D.
Tex. 1982)    37: 63, 65
—558 F. Supp. 507 (S.D. Tex. 1983)
38: 103
Sedlacek v. Hach, 752 F.2d 333, 36 FEP
1253 (8th Cir. 1985)    30: 1, 10, 19
Seep v. Commercial Motor Freight, 575
F. Supp. 1097, 45 FEP 203 (S.D. Ohio
1983)    38: 10
Segar v. Civiletti, 516 F. Supp. 314, 32
FEP 1308 (D.D.C. 1981), *aff'd sub nom.*
Segar v. Smith, 28 FEP 935 (D.D.C.
1982) *and* 738 F.2d 1249, 35 FEP 31
(D.C. Cir. 1984), *cert. denied*, 471 U.S.
1115, 37 FEP 1312 (1985)    1: 8; 6: 15;
15: 119; 17: 29, 32; 36: 9, 104, 124,
128, 134, 136, 172, 186, 261, 276;
37: 32, 53; 38: 50, 121, 122, 124, 125,
126, 132, 135

Seid v. Pacific Bell, 121 LRRM 2349 (S.D.
Cal. 1985)    1: 165; 23: 4, 6, 41, 42
Seidel v. Chicago Sav. & Loan Ass'n,
544 F. Supp 508, 34 FEP 297 (N.D.
Ill. 1982)    14: 223
Sellers v. Delgado College, 781 F.2d 503,
39 FEP 1766 (5th Cir. 1986), *appeal
after remand, judgment aff'd in part
and vacated in part*, 839 F.2d 1132, 46
FEP 464 (5th Cir. 1988)    37: 27;
38: 100
Senkow v. Department of Energy, 35 FEP
26 (D.D.C. 1984), *aff'd*, 762 F.2d 138,
38 FEP 672 (D.C. Cir. 1985)    14: 89,
93
Serafin v. City of Lexington, Neb., 547
F. Supp. 1118, 115 LRRM 5151 (D.
Neb. 1982), *aff'd*, 716 F.2d 909 (8th
Cir. 1983)    23: App B
Seredinski v. Litton Sys., Clifton Precision Prods. Co. Div., 776 F.2d 56, 39
FEP 248 (3d Cir. 1985)    28: 1
Seritis v. Hotel & Restaurant Employees
Local 28, 167 Cal.App.3d 78, 213 Cal.
Rptr. 588, 37 FEP 1501, *reh'g denied
and ordered not to be officially published*, 120 LRRM 2342 (Cal. 1985),
*cert. denied*, 474 U.S. 1060, 121 LRRM
2208 (1986)    1: 165; 12: 230; 23: 4,
6, 41, 42
Serpe v. Four-Phase Sys., 718 F.2d 935,
33 FEP 178 (9th Cir. 1983)    28: 41
Sessum v. Houston Community College,
94 F.R.D. 316, 32 FEP 1172 (S.D. Tex.
1982)    35: 26
Setser v. Novak Inv. Co., 638 F.2d 1137,
24 FEP 1793 (8th Cir.), *cert. denied*,
454 U.S. 1064 (1981)    21: 47
Seville v. Martin Marietta Corp., 638 F.
Supp. 590, 41 FEP 572 (D. Md.
1986)    12: 110
Sewell Mfg. Co., 138 NLRB 66, 50 LRRM
1532 (1962)    22: 1
Shaare Tefila Congregation v. Cobb, 481
U.S. 615, 43 FEP 1309 (1987)    1: 102,
103; 10: 4, 8; 21: 7, 9    •
Shadis v. Beal, 685 F.2d 824 (3d Cir.),
*cert. denied*, 459 U.S. 970 (1982)
39: 25
Shaffer v. Globe Protection, 721 F.2d
1121, 33 FEP 450 (7th Cir. 1983)
37: 59, 61, 62
Shaffer v. National Can Corp., 565 F.
Supp. 909, 34 FEP 172 (E.D. Pa. 1983),
*reconsideration denied*, 35 FEP 840
(E.D. Pa. 1984)    12: 229; 23: 8; 28: 2

Shrock v. Altru Nurses Registry—*Contd.*
*vacated and remanded in part*, 810 F.2d
658, 42 FEP 1393 (7th Cir.
1987) 27: 41; 39: 82

Shultz v. Dempster Sys., 561 F. Supp.
1230, 32 FEP 1766 (E.D. Tenn.
1983) 14: 62, 89, 93

Shuster v. Federated Dep't Stores, 508 F.
Supp. 118, 29 FEP 324 (N.D. Ga.
1980) 14: 85

Sias v. City Demonstration Agency, 588
F.2d 692, 18 FEP 981 (9th Cir.
1978) 38: 87

Silvas v. Dow Chem. Co., 36 FEP 105
(S.D. Tex. 1984) 18: 14

Silverman's Men's Wear; NLRB v., 656
F.2d 53, 26 FEP 876, 107 LRRM 3273
(3d Cir. 1981) 22: 1

Silverstein v. United Men's Store, No.
85-2838, slip op. (E.D. Pa. Oct. 25,
1985) 28: 1

Sime v. California State Univ. & Colleges
Trustees, 526 F.2d 1112, 11 FEP 1104
(9th Cir. 1975) 2: 10

Simi Valley, Cal., City of v. Fair Employment & Hous. Comm. of Cal., 172
Cal.App.3d 1254, 39 FEP 863
(1985) 16: 3

Simmons v. Brown, 611 F.2d 65, 26 FEP
447 (4th Cir. 1979) 34: 32

Simmons v. Camden County Bd. of Educ.,
757 F.2d 1187, 37 FEP 795 (11th Cir.),
*cert. denied*, 474 U.S. 981, 39 FEP 384
(1985) 15: 95, 117

Simmons v. South Carolina State Ports
Auth., 694 F.2d 63, 30 FEP 457 (4th
Cir. 1982) 28: 42

Simon v. Wiremold Co., 35 FEP 1819
(W.D. Pa. 1984) 14: 129

Simpson v. Reynolds Metals Co., 629 F.2d
1226, 23 FEP 868 (7th Cir. 1980)
8: 57, 91, 93

Sims v. Cleland, 813 F.2d 790, 43 FEP
362 (6th Cir. 1987) 36: 71

Sims v. Heckler, 725 F.2d 1143, 33 FEP
1786 (7th Cir. 1984) 15: 1

Sims v. Mme. Paulette Dry Cleaners, 580
F. Supp. 593, 34 FEP 305 (S.D.N.Y.
1984), *remedies determined*, 638 F.
Supp. 224, 41 FEP 193 (S.D.N.Y.
1986) 15: 66, 101; 38: 75, 76

Sinclair v. Automobile Club of Okla., 733
F.2d 726, 34 FEP 1206 (10th Cir.
1984) 38: 19, 65, 110

Singer v. Uni-Marts, 37 FEP 1197 (W.D.
Pa. 1985) 14: 17, 141, 146, 309;
39: 83

Singh v. Bowsher, 609 F. Supp. 454, 41
FEP 202 (D.D.C. 1984), *aff'd*, 786 F.2d
432 (D.C. Cir. 1986) 15: 87

Singh v. Cities Serv. Oil Co., 554 P.2d
1367 (Okla. 1986) 23: App. B

Sioux Falls Rent-A-Car (Hertz), *see* Tombollo v. Dunn

Sisco v. J.S. Alberici Constr. Co., 733
F.2d 55, 34 FEP 1306 (8th Cir.
1984) 39: 72

Sivell v. Conwed Corp., 605 F. Supp.
1265 (D. Conn. 1985) 23: App. B

Skadegaard v. Farrell, 578 F. Supp. 1209,
33 FEP 1528 (D.N.J. 1984) 21: 28

Sklios v. Teamsters Local 70, 503 F. Supp.
123, 115 LRRM 3133 (N.D. Cal.
1980) 23: 42

Sky Chefs, *see* Jones v. Flagship Int'l

Slanina v. William Penn Parking Corp.,
106 F.R.D. 419, 34 FEP 1426 (W.D.
Pa. 1984) 34: 26, 34, 46

Slater v. Guest Servs., 33 FEP 886 (D.D.C.
1981) 16: 3

Sledge v. J.P. Stevens & Co., 585 F.2d
625, 18 FEP 261 (4th Cir. 1978), *cert.
denied*, 440 U.S. 981, 19 FEP 467
(1979) 38: 13, 56, 134

Slenkamp v. Borough of Brentwood, 603
F. Supp. 1298, 38 FEP 73 (W.D. Pa.
1985), *aff'd*, 826 F.2d 1057, 45 FEP
299 (3d Cir. 1987) 14: 93

Slevin v. Safeguard Business Sys., 31 FEP
193 (N.D. Ill. 1982) 28: 43

Slohoda v. United Parcel Serv. (I), 193
N.J. Super. 586, 475 A.2d 618 (App.
Div. 1984), (II), *appeal after remand*,
207 N.J. Super. 145, 504 A.2d 53 (App.
Div.), *certification denied*, 104 N.J. 400,
517 A.2d 403 (1986) 23: 39, 40, 47

Small v. Bethlehem Steel Corp., 33 FEP
414 (D. Md. 1983) 14: 60; 30: 8

Smallwood v. United Airlines, 661 F.2d
303, 26 FEP 1376 (4th Cir. 1981), *cert.
denied*, 456 U.S. 1007, 28 FEP 1656
(1982) 14: 186
—728 F.2d 614, 34 FEP 217 (4th Cir.),
*cert. denied*, 469 U.S. 832, 35 FEP
1608 (1984) 14: 247; 36: 40; 38: 2,
11, 42, 52

Smith v. Administrator, Veterans Affairs,
32 FEP 986 (C.D. Cal. 1983) 8: 85

Smith v. American Serv. Co. of Atlanta,
611 F. Supp. 321, 35 FEP 1552 (N.D.
Ga. 1984), *later proceeding*, 38 FEP
377 (N.D. Ga. 1985), *aff'd in part, vacated and remanded in part*, 796 F.2d
1430, 41 FEP 802 (11th Cir.

Stevens, J.P. & Co. v. Perry—*Contd.*
136, 32 FEP 40 (4th Cir. 1983)   26: 94, 96

Steward v. Holiday Inn, 609 F. Supp. 1468, 40 FEP 191 (E.D. La. 1985)   28: 55

Stewart v. CPC Int'l, 679 F.2d 117, 33 FEP 1680 (7th Cir. 1982)   36: 69

Stewart v. General Motors Corp., 542 F.2d 445, 13 FEP 1035 (7th Cir. 1976), *cert. denied*, 433 U.S. 919, 15 FEP 31 (1977)   38: 13, 56, 134
—756 F.2d 1285 (7th Cir. 1985)   37: 79

Stewart v. Hannon, 675 F.2d 846, 28 FEP 1268 (7th Cir. 1982)   27: 21

Stewart v. Immigration & Naturalization Serv., 762 F.2d 193, 37 FEP 1357 (2d Cir. 1985)   30: 48; 33: 25; 37: 61

Stewart v. Thomas, 538 F. Supp. 891, 30 FEP 1609 (D.D.C. 1982)   12: 193, 226; 23: 45, App. B, App. C; 33: 41

Stiessberger v. Rockwell Int'l Corp., 29 FEP 1273 (E.D. Wash. 1982)   15: 1

Stinson v. Hornsby, 821 F.2d 1537, 44 FEP 594 (11th Cir. 1987)   27: 61; 33: 1

Stitzer v. University of P.R., 617 F. Supp. 1246, 38 FEP 1419 (D.P.R. 1985)   21: 53

Stoecklein v. Illinois Tool Works, 589 F. Supp. 139, 36 FEP 1154 (N.D. Ill. 1984)   14: 68

Stokes v. New York State Dep't of Correctional Servs., 569 F. Supp. 918, 33 FEP 1074 (S.D.N.Y. 1982)   10: 2

Stoller v. Marsh, 682 F.2d 971, 29 FEP 85 (D.C. Cir. 1982), *cert. denied*, 460 U.S. 1037, 31 FEP 368 (1983)   7: 61

Stone v. Mission Bay Mortgage Co., 99 Nev. 802, 672 P.2d 629, 116 LRRM 2917 (1983)   23: 19

Stone Container Corp.; EEOC v., 548 F. Supp. 1098, 30 FEP 134 (W.D. Mo. 1982)   38: 2, 39

Stones v. Los Angeles Community College Dist., 572 F. Supp. 1072, 36 FEP 275 (C.D. Cal. 1983), *aff'd*, 796 F.2d 270, 41 FEP 710 (9th Cir. 1986)   17: 28

Storey v. University of Wis. Sys. Bd. of Regents, 604 F. Supp. 1200, 37 FEP 701 (W.D. Wis. 1985)   38: 6

Stotts v. Memphis Fire Dep't, *see* Firefighters Local 1784 v. Stotts

Stoutt v. Southern Bell Tel. & Tel. Co., 598 F. Supp. 1000, 36 FEP 1778 (S.D. Fla. 1984)   21: 13

Stover v. Alabama Farm Bureau Ins. Co., *see* Murphree v. Alabama Farm Bureau Ins. Co.

Strathie v. Department of Transp., 716 F.2d 227, 32 FEP 1561 (3d Cir. 1983)   8: 116, 117

Strauss v. A.L. Randall Co., 144 Cal.App.3d 514, 194 Cal. Rptr. 520, 37 FEP 1531 (1983)   23: 4, 9, 41

Streckfus v. Gardenside Terrace Coop., 504 N.E.2d 273 (Ind. 1987)   23: App. B

Strickland v. American Can Co., 575 F. Supp. 1111, 34 FEP 542 (N.D. Ga. 1983)   26: 11, 100

Stroud v. Delta Air Lines, 544 F.2d 892, 14 FEP 206 (5th Cir.), *cert. denied*, 434 U.S. 844, 15 FEP 1184 (1977)   12: 155

Stroud v. Seminole Tribe of Fla., 606 F. Supp. 678 (S.D. Fla. 1985)   11: 4

Struble v. Lacks Indus., 157 Mich. App. 169, 403 N.W.2d 71 (1986)   23: 61, App. B

Studint v. LaSalle Ice Cream Co., 623 F. Supp. 232, 39 FEP 1055 (E.D.N.Y. 1985)   23: App. A

Stumph v. Thomas & Skinner, 770 F.2d 93, 38 FEP 1114 (7th Cir. 1985)   14: 146, 309, 328

Stutts v. Freeman, 694 F.2d 666, 30 FEP 1121 (11th Cir. 1983)   4: 13; 8: 114

Suarez v. Little Havana Activities & Nutrition Centers of Dade County, 721 F.2d 338, 33 FEP 806 (11th Cir. 1983)   28: 69, 79

Sullivan v. Boron Oil Co., 831 F.2d 288, 8 EBC 2590 (3d Cir. 1987)   1: 66, 67; 14: 210; 40: 6

Sullivan v. Crown Paper Bd. Co., 719 F.2d 667, 33 FEP 13 (3d Cir. 1983)   14: 277; 39: 73

Sullivan v. Heritage Found., 399 A.2d 856, 115 LRRM 4621 (D.C. Ct. App. 1979)   23: App. B

Sullivan v. School Bd. of Pinellas County, 773 F.2d 1182, 39 FEP 53 (11th Cir. 1985)   21: 47

Sumitomo Shoji Am. v. Avigliano, 457 U.S. 176, 28 FEP 1753 (1982), *on remand*, 103 F.R.D. 562, 38 FEP 561 (S.D.N.Y. 1984)   27: 10, 11, 91; 34: 12, 25, 56

Summers v. Allis-Chalmers, 568 F. Supp. 33, 41 FEP 824 (N.D. Ill. 1983)   15: 110

Sumner v. San Diego Urban League, 681 F.2d 1140, 29 FEP 707 (9th Cir. 1982)   2: 4

Sunbeam Appliance Co. v. Kelly, 532 F.

Taylor v. Secretary of the Army, 583 F. Supp. 1503, 38 FEP 1408 (D. Md. 1984) 17: 14

Taylor v. Teletype Corp., 550 F. Supp. 781, 34 FEP 1385 (E.D. Ark. 1982) 36: 131

Taylor Instrument Co., *see* Giandonato v. Sybron Corp.

Teamsters v. United States, 431 U.S. 324, 14 FEP 1514 (1977), *appeal after remand sub nom.* EEOC v. T.I.M.E.-D.C. Freight, 659 F.2d 690, 27 FEP 10 (5th Cir. 1981) 3: 4, 30; 12: 71; 19: 27; 27: 21; 30: 18; 36: 103, 143, 172; 38: 2, 12, 24

Teamsters Local 988 v. Sabala, *see* Sabala v. Western Gillette

Tecumseh Prods. Co.; EEOC v., 33 FEP 1437 (W.D. Tenn. 1983) 14: 147

Tedeschi v. Smith Barney, Harris Upham & Co., 548 F. Supp. 1172 (S.D.N.Y. 1982), *related proceeding*, 579 F. Supp. 657 (S.D.N.Y. 1984), *aff'd*, 757 F.2d 465 (2d Cir.), *cert. denied*, 474 U.S. 850 (1985) 23: 54

Tellez v. Pacific Gas & Elec. Co., 817 F.2d 536, 125 LRRM 2481, 2 IER 310 (9th Cir.), *cert. denied*, 484 U.S. ___, 126 LRRM 2696, 2 IER 960 (1987) 23: 4, 5, 41

Templeton v. Veterans Admin., 540 F. Supp. 695, 31 FEP 900 (S.D.N.Y. 1982) 33: 40

Teneyuca v. Bexar County, 767 F.2d 148, 38 FEP 989 (5th Cir. 1985) 27: 43, 87

Tennessee, University of v. Elliott, *see* Elliott v. University of Tennessee

Terbovitz v. Fiscal Court of Adair County, Ky., 825 F.2d 111, 44 FEP 841 (6th Cir. 1987) 2: 12

Terrell v. United States Pipe & Foundry Co., 644 F.2d 1112, 25 FEP 1262 (5th Cir. 1981), *reh'g denied*, 655 F.2d 235 (5th Cir. 1982) 19: 8

—696 F.2d 1132, 30 FEP 1515 (5th Cir. 1983), *on remand*, 39 FEP 571 (N.D. Ala. 1985) 3: 15

Terry v. Northrop Worldwide Aircraft Servs., 628 F. Supp. 212, 39 FEP 1185 (N.D. Ala. 1984), *vacated and remanded*, 786 F.2d 1558, 40 FEP 985 (11th Cir. 1986) 25: 94; 26: 12, 46

Texas, Univ. of, at Austin, In re, 38 FEP 886 (1985) 25: 48, 83; 28: 21; 29: 50

Texas Dep't of Community Affairs v. Burdine, 450 U.S. 248, 25 FEP 113

(1981) 1: 3; 2: 2; 10: 149; 13: 141, 143; 14: 143; 17: 10; 18: 2; 36: 2, 18; 37: 2

Texas Health Science Center at San Antonio, Univ. of; EEOC v., 710 F.2d 1091, 32 FEP 944 (5th Cir. 1983) 14: 186

Texas Indus.; EEOC v., 782 F.2d 547, 40 FEP 118 (5th Cir. 1986) 12: 50, 120

Thames v. Oklahoma Historical Soc'y, 646 F. Supp. 13 (W.D. Okla. 1985), *aff'd*, 809 F.2d 699 (10th Cir. 1987) 32: 6

Theiss v. John Fabick Tractor Co., 532 F. Supp. 453, 34 FEP 266 (E.D. Mo. 1982) 15: 91, 117

Thomas v. Barry, 34 FEP 402 (D.D.C. 1984) 14: 141, 151, 152

Thomas v. Brown & Root, 745 F.2d 279, 35 FEP 1648 (4th Cir. 1984) 14: 9, 83

Thomas v. City of Evanston, 610 F. Supp. 422, 42 FEP 1795 (N.D. Ill. 1985) 4: 34, 83, 105, 106, 113, 114; 38: 63

Thomas v. Cooper Indus., 627 F. Supp. 655, 39 FEP 1826 (W.D.N.C. 1986) 17: 29; 38: 91

Thomas v. Jack Marshall Foods, 37 FEP 1607 (N.D. Ala. 1983) 37: 27; 38: 101

Thomas v. KATV Channel 7, 692 F.2d 548, 30 FEP 231 (8th Cir. 1982), *cert. denied*, 460 U.S. 1039, 31 FEP 368 (1983) 28: 71; 32: 8

Thomas v. Menley & James Laboratories, 34 FEP 71 (N.D. Ga. 1984) 21: 47; 38: 108

Thomas v. Metroflight dba Metro Airlines, 814 F.2d 1506, 43 FEP 703 (10th Cir. 1987) 12: 64, 151; 39: 82

Thomas v. Petrulis, 125 Ill.App.3d 415, 465 N.E.2d 1059, 35 FEP 190 (1984) 12: 220, 223, 224, 234, 244

Thomas v. Resort Health Related Facility, 539 F. Supp. 630, 31 FEP 65 (E.D.N.Y. 1982) 21: 47; 30: 94, 96; 38: 2, 29

Thomas v. Rohner-Gehrig & Co., 582 F. Supp. 669, 34 FEP 887 (N.D. Ill. 1984) 10: 10

Thomas v. Zamberletti, 134 Ill.App.3d 387, 480 N.E.2d 869 (4th Dist. 1985) 23: 40, 47

Thompkins v. Morris Brown College, 752 F.2d 558, 37 FEP 24 (11th Cir. 1985) 1: 4, 5; 18: 9; 36: 7, 35, 41, 60

Thompson v. Department of Labor, 813 F.2d 48 (3d Cir. 1987) 25: 34

Wisner—*Contd.*
 Saunders Leasing Sys., 784 F.2d 1571, 40 FEP 613 (11th Cir. 1986)  7: 37
Witten v. A.H. Smith & Co., 100 F.R.D. 446, 33 FEP 1238, *later proceedings on other issues*, 104 F.R.D. 398, 36 FEP 268 *and* 36 FEP 271 (D. Md. 1984), *aff'd mem.*, 785 F.2d 306, 46 FEP 1222 (4th Cir. 1986)  25: 112, 113, 114; 35: 2, 9
Wolber v. Service Corp. Int'l, 40 EPD ¶42,359 (D. Nev. 1985)  23: 45, App. B, App. C
Wolcowicz v. Intercraft Indus. Corp., 133 Ill.App.3d 157, 478 N.E.2d 1039 (1st Dist. 1985)  23: 40, 47
Wolf v. J.I. Case Co., 617 F. Supp. 858, 38 FEP 1647 (E.D. Wis. 1985)  14: 10, 11, 12, 13; 15: 138; 23: App. A
Wolfolk v. Rivera, 729 F.2d 1114, 34 FEP 468 (7th Cir. 1984)  33: 5, 45, 47
Wolk v. Saks Fifth Ave., 728 F.2d 221, 34 FEP 193, 115 LRRM 3064 (3d Cir. 1984)  23: 4, 5, 9, 41
Womack v. Shell Chem. Co., 514 F. Supp. 1062, 28 FEP 224 (S.D. Ala. 1981)  6: 27
Women in City Gov't United v. City of New York, 515 F. Supp. 295, 25 FEP 927 (S.D.N.Y. 1981)  12: 90
Wood v. Lucy, Lady Duff-Gordon, 222 N.Y. 88, 118 N.E. 214 (1917)  23: 12, 26, 35, 36
Wood v. Regan, 622 F. Supp. 399, 38 FEP 1480 (E.D. Pa. 1985)  39: 16
Woodard v. Lehman, 530 F. Supp. 139, 31 FEP 304 (D.S.C. 1982), *aff'd*, 717 F.2d 909, 32 FEP 1441 (4th Cir. 1983)  17: 19, 25; 28: 34, 36; 36: 147
Woodfield v. Heckler, 591 F. Supp. 1390, 36 FEP 457 (E.D. Pa. 1984)  14: 141, 146, 151, 152, 155, 309
Woods v. Missouri Dep't of Mental Health, Kansas City Regional Diagnostic Center, 581 F. Supp. 437, 35 FEP 1587 (W.D. Mo. 1984)  32: 4
Woods v. New York Life Ins. Co., 686 F.2d 578, 29 FEP 1160 (7th Cir. 1982)  14: 135, 136
Woodworkers Local 5-376 v. Champion Int'l Corp., 752 F.2d 163, 43 FEP 383 (5th Cir. 1985), *aff'd sub nom.* Crawford Fitting Co. v. J.T. Gibbons, Inc., 482 U.S. 437, 43 FEP 1775 (1987)  39: 37, 87

Woolley v. Hoffman-LaRoche, 99 N.J. 284, 491 A.2d 1257 (1985)  23: 21, App. B
Wooster Brush Co. Employees Relief Ass'n; EEOC v., 727 F.2d 566, 33 FEP 1823 (6th Cir. 1984)  12: 50, 143; 27: 56; 37: 20
Worsowicz v. Nashua Corp., 612 F. Supp. 310, 38 FEP 1444 (D.N.H. 1985)  14: 23
Wrenn v. New York City Health & Hosps. Corp., No. 82-CIV 6363, slip op. (S.D.N.Y. 1986)  15: 1
Wright v. Newport News Shipbuilding, slip op. No. 83-C-7935 (N.D. Ill. 1984)  30: 82, 83, 84, 85
Wright v. Olin Corp., 697 F.2d 1172, 30 FEP 889 (4th Cir. 1982), *on remand*, 585 F. Supp. 1447, 34 FEP 1226 (W.D.N.C.), *vacated without opinion*, 767 F.2d 915, 40 FEP 192 (4th Cir. 1984)  1: 15; 12: 50, 74, 144; 17: 4; 31: 22; 36: 134, 167, 172, 186, 199
Wright v. Southwest Bank, 648 F.2d 266, 28 FEP 1040 (5th Cir. 1981)  18: 32
Wright v. Udell Dental Lab, 35 FEP 668 (D. Minn. 1984)  15: 87
Wrighten v. Metropolitan Hosps., 726 F.2d 1346, 33 FEP 1714 (9th Cir. 1984)  15: 28; 28: 63; 30: 5; 39: 90
Wust v. Northwest Airlines, 29 FEP 1435 (W.D. Wash. 1979)  19: 16
Wycoff v. Menke, 773 F.2d 983 (8th Cir. 1985), *cert. denied*, 475 U.S. 1028 (1986)  21: 34
Wygant v. Jackson Bd. of Educ., 746 F.2d 1152, 36 FEP 153 (6th Cir. 1984), *aff'g* 546 F. Supp. 1195, 29 FEP 1359 (E.D. Mich. 1982), *rev'd*, 476 U.S. 267, 40 FEP 1321 (1986)  1: 34, 37, 38, 135, 145; 3: 34, 36, 37, 38, 39, 41, 43; 19: 27; 24: 10, 70, 71, 72, 74, 75, 76, 77, 78, 79, 80, 81, 82, 83, 84, 85, 86, 87, 88, 123, 124, 137, 138, 148
Wyman v. Osteopathic Hosp. of Me., 493 A.2d 330, 119 LRRM 3438 (1985)  23: App. B
Wynn v. North Am. Sys., 608 F. Supp. 30, 34 FEP 1869 (N.D. Ohio 1984)  29: 17
Wyoming; EEOC v., 514 F. Supp. 595, 25 FEP 1392 (D. Wyo. 1981), *rev'd*, 460 U.S. 226, 31 FEP 74 (1983), *later proceeding*, 32 FEP 1270 (D. Wyo. 1983)  14: 25, 26, 30; 32: 8
Wyoming Retirement Sys.; EEOC v., 771